GLEIM®

27TH EDITION FEDERAL TAX

EXAM QUESTIONS & EXPLANATIONS

by

Irvin N. Gleim, Ph.D., CPA, CIA, CMA, CFM

and

James R. Hasselback, Ph.D.

Gleim Publications, Inc.
P.O. Box 12848
University Station
Gainesville, Florida 32604
(800) 87-GLEIM or (800) 874-5346
(352) 375-0772
Website: www.gleim.com
Email: admin@gleim.com

For updates to the first printing of the twenty-seventh edition of *Federal Tax Exam Questions and Explanations*

Go To: www.gleim.com/updates

Or: Email update@gleim.com with **TAX EQE 27-1** in the subject line. You will receive our current update as a reply.

Updates are available until the next edition is published.

ISSN: 1092-4191
ISBN: 978-1-61854-109-3

ACKNOWLEDGMENTS

Material from Uniform Certified Public Accountant Examination questions and unofficial answers, Copyright © 1972-2017 by the American Institute of Certified Public Accountants, Inc., is reprinted and/or adapted with permission.

The authors appreciate and thank the Institute of Certified Management Accountants for permission to use problem materials from past CMA examinations, Copyright © 1981-2017 by the Institute of Certified Management Accountants.

The authors also appreciate and thank the Internal Revenue Service for its cooperation. Questions have been used from the 1977-2005 Special Enrollment Examinations.

The authors also appreciate questions contributed by the following individuals: David B. Bradley, Sandra Byrd, C.K. Craig, D.L. Crumbley, Edmund D. Fenton, Jr., Ramon Fernandez, Edsel Grams, Peggy A. Hite, P.J. Markou, Kyle G. McMullen, Gerald W. Rosson, John M. Ruble, C.J. Skender, James P. Trebby, Michael J. Whiteman, and Mary Yates. Each question submitted by these individuals can be noted by viewing the question source, which appears in the first line of its answer explanation in the column to the right of the question.

ABOUT THE AUTHORS

Irvin N. Gleim is Professor Emeritus in the Fisher School of Accounting at the University of Florida and is a member of the American Accounting Association, Academy of Legal Studies in Business, American Institute of Certified Public Accountants, Association of Government Accountants, Florida Institute of Certified Public Accountants, The Institute of Internal Auditors, and the Institute of Management Accountants. He has had articles published in the *Journal of Accountancy*, *The Accounting Review*, and *The American Business Law Journal* and is author/ coauthor of numerous accounting books, aviation books, and CPE courses.

James R. Hasselback is Professor of Accounting at Clarion University of Pennsylvania. A member of the American Accounting Association and the American Taxation Association, he has published over 160 papers in professional and academic journals, including *The Accounting Review*, *The Tax Adviser*, *Financial Management*, *Journal of Real Estate Taxation*, and the *American Business Law Journal*. Dr. Hasselback has presented papers at many national and regional professional meetings and has served as chairman at tax sessions of professional conferences. He regularly presents continuing education seminars for certified public accountants. In addition, he has been coauthor and technical editor of a two-volume introductory taxation series published by CCH, Inc., for the past 30 years and has served as technical editor of several publications by CCH and Harper-Collins. Dr. Hasselback has compiled over 40 editions of the *Accounting Faculty Directory*.

REVIEWERS AND CONTRIBUTORS

Garrett W. Gleim, B.S., CPA (not in public practice), is a graduate of The Wharton School at the University of Pennsylvania and is one of our vice presidents. Mr. Gleim coordinated the production staff, reviewed the manuscript, and provided production assistance throughout the project.

Scott Lawton, B.S., is a graduate of Brigham Young University-Idaho and Utah Valley University and has passed the EA exam. Mr. Lawton performed preliminary technical edits and followed up on the authors' review.

Yiqian Zhao, MAcc., is a graduate from the Fisher School of Accounting at the University of Florida and has passed the CPA exam. Ms. Zhao participated in the technical editing of the manuscript.

A PERSONAL THANKS

This manual would not have been possible without the extraordinary effort and dedication of Julie Cutlip, Blaine Hatton, Belea Keeney, Kelsey Olson, Bree Rodriguez, Teresa Soard, Justin Stephenson, Joanne Strong, Elmer Tucker, and Candace Van Doren, who typed the entire manuscript and all revisions and drafted and laid out the diagrams, illustrations, and cover for this book.

The authors also appreciate the production and editorial assistance of Jacob Bennett, Melody Dalton, Jim Harvin, Jessica Hatker, Kristen Hennen, Katie Larson, Diana León, Jake Pettifor, Shane Rapp, Drew Sheppard, and Alyssa Thomas.

The authors also appreciate the critical reading assistance of Felix Chen, Corey Connell, Solomon Gonite, Jared Halper, Nichole Hyde, Andrew Johnson, Jacey Johnson, Jessica Joseph, Dean Kingston, Josh Lehr, Melissa Leonard, Ross Li, Monica Metz, Sharon Sabbagh, and Diana Weng.

Finally, we appreciate the encouragement, support, and tolerance of our families throughout this project.

IF YOU HAVE QUESTIONS

Gleim has an efficient and effective way for users to submit an inquiry and receive a response regarding Gleim materials directly through their Test Prep. This system also allows you to view your Q&A session in your Gleim Personal Classroom.

Questions regarding the information in the Introduction (study suggestions, studying plans, exam specifics) should be emailed to personalcounselor@gleim.com.

Questions concerning orders, prices, shipments, or payments should be sent via email to customerservice@gleim.com and will be promptly handled by our competent and courteous customer service staff.

For technical support, you may use our automated technical support service at www.gleim.com/support, email us at support@gleim.com, or call us at (800) 874-5346.

Returns of books purchased from bookstores and other resellers should be made to the respective bookstore or reseller. For more information regarding the Gleim Return Policy, please contact our offices at (800) 874-5346 or visit www.gleim.com/returnpolicy.

TABLE OF CONTENTS

vi

DETAILED TABLE OF CONTENTS

PREFACE FOR ACCOUNTING STUDENTS

The purpose of this book is to help you understand federal taxation concepts and their applications. These skills will help you perform better on your academic exams and familiarize you with professional certification exams.

A major benefit of this study guide is its comprehensive coverage of virtually all topics studied in typical college or university tax courses. Appendix A includes a list of cross-references.

The question-and-answer format is designed to facilitate effective study. To get the most from this text, choose a response for each question before referring to the answer to the immediate right. Or you can overcome the temptation to peek at the answer by using our EQE Test Prep, which is packed with features and priced with a student's budget in mind.

The majority of the questions are from past CPA, CMA, and EA exams; however, questions have been modified to accommodate changes in professional pronouncements, to clarify questions, and/or to emphasize a federal taxation concept or its application. In addition, hundreds of publisher-written questions are provided to adequately test areas covered in current textbooks.

Note that this study guide should not be relied upon exclusively to prepare for professional exams, as this book is specifically designed to cover topics in your tax textbooks. You should primarily use review systems specifically developed for each exam. The Gleim CPA, CIA, CMA, and EA Review Systems are up-to-date and comprehensively cover all material necessary for successful completion of these exams. Further descriptions of these exams and our review materials are provided in the Introduction. To obtain any of these materials, order online at www.gleim.com/students or call us at (800) 874-5346.

The questions in general have been written in terms of calendar-year 2017. All tax rates, personal exemptions, standard deductions, itemized deduction and personal exemption phaseouts, automobile standard mileage rates, etc., used in the questions and answers include 2017 amounts except where noted.

Thank you for your interest in this book. We deeply appreciate the many emails and suggestions received from accounting students and educators, as well as from CPA, CIA, CMA, and EA candidates. Please go to www.gleim.com/feedbackTAX to share your suggestions on how we can improve this edition.

Please read the Introduction carefully. It is short but very important.

Good Luck on Your Exams,

Irvin N. Gleim
James R. Hasselback

March 2017

INTRODUCTION

This innovative accounting text provides students with a well-organized, extensive collection of multiple-choice questions covering the topics taught in typical tax courses.

The Gleim *Exam Questions and Explanations* series will help you to pretest yourself before class to determine whether you are strong or weak in the assigned area. Then test yourself after class to reinforce the concepts. The questions in these books cover **all** topics in your related courses, so you will encounter few questions on your exams for which you will not be well prepared.

The titles and organization of Study Units 1 through 23 are based on the current tax textbooks listed in Appendix A, which contains a comprehensive cross-reference of your textbooks to Gleim study units and subunits. If you are using a textbook that is not included in our list or if you have any suggestions on how we can improve these cross-references to make them more useful, please submit your request/feedback at www.gleim.com/crossreferences/TAX or email them to TAXcrossreferences@gleim.com.

FEATURES

Use the Gleim EQE series to ensure your understanding of each topic you study in your courses. Access the largest bank of exam questions (including thousands from past certification exams) that is widely used by professors. Get immediate feedback on your study effort while you take your practice tests.

- Each book or EQE Test Prep question bank contains over 1,000 multiple-choice questions with correct and incorrect answer explanations and can be used in two or more classes.
- Exhaustive cross-references are presented for all related textbooks so that you can easily determine which group of questions pertains to a given chapter in your textbook.
- You absorb important information more efficiently, more quickly, and more permanently through *"programmed learning."*
- Questions taken directly from professional certification exams demonstrate the standards to which you will be held as a professional accountant and help prepare you for certification exams later.
- Titles include Auditing & Systems, Cost/Managerial Accounting, Financial Accounting, Federal Tax, and Business Law & Legal Studies. Go to www.gleim.com/eqe for more details.

After graduation, you will compete with graduates from schools across the country in the accounting job market. Make sure you measure up to standards that are as demanding as the standards of your counterparts at other schools. These standards will be tested on professional certification exams.

USE OF SUBUNITS

Each study unit of this book is divided into subunits to portion overwhelming topics into more manageable study components.

Topics and questions may overlap among subunits. The number of questions offers comprehensive coverage but does not present an insurmountable task. We define each subunit narrowly enough to cover a single topic but broadly enough to prevent questions from being repetitive.

True/false questions appear at the end of most subunits to use as a useful study tool.

QUESTION SOURCES

Past CMA, CPA, and EA (Enrolled Agent) exams and sample questions are the primary sources of questions included in this study guide. The EA exam is also referred to as the IRS Special Enrollment Examination (SEE).

In addition, Gleim Exam Prep prepares questions (coded in this text as *Publisher, adapted*) based on the content of tax textbooks. Professionals and professors from schools around the country also have contributed to provide a more thorough bank of questions. Page ii lists their names.

The source of each question appears in the first line of its answer explanation in the column to the right of the question. Summary of source codes:

CMA	Certified Management Accountant Examination
CPA	Uniform Certified Public Accountant Examination
SPE or SEE	IRS Special Enrollment Examination
Publisher	EQE TAX authors
Individual's name	Name of professional or professor who contributed the question

If you, your professor, or your classmates wish to submit questions, we will consider using them in future editions. Please email questions you develop, complete with answers and explanations, to professor.relations@gleim.com.

Writing and analyzing multiple-choice questions is an excellent way to prepare yourself for your exams. We will make every effort to consider, edit, and use questions you submit. However, we ask that you send us only serious, complete, carefully considered efforts.

MULTIPLE-CHOICE QUESTIONS

The major advantage of multiple-choice questions is their ability to cover a large number of topics with little time and effort in comparison to essay questions and/or computational problems.

The advantage of multiple-choice questions over true/false questions is that they require more analysis and result in a lower score for those with little or no knowledge.

Students and professors both like multiple-choice questions. Students find them relatively easy to answer because only one of the answer choices needs to be selected. Professors like them because they are easy to grade and much more material can be tested in the same period of time. Most professors also will ask students to complete essays or computational questions.

Note that the detailed Gleim answer explanations also can help students prepare for the inevitable essay questions.

ANSWER EXPLANATIONS ALONGSIDE THE QUESTIONS

The format of our book presents multiple-choice questions side by side with their answer explanations. The example below is publisher-developed.

All of the following income items are includible in an employee's gross income except

A. Severance pay for cancelation of employment.

B. Vacation allowance.

C. Payments from employer while sick or injured.

D. Medical insurance premium paid by employer for employee and spouse.

Answer (D) is correct. *(Publisher, adapted)*
REQUIRED: The item that is not includible in an employee's gross income.
DISCUSSION: Gross income includes all income from whatever source derived unless specifically excluded. Section 106 excludes contributions by an employer to accident or health plans for employees. Regulation 1.106-1 extends the exclusion to contributions for the employee's spouse or dependents.
Answer (A) is incorrect. No provision excludes severance pay for cancelation of employment from gross income. Answer (B) is incorrect. No provision excludes vacation allowance from gross income. Answer (C) is incorrect. No provision excludes payments from employer while sick or injured from gross income.

This format is designed to make studying more efficient by eliminating the need to turn pages back and forth from questions to answers.

Be careful, however. Do not misuse this format by consulting the answers before you have answered the questions. Misuse of the readily available answers will give you a false sense of security and will result in poor performance on your actual exams.

STUDY SUGGESTIONS

The emphasis in the next few pages is on developing strategies, approaches, and procedures to learn and retain the material in less time.

Using Tests to Study

Tests, especially quizzes and midterms, provide feedback on your study and test-taking procedures. It is extremely important to diagnose your mistakes on quizzes and tests at the beginning of the term so you can take corrective action on subsequent tests, including your final exam.

When your test is returned, determine how you did relative to the rest of your class and your professor's grading standards. Next, analyze your relative performance between types of questions (essay vs. multiple-choice) and types of subject matter (topics or study units). The objective is to identify the areas where you should take corrective action.

Using Multiple-Choice Questions to Study

Experts on testing continue to favor multiple-choice questions as a valid means of examining various levels of knowledge. Using these questions to study for academic exams is an important tool not only for obtaining good grades, but also for long-range preparation for certification and other exams. The following suggestions will help you study in conjunction with each Gleim *Exam Questions and Explanations* book and EQE Test Prep (visit www.gleim.com/students):

1. Locate the study unit that contains questions on the topic you are currently studying. Each *Exam Questions and Explanations* book and EQE Test Prep contains cross-references to the tables of contents of the most commonly used textbooks.

2. Work through a series of questions, selecting the answers you think are correct.

3. **If you are using the Gleim book, do not consult the answer or answer explanations on the right side of the page until after you have chosen and written down an answer.**

    a. It is crucial that you cover the answer explanations and intellectually commit yourself to an answer. This method will help you understand the concept much better, even if you answered the question incorrectly. Our EQE Test Prep prevents you from consulting the answer, which allows you to study in an exam-like environment.

4. Study the explanations to the correct and incorrect answer choices for each question you answered incorrectly. In addition to learning and understanding the concept tested, analyze **why** you missed the question. Reasons for missing questions include

    - Misreading the requirement (stem)
    - Not understanding what is required
    - Making a math error
    - Applying the wrong rule or concept
    - Being distracted by one or more of the answers
    - Incorrectly eliminating answers from consideration
    - Not having any knowledge of the topic tested
    - Employing bad intuition when guessing

    Studying the important concepts that we provide in our answer explanations will help you understand the principles to the point that you can answer that question (or any other like it) successfully.

5. Identify your weaknesses in answering multiple-choice questions and take corrective action (before you take a test). The EQE Test Prep provides a detailed performance analysis.

    The analysis will show your weaknesses (areas needing more study) and also your strengths (areas of confidence). You can improve your performance on multiple-choice questions both by increasing your percentage of correct answers and by decreasing the time spent per question.

Multiple-Choice Question-Answering Technique

The following series of steps is suggested for answering multiple-choice questions. The important point is that you need to devote attention to and develop **the technique that works for you**. Personalize and practice your answering technique on questions in this study guide. Begin now to develop **your** control system.

1. **Budget your time.**

    a. We make this point with emphasis – **finish your exam before time expires**.
    b. Calculate the time allowed for each multiple-choice question after you have allocated time to the other questions (e.g., essays) on the exam. If 20 multiple-choice questions are allocated 40 minutes on your exam, you should spend a little under 2 minutes per question (always budget extra time for transferring answers to answer sheets, interruptions, etc.).
    c. Before beginning a series of multiple-choice questions, write the starting time on the exam near the first question.
    d. As you work through the questions, check your time. Assuming a time allocation of 120 minutes for 60 questions, you are fine if you worked 5 questions in 9 minutes. If you spent 11 minutes on 5 questions, you need to speed up. Remember that your goal is to answer all questions and achieve the maximum score possible.

2. **Answer the items in consecutive order.**

    a. Do **not** agonize over any one item. Stay within your time budget.
    b. Mark any questions you are unsure of and return to them later as time allows.
    c. Never leave a question unanswered **if** you will not be penalized for incorrect answers. Make your best guess in the time allowed.

3. **For each multiple-choice question,**

    a. **Ignore the answer choices.** Do not allow the answer choices to affect your reading of the question.

        1) If four answer choices are presented, three of them are incorrect. These incorrect choices are called **distractors** for good reason. Often, distractors are written to appear correct at first glance until further analysis.

        2) In computational items, distractors are carefully calculated so they are the result of common mistakes. Be careful, and double-check your computations if time permits.

    b. **Read the question carefully** to determine the precise requirement.

        1) Focusing on what is required enables you to ignore extraneous information and to proceed directly to determining the correct answer.

            a) Be especially careful to note when the requirement is an **exception**; e.g., "Which of the following is **not** an itemized deduction?"

    c. **Determine the correct answer** before looking at the answer choices.

    d. **Read the answer choices carefully.**

        1) Even if the first answer appears to be the correct choice, do **not** skip the remaining answer choices. Questions often ask for the "best" choice provided. Thus, each choice requires your consideration.

        2) Treat each answer choice as a true/false question as you analyze it.

    e. **Select the best answer.**

        1) If you are uncertain, guess intelligently (see "If You Don't Know the Answer" below). Improve on your 25% chance of getting the correct answer with blind guessing.

        2) For many multiple-choice questions, two answer choices can be eliminated with minimal effort, thereby increasing your educated guess to a 50-50 proposition.

4. **Transfer your answers to the answer sheet**, if one is provided.

    a. Make sure you are within your time budget so you will be able to perform this vital step in an unhurried manner.

    b. Do not wait to transfer answers until the very end of the exam session because you may run out of time.

    c. Double-check that you have transferred the answers correctly; e.g., recheck every 5th or 10th answer from your test paper to your answer sheet to ensure that you have not fallen out of sequence.

If You Don't Know the Answer

If the exam you are taking does not penalize incorrect answers, you should make an educated guess. First, rule out answers that you think are incorrect. Second, speculate on what the examiner is looking for and/or the rationale behind the question. Third, select the best answer or guess between equally appealing answers. Mark the question with a "?" in case you have time to return to it for further analysis.

If you cannot make an educated guess, read the stem and each answer, and pick the best or most intuitive answer. It's just a guess! Do **not** look at the previous answer to try to detect an answer. Answers are usually random, and it is possible to have four or more consecutive questions with the same answer letter, e.g., answer (B).

NOTE: Do not waste time beyond the amount you budgeted for each question. Move forward and stay on or ahead of schedule.

Examination Summary

	CPA (Certified Public Accountant)	CIA (Certified Internal Auditor)	CMA (Certified Management Accountant)	EA (IRS Enrolled Agent)
Sponsoring Organization	American Institute of Certified Public Accountants	Institute of Internal Auditors	Institute of Management Accountants	Internal Revenue Service
Contact Information	www.aicpa.org (888) 777-7077	www.theiia.org (407) 937-1111	www.imanet.org (800) 638-4427	www.irs.gov (313) 234-1280
Exam Parts	Auditing and Attestation (4 hrs.); Business Environment and Concepts (4 hrs.); Financial Accounting and Reporting (4 hrs.); Regulation (4 hrs.)	1 – Internal Audit Basics (2.5 hrs.); 2 – Internal Audit Practice (2 hrs.); 3 – Internal Audit Knowledge Elements (2 hrs.)	1 – Financial Reporting, Planning, Performance, and Control (4 hrs.); 2 – Financial Decision Making (4 hrs.)	1 – Individuals (3.5 hrs.); 2 – Businesses (3.5 hrs.); 3 – Representation, Practices, and Procedures (3.5 hrs.)
Exam Format	AUD: 72 multiple-choice questions 8 TBS; BEC: 62 multiple-choice questions 4 TBS 3 written communications; FAR: 66 multiple-choice questions 8 TBS; REG: 76 multiple-choice questions 8 TBS	Part 1: 125 multiple-choice questions; Parts 2 and 3: 100 multiple-choice questions	Parts 1 and 2: 100 multiple-choice questions 2 essays	Parts 1, 2, and 3: 100 multiple-choice questions
Avg. Pass Rate	AUD – 46% BEC – 57% FAR – 46% REG – 49%	1, 2, 3 – 39%	1 – 35% 2 – 50%	1 – 72% 2 – 57% 3 – 88%
Testing Windows	January-March 10 April-May July-September 10 October-December 10	On demand throughout the year	January-February May-June September-October	May-February (e.g., 5/01/2017-2/28/2018)
Resources	gleimcpa.com	gleimcia.com	gleimcma.com	gleimea.com
Available Prep Course Discounts	Up to 20%	Up to 20%	Up to 20%	Up to 20%

ACCOUNTING CERTIFICATION PROGRAMS--OVERVIEW

The CPA (Certified Public Accountant) exam is the grandparent of all professional accounting exams. Its origin was in the 1896 public accounting legislation of New York. In 1917, the American Institute of CPAs (AICPA) began to prepare and grade a uniform CPA exam. It is currently used to measure the technical competence of those applying to be licensed as CPAs in all 50 states, Guam, Puerto Rico, the Virgin Islands, the District of Columbia, the Commonwealth of the Northern Mariana Islands, and an ever-expanding list of international locations.

The CIA (Certified Internal Auditor), CMA (Certified Management Accountant), and EA (IRS Enrolled Agent) exams are relatively new certification programs compared to the CPA. The CMA exam was first administered in 1972 and the first CIA exam in 1974. The EA exam dates back to 1959. Why were these other exams initially created? Generally, the requirements of the CPA designation instituted by the boards of accountancy (especially the necessity for public accounting experience) led to the development of the CIA and CMA programs, which allow for professionals to show proficiency in specific job functions. The EA designation is available for persons specializing in tax.

The table of selected CPA, CIA, CMA, and EA exam data on the preceding page provides an overview of these accounting exams.

ACCOUNTING CERTIFICATION PROGRAMS--PURPOSE

The primary purpose of professional exams is to measure the technical competence of candidates. Competence includes technical knowledge, the ability to apply such knowledge with good judgment, comprehension of professional responsibility, and ethical considerations. Additionally, the nature of these exams (low pass rate, broad and rigorous coverage, etc.) has several very important effects:

1. Candidates are forced to learn all of the material that should have been presented and learned in a good accounting education program.

2. Relatedly, candidates must integrate the topics and concepts that are presented in individual courses in accounting education programs.

3. The content of each exam provides direction to accounting education programs; i.e., what is tested on the exams will be taught to accounting students.

Certification is important to professional accountants because it provides

1. Participation in a recognized professional group
2. An improved professional training program arising out of the certification program
3. Recognition among peers for attaining the professional designation
4. An extra credential to enhance career opportunities
5. The personal satisfaction of attaining a recognized degree of competency

These reasons hold true in the accounting field due to wide recognition of the CPA designation. Accountants and accounting students are often asked whether they are CPAs when people learn they are accountants. Thus, there is considerable pressure for accountants to become **certified.**

A newer development is multiple certifications, which is important for the same reasons as initial certification. Accounting students and recent graduates should look ahead and obtain multiple certifications to broaden their career opportunities.

When to Sit for the Certification Exams

Sit for all exams as soon as you can. Candidates are allowed to sit for the exam and then complete the requirements within a certain time period. The CIA program allows full-time students in their senior year to sit for the exam, and the CMA program offers a 7-year window for submission of educational credentials. The CIA and CMA exams are offered at a reduced fee for students. The requirements for the CPA vary by jurisdiction, but many state boards allow candidates to sit for the exam before they have completed the required hours. However, you will not be certified until you have met all requirements.

Register to take the parts of each exam that best match up to the courses you are currently taking. For example, if you are taking a Business Law course and a Federal Tax course this semester, schedule your CPA Regulation date for the week after classes end.

Steps to Passing Certification Exams

❶ Become knowledgeable about the exam you will be taking, and determine which part you will take first.

❷ Purchase the complete Gleim Premium Review System to thoroughly prepare yourself. Commit to systematic preparation for the exam as described in our review materials.

❸ Apply for membership in the exam's governing body and/or in the certification program as required.

❹ Register online to take the desired part of the exam.

❺ Schedule your test with the testing center in the location of your choice.

❻ Sit for and PASS the exam. Gleim guarantees success!

❼ Email or call Gleim with your comments on our study materials and how well they prepared you for the exam.

❽ Enjoy your career, pursue multiple certifications (CPA, CIA, CMA, EA, etc.), and recommend Gleim to others who are also taking these exams. Stay up-to-date on your Continuing Professional Education requirements with Gleim CPE.

STUDY UNIT ONE
GROSS INCOME

1.1 Identification of Items Included

1.1.1. Which of the following does not have to be included in gross income?

A. Unemployment compensation.

B. Damages from personal injury suit involving back injuries.

C. Prize from church raffle.

D. Free tour from travel agency for organizing a group of tourists.

Answer (B) is correct. *(Publisher, adapted)*
REQUIRED: The item that does not have to be included in gross income.
DISCUSSION: Gross income means all income from whatever source derived unless specifically excluded (Sec. 61). This is an intentionally broad and all-encompassing definition. Section 104(a)(2) includes punitive damages in gross income, even in connection with a physical injury or physical sickness. However, Sec. 104(a)(2) excludes nonpunitive damages awarded for personal injuries involving physical injury or physical sickness.
Answer (A) is incorrect. Unemployment compensation is included in gross income under Sec. 85. Answer (C) is incorrect. A prize received in a raffle (whether from a church or any other organization) is included in gross income under Sec. 74. Answer (D) is incorrect. The fair market value of a free tour is the receipt of an economic benefit, which is included in gross income as compensation since no provision excludes it.

1.1.2. During the current year, Mr. French received state unemployment benefits of $2,500 and $700 of supplemental unemployment benefits from a company financed fund. The union paid Mr. French an additional $2,000 out of regular union dues. What amount must Mr. French include in income for the current year?

A. $2,500

B. $3,200

C. $4,500

D. $5,200

Answer (D) is correct. *(SEE, adapted)*
REQUIRED: The amount of the items listed that must be included in gross income.
DISCUSSION: Gross income is defined under Sec. 61 as all income from whatever source derived that is not specifically excluded. There is no exclusion for unemployment compensation benefits (prior to 1987, all or part could be excluded, and in 2009, $2,400 could be excluded). Since there is no exclusion, all of the state unemployment compensation benefits of $2,500 must be included in Mr. French's gross income [Sec. 85(a)].
Regulation 1.85-1(b)1(i) provides that amounts paid pursuant to private nongovernmental unemployment compensation plans are includible in income without regard to Sec. 85. Thus, the $700 from the company-financed fund and the $2,000 from the union must also be included in gross income.
Answer (A) is incorrect. The $700 from the company-financed fund and the $2,000 from the union must also be included in gross income. Answer (B) is incorrect. The $2,000 from the union must be included in gross income. Answer (C) is incorrect. The $700 from the company-financed fund must be included in gross income.

1.1.3. Which of the following is not subject to federal income tax?

A. Interest on U.S. Treasury bills, notes, and bonds issued by an agency of the United States.

B. Interest on federal income tax refund.

C. Interest on New York State bonds.

D. Discount income in installment payments received on notes bought at a discount.

Answer (C) is correct. *(SEE, adapted)*
    REQUIRED: The item of income that is not subject to federal income tax.
    DISCUSSION: Gross income is defined under Sec. 61 as all income from whatever source derived which is not specifically excluded. Section 103 specifically excludes from gross income interest on most obligations of a state or any political subdivision thereof.
    Answer (A) is incorrect. The exclusion under Sec. 103 does not apply to obligations of the federal government. Answer (B) is incorrect. The exclusion under Sec. 103 does not apply to interest on a federal income tax refund. Answer (D) is incorrect. Discount income (the excess of the face amount of a debt over the purchase price) is a form of interest income included in gross income by Secs. 61 and 1272.

1.1.4. Generally, which of the following should be included in gross income?

A. Life insurance proceeds.

B. Child support payments.

C. Cash rebate from a dealer when a car is purchased.

D. Reimbursements from your employer of a moving expense you properly deducted on last year's tax return.

Answer (D) is correct. *(SEE, adapted)*
    REQUIRED: The item that must be included in gross income.
    DISCUSSION: Section 82 specifically provides that, except as provided in Sec. 132(a)(6), gross income includes amounts received as reimbursement of moving expenses that are attributable to employment. Under Sec. 132(a)(6), the reimbursement is excluded if the expense would be deductible under Sec. 217 if paid by the employee. It may not be excluded, however, if the expense was actually deducted on the individual's return for any prior tax year.
    Answer (A) is incorrect. Life insurance proceeds are specifically excluded under Sec. 101(a). Answer (B) is incorrect. Section 71(c) excludes payments for the support of children. Answer (C) is incorrect. A rebate on a new automobile is merely a reduction of the purchase price of the automobile, not income.

1.1.5. Which of the following should not be included in Mr. W's gross income for the current year?

A. $200 in dental work Mr. W received in exchange for repairs made by Mr. W to his dentist's residence.

B. $5,000 in executor fees received from the estate of Mr. W's brother.

C. Life insurance proceeds of $10,000 received as a beneficiary as a result of the death of Mr. W's brother who owned the policy.

D. A new car worth $7,000 given to Mr. W by his employer for his valuable services.

Answer (C) is correct. *(SEE, adapted)*
    REQUIRED: The item that is excluded from gross income.
    DISCUSSION: Although life insurance proceeds would fall within the broad definition of gross income, Sec. 101(a) specifically excludes from gross income amounts received under a life insurance contract if such amounts are paid by reason of death of the insured.
    Answer (A) is incorrect. If services are paid for with property, the fair market value of the property received in payment must be included in income as compensation [Reg. 1.61-2(d)]. Mr. W should include $200 in income. Answer (B) is incorrect. Compensation for services, including executor fees, is included in gross income. Answer (D) is incorrect. If services are paid for with property, the fair market value of the property received in payment must be included in income as compensation [Reg. 1.61-2(d)]. Mr. W received the new car because of his services, so $7,000 must be included in his gross income.

1.1.6. Which of the following payments received by a member of a U.S. military service is not taxable?

A. Reenlistment bonus.

B. Family separation allowances because of overseas assignments.

C. Armed services academy pay.

D. Reserve training pay.

Answer (B) is correct. *(SEE, adapted)*
    REQUIRED: The item of income that is not taxable.
    DISCUSSION: Gross income means all income from whatever source derived unless specifically excluded by a provision in the Internal Revenue Code (Sec. 61). Some forms of compensation to armed forces personnel are excluded. Most are "fringe benefit" type items. In addition to subsistence, uniform, and quarters allowances, family separation allowances as a result of overseas duty are specifically excluded (Reg. 1.61-2(b) and Rev. Rul. 70-281).
    Answer (A) is incorrect. In general, military pay is included in gross income. Bonuses to enlist or reenlist are included. Answer (C) is incorrect. Armed services academy pay is included in gross income. Answer (D) is incorrect. In general, military pay is included in gross income as well as pay received while in reserve training.

1.1.7. Which of the following is not considered actual receipt or "constructive receipt" of income in the current year?

A. Taxpayer A was informed his check for services rendered was available on December 15 of the current year, but he waited until January 15 of the following year to pick up the check.

B. A payment on a sale of real property was placed in escrow on December 15 of the current year but not received by Taxpayer A until January 10 of the following year, when the transaction was closed.

C. Earned income of Taxpayer A was received by his agent on December 29 of the current year but not received by A until January 5 of the following year.

D. Taxpayer B received a check on December 30 of the current year for services rendered but was unable to make a deposit until January 4 of the following year.

1.1.8. Colin Rosson is a freelance writer who reports income on the cash basis. Some of his current-year transactions follow:

Cash fees received for articles, etc.	$55,000
TV won in resort promotion (had to attend promotion to win)	300
Loss on sale of business furniture	(100)
Appreciation on investment property	1,000

What is Colin's gross income?

A. $55,000
B. $55,900
C. $55,300
D. $55,200

1.1.9. Based on the following, how much should Mr. Big include in income in his federal income tax return?

Punitive damages awarded by jury related to a leg injury from an accident	$10,000
Kickbacks received on sale of goods (not treated as a reduction elsewhere)	5,000
Money borrowed from a bank	8,000
Increase in the value of an asset	1,000

A. $10,000
B. $15,000
C. $16,000
D. $23,000

Answer (B) is correct. *(SEE, adapted)*
REQUIRED: The occurrence that is not considered "constructive receipt" of income.
DISCUSSION: Income, although not actually in a taxpayer's possession, is constructively received in the taxable year during which it is credited to his or her account, set apart for him or her, or otherwise made available so that (s)he may draw upon it at any time, or so that (s)he could have drawn upon it during the taxable year if notice of intention to withdraw had been given (Reg. 1.451-2). However, income is not constructively received if the taxpayer's control of its receipt is subject to substantial limitations or restrictions. Since the taxpayer's control of the receipt of the funds in the escrow account is substantially limited until the transaction has closed, the taxpayer has not constructively received the income until the closing of the transaction in the following year.
Answer (A) is incorrect. The check (and therefore the funds) for services rendered was made available to the taxpayer during the current year. Answer (C) is incorrect. The receipt of the income by the taxpayer's agent makes it available to the taxpayer, and therefore it is constructively received. Answer (D) is incorrect. The receipt of a check is the receipt of the income, regardless of the ability to cash or deposit it.

Answer (C) is correct. *(G.W. Rosson)*
REQUIRED: The taxpayer's gross income from the listed transactions.
DISCUSSION: Under Sec. 61, gross income includes income from whatever source derived. The cash fees are compensation for services. The TV won in the promotion is a prize included in gross income under Sec. 74. These two items total $55,300.
Appreciation on property is not included in gross income until there is a sale or exchange or some other event causing the taxpayer to realize or receive the economic benefit. Losses (if deductible) are deducted from gross income; i.e., they do not affect the computation of gross income.
Answer (A) is incorrect. Gross income also includes prizes received from a promotion. Answer (B) is incorrect. Gross income does not include the loss on a sale of business property or appreciation on investment property until such property is sold or exchanged. However, gross income does include prize money. Answer (D) is incorrect. Gross income does not include the loss on a sale of business property.

Answer (B) is correct. *(SEE, adapted)*
REQUIRED: The amount of the items listed that must be included in gross income.
DISCUSSION: Punitive damages are included in gross income under the broad concept of Sec. 61, which includes all income from whatever source derived unless specifically excluded. Punitive damages are unlike damages for personal injury or property damage, which are considered a return of capital. Section 104(a) includes punitive damages in gross income whether or not they relate to physical injury or physical sickness. Kickbacks on the sale of goods are also included in gross income (even if illegal) since they are not specifically excluded from gross income (and often represent payment for services). Mr. Big should include $15,000 in gross income ($10,000 punitive damages + $5,000 kickbacks).
Money borrowed from a bank is not included in gross income because there is a legal obligation to return it. The increase in the value of an asset is not included in income because there has been no event causing the taxpayer to realize or receive the economic benefit.
Answer (A) is incorrect. Gross income includes kickbacks. Answer (C) is incorrect. Gross income does not include an increase in the value of an asset until the gain is realized by sale or exchange. Answer (D) is incorrect. Money borrowed is not included in gross income.

1.1.10. Ruby Diaz is a commissioned salesperson. She is a cash-method taxpayer. At the end of the year, her earnings for the year were $75,000. During the year, she also received $10,000 in advances on future commissions and repaid $8,000. How much income should Ruby report for the year?

A. $77,000

B. $75,000

C. $87,000

D. $85,000

Answer (A) is correct. *(SEE, adapted)*
REQUIRED: The income reported for a cash-basis taxpayer.
DISCUSSION: Both cash- and accrual-basis taxpayers must include amounts in gross income upon actual or constructive receipt if the taxpayer has an unrestricted claim to such amounts under Reg. 1.61-8(b). All commissions received should be included in the current year's gross income. The $8,000 repaid reduces gross income. Ruby should report $77,000 ($75,000 + $10,000 – $8,000).
Answer (B) is incorrect. Ruby must include the amount of advances on future commissions that she did not repay as income on her return. Answer (C) is incorrect. The amount of advanced future commissions is not included in income to the extent that it has been repaid. Answer (D) is incorrect. The $8,000 repaid reduces gross income.

1.1.11. Trish Durwood works for a small retail clothing store. She earned $26,000 during the year. Because of a cash flow problem in April, Trish did not receive her $500 weekly check but instead was given a credit of $500 on the purchased clothing for her family. How much income should be shown on her Form W-2 and reported on her Form 1040?

A. $26,000

B. $25,500

C. $26,500

D. $25,000

Answer (A) is correct. *(SEE, adapted)*
REQUIRED: The amount of income reported on Form W-2 and Form 1040 for compensation of services.
DISCUSSION: Section 61(a)(1) specifically provides that compensation for services is to be included in gross income. Due to the relationship between an employee and an employer, almost everything received by the employee from the employer is included in gross income as compensation.
Answer (B) is incorrect. The $500 applied to Trish's account should also be included as income. Answer (C) is incorrect. The $500 applied to Trish's account is not additional compensation. It is compensation in lieu of receiving her paycheck. Answer (D) is incorrect. The $500 applied to Trish's account is income in lieu of her receiving a check. This event does not reduce her income.

1.1.12. In the current year, Emil Gow won $5,000 in a state lottery and spent $400 for the purchase of lottery tickets. Emil elected the standard deduction on his current-year income tax return. The amount of lottery winnings that should be included in Emil's current-year gross income is

A. $0

B. $700

C. $4,600

D. $5,000

Answer (D) is correct. *(CPA, adapted)*
REQUIRED: The amount of state lottery winnings included in gross income.
DISCUSSION: Under Sec. 61, gambling winnings (whether legal or illegal) are included in gross income. Therefore, Emil must include the full $5,000 in gross income. Gambling losses, i.e., amounts spent on nonwinning tickets, may be deductible, but only as an itemized deduction after the total gambling winnings are included in gross income [Sec. 165(d)]. Since Emil elected the standard deduction, the gambling losses do not reduce taxable income.
Answer (A) is incorrect. All gambling winnings constitute gross income. Answer (B) is incorrect. Although the standard deduction may reduce taxable income, it does not reduce the amount of gambling winnings included in gross income. Answer (C) is incorrect. If the standard deduction is claimed, itemized deductions are not allowed.

1.1.13. During the previous year, Carrie paid $500 of estimated state income tax payments, which she also deducted for federal income tax purposes. Early in the current year, Carrie received a refund of $300 of these state tax payments. Carrie immediately placed an illegal bet at 5-to-1 odds and won an additional $1,500. Later in the year, Carrie was short of money and robbed a tavern of $4,000. How much should Carrie include in her income for the current year?

A. $0

B. $1,500

C. $1,800

D. $5,800

Answer (D) is correct. *(Publisher, adapted)*
REQUIRED: The amount that the recipient of a state tax refund and illegally obtained money must include in gross income.
DISCUSSION: All of the amounts received, which total $5,800, must be included in gross income. The state tax refund is included in income since it was previously deducted when paid. Under Sec. 111 (known as the "tax benefit rule"), recovery of previously paid taxes is excluded from gross income only if the prior deduction did not reduce the taxpayer's federal income tax. Income from betting, whether legal or illegal, must be included in gross income. Likewise, the $4,000 of proceeds from the robbery must also be included in gross income. Carrie took the money with an expectation of an unrestricted right to it ("claim of right" doctrine).
Answer (A) is incorrect. Gross income includes gambling money, state tax refunds for taxes deducted in a prior year, and robbery proceeds. Answer (B) is incorrect. Gross income includes state tax refunds for taxes deducted in a prior year and robbery proceeds. Answer (C) is incorrect. Gross income includes robbery proceeds.

1.1.14. Clark filed Form 1040EZ for the previous tax year. In the current year, Clark received a state income tax refund of $900, plus interest of $10, for overpayment of the previous year's state income taxes. In addition, Clark received a $1,000 income tax refund from the IRS. How much income must Clark include in his current-year federal tax return as a result of these refunds?

A. $10
B. $900
C. $910
D. $1,910

Answer (A) is correct. *(CPA, adapted)*
REQUIRED: The amount of income from the tax refunds that must be included in gross income.
DISCUSSION: Under Sec. 111, recovery of previously deducted taxes is excluded from gross income only if the prior deduction did not reduce the taxpayer's federal income tax. Since federal income taxes are not deductible, the refund of them is not included in income. Because the state taxes did not reduce federal income taxes (since Clark cannot itemize when he uses Form 1040EZ to report his previous-year income), their refund is not included in income. The interest earned on the state tax refund is, however, included in gross income under Sec. 61.
Answer (B) is incorrect. The state income taxes did not reduce the federal income taxes. The $10 interest is taxable interest income. Answer (C) is incorrect. The state income taxes did not reduce the federal income taxes. Answer (D) is incorrect. Federal income taxes were not deductible, and the state income taxes did not reduce the federal income taxes.

1.1.15. Roger b, age 19, is a full-time student at Marshall College and a candidate for a bachelor's degree. His tuition and fees are $4,000 per year. During the current year, he received the following payments:

State scholarship for 10 months	$3,600
Loan from college financial aid office	1,500
Cash support from parents	3,000
Cash dividends on investments	700
Cash prize awarded in newspaper contest	500
	$9,300

What is Burrow's gross income for the current year?

A. $1,100
B. $1,200
C. $4,800
D. $9,300

Answer (B) is correct. *(CPA, adapted)*
REQUIRED: The taxpayer's gross income for the current year.
DISCUSSION: Gross income includes all income from whatever source derived unless specifically excluded. Section 117 excludes, to the extent of actual tuition and fees, amounts received as a scholarship from a government or other qualified organization. Therefore, the $3,600 state scholarship is excluded from gross income. The $1,500 loan is not considered income as long as there is a bona fide obligation to repay it. The cash support from the parents of $3,000 is a gift that is excluded from gross income under Sec. 102(a). The $700 of dividends should be included in gross income in full. The cash prize of $500 is specifically included by Sec. 74. The taxpayer's total gross income is $1,200 ($700 dividends + $500 prize).
Answer (A) is incorrect. A $100 dividend exclusion is no longer available for individual taxpayers. Answer (C) is incorrect. The state scholarship money is not considered gross income since the outlays for tuition and fees exceeded the amount received. Answer (D) is incorrect. The state scholarship money, the loan, and the cash support from the parents are not considered gross income.

1.1.16. Morbid was always interested in making a "fast buck." When Morbid's father was very ill and unlikely to live very much longer, Morbid purchased an existing life insurance policy on his father's life from a brother who acquired the policy several years ago and was not aware of the serious illness. Morbid paid $10,000 for the policy and received $20,000 in proceeds shortly thereafter when his father died. Under his father's will, all of his property was bequeathed to Morbid's mother, except that the income earned from the property during the administration of the estate was bequeathed to Morbid. The estate had $15,000 of income, which was distributed to Morbid in the same year as the insurance proceeds. How much must Morbid include in his income for the year?

A. $0
B. $10,000
C. $15,000
D. $25,000

Answer (D) is correct. *(Publisher, adapted)*
REQUIRED: The amount of gross income from the life insurance proceeds and the inheritance of income.
DISCUSSION: Although life insurance proceeds payable by reason of death are generally excluded under Sec. 101(a), when a life insurance policy has been assigned for valuable consideration, the amount excluded by the assignee may not exceed the amount paid for the policy. Therefore, $10,000 from the life insurance policy ($20,000 proceeds – $10,000 purchase price) must be included in Morbid's gross income.
Property received by gift or inheritance is generally excluded from gross income under Sec. 102(a). However, the income from such property is not excluded, and Sec. 102(b) requires a gift or inheritance of income from property to be included in gross income. Morbid must include $25,000 in gross income ($10,000 life insurance proceeds + $15,000 inheritance of income).
Answer (A) is incorrect. Income from bequeathed property and insurance proceeds in excess of the price paid for the insurance policy must be included in gross income. Answer (B) is incorrect. Gross income also includes the income earned from bequeathed property. Answer (C) is incorrect. Gross income also includes insurance proceeds in excess of the amount paid to acquire the policy from another person.

1.1.17. Wheeler purchased two parcels of real property for $10,000 each in Year 1 and held the property for investment. These properties appreciated in value and were reassessed for property tax purposes at $15,000 each in Year 2. In Year 3, Wheeler sold one parcel for $20,000 to Dealer and, in a taxable exchange, traded the other parcel for a lot on an island in Maine on which he planned to build his vacation home, which was worth $22,000. Which of the following is a true statement of the amount and time when Wheeler recognized income from the property transactions?

A. $10,000 in Year 3 only.

B. $22,000 in Year 3 only.

C. $10,000 in Year 2 and $12,000 in Year 3.

D. $10,000 in Year 2 and $5,000 in Year 3.

Answer (B) is correct. *(Publisher, adapted)*
REQUIRED: The amount and time of recognition of income from transactions in property.
DISCUSSION: Income is realized when there is a transaction, event, or occurrence which is sufficient to give rise to an economic benefit. It does not include mere appreciation in value. For property, there generally must be a sale or exchange for there to be realization. Therefore, Wheeler realized income in Year 3 when the properties were sold and exchanged. The gain realized that must be recognized is determined under Sec. 1001 as the sum of money received, plus the fair market value of other property received, less the adjusted basis in the property given up. On the first property, $10,000 was realized ($20,000 cash − $10,000 basis). On the second property, $12,000 was realized ($22,000 fair market value received − $10,000 basis), for a total of $22,000.
Answer (A) is incorrect. A $12,000 gain on the exchange of land for the vacation home must also be recognized in Year 3. Answer (C) is incorrect. The $10,000 is not recognized until Year 3 when the sale of the land occurs. Answer (D) is incorrect. The $10,000 gain is not recognized until Year 3 when the land is sold. A $12,000 gain on the exchange of the land for the vacation home is also recognized in Year 3. Appreciation in value for each parcel of land at the end of Year 2 is $5,000; it is not recognized until a sale or exchange occurs.

1.1.18. Optimistic borrowed $20,000 to buy a machine for his printing business. Shortly thereafter, the economy went into a deep recession, and Optimistic was not able to repay the debt, although he was not insolvent. In the current year, the creditor reduced the debt by $10,000 so Optimistic could afford to pay it. The creditor was not the seller of the machine. As a result of this reduction of debt,

A. The purchase price of the machine is adjusted to reduce Optimistic's basis in the machine.

B. Optimistic has $10,000 of income.

C. The debt is a qualified business indebtedness and the basis of the machine must be reduced.

D. Any tax effect from the reduction of the debt is deferred until final payment by Optimistic.

Answer (B) is correct. *(Publisher, adapted)*
REQUIRED: The tax effect of a reduction of a debt from the purchase of business property.
DISCUSSION: The cancelation of indebtedness is included in gross income under Sec. 61(a)(12). Under Sec. 108, the discharge of indebtedness is excluded from gross income if the debtor is insolvent, in bankruptcy reorganizations, a farmer, or a taxpayer other than a C corporation that has invested in real property. The canceled debt can also be excluded if it relates to a purchase-money debt reduction. Since none of these apply, the $10,000 reduction of debt is included in Optimistic's income.
Answer (A) is incorrect. A reduction of purchase-money debt is treated as a purchase price adjustment only if the creditor is the seller of the property. Answer (C) is incorrect. The reduction of basis for qualified business indebtedness is not available after 1986. Answer (D) is incorrect. The discharge of indebtedness causes immediate recognition of income by a solvent taxpayer who is not a farmer or a taxpayer other than a C corporation that has invested in real property.

1.1.19. Shifty borrowed $10,000 from Easy. When Easy tried to collect the debt, she discovered that Shifty had moved to another state. Easy tracked Shifty down and demanded payment. Knowing it would cost Easy a substantial amount of time and money to collect the debt, Shifty offered to pay $5,000 on the condition that Easy cancel the remainder of the debt. Easy agreed to accept the $5,000 and cancel the remaining $5,000 of the debt. Which of the following statements is true?

A. Shifty has $5,000 of income when Easy cancels the debt.

B. Easy has $5,000 of income upon collection of half of the debt.

C. Shifty had $10,000 of income upon obtaining the loan.

D. Neither Shifty nor Easy has any income from this transaction.

Answer (A) is correct. *(Publisher, adapted)*
REQUIRED: The true statement of income recognized from a loan and settlement of the debt at a lesser amount.
DISCUSSION: Under Sec. 61(a)(12), gross income includes income from the discharge of indebtedness. When Easy canceled the remainder of the debt, Shifty was relieved of an obligation and must recognize $5,000 of income.
Answer (B) is incorrect. The receipt of payment on a debt is merely the return of capital, not income. Answer (C) is incorrect. The receipt of a loan is not income since there is an obligation to repay it. Answer (D) is incorrect. Shifty must recognize $5,000 of income from the cancelation of indebtedness.

1.1.20. The forgiveness of a student loan may not be excluded from gross income if the discharge comes from which of the following?

    A. A federal government agency.

    B. A tax-exempt organization.

    C. An educational organization under a government-sponsored program.

    D. A private lending institution.

Answer (D) is correct. *(Publisher, adapted)*
    REQUIRED: The organization(s) from which the forgiveness of a student loan may not be excluded from gross income.
    DISCUSSION: Section 108(f) identifies the organizations from which the forgiveness of a student loan may be excluded from gross income. Prior to the Taxpayer Relief Act of 1997, only the forgiveness of loans from governmental agencies and educational organizations under a government-sponsored program could be excluded from gross income. However, the 1997 act expanded Sec. 108(f) to include tax-exempt charitable organizations.
    Answer (A) is incorrect. A federal government agency meets the requirements prescribed in Sec. 108(f). Answer (B) is incorrect. A tax-exempt organization meets the requirements prescribed in Sec. 108(f). Answer (C) is incorrect. An educational organization under a government-sponsored program meets the requirements prescribed in Sec. 108(f).

1.1.21. Sally, a calendar-year, cash-basis taxpayer, operates a used furniture business in a building she owns. At the end of the current year, her basis in the building is $175,000, and the difference between the building's $100,000 value and the $150,000 mortgage reflects countrywide declining real property values. Because Sally's ability to make full payments on the mortgage that was taken out 2 years ago has decreased with demand for her inventory, the lender reduced the principal amount of the mortgage to $120,000 at year end. Which of the following statements is most accurate regarding the mortgage principal adjustment?

    A. The $30,000 adjustment is not includible in gross income for the current year.

    B. Sally must report $30,000 of gross income on her current-year tax return.

    C. Sally must reduce the property's basis on the first day of her next tax year.

    D. Sally must either report $30,000 of gross income for the current year or reduce the property's basis next year.

Answer (D) is correct. *(Publisher, adapted)*
    REQUIRED: The true statement regarding discharged debt on a building used in the taxpayer's trade or business.
    DISCUSSION: Discharge of debt is gross income [Sec. 61(a)(12)]. Sally is not insolvent, so the debt discharged is not excluded under Sec. 108(a)(1)(B). However, under Sec. 108(a)(1)(D), a taxpayer may elect to exclude discharged debt incurred or assumed in connection with the purchase of real property used in a trade or business. The discharged debt may be excluded to the extent the taxpayer reduces his or her basis in the property. The basis reduction is limited to the lesser of (1) the adjusted basis of real estate held by the taxpayer or (2) the excess of the debt principal before discharge over the fair market value of the property that secures the debt. Thus, Sally must either report gross income or reduce the property's basis in the amount of $30,000. Basis reduction is made at the beginning of the year following discharge.
    Answer (A) is incorrect. Sally may elect to report gross income of $30,000. Answer (B) is incorrect. Sally may elect, in lieu of reporting gross income of $30,000, to reduce the basis in the qualified real property. Answer (C) is incorrect. Debt discharged constitutes gross income unless the basis reduction election is made [Sec. 61(a)(12)].

1.1.22. Photo Gray worked as an employee in a camera store and made $15,000 each year. Photo also had a one-third interest in a calendar-year partnership. The partnership had $9,000 of ordinary income for the year, none of which was distributed to the partners. Photo was also one of two beneficiaries of a simple trust set up by her rich uncle. The trust earned $4,000 of income, and it was all distributed to Photo during the year. Photo's gross income for the year is

    A. $15,000

    B. $18,000

    C. $19,000

    D. $22,000

Answer (D) is correct. *(Publisher, adapted)*
    REQUIRED: The employee's gross income from salary, a partnership, and a trust.
    DISCUSSION: An employee's salary is fully included in gross income under Sec. 61(a)(1). A partner's share of partnership income is included in the partner's gross income, whether distributed or not, under Sec. 702(a). The beneficiary of a trust is also required to include the total amount distributed from the trust to the extent of the trust's income. It does not matter that there was another beneficiary since all the income was distributed to Photo. Therefore, Photo must include $22,000 in gross income ($15,000 salary + $3,000 share of partnership income + $4,000 trust income).
    Answer (A) is incorrect. Gross income includes a partner's share of ordinary income and income distributed by a trust. Answer (B) is incorrect. Gross income includes income distributed by a trust. Answer (C) is incorrect. Gross income includes the wages, trust income, and the partner's share of the partnership's ordinary income.

1.1.23. In Year 3, the Rox Company has gross income of $185,000, a bad debt deduction of $7,000, and other allowable deductions of $181,000. Rox carried back the Year 3 NOL of $3,000 to Year 1, and it was used in full to lower Rox's tax for Year 1. In Year 4, Rox recovered $5,000 of the bad debt deducted in Year 3. What is the amount of the bad debt recovery that Rox should include in income for Year 4?

A. $0

B. $1,000

C. $4,000

D. $5,000

Answer (D) is correct. *(SEE, adapted)*
REQUIRED: The amount of bad debt recovery that must be included in gross income.
DISCUSSION: The recovery of an amount previously deducted as a bad debt is included in gross income to the extent that the prior deduction reduced taxes (Sec. 111). Since the prior deduction reduced taxable income by $7,000, the full amount of the $5,000 recovery is included in gross income.
Answer (A) is incorrect. Bad debt recovery must be included in Rox Company's gross income. Answer (B) is incorrect. Only the recovered amount allocated to Year 1 (not the correct amount of the bad debt recovery included in gross income) is $1,000. Answer (C) is incorrect. Only the amount allocated to Year 3 (not the correct amount of the bad debt recovery included in gross income) is $4,000.

1.1.24. A scholarship received by a student that represents compensation for his or her past, present, or future services is includible in gross income.

A. True.

B. False.

Answer (A) is correct. *(SEE, adapted)*
DISCUSSION: Although Sec. 117 excludes from gross income amounts received as qualified scholarships to be used for tuition and related expenses, this exclusion does not apply to any amount received that represents compensation for past, present, or future services [Sec. 117(c)].

1.1.25. Medical expenses recovered after being claimed as a deduction in the previous year must be included in your income in the year of recovery to the extent that the deductions decreased the federal income taxes paid in the year they were deducted.

A. True.

B. False.

Answer (A) is correct. *(SEE, adapted)*
DISCUSSION: If a taxpayer obtains a deduction for an item in one year that reduces taxes and later recovers all or a portion of the prior deduction, the recovery is included in gross income in the year it is received [Sec. 111 and Reg. 1.213-1(g)]. Note that to the extent the expense did not reduce federal income taxes in the earlier year, the recovery is excluded from income.

1.1.26. Dr. Y, a cash-basis taxpayer, received a check for $250 after banking hours on December 31 of the current year from a patient. Since Dr. Y could not deposit the check in his business checking account until January 3 of the next year, the fee of $250 is not included in his current-year income.

A. True.

B. False.

Answer (B) is correct. *(SEE, adapted)*
DISCUSSION: A check is the equivalent of cash; therefore, a cash-basis taxpayer must report income received in the form of a check in the year in which the check is received. The ability to cash or deposit the check is not relevant unless the check is known to be worthless.

1.1.27. You must include in income, at the time received, the fair market value of property or services you receive in bartering.

A. True.

B. False.

Answer (A) is correct. *(SEE, adapted)*
DISCUSSION: Bartering involves the sale or exchange of property or services (but not for cash). Regulation 1.61-2(d)(1) provides that, if services are paid for with property, the fair market value of the property must be included in income as compensation. If services are paid for by exchanging other services, the fair market value of such other services must be included in income as compensation. If property or services are received in exchange for other property, the taxpayer must compute gain or loss as if the property had been sold.

1.1.28. Compensation for personal injury or illness is taxable.

A. True.

B. False.

Answer (B) is correct. *(SEE, adapted)*
DISCUSSION: Compensation for personal injury or illness is paid to replace the personal capital destroyed. Section 104(a)(2) specifically excludes such compensation from income. However, the exclusion does not apply to any punitive damages.

1.2 Income from Employment

1.2.1. For the current year, Dan's employer paid the following:

Premium on $30,000 of nondiscriminatory group-term life insurance of which Dan's wife was the sole beneficiary	$ 400
Premiums on $30,000 nondiscriminatory ordinary life insurance of which Dan's wife was the sole beneficiary	800
Rental of car used by Dan for commuting to and from work	1,500

In addition, the union to which Dan belonged went on strike and Dan received $1,000 of strike benefits from the union. What amount must Dan include in gross income for the current year?

  A. $1,200

  B. $1,500

  C. $3,300

  D. $3,700

Answer (C) is correct. *(SEE, adapted)*
  REQUIRED: The amount of fringe benefits and union strike benefits includible in gross income for the current year.
  DISCUSSION: Fringe benefits received from an employer must be included in the employee's gross income unless specifically excluded. Section 79 specifically excludes premiums paid by an employer for up to $50,000 of nondiscriminatory group-term life insurance for each employee. However, the $800 of premiums on the ordinary life insurance must be included in Dan's income. The cost of commuting to and from work is considered a personal expense, so the car rental must be included in gross income. Strike benefits are also included in gross income unless considered to be a gift and excluded under Sec. 102.

Ordinary life insurance premiums	$ 800
Car rental	1,500
Strike benefits	1,000
Gross income	$3,300

  Answer (A) is incorrect. The premium on the group-term life insurance should not be included in gross income. Instead, the car rental cost and strike benefits should be included in gross income. Answer (B) is incorrect. Gross income should also include the premiums on the ordinary life insurance and the strike benefits. Answer (D) is incorrect. The premiums on the group-term life insurance should not be included in gross income.

1.2.2. All of the following income items are includible in an employee's gross income except

  A. Severance pay for cancelation of employment.

  B. Vacation allowance.

  C. Payments from employer while sick or injured.

  D. Medical insurance premium paid by employer for employee and spouse.

Answer (D) is correct. *(Publisher, adapted)*
  REQUIRED: The item that is not includible in an employee's gross income.
  DISCUSSION: Gross income includes all income from whatever source derived unless specifically excluded. Section 106 excludes contributions by an employer to accident or health plans for employees. Regulation 1.106-1 extends the exclusion to contributions for the employee's spouse or dependents.
  Answer (A) is incorrect. No provision excludes severance pay for cancelation of employment from gross income. Answer (B) is incorrect. No provision excludes vacation allowance from gross income. Answer (C) is incorrect. No provision excludes payments from employer while sick or injured from gross income.

1.2.3. Bill Walden received a $2,100 grant from his employer and, as required by his employer, used all of the money for tuition and fees to take three graduate-school courses during the period September 1 to December 31 of the current year. Walden is not a candidate for a degree and has never received a scholarship or fellowship grant before. He had previously met the minimum educational requirements for his employment position; however, due to new requirements established by his employer, these courses were necessary for him to retain his job. In computing his current-year taxable income, Walden should include

  A. Gross income of $2,100 and an education expense deduction of $2,100.

  B. Gross income of $2,100 and no education expense deduction.

  C. No gross income and no education expense deduction.

  D. Gross income of $0 and an education expense of $2,100.

Answer (A) is correct. *(CPA, adapted)*
  REQUIRED: The proper treatment of an educational grant from an employer used for courses to retain a job.
  DISCUSSION: The grant was received from an employer by reason of employment and therefore is included in income as compensation for services. It does not qualify for exclusion under Sec. 117 as a scholarship or fellowship. The educational assistance plan must be nondiscriminatory, and the benefits cannot exceed $5,250 for the tax year. Graduate-level courses are eligible for the exclusion.
  Answer (B) is incorrect. The education expense is deductible. Answer (C) is incorrect. The $2,100 payment is not excludable from gross income. Qualified education expenses are deductible. Answer (D) is incorrect. The $2,100 payment must be recognized in gross income.

1.2.4. Corporation X made the following payments to or on behalf of Mr. B, a cash-basis taxpayer:

Note received in lieu of bonus (fair market value $3,000, no payments received on note in current year)	$5,000
Advance commissions for services to be performed in the future	600
Ham received at Christmas party	20
Sick pay due to illness paid directly by Corporation X	1,000
Group-term life insurance premium paid by Corporation X on nondiscriminatory insurance coverage of $50,000	100

What amount should Mr. B report as income?

   A. $4,600

   B. $4,620

   C. $4,720

   D. $6,720

Answer (A) is correct. *(SEE, adapted)*
   REQUIRED: The amount received from an employer that an employee must include in gross income.
   DISCUSSION: Section 61(a)(1) specifically provides that compensation for services is to be included in gross income. Due to the relationship between an employee and an employer, almost everything received by the employee from the employer is included in gross income as compensation. As a cash-basis taxpayer, Mr. B must include the fair market value of the note in gross income in the current year. When the note is subsequently paid, an additional $2,000 will be included ($5,000 – $3,000). The advance commissions of $600 are also included in gross income regardless of when the services are to be performed. Sick pay is included in gross income as part of the employee's compensation for not working when sick. These three amounts total $4,600 and should be reported by Mr. B as income.
   The ham worth $20 is not included in gross income under Sec. 132(a)(4), which excludes de minimis fringe benefits. Under Sec. 79, the cost of up to $50,000 of nondiscriminatory group-term life insurance coverage paid by an employer on behalf of employees is not included in the employees' gross incomes.
   Exception: Notes received only as evidence of the obligation to pay compensation are not income to cash-basis taxpayers.
   Answer (B) is incorrect. The cost of the ham is a de minimis fringe benefit, which should not be included in gross income. Answer (C) is incorrect. The cost of the ham and the premiums on up to $50,000 of group-term life insurance are not considered gross income. Answer (D) is incorrect. The note should be included in gross income at its fair market value, and the cost of the ham and the premiums on up to $50,000 of group-term life insurance should not be included in gross income.

1.2.5. During the current year, Hal Leff sustained a serious injury in the course of his employment. As a result of this injury, Hal received the following payments during the year:

Workers' compensation	$2,400
Reimbursement from his employer's accident and health plan for medical expenses paid by Hal and not deducted by him	1,800
Damages for personal injuries	8,000

The amount to be included in Hal's gross income for the current year should be

   A. $12,200

   B. $8,000

   C. $1,800

   D. $0

Answer (D) is correct. *(CPA, adapted)*
   REQUIRED: The amount of gross income from the payments received as a result of the injury.
   DISCUSSION: Section 104(a) excludes from gross income compensation for personal injuries and sickness whether received as workers' compensation benefits, accident or health insurance benefits, or damages received by suit or agreement. Therefore, none of the payments should be included by Hal in gross income. Note that Sec. 104(a) includes in gross income punitive damages received, whether as a result of physical injury or not.
   Answer (A) is incorrect. The total amount of payments Hal received during the year as a result of his injury is $12,200, and it is excluded from gross income. Answer (B) is incorrect. The amount of $8,000 is damages Hal received for personal injuries, and it is excluded from gross income. Answer (C) is incorrect. The amount of $1,800 is reimbursement from Hal's employer's accident and health plan for medical expenses paid by Hal and not deducted by him. This amount is excluded from Hal's gross income.

1.2.6. Roberta Warner and Sally Roger formed the Acme Corporation in the current year. On the same date that Roberta and Sally purchased Acme stock, Warner paid $75,000 cash to Acme for 750 shares of its common stock. Simultaneously, Roger received 100 shares of Acme's common stock for services rendered as an employee. How much should Roger include as taxable income for the current year, and what will be the basis of her stock?

	Taxable Income	Basis of Stock
A.	$0	$0
B.	$0	$10,000
C.	$10,000	$0
D.	$10,000	$10,000

Answer (D) is correct. *(CPA, adapted)*
   REQUIRED: The amount of taxable income and the basis of stock received in exchange for services rendered.
   DISCUSSION: Section 83 provides that, if property is received in exchange for the performance of services, the excess of the fair market value of such property over the amount paid for such property is included in gross income. Since Roger did not pay anything for the stock, the fair market value of the stock ($10,000) is included in her gross income as payment for her services. The basis of property is its "tax cost basis," the amount paid for the property ($0) increased by the amount that was included in income ($10,000) [Reg. 1.61-2(d)(2)]. Therefore, Roger's basis in the stock is her tax cost of $10,000.
   Answer (A) is incorrect. The stock is recognized as income, and this recognition increases basis. Answer (B) is incorrect. The stock is recognized in income. Answer (C) is incorrect. The basis is increased by the amount included in income.

1.2.7. In Year 1, Alex Burg, a cash-basis taxpayer, earned an annual salary of $80,000 at Ace Corporation but elected to take only $50,000. Ace, which was financially able to pay Burg's full salary, credited the unpaid balance of $30,000 to Burg's account on the corporate books in Year 1 and actually paid this $30,000 to Burg in Year 2. How much of the salary is taxable to Burg in Year 1?

    A. $50,000

    B. $60,000

    C. $65,000

    D. $80,000

Answer (D) is correct. *(CPA, adapted)*
    REQUIRED: The amount of salary from an employer that an employee must include in gross income when received over 2 years.
    DISCUSSION: Section 61(a)(1) specifically provides that compensation for services is to be included in gross income. Here, Burg must report the full $80,000 in Year 1 because it was his and not the employer's choice to receive only a portion of it in Year 1. The $30,000 that was not actually received until Year 2 is considered to have been constructively received in Year 1. Under the general rule of Sec. 451(a) and Reg. 1.451-1(a), a taxpayer using the cash method of accounting includes an item in gross income when it is actually or constructively received.
    Answer (A) is incorrect. The amount of salary that Burg elected to take is $50,000, but it is not the amount of salary taxable to him in Year 1. Answer (B) is incorrect. Only the amount of salary that Burg elected to take in Year 1 plus 1/3 of the Year 2 payment [($30,000 ÷ 12 months) × 4 months (Jan. - Apr.)] constructively received in Year 1 (not the correct amount of salary taxable to Burg in Year 1) is $60,000. Answer (C) is incorrect. Only the amount of salary that Burg elected to take in Year 1 plus 1/2 of the Year 2 payment constructively received in Year 1 (not the correct amount of salary taxable to Burg in Year 1) is $65,000.

1.2.8. An ordained minister cannot exclude the following from gross income:

    A. Rental allowance.

    B. Fees for marriages, baptisms, and funerals.

    C. Fair rental value of parsonage.

    D. Actual cost to provide a home.

Answer (B) is correct. *(SEE, adapted)*
    REQUIRED: The income an ordained minister cannot exclude.
    DISCUSSION: Under Sec. 61, salaries and fees for personal services are always included in gross income. A minister should include his salary; the offerings given directly to him for marriages, baptisms, funerals, etc.; and the other outside earnings donated by him to the organization in his gross income. Regulation 1.107-1 excludes from gross income the rental value of a home, or a rental allowance to the extent it is used to rent or provide a home, furnished to a minister as a part of his or her compensation. A minister is entitled to deduct mortgage interest and real property taxes paid on a personal residence even if the amounts are derived from an allowance that is excluded from gross income.
    Answer (A) is incorrect. Rental allowance is specifically excluded under Reg. 1.107-1. Answer (C) is incorrect. The fair rental value of parsonage is specifically excluded under Reg. 1.107-1. Answer (D) is incorrect. The actual cost to provide a home is specifically excluded under Reg. 1.107-1.

1.2.9. Mr. A works as an employee for Never Peel Painting Company. While on vacation, Mr. A painted the residence of his dentist in exchange for dental services having a fair market value of $1,500. His dentist provided all of the paint and supplies. For income tax purposes, Mr. A has

    A. No income or expense.

    B. $1,500 in wages and $1,500 in medical expenses.

    C. $1,500 in self-employment income and $0 in medical expense.

    D. $1,500 in self-employment income and $1,500 in medical expense.

Answer (D) is correct. *(SEE, adapted)*
    REQUIRED: The income and expense due to an exchange of services.
    DISCUSSION: Regulation 1.61-2(d)(1) provides that, if services are paid for with other services, the fair market value of such other services must be included in income as compensation. Since Mr. A provided services and received dental services with a fair market value of $1,500, he must include that amount in his income.
    At the same time, Mr. A is treated as having paid $1,500 for the dental services. Dental services are medical expenses generally deductible subject to certain limits.
    Answer (A) is incorrect. Mr. A does have income and expenses from these transactions. Answer (B) is incorrect. The amount of $1,500 is self-employment income (not wages). Answer (C) is incorrect. Mr. A has medical expenses.

1.2.10. Carl Slater was the sole proprietor of a drug store that he owned for 25 years before he sold it to Statewide Drug Stores, Inc., in the current year. Besides the $800,000 selling price for the store's tangible assets and goodwill, Slater received a lump sum of $60,000 in the current year for his agreement not to operate a competing enterprise within 10 miles of the store's location for a period of 6 years. How will the $60,000 be taxed to Slater?

A. As $60,000 ordinary income in the current year.

B. As ordinary income of $10,000 a year for 6 years.

C. As part of the gain on the sale of the store.

D. It is excluded since it was not for the performance of services.

Answer (A) is correct. *(CPA, adapted)*
REQUIRED: The tax treatment of an amount received for a covenant not to compete.
DISCUSSION: The taxpayer received the $60,000 as compensation for agreeing not to enter into an income producing activity. Since this payment replaces what would otherwise be ordinary income, the $60,000 is treated as ordinary income in the year received under Sec. 61. Income received in advance is included in gross income when received.
Answer (B) is incorrect. Income received in advance is included in gross income when received. Answer (C) is incorrect. The payment replaces what would be income. Answer (D) is incorrect. The payment is included in income, even though it was not for the performance of services.

1.2.11. Dr. Chester is a cash-basis taxpayer. His office visit charges are usually paid on the date of visit or within 1 month. However, services rendered outside the office are billed to insurance companies weekly and are usually paid within 2 months. Information relating to the current year is as follows:

Cash received at the time of office visits	$ 35,000
Collections on accounts receivable	130,000
Accounts receivable, January 1	16,000
Accounts receivable, December 31	20,000

Dr. Chester's gross income from his medical practice for the current year is

A. $165,000

B. $169,000

C. $181,000

D. $185,000

Answer (A) is correct. *(CPA, adapted)*
REQUIRED: The amount of gross income from the medical practice of a cash-basis taxpayer.
DISCUSSION: Since Dr. Chester is a cash-basis taxpayer, income is recognized at the time cash is actually or constructively received, whichever is earlier. Dr. Chester's current-year income consists of the $35,000 received at the time of office visits plus the $130,000 collected on accounts receivable, for a total of $165,000.
Since Dr. Chester is not an accrual-basis taxpayer, the amount of accounts receivable at the beginning and end of the year do not affect his gross income.
Answer (B) is incorrect. Only the cash received in the current year is included in income. Answer (C) is incorrect. The amount of cash that Dr. Chester received during the current year is less than $181,000. Answer (D) is incorrect. The amount of cash that Dr. Chester received during the current year is less than $185,000.

1.2.12. M, an accrual-method taxpayer using the calendar year, had the following transactions during the current year:

Recovery of an account receivable written off in a prior year but that did not reduce his taxes	$ 5,000
Sales to a customer who is directed to transmit the payment to M's brother	3,500
Amounts received in settlement of a breach of contract suit	22,500

What amount must M include in gross income in the current year?

A. $8,500

B. $26,000

C. $27,500

D. $31,000

Answer (B) is correct. *(SEE, adapted)*
REQUIRED: The amount the taxpayer must include in gross income in the current year.
DISCUSSION: Since the taxpayer's tax was not reduced in the year the account receivable was written off, no income is recognized upon the recovery of the receivable (Sec. 111). The taxpayer must include in his or her gross income the $3,500 from the sale to the customer since income cannot be avoided by assigning the right to collection of the income to another. The amounts received in the settlement of the breach of contract suit represent lost income, so the $22,500 must be included in gross income. Therefore, the taxpayer must include $26,000 ($3,500 sale to customer + $22,500 settlement) in gross income.
Answer (A) is incorrect. Recovery of a write-off made in a prior year that did not reduce taxes is not gross income. However, amounts received from a settlement are included in gross income. Answer (C) is incorrect. Recovery of a write-off made in a prior year that did not reduce taxes is not gross income. However, sales with an assignment of the collection amount are included in gross income. Answer (D) is incorrect. Recovery of a write-off made in a prior year that did not reduce taxes is not gross income.

1.2.13. On January 1 of Year 1, Corporation Y, a cash-basis taxpayer, entered into a contract to pay Mr. A, a cash-basis taxpayer, for his services to be rendered in Year 1. Mr. A is to receive 200 shares of Y's common stock: 100 shares on July 1, Year 1, and 100 shares on February 1, Year 2. The fair market value of the stock on the relevant dates is

January 1, Year 1	$50 per share
July 1, Year 1	$75 per share
February 1, Year 2	$40 per share

Mr. A must report $15,000 as compensation from Corporation Y in Year 1.

  A. True.

  B. False.

Answer (B) is correct. *(SEE, adapted)*
  DISCUSSION: If property is received in connection with the performance of services, the fair market value of such property (at the time of inclusion in income) is included in the taxpayer's gross income under Sec. 83. Since Mr. A is a cash-basis taxpayer, the compensation is included in gross income when actually or constructively received (as long as it is not subject to a substantial risk of forfeiture under Sec. 83). Mr. A must include the fair market value of the shares received in Year 1 in his Year 1 gross income at the July 1 value (100 shares × $75 = $7,500). In Year 2, he must include the fair market value of the shares received in Year 2 at the February 1 value (100 shares × $40 = $4,000).

1.2.14. Highly compensated persons must include in their income excess reimbursements from a self-insured medical reimbursement plan that discriminates in favor of highly compensated persons. These excess reimbursements must be included in the taxpayer's income in the tax year in which the plan year ends, regardless of when they are received.

  A. True.

  B. False.

Answer (A) is correct. *(SEE, adapted)*
  DISCUSSION: The Sec. 105 exclusion for medical expense reimbursements from an employer does not apply to discriminatory amounts paid to a highly compensated individual under a self-insured medical reimbursement plan that discriminates in favor of highly compensated persons. These excess reimbursements are included in the taxpayer's income in the tax year in which the plan year ends.

1.2.15. In the current year, Mr. L, a cash-basis attorney, provided services for Corporation M. In return he received 1% of M's common stock, which had a fair market value of $4,000. Mr. L must report this $4,000 as income on his current-year tax return.

  A. True.

  B. False.

Answer (A) is correct. *(SEE, adapted)*
  DISCUSSION: Compensation for services is gross income under Sec. 61. If services are paid for with property, the fair market value of the property taken in payment must be included in gross income as compensation (Sec. 83).

1.2.16. Abe set up the accounting system for John's construction business. They agree that John will furnish material and build a shed in Abe's yard in exchange for the service. Abe usually charges $500 for this type of service and that seems fair to John. Abe must include $500 in his gross income for this transaction.

  A. True.

  B. False.

Answer (A) is correct. *(SEE, adapted)*
  DISCUSSION: Bartering involves the sale or exchange of property or services (but not for cash). Regulation 1.61-2(d)(1) provides that, if services are paid for with property or by exchanging other services, the fair market value of such property or services must be included in gross income as compensation.

1.3 Interest Income

1.3.1. All of the following are taxable interest income except

  A. Interest on a federal tax refund.

  B. Interest on an IRA before its withdrawal.

  C. Interest on GI insurance dividends.

  D. Interest on U.S. Treasury bills.

Answer (B) is correct. *(SEE, adapted)*
  REQUIRED: The type of interest income that is excluded from gross income.
  DISCUSSION: Interest income is included in gross income under Sec. 61 unless specifically excluded in another section. Section 408 provides in most cases that individual retirement accounts (IRAs) are taxed to the owner only on distribution.
  Answer (A) is incorrect. Taxable interest income includes interest on a federal tax refund. Answer (C) is incorrect. There is no exclusion for interest on U.S. government obligations derived from GI insurance. Answer (D) is incorrect. Taxable interest income includes interest on U.S. Treasury bills.

1.3.2. During the current year, Clark received the following interest income:

On Veterans Administration insurance dividends left on deposit with the VA	$20
On state income tax refund	30

What amount should Clark include for interest income in his current-year return?

   A. $50

   B. $30

   C. $20

   D. $0

Answer (B) is correct. *(CPA, adapted)*
REQUIRED: The amount of interest income the taxpayer should include on his current-year tax return.
DISCUSSION: Interest income is included in gross income under Sec. 61 unless specifically excluded in another section. Although Sec. 103 provides an exclusion for interest on certain obligations of states and municipalities, it does not apply to interest on state income tax refunds. Therefore, the interest on the state income tax refund is included in Clark's gross income. The interest on Veterans Administration insurance dividends left on deposit with the Veterans Administration is excluded from gross income (Rev. Rul. 91-14). Therefore, Clark should include only the state income tax refund interest ($30) in gross income on his current-year tax return.
Answer (A) is incorrect. The interest on VA insurance dividends is excluded from gross income; therefore, it can not be considered interest income. Answer (C) is incorrect. Interest on a state income tax refund, not interest on VA dividends, is considered interest income for tax purposes. Answer (D) is incorrect. Interest on state income tax refunds is considered interest income.

1.3.3. In the current year, Uriah Stone received the following interest payments:

Interest of $400 on refund of federal income tax for a previous year
Interest of $300 on award for personal injuries sustained in an automobile accident in a previous year
Interest of $1,500 on municipal bonds
Interest of $1,000 on United States savings bonds (Series HH)

What amount, if any, should Stone report as interest income on his current-year tax return?

   A. $0

   B. $700

   C. $1,700

   D. $3,200

Answer (C) is correct. *(CPA, adapted)*
REQUIRED: The amount the taxpayer should include as interest income on his current-year tax return.
DISCUSSION: Unless otherwise excluded in another section, Sec. 61 includes interest in gross income. Section 103 excludes from gross income interest on most obligations of states or political subdivisions of a state (e.g., municipal bonds). This exclusion does not apply to the obligations of the United States. Therefore, the taxpayer's interest income includes the $400 of interest on the refund of federal income taxes and the $1,000 of interest on the United States Series HH savings bonds, which is paid by check semiannually. Although an award for personal injuries is tax-exempt under Sec. 104, the interest income earned on the award is not tax-exempt. A total of $1,700 ($400 + $1,000 + $300) is included in gross income.
Answer (A) is incorrect. Stone has interest income and should report it on his current-year tax return. Answer (B) is incorrect. Interest income also includes interest on U.S. savings bonds (Series HH). Answer (D) is incorrect. Interest income does not include interest on municipal bonds.

1.3.4. From the items listed below, determine the interest income includible on Mr. F's tax return for the current year:

Received on deposits in a federal savings and loan association	$320
Received on share accounts in a credit union	125
Received on money market certificates at fixed intervals of 1 year or less	50
Toaster received for opening an account in a mutual savings bank	16
Increase in the value of prepaid premiums applied to the payment of premiums due on a life insurance policy	95

   A. $445

   B. $465

   C. $511

   D. $606

Answer (D) is correct. *(SEE, adapted)*
REQUIRED: The amount of interest income includible in the taxpayer's tax return for the current year.
DISCUSSION: Section 61 includes interest in gross income, whether received in cash or property, unless specifically excluded in another section. None of the items listed is excluded from income. A toaster received to open an account is equivalent to interest since it is paid to induce a deposit, i.e., a payment for the use of money by the bank. De minimis gifts with a fair market value of $10 or less are not included in income. The increase in value of prepaid premiums is due to interest on the prepayments. It is taxable even though not directly received, since Mr. F has the benefit of it. Therefore, all of the items listed are includible interest income and total $606.
Answer (A) is incorrect. Interest income includes the value of a toaster received for opening an account, interest received on money market certificates, and the increase in value of prepaid premiums. Answer (B) is incorrect. Interest income also includes interest received on share accounts and the value of a toaster received for opening an account. Answer (C) is incorrect. Interest income also includes the increase in value of prepaid premiums.

1.3.5. In the current year, Ms. Smith withdrew her funds from a time-savings account before maturity and was charged a penalty of $2,000 for early withdrawal. The interest earned on the account in the current year was $1,600. Ms. Smith had no other interest income. How should Ms. Smith report this transaction on her current-year individual income tax return?

A. Report $1,600 interest income; the $2,000 penalty is not deductible.

B. Report $1,600 interest income; deduct penalty of $2,000 as an adjustment to gross income to arrive at adjusted gross income.

C. Report $1,600 interest income; deduct penalty of $2,000 as an itemized deduction.

D. Report $1,600 interest income; deduct penalty of $1,600 as an adjustment to gross income to arrive at adjusted gross income.

Answer (B) is correct. *(SEE, adapted)*
REQUIRED: The correct way to report interest earned on a time savings account and the penalty for its early withdrawal.
DISCUSSION: Interest income earned must be reported in full. The $1,600 of interest must be included in gross income. The $2,000 interest penalty is a deduction for adjusted gross income under Sec. 62(a)(9).
Answer (A) is incorrect. The $2,000 penalty is deductible. Answer (C) is incorrect. The $2,000 penalty is not an itemized deduction. Answer (D) is incorrect. The full amount of the penalty is deductible; i.e., the deduction is not limited to the interest income.

1.3.6. All of the following are considered interest to be included in gross income:

(1) Dividends on share accounts in a mutual savings bank.
(2) Fair market value of gift received for opening an account with a savings institution.
(3) Interest received on obligations of a state.
(4) Interest charged at an illegal rate. State law does not require application of amount to principal.

A. True.

B. False.

Answer (B) is correct. *(SEE, adapted)*
DISCUSSION: Section 103 excludes from gross income interest on most obligations of states or any political subdivision of a state, so (3) would not be included in gross income. Dividends on share accounts in a mutual savings bank are considered interest, and gifts received for opening an account are also considered equivalent to interest since they are made to induce a deposit. Illegal income must also be included in gross income, and interest in excess of the legal rate is still interest.

1.3.7. At the end of the current year, Mr. B's bank credited his savings account with interest earned from October 1 through December 31. The bank posted this interest to Mr. B's passbook in the following year when he made a withdrawal. Mr. B, a calendar-year, cash-method taxpayer, must report this interest on his current-year income tax return.

A. True.

B. False.

Answer (A) is correct. *(SEE, adapted)*
DISCUSSION: A depositor in a bank is required to report interest income under the doctrine of "constructive receipt" when his or her account is credited with the interest by the bank. That is when the depositor is entitled to the interest. When the interest is posted to the depositor's passbook or when a withdrawal is made is irrelevant. Since the interest was credited to Mr. B in the current year, he is required to report it in the current year.

1.3.8. U.S. Treasury bills are issued at a discount. The difference between the issue price and the face value at maturity is taxable interest income to the holder reported when the bill is paid at maturity.

A. True.

B. False.

Answer (A) is correct. *(SEE, adapted)*
DISCUSSION: Section 454(b) provides that, for a U.S. obligation issued on a discount basis and payable without interest at a fixed maturity date not exceeding 1 year from the date of issue, the amount of discount shall not be considered to accrue until the obligation is paid at maturity, sold, or otherwise disposed of. U.S. Treasury bills generally are issued with a maturity date 1 year or less from the issue date.

1.3.9. In the current year, Mr. Black received a condemnation award from the state of Texas for land to be used as a state park. With the award, Mr. Black received interest of $4,000. The interest received on a condemnation award of a state is tax exempt interest.

A. True.

B. False.

Answer (B) is correct. *(SEE, adapted)*
DISCUSSION: Although Sec. 103 excludes from gross income interest received on obligations of a state, interest on such an obligation is not excluded if the obligation is not issued in registered form [Sec. 103(b)(3)]. Since the interest on the condemnation award is not interest on a state obligation issued in registered form, the interest is not excluded under Sec. 103.

1.3.10. Mr. D received a form 1099-INT from his local bank in the amount of $2,400 for the current taxable year. The state where the bank is located has placed limits on withdrawals because other banks in the state are insolvent. Mr. D was permitted to withdraw only $2,000 during the current year. Under these circumstances, Mr. D must exclude from gross income the entire $2,400 of interest income received from this bank on his current-year income tax return.

A. True.

B. False.

Answer (B) is correct. *(SEE, adapted)*
DISCUSSION: Interest credited on a frozen deposit in a qualified financial institution is includible in gross income only to the extent of the sum of net withdrawals made during the tax year and amounts that are in fact withdrawable at the close of the tax year [Sec. 451(g)]. If no withdrawals are allowed during the year, then the full amount of interest is excludable from gross income. A deposit is frozen if any part of it may not be withdrawn due to any requirement imposed by the state in which the institution is located because of insolvency of any financial institution in the state [Sec. 451(g)(4)(B)].

1.4 Income from Stocks and Bonds

NOTE: See Study Unit 2 for certain dividend and interest exclusions and Study Unit 17 for distributions to shareholders.

1.4.1. Mr. Z owned 200 shares of Corporation K common stock. During the current year, Mr. Z received distributions from Corporation K of $600 in cash dividends, 100 additional shares of K's common stock, and rights to purchase 100 more shares. The distributions were not disproportionate and the shareholders were not given an option to receive cash instead of the stock and stock rights. The fair market value of the total stock dividend shares and the total stock rights were $200 and $100, respectively. What is the amount of income from these distributions that is includible in Mr. Z's income for the current year?

A. $600

B. $700

C. $900

D. $1,000

Answer (A) is correct. *(SEE, adapted)*
REQUIRED: The amount of income a shareholder must report from dividends of cash, stock, and rights to purchase the stock.
DISCUSSION: The $600 in cash dividends are included in taxable income under the general rule of Sec. 61(a)(7). Cash dividends from taxable domestic corporations are included in income provided they are paid out of earnings and profits (which is assumed unless information is given otherwise in the question). However, under Sec. 305(a), gross income generally does not include a stock dividend. Rights to purchase stock are also treated as a stock dividend for this purpose. There are exceptions under Sec. 305(b), but the usual stock dividend paid on common stock falls within the general rule and is not included in the shareholder's income. Therefore, Mr. Z does not have to include any gross income from the stock dividend or distribution of stock rights.
Mr. Z's total taxable income from these distributions is the $600 of cash dividends. Note that, under Sec. 307(a), Mr. Z will be required to allocate some of the basis of his original shares of common stock to the shares of stock received as a dividend. A basis allocation may be needed to the stock rights received as distributions depending upon the relative value of the stock rights and the underlying stock.
Answer (B) is incorrect. The FMV of the stock rights should not be included in gross income. Answer (C) is incorrect. The FMV of stock dividends and stock rights should not be included in gross income. Answer (D) is incorrect. Gross income only includes the value of cash dividends.

1.4.2. Bob owned stock in a corporation that has a dividend reinvestment plan. Bob chose to participate in the plan and, during the current year, the corporation paid dividends. The plan allowed Bob to use the $5,000 to buy 50 additional shares of stock at $100 per share when the fair market value of the stock was $120 per share. How much dividend income must Bob report on his current-year income tax return?

A. $6,000

B. $5,000

C. $1,000

D. $0

Answer (A) is correct. *(SEE, adapted)*
REQUIRED: The amount of dividend income under a dividend reinvestment plan.
DISCUSSION: Dividends are gross income [Sec. 61(a)(7)]. A shareholder who elects to receive shares of greater value than his or her otherwise cash dividend under a dividend reinvestment plan receives a taxable distribution under Sec. 301(a) to the extent of the value of the shares [Rev. Rul. 78-375]. The Sec. 301(a) distribution is generally a taxable dividend to the extent of the corporation's earnings and profits. Bob reports dividend income of $6,000 (50 × $120).
Answer (B) is incorrect. The amount of $5,000 is only the per-share value offered to Bob (not the correct amount of dividend income Bob must report). Answer (C) is incorrect. The amount of $1,000 is only the excess of the FMV over the per-share value offered to Bob (not the correct amount of dividend income Bob must report). Answer (D) is incorrect. Bob must report dividend income from the shares received.

1.4.3. Ms. X, a cash-method taxpayer, received notice from her mutual fund that it has realized a long-term capital gain on her behalf in the amount of $2,500. It also advised her that it has paid a tax of $500 on this gain. The mutual fund indicated that it will not distribute the net amount but will credit the amount to her account. All of the following statements are true except

A. X must report a long-term capital gain of $2,500.

B. X is allowed a $500 credit for the tax since it is considered paid by X.

C. X is allowed to increase her basis in the stock by $2,000.

D. X does not report a long-term capital gain because nothing was paid to her.

Answer (D) is correct. *(SEE, adapted)*
REQUIRED: The false statement concerning an undistributed long-term capital gain in a mutual fund.
DISCUSSION: A mutual fund is a regulated investment company, the taxation of which is determined by Sec. 852. Shareholders are taxed on dividends paid by the mutual fund. If part or all of the dividend is designated as a capital gain dividend, it must be treated as such by the shareholders. Undistributed capital gains must also be included in income by shareholders, but they are allowed a credit for their proportionate share of any tax on the capital gain paid by the mutual fund.
Answer (A) is incorrect. X must include the undistributed capital gain in income. Answer (B) is incorrect. X is allowed a credit for her share of the tax paid by the mutual fund on the capital gain. Answer (C) is incorrect. X does increase her basis by the difference between the amount of such includible gains and the tax deemed paid by X [Sec. 852(b)(3)(D)(iii)].

1.4.4. Oliver purchased a bond on September 20 of the current year for $1,100. Of the $1,100, $100 represented accrued interest. He received $110 in interest income on the bond on December 1 of the current year. What is the proper treatment of the $110 of interest income for federal income tax purposes?

A. Oliver may elect to include the $110 as interest income in the current year or defer the reporting until he cashes in the bond.

B. Oliver reports the total payment as taxable interest, then shows the $100 as an adjustment on Schedule B.

C. $100 represents a return of capital, and the $10 can be currently included as interest income or deferred until the bond is cashed.

D. $100 is taxable as interest income.

Answer (B) is correct. *(SEE, adapted)*
REQUIRED: The proper treatment of interest income from a bond purchased between interest dates.
DISCUSSION: When bonds are purchased between interest dates, the taxpayer theoretically pays an amount equal to the accrued interest on the bond for the right to receive the entire interest payment. When the interest payment is received, the total payment is reported as income, and the amount paid for the right to receive that interest is deducted as a return of capital. In this manner, the seller is taxed on the interest accrued before the sale, and the purchaser is taxed on the interest accrued after the sale.
Answer (A) is incorrect. Only $10 is taxable interest income, and it must be reported in the current year. Answer (C) is incorrect. The $10 of interest income must be included in the current year's gross income. Answer (D) is incorrect. The $100 represents a return of capital, not interest income.

1.4.5. In the current year, Joe Green purchased XYZ Corporation's 10-year, 10% bonds at original issue for $12,000. The bonds had a stated redemption price of $15,000. How much original issue discount must Green include in gross income in the current year assuming a current market yield for bonds of similar quality of 14%?

A. $120

B. $180

C. $300

D. $420

Answer (B) is correct. *(Publisher, adapted)*
REQUIRED: The amount of original issue discount includible in gross income in the current year.
DISCUSSION: For original issue discount bonds issued after July 1, 1982, Sec. 1272(a) requires the inclusion in gross income of an amount equal to the sum of the daily portions of the original issue discount for each day during the taxable year the instrument was held. The daily portions are determined under Sec. 1272(a)(3) as the ratable portion of the excess of the product of the bond's yield to maturity and its adjusted issue price over the interest payable for the bond year. The adjusted issue price is the original issue price adjusted for the original issue discount previously taken into income (which is zero in the current year).

Yield times adjusted issue price ($12,000 × 14%)	$1,680
Less interest payable ($15,000 × 10%)	(1,500)
Ratable portion (entire year)	$ 180

Answer (A) is incorrect. The amount of $120 is 1% of the original issue price of $12,000. Answer (C) is incorrect. The amount of $300 is 10% of the $3,000 bond discount. Answer (D) is incorrect. The amount of $420 is 14% of the $3,000 bond discount.

1.4.6. The income tax rules for reporting original issue discount (OID) on publicly offered instruments apply to which one of the following?

- A. U.S. savings bonds (long-term).
- B. Zero-coupon bonds (long-term).
- C. Tax-exempt obligations that are not stripped bonds or coupons (long-term).
- D. Short-term obligations (fixed maturity date of 1 year or less from date of issue).

Answer (B) is correct. *(SEE, adapted)*
REQUIRED: The instrument to which the income tax rules for reporting original issue discount (OID) apply.
DISCUSSION: Zero-coupon bonds bear no stated rate of interest and are issued at a discount. As the stated redemption price at maturity exceeds the issue price, the provisions of Sec. 1272(a) with regard to original issue discount are applicable.
Answer (A) is incorrect. Section 1272(a)(2) provides an exception for tax-exempt U.S. savings bonds. They would not be subject to the income tax rules for reporting original issue discount. Answer (C) is incorrect. Section 1272(a)(2) provides an exception for tax-exempt obligations. They would not be subject to the income tax rules for reporting original issue discount. Answer (D) is incorrect. Section 1272(a)(2) provides an exception for short-term obligations with a fixed maturity date of 1 year or less from the date of issue. They would not be subject to the income tax rules for reporting original issue discount.

1.4.7. On January 1, Year 1, Ira Ostire, who is not a dealer, purchased 10 $1,000, 5% bonds of the state of California for $10,400 (maturity date of January 1, Year 21). Interest is payable January 1 and July 1 each year. On December 31, Year 4, he sold four of the bonds at a total price of $4,386 exclusive of interest. In computing Mr. Ostire's Year 4 taxable income, the receipt of interest on the bonds and the sale of the bonds will increase his gross income by

- A. $386
- B. $258
- C. $226
- D. $0

Answer (B) is correct. *(CPA, adapted)*
REQUIRED: The amount by which the receipt of interest on the bonds and the sale of the bonds will increase the taxpayer's adjusted gross income.
DISCUSSION: The bonds are obligations of a state, the interest of which is generally tax-exempt under Sec. 103. Therefore, the interest received on the bonds will not increase adjusted gross income. The gain on the sale of the bonds is long-term capital gain since the bonds were not issued at a discount (they were issued at a premium). The bond premium (at $40 per bond) must be amortized to determine the basis of the bonds under Sec. 1016(a)(5); however, the amortization is not deductible under Sec. 171 because they are tax-exempt bonds. The amortization for the four bonds is $32 ($160 premium for the bonds divided by 20-year life of the bonds, times 4-year holding period). Therefore, the basis of the bonds is $4,128 ($4,160 – $32). The effect on gross income is as follows:

Sales price	$4,386
Less: Adjusted basis	(4,128)
Gain included in gross income	$ 258

Answer (A) is incorrect. Interest is not included in income. Answer (C) is incorrect. The basis must be reduced by the amortization of the premium. Answer (D) is incorrect. Gross income will be affected by the sale of the bonds.

1.4.8. Mr. P invested in Park Place Corporation, a real estate investment trust (REIT). Park Place declared a dividend on October 1 of Year 1 and made it payable to its shareholders of record on October 17 of Year 1. Park Place actually paid the dividend on January 5 of Year 2. Mr. P received $1,500. How should P report this dividend for federal income tax purposes?

- A. $1,500 in taxable income for Year 1.
- B. $1,500 in taxable income for Year 2.
- C. $1,125 in taxable income for Year 1, $375 in taxable income for Year 2.
- D. $1,000 in taxable income for Year 1, $500 in taxable income for Year 2.

Answer (A) is correct. *(SEE, adapted)*
REQUIRED: The correct reporting of a dividend from a REIT declared and made payable in Year 1 and paid in Year 2.
DISCUSSION: Dividends declared by a REIT in October, November, or December and made payable to shareholders of record in these months are deemed to have been paid by the REIT and received by its shareholder on December 31 of the same year, provided that the dividends are actually paid in January of the following year [Sec. 857(b)(8)].
Answer (B) is incorrect. Reporting $1,500 in taxable income for Year 2 is an improper accounting treatment of the dividend income. Answer (C) is incorrect. Reporting $1,125 in taxable income for Year 1 and $375 in taxable income for Year 2 does not properly account for the dividend income for federal income tax purposes. Answer (D) is incorrect. Reporting $1,000 in taxable income in Year 1 and $500 in taxable income in Year 2 is an improper accounting treatment of the dividend income.

1.4.9. Dacey Corporation issued a stock option in Year 1 to Crown, an employee, to purchase 100 shares of Dacey stock at $10 per share. Dacey stock was not traded on an exchange, but it was estimated that its stock was worth $9 per share. The stock options were considered not to have a readily ascertainable value. In Year 3, Crown exercised the stock options when it was determined that the stock was worth $18 per share based on several offers by competitors to buy out the company. How much and when must Crown report income from the receipt and exercise of the stock options?

    A. No income or loss.

    B. $100 loss in Year 1.

    C. $800 income in Year 3.

    D. $900 income in Year 3.

Answer (C) is correct. *(Publisher, adapted)*

REQUIRED: The employee's income from a nonqualified and nonstatutory stock option that does not have a readily ascertainable value.

DISCUSSION: The rules for taxation of nonqualified and nonstatutory stock options are contained in Reg. 1.83-7. When a stock option does not have a readily ascertainable value, the employee is not taxed until the option is exercised. At that time, the amount of income is measured by the difference between the stock's fair market value and the amount paid for the stock under the option. It is considered ordinary income. Therefore, Crown must report $800 of ordinary income in Year 3 [100 shares × ($18 – $10) = $800].

Note that if the option is subject to restrictions, no income will be recognized until the restrictions lapse (Sec. 83).

Answer (A) is incorrect. Income will be reported from the receipt and exercise of the stock options. Answer (B) is incorrect. Stock options without readily ascertainable fair market values do not create income until the option is exercised. Therefore, no income or loss would be recognized in Year 1. Answer (D) is incorrect. The amount of $900 would be the gain reported in Year 3 if the stock were valued at the $9 per share price in Year 1 when figuring the difference between price paid and FMV. However, the stock had no readily ascertainable FMV in Year 1.

1.4.10. In Year 1, Bea was granted an incentive stock option (ISO) by her employer as part of an executive compensation package. Bea exercised the ISO in Year 2 and sold the stock in Year 4 at a gain. Bea's profit was subject to the income tax for the year in which the

    A. ISO was granted.

    B. ISO was exercised.

    C. Stock was sold.

    D. Employer claimed a compensation deduction for the ISO.

Answer (C) is correct. *(CPA, adapted)*

REQUIRED: The year in which the taxpayer's profit on an ISO is subject to the income tax.

DISCUSSION: Under Sec. 422, an employee will have no income tax consequences on the grant date or the exercise date of an incentive stock option if that employee meets two requirements. First, the employee cannot dispose of the stock within 2 years after the grant date nor within 1 year after the exercise date. Second, the employee must be employed by the company on the grant date. Since Bea meets these requirements, she is not subject to any tax on the grant or exercise dates. Bea did, however, recognize a capital gain when she sold the stock in Year 4.

Answer (A) is incorrect. There are no income tax consequences on the grant date. Answer (B) is incorrect. There are no income tax consequences on the exercise date. Answer (D) is incorrect. An employer may not take a deduction for the amount of the profit on an incentive stock option.

1.4.11. Mr. T, a cash-basis taxpayer, may either defer reporting the interest on Series EE bonds until he cashes in the bonds, or he may choose to report the increase in redemption value as interest each year.

    A. True.

    B. False.

Answer (A) is correct. *(SEE, adapted)*

DISCUSSION: Series EE bonds are savings bonds issued at a discount and are redeemable for fixed amounts that increase at stated intervals. The income from these bonds is received when the bonds are redeemed and is equal to the difference between the purchase price and the amount received. No interest payments are made while the bond is held. Section 454(a) allows a cash-basis taxpayer to elect to either include in gross income the annual increment in redemption value or defer recognition of any interest income until the bond is redeemed.

1.4.12. The basis of stock received as a result of a dividend reinvestment plan is fair market value, even if purchased at a discounted price.

    A. True.

    B. False.

Answer (A) is correct. *(SEE, adapted)*

DISCUSSION: The value of the stock received equals its fair market value on the date of distribution. The basis of the stock is equal to the amount of the distribution, measured by the fair market value of the stock on the date of the distribution (Rev. Rul. 76-53). Starting January 1, 2011, the basis of stock acquired in connection with a dividend reinvestment plan may be determined using a method other than the taxpayer's default method if the taxpayer elects to do so (Reg. 1.1021-1).

1.4.13. A cash-basis taxpayer must report interest received on Series HH United States Savings Bonds, issued at face value, as income in the year received.

A. True.

B. False.

Answer (A) is correct. *(SEE, adapted)*
DISCUSSION: Interest on United States bonds is taxable. The interest must be reported in the year received. Only for U.S. Savings Bonds issued at a discount and redeemable for fixed amounts increasing at stated intervals is the interest not reported currently. It is reported when the bond is redeemed because that is when the interest is received (although an election is available for a cash-basis taxpayer to report the interest as the bond increases in redemption value).

1.4.14. When bonds are sold between interest dates, a portion of the sales price is accrued interest. The seller does not report the interest income. The purchaser will report the total interest income and deduct the accrued interest payment as a return of capital.

A. True.

B. False.

Answer (B) is correct. *(SEE, adapted)*
DISCUSSION: The purchaser has theoretically paid an amount equal to the accrued interest on the bond for the right to receive the entire interest payment. The seller reports this amount as interest income. When the purchaser receives the interest payment, the amount paid for the right to receive that interest is deducted as a return of capital adjustment on Schedule B. In this manner, the seller is taxed on the interest accrued before the sale, and the purchaser is taxed on the interest accrued after the sale.

1.4.15. On March 5 of Year 2, Mr. B purchased a corporate bond for $8,200. The bond, which was issued January 1 of Year 1, has a face value of $10,000, no stated interest, and will mature December 31 of Year 3. Mr. B's gross income for Year 2 and Year 3 should include a portion of the original issue discount on the corporate bond.

A. True.

B. False.

Answer (A) is correct. *(SEE, adapted)*
DISCUSSION: Under Sec. 1272(a), the original issue discount on bonds issued after July 1, 1982, must be included in gross income and computed on a daily basis using the "yield" method.

1.5 Income from Annuities

Questions 1.5.1 through 1.5.4 are based on the following information.

The next column contains a simplified annuity table for employee annuity contracts that start after November 18, 1996.

Age of Primary Annuitant on the Annuity Starting Date	Number of Anticipated Payments
55 and under	360
56-60	310
61-65	260
66-70	210
71 and over	160

1.5.1. Mr. Kitten, age 72, will be receiving an annuity through his employer. His contribution to the annuity is $80,000. He is to receive $1,500 per month starting April 1 of the current year and continuing for life. Mr. Kitten's reportable annuity income for the current year is

A. $4,500

B. $9,000

C. $12,000

D. $13,500

Answer (B) is correct. *(Publisher, adapted)*
REQUIRED: The taxpayer's income in the first year of a life annuity.
DISCUSSION: Amounts received as an annuity are included in gross income under Secs. 61 and 72. However, under the simplified method to determine basis for annuity contracts, Mr. Kitten would exclude $500 per month as a return of capital. This amount is calculated by dividing the $80,000 investment in the contract by 160 anticipated payments as determined by his age group (age 71 and up). Accordingly, Mr. Kitten's annuity income for the current year is $9,000 [($1,500 – $500) × 9 months].
Answer (A) is incorrect. Mr. Kitten would exclude only $500 per month. Answer (C) is incorrect. The payments are only received in 9 months of the current year. Answer (D) is incorrect. A portion of the payment is excludable as a return of capital.

1.5.2. Tina retired at age 65 at the end of last year. Her employer-sponsored pension is $500 a month starting on March 1 of the current year. Her pension cost was $6,500. The amount of the pension to be included as income on Tina's current-year tax return is

A. $5,750

B. $5,700

C. $4,750

D. $250

Answer (C) is correct. *(Publisher, adapted)*
REQUIRED: The amount of pension received by an employee to be included in gross income in the first year of receipt.
DISCUSSION: Amounts received as an annuity are included in gross income under Secs. 61 and 72. However, the 1996 Small Business Act allows an annuitant to receive a tax-free return of capital from a qualified plan. Tina can exclude $25 per month as a return of capital. This is calculated by dividing $6,500 by 260 anticipated payments. Tina will need to include $4,750 [($500 − 25) × 10 months] on her current-year return.
Answer (A) is incorrect. The amount of $5,750 includes payments for all 12 months of the year less the excludable amount for 10 months. Answer (B) is incorrect. The amount of $5,700 includes payments less the excludable amount of all 12 months of the year. Answer (D) is incorrect. The amount excluded from income is $250.

1.5.3. Mr. Jones, age 74, retired on May 31 of the current year and receives a monthly pension benefit of $800 payable for life. The first pension check was received on June 15 of the current year. During his years of employment, Mr. Jones contributed $27,200 to the cost of his company's pension plan. How much of the pension amounts received may Mr. Jones exclude from taxable income in the current year?

A. $1,190

B. $1,360

C. $4,410

D. $5,600

Answer (A) is correct. *(Publisher, adapted)*
REQUIRED: The amount of pension payments an employee may exclude from taxable income.
DISCUSSION: The 1996 Small Business Act requires the simplified method for determining nontaxable returns of capital for annuity contracts. Under the simplified method, the portion of each payment that represents the tax-free return of capital is determined by dividing the investment in the contract (at the annuity starting date) by the anticipated payments. Mr. Jones is 74 years old, so he is deemed to anticipate 160 payments. Mr. Jones can exclude $170 ($27,200 ÷ 160 payments) of his monthly pension benefit of $800 from his gross income. For the current year, Mr. Jones can exclude a total of $1,190 ($170 × 7 months) from his income.
Answer (B) is incorrect. Only 7 months are considered in calculating the total amount to exclude in the current year. Answer (C) is incorrect. The amount of $630 per month is included in taxable income. Answer (D) is incorrect. The amount of $5,600 excludes 100% of payments from taxable income in the current year.

1.5.4. Tony, age 72, retired on June 30 of Year 1. Tony received $500 a month from a life annuity beginning August 1. During his working years, Tony paid in a total of $32,000 as his contribution to the retirement plan, which did not have a refund feature. If Tony dies on October 2 of Year 7, how much can be deducted on his final tax return?

A. $15,000

B. $15,200

C. $17,000

D. $18,600

Answer (C) is correct. *(Publisher, adapted)*
REQUIRED: The amount of the annuity investment allowed to be deducted on a final tax return.
DISCUSSION: The 1996 Small Business Act allows an annuitant to receive a tax-free return of capital from a qualified plan. Tony can exclude $200 ($32,000 contribution ÷ 160 expected payments) per month as a return of capital. Generally, if an annuitant dies before receiving the full amount of his or her contributions, the amount not recovered may be deducted on the decedent's final tax return. Tony received an annuity payment for 75 months, for a total return of capital of $15,000 ($200 × 75 months). The remaining contribution of $17,000 ($32,000 − $15,000) can be deducted on Tony's final tax return.
Answer (A) is incorrect. The amount of $15,000 represents the total return of capital from the annuity payments Tony received prior to death. Answer (B) is incorrect. The amount of $15,200 is the return of capital prior to death if the annuity payments had started immediately following his retirement date (July 1). Answer (D) is incorrect. The correct amount that could be deducted on Tony's final tax return if he had only received 67 payments before his death is $18,600.

1.5.5. Roger, who is 67 years old, received a lump-sum distribution from a qualified pension plan in May of the current year. All of the following options on how to treat the distribution are available except

    A. Roll over all or part of the distribution.

    B. Report the entire taxable portion as ordinary income.

    C. Report the part of the distribution from pre-1974 participation as capital gain.

    D. If the distribution is less than $50,000, report the present value of a 10-year annuity using the federal tax rate applicable at the date of distribution.

Answer (D) is correct. *(SEE, adapted)*
    REQUIRED: The option that is not available for treatment of a lump-sum distribution.
    DISCUSSION: The taxable portion of a lump-sum distribution is generally includible in ordinary income. The 10-year forward averaging rules (including capital gains treatment in some instances) apply to people reaching age 50 before January 1, 1986. Section 402(c) provides that a lump-sum distribution from a qualified plan may be rolled over and thus excluded from gross income.
    Answer (A) is incorrect. Rolling over all or part of the distribution is an available option with regard to treatment of a lump-sum distribution from a qualified pension plan. Answer (B) is incorrect. Reporting the entire taxable portion as ordinary income is an available option with regard to treatment of a lump-sum distribution from a qualified pension plan. Answer (C) is incorrect. Reporting the part of the distribution from pre-1974 participation as capital gain is an available option with regard to treatment of a lump-sum distribution from a qualified pension plan.

1.5.6. Peter has made contributions to an IRA for a number of years, including both deductible and nondeductible contributions. He retires in the current year and decides to withdraw the balance of the IRA as an annuity. Which of the following statements is true about the taxability of the distribution?

    A. Peter is taxed on the entire amount he receives.

    B. Peter can exclude the portion of each annuity payment received in the current year equal to his investment (nondeductible IRA contributions) in the contract divided by the annuity's expected return.

    C. Peter can exclude the portion of each annuity payment received in the current year equal to his total contributions to the IRA divided by the annuity's expected return.

    D. Peter is not taxed on any amount he receives.

Answer (B) is correct. *(Publisher, adapted)*
    REQUIRED: The amount the taxpayer must include in his income as a result of receiving an annuity from his IRA.
    DISCUSSION: The IRA distribution received after 1986 is taxed under the rules of Sec. 72 [as modified by Sec. 408(d)(2)]. If the benefits payable by an IRA are in the form of an annuity, then the recipient can exclude the amount of the payments received times the ratio that his investment in the contract (his nondeductible contributions to the IRA) bears to the annuity's expected return.
    Answer (A) is incorrect. The distribution is taxed as an annuity, and Peter has an investment in the annuity from his nondeductible contributions. Answer (C) is incorrect. Only nondeductible contributions provide Peter with an investment in the annuity. Answer (D) is incorrect. IRA distributions generally are taxable except when there is an investment in the annuity.

1.5.7. On December 31 of last year, Emmanuel had a $4,000 basis in his IRA. On January 2 of the current year, he withdrew $8,000 from his IRA. On April 15 of the current year, he made a $2,000 nondeductible contribution for the current year to the IRA, bringing his total of nondeductible contributions to $6,000. On December 31 of the current year, the fair market value of his IRA account was $12,000. How much of the $8,000 that Emmanuel withdrew is included in his ordinary income on his current-year individual income tax return?

    A. $0

    B. $2,000

    C. $2,400

    D. $5,600

Answer (D) is correct. *(SEE, adapted)*
    REQUIRED: The amount the taxpayer must include in his income as a result of receiving a nonannuity distribution from his IRA.
    DISCUSSION: If an IRA distribution is not in the form of an annuity, Sec. 408(d)(1) provides that it will be taxed under Sec. 72(e). The excluded portion of Emmanuel's payments equal the amount distributed in the year times the ratio that Emmanuel's investment in the contract (his nondeductible contributions to the IRA) bears to the sum of the value of the IRA at the end of the year plus the amounts distributed from the IRA during the year. The excludable portion of the current year payments equals $6,000 ÷ ($12,000 current-year year-end value + $8,000 current-year distributions) = 0.30. Emmanuel's exclusion equals $2,400 ($8,000 × 0.30); therefore, his gross income inclusion is $5,600 ($8,000 − $2,400).
    Answer (A) is incorrect. A portion of the distribution will be taxed since it is not in the form of an annuity. Answer (B) is incorrect. The amount of $2,000 is the result of excluding the full amount of the nondeductible contributions from the distribution. Answer (C) is incorrect. The amount of $2,400 is the excludable portion of the current-year distribution.

1.6 Rental Income

1.6.1. Paul Bristol, a cash-basis taxpayer, owns an apartment building. The following information was available for the current year:

- An analysis of the bank deposit slips showed recurring monthly rents received totaling $50,000 for the current year.
- On March 1, the tenant in apartment 2B paid Bristol $2,000 to cancel the lease expiring on December 31 of the current year.
- The lease of the tenant in apartment 3A expired on December 31 of the current year and the tenant left improvements valued at $1,000. The improvements were not in lieu of any required rent.

In computing net rental income for the current year, Bristol should report gross rents of

A. $50,000

B. $51,000

C. $52,000

D. $53,000

Answer (C) is correct. *(CPA, adapted)*
REQUIRED: The amount of gross rents given monthly rents, leasehold improvements, and a cancelation payment.
DISCUSSION: Gross rents include the $50,000 of recurring rents plus the $2,000 lease cancelation payment. The cancelation payment is in lieu of rent so it must be included in income like rent.
The $1,000 of leasehold improvements are excluded from income since they were not in lieu of rent (Sec. 109).
Answer (A) is incorrect. The $2,000 to cancel the lease is reported in gross rents. Answer (B) is incorrect. The improvements are not in lieu of rent, so they should not be reported as gross rents. Instead, the lease cancelation payment should be reported in gross rents. Answer (D) is incorrect. The improvements are not in lieu of rent and should not be reported in gross rents.

1.6.2. Gewald enters into an agreement to lease a house to Dorschuk. Although the fair rental value of the house is $5,000 per year, Dorschuk is required to pay only $3,000 per year in return for building a patio and a sundeck and for installing a hot tub, which will be left on the premises at the end of the lease. The lease is to last for 2 years. Dorschuk finishes all the improvements in the first year of the lease. How much and when must Gewald recognize rental income from this transaction?

A. $3,000 in the first year and $3,000 in the second year.

B. $5,000 in the first year and $5,000 in the second year.

C. $7,000 in the first year and $3,000 in the second year.

D. $3,000 in the first year and $7,000 in the second year.

Answer (C) is correct. *(Publisher, adapted)*
REQUIRED: The amount and timing of rental income when the lessee makes improvements in lieu of rent.
DISCUSSION: Section 61(a)(5) includes rents in gross income whether received in cash, property, or as services. Improvements made by a lessee on the lessor's property are generally excluded from income under Sec. 109 unless they are made in lieu of rent. In this case, the improvements made by Dorschuk are made in lieu of $2,000 of rent in the first year of the lease and $2,000 of rent in the second year of the lease. Improvements in lieu of rent are included in the lessor's income when the improvements are completed or placed on the property (the same as if cash rent had been received at that time). Since Dorschuk paid $3,000 in cash in the first year and completed the improvements in the first year, Gewald must recognize $7,000 of rental income in the first year. Gewald must also recognize $3,000 of rental income in the second year when it is received.
Answer (A) is incorrect. The improvements were made in lieu of rent, so their value should be recognized in the year when they were completed. Answer (B) is incorrect. The value of the improvements should be recognized in the year they are completed. Answer (D) is incorrect. The value of the improvements should be recognized in the year they are completed, not in the last year of the lease.

1.6.3. An amount called a security deposit, which is to be used as a final payment of rent, should not be included in rental income in the year received but should be included in income in the year the lease expires.

A. True.

B. False.

Answer (B) is correct. *(SEE, adapted)*
DISCUSSION: Advance rental payments are included in gross income in the year of receipt regardless of the period covered or the method of accounting employed by the taxpayer [Reg. 1.61-8(b)]. Therefore, if a security deposit is intended as an advance rent payment, it must be included in income in the year received.

1.6.4. In the current year, Mrs. G received $5,000 in advance payments under a 50-month lease agreement. The $5,000 represented the entire amount due under the lease. There were no restrictions on the use or enjoyment of the payments. Mrs. G must include the $5,000 as income in the current year.

A. True.

B. False.

Answer (A) is correct. *(SEE, adapted)*
   DISCUSSION: Rent is included in gross income under Sec. 61. Furthermore, gross income includes advance rentals, which must be included in income for the year of receipt regardless of the period covered or the method of accounting employed by the taxpayer [Reg. 1.61-8(b)]. Therefore, in the current year, Mrs. G must include the $5,000 of advance rent in income.

1.7 Income from a Divorce

1.7.1. Which of the following items may be considered alimony?

A. Noncash property settlement.

B. Payments Mr. Stone made under a written separation agreement for the mortgage and real estate taxes on a home he owned by himself and in which his former spouse lived rent-free.

C. Payments made to a third party on behalf of the former spouse for the former spouse's medical expenses.

D. Payments made for the 3-month period after the death of the recipient spouse.

Answer (C) is correct. *(SEE, adapted)*
   REQUIRED: The item that may be considered alimony.
   DISCUSSION: Payments of cash to a third party made at the written request of the payee spouse will qualify as alimony. Payments are often made on behalf of the payee spouse, such as payments for mortgages, rent, medical costs, or education.
   Answer (A) is incorrect. Noncash property settlements are specifically excluded from qualifying as alimony. Answer (B) is incorrect. Neither the mortgage payments nor the real estate taxes paid will qualify as alimony when the payor is the property owner. Answer (D) is incorrect. Alimony payments must cease at the death of the recipient.

1.7.2. Stan and Anne were divorced in January of the current year. The requirements of the divorce decree and Anne's performance follow:

Transfer the title in their resort condominium to Stan. At the time of the transfer, the condominium had a basis to Anne of $75,000 and a fair market value of $95,000; it was subject to a mortgage of $65,000.

Anne is to make the mortgage payments for 17 years regardless of how long Stan lives. Anne paid $8,000 in the current year.

Anne is to pay Stan $1,000 per month, beginning in February, for 10 years or until Stan dies. Of this amount, $300 is designated as child support. Anne made five payments of $900 each in the current year (February – June).

What is the amount of alimony from this settlement that is includible in Stan's gross income for the current year?

A. $3,000

B. $3,500

C. $11,000

D. $38,000

Answer (A) is correct. *(SEE, adapted)*
   REQUIRED: The amount included in Stan's gross income in the current year as alimony.
   DISCUSSION: Section 71(a) provides that gross income includes amounts received as alimony or separate maintenance payments. Alimony is a payment in cash if such payment is received by a spouse under a divorce decree entered after 1984, but subject to certain requirements. Stan's receipt of title to the resort condominium does not qualify as alimony since the payment was not in cash. The mortgage payments could be considered alimony, even though paid to a third party, since they are for the benefit of the payor's ex-spouse. Since they are required even if Stan dies, they are not alimony.
   The monthly payments to Stan would normally be alimony to the extent of $700 per month (the amount in excess of that specified for child support). However, Anne did not pay the full amount of any of the payments in the current year. Section 71(c)(3) provides that, if any payment is less than the amount specified in the instrument, the payment should first be considered child support, and any excess will be alimony. Stan received alimony of $600 for each of the five payments, for a total of $3,000 ($600 × 5) of alimony in the current year.
   Answer (B) is incorrect. When a payment includes alimony and child support and the payment is less than agreed, the remainder of a payment after deducting child support is alimony. Therefore, only $600 of each payment is alimony. Answer (C) is incorrect. The mortgage payments are not alimony since they are not restricted to the life of the ex-spouse. Answer (D) is incorrect. The equity in the house and the mortgage payments are not considered alimony.

1.7.3. Jim and Ann were divorced in Year 1, and the following alimony payments were made by Jim to Ann under their divorce decree:

> $45,000 in Year 1
> $30,000 in Year 2
> $10,000 in Year 3

How much must Jim include in gross income in Year 3?

A. $0

B. $5,000

C. $17,500

D. $25,000

Answer (C) is correct. *(Publisher, adapted)*
REQUIRED: The excess alimony payments included in the payor's gross income in the third year.
DISCUSSION: To prevent the front loading of alimony payments for early tax deductions, excess alimony payments from the first and second years are included in the payor's income in the third year (and are deductible by the recipient in the third year) [Sec. 71(f)].
Excess alimony in the second year is alimony paid in the second year – the sum of the statutory amount of $15,000 plus alimony paid in the third year. For Jim this is $5,000 [$30,000 – ($15,000 + $10,000)].
Excess alimony in the first year is alimony paid in the first year minus the sum of (1) $15,000 plus (2) the average of (a) alimony paid in the second year less excess alimony in the second year plus (b) alimony paid in the third year. For Jim, this is calculated as follows:

1st-year alimony paid		$45,000
Less: statutory amount		(15,000)
Less average of:		
2nd-year alimony paid	$30,000	
Less: 2nd-year excess alimony	(5,000)	
3rd-year alimony paid	10,000	
	$35,000	
Divided by 2	÷ 2	(17,500)
1st-year excess alimony		$12,500

The total excess alimony amount of $17,500 ($5,000 + $12,500) is included in Jim's gross income in Year 3.
Answer (A) is incorrect. Jim's Year 3 gross income is affected by excess alimony payments to Ann in Years 1 and 2. Jim must include alimony payments in gross income in Year 3. Answer (B) is incorrect. This amount is the excess alimony in the second year. Answer (D) is incorrect. The amount of $25,000 is the result of subtracting the $5,000 excess payment in Year 2 from the amount paid in Year 2.

1.7.4. Richard and Alice Kelley lived apart during the current year and did not file a joint tax return for the year. Under the terms of the written separation agreement they signed on July 1 of the current year, Richard was required to pay Alice $1,500 per month of which $600 was designated as child support. He made six such payments in the current year. Additionally, Richard paid Alice $1,200 per month for the first 6 months of the year, no portion of which was designated as child support. Assuming that Alice has no other income, her tax return for the current year should show gross income of

A. $0

B. $5,400

C. $9,000

D. $12,600

Answer (B) is correct. *(CPA, adapted)*
REQUIRED: The taxpayer's gross income arising from periodic payments from her spouse.
DISCUSSION: Section 71(b)(2) requires the recipient of cash payments made pursuant to a written separation agreement (entered into after 1984) to include these payments in gross income if they do not live together and if the payments are not required after the death of the recipient spouse. If the agreement specifies that a fixed portion is for support of a minor child, then that portion is excluded from gross income [Sec. 71(c)]. Since $600 was specifically designated as child support, only $900 ($1,500 – $600) of each monthly payment is included in Alice's gross income for a total of $5,400 ($900 × 6 months). The $1,200 per month paid for the first 6 months of the current year is not included in Alice's gross income since these payments were made before the written separation agreement [Sec. 71(b)].
Answer (A) is incorrect. A portion of the periodic payments is included in income. Answer (C) is incorrect. The amount of $600 was specifically designated as child support. Answer (D) is incorrect. The $1,200 per month paid for the first 6 months of the current year is not included.

1.7.5. Ed and Ann Ross were divorced in January of the current year. In accordance with the divorce decree, Ed transferred the title in their home to Ann. The home, which had a fair market value of $150,000, was subject to a $50,000 mortgage that had 20 more years to run. Monthly mortgage payments amount to $1,000. Under the terms of settlement, Ed is obligated to make the mortgage payments on the home for the full remaining 20-year term of the indebtedness, regardless of how long Ann lives. Ed made 12 mortgage payments in the current year. What amount is taxable as alimony in Ann's current-year return?

- A. $0
- B. $12,000
- C. $100,000
- D. $112,000

Answer (A) is correct. *(CPA, adapted)*
REQUIRED: The amount taxable as alimony in Ann's gross income.
DISCUSSION: The monthly payments to Ann would normally be alimony to the extent of $1,000 a month. However, since they are required even if Ann dies, they are not alimony [Sec. 71(b)]. In addition, receipt of the home does not qualify as alimony since it is not a cash payment.
Answer (B) is incorrect. The $12,000 in mortgage payments paid are not considered alimony because they are not restricted to the life of the ex-spouse. Answer (C) is incorrect. The house is not considered alimony because it is not a cash payment. Answer (D) is incorrect. The house and the mortgage payments are not considered alimony.

1.7.6. A provision agreed to by both parties in a divorce instrument, that payments otherwise qualifying as alimony will not be so treated for tax purposes, will be recognized and followed for federal income tax purposes.

- A. True.
- B. False.

Answer (A) is correct. *(SEE, adapted)*
DISCUSSION: Payments to former spouses under a divorce decree entered after 1984 are treated as alimony if made in cash and if the divorce decree does not designate the payments as not included in gross income [Sec. 71(b)]. If the divorce instrument (decree) specifies that payments will not be treated as alimony (included in the recipient's gross income), this provision will be recognized and followed for federal income tax purposes.

1.8 Assignment of Income

1.8.1. Janice purchased $10,000 in Series HH bonds with her own money and had them issued in her and her son's name as co-owners. During the current year, Janice and her son received $600 in interest on the bonds. Janice allowed her son Mark to keep the full $600 of interest income. For the current year, how should the interest be reported for federal income tax purposes?

- A. Neither Janice nor Mark have to report interest income.
- B. $300 by Janice and $300 by Mark.
- C. $600 by Janice.
- D. $600 by Mark.

Answer (C) is correct. *(SEE, adapted)*
REQUIRED: The correct reporting of interest income received by the co-owners of Series HH bonds.
DISCUSSION: The IRS's position is that, when one person purchases U.S. Savings Bonds solely with his or her own money and names another person as co-owner, the interest is taxable to the person who furnished the money, even if the other co-owner redeems the bond and keeps all of the proceeds. Therefore, Janice must report the entire $600 of interest income for federal income tax purposes.
Answer (A) is incorrect. Interest income from bonds is taxable to the person(s) who own(s) it. Answer (B) is incorrect. The IRS's position is that, when one person purchases U.S. Savings Bonds solely with his or her own money and names another person as co-owner, the interest is taxable to the person who furnished the money, even if the other co-owner redeems the bond and keeps all of the proceeds. Therefore, Janice and Mark cannot split the proceeds of the interest for federal income tax purposes. Answer (D) is incorrect. Janice owns half of the bonds, so she is taxed on half of the interest. Alternatively, if one assumes that a completed gift of one-half of the bonds is not made until Janice does more than make Mark a co-owner, then all $600 is reported by Janice.

1.8.2. Big Bucks owns corporate bonds with detachable interest coupons. Interest of $1,000 is payable each January 1 and July 1. On December 31 of Year 1, Big Bucks gave his son the coupons for the interest payments due on January 1 and July 1 of Year 2. When the interest is received by his son in Year 2, how is it taxed?

A. $1,000 to Big Bucks and $1,000 to his son.

B. $2,000 to his son.

C. $2,000 to Big Bucks.

D. None, since $2,000 was taxed to Big Bucks in Year 1.

Answer (C) is correct. *(Publisher, adapted)*
REQUIRED: The taxation of interest from coupons transferred by gift.
DISCUSSION: Income earned from property is taxed to the person who owns the property. Interest coupons only represent the income and are not the property that earns the income. The corporate bonds are considered to be the property that earns the interest. Therefore, Big Bucks was merely assigning income when he gave the coupons to his son. The entire $2,000 is taxed to Big Bucks when it is received by his son since he still owns the bonds.
This is known as the fruit and the tree doctrine. The fruit (income) cannot be separated from the tree (property).
Answer (A) is incorrect. The amount of $1,000 is not taxable to the son since he does not own the bond. Answer (B) is incorrect. The amount of $2,000 is not taxable to the son since he does not own the bond. Answer (D) is incorrect. Big Bucks will be taxed.

1.8.3. Carter obtained a new job in Washington, D.C., in which she was to receive a substantially larger salary than before. Carter decided to give one-half of this salary to her spouse, and they executed a legal document under which Carter's spouse was required to receive one-half of her salary. This document was given to Carter's employer with directions to issue two checks each pay period, one to Carter and one to Carter's spouse. Carter's salary for the year is $100,000. What are the tax consequences of this transaction?

A. Carter must include $50,000 in gross income, and Carter's spouse must include $50,000 in gross income.

B. Carter must include $100,000 in gross income.

C. Carter has made a taxable gift of $50,000.

D. The person actually receiving the checks must include them in his or her gross income.

Answer (B) is correct. *(Publisher, adapted)*
REQUIRED: The tax effect of an assignment of an employee's salary to his or her spouse.
DISCUSSION: The person who earns income is taxed on it. Although the money or property received as income can be legally assigned, the person who earned the income still must report it as his or her gross income. The amount that the assignee then receives may be a gift. Since Carter earned the $100,000 of salary, Carter must include all of it in gross income.
Answer (A) is incorrect. Carter's spouse cannot include any amount in gross income. Answer (C) is incorrect. There is a deduction for gifts to a spouse in computing taxable gifts under Sec. 2523. If Carter assigned part of her salary to another person, a taxable gift might be made. Answer (D) is incorrect. The person who earns the salary must include it in income, not the person who receives the checks.
Note that in states with community property law (AZ, CA, ID, LA, NV, NM, TX, WA, WI), each spouse is usually considered to earn one-half of each other's earnings. This is valid for income tax purposes also.

1.8.4. During Year 1, Mr. P furnished the money to buy Series EE U.S. Savings Bonds issued in his name and his brother's name (as co-owners). No election was made to report the interest earned in income each year. During Year 5, P's brother cashed the bonds and kept all of the proceeds for his personal use. Mr. P's brother must include the interest earned on the bonds in his gross income for Year 5.

A. True.

B. False.

Answer (B) is correct. *(SEE, adapted)*
DISCUSSION: The IRS takes the position that when one person purchases Series EE U.S. Savings Bonds solely with his or her own money and names another person as co-owner, the interest is taxable to the person who furnished the money even if the other co-owner redeems the bond and keeps all of the proceeds. Therefore, in the question, all of the interest would be taxed to Mr. P since he furnished the money to buy the bond (Rev. Rul. 54-143).
If it can be proven that a gift was made equal to one-half the value of the bond when the bond is issued in both names, then one-half interest should be taxable to each co-owner. This might be proven by a written and signed declaration of gift, filing a gift tax return, etc.

1.9 Income on Final Returns

1.9.1. All of the following items of income are reported on a cash-basis decedent's final income tax return except

A. Paycheck received 1 day before death, cashed 1 week after death.

B. Cash dividend declared before death and received 2 days after death.

C. Distributive share of partnership income for the partnership's tax year ending within or with the decedent's last tax year.

D. Earnings on certificate of deposit credited to decedent's account before death.

Answer (B) is correct. *(SEE, adapted)*
REQUIRED: The income item not reported on a cash-basis decedent's final income tax return.
DISCUSSION: For a cash-basis taxpayer, only those amounts actually or constructively received prior to death are included in the final return. A cash dividend declared before death and received after death would not be actually or constructively received before death and would not be reported on the decedent's final tax return.
Answer (A) is incorrect. The paycheck to the date of death would be considered constructively received and would be reported as income on the final return. Answer (C) is incorrect. Under Sec. 706(a), a partner would include his or her distributive share of partnership income if the partnership's taxable year ends within the partner's taxable year. Answer (D) is incorrect. The interest earnings to the date of death would be considered constructively received and would be reported as income on the final return.

1.9.2. Mr. K, a calendar-year, cash-basis taxpayer, died on September 30 of the current year. From the following transactions, determine the amount of gross income that would not be includible in Mr. K's final income tax return.

Salary received January 1 until his death	$ 8,000
Commission earned that was not received in the current year	10,000
Rental income due September 30, collected October 15	3,350
Passbook savings account interest income credited to K from January 1 to September 30	930
Passbook savings account interest credited to K for the period October 1 to December 31	200

A. $8,000

B. $8,930

C. $13,550

D. $22,280

Answer (C) is correct. *(SEE, adapted)*
REQUIRED: The amount of gross income that is not included on the decedent's final return.
DISCUSSION: As a cash-basis taxpayer, Mr. K recognized income only when actually or constructively received. Therefore, only those amounts actually or constructively received prior to his death are included in his final return. The items that are not included in his final return are the commission paid after death, the rental income collected after death, and the passbook savings interest accruing after death.

Commission	$10,000
Rental income	3,350
Interest after September 30	200
Income not in final return	$13,550

Answer (A) is incorrect. This amount is the salary that is included in gross income. The commission, the rental income, and the interest earned after September 30 should not be included in the final income tax return. Answer (B) is incorrect. The salary and interest earned before October 1 are included in the final income tax return. Answer (D) is incorrect. The interest earned after September 30 and the commission are excluded from the final tax return, not the salary and interest earned before October 1.

1.9.3. B, a calendar-year taxpayer, had received wages before his death on February 15, Year 2. B's Year 1 individual income tax return had not been filed before his date of death. The Year 2 Form 1041 is considered to be the final return for the decedent.

A. True.

B. False.

Answer (B) is correct. *(SEE, adapted)*
DISCUSSION: The final return for a decedent reports the income earned from the beginning of the year up to the date of death. Since income was earned by B in Year 2, the final return will be B's Year 2 Form 1040. Form 1041 is filed for the Year 2 and later income reported by the decedent's estate.

STUDY UNIT TWO
EXCLUSIONS FROM GROSS INCOME

2.1 Dividends, Interest, and Other Items

2.1.1. Gary and Gladys invest in bonds. In the current year, they received the following interest:

California general revenue bonds	$ 800
New York City sanitation fund bonds	1,000
Seattle School District bonds	400
AT&T 20-year bonds	600

The state and local bonds are neither private activity bonds nor arbitrage bonds. How much interest income may Gary and Gladys exclude from gross income on their joint return?

A. $0

B. $800

C. $1,800

D. $2,200

Answer (D) is correct. *(Publisher, adapted)*
REQUIRED: The amount of interest income from bonds excludable from gross income.
DISCUSSION: Under Sec. 103, gross income does not include interest on obligations of a state or any political subdivision thereof. The use of the proceeds of the bonds does not ordinarily change the taxation of the interest (although special rules apply in the case of private activity bonds and arbitrage bonds).
Therefore, Gary and Gladys may exclude the interest from all the state and local bonds (as listed below) but must include the $600 of interest from the AT&T bonds in gross income.

California general revenue bonds	$ 800
New York City sanitation fund bonds	1,000
Seattle School District bonds	400
Total excluded interest	$2,200

Answer (A) is incorrect. Gary and Gladys may exclude state and municipal interest income on their joint return. Answer (B) is incorrect. Interest on obligations of any municipality is also excluded from gross income. Answer (C) is incorrect. Interest from all municipal (local) bonds is excluded from gross income.

2.1.2. Which of the following distributions is nontaxable?

A. Mutual fund distribution from its net realized long-term capital gains in the amount of $1,000. You have an adjusted basis of $10,000 in the mutual fund.

B. Return of capital distribution from a utility company in the amount of $2,000. You have a zero basis in this stock.

C. Dividend on insurance policy in the amount of $1,000. As of the date of this dividend, your net premiums exceed the total dividends by $3,500.

D. Your $25,000 share of ordinary income earned in the current year by an S corporation.

Answer (C) is correct. *(SEE, adapted)*
REQUIRED: The distribution that is nontaxable.
DISCUSSION: Dividends on insurance policies are reported using the Sec. 72(e) rules. They are excluded from gross income when the cumulative dividends do not exceed the cumulative premiums (provided the cash value does not exceed the net investment, which it normally does not).
Answer (A) is incorrect. Mutual fund (regulated investment company) distributions of capital gains are included in the shareholders' incomes (Sec. 852). Answer (B) is incorrect. A return of capital distribution is taxable as a gain when it exceeds basis. Answer (D) is incorrect. The ordinary income earned by an S corporation is taxable to the shareholder in the year earned whether or not it is distributed.

2.1.3. Which of the following bonds can be a tax-exempt bond if issued in the current year so that the interest therefrom may be excluded from gross income?

A. $1 million of bonds issued by a municipality with 50% of the proceeds to be used by a private developer to create an industrial neighborhood of offices and warehouses. The developer will use sales and rents to repay 50% of the bond issue.

B. $1 million of bonds issued by a city with 50% of the proceeds to be invested in higher-yielding corporate bonds.

C. $1 million of bonds issued by a state with all the proceeds to be used to finance student loans.

D. $1 million of bonds issued by a city with all the proceeds to be used to help finance a sports stadium owned by a nongovernment company.

Answer (C) is correct. *(Publisher, adapted)*
REQUIRED: The bond issued in the current year that may qualify as tax-exempt.
DISCUSSION: Under Sec. 103, interest on a state or local government bond is tax-exempt if the bond is not a private activity bond (unless it meets certain qualifications), if it is not an arbitrage bond, and if it is properly registered. If the proceeds are used to finance student loans, it might be a private activity bond if the loans are provided through private banks. But even if it is a private activity bond, it is tax-exempt because the proceeds are used for student loans [Sec. 144(b)].
Answer (A) is incorrect. It describes a private activity bond (more than 10% of the proceeds are for a nongovernmental trade or business and are to be repaid by such business) to be used for nonqualified industrial development purposes (Sec. 141). Answer (B) is incorrect. It describes an arbitrage bond; i.e., funds acquired through low-interest bonds are reinvested in higher-yielding bonds (Sec. 148). Answer (D) is incorrect. It describes a private activity bond (more than 10% of the proceeds are for a nongovernmental trade or business and are to be repaid by such business) to be used for nonqualified industrial development purposes (Sec. 141).

2.1.4. In December 2017, Fred and Tina, a married couple, cashed qualified Series EE U.S. Savings Bonds, which they had purchased in January 2016. The proceeds were used to help pay for their son's 2017 college tuition. They received gross proceeds of $3,500, representing principal of $3,000 and interest of $500. The qualified higher educational expenses they paid during 2017 totaled $2,100. Their modified adjusted gross income for 2017 was $110,000. How much of the $500 interest can Fred and Tina exclude from income for 2017?

A. $200

B. $350

C. $300

D. $500

Answer (C) is correct. *(SEE, adapted)*
REQUIRED: The amount of interest that can be excluded from a Series EE U.S. Savings Bond.
DISCUSSION: Section 135 provides an exclusion for interest on Series EE bonds to the extent spent on higher education expenses for the year. The bonds must be issued after 1989 and must be purchased by the owner. The portion of the interest excluded is based on the ratio of qualified higher education expenses to the total amount of principal and interest. The exclusion is reduced if modified adjusted gross income in 2017 exceeds $78,150 ($117,250 for joint filers). The excludable portion of the 2017 interest equals 60% ($2,100 qualified expenses ÷ $3,500 principal and interest). Fred and Tina's exclusion equals $300 ($500 × 60%).
Answer (A) is incorrect. The amount of interest that is included in income is $200. Answer (B) is incorrect. The amount of $350 is the result of using the exclusion ratio of qualified expenses to the principal instead of the principal and the interest. Answer (D) is incorrect. The full amount of interest is excludable only if the combined principal and interest amount does not exceed the qualified educational expenses.

2.1.5. In the current year, Janine received a rent reduction that is to be used to make improvements to her sporting goods store. The lease is considered for the occupancy or use of retail space and has a duration of 20 years. The improvements cost $2,000, and Janine's rent reduction equals $2,500. How much of the rent reduction can Janine exclude from gross income?

A. $0

B. $500

C. $2,000

D. $2,500

Answer (A) is correct. *(Publisher, adapted)*
REQUIRED: The amount of a rent reduction that may be excluded from gross income.
DISCUSSION: A retail tenant may exclude from gross income a rent reduction that is used for improvements to the rented retail space. The exclusion may not exceed the cost of the improvements. However, the lease term must be considered "short-term" to allow the exclusion from gross income. A short-term lease has a duration of 15 years or less.
Answer (B) is incorrect. Janine does not have a short-term lease on the retail space. Answer (C) is incorrect. The lease term must be for 15 years or less. Answer (D) is incorrect. The exclusion may not exceed the cost of improvements and must be for a short-term lease.

2.2 Compensation for Injuries or Sickness

2.2.1. Which of the following is not excluded from gross income of the recipient taxpayer?

A. Workers' compensation benefits.

B. Payments in lieu of wages (while not able to work due to an injury) from an insurance policy paid for by the taxpayer.

C. Payments in lieu of wages (while not able to work due to an injury) from an insurance policy paid for by the taxpayer's employer.

D. Lump-sum payment from an insurance policy for loss of a hand in an automobile accident.

Answer (C) is correct. *(Publisher, adapted)*
REQUIRED: The item included in the gross income of the recipient taxpayer.
DISCUSSION: Section 104 generally excludes amounts received through accident or health insurance for personal injuries or sickness (other than punitive damages). However, Sec. 105 provides that amounts received by an employee through accident or health insurance paid for by the employer are included in the employee's gross income unless the amounts are for medical care or loss of a body part. Therefore, the payments in lieu of wages from an insurance policy paid for by the taxpayer's employer must be included in the employee's gross income.
Answer (A) is incorrect. Section 104(a) specifically exempts workers' compensation benefits for personal injuries or sickness. Answer (B) is incorrect. Section 104(a) specifically exempts amounts received through accident or health insurance for personal injuries or sickness provided the insurance policy is not paid for by the employer. Answer (D) is incorrect. Section 104(a) specifically exempts amounts received through accident or health insurance for personal injuries, and Sec. 105(c) exempts payments for loss of a body part even if the insurance is paid for by the employer.

2.2.2. In Year 1, John incurred $2,000 of medical expenses but was able to deduct only $500 of them because of the medical deduction floor. In Year 2, John received a reimbursement from his insurance company (he pays his own premiums) of $1,600 of his Year 1 medical expenses. How much of the insurance reimbursement can John exclude?

A. $0

B. $1,100

C. $1,500

D. $1,600

Answer (B) is correct. *(Publisher, adapted)*
REQUIRED: The amount of an insurance reimbursement for medical expenses that can be excluded when part of the expenses were previously deducted.
DISCUSSION: Section 104(a) specifically excludes amounts received through accident or health insurance for personal injuries or sickness (other than punitive damages) but not to the extent that the medical expenses were deducted in a prior year. Since John deducted $500 of the medical expenses in Year 1, only $1,100 of the insurance reimbursement ($1,600 – $500) is excluded in Year 2. John must include the other $500 of the reimbursement in gross income.
Answer (A) is incorrect. A portion of the insurance reimbursement may be excluded. Answer (C) is incorrect. The amount of medical expenses incurred and not deducted in Year 1 is $1,500. Answer (D) is incorrect. The amount of $1,600 is the full reimbursement; only a portion of this amount may be excluded.

2.2.3. Mrs. R is covered under her employer's medical insurance policy. The annual premium for Mrs. R's coverage is $2,000, of which Mrs. R's employer pays 75%. Mrs. R pays the rest. In the current year, Mrs. R received reimbursement of $200 from the insurance company in excess of her actual medical expenses. What amount must Mrs. R include in her gross income?

A. $0

B. $50

C. $150

D. $200

Answer (C) is correct. *(SEE, adapted)*
REQUIRED: The amount of health insurance reimbursement to be included in gross income.
DISCUSSION: Section 105(a) provides that amounts received by an employee through accident and health insurance shall be included in gross income to the extent such amounts (1) are attributable to contributions by the employer that were not includible in the gross income of the employee or (2) are paid by the employer. Section 105(b) excludes amounts that would normally be included in gross income under Sec. 105(a) if such amounts are paid to reimburse the taxpayer for expenses incurred for medical care. Since Mrs. R received reimbursement of $200 in excess of her medical expenses, Sec. 105(a) requires that 75% of this amount ($150) be included in her income.
Answer (A) is incorrect. Mrs. R must include a portion of the excess amount in her gross income. Answer (B) is incorrect. The amount of reimbursement excluded from gross income is $50. Answer (D) is incorrect. The full amount of the reimbursement is $200, and only a certain portion of it is included in gross income.

2.2.4. Ivan Turner, a truck driver, was injured in an accident in the course of his employment in the current year. As a result of injuries sustained, he received the following payments in the current year:

Damages for back injuries	$5,000
Workers' compensation	500
Reimbursement from his employer's accident and health plan for medical expenses paid by Turner in the current year (the employer's contribution to the plan was $475 in the current year)	750

The amount to be included in Turner's gross income for the current year should be

   A. $5,000

   B. $750

   C. $475

   D. $0

Answer (D) is correct. *(CPA, adapted)*
   REQUIRED: The amount included in gross income arising from payments received from a job-related accident.
   DISCUSSION: Section 104(a) specifically excludes from gross income amounts received under workers' compensation acts as compensation for personal injuries or sickness and the amount of any damages received (whether by suit or agreement) on account of personal injuries or sickness. Therefore, the damages for personal injuries and workers' compensation Turner received would not be included in gross income. Punitive damages are not excluded under Sec. 104(a). Section 105(b) excludes payments received from an employer as medical expense reimbursements except to the extent such amounts relate to medical expenses which were deducted by the taxpayer in a prior year. Therefore, Turner's gross income should include none of the payments listed.
   Answer (A) is incorrect. The amount of $5,000 is the payment Ivan received for damages for back injuries. Damages for personal injuries are excluded from gross income. Answer (B) is incorrect. Medical reimbursements are excluded from gross income unless some expenses were deducted in a prior year. Answer (C) is incorrect. The amount of $475 is the employer's contribution to the health plan.

2.2.5. Donald, an accountant, was falsely accused of fraud by a local newspaper. He sued the newspaper for libel claiming damages both to his personal reputation in the community and to his business. In December of the current year, the jury awarded Donald the following:

$10,000 for his personal reputation
$70,000 for his business loss
$70,000 as punitive damages (to punish the newspaper)

How much can Donald exclude from gross income?

   A. $0

   B. $10,000

   C. $70,000

   D. $80,000

Answer (A) is correct. *(Publisher, adapted)*
   REQUIRED: The amount of a recovery from a libel lawsuit that may be excluded from gross income.
   DISCUSSION: Section 104(a)(2) makes punitive damages that are otherwise excludable under Sec. 104(a)(2) includible in gross income. These rules generally apply to amounts received after August 20, 1996. Damages received on account of a nonphysical injury or sickness (e.g., injury to reputation) are also not excludable from gross income. The $70,000 of punitive damages are not generally excludable under Sec. 104(a)(2). The $70,000 for business loss is taxable to Donald as a substitute for compensation he would have otherwise earned.
   Answer (B) is incorrect. This amount is excluded from gross income. Answer (C) is incorrect. Only the damages received for personal injuries (i.e., damage to personal reputation) or sickness are excluded from gross income. Answer (D) is incorrect. Punitive damages are excluded only if they are in conjunction with physical injury or sickness.

2.2.6. Mr. Smith received accelerated life insurance proceeds of $20,000 in the current year. Mr. Smith's qualified long-term care expenses for the year were $26,000. Insurance reimbursed $14,000 of those payments. If Mr. Smith is terminally ill, what amount of the accelerated life insurance must be included in gross income?

   A. $0

   B. $8,000

   C. $12,000

   D. $14,000

Answer (A) is correct. *(Publisher, adapted)*
   REQUIRED: The amount of accelerated life insurance proceeds included in gross income of a terminally ill patient.
   DISCUSSION: When an insured person is terminally ill, amounts received after 1996 under a life insurance contract may be excluded from income [Sec. 101(g)]. A "terminally ill individual" is a person for whom the insurer has obtained certification from a physician that the individual has an illness or physical condition which is reasonably expected to result in death within 24 months of the date of certification. Since Mr. Smith is terminally ill, he may exclude the entire proceeds from his gross income.
   Answer (B) is incorrect. The amount of $8,000 is the excess of Mr. Smith's insurance proceeds over the net of care expenses less the reimbursement. The amount of proceeds included in gross income is affected by Mr. Smith's terminal illness. Answer (C) is incorrect. The amount of $12,000 is the difference between Mr. Smith's qualified long-term care expenses and the insurance reimbursement. Answer (D) is incorrect. The amount of $14,000 is the insurance reimbursement for long-term care expenses Mr. Smith paid. The amount of proceeds included in gross income is affected by Mr. Smith's terminal illness.

2.2.7. Rudy retired on disability in July of the current year. He had earned wages of $20,000 before his retirement and received $10,000 in disability benefits after his retirement. The disability benefits were received from an accident and health insurance plan that was paid for by Rudy's employer. He also received a lump-sum payment for accrued annual leave of $5,000, which was paid in the current year due to his disability retirement in that year. How much income should Rudy report in the current year?

A. $20,000

B. $25,000

C. $30,000

D. $35,000

Answer (D) is correct. *(SEE, adapted)*
REQUIRED: The amount included in gross income.
DISCUSSION: Section 61 provides for the inclusion of wages in gross income. Section 105 provides that amounts received by an employee through accident or health insurance paid for by the employer are included in the employee's gross income unless the amounts are for medical expenses. Lump-sum payments for accrued annual leave are includible in gross income as compensation.
Answer (A) is incorrect. The $10,000 of disability benefits and the $5,000 lump-sum leave payment are also includible in gross income. Answer (B) is incorrect. The $10,000 of disability benefits is also includible in gross income. Answer (C) is incorrect. The $5,000 lump-sum payment is also includible in gross income.

2.2.8. In 2017, Pete Smith receives $370 per day in benefits from a qualified long-term care insurance contract. He can substantiate that he actually incurred $380 of unreimbursed long-term care services each day. How much can he exclude from gross income for 2017?

A. $0

B. $131,400

C. $135,050

D. $138,700

Answer (C) is correct. *(Publisher, adapted)*
REQUIRED: The amount of qualified long-term care insurance proceeds excludable from gross income in 2017.
DISCUSSION: A qualified long-term care insurance contract will generally be treated as an accident and health insurance contract. Therefore, amounts received under a long-term care insurance contract are excluded as amounts received for personal injuries and sickness [Sec. 7702B(d)(4)]. This exclusion is capped at $360 per day on per diem contracts in 2017, and this amount is adjusted yearly for inflation. This contract pays a greater amount ($370) than the per diem rate. Since the actual expenses exceed the reimbursed amount, the entire reimbursement is excluded. Hence, the entire amount of $135,050 ($370 × 365 days) is excludable because Smith can show that he actually incurred more than this amount in expenses.
Answer (A) is incorrect. Amounts received under a long-term care insurance contract are excluded as amounts received for personal injuries and sickness. Answer (B) is incorrect. The amount of $131,400 ($360 × 365 days) does not consider that Smith can show that he paid $380 a day for actual expenses. Answer (D) is incorrect. Exclusions are limited to actual amounts received.

2.2.9. Mr. Doe was in a car accident. As a result of his injuries, he received an insurance check for $8,000 from a self-insured plan. His medical bills relating to the accident were $5,000 and were taken as a deduction on his tax return this year. How much of this amount can Mr. Doe exclude from gross income?

A. $0

B. $3,000

C. $5,000

D. $8,000

Answer (B) is correct. *(Publisher, adapted)*
REQUIRED: The amount of benefits from a self-insured plan that may be excluded from gross income.
DISCUSSION: Section 104(a)(3) provides an exclusion from gross income for amounts received under a self-insured plan. However, the exclusion is limited to amounts that are not deducted under Sec. 213. Since the $5,000 medical expenses are deductible, the exclusion is limited to $3,000.
Answer (A) is incorrect. Mr. Doe is allowed a limited exclusion of the $8,000 insurance check. Answer (C) is incorrect. The amount of Mr. Doe's medical bills relating to the accident is $5,000. This amount was taken as a deduction. Answer (D) is incorrect. The amount of the insurance check Mr. Doe received is $8,000. The exclusion is less than this amount.

2.2.10. Payments received by an airline pilot in settlement of an age discrimination suit brought against his former employer under the Age Discrimination in Employment Act (ADEA), which resulted in an award of back pay, are excludable from gross income as damages received on account of personal injuries.

A. True.

B. False.

Answer (B) is correct. *(Publisher, adapted)*
DISCUSSION: Damages received pursuant to the ADEA do not meet the requirements of Sec. 104(a)(2) and Reg. 1.104-1, which define damages received on account of personal injuries or physical sickness as those arising from a legal suit or action based upon tort or tort type rights [Erich E. Schleier, 115 S.Ct. 2159 (1995)]. Damages awarded under ADEA satisfy neither test. Back pay does not compensate for a personal injury; liquidated damages do not serve to establish that age discrimination is a tort and do not compensate for personal injuries or sickness.

2.3 Employee Benefits

2.3.1. Mr. Hawk, a factory assembly line worker, received the following benefits from his employer:

Medical insurance plan policy	$250
Christmas bonus	125
Reimbursement for college undergraduate physics course beginning January 10, 2017, under a nondiscriminatory written plan	450
$40,000 nondiscriminatory group term life insurance policy	475
Membership in a local health club	550

How much is includible in Mr. Hawk's income for the current year?

- A. $675
- B. $925
- C. $1,050
- D. $1,125

2.3.2. Under a "cafeteria plan" maintained by an employer,

- A. Participation must be restricted to employees and their spouses and minor children.
- B. At least 3 years of service are required before an employee can participate in the plan.
- C. Participants may select their own menu of benefits.
- D. Provision may be made for deferred compensation other than 401(k) plans.

2.3.3. Eagle Airlines operates solely as an air carrier. It allows all its employees to fly at no charge on any of its flights provided that paying customers are not displaced. Eagle has a reciprocal agreement with Diversified, Inc. (which is in both the airline and hotel businesses), under which the employees of one company may use the facilities of the other without charge provided that paying customers are not displaced. Which of the following benefits may an Eagle employee exclude from gross income?

- A. A use of Diversified hotels.
- B. A flight on an Eagle airplane or a Diversified airplane.
- C. A flight on either company's airplane and use of Diversified's hotels.
- D. None. Services provided by an employer are income.

Answer (A) is correct. *(Publisher, adapted)*
REQUIRED: The amount of fringe benefits includible in gross income.
DISCUSSION: Benefits received from an employer are compensation for services and included in gross income under Sec. 61 unless provided otherwise. Section 106 excludes from gross income contributions to accident or health plans (a medical insurance plan) made by an employer on behalf of the employee. Section 79 provides for the inclusion in gross income of the cost of group term life insurance paid by the employer but only to the extent that such cost exceeds the cost of $50,000 of such insurance provided the plan is not discriminatory. Hence, the cost of Mr. Hawk's group term life insurance is not included in gross income.
Section 127, which provides an exclusion of payments up to $5,250 per year made to reimburse an employee for educational expenses, was made permanent by the American Taxpayer Relief Act of 2012 including coverage of expenses for both undergraduate and graduate courses. Therefore, the reimbursement for the physics course is excluded. There is no provision excluding Christmas bonuses or memberships in off-premises health clubs, so $675 ($125 bonus + $550 membership) is includible in gross income.
Answer (B) is incorrect. Medical insurance paid by the employer is not included in gross income. Answer (C) is incorrect. Reimbursement for classes and costs of the group-term life insurance policy are not included in gross income. However, the membership dues for the health club are included in gross income. Answer (D) is incorrect. Reimbursement for classes is not included in gross income.

Answer (C) is correct. *(CPA, adapted)*
REQUIRED: The true statement with regard to cafeteria plans.
DISCUSSION: Section 125 defines a cafeteria plan as a written plan under which all participants are employees and the participants may choose among benefits consisting of cash and qualified benefits.
Answer (A) is incorrect. Participation is limited to employees. Answer (B) is incorrect. There is no minimum service requirement for participation. Answer (D) is incorrect. Cafeteria plans do not include plans that provide for deferred compensation.

Answer (B) is correct. *(Publisher, adapted)*
REQUIRED: The no-additional-cost service that may be excluded from gross income.
DISCUSSION: Section 132(a)(1) excludes from gross income no-additional-cost services provided by an employer to an employee. The service must be one normally sold to customers in the ordinary course of business and in the same line of business in which the employee works. Also, the employer must not incur substantial additional costs. Employees may also exclude the same type of services provided by another related employer if the employers have a reciprocal agreement. Since an Eagle employee works in the airline business, (s)he may exclude a flight provided by Eagle or Diversified.
Answer (A) is incorrect. An Eagle employee does not work in the hotel business, so (s)he cannot exclude use of one of Diversified's hotels. Answer (C) is incorrect. Even though the flights may be excluded, an Eagle employee does not work in the hotel business, so (s)he cannot exclude use of one of Diversified's hotels. Answer (D) is incorrect. Section 132 permits the exclusion of services provided by an employer to the employee as a fringe benefit.

2.3.4. Midwest Department Stores allows all its employees to purchase goods worth up to $1,000 in retail value each year at a 50% discount. Mark, an employee of Midwest, took full advantage of this policy one year and received a $500 discount. Midwest's gross profit percentage on sales to customers is 45%. The normal industry discount was only 30%. How much must Mark include in gross income?

A. $0

B. $50

C. $200

D. $500

Answer (B) is correct. *(Publisher, adapted)*
REQUIRED: The amount of an employee discount that must be included in gross income.
DISCUSSION: Section 132(a)(2) provides an exclusion from gross income for qualified discounts provided by an employer to an employee. The amount of the discount must not exceed the employer's gross profit percentage based on the price normally sold to customers. Since Midwest's gross profit percentage is normally 45%, any discount in excess of 45% must be included in the employee's gross income. Here the excess discount is 5% (50% − 45%). Accordingly, Mark must include $50 in his gross income ($1,000 × 5%).
Answer (A) is incorrect. Mark's gross income is affected by the excessive discount. Answer (C) is incorrect. The includible portion is based on the excess of the discount percentage over the gross profit percentage of the employer, not the industry discount percentage. Answer (D) is incorrect. Only the portion of the discount in excess of the gross profit percentage of the employer times the purchases is includible in gross income.

2.3.5. Mary is a CPA who works for a public accounting firm. How much of the following fringe benefits are excluded from her gross income if paid for or provided by her employer?

Membership in CPA association	$ 75
Subscription to a banking association journal (she has several bank clients)	40
Parking at her office	255
Personal photocopying on office machine	10
Coffee and doughnuts	20

A. $135

B. $295

C. $390

D. $400

Answer (D) is correct. *(Publisher, adapted)*
REQUIRED: The amount of fringe benefits excludable by an employee from gross income.
DISCUSSION: Section 132 provides an exclusion from gross income of an employee for working condition fringe benefits and de minimis fringe benefits provided by an employer. A CPA's membership in a CPA association and a subscription to a banking association journal for someone who has bank clients are considered working condition fringe benefits. Parking is specifically listed as a qualified transportation fringe benefit under Secs. 132(f)(1) and (2). Employers may offer their employees cash instead of free parking. If employees choose the cash option, the cash received is included in gross income. Personal use of a photocopy machine and free coffee and doughnuts are examples of de minimis fringe benefits. Hence, all of the fringe benefits listed are excludable from Mary's gross income. These benefits total $400.
Answer (A) is incorrect. Personal photocopying and parking are excluded from gross income. Answer (B) is incorrect. Memberships in associations, personal photocopying, and coffee and doughnuts are excluded from gross income. Answer (C) is incorrect. Personal photocopying is a de minimis fringe benefit and is excluded from gross income.

2.3.6. From the items listed below, determine the amount of income to be included in Mr. E's tax return for the current year.

Medical insurance premium paid by employer under a plan	$375
Nondiscriminatory group permanent life insurance premiums paid by employer on face amount exceeding $50,000	225
The excess of fair market value over the purchase price paid for property acquired from employer (not a qualified discount)	400
Amount of interview expense allowance received from employer in excess of actual expenses	250

A. $475

B. $650

C. $875

D. $1,250

Answer (C) is correct. *(SEE, adapted)*
REQUIRED: The amount of income includible in Mr. E's tax return.
DISCUSSION: Mr. E would include in gross income the premiums paid by his employer for group permanent life insurance ($225) since Sec. 79 excludes such premiums only if paid for group term life insurance (up to $50,000). The excess of fair market value over the purchase price for property acquired from the employer ($400) is additional compensation for services rendered. The excess reimbursement for interview expenses ($250) is also income. If Mr. E made an adequate accounting to his employer for his interview expenses, he may report the excess reimbursement as miscellaneous income and would not have to include the full amount of reimbursement in gross income with a corresponding deduction for the actual expenses [Reg. 1.162-17(b)(2)]. These three amounts total $875.
The medical insurance premiums paid by the employer are excluded from gross income under Sec. 106.
Answer (A) is incorrect. The excess of fair market value over the purchase price paid for property acquired from an employer is included in income. Answer (B) is incorrect. Nondiscriminatory group permanent life insurance premiums paid by an employer are included in income. Answer (D) is incorrect. Medical insurance premiums paid by an employer are not included in income.

2.3.7. All of the following statements about fringe benefits for 2017 are true except

A. An employer can exclude qualified transportation fringe benefits from an employee's wages even if they are provided in place of pay.

B. Holiday gift certificates given to employees are not excluded from income.

C. Employee wages do not include the value of any property or service that has so little value that accounting for it would be unreasonable or administratively impracticable.

D. An employer can treat all meals furnished to employees on their premises as furnished for the employer's convenience if half of these employees are furnished the meals for a substantial nonpay business reason.

Answer (D) is correct. *(SEE, adapted)*
REQUIRED: The false statement about fringe benefits.
DISCUSSION: More than one-half of all meals furnished to employees on an employer's premise must be furnished for a substantial nonpay business reason.
Answer (A) is incorrect. An employer can exclude qualified transportation fringe benefits from an employee's wages even if they are provided in place of pay. Answer (B) is incorrect. The IRS has ruled in TAM 200437030 that gift certificates are the equivalent of cash. Answer (C) is incorrect. Employee wages do not include the value of any property or service that has so little value that accounting for it would be unreasonable or administratively impracticable.

2.3.8. Mr. T has been a night watchman at Y Company for 10 years. During the current year, he received the following payments from Y Company:

Salary	$15,000
Hospitalization insurance premiums	3,600
Required lodging on Y's premises for Y's convenience as a condition to T's employment	2,400
Reward for preventing a break-in	1,000
Christmas ham (value)	15

What amount is includible in Mr. T's gross income in the current year?

A. $17,400

B. $16,015

C. $16,000

D. $15,000

Answer (C) is correct. *(SEE, adapted)*
REQUIRED: The amount includible in Mr. T's gross income.
DISCUSSION: The hospitalization insurance premiums paid by Mr. T's employer are excluded from gross income under Sec. 106. Since Mr. T was required to live on Y's premises both for Y's convenience and as a condition for his employment, the cost of such lodging is excluded from gross income under Sec. 119. The Christmas ham is excluded from gross income under Sec. 132 as a de minimis fringe. Therefore, Mr. T's salary of $15,000 and the reward of $1,000 are the only items included in gross income as compensation for services rendered (Sec. 61).
Answer (A) is incorrect. Required lodging is excluded from gross income. However, the reward for preventing a break-in is included in gross income. Answer (B) is incorrect. The ham is a de minimis fringe benefit and is excluded from gross income. Answer (D) is incorrect. Gross income also includes the reward for preventing the break-in.

2.3.9. Employee Y, who is 55 years old, is provided with $120,000 of nondiscriminatory group term life insurance by his employer. Based on the IRS uniform premium cost table, the total annual cost of a policy of this type is $9 per $1,000 of coverage. Y's required contribution to the cost of the policy is $2 per $1,000 of coverage per year. Y was covered for the entire year. How much of the cost must Y include in his income?

A. $0

B. $390

C. $630

D. $840

Answer (B) is correct. *(SEE, adapted)*
REQUIRED: The amount of premium for group term life insurance that is included in the employee's gross income.
DISCUSSION: Under Sec. 79, the cost of qualified group term life insurance paid by an employer is included in the employee's gross income to the extent that such cost exceeds the cost of $50,000 of such insurance. The includible cost is determined on the basis of uniform premiums prescribed by regulations, rather than actual cost. Therefore, we do not need to know what the actual premiums were in order to compute the answer.
The includible cost is the total cost (based on uniform premiums prescribed by regulations minus the employee's contribution) of the employer less the amount otherwise excluded. The total cost of the employer based on the IRS tables is $7 per $1,000 of insurance per year because Y is paying $2. The excludable cost is $9 per $1,000 for the first $50,000 of insurance. Computation is below.

Employer's cost of policy ($7 × 120)	$840
Less: excludable portion ($9 × 50)	(450)
Amount included in Y's income	$390

Answer (A) is incorrect. The employee's gross income is affected by the excess of the employer's cost over the excludable portion of the policy cost. Answer (C) is incorrect. The portion excludable is $450. Answer (D) is incorrect. The amount of $840 equals the employer's cost of the policy. A portion of this amount is excludable from gross income.

2.3.10. Which of the following will not be a characteristic (not considering cost-of-living adjustments) of a highly compensated individual for self-insured medical expense reimbursement plans?

A. Owns more than 10% in value of the employer's stock.

B. Receives compensation in excess of $120,000.

C. Is one of the five highest-paid officers.

D. Is among the highest-paid 25% of all employees (excluding all employees who are not plan participants).

Answer (B) is correct. *(Publisher, adapted)*
REQUIRED: The characteristic that will not identify a highly compensated individual.
DISCUSSION: A highly compensated individual is a term used to identify certain employees to determine if employee benefits are discriminatory. For purposes of self-insured medical expense reimbursement plans, Section 105(h)(5) defines a highly compensated employee as one of the five highest-paid officers, a shareholder who owns more than 10% of the value of an employer's stock, or one who is among the highest-paid 25% of all employees (excluding nonparticipants). Receiving compensation in excess of $120,000 is a characteristic of a highly compensated employee for retirement plans, not for self-insured medical reimbursement plans.
Answer (A) is incorrect. For purposes of Sec. 105, a highly compensated individual owns more than 10% in value of the employer's stock. Answer (C) is incorrect. For purposes of Sec. 105, a highly compensated individual is one of the five highest-paid officers. Answer (D) is incorrect. A highly compensated individual for purposes of Sec. 105 is among the highest-paid 25% of all employees (excluding employees who are not plan participants).

2.3.11. Ginger Corporation provides a nondiscriminatory plan under which its employees are able to choose their fringe benefits up to $2,000 in value per year from the following:

Cash
Medical reimbursements
Premiums on major medical insurance
Premiums on up to $50,000 of group term life
  insurance

If an employee chooses major medical insurance premiums worth $950, medical reimbursements of $300, group term life insurance premiums of $50, and cash of $700, how much may the employee exclude from gross income?

A. $0

B. $300

C. $1,250

D. $1,300

Answer (D) is correct. *(Publisher, adapted)*
REQUIRED: The amount of benefits from a cafeteria plan that an employee may exclude from gross income.
DISCUSSION: The cafeteria plan is one in which the employees may choose among their fringe benefits. Under Sec. 125, the use of a cafeteria plan does not cause the benefits to be included in the gross income of the participants, provided the plan does not discriminate in favor of highly compensated or key employees. However, the only benefits allowed under the cafeteria plan are cash and qualified benefits (not allowed are scholarships and fellowship grants or tuition reductions under Sec. 117, educational assistance under Sec. 127, or fringe benefits under Sec. 132). Since only cash and qualified benefits are allowed, Ginger's cafeteria plan qualifies. The taxation of the benefits depends on which are chosen. Medical reimbursements by an employer are excluded from gross income under Sec. 105(b), and major medical insurance premiums paid by an employer are excluded under Sec. 106. Premiums on up to $50,000 of qualified group term life insurance are excluded by Sec. 79. There is no exclusion for cash payments to an employee. Therefore, the employee who chooses major medical insurance premiums worth $950, medical reimbursements of $300, and group term life insurance premiums of $50 may exclude this $1,300 from gross income.
Answer (A) is incorrect. The employee may not exclude the entire amount from gross income. Answer (B) is incorrect. Medical insurance premiums and group term life insurance premiums may be excluded from gross income. Answer (C) is incorrect. Group term life insurance premiums may be excluded from gross income.

2.3.12. Which of the following income items may not be excluded from gross income?

A. Housing received by a medical research student at an academic health center. The monthly charge is 25% of the housing's fair market value.

B. Military pay received while serving in a combat zone.

C. Christmas bonus of $100 in cash received at the end of the year.

D. Adoption expenses incurred by an employee that are reimbursed by an employer.

Answer (C) is correct. *(Publisher, adapted)*
REQUIRED: The item that cannot be excluded from gross income.
DISCUSSION: Benefits received from an employer as compensation for services are included in gross income under Sec. 61 unless provided otherwise. There is no provision excluding a cash Christmas bonus; therefore, the bonus must be included in income.
Answer (A) is incorrect. Section 119(d)(4) specifically excludes employee housing at an academic health center if the rent paid by the employee exceeds 5% of the fair market value of the housing. Answer (B) is incorrect. Section 112 specifically excludes military pay received while serving in a combat zone. Answer (D) is incorrect. Section 137(a) specifically excludes up to $13,570 of reimbursed qualified adoption expenses.

2.3.13. The Rosco Corporation has a medical reimbursement plan under which employees are reimbursed for their medical expenses directly by the corporation. In order for the amount received by a highly compensated employee to be entirely excluded from income, which of the following is true?

A. A self-insured plan may not discriminate, but an insured plan may.

B. The plan must be insured.

C. All employees must be covered by the plan.

D. Both diagnostic medical procedures and those to treat, cure, or test a known illness must be provided in a nondiscriminatory manner.

Answer (A) is correct. *(Publisher, adapted)*
REQUIRED: The true statement regarding the exclusion of medical reimbursements from the income of a highly compensated employee.
DISCUSSION: Section 105(b) excludes from an employee's gross income amounts that are paid, directly or indirectly, to the employee as reimbursements for expenses incurred by the employee, spouse, and dependents for medical care. Section 105(h) provides that a self-insured medical expense reimbursement plan may not discriminate in favor of highly compensated employees. If the plan is discriminatory, the discriminatory portion of the reimbursements will be included in the income of the highly compensated employees. The nondiscriminatory provisions of Sec. 105 apply only to self-insured plans, however, and an insured medical reimbursement plan may discriminate in favor of highly compensated employees. Therefore, an amount received by a highly compensated employee under an insured plan would be excluded from income under Sec. 105 regardless of whether the plan was nondiscriminatory or not.
Answer (B) is incorrect. A medical reimbursement plan may be insured or self-insured and still come within the provisions of Sec. 105. Answer (C) is incorrect. An insured plan may cover any employees, even in a discriminatory manner, and even a self-insured plan can exclude certain employees from coverage (i.e., part-time, seasonal, and employees under age 25). Answer (D) is incorrect. The nondiscriminatory provisions of Sec. 105 apply only to self-insured medical reimbursement plans.

2.3.14. Which of the following qualifications is not necessary in an employer's self-insured accident and health plan to prevent the plan from being considered discriminatory?

A. All benefits provided for participants who are highly compensated individuals must be provided for all other participants.

B. The plan may not discriminate in favor of highly compensated individuals as to eligibility to participate.

C. All employees having completed 3 years of service must be participants in the plan.

D. The plan must not discriminate in favor of highly compensated individuals as to benefits provided under the plan.

Answer (C) is correct. *(Publisher, adapted)*
REQUIRED: The qualification not needed to prevent an employer's accident and health plan from being considered discriminatory.
DISCUSSION: Section 105(h) provides the requirements a plan must meet in order to be considered nondiscriminatory. In determining whether eligibility to participate in the plan is discriminatory, certain employees, such as part-time or seasonal employees or employees who have not attained the age of 25, are excluded from consideration. Therefore, it is not a necessary qualification for a plan to be considered nondiscriminatory.
Answer (A) is incorrect. A requirement of a nondiscriminatory plan as outlined in Sec. 105(h) is that all benefits provided for participants who are highly compensated individuals must be provided for all other participants. Answer (B) is incorrect. A requirement of a nondiscriminatory plan as outlined in Sec. 105(h) is that the plan may not discriminate in favor of highly compensated individuals as to eligibility to participate. Answer (D) is incorrect. A nondiscriminatory plan as outlined in Sec. 105(h) requires the plan not to discriminate in favor of highly compensated individuals as to benefits provided under the plan.

2.3.15. Elmer has been a faithful employee of the Bold Dairy Co. for 25 years. In recognition of Elmer's length of service, Bold Dairy held a banquet and presented Elmer with a gold watch and a brass cow, with a cost and value of $500. The award was not a qualified plan award. Elmer's meal at the banquet was valued at $30. Bold Dairy was able to expense the banquet in full and $400 of the award. Later in the year, Elmer received a cash Christmas gift of $50 (as did other employees), and Bold Dairy was able to expense $25. How much income must Elmer report?

A. $0

B. $150

C. $475

D. $550

Answer (B) is correct. *(Publisher, adapted)*
REQUIRED: The amount an employee must include in income from gifts and awards from the employer.
DISCUSSION: An employee may exclude from gross income the value of an employee achievement award to the extent the employer may deduct it under Sec. 274(j). Elmer must include the excess of the $500 award over the $400 employer deduction, or $100 [Sec. 74(c)]. The value of the meal is excluded as a de minimis fringe benefit under Sec. 132. The entire $50 Christmas gift must be included in Elmer's income under Sec. 102(c), which disallows an exclusion for gifts by an employer to an employee. The cash gift is not de minimis because it is in cash and easily accounted for.
Answer (A) is incorrect. Elmer's income is affected by the gift and award. Answer (C) is incorrect. The portion of the award's FMV that was deductible to the employer ($400) is not included in gross income. Additionally, the value of the meal is excluded as a de minimis fringe benefit. Answer (D) is incorrect. Only the FMV of the award in excess of the employer's deduction is included in gross income, not the whole value of the award.

2.3.16. During the current year, Employee A received tangible personal property as a safety achievement award from her employer. The award was not a qualified plan award. The property cost the employer $500 and had a fair market value of $600. How much must A include in her gross income?

A. $0

B. $200

C. $500

D. $600

Answer (B) is correct. *(SEE, adapted)*
   REQUIRED: The amount an employee must include in income from a safety achievement award.
   DISCUSSION: Section 74(c) allows an employee to exclude from gross income the value of an employee achievement award to the extent the employer may deduct it under Sec. 274(j). An employee achievement award is an item of tangible personal property provided by an employer for length of service achievement or for safety achievement. Section 274(j) allows a deduction of up to $400 per award (or up to $1,600 under a qualified plan) provided the average awards do not exceed $400. Since the award was not a qualified plan award, the limitation is $400. Any excess value received by an employee must be included in gross income. Therefore, A must include $200 ($600 value – $400 excludable) in gross income.
   Answer (A) is incorrect. Employee A's gross income is affected by the excess of the FMV of the award over the employer's deduction. Answer (C) is incorrect. An exclusion of up to $400 is allowed. However, the excess is based on the FMV, not the cost to the employer. Answer (D) is incorrect. The equivalent of the employer's deduction may be excluded from gross income.

2.3.17. Zippy worked at the Maxwell Hotel as a desk clerk. Since there was no one to replace him during the dinner hour, the Maxwell Hotel provided Zippy's meal out of the dining room free of charge. Zippy was allowed to go and eat elsewhere but was encouraged to eat at the hotel and mind the desk. The cost of the meals to the Maxwell Hotel was $450, and the fair market value of the meals was $800. How much must Zippy include in gross income?

A. $0

B. $350

C. $450

D. $800

Answer (A) is correct. *(Publisher, adapted)*
   REQUIRED: The amount that an employee must include in gross income for meals furnished by an employer.
   DISCUSSION: Section 119 provides an exclusion for meals furnished on the business premises of the employer if they are furnished to the employee for the convenience of the employer. The convenience of the employer is served by keeping Zippy at the desk during dinner. In the case of meals, the fact that the employee may accept or decline such meals is not taken into account. Therefore, Zippy may exclude the entire amount of the meals from his gross income. Note that the relevant amount Zippy would have to include in gross income if the meals did not meet the requirements of Sec. 119 is the fair market value of the meals.
   Answer (B) is incorrect. The difference between the cost of the meals and the FMV of the meals is $350. The FMV of the meals is excluded from gross income when provided on the business premises and for the convenience of the employer. Answer (C) is incorrect. The cost of the meals is $450. The FMV of the meals is excluded from gross income when provided on the business premises and for the convenience of the employer. Answer (D) is incorrect. The FMV of the meals is $800. This amount would be included in gross income if the meals did not meet the exclusion requirements.

2.3.18. Hansel and Gretel were employed as managers of a motel. Part of their job requirements was to live on the premises so that they would be available to watch the desk and take care of any guest's problems. They were provided with living quarters and groceries free of charge. The living quarters were worth $3,000 per year, and the groceries were worth $2,500 per year. How much must Hansel and Gretel include in gross income?

A. $0

B. $2,500

C. $3,000

D. $5,500

Answer (B) is correct. *(Publisher, adapted)*
   REQUIRED: The amount that an employee must include in gross income from an employer who provides living quarters and groceries.
   DISCUSSION: Section 119 provides an exclusion for meals and lodging furnished on the business premises of the employer if they are furnished for the convenience of the employer. Having motel managers remain on the premises to register and take care of guests is for the convenience of the employer. For lodging (but not meals), the employee must be required to accept the lodging as a condition of employment. Since these requirements are met for Hansel and Gretel, they may exclude the entire value of their living quarters. However, while the value of meals may be excluded, there is no exclusion for groceries. Therefore, Hansel and Gretel must include the value of groceries ($2,500) in their gross income.
   Answer (A) is incorrect. Their gross income is affected by some of the provisions provided. Answer (C) is incorrect. Groceries may not be excluded from gross income, but the FMV of the lodging may be excluded from gross income. Answer (D) is incorrect. Gross income does not include the FMV of the lodging when it is provided for the employer's convenience.

2.3.19. Mr. J, a highly compensated employee, has group term life insurance coverage of $100,000 paid for by his employer. The plan discriminates in favor of key employees. J must include the actual cost of the entire $100,000 of coverage in his income.

A. True.

B. False.

Answer (A) is correct. *(SEE, adapted)*
DISCUSSION: Under Sec. 79, the cost of up to $50,000 of group term life insurance in a nondiscriminatory plan may be excluded from each employee's income. If the plan discriminates in favor of key employees, the key employees are not eligible for the exclusion and must include in gross income the greater of the actual premiums paid or the amount calculated from the Uniform Premiums Table provided at Reg. 1.79-3. Key employees are defined in Sec. 416(i)(1) as being certain highly compensated owners and officers.

2.3.20. Dependent care assistance paid by an employer to an employee must be included in the employee's income.

A. True.

B. False.

Answer (B) is correct. *(Publisher, adapted)*
DISCUSSION: Under a qualified program, up to $5,000 of dependent care assistance may be excluded (Sec. 129) on a joint return.

2.3.21. During the current year, ZM&T, under a qualified plan for educational assistance, paid for an employee's graduate-level course in computer telecommunications. The exclusion from gross income for educational assistance program benefits applies to payments for graduate-level courses.

A. True.

B. False.

Answer (A) is correct. *(SEE, adapted)*
DISCUSSION: Section 127 allows up to a $5,250 exclusion from an employee's gross income of amounts paid by the employer for educational assistance for undergraduate and graduate courses. The payments must be made pursuant to an educational assistance program as defined in that section.

2.3.22. During the current year, Mrs. P worked as a secretary for a university that has a qualified tuition reduction program. Her son, an undergraduate, whom she is entitled to claim as a dependent, received a tuition reduction of $5,500. The $5,500 is taxable income to Mrs. P's son for federal income tax purposes.

A. True.

B. False.

Answer (B) is correct. *(SEE, adapted)*
DISCUSSION: The amount of any qualified tuition reduction provided for an employee, the employee's spouse, or the employee's dependent child is excluded from gross income under Sec. 117(d). The tuition reduction may be used toward undergraduate and graduate education.

2.4 Social Security Benefits

2.4.1. With regard to the inclusion of Social Security benefits in gross income, which of the following statements is true?

A. The Social Security benefits in excess of modified adjusted gross income are included in gross income.

B. The Social Security benefits in excess of one-half the modified adjusted gross income are included in gross income.

C. 85% of the Social Security benefits is the maximum amount of benefits to be included in gross income.

D. The Social Security benefits in excess of the modified adjusted gross income over $32,000 are included in gross income.

Answer (C) is correct. *(CPA, adapted)*
REQUIRED: The true statement with regard to the inclusion of Social Security benefits in gross income.
DISCUSSION: The taxable portion of Social Security benefits will depend upon the amount of provisional income in relation to the base amount and the adjusted base amount. If provisional income exceeds the adjusted base amount, up to 85% of Social Security benefits may be taxable.
Answer (A) is incorrect. A total of 85% of Social Security benefits is the maximum amount includible in gross income. This amount cannot be found simply by taking the excess of provisional income over modified AGI. Answer (B) is incorrect. A total of 85% of Social Security benefits is the maximum amount includible in gross income. This amount cannot be found simply by taking one-half of modified AGI. Answer (D) is incorrect. A total of 85% of Social Security benefits is the maximum amount includible in gross income. This amount cannot be found simply by taking modified AGI over $32,000.

2.4.2. Ms. Green is single and over 65 years old. She received the following income in the current year:

Interest from certificates of deposit	$ 3,000
Tax-exempt interest	6,000
Taxable dividends	5,000
Taxable pension	20,000
Wages from consulting work	9,000
Social Security	14,000

She did not have any adjustments to income. What is the taxable amount of Ms. Green's Social Security?

    A. $7,000

    B. $11,900

    C. $14,000

    D. $18,100

Answer (B) is correct. *(SEE, adapted)*
    REQUIRED: The amount of Social Security benefits included in gross income.
    DISCUSSION: If the sum of a single individual's modified adjusted gross income plus 50% of the Social Security benefits exceeds $25,000, part of the Social Security benefits is included in gross income. The includible portion is the lesser of 50% of Social Security benefits or 50% of the excess as noted above. Modified adjusted gross income equals adjusted gross income plus tax-exempt interest. A second threshold exists if the sum of the modified adjusted gross income plus 50% of Social Security benefits exceeds $34,000 for a single taxpayer. The includible portion is the lesser of 85% of Social Security benefits or 85% of the excess plus the smaller of $4,500 ($9,000 incremental base amount × 50%) or the amount included under present law (50% rules). Ms. Green's modified adjusted gross income is $43,000 ($20,000 pension + $3,000 taxable interest + $6,000 tax-exempt interest + $5,000 dividends + $9,000 consulting wages). The taxable portion of Social Security is $11,900 because it is less than 85% of the excess of modified AGI plus 50% of Social Security benefits over $34,000, plus $4,500.

Modified AGI	$43,000
One-half of Social Security benefits	7,000
Less: $34,000 base amount	(34,000)
	$16,000
85% of Social Security ($14,000 × 85%)	$11,900
85% of excess ($16,000 × 85%)	$13,600
Plus smaller of:	
$4,500 or $7,000 ($14,000 × 50%)	4,500
	$18,100

    Answer (A) is incorrect. The amount of $7,000 would be the includible portion of Social Security only if modified adjusted gross income plus 50% of the Social Security benefits was more than $25,000 but less than $34,000. Answer (C) is incorrect. Only 85% of the benefits are included in gross income. Answer (D) is incorrect. The taxable amount cannot exceed the $14,000 of Social Security benefits.

2.4.3. Mr. and Mrs. Birch are both over 65 years of age and are filing a joint return. Their income for the current year consisted of the following:

Taxable interest	$ 6,000
Taxable dividends	8,000
Social Security payments	
(Mr. and Mrs. Birch combined)	15,000
Tax-exempt interest	4,000
Taxable pension	15,000

They did not have any adjustments to income. What amount of Mr. and Mrs. Birch's Social Security benefits is taxable?

    A. $0

    B. $4,250

    C. $7,500

    D. $8,500

Answer (B) is correct. *(SEE, adapted)*
    REQUIRED: The amount of Social Security benefits included in gross income.
    DISCUSSION: Under Sec. 86, if the sum of the "modified" adjusted gross income plus one-half of Social Security benefits exceeds $32,000 on a joint return but does not exceed $44,000, part of the Social Security benefits will be included in gross income. Modified adjusted gross income equals adjusted gross income plus tax-exempt interest [Sec. 86(b)(2)]. The includible portion of Social Security benefits is the lesser of one-half of the Social Security benefits or one-half of the excess as noted above. Mr. and Mrs. Birch would include $4,250 since it is less than one-half of the Social Security benefits ($15,000 × 50% = $7,500).

Modified AGI	
($6,000 + $8,000 + $4,000 + $15,000)	$33,000
One-half of Social Security benefits	7,500
Less: $32,000 base amount	(32,000)
	$ 8,500
50% of excess or	$ 4,250
50% of Social Security ($15,000 × 50%)	$ 7,500

    Answer (A) is incorrect. An amount of Mr. and Mrs. Birch's Social Security benefit is taxable. Answer (C) is incorrect. The amount of $7,500 is 50% of the Social Security payments, which is not less than 50% of the excess. Answer (D) is incorrect. The includible portion of the Social Security payments is the lesser of one-half of the payment or one-half of the excess as determined in the problem.

2.4.4. After Hughes died, his daughter Jane was entitled to receive Social Security benefits for education. During the year, she received $2,800 for tuition. However, she also earned $27,000 from part-time work. How much of the Social Security benefits must Jane include in her income?

A. $0

B. $1,400

C. $1,700

D. $2,800

Answer (B) is correct. *(Publisher, adapted)*
   REQUIRED: The Social Security educational benefits includible by a surviving child.
   DISCUSSION: Social Security educational benefits provided to survivors are excluded from gross income to the extent not required to be included under Sec. 86. If a single individual's provisional income (modified adjusted gross income plus 50% of the Social Security benefits) exceeds $25,000, part of the Social Security benefits are included in gross income. Until the single individual's provisional income exceeds $34,000, the includible portion is the lesser of 50% of Social Security benefits or 50% of the excess as noted above. Jane's includible portion is $1,400 ($2,800 Social Security benefits × 50%) because it is less than the result of the computation below.

Modified AGI	$27,000
One-half of Social Security benefits	1,400
Less: $25,000 base amount	(25,000)
	$ 3,400
50% of excess or	$ 1,700
50% of Social Security benefits	$ 1,400

   Answer (A) is incorrect. An amount of Social Security benefits must be included in Jane's income. Answer (C) is incorrect. The amount of $1,700 is 50% of the excess and it is greater than 50% of the Social Security benefits. Answer (D) is incorrect. The amount of $2,800 is the total Social Security benefits. An exclusion is allowed for part of the benefits.

2.4.5. During the current year, Mr. A, who is 67 years old, received Social Security benefits of $12,000. This amount was reported to him at year end on a Form SSA-1099. Because he received a Form SSA-1099, Mr. A must include this amount as income on his income tax return.

A. True.

B. False.

Answer (B) is correct. *(SEE, adapted)*
   DISCUSSION: Social Security benefits are not taxed unless provisional income (the sum of one-half of the Social Security benefits plus modified adjusted gross income) exceeds a base amount. This base amount is $32,000 for a joint return and $25,000 for a single return. The base amount for a married person filing separately is $0. Receiving a Form SSA-1099 does not require Social Security benefits to be included in gross income.

2.5 Payments Made at Death

2.5.1. Mrs. Dee's husband died in the current year. She chose to receive the proceeds of her husband's $100,000 life insurance policy over a 10-year period. The monthly installments are $1,200 each. What is the amount of the annual payments that represents gross income to Mrs. Dee?

A. $0

B. $2,000

C. $4,400

D. $14,400

Answer (C) is correct. *(SEE, adapted)*
   REQUIRED: The surviving spouse's annual gross income from a life insurance policy received in installments if the spouse died after October 22, 1986.
   DISCUSSION: Mrs. Dee will receive $10,000 ($100,000 ÷ 10 years) of the insurance proceeds per year and may exclude this amount each year from gross income. The remaining $4,400 [($1,200 × 12) – $10,000] received each year is interest. The 1986 TRA repealed the Sec. 101(d) exclusion of $1,000 of interest on installment payments of life insurance for surviving spouses when the deceased died after October 22, 1986. Since Mrs. Dee's husband died after October 22, 1986, she must include the entire $4,400 of interest in her gross income each year.
   Answer (A) is incorrect. An amount in excess of the face value of the annual payments will affect gross income to Mrs. Dee. Answer (B) is incorrect. The amount of $2,000 excludes 2 months of installments. Answer (D) is incorrect. The amount of $14,400 is the total payments received in a year. The amount not attributable to interest is excluded from income.

2.5.2. In the current year, Dennis was killed in an automobile accident. In October 2017, his widow received a lump-sum death benefit from his employer in the amount of $15,000. Dennis had no right to the $15,000 prior to death. For 2017, what amount should his widow include in gross income?

A. $0

B. $10,000

C. $14,000

D. $15,000

Answer (D) is correct. *(CPA, adapted)*
  REQUIRED: The amount of a lump-sum death benefit that must be included in gross income.
  DISCUSSION: Since Dennis died in the current year, Dennis's widow would include the full $15,000 in gross income.
  Answer (A) is incorrect. The widow should include the full amount of the proceeds in gross income. Answer (B) is incorrect. The amount of the lump-sum benefit Dennis's widow received is $15,000, and the exclusion no longer applies. Answer (C) is incorrect. The full amount is included in income.

2.5.3. When Sylvester was 16 years old, his uncle died and left him $100,000. After Sylvester received the $100,000, interest income of $10,000 was earned before the end of the year. Sylvester's uncle also left $1 million to a charity, but Sylvester was to receive the income from the money for a period of 5 years. It produced $80,000 worth of income before year end. How much must Sylvester include in his gross income for the year?

A. $0

B. $80,000

C. $90,000

D. $110,000

Answer (C) is correct. *(Publisher, adapted)*
  REQUIRED: The amount of income a beneficiary of a bequest of property and a bequest of income must include in gross income.
  DISCUSSION: Under Sec. 102(a), income does not include the value of property acquired by gift, bequest, or inheritance. Therefore, the bequest of $100,000 to Sylvester is excluded from gross income. Section 102(b) provides, however, that both income from a bequest or inheritance of property and from a bequest or inheritance of income are included in gross income. Therefore, the $10,000 of interest income earned on the bequest is included in Sylvester's gross income, as well as the $80,000 income received from the bequest made to charity. Sylvester must include a total of $90,000 in gross income for the year.
  Answer (A) is incorrect. Sylvester's gross income is affected by interest income and income from the charitable bequest. Answer (B) is incorrect. The amount of $80,000 excludes the effect of interest income on Sylvester's gross income. Answer (D) is incorrect. The $100,000 inheritance is not included in gross income. Only the income earned from an inheritance is included in gross income. In addition, income from other bequests (e.g., charitable) also affects gross income.

2.5.4. Mrs. D, a widow since January 1986, elected to receive the proceeds of her deceased husband's $300,000 life insurance policy in 40 yearly installments of $10,000 instead of a lump-sum payment. The payments are based on a guaranteed interest rate. What amount of interest should Mrs. D include in her gross income in 2017?

A. $0

B. $500

C. $1,500

D. $2,500

Answer (C) is correct. *(SEE, adapted)*
  REQUIRED: The surviving spouse's annual gross income from a life insurance policy received in installments if the spouse died on or before October 22, 1986.
  DISCUSSION: The proceeds of a life insurance policy, if paid by reason of the death of the insured, are excluded from gross income under Sec. 101(a). Mrs. D will receive $7,500 ($300,000 ÷ 40 years) of the insurance proceeds per year, and she may exclude this amount each year from gross income. Section 101(d) permits a surviving spouse to exclude the first $1,000 of interest collected on the proceeds of an insurance policy paid in installments if the spouse died on or before October 22, 1986. (The current code contains the law applicable to post-October 1986 deaths; however, the pre-October 1986 death rules apply to the pre-October 1986 deaths.) In addition to the $7,500 exclusion, Mrs. D may also exclude $1,000 of interest each year. Therefore, she must include $1,500 ($10,000 − $7,500 − $1,000) each year.
  Answer (A) is incorrect. Mrs. D must include part of the interest in gross income. Answer (B) is incorrect. The amount of $500 excludes an excessive amount of interest income. Answer (D) is incorrect. The amount of $2,500 fails to exclude up to the limit for deaths before October 22, 1986.

2.6 Scholarships and Fellowships

2.6.1. Scholarships and fellowships awarded to degree candidates are not taxable unless they are used for

- A. Tuition.
- B. Room and board.
- C. Books.
- D. Supplies required for the course of study.

Answer (B) is correct. *(SEE, adapted)*
REQUIRED: The items that provide an exclusion from gross income for amounts received as a scholarship or fellowship.
DISCUSSION: Section 117 provides an exclusion from gross income for amounts received as a scholarship or fellowship grant by a degree candidate. But only amounts provided and actually used for tuition, fees, books, supplies, and equipment required for instruction qualify for this exclusion. Room and board does not qualify.
Answer (A) is incorrect. Amounts provided and actually used for tuition are specifically excluded from gross income under Sec. 117. Answer (C) is incorrect. Amounts provided and actually used for books are specifically excluded from gross income under Sec. 117. Answer (D) is incorrect. Amounts provided and actually used for supplies required for the course of study are specifically excluded from gross income under Sec. 117.

2.6.2. In Year 1, Lee was beginning his undergraduate education. In January of Year 1, Lee was awarded a scholarship of $500 per month from a tax-exempt educational foundation to continue as long as Lee was a full-time student until he received his degree. Lee remained a full-time student and graduated at the end of August of Year 5. Lee received the scholarship each month from January of Year 5 through August of Year 5 and spent $2,400 for tuition, fees, books, and supplies. How much must Lee include in gross income from the scholarship in Year 5?

- A. $0
- B. $1,600
- C. $2,400
- D. $4,000

Answer (B) is correct. *(Publisher, adapted)*
REQUIRED: The amount of income the recipient of a scholarship who is a candidate for a degree must include in gross income.
DISCUSSION: A candidate for a degree may exclude the amount received as a scholarship at an educational organization. There is no limit on the time for which the scholarship may be received. Only amounts actually used for tuition, course-related fees, books, supplies, and equipment required for instruction qualify for this exclusion. Therefore, Lee needs to include $1,600 in gross income from the scholarship as calculated below:

Monthly payment	$ 500
Times: Number of payments	× 8
Amount received	$4,000
Less: Qualified expenditures	(2,400)
Gross income inclusion	$1,600

Answer (A) is incorrect. Scholarship money is excluded from income provided it is spent on requisite items. Answer (C) is incorrect. The amount of qualified expenditures to be deducted is $2,400. Answer (D) is incorrect. The total amount of scholarship money received in Year 5, all of which is excluded from income, is $4,000.

2.6.3. Mr. P received a fellowship grant from the State of Virginia in December of Year 1 for a special research project on education. During Year 2, he received $700 per month for the period June 1 to December 31. P is not a candidate for a degree. What amount of the fellowship may P exclude from gross income?

- A. $0
- B. $2,100
- C. $3,500
- D. $4,900

Answer (A) is correct. *(SEE, adapted)*
REQUIRED: The amount of a fellowship granted to a nondegree candidate that may be excluded from gross income.
DISCUSSION: Section 117 excludes from gross income scholarships and fellowship grants provided that the payments are not made for services of the recipient, the grants are not made primarily for the benefit of the grantor, and the recipient is a candidate for a degree. Since Mr. P is not a candidate for a degree, none of the fellowship may be excluded.
Answer (B) is incorrect. The amount P received for 3 months from the fellowship grant is $2,100. The exclusion is affected by a taxpayer's status as a candidate for a degree. Answer (C) is incorrect. The amount P received for 5 months from the fellowship grant is $3,500. The exclusion is affected by a taxpayer's status as a candidate for a degree. Answer (D) is incorrect. The amount P received for June 1 to December 31 of Year 2 from the fellowship grant is $4,900. The exclusion is affected by a taxpayer's status as a candidate for a degree.

2.7 Foreign Income Exclusions

2.7.1. On January 1, 2017, Gary, a vice president of Dearborn National Bank (DNB), was transferred to France to work in a French subsidiary of DNB. Gary has qualified as a bona fide foreign resident of France since his arrival in the country. During 2017, Gary was paid a salary of $81,500 and had interest income of $24,000 from U.S. savings accounts. Gary's U.S. gross income for the year is

A. $0

B. $24,000

C. $81,500

D. $105,500

Answer (B) is correct. *(Publisher, adapted)*
   REQUIRED: The gross income of a U.S. citizen who has earned income from a foreign country and is a bona fide foreign resident.
   DISCUSSION: Under Sec. 911, a qualified individual may elect to exclude from gross income any foreign earned income for the taxable year up to a maximum of $102,100 for 2017. A qualified individual includes someone whose tax home is in a foreign country, who is a citizen of the United States, and who is a bona fide resident of the foreign country for an uninterrupted period that includes an entire taxable year or is physically present in foreign countries for at least 330 days of a consecutive 12-month period. Earned income is wages, salaries, professional fees, and other amounts received as compensation for personal services rendered. Since Gary is a qualified individual, foreign earned income of $81,500 can be excluded from gross income since it is less than the $102,100 limitation. Therefore, gross income for the year is the $24,000 of interest income from the U.S. savings accounts.
   Answer (A) is incorrect. Gary's gross income is affected by interest. Answer (C) is incorrect. The amount of $81,500 is foreign earned income, which is excluded from gross income. Answer (D) is incorrect. The salary is foreign earned income, which is excluded from gross income up to $102,100 in 2017.

2.7.2. During all of 2015, 2016, and 2017, Una Dostres, a U.S. employee of Math Corporation, lived in Spain and worked in a Spanish subsidiary of Math. She spent no time in the United States during the 3 years in question. In 2017, Una received a $102,700 salary plus a housing allowance from her employer for her actual qualifying housing costs of $17,336. Una's gross income to be reported on her U.S. tax return is

A. $0

B. $600

C. $16,936

D. $17,936

Answer (C) is correct. *(Publisher, adapted)*
   REQUIRED: The U.S. gross income of an individual who works in a foreign country and receives a housing allowance.
   DISCUSSION: Under Sec. 911, a qualified individual may elect to exclude foreign earned income and a housing allowance. A qualified individual includes someone who is a citizen or resident alien of the U.S. who either is a bona fide resident of a foreign country for an entire tax year or is present in foreign countries for at least 330 days of a consecutive 12-month period. Una meets this second test, if not also the first.
   The foreign earned income exclusion is limited to $102,100 in 2017, so Una must include $600 of her $102,700 salary. The housing allowance exclusion is limited to the qualifying housing costs ($17,336) less the base amount of $16,336, so Una's exclusion is limited to $1,000 ($17,336 – $16,336). Therefore, she must include $16,936 ($16,336 of her housing allowance + $600 of earned income) for 2017.
   Answer (A) is incorrect. Una's gross income is affected by unearned income and the housing allowance. Answer (B) is incorrect. U.S. gross income also includes the housing allowance base amount for 2017 of $16,336. Answer (D) is incorrect. A portion of the housing allowance may be excluded from gross income.

2.7.3. Mr. H is a foreign student studying for a degree in the United States. There is no income tax treaty between his country and the United States. During the 9 months of the school year, Mr. H is employed part-time by a corporation incorporated in his home country doing business in the United States. During summer vacation, Mr. H returns home, where he is employed by the same company. Which of the following statements is true regarding U.S. taxes?

A. All income is taxable on a U.S. tax return.

B. All income is excludable, and filing a U.S. tax return is not required.

C. Only income earned for services in the United States is taxable.

D. All income is taxable on a U.S. tax return, and credit is allowed for foreign taxes paid on his summer income.

Answer (C) is correct. *(SEE, adapted)*
   REQUIRED: The U.S. taxation of compensation earned both in the U.S. and abroad by a foreign student in the United States.
   DISCUSSION: Under Sec. 871, income from U.S. sources that is effectively connected with a U.S. trade or business must be included in a nonresident alien's U.S. gross income. The performance of personal services in the United States constitutes a trade or business in the United States (Sec. 864). Therefore, the income earned by Mr. H while employed part-time in the United States is taxable.
   Answer (A) is incorrect. Not all the income is taxable. Answer (B) is incorrect. The income earned in the United States is taxable. Answer (D) is incorrect. A nonresident alien has no U.S. income when the personal services income is earned outside the United States and is not connected with the conduct of a U.S. trade or business.

2.7.4. Jean Blanc, a citizen and resident of Canada, is a professional hockey player with a U.S. hockey club. Under Jean's contract, he received $68,500 for 165 days of play during the current year. Of the 165 days, he spent 132 days performing services in the United States and 33 playing hockey in Canada. What is the amount to be included in Jean's gross income on his Form 1040NR?

A. $0

B. $34,250

C. $54,800

D. $68,500

Answer (C) is correct. *(SEE, adapted)*
REQUIRED: The U.S. gross income of a nonresident alien who performs services in the U.S. for part of the year.
DISCUSSION: A nonresident alien must include in U.S. gross income that income from U.S. sources which is effectively connected with the conduct of a trade or business in the United States (Sec. 871). Under Sec. 864, the performance of personal services in the U.S. constitutes a trade or business in the United States. If income is derived therefrom, it is considered to be from a U.S. source. According to the IRS and the courts, services of a professional hockey player are allocable to U.S. and non-U.S. time periods during the pre-season training camp, the regular season, and post-season playoffs, but not the off-season. Therefore, Jean must include the portion of his income that is attributable to the performance of personal services in the U.S., i.e., 80% (132 ÷ 165 days). Eighty percent of $68,500 is $54,800, which must be reported as U.S. income.
Answer (A) is incorrect. Jean's gross income is affected by days of service in each country. Answer (B) is incorrect. Income must be apportioned based on the time spent in the United States and in Canada. The income cannot simply be divided in half. Answer (D) is incorrect. The total amount of income is $68,500. Income must be apportioned between the two countries.

2.7.5. An executive was assigned to work in his company's Paris office for an 18-month period from April 1, Year 1, through September 30, Year 2. He retained his United States residence and returned home each month for 4 days. A portion of the income earned in Paris may be excluded from gross income.

A. True.

B. False.

Answer (B) is correct. *(SEE, adapted)*
DISCUSSION: Under Sec. 911, a U.S. citizen or resident alien may exclude earned foreign income (up to certain limits) if his or her tax home is in a foreign country and (s)he either is a bona fide resident of a foreign country for an uninterrupted period including an entire tax year or is present in a foreign country for at least 330 days during 12 consecutive months.
The executive apparently does not meet the bona fide foreign resident test because the retention of the U.S. residence and the frequent visits to the United States indicate a lack of assimilation into French life. (Visits to the United States do not, per se, preclude establishing bona fide foreign residence.) In addition, the executive was not a resident of France for an entire tax year. The executive also fails the 330-day test since his French physical presence has not included 330 days during 12 consecutive months (365 days – 48 days = 317 days).

2.7.6. Vesco, a U.S. citizen working abroad, qualifies for the foreign earned income exclusion in 2017. Vesco has a $76,000 salary plus $7,000 in interest earned in U.S. banks. Employer-provided housing occupied as a condition of his employment is valued at $10,000. The tax due on the interest income is calculated using the highest individual tax rate.

A. True.

B. False.

Answer (B) is correct. *(Publisher, adapted)*
DISCUSSION: The rate at which an individual's taxable income is taxed is the rate for the amount of his or her income plus foreign income exclusions. The amount of taxable income is gross income reduced by any exclusions. Section 911 provides an exclusion of up to $102,100 for foreign earned income in 2017. Section 911 also provides an exclusion for the employer-provided housing in excess of $16,336; therefore, the $10,000 of housing is taxable income. An individual with only $93,000 of gross income would not be in the highest tax bracket.

2.8 Gifts and Prizes

2.8.1. Rupert wanted to give his son and daughter a gift of $10,000 each. However, the son was not trustworthy enough to receive such a large sum of money at one time. Therefore, Rupert decided to invest $10,000 and only give the son the income each year. In the current year, this income amounted to $1,200, which Rupert transferred to the son. Rupert's daughter received her $10,000 outright in the current year. How much gross income must the son and daughter report, respectively, in the current year as a result of the gift?

	Son	Daughter
A.	$0	$0
B.	$1,200	$0
C.	$1,200	$10,000
D.	$10,000	$10,000

Answer (A) is correct. *(Publisher, adapted)*
REQUIRED: The amount of gross income recognized by the recipients of a gift.
DISCUSSION: Section 102(a) excludes the value of property acquired by gift from gross income. However, Sec. 102(b) provides that income from property acquired by gift or a gift of income from property is not excluded from gross income. The $10,000 received by the daughter is a gift under Sec. 102(a) and is excluded from her gross income. The $1,200 received by the son is also a gift of property that is excluded from his gross income. It is not income from a gift of property or a gift of income because the $10,000 was never given or legally set aside for the son. Rupert simply made a gift of $1,200, which happened to be determined by the amount of income earned on $10,000. Rupert must include the $1,200 in his income, and the son does not include any of the gift amount in his income.
Answer (B) is incorrect. The $1,200 is a gift to the son and is excluded from his gross income. Answer (C) is incorrect. The $1,200 and $10,000 are gifts to the son and daughter, respectively, and are not included in gross income. Answer (D) is incorrect. The son received a gift of $1,200, which is excluded from gross income. The $10,000 is a gift to the daughter, which is excluded from gross income.

2.8.2. J. Ripper spent several years studying the human body. Finally, her research provided a new method for making surgical incisions that left no scars. Much to Ripper's astonishment, she was awarded a Nobel Prize that year. Ripper was awarded $50,000 outright (which was paid directly to a recognized charity designated by Ripper) and another $75,000 on the condition that she continue her research. How much must Ripper include in gross income for the year?

A. $0

B. $50,000

C. $75,000

D. $125,000

Answer (C) is correct. *(Publisher, adapted)*
REQUIRED: The amount that the recipient of a scientific prize must include in gross income.
DISCUSSION: Section 74(b) excludes from gross income prizes and awards made primarily in recognition of charitable, scientific, educational, etc., achievement if the recipient was selected without any action on his or her part, (s)he is not required to render substantial future services as a condition of receiving the prize or award, and the payor transfers it to a governmental unit or a charity designated by the award recipient. Ripper received a Nobel Prize in recognition of scientific achievement, she did not take any action to enter the proceeding, and she assigned $50,000 of it to charity. However, $75,000 of the prize was awarded on the condition that substantial future services be rendered. Therefore, only $50,000 is excluded, and Ripper must include the $75,000 in gross income.
Answer (A) is incorrect. A portion of the Nobel Prize is included in gross income. Answer (B) is incorrect. The $50,000 was assigned directly to charity and excluded from gross income. Answer (D) is incorrect. The total amount of the prize is $125,000, and some of it is excluded from gross income.

2.8.3. Sally became a contestant on a daytime television game show. Sally was lucky and won a fur coat with a retail price of $3,000 and a television with a fair market value of $400. Sally lived in Florida, so she sold the fur coat the next day but received only $2,500 for it. One month later, the television broke and Sally discovered there was no warranty on it. How much must Sally include in gross income for the year?

A. $0

B. $2,500

C. $2,900

D. $3,400

Answer (C) is correct. *(Publisher, adapted)*
REQUIRED: The amount that the recipient of prizes must include in gross income.
DISCUSSION: Amounts received as prizes or awards are generally included in the recipient's gross income (Sec. 74). The fair market value of the fur coat was $2,500 (the amount Sally could receive for it) since most products are no longer worth their retail price once taken out of the store. The fair market value of the television was $400 regardless of events occurring after receipt, such as its breaking. Therefore, Sally must include $2,900 in gross income from the prizes.
Answer (A) is incorrect. Sally's gross income is affected by the FMV of the prizes. Answer (B) is incorrect. Gross income includes the FMV of the television. Answer (D) is incorrect. The fur coat should be reported at its FMV.

2.8.4. Brain invented a new product but did not know who would be willing to market it. Brain asked her friend Rooster for some help. Rooster recommended someone who would be likely to market the product. The product turned out to be a success, and Brain was so happy that she went to Rooster and said, "I want to make you a gift since you were so good to me." Brain gave Rooster $5,000. Which of the following statements is true?

A. Rooster must include the $5,000 in gross income.

B. Rooster may exclude the $5,000 as a gift.

C. Rooster may exclude the $5,000 as a prize.

D. Rooster must pay the gift tax on the $5,000.

Answer (A) is correct. *(Publisher, adapted)*
REQUIRED: The true statement concerning a gratuitous transfer of money for help received in producing income.
DISCUSSION: Section 102(a) excludes from gross income the value of property acquired by gift. Under the Duberstein case, 363 U.S. 278 (1960), a gift must be made from "detached and disinterested generosity." In this situation, Brain did not make the "gift" out of detached and disinterested generosity; rather, the "gift" was made in return for the information Rooster gave. Therefore, Rooster must include the $5,000 in his gross income.
Answer (B) is incorrect. The $5,000 is not considered a gift under the Duberstein case. Answer (C) is incorrect. The $5,000 is not a prize, and prizes are included in gross income as a general rule anyway. Answer (D) is incorrect. There is no gift on which to pay gift tax. Even if the $5,000 were a gift, the donor would be liable for the gift tax.

2.8.5. DAC Foundation awarded Kent $75,000 in recognition of lifelong literary achievement. Kent was not required to render future services as a condition to receive the $75,000. What condition(s) must have been met for the award to be excluded from Kent's gross income?

I. Kent was selected for the award by DAC without any action on Kent's part.

II. Pursuant to Kent's designation, DAC paid the amount of the award either to a governmental unit or to a charitable organization.

A. I only.

B. II only.

C. Both I and II.

D. Neither I nor II.

Answer (C) is correct. *(CPA, adapted)*
REQUIRED: The conditions under which an award may be excluded from a taxpayer's gross income.
DISCUSSION: Prizes and awards made primarily in recognition of charitable, scientific, educational, etc., achievement are excluded from gross income only if the recipient was selected without any action on his or her part, is not required to render substantial future services as condition of receiving the prize or award, and assigns it to charity.
Answer (A) is incorrect. Kent must also assign the award to charity. Answer (B) is incorrect. Kent must have been selected without any action on his or her part. Answer (D) is incorrect. Prizes and awards made primarily in recognition of charitable, scientific, educational, etc., achievement are excluded from gross income only if the recipient was selected without any action on his or her part, is not required to render substantial future services as condition of receiving the prize or award, and assigns it to charity.

Use **Gleim Test Prep** for interactive study and easy-to-use detailed analytics!

STUDY UNIT THREE
BUSINESS EXPENSES AND LOSSES

3.1 Ordinary and Necessary Expenses

3.1.1. State X imposes a tax based upon the amount of fixed assets a business owns. An individual proprietor would deduct this tax on which schedule?

A. Schedule A.

B. Schedule C.

C. Schedule E.

D. Schedule SE.

Answer (B) is correct. *(SEE, adapted)*
REQUIRED: The schedule on which an individual proprietor should deduct a state tax imposed upon the business's fixed assets.
DISCUSSION: A tax imposed on business assets is an expense of that business and is deductible under Sec. 162. As an ordinary and necessary expense of the business, it is reported on Schedule C, which is used to report the income and expenses of a sole proprietorship, the net income (or loss) of which is carried onto page 1 of Form 1040.
Answer (A) is incorrect. Schedule A is used to compute itemized deductions. Answer (C) is incorrect. Schedule E is used to report supplemental income such as rents and royalties, and income from partnerships, estates and trusts. Answer (D) is incorrect. Schedule SE is used for computation of the Social Security self-employment tax.

3.1.2. George, a sole proprietor, may deduct various taxes imposed by federal, state, local, and foreign governments, if he incurs them in the ordinary course of his business. All of the following are deductible on Schedule C, Form 1040, except

A. Real estate taxes on real property used in his business.

B. State and local income taxes on net income.

C. Personal property taxes on personal property used in his business.

D. Gasoline taxes included in the cost of fuel used in his business.

Answer (B) is correct. *(SEE, adapted)*
REQUIRED: The tax that is not deductible on Schedule C, Form 1040.
DISCUSSION: State income taxes are imposed on an individual after income from all taxable sources is aggregated. State income taxes are a personal expense (deductible under Sec. 164) and not an expense of the source of income, e.g., a sole proprietorship. They are deducted from adjusted gross income and are reported as an itemized deduction on Schedule A.
Answer (A) is incorrect. Real estate taxes on real property used in a business are deductible on Schedule C, Form 1040. Answer (C) is incorrect. Personal property taxes on personal property used in a business are deductible on Schedule C, Form 1040. Answer (D) is incorrect. Gasoline taxes included in the cost of fuel used in a business are deductible on Schedule C, Form 1040.

3.1.3. Jim Domuch, a calendar-year taxpayer, operates a novelty shop as a sole proprietor. During the current year, he incurred the following expenses in his business. Which is not deductible in the current year?

A. Property tax paid on business premises.

B. Sales taxes on the purchase of $50,000 of equipment used in the business.

C. Sales taxes on the purchase of supplies used in the business.

D. Business license tax imposed by the city.

Answer (B) is correct. *(Publisher, adapted)*
REQUIRED: The tax that is not deductible by a business in the current year.
DISCUSSION: Section 164(a) lists the taxes that may be deducted by any person. Section 164(a) also provides that taxes not listed but paid or accrued in a trade or business may be deducted, except that any tax not listed that is paid or accrued with respect to a property purchase is treated as part of the cost of the property. Therefore, the sales tax on the equipment must be capitalized and only deducted as depreciation over the recovery period of the asset.
Answer (A) is incorrect. Property taxes are listed in Sec. 164 as a deductible tax. Answer (C) is incorrect. Although the sales taxes on the purchase of supplies must be treated as part of the cost of supplies, this entire cost is deductible as an ordinary and necessary expense. Answer (D) is incorrect. The occupational license tax is an ordinary and necessary business expense.

3.1.4. Which of the following insurance premiums paid for policies related to a business is deductible as a business expense?

- A. Owner's share of premiums on a split dollar life insurance plan.
- B. Employee fidelity or performance bonds.
- C. Self-insurance reserve funds.
- D. Insurance against loss of employer's earnings due to sickness or disability.

Answer (B) is correct. *(SEE, adapted)*
REQUIRED: The insurance premium that is deductible as a business expense.
DISCUSSION: Section 162(a) allows a deduction for all ordinary and necessary expenses paid or incurred during the taxable year in carrying on any trade or business. An expense is ordinary if it is customary in the kind of business conducted by the taxpayer and is not capital in nature. An expense is necessary if it is appropriate and helpful. Insurance to cover losses from employee malfeasance or nonperformance qualifies as such an expense.
Answer (A) is incorrect. The policy-owner's share of life insurance premiums is a personal (not business) expenditure. Answer (C) is incorrect. Self-insurance reserve funds are not deductible until paid out and only then if for a deductible loss. Answer (D) is incorrect. Insurance on the loss of the employer's earnings is not a deductible expense. Only if it were for the reimbursement of overhead expenses would such premiums be deductible.

3.1.5. All of the following insurance premiums are ordinarily deductible as a business expense except

- A. Workers' compensation on behalf of partners in a business partnership.
- B. Life insurance on the life of an employee with the employee's wife as the beneficiary.
- C. Group health insurance that does not contain continuation coverage to employees.
- D. Malpractice insurance covering a professional's personal liability for negligence resulting in injury to business clients.

Answer (A) is correct. *(SEE, adapted)*
REQUIRED: The insurance premium not ordinarily deductible as a business expense.
DISCUSSION: Workers' compensation insurance premiums paid on behalf of employees are deductible as a business expense. However, for this purpose, partners are not considered employees of the partnership (they are considered self-employed owners) and the insurance premiums on their behalf are not deductible.
Answer (B) is incorrect. Life insurance premiums paid on the life of an employee are deductible as long as the employer is not the beneficiary. These life insurance premiums are effectively compensation to the employee unless excluded as part of a group term life insurance plan. Answer (C) is incorrect. The premiums are deductible by the employer. However, there is an excise tax imposed under Sec. 4980B if an employer has group health insurance not containing continuation coverage for employees. Answer (D) is incorrect. Malpractice insurance is deductible as an ordinary business expense.

3.1.6. Mr. C operates a business as a calendar-year, cash-basis proprietorship. During the current year, C purchased the following insurance policies:

Description of Policy	Total Cost	Date Paid
One-year policy that pays C for lost earnings owing to sickness or disability effective January 1	$ 600	January 5
One-year life insurance policy on a key employee of which C is beneficiary effective January 1	360	January 5
One-year life insurance policy on his own life required by bank for C to obtain a business loan	240	June 30
Two-year fire and theft policy effective December 1	2,400	January 6 of next year

What is C's deductible insurance expense for the current year?

- A. $0
- B. $360
- C. $840
- D. $2,400

Answer (A) is correct. *(SEE, adapted)*
REQUIRED: The taxpayer's ordinary and necessary business insurance deduction for the current year.
DISCUSSION: Section 162(a) allows a deduction for all ordinary and necessary expenses paid or incurred during the taxable year in carrying on any trade or business. Insurance premiums paid for carrying on a trade or business are deductible. The 1-year policy that pays C for lost earnings is personal; thus, the premiums are not deductible as a trade or business expense. The premiums paid for the 1-year life insurance policy on the key employee are not deductible since C is the beneficiary [Sec. 264(a)]. The premiums on the 1-year life insurance policy on C's own life are also not deductible because the policy is personal even though required by the bank for C to obtain a business loan. The premiums paid on the 2-year fire and theft policy will be deductible, but since C is a cash-basis taxpayer, the premiums are not deductible until paid in the next year. Furthermore, the premiums will have to be apportioned over the 2-year period of the policy but cannot be deducted before they are paid.
Answer (B) is incorrect. Premiums paid on a life insurance policy on a key employee when the company is the beneficiary are not deductible. Answer (C) is incorrect. Both policies are personal and not deductible as a trade or business expense. Answer (D) is incorrect. The fire policy was paid in the next year and, since the taxpayer uses the cash method of accounting, he cannot deduct the apportioned premiums until next year.

3.1.7. Which of the following tests does not need to be met for an employee's pay to be deductible as an expense?

A. Payments for services employee rendered are reasonable. This test is based on the circumstances at the time the taxpayer contracts for the services, not those existing when the amount of pay is questioned.

B. The taxpayer has control over the employee.

C. Payments are made for services actually performed.

D. Depending upon the taxpayer's method of accounting, payments are made or expenses are incurred for services rendered during the year.

Answer (B) is correct. *(SEE, adapted)*
REQUIRED: The item not used to determine whether an employee's pay is deductible.
DISCUSSION: Section 162(a)(1) allows a deduction for a reasonable allowance of salaries or other compensation for personal services actually rendered. There is no requirement that the employer have legal control over the individual. A concept of controlling the individual goes to whether the person is an employee or independent contractor.
Answer (A) is incorrect. Section 162(a)(1) specifically requires the amount to be reasonable in order to deduct compensation. Answer (C) is incorrect. Section 162(a)(1) specifically requires the services to be actually rendered in order to deduct compensation. Answer (D) is incorrect. Section 162 requires the expense to be paid or incurred during the year.

3.1.8. Carbozo was an officer of a corporation in the business of selling hospital supplies. Due to stiff competition, the corporation went bankrupt. Carbozo contracted with Hoover Corporation to purchase hospital supplies for it on commission. In order to reestablish relations with suppliers of hospital supplies that Carbozo had known in his previous capacity and to solidify his credit standing, Carbozo decided to pay certain debts of the former corporation that went bankrupt. Which of the following statements is true concerning these payments?

A. The payments are not deductible because they are not necessary.

B. The payments are not deductible because they are not ordinary.

C. The payments are deductible as ordinary and necessary business expenses.

D. The payments are not deductible because they were not Carbozo's debts.

Answer (B) is correct. *(Publisher, adapted)*
REQUIRED: The true statement concerning a deduction for payment of another's debts.
DISCUSSION: Section 162(a) allows a deduction for the ordinary and necessary expenses paid or incurred in carrying on a trade or business. Courts have held that ordinary does not mean habitual or normal in terms of frequency, rather that it is the common and accepted means of dealing with the situation. Courts have also held that the payment of debts of others without legal obligation or a definite business requirement is not considered ordinary and is not deductible.
Answer (A) is incorrect. Necessary has generally been defined as useful and helpful, which the payments made by Carbozo were. Answer (C) is incorrect. The payments are not deductible since they are not ordinary. Answer (D) is incorrect. The mere fact that Carbozo was not liable did not make the debts nondeductible. If the payments had been required by the suppliers in order for Carbozo to continue in business, they may have been considered ordinary even though they were not his legal obligations.

3.1.9. AMJ Enterprises is a small book publisher. It incurred the following as its miscellaneous expenses:

Bank service charges	$ 70
Office supplies	100
Advertising	600
Fees to attorneys and CPAs	2,400
Interest for the entire period of a 5-year loan taken out on January 1	2,500

How much of the above may AMJ Enterprises deduct for the current year?

A. $770

B. $3,570

C. $3,670

D. $5,670

Answer (C) is correct. *(Publisher, adapted)*
REQUIRED: The amount that a business can deduct for the miscellaneous expenses listed.
DISCUSSION: Professional fees are deductible under Sec. 162, the same as compensation to an employee, provided they are reasonable in amount. Advertising and bank service charges are deductible as general expenses. Office supplies are also deductible under Reg. 1.162-3. Sec. 461(g) requires prepaid interest to be capitalized and allocated to the periods to which it relates. Since the interest was prepaid for 5 years, only one-fifth of the interest may be deducted in the current year.

Bank service charges	$ 70
Office supplies	100
Advertising	600
Professional fees	2,400
Interest (1/5 × $2,500)	500
Deductible business expenses	$3,670

Answer (A) is incorrect. Attorney and CPA fees and the current year's proportion of the prepaid interest are deductible. Answer (B) is incorrect. Office supplies are deductible. Answer (D) is incorrect. The prepaid interest must be capitalized and allocated to each year of the loan.

3.1.10. Frank Fronton decided to become a professional jai alai player. In January, Fronton joined a jai alai club where he could train to become a jai alai player. After training for the first 7 months of the year, Fronton received a contract and began to play professionally; however, he continued to use the club for ongoing training and practice. Fronton paid $12,000 for the use of the club during the year ($1,000 per month). He purchased equipment in January costing $1,500. Replacement equipment after receiving the contract cost $500, and transportation to out-of-town games cost $800 for the remainder of the year. How much can Fronton deduct as business expenses?

A. $800

B. $6,300

C. $7,800

D. $12,800

Answer (B) is correct. *(Publisher, adapted)*
REQUIRED: The amount that a person entering a new business may deduct as business expenses.
DISCUSSION: The playing of professional jai alai would be considered a trade or business; however, the preparation for entering that business is not conducting that trade or business.
Therefore, the $1,000 monthly club dues for the first 7 months are not deductible, whereas the dues for the last 5 months are deductible. The $1,500 initially spent for equipment is also not deductible since it is a depreciable asset. Replacement equipment is deductible assuming it does not have a life substantially longer than the current year. Transportation expenses are also deductible provided there is adequate documentation.

Training club dues ($1,000 × 5 months)	$5,000
Replacement equipment	500
Transportation	800
Total business deductions	$6,300

Answer (A) is incorrect. Five months of training club dues and the cost of replacement equipment are also deductible business expenses. Answer (C) is incorrect. The $1,500 spent on acquiring the initial equipment is not a deductible business expense because it is a depreciable asset. Answer (D) is incorrect. The training club dues paid for the 7 months prior to employment are not deductible; however, the cost of replacement equipment after employment is deductible.

3.1.11. Mr. B paid the following amounts in the current year in connection with his business property:

New motor purchased in December for a truck that extended its useful life by 3 years	$ 600
Replacement parts to maintain machinery in efficient operating condition	3,000
Labor to maintain the above equipment	1,800
Cost of replacing gravel driveway with heavy-duty concrete	12,000
Cost of repainting factory building	1,400

What is Mr. B's allowable deduction for repairs and maintenance expense on his current year Schedule C, Form 1040?

A. $2,400

B. $6,200

C. $6,800

D. $18,800

Answer (B) is correct. *(SEE, adapted)*
REQUIRED: The taxpayer's allowable deduction for repairs and maintenance expense.
DISCUSSION: Repairs and maintenance that do not materially add to the value of property or prolong its life may be deducted. All other expenditures should be capitalized and depreciated (Reg. 1.162-4). The expenditures made for a new truck motor with a useful life of 3 years and the cost of replacing the driveway should be capitalized. The $3,000 cost of replacement parts and the $1,800 in labor costs to maintain the equipment in operating condition are deductible. The $1,400 cost of repainting the factory building is also deductible as a repair and maintenance item. These costs total $6,200 for repair and maintenance expenses, which are deductible in the current year.
Answer (A) is incorrect. The cost of repairs and maintenance also includes the cost of repainting the factory and the cost of replacement parts; however, it does not include the cost of the new truck motor. Answer (C) is incorrect. The cost of a new motor should be capitalized and depreciated, not deducted with repairs and maintenance. Answer (D) is incorrect. The cost of a new truck motor and the cost of replacing a driveway are not repairs and maintenance expenses.

3.1.12. Mr. R is a self-employed over-the-road trucker who uses the cash method of accounting. Which one of the following expenses paid during the current year would be deductible on Mr. R's Schedule C?

A. Penalty for late delivery of cargo paid to Corporation V.

B. Fine for speeding in business truck paid to City A.

C. Overweight fine paid to State B.

D. Contribution to Bull Moose political party in an attempt to receive a trucking contract.

Answer (A) is correct. *(SEE, adapted)*
REQUIRED: The deductible business expense.
DISCUSSION: Although fines and penalties paid to a government are generally not deductible, the payment of a penalty for nonperformance of a contract is generally deductible. This penalty usually represents damages that one contracting party was willing to incur in order to avoid performing under the contract. This is a business decision, and the damages are deductible under Sec. 162(a).
Answer (B) is incorrect. A fine paid to City A for speeding in a business truck is a fine paid to a governmental agency and is specifically not deductible under Sec. 162(f). Answer (C) is incorrect. An overweight fine paid to State B is a fine paid to a government and is specifically not deductible under Sec. 162(f). Answer (D) is incorrect. Political contributions are not deductible as business expenses.

3.1.13. Mr. M, a cash-basis sole proprietor, secured two business loans from two different banks. The following information pertains to the loans. Assume all costs have been paid by M.

	Loan 1	Loan 2
Date of loan	1/1/Yr 1	1/1/Yr 3
Term	10 years	10 years
Loan origination fee	$1,000	$2,000
Mortgage commission	250	500
Abstract fees	150	300
Recording fees	100	200
Interest for Year 3	5,000	7,000

On December 31, Year 3, Mr. M paid off Loan 1 and had to pay a prepayment penalty of $1,500. What deductions can Mr. M take in Year 3 with respect to these loans?

	Interest Expense	Other Costs
A.	$14,500	$500
B.	$14,000	$2,500
C.	$13,500	$3,000
D.	$12,000	$4,500

Answer (A) is correct. *(SEE, adapted)*
REQUIRED: The amount and character of deductions for miscellaneous loan costs.
DISCUSSION: Interest is deductible under Sec. 163 as well as other payments made in lieu of interest. The prepayment penalty is in lieu of interest. The loan origination fees are also in lieu of interest since they are unreasonably large to be actual fees for processing a loan. As prepaid interest, the loan origination fees must be amortized over the period of each loan, but the balance of unpaid origination fees on Loan 1 is deductible in Year 3 when the loan was paid off.

All other expenditures are costs of obtaining a loan and are deductible over the period of each loan as Sec. 162 business expenses. The balance of the costs on Loan 1 is deductible in Year 3 when the loan was paid off.

Stated interest on both loans	$12,000
Prepayment penalty on Loan 1	1,500
Remainder of Loan 1 origination fee ($1,000 – $200 amortized in Year 1 and Year 2)	800
Loan 2 origination fees amortized in Year 3 ($2,000 ÷ 10 years)	200
Total Year 3 deductible interest	$14,500

Remainder of Loan 1 fees ($500 – $100 amortized in Year 1 and Year 2)	$ 400
Loan 2 fees ($1,000 ÷ 10 years) amortized in Year 3	100
Other deductible costs	$ 500

Answer (B) is incorrect. The origination costs should be included in interest expense. Other costs should only include the unamortized miscellaneous costs for the loan and the first-year amortization. Answer (C) is incorrect. The origination fees should also be included in interest expense. Other costs of $3,000 is incorrect because this is the full amount of the origination fees and other fees for Loan 2. Origination fees should be amortized with interest expense, and the other fees should be amortized with other costs and the remaining costs from Loan 1. Answer (D) is incorrect. The prepayment penalty and the loan origination fees are considered interest expenses. Other costs should contain the amortized portions of the other fees associated with the loans.

3.1.14. The Saturn Titans of the Planetary Football League have a team spaceship. The spaceship developed a leak between the power source and living area causing dangerous fumes to enter occasionally. This was fixed at a cost of $100,000. The power source also needed an overhaul, which was done at a cost of $500,000. As a result of the overhaul, the useful life of the spaceship was not changed, but it can now make the trip to the players' home in the United States on Earth in half the former time and at a substantial fuel savings. How should these expenditures be treated?

A. The repair of the leak should be deducted, while the overhaul should be capitalized.

B. The overhaul should be deducted, and the repair of the leak should be capitalized.

C. Both the repair of the leak and the overhaul should be deducted.

D. Both the repair of the leak and the overhaul should be capitalized.

Answer (A) is correct. *(Publisher, adapted)*
REQUIRED: The proper treatment of expenditures for repair and maintenance of business property.
DISCUSSION: Repairs and maintenance that do not materially add to the value of property or prolong its life may be deducted. All other repair and improvement expenditures should be capitalized and depreciated (Reg. 1.162-4). Expenditures to repair damage and put the property back in the same condition as it was before the damage are generally deductible as repairs, provided that they do not materially add to the value of the property or prolong its life. The expenditure for fixing the leak would be deductible. However, the cost of a major overhaul that changes the operation of a vehicle, such as increasing its speed and saving fuel costs, would be considered to add materially to the value of the property. Therefore, the overhaul of the power source in the spaceship may not be deducted. It must be capitalized and depreciated. Answer (B) is incorrect. The repair of the leak should be deducted since it restored the property to its previous condition. Additionally, the overhaul should be capitalized because it added to the value of the property. Answer (C) is incorrect. The overhaul should be capitalized because it added to the value of the property. Answer (D) is incorrect. The repair of the leak should be deducted since it restored the property to its previous condition.

3.1.15. During the current year, Mr. C was forced to permanently abandon business property in a foreign country. The property consisted of the following items:

	Fair Market Value	Cost	Adjusted Basis
Truck	$ 5,000	$ 7,000	$ 3,000
Furniture	2,000	3,000	1,000
Building	45,000	50,000	40,000

Mr. C's abandonment loss for the current year is

A. $0

B. $44,000

C. $52,000

D. $60,000

Answer (B) is correct. *(SEE, adapted)*
REQUIRED: The taxpayer's deductible loss arising from the forced abandonment of business property in a foreign country.
DISCUSSION: Section 165 allows a deduction for an uncompensated loss sustained during the year that is incurred in a trade or business. A loss from abandonment of assets is deductible in the year the assets are actually abandoned with no claim for reimbursement [Reg. 1.165-2 and Reg. 1.167(a)-8]. The amount of the loss is the adjusted basis of the property provided in Sec. 1011 for determining the loss from the sale or other disposition of property. The taxpayer's adjusted basis in the property was $3,000 for the truck, $1,000 for the furniture, and $40,000 for the building. The total loss is $44,000.
Answer (A) is incorrect. Mr. C has a deductible loss for the year for all three assets. Answer (C) is incorrect. The amount of $52,000 incorrectly uses the FMV to determine the abandonment loss. Answer (D) is incorrect. The amount of $60,000 incorrectly uses the FMV to determine the abandonment loss.

3.1.16. Mr. March, a medical equipment manufacturer, paid and incurred the following expenses during the current year:

Raw materials	$60,000
Direct labor	50,000
Materials and supplies	50,000
Freight-in on raw materials	1,000
Freight on shipments of finished goods	1,000
Allocable overhead expenses for production	10,000
Cost of inventory donated to charity	1,000
Fair market value of inventory donated	3,000
Beginning inventory	20,000
Ending inventory	30,000

The inventory donated to charity was included in the beginning inventory and is not eligible for special treatment under Sec. 170(e)(3). What was the amount of Mr. March's cost of goods sold for the current year?

A. $161,000

B. $160,000

C. $159,000

D. $158,000

Answer (B) is correct. *(SEE, adapted)*
REQUIRED: The taxpayer's cost of goods sold.
DISCUSSION: Cost of goods sold is computed by starting with the beginning inventory, adding the cost of materials purchased during the year and the cost of production, and subtracting the ending inventory. Under Sec. 263A, manufacturers are required to use the full absorption method of costing, which means that both direct and indirect production costs must be included. Freight charges are always added to the cost of the goods purchased.
Costs to ship to the purchaser are selling expenses, not costs of inventory. Goods included in beginning inventory that are donated to charity reduce the goods available for sale in the amount of their adjusted basis [Reg. 1.170A-1(c)(4)].

Beginning inventory		$ 20,000
Raw materials and labor:		
Direct labor	$50,000	
Raw materials	61,000	
Materials and supplies	50,000	
Production overhead	10,000	171,000
Goods available for sale		$191,000
Less: inventory donated to charity		(1,000)
Less: ending inventory		(30,000)
Cost of goods sold		$160,000

Answer (A) is incorrect. The cost of the inventory donated to charity must be subtracted from the goods available for sale to determine cost of goods sold. Answer (C) is incorrect. Freight on shipment of finished goods should be included in selling expenses, not cost of goods sold. Answer (D) is incorrect. The cost of the donated inventory, not the FMV, should be subtracted from goods available for sale to determine cost of goods sold.

3.1.17. All of the following expenses incurred in the course of operating a business are deductible business expenses except

A. Cost of sending communications to members of a city council regarding legislation.

B. Public service advertising that keeps the name of the business before the public.

C. Advertising in a concert program the local church is sponsoring.

D. Advertising in a convention program of a political party. The proceeds from the publication of the program are for the local use of the political party.

Answer (D) is correct. *(SEE, adapted)*
REQUIRED: The expense not deductible as a business expense.
DISCUSSION: Section 276 provides that advertising in a publication of a political party is not deductible as a business expense. The proceeds from the convention program are for the use of a political party. Therefore, the expenses incurred to advertise in that program are not deductible.
Answer (A) is incorrect. The cost of communications with local governing bodies with respect to legislation of interest to the taxpayer is deductible. Answer (B) is incorrect. Public service advertising that keeps the name of the business before the public is a deductible expense under Sec. 162. Answer (C) is incorrect. Advertising in a concert program the local church is sponsoring is a deductible expense under Sec. 162.

3.1.18. Which of the following expenditures incurred in the operation of a business is not required to be capitalized?

A. Cost of replacing an old shingle roof with a new tile roof.

B. Cost of changing from one heating system to another.

C. Cost of replacing an old truck used for business delivery.

D. Cost of replacing small tools.

Answer (D) is correct. *(SEE, adapted)*
REQUIRED: The expenditure that should not be capitalized.
DISCUSSION: Small tools used in a business normally do not have to be capitalized under the theory that either they do not have a useful life substantially beyond the taxable year or their cost is so small as not to materially distort income. Items costing a small amount may normally be expensed as long as a consistent policy is followed. Expenditures for property having a useful life substantially beyond the taxable year should be capitalized [Reg. 1.263(a)(2)].
Answer (A) is incorrect. The cost of replacing an old shingle roof with a new tile roof is an expenditure for property having a useful life substantially beyond the taxable year [Reg. 1.263(a)(2)]. Answer (B) is incorrect. The cost of changing from one heating system to another is an expenditure for property having a useful life substantially beyond the taxable year [Reg. 1.263(a)(2)]. Answer (C) is incorrect. The cost of replacing an old truck used for business delivery is an expenditure for property having a useful life substantially beyond the taxable year [Reg. 1.263(a)(2)].

3.1.19. Mr. E, a sole proprietor, made the following payments in the current year. Which payment is not a capital expenditure?

A. Freight paid on new equipment purchased.

B. Cost of rewiring a building to install a new computer.

C. A payment made to eliminate competition for 5 years.

D. A payment to have machinery moved from one location to another.

Answer (D) is correct. *(SEE, adapted)*
REQUIRED: The payment that is not a capital expenditure.
DISCUSSION: Capital expenditures include those that add to the value or prolong the life of property, or adapt the property to a new or different use. Moving machinery to a new location does not increase the value of the machinery, prolong its life, or adapt it to a new or different use. Therefore, the cost of moving the machinery is not a capital expenditure (it is deductible under Sec. 162).
Answer (A) is incorrect. Freight paid on new equipment purchased is a cost of acquisition, which is a capital expenditure. Answer (B) is incorrect. The cost of rewiring a building to install a new computer adapts the building to a new or different use, which is a capital expenditure. Answer (C) is incorrect. A payment made to eliminate competition increases the value of the business and is a capital expenditure.

3.1.20. All of the following expenses paid or incurred in the course of operating a business are deductible as business expenses except

A. Costs incurred by a public utility company in connection with an appearance at a public utility commission rate making hearing.

B. Political contributions.

C. Penalty for nonperformance of a contract.

D. Reimbursements to job applicants in connection with interviews.

Answer (B) is correct. *(SEE, adapted)*
REQUIRED: The expense not deductible as a business expense.
DISCUSSION: Contributions to a political party or candidate are not deductible as business expenses under Sec. 162(e).
Answer (A) is incorrect. Costs to appear at a hearing of a state agency are deductible business expenses under Sec. 162. Answer (C) is incorrect. Penalties for nonperformance of a contract are deductible business expenses under Sec. 162. Answer (D) is incorrect. Reimbursements to job applicants in connection with interviews are deductible business expenses under Sec. 162.

3.1.21. Drew, a cash-basis, calendar-year taxpayer, runs an auto repair shop and has a self-employed insurance plan. His wife Sherry works for an employer who, this year, started health insurance coverage for Sherry and Drew on August 15. Drew's net profit, before health insurance, was $50,000. Drew paid $500 a month for all 12 months of the year for his health insurance plan because of pre-existing illnesses. Drew and Sherry file a joint return. What is the amount of their deduction for self-employed health insurance for the year?

A. $6,000

B. $3,500

C. $2,450

D. $0

Answer (B) is correct. *(SEE, adapted)*
REQUIRED: The current year deduction for self-employed health insurance.
DISCUSSION: Self-employed individuals may deduct 100% of the health insurance costs incurred after 2002 for themselves, their spouses, and their dependents [Sec. 162(l)(1)]. However, Drew can make the deduction only for the 7 months of premiums that he was not covered under his wife's plan.
Answer (A) is incorrect. This amount equals the premiums for 12 months. They are only allowed the deduction for part of the year. Answer (C) is incorrect. The deduction percentage was 70% for 2002. Answer (D) is incorrect. Drew and Sherry may take a deduction for self-employed health insurance for part of the year.

3.1.22. On September 1 of the current year, Mr. Z, a cash-basis, calendar-year, self-employed mechanic, borrowed $10,000 at 10% for 5 years to purchase equipment with a useful life of 10 years. Z paid the lender a loan origination fee of $3,000 on the loan date. This fee was solely for the use of the money. How much of the $3,000 fee may Z deduct on his Schedule C for the current year?

A. $100

B. $200

C. $600

D. $3,000

Answer (B) is correct. *(SEE, adapted)*
   REQUIRED: The current-year deduction for points paid to obtain a loan.
   DISCUSSION: Loan origination fees or points are effectively interest paid in advance. Prepaid interest is not deductible in advance except for the ordinary points paid on a home mortgage. The points must be amortized over the period of the loan. The loan is for a 5-year period, so the points should be amortized over 60 months (5 years × 12 months). Since 4 months are left in the current year after the loan is taken out, $200 ($3,000 ÷ 60 months × 4 months) is deductible as interest expense in the current year.
   Answer (A) is incorrect. The monthly amortization of the loan origination fee amount is based on the term of the loan (5 years) and not the useful life of the equipment (10 years). Answer (C) is incorrect. The loan origination fee is amortized on a monthly basis, rather than deducting one-fifth of the fee in the year it is incurred. Answer (D) is incorrect. The loan origination fee is amortizable over the term of the loan (5 years) and is not deductible in the year that it is incurred.

3.1.23. Barney, who is self-employed, spent $7,000 for medical insurance for himself and his family. Barney's wife is not employed. Barney's records for this year reflect the following:

Profit on Schedule C, Form 1040	$2,000
Contribution to Keogh plan	500
Alimony paid to former wife	6,000

What is the amount of Barney's self-employed health insurance deduction for this year?

A. $1,478

B. $2,000

C. $4,900

D. $7,000

Answer (A) is correct. *(SEE, adapted)*
   REQUIRED: The amount deductible for self-employed health insurance in the current year.
   DISCUSSION: Self-employed persons may deduct up to 100% of the amount paid for medical insurance covering the self-employed individual and his family from gross income as a business expense. The deduction is limited to the earnings of the business for which the insurance plan was established. The balance of the medical insurance premiums not deducted as a business expense are treated as medical expenses and subject to the 10%-of-AGI floor. Barney's self-employed health insurance deduction is computed below.

Amount paid for medical insurance in the current year	$7,000
Deduction percentage (100%)	× 1.0
Tentative deduction	$7,000

The deduction is limited to the lesser of $7,000 or earned income {net earnings from self-employment from the trade or business less one-half of the self-employment tax deductible under Sec. 164(f) and the 20% contribution to Keogh plans deductible under Sec. 404 [Secs. 162(l)(2) and 401(c)(2)(A)]}.

Schedule C profit	$2,000
Less:	
Self-employment taxes ($2,000 × .1530 × 1/2)	(153)
Keogh contribution [($2,000 – $153) × 0.20]	(369)
Earned income limitation	$1,478

Barney's deduction for this year is $1,478.
   Answer (B) is incorrect. The amount of earned income before self-employment taxes and Keogh plan contributions are subtracted is $2,000. Answer (C) is incorrect. This amount was the deduction limit using 2002 rates if earned income is greater than the maximum deduction. Answer (D) is incorrect. The deduction is limited to the lesser of $7,000 or $1,478.

3.1.24. Lisa Johnson started a dry cleaning business in June. In April of the same year, prior to beginning business operations, she incurred costs totaling $1,500 for the purpose of securing prospective suppliers and customers. The $1,500 is a capital expenditure that cannot be deducted as an expense or amortized.

A. True.

B. False.

Answer (B) is correct. *(SEE, adapted)*
   DISCUSSION: The cost of securing suppliers and customers before going into business is a start-up expense that, generally, must be capitalized. It is not a business expense because the business has not yet begun. Such costs may be amortized over a period of 180 months starting with the month in which she commenced business (Sec. 195). However, since the expenses are less than $5,000, they may be expensed in the first year.

3.1.25. An employer may deduct premiums paid on an ordinary life insurance policy covering the life of an officer-employee if the employer is the direct beneficiary.

A. True.

B. False.

Answer (B) is correct. *(SEE, adapted)*
DISCUSSION: Section 264 disallows a deduction for premiums paid on any life insurance policy covering the life of any person financially interested in the trade or business carried on by the taxpayer, when the taxpayer is directly or indirectly a beneficiary under such policy.

3.1.26. In the current year, Mr. X incurred $12,000 in qualified expenses to make a public transportation vehicle used in his business more accessible to handicapped people. Mr. X may deduct the expenses in the current year.

A. True.

B. False.

Answer (A) is correct. *(SEE, adapted)*
DISCUSSION: Section 190 allows a taxpayer to elect to deduct up to $15,000 of qualified expenditures that remove architectural and transportation barriers to the handicapped and the elderly. Section 44 permits a disabled access credit to be claimed for qualified expenditures incurred by an eligible small business to remove architectural and transportation barriers to the handicapped and the elderly. The available credit is 50% of eligible expenditures in excess of $250 but not in excess of $10,250. Any amounts for which a credit is claimed cannot be deducted under Sec. 190 [Sec. 44(d)(7)]. Since the Sec. 190 limit of $15,000 exceeds the Sec. 44 limit of $10,000, some of the expenditures will be deducted under Sec. 190 even though the credit election is made for the $10,000 limit.

3.1.27. During the current year, DN Corporation constructed a building for use in its business. DN borrowed $200,000 during the production period that was used to pay construction costs. The wages paid to employees to construct the building and the entire amount of interest paid on the production period loan can be deducted as a current operating expense.

A. True.

B. False.

Answer (B) is correct. *(SEE, adapted)*
DISCUSSION: The Uniform Capitalization Rules of Sec. 263A apply to real or tangible personal property produced by the taxpayer for use in a business [Sec. 263A(b)(1)]. Section 263A requires all direct costs and a proper share of indirect costs allocable to property produced by the taxpayer to be capitalized. Wages paid to employees for constructing a new building would be direct costs allocable to that building and have to be capitalized [Sec. 263A(a)(2)]. Section 263A(f) requires interest paid or incurred during the production period on real property produced by the taxpayer to be capitalized. These costs are depreciated as part of the cost of the building.

3.1.28. In the current year, if you are self-employed, you can deduct, as a business expense, 100% of the amount you pay for medical insurance for yourself and your family, as an adjustment to arrive at adjusted gross income on your individual income tax return.

A. True.

B. False.

Answer (A) is correct. *(SEE, adapted)*
DISCUSSION: Section 162(l)(1) permits a deduction of 100% of amounts paid for health insurance by self-employed persons for themselves, their spouses, and their dependents.

3.1.29. Mr. Z purchased an apartment building. As part of a major restoration plan to make the apartments suitable for tenants, he painted all of the rooms. Mr. Z can deduct the cost of the paint as a repair expense.

A. True.

B. False.

Answer (B) is correct. *(SEE, adapted)*
DISCUSSION: Since the painting was done as part of a major restoration, the cost of the paint should be capitalized as an amount paid for permanent improvements or betterments made to increase the value of the apartment building [Sec. 263(a)(1)].

3.1.30. Real estate assessments by a municipal government against business property for construction of public parking facilities benefiting the business are not deductible by the business as a tax expense.

A. True.

B. False.

Answer (A) is correct. *(SEE, adapted)*
DISCUSSION: Real property taxes do not include assessments for local benefit, e.g., streets, sidewalks, curbing, and other like improvements, since such assessments tend to increase the value of the property (Reg. 1.164-4). The cost of such assessments is added to the adjusted basis of the taxpayer's property. According to the IRS and the courts, the public parking facilities are a similar improvement.

3.1.31. Trust Me Company, a sole proprietorship, paid Mr. J, an employee of Trust Me, $35,000 in the current year to compensate him for injuries sustained while at work. The company was reimbursed for $15,000 by its insurance carrier. Trust Me can deduct $20,000 on its current-year income tax return as an ordinary and necessary business expense.

A. True.

B. False.

Answer (A) is correct. *(SEE, adapted)*
DISCUSSION: Under Sec. 162(a), a business may deduct, as an ordinary and necessary business expense, reasonable amounts paid for sickness, injury, or disability benefits. In this case, Trust Me Company paid Mr. J $35,000 to compensate him for injuries sustained while at work. Trust Me was reimbursed for $15,000 by its insurance company; thus, the $20,000 of unreimbursed expenditures is deductible.

3.1.32. Mr. C, owner of a sole proprietorship, purchased an insurance policy that will pay for business overhead expenses in the event he is disabled for a long time. The premiums on this policy are deductible as an insurance expense.

A. True.

B. False.

Answer (A) is correct. *(SEE, adapted)*
DISCUSSION: The premiums on an insurance policy that will pay for business overhead expenses in the event the sole proprietor is disabled for a long time are an ordinary and necessary business expense. The premiums paid are deductible under Sec. 162(a).

3.1.33. Mr. C considers it necessary to his business to pay kickbacks to the purchasing agents of his customers. The employers of the purchasing agents are unaware of these payments. The kickbacks are in violation of the law in the state in which Mr. C resides and the law is generally enforced. Mr. C may deduct the kickbacks as a business expense.

A. True.

B. False.

Answer (B) is correct. *(SEE, adapted)*
DISCUSSION: Illegal bribes and kickbacks are specifically disallowed as deductions under Sec. 162(c)(2), provided the law is generally enforced.

3.1.34. Since the seller gets capital gain treatment on the sale of goodwill, the buyer must amortize the value of purchased goodwill over not less than 60 months.

A. True.

B. False.

Answer (B) is correct. *(SEE, adapted)*
DISCUSSION: An intangible asset acquired by a taxpayer that meets the requirements of an amortizable Sec. 197 asset, is held by the buyer in connection with a trade or business or income-producing activity, and was acquired on or after August 6, 1993, is amortizable over a 15-year period (180 months). Goodwill is included in the definition of an amortizable Sec. 197 asset [Sec. 197(d)(1)]. The seller of a business gets capital gain treatment on the sale of the goodwill, but that is irrelevant to eligibility for amortization by the purchaser.

3.1.35. Interest and penalties paid on an individual income tax deficiency are deductible as a business expense if the deficiency was related to income from a business.

A. True.

B. False.

Answer (B) is correct. *(SEE, adapted)*
DISCUSSION: After 1990, personal interest is nondeductible [Sec. 163(h)(1) and Reg. Sec. 1.163-9T(b)(2)]. The Tax Court in *J.E. Redlark* (106 TC 31) disagreed with the regulation and permitted an interest deduction related to a tax deficiency on the taxpayer's unincorporated business. However, the Ninth Circuit overturned the Tax Court decision. Several other circuits have upheld the temporary regulation and disallowed an interest deduction as being related to personal interest in a situation involving a tax deficiency incurred in a taxpayer's farming business. Were the interest incurred by a corporate taxpayer, it would be deductible as a business expense since the personal interest rules are not applicable to corporations. Penalties paid are not deductible [Sec. 162(f)].

3.1.36. If part of the purchase price of a business is clearly for a covenant not to compete, and the covenant is for a fixed number of years, the amount paid for it is deductible as a business expense proportionately over a 15-year period.

A. True.

B. False.

Answer (A) is correct. *(SEE, adapted)*
    DISCUSSION: An intangible asset acquired by a taxpayer that meets the requirements of an amortizable Sec. 197 asset, is held by the taxpayer in connection with a trade or business or income-producing activity, and was acquired on or after August 6, 1993, is amortizable over a 15-year period. A covenant not to compete is included in the definition of an amortizable Sec. 197 asset [Sec. 197(d)(1)(E)].

3.1.37. Mr. X purchased a vacant lot he plans to use later as a parking lot for his business. While the lot remains vacant and unimproved, Mr. X must capitalize the annual taxes and mortgage interest that are otherwise currently deductible.

A. True.

B. False.

Answer (B) is correct. *(SEE, adapted)*
    DISCUSSION: Interest and taxes paid on vacant land that is held for investment, or merely waiting to be improved, are deductible.

3.1.38. Fourteen years ago, Mr. H bought a building for use in his business. He demolished the building in the current year at a cost of $5,000 because repairs were abnormally high and he had an opportunity to rent the land at an acceptable fee. Mr. H can deduct the $5,000 as an ordinary expense, and he can claim the undepreciated basis of the building as a loss.

A. True.

B. False.

Answer (B) is correct. *(SEE, adapted)*
    DISCUSSION: All costs of demolishing structures, and any losses sustained, must be allocated to the land (Sec. 280B). Therefore, the $5,000 cost to demolish the building must be capitalized. Neither this $5,000 nor the undepreciated basis of the building demolished is deductible.

3.1.39. Scott Kyzar is a self-employed, cash-basis restaurant owner. During the current year, he paid off the mortgage on his restaurant building, and he had to pay the lending bank a penalty for early payment. Scott may deduct the penalty as interest on his Schedule C for the current year.

A. True.

B. False.

Answer (A) is correct. *(SEE, adapted)*
    DISCUSSION: When a person pays off a mortgage early and is required to pay the lender a penalty for doing so, the penalty is deductible under Sec. 163 in the year the interest is paid.

3.1.40. On July 1, Mr. K, a calendar-year, cash-basis sole proprietor, paid $3,000 in commitment fees to his bank to have business funds made readily available to him over a period of 3 years as needed. Mr. K did not borrow any of these funds in the current year. Mr. K may deduct $500 of these fees as interest on his Schedule C for the current year.

A. True.

B. False.

Answer (B) is correct. *(SEE, adapted)*
    DISCUSSION: Loan commitment fees are a cost of obtaining a loan. They are deductible over the period of the loan. If the loan is never taken out, a loss is deductible for the loan commitment fees in the year the right to borrow the funds expires. Therefore, Mr. K cannot deduct any loan commitment fees in the current year, since he did not take out a loan and the right to borrow the funds has not yet expired.

3.1.41. Mr. N cannot get business insurance coverage for certain business risks; therefore, he periodically contributes to a reserve he set up for self-insurance. Mr. N may deduct these periodic payments as an expense.

A. True.

B. False.

Answer (B) is correct. *(SEE, adapted)*
    DISCUSSION: Section 162 allows a deduction for ordinary and necessary trade or business expenses only if they were paid or incurred during the taxable year. Since no expense is paid or incurred when a reserve is set aside for self-insurance, no deduction is allowed.

3.1.42. Mr. H established a self-insured medical reimbursement plan that covers medical expenses for all eligible employees. The plan has eligibility requirements that favor highly compensated individuals of the company. Mr. H may not deduct payments under the plan.

    A. True.

    B. False.

Answer (B) is correct. *(SEE, adapted)*
    DISCUSSION: The cost of a medical reimbursement plan is deductible under Sec. 162(a) regardless of whether the plan discriminates in favor of highly compensated employees. Under Sec. 105(h), however, such highly compensated employees who receive payments under this plan may not be able to exclude all the payments from gross income.

3.1.43. The taxpayer is ordered to pay $90,000 in treble damages. The award originated from a civil suit by a customer under the Clayton Antitrust Act. The taxpayer also pleaded guilty to an antitrust violation in criminal proceedings. The taxpayer may not deduct any of the payment.

    A. True.

    B. False.

Answer (B) is correct. *(Publisher, adapted)*
    DISCUSSION: If a taxpayer is convicted of a criminal violation of the antitrust laws or enters a plea of nolo contendere to a charged violation, no deduction is allowable for only two-thirds of the amount paid to satisfy the judgment or in settlement of a civil suit brought under the Clayton Antitrust Act.

3.1.44. The taxpayer is ordered to pay $60,000 in treble damages. The award originated from a civil suit by a customer under the Clayton Antitrust Act. No criminal proceedings for the antitrust violation ever occurred. The taxpayer may deduct the entire payment.

    A. True.

    B. False.

Answer (A) is correct. *(Publisher, adapted)*
    DISCUSSION: The treble damage payment is entirely deductible because no criminal proceeding for the antitrust violation ever occurred. Moreover, the damages were paid to a private person, not to the government.

3.2 Manufacturing Deductions

3.2.1. Venus Motor Company has two plants from which it manufactures cars: Nevada and Mexico. In addition, all executives of Venus and its subsidiaries are offered a discount when they lease cars from the company. All gross receipts are from the sales and leases of cars produced by Venus. In addition, all car leases are leases of cars produced in the Nevada plant. The following reflects the gross receipts from the various business activities:

Sale of cars produced in Nevada	$1,700,000
Sale of cars produced in Mexico	450,000
Leasing cars to customer	400,000
Leasing cars to executives of the subsidiaries of Venus	250,000
Leasing cars to executives of Venus Motor Company	100,000
Sale of cars produced in Nevada to executives of Venus and its subsidiaries	50,000

What is the amount of gross receipts that qualify as domestic production gross receipts (DPGR)?

    A. $2,100,000

    B. $2,150,000

    C. $2,400,000

    D. $2,500,000

Answer (B) is correct. *(Publisher, adapted)*
    REQUIRED: The gross receipts that are considered DPGR.
    DISCUSSION: Section 199 states that gross receipts from the sale or lease of personal property that is manufactured in the U.S. are considered DPGR. However, gross receipts from the lease, rental, or license of property to a related party does not qualify as DPGR. Employees are considered related parties to an employer. In addition, all employees of a company and its subsidiaries are considered to be employed by a single employer. Thus, the gross receipts from all leases to the executives of Venus Motor Co. and its subsidiaries, as well as the sale of cars produced in Mexico, are not included in DPGR. The gross receipts from the sale of a qualified product manufactured by the taxpayer in the U.S. to a related person are included in DPGR. The resulting DPGR is $2,150,000 ($1,700,000 + $400,000 + $50,000).
    Answer (A) is incorrect. Gross receipts from the sale of a qualified product manufactured by the taxpayer in the U.S. to a related person are included in DPGR. Answer (C) is incorrect. The executives of the subsidiaries are considered related parties, so the gross receipts from these leases would not be included in DPGR. Answer (D) is incorrect. The executives of Venus Motor and its subsidiaries are considered related parties, so the gross receipts from these leases would not be included in DPGR.

3.2.2. The gross receipts from which of the following activities would not qualify as domestic production gross receipts (DPGR)?

A. Sale of a qualified movie that was filmed by the taxpayer in Minnesota.

B. Sale of a house that was constructed in Miami, FL, by the taxpayer.

C. Receipts from an architectural consultation by the taxpayer in Austin, TX, about the construction of a building in Mexico.

D. Sale of corn grown in Durand, MI, when the taxpayer participated in 95% of the procedures required to grow the corn.

Answer (C) is correct. *(Publisher, adapted)*
REQUIRED: The gross receipts that qualify as domestic production gross receipts.
DISCUSSION: Section 199 defines DPGR as gross receipts that are derived from

1. The sale, exchange, or other disposition, or any rental, lease, or licensing of

   a. Qualified production property that is manufactured, produced, grown, or extracted in the United States by the taxpayer in whole or in significant part.

   b. Any qualified film produced by the taxpayer in the United States.

   c. Electricity, natural gas, or potable water produced by the taxpayer in the United States.

2. Construction performed in the United States.

3. Engineering and architectural services performed in the United States for a construction project located in the United States.

   Qualified production property generally includes tangible personal property, computer software, and sound recordings. Thus, the gross receipts from the architectural consultation in Austin, TX, about the construction of a building in Mexico do not qualify as DPGR because the construction of the building will not take place in the United States.
   Answer (A) is incorrect. Gross receipts from a qualified movie that was filmed in the U.S. qualifies as DPGR. Answer (B) is incorrect. Construction performed in the U.S. qualifies as DPGR. Answer (D) is incorrect. Gross receipts from qualified production property that is grown in whole or significant part by the taxpayer qualify as DPGR. Since the taxpayer participated in 95% of the growth of the corn, (s)he is considered to have significantly participated in growing the corn.

3.2.3. Woodburg, Inc., has domestic production gross receipts (DPGR) of $200,000. Its total expenses include $100,000 of cost of goods sold and $40,000 of other expenses. The portion of cost of goods sold and other expenses that are allocable to domestic production is 60%. Woodburg's taxable income is $150,000, and the W-2 wages for 2017 are equal to $240,000. What is Woodburg's deduction for income attributable to domestic activities?

A. $10,440

B. $10,800

C. $13,500

D. $18,000

Answer (A) is correct. *(Publisher, adapted)*
REQUIRED: The deduction for income attributable to domestic activities.
DISCUSSION: The deduction for income attributable to domestic gross income for 2017 is equal to 9% of the lesser of the following:

1. The qualified production activities income (QPAI),
2. The taxable income of the taxpayer, or
3. 50% of the W-2 wages for the year.

QPAI is calculated by taking the DPGR and subtracting the sum of the following from it:

1. The cost of goods sold allocable to DPGR,

2. Other deductions, expenses, or losses that are directly allocable to DPGR, and

3. A proper share of other deductions, expenses, or losses that are not directly allocable to DPGR or another class of income.

   Thus, Woodburg's QPAI is equal to $116,000 {$200,000 − [($100,000 × 60%) + ($40,000 × 60%)]}. Since this is less than the taxable income ($150,000) and 50% of the W-2 wages ($120,000), the deduction for income attributable to domestic gross income is 9% of the QPAI, or $10,440 ($116,000 × 9%).
   Answer (B) is incorrect. The deduction is 9% of the lesser of QPAI, taxable income, or 50% of the W-2 wages. QPAI is less than 50% of the W-2 wages. Answer (C) is incorrect. The deduction is 9% of the lesser of QPAI, taxable income, or 50% of the W-2 wages. QPAI is less than the taxable income. Answer (D) is incorrect. The allocable portion of the cost of goods sold and the expenses should be deducted from DPGR before the 9% for the deduction is taken.

3.2.4. Chassis, Inc., located in Detroit, MI, sells a new type of automobile chassis, which is produced by Auto Manufacturing, Inc., in East Lansing, MI. Chassis can utilize the 9% manufacturing deduction in 2017.

    A. True.

    B. False.

Answer (B) is correct. *(Publisher, adapted)*
    DISCUSSION: The U.S. Production Deduction applies to firms that manufacture, produce, and extract activities in the United States. Chassis does not produce the chassis; it only sells it. Therefore, Chassis cannot take the U.S. production deduction.

3.2.5. When determining the income attributable to domestic activities, a company can never include the gross receipts from nondomestic production in the domestic production gross receipts (DPGR).

    A. True.

    B. False.

Answer (B) is correct. *(Publisher, adapted)*
    DISCUSSION: When determining the income attributable to domestic activities, a company generally does not include any gross receipts from nondomestic production in the calculation of DPGR. However, if the nondomestic production gross receipts are less than 5% of the total gross receipts for the company, then the company may treat all gross receipts as though they are DPGR.

3.3 Bad Debt Expense

3.3.1. Which of the following may be deducted as a business bad debt by Mr. Leonard, a cash-basis taxpayer?

    A. A worthless corporate security.

    B. A note evidencing a worthless personal loan to a friend.

    C. A loss from uncollected accounts receivable.

    D. A note evidencing an uncollectible business loan.

Answer (D) is correct. *(SEE, adapted)*
    REQUIRED: The item deductible as a business bad debt by a cash-basis taxpayer.
    DISCUSSION: An uncollectible business loan is a business bad debt under Sec. 166. Therefore, it is deductible.
    Answer (A) is incorrect. A worthless corporate security is not considered a bad debt [Sec. 166(e)]. Answer (B) is incorrect. A loan to a friend is not a business debt. Answer (C) is incorrect. A cash-basis taxpayer does not include accounts receivable in income. Therefore, no deduction will arise from their uncollectibility.

3.3.2. Landon, a sole proprietor, made the following loans during the year. Two loans were closely related to his business operation, and the other two were personal.

To	Loan Amount	Type	Unrecoverable Debt Written Off Landon's Books during the Year
A	$2,000	Nonbusiness	$1,000
B	$1,000	Nonbusiness	$1,000
C	$3,000	Business	$1,000
D	$5,000	Business	$2,000

The unpaid balance of each loan that is not recoverable has been written off. What is the total maximum tax deduction Landon can take for business and nonbusiness worthless debt for the year?

    A. $2,000

    B. $3,000

    C. $4,000

    D. $5,000

Answer (C) is correct. *(SEE, adapted)*
    REQUIRED: The maximum deduction available for the business and nonbusiness bad debts.
    DISCUSSION: A partially worthless nonbusiness debt is not deductible (Reg. 1.166-5), and a wholly worthless nonbusiness debt is treated as a loss from the sale or exchange of a capital asset held for 1 year or less, i.e., a short-term capital loss [Sec. 166(d)]. Notice that the Sec. 1211 limit of $3,000 for a capital loss deduction is not reached in this problem since only the loan to B creates a capital loss. Partially worthless business debts may be deducted under Sec. 166(a) to the extent they are specifically written off. Landon's bad debt deduction is

A	$ 0
B	1,000
C	1,000
D	2,000
Deduction	$4,000

Of the loss, $1,000 is a short-term capital loss and $3,000 is a business bad debt deduction that reduces ordinary income.
    Answer (A) is incorrect. Wholly worthless nonbusiness debts and partially worthless business debts are deductible. Therefore, the losses from the loans to B and C are also deductible. Answer (B) is incorrect. Wholly worthless nonbusiness debts are deductible. Therefore, the loan to B is also deductible. Answer (D) is incorrect. Partially worthless nonbusiness debt (the loan to A) is not deductible.

3.3.3. Patsy lent money to Scarlett in Year 1. Scarlett signed a loan agreement and made the agreed-upon monthly payments until May Year 3, when she stopped making payments. Patsy called Scarlett and wrote her a letter requesting payment but received no response. Then Patsy read in the newspaper that Scarlett had filed for bankruptcy with no assets. Patsy can take a deduction for a bad debt

A. Only on her timely filed Year 3 return.

B. By amending her Year 3 return within 3 years.

C. By amending her Year 1 return.

D. On her timely filed Year 3 return or by amending her Year 3 return within 7 years.

Answer (D) is correct. *(SEE, adapted)*
   REQUIRED: The action required to take a deduction for a bad debt.
   DISCUSSION: A nonbusiness bad debt is defined as any debt other than one acquired in connection with the taxpayer's trade or business [Sec. 166(d)(2)]. Bad debts must be deducted in the year they become worthless. Furthermore, the statute of limitations to take a deduction for bad debts and worthless securities is 7 years.
   Answer (A) is incorrect. Year 3 is not the only year in which the bad debt may be deducted. Answer (B) is incorrect. The statute of limitations for bad debts and worthless securities is 7 years. Answer (C) is incorrect. The bad debt did not occur until Year 3. Thus, Patsy may not amend her Year 1 return for the bad debt.

3.3.4. CW Enterprises is having financial difficulties. It manufactures seagull-shaped sports cars for the jet set. The board of directors is highly paid by CW, and all members lent funds to the company hoping to retain their positions (they own no stock in the company). They instituted a policy requiring the assembly line workers to lend 5% of their wages or face discharge. The officers have all made voluntary loans to the company. In addition, the majority shareholder, who is not employed by CW, made a substantial loan. If CW defaults on all these loans, who is not entitled to a business bad debt deduction?

A. The assembly line workers.

B. The officers.

C. The board of directors.

D. The majority shareholder.

Answer (D) is correct. *(Publisher, adapted)*
   REQUIRED: The person(s) who is(are) not entitled to a bad debt deduction for loans to a company.
   DISCUSSION: A loss from a business debt is an ordinary loss, while a loss from a nonbusiness debt is treated as a short-term capital loss (Sec. 166). A nonbusiness bad debt is a debt other than one incurred or acquired in connection with the trade or business of the taxpayer. An investment is not considered a trade or business, and a shareholder who makes a loan to a corporation to protect his or her investment is not considered to have made a business loan. Therefore, the majority shareholder's bad debt likely will be deductible as a short-term capital loss.
   Employment has been held to constitute an employee's trade or business, and loans made primarily to protect an employee's job (instead of protecting an investment) are considered business loans. Therefore, such loans will be considered a business bad debt if not paid.
   Answer (A) is incorrect. The assembly line workers would be entitled to a business bad debt deduction. Employment has been held to constitute an employee's trade or business, and loans made primarily to protect an employee's job (instead of protecting an investment) are considered business loans. Therefore, such loans will be considered a business bad debt if not paid. Answer (B) is incorrect. The officers would be entitled to a business bad debt deduction if CW defaults. Employment has been held to constitute an employee's trade or business, and loans made primarily to protect an employee's job (instead of protecting an investment) are considered business loans. Therefore, such loans will be considered a business bad debt if not paid. Answer (C) is incorrect. The board of directors would be entitled to a business bad debt deduction. Employment has been held to constitute an employee's trade or business, and loans made primarily to protect an employee's job (instead of protecting an investment) are considered business loans. Therefore, such loans will be considered a business bad debt if not paid.

3.3.5. Which of the following may be deducted as a business bad debt by Mr. G, an accrual-basis taxpayer?

A. Worthless trade receivable.

B. Worthless loan to his partner, which was used to buy a house.

C. Worthless loan to his sister, who used the proceeds in her business.

D. Worthless corporate security.

Answer (A) is correct. *(SEE, adapted)*
   REQUIRED: The item deductible as a business bad debt by an accrual-basis taxpayer.
   DISCUSSION: An accrual-basis taxpayer includes trade receivables in gross income, and a worthless trade receivable is deductible as a business bad debt under Sec. 166(a).
   Answer (B) is incorrect. Worthless loans to the taxpayer's partner may not be bona fide debts and are not business debts in any event. Answer (C) is incorrect. Worthless loans to the taxpayer's sister may not be bona fide debts and are not business debts in any event. Answer (D) is incorrect. A worthless corporate security is not considered a bad debt [Sec. 166(e)]; it is treated as a worthless security loss under Sec. 165(g).

3.3.6. On January 1, Ms. C lent $10,000 to her son to pay tuition expenses for college. Her son repaid $2,000 on July 1, and Ms. C forgave the balance upon her son's agreement to enter her business. What is the amount and character of the loss that Ms. C may deduct on her individual income tax return?

- A. $0
- B. $4,000 short-term capital loss.
- C. $4,000 long-term capital loss.
- D. $8,000 nonbusiness bad debt.

Answer (A) is correct. *(SEE, adapted)*
REQUIRED: The amount deductible for a forgiven debt owed by a related party.
DISCUSSION: A bad debt deduction may be taken only for a bona fide debt arising from a valid debtor-creditor relationship based upon a valid and enforceable obligation to pay a fixed or determinable sum of money [Reg. 1.166-1(c)]. The taxpayer either made a gift to her son of the balance of the debt owed or released the debt in consideration of her son's agreement to enter the business. Therefore, no bad debt exists, and no deduction is available.
Answer (B) is incorrect. Ms. C does not have a capital loss from this transaction due to requirements for a bona fide debt. Answer (C) is incorrect. A bona fide debt arising from a valid debtor-creditor relationship is not present in this transaction. Answer (D) is incorrect. Ms. C does not have an $8,000 nonbusiness bad debt due to requirements for a bona fide debt.

3.3.7. Dr. K, a dentist and calendar-year taxpayer, has consistently reported income and expenses from his business on the cash basis. All cash and checks he receives are deposited and included in income. K's records for the current year reflect the following information:

Uncollectible receivables	$2,000
Patients' uncollectible returned checks	500
Recovery of an uncollectible receivable from 3 years ago	1,000
Business-related loan to a supplier that became totally worthless	3,000

What is the amount of K's bad debt expense for the current year?

- A. $2,500
- B. $3,500
- C. $4,500
- D. $5,500

Answer (B) is correct. *(SEE, adapted)*
REQUIRED: The amount of bad debt expense.
DISCUSSION: Dr. K has consistently reported income and expenses on the cash basis, and cash and checks received are deposited and included in income. Therefore, the $2,000 in accounts receivable has not been included in income, and accordingly, no deduction will arise from uncollectible receivables. The recovery of an uncollectible receivable from 3 years ago of $1,000 will be included in income and will not be netted against bad debt expense. Bad debt expense for the current year will be $3,500; the $500 in returned checks has been included in income, so a bad debt deduction is proper, and the $3,000 business bad debt is also deductible.
Answer (A) is incorrect. The receivables have not been included in income and a deduction cannot be claimed yet for the uncollectible receivables. However, the totally worthless business bad debt (loan to the supplier) may be deducted. Answer (C) is incorrect. The recovery of a bad debt does not increase bad debt expense. Instead, it is added to gross income. Answer (D) is incorrect. Uncollectible receivables should not be included in bad debt expense unless they were realized as income.

3.3.8. All of the following statements regarding the nonaccrual-experience method of accounting for bad debts are true except

- A. Under this method, you do not have to accrue income that you do not expect to collect.
- B. This method cannot be used if interest or penalties are required to be paid for late payments.
- C. This method can only be used for amounts to be received that are earned by performing services.
- D. This method can be used for amounts to be received that are earned from any source.

Answer (D) is correct. *(SEE, adapted)*
REQUIRED: The false statement regarding the nonaccrual-experience method of accounting for bad debts.
DISCUSSION: An accrual method of accounting taxpayer meeting certain qualifications may use the nonaccrual-experience method of accounting for bad debts [Sec. 448(d)(5)]. The nonaccrual-experience method may be used only for amounts to be received for the performance of services that would otherwise be included in income. This method may not be used for amounts to be received from activities other than the performance of services. Amounts arising from lending money, selling goods, or acquiring receivables from other parties would not be eligible for treatment under the nonaccrual-experience method.
Answer (A) is incorrect. Under the nonaccrual-experience method of accounting for bad debts, you do not have to accrue income that you do not expect to collect. Answer (B) is incorrect. The nonaccrual-experience method of accounting for bad debts cannot be used if interest or penalties are required to be paid for late payments. Answer (C) is incorrect. The nonaccrual-experience method of accounting for bad debts can only be used for amounts to be received that are earned by performing services.

3.3.9. Mr. Benson, who operates a small tools supply company, guaranteed payment of a $10,000 note for Black Hardware store, one of Mr. Benson's largest clients. Black Hardware later filed for bankruptcy and defaulted on the loan. Mr. Benson made full payment to satisfy the note. Mr. Benson's payment should be considered a(n)

A. Business bad debt.

B. Nonbusiness bad debt.

C. Gift.

D. Investment.

Answer (A) is correct. *(SEE, adapted)*
REQUIRED: The characterization of a loss on a guarantee of a customer's debt.
DISCUSSION: A business bad debt is deductible in full as an ordinary loss under Sec. 166. A loss on a guarantee of a debt is treated the same as a primary debt in determining whether it is business or nonbusiness. To be a business bad debt, it must be closely related to one's trade or business. However, guaranteeing the debt of a primary customer does not necessarily make it a business debt. If making the guarantee was required to retain the customer, the payment on the guarantee would be a business bad debt.
Authors' note: This question does not specify that the guarantee was required to retain the customer. But the Special Enrollment Exam seems to assume that guaranteeing the debt of a primary customer is closely related to one's trade or business. On that basis, it would be a business bad debt.
Answer (B) is incorrect. Guaranteeing a debt of a primary customer (a bona fide debt from a trade or business) would not be considered a nonbusiness bad debt. Answer (C) is incorrect. Gifts do not occur from bona fide debts from a trade or business. Answer (D) is incorrect. Mr. Benson's payment is not an investment.

3.3.10. Under the specific charge-off method of computing bad debts, partially worthless bad debts may be deducted for tax purposes even though no charge-off is taken on the books.

A. True.

B. False.

Answer (B) is correct. *(SEE, adapted)*
DISCUSSION: Partially worthless bad debts are deductible under Sec. 166(a)(2). When satisfied that a debt is recoverable only in part, the amount not in excess of the part charged off within the taxable year is allowed as a deduction.

3.3.11. Mr. E is an accrual-basis taxpayer. In Year 1, E charged off $1,000 from K's outstanding account that totaled $5,000. E received property worth $3,000 from K as final payment in Year 2. This property had an adjusted basis of $2,000 to K. The remaining amount owed was determined to be worthless in Year 2. E can deduct only $1,000 as a bad debt loss in Year 2.

A. True.

B. False.

Answer (A) is correct. *(SEE, adapted)*
DISCUSSION: Worthless debts are deductible only to the extent of the adjusted basis of the debt [Sec. 166(b)]. Since Mr. E is on the accrual basis, he apparently included $5,000 in income without receiving payment, so he has a $5,000 basis in the debt. He recovered $1,000 in Year 1, and $3,000 in Year 2, leaving a balance of $1,000. E can deduct this $1,000 as a bad debt loss in Year 2 since the remaining amount owed was determined to be worthless in Year 2.

3.4 Business Travel and Entertainment

3.4.1. In which of the following situations would the employee not be required to keep documentation for expenses?

A. The employee claims deductions for expenses that are more than reimbursements.

B. The employee's expenses are reimbursed under a nonaccountable plan.

C. The employee is related to his or her employer.

D. The employee gives records and documentation to his or her employer and is reimbursed in full.

Answer (D) is correct. *(SEE, adapted)*
REQUIRED: The situation in which an employee would not be required to keep documentation for expenses.
DISCUSSION: When the taxpayer is reimbursed for expenses, the 50% limitation is imposed on the party making reimbursement, not the taxpayer. The burden of substantiation is on the party making the deductions subject to the 50% limitation. In effect, there is no difference in tax liability for the employee because the reimbursement is included in gross income and then deducted.
Answer (A) is incorrect. Deductions for amounts of unreimbursed expenses should be substantiated with adequate documentation. Answer (B) is incorrect. Expenses reimbursed under a nonaccountable plan must be substantiated with adequate documentation. Answer (C) is incorrect. The relationship of the parties does not affect the substantiation requirement for deductible expenses.

3.4.2. Mr. Pine, a self-employed engineer in Boston, traveled to Chicago in order to attend a course on new engineering techniques. He spent 2 weeks attending the course and remained in Chicago for an additional 6 weeks on personal matters. The air flight cost $200, hotel $600, meals $320, and the tuition for the course $500. How much of these expenses may Mr. Pine deduct on his return?

A. $500

B. $690

C. $714

D. $890

Answer (B) is correct. *(SEE, adapted)*
REQUIRED: The deductible amount of travel expenses incurred for both business and personal activities.
DISCUSSION: A deduction for adjusted gross income is allowed for travel expenses while away from home in connection with a trade or business [Sec. 162(a)]. However, transportation is deductible only if the trip is primarily related to the taxpayer's trade or business (Reg. 1.162-2). If more days are spent for personal purposes than for business purposes, none of the transportation is deductible. Since Mr. Pine spent 6 out of his 8 weeks in Chicago on personal matters, the cost of the flight to Chicago is not deductible. Meals and lodging must always be allocated between personal and business. Under Sec. 274(n), business meals are deductible at only 50% of their cost. The expenses for 2 weeks out of 8 weeks are deductible. Educational expenses are deductible if the education maintains or improves skills required in the taxpayer's business (Reg. 1.162-5).

Hotel ($600 × 2 ÷ 8)	$150
Meals ($320 × 50% × 2 ÷ 8)	40
Tuition	500
Total deduction	$690

Answer (A) is incorrect. The business portion of the hotel and meals is also deductible. Answer (C) is incorrect. The cost of meals incurred is only 50% deductible, not 80% deductible. Answer (D) is incorrect. None of the airfare is deductible since the trip is primarily personal.

3.4.3. Willy, a self-employed laboratory consultant, flew to Buffalo where he stayed 3 days (2 days were on business). Airfare was $300. Meals were $20 per day, and lodging was $20 per day. From Buffalo, Willy flew to Vancouver, Canada, where he spent 2 weeks on business and 1 week with relatives. Airfare to Vancouver and back home was $600. In Vancouver, food was $100 per week, and lodging was $200 per week. What is Willy's deductible travel expense for the trip?

A. $680

B. $1,260

C. $1,332

D. $1,920

Answer (B) is correct. *(Publisher, adapted)*
REQUIRED: The travel expense deduction for both domestic and foreign travel.
DISCUSSION: Under Reg. 1.162-2(b), on a trip made primarily for business, the entire amount for transportation may be deducted, but the food and lodging must be allocated between business and personal time. However, under Sec. 274(c) and Reg. 1.274-4, travel outside the United States must be allocated between business and personal (including the transportation) if the travel is in excess of 1 week when more than 25% of the time is for nonbusiness activity.
The airfare on the trip to Buffalo is entirely deductible, while food and lodging are deductible for only 2 days. On the trip to Vancouver, the airfare must be apportioned (2/3 business) as well as the food and lodging. Under Sec. 274(n), meals are deductible at only 50% of their cost. Assuming Willy's meals met the requirements for business meals, his business deduction is

Buffalo:	
Airfare	$ 300
Lodging ($20 × 2 days)	40
Meals ($20 × 50% × 2 days)	20
Vancouver:	
Airfare ($600 × 2 ÷ 3)	400
Lodging ($200 × 2 weeks)	400
Meals ($100 × 50% × 2 weeks)	100
Total travel expense deduction	$1,260

Answer (A) is incorrect. The full airfare to Buffalo (not just two-thirds) is deductible while the 2 days of meals in Buffalo are only 50%, not 100%, deductible. In addition, 2 weeks of lodging and meals in Buffalo are also deductible. Answer (C) is incorrect. The deduction for meals is 50%, not 80%. Answer (D) is incorrect. This amount is the total expenses for personal and business purposes. Only the business expenses are deductible, subject to a limitation on meals.

3.4.4. Hugh Jeego is actively engaged in the oil business and owns numerous oil leases in the Southwest. During the current year, he made several trips to inspect oil wells on the leases and to consult about future oil wells to be drilled on these sites. As a result of these overnight trips, he paid the following:

Plane fares	$4,000
Hotels	1,000
Meals	800
Entertaining lessees	500

Of the $6,300 in expenses incurred, he can claim as deductible expenses

  A. $6,300

  B. $6,040

  C. $5,650

  D. $5,000

Answer (C) is correct. *(CPA, adapted)*
REQUIRED: The amount of expenses incurred on overnight trips that are deductible.
DISCUSSION: A deduction is allowed for travel expenses while the taxpayer is away from home in the pursuit of a trade or business [Sec. 162(a)]. Meals are deductible under Sec. 162 provided they are currently related to the active conduct of a trade or business, the expense is not lavish or extravagant under the circumstances, and the taxpayer (or an employee) is present during the meals. Entertainment expenses must be directly related to, or associated with, business to be deductible. Under Sec. 274(n), both meal and entertainment expenses are limited to 50% of their cost. Also, all these expenditures must be substantiated under Sec. 274(d). Assuming that Jeego's expenses meet the above requirements, his total deduction is as follows:

Plane fares	$4,000
Hotels	1,000
Meals ($800 × 50%)	400
Entertainment ($500 × 50%)	250
Total deduction	$5,650

Answer (A) is incorrect. The deduction for meals and entertainment is limited. Answer (B) is incorrect. The deduction for meals and entertainment is limited to less than 80%. Answer (D) is incorrect. This amount excludes the limited allowable deduction for meals and entertainment.

3.4.5. Bob, a calendar-year, cash-basis taxpayer, owns an insurance agency. Bob has four people selling insurance for him. The salesmen incur ordinary and necessary meal and entertainment expenses for which Bob reimburses them monthly. During the current year, Bob reimbursed his agents $10,000 for meals and $26,000 for entertainment. How much of the reimbursement can Bob deduct for meal and entertainment expenses on his current-year federal income tax return?

  A. $18,000

  B. $28,800

  C. $30,800

  D. $36,000

Answer (A) is correct. *(SEE, adapted)*
REQUIRED: The amount an employer may deduct for meal and entertainment expenses.
DISCUSSION: Under Sec. 162(a), an employer may deduct reimbursements to an employee subject to the restrictions of Sec. 274. There is a 50% limitation for meals and entertainment when the employer does not treat the expenses as compensation; thus, Bob's deduction for meals and entertainment expenses is $18,000 [($10,000 + $26,000) × 50%].
Answer (B) is incorrect. The amount of $28,800 would be the deduction if there were only an 80% limit on meals and entertainment. Answer (C) is incorrect. The amount of $30,800 is the result of deducting all of the meal costs and 80% of the entertainment costs. The ceiling applicable to both is lower than 80%. Answer (D) is incorrect. The deductible amount of meals and entertainment expenses is limited to a ceiling.

3.4.6. In January 2017, Mr. D, who is self-employed, purchased a new automobile, which he uses 100% for business. During 2017, he drove the car 14,000 miles. Mr. D also owns another automobile, which he uses occasionally for business but primarily for personal purposes. During 2017, he drove the second car 2,000 business miles. The second car is not fully depreciated. What is the amount of Mr. D's automobile expense deduction using the standard mileage rate?

  A. $7,560

  B. $7,490

  C. $8,640

  D. $8,560

Answer (D) is correct. *(SEE, adapted)*
REQUIRED: The allowable automobile expense deduction using the standard mileage rate.
DISCUSSION: Automobile expenses pertaining to a trade or business are deductible under Sec. 162 as ordinary and necessary business expenses. The taxpayer may either deduct the portion of actual operating cost of the automobile attributed to business use or compute the deduction based on the standard mileage rate. For 2017, the standard mileage rate is $0.535 per mile for all miles of business use. Mr. D's deduction for 2017 is $8,560 (16,000 miles × $0.535). The standard mileage rate is adjusted annually by the IRS to the extent warranted.
Answer (A) is incorrect. The standard mileage rate for 2016 is $0.54. In addition, this amount excludes the deductible miles of the second car. Answer (B) is incorrect. The business mileage on the second car should also be deducted. Answer (C) is incorrect. The amount of automobile expense deduction using the standard mileage rate for 2016 is $8,640.

3.4.7. Terry, a self-employed laboratory consultant specializing in white mice, attended a convention in Paris concerning the care and feeding of white mice. The convention was held in Paris since most of the white mice specialists in the world are located in France. Terry's expenses were $1,600 for airfare, $400 for food, and $400 for lodging. Terry spent 5 days at the convention and 3 days visiting friends. How much can she deduct for the trip?

A. $0

B. $1,375

C. $1,450

D. $2,400

Answer (B) is correct. *(Publisher, adapted)*
REQUIRED: The amount that a taxpayer can deduct for travel to a convention outside of North America.
DISCUSSION: Section 274(h) provides that no deduction is allowed for travel expenses for a person to attend a convention held outside North America, unless the meeting is directly related to the active conduct of his or her trade or business, and it is as reasonable for the meeting to be held outside North America as within. Terry's convention in France will satisfy these tests.

However, this trip is still subject to the rules under Sec. 274(c), which require all foreign travel for more than 1 week to be allocated between business and personal time when more than 25% of the time is spent on nonbusiness affairs. Therefore, Terry may deduct only 5/8 of the transportation, food, and lodging expenses. Meals are limited to 50% of total cost. Her deduction is as follows:

Airfare ($1,600 × 5 ÷ 8)	$1,000
Lodging ($400 × 5 ÷ 8)	250
Meals ($400 × 50% × 5 ÷ 8)	125
Total travel expense deduction	$1,375

Answer (A) is incorrect. Terry can deduct a portion of the expenses for the trip. Answer (C) is incorrect. The deduction for meals is 50% of their cost, not 80%. Answer (D) is incorrect. The total expenses for the trip is $2,400. Only the business portion is deductible.

3.4.8. Partiers Unlimited sent one of its employees to attend an association meeting on behalf of the company. It is customary, and good for business, for spouses to attend these meetings and participate in the social activities in the evenings. The employee took her spouse along for this purpose. Airfare for the employee was $200, food was $100, and lodging was $200. Airfare for the spouse was $200, food was $100, and lodging was $150. Partiers reimbursed its employee for these amounts but included $450 on the employee's W-2 as compensation at the end of the year. How much and in what manner should Partiers deduct for these expenses?

A. $450 as travel expense.

B. $900 as travel expense.

C. $450 as travel expense and $450 as compensation.

D. $650 as travel expense and $250 as compensation.

Answer (C) is correct. *(Publisher, adapted)*
REQUIRED: The amount and method of deducting travel expenses for an employee and spouse.
DISCUSSION: An employer may deduct reimbursements to an employee for business travel under Sec. 162(a) subject to the restrictions in Sec. 274. However, the expenses of an employee's spouse on a trip are not deductible, unless the spouse is an employee of the taxpayer, the travel of the spouse is for a bona fide purpose, and such expenses would otherwise be deductible by the spouse [Sec. 274(m)(3)]. It is not sufficient that the spouse is along for customary social activities. Therefore, the expenses relating to the spouse in this question are not deductible.

Under Sec. 274(e), if an employer treats the nondeductible travel expenses as compensation to the employee, they may be fully deducted as compensation. Treating them as compensation requires withholding income tax, including the amounts on the employee's W-2, and deducting them in the employer's tax return as compensation. When the employee is reimbursed for the cost of meals and entertainment, the 50% limitation applies to the party making the reimbursement. Therefore, Partiers may deduct the following:

Spouse's expenses as compensation	$450

Employee's expenses as travel	
Airfare	$200
Meals ($100 × 50%)	50
Lodging	200
Deductible amount	$450

Answer (A) is incorrect. Partiers may also deduct the spouse's expenses. Answer (B) is incorrect. The amount of $900 cannot be accounted for totally as travel expenses. Answer (D) is incorrect. Deducting $650 as travel expense and $250 as compensation misappropriates $200.

3.4.9. The 50% limit on deductibility of business-related expenses applies to which of the following?

A. Meals and entertainment while traveling away from home on business.

B. Employee's reimbursed expenses.

C. Entertaining customers at your place of business.

D. Meals and entertainment while traveling away from home on business and entertaining customers at your place of business.

Answer (D) is correct. *(SEE, adapted)*
REQUIRED: The item for which the 50% limit on deductibility of business-related expense applies.
DISCUSSION: When the taxpayer is reimbursed for the meal or entertainment expense, the limitation is imposed on the party making reimbursement, not the taxpayer. For employees whose expenses are not reimbursed, the 50% limitation is applied.
Answer (A) is incorrect. The limit also applies to entertainment expenses incurred at your place of business. Answer (B) is incorrect. It is not an expense to which the limit applies. Answer (C) is incorrect. The limit also applies to meals and entertainment expenses while traveling away from home on business.

3.4.10. Happy Lucky drove her car a total of 18,000 miles during 2017. Of this, 12,000 miles was related to business for JR Enterprises. Happy paid $4,500 for gas, $5,500 for repairs, and $500 for tires during the year. Happy accounted to JR for these actual expenses and received a reimbursement for the business portion. How much may JR deduct as travel and transportation expense?

A. $0

B. $3,500

C. $7,000

D. $10,500

Answer (C) is correct. *(Publisher, adapted)*
REQUIRED: The amount an employer may deduct for reimbursed automobile expenses paid to an employee.
DISCUSSION: Under Sec. 162(a), an employer may deduct reimbursements paid to an employee for use of his or her personal car, subject to the substantiation rules of Sec. 274. Although an employee is allowed to report to an employer either the actual expenses or a standard mileage rate for the business miles driven, the employer is allowed to deduct only what is actually reimbursed to the employee. JR reimbursed Happy $7,000 [$10,500 × (12,000 miles ÷ 18,000 miles)]. This represented an allocation of Happy's total automobile expenses, based on the number of business miles driven as compared to the total miles driven. JR may only deduct $7,000.
Answer (A) is incorrect. JR Enterprises is entitled to deduct an amount related to business of the travel and transportation expense. Answer (B) is incorrect. The amount of $3,500 is the personal use portion of the automobile expense, which is not deductible. Answer (D) is incorrect. The total amount of automobile expenses for the year is $10,500.

3.4.11. Which of the following is a true statement with respect to the business use of automobiles and other property placed in service during the year?

A. The maximum purchase price of an automobile is $15,800.

B. The business use of both transportation and entertainment property must exceed 25% to claim the Sec. 179 expensing deduction.

C. The business use of automobiles must exceed 50% to deduct depreciation at an accelerated rate.

D. Depreciation on automobiles and entertainment property is limited per year for each item.

Answer (C) is correct. *(Publisher, adapted)*
REQUIRED: The true statement with respect to the business use of automobiles and other property placed in service during the year.
DISCUSSION: Section 280F(b)(2) provides that, if the business use of an automobile does not exceed 50%, the alternative depreciation system under Sec. 168(g) must be used (i.e., straight-line method).
Answer (A) is incorrect. There is no maximum purchase price for an automobile, although the limitations on depreciation are equivalent to depreciation on a $15,800 asset. Answer (B) is incorrect. The Sec. 179 expensing deduction is available only when business use for the property is the predominant use. Answer (D) is incorrect. Only luxury automobiles are limited in depreciation each year.

3.4.12. Charlie, who is self-employed, paid $7,500 to rent a 10-seat skybox at X stadium for three baseball games. The cost of regular nonluxury box seats at each game was $20 a seat. What is the amount Charlie can deduct as entertainment expense after any limitations?

A. $300

B. $600

C. $3,750

D. $7,500

Answer (A) is correct. *(SEE, adapted)*
REQUIRED: The taxpayer's allowable deduction for entertainment.
DISCUSSION: The deductible portion of entertainment expenses paid in connection with a trade or business is limited to 50% of the expense. In addition, the cost of a skybox that is leased for more than one event is disallowed to the extent that it exceeds the cost of nonluxury box seat tickets multiplied by the number of seats in the skybox [Sec. 274(l)(2)]. The allowable deduction is therefore $300, which is equal to $600 × 50% (10 × $20 × 3).
Answer (B) is incorrect. The deduction is limited to 50% of the $600 cost. Answer (C) is incorrect. The amount of $3,750 is the result of multiplying $7,500 × .50. This ignores the skybox limitation. Answer (D) is incorrect. The actual cost of $7,500 is disallowed according to the above limitations.

3.4.13. Which of the following elements is not part of the directly related test for entertainment?

A. The main purpose of the entertainment was the active conduct of business.

B. You did engage in business with the person during the entertainment period.

C. You had more than a general expectation of getting income or some other specific business benefit.

D. The entertainment took place directly before or after a business discussion.

Answer (D) is correct. *(SEE, adapted)*
    REQUIRED: The false statement about the directly related test for entertainment.
    DISCUSSION: The directly related test for entertainment requires the entertainment expense to be incurred in a clear business setting. Entertainment that occurs directly before or after a business discussion does not satisfy this test. It would, however, meet the requirements for the "associated with" test for entertainment. The directly related test requires business to be actually conducted during the entertainment period for the purpose of receiving some business benefit.
    Answer (A) is incorrect. Part of the directly related test for entertainment is that the main purpose of the entertainment was the active conduct of business. Answer (B) is incorrect. The directly related test requires business to be actually conducted during the entertainment period for the purpose of receiving some business benefit. Answer (C) is incorrect. Having more than a general expectation of getting income or some other specific business benefit is part of the directly related test for entertainment.

3.4.14. Which of the following is not required to substantiate a business entertainment expense deduction?

A. Social Security number of the person entertained.

B. Date the entertainment took place.

C. Type of entertainment, name of person entertained, and name and address or location where it took place.

D. Reason for the entertainment or nature of business derived or expected to be derived.

Answer (A) is correct. *(SEE, adapted)*
    REQUIRED: The information not required to substantiate a business entertainment expense deduction.
    DISCUSSION: Section 274(d) disallows a deduction for business entertainment expenses unless the taxpayer substantiates the expenditure by adequate records or corroborating evidence showing the amount, time, place, business purpose, and the business relationship to the taxpayer of each person entertained. The Social Security number of the person entertained is not required to substantiate a business entertainment expense. The business entertainment expense is not deductible unless it is substantiated.
    Answer (B) is incorrect. The date the entertainment took place is required to substantiate a business entertainment expense deduction. Answer (C) is incorrect. The type of entertainment, name of person entertained, and name and address or location where it took place are required to substantiate a business entertainment deduction. Answer (D) is incorrect. The reason for the entertainment or nature of business derived or expected to be derived is required to substantiate a business entertainment expense deduction.

3.4.15. Which one of the following statements concerning the recordkeeping requirements for travel and entertainment is true?

A. Social Security numbers of business guests must be recorded to support entertainment expenses.

B. If the business purpose of a meal is not recorded, other evidence may be used to substantiate the business purpose.

C. Receipts must be kept for all transportation expenditures over $75.

D. A canceled check, by itself, is adequate evidence to support an entertainment expense.

Answer (B) is correct. *(SEE, adapted)*
    REQUIRED: The true statement of recordkeeping requirements for travel and entertainment expenses.
    DISCUSSION: Section 274(d) requires the taxpayer to substantiate by adequate records or by sufficient corroborating evidence any deduction for travel and entertainment.
    Answer (A) is incorrect. The Social Security numbers of business guests are not required. Answer (C) is incorrect. Receipts for transportation expenditures are not required even if over $75. Answer (D) is incorrect. A canceled check alone is not proper documentary evidence for recordkeeping requirements.

3.4.16. Mr. C, a self-employed insurance salesman, maintains a country club membership. He establishes by appropriate documentation the following for the current year:

Of the use of the club, 20% is directly related to his insurance sales.
An additional 35% of the use of the club is associated with his insurance sales.
Club dues are $100 per month for the current year. Other expenses incurred at the club for meals, golf, and other events were $1,800, of which $1,200 is bona fide business entertainment.

What is the total amount in club dues and other entertainment expenditures that Mr. C can deduct on his Schedule C, Form 1040, for the current year?

A. $600

B. $960

C. $1,488

D. $1,584

Answer (A) is correct. *(SEE, adapted)*
REQUIRED: The total amount of club dues and entertainment expenses deductible on Schedule C.
DISCUSSION: Schedule C is used to report the profit or loss from the business of a sole proprietor. Section 274 disallows a deduction for expenditures made with respect to a facility used in connection with entertainment or recreation (e.g., a country club). The bona fide business entertainment is deductible as long as it is properly documented, i.e., $600 ($1,200 × 50%).
Answer (B) is incorrect. The amount of $960 is based on an 80% limit on deductible meals and entertainment. Answer (C) is incorrect. The amount of $1,488 includes the 80% limit for 55% of the club dues related to business and 80% of the $1,200 bona fide business entertainment expenses. Club dues are no longer deductible. Answer (D) is incorrect. Only the bona fide business entertainment expenses are deductible, subject to a 50% ceiling. Club dues are no longer deductible.

3.4.17. A membership or initiation fee is paid once to join a country club for business use. The membership is sold when the holder terminates his or her membership in the club, with the individual retaining the proceeds. The membership is a capital expenditure, which is not currently deductible.

A. True.

B. False.

Answer (A) is correct. *(SEE, adapted)*
DISCUSSION: Section 274 disallows a deduction for expenditures made with respect to a facility used in connection with entertainment or recreation. The membership or initiation fee is a personal use capital asset. Any gain on a sale would be taxable, and any loss would be nondeductible.

3.4.18. One of the requirements that must be met for meal and entertainment expenses to meet the directly related test is that the taxpayer must show that business income or business benefit actually resulted from each meal or entertainment expense.

A. True.

B. False.

Answer (B) is correct. *(SEE, adapted)*
DISCUSSION: The requirements for meal and entertainment expenses to meet the directly related test are set out in Reg. 1.274-(2)(c)(3). No deduction shall be allowed for any expenditure for entertainment unless the taxpayer establishes the expenditure was directly related to the active trade or business. This means the taxpayer had more than a general expectation of deriving income or some other business benefit. It is not required that business income or other benefit result from each entertainment expense.

3.4.19. Randy Donain lives with his family in Oberlin, Ohio, but for the last 3 years, he has worked in Cleveland where he resides in a hotel and eats in restaurants Monday through Friday. On weekends he returns to his Oberlin home. Randy's tax home is in Oberlin, and he can deduct his expenses for travel, meals, and lodging in Cleveland.

A. True.

B. False.

Answer (B) is correct. *(SEE, adapted)*
DISCUSSION: A person's tax home is his or her residence in the same general locale as his or her principal place of duty, post, or station regardless of the location of the family home. Because the duration of the job in Cleveland is indefinite, Randy's tax home is Cleveland. Since his trips to Oberlin are for personal reasons, they are not deductible. The IRS has provided guidance about this question in Rev. Rul. 93-86 (1993-2 C.B. 71). The nature of the taxpayer's employment as temporary or indefinite is determined at the time the employment commences. Employment away from home that is expected to last less than 1 year is generally temporary even if it ultimately lasts more than 1 year. Employment away from home that is expected to last more than 1 year is generally indefinite even if it ultimately lasts less than 1 year. Employment that is expected to be temporary but that becomes indefinite is considered to be indefinite from the point at which the employment time becomes indefinite.

3.4.20. Mr. Austin, owner of an advertising firm, paid $300 for entertainment in a hospitality room at a business convention. Mr. Austin used the convention to display and discuss his products with potential clients. The entertainment is not directly related entertainment.

A. True.

B. False.

Answer (B) is correct. *(SEE, adapted)*
    DISCUSSION: Section 274 allows a deduction for 50% of the costs of entertainment expenses if the entertainment is directly related to or associated with business. Directly related entertainment includes expenditures in a clear business setting and directly in furtherance of the taxpayer's trade or business. A hospitality room to display and discuss products is an example given in Reg. 1.274-2(c)(4).

3.4.21. Mr. G, a businessman, entertains his customer, Mr. C, by taking him to a cocktail party at a city bar and afterward to the theater. No business discussions took place during the party or at the theater. However, Mr. G and Mr. C had spent several hours earlier in the evening discussing new product lines. Mr. G may deduct as an entertainment expense 50% of the cost of entertaining Mr. C.

A. True.

B. False.

Answer (A) is correct. *(SEE, adapted)*
    DISCUSSION: The cost of entertaining Mr. C is considered an associated business expense because it occurs directly after a substantial business discussion. Expenses associated with business entertainment must serve a clear business purpose such as to obtain new business or continue existing business. The expenditures qualify for deduction at the rate of 50% of the cost if they directly precede or follow a bona fide business discussion [Reg. 1.274-2(d)(3)(ii)].

3.4.22. Ms. Painter, an attorney, rented a skybox for only one football game at the local sports stadium during the current year. Ms. Painter invited and entertained 10 of her best clients. Business discussions took place both before and during the game. Fifty percent of the cost for renting the skybox is an allowable entertainment expense.

A. True.

B. False.

Answer (A) is correct. *(SEE, adapted)*
    DISCUSSION: The cost of tickets and entertaining clients and business customers at sporting events is an entertainment expense. The deduction for entertainment expenses is limited to 50% of the otherwise allowed expense [Sec. 274(n)]. Although Sec. 274(l)(2) contains other limitations on the deduction of skybox rental, that provision applies only when a skybox is leased for more than one event. Since Ms. Painter rented the skybox for only one football game, the additional dollar limitations do not apply, and 50% of the cost is deductible as an entertainment expense.

3.4.23. Mr. O, a real estate broker, went to Paris to attend a convention on "Art as an Investment." Mr. O spent $2,000 on travel expenses on his trip. Mr. O may deduct the cost of the trip on his Schedule C for the current year.

A. True.

B. False.

Answer (B) is correct. *(SEE, adapted)*
    DISCUSSION: A convention on investing in art is not an ordinary and necessary expense of carrying on a real estate trade or business. It would only be deductible as an expense related to the production of income. These types of investment seminars and conventions are no longer deductible under Sec. 274(h)(7).

3.5 Business Gifts

3.5.1. Mr. White is a self-employed artist, his wife is a self-employed designer, and they file calendar-year joint returns. During the current year, Mr. White gave four of his clients gifts costing $40 each. In addition, he gave his accountant, Marianne (who is not his employee), a gift costing $95. During the current year, Mrs. White gave nine of her clients gifts costing $50 each. None of Mrs. White's clients were Mr. White's clients and vice versa. However, Mrs. White used the same accountant, Marianne, and gave her a gift costing $65. What is the amount of the Whites' deductible business gift expense in the current year?

A. $770

B. $485

C. $375

D. $350

Answer (D) is correct. *(SEE, adapted)*
    REQUIRED: The deduction allowed for the business gifts listed.
    DISCUSSION: Section 274(b) limits the deduction for gifts to $25 per recipient per year. Husbands and wives are considered to be a single taxpayer and are subject to a single $25 limit. Therefore, the $160 of gifts given to Marianne is limited to $25. The total deduction allowable is $350 (Mr. White's 4 gifts × $25) + (Mrs. White's 9 gifts × $25) + (Marianne's $25).
    Answer (A) is incorrect. The total amount of gifts ($770) is limited to $350. Answer (B) is incorrect. Marianne is not an employee; therefore, the special rule found in Sec. 274(b) that permits a deduction in excess of $25 for "gifts" that are taxable to an employee under Sec. 102(c) does not apply. Answer (C) is incorrect. The Whites are limited to a single $25 deduction (instead of $25 to each donor) for the gifts given to Marianne.

3.5.2. During the current year, Ashley Corporation charged the following payments to miscellaneous expense:

Travel expense of $300 for the company president to offer voluntary testimony at the state capital against proposed legislation regarded as unfavorable to its business
Christmas gifts to 20 customers at $75 each
Contribution of $600 to local political candidate

The maximum deduction that Ashley can claim for these payments is

- A. $800
- B. $1,400
- C. $1,800
- D. $2,400

Answer (A) is correct. *(CPA, adapted)*
REQUIRED: The maximum deduction available for the listed payments.
DISCUSSION: The travel expenses of $300 incurred to provide testimony with regard to legislation are deductible. A denial of a deduction for influencing legislation under Sec. 162(e)(1)(A) does not occur since up to $2,000 of direct costs allocable to influencing state and federal legislation is deductible under the de minimis exception of Sec. 162(e)(5)(B). Christmas gifts to customers are also deductible as ordinary and necessary business expenses. Section 274(b) limits the deduction for business gifts to $25 per donee in a single year. Accordingly, the taxpayer may deduct only $500 (20 customers × $25) for the Christmas gifts. No deduction is allowed for political contributions. The maximum deduction Ashley can claim is $800.
Answer (B) is incorrect. Contributions to political candidates are not deductible. Answer (C) is incorrect. Business gifts are limited to $25 per donee per year. Answer (D) is incorrect. Contributions to political candidates are not deductible. Furthermore, business gifts are limited to $25 per donee per year.

3.5.3. Gulp Oil Company gives miniature souvenir oil rigs with its name imprinted on them to its suppliers and customers. Each costs the company $2 and is worth $5. Sometimes Gulp Oil gives large quantities of these oil rigs to major wholesalers to be given out to retail customers. Gulp Oil also furnishes display racks to dealers that can be used for both Gulp products and other products. These display racks cost the company $40 and are worth $50. In the current year, 20,000 oil rigs and 500 display racks were given away. How much can Gulp Oil deduct for these gifts?

- A. $52,500
- B. $60,000
- C. $112,500
- D. $125,000

Answer (B) is correct. *(Publisher, adapted)*
REQUIRED: The amount a taxpayer may deduct for business gifts of small items and display racks.
DISCUSSION: Gifts can constitute a business deduction under Sec. 162(a). They are limited by Sec. 274(b) to $25 per recipient per year. There are exceptions for items that do not cost the taxpayer in excess of $4, and on which the name of the taxpayer is clearly imprinted, and for signs and display racks to be used on the recipient's business premises. These may be given without limit as long as they meet the ordinary and necessary test under Sec. 162(a). Since the miniature oil rigs did not cost more than $4, there is no limit on the deduction for giving them away. Similarly, the display racks are not limited to $25 per recipient. Consequently, the cost of these items may be deducted in full. The total deduction is $60,000 [(20,000 × $2 per oil rig) + (500 × $40 per display rack)].
Answer (A) is incorrect. This would be the answer if the racks were limited to $25 per donee like other business gifts. Answer (C) is incorrect. The FMV of the souvenir rigs should not be used, and the racks are not limited to $25 per donee like other business gifts. Answer (D) is incorrect. The FMV of the rigs and display racks should not be used when determining the deduction.

3.5.4. If Mihalick Company gives gift certificates of $30 each to its employees for Christmas in the current year, only $25 per employee is deductible by Mihalick.

- A. True.
- B. False.

Answer (B) is correct. *(Publisher, adapted)*
DISCUSSION: Section 274(b) limits the deduction for gifts to $25 per recipient per year. However, this section applies only to items excludable under Sec. 102. After 1986, "gifts" to employees are not excludable under Sec. 102. Therefore, the entire $30 per employee is deductible as compensation and must be included in income by each employee, unless it can be considered to be a de minimis fringe benefit under Sec. 132(e).

3.5.5. If a partnership gives business gifts, the partnership and the partners are treated as one taxpayer for figuring the $25 per recipient limitation.

- A. True.
- B. False.

Answer (B) is correct. *(SEE, adapted)*
DISCUSSION: The deduction for business gifts is generally limited to $25 per recipient under Sec. 274(b). In the case of a partnership, the $25 limitation applies first at the partnership level and then to each partner. This is not the same as treating both the partnership and partners as one taxpayer.

3.5.6. To take a deduction for business gifts, you must prove all the following elements: cost, date of gift, description of gift, reason for giving gift, and business relationship of person receiving gift.

A. True.

B. False.

Answer (A) is correct. *(SEE, adapted)*
    DISCUSSION: Section 274(d) disallows a deduction for any business gift unless the taxpayer substantiates by adequate records the amount (cost) of the gift, the date and description of the gift, the business purpose of the gift, and the business relationship to the taxpayer of the person receiving the gift.

3.5.7. Calvin gave two tickets to a theater performance to a business customer. The tickets cost $50 each. Calvin did not go with his customer to the performance. He can choose to treat the tickets as either a gift or an entertainment expense.

A. True.

B. False.

Answer (A) is correct. *(SEE, adapted)*
    DISCUSSION: Section 274 does not specify that the taxpayer providing the entertainment for a business customer must be present at the entertainment event (as is required in the case of meals). However, the taxpayer must establish that the entertainment was directly related to, or associated with, the active conduct of the taxpayer's trade or business. The taxpayer has the option of treating the entertainment tickets as a gift, but under Sec. 274(b), the limit for deduction is $25 per person per year. If the taxpayer treats the tickets as entertainment, the deduction is limited to 50% of the cost of the tickets.

3.6 Employee Compensation

3.6.1. Flora Corporation made the following awards of tangible personal property to employees during the current year under a written, qualified, nondiscriminatory plan:

Name	Reason for Award	Value Received
Mike	20 years' employment	$250
Kurt	20 years' employment	250
Steve	35 years' employment	450
Casey	40 years' employment	550
George	5-year safety award	200

No other safety awards were awarded during the current year. The amount Flora can deduct related to these awards is

A. $400

B. $1,300

C. $1,500

D. $1,700

Answer (D) is correct. *(Publisher, adapted)*
    REQUIRED: The amount an employer can deduct for awards to employees under a qualified plan.
    DISCUSSION: Section 274(j) limits the deduction for employment achievement awards (tangible personal property awarded to an employee by reason of length of service or safety achievement) to $400 per employee per year or $1,600 per employee per year if it is a qualified plan award. A qualified plan award is an item awarded as part of a permanent, written plan or program that does not discriminate in favor of highly compensated employees. An item may not be treated as a qualified plan award if the average cost of all items awarded exceeds $400. Under Sec. 274(j)(4), further limitations on employee awards are provided whereby length-of-service awards must not be awarded until after the recipient has worked over 5 years. Also, the recipient must not have received any such award during the applicable year or any of the 4 prior years. Safety achievement awards are also not deductible if, during the taxable year, such awards have previously been awarded to more than 10% of the other employees or to a manager, clerical employee, or other professional employee. Here, since all the requirements of a qualified plan award are met, the full amount of each award, or a total of $1,700, is deductible.
    Answer (A) is incorrect. The amount of $400 is the deductible limit per employee per year for employment achievement awards that are not qualified plan awards. For qualified plan awards, the actual cost is deductible if the average cost of the award is $400 or less. Answer (B) is incorrect. All of the awards qualify for a deduction, even though they may exceed $400, since it is a qualified plan. Answer (C) is incorrect. George's safety award also qualifies for a deduction since safety awards have not been awarded to at least 10% of the work force.

3.6.2. Mr. Z, the sole proprietor of Z's Wholesale, transferred an automobile used in his business to Mr. Y, an employee of Z's Wholesale, for business related services rendered during the current year. Z's adjusted basis in the automobile was $6,000 and the fair market value was $8,000 at the time of the transfer. Z had purchased the automobile 2 years ago for $11,000. During the current year, Z paid $80,000 in employee salaries, not including the automobile given to Mr. Y. Z is a cash-basis taxpayer. What is his total salary and wage deduction for the current year?

A. $48,000

B. $80,000

C. $86,000

D. $88,000

Answer (D) is correct. *(SEE, adapted)*
REQUIRED: The amount of the employer's deduction for property paid to an employee.
DISCUSSION: Section 162(a)(1) allows a deduction for reasonable compensation for personal services actually rendered. Section 83(a) allows the deduction to an employer equal to the fair market value of property given to the employee when the property is transferable or is not subject to a substantial risk of forfeiture. Therefore, Mr. Z's salary and wage deduction is $88,000 ($80,000 + $8,000 FMV of car).
Answer (A) is incorrect. The amount of $48,000 only includes one-half of deductible salaries paid in cash. Answer (B) is incorrect. The automobile is also deductible. Answer (C) is incorrect. The FMV of the automobile, not the adjusted basis, should be deducted as reasonable compensation for services rendered.

3.6.3. Oscar Cinema Studios rewards its retiring officers with miniature gold statuettes if the officers complete at least 10 years of service. Each statuette costs Oscar $400 and is worth $600. Rank-and-file employees receive plastic replicas of the studio's back lot when they retire and have completed 30 years of devoted service. These plastic replicas cost $50 a piece and are each worth $70. In the current year, Oscar gave two retiring officers each a miniature statuette during a meaningful presentation. How much can Oscar deduct for these gifts?

A. $50

B. $100

C. $800

D. $1,200

Answer (C) is correct. *(Publisher, adapted)*
REQUIRED: The amount that an employer may deduct for gifts to employees by reason of length of service.
DISCUSSION: Section 274(j) limits the deduction for employee achievement awards. These are items of tangible personal property awarded to an employee by reason of length of service or safety achievement, and the award is given as part of a meaningful presentation and under circumstances that do not create a significant likelihood that the payment is disguised compensation. The deduction limit is $1,600 per employee per year if it is a qualified plan award (which requires a permanent written plan or program that does not discriminate in favor of highly compensated employees).
In this case, the plan does discriminate in favor of officers, so the deduction is limited to $400 per recipient. Since each statuette costs the company $400, the amount is deductible in its entirety. The total deduction is $800.
Answer (A) is incorrect. The allowable deduction for employee achievement awards is $400 each, not $25 each like other business gifts. Answer (B) is incorrect. The statuettes costing $400 each were awarded, not the replicas costing $50 each. Answer (D) is incorrect. The $400 cost of each statuette is deducted, not the $600 FMV.

3.6.4. Bunker is an officer of Westerfeld Enterprises. Bunker is provided a car for business use and is reimbursed for travel and entertainment. Bunker also uses the car to commute home. Bunker has not been very careful in documenting his travel and entertainment; therefore, the requirements of Sec. 274(d) are not met. How should Westerfeld Enterprises treat the payments to Bunker in order to obtain the maximum tax advantage?

A. Include the commuting use of the car and nondocumented travel and entertainment in Bunker's W-2 and withhold on it.

B. Include the commuting use of the car and nondocumented travel in Bunker's W-2 and not withhold on it.

C. Include the commuting use of the car in Bunker's W-2 but deduct the rest as travel and entertainment.

D. Deduct everything as car expense and travel and entertainment since this is what the expenditures were for.

Answer (A) is correct. *(Publisher, adapted)*
REQUIRED: The employer's most advantageous treatment of an employee's personal use of a company car and nondocumented travel and entertainment.
DISCUSSION: The employee's personal use of an employer's property is additional compensation to the employee. Commuting to and from work is a personal expense that should be deducted by the employer as additional compensation. Nondocumented travel and entertainment is not deductible by the employer unless treated as additional compensation to the employee under Sec. 274(e)(2). All such forms of compensation are subject to withholding.
Answer (B) is incorrect. Failure to withhold could result in the employer's being liable for the employee's share of withholding and a 100% penalty. Answer (C) is incorrect. The nondocumented travel and entertainment is not deductible under Sec. 274 (except as compensation). Negligent deduction of such items could result in additional taxes, interest, and a 20% penalty. Answer (D) is incorrect. These items must be reported as additional compensation to the employee in order to be deductible by the employer.

3.6.5. During the current year, Mr. Y, a cash-basis sole proprietor, paid the following:

Base wages to his 4 employees	$100,000
Year-end bonuses paid to 2 employees for establishing new sales records	20,000
Christmas gifts to his 4 employees in appreciation for past services ($50 per gift)	200

What is the total amount Mr. Y can deduct on his current-year income tax return?

A. $100,000

B. $120,000

C. $120,100

D. $120,200

Answer (D) is correct. *(SEE, adapted)*

REQUIRED: The deductible amount for salary payments, bonuses, and gifts.

DISCUSSION: Section 162(a)(1) permits a deduction for a reasonable allowance for salaries or other personal services actually rendered, including bonuses. In addition, Sec. 274(b) limits the deduction for gifts up to $25 per recipient per year. However, this section applies only to gifts excludable under Sec. 102. Section 102(c) explicitly disallows an exclusion from income for employee gifts. Thus, the entire $200 of employee gifts is deductible. Generally, such amounts are taxable to the employee as compensation, although they may be tax-exempt as a de minimis fringe benefit or a qualified employee achievement award. Mr. Y may deduct $120,200 on his current-year return ($100,000 base wages + $20,000 bonuses + $200 gifts to employees).

Answer (A) is incorrect. The year-end bonuses and the Christmas gifts are also deductible. Answer (B) is incorrect. The Christmas gifts are also deductible. Answer (C) is incorrect. The Christmas gifts are not limited to $25 per recipient per year as they are for business gifts made to individuals other than employees.

3.6.6. All of the following payments made to employees would be currently deductible as business expenses except

A. Wages paid to employees for constructing a new building to be used in the business.

B. Vacation pay paid to an employee when the employee chooses not to take a vacation.

C. Reasonable salary paid to a corporate officer owning a controlling interest for services she rendered.

D. Lump-sum payment made to the beneficiary of a deceased employee that is reasonable in relation to the employee's past services.

Answer (A) is correct. *(SEE, adapted)*

REQUIRED: The payment to an employee not currently deductible.

DISCUSSION: Normally, Sec. 162(a)(1) allows a deduction for a reasonable allowance for salaries or other compensation for personal services actually rendered. However, Sec. 263A requires all direct costs and a proper share of indirect costs allocable to property produced by the taxpayer to be capitalized. Wages paid to employees for constructing a new building would be direct costs allocable to that building. Those costs are capitalized and depreciated as part of the cost of the building rather than currently deductible.

Answer (B) is incorrect. Vacation pay paid to an employee when the employee chooses not to take a vacation is a currently deductible compensation expense. Answer (C) is incorrect. Reasonable salary paid to a corporate officer owning a controlling interest for services she rendered is a currently deductible compensation expense provided it is not an indirect cost of producing property. Answer (D) is incorrect. A lump-sum payment made to the beneficiary of a deceased employee that is reasonable in relation to the employee's past services is a currently deductible compensation expense.

3.6.7. Clark, quarterback for the Metropolis Superheroes, Inc., football team, is also the majority shareholder. He performs no services other than playing as quarterback for the team. His salary is twice that of the next highest-paid player in the league, even though his performance is below average for a quarterback. What is the most likely treatment of his salary upon audit of the Metropolis Superheroes by the IRS?

A. It is not deductible at all.

B. It is deductible in full.

C. It is deductible up to the amount of the next highest paid player.

D. It is deductible to the amount of the reasonable value of Clark's services.

Answer (D) is correct. *(Publisher, adapted)*

REQUIRED: The correct treatment of a salary paid to a shareholder-employee.

DISCUSSION: Section 162(a)(1) permits a deduction for a reasonable allowance for salaries or other compensation for personal services actually rendered. In determining what is reasonable, it is important to compare what other businesses would pay for similar services under similar circumstances (Reg. 1.162-7). Since Clark is below average in performance, he should receive the fair value of his services and not twice that of the next highest-paid player in the league. This is not an arm's-length transaction, and the IRS would likely impose the reasonable compensation issue.

Answer (A) is incorrect. The salary is deductible to the extent that it is a reasonable allowance for services. Answer (B) is incorrect. The salary is probably not deductible in full due to the shareholder relationship and the extraordinary amount of the salary. Answer (C) is incorrect. There is no reason to measure Clark's salary by that of the next highest-paid player in the league if Clark is not one of the best players.

Authors' note: The Sec. 162(m) limit of $1 million on deductible compensation does not apply to Clark's compensation unless the Superheroes are a publicly held company and Clark is the company's CEO or one of the next four highest-paid executives. This does not appear to be the case.

3.6.8. On February 16 of Year 2, Mr. E paid his employees a $10,000 bonus. Mr. E is an accrual-basis taxpayer on a calendar year, and the employees are not related to him. The amount and date of payment was fixed by agreement dated December 31 of Year 1. Mr. E is entitled to take the bonus deduction on his Year 1 income tax return.

A. True.

B. False.

Answer (A) is correct. *(SEE, adapted)*
DISCUSSION: Section 162(a) allows a deduction for ordinary and necessary business expenses paid or incurred during the taxable year, including a reasonable allowance for salaries or other compensation. Since the amount and date of payment were fixed by an agreement dated prior to the end of the taxable year, all the events had occurred to determine the fact and the amount of the liability. Since the payment occurs within 2 1/2 months of the end of the employer's tax year, it is not considered deferred compensation whose deduction is deferred to the year of payment [Temp. Reg. Sec. 1.404(b)-1T]. Therefore, it is deductible in Year 1 (Reg. 1.461-1).

3.6.9. Mr. Bryan, a calendar-year taxpayer, employs his mother and uses the accrual method of accounting. On December 31 of Year 1, he accrued $10,000 of his mother's salary. She uses the calendar year and the cash method of accounting. The $10,000 accrued salary was paid on March 31 of Year 2. Mr. Bryan can deduct the accrued salary on his Year 1 tax return.

A. True.

B. False.

Answer (B) is correct. *(SEE, adapted)*
DISCUSSION: Section 267(a)(2) provides that payments otherwise deductible (e.g., salary) made to a related person are not deductible until includible in the income of the recipient. The effect is to prevent an accrual-basis taxpayer from deducting payments made to a related cash-basis taxpayer until the payments are made. Related persons include members of a family, so Mr. Bryan cannot deduct the salary to his mother until Year 2.

3.6.10. If an employee is required to include the fair market value of a noncash fringe benefit in his or her gross income, the employer can deduct that amount as compensation for services.

A. True.

B. False.

Answer (B) is correct. *(SEE, adapted)*
DISCUSSION: It is the position of the IRS (and the Special Enrollment Exam) that only the cost of noncash fringe benefits (such as meals) provided to employees may be deducted. However, note that under Sec. 83(a), an employee includes property received for services in income at the fair market value of the property. Under Sec. 83(h), the employer is entitled to an equivalent deduction. However, if the employer did take a deduction for the fair market value of the property provided to an employee, the employer would also have to recognize income for the excess of the property's fair market value over its cost, so the net effect is that the employer winds up with a deduction equal to the cost.

3.7 Rental Expense

3.7.1. On April 1 of the current year, Sam, a cash-basis taxpayer, leased office space from Executive Plaza for 5 years, beginning May 1 of the current year, for $700 per month. During the year, he paid $7,000, of which $1,400 was for advance rent, to Executive Plaza. What is the amount Sam can deduct for the current year?

A. $5,600

B. $6,300

C. $7,000

D. $8,400

Answer (A) is correct. *(SEE, adapted)*
REQUIRED: The amount of rent deduction when rent has been prepaid.
DISCUSSION: Prepaid rent may not be deducted by either a cash-basis or accrual-basis taxpayer. To do so would violate the requirement that the taxpayer's method of accounting must clearly reflect income [Sec. 446(b)]. Furthermore, an expenditure that creates an asset having a useful life extending substantially beyond the close of the taxable year is not deductible [Reg. 1.461-1(a)]. Only the $5,600 of rental expense allocable to the current year ($7,000 − $1,400) is deductible in the current year.
Answer (B) is incorrect. The amount of $6,300 would have been the current year's expense if 50% of the prepaid rent had been deductible. Answer (C) is incorrect. The $1,400 of prepaid rent is not deductible in the current year. Answer (D) is incorrect. Only $7,000 was actually paid, of which $1,400 was prepaid rent.

3.7.2. On January 2 of the current year, Melanie paid $9,000 to acquire a lease on a new building for a term of 20 years. At her request, the lease also included two renewal options of 5 years each. Of the above cost, $6,000 was for the original lease and $1,500 for each of the two renewal options. Melanie is a cash-basis taxpayer. What is her allowable deduction for the current year?

A. $0

B. $300

C. $450

D. $9,000

Answer (B) is correct. *(SEE, adapted)*
REQUIRED: The allowable deduction in the year of acquisition for the cost of acquiring a long-term lease.
DISCUSSION: A cash-basis taxpayer normally deducts expenses in the year paid. However, the lease is an asset with a useful life that extends substantially beyond the close of the taxable year, so the cost of it must be capitalized and amortized over the life of the lease [Reg. 1.461-1(a)]. Since less than 75% of the cost of acquiring the entire lease is attributable to the basic or initial term of the lease ($6,000 ÷ $9,000 = 67%), the term of the lease is treated as including all periods for which the lease may be renewed (Sec. 178). The taxpayer's allowable deduction in the current year is $300 ($9,000 ÷ 30-year useful life).
Answer (A) is incorrect. Melanie has an allowable deduction in the current year equal to its amortized cost of the lease for the current year. Answer (C) is incorrect. The useful life of the lease is 30 years, not 20 years. Less than 75% of the lease cost is attributable to the initial lease. Answer (D) is incorrect. The cost of the lease must be amortized over a 30-year useful life. Only the amortized cost for the current year is currently deductible.

3.7.3. In Year 1, Paige signed a 6-year lease for a building to use in her business. In Year 3, she installed shelves and made other leasehold improvements to the building for a total of $3,200. She can

A. Deduct the $3,200 as a current expense.

B. Depreciate the $3,200 using regular MACRS depreciation.

C. Depreciate the $3,200 using the alternative depreciation system.

D. Amortize the $3,200 over the remaining term of the lease.

Answer (B) is correct. *(SEE, adapted)*
REQUIRED: The correct treatment of leasehold improvements.
DISCUSSION: Under prior law, leasehold improvements made by a lessee were deductible over the shorter of the property's ACRS recovery period or the portion of the lease term remaining on the date the property was acquired. After 1986, the lessee recovers capital costs under the general MACRS depreciation rules in every case.
Answer (A) is incorrect. After 1986, the $3,200 of leasehold improvements should be depreciated. Answer (C) is incorrect. After 1986, the $3,200 of leasehold improvements should be depreciated but not using the alternative depreciation system. Answer (D) is incorrect. After 1986, the $3,200 of leasehold improvements should not be amortized over the remaining term of the lease.

3.7.4. An agreement may be considered a conditional sales contract rather than a lease if any of the following are true except

A. You pay rent that is much more than current fair rental value for the property.

B. At the end of the lease, you obtain title to the property by paying its fair market value.

C. The agreement applies part of each "rent" payment toward an equity interest that you will receive.

D. The lease designates some part of the "rent" payments as interest.

Answer (B) is correct. *(SEE, adapted)*
REQUIRED: The factor that would not cause an agreement to be considered a conditional sales contract rather than a lease.
DISCUSSION: By having to pay the fair market value of the property and not just a nominal payment at the end of the lease, the agreement would not be considered a conditional sales contract since the actual sale would not take place until the lease is over. Any rental payments throughout the life of the lease would be deductible as rent and not capitalized as payments toward ownership of the property.
Answer (A) is incorrect. The average person would not pay well above the current fair rental value for property unless such person expected an additional interest in the property. Answer (C) is incorrect. Under such agreement, the lessee gets an increasing interest in the property with each payment. Answer (D) is incorrect. Such a situation would be treated as if the lessee is actually financing the property with the lessor.

3.7.5. In the current year, Jack built a warehouse on property he leased from Max. At the time the warehouse was constructed, there were 12 years remaining on the term of the lease. Jack may not amortize the cost of the improvements over the remaining term of the lease. He must depreciate the cost using the MACRS rules.

A. True.

B. False.

Answer (A) is correct. *(SEE, adapted)*
DISCUSSION: Improvements made or erected on leased property after 1986 are amortized under the general MACRS depreciation rules in every case. Therefore, the remaining term of the lease is not a factor in computing the amortization (depreciation). The recovery class or class life of the improvements determines the recovery period.

3.7.6. Mr. B leased a sprinkler system for his warehouse. The system had an estimated useful life of 40 years and a cost to the lessor of $20,000. Under the agreement, Mr. B will rent the system for 5 years at a yearly rate of $5,000 for a total rent of $25,000. Mr. B must insure the system for an amount at least equal to the total rentals and will bear the risk of any loss. The lessor's liability for any defect is limited to $1,000. The lease may be renewed for another 5-year period at $200 a year. The lease payments may be deducted by Mr. B as rent expense.

A. True.

B. False.

Answer (B) is correct. *(SEE, adapted)*
DISCUSSION: Although the transaction takes the form of a rental, it is in substance a financed sale since the taxpayer is required to provide insurance and maintenance for the system and bear the risk of loss. The lessor has almost no liability for the system. Furthermore, the rentals for the renewal period of the lease are a nominal amount, indicating that the system has already been paid for. In essence, Mr. B has made a capital expenditure for which Sec. 263 disallows a deduction. Instead, he must capitalize and amortize or depreciate the asset over its useful life.

3.7.7. A lease that provides for 85% of the periodic payments to be applied to the purchase price upon exercise of a purchase option by the lessee will normally constitute a conditional sale, and the purchase price (net of interest) should be capitalized.

A. True.

B. False.

Answer (A) is correct. *(SEE, adapted)*
DISCUSSION: A transaction in the form of a lease but in substance a purchase is treated as a purchase so that the rent is not deductible and the purchase price must be capitalized and depreciated. When a substantial portion of the payments can be applied to acquire title, the transaction is considered to be a purchase.

3.8 Farm Expense

3.8.1. On May 4 of the current year, Taxpayer A expected a yield of 50,000 bushels of corn from his farm. The December futures price at that time was $2.05 a bushel. To protect himself against a loss, he sold 10 December futures contracts of 5,000 bushels each. The price did not drop but rose to $2.25 a bushel. He sold his 50,000 bushels of raised corn for $2.25 a bushel. He also purchased his futures obligations of corn at $2.25 a bushel to close out the futures transactions. He paid a broker's commission of $500 for the in and out futures transactions. What is his loss on these futures transactions?

A. $10,000

B. $10,500

C. $12,500

D. $102,500

Answer (B) is correct. *(SEE, adapted)*
REQUIRED: The taxpayer's loss incurred on the sale and purchase of futures contracts.
DISCUSSION: Taxpayer A has engaged in a short sale generally regulated under Sec. 1233. A short sale occurs when securities (e.g., commodity futures) are sold now to be delivered in the future. The price of the commodity used to cover (deliver) the prior short sale determines the gain or loss as compared to the selling price in the short sale. Taxpayer A incurred a loss of $10,500 [(50,000 bushels × $0.20 price increase) + $500 commission]. This was a hedging transaction, which farmers engage in to protect against price drops in the commodity. Because the hedge was made to protect ordinary income from farming, the loss is also ordinary (Reg. 1.1221-2).

Section 1259, which was added by the 1997 act, requires constructive sales treatment for appreciated financial positions. It does not apply here since it is only applicable to certain transactions involving stock, debt instruments, and partnership interests.

Answer (A) is incorrect. The loss on the futures transactions also includes the broker's commission. Answer (C) is incorrect. The loss is only $0.20 per bushel of corn (not $0.25 per bushel) and also includes the $500 broker's commission. Answer (D) is incorrect. The December futures price for the 50,000 bushels is $102,500.

3.8.2. In the current year, Taxpayer A had gross income from Farms X and Y of $20,000 ($10,000 from each). During the current year, A spent $12,000 on Farm X on deductible soil and water conservation expenditures under a plan approved by his state's Soil Conservation Service of the Department of Agriculture. How much of the soil and water conservation expenditures can Taxpayer A deduct for the current year?

A. $2,500

B. $5,000

C. $10,000

D. $12,000

Answer (B) is correct. *(SEE, adapted)*
   REQUIRED: The deductible amount of soil and water conservation expenditures.
   DISCUSSION: Section 175 allows a taxpayer engaged in the business of farming to treat expenditures for the purpose of soil or water conservation on land used for farming as deductible expenses rather than capital expenditures, provided the expenditures are approved by the Soil Conservation Service of the Department of Agriculture for the area in which the land is located. The deduction for any year is limited to 25% of the gross income derived from farming during the year. The gross income includes that from all the taxpayer's farming, not just from the land on which the soil and water conservation expenditures were made. Taxpayer A may deduct $5,000 ($20,000 × 25%) of the soil and water conservation expenditures. The remaining $7,000 may be carried over and deducted in succeeding taxable years subject to the 25% limit each year.
   Answer (A) is incorrect. The 25% limit on soil and water expenditures is on the gross income of all farming property, not just on the property that had the work done. Answer (C) is incorrect. The deduction is not limited to the amount of income earned on the property for which the soil and water conservation expenditures were made. Answer (D) is incorrect. The full amount of the expenditure should not be deducted. The deduction is limited to 25% of gross income from all farming property.

3.8.3. In the current year, Frankie had gross income from farming of $60,000 and taxable income from farming of $25,000. Frankie spent $6,500 on land clearing expenses during the current year. How much of the land clearing expenses can Frankie deduct in the current year?

A. $0

B. $3,250

C. $5,000

D. $6,500

Answer (A) is correct. *(SEE, adapted)*
   REQUIRED: The amount of land clearing expenses deductible in the current year.
   DISCUSSION: A taxpayer engaged in the business of farming may no longer elect to treat expenditures to clear land for the purpose of making such land suitable for farming as deductible expenses rather than capital expenditures because Sec. 182 has been repealed. Land clearing expenses incurred after 1986 must be capitalized.
   Answer (B) is incorrect. Land clearing expenses incurred after 1986 must be capitalized, not deducted. In addition, $3,250 is only 50% of the amount to be capitalized. Answer (C) is incorrect. Land clearing expenses incurred after 1986 must be capitalized, not deducted. In addition, $5,000 is not the full amount to be capitalized. Answer (D) is incorrect. The full amount of land clearing expenses incurred after 1986 must be capitalized, not deducted.

3.8.4. Mr. Cryzer, a calendar-year taxpayer who itemizes his deductions, raises cows in his spare time and on weekends. In the current year, he sold 25 cows for a total of $7,000 and incurred the following expenses directly related to raising those cows:

Medicine and veterinarian bills	$2,000
Taxes	1,000
Feed	5,000
Depreciation	1,000

What is Mr. Cryzer's net profit or loss to be included in his individual income tax return, assuming that the activity is not engaged in for profit?

A. $(2,000) loss.

B. $(1,000) loss.

C. $0

D. $1,000 profit.

Answer (C) is correct. *(SEE, adapted)*
   REQUIRED: The profit or loss of a taxpayer who raises cows as a hobby.
   DISCUSSION: A farmer or cattleman deducts expenses under Sec. 162 for a trade or business, or under Sec. 212 for the production or collection of income. However, if the activity is merely a hobby and not engaged in for profit, Sec. 183 limits the deductions to the gross income from the activity. Mr. Cryzer's gross income from raising cows was $7,000, and his expenses were $9,000. He may deduct $7,000, so he has no profit or loss.
   In order to determine whether an activity is a hobby or engaged in for profit, the presumption of Sec. 183(d) may be used; if a profit is made for 3 or more of 5 consecutive taxable years, the activity will be presumed to have been engaged in for profit.
   Answer (A) is incorrect. A $2,000 loss would occur if all expenses were allowed to be deducted; however, deductible expenses are limited to hobby income. Answer (B) is incorrect. Expenses (other than depreciation) are still in excess of hobby income and are not deductible. Answer (D) is incorrect. Expenses are more than income, so there would be a loss; however, deductible expenses for hobbies are limited to hobby income.

3.8.5. Alma Knack is a calendar-year, cash-basis farmer who grows corn and raises hogs on a large farm in Iowa. On December 26 of the current year, Alma purchased a 6-month supply of feed for the hogs costing $4,000. At the same time, she also purchased a new hybrid variety of seed costing $1,000 for the spring planting period. Her other farm expenses for the year were $9,000. Of the feed and seed purchased on December 26, Alma may deduct in the current year

A. Only $1,000.

B. Only $4,000.

C. Only $4,500.

D. All $5,000.

Answer (C) is correct. *(Publisher, adapted)*

REQUIRED: The amount that a farmer can deduct for prepaid feed and seed.

DISCUSSION: Under Reg. 1.162-12, farmers are allowed to deduct prepaid feed and seed that will not be used until subsequent years. However, this must be a consistent method of accounting from year to year, and after 1986 the deduction for prepaid expenses may not exceed 50% of other farming expenses. Therefore, Alma can deduct only $4,500 ($9,000 × 50%).

Note that a farming syndicate (any business enterprise, other than a regular corporation, an interest in which is a security subject to regulation by the SEC) may not deduct prepaid feed and seed; these are only deductible when actually used or consumed (Sec. 464). These and other restrictions on deductions by farming syndicates are designed to curb their use as tax shelters.

Answer (A) is incorrect. The amount of $1,000 is the cost of the hybrid seed. The $1,000 cost is less than the deduction limit for prepaid feed and seed, which is 50% of other farm expenses. Answer (B) is incorrect. The amount of $4,000 is the cost of the feed for the hogs, which is less than the deduction limit for prepaid feed that is 50% of other farm expenses. Answer (D) is incorrect. The full amount of prepaid feed and seed costs is $5,000. It is limited to 50% of other farming expenses.

3.8.6. A farmer trading in commodity future contracts within the range of his production can deduct a $5,000 loss on such contracts on Schedule F as an ordinary business expense.

A. True.

B. False.

Answer (A) is correct. *(SEE, adapted)*

DISCUSSION: A farmer who trades in commodity futures within the range of his or her production (both amount and type of commodity) is considered to be engaged in hedging to protect against loss in the event of a decline in the price of the commodity farmed. As such, the hedging is deemed a part of the farming operation, and any gain or loss is considered ordinary [Reg. 1.1221-2(c)].

Section 1259, which was added by the 1997 act, requires constructive sales treatment for appreciated financial positions. It does not apply here since it is only applicable to certain transactions involving stock, debt instruments, and partnership interests.

3.8.7. If you rent a farm for farming, the rental expense that represents the fair rental value of the farm residence is not deductible.

A. True.

B. False.

Answer (A) is correct. *(SEE, adapted)*

DISCUSSION: The rental value of the farm residence is a personal expense, which is not deductible. Only that portion of the rental expense attributable to the land and buildings actually used for farming is deductible.

3.8.8. Morgan Donegan, a cash-basis farmer, sold cattle that he had raised for $8,000. His feed, veterinarian fees, and other costs of raising the cattle totaled $4,000. His gross income from this sale is $4,000.

A. True.

B. False.

Answer (B) is correct. *(SEE, adapted)*

DISCUSSION: Gross income from the sale of cattle is the amount received, or $8,000. Furthermore, a farmer's expenses of raising the cattle are generally deducted from gross income, not capitalized, and deducted as part of cost of sales.

3.8.9. Michael Wright purchased several brood mares in Year 1, expecting to breed them and sell their offspring. His Schedule C reflected the following:

Year 1	$ 5,000	loss
Year 2	9,900	loss
Year 3	3,500	loss
Year 4	10,800	profit
Year 5	4,250	loss
Year 6	2,700	loss
Year 7	17,250	profit

Wright's activity is presumed to be for profit.

A. True.

B. False.

Answer (A) is correct. *(SEE, adapted)*
    DISCUSSION: Section 183 applies to activities that are not engaged in for profit and allows a deduction only to the extent of gross income. There is a presumption that an activity is engaged in for profit if it shows a profit in at least 3 of any 5 consecutive years (2 out of 7 years if breeding horses). Since the taxpayer's activity showed a profit in Year 4 and Year 7 that is substantially the same amount as the losses, the horse breeding activity is presumed to be for profit.

3.9 Casualty and Theft Loss

3.9.1. Ernest Kopp started a security guard business. Kopp rented an office and furnished it with used furniture and a typewriter from his home. He also converted one of the family cars to business use. On the second day of operations, the company car was stolen while Kopp was installing a security system. On the third day, the office was burglarized and the typewriter stolen. Kopp's basis in the typewriter was $200 and its fair market value when put in the office was $300. The car had cost Kopp $1,500 but it was worth only $1,000 when converted to business use. What is Kopp's casualty deduction?

A. $1,000

B. $1,100

C. $1,200

D. $1,800

Answer (C) is correct. *(Publisher, adapted)*
    REQUIRED: The casualty loss deduction for property converted from personal to business use.
    DISCUSSION: The adjusted basis for property converted from personal to business use is the lesser of its cost basis or its fair market value on the date of conversion. Under Regs. 1.165-9(b) and 1.165-7(b), the amount of a loss by theft of business property is the property's adjusted basis. Kopp may deduct the total of $1,200 ($200 for the typewriter and $1,000 for the car). The deduction is not subject to the $100 and 10% of adjusted gross income limitations since the property was used in a trade or business.
    Answer (A) is incorrect. The $200 adjusted basis of the typewriter is also part of the casualty loss deduction. Answer (B) is incorrect. The adjusted basis of the typewriter does not have to be reduced by the $100 nondeductible floor since it was being used in a business at the time of the casualty. Answer (D) is incorrect. The typewriter and car are valued at the lesser of their FMV or adjusted basis when converted to business use.

3.9.2. Mr. Smith constructed a building at a cost of $80,000 on land that he leases. He uses half of the building for business purposes and lives in the other half. In the current year, a flood damaged the entire building. Mr. Smith's records reflect the following information:

Cost of building	$80,000
Depreciation properly deducted	4,800
Fair market value of building immediately before the flood	76,000
Fair market value of building immediately after the flood	64,000
Insurance reimbursement received during the current year	8,000
Mr. Smith's adjusted gross income for the current year	50,000

What is the amount of Mr. Smith's business and personal casualty losses after any limitations?

A. $0 business; $0 personal.

B. $2,000 business; $0 personal.

C. $2,000 business; $1,800 personal.

D. $900 business; $2,000 personal.

Answer (B) is correct. *(SEE, adapted)*
    REQUIRED: The deductible loss resulting from a flood of an insured building.
    DISCUSSION: Section 165 allows a deduction for a loss sustained during the taxable year and not compensated for by insurance. Since Mr. Smith uses the building for business purposes 50% of the time, his business casualty loss would be calculated as follows:

Fair market value before flood	$76,000× 50%	=	$38,000
Fair market value after flood	$64,000× 50%	=	(32,000)
Loss due to flood			$ 6,000
Insurance reimbursement	$ 8,000 × 50%	=	(4,000)
Business casualty loss			$ 2,000

This amount was determined under Sec. 165 rules, which state the loss for partial destruction of business property is the lesser of the taxpayer's adjusted basis in the property or the difference between the fair market value of the property immediately before and after the casualty.
    Since Mr. Smith's 50% personal use of the building is subject to the $100 floor for each casualty item, and the total casualty does not exceed 10% of adjusted gross income of the individual, no personal deduction can be claimed [the 10% of AGI limitation of $5,000 ($50,000 × 10%) is greater than the $1,900 personal casualty loss].
    Answer (A) is incorrect. There is a business loss. Answer (C) is incorrect. The personal casualty loss is limited to the 10% of AGI nondeductible floor. Answer (D) is incorrect. The business casualty loss is not $900. Also, the personal casualty loss is limited to 10% of the AGI nondeductible floor.

3.9.3. In April of the current year, Mr. Beach, an accrual-basis taxpayer, had a $25,000 theft loss from inventory items held for sale to customers in the ordinary course of his business. In August of the current year, he received a $25,000 reimbursement from his insurance company to cover the loss. Which of the following is a correct method of reporting the loss and reimbursement on Beach's income tax return?

A. Include the $25,000 in ordinary income; the loss is accounted for in the cost of goods sold.

B. Do not report the loss as a separate item; do not include the $25,000 in ordinary income.

C. Include the $25,000 in ordinary income; decrease the cost of goods sold by the $100 casualty loss rule.

D. Apply the 10% adjusted gross income rule to the loss; the amount of the deductible loss would be the amount of the reimbursement to be included in ordinary income.

Answer (A) is correct. *(SEE, adapted)*
REQUIRED: The correct method of reporting a loss of inventory and an insurance reimbursement.
DISCUSSION: If opening and closing inventories are properly reported, a theft or casualty loss to inventory will automatically be claimed through the increase in cost of goods sold. In such event, an insurance reimbursement must be included in ordinary income. Alternatively, the loss can be shown separately and reduced by the insurance reimbursement. But then either opening inventory or purchases must be adjusted downward so that the loss is also not automatically claimed through cost of goods sold.
Answer (B) is incorrect. If the loss is not reported as a separate item (which means it is automatically claimed through cost of goods sold), then the $25,000 must be included in ordinary income. Answer (C) is incorrect. The $100 casualty loss rule does not apply to inventory; it only applies to personal losses. Answer (D) is incorrect. The 10% of adjusted gross income rule does not apply to business losses; it only applies to personal losses. Also, the deductible loss is not determined by the amount of reimbursement to be included in income.

3.9.4. A machine that Ms. Cunningham used in her business was partially destroyed by a fire. The machine had an adjusted basis of $25,000 and a fair market value of $50,000 just before the fire. The fair market value was $20,000 after the fire and before any repairs were made. Ms. Cunningham's insurance company immediately reimbursed her $35,000. What is her gain or loss from the casualty?

A. $15,000 gain.

B. $10,000 gain.

C. $(15,000) loss.

D. $(30,000) loss.

Answer (B) is correct. *(SEE, adapted)*
REQUIRED: The gain or loss from a casualty when an insurance reimbursement is received.
DISCUSSION: Section 165 allows a deduction for a loss sustained during the taxable year and not compensated for by insurance. The amount of the loss for partial destruction of business property is the lesser of the taxpayer's adjusted basis in the property or the difference between the fair market value of the property immediately before and immediately after the casualty. Ms. Cunningham's adjusted basis in the property was $25,000 while the reduction in the fair market value was $30,000 ($50,000 – $20,000). Therefore, Ms. Cunningham's loss before her insurance recovery was $25,000. Since her insurance recovery was $35,000, she had no deductible loss, but instead a $10,000 gain ($35,000 – $25,000).
Answer (A) is incorrect. A $15,000 gain is from subtracting the insurance reimbursement from the FMV of the machine immediately after the fire. Answer (C) is incorrect. A $15,000 loss is the result of subtracting the insurance reimbursement from the FMV of the machine immediately before the fire. Answer (D) is incorrect. A $30,000 loss is the decrease in FMV after the fire and before the reduction for the insurance reimbursement.

3.9.5. Lynn Newburger owned an office building that she used in her trade or business. A hurricane damaged the building and shrubbery. The building had a fair market value before the hurricane of $100,000 and an adjusted basis of $60,000. After the hurricane, the building had a fair market value of $55,000. The shrubbery had a fair market value of $3,000 before the hurricane and an adjusted basis of $1,000. After the hurricane, the shrubbery had a fair market value of $1,000. Lynn's casualty loss deduction is

A. $46,000

B. $47,000

C. $61,000

D. $62,000

Answer (A) is correct. *(Publisher, adapted)*
REQUIRED: The loss deduction when a building and shrubbery are partially destroyed in one casualty.
DISCUSSION: Under Reg. 1.165-7(b), the amount of a casualty loss deduction is the lesser of the decrease in fair market value or the amount of the adjusted basis of the property destroyed. When there is a casualty loss of real property and improvements not used in a trade or business, the casualty loss is computed on the property as a whole, not each individual part. However, when a loss is incurred in a trade or business, the loss must be computed on each separate item.
Lynn's loss on the building is the decrease in fair market value of $45,000. The loss on the shrubbery is its adjusted basis of $1,000. The total casualty loss deduction is $46,000.
Answer (B) is incorrect. The shrubbery loss is valued at the lesser of the adjusted basis or the decrease in FMV. Answer (C) is incorrect. The building is valued at the lesser of its adjusted basis or the decrease in its FMV. Answer (D) is incorrect. Both properties should be valued at the lesser of their adjusted bases or their decreases in FMV.

3.9.6. Mr. Harvey operates a retail fuel oil distributorship and has several trucks on the road delivering home heating oil to residences. Each year, he determines that he loses 2,500 gallons of fuel oil through spillage. The cost of the fuel oil lost during the current year was determined to be $1,875. Mr. Harvey can claim this loss as a casualty loss on his Schedule C for the current year.

A. True.

B. False.

Answer (B) is correct. *(SEE, adapted)*
   DISCUSSION: The normal casualty or theft loss rules do not apply to inventories [Reg. 1.165-7(a)(4)]. If opening and closing inventories are properly reported, the casualty or theft loss attributable to inventory will automatically be reported through cost of goods sold. In addition, a casualty loss is reported on Form 4684 (and not Schedule C).

3.9.7. Christy embezzled $10,000 from a business operated by Saidy in Year 1. However, the theft was not discovered until Year 2. The insurance recovery in Year 2 was $9,500. Saidy can deduct a $400 casualty loss for Year 1.

A. True.

B. False.

Answer (B) is correct. *(SEE, adapted)*
   DISCUSSION: A loss arising from theft is treated as sustained during the taxable year in which the taxpayer discovers the loss [Sec. 165(e)]. Since the taxpayer discovered the loss in Year 2, it would be deductible in that year. She may claim a casualty loss of $500. The $100 casualty floor does not apply to business thefts.

3.9.8. In the current year, Gus Grizzum, who operates an auto parts store, incurred a $25,000 inventory loss due to fire and submitted an insurance claim for $20,000, his maximum coverage. The insurance reimbursement was not received by the end of the year. Gus could deduct the entire $25,000 loss in the current year and include the insurance proceeds in income in the year received.

A. True.

B. False.

Answer (B) is correct. *(SEE, adapted)*
   DISCUSSION: The normal casualty or theft loss rules do not apply to inventories [Reg. 1.165-7(a)(4)]. If opening and closing inventories are properly reported, the casualty or theft loss to inventory will automatically be reported through cost of goods sold. Because there is the prospect of a $20,000 recovery, either the opening inventory or cost of goods sold must be adjusted downward so that the entire $25,000 loss is not claimed through cost of goods sold until the reimbursement is received or the claim is denied and the loss is deducted.

Use **Gleim Test Prep** for interactive study and easy-to-use detailed analytics!

STUDY UNIT FOUR
LIMITATIONS ON LOSSES

These loss limitations are presented here because, to the extent allowed, the losses reduce income in computing adjusted gross income. For example, an allowable loss either from a direct investment or from a limited partnership is deductible for adjusted gross income. Also, these loss limitations generally apply across the board to varied types of transactions. For other limitations on losses from specific transactions, see

Study Unit 3.9   Casualty and Theft Loss [business]
Study Unit 6.5   Casualty and Theft Losses [personal]
Study Unit 11.7   Capital Loss Limitations and Carryovers
Study Unit 11.8   Sales to Related Parties [capital assets]
Study Unit 12.5   Sales to Related Parties [depreciable property]
Study Unit 14.7   Partnership Losses
Study Unit 16.9   C Corporation Net Operating Losses
Study Unit 17.14   S Corporation Losses

4.1 Net Operating Loss

4.1.1. Which one of the following is deductible in computing a net operating loss for an individual taxpayer?

A. Nonbusiness deductions in excess of nonbusiness income.

B. Loss on disposition of rental property.

C. NOL carryovers from other years.

D. Business capital losses in excess of business capital gains.

Answer (B) is correct. *(SEE, adapted)*
REQUIRED: The item deductible in computing a net operating loss for an individual taxpayer.
DISCUSSION: A loss on the disposition of rental property is allowed in computing a net operating loss (NOL) under Sec. 172.
Answer (A) is incorrect. Nonbusiness deductions in excess of nonbusiness income are nondeductible in computing an NOL under Sec. 172(d). This and other items must be added back to the individual taxpayer's loss as modifications in computing an NOL. Answer (C) is incorrect. NOL carryovers from other years are nondeductible in computing an NOL under Sec. 172(d). This and other items must be added back to the individual taxpayer's loss as modifications in computing an NOL. Answer (D) is incorrect. Business capital losses in excess of business capital gains are nondeductible in computing an NOL under Sec. 172(d). This and other items must be added back to the individual taxpayer's loss as modifications in computing an NOL.

4.1.2. In computing an individual's net operating loss, which of the following is not considered business income or deduction(s)?

A. Wages.

B. Personal casualty loss.

C. Gain on sale of investment property.

D. Gain on sale of business property.

Answer (C) is correct. *(SEE, adapted)*
REQUIRED: The item not considered business income or deductions in computing an individual's net operating loss.
DISCUSSION: Business and nonbusiness income and deductions need to be distinguished because nonbusiness deductions are deductible in computing a net operating loss only to the extent of nonbusiness income [Sec. 172(d)]. Nonbusiness deductions and income are those that are not attributable to or derived from a taxpayer's trade or business. Also, capital losses are only deductible to the extent of capital gains. A gain on the sale of investment property is a capital gain which is nonbusiness income.
Answer (A) is incorrect. Wages are attributable to a trade or business and therefore constitute business income. Answer (B) is incorrect. A personal casualty loss is treated as a business deduction [Reg. 1.172-3(a)(3)]. Answer (D) is incorrect. A gain on the sale of business property is business income.

4.1.3. In computing an individual's net operating loss, all of the following are considered business income or deductions except

- A. Contributions made by a self-employed person to a personal retirement plan.
- B. Moving expenses paid in connection with beginning work at a new principal place of employment.
- C. State income taxes on net income from business profits.
- D. Loss from the rental of property for the year.

Answer (A) is correct. *(SEE, adapted)*
REQUIRED: The item not considered business income or deduction in computing an individual's net operating loss.
DISCUSSION: Contributions made by a self-employed person (or an employee) to a retirement plan are not treated as attributable to the trade or business of the taxpayer [Sec. 172(d)(4)]. Therefore, they are treated as a nonbusiness deduction.
Answer (B) is incorrect. Employment is considered a trade or business. Therefore, employee moving expenses are business expenses [Rev. Rul. 72-195, 1972-1 C.B. 95]. Answer (C) is incorrect. State income taxes on net income from business profits are attributable to the taxpayer's trade or business. Answer (D) is incorrect. The loss from a rental property is a business loss for purposes of Sec. 172.

4.1.4. Mr. Trim sustained a net operating loss (NOL) for 2017. If Trim does not elect to forgo the carryback period, to what years may he carry the NOL?

- A. Back 3 years; forward 7.
- B. Back 2 years; forward 20.
- C. Back 5 years; forward 20.
- D. Back 3 years; forward 15.

Answer (B) is correct. *(SEE, adapted)*
REQUIRED: The years to which a net operating loss may be carried.
DISCUSSION: For 2017, a net operating loss may be carried back to each of the 2 taxable years preceding the taxable year of such loss (oldest first) and may be carried forward to each of the 20 taxable years following the taxable year of the loss. Alternatively, the taxpayer may elect to forgo the carryback entirely and carry forward only the net operating loss [Sec. 172(b)(3)].
Answer (A) is incorrect. Back 3 years is more than the maximum number of years allowed for carryback, and forward 7 years is less than the maximum number of years to which an NOL can be carried forward. Answer (C) is incorrect. Back 5 years is more than the maximum number of years to which an NOL can be carried back. Answer (D) is incorrect. This is not the maximum number of years to which an NOL can be carried back and forward, respectively.

4.1.5. Based on the following information, compute the 2017 net operating loss (NOL) that an individual can carry over to 2018 if the proper election to forgo the carryback is taken.

2016 NOL	$(15,000)
Wages	25,000
S Corporation ordinary loss	(40,000)
Schedule C net profit	7,000
Interest income	500
Standard deduction	6,350
Personal exemptions	4,050

- A. $7,500
- B. $8,000
- C. $17,900
- D. $23,000

Answer (B) is correct. *(SEE, adapted)*
REQUIRED: The taxpayer's 2017 NOL carryover.
DISCUSSION: A net operating loss is defined as the excess of allowable deductions (as modified) over gross income [Sec. 172(c)]. An NOL generally includes only items that represent business income or loss. Personal casualty losses and wage or salary income are included as business items. Nonbusiness deductions in excess of nonbusiness income must be excluded. Interest and dividends are not business income.

Wages	$25,000
Schedule C net profit	7,000
S Corporation ordinary loss	(40,000)
Net operating loss	$ (8,000)

Nonbusiness deductions (the standard deduction) are not allowed because there is only $500 of nonbusiness income. No deduction for personal exemptions is allowed. The NOL carryover from 2016 is not allowed in arriving at the 2017 NOL. If the proper election to forgo the carryback is taken, the entire NOL can be carried over to 2018.
Answer (A) is incorrect. Nonbusiness interest income does not exceed nonbusiness deductions and should not be included in the NOL calculation. Answer (C) is incorrect. The income tax net loss is $17,900. Answer (D) is incorrect. The NOL from 2016 does not increase the amount of the 2017 NOL.

4.1.6. What is the amount of the net operating loss for 2017 based on the following information?

Total income:

Interest on nonbusiness savings	$ 425
Net long-term capital gain on sale of business property	2,000
Salary	1,000

Total deductions:

Net loss from business (sales of $86,000 less expenses of $92,000)	$6,000
Net nonbusiness short-term capital loss on sale of stock	1,000
Personal exemption	4,050
Standard deduction	6,350

A. $0

B. $2,575

C. $3,000

D. $13,975

Answer (C) is correct. *(SEE, adapted)*
REQUIRED: The taxpayer's net operating loss.
DISCUSSION: A net operating loss is defined as the excess of allowable deductions (as modified) over gross income [Sec. 172(c)]. An NOL generally includes only items that represent business income or loss. Personal casualty losses and wage or salary income are included as business items. Nonbusiness income in excess of nonbusiness deductions must be included. Interest and dividends are not business income.

Net loss from business	$(6,000)
Capital gain on business property	2,000
Salary	1,000
Net operating loss	$(3,000)

The nonbusiness capital loss cannot be offset against the business-related capital gain. The nonbusiness deductions (the standard deduction) exceed the nonbusiness income (interest), and both items are excluded from the NOL calculation. No deduction is allowed for the personal exemption in arriving at the NOL.
  Answer (A) is incorrect. A net operating loss is present. Business loss exceeds business income. Answer (B) is incorrect. The nonbusiness interest income does not reduce the amount of the net operating loss since nonbusiness deductions exceed nonbusiness income. Salaries are business income. Answer (D) is incorrect. The nonbusiness interest income, nonbusiness loss on the sale of stock, personal exemption, and standard deduction are not included in the NOL calculation.

4.1.7. Which of the following is not a modification required to calculate an individual's net operating loss?

A. Add back a net operating loss deduction from any other year used in computing taxable income.

B. Add back excess nonbusiness capital losses over nonbusiness capital gains.

C. Add back personal exemptions and dependency exemptions.

D. Add back all itemized deductions.

Answer (D) is correct. *(SEE, adapted)*
REQUIRED: The item that is not a modification required to calculate an individual's net operating loss.
DISCUSSION: In computing a net operating loss, nonbusiness deductions are allowable to the extent of nonbusiness income [Sec. 172(d)]. Itemized deductions are nonbusiness deductions. However, all itemized deductions need not be added back, only those in excess of nonbusiness income.
  Answer (A) is incorrect. Adding back a net operating loss deduction from any other year used in computing taxable income is a modification required to calculate an individual's net operating loss under Sec. 172(d). Answer (B) is incorrect. Adding back excess nonbusiness capital losses over nonbusiness capital gains is a modification required to calculate an individual's net operating loss under Sec. 172(d). Answer (C) is incorrect. Adding back personal exemptions and dependency exemptions is a modification required to calculate an individual's net operating loss under Sec. 172(d).

4.1.8. Which of the following statements about forgoing the net operating loss (NOL) carryback period is false?

A. The election should be made as a written statement attached to the tax return for the NOL year citing the appropriate Internal Revenue Code section.

B. Once the election is made, the taxpayer cannot later revoke it for that tax year.

C. A taxpayer may amend a prior year's return to include the election as long as the election is made before the expiration of the statute of limitations.

D. A taxpayer who wants to forgo the carryback period for more than one NOL must make a separate election for each NOL year.

Answer (C) is correct. *(SEE, adapted)*
REQUIRED: The false statement about forgoing the NOL carryback period.
DISCUSSION: Under Sec. 172(b)(3), an NOL election may be made on an amended return if the return is filed on or before the due date for filing returns for the year the election is sought. An election, once made for any tax year, is irrevocable.
  Answer (A) is incorrect. When forgoing the NOL carryback period, the election should be made as a written statement attached to the tax return for the NOL year citing the appropriate Internal Revenue Code section. Answer (B) is incorrect. When forgoing the NOL carryback period, once the election is made, the taxpayer cannot later revoke it for that tax year. Answer (D) is incorrect. When forgoing the NOL carryback period, a taxpayer who wants to forgo the carryback period for more than one NOL must make a separate election for each NOL year.

4.1.9. Nancy, who is single, started her business in 2017 and had a $40,000 net operating loss for the year. Her 2015 income tax return reflects the following:

Salary	$50,000
Deduction for capital loss	(1,000)
Adjusted gross income	49,000
Charitable contributions	
[$24,500 limit ($49,000 AGI × 50%)]	30,000
Medical expense	
[$5,825 – $4,900 (10% of AGI)]	925
Personal exemption	4,000

Assuming the $40,000 net operating loss is carried back to 2015, what is Nancy's net operating loss to be carried back to 2016?

A. $15,425

B. $16,425

C. $19,425

D. $20,425

Answer (A) is correct. *(SEE, adapted)*
REQUIRED: The amount of the taxpayer's 2017 net operating loss to be carried back to 2016.
DISCUSSION: The entire amount of the net operating loss (NOL) for any taxable year is carried first to the earliest of the taxable years to which it may be carried. The NOL is used to reduce the income (as modified) to zero in such earliest year, and to the extent not so used, it is carried to succeeding years. The modifications to the income of the carryback year are those used in computing NOL, except the deduction for a net operating loss is not disallowed, and nonbusiness deductions are not limited to nonbusiness income [Sec. 172(b)(2)]. When recomputing Nancy's 2015 taxable income, the deductions for the capital loss and personal exemption are not allowed. The limitations on the medical expenses must be recomputed in light of the modified adjusted gross income [Reg. 1.172-5(a)(2)(ii)].

2015 gross income	$ 50,000
Less: NOL/capital loss	(41,000)
AGI	$ 9,000
Less: Charitable contributions	(24,500)
Medical expenses	(925)
Personal exemption	(4,000)
	$(20,425)
Capital loss	1,000
Personal exemption	4,000
	$(15,425)

Answer (B) is incorrect. The $1,000 capital loss should not be deducted from AGI to arrive at the modified income for 2015. Answer (C) is incorrect. The $4,000 personal exemption should not be deducted from AGI to arrive at the modified income for 2015. Answer (D) is incorrect. The $4,000 personal exemption amount and the $1,000 capital loss should not be deducted from AGI to arrive at the modified income for 2015.

4.1.10. Morgan, a single taxpayer, was employed for the first 6 months of 2017 and earned $16,000 in wages. On July 1, 2017, he started a business and sustained a loss of $20,000. Interest income for 2017 was $300. Morgan has a net operating loss for 2017, which he elects to carry back to 2015. His adjusted gross income for 2015 consisted of wages of $16,100 and a capital loss of $1,000. The standard deduction amount for 2015 was $6,300, and the personal exemption amount was $4,000. What is Morgan's 2015 taxable income after the carryback of the net operating loss?

A. $11,100

B. $1,800

C. $1,100

D. $800

Answer (D) is correct. *(SEE, adapted)*
REQUIRED: The taxpayer's taxable income for 2015 after the carryback of the 2017 NOL.
DISCUSSION: First, the net operating loss (NOL) for 2017 must be computed.

Gross income:		
Wages	$ 16,000	
Interest	300	$ 16,300
Modified deductions:		
Business loss	$(20,000)	
Standard deduction limited		
to nonbusiness income	(300)	(20,300)
2017 NOL		$ (4,000)

The 2015 taxable income is then computed with the NOL carryback. Remember, taxable income is adjusted gross income reduced by itemized deductions or the standard deduction and the personal exemption.

Wages	$16,100
Capital loss	(1,000)
2017 NOL carryback	(4,000)
Adjusted gross income	$11,100
Standard deduction	(6,300)
Personal exemption	(4,000)
2015 taxable income	$ 800

Answer (A) is incorrect. The 2015 taxable income needs to be reduced by a $6,300 standard deduction and a $4,000 personal exemption. Answer (B) is incorrect. The 2015 capital loss decreases adjusted gross income and taxable income. Answer (C) is incorrect. The 2017 NOL is increased by a standard deduction limited to the nonbusiness income of $300.

4.1.11. In figuring the amount of a net operating loss that can be absorbed in a carryback or carryforward year, all capital losses incurred in the year to which the net operating loss is carried must be eliminated.

A. True.

B. False.

Answer (B) is correct. *(SEE, adapted)*
DISCUSSION: When carrying an NOL back to an earlier year, modifications to income of the carryback year are those used in computing an NOL except that the deduction for a net operating loss is not disallowed and nonbusiness deductions are not limited to nonbusiness income [Sec. 172(b)(2)]. Capital losses can still be used to offset capital gains or deducted up to the individual limitation ($3,000).

4.1.12. Mr. Folgers was granted an automatic extension for filing his Year 1 calendar-year return. On October 30, Year 2, Mr. Folgers filed his Year 1 return reflecting a net operating loss. On his return, Mr. Folgers made an election to forgo the carryback period. Mr. Folgers is ineligible to make the election to forgo the carryback period.

A. True.

B. False.

Answer (A) is correct. *(SEE, adapted)*
DISCUSSION: A net operating loss (NOL) may be carried back 2 years and forward 20 years. A taxpayer may elect to relinquish the entire carryback period if the election is made by the due date (including extensions of time) for filing the taxpayer's return for the year of the NOL [Sec. 172(b)(3)]. The automatic extension gave an additional 4 months to file the return, thus making it due on October 15, Year 2 (ignoring Saturdays, Sundays, and holidays). Since Mr. Folgers failed to file the return and make the election prior to the due date, he is ineligible to make the election to forgo the carryback period.

4.1.13. If two or more net operating losses are carried back to a tax year, they must be deducted in the order they were incurred.

A. True.

B. False.

Answer (A) is correct. *(SEE, adapted)*
DISCUSSION: A net operating loss (NOL) incurred in Year 3 and Year 4 may be carried back to each of the 2 taxable years preceding the taxable year of such loss (oldest first). If you suffer an NOL in both Year 3 and Year 4, the Year 3 loss must be carried back and must completely offset the income from Year 1 or Year 2 before the Year 4 loss may be carried back to Year 2.

4.2 At-Risk Rules

4.2.1. In the current year, Kathy purchased a small apartment building for $200,000. She used $25,000 of her own money and $25,000 that she borrowed from her father to make the down payment. She signed a note to pay the remainder of the purchase price to the seller. Both the loan from her father and the debt to the seller were nonrecourse, secured only by the apartment building. The terms of both debts were commercially reasonable and on substantially the same terms as loans involving unrelated persons. Kathy's at-risk limitation on losses is

A. $25,000

B. $50,000

C. $175,000

D. $200,000

Answer (D) is correct. *(SEE, adapted)*
REQUIRED: The amount for which an individual is considered at risk for holding real property when there are nonrecourse loans.
DISCUSSION: The first $25,000 that Kathy personally invested is at risk since this is money that she contributed to the activity [Sec. 465(b)(1)(A)]. The $25,000 borrowed from her father comes under the special real property rules. Section 465(b)(6)(A) provides that a taxpayer is at risk with respect to his or her share of any qualified nonrecourse financing that is secured by real property used in the activity. The apartment is used in Kathy's rental activities, so the "used in the activity" requirement is met. Qualified nonrecourse financing means any financing (1) that is borrowed by the taxpayer from a qualified person with respect to the activity of holding real property, (2) that is not convertible debt, and (3) for which no person is personally liable for repayment.
A qualified person is any person who is actively and regularly engaged in the business of lending money and who is not (1) a related person with respect to the taxpayer, (2) a person from whom the taxpayer acquired the property, or (3) a person who receives a fee with respect to the taxpayer's investment in the property [Sec. 49(a)(1)(D)]. Kathy's father is considered a related person. Section 465(b)(6)(D)(ii) permits a related person to be a qualified person if the financing terms are "commercially reasonable and on substantially the same terms as loans involving unrelated persons."
Answer (A) is incorrect. Generally, only the $25,000 would be at-risk, but the amounts from her father and the lender are borrowed under special conditions that allow for inclusion. Answer (B) is incorrect. Since Kathy's father is not actively and regularly engaged in the business of lending money, Kathy is not at risk for the $25,000 loan from her father, even though the terms of the loan are "commercially reasonable." Answer (C) is incorrect. The amount of both loans is $175,000. Each loan is not at-risk for different reasons. The bank loan is nonrecourse.

4.2.2. The at-risk rules

A. Limit a taxpayer's deductible losses from investment activities.

B. Limit the type of deductions in income-producing activities.

C. Apply to business and income-producing activities on a combined basis.

D. Apply at the entity level for partnerships and S corporations.

Answer (A) is correct. *(Publisher, adapted)*
REQUIRED: The true statement concerning the at-risk rules.
DISCUSSION: The at-risk rules are contained in Sec. 465 and limit a taxpayer's deductible losses from each business and income-producing activity to the amount for which the taxpayer is at risk with respect to that activity. Although originally designed to limit deductible losses from tax shelters, the at-risk rules apply across the board to most activities.
Answer (B) is incorrect. It is the losses from each activity that are limited, not the type of deductions. Answer (C) is incorrect. The at-risk rules apply to each business and income-producing activity separately. Answer (D) is incorrect. At-risk rules apply at the partner or shareholder level for "pass-through" entities, such as partnerships and S corporations.

4.2.3. The at-risk rules do not apply to

A. A corporation with five or fewer individuals owning more than 50% during the last half of the year.

B. The holding of real property placed in service in the current year.

C. A closely held corporation for which 50% or more of its gross receipts are from equipment leasing.

D. Exploring for oil and gas resources.

Answer (C) is correct. *(Publisher, adapted)*
REQUIRED: The activity to which the at-risk rules do not apply.
DISCUSSION: The at-risk rules apply to most business and income-producing activities. However, there is an exception for a closely held corporation actively engaged in equipment leasing. A closely held corporation for this purpose is defined as one owned more than 50% during the last half of the year by five or fewer individuals. At least 50% of the gross receipts must be from equipment leasing for the corporation to be considered "actively engaged" in equipment leasing [Sec. 465(c)(4)(B)].
Answer (A) is incorrect. This is the definition of a closely held corporation to which the at-risk rules apply. The at-risk rules do not apply to other C corporations. Answer (B) is incorrect. The holding of real property is generally subject to the at-risk rules after 1986. Answer (D) is incorrect. Exploring for oil and gas resources is an activity specifically included in the at-risk rules by Sec. 465(c)(1)(D).

4.2.4. Mr. Condor began producing picture films in the current year. During the current year, he made the following contributions to his business:

Cash	$10,000
Equipment (adjusted basis to Condor)	15,000
(fair market value)	30,000
Loan from First Bank that he personally promised to repay	20,000
Loan from Second Bank for which he is not personally liable but that is secured by a mortgage on his home	10,000
Loan from Third Bank for which he is not personally liable but that is secured by equipment used in his business	25,000

Under the at-risk rules, Mr. Condor is considered to be at risk in the amount of

A. $45,000

B. $55,000

C. $60,000

D. $80,000

Answer (B) is correct. *(SEE, adapted)*
REQUIRED: The amount for which a taxpayer is considered at risk.
DISCUSSION: A taxpayer is considered at risk for cash contributions to the activity, the adjusted basis of other property contributed to the activity, and amounts borrowed for use in the activity, if the taxpayer is personally liable on the debt or has pledged property not used in the at-risk activity as security for the debt [Sec. 465(b)]. A taxpayer is generally not considered at risk for nonrecourse debt secured by property used in the activity. Mr. Condor is considered at risk for the following:

Cash	$10,000
Basis of property	15,000
Loan from First Bank	20,000
Loan from Second Bank	10,000
Total amount at risk	$55,000

Answer (A) is incorrect. Mr. Condor is at risk with the loan from Second Bank secured by the mortgage on his home. Answer (C) is incorrect. Mr. Condor is at risk for the loan from First Bank, but not for the loan from Third Bank. Answer (D) is incorrect. Mr. Condor is not personally liable for the loan from Third Bank, which is secured by equipment used in the business.

4.2.5. What is the tax treatment of net losses in excess of the at-risk amount for an activity?

A. Any loss in excess of the at-risk amount is suspended and is deductible in the year in which the activity is disposed of in full.

B. Any losses in excess of the at-risk amount are suspended and carried forward without expiration and are deductible against income in future years from that activity.

C. Any losses in excess of the at-risk amount are deducted currently against income from other activities; the remaining loss, if any, is carried forward without expiration.

D. Any losses in excess of the at-risk amount are carried back 2 years against activities with income and then carried forward for 20 years.

Answer (B) is correct. *(CPA, adapted)*
REQUIRED: The tax treatment of net losses in excess of the at-risk amount.
DISCUSSION: The losses are carried forward without expiration and are deductible against income in future years from that activity.
Answer (A) is incorrect. The suspended losses can be deducted before the year in which the activity is disposed of in certain situations. Answer (C) is incorrect. Excess losses cannot be deducted currently against income from other activities; the excess losses are carried forward. Answer (D) is incorrect. Net operating losses, not net losses in excess of the at-risk amount, are carried back 2 years, then carried forward 20 years.

4.2.6. Jill Perry invested $10,000 for a 5% interest in a limited partnership on January 1, Year 1. There is one general partner with a 50% interest. In Year 1, the partnership purchased an office building to rent and incurred a nonrecourse debt of $100,000 to a bank paying interest for only 5 years. The debt has no conversion feature. The partnership incurred a loss of $150,000 in Year 1 and a loss of $200,000 in Year 2. How much can Jill deduct each year, ignoring any passive loss rules?

	Year 1	Year 2
A.	$7,500	$2,500
B.	$7,500	$7,500
C.	$7,500	$10,000
D.	$10,000	$10,000

Answer (B) is correct. *(Publisher, adapted)*
REQUIRED: The at-risk limitation on losses deductible by a limited partner.
DISCUSSION: A limited partner in a partnership is considered to have at risk the amount of cash and adjusted basis of property contributed to the partnership (or used to purchase the partnership interest) and also a share of any qualified nonrecourse financing on real estate (Sec. 465). The existence of a general partner does not affect the fact that Jill will receive a 5% allocation of the nonrecourse debt, provided that no partner has any personal liability on this particular debt. Therefore, Jill's at-risk amount is $15,000 ($10,000 invested + $5,000 share of nonrecourse debt).
Her share of loss in Year 1 is $7,500 ($150,000 loss × 5% interest), which may be deducted in full. Her share of loss in Year 2 is $10,000 ($200,000 loss × 5% interest), but the limitation on the Year 2 deduction is $7,500 ($15,000 at risk – $7,500 deducted in Year 1). Note that there may be further limitations on the deduction of a loss based on the passive loss rules.
Answer (A) is incorrect. Jill's basis is increased by 5% of the nonrecourse debt; therefore, she can deduct losses up to $15,000. She is not limited to the $10,000 initial cash contribution. Answer (C) is incorrect. Jill cannot deduct losses in excess of her $15,000 at-risk amount [$10,000 initial contribution + ($100,000 nonrecourse debt × 5%)]. Answer (D) is incorrect. The partner's share of the Year 1 loss is 5%.

4.2.7. In Year 1, Angie purchased a general partnership interest in Partnership X. Angie was at risk for $20,000. In Year 1, Angie's share of losses was $25,000 and, in Year 2, the partnership broke even. Which of the following is true with respect to the at-risk rules?

A. Angie can deduct $5,000 in Year 2 if she increases her amount at risk by $5,000.

B. Angie can deduct only $2,500 in Year 2 even if she increases her amount at risk by $5,000.

C. Angie cannot deduct any amount in Year 2, even if the partnership incurs recourse debt on tangible personal property, and Angie's share is $10,000.

D. Angie can deduct $5,000 only when her share of the partnership income is at least $5,000.

Answer (A) is correct. *(Publisher, adapted)*
REQUIRED: The carryover of unused loss limited by the at-risk rules.
DISCUSSION: Any loss from an activity not allowed for a taxable year due to the limitations of Sec. 465 may be treated as a deduction in succeeding taxable years [Sec. 465(a)(2)]. In the next taxable year, the at-risk rules will be applied again to the carryover amount. If an individual's at-risk amount increases, the unused loss from a prior year may be deducted to the extent of the increased at-risk amount. Therefore, if Angie's amount at risk is increased by $5,000 in Year 2, she can deduct the $5,000 not deductible in Year 1.
Answer (B) is incorrect. The carryover of unused loss is deductible in full to the extent that the at-risk amount is increased. Answer (C) is incorrect. The at-risk basis will increase if recourse debt is incurred by the partnership with respect to tangible personal property. Answer (D) is incorrect. Angie can increase her at-risk amount by contributions to the partnership, earnings of the partnership, or purchases of additional interest in the partnership, as well as by increasing her share of debt in the partnership.

4.2.8. The at-risk rules limit your losses from most activities to your loss or amount at risk, whichever is less. The at-risk rules must be applied before the passive activity rules.

A. True.

B. False.

Answer (A) is correct. *(SEE, adapted)*
DISCUSSION: The passive loss rules apply only if the taxpayer has usable basis after application of the basis rule limitations (applied first) and the at-risk rules limitations (applied second). A taxpayer is at risk if (s)he is personally liable for repayment of a loan borrowed for use in the activity or if (s)he pledged property as security for a loan (Sec. 465).

4.2.9. The activity of holding real property does not include the provision of any incidental services.

A. True.

B. False.

Answer (B) is correct. *(Publisher, adapted)*
DISCUSSION: The activity of holding real property includes the holding of personal property and the provision of services that are incidental to making the real property available as living accommodations [Sec. 465(b)(6)(E)].

4.3 Passive Activities

4.3.1. If an individual taxpayer's suspended passive losses and credits from an activity other than rental real estate cannot be used in the current year, they may be carried

A. Back 2 years, but they cannot be carried forward.

B. Forward up to a maximum period of 20 years, but they cannot be carried back.

C. Back 2 years or forward up to 20 years, at the taxpayer's election.

D. Forward indefinitely or until the property is disposed of in a taxable transaction.

Answer (D) is correct. *(CPA, adapted)*
REQUIRED: The true statement concerning the carryover or carryback of suspended passive losses and credits from activities other than rental real estate.
DISCUSSION: Suspended passive activity losses (and credits) are carried forward and used to offset passive activity income (and taxes) in later years [Sec. 469(b)]. The carryover is accomplished by treating the disallowed loss from each activity as a deduction for the activity in the following year. In this manner, the carryforward is indefinite. If the entire interest in a passive activity is disposed of in a taxable transaction in a later year, the passive loss may be used at that time. The losses are allowed against income in the following order: (1) income or gain from the passive activity for the year, (2) net income or gain for the year from all other passive activities, (3) any other income or gain.
Answer (A) is incorrect. There is no carryback of disallowed passive losses or credits. However, they may be carried forward. Answer (B) is incorrect. The carryforward is not limited to a maximum period of 20 years. Answer (C) is incorrect. No carryback of disallowed passive losses or credits is allowed, and the carryforward is not limited to a maximum period of 20 years.

4.3.2. Which of the following is a true statement concerning losses from passive activities?

A. Losses from each passive activity are not deductible, regardless of income earned in other passive activities.

B. The losses may offset passive income, such as interest and dividends, but not business income or earned income.

C. The rules apply to losses but not credits.

D. Losses from one passive activity may offset income from another passive activity.

Answer (D) is correct. *(Publisher, adapted)*
REQUIRED: The true statement concerning losses from passive activities.
DISCUSSION: In general, losses from passive activities may not offset nonpassive income, such as salary, interest, dividends, or active business income (Sec. 469). However, deductions from one passive activity may offset income from the same passive activity, and losses from one passive activity may generally offset income from another passive activity.
Answer (A) is incorrect. Losses from a passive activity are deductible to the extent of income from other passive activities. Answer (B) is incorrect. Losses from passive activities may not offset income, such as interest and dividends, which are considered portfolio income. Answer (C) is incorrect. The passive loss rules apply to credits as well as losses.

4.3.3. Which of the following is not an example of a passive activity?

A. The rental of office equipment with no provision of unusual services.

B. A limited partner's interest in a limited partnership.

C. The farming of land when the taxpayer owning the land has hired others to manage operations.

D. A working interest in oil and gas property when the taxpayer-owner has unlimited liability and does not materially participate in the activity.

Answer (D) is correct. *(Publisher, adapted)*
REQUIRED: The activity not considered a passive activity.
DISCUSSION: Passive activities generally include any activity involving the conduct of a trade or business or the production of income and in which the taxpayer does not materially participate (Sec. 469). However, Sec. 469(c)(3) excludes from the passive activity definition any working interest in oil or gas property in which the form of ownership does not limit liability. This is true whether or not the taxpayer-owner materially participates in the activity.
Answer (A) is incorrect. Most rental activities involving personal property are treated as passive activities if no unusual services are provided by the lessors. Answer (B) is incorrect. A limited partnership interest is treated as an activity in which the taxpayer does not materially participate. However, the IRS has provided temporary regulations that provide some exceptions to this rule. Answer (C) is incorrect. A farming operation that others are hired to manage is an example of a passive activity.

4.3.4. Which of the following is treated as income from a passive activity with respect to loss limitations of Sec. 469?

A. Interest on bank accounts.

B. An individual's fees for managing a passive activity.

C. Annuity income from an insurance contract.

D. Rental income from an office building in which the owner earns 80% of her gross income and materially participates for 700 hours of service during the year.

Answer (D) is correct. *(Publisher, adapted)*
REQUIRED: The income treated as passive income.
DISCUSSION: In general, a passive activity is any activity that involves the conduct of a trade or business or the production of income and in which the taxpayer does not materially participate [Sec. 469(c)(1)]. Losses from rental real estate are no longer subject to the passive activity rules if the taxpayer meets two requirements: (1) More than 50% of the individual's personal services are performed in real property trades or businesses in which they materially participate during the year and (2) the individual performs more than 750 hours of service in the real property trades or businesses in which the individual materially participates.
Answer (A) is incorrect. Interest on bank accounts is treated as portfolio income. Portfolio income is excluded from the definition of passive activity income. Answer (B) is incorrect. Income received by an individual in the performance of personal services with respect to a passive activity is not treated as income from a passive activity. Answer (C) is incorrect. Annuity income from an insurance contract is treated as portfolio income. Portfolio income is excluded from the definition of passive activity income.

4.3.5. The rule limiting the allowability of passive activity losses and credits applies to

A. Partnerships.

B. S corporations.

C. Personal service corporations.

D. Widely held C corporations.

Answer (C) is correct. *(CPA, adapted)*
REQUIRED: The type of entity to which passive loss rules apply.
DISCUSSION: Under Sec. 469(a)(2), the passive loss rules apply to individuals, estates, trusts, any closely held C corporation, and any personal service corporation. The passive loss rules do not apply to widely held C corporations [Sec. 465(a)(1)(B)]. The determination of whether an activity is active or passive is made at the partnership or S corporation level. Owners of partnership or S corporation interests (and not the entity) are subject to the passive activity limitations for loss pass-throughs.
Answer (A) is incorrect. Passive loss rules do not apply to partnerships. Answer (B) is incorrect. Passive loss rules do not apply to S corporations. Answer (D) is incorrect. Passive loss rules do not apply to widely held C corporations.

4.3.6. With regard to the passive loss rules involving rental real estate activities, which one of the following statements is true?

A. Passive activity loss limitations do not apply to a rental real estate activity when the individual performs more than 50% of his or her personal services during the year in real property trades or businesses in which (s)he materially participates and at least 750 hours of service are performed in those real property trades or businesses in which (s)he materially participates.

B. Gross investment income from interest and dividends not derived in the ordinary course of a trade or business is treated as passive activity income that can be offset by passive rental activity losses when the "active participation" requirement is not met.

C. Passive rental activity losses may be deducted only against passive income, but passive rental activity credits may be used against taxes attributable to nonpassive activities.

D. The passive activity rules do not apply to taxpayers whose adjusted gross income is $300,000 or less.

Answer (A) is correct. *(CPA, adapted)*
REQUIRED: The true statement with regard to rental real estate activities.
DISCUSSION: Passive activities generally include any activity involving the conduct of a trade or business or the production of income in which the taxpayer does not materially participate (Sec. 469). However, an individual may avoid passive activity limitation treatment on a rental real estate activity if two requirements are met: (1) More than 50% of the individual's personal services performed during the year are performed in the real property trades or businesses in which the individual materially participates and (2) the individual performs more than 750 hours of service in the real property trades or businesses in which the individual materially participates. If 50% or less of the personal services performed are in real property trades or businesses, the individual will be subject to the passive activity limitation rules.
Answer (B) is incorrect. Gross investment income from interest and dividends not derived in the ordinary course of business is not treated as income from passive activities [Sec. 469(e)(1)]. Answer (C) is incorrect. Passive rental activity credits may not be used against taxes attributable to nonpassive activities. Answer (D) is incorrect. The passive activity rules apply to taxpayers without regard to their adjusted gross income.

4.3.7. Mrs. King is a general partner with a 20% interest in a partnership that leases equipment on a long-term basis. She is not regularly involved in the partnership business. During the current year, the partnership has a $200,000 loss, which includes a $250,000 loss from operations and $50,000 of interest income on funds the partnership plans to use to buy more equipment. What is Mrs. King's passive loss for the current year?

A. $0

B. $30,000

C. $40,000

D. $50,000

Answer (D) is correct. *(Publisher, adapted)*
REQUIRED: The partner's passive loss when the passive activity has portfolio income.
DISCUSSION: A passive activity includes a rental activity when the average rental period is not short-term. However, portfolio income of an activity (e.g., interest, dividend, royalty, or annuity income earned on funds set aside for the future use of the activity) is not treated as passive income from the activity [Sec. 469(e)]. Therefore, the $250,000 loss from operations is a loss from a passive activity. Mrs. King's passive loss is $50,000 ($250,000 × 20% interest). Note that the question is asking for the passive loss, not the deduction from the passive loss.
Answer (A) is incorrect. A passive loss is present. Answer (B) is incorrect. The amount of $30,000 is 20% of the "partnership loss" of $200,000, minus the $50,000 of interest income that should be treated as portfolio income. The loss that is passed through is the $250,000 loss from operations. Answer (C) is incorrect. The amount of $40,000 is 20% of the loss from operations netted with the interest income (which is portfolio income).

4.3.8. Barry is a lawyer. He owns 10 apartment buildings that are managed by his brother's real estate business. At the end of the year, the apartment buildings resulted in a $40,000 loss. Barry earned $80,000 in wages. His wife, Claire, earned $20,000 from her part-time job. Their other income included $5,000 in dividends from their mutual funds. They had no other income. How much of the rental loss can Barry use assuming Barry actively participates in the apartment buildings?

A. $0

B. $25,000

C. $40,000

D. None of the answers are correct.

Answer (D) is correct. *(SEE, adapted)*
REQUIRED: The rental loss that can be used if a taxpayer actively participates in rental activities.
DISCUSSION: Any rental activity is a passive activity, whether or not the taxpayer participates in the activity. An individual who actively participates in rental real estate activity may use up to $25,000 of net losses from rental real estate activity to offset other income. The $25,000 is reduced by 50% of the amount by which AGI (determined without regard to Social Security, IRA contributions, or passive losses) exceeds $100,000. Barry has AGI of $105,000 ($80,000 + $20,000 + $5,000). Accordingly, his allowable $25,000 deduction will be reduced by $2,500 [($105,000 – $100,000) × 50%], and is therefore $22,500. If Barry does not actively participate, he is not allowed a deduction.
Answer (A) is incorrect. Barry may use a portion of the rental loss. Answer (B) is incorrect. Barry's loss must be reduced by 50% of the excess of his AGI over $100,000. Answer (C) is incorrect. Barry may not deduct the entire loss.

4.3.9. All of the outstanding stock of Bryant Corporation is owned equally by three individuals. Bryant is not a personal service corporation. During the current year, Bryant had active rental real estate income of $250,000, a passive loss on the rental of an office building (acquired in 1991) of $300,000, and portfolio income of $150,000. The corporation earns more than 60% of its gross receipts from the rental real estate in which it materially participates. How much of Bryant's income may be offset by the rental loss?

- A. $250,000 rental income and $50,000 portfolio income.
- B. $250,000 rental income and $0 portfolio income.
- C. $0 rental income and $150,000 portfolio income.
- D. No income may be offset.

Answer (A) is correct. *(Publisher, adapted)*
REQUIRED: The amount of active business income and portfolio income that may be offset by passive losses for a closely held corporation.
DISCUSSION: Bryant Corporation is a closely held corporation because more than 50% of the value of its stock is held by five or fewer individuals during the last half of the year. After December 31, 1993, a closely held C corporation is not subject to the passive activity loss rules for real estate trades or businesses if during the tax year the corporation derives more than 50% of its gross receipts from the real property trades or businesses in which it materially participates [Sec. 469(c)(7)(D)]. Therefore, Bryant may offset its $300,000 passive loss against active and portfolio income.
Answer (B) is incorrect. A portion of Bryant's portfolio income may be offset by the remainder rental loss. Answer (C) is incorrect. Bryant may use the total loss to offset rental and portfolio income. Answer (D) is incorrect. Bryant is a closely held C corporation and is not subject to passive activity loss rules due to earning more than half of its gross receipts from real property trades or businesses in which it materially participates; therefore, the passive loss may be offset against both types of income.

4.3.10. Don Wolf became a general partner in Gata Associates on January 1 of the current year, with a 5% interest in Gata's profits, losses, and capital. Gata is a distributor of auto parts. Wolf does not materially participate in the partnership business. For the current year, Gata had an operating loss of $100,000. In addition, Gata earned interest of $20,000 on a temporary investment while awaiting delivery of equipment that is presently on order. The investment principal will be used to pay for this equipment. Wolf's passive loss for the current year is

- A. $0
- B. $4,000
- C. $5,000
- D. $6,000

Answer (C) is correct. *(CPA, adapted)*
REQUIRED: The amount treated as a passive loss for the current year.
DISCUSSION: In general, losses arising from one passive activity may be used to offset income from other passive activities but may not be used to offset active or portfolio income (Sec. 469). Wolf's $5,000 operating loss ($100,000 × 5%) may not be used to offset his $1,000 portfolio income (i.e., interest and dividends are portfolio income) ($20,000 × 5%). Therefore, his passive loss is his $5,000 operating loss.
Answer (A) is incorrect. A passive loss is present. Answer (B) is incorrect. The $1,000 portfolio income cannot be netted with the $5,000 passive loss. Answer (D) is incorrect. The amount of $6,000 results from adding the passive loss and portfolio gain instead of offsetting the two.

4.3.11. In Year 7, the Aloha Gardens apartment complex had rental losses of $40,000. Which of the following is true?

- A. Steve and his wife, Barbara, each have a 5% interest in the property and manage the apartments. They had nonpassive income of $30,000 for the year. They may offset their share of the rental loss against their nonpassive income.
- B. T Trust has a 40% interest in the property. The trustee is active in managing the apartments. The trust may offset its portion of the rental loss against other income earned during the year.
- C. John's estate has a 20% interest in the property. John was actively involved in managing the complex from Year 1 until his death in Year 4. His estate may offset its portion of the rental loss against any nonpassive income.
- D. Kathy has an interest as a limited partner in the property. Her nonpassive income for the year is $50,000. She may offset her portion of the rental loss against her nonpassive income up to $25,000.

Answer (A) is correct. *(Publisher, adapted)*
REQUIRED: The true statement concerning the deduction of rental losses by various property owners.
DISCUSSION: In the case of rental real estate activities in which an individual actively participates, up to $25,000 of losses from such activities are allowed each year against nonpassive income [Sec. 469(i)]. Active participation requires only participation such as making management decisions on lease terms, tenant approvals, repair versus replacement decisions, etc., even if an agent handles day-to-day matters. An individual is not treated as actively participating in a rental real estate activity if the individual's and spouse's interests are less than 10% of all interests in the activity [Sec. 469(i)(6)(A)]. Since Steve and his wife together own 10% of the property and manage the apartments, they qualify for allowing up to $25,000 of rental real estate losses against nonpassive income. Their share of the losses is $4,000 ($40,000 × 10%).
Answer (B) is incorrect. Trusts do not qualify for this $25,000 allowance of passive losses against nonpassive income. Answer (C) is incorrect. An estate is considered to participate actively in an activity for only 2 years following the death of a taxpayer who actively participated in the year of death. Answer (D) is incorrect. An interest as a limited partner is usually not treated as an activity in which the taxpayer actively participates.

4.3.12. Maria, a single taxpayer, had losses totaling $30,000 from a rental real estate activity in which she actively participated. Maria also had $15,000 of income from another rental real estate activity in which she actively participated. She acquired both investments in the current year. If Maria has no other passive income and adjusted gross income before passive losses of $70,000, how much loss from rental activities can she use to offset her portfolio and active income?

A. $0

B. $15,000

C. $25,000

D. $30,000

Answer (B) is correct. *(SEE, adapted)*

REQUIRED: The amount of passive losses from rental real estate activities an individual may use to offset other income.

DISCUSSION: The $25,000 allowance of losses from rental real estate activities in which an individual actively participates is applied by first netting the income and losses from all rental real estate activities in which the taxpayer actively participates [Sec. 469(i)]. If there is a net loss for the year from such activities, net passive income (if any) is then applied against it to determine the amount eligible for the $25,000 allowance. Maria's net loss from active participation activities is $15,000 ($15,000 income – $30,000 losses). This is the amount that Maria may use to offset portfolio income and active income. Note that no phaseout of the $25,000 allowance is necessary since Maria's adjusted gross income before passive losses is less than $100,000.

Answer (A) is incorrect. A portion of rental activity losses can be offset against portfolio and active income. Answer (C) is incorrect. The limit for losses from rental activities applied against nonpassive income is $25,000. However, all losses and gains from rental activities must be netted together first before applying the net loss against nonpassive income. Answer (D) is incorrect. The full amount of loss that must first be netted against rental income is $30,000, and then only up to $25,000 of such losses can be offset against nonpassive income.

4.3.13. Dr. J has adjusted gross income for the current year of $130,000 before the deduction for a $2,000 contribution to his IRA and before any potential deduction for $40,000 of losses from rental real estate activities in which he actively participates. How much of the rental losses may he deduct if the rental real estate activities were acquired in the current year?

A. $0

B. $10,000

C. $11,000

D. $25,000

Answer (B) is correct. *(Publisher, adapted)*

REQUIRED: The amount a taxpayer may deduct for losses from active participation in rental real estate activities when adjusted gross income is in excess of $100,000.

DISCUSSION: The $25,000 allowance of losses from active participation in rental real estate activities against nonpassive income is reduced by 50% of the amount by which adjusted gross income (determined without regard to Social Security benefits, IRA contributions, and passive losses) exceeds $100,000 [Sec. 469(i)(3)]. Dr. J's adjusted gross income exceeds $100,000 by $30,000. Therefore, the $25,000 allowance is reduced by $15,000 ($30,000 × 50%). This leaves $10,000 of losses that can be deducted.

Answer (A) is incorrect. A portion of rental losses may be deducted. Answer (C) is incorrect. The phase-out amount was based on AGI after claiming the deduction for the contribution to an IRA ($128,000). Answer (D) is incorrect. AGI exceeds $100,000, so the $25,000 loss allowance must be phased out.

4.3.14. Sandra purchased a limited partnership interest in Year 1. She had nondeductible passive losses of $30,000 in Year 1 and $20,000 in Year 2 from the partnership. If she sells her partnership interest in Year 3 for a $10,000 gain, has $15,000 of income from the partnership up to the date of sale, and has $100,000 of nonpassive income, how much can she deduct in Year 3?

A. $10,000

B. $15,000

C. $25,000

D. $50,000

Answer (D) is correct. *(Publisher, adapted)*

REQUIRED: The amount of previously nondeductible losses that may be deducted when a passive activity is sold.

DISCUSSION: The cumulative total of disallowed losses from an activity are allowed in full when the taxpayer disposes of his or her entire interest in a passive activity in a taxable transaction [Sec. 469(g)]. The losses are allowed against income in the following order: (1) income or gain from the passive activity for the year, (2) net income or gain for the year from all other passive activities, (3) any other income or gain. Sandra may first use the $50,000 of losses to offset both the partnership income of $15,000 and the gain of $10,000 from sale of the partnership interest. She may then use the remaining $25,000 to offset her nonpassive income. Her total deduction for the losses is $50,000 in Year 3.

Answer (A) is incorrect. The passive losses from previous years may also be deducted against the $15,000 of current-year partnership income and the $100,000 of nonpassive income. Answer (B) is incorrect. The passive losses from previous years may be deducted against the $10,000 of gain from the disposition of the interest and the $100,000 of nonpassive income. Answer (C) is incorrect. The passive losses from previous years are not limited to $25,000 since the taxpayer sold the entire interest in the passive activity.

4.3.15. Smith has an adjusted gross income (AGI) of $120,000 without taking into consideration $40,000 of losses from rental real estate activities. Smith actively participates in the rental real estate activities. What amount of the rental losses may Smith deduct in determining taxable income?

A. $0
B. $15,000
C. $20,000
D. $40,000

Answer (B) is correct. *(CPA, adapted)*
REQUIRED: The deductible amount of the passive activity loss.
DISCUSSION: A person who actively participates in rental real estate activity is entitled to deduct up to $25,000 in losses from the passive activity against other than passive income. However, the $25,000 limit is reduced by 50% of that person's MAGI (AGI without regard to passive activity losses, Social Security benefits, and other qualified retirement contributions) over $100,000. Smith has $20,000 of MAGI over $100,000. Accordingly, the $25,000 loss deduction must be reduced by $10,000 ($20,000 MAGI excess × 50%), resulting in $15,000 of deductible loss limitation.
Answer (A) is incorrect. Some of the losses are deductible. Answer (C) is incorrect. This amount is Smith's excess MAGI over $100,000. The $25,000 limit must be reduced by 50% of the excess of a person's MAGI over $100,000. Answer (D) is incorrect. The entire amount of the losses is not deductible.

4.3.16. Kate is married to John, and they lived together all year. They elected to file separate returns. Kate had $70,000 in wages, $15,000 income from a limited partnership, a $26,000 loss from rental real estate activities in which she actively participated, and less than $100,000 of modified adjusted gross income. She can use $15,000 of her $26,000 rental loss to offset her passive income from the partnership and the remaining $11,000 to offset her nonpassive income.

A. True.
B. False.

Answer (B) is correct. *(SEE, adapted)*
DISCUSSION: All rental activity is passive. Material participation is irrelevant except for certain taxpayers who materially participate in real property trade or businesses. A person who actively participates in rental real estate activity may be entitled to deduct up to $25,000 of losses from the passive activity from other than passive income. Single individuals and married individuals filing jointly can qualify for the $25,000 amount. However, married individuals who live together for the entire year and file separately cannot qualify for any part of the $25,000 offset. Income from a limited partnership is passive; therefore, $15,000 of the $26,000 loss can be offset. The remaining $11,000 cannot be used to offset Kate's nonpassive income because of the married individual rule.

4.3.17. David materially participated in one rental real estate activity in Year 3. Seventy-five percent of his personal services for the year were performed in this real estate activity, for a total of 1,500 service hours. David has suspended losses originating in Year 1 and Year 2 from the activity. The deduction for these 2 years of suspended losses may offset David's nonpassive income for Year 3.

A. True.
B. False.

Answer (B) is correct. *(Publisher, adapted)*
DISCUSSION: Individuals are not subject to the passive activity limitation rules on rental real estate activities in which they materially participate if two requirements are met: (1) More than 50% of the individual's personal services for the year are performed in real property trades or businesses in which (s)he materially participates and (2) the individual performs more than 750 hours of service in those real property trades or businesses in which (s)he materially participates. David meets both requirements, so any current loss from the rental real estate activity may offset nonpassive income. The suspended losses, however, are treated as a loss from a former passive activity. Therefore, the deduction for the suspended losses is limited to income from the activity and is not allowed to offset other income (Sec. 469).

4.4 Business Use of Home

4.4.1. Kilgore is a flight instructor who assists in the writing of aviation books. She uses a room in her apartment as an office for her writing, and it constitutes her place of business. It is also used to store personal effects and as an occasional second bedroom. It takes up 25% of the space of the apartment and is used 50% of the time as an office. Kilgore's rent is $400 per month and utilities are $50 per month. How much may Kilgore deduct for this office?

A. $0
B. $675
C. $1,350
D. $2,700

Answer (A) is correct. *(Publisher, adapted)*
REQUIRED: The amount that a self-employed person may deduct for an office in the home.
DISCUSSION: Under Sec. 280A, no deduction is allowable with respect to a dwelling unit used during the year as a residence. There is an exception for regular and exclusive use of a portion of the dwelling unit as a principal place of business of the taxpayer. In this case, Kilgore did not use the bedroom exclusively as an office; therefore, no deduction is allowable.
If Kilgore had used the bedroom exclusively as an office, a ratable portion of the rent and utilities would be deductible since it met the requirements for being her principal place of business.
Answer (B) is incorrect. If the space was used exclusively as an office, the deduction is $675. Answer (C) is incorrect. If the space was used 100% of the time exclusively as an office, the deduction is $1,350. Answer (D) is incorrect. If 100% of the space was used exclusively as an office, the deduction is $2,700.

4.4.2. Mr. G, a plumber, owns his own building, which he uses exclusively in his business. On January 1 of the previous year, Mr. G purchased a residence and began using the entire basement as an office and workshop for his business. The basement constitutes his principal place of business. The size of Mr. G's residence is 2,000 square feet, including the basement, which has an area of 800 square feet. During the current year, Mr. G's net income attributable to the business use of his home (before taking into account expenses of the home) was $10,000. In addition, Mr. G incurred the following costs with respect to his residence:

Mortgage interest	$15,000
Real estate taxes	2,500
Utilities	2,000
Insurance and maintenance expenses	2,500

Assuming $1,500 of depreciation on the basement portion each year, what is Mr. G's depreciation deduction with respect to his residence under the regular method of home office deduction?

- A. $1,500
- B. $1,456
- C. $1,364
- D. $1,200

Answer (D) is correct. *(SEE, adapted)*
REQUIRED: The depreciation that may be deducted for an office in a taxpayer's home.
DISCUSSION: Under Sec. 280A, a deduction for the business use of a dwelling unit also used as a residence is allowed only if a portion of the unit is used exclusively on a regular basis as the principal place of business or as a place of business to meet with patients or customers, or if it is a separate structure that is used in connection with the taxpayer's trade or business.

The expenses of the residence must be apportioned based on the area used exclusively for business. Mr. G's business portion is 40% (800 ÷ 2,000 feet). However, the business deduction is limited to net income from the business activity (not taking into account expenses of the home) less the expenses deductible regardless of the business activity, e.g., interest and taxes. Under Prop. Reg. 1.280A-2(i)(5), expenses deductible only as a result of business use that are not adjustments to basis are deducted first, and then those business deductions affecting basis (e.g., depreciation) are deducted.

Net income	$10,000
Mortgage interest ($15,000 × 40%)	(6,000)
Taxes ($2,500 × 40%)	(1,000)
Utilities ($2,000 × 40%)	(800)
Insurance and maintenance ($2,500 × 40%)	(1,000)
Limitation on depreciation	$ 1,200

Answer (A) is incorrect. The full amount of the depreciation is $1,500. Only a portion of the depreciation is deductible due to business income. Answer (B) is incorrect. The deductible portion of depreciation is limited to the amount remaining after all other deductible expenses have been claimed. A deduction of a ratable share of each of the individual expenses is not allowed. Answer (C) is incorrect. With respect to Mr. G's residence, $1,364 is an excessive depreciation deduction.

4.4.3. Ted Travel is a salesperson. His only office is a converted detached garage at his home, used regularly and exclusively to set up appointments, store product samples, and write up orders and other reports for the companies whose products he sells. Travel's business is selling products to customers at various locations within the metropolitan area where he lives. To make these sales, he regularly visits the customers to explain the available products and to take orders. Ted makes only a few sales from his home office. Ted spends an average of 30 hours a week visiting customers and 12 hours a week working at his home office. Which of the following expenses allocable to Travel's office is(are) deductible?

- A. Real property insurance.
- B. Real property depreciation.
- C. Real property purchase money mortgage interest.
- D. All of the answers are correct.

Answer (D) is correct. *(Publisher, adapted)*
REQUIRED: The deductible expenses allocable to a home office.
DISCUSSION: For a taxpayer to deduct expenses for the business use of his or her home under Sec. 280A, the taxpayer must use part of the home exclusively and regularly (1) as the principal place of business for the trade or business; (2) as a place to meet or deal with patients, clients, or customers in the normal course of the trade or business; or (3) in connection with the trade or business, if a separate structure is used that is not attached to the home. A home office qualifies as a principal place of business if (1) the office is used by the taxpayer to conduct administrative or management activities of the taxpayer's trade or business and (2) there is no other fixed location of the trade or business where the taxpayer conducts substantial administrative or management activities of the trade or business. Since Travel is using a separate structure not attached to his home, regularly and exclusively, in connection with his business, he may deduct expenses allocable to the business use of his home.

Answer (A) is incorrect. Since the office is a separate structure not attached to his home, Travel may deduct expenses allocable to the business use of his home even though the office is not his principal place of business under the *Soliman* decision. Answer (B) is incorrect. In addition to real property depreciation allocable to the business use of Travel's home, real property insurance and real property purchase money mortgage interest may also be deducted. Answer (C) is incorrect. In addition to real property purchase money mortgage interest allocable to the business use of Travel's home, real property insurance and real property depreciation may also be deducted.

4.4.4. B, a barber, is a sole proprietor who uses a room in his residence regularly and exclusively to meet with customers in the normal course of his trade or business throughout Year 1. B determines that the room is 350 sq. ft. and has a cost basis of $10,000. B placed the room in service on January 1, Year 1. B depreciates the room under Sec. 168 as nonresidential real property using the optional depreciation table that corresponds with the general depreciation system, the straight-line method of depreciation, a 39-year recovery period, and the mid-month convention. During the year, B earns $9,000 of gross income from the business and pays the following business expenses:

Supplies	$1,500
Advertising	800
Professional fees	300
Magazines/Subscriptions	700
Postage	100
Total	$3,400

B also pays the following expenses related to his home during the year:

Mortgage interest	$10,000
Real property taxes	3,000
Homeowners' insurance	1,500
Utilities	2,400
Repairs	900
Total	$17,800

Using the simplified option, what amount will B report on Schedule C as "Expenses for business use of your home . . ."?

A. $0

B. $1,500

C. $3,400

D. $13,000

Answer (B) is correct. *(Publisher, adapted)*
REQUIRED: The total of expenses for business use of the home.
DISCUSSION: There are three categories of deductions for taxpayers using all or a portion of their home for business:

1. Itemized deductions

2. Ordinary and necessary business expenses that are unrelated to the qualified business use

3. Expenses for business use of a home

If the simplified option is selected for the third category (i.e., expenses for business use of a home), the taxpayer simply multiplies the square footage of the business-use portion (maximum of 300 sq. ft.) by $5. B's simplified option expenses for business use of his home is $1,500 (300 sq. ft. × $5). No deduction for depreciation is allowed under the simplified option.
Answer (A) is incorrect. The amount of $0 is the allowed depreciation deduction under the simplified option. The question asks for the expenses for business use of a home reported on Schedule C. Answer (C) is incorrect. The "total (business) expenses before expenses for business use of home" reported on Schedule C are $3,400; however, the question asks for "expenses for business use of your home."Answer (D) is incorrect. The otherwise allowable deductions itemized on Schedule A total $13,000 (i.e., mortgage interest and real property taxes).

4.4.5. If a residence is completely converted to business use and not used at all as a dwelling, any carryover "office in home" deductions may be deducted in full regardless of net income.

A. True.

B. False.

Answer (B) is correct. *(Publisher, adapted)*
DISCUSSION: When home office deductions exceed the net income from a business, this excess is carried over to future years. However, these carryover deductions are limited to net income from the business whether or not the dwelling unit is used as a residence during each such succeeding taxable year [Sec. 280A(c)(5)].

4.4.6. A taxpayer who is entitled to a deduction for the use of a portion of his home in his work can base the deduction on the cost to rent equivalent commercial space.

A. True.

B. False.

Answer (B) is correct. *(SEE, adapted)*
DISCUSSION: If the taxpayer is allowed a deduction for the business use of a portion of his or her home, the taxpayer must allocate the total expenses of operating the home between business and personal use. Accordingly, actual allocated expenses are deductible, not the cost of equivalent commercial space.

4.4.7. Amy, a doctor, sees patients at an office in her home 3 days a week. She is entitled to a deduction for a portion of the expenses associated with her basic home phone service, allocable to the business usage.

A. True.

B. False.

Answer (B) is correct. *(Publisher, adapted)*
DISCUSSION: No deduction is allowed for basic charges related to the first telephone of a residence [Sec. 262(b)]. However, additional charges for long-distance calls, equipment, and optional services, such as call waiting and additional lines may be deductible.

4.4.8. Michelle Lee operates a babysitting service out of her home 4 days a week. The state in which she resides has licensed her as a day care center. No part of her home is used exclusively for her business. Michelle Lee is not entitled to claim any depreciation deductions attributable to the business use of her home.

A. True.

B. False.

Answer (B) is correct. *(SEE, adapted)*
DISCUSSION: Under Sec. 280A, a deduction for the business use of a dwelling unit also used as a residence is allowed only if a portion of the unit is used exclusively on a regular basis as the principal place of business, as a place of business to meet with patients or customers, or if it is a separate structure and is used in connection with the taxpayer's trade or business. Section 280A(c)(4) provides an exception to this general rule for any portion of a dwelling unit used in the trade or business of providing day care for children.

4.4.9. An employee who rents a portion of his home to his employer (for the employee to work in) may deduct all expenses allocable to the office space.

A. True.

B. False.

Answer (B) is correct. *(Publisher, adapted)*
DISCUSSION: No deduction is available (except for otherwise allowable interest and taxes) for the business use of a home by an employee when it is rented by the employer [Sec. 280A(c)(6)].

4.4.10. Under the simplified option for home office deduction, amounts in excess of the gross income limitation may be carried forward.

A. True.

B. False.

Answer (B) is correct. *(Publisher, adapted)*
DISCUSSION: Amounts in excess of the gross income limitation may not be carried over.

Use **Gleim Test Prep** for interactive study and easy-to-use detailed analytics!

STUDY UNIT FIVE
OTHER DEDUCTIONS FOR ADJUSTED GROSS INCOME

For other deductions for adjusted gross income (above-the-line), see

Study Unit 3 - Business Expenses and Losses
Study Unit 4 - Limitations on Losses
Study Unit 10 - Depreciation, Amortization, and Depletion
Study Unit 11 - Capital Gains and Losses

5.1 Trade and Business Expenses of Employees

5.1.1. During the current year, Mike Daniel, who is single, had the following income and expenses:

Salary	$50,000
Interest income	4,800
Travel expenses for employer	800
Contribution to IRA	5,500

Mike accounted to his employer for the travel expenses, which were then reimbursed by his employer. Mike Daniel is not an active participant in an employer-provided pension plan. What is Mike's adjusted gross income?

- A. $50,100
- B. $49,700
- C. $49,300
- D. $55,600

Answer (C) is correct. *(Publisher, adapted)*
    REQUIRED: The employee's adjusted gross income when there are reimbursed travel expenses and a contribution to an IRA.
    DISCUSSION: Adjusted gross income is defined in Sec. 62 as gross income minus specified deductions, including reimbursed employee expenses and contributions to an IRA. The employee must account to the employer for the expenses and not receive a reimbursement in excess of the expenses accounted for. Since the travel expenses were accounted for, the reimbursement need not be included in gross income, and the expenses are not deducted. Since Mike is not an active participant in an employer-provided pension plan, he can deduct the $5,500 amount of the IRA contribution. Mike's adjusted gross income is $49,300 ($50,000 salary + $4,800 interest – $5,500 IRA contribution).
    Note that, if the travel expenses were not accounted for (e.g., an expense allowance was received), the expense allowance would be included in gross income, and the expenses would be deductible only as an itemized deduction subject to a 50% limit on meals and entertainment. If any meals and entertainment are included in Mike's $800, it would be the employer, not Mike, for whom the 50% limitation would apply, since the expenses were reimbursed.
    Answer (A) is incorrect. Both the reimbursement and the travel expenses are excluded from the tax calculation since Mike made an adequate accounting to his employer. Answer (B) is incorrect. It is the employer who is denied 50% of the travel expenses should such amounts be related to travel and entertainment. Both the travel expenses and the reimbursement are excluded from the tax calculation since Mike made an adequate accounting to his employer. Answer (D) is incorrect. Mike excludes both the deduction and the reimbursement from his tax return since he made an adequate accounting to his employer, and the IRA contribution is also deductible for AGI.

5.1.2. Justin Peter earned a salary of $30,000 during the current year. During the year, he was required by his employer to take several overnight business trips, and he received an expense allowance of $1,500 for travel and lodging. In the course of these trips, he incurred the following expenses, which were either adjustments to income or deductions from adjusted gross income:

Travel	$1,100
Lodging	500
Entertainment of customers	400

What is Justin's adjusted gross income if he does not account to his employer for the expenses?

A. $29,500

B. $29,900

C. $30,000

D. $31,500

5.1.3. Michelle is a Broadway actress. During the current year, she earned $15,000 from performing in three separately produced plays. She incurred expenses of $2,000 for makeup, costumes, and other expenses attributable to her services as an actress. Assuming she had no other income or expenses, what is her adjusted gross income for the current year?

A. $15,000

B. $14,500

C. $14,000

D. $13,000

Answer (D) is correct. *(CPA, adapted)*
REQUIRED: The taxpayer's adjusted gross income.
DISCUSSION: An employee's business expenses do not need to be included in and deducted from gross income in arriving at AGI if the employee accounts to his or her employer for the expenses and the expenses equal the reimbursement. All other business expenses incurred by employees (except those incurred by a qualified performing artist) are deducted from adjusted gross income [Sec. 62(a)]. Justin's gross income was $31,500 ($30,000 salary + $1,500 expense allowance). When the employee receives an allowance and does not account to the employer for the expenses, the expense allowance is included in gross income, and the expenses are deducted as an itemized deduction.
Therefore, Justin's adjusted gross income is $31,500, and his travel, lodging, and entertainment expenses are deductible from adjusted gross income.
Answer (A) is incorrect. The full amount of the expenses were deducted from the expense allowance when determining AGI. The expenses are instead deducted as an itemized deduction. Answer (B) is incorrect. The travel and lodging expenses were deducted from the expense allowance when determining AGI. The expenses are instead deducted as an itemized deduction. Answer (C) is incorrect. The expense allowance should be included in gross income and then deducted as an itemized deduction.

Answer (D) is correct. *(Publisher, adapted)*
REQUIRED: The adjusted gross income of a performing artist.
DISCUSSION: An exception to the requirement that an employee's business expenses must be reimbursed to be deductible for adjusted gross income is the expenses of a qualified performing artist. Section 62(a)(2)(B) allows the deduction for AGI of expenses incurred relating to the performance of services in the performing arts as an employee if the taxpayer

1. Performs services in the performing arts as an employee for two or more employers during the taxable year,

2. Receives at least $200 from each employer,

3. Has expenses relating to the performance of such services which exceed 10% of the taxpayer's gross income attributable to the performance of such services, and

4. Has adjusted gross income (determined without regard to this deduction) of $16,000 or less [Sec. 62(b)(1)].

Since Michelle meets the above three requirements, she may deduct her expenses of $2,000 in full to arrive at her adjusted gross income of $13,000 ($15,000 – $2,000).
Answer (A) is incorrect. The income without regard to the allowable deduction for the AGI of a qualified performing artist is $15,000. Answer (B) is incorrect. Deducting only $500 of expenses results in $14,500. Answer (C) is incorrect. Deducting only $1,000 of expenses results in $14,000.

5.1.4. Jon is employed by a consulting firm and is required to account to his employer for travel expenses. During the current year, he paid the following business expenses and accounted to his employer for all but the executive search fees:

Travel expenses incurred while away from home overnight	$3,000
Executive search consultant fees paid in securing a new job in the same profession	1,200
Professional society dues	500
Transportation expenses	750

During the current year, Jon received travel expense reimbursements totaling $2,500 from his employer. How much should Jon deduct as employee business expenses in arriving at his adjusted gross income for the current year?

A. $0

B. $500

C. $2,500

D. $3,750

5.1.5. With regard to employer reimbursements under an accountable plan, which of the following statements is false?

A. The expenses must have been paid or incurred while performing services as an employee.

B. The expenses must be adequately accounted for to the employer within a reasonable period of time.

C. Any excess reimbursement must be returned within a reasonable period of time.

D. Any reimbursement paid must be based on a fixed daily amount not to exceed the government's per diem rate.

5.1.6. Dale received $1,000 in the current year for jury duty. In exchange for regular compensation from her employer during the period of jury service, Dale was required to remit the entire $1,000 to her employer. In Dale's current-year income tax return, the $1,000 jury duty fee should be

A. Claimed in full as an itemized deduction.

B. Claimed as an itemized deduction to the extent exceeding 2% of adjusted gross income.

C. Deducted from gross income in arriving at adjusted gross income.

D. Included in taxable income without a corresponding offset against other income.

Answer (C) is correct. *(SEE, adapted)*
REQUIRED: The amount the taxpayer may deduct in arriving at adjusted gross income.
DISCUSSION: Each of the expenses listed is deductible as a trade or business expense under Sec. 162. In the case of an employee, trade and business expenses are deducted from gross income in arriving at adjusted gross income only if they are reimbursed expenses for which the employee accounts to the employer or are incurred by a qualified performing artist [Sec. 62(a)(2)]. If the employee accounts to his or her employer for the expenses, the reimbursement is not included in gross income as long as the expenses equal the reimbursement. If the expenses exceed the reimbursement, the reimbursement is reported as income, and expenses up to the reimbursement amount are deductible from gross income. Excess expenses are deductible from adjusted gross income, subject to the 2% floor.
Therefore, Jon must include the $2,500 reimbursement in gross income and should deduct $2,500 of the travel expenses for AGI. The additional $500 of travel expenses and all the other expenses are deductible from adjusted gross income (subject to limitations, including a deduction of only 50% of any meal expenses included in the $500 of unreimbursed travel expenses).
Answer (A) is incorrect. Qualified deductions for travel expenses are for AGI. Answer (B) is incorrect. Five hundred dollars is the excess that should be deducted from AGI as a miscellaneous itemized deduction subject to limitations. Answer (D) is incorrect. Transportation and a portion of travel expenses are miscellaneous itemized deductions from (not for) AGI.

Answer (D) is correct. *(SEE, adapted)*
REQUIRED: The characteristics of employer reimbursements under an accountable plan.
DISCUSSION: If a reimbursement arrangement between an employee and an employer meets the requirements of a business connection, substantiation, and return of excess payments, then all amounts paid under the arrangement are treated as paid under an accountable plan.
Answer (A) is incorrect. Regarding employer reimbursements under an accountable plan, the expenses must have been paid or incurred while performing services as an employee. Answer (B) is incorrect. Regarding employer reimbursements under an accountable plan, the expenses must be adequately accounted for to the employer within a reasonable period of time. Answer (C) is incorrect. Regarding employer reimbursements under an accountable plan, any excess reimbursement must be returned within a reasonable period of time.

Answer (C) is correct. *(CPA, adapted)*
REQUIRED: The correct treatment of the jury duty fee received in the current year.
DISCUSSION: Section 62(a)(13) allows as a deduction from gross income any jury pay received by the taxpayer that is remitted to the taxpayer's employer in exchange for compensation during the period of jury service.
Answer (A) is incorrect. The jury duty fee may be claimed in full but not as an itemized deduction. Answer (B) is incorrect. The jury duty fee is not claimed as an itemized deduction. Answer (D) is incorrect. The jury duty pay included in taxable income may be offset against a jury duty fee deduction.

5.2 Rental Property Expenses

5.2.1. Mr. Lee rents his vacation home. Given the following information, determine the correct treatment of the rental income and expenses on his current-year return.

Days rented in the current year to unrelated parties at a fair rental price	56
Days used for personal purposes in the current year	18

Total income and (expenses) during the current year:

Gross rental income	$5,000
Allocated interest and taxes	(4,000)
Other allocated expenses	(1,500)
Net rental loss	$ (500)

A. A $500 loss should be shown on Schedule E, Form 1040.

B. The interest and taxes should be deducted on Schedule A, Form 1040, as itemized deductions.

C. Mr. Lee should include none of the income or expenses from the beach house on his current-year income tax return.

D. Rental expenses (other than interest and taxes) are limited to the gross rental income in excess of deductions for interest and taxes allocated to rental use.

Answer (D) is correct. *(SEE, adapted)*
REQUIRED: The correct treatment of the rental income and expenses related to a vacation home.
DISCUSSION: When a dwelling unit is used by the taxpayer as a residence, Sec. 280A disallows a deduction for expenses in excess of the gross income derived from the rents received reduced by the deductions allowable (e.g., taxes and interest), whether or not the unit was used for rental purposes. A taxpayer is deemed to use a dwelling unit as a residence if (s)he uses it for personal purposes for a number of days that exceeds the greater of 14 days or 10% of the number of days during the year for which the unit is rented at fair rental value [Sec. 280A(d)]. These rules apply only if the vacation home is rented for 15 days or more. If the rental is for fewer than 15 days, no rental expenses are deductible (and no rent is includible in gross income) per Sec. 280A(g).
Answer (A) is incorrect. A rental loss is not allowed when the taxpayer personally uses the dwelling unit more than 14 days during the year or 10% of the number of days rented, whichever is greater. Answer (B) is incorrect. Only the interest and taxes not allocated to the rental portion should be deducted as itemized deductions. Answer (C) is incorrect. All income and all deductible expenses must be reported when a dwelling unit is rented for more than 14 days during the year.

5.2.2. Mrs. R owns a beach cottage that she rented out for 3 months, lived in for 1 month, and tried unsuccessfully to rent for the rest of the year. Mrs. R received rental income of $5,600. Her total expenses for the cottage were as follows:

Interest	$3,000
Taxes	1,800
Utilities	1,500
Maintenance	900
Depreciation	2,400

What is Mrs. R's net rental income or loss to be reported on her income tax return?

A. $4,000 loss.

B. $800 income.

C. $0

D. $0 or $800 income.

Answer (D) is correct. *(SEE, adapted)*
REQUIRED: The net rental income or loss to be reported.
DISCUSSION: When a dwelling unit is used by the taxpayer as a residence, Sec. 280A disallows a deduction for expenses exceeding the gross income derived from rents reduced by deductions allowable (e.g., taxes and interest), whether or not the unit was used for rental purposes. Under Reg. 1.280A-3(d)(3), the order of deductions is (1) the allocable portion of expenses deductible regardless of rental activity, (2) deductions not affecting basis, and (3) those that do affect basis.
The allocation of all deductions between rental and personal use is based on the total days actually used per the IRS (i.e., 3/4 of each of R's expenses is deductible as a rental expense, limited to income). However, the case of Bolton, 51 AFTR 2d 83-305 (CA-9, 1982) allocates the interest and taxes based on the total days of the year (i.e., 3/12 of each is deductible as rental expense). The remaining interest and taxes are deductible as an itemized deduction.

	IRS	Bolton
Gross rent	$5,600	$5,600
Interest	(2,250)	(750)
Taxes	(1,350)	(450)
Allowable other deductions	$2,000	$4,400
Utilities and maintenance	(1,800)	(1,800)
Depreciation	(200)	(1,800)
Income	$ 0	$ 800

Answer (A) is incorrect. A $4,000 loss results when the total expenses are deducted from rental income. Answer (B) is incorrect. Depending on which of the two alternative sets of rules is followed, $0 may also be correct. Answer (C) is incorrect. Depending on which of the two alternative sets of rules is followed, $800 income may also be correct.

5.2.3. John offers his beach cottage for rent from June through August 31 (92 days). His family uses the cottage during the last 2 weeks in May (15 days). He was unable to find a renter for the first week in August (7 days). The person who rented the cottage for July allowed him to use it over a weekend (2 days) without any reduction in, or refund of, rent. The cottage was not used at all before May 16 or after August 31. Total income received was $11,000. Total expenses were $4,000. What percentage of the expenses for the cottage can John deduct as rental expenses?

A. 25%

B. 83%

C. 85%

D. 100%

5.2.4. Carla Meehan, a cash-basis taxpayer, owns the Ritz Regency Apartments, which contain 10 identical units. Carla and her husband, Charles, live in Apartment 1 and rent out the remaining apartments. Income and expenses for the current year were reported by their accountant as follows:

Gross rental income	$37,800
Depreciation of building	$12,500
Maintenance and repairs	3,750
Utilities	4,250
Interest and taxes	500
Total expenses	$21,000

What amount of net rental income should be reported by Carla and Charles for the current year?

A. $16,800

B. $17,300

C. $18,900

D. $37,800

5.2.5. Mr. Smith, a cash-basis, calendar-year taxpayer, owns a duplex. He lives in one unit and rents the other unit to an unrelated individual. The two units are approximately equal in size. On July 1, Year 1, Mr. Smith paid the property insurance on the duplex for the 3-year period July 1, Year 1, through June 30, Year 4. The total premium was $360. For Year 1, Mr. Smith's rental expense for this insurance policy is

A. $30

B. $60

C. $120

D. $360

Answer (C) is correct. *(SEE, adapted)*
REQUIRED: The percentage of expenses deductible as rental expense.
DISCUSSION: When a taxpayer has a vacation home, the expenses must be allocated between personal use and rental use. There was a total of 100 days of usage during the year (15 days in May, 92 days from June through August 31, less 7 days unrented in August). The taxpayer had personal usage for the 15 days in May. The 2-day period of personal use in the cottage while it was rented at fair market value does not count as personal use.
Answer (A) is incorrect. There was a total of 100 days of usage during the year, of which 15 were personal use. The expenses must be allocated between personal use and rental use. Answer (B) is incorrect. The 2-day period of personal use in the cottage when it was rented at fair market value does not count as personal use. Answer (D) is incorrect. The expenses must be allocated between personal use and business use.

Answer (C) is correct. *(Publisher, adapted)*
REQUIRED: The amount the taxpayers should report as net rental income.
DISCUSSION: Section 212 allows a deduction for all ordinary and necessary expenses paid or incurred during the taxable year for the production of income. The costs of maintenance, repairs, and utilities are deductible expenses incurred for the production of income under Sec. 212. Section 167 allows a deduction for depreciation on property held for the production of income. Secs. 163 and 164 allow deductions for interest and taxes, respectively. The total amount of these expenses is $21,000 ($12,500 + $3,750 + $4,250 + $500). However, one-tenth of these expenses were personal and may not be deducted as rental expenses (Sec. 262). The net rental income is

Gross rental income	$37,800
Less: expenses ($21,000 × 90%)	(18,900)
Net rental income	$18,900

Note that the $50 of interest and taxes related to the Meehans' apartment is deductible as an itemized deduction (from AGI).
Answer (A) is incorrect. Ten percent of the expenses is personal and may not be deducted as rental expenses. Answer (B) is incorrect. Interest and taxes are eligible expenses, but only 90% of the total expenses is deductible to arrive at net rental income. Answer (D) is incorrect. Ordinary and necessary business expenses related to rental property are deductible.

Answer (A) is correct. *(SEE, adapted)*
REQUIRED: The portion of insurance the taxpayer may deduct as rental expense.
DISCUSSION: Insurance premiums paid on rental property are deductible as rental expenses. However, Sec. 262 disallows a deduction for personal expenses unless otherwise provided in another section. Mr. Smith must allocate the insurance expense between the personal unit and the rented unit. Since the units are approximately equal in size, one-half of the total premium should be allocated to the rental unit ($180). However, only the portion of the premium applying to the current year is deductible in Year 1. The insurance premium is for 3 years or 36 months. The rental portion comes to $5 per month ($180 ÷ 36 months). Since there are 6 months left in Year 1, Mr. Smith's rental expense for the insurance policy is $30 ($5 per month × 6 months).
Answer (B) is incorrect. Sixty dollars includes the personal portion of the property insurance for the applicable half year. Answer (C) is incorrect. Both the business and personal portions of the property insurance for the whole year is $120. Answer (D) is incorrect. Only the current business portion of the property tax is deductible in Year 1.

5.2.6. During the current year, Mr. C had the following expenditures relating to his rental property:

Local assessment for repair of sidewalk	$ 200
Property tax on rental house #1	900
Mr. C's portion of property tax paid on rental house #2 sold in the current year	350
Local assessment for connection to newly constructed sewage system	1,200

What is the amount of the above expenditures that must be capitalized?

- A. $0
- B. $550
- C. $1,200
- D. $1,400

Answer (C) is correct. *(SEE, adapted)*
REQUIRED: The amount of property assessments and taxes that must be capitalized.
DISCUSSION: Property taxes on rental property are deductible under Sec. 164, the same as for any other property. When property is sold during the year, the seller's portion of the property tax is deductible. Assessments tending to increase the value of property are not deductible as taxes [Sec. 164(c)]. However, if the assessment is allocable to maintenance as in the case of the assessment for sidewalk repairs, then it is deductible as a maintenance or repair expenditure. The same concept applies as with the decision to capitalize or deduct any other repair expenses. The fact that it is an assessment from a local government does not affect the determination. Only the assessment for connection to a newly constructed sewage system needs to be capitalized. This payment increases the value of the property and, accordingly, must be capitalized.
Answer (A) is incorrect. The expenditures that substantially increase the value of property must be capitalized. Answer (B) is incorrect. The assessment for repair of the sidewalk and the property taxes on the rental house that was sold are deductible. Answer (D) is incorrect. The assessment for repair of the sidewalk is deductible.

5.2.7. On January 31 of the current year, Mr. Fund, a cash-basis taxpayer, purchased a commercial building in Acorn City. As part of the transaction, he agreed to pay the previous year's property tax of $6,000 due on February 1 of the current year. The city converted the area around the building into a pedestrian mall and financed the construction with 10-year bonds. The full cost was assessed against the affected properties. Mr. Fund's portion of the assessment was $1,100 ($1,000 for principal and $100 for interest on the bonds). On December 31 of the current year, he paid property taxes of $7,600, including the assessment, and $100 of interest. What is the amount of Mr. Fund's real estate tax deduction on this property for the current year?

- A. $5,948
- B. $6,039
- C. $6,600
- D. $12,600

Answer (B) is correct. *(SEE, adapted)*
REQUIRED: The real estate tax deduction for the current year.
DISCUSSION: Section 164 allows a deduction for state and local real property taxes. That section also allows a deduction for real property taxes incurred in carrying on a trade or business or an activity described in Sec. 212 (relating to expenses for production of income). Special assessments for improvements to the land are not deductible but are added to the basis of the land. However, the portion of a "front foot benefit charge" assessed against property benefited by construction of a water system, and added to the taxpayer's real property tax bill that is properly allocated to interest and maintenance charges, is deductible as a tax under Sec. 164 and allocable between the buyer and seller (Rev. Rul. 79-201).
The total real estate tax expense for the current year is $6,600 ($7,600 – $1,000 special principal assessment). Real estate taxes must be apportioned between the buyer and seller based on the number of days the property was held by each in the year of sale. Mr. Fund owned the property for 334 days in the current year (February 1 to December 31). His real estate tax deduction on the property for the current year is $6,039 ($6,600 × 334/365 days). The real estate taxes for the previous year that were paid by Mr. Fund in the current year are not deductible by Mr. Fund since he did not incur the expense. Instead, he must capitalize the $6,000 amount as part of the building's cost.
Answer (A) is incorrect. The $100 of interest on the special assessment is included as part of the offset for the property tax calculation. Answer (C) is incorrect. The $6,600 must be adjusted for the number of days the property is actually owned by Mr. Fund (334 days). Answer (D) is incorrect. The property taxes for the previous year are not deductible by Mr. Fund because he did not incur the expense. In addition, the $6,600 for the current year must be allocated based on the number of days the property was owned by Mr. Fund.

5.2.8. Mrs. W rented a portion of her personal residence to Ms. E, a college student. In allocating the expenses between the rented portion and the personal portion of her residence, it is not necessary for Mrs. W to allocate taxes and mortgage interest.

- A. True.
- B. False.

Answer (B) is correct. *(SEE, adapted)*
DISCUSSION: A taxpayer who rents a portion of a personal residence must allocate all expenses, including taxes and interest, between the rented and personal portions of the residence, because Sec. 62(a)(4) requires expenses attributable to rented property to be deducted for adjusted gross income. The remainder of the interest and taxes is deductible from adjusted gross income under Sec. 63.

5.2.9. Mr. Lee owned a house on a lake. During the current year, he rented out the house for 160 days to unrelated parties. During the current year, he used the house 15 days for personal use. He incurred a $5,000 loss as a result of his rental activities. There is no limit under Sec. 280A to the amount of the loss he may deduct on Schedule E of his income tax return.

A. True.

B. False.

Answer (A) is correct. *(SEE, adapted)*
DISCUSSION: Section 280A restricts the deductions with respect to a dwelling unit used by the taxpayer as a residence. A taxpayer is deemed to use a dwelling unit as a residence if (s)he uses it for personal purposes for a number of days that exceeds the greater of 14 days or 10% of the number of days during the year for which the unit is rented at a fair rental. Since Mr. Lee rented the house for 160 days, he was allowed to use it for personal purposes for 16 days without treating it as a residence. Thus, Mr. Lee's deductible loss is not limited by Sec. 280A. However, the passive loss rules of Sec. 469 may limit the loss deduction.

5.3 Expenses Related to Production of Income

5.3.1. Rickey Spillane earned royalties from writing books on a part-time basis. He did all his writing at home in his kitchen. His expenses included

Paper, pencils, supplies	$ 80
Typing services	700
Rent on apartment (apportioned)	600

Rickey also had to make several trips to the publisher's offices under his royalty contract. Airfare, 50% of the meals, and lodging for these trips cost $900. How much can Rickey deduct for adjusted gross income?

A. $0

B. $780

C. $1,680

D. $2,280

Answer (C) is correct. *(Publisher, adapted)*
REQUIRED: The amount of royalty expenses that can be deducted for adjusted gross income.
DISCUSSION: Expenses incurred in the production of income are deductible under Sec. 212 even if they are not trade or business expenses. However, these expenses may be deductible for adjusted gross income or from adjusted gross income. Royalty expenses are deductible for adjusted gross income under Sec. 62(a)(4).

Rickey can deduct the cost of the paper, pencils, supplies, typing services, and trips to the publisher's office since these are all incurred to produce the royalty income. The total of these expenses is $1,680 (assuming the hobby loss rules do not apply). The rent on the kitchen portion of the apartment is not deductible at all since Sec. 280A requires exclusive use of part of a dwelling for business purposes for the rent allocable thereto to be deductible.

Answer (A) is incorrect. Rickey is allowed a deduction. Answer (B) is incorrect. The $900 in transportation, meals, and lodging costs is also deductible. Answer (D) is incorrect. The rent on the apartment is not deductible.

5.3.2. Dick Mixon was a retired politician who decided to write about his life in politics. In his first year (Year 1), Dick received prepublication royalties. He worked sporadically, and it took 6 years to complete the first draft. In the meantime, he submitted articles to gossip magazines under a pen name. Dick's expenses and income were as follows:

	Income	Expenses
Year 1	$16,000	$2,000
Year 2	50	3,500
Year 3	200	4,000
Year 4	600	4,200
Year 5	900	4,000

How much can Dick deduct as royalty expense in Year 5?

A. $0

B. $50

C. $900

D. $4,000

Answer (C) is correct. *(Publisher, adapted)*
REQUIRED: The business deduction when only 1 year has been profitable.
DISCUSSION: The expenses of an author are deductible under Sec. 162(a) as trade or business expenses or under Sec. 212 as expenses for the production of income. In either case, they are deductible for adjusted gross income under Sec. 62(a)(4). If an activity is not engaged in for profit, however, Sec. 183 limits deductions to those which are allowed regardless of whether the activity is engaged in for profit (e.g., taxes and interest), plus the excess of gross income over the deductions that are allowed regardless of whether the activity is engaged in for profit. An activity is presumed to be engaged in for profit if the gross income from the activity exceeds the deductions attributable to the activity for 3 or more of 5 consecutive taxable years which end with the current taxable year.

Since Mixon earned a profit in only one of the 5 years, he does not satisfy the safe harbor presumption that his activity was engaged in for profit found in Sec. 183(d). His deductions will be limited to the amount of income earned from the activity ($900 in Year 5) unless he can substantiate his profit motive based on the facts and circumstances.

Answer (A) is incorrect. A limited deduction for royalty expenses is allowed. Answer (B) is incorrect. Fifty dollars is the difference between the total of the 6 years' income and expenses. Answer (D) is incorrect. The activity does not meet the rules for profitability of a business since it has been profitable only 1 year in 5. Therefore, not all of the $4,000 of expenses may be deducted.

5.3.3. For the current year, Frances Quinn had a time savings account with the Benevolent Savings Bank. The following entries appeared in her passbook for the year:

March 30, interest credited	$150
June 29, interest credited	160
July 25, penalty forfeiture because of a premature withdrawal	125
September 28, interest credited	80
December 28, interest credited	85

The above information should be reported by Ms. Quinn on her current-year tax return as

A. Interest income of $350.

B. Interest income of $475.

C. Interest income of $475 and an itemized deduction for interest expense of $125.

D. Interest income of $475 and a deduction of $125 in arriving at adjusted gross income.

Answer (D) is correct. *(CPA, adapted)*
REQUIRED: The method of reporting interest income and premature withdrawal penalties.
DISCUSSION: Interest income is included in gross income [Sec. 61(a)(4)] as of the date it is credited to the account and is available for withdrawal. During the taxable year, Ms. Quinn received $475 in interest income ($150 on March 30, $160 on June 29, $80 on September 28, and $85 on December 28). This income must be reported in full and may not be netted with the withdrawal penalty.
Section 165(c)(2) allows an individual to deduct losses incurred during the taxable year on any transaction entered into for profit. The $125 forfeiture penalty is a loss incurred on a transaction entered into for profit and is deductible. The loss is deducted from gross income in arriving at adjusted gross income [Sec. 62(a)(9)].
Answer (A) is incorrect. The $125 withdrawal penalty is a deduction in determining AGI, and not a reduction in the interest income that is reported. Answer (B) is incorrect. In addition to interest income of $475, Ms. Quinn had a $125 deduction. Answer (C) is incorrect. Ms. Quinn's deduction for interest expense of $125 is not itemized.

5.3.4. George opened a 4-year certificate of deposit in January Year 1. He earned $400 in interest for Year 1 and reported this on his Year 1 return. He withdrew all of the funds in October Year 2. However, due to the premature withdrawal provisions, he received only $230 of the Year 1 interest, plus $195 of interest for Year 2. What should he report in Year 2?

A. $195 interest income on Schedule B.

B. $25 interest income on Schedule B.

C. $170 interest expense on Schedule A and $195 interest income on Schedule B.

D. $195 interest income on Schedule B and $170 as an adjustment to gross income.

Answer (D) is correct. *(SEE, adapted)*
REQUIRED: The proper reporting of interest income.
DISCUSSION: Interest income earned must be reported in full. The $400 of interest was included in gross income in Year 1. The $170 ($400 interest earned – $230 interest received) penalty is a deduction for adjusted gross income under Sec. 62(a)(9), and George will deduct it in Year 2 (the year the penalty is incurred). The amount of interest earned and received for Year 2 must also be reported in Year 2.
Answer (A) is incorrect. George can claim an adjustment to gross income for the amount of the penalty paid. Answer (B) is incorrect. The amount of $25 understates George's interest income. Answer (C) is incorrect. The penalty is an adjustment to gross income, not interest expense.

5.3.5. Which of the following is deductible by a calendar-year taxpayer to arrive at adjusted gross income in the current year?

A. Unreimbursed dues to AICPA by an employee of an accounting firm.

B. Unreimbursed union dues by an employee of a company.

C. 100% of the medical insurance expense of a self-employed individual.

D. One-half of a net long-term capital gain in excess of a net short-term capital loss.

Answer (C) is correct. *(CPA, adapted)*
REQUIRED: The item that is deductible from gross income in arriving at adjusted gross income.
DISCUSSION: For tax years after 2002, Sec. 162(l) allows a self-employed individual to deduct 100% of the insurance for family medical insurance expenses as business expenses. Trade and business expenses of an individual other than as an employee are deductible for adjusted gross income [Sec. 62(a)(1)]. This deduction is not available if the taxpayer is eligible for coverage by an employer of the taxpayer or spouse.
Answer (A) is incorrect. Business deductions of employees are deductible for adjusted gross income only if they are accounted for to the employer and reimbursed by the employer or if they are certain expenses of performing artists. The unreimbursed dues may be deducted under Sec. 63 from adjusted gross income as an itemized deduction subject to the 2%-of-adjusted-gross-income floor. Answer (B) is incorrect. Unreimbursed union dues are not deductible for adjusted gross income. Answer (D) is incorrect. There is no long-term capital gain deduction.

5.3.6. Mr. D works full-time as a systems analyst for a consulting firm. In addition, he sells plants that he raises himself in a greenhouse attached to his residence. During the past 5 years, the results from raising and selling the plants have been as follows:

Year	Net Profit (Loss)
Year 1	$(2,000)
Year 2	(1,200)
Year 3	1,000
Year 4	2,500
Year 5	(500)

Lacking evidence to the contrary, this activity is presumed to be an activity carried on for profit, and the $500 loss in Year 5 can be taken on D's Year 5 tax return.

A. True.

B. False.

Answer (B) is correct. *(SEE, adapted)*
DISCUSSION: If an activity is not engaged in for profit, Sec. 183 limits deductions to those allowed regardless of whether the activity is engaged in for profit (e.g., taxes and interest), plus the excess of gross income over the deductions, which are allowed regardless of whether the activity is engaged in for profit. An activity is presumed to be engaged in for profit if the gross income from the activity exceeds the deductions attributable to the activity for 3 or more of 5 consecutive taxable years that end with the current taxable year [Sec. 183(d)]. Mr. D's activity was profitable for only 2 of 5 consecutive years.

5.3.7. Most expenses incurred for the production of income (Sec. 212) are deductible for adjusted gross income.

A. True.

B. False.

Answer (B) is correct. *(Publisher, adapted)*
DISCUSSION: Section 212 allows a deduction for ordinary and necessary expenses paid or incurred for the production or collection of income and for the management, conservation, or maintenance of property held for the production of income. Only those expenses attributable to rents and royalties are deductible for adjusted gross income [Sec. 62(a)(4)]. The other expenses incurred for the production of income that are deductible must be deducted from (not for) adjusted gross income under Sec. 63.

5.4 Alimony

5.4.1. Which one of the following types of allowable deductions can be claimed as a deduction in arriving at an individual's adjusted gross income?

A. Child support payments.

B. Personal casualty losses.

C. Charitable contributions.

D. Alimony payments.

Answer (D) is correct. *(CPA, adapted)*
REQUIRED: The deduction allowable above the line for arriving at adjusted gross income.
DISCUSSION: Section 215 allows the deduction by the payor of amounts includible as alimony in the recipient's gross income. This is a deduction for adjusted gross income (above the line).
Answer (A) is incorrect. Child support payments of an individual are not deductible (either for or from adjusted gross income). Answer (B) is incorrect. Personal casualty losses are an itemized deduction (from adjusted gross income). Answer (C) is incorrect. Charitable contributions are an itemized deduction.

5.4.2. Your divorce decree, which became final last year, requires that you pay $400 a month, of which $250 is specified as child support. During the current year, you pay only $4,000, although in no month did you pay less than $250. What amount may you deduct and must your former spouse report as alimony?

A. $1,000

B. $1,800

C. $2,500

D. $3,000

Answer (A) is correct. *(SEE, adapted)*
REQUIRED: The amount the payor may deduct and the recipient must report as alimony.
DISCUSSION: Any part of a payment that the terms of the decree specify as a sum payable for the support of minor children is not includible in the recipient's gross income and is not deductible by the payor [Sec. 71(c)]. If any payment is less than the amount specified in the decree, it will first be considered child support until all the child support obligation is paid. The decree specified that $250 per month ($3,000) was for child support. The remaining $1,000 is includible in the recipient's gross income and deductible by the payor as alimony.
Answer (B) is incorrect. The deductible amount of alimony if the full amount of the payments were made throughout the year would have been $1,800. Answer (C) is incorrect. Child support of $3,000 must be subtracted to determine the correct amount of deductible alimony. Answer (D) is incorrect. Nondeductible child support is $3,000.

5.4.3. Mr. and Mrs. Wright were legally divorced in 1984. The court decree of divorce was entered into on April 20, 1984. Mr. Wright is required to pay Mrs. Wright $3,000 a month from May 1, 1984, through May 1, 2018. The payments are not subject to contingencies. Mr. Wright also made a voluntary payment of $1,000 to Mrs. Wright on April 1, 2017. Assuming Mr. Wright made all of the payments required by the divorce decree, what is the amount of alimony deductible on his 2017 return?

A. $0

B. $1,000

C. $36,000

D. $37,000

Answer (C) is correct. *(SEE, adapted)*
   REQUIRED: The amount of alimony deductible under a 1984 decree of divorce.
   DISCUSSION: Section 215 allows the payor a deduction for payments that are required to be included in the recipient's gross income as alimony under Sec. 71. For payments under court decrees or separation agreements entered into before 1985, Sec. 71 requires the payments to be periodic, which means they must last for more than 10 years unless they are subject to a contingency. Therefore, the $3,000 per month payable for 34 years is deductible. The voluntary payment of $1,000 on April 1 is considered a gift and not deductible.
   For divorce or separation instruments executed after 1984, the Tax Reform Acts of 1984 and 1986 have amended Sec. 71 and the requirements for alimony and separate maintenance payments.
   Answer (A) is incorrect. Mr. Wright may deduct the $3,000 per month payments starting in May. Answer (B) is incorrect. The $1,000 voluntary payment is considered a gift. However, Mr. Wright may deduct the $3,000 per month payments starting in May. Answer (D) is incorrect. The amount of the monthly payments made for the year plus the $1,000 gift is $37,000. Note that this treatment is a result of pre-1985 court decrees. Deductibility of alimony payments has changed significantly in the 1984 and 1986 tax acts.

5.4.4. Which of the following is not a requirement to be met for a payment received by a spouse or former spouse under a divorce or separation instrument to be considered alimony?

A. The payments must be paid directly to the spouse or former spouse and not to a third party.

B. The payments must be in cash, including checks or money orders.

C. The spouses cannot file a joint return.

D. There must be no liability to make any payment, in cash or property, after the death of the recipient spouse.

Answer (A) is correct. *(SEE, adapted)*
   REQUIRED: The requirement that does not have to be met for a payment to be considered alimony.
   DISCUSSION: Section 71(b)(1) states that the term "alimony or separate maintenance payment" means any payment in cash if (1) such payment is received by (or on behalf of) a spouse under a divorce or separation instrument, (2) the instrument does not designate the payment as not includible in gross income, (3) the payor spouse and the payee spouse are not members of the same household at the time the payment is made, and (4) there is no liability to make such payment after the death of the payee spouse. Assuming these requirements are satisfied, a payment of cash by a payor spouse to a third party under the terms of the divorce or separation agreement will qualify as a payment received "on behalf of" the payee spouse and will be considered alimony (Temp. Reg. 1.71-1T).
   Answer (B) is incorrect. For a payment to be treated as alimony, the payments must be in cash, including checks or money orders. Answer (C) is incorrect. For a payment to be treated as alimony, the spouses cannot file a joint return. Answer (D) is incorrect. For a payment to be treated as alimony, there must be no liability to make any payment, in cash or property, after the death of the recipient spouse.

5.4.5. Mr. K paid $500 a month for 3 months to his estranged wife while they were negotiating a written separation agreement. Mr. K filed a separate return for the current year. An agreement reached June 1 of the current year required Mr. K to pay $300 a month as alimony. Mr. K made payments of $2,100 for the period June 1 to December 31 of the current year. What is Mr. K's alimony deduction for the current year?

A. $900

B. $2,100

C. $3,000

D. $3,600

Answer (B) is correct. *(SEE, adapted)*
   REQUIRED: The taxpayer's alimony deduction for the current year.
   DISCUSSION: Section 215 allows a deduction by the payor of amounts includible in the recipient's gross income as alimony under Sec. 71. Section 71 requires inclusion in the recipient's gross income of cash payments made under a divorce or separation agreement entered into after 1984. The taxpayer may deduct only the $2,100 of payments made under the written separation agreement. The payments made prior to June 1 are neither deductible by Mr. K nor includible in his wife's income.
   Answer (A) is incorrect. The money that would have been paid for the months of March, April, and May if the written agreement had been in force is $900. It is not considered to be alimony. Answer (C) is incorrect. The amount of $3,000 results from treating $900 of the payments made during the 3 months before the agreement was reached as alimony. Answer (D) is incorrect. The $500 payments made during the 3 months before the agreement was reached are not treated as alimony.

5.4.6. Which of the following is deductible as alimony under separation agreements or court decrees entered into before 1985?

A. A periodic payment required under the terms of the divorce decree.

B. A periodic payment that does not arise out of the marital or family relationship.

C. Payment made before the decree of divorce.

D. Lump-sum cash required by a decree of divorce.

Answer (A) is correct. *(SEE, adapted)*
REQUIRED: The payment that is deductible as alimony under agreements and decrees entered into before 1985.
DISCUSSION: Section 215 allows a deduction by the payor of amounts includible as alimony in the recipient's gross income under Sec. 71. To be considered alimony under Sec. 71 (for court decrees and separation agreements entered into before 1985), the payments must be periodic; made under a decree of divorce or separate maintenance, a written separation agreement, or a decree for support; and due to the marital or family relationship.
Answer (B) is incorrect. The periodic payment must arise out of the marital or family relationship. Answer (C) is incorrect. The payment must be required by a court decree or written separation agreement to be deductible. Answer (D) is incorrect. The payment must be periodic (i.e., over more than 10 years or contingent).
NOTE: For divorce or separation instruments executed after 1984, the Tax Reform Acts of 1984 and 1986 have amended Sec. 71 and the requirements for alimony and separate maintenance payments.

5.4.7. Rick and Stacy were divorced in February of the current year. Requirements of the divorce decree and Stacy's performance follow:

Transfer title to their residence to Rick. Stacy's basis was $95,000, the fair market value was $105,000, and the residence was subject to a mortgage of $90,000.

Make the mortgage payments of $1,000 per month (beginning in March) for the remaining 20 years or until Rick dies, if sooner.

Pay Rick $500 per month (beginning in March) for 6 years or until Rick dies, if sooner. Of this amount, $200 is designated as child support.

Stacy's current-year alimony deduction is

A. $3,000

B. $13,000

C. $15,000

D. $18,000

Answer (B) is correct. *(Publisher, adapted)*
REQUIRED: The deduction for alimony paid under a current-year decree of divorce.
DISCUSSION: Section 215 allows a deduction for alimony or separate maintenance payments as defined under Sec. 71. Section 71(b) defines alimony as any payment in cash if (1) it is received under a divorce or separation instrument, (2) the instrument does not designate the payment as not includible in gross income, (3) the payee spouse and payor spouse are not members of the same household at the time the payment is made, and (4) there is no liability to make such payment for any period after the death of the payee spouse.
The transfer of title to the residence is not considered alimony since it is not a payment in cash. The mortgage payments are considered alimony. Even though they are made to a third party, they are for the benefit of Rick. The $500 monthly payment includes $200 of child support that is not includible as alimony [Sec. 71(c)]. Stacy's current-year alimony deduction is $13,000 [($1,000 + $300) × 10 months].
Answer (A) is incorrect. The mortgage payments are also considered alimony. Answer (C) is incorrect. Child support is not deductible and accounts for $2,000 of the $15,000. Answer (D) is incorrect. The child support payments and the alimony payments for the full year are included in $18,000. Payments were made for only 10 months.

5.4.8. On January 2, Year 1, Ms. D divorced her spouse. The divorce decree called for her to pay her former spouse $500 a month as alimony starting in January Year 1. In June Year 1, her former spouse remarried. D was not aware of this and continued to make payments until February of Year 2. Under state law, D's legal obligation to make the payments ended when her former spouse remarried. What are the correct amounts that must be reported on Ms. D's and her former spouse's tax returns for Year 1?

	Ms. D Alimony Deduction	Former Spouse Alimony Income	Other Income
A.	$3,000	$3,000	$0
B.	$3,000	$3,000	$3,000
C.	$6,000	$3,000	$3,000
D.	$6,000	$6,000	$0

Answer (A) is correct. *(SEE, adapted)*
REQUIRED: The amount of alimony income and deduction under a divorce decree.
DISCUSSION: A deduction for alimony is allowed under Sec. 215. Alimony is required to be included in the recipient's income under Sec. 71(a). In order to be considered alimony, payments must be made under a decree of divorce or separate maintenance, a written instrument incident to such a decree, or a written separation agreement. The payments made after Ms. D's legal obligation ended are not alimony. They are treated as gifts. They are neither includible in the recipient's income nor deductible by the payor.
The alimony at $500 per month for 6 months (January through June) equals $3,000.
Answer (B) is incorrect. The $3,000 paid after the remarriage is treated as a gift, not as other income. Answer (C) is incorrect. The $3,000 paid after the remarriage is treated as a gift, not as other income. It is not deducted by the payor. Answer (D) is incorrect. The payor cannot deduct the $3,000 paid after the remarriage, and it is not included in alimony by the payee. It is treated as a gift.

5.4.9. Mr. D is required, under a divorce decree that was entered into 2 years ago, to make cash alimony payments to his former spouse of $30,000 for each of the next 5 years. The payments are to stop if she remarries. Mr. D made cash payments totaling $30,000 in the first year. Last year, his payments totaled only $14,000 because his former wife remarried. Under the recapture rule limiting front-loaded payments, what is the amount of alimony payments Mr. D will have to recapture in the current year?

    A. $0

    B. $8,000

    C. $15,000

    D. $16,000

Answer (A) is correct. *(SEE, adapted)*
    REQUIRED: The amount of alimony payments that must be recaptured in the current year.
    DISCUSSION: Section 71(f) requires a spouse who makes "excess" alimony payments in the first or second post-separation year to recapture part of those payments in the third post-separation year. Section 71(f) supplies a formula for determining the amount of the payments that are considered "excess" and the amount of these payments that must be recaptured by the payor. Section 71(f)(5)(A) provides an exception to the general recapture rule. Under that exception, if either spouse dies before the close of the third post-separation year or if the payee spouse remarries before the close of the third post-separation year, the payor spouse is relieved of the recapture requirement. Because Mr. D's former spouse remarried before the close of the third post-separation year, Mr. D does not have to recapture any of the alimony payments made in the previous years.
    Answer (B) is incorrect. The recapture based on the spouse not remarrying so soon is $8,000. Answer (C) is incorrect. The amount Mr. D will have to recapture in the current year is not $15,000. The recapture amount is affected by the spouse remarrying. Answer (D) is incorrect. The excess of the first year alimony over last year's alimony is $16,000, which is not the correct way of calculating alimony recapture. In addition, the recapture amount is affected by the spouse's remarriage last year.

5.4.10. Mr. A was divorced 3 years ago. Under the court decree, he is to pay his former wife $100,000 in installments of $15,000 a year for 5 years and $5,000 a year for the following 5 years. Other than the provision that the payments shall end at the death of the spouse, the payments are not subject to any contingencies. Mr. A may deduct the $15,000 he paid in the current year as alimony.

    A. True.

    B. False.

Answer (A) is correct. *(SEE, adapted)*
    DISCUSSION: Divorce decrees executed after 1986 are subject to a 3-year recapture rule. "Excess alimony" is recaptured commencing with the third post-separation taxable year. Recapture occurs by having the payor-spouse include such amounts in gross income and the payee-spouse deduct such amounts. Excess alimony is the sum of the excess payments made in the first and second post-separation taxable years according to formulas found in Sec. 71(f)(3) and (4). To be recaptured, the alimony payment must be at least $15,000. Since the payments are constant for the first 5 years and do not exceed $15,000 in the example, we do not have any excess alimony, and even if excess alimony existed, it would not affect the payor's deduction.

5.4.11. Payment of a former wife's medical expenses is deductible as alimony. A divorce decree requires that the husband pay the wife's future medical expenses in addition to qualifying alimony.

    A. True.

    B. False.

Answer (A) is correct. *(SEE, adapted)*
    DISCUSSION: Only those payments that are included in the recipient's income as alimony under Sec. 71 are deductible by the payor under Sec. 215. For a divorce decree entered prior to 1985, payments from the ex-spouse are included in the recipient's income if they are periodic payments in discharge of a legal obligation that arose under the marital or family relationship and that are imposed under the decree of divorce. If the divorce decree requires the husband to pay the wife's future medical expenses, they are periodic since they are contingent, and they are deductible as alimony. For divorce decrees entered after 1984, the payments would have to be made in cash, and there could be no liability to make payments after the former wife's death. If these requirements are met, the medical payments would be deductible as alimony for divorce decrees after 1984.

5.4.12. David and Jane divorced in the current year. They have two children, ages 6 and 11. The divorce decree requires David to pay $800 a month to Jane and does not specify the use of the money. According to the decree, the payments will stop after the children reach 19 or graduate from high school, whichever comes first. David may deduct the payments as alimony.

    A. True.

    B. False.

Answer (B) is correct. *(SEE, adapted)*
    DISCUSSION: Section 71(c) requires that, if a payment to a former spouse will be reduced when a child attains a certain age, that payment shall be treated as an amount payable for the support of the child. Child support payments are not deductible as alimony.

5.5 IRA Plans

5.5.1. Mr. P was eligible for, and set up as his only retirement plan, an individual retirement account for Year 1 on January 27, Year 2. On February 15, Year 2, P contributed $1,700 to his account. Mr. P's income for Year 1 consisted of the following:

Wages	$10,000
Interest income	3,000
Dividend income	2,100

What is P's deduction for Year 1?

A. $0

B. $1,700

C. $3,000

D. $5,500

Answer (B) is correct. *(SEE, adapted)*
REQUIRED: The taxpayer's deduction for his contribution to an IRA.
DISCUSSION: The maximum amount of a contribution to an IRA that a taxpayer may deduct is the lesser of $5,500 or an amount equal to the compensation that is includible in the individual's gross income for the taxable year [Sec. 219(b)]. In Year 1, P had wages of $10,000; thus, his maximum deduction is limited to $5,500. Since P made a contribution of only $1,700, he may deduct only $1,700. The deduction is for adjusted gross income [Sec. 62(a)(7)].
A contribution can be made after year end if it is made on account of the prior year and no later than the due date of the tax return (without extensions) for such prior year.
Answer (A) is incorrect. Mr. P's deductible amount for the IRA contribution is affected by the contribution amount in relation to the gross income and maximum contribution allowable. Answer (C) is incorrect. The maximum amount of a contribution to an IRA that a taxpayer may deduct is the lesser of $5,500 or an amount equal to the compensation that is includible in the individual's gross income for the taxable year [Sec. 219(b)]. The maximum deduction is affected by the contribution made. Answer (D) is incorrect. A taxpayer cannot deduct more than the smaller of the $5,500 IRA contribution ceiling or the amount actually contributed to the account.

5.5.2. Ms. Seburn had the following during the current year:

Taxable alimony received	$ 4,000
Wages	12,000
Net loss from self-employment	(10,000)
Interest income	3,000

For purposes of an IRA, Ms. Seburn had compensation for the current year of

A. $5,500

B. $6,000

C. $16,000

D. $19,000

Answer (C) is correct. *(SEE, adapted)*
REQUIRED: The total amount of compensation for an IRA of an individual.
DISCUSSION: Section 219(f) defines compensation as earned income. Wages is the most common example of earned income. Taxable alimony is included as compensation for this purpose. There is no provision for reducing earned income by net losses from self-employment. Interest income is not earned income. Therefore, Ms. Seburn had compensation for IRA purposes of

Taxable alimony	$ 4,000
Wages	12,000
Total compensation	$16,000

Answer (A) is incorrect. The maximum deduction allowed for contributions to an IRA is $5,500. Answer (B) is incorrect. The self-employment loss is not deducted when determining total compensation. Answer (D) is incorrect. The interest income is not added to the alimony and wages when determining total compensation.

5.5.3. Harry and Sally are married and both are under age 50. During 2017, Harry earned $3,000 and Sally earned $39,500. Neither is covered by an employer retirement plan. What is the maximum amount they can contribute to their individual retirement accounts for 2017?

A. $5,000

B. $5,500

C. $8,500

D. $11,000

Answer (D) is correct. *(SEE, adapted)*
REQUIRED: The maximum amount of contributions to an IRA.
DISCUSSION: Under Sec. 408(a)(1), contributions to an IRA may not exceed $5,500 on behalf of any individual. This limitation applies separately to each spouse who has compensation and makes a contribution to a separate IRA. No other limitations apply because neither taxpayer is an active plan participant. The $5,500 is limited to the amount of compensation includible in the taxpayer's gross income for the year. However, as of 1997, Harry may use Sally's compensation for purposes of obtaining the combined maximum contribution of $11,000. Taxpayers 50 years old or older are allowed to contribute an additional $1,000.
Answer (A) is incorrect. The maximum deduction for an individual in 2012 was $5,000. Answer (B) is incorrect. The amount one individual can contribute to an IRA for a year is $5,500. Answer (C) is incorrect. Harry may use Sally's compensation for purposes of making a contribution to his individual retirement account.

5.5.4. All of the following types of income are considered earned compensation in determining whether an individual retirement account can be set up and contributions made except

    A. Self-employment income.

    B. Partnership income of an active partner providing services to the partnership.

    C. Alimony.

    D. Rental income from a property in which the taxpayer has active participation.

Answer (D) is correct. *(SEE, adapted)*
    REQUIRED: The item not treated as compensation with respect to contributions to an IRA.
    DISCUSSION: Section 219(f) defines compensation as earned income. Rental income is not generally considered earned income, rather it is treated as a passive form of income.
    Answer (A) is incorrect. Self-employment income is a common example of earned income. Answer (B) is incorrect. Partnership income of an active partner providing services to the partnership is a common example of earned income. Answer (C) is incorrect. Alimony is a common example of earned income.

5.5.5. Mr. Knox wants to make contributions to an IRA (spousal IRA) for his wife. For Mr. Knox to be eligible to make such contributions, all of the following requirements must be met except

    A. They must file a joint return for the tax year.

    B. He must have compensation that must be included in his income for the tax year.

    C. They must be married at the end of the tax year.

    D. His wife must have no taxable compensation for the tax year.

Answer (D) is correct. *(SEE, adapted)*
    REQUIRED: The item that is not a requirement for making contributions to an individual retirement account for a spouse.
    DISCUSSION: Section 219(c) provides rules for deducting contributions to a spousal IRA. If one spouse is eligible to make deductible IRA contributions, the other spouse may contribute up to $5,500 if a joint return is filed. The additional $5,500 spousal IRA deduction is available even if the other spouse has no compensation for the year, provided the amount of compensation (if any) of the spouse for whom the election is being made is less than the gross income of the other spouse. Therefore, it is not a requirement that the wife have no compensation for the tax year.
    Answer (A) is incorrect. A requirement that must be met to be eligible to make contributions to a spousal IRA is they must file a joint return for the tax year. Answer (B) is incorrect. A requirement that must be met to be eligible to make contributions to a spousal IRA is Mr. Knox must have compensation that must be included in his income for the tax year. Answer (C) is incorrect. A requirement that must be met to be eligible to make contributions to a spousal IRA is they must be married at the end of the tax year.

5.5.6. Sol and Julia Crane are married and filed a joint return for 2017. Sol earned a salary of $121,000 in 2017 from his job at Troy Corporation, where he is covered by his employer's pension plan. In addition, Sol and Julia earned interest of $4,500 in 2017 on their joint savings account. Julia is not employed, and the couple had no other income. On January 15, 2018, Sol contributed $5,500 to an IRA for himself and $5,500 to an IRA for his spouse. The allowable IRA deduction in the Cranes' 2017 joint return is

    A. $0

    B. $5,500

    C. $10,000

    D. $11,000

Answer (B) is correct. *(CPA, adapted)*
    REQUIRED: The allowable deduction for a contribution to an IRA when the employee is covered by another plan.
    DISCUSSION: Contributions may be made to an individual retirement account and deducted even if an employee is covered by an employer's plan. The Taxpayer Relief Act of 1997 revised the limits for deductions for active plan participants. Since Sol is an active plan participant, and his income exceeds the phaseout range ($99,000 – $119,000) provided in Sec. 219(g)(8) for active plan participants, he is not allowed a deduction. However, since Julia is not an active plan participant (in 1998 and later years), she may deduct her contribution, as long as she does not exceed the AGI limits in Sec. 219(g)(7). The IRA phaseout rules do not apply to Julia since, when one spouse is not an active plan participant, the IRA phaseout does not occur until the couple's AGI is between $186,000 and $196,000, which is not the case in this problem.
    Answer (A) is incorrect. The phaseout for the inactive spouse starts when AGI reaches $186,000. Answer (C) is incorrect. Julia is not an active plan participant, and she may borrow income from Sol for her contribution. Her interest income is not earned income. However, Sol is an active participant and his income exceeds the phaseout. Answer (D) is incorrect. Sol is an active participant, and his income exceeds the phaseout range.

5.5.7. An investment by an IRA in which of the following assets will not be treated as a distribution?

A. A painting valued at $5,000.

B. Gold bullion exceeding the minimum fineness required to satisfy a regulated futures contract.

C. An antique table determined by an appraiser to be worth over $10,000.

D. A stamp that is appraised at over $5,000 and is over 25 years old.

Answer (B) is correct. *(Publisher, adapted)*
REQUIRED: The investment by an IRA not treated as a distribution.
DISCUSSION: Investments in certain platinum coins or in any gold, silver, platinum, or palladium bullion of fineness equal to or exceeding the minimum fineness required for metals that may satisfy a regulated futures contract, subject to regulation by the Commodity Futures Trading Commission, are not considered distributions [Sec. 408(m)(3)]. However, this provision does not apply unless the bullion is in the physical possession of the IRA trustee.
Answer (A) is incorrect. Paintings are treated as distributions. Answer (C) is incorrect. Antiques are treated as distributions. Answer (D) is incorrect. Stamps are treated as distributions.

5.5.8. Gerald, age 50, withdrew $10,000 from his IRA to pay for the graduate school expenses of his son. His son's educational expenses were $10,000, and he received a $2,000 scholarship from the university to help reduce these expenses. What amount of the withdrawal from the IRA is subject to the 10% early withdrawal tax?

A. $10,000

B. $8,000

C. $2,000

D. $0

Answer (C) is correct. *(Publisher, adapted)*
REQUIRED: The amount of a withdrawal from an IRA subject to early withdrawal tax when the distribution is used to pay educational expenses.
DISCUSSION: The 10% early withdrawal tax will not apply to distributions from an IRA if the taxpayer uses the amounts to pay "qualified higher education expenses" of the taxpayer, the taxpayer's spouse, or any child or grandchild of the taxpayer or the taxpayer's spouse. The Committee Report clearly states that qualified higher education expenses include those related to graduate-level courses. However, the amount of qualified higher education expenses is reduced by the amount of any qualified scholarship, educational assistance allowance, or payment (other than by gift, bequest, device, or inheritance) for an individual's educational enrollment, which is excludable from gross income.
Answer (A) is incorrect. The correct amount of the withdrawal subject to the 10% early withdrawal tax is not $10,000. Answer (B) is incorrect. Qualified educational expenses can be paid with early distributions without a penalty assessed. Answer (D) is incorrect. Qualified educational expenses must be reduced by the amount of the scholarship and other tax-exempt support received.

5.5.9. Tony and Carolyn, both age 52 and married, withdrew $10,000 from their IRA to use as a down payment on the purchase of a home for their son, who has lived with them for the last 5 years. The son has never owned his own personal residence before. The transaction closed 31 days after the distribution from the IRA. What amount of the withdrawal from the IRA is subject to the 10% early withdrawal tax?

A. $10,000

B. $5,000

C. $2,417

D. $0

Answer (D) is correct. *(Publisher, adapted)*
REQUIRED: The amount of a withdrawal from an IRA subject to early withdrawal tax when the distribution is used to purchase a first home for a child.
DISCUSSION: The 10% tax on early distributions from an IRA will not apply to qualified first-time homebuyer distributions. Qualified first-time homebuyer distributions are withdrawals from an IRA of up to $10,000 during an individual's lifetime that are used within 120 days of withdrawal to buy, build, or rebuild a "first" home that is the principal residence of the individual; his or her spouse; or any child, grandchild, or ancestor of the individual or spouse.
Answer (A) is incorrect. The amount of a nonqualifying exempt distribution would be $10,000. Answer (B) is incorrect. This is not the correct amount subject to the 10% early withdrawal tax. Answer (C) is incorrect. The withdrawal is a qualified first-time homebuyer distribution.

5.5.10. On April 15, Year 2, Mr. Thomas filed Form 4868, *Application for Automatic Extension of Time to File*, extending the due date for filing his Year 1 income tax return to October 15, Year 2. By what date must he make his IRA contribution to qualify for an IRA deduction on his Year 1 return?

A. December 31, Year 1.

B. April 15, Year 2.

C. June 30, Year 2.

D. October 15, Year 2.

Answer (B) is correct. *(SEE, adapted)*
REQUIRED: The date by which a taxpayer must make his IRA contribution to qualify for an IRA deduction on his Year 1 return.
DISCUSSION: All IRA contributions for a particular year must be made no later than the due date for filing that year's tax return without regard to any filing extensions that may have been granted [Sec. 219(f)(3)].
Answer (A) is incorrect. December 31, Year 1, is prior to the due date by which Mr. Thomas must make his IRA contribution. Answer (C) is incorrect. June 30, Year 2, includes an extension. Answer (D) is incorrect. October 15, Year 2, includes an extension.

5.5.11. Mr. and Mrs. Smith are both employed and file joint federal income tax returns. Both Mr. and Mrs. Smith are covered by their employers' retirement plans. For 2017, Mr. Smith's salary was $39,000 and Mrs. Smith's was $13,000. They both have IRAs, and their combined modified adjusted gross income was $50,000. Mr. Smith contributed $5,500 to his IRA, and Mrs. Smith contributed $2,750 to her IRA. What is the maximum IRA deduction each is entitled to for 2017?

	Mr. Smith	Mrs. Smith
A.	$5,500	$2,750
B.	$2,750	$1,375
C.	$0	$2,750
D.	$0	$0

Answer (A) is correct. *(SEE, adapted)*
REQUIRED: The maximum deduction a husband and wife may claim on their joint tax return for contributions to separate IRAs when each spouse is covered by an employer's retirement plan.
DISCUSSION: Section 219(g) limits the deductions made to IRAs by individuals filing a joint tax return when one or both are covered by their employers' retirement plans. For the taxpayer covered by the plan, the deduction is phased out beginning when AGI exceeds $99,000 in 2017.
Since the Smiths' income does not exceed the phaseout limit for active participants, they may deduct the entire contribution.
Answer (B) is incorrect. The Smiths' deductions are only limited by their respective contribution amounts. Answer (C) is incorrect. Mr. Smith's contribution does not begin phaseout until AGI exceeds $99,000. Answer (D) is incorrect. The Smiths' contributions do not begin phaseout until AGI exceeds $99,000.

5.5.12. A lump-sum distribution from one retirement program may be reinvested in another retirement program. This rollover must be completed within how many days after receipt of the lump-sum distribution?

A. 30

B. 60

C. 90

D. 120

Answer (B) is correct. *(SEE, adapted)*
REQUIRED: The number of days after receipt of a lump-sum distribution in which a rollover must be completed.
DISCUSSION: Under Sec. 408(d), a lump-sum distribution from one retirement program may be treated as a tax-free rollover if the entire amount received is reinvested in another retirement program not later than the 60th day after the day on which the lump-sum distribution is received.
Answer (A) is incorrect. More than 30 days is allowed for the completion of the rollover. Answer (C) is incorrect. Less than 90 days is allowed for completion of the rollover. Answer (D) is incorrect. Less than 120 days is allowed for completion of the rollover.

5.5.13. Larry and Marge Strong are married and living together. They have decided to file joint federal income tax returns for 2017. Larry is an active participant in his employer's pension plan. Marge is not an active participant in any plan. Each contributed $5,500 to an individual retirement account (IRA) on February 1, 2018. Larry's adjusted gross income is $93,000 and Marge's is $98,000. The deductible portion of Marge's contribution to her IRA is

A. $0

B. $1,100

C. $2,750

D. $5,500

Answer (C) is correct. *(SEE, adapted)*
REQUIRED: The deductible portion of contributions made to an IRA by an individual whose spouse is covered by an employer's pension plan.
DISCUSSION: The Taxpayer Relief Act of 1997 revised the limits for deductions for active plan participants. Since Larry is an active plan participant, and his income exceeds the phaseout range provided in Sec. 219(g)(8) for active plan participants, he is not allowed a deduction. However, since Marge is not an active plan participant (in 1998 and later years), she may deduct her contribution as long as she does not exceed the AGI limits in Sec. 219(g)(7). When one spouse is not an active plan participant, the IRA phaseout occurs when the couple's AGI is between $186,000 and $196,000. Since the combined AGI of Larry and Marge equals $189,000, the phaseout limit applies. A shortcut method of calculating the reduced dollar limit is to subtract the AGI from the initial amount at which the deduction is limited to zero ($196,000 in this case) and multiply the difference by .55. Accordingly, the deduction is limited to $2,750 [($196,000 − $191,000) × .55].
If the shortcut calculation of the reduced dollar limit produces a result that is not a multiple of $10, it is rounded to the next highest multiple of $10. However, if the result is less than $200 but more than zero, the reduced limit is $200.
Answer (A) is incorrect. Marge is permitted to deduct a portion of the $5,500 she contributed to the IRA. The deduction is affected by the couple's AGI. Answer (B) is incorrect. An 80% reduction in the deductible portion is $1,100, which assumes an AGI of $194,000. Answer (D) is incorrect. The maximum deduction allowed for contributions to an IRA is $5,500. Not all of Marge's contribution is deductible because one spouse is an active participant in a pension plan provided by his employer and their modified AGI exceeds $186,000.

5.5.14. An individual retirement account (IRA) is a trust or custodial account created by a written document that must meet all of the following requirements, except

    A. The amount in your account must be fully vested.

    B. Money in your account can be used to buy a life insurance policy.

    C. Assets in your account cannot be combined with other property, except in a common trust fund or common investment fund.

    D. You must start receiving distributions from your account by April 1 of the year following the later of the year in which you reach age 70 1/2 or the year of retirement.

Answer (B) is correct. *(SEE, adapted)*
    REQUIRED: The item that is not a requirement for setting up an individual retirement account.
    DISCUSSION: Under Secs. 219(d) and 408, an IRA account must be fully vested at all times, the assets of the trust cannot be commingled with other property except in a common trust fund or common investment fund, and plan distributions must begin by April 1 of the calendar year following the later of (1) the calendar year in which the individual attains age 70 1/2 or (2) the calendar year in which the individual retires. No part of the trust funds can be used to purchase life insurance contracts.
    Answer (A) is incorrect. The amount in your account must be fully vested. Answer (C) is incorrect. Assets in your account cannot be combined with other property, except in a common trust fund or common investment fund. Answer (D) is incorrect. You must start receiving distributions from your account by April 1 of the later of the year following the year in which you reach age 70 1/2 or the year of retirement.

5.5.15. Sunnie is single and under the age of 50 and does not actively participate in her employer's pension plan. She received taxable compensation of $5,000 in 2016 and $5,500 in 2017. Her modified adjusted gross income was $25,000 in both years. For 2016, she contributed $5,500 to her IRA but deducted only $5,000 on her income tax return. For 2017, she contributed $5,000 but deducted $5,500 on her income tax return. Based on this information, which of the following statements is true?

    A. Sunnie must pay an excise tax on the excess contribution for 2016 and also for 2017 since she did not withdraw the excess.

    B. Sunnie must pay an excise tax for 2016 on the $500 excess contribution made in 2016, but since she properly treated the 2016 excess contribution as part of her 2017 deduction, she does not owe the excise tax for 2017.

    C. Sunnie will be assessed a 10% tax for early withdrawals when she withdraws the excess contribution.

    D. Sunnie should claim an IRA deduction of only $5,000 for 2017.

Answer (B) is correct. *(SEE, adapted)*
    REQUIRED: The true statement regarding deductions and contributions to an IRA.
    DISCUSSION: Section 219(b) limits contributions to an IRA to the lesser of $5,500 (2016) and $5,500 (2017) or the amount of compensation includible in the taxpayer's gross income. Sunnie's 2016 contributions should have been limited to $5,000. She therefore had $500 of excess contributions in 2016 ($5,500 – $5,000). Under Sec. 4973, a nondeductible 6% excise tax is imposed on excess contributions to an IRA. Under Sec. 219(b), the deduction for contributions to an IRA is limited to the lesser of $5,500 (2016) and $5,500 (2017) or the amount of compensation that must be included in gross income. Sunnie's $5,000 deduction in 2016 was correct. In 2017, Sunnie contributed only $5,000 but deducted $5,500. Under Sec. 219(f)(6), Sunnie may treat the $500 unused contributions from 2016 as having been made in 2017. Therefore, her allowable deduction for IRA contributions in 2017 is $5,500.
    Answer (A) is incorrect. Sunnie did not make excess contributions in 2016. Answer (C) is incorrect. A 6% excise tax is assessed when the excess contributions are made. Answer (D) is incorrect. Sunnie can claim an IRA deduction of $5,500 for 2017.

5.5.16. In which situation must a taxpayer pay the additional 10% tax on a premature distribution from his IRA?

    A. Taxpayer, age 45, became totally disabled.

    B. Taxpayer, age 50, died and the IRA was distributed to his beneficiaries.

    C. Taxpayer, age 30, withdrew his entire balance in an IRA and invested it in another IRA at another bank 45 days after the withdrawal from the first bank.

    D. Taxpayer, age 40, used the distribution to pay emergency medical bills for his wife. The medical bills equal 5% of the couple's AGI.

Answer (D) is correct. *(SEE, adapted)*
    REQUIRED: The situation in which the taxpayer must pay the additional 10% tax.
    DISCUSSION: Distributions from an IRA to a participant before (s)he reaches age 59 1/2 are subject to a 10% penalty tax. Taxpayers are exempted from this penalty tax if the distribution is attributable to the taxpayer becoming disabled or is made on or after the taxpayer's death. Certain other exceptions apply, but payment of medical expenses is not one of them unless the medical expenses exceed the Sec. 213 nondeductible floor. Since the medical expenses are only 5% of the couple's AGI, they are below the 10%-of-AGI nondeductible floor, and the 10% penalty applies to the entire distribution.
    Answer (A) is incorrect. The distribution is attributable to the taxpayer becoming disabled. Answer (B) is incorrect. The distribution was made after the taxpayer's death. Answer (C) is incorrect. Reinvesting the proceeds of one IRA into another IRA within 60 days qualifies as a tax-free rollover.

5.5.17. Mark established a Roth IRA at age 40 and contributed $2,000 per year to the account for 20 years. He met the income limits for contributing to the account and was therefore eligible to hold a Roth IRA. Mark now wishes to withdraw the $100,000 of accumulated funds from his Roth IRA. What is the amount of the distribution that is included in Mark's gross income?

A. $0

B. $40,000

C. $60,000

D. $100,000

Answer (A) is correct. *(Publisher, adapted)*
REQUIRED: The amount of a distribution from a Roth IRA included in gross income.
DISCUSSION: Qualified distributions from a Roth IRA are not included in the taxpayer's gross income and are not subject to the 10% early withdrawal tax. To be a qualified distribution, the distribution must satisfy a 5-year holding period and must be (1) made on or after the date an individual attains age 59 1/2, (2) made to a beneficiary (or the individual's estate) on or after the individual's death, (3) attributed to the individual being disabled, or (4) used to pay qualified first-time homebuyer expenses. Since Mark has held the funds over 5 years and is over age 59 1/2, he may withdraw the funds tax-free.
Answer (B) is incorrect. The amount of nondeductible contributions is $40,000. This amount is not gross income when distributed since it was gross income when earned and never deducted. Answer (C) is incorrect. The amount of $60,000 would be gross income if Mark maintained the Roth IRA for less than 5 years or had not attained 59 1/2. Answer (D) is incorrect. The requirements for a qualified distribution are met.

5.5.18. Jamal and Ronee Smith are married and filed a joint return for 2017. Jamal earned a salary of $60,000 in 2017 from his job at Sunshine Corporation. Ronee earned $6,500 from her part-time job at Rain Corporation. On March 1, 2017, Jamal contributed $5,500 to a Roth IRA for himself. What is the maximum contribution Ronee may make in 2017 to her Roth IRA?

A. $0

B. $2,750

C. $5,500

D. $11,000

Answer (C) is correct. *(Publisher, adapted)*
REQUIRED: The maximum Roth IRA contribution for a married couple filing in 2017.
DISCUSSION: Roth IRAs are subject to income limits. Since Ronee has earned income of at least $5,500, she is permitted her maximum contribution of $5,500 for a total yearly IRA contribution of $11,000 for the married couple.
Answer (A) is incorrect. Ronee may make an IRA contribution. Answer (B) is incorrect. Ronee may make an IRA contribution that is not phased out because AGI is not over the threshold. Answer (D) is incorrect. The maximum IRA contribution is $5,500 per individual.

5.5.19. Which of the following is not an account requirement for a Coverdell Education Savings Account?

A. Contributions must be made before the trust beneficiary reaches age 18.

B. All contributions must be in cash.

C. Upon the death of the beneficiary, any balance in the fund must not be distributed to the beneficiary's estate.

D. The trustee must be a bank or other qualified individual.

Answer (C) is correct. *(Publisher, adapted)*
REQUIRED: The statement that is not a requirement of a CESA.
DISCUSSION: A CESA is a tax-exempt trust. Seven requirements must be met for a CESA:

(1) No contribution may be accepted by the CESA after the beneficiary attains age 18.

(2) Except in the case of rollover contributions, annual contributions may not exceed $2,000.

(3) Contributions must be in cash.

(4) The trustee must be a bank or other qualified person.

(5) No portion of the trust's assets may be invested in life insurance contracts.

(6) Trust assets must not be commingled with other property, except in a common trust or investment fund.

(7) Upon death of the beneficiary, any balance in the fund must be distributed to the beneficiary's estate within 30 days of death. A similar rule applies to the beneficiary attaining age 30.

Answer (A) is incorrect. An account requirement for a Coverdell Education Savings Account is that contributions must be made before the trust beneficiary reaches age 18. Answer (B) is incorrect. An account requirement for a Coverdell Education Savings Account is that all contributions must be in cash. Answer (D) is incorrect. An account requirement for a Coverdell Education Savings Account is that the trustee must be a bank or other qualified individual.

5.5.20. Thad Manning is a single taxpayer and under the age of 50. In 2017, Thad earned a salary of $139,000 from his job at Rocky Top Corporation. This was his only source of income for the year. What is the maximum contribution Thad can make to a Roth IRA in 2017?

A. $0

B. $2,200

C. $4,400

D. $5,500

Answer (A) is correct. *(Publisher, adapted)*
REQUIRED: The maximum Roth IRA contribution for a single taxpayer in 2017.
DISCUSSION: Roth IRAs are subject to income limits. The maximum yearly contribution that can be made to a Roth IRA is phased out for single taxpayers with adjusted gross income (AGI) between $118,000 and $133,000. Since Thad's AGI exceeds $133,000, Thad is not allowed any portion of the $5,500 maximum yearly contribution. The $5,500 limit represents the total yearly threshold for contributions to all IRAs.
Answer (B) is incorrect. The correct amount of the maximum contribution Thad can make to a Roth IRA if his AGI was $127,000 is $2,200. Answer (C) is incorrect. The correct amount of the maximum contribution Thad can make to a Roth IRA if his AGI was $121,000 is $4,400. Answer (D) is incorrect. Thad's income is above the phaseout level.

5.5.21. Jim and Carolyn, who are married, establish a Coverdell Education Savings Account to pay for the future college expenses of their infant son. They file jointly and have a modified AGI of $80,000. What is the maximum contribution they can make to a CESA in the current year?

A. $8,000

B. $4,000

C. $1,500

D. $2,000

Answer (D) is correct. *(Publisher, adapted)*
REQUIRED: The maximum contribution available for a CESA.
DISCUSSION: Joint filers with modified AGI below $190,000 ($95,000 for singles) may contribute up to $2,000 per beneficiary (child) per year. The amount a taxpayer is able to contribute to a CESA is limited if modified AGI exceeds certain threshold amounts. The limit is phased out for joint filers with modified AGI at or greater than $190,000 and less than $220,000, and for single filers with modified AGI at or greater than $95,000 and less than $110,000.
Answer (A) is incorrect. The maximum contribution available to Jim and Carolyn for a CESA if they had four children (beneficiaries) is $8,000. Answer (B) is incorrect. The maximum contribution available to Jim and Carolyn for a CESA if they had two children (beneficiaries) is $4,000. Answer (C) is incorrect. The maximum contribution available to Jim and Carolyn for a CESA if their AGI is $197,500 is $1,500.

5.5.22. In the current year, Henry started a new business and needed to pledge all his assets to borrow sufficient start-up and working capital. His IRA account was part of the pledged assets. The account was released from collateral by the end of the current year. Which of the following statements is true?

A. Henry did not engage in a prohibited transaction since he did not take a loan from the account.

B. Henry did not engage in a prohibited transaction since the account was not pledged at year end.

C. Henry engaged in a prohibited transaction by pledging the account as security for a loan.

D. Henry did not engage in a prohibited transaction since he pledged the IRA account for the start-up of his own business, and did not take a direct loan or a distribution from the account.

Answer (C) is correct. *(SEE, adapted)*
REQUIRED: The true statement regarding IRAs.
DISCUSSION: Many qualifications must be met for an investment to qualify as an IRA. One qualification outlined in Sec. 408(e)(7) is that using the investment as collateral must be prohibited.
Answer (A) is incorrect. Henry did engage in a prohibited transaction, even though he did not take a loan from the account. Answer (B) is incorrect. Henry did engage in a prohibited transaction, even though the account was not pledged at year end. Answer (D) is incorrect. Henry did engage in a prohibited transaction, by pledging the IRA account for the start-up of his own business even though this is not a direct loan or a distribution from the account.

5.5.23. Which of the following expenses are qualified higher education expenses for purposes of a Coverdell Education Savings Account?

    A. Tuition and fees.

    B. Books and supplies.

    C. Equipment required for enrollment.

    D. All of the answers are correct.

Answer (D) is correct. *(Publisher, adapted)*
    REQUIRED: The expenses that are qualified higher education expenses for a CESA.
    DISCUSSION: Qualified higher education expenses include tuition, fees, books, supplies, and equipment required for the enrollment at an eligible institution. Additionally, room and board may be qualified expenses if they do not exceed the minimum amounts as determined for federal financial aid programs. Beginning in 2002, expenses will include elementary and secondary education expenses, such as tutoring, computer equipment, room and board, uniforms, and extended day program costs.
    Answer (A) is incorrect. Tuition and fees are qualified higher education expenses for purposes of a CESA. Answer (B) is incorrect. Books and supplies are qualified higher education expenses for purposes of a CESA. Answer (C) is incorrect. Equipment required for enrollment is a qualified higher education expense for purposes of a CESA.

5.5.24. On April 8 of the current year, Alan received a lump-sum distribution of $30,000 cash and stock worth $20,000 from his employer's retirement plan. The stock was not stock of his employer. Alan sold the stock for $30,000, and on June 3 of the current year, he rolled over $60,000 in cash to an individual retirement account ($30,000 from the original distribution and $30,000 from the sale of the stock). What is the amount of gain to be included in Alan's gross income for the current year?

    A. $0

    B. $5,000

    C. $10,000

    D. $20,000

Answer (A) is correct. *(SEE, adapted)*
    REQUIRED: The amount of gain to be included in the current-year gross income.
    DISCUSSION: Under Sec. 408(d), a lump-sum distribution from one retirement program may be treated as a tax-free rollover if the entire amount received is reinvested in another retirement program within 60 days after receipt of the lump-sum distribution. In Alan's case, he reinvested the entire amount received from the distribution into an IRA ($30,000 proceeds from the stock sale and the $30,000 cash). Since he did this within 60 days after the distribution, he qualifies for tax-free rollover treatment [Sec. 402(c)(6)(C)]. No gain is recognized.
    Answer (B) is incorrect. The amount of $5,000 is the 10% penalty for early withdrawal of the lump sum distribution of $50,000 ($30,000 cash + $20,000 stock). The total distribution and gain was rolled over to an IRA within 60 days. Answer (C) is incorrect. The correct amount of gain to be included in Alan's gross income for the current year if he had not rolled the $60,000 into an IRA within 60 days is $10,000. Answer (D) is incorrect. Alan rolled the entire $60,000 into an IRA within 60 days.

5.5.25. If a taxpayer creates a Coverdell Education Savings Account for his or her first child but does not use all of the funds in the account for that child's education, the excess may be rolled over into a CESA for a second child.

    A. True.

    B. False.

Answer (A) is correct. *(Publisher, adapted)*
    DISCUSSION: Any amounts in a CESA that are not used by the fund's beneficiary may be distributed and placed in a CESA for another member of the beneficiary's family.

5.5.26. Distributions from Coverdell Education Savings Accounts in excess of qualified education expenses are not taxable.

    A. True.

    B. False.

Answer (B) is correct. *(Publisher, adapted)*
    DISCUSSION: If a taxpayer receives a distribution of monies from a CESA that is in excess of the eligible education expenses, the distributee's gross income will include the portion of the excess distribution that represents income. The tax imposed on the gross income inclusion will be increased by an additional 10% penalty.

5.5.27. Qualified distributions from a Roth IRA are not included in the taxpayer's gross income and are not subject to the additional 10% penalty for early withdrawal.

    A. True.

    B. False.

Answer (A) is correct. *(Publisher, adapted)*
    DISCUSSION: The tax advantages of a Roth IRA are "backloaded." The buildup of interest and dividends in the account may be tax-free if the withdrawal is considered a qualified distribution. To be a qualified distribution, the distribution must satisfy a 5-year holding period and must be (1) made on or after the date on which an individual attains age 59 1/2, (2) made to a beneficiary (or the individual's estate) on or after the individual's death, (3) attributed to the individual being disabled, or (4) used to pay for qualified first-time home buyer expenses [Sec. 408A(d)(2)].

5.5.28. Walter's modified AGI for the current year is $95,000. During the year he transferred $25,000 from a traditional deductible IRA into a Roth IRA. The total amount of the transfer must be included in his gross income (when determining whether he qualifies for the transfer to a Roth IRA).

A. True.

B. False.

Answer (B) is correct. *(Publisher, adapted)*
DISCUSSION: The $100,000 income limitation was removed after 2008.

5.5.29. A deduction is allowable for a contribution of property to an individual retirement account.

A. True.

B. False.

Answer (B) is correct. *(SEE, adapted)*
DISCUSSION: A deduction is provided for in Sec. 219(a) for a qualified retirement contribution. Section 219(e)(1) defines a qualified retirement contribution as cash paid by the individual or on his or her behalf to an IRA. Thus, deductions are not allowable for a contribution of property to an IRA.

5.5.30. Ms. D died on July 5 of the current year. Her son, who is 25 years of age and had compensation of $25,000 in the current year, inherited her IRA. Ms. D's son may treat the IRA as one established on his behalf and deduct payments that he made to the inherited IRA in the current year.

A. True.

B. False.

Answer (B) is correct. *(SEE, adapted)*
DISCUSSION: A person may deduct contributions made to an inherited IRA only if the IRA was inherited from a spouse. Contributions made to an IRA inherited from someone who died after December 31, 1983, and who was not a spouse are not deductible.

5.5.31. Wendy converts to a Roth IRA in May 2017 when her traditional IRA balance is $300,000. In June 2017 she converts back to a traditional IRA when the account is worth $100,000. By September 2017, the account value had risen to $280,000. Wendy can reconvert to a Roth IRA before the end of the tax year.

A. True.

B. False.

Answer (B) is correct. *(Publisher, adapted)*
DISCUSSION: As of January 1, 2000, any taxpayer who converts an amount from their traditional IRA to a Roth IRA during a post-1999 tax year only to reconvert that amount back to a traditional IRA during the same tax year may not reconvert it yet again to a Roth IRA until the beginning of the next tax year.

5.5.32. Frank, in a total distribution from his employer's retirement plan, received $10,000 cash and $20,000 worth of property. Frank decided to keep the property and roll over into an IRA the $10,000 cash received along with an additional $20,000 cash representing the value of the property received. Frank's transaction would qualify as a tax-free rollover.

A. True.

B. False.

Answer (B) is correct. *(SEE, adapted)*
DISCUSSION: Section 408(d) allows a lump-sum distribution from one retirement plan to be treated as a tax-free rollover if the entire amount received is reinvested in another retirement plan. Only the actual money or property received in the distribution may qualify for rollover treatment. Frank used $20,000 cash that did not come from the distribution to try to accomplish the rollover [Sec. 408(d)(3)(A)(i)]. Therefore, the transaction does not qualify for rollover treatment.

5.5.33. If excess contributions are made to an IRA, an excise tax of 10% will be charged on the excess amounts that remain in the IRA for the year of the excess contribution and for each year thereafter unless corrected.

A. True.

B. False.

Answer (B) is correct. *(SEE, adapted)*
DISCUSSION: Under Sec. 4973, a nondeductible 6% penalty tax is imposed on excess contributions to an IRA. A 10% penalty tax is assessed on premature distributions from an IRA.

5.5.34. Mr. Green turned 70 years old and retired on February 20, Year 1. He must take a minimum distribution from his individual retirement account based on the joint life expectancy of himself and his wife, who is his beneficiary. He will be assessed a 50% excise tax on the required minimum amount unless he takes a distribution by no later than April 1, Year 2.

A. True.

B. False.

Answer (A) is correct. *(SEE, adapted)*
DISCUSSION: Retirement payments must begin no later than April 1 following the later of the calendar year in which the individual reaches age 70 1/2 or the year of retirement. Under Sec. 4974, if the amount distributed during the taxable year is less than the minimum required distribution for such taxable year, a tax will be imposed equal to 50% of the amount by which the minimum required distribution exceeds the actual amount distributed during the taxable year.

5.6 Keogh Plans

5.6.1. Mr. Quill, a self-employed individual, has a qualified defined contribution plan. For the current year, Quill's earned income from his business before payment to his plan was $20,000, and his adjusted gross income was $30,000. What is the maximum deduction allowed Quill for the current year?

A. $3,694

B. $4,000

C. $5,000

D. $20,000

Answer (A) is correct. *(SEE, adapted)*
REQUIRED: The maximum amount that a self-employed person may deduct as a contribution to a defined contribution plan.
DISCUSSION: The deduction for contributions on behalf of a self-employed individual is the same as for corporate contributions to an employee plan. Under Sec. 415(c), the contribution limit is 25% of the earned income derived by the self-employed individual from the trade or business, or $54,000, whichever is less. However, Sec. 401(c) requires the earned income to be reduced by the amount of the deductible contribution. This is a circular computation, and the contribution percentage is modified to 20% for convenience. One-half of the self-employment tax rate times the net earnings from self-employment will also reduce the earned income amount that is calculated under Sec. 401(c).
The maximum deduction allowed is calculated as follows:

Earned income as given	$20,000
Less: Self-employment tax adjustment ($20,000 × .1530 × 1/2)	(1,530)
Contribution base	$18,470
Times: 20%	× 0.20
Allowable deduction	$ 3,694

Answer (B) is incorrect. Twenty percent of earned income without the self-employment tax adjustment is $4,000. Answer (C) is incorrect. The amount of $5,000 is 25% of earned income without the self-employment tax adjustment. Due to the circular computation, percentage is set at less than 25%. Answer (D) is incorrect. The total earned income is $20,000. The deduction is only a portion of adjusted earned income.

5.6.2. All of the following statements concerning Keogh plans are true except

A. If a defined contribution plan is a profit sharing plan, the employer can only make contributions for common-law employees out of net profits.

B. If a plan is a defined benefit plan subject to the minimum funding requirements, the employer must make quarterly installment payments of the required contributions.

C. An employer can have more than one Keogh plan.

D. A separate account is set up for each participant under a defined contribution plan.

Answer (A) is correct. *(SEE, adapted)*
REQUIRED: The false statement regarding Keogh plans.
DISCUSSION: Under Sec. 401(a)(27), contributions made by the employer are not required to be based on profits.
Answer (B) is incorrect. With Keogh plans, if a plan is a defined benefit plan subject to the minimum funding requirements, the employer must make quarterly installment payments of the required contributions. Answer (C) is incorrect. An employer can have more than one Keogh plan. Answer (D) is incorrect. With Keogh plans, a separate account is set up for each participant under a defined contribution plan.

5.6.3. Kirk Bennett, a cash-basis taxpayer, is a self-employed accountant. During the current year, he established a qualified defined contribution retirement plan of which he will be the only beneficiary. In examining his records for the current year, the following information is available:

Earned income from self-employment	$40,000
Interest income	6,000
Dividend income	4,000
Net long-term capital gains	10,000
Adjusted gross income	$60,000

What is the maximum amount that Kirk can deduct as a contribution to his qualified retirement plan for the current year?

A. $7,388

B. $7,500

C. $8,000

D. $10,000

Answer (A) is correct. *(CPA, adapted)*
 REQUIRED: The maximum amount that can be deducted as a contribution to the self-employed individual's qualified retirement plan for the current year.
 DISCUSSION: Under Sec. 415(c), the maximum amount that can be deducted for a contribution on behalf of a self-employed individual is the lesser of $54,000 or 25% of the self-employed individual's earned income from the trade or business. Kirk's only income that qualifies as earned income is $40,000. However, Sec. 401(c) requires the earned income to be reduced by the amount of the deductible contribution. This is a circular computation, and the contribution percentage is modified to 20% for convenience. One-half of the self-employment tax rate times the net earnings from self-employment will also reduce the earned income amount calculated under Sec. 401(c).
 The maximum deduction allowed is calculated as follows:

Earned income	$40,000
Less: Self-employment tax adjustment	
($40,000 × .1530 × 1/2)	(3,060)
Contribution base	$36,940
Times: 20%	× 0.20
Allowable deduction	$ 7,388

 Answer (B) is incorrect. The contribution ceiling is the lesser of $30,000 or 25% of earned income, not 25% of the $30,000 ceiling. Answer (C) is incorrect. The amount of $8,000 is 20% of the $40,000 earned income without the self-employment tax adjustment. Answer (D) is incorrect. The amount of $10,000 is 25% of earned income without the self-employment tax adjustment. Due to the circular computation used to determine the deductible contribution, the deduction is only 20% of earned income less the self-employment tax adjustment.

5.6.4. Which of the following distributions would be subject to the 10% additional tax that is imposed upon premature distributions from a Keogh plan prior to an employee having attained age 59 1/2?

A. A distribution made to an employee after separation from service, if the separation occurred during or after the calendar year in which the employee reached age 55.

B. A distribution made to an employee for medical care to the extent that the distribution does not exceed the amount allowable as a medical expense deduction (determined without regard to whether the employee itemizes deductions).

C. A timely made distribution to reduce excess employee or matching employer contributions (excess aggregate contributions).

D. A distribution made to permit the employee to purchase a vacation home.

Answer (D) is correct. *(SEE, adapted)*
 REQUIRED: The situation which would be subject to the 10% additional tax.
 DISCUSSION: Section 72(t)(2) lists many exceptions to the 10% tax on early distributions from qualified retirement plans. Among the exceptions, early distributions received that are qualified first-time homebuyer distributions will not be subject to the additional tax. A qualified first-time homebuyer distribution is a payment received to the extent the payment is used before the close of the 120th day after the day on which the distribution is received to pay qualified acquisition costs with respect to a principal residence of a first-time homebuyer. However, the purchase of a second personal residence does not meet the exception from the additional tax.
 Answer (A) is incorrect. A distribution made to an employee after separation from service, if the separation occurred during or after the calendar year in which the employee reached age 55, is not subject to the 10% additional tax on premature distributions. Answer (B) is incorrect. A distribution made to an employee for medical care to the extent that the distribution does not exceed the amount allowable as a medical expense deduction (determined without regard to whether the employee itemizes deductions) is not subject to the 10% additional tax on premature distributions. Answer (C) is incorrect. A timely made distribution to reduce excess employee or matching employer contributions (excess aggregate contributions) is not subject to the 10% additional tax on premature distributions.

5.6.5. Before a Keogh plan can qualify for special tax benefits, it must meet all of the following requirements except

    A. Plan assets may not be used for, or diverted to, the employer.

    B. Contributions must be for the exclusive benefit of plan participants or their beneficiaries.

    C. There is no minimum number or percentage of the employees that must be covered by a plan.

    D. A plan can require that the employee reach age 21 to participate, regardless of the employee's length of service.

Answer (C) is correct. *(SEE, adapted)*
    REQUIRED: The false statement regarding Keogh plans.
    DISCUSSION: Section 401(a)(26)(A) requires a minimum number of employees to be covered by the plan. The plan must benefit on each day of the plan year the lesser of 50 employees or 40% or more of all the employees of the employer.
    Answer (A) is incorrect. Plan assets may not be used for, or diverted to, the employer in order for a Keogh plan to qualify for special tax benefits. Answer (B) is incorrect. A requirement a Keogh plan must meet to qualify for special tax benefits is that contributions must be made for the exclusive benefit of plan participants or their beneficiaries. Answer (D) is incorrect. A requirement for a Keogh plan must meet to qualify for special tax benefits is that a plan can require that the employee reach age 21 to participate, regardless of the employee's length of service.

5.6.6. All of the following statements with respect to the requirements of a Keogh plan are true except

    A. An employee must be allowed to participate in a company's Keogh plan if the employee is at least age 21, but not over age 65, and has at least 1 year of service (2 years if the plan provides that after not more than 2 years of service the employee has a nonforfeitable right to all of his or her accrued benefit).

    B. The Keogh plan must be in writing and must be communicated to your employees. The provisions must be stated in the plan.

    C. You can either use a prototype plan approved by the IRS or an individually designed plan to meet specific needs.

    D. Advance IRS approval is not required for an individually designed plan. Approval can be obtained by paying a fee and requesting a determination letter.

Answer (A) is correct. *(SEE, adapted)*
    REQUIRED: The false statement regarding Keogh plans.
    DISCUSSION: A Keogh plan is a qualified plan under Sec. 401. All Sec. 401 plans must meet the age and length-of-service requirements of Sec. 410. Under Sec. 410(a)(2), there must be no maximum age that excludes an employee from participating in the plan.
    Answer (B) is incorrect. The Keogh plan must be in writing and must be communicated to your employees. The provisions must be stated in the plan. Answer (C) is incorrect. With Keogh plans, you can either use a prototype plan approved by the IRS or an individually designed plan to meet specific needs. Answer (D) is incorrect. With Keogh plans, advance IRS approval is not required for an individually designed plan. Approval can be obtained by paying a fee and requesting a determination letter.

5.6.7. Only self-employed persons may deduct contributions to a qualified Keogh plan.

    A. True.

    B. False.

Answer (A) is correct. *(SEE, adapted)*
    DISCUSSION: A Keogh plan is for the self-employed, and only self-employed persons may deduct contributions to a Keogh plan. The contributions for employees of a self-employed person (proprietor or a partner in a partnership) are deductible by the self-employed person as a business expense.

5.6.8. If you are an owner-employee, payments to a Keogh plan may be deducted only if you have net earnings from self-employment.

    A. True.

    B. False.

Answer (A) is correct. *(SEE, adapted)*
    DISCUSSION: The deduction for contributions to a Keogh plan are limited to 25% of the earned income derived by the self-employed individual from the trade or business. If an owner-employee does not have net earnings from self-employment, the deduction limitation is zero.

5.6.9. Contributions to defined contribution plans for self-employed persons in excess of the limits for a year may not be carried forward to later years.

    A. True.

    B. False.

Answer (B) is correct. *(SEE, adapted)*
    DISCUSSION: If the contributions to a defined contribution plan for a self-employed person are in excess of the limit for that tax year, any excess will be deductible in each succeeding taxable year under Sec. 404(a)(1)(E), up to the limit in any one year. However, there is a 10% tax on the excess portion of the contribution (Sec. 4972).

5.6.10. If a self-employed individual's contributions to a Keogh plan are less than the deductible limit, (s)he can carry the unused limit over to a later year.

A. True.

B. False.

Answer (B) is correct. *(SEE, adapted)*
 DISCUSSION: Each year, the annual limit on deductions to a Keogh plan start again. If contributions made in a prior year were less than the deductible limit, the unused limitation may not be carried forward to another year.

5.6.11. Participants in a company's Keogh plan may be permitted to make nondeductible voluntary contributions to the plan in addition to their employer's contribution. These contributions are limited to 10% of the participant's compensation received for all years under all plans and must be considered with deductible contributions for purposes of the limits on contributions and benefits.

A. True.

B. False.

Answer (A) is correct. *(SEE, adapted)*
 DISCUSSION: Contributions may be made to qualified self-employed individual retirement plans (Keogh) both by the employer and the participant. Contributions made by employees are nondeductible. The contributions are limited to 10% of the participant's compensation received for all years under all plans. The employer and employee's contributions are considered as part of the annual addition to the plan for purposes of determining if the limit on contributions and benefits has been exceeded.

5.6.12. XYZ, a cash-basis partnership, provides a retirement plan for all its employees. On March 21, Year 2, the partnership made a payment to the plan administrator, with the designation that it was for Year 1. The partnership return for Year 1 was filed on April 15, Year 2, and this payment was included in the retirement plan deduction. This payment was properly included in the Year 1 return.

A. True.

B. False.

Answer (A) is correct. *(SEE, adapted)*
 DISCUSSION: A contribution to a retirement plan is deemed to have been made on the last day of the preceding year if the payment is made on account of such year and no later than the time for filing the return for such year, including extensions of time to file [Sec. 404(a)(6)]. The partnership return for Year 1 was not due until April 15, Year 2, at which time it was filed. Since the contribution was made no later than the time for the filing of the tax return and was designated for Year 1, it was properly deducted in the tax return for Year 1.

5.7 SEP Plans

5.7.1. All of the following statements concerning a simplified employee pension (SEP) plan are true except

A. Employees whose retirement benefits are part of their union's bargaining agreement with their employer do not have to be considered for coverage under their employer's SEP.

B. A leased employee (an employee who is hired by a leasing organization but who performs services for another) may have to be included in the SEP of the organization receiving the services if certain conditions are met.

C. A qualified employee must be at least 21 years old, have worked at least 3 of the prior 5 years for the employer, and have received at least the minimum amount of compensation required by the Internal Revenue Code.

D. An employer who signs SEP arrangements is required to make contributions to the SEP.

Answer (D) is correct. *(SEE, adapted)*
 REQUIRED: The false statement concerning a simplified employee pension plan.
 DISCUSSION: Section 408(k) describes the requirements for Simplified Employee Pensions. The rules do not include the requirement that an employer must make contributions to the SEP if that employer signs SEP arrangements.
 Answer (A) is incorrect. Employees whose retirement benefits are part of their union's bargaining agreement with their employer do not have to be considered for coverage under their employer's SEP. Answer (B) is incorrect. A leased employee may have to be included in the SEP of the organization receiving the services if certain conditions are met. Answer (C) is incorrect. A qualified employee must be at least 21 years old, have worked at least 3 of the prior 5 years for the employer, and have received at least the minimum amount ($600) of compensation required by the Internal Revenue Code.

5.7.2. Doug, who is self-employed, has a simplified employee pension (SEP). Doug has one employee whose compensation for the current year, before Doug's contribution to his employee's SEP-IRA, was $20,000. Doug had net earnings in the current year of $50,000. What is the maximum deductible contribution Doug can make to his employee's SEP-IRA for the current year?

A. $3,000

B. $5,000

C. $6,000

D. $10,000

Answer (B) is correct. *(SEE, adapted)*
REQUIRED: The maximum deductible contribution that can be made to an SEP.
DISCUSSION: Under Sec. 404(h), the amount of deductible contributions for a simplified employee pension shall not exceed the lessor of 25% of the compensation paid to the employee (2017 maximum of $270,000) during the taxable year or $54,000. Doug's maximum deductible contribution is $5,000 ($20,000 × 25%).
Answer (A) is incorrect. Doug's maximum deductible contribution is equal to 25% of his employee's $20,000 compensation, or $5,000. Answer (C) is incorrect. Doug's maximum deductible contribution is equal to 25% of his employee's $20,000 compensation, or $5,000. Answer (D) is incorrect. Doug's maximum deductible contribution is equal to 25% of his employee's $20,000 compensation, or $5,000.

5.7.3. Ahmed Corporation has 25 employees. Its president has created a simplified employee pension (SEP) plan for its employees. The employees are also permitted to make voluntary contributions to the plan. John, an employee of Ahmed, makes a voluntary contribution of $1,750 to his SEP during the year, which is in addition to his employer's 15% contribution. John is not a participant in any other pension plans. Which of the following statements regarding the deductibility of contributions made by Ahmed Corporation and John to the SEP is true?

	Deduction for Employer Contribution	Deduction for Employee Contribution
A.	Deductible	Deductible for AGI
B.	Deductible	Deductible from AGI
C.	Deductible	Nondeductible
D.	Nondeductible	Nondeductible

Answer (A) is correct. *(Publisher, adapted)*
REQUIRED: The tax treatment for contributions made by an employer and an employee to an SEP.
DISCUSSION: Annual contributions made by employers to a SEP are deductible. Annual contributions made by employees to a SEP are subject to the usual rules for IRAs. Since the employee is not a member of any other qualified pension, profit-sharing, stock bonus, or annuity plan, his contributions to the SEP will be deductible for AGI up to $18,000.
Answer (B) is incorrect. A deduction for an employee contribution to a SEP is not deductible from AGI. Answer (C) is incorrect. There is a deduction for employee contribution to a SEP. Answer (D) is incorrect. There are deductions for both employer and employee contributions to a SEP.

5.7.4. If you make contributions to your simplified employee pension IRA (SEP-IRA), you can deduct them the same as contributions to a regular IRA, up to the amount of your deduction limit or 100% of your taxable compensation for the year, whichever is less.

A. True.

B. False.

Answer (B) is correct. *(SEE, adapted)*
DISCUSSION: For purposes of computing contributions and deductions, simplified employee pension IRAs (SEP-IRAs) are deducted up to $54,000 or 25% of your taxable compensation for the year, whichever is less.

5.8 SIMPLE Plans

5.8.1. SIMPLE retirement plans are available to

A. Employers with 50 or fewer employees who received at least $5,000 in compensation from the employer in the preceding year.

B. Employers with 75 or fewer employees who received at least $10,000 in compensation from the employer in the preceding year.

C. Employers with 100 or fewer employees who received at least $5,000 in compensation from the employer in the preceding year.

D. Employers with 100 or fewer employees who received at least $3,000 in compensation from the employer in the preceding year.

Answer (C) is correct. *(Publisher, adapted)*
REQUIRED: The employer eligible to adopt a SIMPLE retirement plan.
DISCUSSION: Employers with 100 or fewer employees who received at least $5,000 in compensation from the employer in the preceding year may adopt a SIMPLE retirement plan if they do not maintain another qualified plan. The plan allows employees to make contributions of up to $12,500 per year (2017) and requires that employers match those contributions. Assets in the account are not taxed until withdrawn, and the employer may usually deduct contributions made to the employees' accounts.
Answer (A) is incorrect. SIMPLE retirement plans are available to employers with more than 50 employees who received at least $5,000 in compensation from the employer in the preceding year. Answer (B) is incorrect. SIMPLE retirement plans are not available to employers with 75 or fewer employees who received at least $10,000 in compensation from the employer in the preceding year. Answer (D) is incorrect. SIMPLE retirement plans are available to employers with 100 or fewer employees who received at least $5,000 in compensation from the employer in the preceding year.

5.8.2. The SIMPLE plan must be available to every employee who

A. Received at least $5,000 in compensation from the employer during each of the 2 preceding years and is reasonably expected to receive at least $5,000 in compensation during the current year.

B. Received at least $5,000 in compensation from the employer during either of the 2 preceding years and is reasonably expected to receive at least $5,000 in compensation during the current year.

C. Received at least $5,000 in compensation from the employer during the 2 preceding years.

D. Is reasonably expected to receive at least $5,000 in compensation during the current year.

Answer (A) is correct. *(Publisher, adapted)*
REQUIRED: The employee who is eligible to participate in a SIMPLE plan.
DISCUSSION: The SIMPLE plan must be available to every employee who (1) received at least $5,000 in compensation from the employer during any 2 preceding years and (2) is reasonably expected to receive at least $5,000 in compensation during the current year. Individuals that are self-employed may also participate in a SIMPLE plan. However, certain nonresident aliens and employees who are covered by a collective bargaining agreement may be unable to participate.
Answer (B) is incorrect. An individual is required to have received at least $5,000 in compensation from the employer during both of the preceding years. Answer (C) is incorrect. An individual who is not reasonably expected to receive at least $5,000 in compensation during the current year is unable to participate in a SIMPLE plan. Answer (D) is incorrect. An individual who did not receive at least $5,000 in compensation during the current year is unable to participate in a SIMPLE plan.

5.8.3. Participants of SIMPLE plans who take early withdrawals are generally subject to

A. A 10% withdrawal penalty.

B. A 25% withdrawal penalty.

C. A 25% withdrawal penalty on the first $10,000 and a 10% withdrawal penalty on the remainder.

D. A 25% withdrawal penalty on withdrawals made during the 2-year period beginning on the date the participant began participating in the plan, and a 10% withdrawal penalty on all other early distributions.

Answer (D) is correct. *(Publisher, adapted)*
REQUIRED: The applicable early withdrawal penalty for SIMPLE plans.
DISCUSSION: Participants are considered to have taken early withdrawals if the distributions are made before age 59 1/2. These distributions are generally subject to a 10% early withdrawal penalty. However, employees who withdraw contributions during the 2-year period beginning on the date the participant began participating in the SIMPLE plan will be assessed a 25% early withdrawal penalty tax.
Answer (A) is incorrect. The 10% withdrawal penalty is only applicable to early withdrawals after the first 2 years the employee participates in the plan. Though this is not a false answer, it is not the best (most complete) choice. Answer (B) is incorrect. Participants of SIMPLE plans who take early withdrawals are only subject to a 25% withdrawal penalty during the first 2 years of plan participation. Answer (C) is incorrect. Participants of SIMPLE plans who take early withdrawals are subject to the various penalties based on time as a plan participant.

5.8.4. All of the following are characteristics of a SIMPLE 401(k) plan except

A. An employer that employs over 100 employees or maintains another qualified plan may not adopt a SIMPLE plan as part of a 401(k) arrangement.

B. An employer has the option of reducing the matching contribution to less than 3% of an employee's compensation.

C. A SIMPLE 401(k) plan is deemed to satisfy the special nondiscrimination test applicable to employee elective deferrals and employer matching contributions if the plan satisfies the contribution requirements applicable to SIMPLE plans.

D. A SIMPLE 401(k) plan is not subject to the top-heavy rules for any year the plan satisfies the contribution requirements applicable to SIMPLE plans.

Answer (B) is correct. *(Publisher, adapted)*
REQUIRED: The false statement regarding characteristics of a SIMPLE 401(k) plan.
DISCUSSION: An employer does not have the option, as under a SIMPLE plan structured like an IRA, of reducing the matching contribution to less than 3% of an employee's contribution.
Answer (A) is incorrect. A characteristic of a SIMPLE 401(k) plan is that an employer that employs over 100 employees or maintains another qualified plan may not adopt a SIMPLE plan as part of a 401(k) arrangement. Answer (C) is incorrect. A SIMPLE 401(k) plan is deemed to satisfy the special nondiscrimination test applicable to employee elective deferrals and employer matching contributions if the plan satisfies the contribution requirements applicable to SIMPLE plans. Answer (D) is incorrect. A SIMPLE 401(k) plan is not subject to the top-heavy rules for any year the plan satisfies the contribution requirements applicable to SIMPLE plans.

5.8.5. All of the following are true statements about the rollover characteristics of a SIMPLE plan except

A. A participant may roll over distributions from one SIMPLE account to another SIMPLE account tax-free.

B. A participant may roll over distributions from a SIMPLE account to a qualified plan tax-free.

C. A participant may roll over distributions from a SIMPLE account to an IRA without penalty if the individual has participated in the SIMPLE plan for 2 years.

D. A participant may not roll over distributions from a SIMPLE account to a tax-sheltered annuity arrangement tax-free.

Answer (B) is correct. *(Publisher, adapted)*
REQUIRED: The false statement about the rollover consequences of a SIMPLE account.
DISCUSSION: A participant may roll over distributions tax-free from one SIMPLE account to another SIMPLE account. In addition, a participant may roll over distributions from a SIMPLE account to an IRA without penalty if the individual has participated in the SIMPLE plan for at least 2 years. A participant may not, however, roll over tax-free distributions from a SIMPLE account to a qualified plan.
Answer (A) is incorrect. A participant may roll over distributions from one SIMPLE account to another SIMPLE account tax-free. Answer (C) is incorrect. A participant may roll over distributions from a SIMPLE account to an IRA without penalty if the individual has participated in the SIMPLE plan for 2 years. Answer (D) is incorrect. Distributions from a SIMPLE account cannot be rolled over to a tax-sheltered annuity arrangement free of tax.

5.8.6. All of the following are true statements about contributions to SIMPLE IRA plans except

A. Employee contributions have to be expressed as a percentage of the employee's compensation and cannot exceed $12,500 in 2017.

B. Unless an election is made otherwise, the employer must match the elective contribution of an employee in an amount not exceeding 3% of the employee's compensation.

C. A SIMPLE IRA contribution cannot be made directly to the employee in cash.

D. An employer may elect to limit its matching contribution, for all eligible employees, to a smaller percentage of compensation, but not less than 1%.

Answer (C) is correct. *(Publisher, adapted)*
REQUIRED: The false statement regarding contribution requirements to a SIMPLE IRA plan.
DISCUSSION: A SIMPLE IRA must allow each eligible employee to elect to have the employer make payments either directly to the employee in cash or as a contribution, expressed as a percentage of compensation, to the SIMPLE account. Elective contributions are limited to $12,500 in 2017. The employer must match the elective contribution of an employee in an amount not exceeding 3% of the employee's compensation. However, an employer may elect to limit its match to a smaller percentage of compensation not to fall below 1%.
Answer (A) is incorrect. Employee contributions to a SIMPLE IRA plan have to be expressed as a percentage of the employee's compensation and cannot exceed $12,500 in 2017. Answer (B) is incorrect. Unless an election is made otherwise, the employer must match the elective contribution of an employee to a SIMPLE IRA in an amount not exceeding 3% of the employee's compensation. Answer (D) is incorrect. An employer may elect to limit its matching contribution to a SIMPLE IRA, for all eligible employees, to a smaller percentage of compensation, but not less than 1%.

5.8.7. Contributions to the SIMPLE account are deductible by a participant in the year the contributions are made. Distributions from a SIMPLE account are excludable from an employee's gross income when received.

A. True.

B. False.

Answer (B) is correct. *(Publisher, adapted)*
DISCUSSION: Contributions to the SIMPLE account are excludable from an employee's income. Distributions from a SIMPLE account are includible in a participant's income when withdrawn from the account.

5.9 Archer Medical Savings Accounts

5.9.1. Archer medical savings account (MSA) contributions are subject to an annual limitation, which is

A. Only the income earned from the business in the case of a self-employed individual.

B. Only the compensation earned from the employer.

C. Only the compensation earned from the employer or the income earned from the business, in the case of the self-employed.

D. A percentage of the required "high deductible" health plan amount.

Answer (D) is correct. *(Publisher, adapted)*
REQUIRED: The annual limitation of contributions to an Archer MSA.
DISCUSSION: Participation in an Archer MSA is conditioned upon coverage under a high-deductible plan [Sec. 220(c)(2)]. Contributions are subject to an annual limitation that is a percentage of the deductible of the required high-deductible health plan. For individual coverage, the annual limit is 65% of the deductible. For family coverage, the annual limit is 75% of the deductible. If one spouse has family coverage, they both fall under the 75% limit and must split the amount between themselves. No deduction is allowed if an individual received excludable employer contributions.

5.9.2. Who is eligible for an Archer medical savings account (MSA) in 2017?

A. All individuals that elected coverage in a high-deductible health plan.

B. A maximum of 750,000 individuals who have elected coverage in a high-deductible health plan and are only self-employed.

C. All individuals that elected coverage in a high-deductible health plan and are only employed by a small employer with no more than 50 workers when the Archer MSA is established.

D. A maximum of only 750,000 individuals who have elected coverage in a high-deductible health plan and are either self-employed or employed by a small employer with no more than 50 workers when the Archer MSA is established.

Answer (D) is correct. *(Publisher, adapted)*
REQUIRED: The individual who is eligible for an Archer MSA.
DISCUSSION: The 1996 act limited the availability of Archer MSAs during the pilot period (1997-2007) to 750,000 individuals who buy a high-deductible health insurance plan and are either self-employed or employed by a small employer. The law defines a small employer as one with no more than 50 workers. However, the law provides relief for businesses that are qualified to provide Archer MSAs but then grow to employ up to 200 workers.
Answer (A) is incorrect. Not all individuals that elected coverage in a high-deductible health plan are eligible for an Archer medical savings account. Answer (B) is incorrect. The individual can either be self-employed or employed by a small employer. Answer (C) is incorrect. The individual can also be self-employed.

5.9.3. Employer contributions to an Archer medical savings account (MSA) are

A. Not included in the income of the employee and not included on the employee's W-2.

B. Not included in the income of the employee unless made through a cafeteria plan, and included on the employee's W-2.

C. Included in income unless made through a cafeteria plan.

D. None of the answers are correct.

Answer (B) is correct. *(Publisher, adapted)*
REQUIRED: The treatment of employer contributions to an Archer MSA.
DISCUSSION: Archer MSAs are like IRAs created to defray unreimbursed medical expenses. Contributions to the account by an individual are deductible from adjusted gross income, and contributions made by the employer are excluded from income (unless made through a cafeteria plan). Employee contributions must be reported on the employee's W-2. Earnings of the fund are not included in taxable income for the current year.
Answer (A) is incorrect. Employer contributions are reported on the W-2. Answer (C) is incorrect. Employer contributions are not included in income. Answer (D) is incorrect. Employer contributions are not included in income but are reported on the W-2.

5.9.4. When funds from an Archer MSA are distributed for qualified medical expenses, these funds are

A. Generally included in the income of the taxpayer.

B. Allocated between contributions made by the employer and the employee, and only the amount attributed to the contributions of the employee are included in income of the taxpayer.

C. Generally excluded from the income of the taxpayer.

D. Always included in the income of the taxpayer.

Answer (C) is correct. *(Publisher, adapted)*
    REQUIRED: The proper treatment of distributions from an Archer medical savings account (MSA).
    DISCUSSION: Distributions for qualified medical expenses incurred for the benefit of the individual, a spouse, or dependents are generally excluded from income. Qualified medical expenses usually are unreimbursed expenses that would be eligible for the medical expenses deduction. However, no exclusion is available if the medical care expense is incurred during a month when the individual is not eligible to participate in an Archer MSA or if the individual's contributions have been made to the Archer MSA for that year.
    Answer (A) is incorrect. Distributions are generally excluded from income. Answer (B) is incorrect. Funds from an Archer MSA distributed for qualified medical expenses are not allocated between contributions made by the employer and the employee, with only the amount attributed to the contributions of the employee being included in income. Answer (D) is incorrect. These distributions usually are excluded from income.

5.9.5. The deduction for Archer medical savings accounts is properly included with other medical insurance and medical expenses as an itemized deduction subject to the 10% limitation.

A. True.

B. False.

Answer (B) is correct. *(SEE, adapted)*
    DISCUSSION: Archer medical savings accounts are like IRAs created to defray unreimbursed medical expenses. Contributions to the account by an individual are deductible from gross income, and contributions made by the employer are excluded from income (unless made through a cafeteria plan). Employee contributions must be reported on the employee's W-2. Earnings of the fund are not included in taxable income for the current year.

5.10 Moving Expenses

5.10.1. Which of the following is a deductible moving expense?

A. Cost of lodging while in transit.

B. Loss on sale of your personal residence.

C. Attorney fees to sell personal residence.

D. Real estate commissions to sell personal residence.

Answer (A) is correct. *(Publisher, adapted)*
    REQUIRED: The item that is a deductible moving expense.
    DISCUSSION: Reasonable expense of traveling, including lodging, from the former residence to the new residence is a moving expense under Sec. 217(b)(1)(B).
    Answer (B) is incorrect. The loss on the sale of a personal use asset is not deductible. Answer (C) is incorrect. Expenses incidental to the sale or exchange of the former residence are not deductible. Answer (D) is incorrect. Expenses incidental to the sale or exchange of the former residence are not deductible.

5.10.2. Marc Clay was unemployed for all of Year 1. In January of Year 2, Clay obtained full-time employment 60 miles away from the city where he had resided during the 10 years preceding Year 2. Clay kept his new job for all of Year 2. In January of Year 2, Clay paid direct moving expenses of $3,000 in relocating to his new city of residence, but he received no reimbursement for these expenses. In his Year 2 income tax return, Clay's direct moving expenses are

A. Not deductible.

B. Fully deductible only if Clay itemizes his deductions.

C. Fully deductible from gross income in arriving at adjusted gross income.

D. Deductible subject to a 2% threshold if Clay itemizes his deductions.

Answer (C) is correct. *(CPA, adapted)*
    REQUIRED: The proper tax treatment of unreimbursed moving expenses.
    DISCUSSION: Section 217 provides that an employee may deduct as an above-the-line deduction in arriving at adjusted gross income under Sec. 62(a)(15) the reasonable expenses of moving himself and his family from one location to another, provided that the move is related to the commencement of work in a new location. To be eligible for the deduction, the new place of work must be at least 50 miles farther from the taxpayer's old residence than his old place of work was from his old residence. Also, the taxpayer must be employed full-time for at least 39 weeks during the 12-month period following the move. As Clay has met the commencement-of-work test, the distance test, and the length of employment test and has received no reimbursement, he may deduct the moving expenses as a deduction that reduces gross income to arrive at adjusted gross income.
    Answer (A) is incorrect. The expenses are deductible. Answer (B) is incorrect. Unreimbursed moving expenses are above-the-line deductions after December 31, 1993. Answer (D) is incorrect. Moving expenses are not itemized deductions; they are deducted when determining AGI.

5.10.3. Which of the following expenses qualifies as a deductible moving expense?

- A. Settling your lease at the old location.
- B. Cost of moving personal goods.
- C. Real estate commission.
- D. Improvements to enhance salability of old residence.

Answer (B) is correct. *(Publisher, adapted)*
REQUIRED: The expense associated with selling or moving from a residence that qualifies as a deductible moving expense.
DISCUSSION: The definition of moving expenses under Sec. 217(b) includes only reasonable expenses of moving household goods and personal effects, and of travel (including lodging) from the former residence to the new residence [Sec. 217(b)(1)]. Improvements to enhance the salability of an old residence, selling fees, and lease settlement costs do not qualify as moving expenses.
Answer (A) is incorrect. Settling your lease at the old location is not an eligible moving expense. Answer (C) is incorrect. Real estate commission is not an eligible moving expense. Answer (D) is incorrect. Improvements to enhance salability of old residence is not an eligible moving expense.

5.10.4. All of the following will qualify as a moving expense for computing the allowable moving expense deduction except

- A. Cost of transporting members of the taxpayer's family to the new home.
- B. Amount of security deposit placed on an apartment at the new location.
- C. Cost of lodging while traveling to new location.
- D. Cost of moving personal and household articles to the new residence.

Answer (B) is correct. *(Publisher, adapted)*
REQUIRED: The item not qualifying as a deductible moving expense.
DISCUSSION: Regulation 1.217-2(b)(7)(iv) specifically provides that no deduction is permitted for payment or prepayments of rent or for payments representing the cost of a security or other similar deposit. Further, after December 31, 1993, indirect moving expenses are not deductible.
Answer (A) is incorrect. Travel expense of individuals for whom both the old and the new residences are the principal place of abode is a deductible moving expense under Sec. 217(b)(2). Answer (C) is incorrect. It is a deductible moving expense under Sec. 217(b)(1). Answer (D) is incorrect. It is a deductible moving expense under Sec. 217(b)(1).

5.10.5. Mr. P and his nonworking spouse made a move that qualifies for the moving expense deduction. They paid the following expenses in the current year after Mr. P got his new job:

Transportation of household goods	$8,000
Pre-move travel for housshunting	900
Travel from old residence to new	400
Temporary living expenses for 20 consecutive days in new location	1,900
Real estate commission on sale of old residence	4,800

What is their moving expenses deduction?

- A. $3,000
- B. $8,400
- C. $11,200
- D. $16,000

Answer (B) is correct. *(SEE, adapted)*
REQUIRED: The taxpayers' allowable moving expense deduction.
DISCUSSION: Section 217(a) allows a deduction for moving expenses paid or incurred in connection with the commencement of work by the taxpayer at a new place of work. The expenses of actually moving the taxpayer, family, and household goods are deductible without limit. After December 31, 1993, indirect moving expenses, including a househunting trip, temporary living expenses, and expenses related to the sale, purchase, or lease of a residence are no longer deductible. In addition, meals during the move are no longer deductible. Mr. and Mrs. P's deduction for moving expense is limited to $8,400.

Expenses of the actual move:	
Household goods	$8,000
Family	400
Moving expense deduction	$8,400

Answer (A) is incorrect. The amount of $3,000 was the limit for house-hunting trips, qualified residence acquisition costs, and temporary living costs under the old rules that applied to tax years 1993 and before. Answer (C) is incorrect. Indirect moving expenses are no longer deductible; therefore, the extra $3,000 should not be included. Answer (D) is incorrect. Only direct moving expenses are deductible.

5.10.6. All of the following statements regarding moving expenses are true except

    A. If you are an employee, you must work full-time for at least 39 weeks during the first 12 months after arrival in the new job area.

    B. If you are self-employed, you must work full-time for at least 39 weeks during the first 12 months and for a total of at least 78 weeks during the first 24 months after arrival in the new job area.

    C. You do not have to meet the time test to deduct your moving expenses if you moved to the United States because you retired.

    D. If you are married and file a joint return and both you and your spouse work full-time, either of you may satisfy the full-time work test, and you can add the weeks your spouse worked to those you worked to satisfy the test.

Answer (D) is correct. *(SEE, adapted)*
    REQUIRED: The false statement regarding moving expenses.
    DISCUSSION: If the taxpayer is married and files a joint return, either spouse can meet the full-time requirement, but weeks worked by both spouses cannot be combined to satisfy the test.
    Answer (A) is incorrect. Regarding moving expenses, if you are an employee, you must work full-time for at least 39 weeks during the first 12 months after arrival in the new job area. Answer (B) is incorrect. Regarding moving expenses, if you are self-employed, you must work full-time for at least 39 weeks during the first 12 months and for a total of at least 78 weeks during the first 24 months after arrival in the new job area. Answer (C) is incorrect. Regarding moving expenses, you do not have to meet the time test to deduct your moving expenses if you moved to the United States because you retired.

5.10.7. Which of the following is not allowed as a deductible moving expense?

    A. Moving household goods and personal effects.

    B. In-transit storage expenses for household goods and personal effects.

    C. Meal expense incurred in traveling to a new home.

    D. Traveling, including lodging, to a new home.

Answer (C) is correct. *(SEE, adapted)*
    REQUIRED: The cost not deductible as a moving expense.
    DISCUSSION: The definition of moving expenses under Sec. 217(b) includes only reasonable expenses of moving household goods and personal effects and of travel (including lodging) from the former residence to the new residence [Sec. 217(b)(1)]. Indirect moving expenses, including meals during the move, are not deductible.
    Answer (A) is incorrect. Moving household goods and personal effects is an allowable moving expense as provided for under Sec. 217(b)(1). Answer (B) is incorrect. In-transit storage expenses for household goods and personal effects are allowable moving expenses as provided for under Sec. 217(b)(1). Answer (D) is incorrect. Traveling, including lodging, to a new home is an allowable moving expense as provided for under Sec. 217(b)(1).

5.10.8. Mr. B, a single taxpayer, moved to a new city in Year 1 to start a new job and properly deducted moving expenses on his Year 1 income tax return. In Year 2, the expenses became nondeductible because Mr. B failed to meet the full-time work test when he voluntarily quit the job. Which of the following is the proper action to take?

    A. Mr. B can secure an extension for the 39-week test.

    B. Mr. B must include the expenses in gross income on his return in the year he returns to work.

    C. Mr. B must either amend his Year 1 return or report the amount previously deducted as income on his Year 2 return.

    D. Mr. B must amend his Year 1 return but can reduce the gain on the sale of his residence by the amount of the moving expenses.

Answer (C) is correct. *(SEE, adapted)*
    REQUIRED: The proper action when a taxpayer becomes ineligible after deducting moving expenses.
    DISCUSSION: To be eligible for a moving expense deduction, an employee must be employed on a full-time basis at the new location for 39 weeks in the 12-month period following the move [Sec. 217(c)(2)]. Regulation 1.217-2(d)(3) provides that a taxpayer, who deducts moving expenses and then is no longer able to satisfy the minimum period of employment condition, may either include the amount previously deducted in the current year's gross income or file an amended return for the year in which the deduction was taken and not claim the deduction.
    Answer (A) is incorrect. The 39-week test may not be extended. Answer (B) is incorrect. If the prior tax return is not amended, the expenses must be included in gross income in the current year. Answer (D) is incorrect. The prior year's tax return need not be amended, and moving expenses may not reduce the gain on the sale of a residence unless they are selling expenses.

5.10.9. Ms. C, a single taxpayer, accepted a new job that required a move from Chicago, Illinois, to Miami, Florida, in the current year. She incurred and paid the following moving expenses:

Real estate commission on sale of residence	$2,000
Cost of moving household and personal goods	2,200
Travel expenses to new residence	550
Cost of decorating new apartment residence	1,200
Temporary (15 days) living expenses at new location	750
Loss of membership in the country club at old residence	1,000

Ms. C was reimbursed $2,500 by her employer who did not include this amount in the wages reported on her W-2 form for the current year. Assume the distance and time requirements were properly met. What is Ms. C's allowable moving expense deduction for the current year?

A. $250

B. $2,200

C. $2,750

D. $4,750

Answer (A) is correct. *(SEE, adapted)*
REQUIRED: The taxpayer's allowable moving expense deduction for the current year.
DISCUSSION: The deduction for the moving expenses is provided in Sec. 217 when a taxpayer commences employment at a new place of work that is at least 50 miles farther from the old residence than was the old place of work.

The deductibility of indirect moving expenses, including expenses of househunting trips; temporary living costs; meals; and expenses related to the sale, purchase, or lease of a residence, were eliminated after December 31, 1993. Ms. C's moving expense deduction is

Moving household goods	$2,200
Travel to new residence	550
	$2,750

A reimbursement for moving expenses must be included in gross income under Sec. 82. However, qualified moving expenses reimbursed by an employer are excluded from the employee's gross income as a qualified fringe benefit under Sec. 132 to the extent that they are a reimbursement for expenses that are deductible moving expenses under Sec. 217 if directly paid or incurred by an employee. No adjustment needs to be made to the amount of the gross income that is reported by Ms. C since the reimbursement offsets a portion of the otherwise deductible moving expenses. Because the reimbursement is excluded from gross income, only the $250 of deductions that are in excess of the reimbursement ($2,750 – $2,500) is deductible as a for-AGI expense.
Answer (B) is incorrect. Travel expenses to the new residence are deductible. However, the qualified expenses must first be offset against the reimbursement. Answer (C) is incorrect. All of the moving expenses that qualify for a deduction are $2,750. Answer (D) is incorrect. The real estate commission is an indirect expense and therefore not deductible.

5.10.10. Rich and Lisa moved in May of the current year because Lisa was starting a new job in June. The following distances relate to the move:

Miles from former home to former job	10
Miles from new home to former job	57
Miles from new home to new job	7
Miles from former home to new job	51

Rich and Lisa have met the distance test for deducting their moving expenses.

A. True.

B. False.

Answer (B) is correct. *(SEE, adapted)*
DISCUSSION: Section 217 allows a deduction only if the taxpayer's new principal place of work is at least 50 miles farther from the old residence than was the former principal place of work.

Former home to new job	51 miles
Less: former home to former job	(10 miles)
Difference	41 miles

Rich and Lisa have failed to meet the distance test for deducting moving expenses as the new principal place of work is only 41 miles farther from the old residence than was the former principal place of work.

5.10.11. Fred lived in Michigan and attended a local university. Upon graduation, he secured a job in Houston, Texas. This will be Fred's first full-time job. Fred's moving expenses are not deductible.

A. True.

B. False.

Answer (B) is correct. *(SEE, adapted)*
DISCUSSION: Section 217(c) requires the taxpayer's new principal place of work to be at least 50 miles farther from his or her former residence than the former principal place of work was. However, if the taxpayer had no former principal place of work, the new place of work must be at least 50 miles from his or her former residence. There are no other requirements concerning a former place of work.

5.11 Interest on Education Loans

5.11.1. Kathy paid $8,000 of interest on qualified education loans in 2017. Kathy is not claimed as a dependent by another taxpayer. Since she graduated from medical school 7 years ago, she has faithfully paid the minimum interest due each month. What is the maximum deduction available to her for education loan interest in 2017?

A. $0

B. $500

C. $2,500

D. $8,000

Answer (C) is correct. *(Publisher, adapted)*
REQUIRED: The amount of qualified education loan interest available for a deduction to arrive at AGI.
DISCUSSION: Beginning in 1998, individuals are allowed to deduct interest paid during the tax year on any qualified education loan. The maximum amount that may be deducted is $2,500 after 2000 under Sec. 221(b).
Answer (A) is incorrect. Kathy qualifies to deduct qualified education loan interest. Answer (B) is incorrect. The amount of $500 fails to maximize the amount of qualified education loan interest Kathy is allowed to deduct. Answer (D) is incorrect. Qualified education loan interest deduction is limited. The amount of $8,000 exceeds the limit.

5.11.2. Rebecca graduated from college in 2015. She refinanced her qualified education loans in 2016 with another loan. She is not claimed as a dependent by another taxpayer. What is the maximum deduction available to her for the $3,000 paid for education loan interest in 2017?

A. $0

B. $2,000

C. $2,500

D. $3,000

Answer (C) is correct. *(Publisher, adapted)*
REQUIRED: The maximum for-AGI deduction available to an individual who refinances qualified education loan interest.
DISCUSSION: Beginning in 1998, individuals are allowed to deduct interest paid during the tax year on any qualified education loan. The maximum deduction for 2017 is $2,500 [Sec. 221(b)]. A qualified education loan also encompasses debt used to refinance the qualified education loan. Note, however, that if a homeowner obtains a home equity loan to refinance the qualified education debt, the homeowner may not utilize both the mortgage interest deduction and the education loan interest deduction.
Answer (A) is incorrect. Rebecca qualifies to deduct qualified education loan interest. Qualified education loan encompasses debt used to refinance the loan. Answer (B) is incorrect. The maximum deduction available to Rebecca is not $2,000. Answer (D) is incorrect. The amount of $3,000 exceeds the maximum deduction available to Rebecca in 201.

5.11.3. All of the following are requirements for a qualified education loan interest deduction except

A. The loan is incurred to pay the costs of attending an eligible educational institution, less adjustments for certain nontaxable educational benefits.

B. An eligible educational institution includes post-secondary educational institutions, certain vocational schools, and an institution conducting an internship or residency program leading to a degree or certificate awarded by an institution of higher education, a hospital, or a health care facility that offers postgraduate training.

C. The deduction for interest on qualified education loans is allowed only with respect to interest paid on the loan during the first 60 months in which interest payments could be made, regardless of whether the payment is deferred or not.

D. The deduction for interest on qualified education loans is an "above-the-line" (for-AGI) deduction that is allowed whether or not the taxpayer itemizes other deductions on Schedule A of Form 1040.

Answer (C) is correct. *(Publisher, adapted)*
REQUIRED: The item that is not required for a deduction of qualified education loan interest.
DISCUSSION: The deduction for interest on a qualified education loan must no longer meet the 60-month requirement after 2002.
Answer (A) is incorrect. A requirement for a qualified education loan interest deduction is that the loan is incurred to pay the costs of attending an eligible educational institution, less adjustments for certain nontaxable educational benefits. Answer (B) is incorrect. A requirement for a qualified education loan interest deduction is that an eligible educational institution includes post-secondary educational residency program leading to a degree or certificate awarded by an institution of higher education, a hospital, or a health care facility that offers postgraduate training. Answer (D) is incorrect. A qualified education loan interest deduction is an "above-the-line" (for-AGI) deduction that is allowed whether or not the taxpayer itemizes other deductions on Schedule A of Form 1040.

5.12 Educator Classroom Expenses

5.12.1. During 2017, Caitlin served as a kindergarten aide for 1,000 hours. She incurred $350 in expenses for books and supplies used in the classroom and was not reimbursed by the school. What amount is Caitlin entitled to deduct as an education expense on her 2017 income tax return?

A. $175

B. $250

C. $350

D. $0

Answer (B) is correct. *(Publisher, adapted)*
REQUIRED: The amount that may be deducted as a higher education expense.
DISCUSSION: Primary and secondary school educators may claim an above-the-line deduction for up to $250 annually in unreimbursed expenses paid or incurred for books and supplies used in the classroom. An eligible educator is an individual who, for at least 900 hours during a school year, is a kindergarten through grade 12 teacher, instructor, counselor, principal, or aide. Therefore, Caitlin may deduct $250 as an education expense.
Answer (A) is incorrect. The deduction is not limited to 50% of Caitlin's unreimbursed expenses. Answer (C) is incorrect. The classroom education expense deduction is limited to an amount below $350. Answer (D) is incorrect. Caitlin qualifies for a deduction.

5.12.2. A married couple may deduct up to $500 on a joint return for educator expenses.

A. True.

B. False.

Answer (A) is correct. *(Publisher, adapted)*
DISCUSSION: If a joint return is filed and both spouses are eligible educators, the maximum deduction is $500. However, neither spouse may deduct more than $250 of his or her qualified expenses.

5.12.3. Home schooling expenses may be deductible as educator classroom expenses.

A. True.

B. False.

Answer (B) is correct. *(Publisher, adapted)*
DISCUSSION: Qualified educator expenses do not include expenses for home schooling or for nonathletic supplies for courses in health or physical education.

Use **Gleim Test Prep** for interactive study and easy-to-use detailed analytics!

STUDY UNIT SIX
DEDUCTIONS FROM AGI

6.1 Medical Expenses

6.1.1. Which one of the following expenses does not qualify as a deductible medical expense?

A. Cost of long-term care for a developmentally disabled person in a relative's home.

B. Special school for a deaf child to learn lip reading.

C. Cost of elevator installed for individual who had heart bypass surgery (in excess of increase in value of individual's home).

D. Cost and care of guide dogs used by a blind person in his business.

Answer (A) is correct. *(SEE, adapted)*
REQUIRED: The expense that does not qualify as a deductible medical expense.
DISCUSSION: Section 213 allows a deduction for expenses paid for medical care of the taxpayer, spouse, and dependents to the extent such expenses exceed 10% of adjusted gross income. The term medical care includes amounts paid for the diagnosis, cure, mitigation, treatment, or prevention of a disease or physical handicap, or for the purpose of affecting any structure or function of the body [Sec. 213(d)]. The cost of keeping a developmentally disabled person in a relative's home is an expenditure for the support of the person and does not fall within the definition of medical care. The cost of institutional care could be deductible as a medical expense. If the developmentally disabled person met the definition of "chronically ill," the care would qualify as a deductible medical expense.
Answer (B) is incorrect. Cost of a special school for a deaf child to learn lip reading is an expenditure for the mitigation of a physical handicap. Therefore, it is a deductible medical expense. Answer (C) is incorrect. Cost of an elevator installed for an individual who had heart bypass surgery (in excess of increase in value of individual's home) is an expenditure for mitigation of a disease. Therefore, it is a deductible medical expense. Answer (D) is incorrect. Cost and care of guide dogs used by a blind person in his business is an expenditure for the mitigation of a physical handicap, and is a deductible medical expense.

6.1.2. Which of the following qualify as deductible medical expenses?

1. Payments to physician

2. Payments for elective cosmetic face-lifting operation

3. Medical portion of your auto insurance premium (although not separately stated)

4. Payments for acupuncture service

5. Domestic help

A. 1, 3, and 5.

B. 1 and 5.

C. 1, 2, and 4.

D. 1 and 4.

Answer (D) is correct. *(SEE, adapted)*
REQUIRED: The expenditure(s) qualifying as deductible medical expenses.
DISCUSSION: Payments to a physician and payments for acupuncture service are both expenditures made for the diagnosis, cure, mitigation, treatment, or prevention of disease, or for the purpose of affecting any structure or function of the body. Accordingly, they fall within the definition of medical care under Sec. 213 and are deductible expenses.
Expenditure 2 is not a deductible expense under Sec. 213 unless the procedure was necessary to "ameliorate a deformity arising from, or directly related to, a congenital abnormality, a personal injury resulting from an accident or trauma, or disfiguring disease." Expenditures 3 and 5 are also not deductible medical expenses. Although insurance covering medical care is a deductible medical expense, if the insurance contract covers losses other than medical care and the charge for the medical insurance is not separately stated, no portion of the premium may be deducted as a medical expense. Domestic help does not fall within the definition of medical care under Sec. 213(d) and is not deductible.
Answer (A) is incorrect. The medical portion of the auto insurance premium and the domestic help are not deductible medical expenses. Answer (B) is incorrect. The domestic help does not qualify as a deductible medical expense. Answer (C) is incorrect. The payment for cosmetic face-lifting does not qualify as a deductible medical expense.

6.1.3. Which one of the following expenditures qualifies as a deductible medical expense for tax purposes?

    A. Vitamins for general health not prescribed by a physician.

    B. Health club dues.

    C. Transportation to physician's office for required medical care.

    D. Mandatory employment taxes for basic coverage under Medicare A. Taxpayer is covered by Social Security.

Answer (C) is correct. *(CPA, adapted)*
    REQUIRED: The expenditure that qualifies as a deductible medical expense for tax purposes.
    DISCUSSION: Section 213(d) defines medical care as including transportation for needed medical care.
    Answer (A) is incorrect. Vitamins for general health not prescribed by a physician are not for the purpose of curing any specific ailment or disease and do not qualify as a deductible medical expense for tax purposes. Answer (B) is incorrect. Health club dues are costs incurred for the purpose of improving the taxpayer's general health and not for the purpose of curing any specific ailment or disease, which disqualifies them as deductible medical expenses for tax purposes. Answer (D) is incorrect. Medicare A premiums are not deductible unless voluntarily paid by a taxpayer otherwise ineligible for coverage (Rev. Rul. 79-175). The amounts withheld from wages (or paid on self-employment income) under Medicare A are considered to be paid as taxes.

6.1.4. Which of the following is deductible as medical insurance?

    A. Medical portion of auto insurance policy that provides coverage for all persons injured in or by the taxpayer's car.

    B. Insurance policy that pays you $50 a day if you are unable to work due to illness or injury.

    C. Medicare Part B.

    D. None of the answers are correct.

Answer (C) is correct. *(SEE, adapted)*
    REQUIRED: The item deductible as medical insurance.
    DISCUSSION: To qualify for a deduction, a medical expense must be paid during the taxable year for the taxpayer, the taxpayer's spouse, or a dependent and must not be compensated for by insurance or otherwise during the taxable year. The basic cost of Medicare insurance (Medicare Part A) is not deductible unless voluntarily paid by the taxpayer for coverage. However, the extra cost of Medicare (Medicare Part B) is deductible.
    Answer (A) is incorrect. If an insurance contract covers both medical care and nonmedical care, none of the insurance premium is deductible unless the amount of the premium allocable to medical care insurance is separately stated. Answer (B) is incorrect. Premiums paid on a policy that merely pays the insured a specified amount per day are not deductible. Answer (D) is incorrect. Medicare Part B is deductible as medical insurance.

6.1.5. Scott is an 8-year-old with a rare lung problem. His doctor wants him to be examined by a specialist at the Mayo Clinic. Scott and his mother travel to Rochester, Minnesota. Scott is not sick enough to be admitted to the hospital, so he stays in a nearby hotel from which he can go to the hospital daily for the specialist to monitor his reaction to a new drug. Scott and his mother have separate rooms so that Scott can rest properly. They remain for 10 nights and the rooms each cost $60 per night. How much is allowable as a medical expense?

    A. $500

    B. $600

    C. $1,000

    D. $1,200

Answer (C) is correct. *(Publisher, adapted)*
    REQUIRED: The amount paid for lodging away from home that is deductible as a medical expense.
    DISCUSSION: Section 213(d)(2) provides special rules for amounts paid for lodging away from home related to medical care. The amounts paid for lodging will be considered paid for medical care if the medical care is provided by a physician in a licensed hospital and if there is no significant element of personal pleasure, recreation, or vacation in the travel away from home. The amount for lodging is limited to $50 for each night for each individual (including a parent with his or her child). Therefore, Scott and his mother are limited to $100 per night for 10 nights, or $1,000.
    Answer (A) is incorrect. The maximum medical expense allowed for one person for the 10 days is $500; however, expenses incurred by a parent are also deductible. Answer (B) is incorrect. The total medical expense incurred for one person is $600. The deductible amount for lodging is limited to $50 per night per person. Answer (D) is incorrect. The total expenses incurred for the medical trip is $1,200. The deductible amount for lodging is limited to $50 per night per person.

6.1.6. Josef had to have the following improvements made to his home in the current year because he was handicapped:

Cost of ramps (January 1)	$ 300
Increase in value of home due to ramps	0
Cost of decorative lattice work over ramp area (January 2)	100
Increase in value of home due to lattice work	0
Cost of chair lift on stairs (January 2)	2,500
Increase in value of home due to chair lift	1,500
Cost of repairing ramps (December 1)	50
Cost of repairing chair lift (December 1)	200

None of the expenses were covered by insurance. How much would qualify as a deductible medical expense in the current year (before any limitations)?

A. $1,450

B. $1,550

C. $2,800

D. $3,050

Answer (B) is correct. *(SEE, adapted)*
REQUIRED: The amount of home improvements deductible as a medical expense.
DISCUSSION: Capital expenditures are generally not deductible as medical expenses [Reg. 1.213-1(e)(1)(iii)]. However, a capital expenditure related to the care of a sick person is deductible. The IRS's position is that home-related capital expenditures incurred by a physically handicapped individual are deductible only to the extent the expenditures exceed any increase in the value of the property. The repair costs are also deductible. Therefore, Josef may deduct only $1,550.

Cost of ramps	$ 300
Cost of chairlift	2,500
Less: Increased home value	(1,500)
Cost of repairing ramps	50
Cost of repairing chairlift	200
	$1,550

Decorative latticework would not be a medical expense.
The Committee Reports to the 1986 TRA indicated an intent to allow a deduction for the full cost of such expenditures, but such a provision was not included in the law. Nevertheless, the IRS did publish a list of certain capital expenses that it feels do not ordinarily increase the value of a residence. Two of the items on this list are constructing ramps and widening doorways. Since the facts of the question indicate a definite increase in value, only the excess is deductible.
Answer (A) is incorrect. The cost of the lattice work is not deductible, but the cost of repairing the chair lift is deductible. Answer (C) is incorrect. The increase in home value due to the chair lift is the only item that is not a deductible medical expense. Answer (D) is incorrect. The increase in home value from the chair lift should be subtracted from expenditures when determining the deductible medical expense.

6.1.7. Mr. E, a 50-year-old, single taxpayer, had an adjusted gross income of $10,000 for the current year. In addition, he paid the following expenses:

Surgeon's fee (outpatient)	$600
Psychiatrist's fee	700
Hospital bill as follows:	
Medical services	300
Meals in hospital	200
Hospital room charge	500
Transportation to/from doctor's office and hospital	50
Contact lenses	200
Prescription drugs	80
Vitamins for general health	60
Weight-loss program	300
Chiropractor's fee	400

Mr. E also paid $900 for medical insurance premiums and received reimbursement of $850 from the insurance company on claims for the above expenses. Compute Mr. E's current-year medical deduction for Schedule A.

A. $1,930

B. $2,080

C. $2,580

D. $3,080

Answer (B) is correct. *(SEE, adapted)*
REQUIRED: The medical expense deduction for the current year on Schedule A.
DISCUSSION: Section 213 allows a deduction for medical care expenses to the extent that they exceed 10% of adjusted gross income. Medicine and drugs are limited to prescription drugs and insulin. Vitamins and the weight-loss program are not deductible because they are for the purpose of improving the taxpayer's general health and not for a specific ailment. The total amount of expenses paid during the year must be reduced by the amount of insurance reimbursements received.

Surgeon's fee	$ 600
Psychiatrist's fee	700
Hospital bills ($300 + $200 + $500)	1,000
Transportation	50
Contact lenses	200
Prescription drugs	80
Chiropractor's fee	400
Medical insurance premium	900
	$3,930
Less: insurance reimbursement	(850)
	$3,080
Less: 10% of AGI	(1,000)
Medical expense deduction	$2,080

Answer (A) is incorrect. The full cost of the hospital medical services should be included, not just 50%. Answer (C) is incorrect. The weight loss program is not deductible, and the medical insurance premiums are deductible. Additionally, the amount of medical expenses should be reduced by the amount of the reimbursement and by the 10%-of-AGI limit. Answer (D) is incorrect. The total medical expenses is $3,080, which should be reduced by the 10%-of-AGI limit.

6.1.8. Al Daly's adjusted gross income for the year ended December 31, Year 1, was $20,000. He was not covered by any medical insurance plan. During Year 1, he paid $600 to a physician for treatment of a heart condition. He also owed the physician $900 for an operation performed in December Year 1, which he paid in January Year 2. In addition, Daly incurred a $1,900 hospital bill in Year 1, which he charged to his bank credit card in December Year 1, and paid to the bank in January Year 2. Daly's total allowable medical deduction for Year 1 is

A. $0

B. $500

C. $1,500

D. $2,500

Answer (B) is correct. *(CPA, adapted)*
REQUIRED: The allowable medical expense deduction for Year 1.
DISCUSSION: The taxpayer may only deduct medical expenses that were paid during the year. The taxpayer may not deduct as a medical expense the balance owed for an operation performed during the year, but it will be deductible in Year 2 when paid. The taxpayer may deduct the medical expense charged on a bank credit card, even though the bank was not paid until the following year. Daly's total allowable medical expense deduction is

Payment to physician	$ 600
Hospital bill	1,900
Total expenses	$2,500
Less: 10% AGI	(2,000)
Allowable medical expense deduction	$ 500

Answer (A) is incorrect. Daly is entitled to a medical deduction. Answer (C) is incorrect. The result of subtracting a 5%-of-AGI (and not a 10%-of-AGI) nondeductible floor is $1,500. Answer (D) is incorrect. The amount of medical expenses that qualify for a deduction before deducting the 10%-of-AGI nondeductible floor is $2,500.

6.1.9. Gail and Jeff Payne are married and filed a joint return for the current year. During the year, they paid the following doctors' bills:

For Gail's mother, who received over half of her support from Gail and Jeff but who does not live in the Payne household and who earned $2,000 in the current year for baby-sitting	$700
For their unmarried 26-year-old son, who earned $4,000 in the current year but was fully supported by his parents. He is not a full-time student	500

Disregarding the adjusted gross income percentage test, how much of these doctors' bills may be included on the Paynes' joint return in the current year as qualifying medical expenses?

A. $0

B. $500

C. $700

D. $1,200

Answer (D) is correct. *(CPA, adapted)*
REQUIRED: The total amount of qualifying medical expenses.
DISCUSSION: Section 213(a) allows a deduction for expenses paid for medical care of the taxpayer, his or her spouse, or a dependent. Dependent is defined in Sec. 152 to include the mother of the taxpayer and the son of the taxpayer if each received over half of his or her support from the taxpayer. Gail's mother and son are thus considered dependents for purpose of the medical deduction, regardless of their gross income or filing status (these other factors do affect the availability of the dependency exemption). Therefore, all the medical expenses incurred by Gail and Jeff ($1,200) for their son and Gail's mother are considered qualifying medical expenses.
Answer (A) is incorrect. There are qualifying medical expenses. Answer (B) is incorrect. The expenses incurred by Gail's mother are also deductible. Answer (C) is incorrect. The son's medical expenses are also deductible.

6.1.10. During Year 2, Scott charged $4,000 on his credit card for his dependent son's medical expenses. Payment to the credit card company had not been made by the time Scott filed his income tax return in Year 3. However, in Year 2, Scott paid a physician $2,800 for the medical expenses of his wife who died in Year 1. Disregarding the adjusted gross income percentage threshold, what amount could Scott claim in his Year 2 income tax return for medical expenses?

A. $0

B. $2,800

C. $4,000

D. $6,800

Answer (D) is correct. *(CPA, adapted)*
REQUIRED: The deductible amount of medical expenses paid for a spouse who died in the prior year and also a son.
DISCUSSION: Section 213(a) allows a deduction for expenses paid for medical care of the taxpayer, his or her spouse, or a dependent. Therefore, the $4,000 of medical expense paid for the son is deductible. The fact that it was charged on a credit card does not affect the deduction. Medical expenses are deductible in the year in which they are paid. Therefore, the $2,800 of medical expenses paid for the wife who died in the prior year is deductible in Year 2. Scott's total deductible expenses before the limitation is $6,800 ($4,000 + $2,800).
Answer (A) is incorrect. There are qualifying medical expenses that can be claimed. Answer (B) is incorrect. The bills charged to the credit card also qualify for the medical expense deduction. Answer (C) is incorrect. The wife's medical expenses also qualify for the medical expense deduction since medical expenses are deductible in the year in which they are paid.

6.1.11. Ruth and Mark Cline are married and will file a joint income tax return this year. Among their expenditures during this year were the following discretionary costs that they incurred for the sole purpose of improving their physical appearance and self-esteem:

Face-lift for Ruth, performed by a licensed surgeon	$5,000
Hair transplant for Mark, performed by a licensed surgeon	3,600

Disregarding the adjusted gross income percentage threshold, what total amount of the aforementioned doctors' bills may be claimed by the Clines in their current-year return as qualifying medical expenses?

A. $0

B. $3,600

C. $5,000

D. $8,600

Answer (A) is correct. *(CPA, adapted)*
REQUIRED: The amount deductible as medical expense.
DISCUSSION: Cosmetic surgery is defined as "any procedure which is directed at improving the patient's appearance and does not meaningfully promote the proper function of the body or prevent or treat illness or disease" [Sec. 213(d)(9)(B)]. The cost of cosmetic surgery is not deductible under Sec. 213(d)(9), unless it is necessary to ameliorate a deformity arising from, or directly related to, a congenital abnormality, a personal injury resulting from an accident or trauma, or disfiguring disease.
Answer (B) is incorrect. The cost of the hair transplant is not a qualifying medical expense since it represents cosmetic surgery. Answer (C) is incorrect. The cost of the face lift is not a qualifying medical expense since it represents cosmetic surgery. Answer (D) is incorrect. The cost of the hair transplant and the cost of the face lift are not qualifying medical expenses since they represent cosmetic surgery.

6.1.12. The cost and maintenance of a guide dog for a blind person is a qualified medical expense.

A. True.

B. False.

Answer (A) is correct. *(SEE, adapted)*
DISCUSSION: Section 213(d) includes in the definition of medical expense amounts paid for the mitigation of disease or handicap. The cost and maintenance of a guide dog for a blind person is an expenditure made for the mitigation of the taxpayer's handicap.

6.1.13. During the current year, Mr. R paid medical expenses for his wife who died last year. He remarried and is filing a joint return for the current year with his second wife. Mr. R may not include the medical expenses for his first wife on the joint return with his second wife.

A. True.

B. False.

Answer (B) is correct. *(SEE, adapted)*
DISCUSSION: Medical expenses are deductible in the year in which they are paid. Since Mr. R incurred the expenditures for the medical care of his first wife in the previous year, he may deduct the expenditures in the year they are paid [Reg. 1.213-1(a)], even on a joint return filed with his second wife.

6.1.14. Last year, Joe's niece was his dependent. This year, she no longer qualifies as his dependent. However, he paid $800 this year for medical expenses she incurred last year when she was his dependent. Joe can include the $800 in figuring this year's medical expense deduction.

A. True.

B. False.

Answer (A) is correct. *(SEE, adapted)*
DISCUSSION: The deduction is allowed for a person who was either a spouse or a dependent at the time medical services were rendered or at the time the expenses were actually paid. Since Joe's niece was his dependent at the time the medical services were rendered, he can deduct the $800 of medical expenses for his niece.

6.1.15. Kathy and Rob have been legally divorced for 2 years. Their son, Tommy, lived with Kathy for all of the current year. Kathy and Rob provide 100% of Tommy's support. Kathy, as the custodial parent, was allowed to claim Tommy as a dependent on her current-year federal income tax return. Rob paid for $1,000 of Tommy's medical expenses. Rob cannot include the $1,000 as a medical expense on his current-year federal income tax return because he was not allowed the exemption for Tommy.

A. True.

B. False.

Answer (B) is correct. *(SEE, adapted)*
DISCUSSION: Section 213(d)(5) provides that any child of divorced or separated parents shall be treated as a dependent of both parents for purposes of the medical expense deduction.

6.1.16. For the current year, Mr. Q had adjusted gross income of $10,000. His itemized deductions included qualifying medical expenses of $1,000. A reimbursement of the previous year's medical expenses in the amount of $400 was received this year. If Mr. Q itemizes his deductions in the current year, he must reduce his medical expenses by the $400 reimbursement received.

A. True.

B. False.

Answer (B) is correct. *(SEE, adapted)*
   DISCUSSION: Regulation 1.213-1(g)(1) provides that, when a reimbursement for medical expenses is received in a taxable year subsequent to a year in which the expense was deducted, the reimbursement must be included in gross income in the year received. This amount may be excluded from gross income if no tax benefit was received for the deduction (e.g., the taxpayer claimed a standard deduction in the previous year).

6.1.17. In the previous year, Mrs. D installed an elevator in her house on the advice of her doctor because of a persistent heart condition. The elevator cost $10,000, and the fair market value of Mrs. D's house increased $4,000 due to the elevator being installed. In the current year, Mrs. D paid $1,000 for repairs to the elevator. Since the cost of the elevator was not entirely deductible in the previous year, Mrs. D may only deduct a portion of the $1,000 as a medical expense deduction for the current year.

A. True.

B. False.

Answer (B) is correct. *(SEE, adapted)*
   DISCUSSION: Home-related capital expenditures incurred by a physically handicapped individual are deductible. An example is an elevator needed for someone with a heart condition. Once a capital expense qualifies as a medical expense, amounts paid for the operation and upkeep also qualify as a medical expense. This is true even if the original capital expenditure was not entirely deductible (because it may have increased the fair market value of the residence). Therefore, the entire $1,000 for repairs to the elevator is deductible as a medical expense.

6.2 Taxes

6.2.1. Taxes deductible as an itemized deduction include all of the following except

A. Real estate taxes based on the assessed value of the property and charged uniformly against all property.

B. State and local income taxes.

C. Taxes that the taxpayer paid on property owned by his or her parents or children.

D. Personal property taxes based on the value of the personal property.

Answer (C) is correct. *(SEE, adapted)*
   REQUIRED: The tax that is not deductible as an itemized deduction.
   DISCUSSION: Section 164(a) lists the taxes that are deductible from adjusted gross income; state and local income taxes withheld, real estate taxes paid, and personal property taxes are deductible as itemized deductions. However, taxes paid on another person's property are not deductible because the tax liability is the liability of the other person.
   Answer (A) is incorrect. Under Sec. 164(a), real estate taxes based on the assessed value of the property and charged uniformly against all property, are taxes deductible as an itemized deduction. Answer (B) is incorrect. State and local income taxes are deductible as an itemized deduction under Sec. 164(a). Answer (D) is incorrect. Personal property taxes based on the value of the personal property are deductible as an itemized deduction under Sec. 164(a).

6.2.2. All of the following taxes are deductible on Schedule A (Form 1040) except

A. State or local inheritance tax.

B. State income tax.

C. State real estate tax on a personal residence.

D. Occupational tax charged at a flat rate by a locality for the privilege of working there.

Answer (A) is correct. *(SEE, adapted)*
   REQUIRED: The tax not deductible on Schedule A of Form 1040.
   DISCUSSION: No deduction is allowed for state or local inheritance taxes. On the federal estate tax return, a deduction may be allowed, but for income tax purposes, no deduction is available.
   Answer (B) is incorrect. Section 164(a) specifically lists state income taxes as a deduction. Answer (C) is incorrect. Section 164(a) also specifically lists state and local (and foreign) real property taxes as a deduction. Answer (D) is incorrect. Section 164(a) provides a deduction for taxes paid or accrued in carrying on a trade or business or activity related to the production of income. An occupational tax paid by an employee would be deductible on Schedule A (subject to the 2% floor on miscellaneous itemized deductions). A similar tax paid by a self-employed individual is deductible on Schedule C.

6.2.3. Which of the following taxes may be deducted on Form 1040, Schedule A?

A. Homeowners' association charges.

B. Assessments for sewer lines.

C. State income taxes on municipal bond interest.

D. State and local taxes on gasoline.

6.2.4. George Burke, a salaried taxpayer, paid the following taxes which were not incurred in connection with a trade or business during the current year:

Federal income tax (withheld by employer)	$1,500
State income tax (withheld by employer)	1,000
FICA tax (withheld by employer)	700
State sales taxes	900
Federal auto gasoline taxes	200
Federal excise tax on telephone bills	50

What taxes are allowable deductions from Burke's adjusted gross income for the current year?

A. $2,850

B. $2,550

C. $1,900

D. $1,000

6.2.5. During the current year, Paul and Mary Davis, cash-basis taxpayers, paid the following taxes:

State income taxes withheld	$ 300
Estimated federal income tax	250
Estimated state income tax	1,500
Sales tax on new auto used 60% for business	1,400
State gift tax	1,000
Property tax, including $50 for trash pickup	2,600
Property tax on their vacation home in Canada	1,000

What amount can Mary and Paul claim as an itemized deduction on their current-year federal income tax return?

A. $4,350

B. $5,350

C. $6,350

D. $6,400

Answer (C) is correct. *(SEE, adapted)*
REQUIRED: The tax that may be deducted on Form 1040, Schedule A.
DISCUSSION: Section 164(a) allows a deduction for state income taxes (even if the income is exempt from federal tax). Since this is not allowed as a deduction in arriving at adjusted gross income as defined in Sec. 62, it is an itemized deduction as defined in Sec. 63(d) and is reported on Schedule A.
Answer (A) is incorrect. Homeowners' association charges are not a tax; they are a type of private dues for services provided. Answer (B) is incorrect. An assessment for sewer lines is a payment for a special benefit tending to increase the value of the property and is not deductible under Sec. 164. Answer (D) is incorrect. Gasoline taxes are not deductible except as a business expense.

Answer (D) is correct. *(CPA, adapted)*
REQUIRED: The taxes that are allowable deductions from adjusted gross income.
DISCUSSION: Section 164(a) lists the taxes that are deductible from adjusted gross income. These include the state income tax of $1,000.
Section 164 does not allow a deduction for federal income taxes in any case. FICA tax, federal gasoline taxes, and federal excise taxes are deductible only if incurred as trade or business expenses or for the production of income. Taxpayers are allowed an itemized deduction for the higher of the state income tax or the state sales tax. Since the state income tax is greater, Burke would deduct it instead of the sales tax.
Answer (A) is incorrect. FICA tax, federal auto gasoline taxes, and federal excise taxes are not deductible. The sales tax is deductible only in lieu of state income tax. Answer (B) is incorrect. Federal income tax and federal excise taxes are not deductible. Answer (C) is incorrect. State sales taxes are only deductible in lieu of state income tax.

Answer (B) is correct. *(SEE, adapted)*
REQUIRED: The amount of taxes paid that can be claimed as an itemized deduction.
DISCUSSION: Section 164(a) allows a deduction for state, local, and foreign real property taxes. This would include $1,000 tax on the vacation home and $2,550 of other property taxes ($2,600 – $50 trash pickup fee). A deduction is also allowed for state income taxes. This would include the $300 of state income taxes withheld and the $1,500 of estimated state income taxes. Section 164 does not allow a deduction for federal income taxes in any case. The business portion of the sales tax paid on the automobile would be deducted as a business expense on the taxpayer's Schedule C through the claiming of a depreciation deduction, not as an itemized deduction on Schedule A and the personal portion of the sales tax could be deductible as an itemized deduction. An itemized deduction is allowed for the higher of the state income tax or the state sales tax. Section 164 does not allow a deduction for gift taxes. The $50 fee paid for trash pickup would not be allowed as an itemized deduction.

State income taxes withheld	$ 300
Estimated state income tax	1,500
Property tax ($2,600 – $50 trash pickup)	2,550
Property tax -- vacation home	1,000
	$5,350

Answer (A) is incorrect. The property tax on the vacation home is also deductible. Answer (C) is incorrect. State gift tax is not deductible. Answer (D) is incorrect. The trash pick-up fee and state gift tax are not deductible.

6.2.6. During the current year, Jack and Mary Bronson paid the following taxes:

Taxes on residence (for period January 1 to September 30 of the current year)	$2,700
State motor vehicle tax on value of the car	360

The Bronsons sold their house on June 30 of the current year under an agreement in which the real estate taxes were not prorated between the buyer and sellers. What amount should the Bronsons deduct as taxes in calculating itemized deductions for the current year?

A. $1,800

B. $2,160

C. $2,700

D. $3,060

Answer (B) is correct. *(CPA, adapted)*
REQUIRED: The amount the taxpayers can deduct as taxes in calculating itemized deductions.
DISCUSSION: Section 164(a) allows a deduction for state, local, and foreign real property taxes, and for state and local personal property taxes. Real estate taxes must be apportioned between the buyer and the seller on the basis of the number of days the property was held by each in the year of sale, regardless of an agreement not to prorate them [Sec. 164(d)]. The taxpayers held the property for 6 months of the 9-month period the taxes covered. The amount of the taxes apportioned to the Bronsons is $1,800 [$2,700 × (6 ÷ 9)]. The state motor vehicle tax on the value of the car is a tax on the value of personal property, so the $360 may also be deducted. The taxpayers may deduct a total of $2,160 as taxes in calculating their itemized deductions.
Answer (A) is incorrect. The state motor vehicle tax may also be deducted. Answer (C) is incorrect. The amount of the taxes apportioned to the Bronsons and the state motor vehicle tax may be deducted. Answer (D) is incorrect. All of the taxes on the residence may not be deducted.

6.2.7. In the current year, Smith paid $6,000 to the tax collector of Big City for realty taxes on a two-family house owned by Smith's mother. Of this amount, $2,800 covered back taxes for the previous year, and $3,200 covered the current-year taxes. Smith resides on the second floor of the house, and his mother resides on the first floor. In Smith's itemized deductions on his current-year return, what amount was Smith entitled to claim for realty taxes?

A. $6,000

B. $3,200

C. $3,000

D. $0

Answer (D) is correct. *(CPA, adapted)*
REQUIRED: The amount of deductible property taxes paid by a person who does not own the property but resides in half of the property.
DISCUSSION: Taxes may be deducted only by the person on whom they are legally levied. Since Smith does not own the house, none of the taxes paid by Smith can be deducted by Smith. Smith's mother is entitled to the deduction only if she pays the taxes.
Answer (A) is incorrect. Smith paid $6,000 for realty taxes on the home owned by Smith's mother. Deductibility of taxes is affected by ownership. Answer (B) is incorrect. Current-year realty taxes are $3,200 on Smith's mother's home. Deductibility of taxes is affected by ownership. Answer (C) is incorrect. Half of the total amount Smith paid for his mother is $3,000. Deductibility of taxes is affected by ownership.

6.2.8. Ms. L, a cash-basis taxpayer, lives in a county where the real estate tax year runs from July 1 to June 30. The tax bills are due in two installments-- July 1 and January 1. Ms. L purchased her first house on September 1 of the current year. As part of her purchase price, she reimbursed the sellers $700 for her share of the current-year real estate taxes. At the date of purchase, she also paid her mortgage company $450, which was credited to her tax escrow account. From her monthly mortgage payments in the current year, a total of $600 was credited to her tax escrow account. On January 4 of the following year, the bank paid the escrow balance to the county tax office. L's real estate tax deduction for the current year is

A. $450

B. $700

C. $1,150

D. $1,750

Answer (B) is correct. *(SEE, adapted)*
REQUIRED: The real estate tax deduction for the current year.
DISCUSSION: Section 164(d) provides for the apportionment of taxes on real property between sellers and purchasers. Ms. L paid her share of the real estate taxes in the current year ($700). The amounts credited to her account by the mortgage company and held in escrow are not deductible as taxes until the tax is actually paid. The $1,050 ($450 + $600) held by the mortgage company in escrow will be deductible by Ms. L in the following year, the year paid.
Answer (A) is incorrect. The amount placed in escrow at the purchase date is not deductible until the tax is actually paid. Answer (C) is incorrect. The $450 placed in escrow at the purchase date is not deductible. Answer (D) is incorrect. Amounts placed in escrow ($450 and $600) will not be deductible until the following year.

6.2.9. Mr. and Mrs. Smith's real property tax year is the calendar year. Real estate taxes for the previous year are assessed in their state on January 2 and become due on May 1 and October 1. The tax becomes a lien on May 1. The Smiths bought a home on July 1 of the current year. The real estate taxes on the home for the previous year, which became due in the current year, were $1,000. The Smiths agreed to pay the $1,000 after the sale. They paid $500 in late taxes on August 1 and $500 on October 1. How should the Smiths treat the tax payments for federal income tax purposes for the current year?

A. The entire $1,000 is deductible.

B. They may deduct only the $500 payment made on October 1.

C. They may not deduct any amount but must add the $1,000 to the cost of their home.

D. They may deduct only the $500 payment made on August 1 as a settlement fee or closing cost.

Answer (C) is correct. *(SEE, adapted)*
REQUIRED: The correct tax treatment of the payment of back taxes by the purchasers of real property.
DISCUSSION: Real property taxes are generally deductible only by the person against whom the tax is imposed. Section 164(d) requires real estate taxes to be apportioned between the buyer and the seller based on the number of days in the real property tax year that the property was held by each. If the buyer pays the seller's taxes, they are capitalized as an additional cost of the property. The Smiths paid $1,000 in real estate taxes for the previous year after they purchased the property in the current year. They have, in effect, paid taxes owed by the seller and will not be able to deduct any of the amount and instead must add the $1,000 to the basis of the property.
Answer (A) is incorrect. The entire $1,000 in taxes was levied on the prior owner. Answer (B) is incorrect. The $500 payment made on October 1 was levied on the prior owner. Answer (D) is incorrect. They may not deduct the $500 payment made on August 1 because it was levied on the prior owners.

6.2.10. In certain circumstances, it is possible to have two taxpayers deduct the same state tax. Which of the following is such an example?

A. A retailer separates the state sales tax collected from his revenues. Both he and the consumer may deduct the tax on their federal returns.

B. A retailer separates the state sales tax on gasoline sold from his revenues. The consumer claims a state tax on gasoline on his federal return.

C. A retailer includes the state tax on gasoline in his revenues and claims a deduction for the tax. The consumer claims the tax as a proper business expense.

D. A retailer includes the state tax on gasoline in his revenues and claims a deduction for the tax. The consumer claims the tax as a personal deduction on his federal return.

Answer (C) is correct. *(Publisher, adapted)*
REQUIRED: The circumstances under which the same state taxes may be deducted by two taxpayers.
DISCUSSION: When a retailer includes state gasoline taxes in his gross revenues, he may deduct the amount as a tax on his return. The consumer who claims the gasoline purchase as business expense may show the tax portion separately as a tax. Note, however, that including the tax in gross revenue is not a proper method of accounting by the retailer.
Answer (A) is incorrect. The retailer may not deduct the state sales tax if he has not included it in his total revenues. Answer (B) is incorrect. The retailer may not deduct the state sales tax on gasoline sold if he has not included it in his total revenues. Answer (D) is incorrect. The consumer may not claim the state tax on gasoline as a personal deduction.

6.2.11. Fred Harvey, a cash-basis taxpayer, elected to itemize his deductions on his Year 2 income tax return. Harvey plans to itemize again in Year 3. The following information relating to his state income taxes is available:

Taxes withheld in Year 3	$2,500
Refund received in Year 3 of Year 2 tax	500
Assessment paid in Year 3 of Year 1 tax	700

The above information should be reported by Harvey in his Year 3 tax return as

A. State and local income taxes of $2,500.

B. State and local income taxes of $2,700.

C. State and local income taxes of $3,200.

D. State and local income taxes of $3,200 and gross income from state and local income tax refund of $500.

Answer (D) is correct. *(CPA, adapted)*
REQUIRED: The correct tax treatment of state income tax withholdings, refund, and assessment.
DISCUSSION: State and local income taxes are deductible under Sec. 164. A cash-basis taxpayer is entitled to deduct state income taxes withheld by his or her employer in the year such amounts are withheld. Assessments of state income taxes are deductible in the year of payment by a cash-basis taxpayer even if the payments relate to prior years. A refund of a prior year's tax payment must be included in the taxpayer's gross income in the year received if the taxpayer deducted the taxes in an earlier year.
In Year 3, Harvey should deduct the taxes withheld of $2,500 and the assessment paid of $700. He should include the $500 refund he received in gross income.
Answer (A) is incorrect. State and local income taxes reported in Year 3 includes assessment paid. Gross income is affected by refunds. Answer (B) is incorrect. The amount of state and local income taxes withheld in Year 3 plus the difference between the assessment paid in Year 3 of Year 1 tax and the refund received in Year 3 of Year 2 tax is $2,700. These taxes are not netted for reporting purposes. Answer (C) is incorrect. Harvey should not only report state and local income taxes paid of $3,200 in his Year 3 tax return. Refunds affect gross income.

6.2.12. Last year, Mrs. R, an accrual-method taxpayer, was assessed real property taxes. During that year, she filed a formal protest with Z County in accordance with local law. Mrs. R paid the contested liability in the current year and is entitled to a deduction in the year of payment.

A. True.

B. False.

Answer (A) is correct. *(SEE, adapted)*
DISCUSSION: When a liability is honestly disputed, an accrual-method taxpayer may not deduct the amount until the dispute is settled or adjudicated under general accrual principles. But Sec. 461(f) allows the deduction when the amount is paid, even if an honest dispute continues after the payment.

6.2.13. State and local income taxes for a sole proprietor are deductible only on Schedule A, Form 1040, even if the only source of income is from a business.

A. True.

B. False.

Answer (A) is correct. *(SEE, adapted)*
DISCUSSION: State and local income taxes are deducted from adjusted gross income and are reported on Schedule A regardless of whether the source of the income is from a business or not.

6.2.14. If state law imposes the sales tax on the seller or retailer and allows the seller or retailer to state it separately or pass it on to the consumer, the consumer may deduct the sales tax paid in purchasing a business asset in the current year as a business expense.

A. True.

B. False.

Answer (B) is correct. *(SEE, adapted)*
DISCUSSION: If the sales taxes were incurred in connection with the acquisition of property, the taxes must be capitalized and recovered through depreciation or amortization.

6.3 Interest Expense

6.3.1. On June 30, Jeff, who uses the cash method of accounting, borrowed $25,000 from a bank for use in his business. Jeff was to repay the loan in one payment with interest on December 30 of the same year. On December 30, he renewed that loan plus the interest due. The new loan was for $27,000. What amount of interest expense can Jeff deduct for the current year?

A. $0

B. $333

C. $1,000

D. $2,000

Answer (A) is correct. *(SEE, adapted)*
REQUIRED: The amount of interest expense deductible.
DISCUSSION: Under the cash method of accounting, expenses are deductible when they are actually paid. Since Jeff paid no interest on the loan in the current year, no interest expense is deductible for the current year.
Answer (B) is incorrect. This amount is the $2,000 excess of the new loan allocated over the 6 months in the current year. Interest is deductible in the year paid. Answer (C) is incorrect. The correct amount of interest expense Jeff may deduct for the current year is not $1,000. Answer (D) is incorrect. This amount is the excess of the new loan over the original loan. No interest is paid in the current year.

6.3.2. Which of the following is treated as personal interest of Individual A?

A. Interest incurred on refinancing A's home if the funds are used for a vacation.

B. Interest incurred to purchase bonds as an investment.

C. Interest incurred by a limited partnership in which A is a limited partner.

D. Interest incurred on an ordinary bank loan if the funds are used to provide medical care for a dependent of A.

Answer (D) is correct. *(Publisher, adapted)*
REQUIRED: The interest expense treated as personal interest.
DISCUSSION: Personal interest is defined in Sec. 163(h)(2) as any interest other than qualified residence interest, investment interest, interest taken into account in computing income or loss from a passive activity, interest in connection with a business, qualified student loan interest, and interest during certain extensions of time to pay the estate tax. Interest on an ordinary bank loan incurred for medical care is personal interest. Personal interest is not deductible.
Answer (A) is incorrect. Interest on debt secured by one's residence may be qualified residence interest regardless of the use of the funds. Answer (B) is incorrect. Interest incurred to purchase bonds as an investment is investment interest. Answer (C) is incorrect. A limited partnership is generally a passive activity, and the interest is deductible subject to the passive activity loss limitations rules.

6.3.3. In the current year, Mr. A, a sole proprietor, made interest payments of $800 on his personal credit cards, $650 on his business truck loan, $3,000 to the bank for a loan origination fee (charge for services) for his Veterans Administration mortgage, and $8,000 on his home mortgage. What is the total allowable interest deduction on Schedule A, Form 1040?

A. $12,450
B. $11,800
C. $9,450
D. $8,000

Answer (D) is correct. *(SEE, adapted)*
REQUIRED: The allowable interest deduction on Schedule A.
DISCUSSION: Personal interest is no longer allowed as an itemized deduction. Therefore, the $800 of credit card interest is not deductible. The $650 interest on the business truck loan probably may be deducted as business interest on Schedule C; it is not a deduction on Schedule A. Points paid on a Veterans Administration loan are not deductible as interest. Note also that points charged as compensation for services are not deductible as interest. Therefore, none of the $3,000 loan origination fees (points) are deductible as interest. The $8,000 of home mortgage interest is deductible in full. Mr. A's interest deduction on Schedule A for the current year is $8,000.
Answer (A) is incorrect. Personal interest, business interest, and loan origination fees in the form of services are not deductible as itemized deductions on Schedule A. Answer (B) is incorrect. Personal interest and loan origination fees in the form of services are not deductible as itemized deductions on Schedule A. Answer (C) is incorrect. Personal and business interest expenses are not deductible as itemized deductions.

6.3.4. Which of the following types of interest payments, not allowed because of one of the limitations, may be carried over to the next year?

A. Interest on a personal car loan.
B. Interest on credit cards.
C. Interest on a personal residence mortgage.
D. Interest on money borrowed to buy stocks.

Answer (D) is correct. *(SEE, adapted)*
REQUIRED: The type of disallowed interest deduction that may be carried over to a subsequent year.
DISCUSSION: The deduction for interest on investment indebtedness is limited by Sec. 163(d) to the amount of net investment income. Any disallowed investment interest may be carried over and treated as investment interest paid or accrued in the succeeding taxable year [Sec. 163(d)(2)].
Answer (A) is incorrect. Interest on a personal car loan is a type of personal interest and any disallowed deduction is lost forever. Answer (B) is incorrect. Interest on credit cards is a type of personal interest and any disallowed deduction is lost forever. Answer (C) is incorrect. Any qualified residence interest in excess of the amount deductible is treated as nondeductible personal interest.

6.3.5. On July 1 of Year 1, Correy refinanced his mortgage and obtained a new 30-year loan. He paid $3,600 (1% of the loan value) to obtain an 8% rate. On January 1 of Year 4, Correy sold his home and purchased a new house, with a down payment of $10,000. He paid an additional 1% of the loan value ($3,600) to obtain a 30-year loan with an 8% interest rate. Points are normal business practice and were reasonable in the area in which Correy lived. Assuming mortgage payments were made at the end of the month, how much can Correy deduct as points on his Year 4 tax return?

A. $0
B. $3,300
C. $3,600
D. $6,900

Answer (D) is correct. *(SEE, adapted)*
REQUIRED: The amount Correy can deduct as points on his Year 4 return.
DISCUSSION: Prepaid interest paid in the form of points on a home mortgage to purchase a home is deductible in the year paid as long as points are normal business practice and are reasonable in the area. Points paid to refinance a mortgage are not currently deductible. Instead, the points are deductible over the term of the loan ($3,600 ÷ 360 months = $10/month). If the mortgage is repaid early, the balance of the points is deductible in the year of the repayment. By the repayment date, Correy will have deducted $300 ($10 × 30 months) in points, leaving a $3,300 balance. Thus, Correy's Year 4 point deduction is calculated as follows:

July 1, Year 1, mortgage points	$3,600
Amount previously deducted	(300)
Balance after 30 months	$3,300
Points on purchase of new home	3,600
Total Year 4 points deduction	$6,900

Answer (A) is incorrect. Correy's deduction for points is based on the balance of points from the refinance and the total points on the purchase of the new home. Answer (B) is incorrect. This amount does not include the available points on the new home. Answer (C) is incorrect. The balance of the points from refinancing is also deductible.

6.3.6. Earl took out a mortgage on his home for $250,000 in Year 1. He filed as single for Year 10. In April Year 10, when the home had a fair market value of $430,000, Earl took out a home equity loan for $140,000. He used the proceeds as follows:

1. $90,000 for home improvements
2. $30,000 for payment of credit card debt
3. $20,000 for purchase of securities that produce tax-free income

How much of the $140,000 loan would produce deductible mortgage interest in Year 10?

   A. $0
   B. $90,000
   C. $120,000
   D. $140,000

Answer (C) is correct. *(SEE, adapted)*
REQUIRED: The amount of the home equity loan that would produce deductible mortgage interest.
DISCUSSION: Earl's first mortgage is acquisition indebtedness, which has fully deductible interest. Of the second mortgage, $90,000 is acquisition indebtedness because it was used to improve the residence. The $20,000 used to produce tax-free income is not permitted a mortgage interest deduction. The remaining $30,000 is home equity indebtedness, which is limited to the smaller of $100,000 or the excess of the home's FMV over the acquisition indebtedness [$430,000 – ($250,000 + $90,000)], or $90,000. The home equity portion of the debt ($30,000) meets these limits, and interest on this loan is also fully deductible. Thus, the total amount able to be deducted is $120,000.
Answer (A) is incorrect. The interest from the proceeds of $90,000 for home improvements and $30,000 for credit card debt is deductible. Answer (B) is incorrect. The interest related to the $30,000 credit card debt is also deductible. Answer (D) is incorrect. The interest related to the $20,000 used to purchase tax-free securities is not deductible.

6.3.7. Jo Jackson, who is married and files a joint return, purchased her principal residence for $500,000 in Year 1, and the balance of her original mortgage is $400,000 in July of Year 3. Assume the fair market value of the home is $550,000 in July of Year 3. Which of the following is a true statement of deductibility of interest on additional debt secured by the home?

   A. Interest on a second mortgage (home equity loan) of $120,000 incurred in July of Year 3 is deductible in full as qualified residence interest.

   B. Interest on a second mortgage (proceeds used to make a financial investment) of $85,000 incurred in July of Year 3 is deductible in full as qualified residence interest.

   C. Interest on a second mortgage (home equity loan) of $200,000 incurred in July of Year 3 is limited to $150,000, the difference between the FMV and the acquisition indebtedness on the home.

   D. Interest on a second mortgage of $800,000 incurred in July of Year 3 is fully deductible if the proceeds are used to remodel and add on to the house.

Answer (B) is correct. *(Publisher, adapted)*
REQUIRED: The true statement concerning the deduction for qualified residence interest.
DISCUSSION: Qualified residence interest is deductible in full, subject to limitations, and is defined in Sec. 163(h)(3). For tax years beginning after December 31, 1987, the general rule classifies qualified residence interest as interest on two categories of debt secured by a taxpayer's principal or second residence. Acquisition indebtedness is debt used to purchase, build, or substantially improve the residence. The limit on acquisition indebtedness is $1 million. Home equity indebtedness is any debt secured by the residence other than acquisition indebtedness. Home equity indebtedness is limited to the lesser of $100,000 or the excess FMV of the residence over any acquisition indebtedness ($150,000).
Since Jo's $85,000 home equity debt is less than both the difference between the FMV and acquisition indebtedness of the residence, and the $100,000 home equity indebtedness limitation, the interest paid on the second mortgage is fully deductible. Note that the interest on the $85,000 of debt is deductible as qualified residence interest even if it is also investment interest.
Answer (A) is incorrect. Interest on a second mortgage (home equity loan) of $120,000 incurred in July of Year 3 is not deductible in full as qualified residence interest. Answer (C) is incorrect. Interest on a second mortgage (home equity loan) of $200,000 incurred in July of Year 3 is not limited to the lesser of $100,000 or the difference between the FMV and the acquisition indebtedness on the home. Answer (D) is incorrect. Interest on a second mortgage of $800,000 incurred in July of Year 3 is not fully deductible even if the proceeds are used to remodel and add on to the house. Total acquisition indebtedness is limited to $1.1 million ($1 million acquisition indebtedness plus $100,000 home equity loan).

6.3.8. The amount of investment interest deductible in the current year is limited to

   A. Net investment income.
   B. Net investment income plus $10,000.
   C. Net investment income plus 10% of the excess, limited to $1,000.
   D. Net investment income plus $4,000.

Answer (A) is correct. *(Publisher, adapted)*
REQUIRED: The amount of investment interest deductible in the current year.
DISCUSSION: Section 163(d) limits the deduction for investment interest to the net investment income.
Answer (B) is incorrect. The amount of investment interest deductible in the current year is not increased by $10,000. Answer (C) is incorrect. The amount of investment interest deductible in the current year is not increased by 10% of the net investment income excess, limited to $1,000. Answer (D) is incorrect. The amount of investment interest deductible in the current year is not increased by $4,000.

6.3.9. Which of the following payments may be deducted in full in the current year as interest expense on Form 1040, Schedule A?

1. Mortgage prepayment penalty
2. Interest relating to tax-exempt interest income
3. Installment plan interest for clothes purchases
4. Mortgage interest
5. Credit investigation fees

   A. 1, 3, and 5.

   B. 1 and 4.

   C. 2, 4, and 5.

   D. 3 and 4.

Answer (B) is correct. *(SEE, adapted)*
REQUIRED: The payments that may be deducted as interest expense.
DISCUSSION: Section 163 allows a deduction for certain interest paid or accrued within the taxable year on indebtedness. Interest is compensation for the use or forbearance of money. Personal interest is not deductible, but mortgage interest is generally deductible, provided that it is "qualified residence interest" as defined in Sec. 163(h)(3). Mortgage prepayment penalties have also been held to be compensation for the use of money and are deductible as interest.
Answer (A) is incorrect. Credit investigation fees are not paid as compensation for the use or forbearance of money; they are paid for services to obtain a loan. Also, installment plan interest is not deductible as personal interest. Answer (C) is incorrect. Interest relating to tax-exempt interest income is not deductible (Sec. 265). Also, credit investigation fees are not paid as compensation for the use or forbearance of money; they are paid for services to obtain a loan. Answer (D) is incorrect. Installment plan interest is not deductible as personal interest.

6.3.10. Mr. and Mrs. L are calendar-year, cash-basis taxpayers. They have their own business, which they operate as a sole proprietorship. In addition, they own several investments including a 4-year-old rental property in whose operations they do not materially participate. Mr. and Mrs. L are not involved in a real property trade or business for purposes of Sec. 469. In the current year, the rental property produced a net loss of $40,000 including interest expense of $90,000. In addition, Mr. and Mrs. L paid the following amounts of interest expense:

Interest on home mortgage	$ 4,500
Interest on business loan	35,500
Interest on loan to purchase 10,000 shares of ABC Corporation stock	45,000
	$85,000

Mr. and Mrs. L had no dividend or interest income in the current year. If they file a joint return, what is the total amount deductible as investment interest on their 1040 for the current year?

   A. $0

   B. $2,000

   C. $9,000

   D. $37,500

Answer (A) is correct. *(SEE, adapted)*
REQUIRED: The total investment interest deductible for the year.
DISCUSSION: The deduction for interest on investment indebtedness is limited by Sec. 163(d) to the amount of net investment income. Net investment income is the excess of investment income over investment expenses. Gross income and any net gains on property held for investment are considered investment income to the extent such amounts are not derived from the conduct of a trade or business. Investment income does not include any income derived from a passive activity as defined in Sec. 469(c). Rental of real property is generally considered a passive activity. Investment expenses are those associated with the investment income.
Mr. and Mrs. L's ordinary interest is $40,000 [$4,500 home mortgage (qualified residence interest) + $35,500 business loan]. Their investment interest is only the $45,000 on the loan to purchase stock. The $90,000 interest on the rental property is not considered investment interest under Sec. 163(d)(3)(B) because it is interest taken into account under Sec. 469 in computing income or loss on a passive activity. Since Mr. and Mrs. L have no net investment income, their investment interest deduction is $0.
Answer (B) is incorrect. The amount of $2,000 does not consider the effect of no net investment income. Answer (C) is incorrect. The amount of $9,000 does not consider the effect of no net investment income. Answer (D) is incorrect. The amount of $37,500 does not consider the effect of no net investment income.

6.3.11. Investment interest generally includes

   A. Interest expense for rental activity in which the taxpayer materially participates.

   B. Interest expense for an investment in property subject to a net lease.

   C. Interest expense to acquire a limited partnership interest.

   D. Interest expense to acquire stocks and bonds.

Answer (D) is correct. *(Publisher, adapted)*
REQUIRED: The type of interest expense that constitutes investment interest.
DISCUSSION: Investment interest includes interest paid or accrued on indebtedness incurred or continued to purchase or carry property held for investment, and interest expense for a business activity in which the taxpayer does not materially participate, if that activity is not treated as a passive activity under Sec. 469 [Sec. 163(d)]. Interest to acquire stocks and bonds meets the first part of this definition as interest on indebtedness incurred to purchase property held for investment.
Answer (A) is incorrect. Investment property does not include any interest in a passive activity under Sec. 469 and passive activity includes most rental activities, even those in which the taxpayer materially participates. Answer (B) is incorrect. Investment interest generally does not include interest expense for an investment in property subject to a net lease. Answer (C) is incorrect. A limited partnership interest is also treated as a passive activity in most instances, so it is not investment property under Sec. 163(d).

6.3.12. For the year ending December 31, David Roth, a married taxpayer filing a joint return, reported the following:

Investment income from dividends and interest	$24,000
Long-term capital gains on stock held for investment (Roth elects to treat the gain as ordinary income)	25,000
Investment expenses	4,000
Interest expense on funds borrowed in the current year to purchase investment property	70,000

What amount can Roth deduct this year as investment interest expense?

- A. $22,000
- B. $45,000
- C. $49,000
- D. $70,000

Answer (B) is correct. *(CPA, adapted)*
REQUIRED: The amount of investment interest the taxpayer may deduct in the current year.
DISCUSSION: Section 163(d) limits the deduction on investment interest to the amount of net investment income. Investment income includes gross income from property held for investment and any net gain attributable to the disposition of property held for investment, to the extent that such amounts are not derived from the conduct of a trade or business.
Roth had investment income of $49,000 ($24,000 + $25,000) and investment expenses of $4,000, or net investment income of $45,000. His investment interest deduction is limited to $45,000.
The $25,000 of disallowed investment interest ($70,000 – $45,000 deductible this year) may be carried over and treated as investment interest paid or accrued in the succeeding taxable year [Sec. 163(d)(2)].
Answer (A) is incorrect. Net investment income is the dividends, interest, and capital gains less related investment expenses. A similar amount of interest expense is deductible. Answer (C) is incorrect. The dividends, interest, and long-term capital gains must be reduced by investment expenses to determine the ceiling on the investment interest expense that is deductible. Answer (D) is incorrect. The interest expense is deductible only to the extent that net investment income has been earned.

6.3.13. During the current year, William Clark, an employee of Helton Corporation, was assessed a deficiency on his federal income tax return from the previous year. As a result of this assessment, he was required to pay $1,120, determined as follows:

Additional tax	$900
Late filing penalty	60
Negligence penalty	90
Interest	70

The additional assessment is the result of a deduction claimed with respect to Clark's personal residence. What portion of the $1,120 outlay qualifies as itemized deductions for the current year?

- A. $0
- B. $10
- C. $220
- D. $970

Answer (A) is correct. *(CPA, adapted)*
REQUIRED: The portion of the payment to the IRS which qualifies as an itemized deduction.
DISCUSSION: Federal income taxes and penalties are generally not deductible in any year for the individual taxpayer. The IRS has generally held in Temp. Reg. Sec. 1.163-9T(b)(2) that interest on tax deficiencies is personal interest and therefore nondeductible under Sec. 163. The Tax Court in *Redlark* (106 TC 31) held that interest paid or accrued on a tax deficiency indebtedness allocable to a trade or business (a sole proprietorship) is deductible. The Ninth Circuit Court of Appeals overturned the Tax Court decision in 1998. The Eighth Circuit Court in *Miller* (65 F.3d 687) also held that tax deficiency interest allocable to a trade or business (sole proprietorship) relates to an individual liability and is personal interest and nondeductible whether the income arose from a trade or business or not. Since Clark's $70 of interest is related to a nonbusiness outlay (related to his personal residence), the interest outlay is apparently not directly covered by either *Redlark* or *Miller* and therefore is nondeductible under the temporary regulations.
Answer (B) is incorrect. The additional tax, late filing penalty, negligence penalty, and personal interest are all nondeductible. Answer (C) is incorrect. The late filing penalty, negligence penalty, and personal interest are all nondeductible. Answer (D) is incorrect. The additional tax and personal interest are both nondeductible.

6.3.14. Mr. X, a farmer, borrowed $50,000 from the local bank. The loan was secured by a first mortgage on his farm where he resides. Proceeds from the loan were used to construct an addition to an equipment shed and to pay fertilizer costs for the following spring. How will Mr. X handle the interest paid on his mortgage?

- A. Deduct all interest on Schedule A.
- B. Deduct all interest on Schedule F.
- C. Prorate interest between farm property and residential property and deduct on Schedules A and F accordingly.
- D. Deduct all interest on either Schedule A or F as he chooses.

Answer (B) is correct. *(SEE, adapted)*
REQUIRED: The method of deducting farm interest.
DISCUSSION: Interest on a farm is generally deductible on Schedule F. Since the proceeds of this mortgage were used for farming operations, it is entirely deductible on Schedule F.
If the mortgage had been incurred to purchase the farm, then the interest would have to be prorated between farm property (deducted on Schedule F) and residential property (deducted on Schedule A).
Answer (A) is incorrect. Farm interest is not deducted on Schedule A. Answer (C) is incorrect. The interest paid on the mortgage may not be prorated between farm property and residential property and deducted accordingly on Schedules A and F. Answer (D) is incorrect. Mr. X may not choose the schedule on which to deduct the interest paid on his mortgage.

6.3.15. Charles Wolfe purchased the following long-term investments at par during the year:

$20,000 general obligation bonds of Burlington County (wholly tax-exempt)
$10,000 debentures of Arrow Corporation

Wolfe financed these purchases by obtaining a $30,000 loan from Union National Bank. For the year, Wolfe made the following interest payments:

Union National Bank	$3,600
Qualified residence interest on home mortgage	3,000
Interest on credit card charges	500

Wolfe's net investment income for the year was $10,000. What amount can Wolfe utilize as interest expense in calculating itemized deductions for the year?

   A. $3,000

   B. $4,200

   C. $4,700

   D. $7,100

Answer (B) is correct. *(CPA, adapted)*
   REQUIRED: The amount of interest expense allowed in computing itemized deductions.
   DISCUSSION: Section 163 allows a deduction for certain interest paid or accrued during the year on indebtednesses. Investment interest is deductible up to the taxpayer's net investment income for the year. Personal or consumer interest is not deductible. Qualified residence interest is deductible under Sec. 163(h)(3). Section 265 disallows a deduction for interest on debt incurred to purchase or carry tax-exempt securities. Since Wolfe used two-thirds of the loan from Union National Bank to purchase tax-exempt securities, two-thirds of the interest on this loan is disallowed as a deduction. Wolfe may deduct

Union National Bank ($3,600 × 1/3)	$1,200
Interest on home mortgage	3,000
Interest deduction	$4,200

   Answer (A) is incorrect. Only one-third of the bank loan interest is deductible. Answer (C) is incorrect. None of the credit card interest is deductible. Answer (D) is incorrect. The deductible bank loan interest is limited, and credit card interest is not deductible.

6.3.16. Phil and Joan Crawley made the following payments during the current year:

Interest on bank loan (loan proceeds used to purchase U.S. Series EE savings bonds)	$4,000
Interest on installment charge accounts	500
Interest on home mortgage for period April 1 to December 31	2,700
Points paid to obtain conventional mortgage loan on April 1	900

The Crawleys had net investment income of $3,000 for the year. What is the maximum amount that the Crawleys can deduct as interest expense in calculating itemized deductions for the current year?

   A. $3,600

   B. $6,600

   C. $7,600

   D. $8,100

Answer (B) is correct. *(CPA, adapted)*
   REQUIRED: The maximum amount the taxpayers can deduct as interest expense.
   DISCUSSION: Section 163 allows a deduction for certain interest paid or accrued during the tax year on indebtedness. The interest on U.S. savings bonds is taxable, so Sec. 265 does not deny the interest deduction on the loan to purchase them. Since Sec. 163(d) limits investment interest to net investment income, the Crawleys may deduct only $3,000 of investment interest. The interest on the installment charge accounts is personal interest, none of which is deductible. The home mortgage interest is deductible assuming it is qualified residence interest as defined in Sec. 163(h)(3). Section 461(g) allows the deduction for points on a conventional mortgage loan even though the points represent prepaid interest. The Crawleys' maximum interest deduction is

Interest on bank loan	$3,000
Interest on home mortgage	2,700
Points	900
Interest deduction	$6,600

   Answer (A) is incorrect. The interest on the bank loan is deductible up to the amount of net investment income ($3,000). Answer (C) is incorrect. The interest deduction for the bank loan is limited to the amount of net investment income ($3,000). Answer (D) is incorrect. The total amount of interest the Crawleys paid for the current year is $8,100. However, it may not all be deducted.

6.3.17. During the current year, Ms. Cheung used corporate stock that she held for investment as collateral to borrow funds. The funds were used to purchase personal property for sale in her business. Which of the following statements concerning the interest expense paid or incurred by Ms. Cheung is true?

    A. The expense is limited by the personal interest limitation.

    B. The expense is fully deductible in the year paid or incurred.

    C. The expense is limited by the investment interest limitation.

    D. The expense has to be capitalized.

Answer (B) is correct. *(SEE, adapted)*
    REQUIRED: The true statement regarding interest expense on a loan used to purchase business property when the loan was secured by investment property.
    DISCUSSION: Interest expense incurred in a trade or business is deductible from gross income. It is the use to which borrowed funds are put, not the security behind the obligation, which is the determining factor in deciding whether interest is a business or nonbusiness expense deduction. Ms. Cheung used the borrowed funds to purchase personal property for sale in her business, so the interest expense is deductible as a business expense without regard to the nature of the collateral.
    Answer (A) is incorrect. The interest is not personal interest. Answer (C) is incorrect. The interest is business interest, not investment interest, in spite of the fact that the obligation was secured by an investment property. Answer (D) is incorrect. The provisions of Sec. 263A do not apply to interest expense that is incurred on a loan used to buy property for sale in a trade or business.

6.3.18. All of the following statements regarding deductible interest expense are true except

    A. The day you mail a check for the payment of interest is the date the interest is paid.

    B. "Points" paid by a seller are deductible as interest only by the seller.

    C. A mortgage prepayment penalty is deductible as interest.

    D. "Points" paid by the borrower for the use of money are deductible as interest either ratably as the loan is repaid or in the year of payment.

Answer (B) is correct. *(SEE, adapted)*
    REQUIRED: The false statement concerning deductible interest expense.
    DISCUSSION: Points are generally a fee paid for processing, placing, or finding a loan. Points are deductible as interest if considered compensation to a lender for the use of the money. For many years, points paid by a seller were not deductible as interest because the debt on which they are paid was not the debt of the seller. Instead, they were treated as a reduction of the selling price. The IRS changed its position for seller-paid points paid by cash-method taxpayers. Revenue Procedure 94-27 permits the purchaser to deduct seller-paid points. A basis reduction must be made for the seller paid points that are deducted.
    Authors' note: Revenue Procedure 94-27 does not prohibit the purchaser from adopting the general amortization rules of prepaid interest. In the event the purchaser's standard deduction exceeds his or her itemized deductions, (s)he may elect to amortize the "points" over the duration of the loan.
    Answer (A) is incorrect. Concerning the deduction of interest expense, the day you mail a check for the payment of interest is the date the interest is paid. Answer (C) is incorrect. A mortgage prepayment penalty is deductible as interest. Answer (D) is incorrect. "Points" paid by the borrower for the use of money are deductible as interest, either ratably as the loan is repaid, or in the year of payment.

6.3.19. Mr. O is in the business of constructing houses. Owing to poor market conditions in his area, he offers zero interest financing to his prospective customers. Mr. and Mrs. B purchased one of Mr. O's houses for $40,000 and, as offered, financed their purchase with a noninterest-bearing 10-year mortgage to Mr. O for the purchase price. Since Mr. and Mrs. B's mortgage payments reduce principal only, they are not entitled to deduct any interest expense even if they itemize their deductions on Schedule A.

    A. True.

    B. False.

Answer (B) is correct. *(SEE, adapted)*
    DISCUSSION: Section 483 imputes interest to deferred payments for the sale or exchange of property when there is unstated interest. Unstated interest is the excess of the sum of the payments over the sum of the present values of the payments using a discount rate equal to the appropriate federal rate. Imputed interest is determined in accordance with the original issue discount rules.

6.3.20. On August 18 of the current year, Mr. Q's original home mortgage had a balance of $30,000. On that date, he took out a $20,000 second mortgage. Mr. Q used $5,000 for paving his driveway and $15,000 to buy a new car. After the improvement, Mr. Q's residence has an adjusted basis of $45,000 and a fair market value of $60,000. All of the interest paid by Mr. Q on his first and second mortgages is fully deductible.

A. True.

B. False.

Answer (A) is correct. *(SEE, adapted)*
   DISCUSSION: Mr. Q's first mortgage is acquisition indebtedness which has fully deductible interest. Of the second mortgage, $5,000 is acquisition indebtedness because it was used to improve the residence. The remaining $15,000 is home equity indebtedness, which is limited to excess of the home's FMV over the acquisition indebtedness $25,000 ($60,000 – $35,000) or $100,000. The home equity portion of the debt meets these limits, and interest on this loan is also fully deductible.

6.3.21. On August 1, Year 1, Mr. G borrowed $10,000 in order to meet margin requirements on his investment in the commodities market. On August 5, Year 1, Mr. G bought five contracts of May, Year 2 corn and sold five contracts of June, Year 2 corn. On December 24, Year 1, Mr. G sold the May, Year 2 contracts realizing a loss of $20,000, and bought five contracts of July, Year 2 corn. Interest on the loan amounted to $800, which Mr. G paid in Year 1. Mr. G may deduct the $800 as interest expense on his Year 1 tax return.

A. True.

B. False.

Answer (B) is correct. *(SEE, adapted)*
   DISCUSSION: Under Sec. 263(g), interest on indebtedness incurred or continued to purchase or carry personal property which is part of a straddle is not deductible in general to the extent that interest and other carrying charges exceed ordinary income derived from the straddle property. The interest must be capitalized. Mr. G's corn contracts constitute a straddle because he has offsetting positions; i.e., he has contracts to buy and sell at the same time [Sec. 1092(c)].

6.3.22. Commitment fees that you incur to have business funds made readily available to you over a period of time, but not for actual use of the funds, are not deductible as interest payments. However, these fees are costs of getting your loan, and you can deduct a part of the fees in each tax year during the period of the loan.

A. True.

B. False.

Answer (A) is correct. *(SEE, adapted)*
   DISCUSSION: Commitment fees do not represent interest incurred so they are not deductible under Sec. 163. The expense is, however, deductible as a business expense under Sec. 162. Loan commitment fees in this case are capitalized and deducted ratably over the term of the loan since the outlay relates not to the tax year in which the loan is obtained but to the entire term of the loan.

6.4 Charitable Contributions

6.4.1. Money or property given to the following is deductible as charitable contributions except

A. Nonprofit schools or hospitals.

B. Civic leagues and chambers of commerce.

C. Churches, synagogues, temples, mosques, and other religious organizations.

D. War veterans' groups.

Answer (B) is correct. *(SEE, adapted)*
   REQUIRED: The charitable contribution to which a donation is not deductible.
   DISCUSSION: Charitable contributions are deductible only if they are made to qualified organizations. Qualified organizations can be either public charities or private foundations. (Generally, a public charity is one that derives more than one-third of its support from its members and the general public.) Donations can be made in the form of cash or noncash property.
   Answer (A) is incorrect. Nonprofit schools or hospitals are qualified charitable organizations as provided for under Sec. 170(c) to which deductible charitable contributions can be made. Answer (C) is incorrect. Churches, synagogues, temples, mosques, and other religious organizations are qualified charitable organizations as provided for under Sec. 170(c) to which deductible charitable contributions can be made. Answer (D) is incorrect. War veterans' groups are qualified charitable organizations as provided for under Sec. 170(c) to which deductible charitable contributions can be made.

6.4.2. Donations to all of the following organizations are deductible as charitable contributions except a

- A. Charitable community chest.
- B. Local chamber of commerce.
- C. Nonprofit hospital.
- D. Charitable fund of a domestic fraternal society operating under the lodge system.

Answer (B) is correct. *(SEE, adapted)*
REQUIRED: The organization that is not a qualified charitable organization.
DISCUSSION: A contribution is deductible only if made to an organization described in Sec. 170(c). The organizations listed include a state or possession of the United States or any subdivisions thereof; a corporation, trust, community chest, fund, or foundation that is situated in the United States and is organized and operated exclusively for religious, charitable, scientific, literary, or educational purposes, or for the prevention of cruelty to children or animals; a veterans' organization; a fraternal organization operating under the lodge system; or a cemetery company. The Chamber of Commerce does not fall within these categories.
Answer (A) is incorrect. A charitable community chest meets the criteria of a qualified organization described in Sec. 170(c). Answer (C) is incorrect. A nonprofit hospital meets the criteria of a qualified organization described in Sec. 170(c). Answer (D) is incorrect. A charitable fund of a domestic fraternal society operating under the lodge system meets the criteria of a qualified organization described in Sec. 170(a).

6.4.3. On December 20 of the current year, Mr. and Mrs. Garrison purchased four tickets for a New Year's Eve party at their church, a qualified charitable organization. Each ticket cost $75 and had a fair market value of $50. The Garrisons gave two of the tickets to a needy family in the community. Mr. Garrison tended bar at the party from 8 p.m. to 4 a.m. and was paid $40. The usual charge for such services is $80. Immediately before midnight, Mr. Garrison pledged $200 to the building fund and delivered a check for that amount on January 2 of the following year. Of the amounts described above, the total amount which the Garrisons can include as a charitable contribution deduction for the current year on a joint return is

- A. $340
- B. $140
- C. $100
- D. $50

Answer (C) is correct. *(CPA, adapted)*
REQUIRED: The total amount the taxpayers can include as a charitable contribution deduction for the current year on a joint return.
DISCUSSION: The taxpayers may deduct as a charitable contribution the excess of what they gave over the probable fair market value of what they received, or $100. The taxpayers gave $300 (4 tickets × $75 per ticket) to a qualified charitable organization in return for property with a fair market value of $200 (four tickets with a fair market value of $50 each).
The donation of the two tickets to the needy family was not a donation to a qualified organization and therefore was not deductible. No deduction is allowable for a contribution of services [Reg. 1.170A-1(g)], so the taxpayer may not deduct the value of his time. The pledge of $200 is not deductible until actually paid, i.e., in the following year.
Answer (A) is incorrect. The $200 pledge and the services donated are not deductible charitable contributions. Answer (B) is incorrect. The services donated are not deductible. Answer (D) is incorrect. The difference between the cost of the tickets to the taxpayer and the FMV of the tickets is the deductible charitable contribution.

6.4.4. During the current year, Vincent Tally gave to the municipal art museum title to his private collection of rare books that was appraised and valued at $60,000. However, he reserved the right to the collection's use and possession during his lifetime. For the current year, he reported an adjusted gross income of $100,000. Assuming that this was his only contribution during the year, and that there were no carryovers from prior years, what amount can he deduct as contributions for the current year?

- A. $0
- B. $30,000
- C. $50,000
- D. $60,000

Answer (A) is correct. *(CPA, adapted)*
REQUIRED: The current deduction for a contribution when the donor reserves the right to use the property during his or her lifetime.
DISCUSSION: Payment of a charitable contribution that consists of a future interest in tangible personal property is treated as made only when all intervening interests and rights to the actual possession and enjoyment of the property have expired or are held by persons other than the taxpayer or those related to the taxpayer [Sec. 170(a)(3) and (f)(3)]. Therefore, the contribution of the rare books will be treated as made only when Tally's intervening lifetime right to use and possess the books has terminated, i.e., at his death.
Answer (B) is incorrect. The 30%-of-AGI charitable contribution limitation is irrelevant if rights to property are retained. Answer (C) is incorrect. The 50%-of-AGI charitable contribution limitation is irrelevant if rights to property are retained. Answer (D) is incorrect. Vincent Tally still retains the right to possess and enjoy the property.

6.4.5. During the current year, Mr. K, who is single and 45 years of age, made cash contributions of $500 to his church. Mr. K is taking the standard deduction on his current-year return. What is the amount of Mr. K's deduction for charitable contributions?

A. $500

B. $300

C. $75

D. $0

Answer (D) is correct. *(SEE, adapted)*
REQUIRED: The deduction for charitable contributions when the standard deduction is taken.
DISCUSSION: Charitable contributions are allowed in Sec. 170 as itemized deductions (below the line to arrive at taxable income). Itemized deductions are an election in lieu of taking the standard deduction. Since Mr. K claimed the standard deduction, he is not entitled to any additional deduction for a charitable contribution.
Answer (A) is incorrect. Mr. K elected to take the standard deduction. Answer (B) is incorrect. Even though Mr. K's charitable deduction is not reduced by 40%, it is an itemized deduction. Answer (C) is incorrect. Even though Mr. K's charitable deduction is not limited to $75, it is an itemized deduction.

6.4.6. Mr. Q's records for the current year contain the following information:

● Donated stock having a fair market value of $1,000 to a qualified charitable organization. He acquired the stock 5 months previously at a cost of $800.

● Paid $3,000 to a church school as a requirement for the enrollment of his daughter.

● Paid $200 for annual homeowner's association dues.

● Drove 300 miles in his personal auto that were directly related to services he performed for his church. Actual costs were not available.

● Paid $40 in parking fees and tolls in connection with the 300 miles.

What is Mr. Q's charitable contribution deduction for the current year?

A. $882

B. $1,082

C. $4,042

D. $4,082

Answer (A) is correct. *(SEE, adapted)*
REQUIRED: The portion of the contributions deductible for the year.
DISCUSSION: The amount of a charitable contribution of ordinary income property is the fair market value of the property reduced by the amount of gain which would not have been long-term capital gain if the property had been sold by the taxpayer at its fair market value [Sec. 170(e)(1)(A)]. Accordingly, Q will be allowed a deduction of $800 ($1,000 – $200) on the contribution of the stock. The 300 miles driven in the personal auto were directly related to services performed for the church and would, therefore, constitute a deductible contribution. For tax years beginning after December 31, 1997, the amount of the contribution would be $42 (300 × $.14) [Sec. 170(i)]. The $40 in parking fees and tolls associated with the travel would also qualify as a charitable contribution (Rev. Proc. 97-58).

Contribution of stock ($1,000 – $200)	$800
Mileage (300 × $.14)	42
Parking fees and tolls	40
Total	$882

The tuition payments of $3,000 are required for the daughter's enrollment and do not qualify as a charitable contribution. Neither are the homeowner's association dues considered a charitable contribution under Sec. 170.
Answer (B) is incorrect. The homeowner's dues are not deductible. Answer (C) is incorrect. Tuition payments and the homeowner's dues are not deductible, but the parking fees are deductible. Answer (D) is incorrect. Neither the homeowner's dues nor the tuition payments are deductible.

6.4.7. Under a written agreement between Mrs. Norma Lowe and an approved religious exempt organization, a 10-year-old girl from Vietnam came to live in Mrs. Lowe's home on August 1 of the current year in order to be able to start school in the U.S. on September 3 of the same year. Mrs. Lowe actually spent $500 for food, clothing, and school supplies for the student during the year, without receiving any compensation or reimbursement of costs. What portion of the $500 may Mrs. Lowe deduct on her current-year income tax return as a charitable contribution?

A. $0

B. $200

C. $250

D. $500

Answer (B) is correct. *(CPA, adapted)*
REQUIRED: The portion of the expenditures for the student's maintenance the taxpayer may deduct as a charitable contribution for the year.
DISCUSSION: Amounts paid by a taxpayer to maintain an individual other than a dependent as a member of his or her household under a written agreement between the taxpayer and a qualified organization to provide educational opportunity for pupils or students in private homes are deductible up to $50 per month [Sec. 170(g)]. The student must attend full-time in the 12th or any lower grade of a qualified educational organization located in the United States. The deduction is only available for the months the child is a full-time student, which is 4 months in this case: September – December. Mrs. Lowe's expenditures qualify under this provision as a charitable contribution deduction of $200 ($50 × 4 months in the current year).
Answer (A) is incorrect. A deduction is permitted. Answer (C) is incorrect. A deduction is only available for the 4 months the child actually is in school. Answer (D) is incorrect. A $50 per month limit applies to the donation. Actual expenses are ignored in determining the deduction amount.

6.4.8. Mr. U is actively involved in church activities in his community. During the current year, he incurred the following church-related expenses:

Cash contributed to the church	$2,000
Round-trip mileage to attend church services (400 miles × $.14)	56
Round-trip mileage to do church volunteer work (500 miles × $.14)	70
Fair market value of used clothing given to church mission	500
Raffle tickets purchased from the church	200
Value of time and services contributed to the church	400

Mr. U's adjusted gross income is $25,000, and he itemizes his deductions on his tax return. What is his charitable contribution deduction?

A. $2,500

B. $2,570

C. $2,770

D. $3,226

Answer (B) is correct. *(SEE, adapted)*
REQUIRED: The amount of the charitable contribution deduction for the current year.
DISCUSSION: The cash contribution of $2,000 to the church will be fully deductible. The $70 at the standard mileage rate for church-related volunteer work will also be deductible [Sec. 170(i)]. The clothing donated is capital gain property, and the donation would be $500.

Cash	$2,000
Mileage for volunteer work	70
Value of used clothing	500
Total	$2,570

The mileage to and from church does not constitute a charitable contribution for Mr. U. The purchase price of raffle tickets, also, is not a deductible charitable contribution. The value of a service rendered to a charitable organization is not deductible as a contribution either. Mr. U may not deduct, then, the $56 in mileage to attend church services, the cost of the raffle tickets, or the $400 in services contributed to the church.
Answer (A) is incorrect. The mileage for volunteer work is deductible. Answer (C) is incorrect. The raffle tickets are not deductible. Answer (D) is incorrect. The raffle tickets and the value of time and services are not deductible.

6.4.9. An individual may deduct contributions to most charities up to 50% of adjusted gross income. However, some contributions have other limits. These limits are

A. 40% and 30%.

B. 30% and 10%.

C. 30% and 20%.

D. 40% and 20%.

Answer (C) is correct. *(SEE, adapted)*
REQUIRED: The percentage limitations for charitable contributions other than the 50% limitation.
DISCUSSION: The annual limit for the deduction of an individual's contributions to most charities is 50% of adjusted gross income for the year [Sec. 170(b)(1)(A)]. Another limitation is 30% of adjusted gross income for contributions to charities to which the 50% limitation does not apply [Sec. 170(b)(1)(B)], and also for contributions of long-term capital gain property, which is included at full fair market value and not reduced by any of its appreciation [Sec. 170(b)(1)(C)]. The third limitation is 20% of the taxpayer's adjusted gross income for long-term capital gain property given to charities to which the 50% limitation does not apply (e.g., private nonoperating foundations) [Sec. 170(b)(1)(D)].
Answer (A) is incorrect. The charitable contribution limits do not include 40%. Answer (B) is incorrect. The charitable contribution limits do not include 10%. Answer (D) is incorrect. Forty percent is not a charitable contribution limit.

6.4.10. On December 15 of the current year, Donald Calder made a contribution of $500 to a qualified charitable organization by charging the contribution on his bank credit card. Calder paid the $500 on January 20 of the following year, upon receipt of the bill from the bank. In addition, Calder issued and delivered a promissory note for $1,000 to another qualified charitable organization on November 1 of the current year, which he paid upon maturity 6 months later. If Calder itemizes his deductions, what portion of these contributions is deductible in the current year?

A. $0

B. $500

C. $1,000

D. $1,500

Answer (B) is correct. *(CPA, adapted)*
REQUIRED: The amount of contributions that is deductible in the current year.
DISCUSSION: Charitable contributions are deductible under Sec. 170 in the year in which payment is made. A promissory note is not payment of a charitable contribution until the note is paid, since it is merely a promise made by the donor to the charitable organization. However, a contribution made by bank credit card is considered payment in the year charged even though the credit card obligation may not be paid until the following year. The IRS is currently requiring that the credit card charge be processed by the charity by year end in order to be deductible in the year that the contribution is made. This is because the charitable organization is entitled to the funds and the donor is obligated to a third party (the bank). As a result, $500 of the contributions are deductible in the current year for the credit card charge, but none for the promissory note until it is paid.
Answer (A) is incorrect. A deduction is permitted. Answer (C) is incorrect. A deduction is permitted for the donation paid by the credit card charge, but not for the amount paid by giving the promissory note. Answer (D) is incorrect. A deduction is not permitted for the donation paid by giving the promissory note.

6.4.11. For the year, Ms. Shickle had adjusted gross income of $40,000. She contributed $24,000 cash to a church and $6,000 cash to a private nonoperating foundation which is subject to the 30% limitation. What is the amount of Shickle's charitable contribution deduction for the year and the amount to be carried over?

	Deduction for the Year	Carryover
A.	$20,000	$0
B.	$20,000	$6,000
C.	$20,000	$10,000
D.	$26,000	$0

Answer (C) is correct. *(SEE, adapted)*
REQUIRED: The charitable contribution deduction for the current year and the amount to be carried over to the following year.

DISCUSSION: All $30,000 ($24,000 + $6,000) of contributions made by Ms. Shickle are deductible contributions. However, the deduction allowed in any tax year is limited to a percentage of the taxpayer's "contribution base" (AGI computed without regard to NOL carrybacks). The percentage is determined by the type of property contributed and the type of organization to which the property is contributed [Sec. 170(b)(1)]. The $24,000 in contributions to a church would be subject to a 50% limitation, while the other $6,000 in contributions is subject to a 30% limitation.

Contribution to church	$24,000
Contribution to nonoperating foundation subject to $12,000 ($40,000 × 30%) limitation	6,000
Total contributions	$30,000
Less: deduction for current year subject to 50% limitation $20,000 ($40,000 × 50%)	(20,000)
Carryforward to next year	$10,000

Note that the carryforward to next year would consist of the following amounts and can be carried forward up to 5 years.

Contribution subject to 50% limitation	$ 4,000
Contribution subject to 30% limitation	6,000
Total carryforward	$10,000

The cash contributions to the 50% charities are considered first for limitation purposes. Since $24,000 contributions exceed the $20,000 overall limitation, $4,000 of the contributions to the 50% charities is carried over. All of the contributions to the 30% charities are also carried over, since the overall limit has already been exceeded.

Answer (A) is incorrect. Ms. Shickle has a carryover of the charitable contribution deduction. Answer (B) is incorrect. The $6,000 carryover is subject to the 30% limitation. Part of the contribution to the church is also carried over. Answer (D) is incorrect. Ms. Shickle may not deduct $26,000 as a charitable contribution in the current year. Part of her charitable contribution deduction will be carried over.

6.4.12. For the year, Mrs. Lynn had adjusted gross income of $30,000. During the year, she contributed $9,000 in cash to her church, $10,000 in cash to qualified public charities, and a painting she has owned for 8 years with a fair market value of $16,000 and a $4,000 adjusted basis to her city's library. What is the amount of Mrs. Lynn's allowable charitable contributions deduction for the year?

A. $15,000

B. $19,000

C. $30,000

D. $35,000

Answer (A) is correct. *(SEE, adapted)*
REQUIRED: The taxpayer's allowable charitable contribution deduction.

DISCUSSION: Mrs. Lynn's charitable deduction limitation is $15,000 (50% of her adjusted gross income). All of her contributions qualify under Sec. 170; thus the amount of her contribution is $35,000. However, the amount of her allowable charitable contribution deduction for the year is limited to $15,000. The excess $20,000 can be carried forward and deducted in the 5 succeeding tax years [Sec. 170(d)]. The amount of the contribution of the painting is its $16,000 FMV. The fair market value is not reduced by what would have been long-term capital gain had Mrs. Lynn sold it because it is presumed that the property is used in connection with the library's tax-exempt purpose. Even though no reduction occurs, the 30% limitation on contributions of capital gain property is applicable.

Answer (B) is incorrect. The FMV of the painting is a charitable contribution, but the deduction is limited to 50% of AGI in the current year, with the excess creating a carryover. Answer (C) is incorrect. The total amount of AGI is $30,000. Answer (D) is incorrect. The total charitable contribution is $35,000, all of which is not deductible in the current year.

6.4.13. Stuart Green had adjusted gross income during the year of $200,000 and made contributions to qualified charities as follows:

	Basis	FMV
Cash	$10,000	$10,000
Inventory	6,000	8,000
IBM stock	8,000	5,000

Green's charitable contribution deduction is

A. $21,000

B. $23,000

C. $24,000

D. $26,000

Answer (A) is correct. *(I.S. Greenberg)*
REQUIRED: The charitable contribution deduction for the property contributed.
DISCUSSION: The taxpayer is allowed a deduction for the full amount of the cash contributed ($10,000). Inventory contributed to a charitable organization is considered ordinary income property. If such property is contributed, Sec. 170(e)(1)(A) limits the deduction to its fair market value less the amount of ordinary income that would have been reported if the property had been sold (in most instances, the deduction is limited to the cost basis of the property). The deduction for inventory is thus limited to $6,000. The IBM stock is valued at its fair market value ($5,000) because there would be no long-term capital gain if sold at its FMV. Green's total deduction is $21,000 ($10,000 cash + $6,000 inventory + $5,000 IBM stock).
Note that Green will not be able to deduct the loss on the stock (FMV less than basis). Thus, such assets may not make a good choice for a charitable contribution.
Answer (B) is incorrect. The inventory should be valued at its $6,000 adjusted basis. Answer (C) is incorrect. The stock should be valued at its $5,000 FMV. Answer (D) is incorrect. The inventory and the stock are not valued correctly for calculating Green's contribution deduction.

6.4.14. Mr. Q is single and has adjusted gross income of $7,250 in the year. He made the following contributions in December of the year:

Appraisal fee on donated property	$ 250
Nonprofit hospital, cash	400
War veterans' organization, land held as inventory: fair market value	4,000
basis	2,200
Domestic fraternal society (to be used exclusively for a qualified charitable purpose), cash	850
Value of land used for church picnic	300

What is his allowable contribution deduction?

A. $2,575

B. $3,625

C. $3,700

D. $4,000

Answer (A) is correct. *(SEE, adapted)*
REQUIRED: The taxpayer's allowable charitable contribution deduction.
DISCUSSION: An appraisal fee paid on donated property is not an amount paid to a qualified organization and therefore is not deductible as a charitable contribution (Rev. Rul. 67-461). It is deductible as a miscellaneous itemized deduction subject to the 2% limitation. The value of the use of the taxpayer's land is also not deductible [Sec. 170(f)(1)]. The land is ordinary income property and deductible in the amount of the property's fair market value minus the amount of ordinary income that would be recognized if the property had instead been sold ($2,200 = $4,000 − $1,800). The deduction for the $2,200 contribution to the war veterans' organization and the $850 contribution to the domestic fraternal society are limited to 30% of the taxpayer's adjusted gross income [Sec. 170(b)(1)(B)], since these are charitable organizations to which the 50% limit does not apply. The taxpayer may also deduct the $400 contribution to the nonprofit hospital (a 50% charity).

War veterans' organization	$2,200	
Fraternal society	850	
Limited to 30% of AGI ($7,250)	$3,050	$2,175
Nonprofit hospital		400
Allowable contribution deduction (limited to 50% of $7,250 = $3,625)		$2,575

Answer (B) is incorrect. The 50% of AGI charitable contribution deduction limit is $3,625. Answer (C) is incorrect. This amount includes the appraisal fee, which is a miscellaneous itemized deduction, and does not consider the 30% or 50% of AGI limits. Answer (D) is incorrect. The FMV of the land is $4,000, which is deductible only for its adjusted basis. Omitted are the two cash contributions and the effect of the 30% of AGI limitation.

6.4.15. Ruth Lewis has adjusted gross income of $100,000 for the year and itemizes her deductions. On March 1, Year 1, she made a contribution to a private nonoperating foundation (not a 50% charity) of exchange-traded stock held for investment for 2 years that cost $25,000 and had a fair market value of $70,000. The foundation sold the stock for $70,000 on the same date. Assume that Lewis made no other contributions during the year. How much should Lewis claim as a charitable contribution deduction for this year?

A. $50,000

B. $30,000

C. $25,000

D. $20,000

Answer (D) is correct. *(CPA, adapted)*
REQUIRED: The amount of charitable contribution deduction for stock contributed to a private nonoperating foundation.
DISCUSSION: Generally, contributions to private operating foundations are limited to 30% of the taxpayer's adjusted gross income. But contributions of long-term capital gain property to private nonoperating foundations are limited to 20% of the taxpayer's adjusted gross income [Sec. 170(b)(1)(D)]. Lewis's charitable contribution deduction should be limited to $20,000 ($100,000 × 20%).

For deduction purposes, the contribution is equal to $25,000 ($70,000 fair market value – $45,000 long-term capital gain) because it is being made to a private nonoperating foundation [Sec. 170(e)(1)(B)]. The amount of $20,000 can be deducted in this year. The remaining $5,000 can be carried forward for up to 5 years. The deduction for stock contributed to private foundations would be $70,000 provided the stock is publicly traded. However, the deduction is still limited to $20,000, with $50,000 being carried forward.

Answer (A) is incorrect. The 50%-of-AGI limit is $50,000, but the private nonoperating foundation is not a 50% charity. Answer (B) is incorrect. The 30%-of-AGI limit is $30,000, but the private nonoperating foundation is not a 30% charity. Answer (C) is incorrect. The $25,000 adjusted basis is the total charitable contribution.

6.4.16. In Year 1, T contributed $8,000 cash and also some appreciated intangible capital gain property, which T had held for 2 years, to the University of Illinois. The appreciated capital gain property had a basis to T of $3,000 and a FMV of $5,000. In Year 2, T contributed $1,000 cash to the University. For Year 1 and Year 2, T had AGI of $20,000 and $8,000, respectively. T itemized his deductions in both years. What is T's charitable deduction carryforward, if any, to Year 3?

A. $0

B. $600

C. $2,400

D. $3,400

Answer (B) is correct. *(Publisher, adapted)*
REQUIRED: The charitable contribution carryforward to Year 3.
DISCUSSION: All contributions were made to a public charitable organization. Under Sec. 170(b)(1)(C), intangible long-term capital gain property is subject to a 30% limitation that also applies to carryforwards. (Note that the taxpayer can elect the 50% limitation with a contribution amount of the fair market value minus the long-term capital gain.)

Calculation for Year 1

Cash	$ 8,000
Capital gain property subject to $6,000 ($20,000 × .30) limitation	5,000
	$13,000
Deduction subject to $10,000 ($20,000 × .50) limitation	(10,000)
Carryforward subject to 30% limit	$ 3,000

Calculation for Year 2

Cash	$ 1,000
$3,000 carryforward with $2,400 ($8,000 × .30) limitation	2,400
Deduction subject to $4,000 ($8,000 × .50) limitation	$ 3,400

The $2,400 limitation for the capital gain property results in a carryforward to Year 3 of

Carryover from Year 1	$ 3,000
Year 2 deduction of Year 1 carryforward	(2,400)
Carryforward to Year 3 still subject to a 30% limitation	$ 600

Answer (A) is incorrect. There is a charitable deduction carryforward. Answer (C) is incorrect. The 30%-of-AGI limit in Year 2 is $2,400. Answer (D) is incorrect. The total charitable deduction allowed in Year 2 is $3,400.

6.4.17. All of the following statements relating to a contribution of $500 or more of charitable deduction property (property other than money or publicly traded securities) are true except

A. An organization that received such property in July of the current year and sells it in December of the following year must file a special return Form 8282, *Donee Information Return*, within 90 days after the disposition.

B. An organization selling such property must provide the donor with a copy of Form 8282 or be subject to a penalty.

C. The donor of such property is required to get a qualified appraisal if the claimed value of the property exceeds $1,000.

D. The organization receiving such property is not a qualified appraiser for the purpose of making a qualified appraisal.

Answer (C) is correct. *(SEE, adapted)*
REQUIRED: The false statement concerning a noncash charitable contribution.
DISCUSSION: A donor of noncash charitable contributions is not required to obtain a qualified appraisal unless the value of the property exceeds $5,000. If the value of the property exceeds $500 but is not over $5,000, then the person making the contribution must retain a description of the property including its fair market value and how the fair market value was computed (Reg. 1.170A-13). Contributions of single items of clothing and household items, for which a deduction of $500 or more is claimed, must be accompanied by an appraisal.
Answer (A) is incorrect. An organization that received a contribution of $500 or more of charitable deduction property (property other than money or publicly traded securities) in July of the current year and sells it in December of the following year must file a special return Form 8282, *Donee Information Return*, within 90 days after the disposition. Answer (B) is incorrect. An organization selling a contribution of $500 or more of charitable deduction property (property other than money or publicly traded securities) must provide the donor with a copy of Form 8282 or be subject to a penalty. Answer (D) is incorrect. The organization receiving a contribution of $500 or more of charitable deduction property (property other than money or publicly traded securities) is not a qualified appraiser for the purpose of making a qualified appraisal.

6.4.18. In the current year, Mr. F, a farmer, contributed a mower that he used on his farm to a church. The fair market value of the mower is $400. Mr. F purchased it 3 years ago for $600 and has claimed $300 depreciation. The amount of Mr. F's contribution deduction is $100.

A. True.

B. False.

Answer (B) is correct. *(SEE, adapted)*
DISCUSSION: The amount of any charitable contribution of property must be reduced by the amount of gain that would not have been long-term capital gain if the property had been sold [Sec. 170(e)]. If the taxpayer had sold the mower for its fair market value of $400, he would have realized a gain of $100 ($400 realized – $300 basis). This $100 gain would have been characterized as ordinary income under the recapture provisions of Sec. 1245. Thus, the $400 FMV of the mower is reduced by the $100 of gain that would not be long-term capital gain if Mr. F sold the property, giving him a charitable contribution deduction of $300.

6.4.19. Farmer A donated a hog that he had raised and was holding for sale to his church for its annual picnic on July 3 of the current year. Farmer A can deduct the fair market value of the hog as a charitable contribution on his current-year return.

A. True.

B. False.

Answer (B) is correct. *(SEE, adapted)*
DISCUSSION: Inventory contributed to a charitable organization is considered ordinary income property. Section 170(e) limits the deduction to its fair market value less the amount of ordinary income that would have been reported if the property had been sold (in most instances, the deduction is limited to the cost basis of the property). However, the Pension Protection Act of 2006 enhanced the deduction to the lesser of (1) two times the item's basis, or (2) the item's basis plus 1/2 of the appreciation. A farmer who raises animals generally has no cost basis in them because the cost of raising animals is deducted currently. Therefore, Farmer A would have no basis in the hog and would not be able to claim any deduction for the charitable contribution.

6.4.20. The Veterans of Foreign Wars of the United States is a qualified charitable organization.

A. True.

B. False.

Answer (A) is correct. *(SEE, adapted)*
DISCUSSION: A post or organization of war veterans organized in the United States and no part of the net earnings of which inures to the benefit of any private shareholder or individual is a qualified organization [Sec. 170(c)(3)].

6.4.21. Mr. C contributed $100 to the presidential campaign in the current year. Mr. C can deduct the $100.

A. True.

B. False.

Answer (B) is correct. *(SEE, adapted)*
DISCUSSION: Section 170(c)(2)(D) specifically provides that an organization is not qualified if it participates in any political campaign on behalf of (or in opposition to) any candidate for public office.

6.4.22. An individual donates land that he has held for 2 years to his town. The fair market value of this land may qualify as a charitable contribution.

A. True.

B. False.

Answer (A) is correct. *(SEE, adapted)*
DISCUSSION: The charitable contribution of property is valued at fair market value, although the annual deduction for long-term capital gain property is limited to 30% of the taxpayer's contribution base (adjusted gross income computed without regard to a net operating loss carryback) [Sec. 170(b)(1)(C)].

6.4.23. Mrs. S donated two pints of her blood to the Red Cross. The fair market value per pint on the dates the blood was given was $25 and $30. The $55 is deductible by Mrs. S as a noncash contribution.

A. True.

B. False.

Answer (B) is correct. *(SEE, adapted)*
DISCUSSION: A person has no basis in one's own blood. If sold, the gain would not be long-term capital gain according to the IRS. Therefore, the contribution is reduced by the entire gain, i.e., its value, under Sec. 170(e)(1)(A).

6.4.24. Child care expenses that are incurred while you perform services for a qualified charitable organization are not deductible.

A. True.

B. False.

Answer (A) is correct. *(SEE, adapted)*
DISCUSSION: Expenses incurred by taxpayers in caring for their children while performing gratuitous services for charitable organizations are nondeductible personal expenses under Sec. 262 and, therefore, not deductible as charitable contributions (Treasury Information Release 1267).

6.4.25. Jerry attended a charity auction and purchased a piano for $5,000 which had a FMV of $3,000. The charity must issue Jerry a receipt for a $5,000 donation.

A. True.

B. False.

Answer (B) is correct. *(Publisher, adapted)*
DISCUSSION: Charitable organizations must inform donors that quid pro quo contributions in excess of $75 are only deductible to the extent the contribution exceeds the FMV of the goods purchased. The organization must provide a written statement which informs the donor of the actual amount of the contribution of $2,000 ($5,000 cash payment – $3,000 FMV of the piano).

6.5 Casualty and Theft Losses

NOTE: See Study Unit 3 for casualty and theft loss incurred in a business.

6.5.1. A flood completely destroyed Mr. and Mrs. Washington's home on November 30 of the current year. The home was located in a federally declared disaster area. They claimed the loss on their current-year tax return. Based on the following facts, what is the amount of loss Mr. and Mrs. Washington can deduct for the current year?

Basis (contents not considered for this purpose)	$110,000
Fair market value before flood	150,000
Fair market value after flood	30,000
Insurance reimbursement received February 15 of the following year	80,000
Replacement February 1 of the following year (property provided under disaster relief programs of government agencies)	8,000
Adjusted gross income for the current year	40,000

A. $0

B. $17,900

C. $27,900

D. $35,900

Answer (B) is correct. *(SEE, adapted)*
REQUIRED: The total casualty loss deduction for the year.
DISCUSSION: Section 165(h) allows a casualty deduction for nonbusiness casualty losses to the extent that each uninsured loss exceeds $100 and the aggregate of all such losses during the year exceeds 10% of AGI. The amount of a loss is the lesser of the decrease in the fair market value of the property resulting from the casualty or the property's adjusted basis. If any insurance reimbursements result in casualty gains, the gains are netted against casualty losses before computing the casualty loss deduction. In any case, a deduction for casualty losses is allowed to the extent of any casualty gain, without regard to the 10% test.

Lesser of adjusted basis [$110,000 or decrease in FMV ($120,000)]	$110,000
Less: Insurance reimbursement	(80,000)
Replacement property	(8,000)
$100 per occurrence	(100)
10% of AGI	(4,000)
Deductible casualty loss	$ 17,900

Answer (A) is incorrect. A loss can be deducted in the current year. Answer (C) is incorrect. The loss on the nonbusiness property should be based on the adjusted basis ($110,000) since it is less than the decrease in FMV ($120,000) due to the flood. Answer (D) is incorrect. The loss on the property should be based on the adjusted basis. Additionally, the $8,000 replacement property reduces the deductible loss.

6.5.2. Which of the following events is a casualty loss that is deductible?

   A. Damage to a house from wood rotting.

   B. Decline in value of a home due to mudslides which damaged only neighboring homes.

   C. Damage to a building from a fire which was intentionally set by an enemy of the taxpayer.

   D. Loss of a seawall from the waves continually striking it.

Answer (C) is correct. *(Publisher, adapted)*
  REQUIRED: The event that is a casualty for tax deduction purposes.
  DISCUSSION: A casualty is defined as the complete or partial destruction of property from a sudden, unexpected, or unusual cause. A fire is a sudden and unexpected event causing damage to a building. It does not matter that the fire was intentionally set as long as it was not intentionally set by the taxpayer incurring the loss.
  Answer (A) is incorrect. Damage from rotting wood is not considered a loss from a sudden event. Answer (B) is incorrect. It has been held that physical damage to the taxpayer's property must occur to sustain a casualty loss. Answer (D) is incorrect. The loss of or damage to a seawall from the continual pounding by waves is not from a sudden or unexpected event.

6.5.3. Which of the following are casualty losses for tax purposes?

1. Damage to fur coat by moths
2. Water damage to rugs caused by bursting water heater
3. Damage to old water heater that burst
4. Damage to residence by earthquake
5. Citrus trees killed by a freeze

   A. 1, 3, and 5.

   B. 2, 3, and 4.

   C. 2, 4, and 5.

   D. 2, 3, 4, and 5.

Answer (C) is correct. *(SEE, adapted)*
  REQUIRED: The losses that are casualty losses for tax purposes.
  DISCUSSION: A casualty is defined as the complete or partial destruction of property resulting from a sudden, unexpected, or unusual cause. Water damage to rugs caused by a bursting water heater, damage to a residence by earthquake, and freeze damage to citrus trees are all losses resulting from sudden and unexpected events. Each is a casualty loss for tax purposes.
  Answer (A) is incorrect. Items 1 and 3 are not sudden events. Damage to a fur coat by moths and damage to an old water heater that burst are losses from events that occur slowly over time. Hence, they are not casualty losses for tax purposes. Answer (B) is incorrect. Item 3 is not a sudden event. Damage to an old water heater that burst is a loss that occurs slowly over time. Hence, it is not a casualty loss for tax purposes. Answer (D) is incorrect. Item 3 is not a sudden event. Damage to an old water heater that burst is a loss that occurs slowly over time. Hence, it is not a casualty loss for tax purposes.

6.5.4. Several years ago, Mr. B purchased an antique vase for his personal use at a flea market sale for $500. This vase was stolen on July 1 of this year, when its fair market value was $1,000. Mr. B had insurance on the vase, but only for $300 with no deductible amount. B had no other casualty or theft losses. What is the amount of B's allowable casualty and theft loss for this year, disregarding the limitation based on adjusted gross income?

   A. $100

   B. $200

   C. $500

   D. $600

Answer (A) is correct. *(SEE, adapted)*
  REQUIRED: The amount of the casualty and theft loss deduction for this year without regard to the adjusted gross income limitation.
  DISCUSSION: Disregarding the adjusted gross income limitation, Mr. B's casualty and theft loss deduction would be $100 computed as follows:

Adjusted basis in vase	$500
Less: insurance reimbursement	(300)
Loss sustained	$200
Less: floor amount for casualty losses	(100)
Casualty and theft loss deduction	$100

Note that casualty and theft losses are generally limited to the amount that each loss exceeds $100. After the $100-floor limitation is applied to each loss, all losses are aggregated and are deductible to the extent that they exceed 10% of the taxpayer's adjusted gross income [Sec. 165(h)(2)].
  Answer (B) is incorrect. The loss sustained without reduction for the $100 nondeductible floor amount for casualty losses is $200. Answer (C) is incorrect. The adjusted basis in the vase is $500. The reimbursement and the $100 nondeductible floor should be subtracted from the basis. Answer (D) is incorrect. The FMV of the vase less the reimbursement and the $100 nondeductible floor is $600. The adjusted basis, not the FMV, should be used.

6.5.5. Mr. A lives in an area that had been hit by a flood in the current year. Mr. A's house was not damaged. An appraisal of A's property indicates the following:

Cost	$50,000
Improvements	5,000
Fair market value, December 31 of the current year	45,000

In addition, A spent $3,500 for a drainage system around his house because of potential flooding. Without considering any limitations, what is the amount of A's deductible casualty loss for the current year?

A. $0
B. $3,500
C. $10,000
D. $13,500

6.5.6. A deductible loss would result from which of the following?

A. Valuable sound equipment stolen from your home by unknown persons.

B. Damage to your home caused by termites over an extended period of time.

C. Damage to your automobile caused by the willful negligence of a friend who was driving your automobile.

D. A valuable piece of art destroyed by your household pet.

6.5.7. Which of the conditions below is not required for a taxpayer to claim a casualty loss deduction if his or her personal residence is demolished or relocated after a disaster?

A. The residence is damaged as a result of the disaster.

B. The residence is located in an area designated to warrant assistance under the Disaster Relief Act of 1974.

C. The residence has been rendered unsafe for use as a residence owing to the disaster.

D. Within 120 days of the disaster relief determination, the state or local government orders the residence demolished or relocated.

Answer (A) is correct. *(SEE, adapted)*
REQUIRED: The deductible casualty loss for reduced value in a residence from neighborhood flooding.
DISCUSSION: A casualty is defined as the complete or partial destruction of property from a sudden, unexpected, or unusual cause. Although a flood is a sudden cause, it has been held that physical damage to the taxpayer's property must occur to sustain a casualty loss. Since the value of Mr. A's property decreased only because there was a flood in the surrounding area and not because the house was actually flooded itself, no casualty loss is available. The amount spent to add a drainage system around the house is a capital improvement which increases the cost basis in his residence.
Answer (B) is incorrect. The amount Mr. A spent for a drainage system around his house because of potential flooding is $3,500. Potential flooding is not casualty damage/loss. Answer (C) is incorrect. The $10,000 difference between adjusted basis and FMV is not caused by qualifying casualty damage. Answer (D) is incorrect. Physical damage to a taxpayer's property must occur to sustain a casualty loss.

Answer (A) is correct. *(SEE, adapted)*
REQUIRED: The event that would result in a loss.
DISCUSSION: Any loss from theft is a deductible loss in the year it is discovered.
Answer (B) is incorrect. A casualty is defined as the complete or partial destruction of property from a sudden, unexpected, or unusual cause. This event does not fall within this definition. Answer (C) is incorrect. A casualty loss is sustained when an automobile owned by the taxpayer is damaged and when the damage results from the faulty driving of the taxpayer or other person operating the automobile but such damage cannot be due to a willful act or willful negligence of the taxpayer or someone acting on his or her behalf. Answer (D) is incorrect. A casualty is defined as the complete or partial destruction of property from a sudden, unexpected, or unusual cause. This event does not fall within this definition.

Answer (A) is correct. *(S. Byrd)*
REQUIRED: The condition that is not a requirement for a casualty loss deduction if a personal residence is demolished or relocated after a disaster.
DISCUSSION: Section 165(k) allows a casualty loss deduction to taxpayers who are ordered to have their personal residences demolished or relocated as a result of a disaster. The requirements for the casualty loss treatment are that the residence be located in an area designated to warrant assistance under the Disaster Relief Act of 1974, the residence has been rendered unsafe for use as a residence owing to the disaster, and the taxpayer has been ordered by the state or local government, not later than 120 days after the federal determination, to demolish or relocate the residence.
However, there is not a requirement that the residence actually be damaged.
Answer (B) is incorrect. The residence being located in an area designated to warrant assistance under the Disaster Relief Act of 1974 is a requirement for a casualty loss deduction if the personal residence is demolished or relocated after a disaster. Answer (C) is incorrect. The residence being rendered unsafe for use as a residence owing to the disaster is a requirement for a casualty loss deduction if the personal residence is demolished or relocated after a disaster. Answer (D) is incorrect. A requirement for a casualty loss deduction, if the personal residence is demolished or relocated after a disaster, is that the order must be made by the state or local government within 120 days of the disaster relief determination.

6.5.8. Kultchurd went to a museum wearing a very expensive ring. Upon leaving the museum, she realized the ring was missing. Kultchurd had bought the ring several years earlier for $5,000 and its fair market value before it was lost was $9,000. What is Kultchurd's theft loss deduction?

A. $0

B. $4,900

C. $5,000

D. $8,900

Answer (A) is correct. *(Publisher, adapted)*
REQUIRED: The theft loss deduction for lost property.
DISCUSSION: Theft includes larceny, embezzlement, and robbery [Reg. 1.165-8(d)]. It does not include misplacing property or other loss by inadvertence. Without some proof or specific indication that a theft actually occurred, there can be no deduction for a theft loss.

Answer (B) is incorrect. The adjusted basis in the ring less the $100 nondeductible floor for casualty losses is $4,900. The loss must qualify as theft. Answer (C) is incorrect. The adjusted basis in the ring is $5,000, not Kultchurd's theft loss deduction. The loss must qualify as theft. Answer (D) is incorrect. The FMV of the ring less the $100 nondeductible floor amount for casualty losses is $8,900. The loss must qualify as theft.

6.5.9. Keith wrecked his speedboat on Lake George during the summer of the current year. Damage to the boat was estimated at $30,000. Original cost was $25,000. The boat was partially insured, and Keith received an insurance reimbursement of $15,000. Keith's adjusted gross income is $50,000, and he had no other losses during the year. What amount can Keith deduct on his tax return for this year?

A. $4,900

B. $5,000

C. $9,900

D. $14,900

Answer (A) is correct. *(Publisher, adapted)*
REQUIRED: The amount of a casualty loss to be deducted on the current-year tax return.
DISCUSSION: Personal losses are allowed only to the extent that total losses exceed 10% of adjusted gross income and to the extent that each loss exceeds $100. The amount of the casualty loss is the lesser of the asset's basis ($25,000) or the decrease in fair market value ($30,000). Hence, the loss is limited to $25,000, reduced by the insurance reimbursement of $15,000, the $100 floor, and 10% of AGI.

Loss	$25,000
Less: Insurance	(15,000)
$100 floor per casualty	(100)
10% of AGI	(5,000)
Deductible casualty loss	$ 4,900

Answer (B) is incorrect. The amount of $5,000 does not include the reduction for the $100 nondeductible floor. Answer (C) is incorrect. The amount of $9,900 does not include the reduction for 10% of AGI that is nondeductible. Answer (D) is incorrect. The difference between the FMV and the insurance reimbursement reduced by the $100 floor is $14,900. The difference between the boat's adjusted basis and the reimbursement should be reduced by the $100 nondeductible floor and 10% of AGI.

6.5.10. The following information pertains to Cole's personal residence, which sustained casualty fire damage in the current year:

Adjusted basis	$150,000
Fair market value immediately before the fire	200,000
Fair market value immediately after the fire	180,000
Fire damage repairs paid for by Cole in the current year	10,000

The house was uninsured. Before consideration of any "floor" or other limitation on tax deductibility, the amount of the casualty loss was

A. $30,000

B. $20,000

C. $10,000

D. $0

Answer (B) is correct. *(CPA, adapted)*
REQUIRED: The casualty loss (before any limitations) when a residence is damaged by fire.
DISCUSSION: The amount of a casualty loss under Sec. 165 is the lesser of the decrease in the fair market value of the property resulting from the casualty or the taxpayer's adjusted basis in the property. The decrease in the fair market value of Cole's residence is $20,000 ($200,000 – $180,000). This is less than the adjusted basis, so the casualty loss is $20,000.

The repairs paid by Cole are not an additional loss. Instead, they are an effort by Cole to replace the loss which has already occurred.

Answer (A) is incorrect. The difference between the adjusted basis and the FMV after the fire is $30,000. The amount of a casualty loss is the lesser of the decrease in FMV caused by the casualty or the adjusted basis of the property. Answer (C) is incorrect. The cost of the repairs is $10,000. The amount of a casualty loss is the lesser of the decrease in FMV caused by the casualty or the adjusted basis of the property. Answer (D) is incorrect. The casualty loss deduction is affected by the fluctuation in FMV caused by the casualty, or the adjusted basis of the property.

6.5.11. Ms. Gray owned a building that was built on leased land. She used half the building in her business and lived in the other half. In April of the current year, the building was completely destroyed by a fire caused by faulty wiring. What is the amount of Ms. Gray's business and personal casualty losses, after any limitations, based on the following information?

Cost of building	$100,000
Depreciation properly deducted	20,000
Fair market value of building immediately before the fire	120,000
Insurance reimbursement, October of the current year	50,000
Ms. Gray's adjusted gross income for the current year	50,000

	Business Loss	Personal Loss
A.	$0	$0
B.	$0	$19,900
C.	$5,000	$24,900
D.	$5,000	$19,900

Answer (D) is correct. *(SEE, adapted)*
REQUIRED: The taxpayer's deductible business and personal casualty losses for the current year.
DISCUSSION: Personal casualty losses of an individual are deductible to the extent that the loss from each casualty exceeds $100. The amount of a personal casualty loss is the lesser of the decrease in fair market value or the adjusted basis of the property, less any insurance reimbursement. The amount of a business casualty loss from total destruction of business property is the property's adjusted basis, less any insurance reimbursement. If there are no personal casualty gains, the aggregate of all personal casualty losses for the year are deductible only to the extent they exceed 10% of adjusted gross income [Sec. 165(h)(2)]. Business casualty losses are not subject to the $100 per casualty limit or the 10%-of-AGI limit.

Business

Adjusted basis ($50,000 – $20,000 = $30,000)	$30,000
Less: insurance reimbursement	(25,000)
Deductible casualty loss	$ 5,000

Personal

Lesser of adjusted basis ($50,000) or decrease in FMV ($60,000)	$50,000
Less: Insurance reimbursement	(25,000)
$100 per occurrence	(100)
10% of AGI	(5,000)
Deductible casualty loss	$19,900

Answer (A) is incorrect. Since there are two separate properties for tax purposes, Ms. Gray has both a business loss and a personal loss. Answer (B) is incorrect. Since there are two separate properties for tax purposes, Ms. Gray has a business loss. Answer (C) is incorrect. Ms. Gray does not have a personal loss of $24,900, which does not take into account the 10%-of-AGI limit.

6.5.12. In October of the current year, John Dill's wife was involved in an accident while driving the family automobile. Damage to the automobile was estimated at $300. Though fully insured, Dill was fearful that his automobile insurance rates would rise as a result of the accident. He did not notify his insurance company and had the automobile repaired at his own expense. What amount can he deduct as a casualty loss on his income tax return for the current year if his adjusted gross income is $1,000?

A. $0

B. $100

C. $200

D. $300

Answer (A) is correct. *(CPA, adapted)*
REQUIRED: The amount the taxpayer may deduct as a casualty loss when an insurance claim is not made.
DISCUSSION: A deduction for a personal casualty loss is allowed by Sec. 165(c). However, any loss is deductible only to the extent it is not compensated for by insurance or otherwise. Since Dill's automobile was fully insured, the loss he sustained resulted from his choice not to collect the insurance proceeds rather than from a casualty. Section 165(h)(4)(E) requires an insurance claim to be timely filed if the loss is covered by insurance.

Answer (B) is incorrect. The nondeductible floor for casualty losses is $100. Answer (C) is incorrect. The estimated amount of damage to the automobile less the $100 nondeductible floor for casualty losses is $200. The allowable deduction is affected by the insurance coverage. Answer (D) is incorrect. The estimated amount of damage to the automobile is $300. The allowable deduction is affected by the insurance coverage.

6.5.13. Determine the deductible casualty loss for Mr. J for the year. Mr. J's adjusted gross income is $40,000.

Asset	J's Adj. Basis	FMV Before	FMV After	Insurance Reimbursement
T	$ 300	$ 2,000	$ 500	$ 50
O	14,000	10,000	4,000	1,000
P	600	3,000	2,775	125

Each asset was damaged in a separate casualty during the year. All casualty losses were nonbusiness personal property losses and none occurred in a federally declared disaster area.

   A. $13,725

   B. $9,725

   C. $2,550

   D. $1,050

Answer (D) is correct. *(SEE, adapted)*
   REQUIRED: The deductible casualty loss for the year.
   DISCUSSION: Each loss must be calculated separately, and the $100 limitation applies to each loss [Sec. 165(h)].

	Asset		
	T	O	P
Loss amount (lesser of decrease in FMV or adjusted basis)	$300	$6,000	$225
Less: Insurance	(50)	(1,000)	(125)
$100 floor	(100)	(100)	(100)
Casualty loss	$150	$4,900	$ 0

   The total casualty loss of $5,050 ($150 + $4,900 + $0) is deductible to the extent it exceeds $4,000 ($40,000 adjusted gross income × 10%). Accordingly, J's deduction for the year is $1,050.
   Answer (A) is incorrect. The adjusted basis of each property was used to find the casualty loss. Since each loss involves a nonbusiness property, the lesser of the adjusted basis or the decline in FMV due to casualty should be used for each property. Additionally, the $100 nondeductible floor must be subtracted for each property ($300), and the 10%-of-AGI nondeductible floor ($4,000) must be subtracted to find the deductible casualty loss. Answer (B) is incorrect. The adjusted basis of each property was used to find the casualty loss. Since each loss involves a nonbusiness property, the lesser of the adjusted basis or the decline in FMV due to the casualty should be used for each property. Additionally, the $100 nondeductible floor must be subtracted for each property ($300). Answer (C) is incorrect. The decline in the FMV of each property was used to find the casualty loss. Since each loss involves a nonbusiness property, the lesser of the adjusted basis or the decline in FMV due to the casualty should be used for each property. Additionally, the $100 nondeductible floor must be subtracted for each property ($300).

6.5.14. Ed can reasonably estimate his loss from a savings account deposit in a bankrupt qualified financial institution. Ed can choose to treat the amount as either a casualty loss or an ordinary loss in the current year, or wait until the year of final determination and treat the loss as a nonbusiness bad debt.

   A. True.

   B. False.

Answer (A) is correct. *(SEE, adapted)*
   DISCUSSION: Section 165(l) provides that a taxpayer incurring a loss on deposits in a bankrupt or insolvent financial institution may choose to treat the loss as an ordinary loss or casualty loss rather than as a nonbusiness bad debt. This treatment is allowed provided that the taxpayer is not at least a 1% owner or officer of the financial institution or related to that owner or officer. The casualty loss alternative is subject to the $100 floor and 10%-of-AGI limitations.

6.5.15. While driving home from work, Mr. B's car unavoidably skidded on ice and struck the car in front of him, causing extensive damage to both cars. Mr. B may not deduct a casualty loss since the accident was solely his fault.

   A. True.

   B. False.

Answer (B) is correct. *(SEE, adapted)*
   DISCUSSION: A casualty is defined as the complete or partial destruction of property resulting from some sudden, unexpected, or unusual cause. An auto accident meets this definition if it was not caused by the taxpayer's willful act or willful negligence. The damage to Mr. B's car is deductible as a casualty loss [Reg. Sec. 1.165-7(a)(3)(i)].

6.5.16. For purposes of determining a casualty loss, the amount offered for a vehicle as a trade-in on a new vehicle is the acceptable measure of fair market value.

   A. True.

   B. False.

Answer (B) is correct. *(SEE, adapted)*
   DISCUSSION: Under Reg. 1.165-7(a)(2), fair market value must generally be ascertained by appraisal. The loss can also be determined by the cost of repairs if they are necessary, not excessive, and do not increase the value of the property. Trade-in offers are often inflated to generate business.

6.5.17. Mr. T's boat was damaged by a storm last year. Due to some financial difficulty, he put off having the boat repaired until this year. Mr. T may claim the casualty loss on the boat this year.

A. True.

B. False.

Answer (B) is correct. *(SEE, adapted)*
   DISCUSSION: A deduction for a casualty loss is allowed only for the taxable year in which loss is sustained unless there exists a claim for reimbursement with a reasonable prospect for recovery, but about which there is some uncertainty. In such a case, the loss is deducted when it can be ascertained with reasonable certainty whether such reimbursement will be received [Reg. 1.165-1(d)]. Mr. T must deduct the casualty loss in the previous year.

6.5.18. An election exists whereby a loss in a federally declared disaster area can be deducted on the tax return for the year immediately preceding the year in which the disaster occurred.

A. True.

B. False.

Answer (A) is correct. *(SEE, adapted)*
   DISCUSSION: Section 165(i) provides that a taxpayer who has suffered a disaster loss that is allowable as a deduction under Sec. 165(a) may, if the disaster is in an area that warrants assistance from the federal government under the Disaster Relief and Emergency Assistance Act, elect to deduct such loss for the taxable year immediately preceding the taxable year in which the disaster occurred.

6.5.19. In July of the current year, Mr. P, a calendar-year taxpayer, incurred a casualty loss as a result of an event declared to be a federal disaster. He can claim the loss on his prior-year return if he amends the prior-year return within 3 years of its filing date or due date, whichever is later.

A. True.

B. False.

Answer (B) is correct. *(SEE, adapted)*
   DISCUSSION: Under Sec. 165(i), a loss attributable to a disaster occurring in an area declared by the federal government to be a disaster area may be deducted in the year prior to the disaster if the taxpayer so elects. In order to make this election, a statement indicating the election must be filed with the IRS by the later of the due date (without extensions) of the tax return for the year when the loss occurred or the due date (with extensions) of the prior-year return. Mr. P would generally have to file the election by April 15 of next year.

6.5.20. The amount of a nonbusiness casualty loss must be reduced by the expected insurance recovery even though the insurance proceeds are not received until a later year.

A. True.

B. False.

Answer (A) is correct. *(SEE, adapted)*
   DISCUSSION: A casualty loss must be reduced by any insurance recovery that is expected to be received even if the proceeds are not received until a later year. If the reimbursement actually received is less than expected, the difference is claimed as a loss in such later year. If the reimbursement actually received is more than expected, the difference is included in income at such later year.

6.6 Other Itemized Deductions

6.6.1. Which of the following expenses is not deductible in full as an itemized deduction?

A. Property taxes.

B. Reimbursed business expenses of an employee which are not substantiated to the employer.

C. Expenses of a handicapped individual to be able to work.

D. Gambling losses to the extent of gambling winnings.

Answer (B) is correct. *(Publisher, adapted)*
   REQUIRED: The itemized deduction not allowed in full.
   DISCUSSION: Some itemized deductions are allowed in full, and some itemized deductions are deductible only to the extent that they exceed 2% of adjusted gross income. Therefore, we call those deductible in full, first-tier itemized deductions, and those subject to the 2%-of-adjusted-gross-income floor, second-tier itemized deductions. Employee business expenses must be substantiated to the employer and reimbursed to be deductible for adjusted gross income. Otherwise, they are deductible as second-tier itemized deductions.
   Answer (A) is incorrect. Property taxes are a first-tier itemized deduction. Answer (C) is incorrect. Expenses of a handicapped individual to be able to work are a first-tier itemized deduction. Answer (D) is incorrect. Gambling losses to the extent of gambling winnings are a first-tier itemized deduction.

6.6.2. Which one of the following statements is true with regard to an individual taxpayer who has elected to amortize the premium on a bond that yields taxable interest?

A. The amortization is treated as an itemized deduction.

B. The amortization is not treated as a reduction of taxable income.

C. The bond's basis is reduced by the amortization.

D. The bond's basis is increased by the amortization.

Answer (C) is correct. *(CPA, adapted)*
REQUIRED: The true statement regarding bond premiums amortized on a bond yielding taxable interest income.
DISCUSSION: Section 171 permits an election to be made to amortize the premium on a bond yielding taxable interest income. Section 1016(a)(5) requires the basis of the bond to be reduced by the amount of premium that is amortized.
Answer (A) is incorrect. For bonds issued after 1987, the bond premium amortized is an offset against the interest income from the bond. (Amortization is not treated as an itemized deduction.) Answer (B) is incorrect. For bonds issued after 1987, the bond premium amortized is an offset against the interest income from the bond. (Amortization is not treated as a reduction of taxable income.) Answer (D) is incorrect. The basis of the bond is not increased by the amortization.

6.6.3. Which of the following is a true statement concerning miscellaneous itemized deductions?

A. Most miscellaneous itemized deductions are allowed only to the extent they exceed 2% of adjusted gross income.

B. Most miscellaneous itemized deductions are limited to 2% of adjusted gross income.

C. Reimbursed employee business expenses are deductible as miscellaneous itemized deductions, but unreimbursed employee business expenses are not deductible.

D. Moving expenses are itemized deductions.

Answer (A) is correct. *(Publisher, adapted)*
REQUIRED: The true statement regarding miscellaneous itemized deductions.
DISCUSSION: Some miscellaneous itemized deductions are available in full and some are allowed only to the extent that they exceed 2% of adjusted gross income. The first group we call first-tier itemized deductions and the second group (subject to the 2% floor) we call second-tier itemized deductions.
Answer (B) is incorrect. Most miscellaneous itemized deductions are second-tier and are allowed only to the extent in total they exceed 2% of adjusted gross income. Answer (C) is incorrect. Reimbursed employee business expenses are still deductible for adjusted gross income (above the line) provided the employee substantiates the expenses to the employer. Unreimbursed employee business expenses are second-tier itemized deductions. Answer (D) is incorrect. Moving expenses are deductible for AGI deductions, rather than itemized deductions.

6.6.4. All of the following expenses may be claimed on Schedule A as an expense of producing income except

A. Investment counsel fee paid for managing your investments.

B. Trustee's administrative fees that are billed separately and paid in connection with your individual retirement arrangement.

C. Custodian fees and service charges to subscribers in a dividend reinvestment plan.

D. Fee paid to a broker to buy investment property such as stocks or bonds.

Answer (D) is correct. *(SEE, adapted)*
REQUIRED: The expense not allowable as an expense of producing income.
DISCUSSION: A fee paid to a broker to acquire stocks or bonds is a cost of acquiring the property that should be included in the basis of the stocks or bonds under Sec. 1012. A cost to acquire property which is included in the basis of the property is not deducted.
Answer (A) is incorrect. An investment counsel fee paid for managing your investments is allowable as a deduction under Sec. 212 for an ordinary and necessary expense paid or incurred for the production or collection of income, or for the management, conservation, or maintenance of property held for the production of income. However, this expense is considered a second-tier itemized deduction and is deductible to the extent that total second-tier itemized deductions exceed 2% of AGI. Answer (B) is incorrect. Trustee's administrative fees that are billed separately and paid in connection with your individual retirement arrangement are allowable as a deduction under Sec. 212. However, this expense is considered a second-tier itemized deduction and is deductible to the extent that total second-tier itemized deductions exceed 2% of AGI. Answer (C) is incorrect. Custodian fees and service charges to subscribers in a dividend reinvestment plan are allowable as a deduction under Sec. 212. However, this expense is considered a second-tier itemized deduction and is deductible to the extent that total second-tier itemized deductions exceed 2% of AGI.

6.6.5. All of the following items are nondeductible miscellaneous expenses except

   A. Adoption expenses for children with special needs.

   B. Expenses generating tax-exempt income.

   C. Governmental fines and penalties, such as parking tickets.

   D. Subscriptions to professional journals and trade magazines related to your work as an employee.

Answer (D) is correct. *(SEE, adapted)*
   REQUIRED: The item that is deductible as a miscellaneous expense.
   DISCUSSION: Amounts paid by an individual for work-related professional journals and trade magazines would be deductible as unreimbursed employee business expenses. Such expenses are second-tier itemized deductions and subject to the 2%-of-AGI floor.
   Answer (A) is incorrect. Adoption expenses can be claimed as a nonrefundable credit of up to $13,570. However, this credit is phased out when modified adjusted gross income is between $203,540 and $243,540. Answer (B) is incorrect. A deduction is not allowed under Sec. 265 for any expense allocable to the earning of tax-exempt income. Answer (C) is incorrect. Penalties and fines are not deductible, as such a deduction would tend to frustrate public policy [Reg. 1.212-1(p)].

6.6.6. Each of the following expenses is considered a deductible employee expense on Schedule A (Form 1040), except

   A. Firefighter's uniform.

   B. Union membership dues.

   C. Small tools used for work.

   D. Painter's work clothing and standard shoes required by the union.

Answer (D) is correct. *(SEE, adapted)*
   REQUIRED: The expenses incurred that are not deductible as itemized deductions.
   DISCUSSION: A deduction is allowed under Sec. 212 for all ordinary and necessary expenses paid or incurred during the taxable year for the production or collection of income. The items in the other answer choices are deductible under Sec. 212 as second-tier deductions. Protective clothing and equipment are also deductible if they are required as a condition of employment and are not adaptable to regular wear. A firefighter's uniform qualifies under this definition, but a painter's work clothing and standard shoes do not.
   Answer (A) is incorrect. A firefighter's uniform is considered a deductible employee expense. Answer (B) is incorrect. Union membership dues are considered a deductible employee expense. Answer (C) is incorrect. Small tools used for work are considered deductible employee expenses.

6.6.7. Which of the following miscellaneous itemized deductions is subject to the 2%-of-adjusted-gross-income limit?

   A. Unrecovered investment in a pension plan.

   B. Gambling losses to the extent of gambling winnings.

   C. Tax advice and preparation fees.

   D. Impairment-related work expenses of persons with disabilities.

Answer (C) is correct. *(SEE, adapted)*
   REQUIRED: The itemized deduction subject to the 2%-of-AGI floor.
   DISCUSSION: Section 67 provides that certain itemized deductions are only allowed to the extent the aggregate of such deductions exceeds 2% of adjusted gross income. The itemized deductions subject to this 2% floor are those other than ones listed in 67(b). Tax return preparation fees are an itemized deduction allowed by Sec. 212 and not listed in 67(b). Therefore, it is only deductible to the extent it exceeds 2% of AGI.
   Answer (A) is incorrect. The unrecovered investment in a pension annuity that is deductible under Sec. 72(b)(3) is specifically excluded from the 2% rule by Sec. 67(b)(10). Answer (B) is incorrect. Gambling losses are deductible to the extent of gambling winnings as a loss under Sec. 165(d). Section 67(b)(3) specifically excludes such losses from the 2% rule. Answer (D) is incorrect. Impairment-related work expenses are expenses of a handicapped individual for care at the individual's place of employment that are necessary for such person to be able to work. These expenses are deductible under Sec. 162 [Sec. 67(b)(6)].

6.6.8. Mr. and Mrs. Storm's adjusted gross income for the year was $75,000. During the year, they incurred and paid the following:

Investment fees and expenses	$ 750
Tax return preparation fee	250
Union dues	1,500
Gambling losses	3,000
Employment agency fees looking for a new job	2,500
IRA trustee's fees	100

Assuming they itemize, how much can Mr. and Mrs. Storm deduct as miscellaneous itemized expenses?

- A. $6,600
- B. $4,100
- C. $3,600
- D. $3,500

Answer (C) is correct. *(SEE, adapted)*
REQUIRED: The deductible amount of various expenses.
DISCUSSION: Gambling losses are deductible to the extent of winnings (Reg. 1.165-10). They are first-tier deductions without further limitation. Investment fees and expenses, employment agency fees, IRA trustee fees, union dues, and tax return preparation fees are second-tier itemized deductions. However, they are only deductible to the extent they exceed 2% of adjusted gross income. The computation is shown below.

First-tier deduction		
Gambling losses (limited to winnings)		$ 0
Second-tier deductions		
Investment fees and expenses	$ 750	
Tax return preparation fee	250	
Union dues	1,500	
Employment agency fees	2,500	
IRA trustee's fees	100	
	$5,100	
Less: 2% of AGI	(1,500)	3,600
Total deductible expenses		$3,600

Answer (A) is incorrect. The gambling losses are only included to the extent of winnings. Answer (B) is incorrect. Miscellaneous itemized deductions include investment fees and tax return preparation fees. Also, 2% of AGI should be subtracted to determine the deductible portion. Answer (D) is incorrect. The IRA trustee fees are deducted as miscellaneous itemized deductions.

6.6.9. Which of the following expenses may be claimed as a miscellaneous itemized deduction subject to the 2%-of-AGI limit?

- A. Legal expenses to collect taxable alimony.
- B. Expenses of attending shareholders' meeting.
- C. Bar exam fees.
- D. Management fees paid to an investment firm in connection with managing a tax-exempt bond portfolio.

Answer (A) is correct. *(SEE, adapted)*
REQUIRED: The expense that may be deducted subject to the 2%-of-AGI floor.
DISCUSSION: Legal expenses incurred to collect taxable alimony would be allowed as a miscellaneous itemized deduction subject to the 2%-of-adjusted-gross-income limit. Because the alimony is taxable income, legal costs incurred in the collection of the income may be deducted under Sec. 212.
Answer (B) is incorrect. The expense of attending a shareholders' meeting is not directly related to the production or collection of income but, rather, is generally a personal expense and disallowed under Sec. 262. Answer (C) is incorrect. Bar exam fees are also personal expenses and are not deductible under Sec. 262. Answer (D) is incorrect. Fees paid to an investment firm in connection with managing a tax-exempt bond portfolio are nondeductible under Sec. 265 since they are related to the production of tax-exempt income.

6.6.10. Mr. and Mrs. White's adjusted gross income for the current year was $100,000. During the year, they incurred and paid the following:

Business publications	$ 200
Tax return preparation fee	600
Fees for will preparation	1,000
Life insurance premiums	2,000
Union dues	2,400

Assuming they can itemize, how much should the Whites claim as miscellaneous deductible expenses?

- A. $1,200
- B. $3,200
- C. $4,200
- D. $6,000

Answer (A) is correct. *(SEE, adapted)*
REQUIRED: The amount taxpayers can claim as miscellaneous itemized deductions.
DISCUSSION: Under Sec. 262, life insurance premiums and the preparation of a will are personal expenses for which a deduction is disallowed. The business periodicals ($200), tax return preparation fee ($600), and union dues ($2,400) are deductible under Sec. 212 as "second-tier" itemized deductions, to the extent they exceed 2% of AGI. Total deductible items thus amount to $1,200 [$3,200 – ($100,000 × .02)].
Answer (B) is incorrect. Life insurance premiums are not miscellaneous itemized deductions. Answer (C) is incorrect. Life insurance premiums and will preparation fees are not miscellaneous itemized deductions. Answer (D) is incorrect. Life insurance premiums and will preparation fees are not miscellaneous itemized deductions; however, business publications are itemized deductions. A reduction for the 2%-of-AGI nondeductible floor should be made.

6.6.11. Education expenses may be deductible as a miscellaneous itemized deduction as well as any related travel and transportation expenses. Which of the following may also be true concerning education expenses?

    A. The education expense is deductible, even though it may qualify one for an additional trade or business as long as it improves one's skills in an established trade or business.

    B. The expenses related to education are deductible if the education is primarily to bring one up to the minimum level of knowledge or skills required by the employer.

    C. As long as one has met the minimum knowledge or skill requirements for one's established employment, trade, or business, all additional expenses are deductible.

    D. Education expenses are for the most part deductible as long as one has already met the minimum requirements for one's established employment, trade, or business; the education does not qualify one for a new trade or business; and either the education is necessary to keep a present job status or pay rate, or it maintains or improves skills needed in present work.

Answer (D) is correct. *(Publisher, adapted)*
    REQUIRED: The true statement concerning education expenses.
    DISCUSSION: Expenditures made by an individual for education include amounts spent on correspondence courses, travel and transportation costs, supplies and books, and tuition. They are deductible as second-tier itemized deductions if the education maintains or improves skills required of the individual in his or her employment or other trade or business, or if it meets the express requirements of the individual's employer or the requirements of applicable law or regulations imposed as a condition to the retention by the individual of an established employment relationship, status, or rate of compensation [Reg. 1.162-5(a)]. Note that travel itself as a form of education is not a deductible expense.
    Answer (A) is incorrect. Education that qualifies one for a new trade or business is not deductible. Answer (B) is incorrect. One of the requirements for education expense to be deductible is to have already met the minimum level of education or skills required of employment. It is the additional education which may be deductible. Answer (C) is incorrect. This is only one requirement and does not guarantee the deduction, e.g., if the education does qualify one for a new trade or business, it is not deductible even if one does not intend to enter the new trade or business.

6.6.12. Sharon, who had completed 2 years of a normal 3-year law school course leading to a Bachelor of Laws degree (LL.B.), was hired by a law firm to do legal research and perform other functions on a full-time basis. As a condition to continued employment, Sharon was required to obtain an LL.B. and pass her state bar examination. Sharon completed her law school education by attending law school at night. She incurred the following expenses from January through May:

Tuition	$5,000
Books	500
Transportation costs	300
Word processing expenses	100

Sharon also took a bar review course in order to prepare for the state bar examination. She paid $2,000 on May 10 for the review course given in June. How much can Sharon deduct as educational expense before any limitation for miscellaneous deductions or adjusted gross income?

    A. $0

    B. $5,600

    C. $5,900

    D. $7,900

Answer (A) is correct. *(SEE, adapted)*
    REQUIRED: The deductible amount of educational expenses.
    DISCUSSION: The law courses and bar review course constitute education required to meet minimum educational requirements for qualification in Sharon's trade or business; thus, the expenditures for such courses are not deductible [Reg. 1.162-5(b)(2)(iii)].
    Answer (B) is incorrect. The amount of $5,600 includes tuition, books, and word processing expenses. Allowance of the deduction is affected by the purpose of the education. Answer (C) is incorrect. The total amount of Sharon's expenses from January through May is $5,900. Allowance of the deduction is affected by the purpose of the education. Answer (D) is incorrect. The total amount of Sharon's educational expenses is $7,900. Allowance of the deduction is affected by the purpose of the education.

6.6.13. On January 1 of this year, John received $7,250 from his employer as part of a qualified educational assistance plan. His employer included $2,000 of this payment on John's W-2 for this year. John used the $7,250 to pay for work-related, qualified educational expenses (tuition and books). If John is single and has AGI in excess of $80,000, what can he list on his Schedule A as a miscellaneous deduction subject to the 2% limitation for this year?

A. $0

B. $1,000

C. $2,000

D. $7,250

Answer (C) is correct. *(SEE, adapted)*
REQUIRED: The amount that may be deducted as a miscellaneous itemized deduction.
DISCUSSION: Payments of up to $5,250 per year received by an employee for a qualified educational assistance program can be excluded from gross income under Sec. 127(a). Any excess (the $2,000) is includible in the employee's gross income. This excess is deductible as a miscellaneous itemized deduction if used for work-related education expenses.
Answer (A) is incorrect. John's miscellaneous itemized deduction is affected by the excess of assistance over the annual exclusion. Answer (B) is incorrect. The amount $1,000 is only 50% of the excess of assistance over the annual exclusion. Answer (D) is incorrect. The amount of $7,250 is 100% of qualified expenses John can list on his Schedule A as a miscellaneous itemized deduction; however, it is affected by the limited annual exclusion.

6.6.14. Betty Brunett, who is single, spent $2,000 in unreimbursed business expenses associated with her $20,000 annual salary. Included in those expenses were $1,000 of travel and $1,000 of dues and subscriptions. Because of $5,000 of interest expense on her home, she will be filing Schedule A of Form 1040. In the current year, how much of her $2,000 expenses will be deductions "for" and "from" AGI?

	For	From
A.	$0	$1,600
B.	$1,000	$1,000
C.	$0	$2,000
D.	$1,000	$600

Answer (A) is correct. *(P. Hite)*
REQUIRED: The deduction for second-tier itemized deductions.
DISCUSSION: Unreimbursed business expenses of an employee are deductible as miscellaneous itemized deductions. They are second-tier itemized deductions and only allowed to the extent that, in total, they exceed 2% of adjusted gross income. Since Brunett's adjusted gross income was $20,000, the unreimbursed business expenses are deductible only to the extent they exceed $400 ($20,000 × 2%). Therefore, $1,600 of the expenses ($2,000 – $400) are deductible from adjusted gross income. None of the expenses are deductible for adjusted gross income.
Answer (B) is incorrect. The correct amount of the "for" and "from" AGI deductions is not $1,000. Answer (C) is incorrect. The correct amount of the "from" AGI deduction is not $2,000. Answer (D) is incorrect. These are not the correct amounts of the "for" and "from" AGI deductions.

6.6.15. Mr. G, a full-time accountant with a CPA firm, incurred the following deductible educational expenses in the current year and substantiated them to his employer:

Travel and transportation	$1,000
Tuition	2,000
Books	600

Mr. G's employer reimbursed him $1,600 for these expenses and included the reimbursement on G's Form W-2 for the current year. What amount may G list on Schedule A for the current year as a miscellaneous deduction subject to the 2% limitation?

A. $3,600

B. $2,600

C. $2,000

D. $0

Answer (C) is correct. *(SEE, adapted)*
REQUIRED: The amount that may be deducted for tuition and books as a miscellaneous itemized deduction.
DISCUSSION: Education expenses include books, tuition, and transportation and travel. They are deductions from adjusted gross income unless the employee substantiates the expenses to the employer and is reimbursed by the employer. G received a reimbursement of $1,600, which should be applied to each of the expenses proportionately when it is not a reimbursement for a specific expense. The tuition and books are 72% ($2,600 ÷ $3,600) of the total expenses, so $1,152 ($1,600 × 72%) of the reimbursement is treated as for tuition and books. The travel and transportation are 28% ($1,000 ÷ $3,600) of total expense, so $448 ($1,600 × 28%) of the reimbursement is treated as for travel and transportation. Therefore, G may deduct $1,600 ($1,152 + $448) for tuition, books, travel, and transportation to arrive at AGI. The remaining $1,448 of tuition and books and $552 of travel and transportation, totaling $2,000, are deductible from AGI as a second-tier itemized deduction to the extent that total second-tier deductions exceed 2% of AGI.
Answer (A) is incorrect. The total educational expense is $3,600, which must be apportioned between for AGI deductions and miscellaneous itemized deductions. Answer (B) is incorrect. The travel and transportation expenses are deductible but must be apportioned between for AGI deductions and miscellaneous itemized deductions. Answer (D) is incorrect. Mr. G's miscellaneous itemized deductions are affected by all of the expenses.

6.6.16. Mr. B uses the standard mileage rate in calculating the expense of operating his car for business purposes. He is an employee who is not reimbursed for his transportation expenses. B purchased the car in 2013 and has driven the car 15,000 business miles each year through 2016. In 2017, B drove 20,000 business miles, and his adjusted gross income is $40,000. Mr. B had no other miscellaneous deductions. B has a

A. $9,900 miscellaneous itemized deduction.

B. $10,800 miscellaneous itemized deduction.

C. $10,000 miscellaneous itemized deduction.

D. $10,700 miscellaneous itemized deduction.

Answer (A) is correct. *(SEE, adapted)*
REQUIRED: The deduction for use of an automobile in business.
DISCUSSION: Automobile expenses pertaining to a trade or business are deductible under Sec. 162 as ordinary and necessary business expenses. The taxpayer may either deduct the portion of actual operating cost of the automobile attributed to business use or compute the deduction based on the standard mileage rate. For 2017, the standard mileage rate is $.535 per mile for miles of business use. The deduction for 2017 is $9,900 [(20,000 miles × $.535) – $800 AGI floor]. The deduction is limited to the amount that exceeds 2% of AGI. The standard mileage rate is adjusted by the IRS to the extent warranted.
Answer (B) is incorrect. The standard mileage rate is $.535 per mile, not $.54, for 2017, and the deduction is limited to the amount that exceeds 2% of AGI. Answer (C) is incorrect. The standard mileage rate is $.535 per mile, not $.54, for 2017. Answer (D) is incorrect. The deduction is limited to the amount that exceeds 2% of AGI.

6.6.17. Which of the following is not required when using the standard mileage rate to compute deductible transportation expenses?

A. You may use no more than four cars at a time in the business.

B. You must own or lease the vehicle.

C. You may not use the vehicle for hire, such as a taxi.

D. You must use the vehicle over 50% of the time for business.

Answer (D) is correct. *(SEE, adapted)*
REQUIRED: The item not required when using the standard mileage rate.
DISCUSSION: The standard mileage rate is allowed under IRS Notice 2016.79. Instead of deductions for actual costs, depreciation, etc., a mileage rate is deductible for all business miles driven in 2017. There is no required percentage of business use of the vehicle. The standard mileage rate can be used for any occasional business use of a vehicle. The standard mileage rate is adjusted (to the extent warranted) by the IRS.
Answer (A) is incorrect. A requirement for use of the standard mileage rate is that you may use no more than four cars at a time in the business. Answer (B) is incorrect. A requirement for use of the standard mileage rate is that you must own or lease the vehicle. Answer (C) is incorrect. A requirement for use of the standard mileage rate is that you may not use the vehicle for hire, such as a taxi.

6.6.18. Which one of the following is a deductible transportation expense?

A. Hauling tools and equipment in a vehicle while commuting to and from a regular place of work.

B. Use of a vehicle which displays material that advertises one's business while commuting to and from work.

C. Use of vehicles by Armed Forces Reservists to attend weekend meetings in the general area of their homes.

D. Use of a vehicle to report to and return home each evening from a temporary or minor assignment beyond the general area of one's regular place of work.

Answer (D) is correct. *(SEE, adapted)*
REQUIRED: The item that is a deductible transportation expense.
DISCUSSION: An employee is permitted a deduction for transportation expenses paid in connection with services performed as an employee (Sec. 162). The use of a vehicle to report to and return home each evening from a temporary or minor assignment beyond the general area of one's regular place of work would qualify as a deductible transportation expense under Sec. 162. Rev. Rul. 94-47 has extended the transportation expense deduction to include the cost of any travel by a taxpayer having a regular place of business between home and temporary work stations, regardless of the distances. Thus, not only the costs mentioned in this answer, but also costs related to assignments in the same metropolitan area of one's regular place of business are now deductible.
Answer (A) is incorrect. A taxpayer may not deduct the costs of commuting to and from work as a transportation expense even if hauling tools and equipment (extra costs, such as renting a trailer to haul equipment can be deducted). Answer (B) is incorrect. The use of the car to display advertising for your business will not change the nature of commuting from personal use to business use. Answer (C) is incorrect. The cost of transportation to an armed forces reserve meeting in the general area of the taxpayer's home is commuting expense, which is not deductible.

6.6.19. In all of the following situations, an individual can deduct transportation costs, except

A. From a place of business for employer A to a place of business for employer B.

B. From home to a temporary training site in the same city as the individual's regular office.

C. From a legitimate home office to a client's place of business.

D. From an employee's regular place of business to the employee's home within the same metropolitan area.

Answer (D) is correct. *(SEE, adapted)*
REQUIRED: The situation in which an individual cannot deduct transportation costs.
DISCUSSION: Commuting expenses between a taxpayer's residence and a business location within the area of a taxpayer's home are not deductible when they are in the same metropolitan area (Rev. Rul. 94-47).
Answer (A) is incorrect. A transportation deduction is allowed from a place of business for employer A to a place of business for employer B. Answer (B) is incorrect. A transportation deduction is allowed from home to a temporary training site in the same city as the individual's regular office. Answer (C) is incorrect. A transportation deduction is allowed from a legitimate home office to a client's place of business.

6.6.20. In 2017, Mr. L, a salesperson, drove his car 36,000 miles, of which 24,000 miles pertained to business. The total operating costs and other costs were as follows:

Gas and oil	$10,250
Auto license tag	50
Insurance	580
Repairs	920
Tires	200
Parking (incurred during business use)	175
Depreciation for business use of car	2,000

What is Mr. L's greatest allowable auto expense deduction?

A. $10,175

B. $12,840

C. $13,015

D. $19,435

Answer (C) is correct. *(SEE, adapted)*
REQUIRED: The salesperson's maximum automobile expense deduction.
DISCUSSION: Mr. L's automobile expenses must be allocated between business use and personal use. One method is to take the business portion of the general expenses and add the direct business expenses. L's general expenses of gas and oil, license, insurance, repairs, and tires total $12,000. The business use of the automobile is two-thirds of total use (24,000 ÷ 36,000 miles), so the deductible part of these expenses is $8,000 (2/3 × $12,000). Parking and depreciation are direct business expenses which total $2,175. Operating costs total $10,175.
Alternatively, L can use the standard mileage rate authorized by the IRS. Direct business (other than depreciation) expenses may be added to this, e.g., parking of $175. The standard mileage rate of $12,840 (24,000 × $.535) plus parking equals $13,015. Since this amount is greater than actual operating costs, $13,015 will be deducted.
Answer (A) is incorrect. The amount of $10,175 is the total of the actual operating costs, which is less than the standard mileage rate (24,000 × $.535) plus nonautomobile expenses ($175). Answer (B) is incorrect. The amount of $12,840 is the standard mileage rate at $.535 per mile. For 2017, a $.535 per mile mileage rate should be used, and nonautomobile expenses should also be included. Answer (D) is incorrect. The amount of $19,435 is parking plus the standard mileage rate without subtracting the mileage associated with nonbusiness travel.

6.6.21. Paul Dunyan worked for a logging company the last 9 months of 2017. He uses the standard mileage rate of $.535 per mile for all business use of his car. During 2017, Paul incurs the following:

Mileage commuting to and from work	2,400
Mileage on inspection jobs at work	3,000
Mileage to testify for the company on new state timber regulations	600
Airfare to visit another company facility for a day	$350

How much can Paul Dunyan deduct as transportation expenses before the 2%-of-AGI limitation (round to nearest dollar)?

A. $350

B. $1,955

C. $2,276

D. $3,590

Answer (C) is correct. *(Publisher, adapted)*
REQUIRED: The amount the employee can deduct as transportation expenses.
DISCUSSION: An employee is permitted a deduction from adjusted gross income for transportation expenses paid in connection with services performed as an employee (Sec. 162). Transportation expenses include the cost of transporting the employee from one place to another in the course of employment while not away from home in a travel status. The cost of commuting to and from work is not deductible because it is considered a personal rather than a business expense. Since the mileage connected with new state timber regulations does not constitute "lobbying" under Sec. 162(e), the expenses (e.g., mileage) related to such efforts are deductible.
Dunyan's transportation expenses are $2,276 [$350 airfare + (3,600 miles × $.535)].
Answer (A) is incorrect. The mileage on inspection jobs at work and the mileage to testify are also deductible. Answer (B) is incorrect. Mileage to testify for the company on new state timber regulations is also deductible. Answer (D) is incorrect. The mileage for commuting is not deductible.

6.6.22. Mr. Mack, a self-employed engineer, traveled to Boston for a 5-day seminar concerning engineering techniques. Mack took his wife, who performed minor entertainment services, and the two of them stayed an extra 10 days to visit family. Mr. Mack paid the following expenses:

Airfare ($500 each)	$1,000
Hotel (single occupancy for 15 days would have cost $1,500)	1,650
Meals for 15 days (Mr. Mack $450; Mrs. Mack $400)	850

What is the amount of travel expenses Mr. Mack can deduct on his income tax return?

 A. $0

 B. $500

 C. $575

 D. $620

Answer (C) is correct. *(SEE, adapted)*
 REQUIRED: The amount of travel expenses to be deducted by the taxpayer.
 DISCUSSION: Travel expenses are deductible if incurred in the pursuit of a trade or business activity or are related to the taxpayer's employment. If the purpose for the travel is primarily personal, no deduction is permitted except for the specific expenditures directly related to the trade or business or employment related activity. As Mr. Mack attended the seminar for 5 days and stayed for 10 additional personal days, none of the airfare to and from Boston would be deductible. In addition, Sec. 274(m)(3) denies a deduction for expenses paid or incurred with respect to a spouse, dependent, or other individual accompanying a person on a business trip unless (1) the spouse, dependent, or other individual is an employee of the person paying or reimbursing the expenses; (2) the travel of the spouse, dependent, or other individual is for a bona fide business purpose; and (3) the expenses of the spouse, dependent, or other individual would otherwise be deductible. These requirements are not met here, and Mack's deduction is limited to his specific expenditures incurred in his attending the convention. As discussed, no portion of the plane fare or of the expense relating to Mack's spouse will be permitted as a deduction. Mack's deduction is computed as follows:

Hotel ($1,500 × 5/15)	$500
Meals ($450 × 50% × 5/15)	75
Airfare	0
Deductible travel expense	$575

 Answer (A) is incorrect. A portion of the travel expenses is deductible. Answer (B) is incorrect. Fifty percent of the business portion of Mr. Mack's meals is deductible in addition to Mr. Mack's travel. Answer (D) is incorrect. Only 50% of the meals is deductible, not 80% as under pre-1994 law.

6.6.23. During the current year, Mr. H, an employee of Corporation Z, flew to Seattle to meet with a client and incurred the following expenses that were directly related to his business:

Airfare	$500
3 days' lodging	400
Meals	120
Theater tickets with a face value of $40 each for H and his client	240

Mr. H's employer reimbursed him $500 for airfare, $400 for lodging, and $120 for meals after Mr. H submitted the necessary accounting of his expenses. The reimbursement was not included on Mr. H's W-2. What is the amount of the deduction Mr. H may claim on his current-year return, disregarding the 2%-of-adjusted-gross-income limitation?

 A. $0

 B. $40

 C. $64

 D. $240

Answer (B) is correct. *(SEE, adapted)*
 REQUIRED: The amount of the deduction related to partially reimbursed business expenses not included on the taxpayer's W-2 form.
 DISCUSSION: No deduction will be allowed for the expenses incurred by Mr. H that were reimbursed by his employer. Therefore, no deduction will be allowed relating to the airfare ($500), the lodging ($400), and $120 of meals. Additionally, the deduction relating to the cost of a ticket for an entertainment activity is limited to the face value of the ticket. The total deduction for entertainment expense is limited to 50%. Thus, the allowed deduction is $40 ($80 × 50%).
 Answer (A) is incorrect. Mr. H can claim a deduction. Answer (C) is incorrect. The tickets are deductible at 50%, not 80%, of their total cost. Answer (D) is incorrect. The tickets are deductible at their face values, less a 50% nondeductible amount.

6.6.24. During the current year, Joe spent $1,000 in travel expenses to attend the annual shareholders' meeting for ABC Corporation. Joe holds his less-than-1% interest in the ABC stock for investment purposes only. How much of the travel expense can Joe deduct in the current year if his adjusted gross income is $20,000?

A. $0

B. $500

C. $600

D. $1,000

Answer (A) is correct. *(SEE, adapted)*
REQUIRED: The amount of the deduction for travel expenses incurred in attending shareholder meetings.
DISCUSSION: Transportation and other expenses paid to attend shareholders' meetings of companies in which the taxpayer owns stock but has no other interest are not deductible travel expenses. In general, no expenses of attending conventions, seminars, or similar meetings for investment purposes may be deducted. Joe will not be permitted a deduction for travel expenses in this situation.
Answer (B) is incorrect. Fifty percent of the cost is $500. Allowance for travel expense deductions is affected if expenses are for investment purposes. Answer (C) is incorrect. The excess of expenses after applying a 2%-of-AGI floor is $600. Allowance for travel expense deductions is affected if expenses are for investment purposes. Answer (D) is incorrect. The total amount Joe spent in travel expenses is $1,000. Allowance for travel expense deductions is affected if expenses are for investment purposes.

6.6.25. In determining which place of business constitutes an individual's tax home, all of the following factors are taken into account except

A. Total time spent at each place of business.

B. Amount of expenses incurred at each place of business.

C. The degree of business activity at each place of business.

D. The relative income earned at each place of business.

Answer (B) is correct. *(SEE, adapted)*
REQUIRED: The factor not determinative of what constitutes an individual's tax home.
DISCUSSION: Traveling expenses while away from home in pursuit of a trade or business are deductible. The taxpayer's home is his or her principal place of business when (s)he has more than one (Rev. Rul. 71-267). Important factors in determining which of two places of business is the principal one include (1) the time spent performing duties at each place, (2) the degree of the taxpayer's business activity in each area, and (3) the relative significance of the financial return from each area. This is referred to as the Markey test. Expenses incurred at each place of business are not taken into account.
Answer (A) is incorrect. Total time spent at each place of business is a factor used when determining an individual's tax home. Answer (C) is incorrect. The degree of business activity incurred at each place of business is a factor used when determining an individual's tax home. Answer (D) is incorrect. The relative income earned at each place of business is a factor used when determining an individual's tax home.

6.6.26. Which of the following items is a deductible travel expense if not substantiated to and reimbursed by the employer?

A. Mr. A pays taxi fares to and from his job and home each day.

B. Mr. B, an employee of an insurance company, incurs the cost of meals on days when he services clients 15 miles from his office.

C. Mr. C, an employee, incurred an expense for meals while returning from a 6-hour business trip.

D. Mr. D, a Pittsburgh lawyer, incurred laundry expenses while in Boston defending a client.

Answer (D) is correct. *(SEE, adapted)*
REQUIRED: The expenditure that is deductible as a travel expense.
DISCUSSION: A deduction is allowed for travel expenses, including amounts spent for meals and lodging, while away from home in the performance of services as an employee (Sec. 162). Travel expenses are those incurred while away from home overnight or for a period of time long enough to require a rest period. Travel expenses include transportation, meals, lodging, and expenses incident to travel, including reasonable laundry expenses, and are subject to the 2%-of-adjusted-gross-income floor.
Answer (A) is incorrect. Commuters' taxi fares are not considered business expenses and are not deductible [Reg. 1.162-2(e)]. Answer (B) is incorrect. The taxpayer has not met the overnight test and thus has not incurred travel expenses (which is necessary to deduct the cost of meals). Answer (C) is incorrect. The length of Mr. C's trip did not meet the requirement to qualify as travel.

6.6.27. For the current year, Mr. G, a construction worker, had adjusted gross income of $30,000. He incurred the following employment-related and investment-related miscellaneous expenses:

Safety shoes	$ 100
Union initiation fee	2,000
Union dues	300
Life insurance	800
Jeans and flannel shirts used for work	200
Management fees on investments producing taxable income	1,200
Legal expenses for drafting a will	200

The union initiation fee and dues had to be paid before commencing to work. He was not reimbursed for any of the employment-related expenses. What is the amount of his miscellaneous expense deduction after any limitations?

A. $4,200

B. $3,600

C. $3,200

D. $3,000

6.6.28. Mr. Jones owns a race car that he drives in his spare time and on weekends. His records regarding this activity reflect the following for the current year:

Income	$3,500
Expenses:	
Entry fees	1,000
Depreciation on car	700
Tires (have a life of 6 months)	200
Interest on loan for race car	800
Insurance premiums	1,000

What is the allowable deduction for depreciation, assuming that this activity is not engaged in for profit and Mr. Jones can itemize his deductions?

A. $0

B. $400

C. $500

D. $700

Answer (D) is correct. *(SEE, adapted)*
REQUIRED: The amount of the miscellaneous expense deduction after limitations.
DISCUSSION: Dues and initiation fees paid for union membership and the cost of safety shoes are unreimbursed employee business expenses and are deductible as second-tier itemized deductions subject to the 2%-of-AGI limitation. Management fees on investments producing taxable income are other expenses also deductible as second-tier deductions, subject to the 2%-of-AGI floor. The cost of life insurance, clothing suitable for normal wear (jeans and flannel shirts), and legal expenses for drafting a will are all personal expenditures and may not be included in itemized deductions (Sec. 262). Mr. G's deduction is calculated as follows:

Safety shoes	$ 100
Union initiation fees	2,000
Union dues	300
Management fees on investments	1,200
	$3,600
Less: AGI floor ($30,000 × .02)	(600)
Miscellaneous expense deduction after limitation	$3,000

Answer (A) is incorrect. Life insurance, jeans and flannel shirts for work, and legal expenses for a will are not deductible as miscellaneous itemized deductions. Answer (B) is incorrect. The total miscellaneous itemized deduction before subtracting the 2%-of-AGI nondeductible floor is $3,600. Answer (C) is incorrect. Legal expenses for drafting a will are not deductible as miscellaneous itemized deductions.

Answer (D) is correct. *(SEE, adapted)*
REQUIRED: The depreciation deduction for an asset used in an activity not engaged in for profit.
DISCUSSION: The activity engaged in by Mr. Jones would be considered a "hobby" as it is an activity not engaged in for profit. Expenses and losses of such an activity, known as hobby losses, are deductible only to the extent of any income produced by the hobby activity (Sec. 183; Reg. 1.183-1 through 1.183-4). Certain expenses are deductible even if they exceed hobby income, such as taxes, interest, and casualty losses. The deduction of these expenses, though, reduces the amount of hobby income against which hobby expenses may be offset. After deducting these amounts, hobby expenses are applied to hobby income in the following order: (1) operating expenses other than depreciation and (2) depreciation and other basis adjustment items. The calculation for Mr. Jones follows:

Hobby income	$ 3,500
Interest on race car loan	0
Entry fees	(1,000)
Tires	(200)
Insurance premiums	(1,000)
Remaining hobby income (against which depreciation may be deducted)	$ 1,300

The full $700 depreciation deduction would be available for Mr. Jones because the $800 interest on the race car loan is personal interest and nondeductible.

Answer (A) is incorrect. There is an allowable deduction for depreciation up to the lesser of depreciation or hobby income after allowable deductions before depreciation. Answer (B) is incorrect. This amount assumes an additional $900 of deductions before depreciation. Answer (C) is incorrect. The interest expense is personal and therefore not deductible.

6.6.29. Unreimbursed employee business expenses not reported on a Form W-2 or Form 1099 are deducted as a miscellaneous itemized deduction subject to a 2%-of-adjusted-gross-income floor.

A. True.

B. False.

Answer (A) is correct. *(SEE, adapted)*

DISCUSSION: Unreimbursed employee business expenses are deductible from AGI. The unreimbursed expense relating to meals and entertainment are subject to the 50% rule, and all unreimbursed employee expenses are subject to the 2%-of-AGI floor.

6.6.30. You may deduct, as miscellaneous itemized deductions, fees paid to a broker, a bank, or a similar agent to collect your bond interest or dividends on stock. But you may not deduct as a miscellaneous itemized deduction a fee you paid to a broker to buy investment property, such as stocks or bonds.

A. True.

B. False.

Answer (A) is correct. *(SEE, adapted)*

DISCUSSION: The fees paid to a broker to buy investment property such as stocks or bonds are added to the cost of such property and recovered upon its sale or other disposition. Note that the deductible fees are second-tier miscellaneous itemized deductions, subject to the 2%-of-AGI limitation.

6.6.31. Mr. A, a practicing CPA with a large accounting firm, uses one room in his home to read financial periodicals and reports, clip bond coupons, and perform similar investment activities. Mr. A uses this room regularly and exclusively for this purpose. These activities are not a part of Mr. A's trade or business. Mr. A can take a miscellaneous deduction on Schedule A for the use of this room.

A. True.

B. False.

Answer (B) is correct. *(SEE, adapted)*

DISCUSSION: No deduction is allowed for an in-home office unless a portion of the residence is used exclusively on a regular basis as the taxpayer's principal place of business or as a place of business to meet with patients, clients, or customers (Sec. 280A). Investing is a production-of-income activity, not a business.

6.6.32. For the current year, the allocated investment expenses of "publicly offered" mutual funds are not subject to the 2%-of-adjusted-gross-income limit.

A. True.

B. False.

Answer (A) is correct. *(SEE, adapted)*

DISCUSSION: Section 67(c)(1) prevents taxpayers from claiming deductions by using pass-through entities to obtain a tax benefit for amounts that are not allowable as a deduction because of the 2% floor on miscellaneous itemized deductions when such amounts are directly paid or incurred by an individual. An exception to this general disallowance rule is found in Sec. 67(c)(2), which permits investment expenses of "publicly offered" regulated investment companies (such as mutual funds) to be deducted by individuals without regard to the 2% floor.

6.6.33. Employment agency fees in seeking employment in a new trade or business are deductible if employment is secured.

A. True.

B. False.

Answer (B) is correct. *(SEE, adapted)*

DISCUSSION: Although employment agency fees for seeking employment in the same trade or business are deductible under Sec. 212 whether or not a new job is secured, such expenses incurred in seeking employment in a new trade or business are not deductible regardless of whether employment is secured.

6.6.34. B, a trust officer in a bank, is required by the bank to get a law degree. B registered at the local university's law school in the current year for the regular curriculum that leads to a law degree. For the current year, B paid $7,000 for tuition, etc., which the bank reimbursed in full. The bank included the $7,000 on B's W-2. The $7,000 is deductible by B as an education expense.

A. True.

B. False.

Answer (B) is correct. *(SEE, adapted)*

DISCUSSION: The education expenditures incurred in earning a law degree are not deductible because they qualify the taxpayer for a new trade or business, that of being a lawyer. The fact that the law degree was required by B's employer to retain his employment status does not cause the expenditures to be deductible.

6.6.35. Ms. Q is a college professor with a master's degree. She takes additional courses toward a doctorate that is needed to qualify her for an appointment as president of a junior college. Ms. Q may deduct her educational expenses for the additional courses leading toward the doctorate.

A. True.

B. False.

Answer (A) is correct. *(SEE, adapted)*
DISCUSSION: All teaching and related duties are considered the same general kind of work. This includes a teacher whose duties change from classroom teacher to school administrator. Since Ms. Q's educational expenses to qualify as president of a junior college are not considered as qualifying her for a new trade or business, they are deductible.

6.6.36. Mr. Good holds a permanent teaching certificate in State A and was employed as a teacher by that state for several years. In August of the current year, he moved to State B and was promptly hired by a local school district to teach school. He is required, however, to complete certain prescribed courses to get a permanent teaching certificate in State B. Mr. Good may deduct his educational expenses for the additional courses to get a permanent teaching certificate in State B.

A. True.

B. False.

Answer (A) is correct. *(SEE, adapted)*
DISCUSSION: Teaching educational courses in one state is considered the same kind of work as teaching educational courses in another state. Therefore, completing courses for a teaching certificate in a new state is not considered qualifying the individual for a new trade or business. The cost of these additional courses is deductible.

6.6.37. Jody is a high school Spanish teacher. During her summer vacation in the current year, Jody traveled around Spain to improve her knowledge of the Spanish language. She took pictures to use in her classroom, visited Spanish schools, and attended movies and plays to improve her Spanish language skills. Jody may deduct the cost of the trip to Spain because it is directly related to her work.

A. True.

B. False.

Answer (B) is correct. *(SEE, adapted)*
DISCUSSION: Under Sec. 274(m)(2), no deduction is generally allowed for travel as a form of education. A travel deduction, which would otherwise be allowed on the grounds that the travel itself served an educational purpose, is not permitted by Sec. 274(m).

6.6.38. Mr. W attends classes at the local university two nights a week and on Saturdays. His qualifying educational expenses are deductible. On Tuesday and Thursday nights, Mr. W goes directly from work to his night classes. On Saturday, he goes from his home to his classes. Mr. W may deduct all of the transportation expenses incurred in going from work to his classes and from home to classes.

A. True.

B. False.

Answer (B) is correct. *(SEE, adapted)*
DISCUSSION: Education expenses include books, tuition, transportation, and travel. However, the cost of local transportation between home and school on a nonworking day is treated as a personal commuting expense and is not deductible.

6.6.39. An individual may use the standard mileage rate for a car used for business whether (s)he leases or owns it.

A. True.

B. False.

Answer (A) is correct. *(SEE, adapted)*
DISCUSSION: The standard mileage rate may be used for any vehicle that is leased. The taxpayer may operate only one vehicle at a time for business purposes (Rev. Proc. 2001-54).

6.6.40. If an individual changes from the standard mileage rate to the actual-cost method to compute auto expenses before the auto is considered fully depreciated, the individual must estimate the useful life of the auto and use straight-line depreciation.

A. True.

B. False.

Answer (A) is correct. *(SEE, adapted)*
    DISCUSSION: According to Rev. Proc. 97-58, if the taxpayer elects to use the standard mileage rate in the first year of business use, the taxpayer is considered to have made an election not to use ACRS or MACRS depreciation. Thus, if the taxpayer changes to the actual-cost method in a later year before the car is fully depreciated, the taxpayer must use straight-line depreciation over the car's useful life.

6.6.41. During the current year, Joe sometimes used his cell phone to discuss business with clients while driving to and from his home and regular place of business. Joe's transportation expenses relating to the trips he used the phone are deductible.

A. True.

B. False.

Answer (B) is correct. *(SEE, adapted)*
    DISCUSSION: Commuting expenses between a taxpayer's residence and regular place of business are not deductible as transportation expenses under Sec. 162.

6.6.42. If you work at two places in 1 day for two employers, you may deduct the expense of getting from one place of employment to the other.

A. True.

B. False.

Answer (A) is correct. *(SEE, adapted)*
    DISCUSSION: An employee is permitted a deduction from adjusted gross income for unreimbursed transportation expenses paid in connection with services performed as an employee (Sec. 162). Transportation expenses include only the cost of transporting the employee from one place to another in the course of employment while not away from home in a travel status. The expense of getting from one job to another is deductible, while the expense of commuting to and from home or between the taxpayer's home and one or more regular places of employment or business, unless they are temporary workstations that are not the taxpayer's regular place of business, is not deductible (Rev. Ruls. 90-23 and 94-47).

6.6.43. Mr. A, a steamfitter, has a temporary assignment beyond the general area of his tax home (place of employment). He leaves his tax home early each morning and returns home each evening. Mr. A cannot deduct the daily round-trip transportation expenses because they are commuting expenses and are nondeductible personal expenses.

A. True.

B. False.

Answer (B) is correct. *(SEE, adapted)*
    DISCUSSION: Transportation expenses associated with temporary assignments beyond the general area of the tax home are an exception to the general rule that commuting expenses are nondeductible. The reason is that, as long as the assignment is temporary, the employee's tax home (place of employment) has not changed, and the transportation is not between his personal home and his tax home (which is a personal commuting expense) (Rev. Rul. 90-23).

6.6.44. Mr. C, a construction worker who does not work beyond the general area of his employment, hauls his tools in his automobile between his residence and the job site each day. He incurs no additional costs in doing so. Mr. C can use the standard mileage rate to deduct the daily round trip between his home and the job site, providing he maintains the necessary records.

A. True.

B. False.

Answer (B) is correct. *(SEE, adapted)*
    DISCUSSION: An employee who uses an automobile to transport tools to work will be allowed a deduction for transportation expenses only if additional costs are incurred, such as renting a trailer. A deduction is allowed only for the additional costs incurred to transport the tools to work. Therefore, Mr. C is not entitled to a deduction for transporting his tools.

6.7 Limitation on Itemized Deductions for High-Income Taxpayers

6.7.1. Paul and Jodi, age 40 and 45, are married taxpayers who file jointly. Their adjusted gross income for 2017 is $413,800. They also had the following itemized deductions:

Medical expenses
  (after 10%-of-AGI floor) $12,000
Mortgage interest   2,500
Investment interest   4,500
State income taxes   1,500
                          $20,500

What amount may Paul and Jodi deduct as itemized deductions in determining taxable income?

- A. $20,500
- B. $17,500
- C. $17,300
- D. $3,200

Answer (B) is correct. *(Publisher, adapted)*
   REQUIRED: The amount of the taxpayers' itemized deductions allowed in 2017.
   DISCUSSION: Taxpayers with adjusted gross income in excess of a threshold amount must reduce the amount of itemized deductions allowed by 3% of that excess. The total reduction may not exceed 80% of the total itemized deductions allowed, not including deductions arising from medical expenses, investment interest, casualty and theft losses, or wagering losses to the extent of wagering gains. For 2017, the threshold amount for married taxpayers filing jointly is $313,800. The total itemized deduction that is allowed is computed as follows:

Taxpayer's AGI	$ 413,800
Less: threshold amount	(313,800)
Excess over threshold amount	$ 100,000
Limitation percentage	× .03
Tentative reduction	$ 3,000

The reduction for 2017 will be equal to the lesser of $3,000 or 80% of the total itemized deductions allowed. Note that, for purposes of the overall 80% limitation, medical expenses, investment interest, casualty and theft losses, and wagering losses to the extent of wagering gains are not included.

Total deductions allowed ($2,500 + $1,500)	$4,000
Times: Overall limitation percentage	× .80
Overall limit on reduction	$3,200

The taxpayers' reduction then is $3,000 for 2017, and they may claim a total of $17,500 ($20,500 – $3,000) in itemized deductions for 2017.
   Answer (A) is incorrect. The amount of $20,500 is the total itemized deductions before any reductions are applied. Answer (C) is incorrect. The 80% reduction limit of $3,200 is greater than the 3% of AGI in excess of the threshold amount. Answer (D) is incorrect. The limit is the lesser of 3% of AGI in excess of a threshold amount or 80% of itemized deductions. In addition, the 80% of itemized deductions limit is based on total itemized deductions, excluding medical expenses and investment interest.

6.7.2. Which of the following deductions is not subject to the limitation on itemized deductions when incurred by a single taxpayer whose adjusted gross income is more than $261,500 for 2017?

- A. Home mortgage interest.
- B. Investment interest.
- C. Miscellaneous itemized deductions.
- D. State income and real estate taxes.

Answer (B) is correct. *(SEE, adapted)*
   REQUIRED: The deduction not limited by a gross income threshold.
   DISCUSSION: An individual whose adjusted gross income exceeds a threshold amount is required to reduce the amount of allowable itemized deductions by the lesser of 3% of the excess of the threshold amount (Sec. 68) or 80% of itemized deductions reduced by medical expenses, investment interest, casualty and theft losses, and wagering losses. No reduction is required in the case of investment interest, medical expenses, and casualty, theft, or wagering losses to the extent of wagering gains.
   Answer (A) is incorrect. Home mortgage interest is subject to the limitation on itemized deductions when AGI exceeds a threshold amount. Answer (C) is incorrect. Miscellaneous itemized deductions are subject to the limitation on itemized deductions when AGI exceeds a threshold amount. Answer (D) is incorrect. State income and real estate taxes are subject to the limitation on itemized deductions when AGI exceeds a threshold amount.

6.7.3. For married taxpayers filing joint returns, the threshold amount beyond which a reduction in itemized deductions will occur under Sec. 68 is $313,800 for 2017.

A. True.

B. False.

Answer (A) is correct. *(Publisher, adapted)*

DISCUSSION: Section 68 provides for a reduction in the amount of itemized deductions allowed for taxpayers whose adjusted gross income exceeds a specified threshold amount. In 2017, the threshold amount for married taxpayers filing jointly is $313,800.

6.7.4. The reduction in itemized deductions for high-income taxpayers provided for in Sec. 68 is applied only after taking into account other Code provisions determining the amount of a particular type of expense which may be deducted, such as the 2%-of-AGI floor on miscellaneous deductions.

A. True.

B. False.

Answer (A) is correct. *(Publisher, adapted)*

DISCUSSION: The reduction in itemized deductions provided for under Sec. 68 is applied only after taking into account other Code provisions limiting deductions, such as the 2% floor on miscellaneous itemized deductions. Furthermore, in determining the correct treatment of state income tax refunds, the tax benefit rule will continue to apply in the same manner as it did prior to the enactment of Sec. 68.

6.7.5. Manuel, a single taxpayer, has AGI of $170,000 for the 2017 tax year. He had $3,000 of gambling losses not in excess of gambling winnings for the year, and he paid $2,000 in 2017 to determine his 2016 state and federal income tax liability. These were the only amounts that might qualify as itemized deductions on Manuel's 2017 return. The amount of expense for determining his 2017 tax liability is deductible in full up to the excess of 2% of his AGI, or $3,400.

A. True.

B. False.

Answer (B) is correct. *(Publisher, adapted)*

DISCUSSION: Gambling losses and taxes are not miscellaneous itemized deductions subject to the 2% of AGI reduction.

Use **Gleim Test Prep** for interactive study and easy-to-use detailed analytics!

STUDY UNIT SEVEN
INDIVIDUAL TAX COMPUTATIONS

7.1 Personal Exemptions

7.1.1. Which of the following is included in determining the total support of a dependent who is a qualifying relative?

A. Fair rental value of lodging provided.

B. Allocable portion of mortgage payment on lodging facility.

C. Social Security benefits added to savings account.

D. Life insurance premiums.

Answer (A) is correct. *(SEE, adapted)*
REQUIRED: The item considered in determining the total support of a dependent.
DISCUSSION: A taxpayer must provide over one-half of the support for a person to be considered a dependent [Sec. 152(a)]. The term support includes food, shelter, clothing, medical and dental care, education, and other items contributing to the individual's maintenance and livelihood [Reg. 1.152-1(a)(2)]. Shelter or lodging is determined as the fair rental value of the room, apartment, or house in which the person lives.
Answer (B) is incorrect. The fair rental value of lodging is used for support instead of an allocable portion of mortgage payments. Answer (C) is incorrect. Amounts added to savings are not part of support. Support refers to amounts spent for an individual's maintenance and livelihood. Answer (D) is incorrect. Life insurance premiums do not contribute to the maintenance and livelihood of an individual.

7.1.2. When figuring if a dependent child who is a full-time student meets the support test, all of the following items are taken into account in determining total support except

A. Food.

B. Scholarships.

C. Recreation.

D. Birthday presents.

Answer (B) is correct. *(SEE, adapted)*
REQUIRED: The item not taken into account in determining total support of a dependent child who is a full-time student.
DISCUSSION: To determine whether an individual has not provided more than one-half of his or her own support, the amount of support provided by the qualifying child is compared to the entire amount of support received from all sources. However, amounts received as a scholarship are not taken into account in determining whether the individual provided more than half of his or her own support [Sec. 152(d)].
Answer (A) is incorrect. Food constitutes an expense of support. Answer (C) is incorrect. Recreation constitutes an expense of support. Answer (D) is incorrect. Birthday presents constitute expenses of support.

7.1.3. All of the following are included in calculating the total support of a dependent who is a qualifying relative except

A. Child care even if you are claiming the credit for the expense.

B. Amounts veterans receive under the GI bill for tuition and allowances while in school.

C. Medical insurance benefits, including basic and supplementary Medicare benefits received.

D. Tax-exempt income, savings, or borrowed money used to support a person.

Answer (C) is correct. *(SEE, adapted)*
REQUIRED: The item not taken into account in determining total support of a dependent who is a qualifying relative.
DISCUSSION: A taxpayer must provide over one-half of the support for a person to be considered a qualifying relative [Sec. 152(a)]. The term support includes food, shelter, clothing, medical and dental care, education, and other items contributing to the individual's maintenance and livelihood [Reg. 1.152-1(a)(2)]. Although medical care is an item of support, medical insurance benefits are not included. Medical insurance premiums are included.
Answer (A) is incorrect. Child care contributes to the maintenance and livelihood of the individual and is considered support. Answer (B) is incorrect. Education contributes to the maintenance and livelihood of the individual and is considered support. Answer (D) is incorrect. Any funds used to support a person, whether tax exempt, borrowed, or from savings, contribute to the maintenance and livelihood of the individual and are considered support.

7.1.4. In which of the following situations will the divorced custodial parent be entitled to the dependency exemption for the child?

    A. The noncustodial parent provides $1,500 of support for the child and the custodial parent provides $1,200.

    B. The custodial and noncustodial parent both provide $1,500 of support for the child.

    C. The custodial parent provides $1,500 of support for the child and the noncustodial parent provides $1,200.

    D. All of the answers are correct.

Answer (D) is correct. *(SEE, adapted)*
    REQUIRED: The situation(s) in which a divorced custodial parent will receive the dependency exemption for a child.
    DISCUSSION: Assuming the child is under the age of 19 or a student under the age of 24, the child meets the definition of a qualifying child and the custodial parent is allowed the exemption. The amount of support provided by each parent is not a factor unless the child provides more than one-half of his or her own support. The noncustodial parent may only claim the exemption for the child if one of the following occurs:

1. The divorce decree declares the noncustodial parent the recipient of the exemption of the child.

2. The custodial parent signs a written declaration that the custodial parent will not claim the child as a dependent and the noncustodial parent attaches the written declaration to his or her tax return.

There is no dollar requirement for support under these rules, but the child's support must come from the parents combined.
    Answer (A) is incorrect. Situations in which the divorced custodial parent can be entitled to the dependency exemption also include the following: (1) The custodial and noncustodial parent both provide $1,500 of support for the child, and (2) the custodial parent provides $1,500 of support for the child and the noncustodial parent provides $1,200 of support for the child. Answer (B) is incorrect. Situations in which the divorced custodial parent can be entitled to the dependency exemption also include the following: (1) The noncustodial parent provides $1,500 of support for the child and the custodial parent provides $1,200, and (2) the custodial parent provides $1,500 of support for the child and the noncustodial parent provides $1,200. Answer (C) is incorrect. Situations in which the divorced custodial parent can be entitled to the dependency exemption also include the following: (1) The noncustodial parent provides $1,500 of support for the child and the custodial parent provides $1,200, and (2) the custodial and noncustodial parent both provide $1,500 of support for the child.

7.1.5. Mr. and Mrs. P are filing a joint return for the current year. They have two children. Marie, who is 18, earned $4,160 from a part-time job. James, who is 24 and attends college as a full-time student, earned $4,100 during the summer. Mr. and Mrs. P provide over one-half of their children's support. Mr. P's mother also lives with them but is self-supporting. How many exemptions can Mr. and Mrs. P claim on their current-year return?

    A. 2

    B. 3

    C. 4

    D. 5

Answer (B) is correct. *(SEE, adapted)*
    REQUIRED: The number of exemptions to which the taxpayers are entitled.
    DISCUSSION: Section 151(c) allows an exemption for each dependent whose gross income for the taxable year is less than the exemption amount ($4,050 in 2017), or who is a child of the taxpayer and either has not attained the age of 19 or is a student under age 24. Mr. and Mrs. P are not permitted an exemption for Mr. P's mother because she is not a dependent (she is self-supporting). They are permitted an exemption for their daughter, Marie, since she has not attained age 19. James is not a qualifying child because he is not under 24. He is not a qualifying relative because he earned more than $4,050 and is not a student under 24. On a joint return, each spouse is entitled to an exemption (Publication 501). The Ps are allowed three exemptions (Mr. P, Mrs. P, and Marie).
    Answer (A) is incorrect. An exemption is also allowed for their daughter. Answer (C) is incorrect. An exemption is not allowed for their son. Answer (D) is incorrect. An exemption is not allowed for the son or Mr. P's mother.

7.1.6. Jim Planter, who reached age 65 on January 1 of the current year, filed a joint return for the year with his wife, Rita, age 50. Mary, their 21-year-old daughter, was a full-time student at a college until her graduation on June 2 of the current year. The daughter had $7,050 of income and provided 25% of her own support during the year. In addition, during the year, the Planters were the sole support for Rita's niece, who had no income and lived with them the entire year. How many exemptions should the Planters claim on their current-year tax return?

A. 2

B. 3

C. 4

D. 5

Answer (C) is correct. *(CPA, adapted)*
REQUIRED: The number of exemptions to which the taxpayers are entitled.
DISCUSSION: Section 151(b) provides an exemption for the taxpayer. On a joint return, there are two taxpayers and an exemption is allowed for each [Reg. 1.151-1(b)]. The Planters are entitled to an exemption for both Mary and the niece because Sec. 151(c) provides an exemption for each dependent whose gross income for the taxable year is less than the exemption amount ($4,050 in 2017) or who is a child of the taxpayer and is a full-time student (under age 24) at an educational organization during at least 5 months of the taxable year. Thus, the Planters are entitled to four exemptions, one for each spouse and one for each dependent.
Answer (A) is incorrect. This answer only includes the exemptions for each spouse. Answer (B) is incorrect. An exemption is permitted for both the daughter, who is a full-time student, and the niece, who lived with them for the entire year. Answer (D) is incorrect. No additional exemptions are permitted because Jim is over 65.

7.1.7. In the current year, Sam Dunn provided more than half the support for his wife, his father's brother, and his cousin. Sam's wife was the only relative who was a member of Sam's household. None of the relatives had any income, nor did any of them file an individual or a joint return. All of these relatives are U.S. citizens. Which of these relatives should be claimed as a dependent or dependents on Sam's current-year joint return?

A. Only his wife.

B. Only his father's brother.

C. Only his cousin.

D. His wife, his father's brother, and his cousin.

Answer (B) is correct. *(CPA, adapted)*
REQUIRED: The relative(s) who could be claimed as a dependent on the taxpayer's return.
DISCUSSION: Section 152(a) lists those relatives who may be claimed as dependents if they receive over half of their support from the taxpayer. The taxpayer's uncle is included in this list, so Sam's father's brother may be claimed by him as a dependent.
Answer (A) is incorrect. Sam's wife is entitled to her own personal exemption and is not classified as a dependent. Answer (C) is incorrect. Section 152(a) does not include cousins in its list of relatives, and Sam's cousin was not a member of the household. Answer (D) is incorrect. Sam's wife is entitled to her own personal exemption and is not classified as a dependent. Also, Sec. 152(a) does not include cousins in its list of relatives, and Sam's cousin was not a member of the household.

7.1.8. Mr. and Mrs. D file a joint return for the current year. Mr. D is 67 years old, and Mrs. D is 52 years old. They provide 80% of the support for their son, Tom. Tom is 17 years old, is single, and had wages of $4,350 in the year. On their respective tax returns for the current year, Mr. and Mrs. D and their son, Tom, should claim which of the following number of personal exemptions?

	Mr. & Mrs. D	Tom
A.	4	1
B.	3	1
C.	3	0
D.	2	1

Answer (C) is correct. *(SEE, adapted)*
REQUIRED: The number of exemptions allowed to the parents and child.
DISCUSSION: Section 151(c) allows an exemption for each qualifying relative whose gross income for the taxable year is less than the exemption amount ($4,050 in 2017). In addition, an exemption is allowed for a qualifying child who is under age 19. Qualifying children are not required to meet the gross income test. Even though Tom has gross income in excess of the exemption amount, Mr. and Mrs. D are entitled to an exemption for him since he has not attained age 19 and meets the other requirements for being a dependent. Each spouse is also entitled to an exemption; therefore, Mr. and Mrs. D are entitled to a total of three exemptions.
Section 151(d)(2) states that no personal exemption may be taken on the return of an individual who can be claimed as a dependent on another taxpayer's return. Since Tom's parents are entitled to claim him as a dependent on their return, Tom is not entitled to a personal exemption himself.
Answer (A) is incorrect. Five exemptions are not possible for three people. Answer (B) is incorrect. If Mr. and Mrs. D claim Tom, then Tom cannot also claim himself on his own return. Answer (D) is incorrect. It would be more advantageous for Mr. and Mrs. D to claim an exemption for their dependent son Tom than for Tom to claim himself as an exemption on his return. Tom cannot be claimed on both returns.

7.1.9. Sara Hance, who is single and lives alone in Idaho, has no income of her own and is supported in full by the following persons:

	Amount of Support	Percent of Total
Alma (an unrelated friend)	$2,400	48
Ben (Sara's brother)	2,150	43
Carl (Sara's son)	450	9
Total	$5,000	100

Under a multiple support agreement, Sara's dependency exemption can be claimed by

A. No one.

B. Alma.

C. Ben.

D. Carl.

Answer (C) is correct. *(CPA, adapted)*
REQUIRED: The person entitled to a dependency exemption under a multiple support agreement.
DISCUSSION: A dependent is defined in Sec. 152(a), which requires the taxpayer to provide over one-half of the support of the individual. An exception to the support test permits one of a group of taxpayers, otherwise eligible to claim the exemption and who together furnish more than one-half of the support of a dependent, to claim a dependency exemption even when no one person provides more than 50% of the support [Sec. 152(c)]. Any such individual who contributed more than 10% of the support is entitled to claim the exemption if each of the other persons in the group who contributed more than 10% signs a written consent filed with the return of the claiming taxpayer.
Ben can claim the dependency exemption because, as Sara's brother, he would otherwise be entitled under Sec. 152(a) to claim her as a dependent, and he contributed over 10% of her support. Carl cannot because he did not contribute over 10%. Alma cannot because she is not related to Sara and Sara did not live in the same place of abode.
Answer (A) is incorrect. A dependency exemption can be claimed by one of the individuals. Answer (B) is incorrect. Alma is not related to Sara and cannot claim the exemption. Answer (D) is incorrect. Carl does not provide over 10% of Sara's support.

7.1.10. Mr. and Mrs. X, both age 50, are filing a joint return and have AGI of $353,800 for 2017. Their son, who is blind, is a full-time student and is entirely supported by Mr. and Mrs. X. Mr. and Mrs. X also contributed more than half of the total support of their daughter, who lived with them until her marriage in November. Their daughter and her husband had gross income for the year of $1,000 and $1,500, respectively, and filed a joint return to recover income tax withheld. What amount can Mr. and Mrs. X claim for exemptions in 2017?

A. $0

B. $5,184

C. $11,016

D. $16,200

Answer (C) is correct. *(Publisher, adapted)*
REQUIRED: The amount which the taxpayers can claim as exemptions in 2017.
DISCUSSION: If a taxpayer's adjusted gross income exceeds a specific threshold amount (based on filing status), the deduction allowed for personal and dependency exemptions is reduced by 2% for each $2,500, or fraction thereof, by which the adjusted gross income exceeds the threshold amount. The threshold amounts are

Joint returns or surviving spouse	$313,800
Head of household	287,650
Single taxpayers	261,500
Married filing separately	156,900

The amount of Mr. and Mrs. X's four exemptions is $16,200 ($4,050 × 4). The amount of the exemptions subject to phaseout is calculated as follows:

Adjusted gross income	$353,800
(Less threshold amount for joint returns)	(313,800)
Excess amount subject to 2% for each $2,500	$ 40,000

The X's exemption amount is reduced by 32%. This results from dividing the excess over the threshold amount ($40,000) by $2,500 and multiplying the result by 2% [($40,000 ÷ $2,500) × 2% = 32%]. As a result, the X's $16,200 exemption is reduced by $5,184 (32% of $16,200). The allowable exemption deduction then becomes $11,016 ($16,200 − $5,184).
Answer (A) is incorrect. A partial exemption may be claimed. Answer (B) is incorrect. The phased-out amount by which the exemption is reduced is $5,184. Answer (D) is incorrect. The exemptions must be phased out when AGI is in excess of $313,800.

7.1.11. Mr. and Mrs. X, both age 50, are filing a joint return and have AGI of $75,000 for 2017. Their son, who is blind, is a full-time student and is entirely supported by Mr. and Mrs. X. Mr. and Mrs. X also contributed more than half of the total support of their daughter, who lived with them until her marriage in November. Their daughter and her husband had gross income for the year of $1,000 and $1,500, respectively, and filed a joint return to recover income tax withheld. What amount can Mr. and Mrs. X claim for exemptions in 2017?

A. $12,150

B. $12,600

C. $16,200

D. $20,250

Answer (C) is correct. *(SEE, adapted)*
REQUIRED: The total amount the taxpayers can claim for exemptions.
DISCUSSION: An exemption is allowed under Sec. 151(c) for each dependent whose gross income for the taxable year is less than the exemption amount ($4,050 in 2017), or who is a child of the taxpayer and has either not attained the age of 19 or is a full-time student under age 24. No additional exemption is allowed for blindness or for being age 65 or over. Also, no exemption is allowed for any dependent who files a joint return with his or her spouse [Sec. 151(c)(2)], unless the joint return is filed solely to receive a refund.
Mr. and Mrs. X are thus entitled to four exemptions, one each for themselves and one for each of their two dependent children. Their daughter qualifies since her joint return was filed solely to receive a refund. No additional exemption is allowed for their son's blindness. The amount of the personal exemption for 2017 is $4,050. The total amount of four exemptions is $16,200 (4 × $4,050).
Answer (A) is incorrect. An exemption is also allowed for the daughter. Answer (B) is incorrect. The personal exemption amount is $4,050. Answer (D) is incorrect. An exemption is not allowed for the daughter's husband.

7.1.12. Mr. and Mrs. P became legally separated under a separate maintenance agreement in the current year. Mr. P provided more than half of the support for the P's child, Cathy, who lived with Mrs. P for all of the year. Mr. P may claim Cathy as an exemption in the year if

A. Mrs. P signs a Form 8332, *Release of Claim to Exemption for Child of Divorced or Separated Parents*, and Mr. P attaches it to his return.

B. Mr. P signs a Form 8332, and Mrs. P attaches it to her return.

C. Mr. P is not allowed to claim Cathy as an exemption because the separate maintenance agreement was post-1984.

D. Mrs. P agrees orally not to claim Cathy as an exemption.

Answer (A) is correct. *(SEE, adapted)*
REQUIRED: The procedure to claim a dependency exemption of a child in a legal separation.
DISCUSSION: Assuming age requirement is met and Cathy does not provide over one-half of her own support, Cathy is a qualifying child of Mrs. P. The noncustodial parent may only claim the exemption for the child if one of the following occurs.

1. The divorce decree declares the noncustodial parent the recipient of the exemption of the child.

2. The custodial parent signs a written declaration that the custodial parent will not claim the child as a dependent and the noncustodial parent attaches the written declaration to his or her tax return.

Answer (B) is incorrect. Mr. P, and not Mrs. P, must attach the form to his return. Answer (C) is incorrect. Mr. P is allowed to claim the exemption with a release Form 8332 signed by Mrs. P. Answer (D) is incorrect. Mrs. P must sign Form 8332; this waiver cannot be granted orally.

7.1.13. All of the following are true except

A. A brother-in-law must live with the taxpayer the entire year to be claimed as a dependent even if the other tests are met.

B. A son, age 21, was a full-time student who earned $4,250 from his part-time job. The money was used to buy a car. Even though he earned $4,250, his parents can claim him as a dependent if the other exemption tests were met.

C. For each person claimed as a dependent, the Social Security number, adoption taxpayer identification number, or individual taxpayer identification number must be listed.

D. If a married person files a separate return, (s)he can take an exemption for his or her spouse if the spouse had no gross income and was not the dependent of another taxpayer.

Answer (A) is correct. *(SEE, adapted)*
REQUIRED: The false statement regarding the relationship requirement.
DISCUSSION: The relationship requirement is satisfied by existence of an extended (by blood) or immediate (by blood, adoption, or marriage) relationship. The relationship need be present to only one of the two married persons who file a joint return. Any relationship established by marriage is not treated as ended by divorce or by death. An individual must satisfy either a relationship or a residence requirement but does not have to satisfy both.
Answer (B) is incorrect. Gross income of the qualifying relative (to be claimed as a dependent) must be less than the amount of the dependency exemption ($4,050 for 2017). However, this test does not apply to a child of the claimant who is either under 19 years of age or a student under 24 years of age. Answer (C) is incorrect. For each person claimed as a dependent, the Social Security number, adoption taxpayer identification number, or individual taxpayer identification number must be listed. Answer (D) is incorrect. If a married person files a separate return, (s)he can take an exemption for his or her spouse if the spouse had no gross income and was not the dependent of another taxpayer.

SU 7: Individual Tax Computations

7.1.14. D provides 20% of her own support. She has four children, daughters K and L and twin sons M and W, who provide the balance of her support. For last year, K provided 40%, L 20%, M 12%, and W 8% of D's support. K and L file joint tax returns with their spouses. M files as a head of household, and W files as a single taxpayer. Taxable income last year, as reported on their returns, was $60,000 for K, $40,000 for L, $60,000 for M, and $60,000 for W. The four siblings come to you on April 1 of this year and inquire about a multiple support agreement. Moreover, if one is able to claim D as a dependent, they want you to determine which individual to choose to maximize tax savings. Which of the following matches the advice you should give to K, L, M, and W?

	Must Be Party to Agreement	Should Claim Exemption
A.	K, L, M, W	W
B.	K and L, or K and M	K
C.	K, L, M	M
D.	K, L, M	K

7.1.15. Mr. C and Ms. D are the divorced parents of one disabled child. Together they provide all the child's support and have custody of the child for more than half the year. Their 1984 divorce decree gives the exemption for the child to C, who is the noncustodial parent. There have been no modifications to the decree. Which of the following requirements must C also meet in order to claim the exemption?

A. He must pay at least $600 in support for the child during the year.

B. He must pay at least $4,050 (in 2017) in support for the child during the year.

C. He must provide over half the support for the child during the year.

D. None of the answers are correct.

7.1.16. Miss V's friend, Miss D, who is single and a U.S. citizen, was a member of V's household during the entire year. V supported D for the entire year since D was unable to find employment and had no gross income. V may claim D as a dependent on her current-year tax return.

A. True.

B. False.

7.1.17. Funds paid into a trust for the purpose of a child's future education are includible in determining support for dependency purposes.

A. True.

B. False.

Answer (C) is correct. *(Publisher, adapted)*
REQUIRED: The correct application of the requirements for a multiple support agreement and an analysis of the structure of the tax rate tables.
DISCUSSION: Section 152(c) sets out the requirements of a multiple support agreement. All individuals who provide over 10% of D's support and are otherwise eligible to claim D as a dependent must agree that one of their number will claim D. No one individual can have provided over 50% of support. K, L, and M must be party to the agreement since each provided over 10% of D's support.
Of the three, M is subject to the highest tax rates since a head of household is subject to higher rates (25%) than a married person filing jointly (15%) when the two individuals have $50,000 of taxable income. Consequently, M will derive the greatest benefit from the exemption.
Form 2120 is used as a declaration that the persons who sign it (K and L) will not claim the individual (D) as a dependent. The taxpayer claiming the exemption (M) files it with his tax return.
Answer (A) is incorrect. Individuals who provide over 10% of the support and are otherwise eligible to claim D as a dependent must be parties to the agreement. This precludes W from being a party to the multiple support agreement. Answer (B) is incorrect. Individuals who provide over 10% of the support may not be excluded from the agreement. Answer (D) is incorrect. K should not claim the exemption.

Answer (A) is correct. *(SEE, adapted)*
REQUIRED: The requirement for a noncustodial parent to claim a dependency exemption pursuant to a 1984 divorce decree.
DISCUSSION: The dependency exemption for a child of divorced taxpayers generally goes to the parent having custody of the child for the greater part of the year. This rule applies only when the child has not provided more than half of his or her own support and was in the custody of one or both parents for more than half the year. Three exceptions exist to the general rule that a custodial parent is entitled to the dependency exemption, one of which is when a pre-1985 divorce decree or separation agreement between the parents grants the exemption to the noncustodial parent. In order for the noncustodial parent to claim the exemption in this situation, (s)he must provide at least $600 of support for the child during the year in question.
Answer (B) is incorrect. C does not have to pay at least $4,050 (in 2017) in support for the child during the year in order to claim a dependency exemption pursuant to a pre-1985 divorce decree. Answer (C) is incorrect. C does not have to provide over half the support for the child during the year in order to claim a dependency exemption pursuant to a pre-1985 divorce decree. Answer (D) is incorrect. The noncustodial parent must pay one of the amounts in the other answer choices towards the support of the child.

Answer (A) is correct. *(SEE, adapted)*
DISCUSSION: Provided the other dependency requirements are met (i.e., gross income is less than his or her personal exemption amount), an individual who has his or her principal place of abode for the entire year in the home of the taxpayer and is a member of the taxpayer's household may be claimed as a dependent [Sec. 152(a)(9)].

Answer (B) is correct. *(SEE, adapted)*
DISCUSSION: Only support provided during the current taxable year is considered in determining whether an individual is a dependent [Sec. 152(a)]. Regulation 1.152-1(a)(2) specifies that only amounts received are taken into account as support. Funds put into trust for future education are not yet received, nor do they provide support during the current year.

7.1.18. Mr. B's 19-year-old son receives a $6,000 scholarship to X University. In the same year, Mr. B provides $4,500 to his son as the only other support. The other dependency tests are met. Mr. B is entitled to claim his son as a dependent on his current-year return.

A. True.

B. False.

Answer (A) is correct. *(SEE, adapted)*
   DISCUSSION: To claim an exemption for a qualifying child, the child must provide less than half of his or her own support [Sec. 152(a)]. Amounts received as scholarships for study at an educational organization are not considered in determining whether the individual has provided less than half of his or her own support [Sec. 152(d)]. Therefore, Mr. B is considered to have supplied the only support for his son and is entitled to claim his son as a dependent.

7.1.19. Mr. T divorced his wife in December of the current year. If he contributed all her support for the year, he can claim her as a dependent on his current-year income tax return.

A. True.

B. False.

Answer (B) is correct. *(SEE, adapted)*
   DISCUSSION: Even if the ex-spouse had her principal place of abode in the home of the taxpayer and was a member of the taxpayer's household during the year, if she was at any time during the taxable year the spouse of the taxpayer, she may not be considered a dependent [Sec. 152(a)(9)].

7.1.20. Roy met all five tests to claim an exemption for his sister, who is single. However, he did not claim an exemption for her. Roy's sister can take an exemption for herself on her own return.

A. True.

B. False.

Answer (B) is correct. *(SEE, adapted)*
   DISCUSSION: If an individual meets the requirements to be classified as a dependent on another person's tax return, that individual (the dependent) is not entitled to the deduction for personal exemptions for himself or herself.

7.1.21. If a child being adopted is eligible to be claimed as a dependent by the adoptive parents, an identifying number must be obtained for the child.

A. True.

B. False.

Answer (A) is correct. *(SEE, adapted)*
   DISCUSSION: An adoption taxpayer identification number (ATIN) is a temporary taxpayer identifying number assigned by the IRS to a child who has been placed in the household of a prospective adoptive parent. Once the adoption becomes final, the adoptive parent must apply for a Social Security number for the child to replace the child's ATIN.

7.1.22. Mr. R is divorced from his wife, who has custody of their child, who is disabled. The divorce decree entered in 1984 provides that Mr. R must pay his former wife $15 per week toward the child's support, which he did throughout the calendar year. The decree also provides that he may claim the child as his exemption. R's former wife can prove that, during the year, she contributed $7,500 toward the support of the child. Mr. R is entitled to claim the exemption for the child in the current year.

A. True.

B. False.

Answer (A) is correct. *(SEE, adapted)*
   DISCUSSION: A noncustodial parent can claim the dependency exemption when the divorce decree was entered before 1985, if it provides for the noncustodial parent to have the exemption, and if the parent not having custody furnished at least $600 for the support of the child during the calendar year [Sec. 152(e)(4)]. Mr. R provided $780 ($15 × 52 weeks) of support, and the divorce decree awarded him the exemption. Mr. R is thus entitled to the exemption in the current year.

7.1.23. Mr. and Mrs. K are filing a joint return for the current year. They provided more than half the support of their daughter and her husband, who lived with them the entire year while they were full-time students at the local university. Neither their daughter nor her husband is required to file a return, but they file a joint return to get a refund of income taxes that were withheld. No tax liability exists for either spouse on separate returns. All are U.S. citizens. Mr. and Mrs. K are entitled to claim their daughter and son-in-law as their dependents.

A. True.

B. False.

Answer (A) is correct. *(SEE, adapted)*
   DISCUSSION: In general, a married child may be claimed as a dependent by his or her parents only if the child does not file a joint return and would otherwise qualify as a dependent. An exception to the general rule exists. A parent may claim a married child and his or her spouse as dependents in spite of their filing a joint return, provided that neither is required to file a return for the year and that the filing was solely for the purpose of obtaining a refund of tax withheld (Rev. Ruls. 54-567 and 65-34).

7.2 Filing Status

7.2.1. For federal income tax purposes, an individual is considered married for the whole year in all of the following situations except

A. On the last day of the tax year, the individual has not remarried after being widowed during the tax year.

B. On the last day of the tax year, the individual is separated under an interlocutory (not final) decree of divorce.

C. The individual lived with another individual over half the year as husband and wife in a state that does not recognize a common-law marriage.

D. The individuals are married with no dependents and lived apart the whole year but are not legally separated under a decree of divorce or separate maintenance.

Answer (C) is correct. *(SEE, adapted)*
REQUIRED: The situation in which an individual would not be considered married for the entire year for tax purposes.
DISCUSSION: For federal income tax purposes, an individual is considered to have been married for the entire year if, on the last day of the tax year, the taxpayer is living in a common-law marriage that is recognized in the state where the taxpayer is currently living or the state where the common-law marriage began. A taxpayer who lived with another individual over half the year as husband and wife in a state not recognizing common-law marriage is not considered to be married for federal income tax purposes.
Answer (A) is incorrect. If, on the last day of the tax year, the individual has not remarried after being widowed during the tax year, the taxpayer would be treated as having been married for the entire tax year. Answer (B) is incorrect. If, on the last day of the tax year, the individual is separated under an interlocutory (not final) decree of divorce, the taxpayer would be treated as having been married for the entire tax year. Answer (D) is incorrect. If the individuals are married with no dependents and lived apart the whole year but are not legally separated under a decree of divorce or separate maintenance, they are treated as having been married for the entire tax year.

7.2.2. A husband and wife can file a joint return even if

A. The spouses have different tax years, provided that both spouses are alive at the end of the year.

B. The spouses have different accounting methods.

C. Either spouse was a nonresident alien at any time during the tax year, provided that at least one spouse makes the proper election.

D. They were divorced before the end of the tax year.

Answer (B) is correct. *(CPA, adapted)*
REQUIRED: The condition under which a husband and wife may file a joint return.
DISCUSSION: There is no provision disallowing spouses to file a joint return because they have different accounting methods.
Answer (A) is incorrect. Section 6013(a)(2) disallows spouses with different tax years from filing a joint return. Answer (C) is incorrect. Section 6013(a)(1) provides that neither spouse can be a nonresident alien during the tax year and still file a joint return. An exception applies if the nonresident alien spouse is married to a U.S. citizen or resident alien at year end and both spouses elect to have the nonresident alien treated as a resident alien [Sec. 6013(g)]. Answer (D) is incorrect. Reg. Section 1.6013-4 states that spouses must be married on the last day of the tax year to be allowed to file a joint return.

7.2.3. Mrs. Doe, by herself, maintains her home in which she and her unmarried daughter resided for the entire year. Her daughter, however, does not qualify as her dependent. Mrs. Doe's husband died last year. What is Mrs. Doe's filing status for the current year?

A. Qualifying widow.

B. Married filing jointly.

C. Head of household.

D. Single.

Answer (D) is correct. *(SEE, adapted)*
REQUIRED: The filing status of a widow whose child does not qualify as a dependent.
DISCUSSION: An unmarried taxpayer who is not a surviving spouse is considered a head of household if the taxpayer maintains as his or her home a household which constitutes the principal place of abode of a child or stepchild of the taxpayer [Sec. 2(b)(1)]. A qualifying child for the purposes of determining filing status is one who has the same place of abode as the taxpayer, is the taxpayer's adopted/foster child, son, daughter, stepson, stepdaughter, brother, sister, stepbrother, stepsister, or a descendant of such an individual, and is under the age of 19 (24 if the child is a student). In addition, a dependent or a spouse who is incapable of caring for himself or herself is a qualifying individual. The Working Families Tax Relief Act of 2004 revised the definition of a child for the purposes of the Head of Household filing status. A child must be a qualifying child or a dependent. Since a taxpayer would be allowed a dependency exemption for a qualifying child, her daughter could not be a qualifying child. Thus, she is ineligible to file as a head of household or qualifying widow without this qualification. Accordingly, Mrs. Doe is a single taxpayer.
Answer (A) is incorrect. A qualifying widow(er) must maintain a home for a child or stepchild with respect to whom the taxpayer is entitled to a dependency exemption under Sec. 151. Answer (B) is incorrect. Mrs. Doe was not married at year end. Answer (C) is incorrect. A head of household must maintain a home for a qualifying child, for whom the taxpayer would be able to claim a dependency exemption, unless the exemption were granted to the noncustodial parent.

7.2.4. Which of the following is not a requirement that must be met in determining whether a taxpayer is considered unmarried for head-of-household filing status purposes?

A. An individual must file a separate return.

B. An individual must pay more than one-half the cost of keeping up a home for the tax year.

C. For the entire year, an individual's home must be the main home of his child, stepchild, or adopted child, whom he or the noncustodial parent can properly claim as a dependent.

D. An individual's spouse must not have lived in their home for the last 6 months of the tax year.

Answer (C) is correct. *(SEE, adapted)*
REQUIRED: The item that is not a requirement in determining if a taxpayer is unmarried for head-of-household filing status purposes.
DISCUSSION: In determining if a taxpayer qualifies for head-of-household filing status, the taxpayer is considered unmarried if the following requirements are met:

1. The taxpayer filed a separate return.
2. The taxpayer paid more than half the cost of keeping up the home for the tax year.
3. The taxpayer's spouse did not live in the home during the last 6 months of the tax year.
4. The home was, for more than half the year, the main home of the taxpayer's child, stepchild, or adopted child, whom the taxpayer or the noncustodial parent can properly claim as a dependent.

Therefore, this answer is correct, as the requirement is that the home must be the main home of the child, stepchild, or adopted child for more than half the year, not the entire year [Sec. 2(b)].
Answer (A) is incorrect. A requirement for the taxpayer to be considered unmarried for the purpose of determining head-of-household filing status is that the individual must file a separate return. Answer (B) is incorrect. A requirement for the taxpayer to be considered unmarried for the purpose of determining head-of-household status is that the individual must pay more than one-half the cost of keeping up a home for the tax year. Answer (D) is incorrect. A requirement for the taxpayer to be considered unmarried for the purpose of determining head-of-household status is that the individual's spouse must not have lived in their home for the last 6 months of the tax year.

7.2.5. James and Edna Smith are a childless married couple who lived apart for all of the current year. On December 31, they were legally separated under a decree of separate maintenance. Which of the following is the only filing status choice available to them for the current year?

A. Married filing joint return.

B. Married filing separate return.

C. Head of household.

D. Single.

Answer (D) is correct. *(SEE, adapted)*
REQUIRED: The filing status of married individuals living apart.
DISCUSSION: According to Sec. 7703(a)(2), an individual who is legally separated under a decree of separate maintenance is not considered married. Neither James nor Edna is eligible to file as head of household. Therefore, each must file as a single person.
Answer (A) is incorrect. Individuals legally separated under a decree of separate maintenance may not file as married filing jointly. Answer (B) is incorrect. Individuals legally separated under a decree of separate maintenance may not file as married filing separately. Answer (C) is incorrect. Individuals legally separated under a decree of separate maintenance are not considered married. In addition, neither taxpayer is eligible to file as a head of household.

7.2.6. During 2017, Robert Moore, who is 50 years old and unmarried, maintained his home, in which he and his widowed father, age 75, resided. His father had $3,900 interest income from a savings account and also received $2,400 from Social Security during the current year. Robert provided 60% of his father's total support for the current year. What is Robert's filing status for the current year, and how many exemptions should he claim on his tax return?

A. Head of household and two exemptions.

B. Single and two exemptions.

C. Head of household and one exemption.

D. Single and one exemption.

Answer (A) is correct. *(CPA, adapted)*
REQUIRED: The filing status and number of exemptions for an unmarried taxpayer who supports his father.
DISCUSSION: Robert's father has less than $4,050 of gross income in the current year, so he qualifies as Robert's dependent [Sec. 151(c)(1)]. Only the interest income is considered when determining the amount of gross income. Since his father qualifies as a dependent, Robert qualifies for head-of-household filing status [Sec. 2(b)]. Robert may file as a head of household with two exemptions (himself and his father).
Answer (B) is incorrect. Robert is eligible for head of household status. Answer (C) is incorrect. Robert may claim an exemption for his father. Answer (D) is incorrect. The head of household status is available to Robert, and he can claim an exemption for his father.

7.2.7. Which of the following is not considered part of keeping up a home for purposes of determining head-of-household filing status?

    A. Real estate taxes.

    B. Allowance for depreciation.

    C. Rent.

    D. Food eaten in the home.

Answer (B) is correct. *(SEE, adapted)*
    REQUIRED: The item not considered part of keeping up a home for head-of-household filing status.
    DISCUSSION: Regulation 1.2-2(d) provides that the cost of maintaining a household for head-of-household status includes the expenses incurred for the mutual benefit of the occupants. The allowance for depreciation of the home is not considered part of keeping up a home since it is not an actual expense.
    Answer (A) is incorrect. Real estate taxes are an expense incurred for the mutual benefit of the occupants. Answer (C) is incorrect. Rent is an expense incurred for the mutual benefit of the occupants. Answer (D) is incorrect. Food eaten in the home is an expense incurred for the mutual benefit of the occupants.

7.2.8. Mrs. Oak was divorced on January 1 of the current year. She had an unmarried son living in her home for the entire year. It cost $3,000 to maintain Mrs. Oak's home for the year, of which she contributed $2,000 and Joe Oak, ex-husband, contributed $1,000 through support payments. Joe Oak, however, provides more than one-half of the son's total support and claims him as his dependent. Which is the most advantageous filing status for which Mrs. Oak can qualify?

    A. Married filing joint return.

    B. Head of household.

    C. Married filing separately.

    D. Single.

Answer (B) is correct. *(SEE, adapted)*
    REQUIRED: The most advantageous filing status for which the taxpayer qualifies.
    DISCUSSION: The determination of whether an individual is married is made as of the close of the taxable year, so Mrs. Oak is unmarried. Mrs. Oak is not a surviving spouse, and the tax rates for a head of household are lower than those for a single taxpayer. To qualify for head-of-household rates, she must maintain (furnish over half the cost of) a household as her home that is the domicile of her unmarried child, regardless of whether she is entitled to the dependency exemption for the son [Sec. 2(b)]. Mrs. Oak meets these requirements for head-of-household status.
    Answer (A) is incorrect. Mrs. Oak is unmarried at year end. Answer (C) is incorrect. Since Mrs. Oak is unmarried at year end, she may not file as married filing separately. Answer (D) is incorrect. Single is not the most advantageous filing status.

7.2.9. Mr. W died early in the current year. Mrs. W remarried in December of the same year and therefore was unable to file a joint return with Mr. W. What is the filing status of the decedent, Mr. W?

    A. Single.

    B. Married filing separate return.

    C. Married filing joint return.

    D. Head of household.

Answer (B) is correct. *(SEE, adapted)*
    REQUIRED: The filing status of a decedent whose spouse remarried in the same year as the decedent's death.
    DISCUSSION: Generally, a surviving spouse may file a joint return for himself or herself and the decedent. In that case, the decedent's filing status on the final return would be married filing jointly. However, a joint return with the deceased spouse may not be filed if the surviving spouse remarried before the end of the year of the decedent's death. In this case, the filing status of the deceased spouse is that of married filing separate return [Sec. 6013(a)(2)].
    Answer (A) is incorrect. The decedent was married up until the time of his death and will not use single filing status. Answer (C) is incorrect. A joint return may not be filed for a deceased taxpayer whose spouse has remarried before the end of the year of the decedent's death. Answer (D) is incorrect. The decedent does not meet the requirements for head-of-household filing status.

7.2.10. Mrs. W's husband died in Year 1. She has not remarried and has maintained a home for herself and her dependent son, whose personal exemption she can claim. In the summer of Year 3, the son was killed in an automobile accident. What is Mrs. W's filing status for Year 3?

    A. Single.

    B. Married filing separate return.

    C. Qualifying widow.

    D. Head of household.

Answer (C) is correct. *(SEE, adapted)*
    REQUIRED: The filing status of a widow whose dependent died during the year.
    DISCUSSION: A qualifying widow(er) is a taxpayer whose spouse died in either of the 2 preceding taxable years and who maintains a household that constitutes the principal place of abode of a dependent who is a child or stepchild of the taxpayer and with respect to whom the taxpayer is entitled to a dependency deduction [Sec. 2(a)]. Regulation 1.2-2(c)(1) provides that a dependent's death during the year will not prevent the taxpayer from qualifying as a surviving spouse. Mrs. W is a qualifying widow and can file as a surviving spouse.
    Answer (A) is incorrect. A surviving spouse may not use the tax rates for a single individual [Sec. 1(c)] and would not want to since single rates are higher. Answer (B) is incorrect. Mrs. W was not married at year end. Answer (D) is incorrect. A surviving spouse is not a head of household [Sec. 2(b)(1)].

7.2.11. Ms. N, who is married, wants to file as a single person for the current year. Which of the following will prevent her from filing as a single person?

A. Her spouse lived in her home for the final 6 months of the current year.

B. She and her husband did not commingle funds for support purposes.

C. She paid more than half the cost of keeping up her home for the tax year.

D. Her home was, for more than 6 months of the year, the principal home of her son whom she can claim as a dependent.

Answer (A) is correct. *(SEE, adapted)*
    REQUIRED: The item that will prevent the taxpayer from filing as a single person.
    DISCUSSION: The determination of whether an individual is married is made as of the close of the taxable year. A taxpayer's filing status is single if the taxpayer is unmarried or is separated from his or her spouse by a divorce or separate maintenance decree and does not qualify for another filing status. As Ms. N is married, the fact that her spouse lived in her home for the final 6 months of the tax year will prevent her from filing as a single person.
    Answer (B) is incorrect. The fact that she and her husband did not commingle funds for support purposes will not prevent her from filing as a single person. Answer (C) is incorrect. Although paying more than half the cost of keeping up a home for the tax year is a requirement that must be met in order to file as a head of household, it would not prevent Ms. N from filing as a single taxpayer. Note, however, that, if all the requirements are met, it would be advantageous for the taxpayer to file as a head of household because lower tax rates apply than for a taxpayer filing as a single person or a married person filing a separate return. Answer (D) is incorrect. Although this requirement must be met in order to file as head of household, it would not prevent Ms. N from filing as a single taxpayer. Note, however, that, if all the requirements are met, it would be advantageous for the taxpayer to file as a head of household because lower tax rates apply than for a taxpayer filing as a single person or a married person filing a separate return.

7.2.12. Mr. A, a calendar-year taxpayer, died January 15 of Year 2. His widow, Mrs. A, remarried December 15 of Year 2. The last year for which a joint return may be filed by or for Mr. and Mrs. A is

A. Year 1.

B. Year 2.

C. Year 3.

D. Year 4.

Answer (A) is correct. *(SEE, adapted)*
    REQUIRED: The last year a joint return may be filed by a decedent whose surviving spouse remarried before year end.
    DISCUSSION: The determination of whether an individual is married is made as of the close of the taxable year, except that, if his or her spouse dies during the taxable year, such determination is made as of the time of the death [Sec. 7703(a)]. Since the decedent was married at the time of his death, he is considered married for purposes of filing status. A decedent (through a personal representative) and a surviving spouse may file a joint return under Sec. 6013(a)(2) unless the surviving spouse remarries before year end. Since Mrs. A remarried prior to the end of Year 2, they may not file a joint return for Year 2. The last year they could file a joint return was Year 1.
    Answer (B) is incorrect. A joint return may be filed only if the widowed spouse does not remarry within that tax year. Answer (C) is incorrect. Mrs. A remarried prior to the end of Year 3. Answer (D) is incorrect. The requirement not to remarry was not met.

7.2.13. All of the following are reasons for not holding the "innocent" spouse liable for the tax (or any later assessments of tax, interest, or penalty) related to a joint return except

A. The innocent spouse did not know, and had no reason to know, that there was a substantial understatement of the tax.

B. Taking into account the facts and circumstances, it would be inequitable to hold the innocent spouse liable.

C. The other spouse's erroneous item resulted in a joint tax understatement.

D. The divorce decree states that the other spouse will be responsible for any amounts due on previously filed joint returns.

Answer (D) is correct. *(R. Fernandez)*
    REQUIRED: The circumstances under which an innocent spouse may be liable for an understatement of tax on a joint return.
    DISCUSSION: If a joint return is filed, husband and wife are jointly and severally (individually) liable for any tax, including any later assessments, related to the joint return. A divorced taxpayer may still be jointly and severally liable for tax, interest, and penalties due on a joint return filed before the divorce, regardless of what the divorce decree says.
    Answer (A) is incorrect. An "innocent" spouse will not be held liable for the tax if (s)he did not know, and had no reason to know, that there was a substantial understatement of the tax [Sec. 6015(b)]. Answer (B) is incorrect. A provision that must be met in order to absolve the innocent spouse from any tax liability resulting from the joint return is taking into account the facts and circumstances; it would be inequitable to hold the innocent spouse liable [Sec. 6015(b)]. Answer (C) is incorrect. An "innocent" spouse will not be held liable for the tax if the other spouse's erroneous income item resulted in a joint tax return understatement [Sec. 6015(b)].

7.2.14. Emil Gow's wife died in Year 1. Emil did not remarry, and he continued to maintain a home for himself and his dependent infant child during Year 2 and Year 3, providing full support for himself and his child during these years. For Year 1, Emil properly filed a joint return. For Year 3, Emil's filing status is

A. Single.

B. Head of household.

C. Qualifying widower with dependent child.

D. Married filing joint return.

Answer (C) is correct. *(CPA, adapted)*
REQUIRED: The filing status of a widower whose wife died during the second preceding year.
DISCUSSION: Emil qualifies as a surviving spouse whose spouse died in either of the 2 preceding tax years, who has not remarried, and who maintains a household that constitutes a principal place of abode of a dependent who is a child or stepchild of the taxpayer [Sec. 2(a)]. A qualifying widow(er) is another term for a surviving spouse, and it is used by the IRS (and sometimes on the CPA exam).
Answer (A) is incorrect. A surviving spouse may not use the tax rates of a single taxpayer and would not want to since the single rates are higher. Answer (B) is incorrect. A surviving spouse is not a head of household [Sec. 2(b)(1)]. Answer (D) is incorrect. Emil was not married at the end of Year 3.

7.2.15. A married couple who files separate returns may change to a joint return any time within 3 years from the original due date of the separate returns.

A. True.

B. False.

Answer (A) is correct. *(SEE, adapted)*
DISCUSSION: Section 6013(b) provides that individuals may file a joint return after filing separate returns if they do so within 3 years from the due date, not including any extensions, of the separate returns.

7.2.16. X and Y were married on December 31 of the current year. This is the first marriage for both. Since they were single for the majority of the tax year, they must file single tax returns for the current year.

A. True.

B. False.

Answer (B) is correct. *(SEE, adapted)*
DISCUSSION: Under Sec. 7703(a), the determination of marital status is made on the last day of the taxable year. Since X and Y were married on the last day of the taxable year, they must file as married.

7.2.17. Mary is unmarried. Her mother, for whom she can claim an exemption, lived in an apartment by herself. She died on November 14. The cost of the upkeep of her apartment for the year until her death was $8,000. Mary paid $5,600, and her brother paid $2,400. Her brother made no other payments towards their mother's support. Mary's mother had no other income. Mary must use single filing status on her tax return.

A. True.

B. False.

Answer (B) is correct. *(SEE, adapted)*
DISCUSSION: In determining if a taxpayer qualifies for head of household filing status, the taxpayer is considered unmarried if the following requirements are met:

1. The taxpayer filed a separate return.

2. The taxpayer paid more than half the cost of keeping up the home for the tax year.

3. The taxpayer's spouse did not live in the home during the last 6 months of the tax year.

4. The home was, for more than half the year, the main home of the taxpayer's child, stepchild, or adopted child, whom the taxpayer or the noncustodial parent can properly claim as a dependent.

In addition, there are two special rules concerning a qualifying person. First, the taxpayer with a dependent parent qualifies even if the parent does not live with the taxpayer. Second, if an unmarried descendant (including adopted child and stepchild) lives with the taxpayer, that descendant need not be the taxpayer's dependent. Otherwise, the IRS maintains that the qualifying individual must occupy the same household (except for temporary absences). Since Mary is not required to live with her dependent parent, she qualifies for head of household filing status.

7.2.18. A and B are married and timely filed a joint return for the current year. They may change to separate returns within 3 years from the due date of the joint return.

A. True.

B. False.

Answer (B) is correct. *(SEE, adapted)*
DISCUSSION: Once a joint return has been filed, separate returns are not allowed after the time for filing the return has expired [Reg. 1.6013-1(a)(1)]. Therefore, A and B may not change to separate returns after the due date of the joint return.

7.2.19. If a taxpayer's marriage is annulled, (s)he must file amended returns, claiming single or head of household filing status for all open years affected by the annulment.

A. True.

B. False.

Answer (A) is correct. *(SEE, adapted)*
 DISCUSSION: If an annulment is obtained, the individual is considered unmarried even if joint returns were filed in the previous years. The individual must file amended returns claiming single or head of household status for all tax years affected by the annulment that are not closed by the statute of limitations for filing a tax return. The statute of limitations generally does not expire until 3 years after the original return was filed.

7.2.20. Mrs. Brown's husband died on February 10 of the current year. On December 30 of the same year, Mrs. Brown married Mr. White. Mrs. White (previously Mrs. Brown), may elect to file a joint return with either the decedent or Mr. White.

A. True.

B. False.

Answer (B) is correct. *(SEE, adapted)*
 DISCUSSION: The determination of whether an individual is married is made at the end of the year [Sec. 7703(a)]. Therefore, a taxpayer who remarries is considered married to the new spouse at year end and may file a joint return only with the new spouse [Sec. 6013(a)]. Note that in this situation the filing status of the deceased spouse would be married filing separately for his final return [Sec. 6013(a)(2)].

7.2.21. Mrs. B filed a timely joint Year 1 income tax return for herself and her husband who died October 1, Year 1. An executor for the decedent was appointed on April 20 of Year 2. The executor can revoke the joint return by filing a separate return for the decedent on or before April 15 of Year 3.

A. True.

B. False.

Answer (A) is correct. *(SEE, adapted)*
 DISCUSSION: A joint return for a decedent must be filed by the personal representative of the estate unless one is not appointed prior to the due date for the surviving spouse's return (April 15). In that case the surviving spouse may file it. Per Sec. 6013(a)(3), if a personal representative is subsequently appointed, (s)he may revoke the joint return by filing a separate return for the decedent within 1 year after the due date of the surviving spouse's return (April 15 of Year 3).

7.2.22. An executor may elect to file a joint return for a decedent and the surviving spouse providing the surviving spouse has not remarried and the spouse elects to file a joint return.

A. True.

B. False.

Answer (A) is correct. *(SEE, adapted)*
 DISCUSSION: A taxpayer whose spouse has died during the taxable year may file a joint return unless (s)he has remarried before year end [Sec. 6013(a)(2)]. Both spouses must elect to file a joint return, but the executor makes this election for the decedent [Sec. 6013(a)(3)].

7.2.23. A person who qualifies as an abandoned spouse (e.g., married, but meets the tests for consideration as unmarried) automatically qualifies to file as head of household.

A. True.

B. False.

Answer (A) is correct. *(R. Fernandez)*
 DISCUSSION: To qualify as an abandoned spouse, the individual must file a separate return and pay more than half the cost of keeping up a home which is his or her home and that of a son or daughter (step or adopted children included) for whom a dependency exemption is or could be claimed. The child must live in the home for more than half the taxable year, and the taxpayer's spouse must not live in the home at any time during the last 6 months of the year [Sec. 7703(b)]. If these requirements are met, an abandoned spouse also qualifies as a head of household [Sec. 2(b)(1)]. A head of household, on the other hand, may or may not qualify as an abandoned spouse.

7.3 Filing Requirements

7.3.1. During 2017, student D, who is single, was claimed as a dependent by his parents. D earned $1,500 from a part-time job at a gas station. How much interest or other unearned income would D have to receive at a minimum to require him to file an income tax return for 2017?

A. $1

B. $351

C. $4,050

D. $8,300

Answer (B) is correct. *(SEE, adapted)*
   REQUIRED: The unearned income that would require filing an income tax return.
   DISCUSSION: In general, an individual must file an income tax return if his or her gross income equals or exceeds the sum of his or her personal exemption and standard deduction [Sec. 6012(a)]. But in the case of an individual who is claimed as a dependent on another's tax return, (s)he must file if unearned income exceeds $1,050 or total income exceeds the standard deduction. For such a person, the standard deduction is limited to the greater of (1) $1,050 or (2) the individual's earned income plus $350 [Sec. 63(c)(5)]. Since D was claimed as a dependent by his parents, his standard deduction is limited to his earned income of $1,500 plus $350 ($1,850). Therefore, if D receives $351 of unearned income, his total income will exceed his standard deduction, and he must file a tax return. Note that D is not entitled to a personal exemption because he was claimed as a dependent by his parents.
   Answer (A) is incorrect. One dollar is not enough to meet the threshold amount required for a dependent to file an income tax return. Answer (C) is incorrect. Although unearned income of $4,050 would require D to file an income tax return, this amount is not the minimum amount required to file an income tax return for 2017. Answer (D) is incorrect. Although unearned income of $8,300 would require D to file an income tax return, this amount is not the minimum amount required to file an income tax return for 2017.

7.3.2. Mr. and Mrs. X plan to file a joint return for 2017. Neither is over 65 or blind, nor do they have any dependents. What is the amount of gross income required before they must file a return?

A. $12,600

B. $14,450

C. $16,750

D. $20,800

Answer (D) is correct. *(SEE, adapted)*
   REQUIRED: The minimum amount of gross income for which a joint return must be filed when there are no dependents.
   DISCUSSION: In general, a return must be filed if a taxpayer's gross income equals or exceeds the sum of the personal exemption to which (s)he is entitled plus the standard deduction amount applicable to the taxpayer's filing status [Sec. 6012(a)(1)]. Section 151 allows a $4,050 exemption for each taxpayer in 2017. For a joint return, the standard deduction is $12,700 in 2017, and no additional standard deductions are allowed for taxpayers who are not over age 65 or blind. The couple must file a return if their gross income equals or exceeds $20,800 ($12,700 + $4,050 + $4,050).
   Answer (A) is incorrect. The amount of $12,700 does not include their two personal exemptions. Answer (B) is incorrect. The amount of $14,450 uses the single standard deduction instead of the married standard deduction. Answer (C) is incorrect. The amount of $16,750 does not include the second personal exemption.

7.3.3. Mr. and Mrs. Jones, both over age 65, elect joint return status. They must file a return for 2017 if their combined gross income equals or exceeds

A. $1

B. $20,800

C. $22,050

D. $23,300

Answer (D) is correct. *(Publisher, adapted)*
   REQUIRED: The minimum amount of gross income for which a joint return must be filed in 2017 when both taxpayers are over age 65.
   DISCUSSION: In general, a return must be filed if the taxpayer's gross income equals or exceeds the sum of his or her personal exemption and standard deduction [Sec. 6012(a)]. Section 151 allows a $4,050 exemption for each taxpayer in 2017. For a joint return, the basic standard deduction is $12,700 in 2017. In addition, Mr. and Mrs. Jones are allowed two additional standard deductions of $1,250 each for being age 65 or over [Sec. 63(f)]. The couple must file a return if their gross income equals or exceeds $23,300 ($12,700 + $1,250 + $1,250 + $4,050 + $4,050).
   Answer (A) is incorrect. A return must be filed if the taxpayer's gross income equals or exceeds the sum of his or her personal exemptions and standard deduction. Answer (B) is incorrect. Two additional standard deductions of $1,250 each should be included. Answer (C) is incorrect. Two additional standard deductions of $1,250 each are allowed for being age 65 or over.

7.3.4. Mr. T is age 21, is single, and cannot be claimed as a dependent by another taxpayer. For 2017, he must file a federal income tax return if he had gross income of at least

A. $1,050

B. $4,050

C. $6,350

D. $10,400

Answer (D) is correct. *(SEE, adapted)*
REQUIRED: The minimum amount of gross income for which a single individual return must be filed.
DISCUSSION: Generally, a taxpayer must file a return if his or her gross income equals or exceeds the sum of the personal exemption to which (s)he is entitled plus the standard deduction amount applicable to the taxpayer's filing status [Sec. 6012(a)(1)]. Section 151 allows a $4,050 exemption for each taxpayer in 2017. For a single taxpayer, the standard deduction is $6,350 in 2017 [Sec. 63(c)]. Mr. T must file a tax return if his gross income is at least $10,400 ($6,350 + $4,050).
Answer (A) is incorrect. Income has to exceed the personal exemption plus the standard deduction. Answer (B) is incorrect. The amount of $4,050 does not include the standard deduction. Answer (C) is incorrect. The amount of $6,350 does not include the personal exemption.

7.3.5. Sam Johnson, a calendar-year taxpayer, applied for and received an extension for filing his Year 1 tax return. Mr. Johnson filed his tax return on June 2 of Year 2 and paid the balance due. The return reflected a tax liability of $50,000 and estimated tax payments made timely of $45,000. Based on these facts, Mr. Johnson owes

	Failure to File Penalty	Failure to Pay Penalty
A.	$0	$50
B.	$0	$25
C.	$500	$50
D.	$250	$25

Answer (A) is correct. *(M. Yates)*
REQUIRED: The taxpayer's penalty when payment of tax is made at the time of filing an extended return.
DISCUSSION: Payment of tax is due by the due date for filing a tax return. The tax return is due April 15 for a calendar-year taxpayer. Since Mr. Johnson received an extension to file his tax return and filed it before the end of the extension period, there is no failure to file penalty.
The penalty for failure to pay tax is 0.5% of the amount due for each month (or fraction thereof) during which such tax remains unpaid. The maximum penalty under this provision is 25% (Sec. 6651). Mr. Johnson's failure to pay penalty is computed as follows:

Additional tax due on return	$5,000
Penalty rate per month	× .005
Penalty for 1 month	$ 25
Number of months past due	× 2
Failure to pay penalty	$ 50

The failure to pay penalty is computed only on the amount of tax due. There is no penalty for failure to pay estimated taxes because 90% of the total tax shown on the current-year return was paid as estimated payments during the year.
Answer (B) is incorrect. The failure to pay penalty is owed for 2 months. Answer (C) is incorrect. The failure to file penalty if the return is not filed timely is $500. Answer (D) is incorrect. The failure to file penalty if the return is 1 month late is $250. Also, $25 is the failure to pay penalty for 1 month.

7.3.6. Silvia House, a calendar-year taxpayer, owed an additional $600 tax on her 2017 tax return, which she filed on June 25 of Year 2. Ms. House failed to request an extension for filing her return. What are her failure to file and failure to pay penalties?

	Failure to File Penalty	Failure to Pay Penalty
A.	$210	$0
B.	$210	$9
C.	$201	$9
D.	$81	$9

Answer (B) is correct. *(M. Yates)*
REQUIRED: The failure to file and failure to pay penalties when a very small amount of additional tax is due.
DISCUSSION: Section 6651(a) normally provides for a penalty of 5% of the tax due per month (or fraction thereof) when a return is not filed timely. In this case, House's penalty is only $90 ($600 × .05 × 3 months), reduced by the failure to pay penalty.
However, Sec. 6651(a) also provides for a failure to file minimum penalty of the lesser of $210 or 100% of the additional tax due for returns that are more than 60 days past due, unless reasonable cause can be shown. When this rule applies, the failure to file penalty is not reduced by the failure to pay penalty. House's failure to file penalty is $210, and her failure to pay penalty is $9 ($600 × .005 × 3 months).
Answer (A) is incorrect. There is a failure to pay penalty. Answer (C) is incorrect. The failure to file penalty is not reduced by the failure to pay penalty when the failure to file minimum amount rule is applied. Answer (D) is incorrect. The failure to file penalty is only reduced by the failure to pay penalty. However, Sec. 6651(a) asserts that, when the failure to file penalty is assessed for tax returns that are more than 60 days past due, the additional failure to pay penalty is not used to reduce the failure to file penalty.

7.3.7. George Webster, a calendar-year taxpayer, filed his 2017 tax return on July 22 of 2018. Mr. Webster did not request an extension for filing this return. The tax liability reflected on the tax return is $10,000. Mr. Webster had $9,000 withheld for federal income taxes by his employer. What are the failure to file and failure to pay penalties for this return?

	Failure to File Penalty	Failure to Pay Penalty
A.	$0	$20
B.	$210	$20
C.	$190	$20
D.	$0	$210

Answer (B) is correct. *(M. Yates)*
REQUIRED: The taxpayer's penalty when a tax return is not filed timely and payment of tax is not made until the return is filed.
DISCUSSION: Mr. Webster's tax return was due on April 15. Since he did not file for an extension of time to file his Year 1 tax return, he is subject to a penalty for failure to file.
Under Sec. 6651, this penalty is normally 5% of the tax due on the return for each month (or fraction thereof) that the return is not filed. In that case, Webster's penalty is only $200 ($1,000 × 0.05 × 4 months), reduced by the failure to pay penalty. However, Sec. 6651(a) also provides for a failure to file minimum penalty of the lesser of $210 or 100% of the additional tax due for returns that are more than 60 days past due, unless reasonable cause can be shown. When this rule applies, the failure to file penalty is not reduced by the failure to pay penalty. Webster's failure to file penalty is $210 and his failure to pay penalty is $20 ($1,000 × 0.05 × 4 months).
Answer (A) is incorrect. A failure to file penalty is also assessed. Answer (C) is incorrect. The failure to file penalty is not reduced by the failure to pay penalty when the failure to file minimum amount rule is applied. Answer (D) is incorrect. There is a failure to file penalty and the failure to pay penalty is not $210.

7.3.8. Which of the following taxpayers must file a return for 2017?

A. Married taxpayers filing jointly who have income of $18,800 for the year and one child who is a dependent.

B. A single taxpayer, age 67, with interest and dividend income of $10,400.

C. A single taxpayer, claimed as a dependent by his parents, who earns $2,000 from a part-time job and has no unearned income.

D. A taxpayer who files as a head of household with two exemptions and who earns $14,150.

Answer (D) is correct. *(Publisher, adapted)*
REQUIRED: The taxpayer who must file a return for 2017.
DISCUSSION: Generally, a taxpayer must file a tax return if the taxpayer's gross income equals or exceeds the sum of his or her personal exemption and standard deduction [Sec. 6012(a)]. Section 151 allows a $4,050 personal exemption for each taxpayer in 2017. Standard deductions in 2017 are $12,700 for married filing jointly, $9,350 for heads of household, and $6,350 for unmarried individuals. A taxpayer who files as a head of household must file a return if his or her gross income equals or exceeds $13,400 ($9,350 + $4,050). The second exemption is not considered.
Answer (A) is incorrect. Gross income is less than the standard deduction plus exemptions. Answer (B) is incorrect. Gross income is less than the standard deduction (basic plus additional for age 65) plus his or her exemption. Answer (C) is incorrect. (S)he has no unearned income and his or her earned income is not greater than his or her standard deduction plus exemptions [Sec. 63(c)(5)].

7.3.9. Mr. R, who is single and under age 65, had the following items of income and expense during 2017:

Gross receipts of sole proprietorship	$11,400
Cost of goods sold of sole proprietorship	4,000
Other expenses of sole proprietorship	1,500
Interest income (personal savings account)	2,000
Cash dividends	600

Mr. R is required to file a return for 2017.

A. True.

B. False.

Answer (A) is correct. *(SEE, adapted)*
DISCUSSION: Generally, a taxpayer must file an income tax return if (s)he has gross income equal to or in excess of his or her standard deduction plus personal exemptions [Sec. 6012(a)]. The gross income of a merchandising business is sales less cost of goods sold [Reg. 1.61-3(a)]. Therefore, Mr. R's total gross income is only $10,000 ($7,400 from sole proprietorship + $2,000 interest + $600 dividends). This amount is less than R's standard deduction of $6,350 plus his 2017 personal exemption of $4,050, so R generally would not be required to file a return.
However, a tax return is also required to report net self-employment income of $400 or more. Mr. R's self-employment income is $5,900 ($11,400 – $4,000 – $1,500).

7.3.10. Taxpayer C's income for the current year was $450 in wages and $250 in tips. Social Security was not collected or reported on the tips. No tax return is required to be filed because total income is less than $1,050.

A. True.

B. False.

Answer (B) is correct. *(SEE, adapted)*
DISCUSSION: If Social Security is not collected or reported on tips, the employee is required to pay the tax [Sec. 3102(c)(4)]. The taxpayer must file a tax return to pay the tax.

7.3.11. During the year 2017, Mr. and Mrs. P had combined gross income of $21,000. Mr. P was 66 on May 3, 2017, and Mrs. P's 65th birthday will be January 1, 2018. They are required to file an individual income tax return.

A. True.
B. False.

Answer (B) is correct. *(SEE, adapted)*
    DISCUSSION: The taxpayers must file an income tax return if their gross income equals or exceeds the sum of their personal exemptions and the standard deduction [Sec. 6012(a)]. Section 151 allows a $4,050 exemption for each taxpayer in 2017. On a joint return, the standard deduction in 2017 is $12,700. Additional standard deductions of $1,250 are available if the taxpayer is blind or is age 65 or over [Sec. 63(f)]. An individual is considered 65 on the first moment of the day preceding his or her 65th birthday. Therefore, Mrs. P is considered age 65 on December 31, 2017. The taxpayers are entitled to $8,100 of exemptions and have a total standard deduction of $15,200 ($12,700 + $1,250 + $1,250). Since the taxpayers' combined gross income of $21,000 is less than $23,300 ($8,100 exemptions + $15,200 standard deduction), they are not required to file a return.

7.3.12. In 2017, a child who may be claimed as a dependent by another taxpayer, and who has earned income of $700 and unearned income of $400, must file a tax return.

A. True.
B. False.

Answer (A) is correct. *(SEE, adapted)*
    DISCUSSION: In the case of an individual who is claimed as a dependent on another's tax return, (s)he must file if unearned income exceeds $1,050 or total income exceeds the standard deduction. For such a person, the standard deduction is limited to the greater of (1) $1,050 or (2) the individual's earned income plus $350 [Sec. 63(c)(5)]. The child who has unearned income of only $400 needs to file a return only if total income exceeds the standard deduction. In this case, the total income of $1,100 exceeds the standard deduction of $1,050 ($700 + $350). The standard deduction is limited to $1,050, since this is earned income plus $350.

7.3.13. Mr. Mercury does not have sufficient gross income to require the filing of a tax return; however, he has $100 in income tax withheld, so he should file a return in order to collect his taxes withheld.

A. True.
B. False.

Answer (A) is correct. *(SEE, adapted)*
    DISCUSSION: Even if the taxpayer is not required to file, a tax return should be filed to get a refund if income tax was withheld from pay or if the taxpayer can take the earned income credit.

7.3.14. The final return of a cash-basis, calendar-year individual must be filed within 3 1/2 months following the month in which (s)he died.

A. True.
B. False.

Answer (B) is correct. *(SEE, adapted)*
    DISCUSSION: The final return of a cash-basis, calendar-year individual must be filed by April 15 of the year following the year of death. There is no requirement that the final return of a decedent be filed any earlier than (s)he would have if (s)he had not died.

7.3.15. An individual may obtain an automatic 6-month extension to file his or her individual income tax return and pay any balance of tax due by filing Form 4868, *Application for Automatic Extension of Time to File U.S. Individual Income Tax Return*.

A. True.
B. False.

Answer (B) is correct. *(SEE, adapted)*
    DISCUSSION: An individual who is required to file an income tax return is allowed an automatic 6-month extension of time to file the return by filing Form 4868. However, no extension of time is allowed for payment of the tax due. A taxpayer desiring an extension of time to file his or her tax return and avoid the failure to pay penalty must file Form 4868, accompanied by the payment of tax estimated to be owed for the year and not yet paid, by the normal due date of the tax return.

7.3.16. If the Internal Revenue Service has granted a taxpayer an extension of time to file beyond the automatic 6-month extension and later justifiably renders the extension null and void, the taxpayer will have to pay the failure to file penalty on any tax not paid by the original due date of the return.

A. True.
B. False.

Answer (A) is correct. *(SEE, adapted)*
    DISCUSSION: A failure to file penalty is not imposed if the taxpayer has validly obtained an extension of time to file. But if the extension of time was not valid and is rendered null and void, the taxpayer must pay the failure to file penalty from the original due date of the return.

7.4 Tax Calculations (Other than the Capital Gains Rules)

NOTE: This subunit includes individual tax calculations other than those involving capital gains. The individual tax calculations including capital gains income can be found in Study Unit 11, Subunit 9.

7.4.1. Which of the following is not true about adjusted gross income (AGI)?

- A. It is a determining factor in the calculation of deductible medical and dental expenses.

- B. It is a determining factor in the calculation of nonbusiness casualty or theft losses.

- C. It may include a deduction for the unreimbursed qualifying educational expenses (tuition and books) of an employee.

- D. It may include a deduction for qualifying alimony payments.

Answer (C) is correct. *(R. Fernandez)*
REQUIRED: The false statement about adjusted gross income.
DISCUSSION: Unreimbursed qualifying educational expenses of an employee are itemized deductions, i.e., deductions from AGI. However, a taxpayer may deduct business expenses that have been substantiated to and reimbursed by an employer in arriving at AGI (Sec. 62). Books do not qualify for AGI deduction.
Answer (A) is incorrect. AGI is used in determining the deduction for medical and dental expenses. Answer (B) is incorrect. AGI is used in calculating nonbusiness theft or casualty losses. Answer (D) is incorrect. Qualifying alimony payments are deductible for AGI.

7.4.2. Scott and Trish Smith are married and file a joint return. In the current year, Scott earned a salary of $48,000 and Trish earned $30,000. They received $600 of interest during the year. They had unreimbursed expenses for moving household goods of $5,000 after both found new jobs across the country. What is their adjusted gross income for the current year?

- A. $52,800
- B. $60,900
- C. $73,600
- D. $78,600

Answer (C) is correct. *(C.J. Skender)*
REQUIRED: The AGI for a couple with salaries, dividend income, and moving expenses.
DISCUSSION: The AGI includes $78,000 of salaries. All $600 of interest is included in AGI. Moving expenses are subtracted from gross income as a for-AGI deduction to the extent the expenses are not reimbursed or paid for by the taxpayer's employer. Therefore, the Smiths' AGI equals $73,600.
Answer (A) is incorrect. AGI minus the Smiths' standard deduction and two personal exemptions is $52,800. Answer (B) is incorrect. AGI minus the Smiths' standard deduction is $60,900. Answer (D) is incorrect. The amount of $78,600 does not take into account the moving expense deduction.

7.4.3. Jerry Samson is single, age 35, and had $306,500 in adjusted gross income for 2017. All of Jerry's income is salary income. His itemized deductions were less than his standard deduction. Jerry claimed one personal exemption of $4,050. Samson's taxable income for 2017 is

- A. $303,908
- B. $297,558
- C. $300,150
- D. $296,100

Answer (B) is correct. *(Publisher, adapted)*
REQUIRED: The taxable income for a single taxpayer in 2017.
DISCUSSION: If a taxpayer's adjusted gross income exceeds a specific threshold amount (based on filing status), the deduction allowed for personal and dependency exemptions is reduced by 2% for each $2,500, or fraction thereof, by which the adjusted gross income exceeds the threshold amount. For a single taxpayer, the threshold amount is $261,500 in 2017. The standard deduction for a single taxpayer is $6,350 in 2017. Samson's taxable income computation is as follows:

Adjusted gross income	$306,500
Standard deduction	(6,350)
Personal exemption	(2,592)
Taxable income	$297,558

The personal exemption amount is calculated as follows:

($306,500 AGI − $261,500) ÷ $2,500 × .02 = 36%

Exemption for 2017	$4,050
Disallowance percentage	× .36
Disallowed exemption amount	$1,458

The deduction for Samson's personal exemption is $2,592 ($4,050 − $1,458).
Answer (A) is incorrect. Samson is entitled to a standard deduction in addition to the personal exemption. Answer (C) is incorrect. The amount of $300,150 assumes a complete phaseout of the personal exemption. Answer (D) is incorrect. The personal exemption is subject to a phaseout due to his AGI being greater than $297,558.

7.4.4. Robert Francis, a single taxpayer, age 30, had adjusted gross income of $23,000 in 2017. Upon examining his records, he listed the following deductions for the year:

Medical expenses	$4,300
Charitable contributions	2,300
State income taxes paid	1,160
Business expenses reimbursed by employer, but not substantiated	1,500

The amount of his allowable itemized deductions for 2017 is

A. $5,460
B. $6,500
C. $6,960
D. $9,260

Answer (B) is correct. *(Publisher, adapted)*
REQUIRED: The taxpayer's allowable itemized deductions for 2017.
DISCUSSION: If a taxpayer's allowable itemized deductions are greater than his standard deduction he may use these itemized deductions in computing his taxable income for the year. Qualifying medical expenses in excess of 10% of AGI may be deducted [Sec. 213(a)]. State and local income taxes (Sec. 164) and qualifying charitable contributions (Sec. 170) also may be deducted. Employee's business expenses must be substantiated to the employer and reimbursed to be deductible above the line. Otherwise, they are a miscellaneous itemized deduction subject to the 2%-of-AGI floor.

Medical expenses	$4,300	
Less: 10% of AGI ($23,000 × .10)	(2,300)	
Allowable medical expenses		$2,000
Charitable contributions		2,300
State income taxes paid		1,160
Business expenses	$1,500	
Less: 2% of AGI	(460)	1,040
		$6,500

Answer (A) is incorrect. Robert is allowed a business expense deduction of $1,040 ($1,500 – 2% of AGI). Answer (C) is incorrect. Robert must subtract 2% of AGI from his business expenses. Answer (D) is incorrect. Robert must subtract 10% of AGI from his medical expenses and 2% of AGI from his business expenses.

7.4.5. Donna Weber, age 24 and single, provided the following information on her 2017 income tax return:

Adjusted gross income	$30,000
Total itemized deductions	5,000
Personal exemption	4,050

Donna should report taxable income for 2017 of

A. $19,600
B. $20,950
C. $23,650
D. $25,950

Answer (A) is correct. *(Publisher, adapted)*
REQUIRED: The taxpayer's taxable income for 2017.
DISCUSSION: Section 63 defines taxable income as adjusted gross income minus the standard deduction (or total itemized deductions) and the deduction for personal exemption(s). For a single taxpayer in 2017, the basic standard deduction is $6,350. Since Donna's itemized deductions do not exceed the standard deduction, she will elect to use the larger amount. Donna's taxable income is

Adjusted gross income	$30,000
Standard deduction	(6,350)
Personal exemption	(4,050)
Taxable income	$19,600

Answer (B) is incorrect. Since Donna's itemized deductions are less than her standard deduction, she should use her standard deduction. Answer (C) is incorrect. Donna is entitled to her personal exemption in addition to her standard deduction. Answer (D) is incorrect. Donna is entitled to both her personal exemption and standard deduction.

7.4.6. George and Lillian Smith are married and file a joint return for 2017. They are both over age 65, and George is legally blind. They have adjusted gross income for the year of $30,000. What is the Smiths' taxable income for 2017?

A. $5,450
B. $9,200
C. $6,700
D. $21,900

Answer (A) is correct. *(Publisher, adapted)*
REQUIRED: The taxpayers' taxable income for 2017.
DISCUSSION: An additional standard deduction of $1,250 is available if, during the taxable year, the taxpayer and/or his or her spouse is age 65 or over, and if the taxpayer and/or his or her spouse is blind. The Smiths will receive three additional standard deductions in 2017. Their taxable income for the year is

Adjusted gross income	$30,000
Basic standard deduction	(12,700)
Additional standard deductions ($1,250 × 3)	(3,750)
Personal exemptions ($4,050 × 2)	(8,100)
Taxable income	$ 5,450

Answer (B) is incorrect. The Smiths are entitled to additional standard deductions of $3,750. Answer (C) is incorrect. The Smiths are entitled to an additional standard deduction of $1,250 for George's legal blindness. Answer (D) is incorrect. The Smiths are entitled to the basic standard deduction of $12,700 and additional standard deductions of $3,750.

7.4.7. For the year 2017, Carolyn earned $80,000 and incurred the following expenses:

Moving expenses	$ 500
Credit card interest	250
Mortgage interest (qualified residence interest)	6,200
Tax return preparation fees	1,100
Unreimbursed employee business expenses	1,750

Assuming she had no other expenses, what are her total allowable itemized deductions for 2017?

A. $7,450

B. $7,460

C. $7,960

D. $9,050

Answer (B) is correct. *(Publisher, adapted)*
REQUIRED: The amount of deductions allowable given gross income and total expenses.
DISCUSSION: Carolyn's moving expenses are deductible in determining AGI. The qualified residence interest is deductible from AGI in full. None of the personal interest (credit card interest) is deductible. Tax return preparation fees and unreimbursed employee business expenses are miscellaneous deductions under Sec. 67 and deductible only to the extent they exceed 2% of AGI.

Salary income		$80,000
Moving expenses		(500)
AGI		$79,500
Mortgage interest		6,200
Tax return preparation fees	$1,100	
Employee business expenses	1,750	
	$2,850	
2% of AGI ($79,500 × .02)	(1,590)	
Allowable misc. itemized deductions		1,260
Total deductions		$ 7,460

Answer (A) is incorrect. The miscellaneous deductions are reduced by 2% of AGI. AGI is affected by the moving expenses. Answer (C) is incorrect. Moving expenses are an above-the-line deduction. Answer (D) is incorrect. The miscellaneous deductions are reduced by 2% of AGI.

7.4.8. Darren Cantrelle, age 21, is a full-time student and receives over half of his support from his parents. His other income is from a part-time job, from which he earned $1,100 in 2017. If Darren's parents claim him as a dependent for the year, what will his standard deduction be in 2017?

A. $0

B. $1,100

C. $1,450

D. $4,050

Answer (C) is correct. *(Publisher, adapted)*
REQUIRED: The standard deduction for a taxpayer claimed as a dependent.
DISCUSSION: If an individual is eligible to be claimed as a dependent (Sec. 151) by another taxpayer for the taxable year, that individual's basic standard deduction cannot exceed the greater of (1) $1,050 or (2) that individual's earned income plus $350. Since Darren's parents claimed him as a dependent for 2017, his 2017 standard deduction will be limited to his earned income of $1,100 plus $350, or $1,450.

Answer (A) is incorrect. Darren is entitled to a standard deduction for 2017. Answer (B) is incorrect. Darren's deduction is equal to his earned income plus $350. Answer (D) is incorrect. The amount of the exemption for Darren that can be claimed on his parents' tax return is $4,050.

7.4.9. For 2017, Frances had an adjusted gross income figure of $60,000. She is single, age 66, and incurred the following expenses:

Medical expenses unreimbursed	$6,500
State income taxes	4,000
Real estate property taxes	1,000
State sales taxes	2,500
Contribution to church	6,000
Credit card interest	1,500
Home mortgage interest	7,000
Auto loan interest (personal)	600

Her allowable itemized deductions for 2017 are

A. $23,000

B. $20,600

C. $19,100

D. $18,500

Answer (D) is correct. *(E. Fenton, Jr.)*
REQUIRED: The amount of itemized deductions allowable for 2017.
DISCUSSION: The medical expense deduction is limited to the portion greater than 10% of AGI [Sec. 213(a)], and the state sales taxes are less than the state income taxes. Consumer personal interest (credit card and auto loan interest) is not allowed as a deduction. The computations are

Medical [$6,500 − ($60,000 × .10)]	$ 500
State income taxes	4,000
Real estate property taxes	1,000
State sales tax	0
Contributions	6,000
Credit card interest	0
Home mortgage interest	7,000
Auto loan interest	0
Allowable itemized deductions	$18,500

Answer (A) is incorrect. The medical expense deduction is limited to the portion greater than 10% of AGI. Answer (B) is incorrect. The credit card interest and auto loan interest are not deductible. Answer (C) is incorrect. The auto loan interest is not deductible.

7.4.10. Harold and Tina Skagg, both over age 65, file a joint return in 2017. They have adjusted gross income for the year of $65,600 and $8,000 of itemized deductions. The Skaggs' tax liability for 2017, rounded to the nearest dollar, is

A. $7,003

B. $6,815

C. $5,788

D. $5,413

7.4.11. Jeff Gibson, who is 26 years old and single, claimed one exemption and provided the following information for his 2017 return:

Salary	$40,000
Charitable contributions	4,000
State income tax paid	2,500

Gibson's taxable income for 2017 is

A. $29,450

B. $29,600

C. $35,950

D. $33,500

7.4.12. Marty and Michelle Hall, both under 65 years of age, file a joint return for 2017. Their adjusted gross income for the year is $55,300, and their itemized deductions amount to $12,900. They claim one child as a dependent. Their income tax liability for 2017, rounded to the nearest dollar, is

A. $3,605

B. $3,635

C. $4,213

D. $5,540

Answer (D) is correct. *(Publisher, adapted)*
REQUIRED: The taxpayers' tax liability for 2017.
DISCUSSION: For taxpayers filing a joint return in 2017, the rates in Sec. 1(a) should be applied to their taxable income, defined in Sec. 63 as adjusted gross income minus the standard deduction (or total itemized deductions if greater) and the deduction for personal exemptions (Sec. 151). The Skaggs will use the standard deduction since it is greater than their itemized deductions. Their standard deduction is the $12,700 basic standard deduction plus two additional standard deductions of $1,250 each because they are over age 65. Each spouse on a joint return is entitled to a $4,050 personal exemption in 2017. The Skaggs' taxable income is $42,300 ($65,600 adjusted gross income − $12,700 basic standard deduction − $2,500 additional standard deductions − personal exemptions). Their tax liability for 2017 is $5,413 [($18,650 × 10%) + ($23,650 × 15%)].
Answer (A) is incorrect. This figure is the amount of tax liability from taxable income calculated by subtracting only the basic standard deduction of $12,700 from gross income of $65,600. Answer (B) is incorrect. This figure fails to deduct the second additional standard deduction and the personal exemptions. Answer (C) is incorrect. This figure is the amount of tax liability from taxable income calculated by subtracting only the basic standard deduction of $12,700 and the personal exemptions of $8,100 from gross income of $65,600.

Answer (A) is correct. *(Publisher, adapted)*
REQUIRED: The taxpayer's taxable income for 2017.
DISCUSSION: Section 63 defines taxable income as adjusted gross income minus (1) the standard deduction (or total itemized deductions if greater) and (2) the deduction for personal exemptions. For a single taxpayer in 2017, the basic standard deduction is $6,350. Since there is a deduction for state and local income tax, he will therefore use the itemized deduction because it exceeds the standard deduction. The amount of the personal exemption in 2017 is $4,050. Gibson's taxable income is

Salary	$40,000
Itemized deduction	(6,500)
Personal exemption	(4,050)
Taxable income	$29,450

Answer (B) is incorrect. The amount of $29,600 is arrived at by using the standard deduction of $6,350 instead of the more beneficial itemized deduction of $6,500. Answer (C) is incorrect. Gibson is entitled to deduct his itemized deductions in addition to his personal exemption. Answer (D) is incorrect. Gibson is entitled to a personal exemption of $4,050 in addition to his itemized deductions.

Answer (A) is correct. *(Publisher, adapted)*
REQUIRED: The taxpayers' tax liability for 2017.
DISCUSSION: For taxpayers filing a joint return for 2017, the rates in Sec. 1(a) should be applied to their taxable income, defined as adjusted gross income minus the standard deduction (or total itemized deductions if greater) and the deduction for personal exemptions (Sec. 63). Each spouse on a joint return in 2017 is entitled to a $4,050 personal exemption and a $4,050 exemption for each dependent [Secs. 151(b) and (c)]. The taxpayers' taxable income is $30,250 ($55,300 adjusted gross income − $12,900 itemized deductions − $12,150 personal exemptions). Since the beginning of the 25% bracket is $75,900 for a married couple filing a joint return, the Halls' tax liability for 2017 is $3,605 [($18,650 × .10) + ($11,600 × .15)].
Answer (B) is incorrect. The amount of $3,635 was calculated using the standard deduction instead of the Halls' itemized deductions. Answer (C) is incorrect. The amount of $4,213 includes only two personal exemptions. Answer (D) is incorrect. The amount of $5,540 does not include a reduction for the itemized deduction.

7.4.13. Mike Law was married and filed a joint return with his wife in 2017. Neither Mike nor his wife is 65 or over or blind. Assuming he does not itemize, what is Mike's standard deduction for 2017?

A. $4,050

B. $8,100

C. $20,800

D. $12,700

Answer (D) is correct. *(Publisher, adapted)*
REQUIRED: The standard deduction for a married taxpayer filing a joint return in 2017.
DISCUSSION: The standard deduction is allowed by Sec. 63 in lieu of itemizing. Additional standard deductions are allowed for those taxpayers who are age 65 or over or blind. In 2017, the basic standard deduction for those married and filing joint returns is $12,700.
Answer (A) is incorrect. The 2017 personal exemption for one individual is $4,050. Answer (B) is incorrect. The 2017 personal exemption total for two individuals is $8,100. Answer (C) is incorrect. The amount of $20,800 includes the Laws' two personal exemptions.

7.4.14. John and Barbara are married, age 46 and 44, respectively, have no dependents, and file a joint return for 2017. The following information is obtained from their 2017 tax return:

John's salary	$197,550
Barbara's salary	182,300
Dividend income (jointly owned stock)	45,000
Itemized deductions	40,000
Personal exemptions ($4,050 × 2)	8,100

The itemized deductions consist of mortgage interest, $30,000; investment interest, $4,000; medical expenses (in excess of 10%-of-AGI limitation), $1,500; and charitable contributions, $4,500. John and Barbara's taxable income for 2017 is

A. $387,291

B. $380,082

C. $383,959

D. $376,750

Answer (A) is correct. *(Publisher, adapted)*
REQUIRED: The amount of the taxpayer's taxable income for 2017.
DISCUSSION: The deduction allowed for personal and dependency exemptions is reduced for taxpayers whose adjusted gross income exceeds a specified threshold amount. Similarly, the amount of itemized deductions allowed is also reduced when the taxpayer's AGI exceeds the same threshold. For married taxpayers filing jointly, the threshold amount is $313,800 for both personal exemptions and itemized deductions.
Note that the total reduction in itemized deductions may not exceed 80% of allowable itemized deductions, not including the deductions for medical expenses, investment interest, casualty and theft losses, or wagering losses to the extent of wagering gains. The overall limitation did not apply in this situation.

Overall limitation on disallowed deductions:	
Mortgage interest	$ 30,000
Charitable contributions	4,500
Total deductions	$ 34,500
Times: disallowance percentage	× .80
Maximum disallowed deduction	$ 27,600

Itemized deduction floor:	
($424,850 AGI − $313,800 threshold) × 3% =	$ 3,332

Total itemized deductions allowed	
($40,000 − $3,332) =	$ 36,668

Exemption limitation:
($424,850 AGI − $313,800) ÷ $2,500 × .02 = 89%

Exemptions for 2017 (2 × $4,050)	$ 8,100
Disallowance percentage	× .89
Disallowed exemption amount	$ 7,209
Total exemption allowed ($8,100 − $7,209)	$ 891

Taxable income:	
John's salary	$197,550
Barbara's salary	182,300
Dividends	45,000
Adjusted gross income	$424,850
Itemized deductions	(40,000)
Exemptions	(8,100)
Disallowed itemized deductions	3,332
Disallowed personal exemptions	7,209
Taxable income	$387,291

Answer (B) is incorrect. The itemized deduction must be reduced by to $3,332. Answer (C) is incorrect. The personal exemptions must be reduced by $7,209. Answer (D) is incorrect. There is a disallowed exemption amount of $7,209 and a disallowed itemized deduction amount of $3,332.

7.5 Unearned Income of a Minor Child

7.5.1. When will a minor's income be taxed at his or her parent's rate?

A. When a child has any income and is under age 19.

B. When a child has net unearned income regardless of his or her age.

C. When a child has unearned income and is under age 19.

D. When a child has net unearned income and is under age 19 with at least one living parent.

Answer (D) is correct. *(Publisher, adapted)*
REQUIRED: The circumstances that require a minor's parent's rates to be used to tax a minor's income.
DISCUSSION: Section 1(g) provides in general that unearned income of certain minor children will be taxed to the child at the top rate of the parents. For this purpose, a minor is any child under 19 years of age or under 24 and a full-time student at the end of the tax year who has at least one living parent. If the minor is 18 or a full-time student under 24 and has earned income that exceeds one-half of their support, the net unearned income will not be taxed at the parent's rate. The provision applies to net unearned income, which is specially defined.
Answer (A) is incorrect. This provision applies only to net unearned income. Answer (B) is incorrect. This provision applies only to children under age 19. Answer (C) is incorrect. This provision applies only to net unearned income, not just unearned income.

7.5.2. Marcy, age 12, earned $300 from babysitting during 2017. Her parents claim her as a dependent. She also had interest and dividends of $2,700 during the year. She did not itemize deductions. What is her net unearned income for 2017?

A. $3,000

B. $2,700

C. $1,650

D. $600

Answer (D) is correct. *(Publisher, adapted)*
REQUIRED: The amount of a child's net unearned income.
DISCUSSION: Net unearned income is defined in Sec. 1(g)(4) as unearned income less the sum of (1) $1,050, plus (2) the greater of $1,050 or, if the child itemizes, the amount of allowable deductions directly connected with the production of the unearned income. However, unearned income may not exceed the child's taxable income. Marcy's unearned income consists of $2,700 of interest and dividends. Her net unearned income is $600 [$2,700 – ($1,050 + $1,050)].
Answer (A) is incorrect. Earned income plus interest and dividends, which are unearned income items, is $3,000. Answer (B) is incorrect. Unearned income, not net unearned income, is $2,700. Answer (C) is incorrect. An additional $1,050 should be subtracted to obtain net unearned income.

7.5.3. Mr. and Mrs. Martinez had joint taxable income of $50,000 in 2017 on which their tax is $6,578. Their marginal tax rate is 15%, and they did not elect to include their children's income in their own income. Their children had the following unearned income: daughter Linda, 17, $3,500; son Fred, 15, $2,700; and son Jose, 13, $2,200. The children had no other income. What is Fred's tax for 2017 (round to the nearest dollar)?

A. $165

B. $90

C. $195

D. $315

Answer (C) is correct. *(Publisher, adapted)*
REQUIRED: The tax on the net unearned income (NUI) of a minor child whose parents have other minor children.
DISCUSSION: The tax imposed on a minor child's income is computed as follows. The child's portion is the allocable parental tax times the ratio of the child's NUI over the total of all NUI of the parent's minor children.

Linda's NUI is $1,400 [$3,500 – ($1,050 + $1,050)].
Jose's NUI is $100 [$2,200 – ($1,050 + $1,050)].
Fred's NUI is $600 [$2,700 – ($1,050 + $1,050)].

Fred's tax is computed as the greater of 1 or 2 below. Since total tax under method 2 is greater, Fred's tax is $195.

1. ($2,700 total income – $1,050 standard deduction) × .10 applicable rate = $165

2. The sum of
   (a) ($2,700 total income – $600 NUI – $1,050 standard deduction) × .10 applicable rate = $105
   Plus
   (b) Parents' tax on $52,100 $ 6,883
       Less parents' tax on $50,000   (6,568)
                          $ 315

       Multiplied by $600
       (Fred's NUI) ÷ $2,100
         total children's NUI   × .29   90
                                  $195

Answer (A) is incorrect. Fred's income tax calculated without regard to Sec. 1(g) equals $165. Answer (B) is incorrect. The allocable parental tax multiplied by the ratio of Fred's NUI to the total is $90. Answer (D) is incorrect. The allocable parental tax is $315.

7.5.4. Jamie is 13 years old. She received income in the current year from the following sources:

Babysitting for neighbor	$ 80
A trust created and funded by her grandparents	2,000
Dividends from stocks given to her by her parents	200
Interest on a bank account (deposits from last year's babysitting)	50

What is Jamie's unearned income for the year?

A. $200

B. $2,200

C. $2,250

D. $2,330

Answer (C) is correct. *(Publisher, adapted)*
REQUIRED: The minor child's unearned income given various sources.
DISCUSSION: Unearned income is simply income that is not earned. The only earned income of Jamie is the $80 from babysitting for neighbors. All the rest of the income is considered unearned income. The source of the unearned income and whether it was from assets provided by third parties or from parents does not matter. Unearned income may commonly come from a trust, from a bank account, or from assets held by a custodian or guardian under the Uniform Gifts to Minors Act. Jamie's unearned income is $2,250 ($2,000 from the trust + $200 from dividends + $50 interest).
Answer (A) is incorrect. Unearned income also includes income from a trust and interest on a bank account. Answer (B) is incorrect. Unearned income also includes interest on a bank account. Answer (D) is incorrect. Unearned income does not include babysitting money.

7.5.5. In 2017, parents may elect to include in their own return income over $2,100 of their children under age 19 who have net unearned income.

A. True.

B. False.

Answer (A) is correct. *(Publisher, adapted)*
DISCUSSION: Section 1(g)(7) allows the parents of a child who is subject to the "kiddie tax" to include the child's income in excess of $2,100 in the parents' own tax return. The purpose is to simplify the inconvenience of the child paying tax on his or her unearned income. Parents will also have to pay a tax equal to the lesser of $105 or 10% of the excess of the child's gross income over $1,050. These amounts are indexed for inflation. This is reported on Form 8814.

7.5.6. If a child's parents elect to include the child's income in the parents' return, the child will still be required to file a return in most cases.

A. True.

B. False.

Answer (B) is correct. *(Publisher, adapted)*
DISCUSSION: Under Sec. 1(g)(7), a child is treated as having no gross income and is not required to file a return if the parents elect to include the child's income in their own return. Once the parents have included the child's income in their own return and paid the additional tax equal to the lesser of $105 or 10% of the excess of the child's gross income over $1,050, there is no need for a child to file a return and pay tax. But if there has been withholding on the child's income or estimated tax payments have been made for the child, the child will need to file a return to recover these amounts.

7.6 Alternative Minimum Tax

7.6.1. For property placed in service after 1998, which of the following is a true statement of the adjustment required for alternative minimum taxable income?

A. The alternative depreciation system of Sec. 168(g) is used in its entirety.

B. For personal property, the alternative depreciation system of Sec. 168(g) is used with the 150%-declining-balance method (switching to straight-line when larger), but the MACRS recovery period that applies for regular tax purposes also applies for AMT purposes.

C. Section 1250 property and other property depreciated under MACRS using the straight-line method are depreciated using the alternative depreciation system of Sec. 168(g).

D. It is the same as for property placed in service prior to 1987.

Answer (B) is correct. *(Publisher, adapted)*
REQUIRED: The true statement concerning the adjustment for depreciation on property placed in service after 1998.
DISCUSSION: The deduction allowed for depreciation of tangible property (personal and real) placed in service after 1998 is generally determined under the alternative depreciation system of Sec. 168(g). However, for personal property, the 150%-declining-balance method is used and switches to a straight-line method in the first year the straight-line method yields a larger deduction. For tax years after 1998, the MACRS recovery period that applies for regular tax purposes also applies for AMT purposes. Therefore, the requirement that the 150%-declining-balance method be used over the applicable ADS recovery period for AMT purposes is no longer necessary. The former rules apply to property placed in service before 1999.
Answer (A) is incorrect. The 150%-declining-balance method is used for personal property. Answer (C) is incorrect. For tax years after December 31, 1998, the AMT adjustment for the MACRS depreciation allowance claimed on Sec. 1250 property and any other property under MACRS using the straight-line method is disregarded. Answer (D) is incorrect. For property placed in service prior to 1987, accelerated depreciation over straight-line is a tax preference item and this applied only to real property and leased personal property.

7.6.2. Alternative minimum tax for individuals requires certain adjustments and preferences. Which of the following is a preference or adjustment item for noncorporate taxpayers?

A. Personal exemptions.

B. Incentive stock options.

C. Tax-exempt interest on certain private activity bonds.

D. All of the answers are correct.

Answer (D) is correct. *(SEE, adapted)*
REQUIRED: The item that is a preference or adjustment item for noncorporate taxpayers.
DISCUSSION: Several adjustments affect only noncorporate taxpayers. Personal exemptions, tax-exempt interest on private activity bonds, which is included in investment income, and incentive stock options are examples of these adjustments.
Answer (A) is incorrect. Incentive stock options and tax-exempt interest on certain private activity bonds are also preference or adjustment items for noncorporate taxpayers when determining the alternative minimum tax. Answer (B) is incorrect. Personal exemptions and tax-exempt interest on certain private activity bonds are also preference or adjustment items for noncorporate taxpayers when determining the alternative minimum tax. Answer (C) is incorrect. Personal exemptions and incentive stock options are also preference or adjustment items for noncorporate taxpayers when determining the alternative minimum tax.

7.6.3. The alternative minimum tax for individuals is the sum of

A. 26% of the tax base that does not exceed $187,800 and 28% of the tax base that exceeds $187,800 reduced by the regular tax.

B. 26% of tax base not exceeding $150,000 plus 28% of the tax base exceeding $150,000.

C. 28% of the tax base exceeding $187,800.

D. 28% of the tax base reduced by the regular tax.

Answer (A) is correct. *(Publisher, adapted)*
REQUIRED: The definition of alternative minimum tax for individuals.
DISCUSSION: The alternative minimum tax is imposed by Sec. 55 for corporations and individuals. The tax base for the alternative minimum tax is the alternative minimum taxable income minus the statutory exemption [Sec. 55(a)]. The tax for individuals is the sum of 26% of the tax base that does not exceed $187,800, and 28% of the tax base that does exceed $187,800. This amount is then reduced by the regular tax amount for the taxable year.
Answer (B) is incorrect. The threshold amount at which the AMT rate changes is not $150,000. Answer (C) is incorrect. The AMT rate is 26% on the tax base that is less than $187,800 and is reduced by the regular tax. Answer (D) is incorrect. The AMT rates change when taxable excess exceeds $187,800 and is reduced by the regular tax.

7.6.4. A single individual may have to pay alternative minimum tax if taxable income for regular tax purposes, plus any adjustments and preference items exceeds

A. $24,100

B. $42,250

C. $54,300

D. $84,500

Answer (C) is correct. *(SEE, adapted)*
REQUIRED: The alternative minimum tax exemption for single individual taxpayers.
DISCUSSION: Section 55(d) provides an exemption amount for individuals for purposes of computing the alternative minimum tax. The amount of this exemption for individuals who are not married and not a surviving spouse is $54,300. As a result, a single individual will not have to pay alternative minimum tax until his or her alternative minimum taxable income exceeds $54,300. Note that this amount would be phased out by reducing the exemption for 25% of the excess of alternative minimum taxable income over a certain amount ($120,700 in the case of a single individual).
Answer (A) is incorrect. This is the exemption for estates and trusts. Answer (B) is incorrect. This is the exemption for married individuals who file separately. Answer (D) is incorrect. This is the exemption for married individuals filing a joint return and surviving spouses.

7.6.5. Which of the following applies to the allowable credit for prior-year minimum tax?

A. Any unused portion may not be carried forward.

B. It is allowed in full against the current year's tax.

C. It may only be carried forward for 5 years.

D. The allowable credit cannot reduce the current year's tax below the current year's tentative minimum tax.

Answer (D) is correct. *(SEE, adapted)*
REQUIRED: The statement that applies to the allowable credit for prior-year minimum tax.
DISCUSSION: A credit is allowed for the amount of adjusted net minimum tax for all tax years reduced by the minimum tax credit for all prior tax years (Sec. 53). The credit may be carried forward indefinitely as a credit against regular tax liability. The credit is limited to the extent that the regular tax liability reduced by other nonrefundable credits exceeds the tentative minimum tax for the year.
Answer (A) is incorrect. Any unused portion of the allowable credit may be carried forward indefinitely. Answer (B) is incorrect. There are specific limitations on the amount of the allowable credit. Answer (C) is incorrect. Any unused portion of the allowable credit may be carried forward indefinitely.

7.6.6. Alternative minimum taxable income is

A. Taxable income increased by tax preferences and increased or decreased by adjustments and other statutory modifications.

B. The sum of all tax preferences.

C. Computed the same for individuals and corporations.

D. Taxable income adjusted by tax preferences and reduced by an exemption amount.

Answer (A) is correct. *(SEE, adapted)*
REQUIRED: The definition of alternative minimum taxable income.
DISCUSSION: Taxable income is adjusted by positive and negative adjustments and various other statutory items to arrive at alternative minimum taxable income. There are numerous adjustments to items taken into account in determining taxable income as well as some additional adjustments. Tax preference items are also added to taxable income to arrive at alternative minimum taxable income.
Answer (B) is incorrect. The sum of all tax preferences is only one adjustment to taxable income to arrive at alternative minimum taxable income. Answer (C) is incorrect. Some of the adjustments differ for individuals and corporations, although many are the same. Answer (D) is incorrect. The exemption amount is subtracted from alternative minimum taxable income to arrive at a tax base before the tax rate is applied.

7.6.7. Scott and Cindy Muir had alternative minimum taxable income of $130,000 in the current year and file a joint return. For purposes of computing the alternative minimum tax, their exemption is

A. $24,100

B. $42,250

C. $54,300

D. $84,500

Answer (D) is correct. *(SEE, adapted)*
REQUIRED: The alternative minimum tax exemption for taxpayers filing a joint return.
DISCUSSION: Section 55(d) provides an exemption amount for individuals for purposes of computing the alternative minimum tax. The amount of this exemption for joint returns is $84,500. Note that this amount would be phased out by reducing the exemption for 25% of the excess of alternative minimum taxable income over a certain amount ($160,900 for married taxpayers filing joint returns). As the Muirs did not exceed this threshold, no reduction in the exemption was made.
Answer (A) is incorrect. The statutory exemption for estates and trusts is $24,100. Answer (B) is incorrect. The statutory exemption for married individuals filing separate returns is $42,250. Answer (C) is incorrect. The statutory exemption for an individual who is not married or is not a surviving spouse is $54,300.

7.6.8. For property placed in service after 1999, which of the following is a true statement of the depreciation adjustment required to compute alternative minimum taxable income?

A. The alternative depreciation system of Sec. 168(g) is used in its entirety.

B. The alternative depreciation system of Sec. 168(g) is used with the 150%-declining-balance method (switching to straight-line when larger) for personal property.

C. There is no adjustment for depreciation on real property.

D. It is the same as for property placed in service prior to 1987.

Answer (B) is correct. *(Publisher, adapted)*
REQUIRED: The true statement concerning the adjustment for depreciation on property placed in service after 1986.
DISCUSSION: The deduction allowed for depreciation of any tangible property (personal and real) placed in service after 1986 is generally determined under the alternative depreciation system of Sec. 168(g). However, for personal property, the 150%-declining-balance method is used and switches to a straight-line method in the first year the straight-line method yields a larger deduction. For nonresidential real and residential rental property, the straight-line method is used over a 40-year recovery period [Sec. 56(a)(1)]. However, for Sec. 1250 property placed in service after 1999, the adjustment is based on the property's regular MACRS recovery period, which eliminates the adjustment.
Answer (A) is incorrect. The 150%-declining-balance method is used for personal property. Answer (C) is incorrect. Real property must generally be depreciated over 40 years for alternative minimum taxable income purposes instead of the shorter 27.5- to 39-year recovery period that is used for regular tax purposes. For Sec. 1250 property placed in service after 1999, however, the adjustment is based on the property's regular MACRS recovery period, which eliminates the adjustment. Answer (D) is incorrect. For property placed in service prior to 1987, accelerated depreciation over straight-line is a tax preference item. This generally only applies to real property.

7.6.9. All of the following are considered adjustments for arriving at alternative minimum taxable income except

A. Real property taxes.
B. Personal exemptions.
C. Home mortgage interest (debt used to purchase, build, or substantially improve a residence).
D. Standard deduction.

Answer (C) is correct. *(SEE, adapted)*
REQUIRED: The item that is not an adjustment for arriving at alternative minimum taxable income.
DISCUSSION: Taxable income must be adjusted to arrive at alternative minimum taxable income. The adjustments are described in Secs. 56 and 58, with tax preferences in Sec. 57. The adjustments with respect to itemized deductions of an individual are contained in Sec. 56(b)(1). The only home mortgage interest adjustment made to taxable income in order to arrive at alternative minimum taxable income is home equity loan interest [Sec. 56(b)(1)(C)(i)].
Answer (A) is incorrect. Real property taxes are not allowed as deductions in arriving at alternative minimum taxable income under Sec. 56(b) and therefore must be added back as adjustments to taxable income for arriving at alternative minimum taxable income. Answer (B) is incorrect. Personal exemptions are not allowed as deductions in arriving at alternative minimum taxable income under Sec. 56(b) and therefore must be added back as adjustments to taxable income for arriving at alternative minimum taxable income. Answer (D) is incorrect. The standard deduction is not allowed as a deduction in arriving at alternative minimum taxable income under Sec. 56(b) and therefore must be added back as an adjustment to taxable income for arriving at alternative minimum taxable income.

7.6.10. Which of the following is a tax preference item to be considered in computing the alternative minimum tax for individuals in the current year?

A. Tax-exempt interest on any municipal bonds.
B. Excess of accelerated depreciation over straight-line depreciation for real property placed in service before 1987.
C. Interest on savings accounts over $10,000.
D. Standard deduction.

Answer (B) is correct. *(SEE, adapted)*
REQUIRED: The item considered a tax preference item in the current year.
DISCUSSION: Tax preference items increase adjusted taxable income to arrive at alternative minimum taxable income [Sec. 55(b)]. Section 57(a)(6) lists excess depreciation as a tax preference item for real property placed in service prior to 1987. Depreciation on assets placed in service after 1986 is specially computed as an adjustment under Sec. 56(a)(1) rather than as a tax preference.
Answer (A) is incorrect. Only tax-exempt interest on private activity bonds issued after August 7, 1986, is a tax preference item. Answer (C) is incorrect. The Code does not list interest on savings accounts over $10,000 as an adjustment or a tax preference item. Answer (D) is incorrect. The standard deduction is an adjustment item and not a tax preference item.

7.6.11. In 2017, Dr. and Mrs. McCoy, both under 65, had four dependent children, filed jointly, and had $150,000 of adjusted gross income and $25,000 of tax-exempt interest on private activity bonds issued in 1993. They took a depreciation deduction of $9,000 for a vacation home placed in service in 1991 (alternative depreciation system would have been $6,000). They also had deductible residence interest of $10,000, property taxes of $4,000, and medical expenses of $19,000. Their regular tax is $18,403. The McCoys' alternative minimum tax for 2017 is

A. $0
B. $2,469
C. $18,403
D. $20,872

Answer (B) is correct. *(Publisher, adapted)*
REQUIRED: The taxpayers' alternative minimum tax for 2017.
DISCUSSION: The minimum tax is the excess of the tentative minimum tax over the regular tax [Sec. 55(a)]. The McCoys' alternative minimum tax for 2017 is computed as follows:

Adjusted gross income	$150,000
Plus tax preferences:	
Tax-exempt interest	25,000
Excess GDS depreciation over ADS	3,000
Less itemized deductions:	
Interest	(10,000)
Medical expenses [$19,000 −	
($150,000 AGI × 10%)]	(4,000)
Alternative minimum taxable income	$164,000
Less exemption (reduced by phaseout)	(83,725)
Alternative minimum tax base	$ 80,275
Alternative minimum tax rate	× .26
Total tentative tax	$ 20,872
Less regular tax	(18,403)
Alternative minimum tax	$ 2,469

Answer (A) is incorrect. Only a portion of the medical expenses are deductible. Answer (C) is incorrect. The alternative minimum tax due is not equal to the regular tax liabilities. Answer (D) is incorrect. The total tentative tax of $20,872 is reduced by the regular tax to arrive at the alternative minimum tax.

7.6.12. Ms. K is a single taxpayer. What is her alternative minimum tax for 2017 based on the following information?

Taxable income	$40,250
Regular income tax before credits	5,801

The following adjustments or preferences have been identified from Ms. K's partially completed tax return:

Miscellaneous itemized deductions after taking account of the 2% floor from Schedule A	$ 2,500
Taxes from Schedule A	3,500
Depreciation adjustment for personal property placed in service after 1986	1,500
Adjustment on passive activity loss on continuing investment	10,000
Depletion preference item	15,000

A. $0

B. $22,500

C. $49

D. $5,850

Answer (C) is correct. *(SEE, adapted)*
REQUIRED: The taxpayer's alternative minimum tax for 2017.
DISCUSSION: The minimum tax is the excess of the tentative minimum tax over the regular tax [Sec. 55(a)]. In computing alternative minimum taxable income, all of the items listed in the question need to be added back to taxable income. In addition, one personal exemption needs to be added back because it was deducted in computing taxable income but is not allowed in computing alternative minimum taxable income. There is a $54,300 statutory exemption available for single taxpayers under the minimum tax. The computation follows:

Taxable income	$40,250
Plus adjustments:	
Personal exemption	4,050
Miscellaneous itemized deductions	2,500
Taxes	3,500
Passive activity loss adjustment	10,000
Depreciation adjustment	1,500
Plus tax preference:	
Depletion	15,000
Alternative minimum taxable income	$76,800
Less exemption	(54,300)
Alternative minimum tax base	$22,500
	× .26
Total tentative tax	$ 5,850
Less regular tax	(5,801)
Alternative minimum tax	$ 49

Answer (A) is incorrect. There is a minimum alternative tax. Answer (B) is incorrect. The alternative minimum tax base amount is $22,500. Answer (D) is incorrect. The total tentative tax is $5,850.

7.6.13. In Year 1, Ron and Cindy had an alternative minimum tax (AMT) liability of $19,000. This is the first tax year in which they ever paid the AMT. They recompute the AMT amount using only exclusion preferences and adjustments, and it results in a $8,500 AMT liability. In Year 2, Ron and Cindy have a regular tax liability of $45,000. Their tentative minimum tax liability is $42,000. What is the amount of Ron and Cindy's minimum tax credit (MTC) carryover to Year 2? What is the amount of the carryover that can be used in Year 2?

	Carryover to Year 2	Carryover Used
A.	$19,000	$3,000
B.	$19,000	$0
C.	$10,500	$3,000
D.	$8,500	$3,000

Answer (C) is correct. *(Publisher, adapted)*
REQUIRED: The taxpayer's MTC carryover for Year 1 and the amount used in Year 2.
DISCUSSION: For the first tax year that the AMT is owed, the MTC is the portion of the AMT attributable to deferral preferences or adjustments. Exclusion preferences or adjustments are disallowed itemized deductions or standard deduction, personal exemptions, excess percentage depletion, tax-exempt interest from private activity bonds, and the 50% excluded gain from the sale of small business stock. In Year 1, the deferral preferences and adjustments result in a $10,500 MTC ($19,000 – $8,500). This credit can be carried over to Year 2 and used to the extent that the regular tax liability exceeds the tentative minimum tax. This amount is $3,000 ($45,000 – $42,000).
Answer (A) is incorrect. The AMT without reduction for exclusion preferences or adjustments is $19,000. Answer (B) is incorrect. There is a carryover, and the $19,000 should be reduced by the exclusion preferences. Answer (D) is incorrect. The exclusion preferences and adjustments amount by which the AMT is reduced is $8,500.

7.6.14. Net operating losses can be used to offset no more than 100% of alternative minimum taxable income.

A. True.

B. False.

Answer (B) is correct. *(Publisher, adapted)*
DISCUSSION: The Sec. 56 adjustments used in computing alternative minimum taxable income provide for an alternative net operating loss (NOL) deduction. The alternative NOL deduction is adjusted for tax preference items and other alternative minimum taxable income adjustments. The alternative NOL deduction and the alternative minimum tax foreign tax credit (if any) cannot offset more than 100% of the tentative minimum tax amount [Sec. 59(a)(2)].

7.6.15. Nonrefundable personal credits can be used to reduce the tentative minimum tax.

A. True.

B. False.

Answer (A) is correct. *(Publisher, adapted)*
DISCUSSION: The personal nonrefundable credits may offset both the regular tax and the minimum tax.

7.7 Estimated Tax Payments

7.7.1. For Year 1, Robert and Martha, calendar-year taxpayers, received all of their gross income of $75,000 from their dairy farm. As of December 31 of Year 1, they had not made any estimated tax payments for Year 1. Which of the following will allow them to avoid the estimated tax penalty (ignoring Saturdays, Sundays, and holidays)?

A. Make one estimated tax payment by January 15 of Year 2.

B. File their Year 1 federal income tax return by March 15 of Year 2.

C. File their Year 1 federal income tax return by April 15 of Year 2, pay all of the tax, and attach a statement that they are qualified farmers.

D. File their Year 1 federal income tax return by March 15 of Year 2, and pay all the tax due.

Answer (A) is correct. *(SEE, adapted)*
REQUIRED: The action that will allow the taxpayers to avoid the estimated tax penalty.
DISCUSSION: Section 6654(i) allows farmers or fishermen who expect to receive at least two-thirds of their gross income from farming or fishing activities, or who received at least two-thirds of their gross income for the prior tax year from farming or fishing, to pay estimated tax for the year in one installment. Because Robert and Martha received all their gross income from farming, they may wait until January 15 of Year 2 to make their Year 1 estimated tax payment without penalty. The entire estimated tax for the year must be paid at that time. However, the January payment date may be ignored provided that the farmer or fisherman files his return for Year 1 and pays the entire tax due by March 1 of Year 2. Farmers and fishermen who satisfy the two-thirds requirement are not subject to the estimated tax requirements for taxpayers experiencing substantial income increases. Note that, when a farmer or fisherman files a joint return, the gross income of the spouse must be considered in determining whether two-thirds of the gross income is from farming or fishing.
Answer (B) is incorrect. Filing their Year 1 federal income tax return by March 15 of Year 2 will be a late return. In addition, payment of the entire tax is due with the return. Answer (C) is incorrect. Filing their Year 1 federal income tax return by April 15 of Year 2, paying all of the tax, and attaching a statement that they are qualified farmers will still be considered a late return. Answer (D) is incorrect. Filing their Year 1 federal income tax return by March 15 of Year 2, and paying all of the tax due will still be considered a late return.

7.7.2. G's Year 2 tax liability after credits was $12,000. Tax withheld by his employer for the year totaled $8,000. G earned his taxable income evenly throughout the year and used the standard deduction. G's Year 1 tax liability per his return was $10,000. Estimated tax payments for Year 2 were made as follows:

Installment	Date of Payment	Amount
1st	April 15, Year 2	$800
2nd	June 30, Year 2	800
3rd	September 15, Year 2	800
4th	January 15, Year 3	800

Assuming there are no circumstances justifying a waiver for the second installment period, what is the underpayment of estimated tax for the second installment payment period?

A. $1,000

B. $600

C. $200

D. $0

Answer (C) is correct. *(SEE, adapted)*
REQUIRED: The underpayment of estimated tax for the second quarter.
DISCUSSION: A penalty is provided in Sec. 6654(a) for the underpayment of estimated taxes. The penalty is avoided by paying quarterly payments that would equal or exceed the lesser of 90% of the current tax liability or 100% of the prior year's tax liability. Ninety percent of the current year's tax liability is $10,800 ($12,000 × 90%). One hundred percent of the prior year's tax liability is $10,000. Therefore, the minimum quarterly payments to avoid the penalty for underpayment of estimated taxes are $2,500 ($10,000 ÷ 4).
Tax withheld by an employer is paid equally on each installment date. Therefore, G is treated as having paid $2,000 ($8,000 ÷ 4) on each estimated tax due date. That leaves $500 of estimated payments required each quarter ($2,500 – $2,000). Since G paid $800 on the first due date of April 15, he overpaid by $300. He did not make his timely payment before or on the June 15 due date, so he underpaid by $200 ($2,500 – $2,000 withheld – $300 carried over from April 15).
Answer (A) is incorrect. The total estimated tax payments that are due for the first two installment periods is $1,000. Answer (B) is incorrect. The overpayment when the $800 estimated tax installment is finally paid on June 30 is $600. Answer (D) is incorrect. There is an underpayment of estimated tax for the second installment payment period based on withholding and carryover from the prior period.

7.7.3. For estimated tax purposes, the calendar year is divided into four payment periods. Which of the following payment periods is incorrect?

A. January 1 through March 31.

B. April 1 through June 30.

C. June 1 through August 31.

D. September 1 through December 31.

Answer (B) is correct. *(SEE, adapted)*
REQUIRED: The months that do not compose a quarter of a calendar year for estimated tax purposes.
DISCUSSION: Section 6654(a) provides a penalty for the underpayment of estimated taxes. In order to avoid the penalty, estimated tax payments are due quarterly. The first payment is due April 15 for the months January through March. The second payment is due June 15 for the months of April and May. The third payment is due September 15 for the months June through August. The fourth payment is due January 15 of the following year for the months September through December.
Answer (A) is incorrect. January 1 through March 31 is a correct payment period. Answer (C) is incorrect. June 1 through August 31 is a correct payment period. Answer (D) is incorrect. September 1 through December 31 is a correct payment period.

7.7.4. A taxpayer does not have to pay estimated taxes if

A. The taxpayer's tax liability for the previous year was less than $1,000.

B. The taxpayer's withholding covers 90% of the tax liability for the previous year.

C. The taxpayer's earned income credit will exceed his or her tax liability for the current year.

D. All of the answers are correct.

Answer (C) is correct. *(SEE, adapted)*
REQUIRED: The situation in which a taxpayer does not have to pay estimated taxes.
DISCUSSION: If tax credits exceed the tax liability, the taxpayer will not owe taxes and thus does not have to pay any estimated taxes. A $1 credit reduces tax liability by $1. Thus, if the earned income credit exceeds the tax liability, no taxes are due.
Answer (A) is incorrect. If the taxes due in the current year are less than $1,000, no estimated payments need to be made. Answer (B) is incorrect. Withholding must cover 100% of the tax liability for the previous year. Answer (D) is incorrect. Only one of the answers is correct.

7.7.5. For 2017, all of the following situations qualify as exceptions to the penalty for underpayment of estimated tax except

A. Total tax shown on the return minus withholdings is less than $1,000.

B. Estimated tax payments were 105% of that shown on the 2016 return, and last year's AGI was $160,000.

C. A U.S. citizen paid no estimated tax because he had no tax liability in the preceding year and the year was a 12-month period.

D. The taxes shown as owed on the return are no more than 10% of the total 2017 tax, all required estimated tax payments were made on time, and 2016 AGI was $100,000.

Answer (B) is correct. *(SEE, adapted)*
REQUIRED: The situation that is not an exception to the penalty for underpayment of estimated tax.
DISCUSSION: According to Sec. 6654(d)(1)(C)(i), adjusted gross income above $150,000 subjects the individual taxpayer to a different safe harbor provision. For 2017, the safe harbor percentage is 110%.
Answer (A) is incorrect. An exception precludes the penalty when taxes owed are less than $1,000. Answer (C) is incorrect. It is an exception to the underpayment rules. Answer (D) is incorrect. It fits within the rules to avoid the penalty.

7.7.6. Ms. W, who is single, determined that her total tax liability for Year 2 would be $10,000. W is required to make estimated tax payments if

A. Her Year 1 tax liability was $12,000 and her Year 2 income tax withholding will be $9,750.

B. Her Year 1 tax liability was $12,000 and her Year 2 income tax withholding will be $9,000.

C. Her Year 1 tax liability was $5,000 and her Year 2 income tax withholding will be $6,000.

D. Her Year 1 tax liability was $9,000 and her Year 2 income tax withholding will be $8,500.

Answer (D) is correct. *(SEE, adapted)*
REQUIRED: The circumstances under which the taxpayer would be required to make estimated tax payments.
DISCUSSION: In general, individuals must make estimated tax payments or be subject to a penalty (Sec. 6654). Amounts withheld from wages are treated as estimated tax payments. The annual estimated payment that must be made is equal to the lesser of (1) 90% of the tax for the current year or (2) 100% of the tax for the prior year. Assuming Ms. W's tax liability for Year 2 is $10,000 and her Year 1 tax liability was $9,000, the $8,500 withheld from her Year 2 wages does not meet the required annual estimated payment.
Answer (A) is incorrect. W would not be required to make estimated tax payments in this case, since she would meet the 90% of the current year's tax liability test. Answer (B) is incorrect. W is not required to make estimated payments if 90% of the current year's tax liability is covered by current year withholding. Answer (C) is incorrect. W would not be required to make estimated tax payments in this case, since she would meet the 100% of the prior year's tax liability test.

7.7.7. Charles is a self-employed attorney and files a joint return. He reported AGI of $80,000 and taxable income of $60,000 in Year 1, and he paid a tax liability of $12,000 after credits. In Year 2, he expects his AGI to increase about 25%. In setting up his estimated tax payments so as to avoid any penalty for underpayment of his Year 2 liability, Charles should

A. Pay quarterly installments of 25% of $12,000.

B. Make only one estimated payment late in Year 2 when he can more clearly estimate his Year 2 income.

C. Pay at least 25% more tax each quarter than he paid in Year 1.

D. Pay quarterly installments of 90% of 25% of $12,000.

Answer (A) is correct. *(Publisher, adapted)*
REQUIRED: The estimated tax payments to avoid an underpayment penalty.
DISCUSSION: Section 6654(a) provides a penalty for the underpayment of estimated taxes. The taxpayer can avoid the imposition of the penalty for underpayment of estimated taxes by paying quarterly installments that would equal or exceed the lesser of 90% of the current year's tax liability or 100% of the prior year's tax liability since his AGI was not greater than $150,000 in the prior year. Thus, Charles could avoid the penalty by paying quarterly installments of 25% of $12,000, his prior year's tax liability.
Answer (B) is incorrect. The installments must be made on a quarterly basis. Answer (C) is incorrect. There is no provision for paying 25% more tax each quarter than paid in the previous year. Answer (D) is incorrect. The quarterly installments must equal or exceed 100% of the prior year's actual tax liability.

7.7.8. Taxpayer C elected to apply his Year 1 overpayment of income tax to his Year 2 estimated tax. The overpayment was more than the amount due on the first installment of the estimated tax owed for Year 2. Therefore, C does not have to make an estimated tax payment until June 15, Year 2.

A. True.

B. False.

Answer (A) is correct. *(SEE, adapted)*
DISCUSSION: An overpayment of tax of a prior year may be applied to the current year's tax. The overpayment will be treated as an estimated payment of tax for the earliest payment due. Even if an overpayment of prior year's tax is determined after the due date of the first estimated payment (e.g., when an extension of time to file the prior tax return has been obtained) the overpayment may be applied to the first estimated payment. June 15 is the due date of the second installment of estimated tax for a calendar-year taxpayer.

7.7.9. Mrs. X files her Year 1 Form 1040 on January 1, Year 2, and pays the balance of the tax due. Mrs. X is not required to pay the last installment of her estimated tax due on January 15, Year 2.

A. True.

B. False.

Answer (A) is correct. *(SEE, adapted)*
DISCUSSION: At the election of the individual, the final installment of the estimated tax may be paid by filing the tax return for the tax year before January 31 following the tax year and paying in full the tax computed on the return [Sec. 6654(h)]. By filing the income tax return on January 1 and paying the balance of the tax due, the taxpayer has paid her last installment prior to the due date.

7.7.10. The penalty for underpayment of estimated tax can be waived for reasonable cause.

A. True.

B. False.

Answer (A) is correct. *(SEE, adapted)*
DISCUSSION: A penalty is imposed on the underpayment of estimated tax under Sec. 6654(a), unless the taxpayer falls within one of the exceptions provided in Sec. 6654(e)(3)(A). A waiver is allowed if, by reason of casualty, disaster, or other unusual circumstance, the imposition of a penalty would be against equity and good conscience.

7.7.11. The tax shown on Janet's 2016 return was $11,000. Her expected tax liability for 2017 is $12,000. Tax expected to be withheld in 2017 is $10,900. Janet will be subject to the estimated tax penalty if she does not adjust her withholding or make estimated tax payments.

A. True.

B. False.

Answer (B) is correct. *(SEE, adapted)*
DISCUSSION: In general, individuals must make estimated tax payments or be subject to a penalty (Sec. 6654). To avoid penalty, the taxpayer must at least pay the lesser of (1) 90% of the tax for the current year or (2) 100% of the tax for the prior year. Since 90% of Janet's 2017 tax liability is lower than 100% of her tax in the prior year, she will compare $10,800 ($12,000 × 90%) to the tax expected to be withheld of $10,900. Because the adjusted estimated tax does not exceed the tax expected to be withheld, Janet will not be subject to the estimated tax penalty.

7.7.12. If you know early in the year that you will realize substantial income late in that year and that the income will be subject to estimated tax, you must make your first payment of estimated tax by April 15.

A. True.

B. False.

Answer (B) is correct. *(SEE, adapted)*
DISCUSSION: If substantial income is to be earned late in the year, estimated tax payments can be annualized [Sec. 6654(d)(2)]. This allows estimated tax payments to be made later in the year when income is earned later in the year.

7.7.13. Ms. B is a waitress at Mary's restaurant. Since she is a good waitress, her tips are substantial. Her regular wages are too small for her employer to withhold the taxes due on the tips. She had previously been giving her employer extra money to pay these taxes. Ms. B may pay estimated tax payments instead of giving her employer the extra money.

A. True.

B. False.

Answer (A) is correct. *(SEE, adapted)*
DISCUSSION: Anyone may make estimated tax payments. The penalty for underpayment of estimated tax is based on the amount of underpayment each quarter after treating amounts withheld from wages as being paid in equal parts on each due date of estimated taxes. Therefore, either withholding or timely payment of estimated taxes will avoid the penalty.

Ms. B's employer is required to withhold income tax and Social Security tax and pay the employer's Social Security tax on tips reported by the employee. Employees must report to the employer cash tips in excess of $20 in a month. If Ms. B receives substantial tips, her employer should be withholding on these tips which should obviate the need to make part or all of the estimated tax payments. Any additional amounts that must be paid in by the employee in excess of the amounts withheld can be paid through quarterly estimated tax payments rather than giving the money to her employer [Sec. 3402(k)].

7.7.14. Mr. John is married and files a joint return. His gross income from farming was $60,000, while his wife's gross income from an unrelated business was $40,000. For purposes of his estimated tax, Mr. John meets the gross income test and qualifies as a farmer.

A. True.

B. False.

Answer (B) is correct. *(SEE, adapted)*
DISCUSSION: Section 6654(i) provides special rules for estimated tax payments by farmers and fishermen. There is only one estimated tax payment due each year and it is not due until January 15 following the end of the tax year. However, to qualify, the taxpayer's gross income from farming or fishing must be at least two-thirds of the total gross income. Mr. John's gross income from farming is only 60% of total gross income to be reported on the joint return.

7.8 Net Investment Income Tax and Additional Medicare Tax

7.8.1. Taxpayers A and B, filing a joint return, earned box 5 Medicare wages of $190,000 and $110,000, respectively. Determine the amount of additional Medicare tax they owe on their final Form 1040.

A. $0

B. $450

C. $2,700

D. $25,650

Answer (B) is correct. *(Publisher, adapted)*
REQUIRED: The applicable amount of additional Medicare tax for this couple filing a joint return.
DISCUSSION: Married filing joint taxpayers owe the additional Medicare tax of 0.9% of excess income when combined income exceeds $250,000. Taxpayers A and B have a combined income of $300,000 ($190,000 + $110,000) and additional Medicare tax liability of $450 [($300,000 − $250,000) × 0.9%].

Answer (A) is incorrect. Neither taxpayer individually exceeds the threshold, but together they do. Therefore, they owe the additional tax. Answer (C) is incorrect. The additional Medicare tax has a floor threshold of $250,000 for MFJ taxpayers. The amount of $2,700 ignores the floor. Answer (D) is incorrect. The total of all three FICA taxes is $25,650 if both the OASDI ceiling and additional Medicare tax floor were ignored.

7.8.2. A taxpayer who earned $190,000 in wages and files as head of household also received $100,000 from a passive activity interest, for a total MAGI of $290,000. How much net investment income tax does the taxpayer owe?

A. $3,420

B. $3,800

C. $7,600

D. $11,020

Answer (A) is correct. *(Publisher, adapted)*
REQUIRED: The NIIT liability.
DISCUSSION: The taxpayer's net investment income is $100,000 (passive activity interest). The NIIT is based on the lower of $90,000 ($290,000 MAGI − $200,000 threshold for head of household filers) or $100,000 (the net investment income). The taxpayer's NIIT liability is $3,420 ($90,000 × 3.8%).

Answer (B) is incorrect. The NIIT is based on the lower of the excess MAGI over the applicable threshold or the net investment income. Answer (C) is incorrect. The amount of $7,600 is derived from applying the rate the head of household threshold. Answer (D) is incorrect. The rate is applied to only the excess MAGI over the threshold for head of household filers.

STUDY UNIT EIGHT
CREDITS

8.1 Earned Income & Child Tax Credits

8.1.1. All of the following individuals, who meet the income and residency requirements, qualify for the Earned Income Credit except

A. A 19-year-old head of household with a qualifying child.

B. A 45-year-old single individual.

C. A 22-year-old married individual whose spouse is 18 years old.

D. A 60-year-old married individual.

Answer (C) is correct. *(Publisher, adapted)*
REQUIRED: The individual who does not qualify for the Earned Income Credit.
DISCUSSION: A taxpayer can be eligible for the Earned Income Credit by having a qualifying child or by meeting three qualifications: (1) The individual must have his or her principal place of abode in the United States for more than one-half of the taxable year, (2) the individual must be at least 25 years old and not more than 64 years old at the end of the taxable year, and (3) the individual cannot be claimed as a dependent of another taxpayer for any tax year beginning in the year the credit is being claimed. A 22-year-old who is married to an 18-year-old without a qualifying child does not meet the requirements for the Earned Income Credit.
Answer (A) is incorrect. A 19-year-old head of household with a qualifying child meets the qualifications for the Earned Income Credit under Sec. 32(c)(1)(A). Answer (B) is incorrect. A 45-year-old single individual meets the qualifications for the Earned Income Credit under Sec. 32(c)(1)(A). Answer (D) is incorrect. A 60-year-old married individual meets the qualifications for the Earned Income Credit under Sec. 32(c)(1)(A).

8.1.2. If a taxpayer qualifies for the Earned Income Credit, such credit can be subtracted from

A. Gross income to arrive at adjusted gross income.

B. Adjusted gross income to arrive at taxable income.

C. The tax owed, or can result in a refund, but only if the taxpayer had tax withheld from wages.

D. The tax owed, or can result in a refund, even if the taxpayer had no tax withheld from wages.

Answer (D) is correct. *(CPA, adapted)*
REQUIRED: The effect of the Earned Income Credit.
DISCUSSION: The Earned Income Credit is a refundable credit for low-income taxpayers under Sec. 32. Having taxes withheld from wages is not a requirement for using the Earned Income Credit.
Answer (A) is incorrect. The Earned Income Credit is not subtracted from gross income to arrive at adjusted gross income. Answer (B) is incorrect. The Earned Income Credit is not subtracted from the adjusted gross income to arrive at taxable income. Answer (C) is incorrect. The taxpayer need not have tax withheld from wages to use the credit.

8.1.3. All of the following statements regarding qualification for the Earned Income Credit are true except

A. The tax return claiming the credit must cover a full 12 months (unless a short period return is required due to the taxpayer's death).

B. The taxpayer's principal residence must be in the United States for more than one-half of the taxable year.

C. The taxpayer's filing status must be either married filing a joint return or head of household.

D. The taxpayer must have received earned income during the year.

Answer (C) is correct. *(SEE, adapted)*
REQUIRED: The item that is not required to qualify for the Earned Income Credit.
DISCUSSION: The Earned Income Credit is a refundable tax credit for low-income taxpayers under Sec. 32. The credit is based on a taxpayer's earned income subject to certain limitations. An individual is eligible for the Earned Income Credit if (s)he has a qualifying child for the tax year or does not have a qualifying child for the tax year and (1) has a principal place of abode in the United States for more than one-half of the tax year, (2) has attained age 25 but not age 65 before the close of the tax year, and (3) is not a dependent of another taxpayer for any tax year beginning in the same calendar year. A qualifying child is one who bears the necessary relationship to the taxpayer, has the same principal place of abode as the taxpayer for more than one-half of the tax year, and meets the requisite age requirements and is one for whom the necessary identification requirements are satisfied. A married taxpayer is eligible for the credit only if (s)he files a joint return or is treated as not married under Sec. 7703(b) (e.g., certain married individuals living apart). Thus, single taxpayers and heads of households may qualify for the Earned Income Credit. Only MFS do not qualify.
Answer (A) is incorrect. The Earned Income Credit is disallowed if the taxpayer's tax year covers a period of less than 12 months, unless the tax year is closed by reason of death. Answer (B) is incorrect. In order to be eligible for the Earned Income Credit, a taxpayer's principal residence must be in the United States for more than one-half of the tax year. Answer (D) is incorrect. The credit is based on earned income, so there must be some earned income during the year.

8.1.4. Which of the following items is considered earned income for the Earned Income Credit?

A. Self-employment income earned from a sole proprietorship.

B. Interest on savings accounts.

C. Capital gains on stock sales.

D. Rental income for which no services are performed.

Answer (A) is correct. *(SEE, adapted)*
REQUIRED: The item of earned income for purposes of the Earned Income Credit.
DISCUSSION: Section 32(c)(2) defines earned income as wages, salaries, tips, and other employee compensation, plus the amount of the taxpayer's net earnings from self-employment. This includes self-employment income earned from a sole proprietorship.
Answer (B) is incorrect. Interest and dividends are prime examples of what is not earned income. Answer (C) is incorrect. Capital gains are not considered earned income. Answer (D) is incorrect. Rental income for which the taxpayer performs no services is not earned income.

8.1.5. In the current year, Alex Burgos, who is 24 years old, paid $600 to Rita, his ex-wife, for child support. Under the terms of his divorce decree, Alex claims the exemption for his 3-year-old son, William, who lived with Rita for the entire year. Alex's only income in the current year was from wages of $16,000, resulting in an income tax of $155. How much is Alex's Earned Income Credit for the current year?

A. $0

B. $510

C. $3,400

D. $5,616

Answer (A) is correct. *(CPA, adapted)*
REQUIRED: The amount of the taxpayer's Earned Income Credit.
DISCUSSION: Section 32(a) allows an Earned Income Credit for an eligible individual. An eligible individual includes one who has a qualifying child or meets three qualifications: (1) The individual has a principal place of abode in the United States for more than one-half of the tax year, (2) the individual is at least 25 years old and not more than 64 at the end of the tax year, and (3) the individual cannot be claimed as a dependent of another taxpayer for the year the credit is being claimed. Since Alex is only 24, he does not meet the qualifications. Also, he does not have a qualifying child since his son does not live with him in the United States for more than one-half of the tax year [Sec. 32(c)(1)].
Answer (B) is incorrect. The maximum amount of the allowable Earned Income Credit for an individual without a qualifying child is $510. Answer (C) is incorrect. The maximum amount of the allowable Earned Income Credit for an individual with one qualifying child is $3,400. Answer (D) is incorrect. The maximum amount of the allowable Earned Income Credit for an individual with two qualifying children is $5,616.

8.1.6. For purposes of claiming the Earned Income Credit, a qualifying child could be any of the following except

A. Your 20-year-old unemployed child.

B. Your child who is less than 19 years old.

C. Your 22-year-old grandson who is a full-time student.

D. Your 40-year-old permanently disabled stepson.

Answer (A) is correct. *(SEE, adapted)*
REQUIRED: The child who is not a qualifying child for the Earned Income Credit.
DISCUSSION: A qualifying child for the Earned Income Credit must be less than 19 at the close of the tax year, be a full-time student under the age of 24, or be permanently and totally disabled. A 20-year-old unemployed child does not qualify.
Answer (B) is incorrect. A child who is less than 19 years old meets the requirements under Sec. 32(c)(3) for a qualifying child. Answer (C) is incorrect. A grandson meets the relationship test for a qualifying child. Answer (D) is incorrect. A 40-year-old permanently disabled stepson meets the requirements under Sec. 32(c)(3).

8.1.7. Which of the following is not disqualified income for purposes of the Earned Income Credit?

A. Net capital gain income.

B. Net rent and royalty income.

C. Income earned from part-time employment.

D. Tax-exempt interest income.

Answer (C) is correct. *(Publisher, adapted)*
REQUIRED: The disqualified income for purposes of the Earned Income Credit.
DISCUSSION: A taxpayer is ineligible to claim the Earned Income Credit if his or her disqualified income for the tax year exceeds $3,450 for 2017 [Sec. 32(i)]. Income earned from part-time employment is not disqualified income. For purposes of the Earned Income Credit, disqualified income includes taxable and tax-exempt interest, dividends, net rental and royalty income, net capital gain income, and net passive income.
Answer (A) is incorrect. Net capital gain income is disqualified income for purposes of the Earned Income Credit. Answer (B) is incorrect. Net rent and royalty income is disqualified income for purposes of the Earned Income Credit. Answer (D) is incorrect. Tax-exempt interest income is disqualified income for purposes of the Earned Income Credit.

8.1.8. Bill and Mary Old have combined wages of $24,930, dividends of $80, and interest of $800 in 2017. They are filing a joint return for the current year. Their 6-year-old son resides with them and qualifies as their dependent. The Old's son has resided in Bill and Mary's household for the entire year. What is their Earned Income Credit for 2017?

A. $0

B. $300

C. $3,100

D. $3,400

Answer (C) is correct. *(Publisher, adapted)*
REQUIRED: The amount of Earned Income Credit in 2017.
DISCUSSION: Section 32(b) allows an eligible individual having one qualifying child a credit equal to 34% of the earned income for the taxable year that does not exceed $10,000 (in 2017). The amount of the credit allowable for 2017 is limited to $3,400, reduced by 15.98% of the taxpayer's adjusted gross income (or earned income if larger) above $23,930 [Sec. 32(b)].
Bill and Mary are eligible individuals because they have a qualifying child. Their earned income consists of the $24,930 of wages. The dividends and interest are excluded from earned income but are included in AGI. Thus, their AGI is $25,810 ($24,930 wages + $800 interest + $80 dividends).

Credit limit ($10,000 × 34%)	$3,400
Less ($25,810 − $23,930) × 15.98%	(300)
Earned Income Credit	$3,100

Answer (A) is incorrect. The Olds are entitled to an Earned Income Credit. Answer (B) is incorrect. The phaseout amount that must be subtracted from the Earned Income Credit limit is $300. Answer (D) is incorrect. The amount of the Earned Income Credit before the phaseout is $3,100.

8.1.9. For which of the following dependent children will a parent not be allowed a child tax credit?

A. 15-year-old daughter.

B. 12-year-old foster child.

C. 19-year-old stepchild.

D. 16-year-old stepchild.

Answer (C) is correct. *(Publisher, adapted)*
REQUIRED: The child who does not qualify for the child tax credit.
DISCUSSION: For purposes of eligibility for the child tax credit, a "qualifying child" is a child, descendant, stepchild, or eligible foster child. The child must also be under 17 years of age and be claimed as a dependent by the taxpayer.
Answer (A) is incorrect. A 15-year-old daughter is a "qualifying child" for the child tax credit. Answer (B) is incorrect. A 12-year-old foster child is a "qualifying child" for the child tax credit. Answer (D) is incorrect. A 16-year-old stepchild is a "qualifying child" for the child tax credit.

8.1.10. Sandy and John Smith have combined wages of $26,530 and interest of $300 in 2017. They made a $500 deductible contribution to an IRA during the year. Their 4-year-old son and 6-year-old daughter reside with them and qualify as their dependents. The Smiths' children have resided with Sandy and John for the entire year. They are filing a joint return for the current year. What is their Earned Income Credit for 2017?

A. $0

B. $548

C. $5,068

D. $5,616

Answer (C) is correct. *(Publisher, adapted)*
    REQUIRED: The amount of the Earned Income Credit for 2017 when the taxpayers have two qualifying children.
    DISCUSSION: Section 32(a) allows an Earned Income Credit for an eligible individual. For taxpayers with two qualifying children, this credit is equal to 40% of the earned income for the taxable year that does not exceed $14,040 in 2017. The amount of the credit allowable for 2017 is limited to $5,616 reduced by 21.06% of the taxpayer's modified adjusted gross income (or earned income if larger) above $23,930 [Sec. 32(b)].
    Sandy and John are eligible for the increased credit rate because they have two qualifying children living with them. The credit reduction is based on the Smiths' earned income ($26,530) since it is larger than their AGI of $26,330 ($26,530 wages + $300 interest – $500 IRA contribution).

Credit limit ($14,040 × 40%)	$5,616
Less ($26,530 – $23,930) × 21.06%	(548)
Earned Income Credit	$5,068

    Answer (A) is incorrect. Sandy and John are entitled to an Earned Income Credit. Answer (B) is incorrect. The phaseout amount is $548. The phaseout is based on the larger of the taxpayer's earned income or AGI minus the phaseout base amount. Answer (D) is incorrect. The Earned Income Credit before being phased out is $5,616.

8.1.11. Jerry and Lori, who are married and file a joint return, have two qualifying children and earned income of $35,900 in 2017. What is the amount of their child tax credit for 2017?

A. $0

B. $1,000

C. $700

D. $2,000

Answer (D) is correct. *(Publisher, adapted)*
    REQUIRED: The amount of the child tax credit for 2017.
    DISCUSSION: The nonrefundable child credit is equal to the lesser of (1) $1,000 times the number of qualifying children or (2) the tax liability limitation (the taxpayer's regular tax liability plus the taxpayer's minimum tax). The nonrefundable credit is calculated as follows:

Earned income	$35,900
Standard deduction	(12,700)
Personal exemptions (4 × $4,050)	(16,200)
Taxable income	$ 7,000

(1) Nonrefundable credit (2 × $1,000)	$2,000
(2) Income (regular) tax on $7,000 taxable income	700
(3) Tentative minimum tax (below exemption)	0
(4) Net regular tax (4) = (2) + (3)	700
(5) Nonrefundable credit allowed [lesser of basic credit ($2,000) or tax liability limitation ($700)]	700

A refundable child credit is equal to the lesser of (1) $1,000 times the number of qualifying children (without regard to the tax liability limitation) or (2) 15% of the taxpayer's earned income in excess of $3,000. The refundable credit is calculated as follows:

(1) Refundable credit	$2,000
(2) 15% of $32,900	4,935
(3) Refundable credit allowed [lesser of basic credit ($2,000) or 15% of earned income in excess of $3,000 ($4,935)]	2,000

The refundable credit allowed reduces the nonrefundable credit allowed, without regard to the tax liability limitation. Thus, $2,000 (2 × $1,000) – $2,000 (refundable credit) = $0 (nonrefundable credit). Jerry and Lori's child tax credit is $2,000, of which $0 is nonrefundable credit and $2,000 is refundable credit.
    Answer (A) is incorrect. A credit is allowed against the net regular tax. Answer (B) is incorrect. The child tax credit for one qualifying child is $1,000. Answer (C) is incorrect. The tax before the child tax credit is $700.

8.1.12. Mike Stone, who is 30 years old, earned wages of $10,340 in 2017. He had no other income and is single with no dependents. Mike has lived in Youngstown, Ohio, all of his life and was not claimed as a dependent on any other tax return. What is the amount of his Earned Income Credit for 2017?

A. $0

B. $153

C. $357

D. $510

Answer (C) is correct. *(Publisher, adapted)*
  REQUIRED: The amount of the Earned Income Credit for 2017.
  DISCUSSION: Section 32(c) allows a taxpayer at least 25 years old and not more than 64 years old, who is not a dependent of another taxpayer and who lives in the U.S. for more than one-half of the year, to be eligible for the Earned Income Credit. For these taxpayers with no qualifying children, the credit is equal to 7.65% of the earned income for the taxable year that does not exceed $6,670 in 2017. The amount of the credit allowed is limited to $510 reduced by 7.65% of the taxpayer's modified adjusted gross income (or earned income if larger) above $8,340 [Sec. 32(b)]. Mike's Earned Income Credit is calculated as follows:

Credit limit ($6,670 × 7.65%)	$510
Less ($10,340 – $8,340) × 7.65%	(153)
Earned Income Credit	$357

  Answer (A) is incorrect. Mr. Stone is entitled to an Earned Income Credit. Answer (B) is incorrect. The phaseout amount of the Earned Income Credit is $153. Answer (D) is incorrect. The amount of the Earned Income Credit before the phaseout is $510.

8.1.13. Sally and Joe Johnson have one child who is a U.S. citizen under the age of 17. Their earned income for all of 2017 was $40,000. What is the amount of child tax credit that they may take in 2017?

A. $0

B. $200

C. $400

D. $1,000

Answer (D) is correct. *(Publisher, adapted)*
  REQUIRED: The amount of the child tax credit allowed in 2017.
  DISCUSSION: A child credit in the amount of $1,000 per child is allowed in 2017. Therefore, the Johnsons are allowed a credit of $1,000.
  Answer (A) is incorrect. Sally and Joe may take a child tax credit. Answer (B) is incorrect. This figure is not the correct amount of the child tax credit Sally and Joe may take. Answer (C) is incorrect. This figure is not the correct amount of the child tax credit Sally and Joe may take.

8.1.14. The child tax credit is a nonrefundable credit.

A. True.

B. False.

Answer (B) is correct. *(Publisher, adapted)*
  DISCUSSION: In 2017, the credit is refundable to the extent of 15% of earned income in excess of $3,000.

8.1.15. Mr. X meets all of the requirements for claiming an Earned Income Credit except he is not entitled to claim the exemption for his child because he released his claim in writing to his ex-wife. Even though X does not meet this requirement, he is still entitled to an Earned Income Credit.

A. True.

B. False.

Answer (A) is correct. *(SEE, adapted)*
  DISCUSSION: A parent's releasing of his claim to the exemption for his child to another parent does not disqualify him for claiming the Earned Income Credit. If the parent meets all the eligibility requirements in Sec. 32(c), then he may still receive the Earned Income Credit, no matter which parent receives the exemption.

8.1.16. Taxpayers who fraudulently claim the Earned Income Credit are prohibited from using future credits for a period of 10 years.

A. True.

B. False.

Answer (A) is correct. *(Publisher, adapted)*
  DISCUSSION: The Taxpayer Relief Act of 1997 states that, if a taxpayer fraudulently claims the Earned Income Credit, (s)he will be prohibited from claiming future Earned Income Credits for a period of 10 years after there is a final determination that the taxpayer fraudulently claimed the credit. The disallowance period is only 2 years if the Earned Income Credit was based on recklessness or intentional disregard of the rules and regulations.

8.1.17. Individuals claiming the earned income tax credit are not required to include taxpayer identification numbers (TINs) for themselves, their spouses (if married), and any qualifying children on the return.

A. True.

B. False.

Answer (B) is correct. *(Publisher, adapted)*
    DISCUSSION: Individuals who claim the earned income tax credit must include TINs (valid Social Security numbers) for themselves, their spouses (if married), and any qualifying children on the return.

8.1.18. Unless the employee is claiming an exemption from withholding on Form W-4, an employer is required to notify an employee not having income tax withheld that (s)he may be eligible for a tax refund because of the Earned Income Credit.

A. True.

B. False.

Answer (A) is correct. *(SEE, adapted)*
    DISCUSSION: Regulation 31.6051-1(h) requires an employer to furnish Notice 797 to an employee who has not had income tax withheld that (s)he may be eligible for a tax refund based on the Earned Income Credit. This does not apply if the employee claimed an exemption from withholding.

8.2 Other Refundable Credits

8.2.1. Which of the following may not be treated as a credit against the income tax or refunded to the taxpayer if in excess of the taxpayer's income tax?

A. Amounts withheld from an employee's wages.

B. Amounts withheld as a tax from nonresident aliens.

C. Amounts paid as a gasoline tax for personal automobiles.

D. Overpayments of the income tax.

Answer (C) is correct. *(Publisher, adapted)*
    REQUIRED: The amount that is neither a tax credit nor refundable if in excess of the income tax.
    DISCUSSION: Amounts paid as a gasoline tax for personal automobiles are personal expenditures and are therefore nondeductible. Certain taxpayers may take a credit for the taxes paid on gasoline used in special circumstances, such as off-road nonrecreational use, e.g., farming [Sec. 34(a)].
    Answer (A) is incorrect. It is a credit against income tax that may be refunded per Sec. 31. Answer (B) is incorrect. It is a credit against income tax that may be refunded per Sec. 1464. Answer (D) is incorrect. It is a credit against income tax that may be refunded per Sec. 35.

8.2.2. Kenny, a sole proprietor, purchases gasoline for a forklift he uses in his business. The forklift is not a highway vehicle and is not required to be registered for highway use. Kenny may claim a credit or refund for the federal excise taxes paid on this gasoline.

A. True.

B. False.

Answer (A) is correct. *(SEE, adapted)*
    DISCUSSION: Section 34(a)(2) provides a credit equal to the amount determined under Sec. 6421 for taxes paid on gasoline used for nonhighway business purposes. Kenny's forklift qualifies for the credit since it is not a highway vehicle.

8.2.3. Mr. A worked for only one employer in 2017. A's salary for 2017 was $128,300, and his employer withheld Social Security (FICA) tax on the entire amount. Mr. A may claim a credit against his income tax for the excess FICA tax withheld.

A. True.

B. False.

Answer (B) is correct. *(SEE, adapted)*
    DISCUSSION: In 2017, FICA tax applies to the first $127,200 of wages or self-employment income. The portion of the FICA taxes (1.45%) or self-employment tax (2.90%) applying to Medicare hospital insurance applies to all the taxpayer's wages. Excess FICA withheld when an employee works for only one employer may not be used as a credit against income taxes. A's employer should adjust the error.

8.3 Child Care Credit

8.3.1. Which of the following statements is not a general requirement to qualify for the child and dependent care credit?

A. The qualifying individual must not provide more than 50% of his or her own support.

B. Your expenditures must be necessary to enable you to be gainfully employed.

C. Your payments for services must not be to dependent relatives.

D. You must be divorced or legally separated when you incur the expense.

Answer (D) is correct. *(SEE, adapted)*
REQUIRED: The statement that is not a general requirement to qualify for the child care and dependent care credit.
DISCUSSION: Section 21 allows a credit for employment-related expenses for an individual who has the same place of abode as one or more qualifying individuals for more than 6 months of the year. A qualifying individual is the taxpayer's child, sibling, half-sibling, or a descendant who is under the age of 13, a dependent of the taxpayer who is physically handicapped, or a spouse of the taxpayer if (s)he is incapable of caring for himself or herself. The qualifying individual must not provide more than 50% of his or her own support. The taxpayer need not be divorced or separated when the expense is incurred.
Answer (A) is incorrect. The child must not provide more than 50% of his or her own support. Answer (B) is incorrect. The credit is for employment-related expenses for the care of a qualifying individual. Answer (C) is incorrect. Payments for services to a dependent relative are not eligible for the credit.

8.3.2. All of the following qualify as work-related expenses for computing the child and dependent care credit except

A. The parent-employer's portion of Social Security tax paid on wages for a person to take care of dependent children while the parents work.

B. Payments to a nursery school for the care of dependent children while the parents work.

C. The cost of meals for a housekeeper who provides necessary care for a dependent child while the parents work.

D. Payments to a housekeeper who provides dependent care while the parent is off from work because of illness.

Answer (D) is correct. *(SEE, adapted)*
REQUIRED: The child or dependent care expense that does not qualify as employment-related.
DISCUSSION: Employment-related expenses are paid for household services and for the care of a qualifying individual [Sec. 21(b)(2)]. Expenses are only classified as work-related if they are incurred to enable the taxpayer to be gainfully employed. An expense is not considered to be work-related merely because it is incurred while the taxpayer is gainfully employed [Reg. 1.44A-1(c)(1)].
Answer (A) is incorrect. The parent-employer's portion of Social Security tax paid on wages for a person to take care of dependent children while the parents work is an expense incurred to enable the taxpayer to be gainfully employed. Answer (B) is incorrect. Payments to a nursery school for the care of dependent children while the parents work are an expense incurred to enable the taxpayer to be gainfully employed. Answer (C) is incorrect. The cost of meals for a housekeeper who provides necessary care for a dependent child while the parents work is an expense incurred to enable the taxpayer to be gainfully employed.

8.3.3. Miss Dunn, a single parent who keeps up a home for herself and her two preschool children, paid work-related expenses of $6,200 for child care at a nursery school. Her adjusted gross income is $25,000, the sole source of which is wages. What amount can she claim as a Child Care Credit?

A. $1,740

B. $1,800

C. $1,860

D. $6,200

Answer (B) is correct. *(SEE, adapted)*
REQUIRED: The amount of the taxpayer's child and dependent care credit.
DISCUSSION: The Child Care Credit is equal to the applicable percentage of employment-related expenses paid during the taxable year [Sec. 21(a)]. The applicable percentage is 35%, reduced (but not below 20%) by one percentage point for each $2,000 (or fraction thereof) by which adjusted gross income exceeds $15,000. Miss Dunn's applicable percentage is 30% {35% − [($25,000 − $15,000) ÷ $2,000]}. The amount of employment-related expenses incurred during any taxable year that may be taken into account in computing the credit may not exceed $3,000 if there is one qualifying individual and $6,000 if there are two or more qualifying individuals [Sec. 21(c)]. Miss Dunn's employment-related expenses are $6,200, which exceeds the $6,000 limit. Therefore, her Child Care Credit is $1,800 ($6,000 maximum employment-related expenses for two qualifying individuals × 30%).
Answer (A) is incorrect. The amount of $1,740 is 29% of $6,000. It is the incorrect percentage to use in this case. Answer (C) is incorrect. The amount of $1,860 is 31% of $6,000. It is the incorrect percentage to use in this case. Answer (D) is incorrect. The amount of $6,200 exceeds the $6,000 limit for two qualifying individuals, and AGI exceeds the threshold amount.

8.3.4. Bethany is single and has adjusted gross income of $40,000. Bethany works full-time and keeps up a home for herself and her dependent father, who is not able to care for himself. She pays a housekeeper $1,100 per month to care for and provide meals to her father. What is the maximum amount of annual housekeeper expenses that Bethany can use to compute her dependent care credit?

A. $1,320

B. $3,000

C. $3,600

D. $6,000

Answer (B) is correct. *(SEE, adapted)*
REQUIRED: The maximum amount of dependent care expenses allowable in computing the dependent care credit.
DISCUSSION: The amount of employment-related expenses incurred during any taxable year for the care of a qualifying individual may not exceed $3,000 if there is one qualifying individual, or $6,000 if there are two or more qualifying individuals, in computing the dependent care credit [Sec. 21(c)]. A qualifying individual includes any dependent of the taxpayer who is physically incapable of caring for himself or herself. Some of the expenses for caring for Bethany's father that are not counted for Child Care Credit purposes may be eligible to be deducted as medical expenses.
Answer (A) is incorrect. The maximum amount of dependent care expenses is not $1,320. Answer (C) is incorrect. The maximum amount of dependent care expenses is not $3,600. Answer (D) is incorrect. The maximum amount of dependent care expenses is $6,000 if there are two or more qualifying individuals.

8.3.5. Mr. and Mrs. Wilson's 5-year-old son, Dennis, goes to kindergarten in the morning. In the afternoon, he attends a day-care center. The cost of sending Dennis to the day-care center for the current year was $3,400. Mr. Wilson's earned income was $40,000, and Mrs. Wilson's earned income was $2,100. Based on the above information, the amount of the Wilson's work-related expenses used to figure the child and dependent care credit for the current year cannot be more than

A. $2,100

B. $3,000

C. $3,400

D. $6,000

Answer (A) is correct. *(SEE, adapted)*
REQUIRED: The maximum amount of expenses used to figure the child and dependent care credit.
DISCUSSION: Section 21(c)(1) allows employment-related expenses of up to $3,000 to be used to calculate the child and dependent care credit. There is a limitation under Sec. 21(d)(1) that the amount used for the calculation cannot exceed the taxpayer's income or, in the case of a married individual, the lesser of such individual's or his or her spouse's earned income for the year. Thus, the amount used in the calculation is limited to Mrs. Wilson's earned income of $2,100.
Answer (B) is incorrect. The expenses related to the dependent care credit cannot exceed the lesser of the credit or the earned income of either spouse. Answer (C) is incorrect. The amount of $3,400 is the cost of the day-care center. Answer (D) is incorrect. The Wilsons only have one qualifying individual.

8.3.6. Mr. Bently works and maintains a home for himself, his wife, and their two children. During the current year, Mr. Bently had earned income of $50,000. They file a joint return and have itemized deductions of $8,200. Mrs. Bently was a full-time student for 5 months in the current year and had no earned income. They paid $3,000 of qualified work-related expenses while Mrs. Bently was a student. What is the amount of child and dependent care credit for the current year?

A. $0

B. $500

C. $625

D. $875

Answer (B) is correct. *(SEE, adapted)*
REQUIRED: The taxpayers' maximum allowable credit for child care.
DISCUSSION: Section 21(a) allows a credit equal to the applicable percentage of employment-related expenses. The applicable percentage is 35%, reduced (but not below 20%) by one percentage point for each $2,000 (or fraction thereof) by which adjusted gross income exceeds $15,000. The Bentlys' adjusted gross income exceeded $15,000 by more than $30,000, so the applicable percentage is 35% – 15% = 20%.
The taxpayers incurred $3,000 of employment-related expenses. However, Sec. 21(d) limits the amount of employment-related expenses to the individual's earned income or the earned income of his or her spouse, whichever is less. A full-time student at an educational institution is deemed to have earned $500 per month while a student with two or more qualifying individuals ($250 per month if only one qualifying individual). Mrs. Bently's deemed earned income is $2,500 ($500 per month × 5 months). Their credit for child care is $500 ($2,500 × 20%).
Answer (A) is incorrect. Mr. Bently and his wife are eligible for a child and dependent care credit. Answer (C) is incorrect. The amount of $625 is 25% of $2,500. The $2,000 amount should be used in this case. Answer (D) is incorrect. The amount of $875 is 20% of $3,000. The actual expenses are limited to the ceiling or either of the spouses' earned income.

8.3.7. Mr. and Mrs. Donegan are filing a joint return for the current year. Mr. Donegan was employed the full year. Mrs. Donegan was a full-time student for 9 months and was not employed at any time during the year. For the 9 months that Mrs. Donegan was a student, she paid $500 per month to a child care center to care for their 4-year-old daughter. For purposes of the Child Care Credit, Mrs. Donegan is considered to have current-year earned income of

A. $2,250
B. $3,000
C. $4,500
D. $6,000

Answer (A) is correct. *(SEE, adapted)*
REQUIRED: The amount of earned income a spouse is treated as having while a full-time student.
DISCUSSION: Section 21(d) limits the amount of employment-related expenses to the individual's earned income or the earned income of his or her spouse (whichever is less). A full-time student at an educational institution is deemed to have earned $250 per month while a student with one qualifying individual. Since Mrs. Donegan was a full-time student for 9 months, her earned income is deemed to be $2,250 ($250 × 9 months).
Answer (B) is incorrect. Dependent care expenses are limited to the lesser of $3,000 (for one individual) or the earned income of either spouse. Answer (C) is incorrect. The figure of $4,500 is the amount of earned income a spouse is treated as having, while a full-time student for 9 months, with two or more qualifying children. Answer (D) is incorrect. The amount of $6,000 is the limit for dependent care expenses for two or more qualifying individuals.

8.3.8. A divorced custodial parent of a 10-year-old child has granted the exemption to the noncustodial parent. However, the custodial parent is entitled to consider the child as a "qualifying person" for purposes of the Child Care Credit as long as more than half of the child's support is received from one or both parents.

A. True.
B. False.

Answer (A) is correct. *(SEE, adapted)*
DISCUSSION: Section 21(a) allows a Child Care Credit to an individual who has the same place of abode as one or more qualifying individuals [a dependent under age 13 for whom the taxpayer is entitled to an exemption under Sec. 151(c)] for more than 6 months of the year. However, a divorced taxpayer having custody of a disabled or under-age-13 child is entitled to the Child Care Credit even though (s)he is not entitled to an exemption [Sec. 21(e)].

8.3.9. A payment to a nursing home for the day care of your disabled and dependent father may qualify as an "employment-related" expense for the disabled dependent care credit.

A. True.
B. False.

Answer (A) is correct. *(SEE, adapted)*
DISCUSSION: The credit is allowed under Sec. 21 with respect to employment-related expenses incurred for services performed outside the household of the taxpayer, but only if the expenses are incurred for the care of a qualifying individual who is a dependent under the age of 13, or someone who spends at least 8 hours per day in the taxpayer's household [Sec. 21(b)(2)(B)]. The payment to the nursing home will qualify, as long as the father comes home for at least 8 hours per day.

8.3.10. Mrs. Neat's daughter, Nancy, is physically handicapped and unable to care for herself. She is 23 years old, and her gross income for 2017 was $4,200. She could be claimed as a dependent by Mrs. Neat except for the gross-income limitation. If Mrs. Neat incurs and pays expenses for Nancy's care so that she (Mrs. Neat) can work, Mrs. Neat can claim the child and dependent care credit.

A. True.
B. False.

Answer (A) is correct. *(SEE, adapted)*
DISCUSSION: A qualifying individual under Sec. 21(b) is a dependent of the taxpayer under age 13 and for whom the taxpayer is entitled to a dependency exemption, a dependent who is physically or mentally incapable of caring for himself or herself, or the spouse of the taxpayer who is physically or mentally incapable of caring for himself or herself. In order to qualify, the qualifying child may not provide more than 50% of his or her own support; otherwise, the taxpayer is not entitled to a dependency exemption for the person. However, a person may qualify as a dependent of the taxpayer and be physically or mentally incapable of caring for himself or herself. There is no gross income test. Nancy qualifies as a dependent, and Mrs. Neat may claim the child and dependent care credit on her return.

8.3.11. To be a qualifying individual for purposes of the Child Care Credit, a dependent under the age of 13 must be the taxpayer's child.

A. True.
B. False.

Answer (B) is correct. *(SEE, adapted)*
DISCUSSION: A qualifying child for the purposes of the Child Care Credit is one who has the same place of abode as the taxpayer for more than 6 months of the year; is the taxpayer's adopted/foster child, son, daughter, stepson, stepdaughter, brother, sister, stepbrother, stepsister, or a descendant of such an individual; and is under the age of 13. In addition, a dependent or a spouse who is incapable of caring for himself or herself is a qualifying individual. Thus, a qualifying child need not be the taxpayer's child.

8.3.12. Steve Steffler, a single taxpayer, earned $10,000 in wages in the current year as a truck driver. He maintains a home for his two dependent children, ages 10 and 12. Steve paid his mother, who is not his dependent, $2,000 to care for his children while he worked. Steve may claim a Child Care Credit on his current-year Form 1040 income tax return.

A. True.

B. False.

Answer (A) is correct. *(SEE, adapted)*
   DISCUSSION: The Child Care Credit is allowed under Sec. 21 for employment-related expenses for the care of a qualifying individual. The term "qualifying individual" includes a dependent of the taxpayer who is under the age of 13 and for whom the taxpayer is entitled to a dependency exemption [Sec. 21(b)(1)]. Although the credit is disallowed if the payments are made to related individuals, for purposes of the credit, a related individual is one for whom the taxpayer is entitled to a dependency exemption or who is a child of the taxpayer under the age of 19 [Sec. 21(e)(6)]. Therefore, Steve remains eligible to claim the credit.

8.3.13. Mr. and Mrs. J hired a housekeeper to care for their 8-year-old and 10-year-old children while they work. The housekeeper spends most of the time taking care of the children and doing the regular household work of cleaning and cooking, and spends 30 minutes a day driving Mr. and Mrs. J to and from work. The total amount ($6,000) paid to the housekeeper would qualify as work-related expenses for computing the child and dependent care credit.

A. True.

B. False.

Answer (A) is correct. *(SEE, adapted)*
   DISCUSSION: Employment-related expenses that are used to calculate the credit include (1) expenses for household services and (2) expenses for the care of qualifying individuals [Sec. 21(b)(2)(A)]. Regulations define expenses for household services as amounts paid for ordinary and necessary services for the maintenance of a household, but only if the expenses are attributable in part to the care of the qualifying individual [Reg. 1.44A-1(c)(2)]. Therefore, the housekeeper's salary qualifies as employment-related expenses for the Child Care Credit. When a portion of the expenses is for other than household purposes, a reasonable allocation must be made. But if the portion for other purposes is de minimis, no allocation is necessary, as in this case for the 30 minutes of chauffeuring [Reg. 1.44A-1(c)(6)].

8.3.14. Jeanne incurs $2,000 of expenses to care for her 3-year-old daughter in order for Jeanne to work. Her employer reimburses Jeanne for $1,200 of these expenses under a plan so the reimbursement is exempt from tax under Sec. 129. Only $800 of Jeanne's expenses will qualify for the Child Care Credit.

A. True.

B. False.

Answer (A) is correct. *(Publisher, adapted)*
   DISCUSSION: The child and disabled dependent care credit is equal to the applicable percentage of the employment-related expenses paid during the taxable year [Sec. 21(a)]. Only those amounts that are not reimbursed under a Sec. 129 plan qualify as child care expenses.

8.4 Credit for the Elderly

8.4.1. All of the following statements regarding the "Credit for the Elderly and the Permanently and Totally Disabled" are true except

A. The amount of the credit is based on age and filing status.

B. Married persons living together must file a joint return to be eligible for the credit.

C. A person under 65 must be retired on disability and must have been permanently and totally disabled upon retirement to be eligible for the credit.

D. The amount of the credit that is not absorbed can be carried back 3 years or carried forward 5 years.

Answer (D) is correct. *(SEE, adapted)*
   REQUIRED: The item that is not true with regard to the credit for the elderly and the permanently and totally disabled.
   DISCUSSION: Section 22 provides a credit for qualified individuals based on age and filing status. Section 22 does not provide for any carryback or carryforward of unused credit. Any credit not currently used expires.
   Answer (A) is incorrect. The amount of the credit for the elderly and the permanently and totally disabled is based on age and filing status. Answer (B) is incorrect. Married persons living together must file a joint return to be eligible for the elderly and permanently and totally disabled credit. Answer (C) is incorrect. A person under 65 must be retired on disability and must have been permanently and totally disabled upon retirement to be eligible for the credit.

8.4.2. Mr. K is 67 years old, single, and retired. During the current year, he received a taxable pension from his former employer in the amount of $4,000. His adjusted gross income is $14,000, and he received $500 of Social Security benefits. His tax before credits is $205. What is Mr. K's credit for the elderly?

    A. $0

    B. $188

    C. $205

    D. $675

Answer (B) is correct. *(Publisher, adapted)*
    REQUIRED: The amount of the taxpayer's credit for the elderly.
    DISCUSSION: An individual who has attained age 65 is allowed a credit equal to 15% of the individual's Sec. 22 amount [Sec. 22(a)]. For a single individual, the initial Sec. 22 amount is $5,000, reduced by any amounts received as Social Security benefits or otherwise excluded from gross income [Sec. 22(c)(3)]. The Sec. 22 amount is also reduced by one-half of the excess of AGI over $7,500 (for a single individual).

Initial Sec. 22 amount	$5,000
Less: Social Security	(500)
Less: AGI limitation	
[($14,000 − $7,500) × 50%]	(3,250)
Section 22 amount	$1,250
	× .15
K's credit for the elderly	$ 188

Since the taxpayer's tax before credits exceeds the credit for the elderly, the entire credit can be claimed.
    Answer (A) is incorrect. Mr. K is eligible for a credit for the elderly. Answer (C) is incorrect. The amount of $205 is Mr. K's tax before credits. Answer (D) is incorrect. There is a limitation that reduces the Sec. 22 amount by one-half of the excess of AGI over $7,500.

8.4.3. Mr. and Mrs. Robinson are both over age 65 and file a joint return. During the current year, they received $700 in nontaxable benefits from Social Security. This was their only nontaxable income. Their adjusted gross income was $23,400. The Robinsons' tax before credits is $8. How much can they claim as a credit for the elderly?

    A. $10

    B. $15

    C. $120

    D. $1,020

Answer (A) is correct. *(SEE, adapted)*
    REQUIRED: The amount the taxpayers may claim as a credit for the elderly.
    DISCUSSION: In the case of an individual who has attained age 65 before the close of the taxable year, Sec. 22(a) allows a credit equal to 15% of the individual's Sec. 22 amount. On a joint return when both spouses are eligible for the credit, the Sec. 22 amount is equal to an initial amount of $7,500 reduced by any amounts received as Social Security benefits or otherwise excluded from gross income [Sec. 22(c)(3)]. The Sec. 22 amount is also reduced by one-half of the excess of adjusted gross income over $10,000 (in the case of a joint return), which is $6,700 [($23,400 − $10,000) × 50%] for the Robinsons.

Initial Sec. 22 amount	$ 7,500
Less: Social Security	(700)
Less: AGI limitation	(6,700)
Section 22 amount	$ 100
	× .15
Robinsons' tentative credit for the elderly	$ 15

Since the Robinsons' tax before credits will be $10, only $10 of the tentative credit for the elderly is claimed.
    Answer (B) is incorrect. The tax liability is smaller than the credit. Answer (C) is incorrect. The amount of $120 exceeds the Robinsons' pre-credit tax liability of $10 and fails to consider the Social Security benefits. Also, Social Security benefits that are excluded from gross income reduce the tax credit base. Answer (D) is incorrect. The reduction of the tax base for 50% of AGI in excess of a statutory limit did not take place.

8.4.4. Mr. and Mrs. Troast are married and filing a joint return. Both are qualified individuals for purposes of credit for the elderly. No Social Security benefits are received by the Troasts. They will not be eligible for the credit if their adjusted gross income is at least

A. $27,500

B. $25,000

C. $20,000

D. $17,500

Answer (B) is correct. *(SEE, adapted)*
REQUIRED: The level of adjusted gross income at which a married couple filing a joint return will lose eligibility for the credit for the elderly.
DISCUSSION: A qualified individual is entitled to a credit of 15% of his or her Sec. 22 amount, so the level at which the credit is no longer allowed is the level at which the Sec. 22 amount becomes zero.
The Sec. 22 amount for Mr. and Mrs. Troast is the initial amount of $7,500 less one-half of the excess of AGI over $10,000. Solve for AGI by setting the initial amount equal to zero.

$$\$7,500 - 1/2(\text{AGI} - \$10,000) = \$0$$
$$1/2 \text{ AGI} = \$12,500$$
$$\text{AGI} = \$25,000$$

Answer (A) is incorrect. The figure of $27,500 is the incorrect amount of adjusted gross income to make the Troasts ineligible for the credit for the elderly. Answer (C) is incorrect. The amount of $20,000 is the limit when one spouse is eligible when filing the joint return. Answer (D) is incorrect. The amount of $17,500 is the limit for single individuals.

8.4.5. Mr. Babyface was a truck driver until he retired on disability in 2008. He has a statement from his doctor that due to a back injury he will never be able to drive a truck again. He is 54 years old and now does volunteer work as a bookkeeper for a charitable organization. He sets his own hours, averaging 20 hours per week, and is not paid. Mr. Babyface is eligible for the credit for the elderly.

A. True.

B. False.

Answer (B) is correct. *(SEE, adapted)*
DISCUSSION: Section 22 allows a credit for individuals who retire on disability and are permanently and totally disabled. Section 22(e)(3) defines permanently and totally disabled as being unable to engage in any substantial gainful activity by reason of any medically determinable physical or mental impairment.

8.4.6. Ms. F, age 65, received a distribution from a qualified individual retirement account that she has contributed to because her employer did not provide a pension plan. The tax on the distribution she received can be reduced by the tax credit for the elderly if she meets all other requirements.

A. True.

B. False.

Answer (A) is correct. *(SEE, adapted)*
DISCUSSION: A distribution from a qualified individual retirement account such as the one described is taxable as income to the recipient. Therefore, since Ms. F meets all the other requirements, she may use the tax credit for the elderly to offset any taxes due on the IRA distribution.

8.5 Interest on Home Mortgage Credit

8.5.1. Judy purchased her first home in January of the current year. She obtained a new mortgage and paid $6,000 of interest during the current year. Her state has elected to issue mortgage credit certificates in lieu of mortgage subsidy bonds. If Judy receives a mortgage credit certificate specifying a 20% credit rate, how much are her income tax credit and interest deduction?

	Credit	Deduction
A.	$1,200	$0
B.	$1,200	$4,800
C.	$1,200	$6,000
D.	$2,000	$4,000

Answer (B) is correct. *(Publisher, adapted)*
REQUIRED: The taxpayer's income tax credit for home mortgage interest and the interest deduction for the current year.
DISCUSSION: Section 25 allows a credit to home purchasers who receive mortgage credit certificates in an amount equal to a specified percentage of the interest that the home purchaser pays or accrues during the taxable year on the mortgage on his or her principal residence. This percentage may not exceed 50% (but may not be less than 10%) of the interest on the qualifying indebtedness. If the percentage exceeds 20%, the credit is limited to $2,000 [Sec. 25(a)(2)]. The amount of the home buyer's interest deduction in any year is reduced by the amount of the mortgage credit certificate interest for that year. Judy is entitled to a credit of $1,200 ($6,000 mortgage interest paid × 20% applicable credit rate). She may deduct the balance of the interest for the year ($4,800) as an itemized deduction.
Answer (A) is incorrect. There is an interest deduction. Answer (C) is incorrect. The $1,200 amount of the credit reduces the interest that is deductible. Answer (D) is incorrect. Judy is only entitled to a 20% credit rate. A $2,000 credit implies a 33% rate.

8.5.2. The maximum credit for interest on a home mortgage is $2,000.

A. True.

B. False.

Answer (B) is correct. *(Publisher, adapted)*
   DISCUSSION: Section 25(a) limits the credit for interest on home mortgages to $2,000 only when the credit rate exceeds 20%. If the credit rate is less than 20%, there is no maximum credit.

8.5.3. If two or more persons hold interests in any residence, the credit shall be allocated among such persons in proportion to their respective interests in the residence.

A. True.

B. False.

Answer (A) is correct. *(Publisher, adapted)*
   DISCUSSION: Section 25(a)(2)(B) provides that, if two or more persons hold interests in any residence, the credit shall be allocated among such persons in proportion to their respective interests in the residence.

8.6 Other Nonrefundable Credits

8.6.1. Which of the following is not a requirement for a student to be eligible for the American Opportunity Tax Credit?

A. Full-time enrollment.

B. One-half time enrollment.

C. Student must be enrolled in a degree program.

D. Married taxpayers must file a joint return to be eligible.

Answer (A) is correct. *(Publisher, adapted)*
   REQUIRED: The requirements for a student to be eligible for the American Opportunity Tax Credit.
   DISCUSSION: To be eligible for the American Opportunity Tax Credit, a student must be enrolled in a program leading to a degree or certificate and must be enrolled at least one-half time. Also, an eligible student must be enrolled in one of the first 4 years of post secondary education and be free of any felony conviction for possessing or distributing a controlled substance. Married taxpayers must file a joint return to be eligible.
   Answer (B) is incorrect. One-half time enrollment is a requirement for the American Opportunity Tax Credit. Answer (C) is incorrect. A requirement for the American Opportunity Tax Credit is that the student must be enrolled in a degree program. Answer (D) is incorrect. A requirement for the American Opportunity Tax Credit is that married taxpayers must file a joint return to be eligible.

8.6.2. Which of the following are eligible expenses for the American Opportunity Tax Credit?

I.   Tuition and fees required for enrollment
II. Course materials
III. Room and board

A. I only.

B. I and II only.

C. II and III only.

D. I, II, and III.

Answer (B) is correct. *(Publisher, adapted)*
   REQUIRED: The expenses eligible for the American Opportunity Tax Credit.
   DISCUSSION: Tuition, fees, and course materials required for enrollment are eligible expenses for the credit. The credit may not be used for room and board, activity fees, athletic fees, insurance expense, or transportation.
   Answer (A) is incorrect. Course materials are now eligible for the credit along with tuition and fees. Answer (C) is incorrect. Room and board are not eligible for the credit. Answer (D) is incorrect. Not all three of these expenses are eligible for the credit.

8.6.3. Joe and Mary Day's daughter Julie is a first-year student in college during 2017. Joe and Mary, who filed jointly, had an adjusted gross income of $128,100, and Julie's eligible expenses were $8,000. What is the amount of the American Opportunity Tax Credit that the Days may use in 2017?

A. $0

B. $2,000

C. $2,500

D. $8,000

Answer (C) is correct. *(Publisher, adapted)*
   REQUIRED: The amount of the American Opportunity Tax Credit allowed in 2017.
   DISCUSSION: The American Opportunity Tax Credit allows taxpayers a 100% credit for the first $2,000 of tuition expenses and a 25% credit for the second $2,000 of tuition expenses per year for the first 4 years of school (Sec. 25). Phaseout of the credit does not begin for joint filers until AGI reaches $160,000 in 2017. Therefore, the Days may use the entire $2,500 credit.
   Answer (A) is incorrect. The Days are eligible for some amount of the American Opportunity Tax Credit. Answer (B) is incorrect. The amount of $2,000 ignores the available credit for the expense in excess of $2,000. Answer (D) is incorrect. Julie's eligible expenses were $8,000. The American Opportunity Tax Credit is limited.

8.6.4. Mr. and Mrs. X had adjusted gross income of $172,000 in 2017. Their daughter's eligible education expenses for her first year of college were $4,500 in 2017. What is the amount of American Opportunity Tax Credit that Mr. and Mrs. X may use in 2017?

A. $0

B. $1,000

C. $1,500

D. $2,500

Answer (B) is correct. *(Publisher, adapted)*
REQUIRED: The amount of American Opportunity Tax Credit allowed in 2017.
DISCUSSION: The American Opportunity Tax Credit allows taxpayers a 100% credit for the first $2,000 of tuition, fees, and books incurred per year for the first 4 years of school, and a 25% credit for the second $2,000 of tuition, fees, and books incurred per year for the first 4 years of school (Sec. 25). However, the credit is phased out when modified AGI exceeds $160,000 for joint filers. The credit phaseout is complete when modified AGI exceeds $180,000. Therefore, the allowable credit for 2016 is reduced by $1,500 [$2,500 × ($172,000 − $160,000) ÷ $20,000]. The credit that can be claimed is $1,000.
Answer (A) is incorrect. Mr. and Mrs. X are eligible for a credit. Answer (C) is incorrect. The figure of $1,500 is the phaseout amount that is reduced from the allowable credit. Answer (D) is incorrect. The figure of $2,500 is the amount of the credit before the reduction of the phaseout.

8.6.5. Which of the following is not a qualifying student for purposes of the lifetime learning credit?

A. A student in a graduate program.

B. A part-time student (less than half-time).

C. A student in a continuing professional education program.

D. None of the answers are correct.

Answer (D) is correct. *(Publisher, adapted)*
REQUIRED: The student not eligible for the lifetime learning credit.
DISCUSSION: The lifetime learning credit can be applied to qualified tuition and related expenses paid during the tax year for all eligible students who are enrolled in eligible educational institutions. The credit is not based on the student's work load, is not limited to the first 4 years of post secondary education, and may be applied to graduate-level courses.
Answer (A) is incorrect. A student in a graduate program is eligible for the lifetime learning credit. Answer (B) is incorrect. A part-time student (less than half-time) is eligible for the lifetime learning credit. Answer (C) is incorrect. A student in a continuing professional education program is eligible for the lifetime learning credit.

8.6.6. Mr. and Mrs. Baker, who file a joint tax return, have an adjusted gross income of $96,000 for 2017. Their son, Tony, began his first year of graduate school on July 15, 2017. The Bakers' expenses incurred in 2017 were $6,000 for tuition. What is the amount of lifetime learning credit the Bakers may claim in 2017?

A. $1,000

B. $1,200

C. $1,500

D. $6,000

Answer (B) is correct. *(Publisher, adapted)*
REQUIRED: The amount of lifetime learning credit allowed for 2017.
DISCUSSION: A lifetime learning credit is allowed in the amount of 20% of the first $10,000 of tuition paid. The lifetime learning credit is available in years the American Opportunity Tax Credit is not claimed. The Bakers' credit for 2017 will be $1,200 ($6,000 × 20%). There is no phaseout of the lifetime learning credit for the Bakers since the credit phase-out for married taxpayers filing jointly commences when modified AGI is $112,000 and ends at $132,000.
Answer (A) is incorrect. The amount of $1,000 is 17% of the tuition paid. Answer (C) is incorrect. The amount of $1,500 is 25% of the tuition paid. Answer (D) is incorrect. The amount of actual tuition expenses is $6,000.

8.6.7. Which of the following is an eligible child for purposes of the adoption credit?

I.   An infant child
II. A 15-year-old child
III. A 19-year-old child mentally incapable of self-care

A. I only.

B. II only.

C. I and II only.

D. I, II, and III.

Answer (D) is correct. *(Publisher, adapted)*
REQUIRED: The child eligible for the adoption credit.
DISCUSSION: An eligible child is a child who has not reached age 18 or a child who is physically or mentally incapable of self-care.
Answer (A) is incorrect. There are other children also eligible for purposes of the adoption credit. Answer (B) is incorrect. The 15-year-old child is not the only child eligible for purposes of the adoption credit. Answer (C) is incorrect. Another child is also eligible for purposes of the adoption credit.

8.6.8. Which of the following are expenses that are not eligible for the adoption credit?

    A. Adoption fees.

    B. Court costs.

    C. Attorneys fees.

    D. Child care expenses.

Answer (D) is correct. *(Publisher, adapted)*
    REQUIRED: The expenses that are eligible for the adoption credit.
    DISCUSSION: Expenses that are eligible for the adoption credit include reasonable and necessary adoption fees, attorneys fees, and court costs related to the legal adoption of an eligible child by the taxpayer. Child care expenses are covered by the Child Care Credit.
    Answer (A) is incorrect. Adoption fees are an eligible expense for the adoption credit. Answer (B) is incorrect. Court costs are an eligible expense for the adoption credit. Answer (C) is incorrect. The attorneys fees are an eligible expense for the adoption credit.

8.6.9. Mr. and Mrs. Greg adopted a child in the current year. During the year, the Gregs' qualified adoption expenses were $14,000, and they had an AGI of $65,000. What is the Gregs' adoption credit for 2017?

    A. $0

    B. $13,460

    C. $13,570

    D. $14,000

Answer (C) is correct. *(Publisher, adapted)*
    REQUIRED: The amount of adoption credit allowed for 2017.
    DISCUSSION: Taxpayers may claim a nonrefundable credit of up to $13,570 for 2017 (Sec. 23). Therefore, since the Gregs' adoption expenses exceeded $13,570, they may take the entire $13,570 credit. If credit allowable exceeds the tax liability, taxpayers may carry remaining credit forward up through the fifth taxable year [Sec. 23(c)].
    Answer (A) is incorrect. Taxpayers are allowed a nonrefundable credit of up to $13,570 for qualified adoption expenses. Answer (B) is incorrect. The credit allowed for 2016 was $13,460. Answer (D) is incorrect. The adoption credit is limited to $13,570 in 2017.

8.6.10. Mr. and Mrs. Hall adopted a special-needs child in the current year. During the year, the Halls' qualified adoption expenses were $8,000, and their adjusted gross income was $208,540. What is the amount of the Halls' adoption credit for the current year?

    A. $11,874

    B. $8,000

    C. $13,570

    D. $15,266

Answer (A) is correct. *(Publisher, adapted)*
    REQUIRED: The amount of adoption credit allowed for the current year.
    DISCUSSION: Taxpayers may claim a nonrefundable credit of up to $13,570 for qualified adoption expenses (Sec. 23). However, the credit is phased out for taxpayers with income exceeding $203,540. The phaseout is completed when AGI exceeds $243,540. The phaseout for the Halls will be $1,696 [$13,570 × ($208,540 − $203,540) ÷ $40,000], resulting in an allowable credit of $11,874 ($13,570 − $1,696) for the current year.
    Answer (B) is incorrect. The credit is not limited by the expenditures for a child with special needs. Answer (C) is incorrect. The allowable credit of $13,570 is reduced by the high income phaseout. Answer (D) is incorrect. The $1,696 reduces the adoption credit, not increases the credit.

8.6.11. If a student is enrolled in college full-time, (s)he may use both the American Opportunity Tax Credit and the lifetime learning credit during the same calendar year.

    A. True.

    B. False.

Answer (B) is correct. *(Publisher, adapted)*
    DISCUSSION: The American Opportunity Tax Credit and lifetime learning credit may not be claimed at the same time. The American Opportunity Tax Credit is available during a student's first 4 years in college. The lifetime learning credit is available in years that the American Opportunity Tax Credit is not taken (for example, fifth and later years of college).

8.6.12. If a student is on a full scholarship to attend college, (s)he is eligible for the American Opportunity Tax Credit.

    A. True.

    B. False.

Answer (B) is correct. *(Publisher, adapted)*
    DISCUSSION: The American Opportunity Tax Credit and lifetime learning credit are only available for out-of-pocket expenses. The credit is not allowed in situations in which the taxpayer can receive a double tax benefit (i.e., an exclusion for the scholarship income and a credit for the payment of expenses from the scholarship).

8.7 Limitations on Nonrefundable Personal Credits

8.7.1. Linda and Jerry Brown have a tax liability for the current year of $2,600 before credits. They have the following tentative credits:

Child care credit	$ 800
Interest on home mortgage credit	2,200

How much of these credits will be available for carryover to the next year, and how will any carryforward be treated?

A. $0. The credits must all be used in the year in which they arise.

B. $400. The carryforward is treated as a general nonrefundable personal credit in applying the limitation next year.

C. $400. The carryforward is treated as a Child Care Credit. The other credits are used first in the current year.

D. $400. The carryforward is treated as an interest on home mortgage credit. It is the only one of these credits that may be carried forward.

Answer (D) is correct. *(Publisher, adapted)*
REQUIRED: The amount of nonrefundable personal credits that may be carried over and used in the next year and the treatment of the carryforward.
DISCUSSION: Section 26(a) limits the amount of nonrefundable personal credits, such as the Child Care Credit, the credit for the elderly, the interest on home mortgage credit, the adoption expenses credit, the child tax credit, the American Opportunity Tax Credit, and the lifetime learning credit, to the excess of taxpayer's regular tax liability for the year over the tentative minimum tax for the taxable year (excluding the alternative minimum tax Foreign Tax Credit) [Sec. 26(a)]. Thus, the Browns are allowed a credit in the current year of only $2,600.
The excess of $400 is carried forward for 3 years as an interest on home mortgage credit. There is no provision to carry forward the Child Care Credit. Section 25(e)(1) provides that the carryover is the amount by which the interest on home mortgage credit exceeds the tax liability less the other nonrefundable personal credits. It is treated as an interest on home mortgage credit in the subsequent year.
Answer (A) is incorrect. The Home Mortgage Interest Credit is permitted to be carried forward to the extent it exceeds the tax liability less the other nonrefundable personal credits. Answer (B) is incorrect. The Home Mortgage Interest Credit is the only nonrefundable credit that may be carried forward. Answer (C) is incorrect. The Home Mortgage Interest Credit carryforward cannot be treated as a Child Care Credit.

8.8 Foreign Tax Credit

8.8.1. For the current year, Gannon Corporation has U.S. taxable income of $500,000, which includes $100,000 from a foreign division. Gannon paid $45,000 of foreign income taxes on the income of the foreign division. Assuming Gannon's U.S. income tax for the current year before credits is $170,000, its maximum Foreign Tax Credit for the current year is

A. $45,000

B. $40,500

C. $34,000

D. $20,250

Answer (C) is correct. *(CMA, adapted)*
REQUIRED: The Foreign Tax Credit that can be claimed in the current year.
DISCUSSION: The Foreign Tax Credit is allowed under Secs. 27 and 901 for foreign income taxes paid or accrued during the year and is limited by Sec. 904(a). The limitation is the proportion of the taxpayer's tentative U.S. income tax (before the Foreign Tax Credit) that the taxpayer's foreign source taxable income bears to his or her worldwide taxable income for the year. The following calculation should be made:

$$\frac{\text{Foreign source taxable income}}{\text{Worldwide taxable income}} \times \text{U.S. income tax} = \text{Foreign tax credit limitation}$$

$$\frac{\$100,000}{\$500,000} \times \$170,000 = \$34,000$$

The unused credit of $11,000 ($45,000 – $34,000) may be carried back 1 preceding year and then forward to the following 10 taxable years [Sec. 904(c)].
Answer (A) is incorrect. The figure of $45,000 is the amount of foreign income taxes Gannon paid. It is not Gannon's maximum Foreign Tax Credit. Answer (B) is incorrect. The Foreign Tax Credit is limited to the lesser of the foreign taxes paid or accrued or the U.S. income tax multiplied by the fraction of foreign source taxable income over worldwide taxable income. Answer (D) is incorrect. The figure of $20,250 is not the correct amount of Gannon's maximum Foreign Tax Credit.

8.8.2. The following information pertains to Wald Corporation's operations for the current year:

Worldwide taxable income	$300,000
U.S. source taxable income	180,000
U.S. income tax before Foreign Tax Credit	96,000
Foreign nonbusiness-related interest earned	30,000
Foreign income taxes paid on nonbusiness-related interest earned	6,000
Other foreign source taxable income	90,000
Foreign income taxes paid on other foreign source taxable income	30,000

What amount of Foreign Tax Credit may Wald claim for the current year?

- A. $28,800
- B. $34,800
- C. $36,000
- D. $38,400

Answer (B) is correct. *(CPA, adapted)*

REQUIRED: The Foreign Tax Credit available when foreign nonbusiness interest income is earned in addition to foreign business income.

DISCUSSION: The Foreign Tax Credit is allowed under Secs. 27 and 901 and is limited by Sec. 904(a). The limitation is the proportion of the taxpayer's tentative U.S. income tax (before the Foreign Tax Credit) that the taxpayer's foreign taxable income bears to his or her worldwide taxable income for the year. Under Sec. 904(d), however, this limitation must be applied separately to nonbusiness-related interest income. For Wald, these limits are

Nonbusiness-related interest income:

($30,000 ÷ $300,000) × $96,000 = $9,600

Foreign business income:

($90,000 ÷ $300,000) × $96,000 = $28,800

The credit for foreign taxes paid on the interest income is limited to the $6,000 in taxes paid. The credit for foreign income taxes paid on business income is limited to $28,800. The $1,200 ($30,000 − $28,800) of excess foreign tax payments can be carried back 1 year and forward 10 years. Total Foreign Tax Credit is $34,800 ($6,000 + $28,800).

Answer (A) is incorrect. The amount of $28,800 is the Foreign Tax Credit limit for the foreign business income. The Foreign Tax Credit equals the total of the limited Foreign Tax Credit amounts for the foreign business income plus the nonbusiness-related interest income. Answer (C) is incorrect. The foreign credit cannot exceed the smaller of the limit or the foreign taxes paid or accrued for each of the two income categories. The business-related interest income credit is limited to the actual taxes paid. Answer (D) is incorrect. The figure of $38,400 is the amount of foreign taxes paid for business and non-business purposes. The actual credit is limited to the smaller of the limit or the foreign taxes paid or accrued for each income category.

8.8.3. Smithco, Inc., a domestic corporation, was paid $20,000 of the total of $100,000 in dividends paid by a foreign corporation this year. Smithco owned 20% of the foreign corporation's stock. The foreign corporation paid $35,000 in foreign taxes and had accumulated profits of $120,000 after payment of its foreign taxes for the last 11 years. Smithco also had $1,000 in taxes withheld by the foreign country on the dividend. Smithco has a Foreign Tax Credit before limitation of

- A. $1,000
- B. $5,833
- C. $6,833
- D. $8,000

Answer (C) is correct. *(Publisher, adapted)*

REQUIRED: The Foreign Tax Credit (before limitation) of a U.S. corporation that received dividends from a foreign corporation subject to foreign taxes on its income.

DISCUSSION: The Foreign Tax Credit is allowed under Secs. 27 and 901(a) for taxes paid by the corporation and those deemed to have been paid under Sec. 902. Section 902(a) provides that a domestic corporation owning at least 10% of the voting stock of a foreign corporation and receiving a dividend is deemed to have paid the foreign taxes that the foreign corporation paid on its profits accumulated after 1986. The dividend must be paid out of profits accumulated after 1986, and the amount of foreign taxes deemed paid is in the same proportion as that of the dividend to the profits accumulated after 1986 in excess of the post-1986 foreign taxes. The amount of taxes deemed paid by Smithco is

$$\frac{\$20,000 \text{ Dividend}}{\$120,000 \text{ Post-1986 undistributed earnings}} \times \$35,000 \text{ post-1986 foreign taxes} = \$5,833 \text{ deemed paid credit}$$

Since Smithco also paid $1,000 in foreign taxes through withholding, the total foreign taxes are $6,833, the Foreign Tax Credit before limitation. In computing its U.S. tax liability, Smithco must add the deemed taxes paid of $5,833 to its $20,000 of foreign source gross income. The dividend payment reduces the post-1986 undistributed earnings amount. The deemed paid taxes reduce the post-1986 foreign-taxes amount.

Answer (A) is incorrect. The figure of $1,000 is only the amount of foreign taxes withheld. Answer (B) is incorrect. The figure of $5,833 is not the correct amount of the Foreign Tax Credit. Answer (D) is incorrect. The figure of $8,000 is the amount of the dividend paid plus the foreign taxes withheld instead of the sum of the foreign taxes withheld plus the deemed paid credit.

8.8.4. Which one of the following statements about the foreign operations of Nora Corporation (a domestic corporation) is true?

A. Nora may take a credit, but not a deduction, for the income taxes paid to a foreign country.

B. Nora may take a deduction, but not a credit, for the income taxes paid to a foreign country.

C. Nora may elect to take either a credit or a deduction, but not both, for the income taxes paid to a foreign country.

D. Nora may exclude both revenues and expenses of the foreign operations from its federal income tax return.

Answer (C) is correct. *(CMA, adapted)*
REQUIRED: The true statement about the foreign operations of a domestic corporation.
DISCUSSION: Section 164 allows a deduction for foreign income taxes paid or accrued during the taxable year. Alternatively, Secs. 27 and 901(a) permit both individual taxpayers and corporations to claim a Foreign Tax Credit on income earned and subject to tax in a foreign country or U.S. possession. One may not claim both the deduction and the credit [Sec. 275(a)(4)].
Answer (A) is incorrect. Nora may take a deduction for the income taxes paid to a foreign country. Answer (B) is incorrect. Nora may take a credit for the income taxes paid to a foreign country. Answer (D) is incorrect. Worldwide income generally must be included on a federal income tax return.

8.9 Research and Experimentation Credit

8.9.1. Which of the following statements regarding the research credit is false?

A. The credit is equal to the larger of 20% of your qualified research expenses for the year over the product of (1) your "fixed base" percentage and (2) the average amount of your annual gross receipts for the 4 preceding tax years, plus 20% of your basic research payments, or an alternative "three-tier" formula that can be elected in the taxpayer's first post-June 30, 1996, tax year.

B. The research credit applies only to research and development work that is incurred in your trade or business.

C. Wages paid to an individual that are used in figuring the work opportunity tax credit may be included in arriving at your research credit.

D. The cost of acquiring someone else's product or process does not qualify for the credit.

Answer (C) is correct. *(SEE, adapted)*
REQUIRED: The item that is false with regard to the research and development credit.
DISCUSSION: Section 41(a) allows a credit against the income tax equal to 20% of the excess of the qualified research expenses for the taxable year over the base period research expenses plus 20% of your basic research payments plus 20% of amounts to an energy research consortium. "Qualified research expenses" means the sum of the in-house research expenses and contract research expenses paid or incurred by the taxpayer during the taxable year in carrying on any trade or business [Sec. 41(b)]. Section 41(b)(2)(D) explicitly excludes wages taken into account in determining the work opportunity tax credit from qualified research expenses. The new three-tier credit formula may prove advantageous when a firm spends more on research activities now than in the 1984-1988 base period.
Answer (A) is incorrect. The research credit is equal to the larger of 20% of your qualified research expenses for the year over the product of (1) your "fixed base" percentage and (2) the average amount of your annual gross receipts for the 4 preceding tax years, plus 20% of your basic research payments, or an alternative "three-tier" formula that can be elected in the taxpayer's first post-June 30, 1996, tax year. Answer (B) is incorrect. The research credit applies only to research and development work that is incurred in your trade or business. Answer (D) is incorrect. The cost of acquiring someone else's product or process does not qualify for the research credit.

8.9.2. Which of the following research expenditures qualify for the Research and Experimentation Credit?

I. Research activities conducted in Brazil by a U.S. company

II. Research funded by the U.S. government

III. Research done by a state university under contract for a U.S. corporation

A. I only.

B. II only.

C. III only.

D. I and III only.

Answer (C) is correct. *(Publisher, adapted)*
REQUIRED: The expenditure(s) that qualify for the Research and Experimentation Credit.
DISCUSSION: Qualified research does not include research conducted outside the United States, research in the social sciences or humanities, and research to the extent funded by any grant, contract, or otherwise by another person or governmental entity [Sec. 41(d)]. However, 20% of cash expenditures by a corporation in excess of the sum of (1) a fixed research floor plus (2) an amount reflecting any decrease in nonresearch giving to qualified organizations as compared to such giving during a fixed base period qualifies for the credit [Sec. 41(e)]. Qualified organizations include institutions of higher education [Sec. 41(e)(6)].
Answer (A) is incorrect. Research conducted outside the U.S. is not qualified. Answer (B) is incorrect. Research funded by a governmental entity is not qualified. Answer (D) is incorrect. Even though a U.S. company conducted the research, it conducted it in Brazil, which disqualifies the research for the credit.

8.9.3. Mihalco Corporation incurs $170,000 of qualified research expenses in the first half of 2017. Mihalco's ratio of total qualified research expenses over total gross receipts for the period 1987-1991 is 0.15. Gross receipts for 2013-2016 are as follows:

Year	Gross Receipts
2013	$500,000
2014	550,000
2015	650,000
2016	700,000

Mihalco Corporation's income tax liability and tentative minimum tax for 2017 are $61,250 and $31,000, respectively. It did not have any other tax credits. For 2017, Mihalco's Research and Development Credit using the basic credit calculation is

A. $13,000

B. $16,000

C. $30,250

D. $34,000

Answer (B) is correct. *(Publisher, adapted)*
REQUIRED: The taxpayer's research and development credit before limitations.
DISCUSSION: Section 41(a) allows a credit equal to 20% of the excess of the qualified research expenses for the taxable year over its base amount. The base amount is defined as the product of (1) the taxpayer's fixed base percentage times (2) the average annual gross receipts for the 4 tax years preceding the credit year. The base amount, however, may not be less than 50% of the qualified research expenses for the credit year. The fixed base percentage is the aggregate of qualified research expenditures for tax years 1987-1991 divided by the aggregate gross receipts of the taxpayer for that period. In this case, Mihalco's Research and Development Credit for 2017, as calculated below, is $16,000.

$$\$16,000 \ = \ \{.20 \times [\$170,000 - (\ .15 \times \frac{\$2,400,000}{4})]\}$$

The full amount of the credit can be claimed since the General Business Credit limitation is $30,250 ($61,250 − $31,000).
    Answer (A) is incorrect. The amount of $13,000 is 20% of the Research and Development Credit expenditures for the second preceding year and fails to properly take into account the incremental nature of the credit calculation. Answer (C) is incorrect. The General Business Credit limitation is $30,250. Answer (D) is incorrect. The amount of $34,000 is 20% of the current year's qualified research expenses and fails to take into account the incremental nature of the credit calculation.

8.9.4. XYZ Company incurs $300,000 of research expenses this year deductible under Sec. 174. These same expenses entitle XYZ to a research credit of $20,000. XYZ will be able to deduct only $280,000 of the research expenses.

A. True.

B. False.

Answer (A) is correct. *(Publisher, adapted)*
DISCUSSION: Section 280C(c) requires the deduction for research expenses under Sec. 174 to be reduced by 100% of the research credit. Alternatively, if the taxpayer elected to capitalize research expenses, the amount capitalized must also be reduced by 100% of the research credit. Since XYZ's research credit is $20,000, XYZ can deduct only $280,000 ($300,000 − $20,000) of the research expenses.

8.9.5. Marcus Manufacturing is a start-up company formed in 2017. It must use a fixed-base percentage of 3% to compute the base amount for the research credit for the first 10 years as a start-up company.

A. True.

B. False.

Answer (B) is correct. *(Publisher, adapted)*
DISCUSSION: A start-up company's fixed-base percentage is 3% for each of the taxpayer's first 5 tax years, beginning after December 31, 1993, for which the taxpayer has qualified research expenses. For the sixth through 10th years, after 1993, the fixed-base percentage will be a portion (one-sixth to five-sixths) of the percentage of qualified research expenses to gross receipts [Sec. 41(c)(3)(B)]. The Small Business Act of 1996 changed the definition of a start-up corporation. Marcus Corporation qualifies as a start-up corporation since the first tax year for which it had gross receipts and expenditures is after December 31, 1983. A corporation could also qualify as a start-up company if there are fewer than 3 tax years beginning after December 31, 1983, and before 1989 in which it had both gross receipts and qualified research expenditures.

8.9.6. The research credit cannot be taken for any of the following:

1) Research to find and evaluate gas and oil deposits
2) Research in the social sciences or humanities
3) Management efficiency surveys
4) Research related to style, taste, cosmetic, or seasonal design factors

A. True.

B. False.

Answer (A) is correct. *(SEE, adapted)*
DISCUSSION: None of the listed work qualifies for the research credit. Section 41(d) defines qualified research as meaning the same as in Sec. 174, and also excludes research in the social sciences or humanities, and efficiency surveys and management studies. Section 174(d) excludes exploration and evaluation of oil and gas deposits. Section 41(d)(3) states that items that do not qualify for research purposes are those that relate to style, taste, cosmetic, or seasonal design factors.

8.9.7. A taxpayer may elect not to take the research credit.

A. True.

B. False.

Answer (B) is correct. *(Publisher, adapted)*
   DISCUSSION: The election not to take the research credit was repealed. A taxpayer can elect to avoid reducing the Sec. 174 deduction by 100% of the credit claimed by electing to reduce the credit by 50% of the credit times the maximum corporate tax rate imposed by Sec. 11(b)(1). The reduction is an annual election that is irrevocable and must be made no later than the filing date for the tax return (including extensions) [Sec. 280C(c)(3)].

8.9.8. Mr. A and Mr. B formed a calendar-year Partnership C in February 2017. The partnership passed through the following items to partners A and B in 2017:

Ordinary loss $50,000
Research credit from qualifying research   11,250

Mr. A has an income tax liability of $20,000 before research credits. Mr. A may claim his proportionate share of the research credit from Partnership C on his 2017 tax return.

A. True.

B. False.

Answer (B) is correct. *(SEE, adapted)*
   DISCUSSION: Section 41(g) limits a partner's use of the research credit passed through from a partnership to the tax attributable to the partner's share of taxable income from the partnership. Since the partnership has no taxable income, neither A nor B may use the research credit in 2017. The unused credit may be carried back or forward to other tax years according to the General Business Credit carryover rules of Sec. 39.

8.9.9. Taxpayers may treat 100% of amounts paid for qualified research as expenses eligible for the Research and Experimentation Credit if the research is conducted through a qualified research consortium.

A. True.

B. False.

Answer (B) is correct. *(Publisher, adapted)*
   DISCUSSION: Taxpayers that conduct qualified research through a research consortium may treat 75% of amounts paid or incurred for qualified research as qualified expenses for the research credit.

8.10 Work Opportunity Tax Credit

8.10.1. On April 1, 2017, Toni Painta hired a qualified ex-felon to perform duties related to her business. Toni Painta paid the employee a total of $6,500 during 2017. The employee worked a total of 800 hours during the year. What is the amount Toni Painta may claim as a work opportunity credit?

A. $0

B. $2,400

C. $2,600

D. $3,000

Answer (B) is correct. *(SEE, adapted)*
   REQUIRED: The amount of the work opportunity credit.
   DISCUSSION: Under Sec. 51, the amount of the work opportunity credit is equal to 40% of the first $6,000 of wages paid to a qualified employee in his or her first year of service. Painta paid the employee $6,500, so the credit is limited to $2,400 ($6,000 × 40%). To be eligible for the work opportunity credit, the employee must have completed a minimum of 120 hours of service. If the employee meets or exceeds the 120-hour minimum requirement but does not perform 400 or more hours of service, the employer is entitled to a credit of 25%. For employees performing 400 or more hours of service, the appropriate percentage is 40%.
   Answer (A) is incorrect. Toni is entitled to a work opportunity credit. Answer (C) is incorrect. The amount of $2,600 is 40% of the actual salary paid. Answer (D) is incorrect. The amount of $3,000 is 50% of the first $6,000 paid.

8.10.2. All the following groups are targeted groups for the work opportunity credit except

A. Trade Readjustment Act beneficiaries.

B. Designated Community Residents.

C. Qualified veterans.

D. Qualified IV-A [Aid to Families with Dependent Children (AFDC)] recipients.

Answer (A) is correct. *(SEE, adapted)*
   REQUIRED: The group not considered a targeted group for purposes of the work opportunity credit.
   DISCUSSION: Section 51(d) provides a list of the groups that are considered targeted groups for purposes of the work opportunity credit. Trade Readjustment Act beneficiaries are not included among the list of targeted groups.
   Answer (B) is incorrect. Designated community residents is a group included as a targeted group in Sec. 51(d). Answer (C) is incorrect. Qualified veterans is a group included as a targeted group in Sec. 51(d). Answer (D) is incorrect. Qualified IV-A AFDC recipients is a group included as a targeted group in Sec. 51(d).

8.10.3. Red Baron hired two employees under a work opportunity program and claimed the following credit in 2016:

Employee X, hired 10/1/16	
($3,000 salary × 40%)	$1,200
Employee Y, hired 9/1/16	
($4,000 salary × 40%)	1,600
	$2,800

On January 10, 2017, Red Baron terminated Employee X for poor job performance. On February 15, 2017, Employee Y was laid off for lack of work in Red's business. What amount, if any, of the credit claimed in 2016 will Red Baron recapture in 2017?

A. $0

B. $600

C. $700

D. $1,400

8.10.4. In 2017, the following amounts were paid by Trusty Grocery for wages:

$3,000 to designated community residents who worked 600 hours from February through June

$1,500 to a qualified veteran in his second year with Trusty Grocery

$2,000 to qualified summer youths, who worked 360 hours for the entire summer (June through August)

$1,000 to a vocational rehabilitation referral, who worked 100 hours during April and May

All of these employees were properly certified, and none were related to the owner of Trusty Grocery. What is the amount that qualifies as work opportunity credit wages?

A. $3,000

B. $4,500

C. $5,000

D. $6,500

8.10.5. Which of the following statements about the work opportunity credit is false?

A. The credit is available to employers for wages paid to long-term family assistance recipients in 2017.

B. The credit is equal to 50% of qualified first-year wages for long-term family assistance recipients.

C. The credit applies to the first $10,000 of wages per qualified employee for each of the first and second years of employment for long-term family assistance recipients.

D. The credit is limited to $9,000 over a 2-year period for long-term family assistance recipients.

Answer (A) is correct. *(SEE, adapted)*
REQUIRED: The amount of credit claimed in 2016 that the taxpayer will recapture in 2017.
DISCUSSION: The work opportunity credit is provided in Sec. 38, and operating rules are contained in Secs. 51 and 52. The purpose of the credit is to provide incentives for employers to hire certain groups of employees who have found it hard to find employment. The credit is equal to the sum of 40% of the first $6,000 of wages paid to each qualified employee in his or her first year of service. Employees must have completed at least 90 days or 120 hours of service to be eligible for a 25% credit or at least 400 hours of service to be eligible for a 40% credit [Sec. 51(i)(3)]. The employer is required to reduce his or her deduction for wages by the amount of the credit. There is no provision for recapture of the credit when an employee is terminated.
Answer (B) is incorrect. The figure of $600 is the incorrect amount of recapture for the work opportunity credit. Answer (C) is incorrect. The figure of $700 is the incorrect amount of recapture for the work opportunity credit. Answer (D) is incorrect. The figure of $1,400 is the incorrect amount of recapture for the work opportunity credit.

Answer (C) is correct. *(SEE, adapted)*
REQUIRED: The amount that qualifies as work opportunity credit wages.
DISCUSSION: The work opportunity credit applies to qualified employees in their first year of service. The credit is equal to 40% of the first $6,000 of wages ($3,000 for qualified summer youths). The credit is reduced to 25% for employees that work at least 120 hours but less than 400 hours. To qualify, the employee must be a member of a targeted group. The designated community residents and the qualified summer youths meet the requirements for the work opportunity credit. The qualified veteran is in his second year, so he does not qualify. The vocational rehabilitation referral did not work for the minimum employment period, so (s)he does not qualify. The total wages that qualify for the credit are $5,000 ($3,000 + $2,000).
Answer (A) is incorrect. The qualified summer youths also qualify. Answer (B) is incorrect. The qualified summer youths also qualify, but the economically disadvantaged veteran does not since he is in his second year. Answer (D) is incorrect. The economically disadvantaged veteran does not qualify since he is in his second year.

Answer (B) is correct. *(Publisher, adapted)*
REQUIRED: The false statement about the work opportunity credit.
DISCUSSION: The credit is equal to 40% of qualified first-year wages and 50% of qualified second-year wages for long-term family assistance recipients.
Answer (A) is incorrect. The work opportunity credit is available to all employers for wages paid to long-term family assistance recipients in 2017. Answer (C) is incorrect. The work opportunity credit applies to the first $10,000 of wages per qualified employee for each of the first and second years of employment for long-term family assistance recipients. Answer (D) is incorrect. The work opportunity credit is limited to $9,000 over a 2-year period for long-term family assistance recipients.

8.10.6. Which of the following are wages for the purpose of the work opportunity credit?

I.   Remuneration for employment
II. Educational assistance program expenses
III. Dependent care expenses

    A. I only.

    B. III only.

    C. II and III.

    D. I, II, and III.

Answer (D) is correct. *(Publisher, adapted)*
    REQUIRED: The definition of wages for the work opportunity credit.
    DISCUSSION: For purposes of the work opportunity credit, wages include the following: remuneration for employment, amounts received under accident and health plans, contributions by employers to accident and health plans, educational assistance, and dependent care expenses.
    Answer (A) is incorrect. Remuneration for employment is not the only item considered wages for the purposes of the work opportunity credit. Answer (B) is incorrect. Dependent care expenses is not the only item considered wages for the purposes of the work opportunity credit. Answer (C) is incorrect. Educational assistance program expenses and dependent care expenses are not the only items considered wages for the purpose of the work opportunity credit.

8.10.7. Jones Corporation hired a new employee on March 12, 2017. The new employee was a long-term family assistance recipient and received qualified first-year wages in the amount of $12,000 during 2017. An additional $3,500 of wages was earned between January 1 and March 11, 2018. What is Jones Corporation's allowable work opportunity credit for 2017?

    A. $4,000

    B. $4,800

    C. $5,000

    D. $6,000

Answer (A) is correct. *(Publisher, adapted)*
    REQUIRED: The amount of work opportunity credit allowed for 2017.
    DISCUSSION: Employers are allowed a credit in the amount of 40% of the first $10,000 of qualified first-year wages paid to employees who are long-term family assistance recipients. Therefore, Jones is allowed a credit of $4,000 for 2017.
    Answer (B) is incorrect. The amount of $4,800 disregards the qualified first-year wages limit. Answer (C) is incorrect. The amount of $5,000 is 50% of the first $10,000 of qualified first-year wages. Answer (D) is incorrect. The amount of $6,000 disregards the qualified first-year wages limit and uses the second-year credit percentage.

8.10.8. Jones Corporation hired a new employee on March 12, 2016. The new employee was a long-term family assistance recipient and received qualified first-year wages in the amount of $12,000 during 2016. An additional $3,500 of wages was earned between January 1 and March 11, 2017. In 2017, Jones paid this employee $15,000 of wages. Of the wages, $11,500 was attributable to the portion of the calendar year after March 11. What is Jones Corporation's allowable work opportunity credit for 2017?

    A. $4,000

    B. $5,000

    C. $5,250

    D. $7,500

Answer (B) is correct. *(Publisher, adapted)*
    REQUIRED: The amount of work opportunity credit allowed for 2017 (the employee's second year of employment).
    DISCUSSION: Employers are allowed a credit in the amount of 50% of the first $10,000 of qualified second-year wages paid to employees who are long-term family assistance recipients. Therefore, Jones Corporation is allowed a credit of $5,000 for 2017. Note that the combined credit for the 2 years may not exceed $9,000 per qualified employee.
    Answer (A) is incorrect. The credit for the first year (2016) is $4,000. Answer (C) is incorrect. The amount of $5,250 is 50% of what was earned after March 11, 2017, ignoring the limit. Answer (D) is incorrect. The amount of $7,500 is 50% of the total earned in 2017.

8.11 Empowerment Zone Employment Credit

8.11.1. Kerry Construction, which is 75% owned by Kerry Von Erich, is located in an empowerment zone in an urban area. Which of the following of Kerry's employees, whose primary residences are all within the empowerment zone, is eligible to be labeled a "qualified zone employee"?

    A. Fritz, who just started work last week.

    B. Kevin, who is Kerry's brother.

    C. Dave, who has worked for Kerry for 2 years.

    D. Mike, who has purchased 5% of Kerry's stock through an employee incentive program.

Answer (C) is correct. *(Publisher, adapted)*
    REQUIRED: The employee who can be a "qualified zone employee."
    DISCUSSION: "Qualified zone employees" are defined in Sec. 1396(d). Any employee who performs substantially all his or her services within the empowerment zone in a trade or business of the employer, and whose principal place of abode is within the zone, can be labeled a "qualified zone employee" except for a few exceptions.
    Answer (A) is incorrect. The individual must be employed for 90 days before becoming a qualified zone employee. Answer (B) is incorrect. The individual cannot be related to a majority owner [Secs. 51(i)(1)(A), (B), and (C)]. Answer (D) is incorrect. The individual cannot own 5% or more of the company according to Sec. 416(i)(1)(B).

8.11.2. Jane works for Dave's Diner, which is located in an empowerment zone. She is a "qualified zone employee." Jane earned $19,500 in wages during the current year. What is the amount of the empowerment zone employee credit Dave's Diner can claim for the year?

    A. $1,950

    B. $3,000

    C. $3,900

    D. $6,000

Answer (B) is correct. *(Publisher, adapted)*
    REQUIRED: The amount of the empowerment zone employee credit.
    DISCUSSION: Only the first $15,000 in wages paid is taken into account when calculating the empowerment zone employee credit. For the years 1994-2001, the applicable percentage is 20% for the nine empowerment zones authorized before the 1997 Tax Act. Thus, the credit is $3,000 ($15,000 × 20%). The 1997 Tax Act added two new urban-area empowerment zones. The 20% rate applies to the two new zones from 2000-2005 for these urban-area zones. Twenty other empowerment zones were authorized with reduced tax incentives. These zones, which were created between August 5, 1997, and January 1, 1999, do not qualify for the empowerment zone wage credit.
    Answer (A) is incorrect. The figure of $1,950 is 10% of wages paid and is not the correct amount for the credit Dave's Diner can claim for the year. Answer (C) is incorrect. The figure of $3,900 is 20% of wages paid and is not the correct amount for the credit Dave's Diner can claim for the year. Answer (D) is incorrect. The figure of $6,000 is 40% of the first $15,000 in wages paid and is not the correct amount for the credit Dave's Diner can claim for the year.

8.11.3. The wages paid to any employee who was terminated for any reason before 90 days do not qualify for empowerment zone employee credits.

    A. True.

    B. False.

Answer (B) is correct. *(Publisher, adapted)*
    DISCUSSION: An employee who works for less than 90 days and who was terminated due to a disability is considered a qualified employee. If the disability is removed before the 90-day period and the employee is not rehired, (s)he is not eligible.

8.11.4. Only employees who are paid an hourly wage can qualify as empowerment zone employees.

    A. True.

    B. False.

Answer (B) is correct. *(Publisher, adapted)*
    DISCUSSION: Both salary and wages qualify as empowerment zone wages.

8.11.5. The amount of the empowerment zone employee credit that a corporation can claim is limited to the corporation's income tax liability in any year.

    A. True.

    B. False.

Answer (B) is correct. *(Publisher, adapted)*
    DISCUSSION: The empowerment zone employee credit is part of the General Business Credits that are limited in total to the taxpayer's net income tax over the greater of (1) its tentative minimum tax or (2) 25% of its regular tax amount in excess of $25,000.

8.12 Disabled Access Credit

8.12.1. Which one of the following statements about the disabled access credit is false?

    A. The credit is available in the current year to only businesses having either gross receipts that were less than $1 million or no more than 30 full-time employees in the preceding tax year.

    B. The credit equals 50% of eligible expenditures in excess of $250 and less than $10,250.

    C. No deduction is allowed for any amount for which the disabled access credit is claimed.

    D. The credit is a refundable credit for eligible small businesses.

Answer (D) is correct. *(Publisher, adapted)*
    REQUIRED: The false statement regarding the disabled access credit.
    DISCUSSION: Under Sec. 44(a), a credit is available to eligible small businesses that make expenditures to provide access to disabled individuals. The disabled access credit is not a refundable credit because it is part of the General Business Credit. Excess General Business Credits may be carried back 1 year or forward 20 years, but not refunded.
    Answer (A) is incorrect. The disabled access credit is available for the current year to only businesses having either gross receipts that were less than $1 million or no more than 30 full-time employees in the preceding tax year. Answer (B) is incorrect. The disabled access credit equals 50% of eligible expenditures in excess of $250 and less than $10,250. Answer (C) is incorrect. No deduction is allowed for any amount for which the disabled access credit is claimed.

8.12.2. Eligible expenditures for the disabled access credit include amounts spent for all but which one of the following?

A. Removing architectural barriers restricting access to a business.

B. Modifying equipment or devices for disabled individuals.

C. Making a new building accessible to the disabled.

D. Providing interpreters for hearing-impaired individuals.

Answer (C) is correct. *(Publisher, adapted)*
REQUIRED: The false statement regarding the disabled access credit.
DISCUSSION: Code Sec. 44(c)(2) states that the disabled access credit is available for certain kinds of expenditures incurred in order to enable small businesses to comply with the Americans with Disabilities Act. Included in eligible expenditures are these related to removing architectural barriers restricting access to a business, for modifications of equipment or devices for disabled individuals, and for providing interpreters for making aurally delivered materials available to individuals with hearing impairments.
Making a new building accessible for the disabled is not an expenditure for which the disabled access credit may be used [Sec. 44(c)(4)]; thus, this answer is the false statement regarding the disabled access credit.
Answer (A) is incorrect. Removing architectural barriers restricting access to a business is an eligible expenditure for the disabled access credit. Answer (B) is incorrect. Modifying equipment or devices for disabled individuals is an eligible expenditure for the disabled access credit. Answer (D) is incorrect. Providing interpreters for hearing-impaired individuals is an eligible expenditure for the disabled access credit.

8.12.3. In the current year, Jones Corporation incurred $25,000 in expenditures in making its existing three-story office building accessible to wheelchair-bound individuals. For the year, its regular tax liability is $61,250 and its tentative minimum tax liability is $40,000. What is the amount of its disabled access credit?

A. $0

B. $5,000

C. $12,500

D. $25,000

Answer (B) is correct. *(Publisher, adapted)*
REQUIRED: The amount of the disabled access credit.
DISCUSSION: The amount of the disabled access credit for any tax year is equal to 50% of the amount of the eligible access expenditures for that year that exceed $250 but do not exceed $10,250. Jones's disabled access credit is $5,000 (lesser of $25,000 actual expenditures or $10,250 limitation minus $250 floor times the 50% credit rate). The disabled access credit is included as part of the General Business Credit and, thus, is subject to the Sec. 38(c) rules that limit the amount of the General Business Credit for any given year. The $5,000 credit is less than the $21,250 ($61,250 net income tax – greater of $40,000 tentative minimum tax or $9,062 that is 25% of the net regular tax liability in excess of $25,000) limitation for the General Business Credit.
Answer (A) is incorrect. Jones Corporation is entitled to a disabled access credit. Answer (C) is incorrect. The amount of $12,500 is 50% of $25,000, and there is a limitation and a floor taken prior to the 50% calculation. Answer (D) is incorrect. The figure of $25,000 is the amount of the full expenditure, and it is subject to the rules involving the disabled access credit.

8.13 Business Energy Credit

8.13.1. Which of the following statements on business energy credit property is false?

A. The property may be used property.

B. The property must be depreciable or amortizable property.

C. The property must be predominantly used in connection with a structure within the United States.

D. The property may be structural components.

Answer (A) is correct. *(SEE, adapted)*
REQUIRED: The false statement about business energy credit property.
DISCUSSION: Energy property is defined in Sec. 48(a)(3). One of the requirements is that the taxpayer claiming the credit must have constructed or erected the property or acquired and have the original use of the property. This means the property must be new, not used [Sec. 48(a)(3)(B)].
Answer (B) is incorrect. Energy property must be property with respect to which depreciation or amortization is allowable [Sec. 48(a)(3)(C)]. Answer (C) is incorrect. Energy property must generally meet the requirements of Sec. 50(b)(1), under which the property may not be used predominantly outside the U.S. Answer (D) is incorrect. Structural components of a building may qualify for the energy credit [Reg. 1.48-9(b)(1)].

8.13.2. In the current year, Mr. L. E. Phant purchased geothermal energy property with a 5-year recovery period for his business from an unrelated firm. The property cost $40,000; Mr. Phant paid $10,000 down and borrowed the remaining $30,000 from First Bank where he had been a customer for years. Mr. Phant had no personal liability on the $30,000 note. The note was due in three annual installments beginning in the following year. Mr. Phant's tentative current-year geothermal energy credit is

A. $0
B. $1,000
C. $2,000
D. $4,000

Answer (D) is correct. *(Publisher, adapted)*
REQUIRED: The tentative energy credit for geothermal property acquired with nonrecourse debt.
DISCUSSION: Under Sec. 49(a)(1)(A), the basis of property included in the qualified investment is limited to the amount for which the taxpayer is at risk with respect to such property. Since Phant has no personal liability on the $30,000, he generally would not be considered at risk for $30,000 of the property. Under an exception, however, a taxpayer is considered at risk on nonrecourse debt if (s)he is at risk with respect to at least 20% of the basis of the property, if the property was not acquired from a related person, and if the borrowed amount is from a qualified person (which includes a bank). Phant meets these requirements. Therefore, the amount borrowed is also considered at risk, and the qualified investment is $40,000. Under Sec. 48(a)(2), the geothermal energy credit is $4,000 ($40,000 × 10%) for the current year.
Answer (A) is incorrect. Phant can claim a geothermal energy credit. Answer (B) is incorrect. The figure of $1,000 is 10% of the $10,000 down payment but is not the correct amount of the credit Phant can claim. Answer (C) is incorrect. The figure of $2,000 is 20% of the $10,000 down payment but is not the correct amount of the credit Phant can claim.

8.13.3. In the current year, Ms. Green purchased solar energy property with a 5-year recovery period for use in her business at a total cost of $10,000. Ms. Green paid $2,000 down and signed a note agreeing to pay the seller the remaining amount plus interest over the next 4 years. The seller had a lien on the solar property to secure the note, but Ms. Green had no personal liability. The tentative energy credit available to Ms. Green in the current year is

A. $0
B. $600
C. $2,400
D. $3,000

Answer (B) is correct. *(Publisher, adapted)*
REQUIRED: The tentative energy credit for property acquired with nonrecourse debt.
DISCUSSION: Property will qualify for the energy credit only to the extent the taxpayer is at risk with respect to it [Sec. 49(a)(1)(A)]. Since Ms. Green does not have any personal liability for $8,000 of the cost of the solar property, only the $2,000 for which she was at risk will qualify. The Sec. 49(a)(1)(D) exception for nonrecourse financing does not apply, even though Ms. Green invested 20% of the property's cost, because the loan was obtained from the seller. The tentative credit in the current year is 30% of the qualified investment of $2,000, which equals $600.
Answer (A) is incorrect. A credit is available. Answer (C) is incorrect. The amount of $2,400 is 30% of the portion of the cost for which Ms. Green is not at risk. Answer (D) is incorrect. Ms. Green is not at risk for the remaining $8,000 since the monies came from the seller, so no credit may be taken against that portion of the cost.

8.13.4. Active solar property installed as a structural component of a building may not qualify for the business energy credit.

A. True.
B. False.

Answer (B) is correct. *(SEE, adapted)*
DISCUSSION: Energy property has included structural components of a building even though such components generally did not qualify as investment tax credit property [Reg. 1.48-9(b)(1)]. Energy property includes active solar property, and active solar property installed as a structural component of a building may qualify for the business energy credit.

8.13.5. For energy property placed in service after 1982, the basis of the property must be reduced by 50% of the business energy credit claimed.

A. True.
B. False.

Answer (A) is correct. *(Publisher, adapted)*
DISCUSSION: Under Sec. 50(c)(3), the basis of energy property must be reduced by 50% of the business energy credit claimed. This basis reduction will, for purposes of Sec. 1245 and Sec. 1250, be treated as depreciation and may therefore result in recapture of ordinary income upon later sale of the property.

8.14 Rehabilitation Credit

8.14.1. Expenditures that can qualify for the tax credit for rehabilitated buildings include

I.   Cost of acquiring a business building that is more than 33 years old

II. Cost of replacing all floors and plumbing in an 83-year-old office building

III. Cost of enlarging a certified historic structure used as a restaurant so that kitchen facilities can be modernized

A. I only.

B. II only.

C. III only.

D. I and III only.

Answer (B) is correct. *(Publisher, adapted)*
REQUIRED: The item(s) qualifying for the tax credit for rehabilitated buildings.
DISCUSSION: Section 47(c)(2) defines qualified rehabilitation expenditures as amounts that are chargeable to capital for nonresidential real property, residential rental property, real property with a class life of more than 12.5 years, or improvements to any of the above-named properties and amounts that are spent in connection with the rehabilitation of a qualified rehabilitated building. The cost of replacing floors and plumbing in an 83-year-old office building is a qualified expenditure since it will be capitalized, and the 83-year-old office building is a qualified rehabilitated building because it was placed in service before 1936 [Sec. 47(c)(1)(B)].
Answer (A) is incorrect. Qualified expenditures do not include the cost of acquiring a building or an interest in a building [Sec. 47(c)(2)(B)]. Answer (C) is incorrect. Qualified expenditures do not include the cost of enlarging a building [Sec. 47(c)(2)(B)]. Answer (D) is incorrect. Neither expenditure qualifies for the tax credit for rehabilitated buildings.

8.14.2. In 2015, Sunset Corporation acquired an 83-year-old building at a cost of $320,000 and used it for 2 years. Sunset had the interior of the building rehabilitated at a cost of $200,000 in 2017 when the adjusted basis of the building was $300,000. All work was completed during 2017 when Sunset moved back into the building. The building was not a certified historic structure. The available tax credit for the rehabilitation before any limitation is

A. $0

B. $30,000

C. $40,000

D. $50,000

Answer (A) is correct. *(Publisher, adapted)*
REQUIRED: The available tax credit for the rehabilitated building.
DISCUSSION: Section 47(c)(1) defines a qualified rehabilitated building for purposes of computing the credit as one placed in service before the rehabilitation began, and one in which 50% or more of the existing external walls are retained as external walls, 75% of existing external walls are retained as internal or external walls, and 75% of existing internal structural framework is retained. In addition, the building must have been placed in service before 1936 if it is not a certified historic structure, and substantial rehabilitation must have occurred. Rehabilitation is substantial if its cost exceeds the greater of the adjusted basis of the property or $5,000.
The basis in the building acquired by Sunset Corporation was $300,000 at the time the rehabilitation began. The cost of the rehabilitation was only $200,000, which does not meet the requirement for substantial rehabilitation. The tax credit will be $0.
Answer (B) is incorrect. The figure of $30,000 is the incorrect amount of the available tax credit for the rehabilitation. Answer (C) is incorrect. The figure of $40,000 is the incorrect amount of the available tax credit for the rehabilitation. Answer (D) is incorrect. The figure of $50,000 is the incorrect amount of the available tax credit for the rehabilitation.

8.14.3. Aged Corporation built an office building in 1931 at a cost of $100,000 to be used as its corporate headquarters. The building was fully depreciated, and it had a basis of $14,000 in the current year when Aged began rehabilitating the structure. Rehabilitation expenditures of $200,000 were incurred during the year, and Aged moved back into the building in December of the same year. Aged's credit for rehabilitation expenditures is

A. $20,000

B. $21,400

C. $32,100

D. $40,000

Answer (A) is correct. *(Publisher, adapted)*
REQUIRED: The taxpayer's credit for rehabilitation expenditures.
DISCUSSION: Aged Corporation rehabilitated a building that had been placed in service before 1936. Substantial rehabilitation has occurred because the cost of rehabilitation exceeded the basis of $14,000 [Sec. 47(c)(1)(C)]. Under Sec. 47(a)(1), the rehabilitation credit for a rehabilitated building other than a certified historic structure is 10%. Thus, Aged's tentative rehabilitation credit is $20,000 ($200,000 rehabilitation expenditures × 10%).
Answer (B) is incorrect. The amount of $21,400 equals the sum of 10% of the $200,000 rehabilitation expenditures and 10% of the basis of $14,000. Answer (C) is incorrect. The figure of $32,100 is not the correct amount of Aged's credit for rehabilitation expenditures. Answer (D) is incorrect. When the building is a certified historic structure, 20% of rehabilitation expenditures is used.

8.14.4. Last year, C. P. Aye acquired a 45-year-old residence, which was a certified historic structure, at a cost of $75,000. In a certified rehabilitation, Aye spent $90,000 converting the house into an office for her accounting practice. Aye completed the rehabilitation this year. Aye's credit for rehabilitation of the building and her basis in the building after the rehabilitation are

A. $18,000 credit and $147,000 basis.
B. $18,000 credit and $156,000 basis.
C. $22,500 credit and $153,750 basis.
D. $22,500 credit and $142,500 basis.

Answer (A) is correct. *(Publisher, adapted)*
REQUIRED: The credit for rehabilitation of a certified historic structure and its basis.
DISCUSSION: Rehabilitation of a certified historic structure results in a credit of 20% of the qualified expenditures [Sec. 47(a)(2)]. Aye invested $90,000 in rehabilitating the structure. Accordingly, she can claim a credit of $18,000 ($90,000 × 20%). The basis of rehabilitated certified historic structures must be adjusted by 100% of the credit claimed. Therefore, Aye's new basis in the building is equal to the original cost of $75,000, plus the amount of the rehabilitation expenditure ($90,000), less 100% of the credit ($18,000), for a total basis of $147,000 [Sec. 50(c)(1)].
Answer (B) is incorrect. The basis is the cost of the building plus rehabilitation costs minus the entire credit amount, not just half the credit amount. Answer (C) is incorrect. The amount of $22,500 is based on a 25% credit rate, and only one-half of the credit is used to reduce the basis. Answer (D) is incorrect. A 25% credit is used.

8.14.5. Which of the following must be true for a building other than a certified historic structure to be considered a qualified rehabilitated building?

A. The building must have been placed in service prior to 1936.
B. At least 50% of existing external walls must remain in place as external walls.
C. At least 75% of existing external walls must remain in place as internal or external walls.
D. All of the answers are correct.

Answer (D) is correct. *(Publisher, adapted)*
REQUIRED: The requirement necessary for a building other than a certified historic structure to be considered a qualified rehabilitated building.
DISCUSSION: Under Sec. 47(c)(1)(B), a building other than a certified historic structure must have been placed in service prior to 1936 to be considered a qualified rehabilitated building. The other two requirements listed in the answer choices (50% and 75% of external walls) are necessary for any building to be considered a qualified rehabilitated building. In addition, at least 75% of existing internal structural framework must remain in place [Sec. 47(c)(1)(A)].
Answer (A) is incorrect. In addition to this requirement, at least 50% of existing external walls must remain in place as external walls, and at least 75% of existing external walls must remain in place as internal or external walls. Answer (B) is incorrect. In addition to this requirement, the building must have been placed in service prior to 1936, and at least 75% of existing external walls must remain in place as internal or external walls. Answer (C) is incorrect. In addition to this requirement, the building must have been placed in service prior to 1936, and at least 50% of existing external walls must remain in place as external walls.

8.14.6. Basis in a building placed in service before 1936 that is not a certified historic structure must be reduced by any credit for rehabilitation expenditures claimed after 1986.

A. True.
B. False.

Answer (A) is correct. *(Publisher, adapted)*
DISCUSSION: Under Sec. 50(c), the basis in a building for which a credit for rehabilitation expenditures is claimed after 1986 must be reduced by the full amount of the credit claimed, even if the building is not a certified historic structure.

8.14.7. Accelerated depreciation can be claimed on qualified rehabilitation expenditures.

A. True.
B. False.

Answer (B) is correct. *(Publisher, adapted)*
DISCUSSION: If a credit is claimed for qualified rehabilitation expenditures, amortization or accelerated methods of depreciation may not be used on the property [Sec. 47(c)(2)(B)(i)].

8.15 ITC Recapture

8.15.1. The investment tax credit (or investment credit) includes all but which of the following?

A. Foreign tax credit.

B. Energy credit.

C. Rehabilitation credit.

D. Advanced coal project credit.

Answer (A) is correct. *(Publisher, adapted)*
    REQUIRED: The type of credit not considered part of the investment tax credit.
    DISCUSSION: The investment tax credit is defined in Sec. 46 as being composed of the qualifying advanced coal project credit, the qualifying gasification project credit, the qualifying advanced energy project credit, the energy credit, and the rehabilitation credit. The Foreign Tax Credit is not part of the investment tax credit.
    Answer (B) is incorrect. The energy credit is part of the investment tax credit. Answer (C) is incorrect. The rehabilitation credit is also part of the investment tax credit. Answer (D) is incorrect. The advanced coal project credit is also part of the investment tax credit.

8.15.2. Which one of the following transactions is not a disposition of property that would cause a recapture of the investment tax credit?

A. Property transferred by gift.

B. Property converted by theft.

C. Property that has been abandoned.

D. Property transferred as security for a loan.

Answer (D) is correct. *(SEE, adapted)*
    REQUIRED: The transaction that does not cause recapture of the investment tax credit.
    DISCUSSION: Under Sec. 50(a)(1)(A), if property is disposed of or otherwise ceases to be owned by the taxpayer, the taxpayer must recapture the investment tax credit. This means his or her tax is increased for the current year by part or all of the credit previously taken. The transfer of property as security for a loan is not considered to be a disposition and would not cause any recapture.
    Answer (A) is incorrect. Property transferred by gift is a disposition of property that causes the recapture of ITC. Answer (B) is incorrect. Property converted by theft is a disposition of property that causes the recapture of ITC. Answer (C) is incorrect. Property that has been abandoned is a disposition of property that causes a recapture of ITC.

8.15.3. Which of the following transactions is not a disposition of property that would cause a recapture of investment tax credit?

A. Business property converted to personal use.

B. Transfer of property by foreclosure.

C. Property transferred by reason of death.

D. Property destroyed by casualty.

Answer (C) is correct. *(SEE, adapted)*
    REQUIRED: The transaction that is not a disposition that causes recapture of the investment tax credit.
    DISCUSSION: Section 50(a)(1)(A) requires the recapture of the investment tax credit if property on which it has been taken is disposed of prematurely. Under Sec. 50(a)(4)(A), a transfer by reason of death is specifically excluded from dispositions that would result in the recapture of the investment tax credit.
    Answer (A) is incorrect. Business property converted to personal use is a disposition of property that causes a recapture of ITC. Answer (B) is incorrect. Transfer of property by foreclosure is a disposition of property that causes a recapture of ITC. Answer (D) is incorrect. Property destroyed by casualty is a disposition of property that causes a recapture of ITC.

8.15.4. On June 3, Year 1, Universal Corporation purchased $50,000 of solar panels. The company claimed the maximum possible solar energy property credit and then the maximum depreciation but did not use the Sec. 179 expensing election. On August 2, Year 3, the equipment was sold for $38,000. Universal Corporation's energy tax credit recapture on the disposition of the solar panels amounts to

A. $0

B. $9,000

C. $12,000

D. $15,000

Answer (B) is correct. *(Publisher, adapted)*
    REQUIRED: The amount of energy tax credit that must be recaptured.
    DISCUSSION: Since 1988, solar energy panels have been entitled to a 30% credit. Thus, in Year 1, Universal Corporation received a $15,000 ($50,000 × .30) energy tax credit. Since Universal sold the property before the full credit had been earned, it must recapture part of the credit and add it directly to its Year 3 tax liability.
    Under Sec. 50(a)(1)(B), the recapture percentage is 100% if the property is disposed of within the first year of being placed in service. For each year thereafter, the recapture percentage declines by 20%. Universal held the property for 2 full years; thus, their recapture percentage is 60% [100% − (20% × 2 years)]. Hence, Universal's energy tax credit recapture is $9,000 ($15,000 × 60%).
    Answer (A) is incorrect. A portion of the energy tax credit must be recaptured. Answer (C) is incorrect. The property was held for 2 years, so 80% of the credit is not recaptured. Answer (D) is incorrect. The full amount of the credit does not have to be recaptured unless the property is disposed of within the first year.

8.15.5. Solo Corporation built an office building in 1931 to be used as its corporate headquarters. The building was rehabilitated 3 years ago with rehabilitation expenditures of $300,000 being incurred. Solo occupied the building in October of that year and claimed a $30,000 credit for its rehabilitation expenditures. Solo Corporation was acquired by Large Corporation in June of the current year. The Solo Corporation corporate headquarters were sold in December of the current year at a $150,000 profit. What is the recapture of the rehabilitation building credit in the current year?

A. $0

B. $12,000

C. $18,000

D. $30,000

Answer (B) is correct. *(Publisher, adapted)*
REQUIRED: The amount of the rehabilitation credit that must be recaptured.
DISCUSSION: The credit for rehabilitation expenditures must be recaptured if the rehabilitated structure is disposed of in less than 5 years. Under Sec. 50(a)(1)(B), the recapture percentage is 100% of the credit taken if the property is disposed of within the first year after being placed in service. For each year the property is held after the first year, the recapture percentage declines by 20%.
Solo Corporation held the property for 3 full years, so they must recapture 40% [100% − (20% × 3 years)] of the original credit amount

Rehabilitation credit	$30,000
Times: Recapture percentage	× .40
Recapture amount	$12,000

Answer (A) is incorrect. A portion of the rehabilitation credit must be recaptured. Answer (C) is incorrect. The property was held for 3 years, not 2 years, so the recaptured amount should not be 60% of the credit. Answer (D) is incorrect. The full amount of the credit does not have to be recaptured when the property has been held for 3 years.

8.15.6. The four partners of the ABCD Partnership share the profits and losses equally. In April of Year 1, ABCD acquired new business assets including solar energy property in the amount of $100,000, and the partners together claimed an energy tax credit of $10,000. In July of Year 4, A sold his interest to Ms. E. Mr. A had properly claimed his full share of the investment credit for Year 1. What is the amount A must add to his Year 4 income tax liability under the energy credit recapture rules?

A. $2,500

B. $2,000

C. $1,500

D. $1,000

Answer (D) is correct. *(SEE, adapted)*
REQUIRED: The amount of energy credit recapture.
DISCUSSION: Under Sec. 50(a)(1)(B), if the energy property in question is sold within 5 years, part of the energy tax credit taken on the property must be recaptured. The recapture percentage is 100% of the credit taken if the property is disposed of within the first year after being placed in service. For each year thereafter, the recapture percentage declines by 20%.
In this case, Mr. A's share of the partnership's credit is $2,500 ($10,000 credit ÷ 4 equal partners). Since A was in the partnership for only 3 years, he must recapture 40% of the credit [100% − (20% × 3 years)]. Therefore, A's recapture amount is $1,000 ($2,500 × 40%). Ms. E may not take an additional investment tax credit as a result of purchasing her interest.
Answer (A) is incorrect. The figure of $2,500 is the full amount of the credit Mr. A claimed. The full amount does not have to be recaptured. Answer (B) is incorrect. The property was held for 3 years, not 1 year, so the recaptured amount is not 80% of the credit. Answer (C) is incorrect. The property was held for 3 years, not 2 years, so the recaptured amount is not 60% of the credit.

8.15.7. In January of Year 1, TexAnn Corporation, an S corporation, purchased solar heating panels for $150,000 from Ark Company. TexAnn paid $35,000 in cash and financed the remaining $115,000 on a recourse basis with Ark Company. TexAnn took an energy credit of $15,000. In January of Year 3, Ark and TexAnn modified their financing arrangement so that TexAnn no longer had any liability for the $75,000 of the debt that was not yet paid. How much of the investment tax credit taken in Year 1 must TexAnn recapture?

A. $0

B. $22,500

C. $27,000

D. $36,000

Answer (B) is correct. *(Publisher, adapted)*
REQUIRED: The amount of energy tax credit taken in Year 1 that must be recaptured.
DISCUSSION: Under Sec. 49(b)(1), if a taxpayer ceases to be at risk with regard to property for which the energy tax credit was previously claimed, it must recapture the amount of credit that would not have been able to be claimed if it had not been at risk with respect to that amount when the property was placed in service. Ark and TexAnn modified their financing arrangement so that TexAnn was no longer liable for $75,000 of the debt. Therefore, $22,500 ($75,000 × 30%) must be recaptured in Year 3.
Answer (A) is incorrect. There is a recapture of the investment tax credit. Answer (C) is incorrect. Only the portion of the original credit for which the taxpayer is not at risk must be recaptured. Answer (D) is incorrect. This figure is not the correct amount of the investment tax credit that must be recaptured.

8.15.8. If you have previously taken an investment credit on qualified property, and later, before the end of its useful life, traded it for other qualified property, there will be a recapture of investment credits for the original property and an investment credit available for the new property in the year of trade.

A. True.

B. False.

Answer (A) is correct. *(SEE, adapted)*
   DISCUSSION: When property on which ITC has been claimed is disposed of, the taxpayer may have to recapture part of the investment tax credit depending on how long the property has been held (Sec. 50). This applies even if the taxpayer trades the original property for other property that qualifies for the credit. When traded before the property has been held for the required period of time, the taxpayer must recapture a portion of the tax credit originally claimed on the original property. A new tax credit may then be claimed for the new qualified property, if such a credit is available.

8.16 Low-Income Rental Housing Credit

8.16.1. Which of the following statements is not a requirement that must be met in order for residential rental property to be eligible for the low-income housing credit?

A. Twenty percent or more of the aggregate residential rental units must be occupied by individuals with incomes of 50% or less of area median income.

B. Forty percent or more of the aggregate rental units must be occupied by individuals with incomes of 60% or less of area median income.

C. The gross rent paid by families in the rent-restricted units may not exceed 30% of the qualifying income for a family of its size.

D. Qualified residential rental properties must remain as rental property and meet the minimum low-income set-aside requirements for 20 consecutive years.

Answer (D) is correct. *(Publisher, adapted)*
   REQUIRED: The false statement regarding eligibility for the low-income housing credit for residential rental property.
   DISCUSSION: Section 42(h)(6) requires that qualified residential rental property remain as rental property and meet the minimum low-income set-aside requirements for 15 consecutive years in order to be eligible for the low-income housing credit.
   Answer (A) is incorrect. It is a minimum low-income set-aside requirement under Sec. 42(g). Note that only the statement "20% or more of the aggregate residential rental units must be occupied by individuals with incomes of 50% or less of area median income" or the statement "40% or more of the aggregate rental units must be occupied by individuals with incomes of 60% or less of area median income," not both, must be met. Answer (B) is incorrect. It is a minimum low-income set-aside requirement under Sec. 42(g). Answer (C) is incorrect. It is a rent limitation that also must be met for 15 years.

8.16.2. On February 1, 2017, Herman placed in service a residential rental apartment building for low-income individuals. The qualified basis of the building is $450,000. The building is not federally subsidized. Assume the monthly low-income housing credit percentage for February 1, 2017, is 6%. How much low-income housing credit may Herman be eligible for this year?

A. $2,700

B. $13,500

C. $27,000

D. $40,500

Answer (C) is correct. *(Publisher, adapted)*
   REQUIRED: The low-income housing credit for rental property.
   DISCUSSION: For buildings placed in service after 1986, Sec. 42 provides a credit that may be claimed by owners of residential rental projects providing low-income housing, in lieu of other credits. The credit is taken over a 10-year period (the credit period) starting in the year the building or a rehabilitation of the building is placed in service. The credit amount is determined by applying a percentage to the qualified basis amount in each year. The percentage in 1987 was 9% for new buildings not federally subsidized and 4% for new buildings that are federally subsidized and also for existing buildings. For buildings placed in service after 1987, the credits are adjusted monthly. But once determined, the credit remains the same for the taxpayer each year. Herman's eligible credit amount is $27,000 ($450,000 × 6%).
   Answer (A) is incorrect. The figure of $2,700 is the amount of the credit taken in each of the 10 years. Answer (B) is incorrect. The figure of $13,500 is not the correct amount of the low-income housing credit Herman may be eligible for this year. Answer (D) is incorrect. The credit rate is not the standard 10% investment credit rate that is used for the rehabilitation credit.

8.16.3. In Year 1, Brian Baseball purchased an apartment complex in which 30% of the basis qualified as low-income rental housing for individuals with incomes of 50% or less of area median incomes. His low-income credit each year is $15,000, but it would have been $10,000 if calculated ratably over 15 years instead. In Year 3, only 24% of the basis of the project qualifies because vacancies have been filled by nonqualifying tenants. What is Brian's recapture of the low-income credit excluding interest?

A. $2,000

B. $3,000

C. $5,000

D. $10,000

Answer (A) is correct. *(Publisher, adapted)*
REQUIRED: The amount of recapture of the low-income housing credit when fewer units are occupied by qualified tenants.
DISCUSSION: Under Sec. 42(j), recapture may occur as a result of one of the following during the 15-year compliance period: noncompliance with the minimum requirements, failure to use part of the building for low-income housing, or sale of the building (unless the original owner posts a bond and it is expected that the building will continue to qualify). The amount of recapture is the accelerated portion of the credit (actual credit in excess of the amount if it had been taken over 15 years) in all prior years attributable to the portion of basis that no longer qualifies.
Low-income use of the complex decreased by 20% (6% ÷ 30%). The accelerated portion of Brian's credit each year was $5,000 ($15,000 – $10,000). His recapture is for 2 years (Year 1 and Year 2). The recapture amount is $2,000 ($5,000 × 20% × 2 years) plus interest.
Answer (B) is incorrect. The amount of $3,000 would be the recapture for 3 years, and the low-income credit has been claimed for only 2 years. Answer (C) is incorrect. The figure of $5,000 is the accelerated portion of the credit each year, not the recapture amount. Answer (D) is incorrect. The figure of $10,000 is the accelerated amount of the credit actually claimed that is in excess of the amount that would be claimed if a ratable allocation of the credit over 15 years had been used.

8.16.4. The low-income rental housing credit is available for rehabilitated as well as new buildings.

A. True.

B. False.

Answer (A) is correct. *(Publisher, adapted)*
DISCUSSION: Low-income housing property costs that qualify for the credit include rehabilitation costs as well as the cost of new buildings [Sec. 42(d)(1) and (2)].

8.16.5. The eligible basis for new and existing buildings includes expenditures incurred before the close of the first tax year in the credit period.

A. True.

B. False.

Answer (A) is correct. *(Publisher, adapted)*
DISCUSSION: The eligible basis for both new and certain existing buildings is determined as of the close of the first tax year in the credit period and is the adjusted basis of such property [Sec. 42(d)(1) and (2)]. Thus, expenditures incurred before the close of the first tax year in the credit period are includible in the eligible basis. The determination of eligible basis is made before any adjustments to basis are made for depreciation allowable in the first tax year.

8.16.6. The qualified basis used to compute the low-income rental housing credit may be based on the proportion of the floor space devoted to low-income units.

A. True.

B. False.

Answer (A) is correct. *(Publisher, adapted)*
DISCUSSION: The qualified basis amounts are computed as the proportion of eligible basis in a qualified low-income building attributable to the low-income rental units. This proportion is the lesser of the proportion of low-income units to all residential rental units, or the proportion of floor space of the low-income units to the floor space of all residential rental units [Sec. 42(c)].

8.16.7. The eligible basis of low-income rental housing includes the cost of land.

A. True.

B. False.

Answer (B) is correct. *(Publisher, adapted)*
DISCUSSION: Eligible basis is the adjusted basis of a new building or the adjusted basis of existing buildings attributable to the cost of acquisition and the cost of rehabilitation, if any, incurred before the close of the first taxable year of the credit. It excludes the cost of land.

8.17 Limitations and Carryovers of the General Business Credit

8.17.1. The maximum amount of income tax liability that can be offset by the General Business Credit is limited to

A. 100% of net income tax liability.

B. 100% of the first $25,000 of net income tax liability and 75% of the amount in excess of $25,000.

C. 100% of excess of net income tax liability over tentative minimum tax amount.

D. 100% of excess of net income tax liability over the greater of (1) the tentative minimum tax amount or (2) 25% of the net regular tax liability in excess of $25,000.

Answer (D) is correct. *(Publisher, adapted)*
REQUIRED: The General Business Credit limitation.
DISCUSSION: The maximum amount of General Business Credit that may be used to offset an income tax liability is 100% of the taxpayer's net income tax over the greater of (1) the tentative minimum tax for the taxable year or (2) 25% of the taxpayer's net regular tax liability exceeding $25,000 [Sec. 38(c)(1)]. The term "net income tax" includes the sum of the regular tax liability and the alternative minimum tax reduced by certain allowable credits.
Answer (A) is incorrect. The maximum amount of income tax liability that can be offset by the General Business Credit is not limited to 100% of net income tax liability. Answer (B) is incorrect. The maximum amount of income tax liability that can be offset by the General Business Credit is not 100% of the first $25,000 of net income tax liability and 75% of the amount in excess of $25,000. Answer (C) is incorrect. The maximum amount of income tax liability that can be offset by the General Business Credit is not limited to 100% of excess net income tax liability over the tentative minimum tax amount.

8.17.2. All of the following credits are applied against income tax before the General Business Credit can be allowed except

A. Credit for household and dependent care.

B. Foreign tax credit.

C. Earned income credit.

D. Interest on home mortgage credit.

Answer (C) is correct. *(SEE, adapted)*
REQUIRED: The tax credit that is not applied against income tax before the General Business Credit can be allowed.
DISCUSSION: Section 38(c)(1) defines the limitation on the General Business Credit and states that the credit shall not exceed the excess of the taxpayer's net income tax over the greater of (1) the tentative minimum tax or (2) 25% of the taxpayer's net regular tax liability exceeding $25,000. Net income tax liability is defined as the sum of the regular tax liability plus the alternative minimum tax reduced by the sum of nonrefundable personal credits and the Foreign Tax Credit. The Earned Income Credit is a refundable personal credit and is applied after the General Business Credit.
Answer (A) is incorrect. The credit for household and dependent care is a nonrefundable personal credit subtracted from the income tax liability to obtain the net income tax liability. Answer (B) is incorrect. The Foreign Tax Credit is subtracted before the General Business Credit. Answer (D) is incorrect. The interest on home mortgage credit is a nonrefundable personal credit subtracted from the income tax liability to obtain the net income tax liability.

8.17.3. During the current year, Frank had a General Business Credit of $80,000. His regular (income) tax liability was $41,000, and his tentative minimum tax figured on Form 6251 was $5,000. What is the maximum amount of General Business Credit Frank can claim in the current year?

A. $36,000

B. $37,000

C. $41,000

D. $80,000

Answer (A) is correct. *(SEE, adapted)*
REQUIRED: The maximum general tax credit that may be taken in the current year.
DISCUSSION: Section 38(c) states that the General Business Credit is limited to the taxpayer's net income tax over the greater of (1) the tentative minimum tax for the taxable year or (2) 25% of the net regular tax liability exceeding $25,000. Applying this formula, Frank's General Business Credit is $41,000 minus the greater of (1) $5,000 or (2) ($41,000 – $25,000) × 25% = $4,000; therefore, Frank's General Business Credit limitation is $41,000 – $5,000 = $36,000.
Answer (B) is incorrect. The figure of $37,000 is not the correct maximum amount of General Business Credit Frank can claim in the current year. Answer (C) is incorrect. The amount of $41,000 should be reduced by the greater of the $5,000 tentative minimum tax or 25% of the net regular tax liability exceeding $25,000. Answer (D) is incorrect. The amount of $80,000 is the General Business Credit that Frank had for the current year, which ignores the limit that he may claim this year.

8.17.4. Celaine, a calendar-year taxpayer, hired two employees from a targeted group on April 1 of the current year. In the current year, the employees each received $14,000 in qualified wages. Celaine has no unused work opportunity credit carried over into the current year. How much of the work opportunity credit is usable in the current year if Celaine had a regular tax liability before credits of $8,000, a tentative minimum tax amount of zero, and a research credit of $2,100?

A. $4,800

B. $5,900

C. $6,000

D. $8,000

Answer (A) is correct. *(SEE, adapted)*
REQUIRED: The allowable amount of work opportunity credit.
DISCUSSION: Under Sec. 51, the work opportunity credit is 40% of the first $6,000 of wages paid to each qualified employee during the first year of service. Therefore, Celaine's tentative work opportunity credit is $4,800 (2 × $6,000 × 40%).
Section 38 combines the work opportunity credit, the research credit, and several other credits as one General Business Credit. The credit allowed is limited to the taxpayer's net income tax over the greater of (1) the tentative minimum tax or (2) 25% of the taxpayer's net regular tax liability exceeding $25,000. Celaine's General Business Credit is thus limited to $8,000 ($8,000 − $0). Her entire $4,800 work opportunity credit is usable because her total General Business Credit of $6,900 ($4,800 + $2,100) is less than the $8,000 limit.
Answer (B) is incorrect. The figure of $5,900 is the incorrect amount of the usable work opportunity credit. Answer (C) is incorrect. The figure of $6,000 is the incorrect amount of the usable work opportunity credit. Answer (D) is incorrect. The figure of $8,000 is the incorrect amount of the usable work opportunity credit.

8.17.5. John Rich is a sole proprietor. During the current year, he purchased business property for $71,000 that qualifies for a 10% business energy credit. He takes the maximum amount of the business energy credit but makes no Sec. 179 election. He also has a $950 Child Care Credit. If Mr. Rich's regular tax liability before credits is $8,000 and tentative minimum tax amount is zero, how much of the General Business Credit may he use this year?

A. $71,000

B. $8,000

C. $7,100

D. $7,050

Answer (D) is correct. *(Publisher, adapted)*
REQUIRED: The amount of the General Business Credit that may be used along with the Child Care Credit.
DISCUSSION: Rich's energy credit is $7,100 ($71,000 × 10%).
Section 38(c) limits the amount of the General Business Credit to the taxpayer's net income tax over the greater of (1) the tentative minimum tax or (2) 25% of the taxpayer's net regular tax liability exceeding $25,000. Rich's net regular tax liability is the regular tax amount ($8,000), reduced by any nonrefundable personal credits or Foreign Tax Credits. The Child Care Credit is a nonrefundable personal credit, which reduces Rich's net tax liability to $7,050. Rich is limited to $7,050 of General Business Credits, which equals 100% of his net tax liability.
Answer (A) is incorrect. The amount of $71,000 is the price of the property. Answer (B) is incorrect. The amount of $8,000 is the regular tax liability before credits. Answer (C) is incorrect. The amount of $7,100 is the energy credit before applying the limit. This amount must be compared to the net tax liability. The lesser amount is the allowable General Business Credit.

8.17.6. Suppose ATO Corporation could not apply the full amount of its General Business Credit this year because the maximum limitation was reached. The excess credit would

A. Expire and could not be applied to any other years.

B. Only be carried forward 20 years.

C. Be carried back 1 year and carried forward 20 years.

D. Be carried forward 21 years if ATO elects not to carry back the credit.

Answer (C) is correct. *(CMA, adapted)*
REQUIRED: The carryback and carryover rules for the General Business Credit.
DISCUSSION: Section 38 combines several business credits and applies the limitations to them as a General Business Credit. Under Sec. 39, if the General Business Credit for a taxable year exceeds the maximum limit, the excess credit may be carried back 1 tax year preceding the current year and carried forward to each of the 20 tax years following the current year.
Answer (A) is incorrect. The credit does not expire unless it goes unused during the carryback and carryover years. Answer (B) is incorrect. The credit cannot only be carried forward 20 years. Answer (D) is incorrect. The credit cannot be carried forward if ATO elects not to carry back the credit. There is no election in this case.

8.17.7. Ms. T, a calendar-year taxpayer, has $3,500 of unused General Business Credit for Year 2 available as a carryback to Year 1. Her income tax for Year 1 was $2,500, and her General Business Credit for Year 1 was $1,000. What amount of the unused credit from Year 2 can be used in Year 1?

A. $250

B. $500

C. $1,000

D. $1,500

Answer (D) is correct. *(SEE, adapted)*
REQUIRED: The unused General Business Credit from Year 2 that may be used in Year 1.
DISCUSSION: Section 38 combines several business credits and applies the limitations to them as a General Business Credit. Section 39 provides that any unused General Business Credit is to be carried back 1 year and forward 20 years. In each year, carryovers are used first, then current business credits, and lastly carrybacks.
In Year 1, Ms. T had a tax liability of $2,500, which was offset by a $1,000 general business tax credit for that year. This leaves $1,500 of tax liability to which the Year 2 tax credit may be applied. The remaining $2,000 of unused credit may be carried forward for 20 years.
Answer (A) is incorrect. The figure of $250 is not the correct amount of unused credit. Answer (B) is incorrect. The figure of $500 is not the correct amount of unused credit. Answer (C) is incorrect. The amount of $1,000 is Ms. T's General Business Credit for Year 1. It is not the correct amount of unused credit.

Use **Gleim Test Prep** for interactive study and easy-to-use detailed analytics!

STUDY UNIT NINE
BASIS

9.1 Purchased Property

9.1.1. During the current year, Mrs. Brown paid $15,000 for the demolition of a warehouse she was using in her business. At the time of the destruction, Mrs. Brown had an adjusted basis in the warehouse of $25,000 and a basis of $12,000 in the land where the warehouse stood. How should Mrs. Brown treat the cost of demolishing the warehouse for federal income tax purposes?

A. $15,000 business expense; $25,000 recognized loss.

B. $15,000 business expense; $25,000 addition to basis of land.

C. $40,000 business expense.

D. $40,000 addition to basis of land.

Answer (D) is correct. *(SEE, adapted)*
 REQUIRED: The tax treatment for demolishing a warehouse.
 DISCUSSION: All costs associated with demolishing structures (and any losses sustained) must be allocated to the land (Sec. 280B). The original cost of the warehouse is added to the basis of the land.

Cost of warehouse	$25,000
Cost of demolition	15,000
Addition to basis of land	$40,000

 Answer (A) is incorrect. The cost of demolishing the warehouse should not be treated as a business expense and a recognized loss for federal income tax purposes. Answer (B) is incorrect. Although Mrs. Brown paid $15,000 to have the warehouse demolished, she does not have a $15,000 business expense as a result. Answer (C) is incorrect. Mrs. Brown does not have a $40,000 business expense resulting from demolishing the warehouse.

9.1.2. Mr. Y purchased a high-volume drug store on January 1 of the current year for a lump-sum price of $963,000 with no liabilities assumed. The fair market values of the assets at the time of the purchase were as follows:

Cash	$200,000
U.S. government securities	250,000
Furniture	56,000
Building	115,000
Equipment	302,000

Mr. Y intends to operate the drug store using the same name as before the purchase. What is Mr. Y's basis for goodwill or going concern value?

A. $0

B. $40,000

C. $96,300

D. $115,560

Answer (B) is correct. *(SEE, adapted)*
 REQUIRED: The basis for goodwill on going concern value acquired as part of the purchase price of a going concern.
 DISCUSSION: Under Sec. 1060, both the buyer and seller involved in a transfer of assets that amount to a trade or business must allocate the purchase price among the assets using the "residual method." The residual method requires the purchase price first to be allocated to cash and cash equivalents; then to near cash items, such as CDs and government securities and other marketable securities; then to accounts receivable, mortgages, and credit card receivables; then to stock in dealer inventory or property held for sale in the ordinary course of business; then to assets not already listed; and then to all Sec. 197 intangibles, except goodwill and going concern value. Any remaining purchase price is allocated to goodwill and/or going concern value.
 In this case, Mr. Y's purchase price of $963,000 is in excess of the fair market value of all the assets listed ($923,000). Therefore, the purchase price is allocated to each asset listed based on its fair market value and the remaining $40,000 ($963,000 purchase price – $923,000 listed assets) is allocated to goodwill or going concern value. The purchased goodwill is amortizable under Sec. 197 over a 15-year period.
 Section 1060 also provides that the transferor and transferee may agree in writing as to the allocation of consideration, or as to the fair market value of any assets. This agreement is binding on the transferor and transferee unless determined inappropriate by the IRS.
 Answer (A) is incorrect. A basis for the goodwill exists. Answer (C) is incorrect. This amount is 10% of the lump-sum price. It is not the basis for goodwill. Answer (D) is incorrect. This amount is 12% of the purchase price.

9.1.3. Mr. Black purchased his first house in March for $41,000. In addition, Mr. Black incurred the following expenses:

$360 for 3 years of casualty insurance
$820 for new driveway
$250 for interior painting
$145 for title insurance
$400 for exterior painting
$405 for new gutters

What is Mr. Black's basis in this house?

   A. $42,225

   B. $42,370

   C. $42,730

   D. $43,020

Answer (B) is correct. *(SEE, adapted)*
   REQUIRED: The purchaser's basis in a house after incurring purchase costs and repair expenses.
   DISCUSSION: Under Sec. 1012, the basis of property is the cost of the property. In addition, basis includes expenditures for major improvements and costs to acquire title. The costs that are not capitalized are the casualty insurance, the interior painting, and the exterior painting. Painting is usually considered ordinary maintenance. Furthermore, these costs are not deductible unless the house is rental property, i.e., unless the costs were incurred for the production of income. Basis is computed as follows:

Purchase price	$41,000
New driveway	820
Title insurance	145
New gutters	405
Basis in house	$42,370

   Answer (A) is incorrect. The basis of the house includes the title insurance. Answer (C) is incorrect. The 3 years of casualty insurance is a nondeductible expense and is not included in basis. Answer (D) is incorrect. Basis does not include the cost of interior and exterior painting.

9.1.4. On January 1 of the current year, Joe purchased new car wash equipment for use in his service station business. Joe's costs in connection with the purchase were as follows:

Cost of the equipment	$43,000
Sales tax on the equipment	3,000
Delivery charges	800
Installation and testing charges	2,000
Current year personal property taxes	1,100

What is the amount of Joe's basis in the car wash equipment?

   A. $45,800

   B. $46,100

   C. $48,800

   D. $49,900

Answer (C) is correct. *(SEE, adapted)*
   REQUIRED: The basis in equipment acquired by purchase.
   DISCUSSION: Under Sec. 1012, the basis of property is the cost of the property. Sales tax paid in connection with the acquisition of property is treated as a cost of the property [Sec. 164(a)]. Delivery, installation, and testing charges are also included as part of the cost of the property. Basis is computed as follows:

Purchase price	$43,000
Sales tax	3,000
Delivery charges	800
Installation and testing charges	2,000
Basis in equipment	$48,800

   Answer (A) is incorrect. The sales tax is included as part of the cost of the property. Answer (B) is incorrect. This amount of basis would incorrectly include the personal property taxes and ignore the delivery charges and sales tax as part of the cost of property. Answer (D) is incorrect. Personal property taxes are not treated as a cost of the property.

9.1.5. Mary purchased stock for $5,000 from her brother Tom. Tom had a basis in the stock of $9,000 but could not recognize his loss on the sale. Mary's basis in the stock is

   A. $1,000

   B. $4,000

   C. $5,000

   D. $9,000

Answer (C) is correct. *(Publisher, adapted)*
   REQUIRED: The purchaser's basis in property acquired from a related party who could not recognize a loss.
   DISCUSSION: A loss on the sale of property to a related party (including siblings) cannot be recognized (Sec. 267). Nevertheless, the purchaser's basis is his or her cost and is not affected by the nonrecognized loss. Mary's basis is $5,000. On a subsequent sale, Mary's gain will be recognized only to the extent it exceeds Tom's unrecognized loss (i.e., since Tom's unrecognized loss is $4,000, if Mary sells the stock for $10,000, her realized gain is $5,000, but she will only recognize $1,000 of it).
   Answer (A) is incorrect. The $5,000 purchase price is not reduced by Tom's $4,000 disallowed loss. Answer (B) is incorrect. This amount is Tom's unrecognized loss and does not affect Mary's basis in the stock. Answer (D) is incorrect. Tom's basis in the stock is $9,000.

9.1.6. The basis of property acquired by purchase includes all of the following except

A. Amount paid in notes to the seller.

B. Freight, installation, and testing charges.

C. Unstated interest on any time-payment plan.

D. Sales tax charged on the purchase.

Answer (C) is correct. *(SEE, adapted)*
REQUIRED: The costs that should be included in the basis of property acquired by purchase.
DISCUSSION: The basis of purchased property does not include unstated interest on time-payment plans. Interest is deductible as an expense.
Answer (A) is incorrect. The amount paid in notes to the seller is part of the cost of the property. Answer (B) is incorrect. Freight, installation, and testing charges are acquisition costs included as part of the cost of the property. Answer (D) is incorrect. Sales tax paid in connection with the acquisition of property is treated as a cost of the property [Sec. 164(a)].

9.1.7. Kathy purchased the Blue Restaurant, an operating business, from Mr. Hungry for $180,000. The following items were included in Kathy's purchase:

Cash	$ 20,000
Inventory	20,000
Equipment	80,000
Real estate	100,000

What is Kathy's basis in the real estate? The inventory, equipment, and real estate are stated at their fair market value.

A. $60,000

B. $70,000

C. $77,778

D. $81,818

Answer (C) is correct. *(SEE, adapted)*
REQUIRED: The allocation of a lump-sum purchase price to real estate.
DISCUSSION: Under Sec. 1060, both the buyer and seller involved in a transfer of assets that amount to a trade or business must allocate the purchase price among the assets using the "residual method." The residual method requires the purchase price first to be allocated to cash and cash equivalents; then to near cash items, such as CDs and government securities and other marketable securities; then to accounts receivable, mortgages, and credit card receivables; then to stock in dealer inventory or property held for sale in the ordinary course of business; then to assets not already listed; and then to all Sec. 197 intangibles, except goodwill and going concern value. Any remaining purchase price is allocated to goodwill and/or going concern value.
In this case, Kathy paid $180,000, which is less than the total fair market value of the assets ($220,000). Twenty thousand is first allocated to cash. The next category is inventory. There is a remaining available purchase price of $160,000, so $20,000 is allocated to inventory. Equipment and real estate are in the same class. Their combined FMV is $180,000 and only $140,000 of the purchase price remains to be allocated to the equipment and the real estate.

$$\frac{\$100,000}{\$180,000} \times \$140,000 = \$77,778$$

Section 1060 also provides that the transferor and transferee may agree in writing as to the allocation of consideration, or as to the fair market value of any assets. This agreement is binding on the transferor and transferee unless determined inappropriate by the IRS.
Answer (A) is incorrect. The amount of $60,000 is 60% of the FMV of the real estate. Answer (B) is incorrect. The amount of $70,000 is 70% of the FMV of the real estate. Answer (D) is incorrect. The amount of $81,818 is the $180,000 purchase price times the fraction of FMV of the real estate divided by the total FMV of cash and noncash assets.

9.1.8. The uniform capitalization method must be used by

I. Manufacturers of tangible personal property

II. Retailers of personal property with $2 million in average annual gross receipts for the 3 preceding years

A. I only.

B. II only.

C. Both I and II.

D. Neither I nor II.

Answer (A) is correct. *(CPA, adapted)*
REQUIRED: The taxpayers required to use UNICAP rules.
DISCUSSION: A taxpayer that produces tangible personal property must capitalize all the direct costs of producing the property and an allocable share of indirect costs regardless of whether the property is sold or used in the taxpayer's trade or business. A retailer that acquires property for resale must capitalize the costs unless the taxpayer's annual gross receipts for the 3 preceding years do not exceed $10 million.
Answer (B) is incorrect. The UNICAP method is not required for retailers of personal property with $2 million in average annual gross receipts for the 3 preceding years. Answer (C) is incorrect. Both groups of taxpayers do not have to use the UNICAP rules. Answer (D) is incorrect. One of the groups of taxpayers must use the UNICAP rules.

9.1.9. Mr. A constructed a factory building costing $1.5 million for use in his business. The construction started on January 2 of Year 1 and was completed and placed in service on July 1 of Year 2. During the construction period, Mr. A incurred and paid interest and real property taxes of $10,000 attributable to the construction. Mr. A must

A. Amortize the $10,000 over a 10-year period starting in Year 1.

B. Amortize the $10,000 over a 10-year period starting in Year 2.

C. Capitalize the $10,000 as part of the building cost. Recover the costs by claiming MACRS depreciation on the building.

D. Capitalize the $10,000 as part of the land cost.

Answer (C) is correct. *(SEE, adapted)*
REQUIRED: The correct treatment of interest and real property taxes during construction of property to be used in a business.
DISCUSSION: Prior to 1987, construction period interest and taxes were amortizable over a 10-year period. However, after 1986, no amortization is allowed and Sec. 263A requires production costs (direct and indirect) to be capitalized. Therefore, the construction period interest and taxes must be capitalized as part of the building cost.
Answer (A) is incorrect. Production costs must be capitalized. Answer (B) is incorrect. Construction period interest and taxes are no longer amortizable over a 10-year period. Answer (D) is incorrect. The construction period interest and taxes should not be capitalized as part of the land.

9.1.10. Mr. X constructed a building in the first quarter of the current year for use in his business. The costs that he incurred were as follows:

Land	$25,000
Wages paid to employees for construction of building	30,000
Building materials	40,000
Architect's fees	10,000
Building permit fees	3,000
Equipment rental for construction	7,000

Mr. X had an allowable work opportunity credit of $1,000 on the wages paid to employees for construction of the building. What is Mr. X's basis in the building?

A. $60,000

B. $89,000

C. $114,000

D. $115,000

Answer (B) is correct. *(SEE, adapted)*
REQUIRED: The costs that should be included in the basis of a constructed building.
DISCUSSION: Under Sec. 1012, the basis of property is defined as its cost. When property is constructed, the cost includes all expenditures necessary to prepare the building for its intended use. The uniform capitalization rules of Sec. 263A apply to the construction of real or tangible personal property to be used in a business. These rules require capitalization of all direct costs and an allocable portion of most indirect costs. Costs (other than the cost of the land) to be capitalized are those for the building materials, compensation paid to the employees constructing the building, rent for equipment used in construction, the architect's fee, and the building permit fees. These costs total $90,000. However, the wages must be reduced by the work opportunity credit that applies to them. Therefore, Mr. X's basis in the building is $89,000 ($90,000 – $1,000 work opportunity credit).
Answer (A) is incorrect. The basis of the building should also include wages paid to construct the building less the work opportunity credit claimed. Answer (C) is incorrect. The basis of the building should not include the basis of the land. Answer (D) is incorrect. The basis of the building does not include the basis of the land and the work opportunity credit claimed should be deducted from the amount of the wages included in the building's basis.

9.1.11. JCN Enterprises exchanged 30% of the stock of a closely held corporation that it owns for improved real property. The real property had a fair market value of $100,000 and an adjusted basis of $75,000 at the date of the exchange. The fair market value of the stock is unknown, although the shareholder's basis was $10,000 at the date of the exchange. What is JCN's basis in the real property after the exchange?

A. $10,000

B. $75,000

C. $100,000

D. $110,000

Answer (C) is correct. *(Publisher, adapted)*
REQUIRED: The basis of property acquired in an exchange when the fair market value of the assets given up is not known.
DISCUSSION: The basis of property is generally its cost (Sec. 1012). In an exchange, the cost of the property acquired is the fair market value of the property given up. If the fair market value of the property given up is not known, it is assumed to be the same as the fair market value of the property received when the transaction is at arm's-length. Since the value of the stock used to buy the land is not known, the value of the stock is assumed to be the fair market value of the property purchased. Therefore, JCN Enterprises will have a basis in the land of $100,000.
JCN will also have a gain of $90,000 ($100,000 received – $10,000 basis) on the disposition of the stock. This transaction is not tax-free because the properties are not like-kind.
Answer (A) is incorrect. This amount is the basis of the stock in JCN's hands. Answer (B) is incorrect. This amount is the adjusted basis of the real property on the seller's books on the date of the exchange. Answer (D) is incorrect. The basis of the real property does not include JCN's basis for the stock and the FMV of the real estate.

9.1.12. Ms. F had an old truck that was not used in her business or held for investment purposes. It had an original cost of $2,700. She traded in the truck on a new one costing $12,800. The dealer allowed Ms. F $4,000, the truck's fair market value, on the old truck, and Ms. F paid $8,800 in cash. What is Ms. F's basis in the new truck that, like the old truck, will not be used in her business or held for investment purposes?

A. $6,700

B. $8,800

C. $11,500

D. $12,800

Answer (D) is correct. *(SEE, adapted)*
REQUIRED: The basis of personal-use property acquired in an exchange.
DISCUSSION: The basis of property is generally its cost (Sec. 1012). In the case of a taxable exchange of property, the cost is the value of the property given up plus any additional cash paid. Ms. F's basis in the new truck is the $4,000 fair market value of the old truck plus $8,800 cash, for a total of $12,800.
Ms. F will also have a gain of $1,300 ($4,000 received for old truck – $2,700 basis). This exchange is taxable because neither the old or new truck was used in a trade or business or held for investment purposes.
Answer (A) is incorrect. The basis of the old truck plus the trade-in value of the old truck is $6,700. Answer (B) is incorrect. The difference between the trade-in value of the old truck and the cost of the new truck is $8,800. Answer (C) is incorrect. The adjusted basis of the truck given up plus any additional cash paid is $11,500.

9.1.13. Mr. G bought 100 shares of Corporation H stock in Year 1 for $5,000. In Year 2, he bought another 100 shares for $11,000. In Year 3, Mr. G gave his son 50 shares he had purchased in Year 2 and purchased an additional 100 shares for $9,000. In Year 5, Mr. G sold 220 shares for $22,500. Mr. G was unable to identify the specific shares sold. What was Mr. G's basis in the 220 shares that were sold?

A. $16,800

B. $17,160

C. $17,800

D. $22,500

Answer (A) is correct. *(SEE, adapted)*
REQUIRED: The basis in shares of stock purchased in several blocks when the shares cannot be specifically identified.
DISCUSSION: Regulation 1.1012-1(c)(1) provides that, if the taxpayer cannot specifically identify the blocks being sold, the taxpayer must assume that the shares of stock are sold using the first-in, first-out (FIFO) basis. Therefore, Mr. G must assume that 100 of his shares were those purchased in Year 1, 50 were of those purchased in Year 2 since he had given away 50 of those that could be specifically identified to the purchase, and the remaining 70 shares were part of those purchased in Year 3 for $9,000. The computation is below.

100 shares	$ 5,000
50 shares ($11,000 × 50%)	5,500
70 shares ($9,000 × 70%)	6,300
Total basis	$16,800

Answer (B) is incorrect. The average cost method may not be used to determine the basis of the shares sold. Answer (C) is incorrect. Only 50 of the shares purchased in Year 2 were available for sale. Answer (D) is incorrect. The amount of money received for the shares is $22,500.

9.1.14. In Year 1, Hilary Leary purchased three blocks of XYZ Company common stock as follows: March 1, 100 shares at $50 per share; June 15, 100 shares at $55; October 1, 100 shares at $60. On January 15 of Year 4, Hilary sold 200 shares at a price of $70 per share. Under IRS regulations, which two of the following cost flow assumptions are acceptable in determining the cost basis to be used in measuring Leary's gain on the sale?

A. FIFO or LIFO.

B. Specific identification or weighted average.

C. FIFO or weighted average.

D. Specific identification or FIFO.

Answer (D) is correct. *(D.B. Bradley)*
REQUIRED: The cost flow methods acceptable for determining the basis to be used in measuring a gain on the sale of stock.
DISCUSSION: Regulation 1.1012-1(c)(1) provides that, if the taxpayer can specifically identify the lots being sold, this method may be used. If they cannot be specifically identified, the taxpayer must assume that they are being sold on the first-in, first-out (FIFO) basis.
Answer (A) is incorrect. The LIFO method may not be used to determine cost basis when selling stock. Answer (B) is incorrect. Weighted average may not be used to determine cost basis when selling stock. Answer (C) is incorrect. Under IRS regulations, both of these cost flow assumptions cannot be used to determine cost basis when selling stock.

9.1.15. Mr. G purchased a tract of land. In order to have city water, he had to pay the water company $5,000 to extend the water line to his property. The $5,000 cost is an addition to the basis of the land.

A. True.

B. False.

Answer (A) is correct. *(SEE, adapted)*
DISCUSSION: Expenditures chargeable to capital are adjustments to basis under Sec. 1016. Since the $5,000 cost for the extended water line would be charged to capital, it is an addition to the basis of the land.

9.1.16. Mr. B purchased a new automobile for $8,000. He received a $1,000 cash rebate from the auto manufacturer. Mr. B should report the $1,000 as taxable income.

    A. True.

    B. False.

Answer (B) is correct. *(SEE, adapted)*
    DISCUSSION: Cash rebates received by a purchaser of property are treated as a reduction in purchase price rather than income. Therefore, Mr. B's basis in the new automobile is $7,000 ($8,000 cost – $1,000 cash rebate).

9.1.17. Mr. B bought land and a building to be used in his business. In connection with this acquisition, he paid $50,000 to the seller as the purchase price of the property, $5,000 to his attorney for reviewing the purchase contract, and $3,000 to the seller for property taxes incurred up to the date of sale. Mr. B's cost basis in the property is $58,000.

    A. True.

    B. False.

Answer (A) is correct. *(SEE, adapted)*
    DISCUSSION: Section 1012 defines the basis of property as its cost. The cost Mr. B incurred in acquiring the land was the $50,000 purchase price, plus $5,000 in attorney's fees and $3,000 for prior property taxes. The property taxes are an acquisition cost and are not deductible because they were pre-purchase taxes not allocated to Mr. B [Sec. 164(a)]. Mr. B's cost basis in the property is $58,000.

9.1.18. The cost of renting construction equipment to build a storage facility for use in your business must be capitalized as part of the cost of the building.

    A. True.

    B. False.

Answer (A) is correct. *(SEE, adapted)*
    DISCUSSION: The uniform capitalization rules of Sec. 263A apply to the construction of real or tangible personal property to be used in a trade or business. The uniform capitalization rules require all direct costs to be capitalized as well as an allocable portion of most indirect costs. The cost of renting construction equipment must be capitalized as part of the cost of the completed building and expensed through depreciation.

9.1.19. The basis for nonbusiness property changed to business use is the greater of the adjusted basis of the property or its fair market value on the date it is converted to business use.

    A. True.

    B. False.

Answer (B) is correct. *(SEE, adapted)*
    DISCUSSION: When nonbusiness property is converted to business use, its basis for determining loss or depreciation is the lesser of the adjusted basis of the property or its fair market value at the date of conversion [Regs. 1.165-9 and 1.167(g)]. There is no similar provision for determining gains, so the basis for gain is the adjusted basis.

9.2 Property Received by Gift

9.2.1. During the current year, Joey received a gift of property from his uncle. At the time of the gift, the property had a fair market value of $120,000 and an adjusted basis to his uncle of $80,000. Joey's uncle paid a gift tax on the property of $24,000. Ignoring the effects of the annual exclusion, what is the amount of Joey's basis in the property?

    A. $80,000

    B. $88,000

    C. $104,000

    D. $128,000

Answer (B) is correct. *(SEE, adapted)*
    REQUIRED: The donee's basis in property on which gift tax was paid.
    DISCUSSION: The basis of property acquired by gift is generally the donor's adjusted basis [Sec. 1015(a)], increased by any gift tax paid applicable to appreciation [Sec. 1015(d)]. The gift tax applicable to appreciation is the appreciation divided by the taxable gift times the gift tax.

Donor's adjusted basis	$80,000
Gift tax*	8,000
Donee's basis	$88,000

$$\frac{\$120,000 - 80,000}{\$120,000} \times \$24,000 = \$8,000^*$$

    Answer (A) is incorrect. The basis must be increased by the gift tax. Answer (C) is incorrect. Only a portion of the gift tax is added to the donor's adjusted basis. Answer (D) is incorrect. The donee's basis is not figured by the fair market value.

9.2.2. Mr. R received bonds as a gift from his mother. At the time of the gift, the bonds had a fair market value of $5,000 and an adjusted basis to R's mother of $6,000. No gift tax was paid. Six months later, R sold the bonds for $6,500. What was R's basis in the bonds for computing gain?

A. $0

B. $5,000

C. $6,000

D. $6,500

Answer (C) is correct. *(SEE, adapted)*
REQUIRED: The donee's basis for computing gain in property received as a gift.
DISCUSSION: The basis of property acquired by gift is generally the donor's adjusted basis [Sec. 1015(a)]. Since the property had a basis in the mother's hands of $6,000, Mr. R's basis in the property is the same. No basis adjustment is required for gift taxes since none were paid on the transfer [Sec. 1015(d)]. The basis of the property for loss purposes is its fair market value on the date of the gift, or $5,000.
Answer (A) is incorrect. A donor's basis exists for the bonds. Answer (B) is incorrect. The FMV on the date of the gift is $5,000. This is the basis of the property for loss purposes. Answer (D) is incorrect. The amount that the bonds were sold for 6 months later is $6,500.

Questions 9.2.3 through 9.2.5 are based on the following information. Laura's father, Albert, gave Laura a gift of 500 shares of Liba Corporation common stock in the current year. Albert's basis for the Liba stock was $4,000. At the date of this gift, the fair market value of the Liba stock was $3,000. No gift tax was paid with respect to the transfer.

9.2.3. If Laura sold the 500 shares of Liba stock in the current year for $5,000, her basis is

A. $5,000

B. $4,000

C. $3,000

D. $0

Answer (B) is correct. *(CPA, adapted)*
REQUIRED: The basis of property acquired by gift and sold at a gain.
DISCUSSION: The basis of property acquired by gift is generally the donor's adjusted basis, plus any gift tax attributable to appreciation (Sec. 1015). This rule applies when the donee determines any gain on a sale of the property. Since no gift tax was paid attributable to appreciation, Laura's basis is the same as her father's, or $4,000.
Answer (A) is incorrect. The amount for which Laura sold the Liba stock is $5,000. Answer (C) is incorrect. The FMV of the Liba stock at the date of the gift is $3,000. Answer (D) is incorrect. Laura has basis in the Liba stock.

9.2.4. If Laura sold the 500 shares of Liba stock in the current year for $2,000, her basis is

A. $4,000

B. $3,000

C. $2,000

D. $0

Answer (B) is correct. *(CPA, adapted)*
REQUIRED: The basis of property acquired by gift and sold at a loss.
DISCUSSION: The basis of property acquired by gift is usually the donor's adjusted basis, plus any gift tax applicable to appreciation (Sec. 1015). For determining loss, however, the basis may not exceed the fair market value of the property at the time of the gift. Since the donor's adjusted basis ($4,000) was greater than the fair market value ($3,000), basis is limited to $3,000.
Answer (A) is incorrect. Laura's father's basis in the stock is $4,000. Answer (C) is incorrect. The amount for which Laura sold the stock is $2,000. Answer (D) is incorrect. Laura has basis in the stock.

9.2.5. If Laura sold the 500 shares of Liba stock in the current year for $3,500, what is the reportable gain or loss in the current year?

A. $3,500 gain.

B. $500 gain.

C. $500 loss.

D. $0 gain or loss.

Answer (D) is correct. *(CPA, adapted)*
REQUIRED: The amount of gain (loss) to be reported upon the sale of property acquired by gift.
DISCUSSION: For determining gain on the sale of property acquired by gift, the basis is the donor's adjusted basis. Laura's sale results in no gain ($3,500 sales price – $4,000 basis = no gain). For determining loss on the sale of property acquired by gift, the basis may not exceed the fair market value of the property at the date of the gift. Hence, there is no loss ($3,500 sales price – $3,000 basis = no loss).
Answer (A) is incorrect. Laura does not have a $3,500 gain from the stock sale. Answer (B) is incorrect. Laura does not have a $500 gain from selling the stock. Answer (C) is incorrect. Laura does not have a $500 loss from the stock sale.

9.2.6. Esther gave an old truck to Lamont for use in his business. Esther's basis in the truck was $2,000 and its fair market value on the date of the gift was $500. Esther paid $90 of gift tax on the transaction. What is Lamont's basis for depreciation?

- A. $500
- B. $590
- C. $2,000
- D. $2,090

Answer (A) is correct. *(Publisher, adapted)*
REQUIRED: The basis in property received as a gift when its fair market value is less than basis and it is converted to business use.
DISCUSSION: Under Sec. 1015, the basis of property received as a gift is the donor's basis prior to the gift. However, if the fair market value is less than the donor's basis, the basis for purposes of computing a loss is the fair market value on the date of the gift. This basis is increased by the amount of gift tax paid attributable to the appreciation in the value of the gift. Since there was no appreciation in the value of the gift, no part of the gift tax may be added to basis.
For purposes of depreciation, the basis of property received by gift is the basis for gain. In this case, that is $2,000. Property Regulation 1.168-2(j)(6) provides, however, that the basis of property that has not been used in a trade or business and that is converted to such use is the fair market value on such date if less than the adjusted basis. For purposes of depreciation, Lamont's basis in the truck is $500.
Answer (B) is incorrect. The basis does not include the gift tax, since there was no appreciation on the donor's gift. Answer (C) is incorrect. Esther's adjusted basis in the truck is $2,000. Answer (D) is incorrect. Esther's adjusted basis plus the gift tax is $2,090.

9.2.7. In the current year, Mr. B received a gift of rental property that had a fair market value of $10,000 at the time of the gift. The donor's adjusted basis (net of previously claimed depreciation) in the property at the time of the gift was $12,000. Mr. B's basis for computing depreciation is $12,000.

- A. True.
- B. False.

Answer (A) is correct. *(SEE, adapted)*
DISCUSSION: Section 1015 provides that the basis of property acquired by gift is the donor's adjusted basis plus the gift tax paid applicable to the appreciation. Since there was no appreciation, there was no addition to basis for gift tax. Therefore, Mr. B's basis is $12,000. For purposes of depreciation, the basis of property received by gift is the basis for gain ($12,000). The limitation of basis to fair market value only applies to determine loss in this situation, not to compute depreciation, since the property was previously used by the transferor as a rental property.

9.2.8. Brent received a gift of Sec. 1250 property from his grandfather. The basis of this property is reduced by the depreciation that was either allowed or allowable to his grandfather. Therefore, Brent must attach a separate statement to his return for the year he received the gift to indicate how his basis in the property was determined.

- A. True.
- B. False.

Answer (A) is correct. *(SEE, adapted)*
DISCUSSION: The basis of property acquired by gift is the donor's adjusted basis. The basis of Sec. 1250 property is adjusted downward for depreciation allowed or allowable. Thus, Brent's basis in the property is equal to his grandfather's basis less the depreciation. Brent must indicate how he determined his basis by attaching a statement to his Form 4562 that is part of his tax return.

9.3 Inherited Property

9.3.1. The basis in property inherited from a decedent may be determined as follows:

- A. The decedent's basis plus any inheritance tax paid on the increased value.
- B. The fair market value at the date of death.
- C. The fair market value at an alternate valuation date.
- D. The fair market value at the date of death or the fair market value at an alternative valuation date.

Answer (D) is correct. *(SEE, adapted)*
REQUIRED: The basis of inherited property.
DISCUSSION: The basis of property received from a decedent is generally the fair market value of the property on the date of the decedent's death [Sec. 1014(a)]. If the executor elects the alternate valuation date for the estate tax return, the basis of the assets is their fair market value 6 months after death or the date of sale or distribution, if earlier.
Answer (A) is incorrect. The decedent's basis plus any inheritance tax paid on the increased value is not a correct method for determining basis in inherited property. Answer (B) is incorrect. The fair market value at the date of death is not the only acceptable method that is listed for determining the basis of inherited property. Answer (C) is incorrect. The fair market value at an alternate valuation date is not the only acceptable method that is listed for determining the basis of inherited property.

9.3.2. On August 15 of the current year, Harold received 100 shares of stock as an inheritance from his mother, Mona, who died on January 20. Mona's adjusted basis in the stock was $45,000. The stock had a fair market value of $50,000 on January 20. On July 20, its value was $65,000 and on the date Harold received it, its value was $48,000. The alternative valuation date was not selected. Harold's basis in the inherited stock is

A. $45,000

B. $48,000

C. $50,000

D. $65,000

Answer (C) is correct. *(SEE, adapted)*
REQUIRED: The basis of inherited property when the alternate valuation date is not elected.
DISCUSSION: The basis of property received from a decedent is generally the fair market value of the property on the date of the decedent's death [Sec. 1014(a)]. If the alternate valuation date for the estate tax return is elected by the executor, the basis of the assets is their fair market value 6 months after death. Harold's basis in the stock is the $50,000 fair market value on January 20 (the date of Mona's death).
Answer (A) is incorrect. Mona's adjusted basis is $45,000. Answer (B) is incorrect. The FMV on the date the stock was received is $48,000. Answer (D) is incorrect. The basis if the alternate valuation date had been selected would be $65,000.

9.3.3. Eric Helton inherited 50 shares of stock in an S corporation from his grandfather. At the date of the grandfather's death, the stock was valued at $20 per share. However, $5 of that value was attributed to income in respect to a decedent. What is Helton's basis in the stock?

A. $0

B. $250

C. $750

D. $1,000

Answer (C) is correct. *(Publisher, adapted)*
REQUIRED: The adjusted basis of inherited stock of an S corporation.
DISCUSSION: Under Sec. 1014, the basis of inherited property is its fair market value at the date of death. However, under Sec. 1367(b)(4)(B), the basis is reduced to the extent that the stock's value consists of income in respect of a decedent. Therefore, Eric Helton's adjusted basis in the stock is $750 [50 shares × ($20 – $5)].
Answer (A) is incorrect. Helton has basis in the stock. Answer (B) is incorrect. This amount is the income in respect of a decedent. Answer (D) is incorrect. This amount is the value of the stock at the date of the grandfather's death.

9.3.4. Mr. More inherited 2,000 shares of Corporation Zero stock from his father, who died on March 4 of the current year. His father paid $10 per share for the stock 30 years ago. The fair market value of the stock on the date of death was $50 per share. On September 4 of the same year, the fair market value of the stock was $60 per share. Mr. More sold the stock for $75 per share on December 3 of the same year. The estate qualified for, and the executor elected, the alternate valuation date. A federal estate tax return was filed. What was Mr. More's basis in the stock on the date of the sale?

A. $100,000

B. $120,000

C. $130,000

D. $150,000

Answer (B) is correct. *(SEE, adapted)*
REQUIRED: The basis of inherited property when the alternate valuation date is elected.
DISCUSSION: The basis of property received from a decedent is generally the fair market value of the property on the date of the decedent's death [Sec. 1014(a)]. If the executor elects the alternate valuation date for the estate tax return, the basis of the assets is their fair market value 6 months after death or the date of sale or distribution, if earlier. Mr. More's basis in the stock is the $120,000 fair market value 6 months after his father's death (2,000 shares × $60 per share).
Answer (A) is incorrect. The amount of $100,000 was the value on the date of death, not on the alternate valuation date. Answer (C) is incorrect. The correct per share value of the stock is $60, not $65. Answer (D) is incorrect. The basis is not calculated by using the sales price per share of $75.

9.3.5. Mrs. N inherited property from a decedent where an estate tax return was not required to be filed. The decedent's adjusted basis in the property at the time of death was $75,000. A local real estate agent, qualified as an appraiser, placed a valuation of $100,000 on the property at the date of death. The appraised value for state inheritance tax purposes was $90,000. What is Mrs. N's basis in the property?

A. $100,000

B. $90,000

C. $75,000

D. $0

Answer (B) is correct. *(SEE, adapted)*
REQUIRED: The basis of inherited property when a federal estate tax return is not required to be filed.
DISCUSSION: The basis of property received from a decedent is generally the fair market value of the property on the date of the decedent's death [Sec. 1014(a)]. The value of the property for basis purposes is normally the value as appraised for the federal estate tax return, but if no federal estate tax return is required to be filed, the value as appraised for state inheritance tax purposes is used [Reg. 1.1014-3(a)]. Therefore, the basis is $90,000.
Answer (A) is incorrect. The amount of $100,000 is the value determined by a qualified appraiser. Answer (C) is incorrect. The decedent's adjusted basis is $75,000. Answer (D) is incorrect. Mrs. N has basis in the inherited property.

9.3.6. Hoss McDonald sold his farm for $200,000. He received $50,000 cash at closing and a promissory note for $150,000 to be paid in equal installments over a 10-year period. Hoss reported the income from the sale on the installment method. After collecting the first payment on the note, Hoss died, leaving all his property to his daughter. The fair market value of the promissory note at Hoss's death was $100,000 and its basis was $45,000. A balance of $135,000 plus interest was still due and owing on the note. What is the daughter's basis in the note for the purpose of selling it or collecting on it?

A. $135,000

B. $100,000

C. $45,000

D. $0

Answer (C) is correct. *(Publisher, adapted)*
REQUIRED: The basis of an installment note received from a decedent.
DISCUSSION: Normally, the basis of property received from a decedent is the fair market value of the property on the date of the decedent's death [Sec. 1014(a)]. This rule does not apply to income in respect of a decedent [Sec. 1014(c)]. Income in respect of a decedent is income that has been earned or created by a decedent but that is not properly included in his or her final tax return. Installment income is an example of income in respect of a decedent since the sale occurred prior to death but all the income was not properly included in the decedent's final tax return. Accordingly, the daughter's basis in the installment note is the decedent's basis of $45,000.
Answer (A) is incorrect. The amount still due on the note is $135,000. Answer (B) is incorrect. The FMV of the note is $100,000. Answer (D) is incorrect. The daughter has basis in the note.

9.3.7. Ten years ago, Edwin Ryan bought 100 shares of a listed stock for $5,000. In June of the current year, when the stock's fair market value was $7,000, Edwin gave it to his sister, Lynn. No gift tax was paid. Lynn died in October of the same year, bequeathing the stock to Edwin, when the stock's fair market value was $9,000. Lynn's executor did not elect the alternate valuation date. What is Edwin's basis for this stock after he inherits it from Lynn's estate?

A. $0

B. $5,000

C. $7,000

D. $9,000

Answer (B) is correct. *(CPA, adapted)*
REQUIRED: The basis of property received from a decedent when the beneficiary had given it to the decedent within the previous year.
DISCUSSION: Section 1014(a) provides that a person who acquires property from a decedent is generally entitled to a basis equal to the fair market value of the property on the date of death. If, however, appreciated property is acquired by the decedent by gift within 1 year of death and passes back to the donor by reason of the decedent's death, the beneficiary's basis in the property is its adjusted basis immediately prior to the decedent's death [Sec. 1014(e)].
Since Lynn received the stock as a gift from Edwin within 1 year of her death, Edwin assumes Lynn's basis ($5,000), which was Edwin's basis when he made the gift. If someone other than Edwin had received the stock following Lynn's death, its adjusted basis would be $9,000.
Answer (A) is incorrect. Edwin has basis in the inherited stock. Answer (C) is incorrect. This amount is the FMV of the stock on the date of the gift. Answer (D) is incorrect. This amount is the FMV of the stock on the date of death.

9.3.8. Freida Farina purchased a rooming house in Waldo, Florida. In order to avoid probate, Freida took title to the rooming house with her daughter, Farrah, as joint tenants with right of survivorship. Freida paid $10,000 cash and signed a promissory note and mortgage for $40,000. Several years later, Freida died when the house was worth $80,000 and there was still a $30,000 mortgage on the property. What is Farrah's basis in the house?

A. $50,000

B. $65,000

C. $80,000

D. $110,000

Answer (C) is correct. *(Publisher, adapted)*
REQUIRED: The daughter's basis after her mother's death in property that they held as joint tenants with right of survivorship.
DISCUSSION: The basis of property in the hands of a person acquiring the property from a decedent is the fair market value of the property on the date of the decedent's death [Sec. 1014(a)]. Since Farrah already had an interest as a joint tenant, it is not clear what she received from the decedent. However, Sec. 1014(b)(9) provides that property acquired from a decedent by reason of form of ownership acquires a basis equal to its fair market value on the date of the decedent's death to the extent the property is required to be included in the decedent's gross estate. Under Sec. 2040(a), property held jointly by nonspouses is included in the decedent's gross estate unless it can be proven that consideration for the property was provided by another joint tenant. Since Farrah provided no consideration for the property, the entire value will be included in Freida's gross estate. Therefore, Farrah will obtain a basis in the house equal to its fair market value of $80,000 on the date of Freida's death. The amount of the mortgage has no effect on the basis.
Answer (A) is incorrect. The amount paid for the house when they acquired it is $50,000. Answer (B) is incorrect. The amount of $65,000 values one-half of the house at the $25,000 cost on the date it was acquired and the other half at its $40,000 FMV on the date of death. Answer (D) is incorrect. The mortgage on the house does not increase the property's basis.

9.3.9. Donora made a gift of a farm to her daughter with the stipulation that Donora would continue to live on and use the land for the rest of her life. Donora's basis in the farm was $40,000 and its fair market value was $160,000 at the date of the gift. When Donora died, the fair market value of the farm was $180,000. The personal representative of the estate elected to value the estate property at the alternate valuation date, 6 months after death. At this date, the fair market value of the farm was $200,000. What is the daughter's basis in the farm?

A. $40,000

B. $160,000

C. $180,000

D. $200,000

Answer (D) is correct. *(Publisher, adapted)*
REQUIRED: The donee's basis in property that was received prior to the donor's death and is included in the donor's gross estate.
DISCUSSION: Section 1014(a) provides that the basis of property received from a decedent is the fair market value of the property on the date of the decedent's death, or on the alternate valuation date if the alternate valuation date is elected. Although the daughter received the gift prior to Donora's death, Sec. 1014(b)(9) provides that property is considered to be acquired from a decedent if the property is required to be included in the decedent's gross estate for estate tax purposes. The farm would be included in Donora's estate under Sec. 2036 because she gave it away without full and adequate consideration and retained the right to use the property for life. Therefore, the daughter is considered to have acquired the farm from a decedent and is entitled to a basis equal to the fair market value of the farm on the alternate valuation date ($200,000).
Answer (A) is incorrect. Donora's basis in the farm is $40,000. Answer (B) is incorrect. The FMV on the date of the gift is $160,000. Answer (C) is incorrect. The $180,000 date of death value would be the basis if the alternate valuation date were not used.

9.3.10. Olympia Husky and her husband, Merlin, lived in Walla Walla, Washington. Their residence was owned by them as community property and has a basis of $60,000. Upon Olympia's death, all her property was bequeathed to Merlin. At the date of death, the fair market value of the residence was $120,000. What is Merlin's basis in the residence?

A. $60,000

B. $75,000

C. $90,000

D. $120,000

Answer (D) is correct. *(Publisher, adapted)*
REQUIRED: The basis to a surviving spouse of property that was community property prior to the decedent's death.
DISCUSSION: Section 1014(a) provides that property acquired from a decedent shall have a basis equal to the fair market value of the property on the date of the decedent's death. Merlin will acquire a basis of $60,000 in the one-half of the property owned by Olympia and bequeathed to him. Section 1014(b)(6) provides that the surviving spouse's one-half share of community property is considered to have been acquired from a decedent (for the purpose of basis) if at least one-half of the entire community property interest was included in the decedent's gross estate. Under Sec. 2031, Olympia's estate would include her one-half share of community property, so Merlin will acquire a basis in his one-half equal to its fair market value on the date of Olympia's death. Merlin's basis in the entire house is $120,000.
Answer (A) is incorrect. The amount of $60,000 is the couple's basis before the wife's death. Answer (B) is incorrect. The amount of $75,000 does not value both spouses' property at its FMV on the date of death. Answer (C) is incorrect. The amount of $90,000 is one-half of the property's basis before the wife's death and one-half of the property's FMV on the date of death.

9.3.11. In Year 1, Mr. Green received a gift of rental property from Mr. Blue. Mr. Blue retained the power to transfer this property to his son in his will. At the time of the gift, Mr. Blue's adjusted basis in the property was $18,000 and its fair market value was $24,000. No gift tax was paid. In Year 1 and Year 2, Mr. Green deducted a total of $2,000 of depreciation. In Year 3, Mr. Blue died but did not exercise his power to transfer the property. The rental property given to Mr. Green was included in the gross estate as a revocable transfer. The value of the rental property for estate tax purposes was the fair market value at Mr. Blue's death, $28,000. What is Mr. Green's basis in the property after Mr. Blue's death?

A. $18,000

B. $22,000

C. $26,000

D. $28,000

Answer (C) is correct. *(SEE, adapted)*
REQUIRED: The basis of property received as a revocable gift before the transferor dies.
DISCUSSION: The basis of property acquired from a decedent is the fair market value of the property at the date of the decedent's death [Sec. 1014(a)]. If the property is acquired before the death of the decedent, the basis is reduced by the depreciation deduction allowed the donee. Mr. Green's basis in the property is

Fair market value at Mr. Blue's death	$28,000
Less depreciation deducted by donee	(2,000)
Basis in the property	$26,000

The property was included in Mr. Blue's taxable estate under Sec. 2038 because he retained the right to revoke the transfer to Mr. Green.
Answer (A) is incorrect. Mr. Blue's adjusted basis at the time of the gift is $18,000. Answer (B) is incorrect. The amount of $22,000 is the FMV on the gift date, reduced by the depreciation claimed by the donee. Answer (D) is incorrect. The FMV on the date of death must be reduced for depreciation claimed by the donee.

9.4 Property Received for Services

9.4.1. Mr. P developed a patent on a machine that could be used in his trade or business. Mr. P made no election to currently deduct any of his developmental expenses. Which of the following expenditures may not be included in the basis of Mr. P's patent?

A. Research expenditures.

B. Drawing fees.

C. Governmental fees.

D. Value of Mr. P's time.

Answer (D) is correct. *(SEE, adapted)*
REQUIRED: The developmental expense that may not be included in the basis of a patent.
DISCUSSION: If no election is made to either expense in the current year or defer and amortize research and experimental expenses, then these expenses are capitalized. Section 1012 defines the basis of property as its cost, and cost is the amount paid for the property in cash or other property. Since Mr. P did not pay for his time in cash or other property, he may not include it in the basis of the patent.
Answer (A) is incorrect. Research expenditures represent an expenditure paid in cash or other property to develop an asset (patent). Therefore, it may be included in the basis of the patent. Answer (B) is incorrect. Drawing fees represent an expenditure paid in cash or other property to develop an asset (patent). Therefore, it may be included in the basis of the patent. Answer (C) is incorrect. Governmental fees represent an expenditure paid in cash or other property to develop an asset (patent). Therefore, it may be included in the basis of the patent.

9.4.2. The basis of property received in exchange for service is determined by which of the following?

A. The value of the services rendered.

B. The basis of the property received.

C. The fair market value of the property received.

D. None of the answers are correct.

Answer (C) is correct. *(SEE, adapted)*
REQUIRED: The item that determines basis of property received in exchange for service.
DISCUSSION: Section 83(a) provides that the receipt of property for services provided is a taxable transaction. Accordingly, the fair market value of the property must be included in gross income as compensation, and the basis of the property will be its fair market value.
Answer (A) is incorrect. The value of the services rendered should be used only if the fair market value of the property is not readily determinable. Answer (B) is incorrect. The transaction is a taxable transaction. Carryover basis applies only to nontaxable transactions. Answer (D) is incorrect. The fair market value of the property received should be used as the basis of property received in exchange for services.

9.4.3. Ms. G performed interior decorating services for Mr. K, and accepted property as payment in lieu of cash. Ms. G and Mr. K originally agreed upon a price of $4,500 for Ms. G's services. At the time of the exchange, the property had an estimated fair market value of $5,000, based on sales of similar property and an adjusted basis to Mr. K of $2,000. What is the amount Ms. G must include in her income and what is her basis in the property received?

	Income	Basis
A.	$5,000	$2,000
B.	$5,000	$5,000
C.	$4,500	$4,500
D.	$4,500	$2,000

Answer (B) is correct. *(SEE, adapted)*
REQUIRED: The amount to be included in gross income and the basis to be taken in property exchanged for services performed.
DISCUSSION: Section 83 provides that the receipt of property for services provided is a taxable transaction. Regulation 1.61-2(d)(1) provides that, if property or services are paid for with property, the fair market value of the property must be included in gross income as compensation. Accordingly, Ms. G would include $5,000 in gross income and take an adjusted basis in the property equal to its fair market value of $5,000.
Answer (A) is incorrect. The adjusted basis of the property is not equal to Mr. K's adjusted basis. Answer (C) is incorrect. The income and basis are not valued as the agreed upon price. Answer (D) is incorrect. The income and the basis are equal to the FMV of the property.

9.4.4. Dr. Brown, a surgeon, performed an operation on Mr. Bell. The usual cost of such service is $5,000. In lieu of cash, Bell deeded to Brown a parcel of real estate with a fair market value of $8,000 encumbered by a $2,000 mortgage. What is Brown's basis in this property?

A. $0

B. $5,000

C. $6,000

D. $8,000

Answer (D) is correct. *(Publisher, adapted)*
REQUIRED: The basis in encumbered property received for services.
DISCUSSION: Under Sec. 83(a), Brown is required to recognize income equal to the fair market value of property received (less any amount paid) for the performance of his services. The $2,000 mortgage is considered an amount paid, so Brown will recognize income of $6,000 ($8,000 FMV – $2,000 liability). Brown then has a basis in the property equal to the amount paid ($2,000 liability) plus the amount of income he recognized on its receipt ($6,000). Brown's total basis in the property is $8,000. The concept of including the amount of income recognized on the receipt of property is known as "tax cost basis." This concept is not provided by statute but is applied in Reg. 1.61-2(d)(2).
Answer (A) is incorrect. The property has basis. Answer (B) is incorrect. This amount is the value of the services performed. Answer (C) is incorrect. The amount of income Brown recognized is $6,000, which should be increased by the liability he assumed to find the basis of the property.

9.4.5. In the current year, Jim paid Roger $8,000 cash and built a boat dock for him in exchange for a boat whose fair market value at the time of the exchange was $11,000. What is the amount, if any, Jim should include in his income and what is his basis in the boat?

	Income	Basis in Boat
A.	$0	$8,000
B.	$3,000	$8,000
C.	$0	$11,000
D.	$3,000	$11,000

Answer (D) is correct. *(SEE, adapted)*
REQUIRED: The amount to be included in gross income and the basis to be taken in property exchanged for services.
DISCUSSION: Under Sec. 83(a), Jim is required to recognize income equal to the fair market value of property received (less any amount paid) for the performance of his services. Jim will recognize income of $3,000 ($11,000 FMV – $8,000 cash paid to Roger). Jim has a basis in the boat equal to the amount paid ($8,000) plus the amount of income he recognized on its receipt ($3,000). Jim's total basis in the boat is $11,000.
Answer (A) is incorrect. Jim has income resulting from the exchange, and $8,000 is the cash paid, which is not the correct amount of Jim's basis in the boat. Answer (B) is incorrect. The amount of $8,000 is the cash paid, which is not the correct amount of Jim's basis in the boat. Answer (C) is incorrect. Jim has income resulting from the exchange.

9.4.6. Ola Associates is a limited partnership engaged in real estate development. Hoff, a civil engineer, billed Ola $40,000 in the current year for consulting services rendered. In full settlement of this invoice, Hoff accepted a $15,000 cash payment plus the following:

	Fair Market Value	Carrying Amount on Ola's Books
3% limited partnership interest in Ola	$10,000	N/A
Surveying equipment	7,000	$3,000

What amount should Hoff, a cash-basis taxpayer, report in his current year return as income for the services rendered to Ola?

A. $15,000

B. $28,000

C. $32,000

D. $40,000

Answer (C) is correct. *(CPA, adapted)*
REQUIRED: The amount to be included in gross income for services rendered.
DISCUSSION: Section 83 requires Hoff to recognize income from services equal to the fair market value of property received ($17,000). Total income received for services is $32,000, which is equal to the $15,000 cash payment plus the $17,000 fair market value of the property.
Answer (A) is incorrect. Income must be recognized for the receipt of the property. Answer (B) is incorrect. The surveying equipment is not valued at its carrying value. Answer (D) is incorrect. The income to be reported is not equal to the amount billed.

9.4.7. During the current year, Bruce, a self-employed attorney, performed legal services for Zoom Corporation. Bruce received 10 shares of Zoom's stock for his services. Which of the following statements concerning this transaction is true?

A. Bruce's basis in the stock is zero, and he does not report any income until he sells the stock.

B. Bruce's basis in Zoom's stock is the amount he usually charges for his services but he does not report any income until he sells the stock.

C. Bruce should include in income the fair market value of the stock on Schedule C (Form 1040) in the current year, and this becomes his basis for the stock.

D. Bruce's basis in the stock is the same as Zoom's basis, and he should include this amount on Schedule C (Form 1040) in the current year.

Answer (C) is correct. *(SEE, adapted)*
   REQUIRED: The proper treatment of stock received for services performed.
   DISCUSSION: Under Sec. 83(a), Bruce is required to recognize income equal to the fair market value of property received (less any amount paid) for the performance of his services. The income is reported in the year the property is received if it is not subject to a substantial risk of forfeiture and there are no restrictions on Bruce's ability to transfer it. Here, Bruce would include in the current year's income the fair market value of the 10 shares of Zoom stock he received for services performed. Schedule C (Form 1040) is used to report profit or loss from business conducted as a sole proprietor. Bruce has a basis in the land equal to the stock's fair market value.
   Answer (A) is incorrect. Bruce has basis in the stock, and he must report income in the current year. Answer (B) is incorrect. Bruce's basis in Zoom's stock is not the amount he usually charges for his services. Also, he must report income in the current year. Answer (D) is incorrect. Bruce's basis in the stock is not the same as Zoom's basis.

9.4.8. Karlyle purchased 100 shares of stock in TB Corporation (her employer) on June 1, Year 1, for $1,000. The fair market value of the stock on the purchase date was $6,000. Karlyle agreed to sell the stock back to TB Corporation at $1,000 should she leave her job within 5 years. During the 5-year period, Karlyle could make no other transfer of the shares. Karlyle made no election under Sec. 83(b). Her basis in the stock on June 1, Year 5, is

A. $0

B. $1,000

C. $4,000

D. $6,000

Answer (B) is correct. *(Publisher, adapted)*
   REQUIRED: The basis of restricted stock in the taxpayer's employer corporation.
   DISCUSSION: The purchase of stock from an employer below fair market value is in essence a bonus paid to the employee. In this case, the stock is restricted so Karlyle has no bonus unless she stays with the company for 5 years and the value of the stock at the end of the 5 years exceeds Karlyle's own investment. Section 83 provides in such a case that Karlyle does not recognize income until the restriction ends, so her basis is equal only to the $1,000 investment. When the restriction ends in Year 6, Karlyle will recognize ordinary income equal to the difference between the fair market value of the stock on that date and the amount she paid for the shares in Year 1. On that date, her basis will increase by the amount of ordinary income recognized.
   Answer (A) is incorrect. Karlyle has basis in the stock. Answer (C) is incorrect. The correct amount of Karlyle's basis in the stock is not $4,000. Answer (D) is incorrect. The FMV at the date of purchase is $6,000.

9.5 Property Received in a Nontaxable Transaction

9.5.1. Kelly Green's automobile, used exclusively for business, had an adjusted basis of $1,600 when she traded it in on a new one. The dealer allowed her $1,800 on the old automobile and she had to pay $3,200 in cash. What is Ms. Green's adjusted basis in her new car that will be used in her business?

A. $3,200

B. $3,400

C. $4,800

D. $5,000

Answer (C) is correct. *(SEE, adapted)*
   REQUIRED: The basis of an automobile received in a like-kind exchange.
   DISCUSSION: The basis of property received in a like-kind exchange is the adjusted basis of the property surrendered, increased by any boot given and any gain recognized, and decreased by any boot received [Sec. 1031(d)]. Boot is generally money or nonlike-kind property. Green's realized gain on the trade would not be recognized since this is a like-kind exchange under Sec. 1031, and gain is recognized only to the extent of boot received. Green's basis in the new automobile is equal to her adjusted basis in the old automobile of $1,600, increased by the $3,200 she gave in cash, for a total of $4,800.
   Answer (A) is incorrect. The adjusted basis in the new car also includes the adjusted basis in the old car. Answer (B) is incorrect. The adjusted basis in the new car does not include the dealer's trade-in amount for the old car. It does, however, include the cash paid for the new car. Answer (D) is incorrect. The basis of the new car includes the basis of the old car, not the dealer's trade-in amount for the old car.

9.5.2. Henry traded a truck with an adjusted basis of $4,000 and a fair market value of $6,000 for another truck that had a list price of $12,000. Henry also paid an additional $5,000 and was eligible for a $500 rebate that will be mailed to him in 4 weeks from the date of purchase. Both trucks will be or have been used in Henry's business. What is Henry's basis in the new truck?

A. $12,000

B. $10,500

C. $9,000

D. $8,500

9.5.3. A fire destroyed Mr. C's business automobile. Mr. C originally paid $8,000 for the automobile and, up to the time of the fire, had been allowed $5,000 in depreciation. Within 3 months, the insurance company replaced the old automobile with a new one that was worth $7,000. What is the basis of the new automobile for purposes of computing depreciation?

A. $3,000

B. $5,000

C. $7,000

D. $8,000

9.5.4. Darwin contributed land with a fair market value of $40,000 and a basis of $45,000 to the Double Dee Partnership for a 50% partnership interest. The partnership assumed a $10,000 liability on the land but had no other liabilities. Darwin's basis in his partnership interest is

A. $30,000

B. $35,000

C. $40,000

D. $45,000

Answer (D) is correct. *(SEE, adapted)*
REQUIRED: The basis of a truck acquired in a like-kind exchange.
DISCUSSION: The basis of property received in a like-kind exchange is equal to the adjusted basis of the property surrendered, decreased by any boot received, and increased by any gain recognized or boot given [Sec. 1031(d)]. Since no boot is received or gain recognized by Henry, his basis in the new truck is equal to his adjusted basis in the old truck of $4,000, increased by the $5,000 he paid in cash and reduced by the $500 rebated for a total of $8,500.
Note that list price does not necessarily equal fair market value.
Answer (A) is incorrect. The list price of the new truck is $12,000. Answer (B) is incorrect. The adjusted basis of the new truck does not include the FMV of the old truck. Answer (C) is incorrect. The basis must also be reduced by the rebate amount.

Answer (A) is correct. *(SEE, adapted)*
REQUIRED: The basis of property received as a replacement for destroyed property.
DISCUSSION: If property is destroyed in an involuntary conversion, the basis of property acquired in replacement is the same as the basis of the property destroyed (decreased by any money received and increased by any gain recognized) if the replacement property (rather than cash) is received for the destroyed property [Sec. 1033(b)]. Since Mr. C did receive the new automobile from the insurance company (instead of receiving cash and buying a new automobile), Mr. C's basis in the new automobile is the same as his $3,000 basis in the old automobile ($8,000 – $5,000 depreciation). Mr. C's holding period of the new automobile will include the holding period of the old automobile because there was a substituted basis.
Answer (B) is incorrect. The amount of depreciation taken on the old auto is $5,000. Answer (C) is incorrect. The amount of $7,000 is the value of the new auto. Answer (D) is incorrect. The amount of $8,000 is the original cost of the old auto.

Answer (C) is correct. *(Publisher, adapted)*
REQUIRED: The basis of a partnership interest acquired in exchange for property that is subject to a debt.
DISCUSSION: The basis of a partnership interest acquired by a contribution of property to the partnership is equal to the adjusted basis of such property to the contributing partner at the time of contribution (Sec. 722). Under Sec. 752, an assumption of an individual partner's liabilities by the partnership is considered a distribution of money to the partner by the partnership, and this reduces the basis of the partner's interest under Sec. 733. The other partners in the Double Dee Partnership assumed $5,000 of Darwin's individual liabilities ($10,000 × 50%). His basis in the partnership interest is equal to the adjusted basis of the land contributed reduced by the liabilities assumed by the other partners ($45,000 – $5,000 = $40,000). No mention is made of partnership liabilities other than Darwin's $10,000 liability. Normally, Darwin would assume an interest in the other partnership liabilities, which would increase his basis.
Answer (A) is incorrect. The FMV of the land reduced by the full liability is $30,000. Answer (B) is incorrect. The basis of the land reduced by the full liability is $35,000. Answer (D) is incorrect. The basis in the land should be reduced by the amount of liabilities assumed by the other partners.

9.5.5. Mr. R owned a printing press with an adjusted basis of $2,000 that he used in his business. On July 17 of the current year, he transferred this property to Ms. A in exchange for the following assets:

	A's Adjusted Basis	Fair Market Value
Printing press (to be used for business)	$4,000	$6,000
Truck (for personal use)	1,000	2,000
Cash	2,000	2,000

What is R's basis in the new printing press and the truck after the exchange?

	New Press	Truck
A.	$2,000	$2,000
B.	$4,000	$1,000
C.	$6,000	$2,000
D.	$6,400	$1,600

Answer (A) is correct. *(SEE, adapted)*
REQUIRED: The basis of two assets acquired in a like-kind exchange.
DISCUSSION: The basis of property received in a like-kind exchange is equal to the adjusted basis of the property surrendered, decreased by any boot received, and increased by any gain recognized or boot given [Sec. 1031(d)]. Since this is a like-kind exchange (one press for another) and Mr. R received boot along with the like-kind property, he will recognize gain to the extent of the lesser of the realized gain or the value of boot received. Mr. R's realized gain is $8,000 ($10,000 total FMV received – $2,000 basis). Of this amount, he recognizes only $4,000, the value of the boot received (the truck plus the cash).
The basis in the new printing press (the like-kind property) will be the basis of the property transferred ($2,000), minus the amount of boot received ($4,000), plus the amount of gain recognized ($4,000), or $2,000. The basis of the truck received will be its fair market value ($2,000).
Answer (B) is incorrect. These amounts are A's adjusted basis in each asset. Answer (C) is incorrect. The amount of $6,000 for the printing press is its fair market value. Answer (D) is incorrect. These amounts are the FMV of the assets prorated based on A's adjusted basis.

9.5.6. A hurricane destroyed a bus owned by the Gator Booster Club. The bus originally cost $10,000, and $4,000 of depreciation had been allowed up to the time of the hurricane. The Gator Booster Club received $9,000 in insurance proceeds that they used to purchase a new bus by paying an additional $3,000 cash. The Gator Booster Club elected to defer gain recognition on the involuntary conversion. What is the basis of the new bus?

A. $6,000

B. $7,000

C. $9,000

D. $12,000

Answer (C) is correct. *(Publisher, adapted)*
REQUIRED: The basis of property purchased with funds received from an involuntary conversion of old property.
DISCUSSION: Under Sec. 1033(b), the basis of replacement property acquired with cash received in payment for an involuntary conversion of old property is the cost of the replacement property decreased by the amount of gain not recognized. The Gator Booster Club realized a gain of $3,000 ($9,000 – $6,000 basis), but it recognized no gain under Sec. 1033(a) since the entire proceeds were reinvested in replacement property similar or related in use. The club's basis in the new bus is $9,000 ($12,000 cost – $3,000 gain not recognized).
Answer (A) is incorrect. This amount is the basis of the old bus. Answer (B) is incorrect. This amount is the depreciation claimed on the old bus plus the additional cash paid. Answer (D) is incorrect. This amount is the cost of the new bus.

9.5.7. Speculator has owned a tract of land for several years. She paid $100,000 for it, and it is now worth $200,000. Speculator decides to form a corporation to subdivide and develop the land. Speculator transfers the land plus $10,000 cash to a newly formed corporation in exchange for all of the stock in the corporation. What is Speculator's basis in the stock?

A. $100,000

B. $110,000

C. $200,000

D. $210,000

Answer (B) is correct. *(Publisher, adapted)*
REQUIRED: The shareholder's basis in stock acquired in exchange for appreciated property.
DISCUSSION: The basis in stock is generally what the shareholder pays for it (Sec. 1012). However, Sec. 358 provides that the basis of stock received by a shareholder without the recognition of gain under Sec. 351 is the same as the basis of the property exchanged. Section 351 provides that no gain or loss is recognized when property is transferred to a corporation solely in exchange for stock in such corporation and immediately after the exchange, such person is in control (80% or more ownership) of the corporation.
Since Speculator owns 100% of the corporation after the exchange, she will not recognize gain on the transfer of the appreciated property to the corporation. Speculator's basis in the stock is $110,000 ($100,000 substituted basis from the land + $10,000 cash).
Answer (A) is incorrect. The stock basis also includes the cash paid. Answer (C) is incorrect. The amount of $200,000 is the FMV of the land. Answer (D) is incorrect. The stock's basis includes the adjusted basis of the land, not its FMV.

9.5.8. Speculator has owned a tract of land for several years. She paid $100,000 for it, and it is now worth $200,000. Speculator decides to form a corporation to subdivide and develop the land. Speculator transfers the land to a newly formed corporation in exchange for all of the stock in the corporation. What is the corporation's basis in the land received from Speculator?

A. $90,000

B. $100,000

C. $190,000

D. $200,000

9.5.9. Mr. C's building, which was used in his business, was partially destroyed in a storm. The building cost $125,000 and had an adjusted basis of $75,000. The fair market value was $85,000 before the storm and $45,000 immediately after. Mr. C received a $20,000 reimbursement from his insurance company. What is the adjusted basis of the building before any repairs are made?

A. $55,000

B. $35,000

C. $30,000

D. $15,000

9.5.10. Ms. H sold her principal residence on June 1 of the current year for $55,000. The residence had been purchased 10 years ago for $30,000. Seven years ago, a garage had been added at a cost of $2,500. Ms. H purchased a new home in August of last year for $48,000. What is the adjusted basis of Ms. H's new residence?

A. $25,500

B. $30,000

C. $32,500

D. $48,000

Answer (B) is correct. *(Publisher, adapted)*
REQUIRED: The corporation's basis in property received in exchange for stock.
DISCUSSION: Section 362 provides that property received by a corporation in a Sec. 351 transaction shall have the same basis as in the hands of the transferor increased by the amount of any gain recognized on the transfer. Since Speculator recognized no gain under Sec. 351 in the previous question, the corporation will take a carryover basis in the land received from Speculator of $100,000.
Answer (A) is incorrect. The land's basis is not reduced by the cash contributed by Speculator. Answer (C) is incorrect. The FMV of the land reduced by the cash contributed by Speculator is $190,000. Answer (D) is incorrect. The FMV of the land is $200,000.

Answer (B) is correct. *(SEE, adapted)*
REQUIRED: The basis in a building that was partially destroyed by storm and for which partial reimbursement was received by insurance.
DISCUSSION: Section 1016 provides that adjustments shall be made to the basis of property for receipts and losses (among other items) properly chargeable to capital. These are, in effect, recoveries of capital for which an adjustment to basis is needed so the taxpayer does not receive a double benefit. Here, there is a $40,000 decline in fair market value ($85,000 – $45,000). The $20,000 unreimbursed loss is a reduction in basis and the $20,000 receipt of insurance proceeds is also a reduction in basis. Mr. C's basis in the building before repairs is $35,000 ($75,000 – $20,000 – $20,000). If repairs are made, the basis will be increased by their cost.
Answer (A) is incorrect. The correct amount of the adjusted basis of the building before any repairs are made is not $55,000. Answer (C) is incorrect. The difference between the adjusted basis of the building before the storm and its FMV after the storm is $30,000. Answer (D) is incorrect. The correct amount of the adjusted basis of the building before any repairs are made is not $15,000.

Answer (D) is correct. *(SEE, adapted)*
REQUIRED: The adjusted basis of a new residence after the sale of an old residence.
DISCUSSION: Ms. H realized a gain of $22,500 on the sale of her old residence.

Sales price		$55,000
Adjusted basis:		
Acquisition cost	$30,000	
Plus: Addition	2,500	(32,500)
Gain realized		$22,500

The Taxpayer Relief Act of 1997 provides a $250,000 exclusion of gain for an individual on the sale of a principal residence after May 6, 1997, provided that the taxpayer has lived there for 2 years. Therefore, Ms. H recognizes no gain on the sale, and her basis in the new house is its cost, $48,000.
Answer (A) is incorrect. The basis of the new residence is not adjusted by the gain realized on the old residence. Answer (B) is incorrect. This amount is the original cost of the old residence. Answer (C) is incorrect. The basis of the new residence is its cost, not the adjusted basis of the old residence.

9.5.11. On September 1 of the current year, Mr. G traded in his old car, which was used 50% for business and 50% for pleasure. His old car originally cost $5,000 and he had claimed $800 of depreciation in earlier years. He was given a $2,000 trade-in allowance on his old car. The sales price on the new car (also to be used 50% for business and 50% for pleasure) is $7,000. The $5,000 difference between the sales price and the trade-in allowance was paid in cash. What is Mr. G's depreciable basis of the new car?

A. $3,500

B. $3,700

C. $4,200

D. $4,600

Answer (C) is correct. *(SEE, adapted)*
REQUIRED: The depreciable basis of a new car used 50% for business and acquired in a like-kind exchange.
DISCUSSION: Sections 167 and 168 define the depreciable basis of an asset as the adjusted basis used for determining gain. Only the portion of the car used for business is depreciable. The business portions of the cars also qualify as a like-kind exchange under Sec. 1031, and no gain or loss is recognized on the disposal of the old car. The basis of the newly acquired asset is the adjusted basis of the property surrendered, plus the boot given, plus gain recognized. These computations only apply to the one-half of the car used for business.

Original cost of old car	$2,500
Less: depreciation	(800)
Adjusted basis of old car	$1,700
Plus boot given (1/2 of $5,000 cash)	2,500
Depreciable basis of new car	$4,200

Answer (A) is incorrect. The unadjusted basis of the business portion of the old car plus one-half of the trade-in allowance is $3,500. Answer (B) is incorrect. The adjusted basis of the business portion of the old car plus the trade-in allowance that was given is $3,700. Answer (D) is incorrect. Only half of the depreciation that was claimed was used to reduce the adjusted basis of the old car.

9.5.12. On September 30, Year 1, Mr. O'Donnell purchased investment land. On April 15, Year 2, Mr. O'Donnell traded his land for some other investment land in a nontaxable exchange. On October 5, Year 2, Mr. O'Donnell sold the land received in the exchange for a gain. His gain will be treated as

A. A short-term capital gain.

B. A long-term capital gain.

C. Part short-term capital gain, part long-term capital gain.

D. Ordinary income.

Answer (B) is correct. *(SEE, adapted)*
REQUIRED: The character of gain on property received in a nontaxable transaction.
DISCUSSION: Under Sec. 1223(1)-(2) and Reg. 1.223-1(a)-(b), if the basis for property is determined in whole or in part by reference to the basis of other property previously held by the taxpayer (a substituted basis), as in the case of a tax-free exchange, the holding period for the new property includes the period during which the other property was held. Accordingly, the holding period on the exchanged land that was sold by Mr. O'Donnell includes the previously held land that was transferred in the tax-free exchange. Since the land was held for over 12 months, the capital gain is long-term.
Answer (A) is incorrect. The holding period for the new property includes the period during which the other property was held. Answer (C) is incorrect. The capital gain cannot be split between short-term and long-term. Answer (D) is incorrect. The gain will be treated as a capital gain.

9.5.13. Mr. A sold a truck used in his business with an adjusted basis of $2,000 for $500 to a salvage yard in the current year. He purchased a replacement truck 2 months later for $8,000. Mr. A's basis in the new truck is $9,500.

A. True.

B. False.

Answer (B) is correct. *(SEE, adapted)*
DISCUSSION: Since Mr. A sold the old truck to a salvage yard and purchased the replacement truck 2 months later, the two transactions are independent and would not qualify as a like-kind exchange under Sec. 1031. Mr. A would fully recognize the loss on the sale of the old business truck, and the basis of the new truck would be its cost of $8,000.

9.5.14. Mrs. K transfers a building with a $140,000 fair market value and a $120,000 adjusted basis to Z Corporation in exchange for 90% of Z's stock valued at $139,000 plus $1,000 in cash. The basis of the building to Z Corporation is $120,000.

A. True.

B. False.

Answer (B) is correct. *(SEE, adapted)*
DISCUSSION: Since this transaction qualifies as nontaxable under Sec. 351, the basis of the building to Z Corporation is determined under Sec. 362. The building has the same basis for Z as in the hands of Mrs. K, plus the amount of gain recognized by Mrs. K on the transfer. Under Sec. 351, any realized gain is recognized to the extent of cash received. A $20,000 gain is realized on the exchange [($139,000 + $1,000) – $120,000]. A gain of $1,000 is recognized under Sec. 351(a). Z's basis for the land is the $120,000 adjusted basis for the land in K's hands plus the $1,000 recognized gain, or $121,000.

9.5.15. B Corporation received land valued at $80,000 from Town E as an incentive to develop an industrial park there. The basis of the land to B Corporation is $0.

A. True.

B. False.

Answer (A) is correct. *(SEE, adapted)*
DISCUSSION: Under Sec. 362(c), property other than money contributed by a nonshareholder to the capital of a corporation has a basis of $0 to the corporation.

9.6 Stock Dividends and Stock Rights

9.6.1. In January of Year 1, Joan Hill bought one share of Orban Corp. stock for $300. On March 1, Year 4, Orban distributed one share of a new class of preferred stock for each share of common stock held. This distribution was nontaxable. On March 1, Year 4, Joan's one share of common stock had a fair market value of $450, while the preferred stock had a fair market value of $150. After the distribution of the preferred stock, Joan's bases for her Orban stocks are

	Common	Preferred
A.	$300	$0
B.	$225	$75
C.	$200	$100
D.	$150	$150

Answer (B) is correct. *(CPA, adapted)*
REQUIRED: The tax bases of common stock and preferred stock received as a nontaxable dividend.
DISCUSSION: Since the preferred stock dividend was nontaxable, the original basis of the common stock would be allocated between the common stock and the preferred stock based on the relative fair market values of each on the date of the stock dividend (Reg. 1.307-1). The market values of Joan's common and preferred stock on the date of the dividend were $450 and $150, respectively. Joan's tax basis in the common stock after the receipt of the dividend is

$$(\$450 \div \$600) \times \$300 = \$225$$

Joan's tax basis in the preferred stock is

$$(\$150 \div \$600) \times \$300 = \$75$$

Answer (A) is incorrect. The basis of the common stock must be allocated between the preferred stock and the common stock. Answer (C) is incorrect. The stock should not be split 66.67%/33.33%. Answer (D) is incorrect. The basis should not be split based on the number of shares held of each type of stock.

9.6.2. Joe Blue owns 200 shares of common stock in the Water Corporation. These were purchased several years ago for $2,000. In the current year, Blue received a nontaxable distribution of stock rights to purchase 20 additional shares of stock in the Water Corporation for $10 each. On the date of distribution, the fair market value of the common stock was $40 per share and the fair market value of the stock rights was $600. What is Blue's lowest basis in the stock rights?

A. $0

B. $70

C. $140

D. $600

Answer (A) is correct. *(Publisher, adapted)*
REQUIRED: The shareholder's basis in stock rights received as a distribution when the stock rights are worth less than 15% of the value of the stock.
DISCUSSION: Under Sec. 307(a), the basis of stock rights received in a nontaxable distribution is generally determined by allocating the basis of the stock between the stock rights and the stock. Section 307(b) provides, however, that if the fair market value of the stock rights at the time of distribution is less than 15% of the fair market value of the stock, the basis of the stock rights is zero unless the shareholder elects to determine the basis under Sec. 307(a). The stock rights in the Water Corporation had a fair market value of $600, which is less than 15% of the $8,000 fair market value of the stock, so Blue's basis in the stock rights is zero (unless he elects to allocate basis).
Answer (B) is incorrect. The amount of $70 is not Blue's lowest basis in the stock rights. Answer (C) is incorrect. The amount of $140 is not Blue's lowest basis in the stock rights. Answer (D) is incorrect. The amount of $600 is the fair market value of the stock rights.

9.6.3. Joe Blue owned 100 shares of common stock in the Sky Corporation previously purchased for $5,000. In the current year, Blue receives a nontaxable distribution of stock rights to purchase 40 additional shares of common stock in Sky. The fair market value of the common stock was $100 per share on the date of distribution and the fair market value of the stock rights was $2,000. What is Blue's basis in the stock rights?

A. $0

B. $833

C. $1,000

D. $2,000

Answer (B) is correct. *(Publisher, adapted)*
REQUIRED: The basis of stock rights received in a distribution from a corporation.
DISCUSSION: Under Sec. 307(a), the basis of stock rights distributed tax-free to a shareholder is determined by allocating the basis of the stock between the stock rights and the stock. Since the fair market value of the rights is at least 15% of the fair market value of the underlying stock, Sec. 307(b) requires a basis allocation to take place. The allocation is based on the relative fair market values of the stock and the stock rights on the date of the distribution. Blue's basis in the stock rights is $833, as computed below.

$$\frac{\$2,000 \text{ FMV stock rights}}{\$10,000 \text{ FMV stock} + \$2,000 \text{ FMV rights}} \times \$5,000 = \$833$$

If Blue lets the rights lapse without being exercised or sold, the basis assigned to the rights reverts back to the common stock.
Answer (A) is incorrect. The stock rights have basis. Answer (C) is incorrect. One-half of the FMV of the stock rights is $1,000. Answer (D) is incorrect. The FMV of the stock rights is $2,000.

9.6.4. In Year 1, Mr. Smith purchased 50 shares of common stock in Corporation D for $1,000. In Year 8, Corporation D declared a stock dividend of two shares of its common stock for each 10 shares held. In Year 11, D's common stock split 2 for 1 at a time when the fair market value was $20 a share. What is Mr. Smith's basis in each of his shares of D's stock (rounded to the nearest dollar) if both distributions were tax-free and all the stock received was identical to the stock purchased?

A. $8 per share.

B. $20 for 100 shares and $0 for all additional shares.

C. $17 for 60 shares and $20 for 60 shares.

D. $20 per share.

Answer (A) is correct. *(SEE, adapted)*
REQUIRED: The shareholder's basis in stock after a stock dividend and a stock split.
DISCUSSION: A distribution of common stock as a stock dividend on common stock is generally a tax-free distribution. The same is true for a stock split. Under Sec. 307(a), the basis of the original stock is allocated between it and the distributed stock based on their relative fair market values. Here, all the stock has the same fair market value, so the basis per share is calculated as total basis divided by total number of shares. Mr. Smith's total number of shares is 120 [(50 + 10) × 2]. His basis per share (rounded to the nearest dollar) is $8 ($1,000 ÷ 120 shares = $8.333).
Answer (B) is incorrect. The basis per share is equal to the total basis divided by the total number of shares. Answer (C) is incorrect. There is no allocation to different blocks of stock. Answer (D) is incorrect. The basis in each share is not equal to the FMV at the time of the stock split.

9.6.5. In Year 1, Alice bought one share of Proud Corporation stock for $100. On April 15, Year 3, Proud declared a common stock dividend of 5%. The fair market value of Alice's stock on April 15, Year 3, was $200. Proud Corporation had a plan by which no fractional shares would be issued. The stock dividend that Alice was entitled to did not amount to a full share, so Proud sold the fractional share on Alice's behalf and paid her $10 for her fractional share stock dividend. What is the basis of Alice's old stock after the dividend (rounded to the nearest dollar)?

A. $95

B. $98

C. $100

D. $110

Answer (A) is correct. *(SEE, adapted)*
REQUIRED: The basis of stock after a stock dividend of a fractional share that is redeemed by the distributing corporation.
DISCUSSION: Calculation of basis:

Original cost	$100.00
Basis allocated to fractional share	(4.76)
Adjusted basis	$ 95.24

The original $100 basis for the single share of Proud Corporation stock is allocated between the original share and the 5% share of Proud stock received as a stock dividend. The basis for the fractional share is $4.76 {[$100 ÷ (1 + .05)] × .05}. This allocation makes the basis of the old Proud stock $95.24 ($100 – $4.76). The $4.76 basis for the fractional share reduces the $10 proceeds for the redemption of the fractional share of stock to produce a $5.24 capital gain [Sec. 302(b)(1)].
Answer (B) is incorrect. The correct amount of the basis is not $98. Answer (C) is incorrect. The original cost of one share of stock is $100. Answer (D) is incorrect. The amount Alice paid for the share and the fractional share stock dividend is $110.

9.6.6. In Year 1, Melanie Tyson bought 100 shares of XYZ stock for $1,000 or $10 a share. In Year 2, she bought 100 shares of XYZ stock for $1,600, or $16 a share. In Year 3, XYZ declared a 2-for-1 stock split. Which of the following is true?

A. Melanie now has 200 shares with a basis of $5 per share.

B. Melanie now has 200 shares with a basis of $8 per share.

C. Melanie now has 400 shares with a basis of $6.50 per share.

D. Melanie now has 200 shares with a basis of $5 per share and 200 shares with a basis of $8 per share.

9.6.7. If nontaxable stock rights are allowed to expire, they have no basis.

A. True.

B. False.

9.7 Adjustments to Asset Basis

NOTE: See Study Unit 10 for depreciation, depletion, and amortization that reduce bases of assets.

9.7.1. On January 1, Mr. D owned rental property that had an adjusted basis to him of $250,000. Mr. M made the following expenditures during the year:

Ordinary painting of the building	$ 5,000
Repair of one section of the roof (useful life not appreciably extended)	2,500
Legal fees paid to defend title	10,000
Property taxes	6,000
Assessment for local improvement of street that increased the value of the property appreciably	15,000

Not considering depreciation, what is Mr. D's basis in the property at year end?

A. $225,000

B. $240,000

C. $260,000

D. $275,000

Answer (D) is correct. *(SEE, adapted)*
REQUIRED: The taxpayer's basis and number of shares after a stock split.
DISCUSSION: A distribution of common stock as a stock split is generally a tax-free distribution. The basis of the original stock is allocated between it and the new stock based on their relative fair market values. The 100 shares purchased in Year 1 have a basis of $1,000 (100 shares × $10 per share), which must be allocated to the additional 100 shares from the stock split. The basis for the Year 1 stocks will be $5 per share ($1,000 ÷ 200). The 100 shares purchased in Year 2 have a basis of $1,600 (100 shares × $16), which must be allocated to the additional 100 shares from the stock split. The basis for the Year 2 stocks will be $8 per share ($1,600 ÷ 200).
Answer (A) is incorrect. The stock split also applies to the second purchase of XYZ stock. Answer (B) is incorrect. The stock split also applies to the first purchase of XYZ stock. Answer (C) is incorrect. Since the stock purchases attribute a different basis to each purchase of the stock, the stock should be separately maintained, and the stock split will not cause an average of basis.

Answer (A) is correct. *(SEE, adapted)*
DISCUSSION: Under Sec. 307, the basis of nontaxable rights is $0 unless the taxpayer elects or is required to allocate part of the basis of the stock. Under Reg. 1.307-1(a), allocation of basis to stock rights can occur only if the rights are sold or exercised.

Answer (D) is correct. *(SEE, adapted)*
REQUIRED: The basis of property at year end after expenditures were made.
DISCUSSION: Under Reg. 1.162-4, repairs are deductible, while improvements that prolong the life of property or materially increase its value must be capitalized. Therefore, the ordinary painting of a building and repair of a roof that does not appreciably extend the useful life are deductible and do not increase basis. Property taxes are also deductible under Sec. 164 and therefore do not increase basis. But assessments for local improvements of the street that increase the value of the property are not deductible and do increase the basis of property [Sec. 164(c)(1)]. Also, expenses paid or incurred in defending or perfecting title of property constitute a part of the cost of property and are not deductible [Reg. 1.212-1(k)]. Therefore, Mr. D's basis in the property is as follows:

Beginning basis	$250,000
Fees to defend title	10,000
Assessment for improvements	15,000
Basis at year end	$275,000

Answer (A) is incorrect. The fees to defend the title and the assessment for improvements should increase, not decrease, the basis of the property. Answer (B) is incorrect. The fees to defend the title should increase, not decrease, the basis. In addition, the assessment for improvements increases the basis. Answer (C) is incorrect. The assessment for improvements also increases the basis.

9.7.2. Kylie purchased a horse farm in Ocala, Florida. Kylie properly allocated $10,000 of the purchase price to the barn. Several months after the purchase, Kylie built an addition to the barn at a cost of $2,000. In the subsequent year, Kylie expended $800 to paint the barn, repair broken windows, and have the inside thoroughly cleaned. What is Kylie's basis in the barn at the end of the second year, excluding depreciation?

A. $10,000

B. $10,800

C. $12,000

D. $12,800

Answer (C) is correct. *(Publisher, adapted)*
REQUIRED: The basis of property on which expenditures have been made for both repairs and improvements.
DISCUSSION: Under Reg. 1.162-4, repairs are deductible, while improvements that prolong the life of property or materially increase its value must be capitalized. Under Sec. 1016(a)(1), expenditures properly chargeable to capital increase the basis of property. An addition to a barn is considered an improvement, but fixing broken windows, painting, and cleaning are generally considered repairs. Kylie's basis (excluding depreciation) is $12,000 ($10,000 purchase price + $2,000 improvements).
Answer (A) is incorrect. The addition to the barn increases the basis. Answer (B) is incorrect. The repairs and maintenance to the barn are deductible and do not increase basis, but the addition to the barn does increase basis. Answer (D) is incorrect. The repairs and maintenance costs are deductible and do not increase basis.

9.7.3. Feld, the sole stockholder of Maki Corp., paid $50,000 for Maki's stock in Year 1. In Year 2, Feld contributed a parcel of land to Maki but was not given any additional stock for this contribution. Feld's basis for the land was $10,000, and its fair market value was $18,000 on the date of the transfer of title. What is Feld's adjusted basis for the Maki stock?

A. $50,000

B. $52,000

C. $60,000

D. $68,000

Answer (C) is correct. *(CPA, adapted)*
REQUIRED: The shareholder's basis in stock after a contribution of property.
DISCUSSION: A shareholder recognizes no gain on the voluntary contribution of capital to a corporation. The contribution of capital merely increases the shareholder's basis in the corporation (Reg. 1.118-1). The shareholder's basis is increased by the basis in the property contributed, not by the fair market value. Feld will recognize no gain on the contribution and his basis for the Maki stock is

Cost of stock	$50,000
Contribution of property (basis)	10,000
Adjusted basis in stock	$60,000

Answer (A) is incorrect. The contribution of land increases the basis of the stock. Answer (B) is incorrect. The basis in the stock is increased by $10,000, not $2,000. Answer (D) is incorrect. The basis in the stock is increased by the adjusted basis of the land, not the fair market value of the land.

9.7.4. Beth owned a large parcel of property. She had purchased it in one transaction for $80,000. In the current year, Beth was badly in need of cash, so she sold one-fourth of the land for $20,000 and sold one-half of the original land for $30,000 to another person, although it was all of approximately equal value. What is Beth's basis in the remaining land that she owns?

A. $20,000

B. $30,000

C. $50,000

D. $80,000

Answer (A) is correct. *(Publisher, adapted)*
REQUIRED: The remaining basis in land after selling three-fourths of an original tract at varying prices.
DISCUSSION: When a part of a larger property is sold, the cost or basis of the entire property must be equitably apportioned among the several parts (Reg. 1.61-6). This is generally done on the basis of the relative fair market values of each part. If all the land is of approximately equal value, the basis is allocated based on the amount of land sold in each transaction. Since Beth sold three-fourths of the land and still owns one-fourth, her basis is $20,000 ($80,000 × 1/4).
Answer (B) is incorrect. Beth cannot use the cost recovery method to treat the $50,000 as a recovery of her investment, thereby leaving $30,000 of unrecovered basis. Answer (C) is incorrect. The amount of $50,000 is the money received for three-fourths of the land. Answer (D) is incorrect. The cost of the land is $80,000. Since three-fourths of the land was sold, the $80,000 basis must be reduced by three-fourths, regardless of the selling price of each portion of land.

9.7.5. A fire in Mr. White's residence resulted in a loss of $22,000. Mr. White recovered only $16,000 from his insurance company and deducted a casualty loss of $2,900 ($6,000 unreimbursed loss, less nondeductible 10% AGI limitation and $100 nondeductible floor on property used for personal purposes). By what amount must Mr. White reduce his basis before considering any reinvestment of the insurance proceeds in repairs on the house?

A. $6,000

B. $16,000

C. $18,900

D. $22,000

Answer (C) is correct. *(SEE, adapted)*
REQUIRED: The adjustment to the basis of a personal residence after a casualty loss.
DISCUSSION: Mr. White received $16,000 in insurance proceeds and recognized a casualty loss of $2,900. These are considered recovered costs for tax purposes, and Mr. White must reduce his basis by $18,900. The remaining $100 loss for which he received no tax benefit, as well as any loss disallowed under the 10% of AGI nondeductible floor, does not reduce Mr. White's basis.
Answer (A) is incorrect. Basis must be reduced by the $16,000 insurance reimbursement and the $2,900 deductible casualty loss. Answer (B) is incorrect. The deductible portion of the casualty loss also reduces basis. Answer (D) is incorrect. The $100 nondeductible portion of the casualty loss does not reduce basis.

9.7.6. Which of the following will decrease the basis of property?

A. Depreciation.

B. Return of capital.

C. Recognized losses on involuntary conversions.

D. All of the answers are correct.

Answer (D) is correct. *(SEE, adapted)*
REQUIRED: The item that will decrease the basis of property.
DISCUSSION: Basis must be reduced by the larger of the amount of depreciation allowed or allowable (even if not claimed). A return of capital is a tax-free distribution that reduces a stock's basis by the amount of the distribution. If a shareholder's basis has been reduced to zero because of a tax-free return of capital, any excess amounts received are treated as a capital gain. Under Sec. 1033(b), the basis of the replacement property from an involuntary conversion is reduced by any gain not recognized.
Answer (A) is incorrect. Return of capital and recognized losses on involuntary conversions will also reduce the basis of property. Answer (B) is incorrect. Depreciation and recognized losses on involuntary conversions will also reduce the basis of property. Answer (C) is incorrect. Depreciation and return of capital will also reduce the basis of property.

9.7.7. In the current year, Mr. A sold an asset that originally cost $7,000. Mr. A incorrectly claimed $4,000 depreciation over a 5-year period. He should have claimed $5,000 depreciation. What was the adjusted basis when sold?

A. $2,000

B. $3,000

C. $5,000

D. $7,000

Answer (A) is correct. *(SEE, adapted)*
REQUIRED: The adjusted basis of an asset that was depreciated by an amount less than the amount allowable.
DISCUSSION: Under Sec. 1016(a)(2), an adjustment is made to the basis of an asset for the amount of depreciation allowed in previous years, but the adjustment cannot be less than the amount allowable under Sec. 167. The amount of depreciation allowable on this asset was $5,000. Mr. A must reduce his basis by this amount. The adjusted basis of the asset when sold was $2,000 ($7,000 − $5,000).
Answer (B) is incorrect. The correct amount of depreciation ($5,000) should be subtracted from the original cost. Answer (C) is incorrect. The amount of depreciation that should be subtracted from the asset's original cost is $5,000. Answer (D) is incorrect. This amount is the original cost, which must be reduced by the correct depreciation.

9.7.8. Which of the following items is not a reduction to the basis of an asset?

A. Casualty loss.

B. Amount received for granting an easement on property.

C. Personal property tax.

D. Rehabilitated building credit.

Answer (C) is correct. *(SEE, adapted)*
REQUIRED: The item that would not cause a reduction in the basis of an asset.
DISCUSSION: Under Sec. 1016, expenditures, receipts, losses, or other items properly chargeable to capital result in an adjustment in the basis of the property. However, there is no adjustment for deductible taxes. A personal property tax is deductible and does not reduce the basis of the asset.
Answer (A) is incorrect. Casualty losses do reduce the basis of an asset. Answer (B) is incorrect. The grant of an easement requires a portion of the basis to be allocated. Answer (D) is incorrect. The basis of an asset is reduced by 100% of the credit for rehabilitation of buildings [Sec. 50(c)].

9.7.9. All of the following items decrease the basis of property except

A. Casualty or theft loss deductions and insurance reimbursements.

B. The cost of defending and perfecting a title.

C. Section 179 deduction.

D. The exclusion from income of subsidies for energy conservation measures.

Answer (B) is correct. *(SEE, adapted)*
REQUIRED: The item that does not decrease the basis of property.
DISCUSSION: According to Reg. 1.212-1(k), the expenses paid or incurred in defending or perfecting title of property constitute a part of the cost of property. The expenses are not deductible, and the cost is added to the basis of the property.
Answer (A) is incorrect. Casualty or theft loss deductions decrease the basis of property. Answer (C) is incorrect. Section 179 deductions decrease the basis of property. Answer (D) is incorrect. Exclusions from income of subsidies for energy conservation measures decrease the basis of property.

9.7.10. All of the following increase the basis of property except

A. The cost of extending utility service lines to the property.

B. The cost of painting the interior of the building.

C. Assessments for items that increase the value of the property.

D. Legal fees for defending title to the property.

Answer (B) is correct. *(SEE, adapted)*
REQUIRED: The item that does not increase the basis of property.
DISCUSSION: Capital expenditures add to the value of property or adapt the property to a new or different use. (Reg. 1.263). Capital expenditures increase the basis of property. The cost of painting the interior of the building is not a capital expenditure. Rather, it is a cost that is deductible as an ordinary and necessary business expense. Therefore, the cost of painting does not increase the basis of the building.
Answer (A) is incorrect. The cost of extending utility service lines increases the value of the property and is a capital expenditure. Answer (C) is incorrect. The assessments that increase the value of the property are capitalized. Answer (D) is incorrect. Fees to defend title are treated as a cost of the property [Reg. 1.212-1(k)].

9.7.11. During Year 8, Julia received a dividend payment from Chipper Corporation in the amount of $1,000 and a return of capital payment in the amount of $1,600. Julia had originally purchased Chipper stock for $4,000 in Year 1 (Block A) and purchased some additional Chipper stock for $2,000 (Block B) in Year 2. She could not definitely identify the shares subject to the return of capital. Julia's basis in the two blocks of stock at the end of Year 8, assuming no other transactions, is

	Block A	Block B
A.	$1,400	$2,000
B.	$2,400	$2,000
C.	$2,933	$1,467
D.	$4,000	$400

Answer (B) is correct. *(SEE, adapted)*
REQUIRED: The return of capital when specific identification of stock is not possible.
DISCUSSION: If a shareholder purchases stock in different lots and at different times and it is impossible to definitely identify the shares subject to a return of capital, the basis of the earliest shares purchased is reduced first [Reg. 1.1012-1(c)]. Therefore, the $1,600 return of capital is applied entirely against Block A, the stock purchased in Year 1. The dividend represents a return on capital and does not reduce the stock basis.
Answer (A) is incorrect. The dividend does not reduce the stock basis. Answer (C) is incorrect. The return of capital is not allocated between the two blocks of stock. Answer (D) is incorrect. The return of capital is applied entirely against Block A, not Block B.

9.8 Holding Period

9.8.1. For sales and exchanges, the holding period for determining long-term capital gains and losses is more than

A. 6 months.

B. 9 months.

C. 12 months.

D. 18 months.

Answer (C) is correct. *(CPA, adapted)*
REQUIRED: The long-term holding period for capital assets sold or exchanged.
DISCUSSION: Under Sec. 1222, capital assets must be held for more than 1 year in order for the gain or loss on sale or exchange to be treated as long-term.
Answer (A) is incorrect. The holding period is longer than 6 months. Answer (B) is incorrect. The holding period is longer than 9 months. Answer (D) is incorrect. Eighteen months is longer than the minimum required holding period for long-term capital gains and losses.

9.8.2. If 100 shares of stock are purchased February 14, Year 1, what is the earliest date on which the stock can be sold and the gain or loss qualify for the long-term holding period?

    A. August 14, Year 2.

    B. February 15, Year 2.

    C. February 14, Year 2.

    D. August 15, Year 2.

Answer (B) is correct. *(SEE, adapted)*
    REQUIRED: The earliest date in which the stock can be sold and the gain/loss qualify for the long-term holding period.
    DISCUSSION: The holding period of an asset for purposes of long-term gain treatment is more than 1 year from the date of acquisition, not including the day of acquisition but including the day of disposition.
    Answer (A) is incorrect. Holding the stock for 6 months does not qualify as a long-term holding period. Answer (C) is incorrect. The holding period of an asset does not include the day of acquisition. Answer (D) is incorrect. An asset does not have to be held for 18 months to qualify for long-term treatment.

9.8.3. Joe contributed land (a capital asset) to a partnership for a 30% partnership interest on March 1, Year 5. Joe had purchased the land on June 15, Year 1, for $25,000, and the land had a fair market value of $50,000 in March Year 5. The partnership sold the land on December 10, Year 5, for $55,000. In April Year 6, Joe sold his partnership interest. The holding period for Joe's partnership interest began

    A. December 10, Year 5.

    B. March 1, Year 5.

    C. June 16, Year 1.

    D. One-half on June 16, Year 1, and one-half on March 1, Year 5.

Answer (C) is correct. *(Publisher, adapted)*
    REQUIRED: The holding period for a partnership interest acquired in exchange for a contributed capital asset.
    DISCUSSION: If the property received in an exchange has the same basis as the property given (substituted basis), the holding period of the property given will be tacked to the period for the property received [Sec. 1223(1)]. This rule applies only if the assets are capital assets or Sec. 1231 assets. Under Sec. 722, the basis of a partnership interest is equal to the adjusted basis of property contributed to the partnership in exchange for such interest. Therefore, Joe's holding period for the partnership interest runs from the day after he acquired the land (capital asset) contributed to the partnership, which was June 16, Year 1.
    Note that the partnership's holding period in the land is also tacked under Sec. 1223(2) since the partnership has a carryover basis under Sec. 723.
    Answer (A) is incorrect. On December 10, Year 5, the partnership sold the land. Answer (B) is incorrect. On March 1, Year 5, Joe contributed the land for a partnership interest. Answer (D) is incorrect. When capital assets are contributed to a partnership, there is a substituted basis for the partnership interest.

9.8.4. On January 1, Year 2, Minogue contributed inventory with a basis of $10,000 and a fair market value of $14,000 to ASTEC Corporation and received 100 shares of ASTEC stock. All the requirements of Sec. 351 were met. Minogue had acquired the inventory on December 1, Year 1, in the normal course of business. By April 15, Year 2, all the inventory was sold. Minogue's holding period for the ASTEC stock

    A. Began December 2, Year 1.

    B. Began January 2, Year 2.

    C. Began April 16, Year 2.

    D. Is always short-term because the stock was received for an ordinary income asset.

Answer (B) is correct. *(Publisher, adapted)*
    REQUIRED: The holding period of stock acquired in a nontaxable exchange for ordinary income property.
    DISCUSSION: When a capital asset or Sec. 1231 property is acquired in exchange for an ordinary income asset in a nontaxable transaction, the holding period begins on the date the capital asset or Sec. 1231 property is acquired. The holding period for an ordinary income asset cannot be included as part of the holding period of a capital asset. Minogue's holding period began on the date of the exchange, January 2, Year 2.
    Answer (A) is incorrect. The holding period for the ASTEC stock did not begin on December 2, Year 1. This is the date Minogue acquired the inventory. Answer (C) is incorrect. The holding period for the ASTEC stock did not begin on April 16, Year 2. This is the date Minogue sold all the inventory. Answer (D) is incorrect. The holding period is not always short-term because the stock was received for an ordinary asset.

9.8.5. On July 1, Year 1, Dora Flora purchased a greenhouse for use in her garden. On September 1, Year 1, she started a nursery business and converted the greenhouse to business use. Dora decided to incorporate the business and transferred all her business assets, including the greenhouse, to the Flora Corporation in exchange for 100% of its stock on June 1, Year 2. Flora Corporation sold the greenhouse on August 1, Year 2. What is Flora Corporation's holding period for the greenhouse?

A. 2 months.

B. 11 months.

C. 13 months.

D. 14 months.

Answer (C) is correct. *(Publisher, adapted)*
REQUIRED: The holding period of property converted from personal to business use, and then transferred to a corporation in exchange for stock.
DISCUSSION: The holding period of property generally begins on the date of acquisition. When property has the same basis in whole or in part as it had in the hands of a prior holder, however, the holding period of the prior holder is tacked to the present owner's holding period [Sec. 1223(2)]. The transfer of business assets by Dora to the Flora Corporation qualified under Sec. 351 as a tax-free exchange and the corporation took Dora's basis in the assets. Therefore, the corporation's holding period also includes Dora's. When Dora converted the greenhouse from personal to business use, the holding period of the greenhouse was not affected. As a result, Flora Corporation's holding period ran from July 2, Year 1, to August 1, Year 2, or 13 months.
Answer (A) is incorrect. The amount of time the asset was held by the corporation before being sold is 2 months. Answer (B) is incorrect. The time that the asset was held before the business was started is 11 months. Answer (D) is incorrect. The property was owned in total by Dora and the corporation for less than 14 months.

9.8.6. In Year 1, Alice Smith bought a diamond necklace for her own use at a cost of $10,000. In Year 5 when the fair market value was $12,000, Alice gave this necklace to her daughter, Julie. No gift tax was due. Julie's holding period for this gift

A. Starts in Year 5.

B. Starts in Year 1.

C. Depends on whether the necklace is sold by Julie at a gain or at a loss.

D. Is irrelevant because Julie received the necklace for no consideration of money or money's worth.

Answer (B) is correct. *(CPA, adapted)*
REQUIRED: The holding period of property acquired by gift.
DISCUSSION: Under Sec. 1015, the basis of property acquired by gift is generally the same as the basis in the hands of the donor. Under Sec. 1223(2), the holding period of property that has a carryover basis (the same basis as the prior holder's) includes the holding period of the prior owner. Julie's holding period, therefore, begins in Year 1 when Alice purchased the necklace.
Answer (A) is incorrect. Julie will tack Alice's holding period on to her own. Answer (C) is incorrect. Fair market value is greater than the basis at the time of the gift, so Julie will always use Alice's basis whether she sells it at a gain or a loss. Answer (D) is incorrect. The holding period is relevant in the event that Julie sells the necklace. The necklace is a capital asset and the holding period affects whether it is a long-term or short-term capital gain or loss.

9.8.7. Webster received 100 shares of Gator Corporation stock as a gift from Aunt Clara on August 1, Year 2, when the fair market value of the stock was $4,000. Clara purchased the stock on June 1, Year 1, for $5,000. On September 15, Year 2, Webster sold the stock for $3,700. Webster's loss and its character are

A. $1,300 long-term capital loss.

B. $1,300 short-term capital loss.

C. $300 long-term capital loss.

D. $300 short-term capital loss.

Answer (D) is correct. *(Publisher, adapted)*
REQUIRED: The amount and character of a loss incurred on the sale of stock acquired by gift.
DISCUSSION: The basis of property acquired by gift (to compute a loss) is the lower of the donor's basis or the fair market value of the property on the date of the gift (Sec. 1015). The FMV on the date of the gift was lower than Aunt Clara's basis, so Webster's basis for purposes of determining loss was $4,000. Webster sold the stock for $3,700 and realized a loss of $300. Since Webster did not receive a carryover basis from Clara, the holding period was not tacked on under Sec. 1223(2). Webster's holding period ran from the date of the gift, which is less than 1 year (from August 1 to September 15), so the character of the loss is short-term (Sec. 1222).
Answer (A) is incorrect. Webster does not have a $1,300 long-term capital loss from this transaction. Answer (B) is incorrect. Webster does not have a $1,300 loss from this stock sale. Answer (C) is incorrect. Webster does not have a long-term loss from this transaction.

9.8.8. On September 30, Year 1, Mr. C purchased investment land. On April 15, Year 2, C traded his land for some other investment land in a nontaxable exchange. On October 5, Year 2, C sold the land received in the exchange for a gain. C's gain will be treated as

A. A short-term capital gain.

B. A long-term capital gain.

C. Part short-term capital gain, part long-term capital gain.

D. Part nontaxable, part long-term capital gain.

Answer (B) is correct. *(SEE, adapted)*
REQUIRED: The character of gain on a sale of land acquired in a like-kind exchange.
DISCUSSION: If property received in an exchange has the same basis in whole or in part as that of the property given and if the property given is a capital asset or a Sec. 1231 asset, the holding period of the property received includes the period for which the property given was held [Sec. 1223(1)]. Since the basis of the land C received is the same as the adjusted basis of the land he traded as adjusted for the factors in Sec. 1031(d), the holding period of the land traded is added to the holding period of the land acquired. Therefore, C is deemed to have held the investment land sold since October 1, Year 1. C's gain will receive long-term capital gain treatment.
Answer (A) is incorrect. The capital gain will not be short-term. Answer (C) is incorrect. The capital gain is not part short-term and part long-term. Answer (D) is incorrect. The transaction is not part nontaxable and part long-term capital gain.

9.8.9. Don invested in Ho Ho Mutual Fund by purchasing 100 shares on March 1, Year 1. On the first day of every month, the Ho Ho fund pays a dividend that Don elected to have reinvested in the Ho Ho fund. Don received five additional shares each month. On April 15, Year 2, Don sold his entire interest (165 total shares) in the Ho Ho fund. How many of the Ho Ho fund shares sold by Don qualify for the long-term holding period?

A. 100

B. 105

C. 110

D. 165

Answer (B) is correct. *(SEE, adapted)*
REQUIRED: The number of shares that qualify for the long-term holding period.
DISCUSSION: The holding period of an asset for purposes of long-term gain treatment is 1 year from the date of acquisition, not including the day of acquisition but including the day of disposition. In this case, the only dividend reinvestment received more than 1 year away from the date of sale was the one received 4/1/Yr 1. The other shares were received less than 1 year from the date of sale.
Answer (A) is incorrect. The five shares that Don received as a dividend on April 1, Year 1, will also qualify for the long-term holding period. Answer (C) is incorrect. Not all 110 shares qualify for the long-term holding period. Answer (D) is incorrect. The total interest Don sold on April 15, Year 2, is 165 shares; however, they do not all qualify for the long-term holding period.

9.8.10. Rollo purchased a new car for use in his business on January 1, Year 1, for $10,000. On July 1, Year 2, a fire destroyed the car. The car was worth $10,000, and $1,000 of depreciation had been claimed. The insurance company replaced the car with another car worth $10,000 on September 1, Year 2. Rollo sold this replacement car on January 1, Year 3. What is Rollo's holding period for the replacement car?

A. 4 months.

B. 5 months.

C. 6 months.

D. 22 months.

Answer (D) is correct. *(Publisher, adapted)*
REQUIRED: The holding period of a car received in an involuntary conversion.
DISCUSSION: Under Sec. 1033(b), the basis of property replaced as a result of a casualty is the same as the basis in the destroyed property (increased by any gain recognized and decreased by any cash received). Under Sec. 1223(1), the holding period for a capital or Sec. 1231 asset acquired in an exchange includes the holding period of the property exchanged if the basis of the acquired property has the same basis in whole or in part as the property exchanged. Section 1223(1)(A) specifically states that an involuntary conversion shall be considered an exchange for purposes of applying the holding period rules.
Rollo's basis in the new car is the same as the basis in the old car. Under Sec. 1223(1), his holding period for the new car includes the holding period for the destroyed car, so his holding period for the new car is 22 months (no asset held during July and August of Year 2).
Answer (A) is incorrect. The holding period for the replacement car is not 4 months. Answer (B) is incorrect. The holding period for the replacement car is not 5 months. Answer (C) is incorrect. The period Rollo had the new car (not the replacement car), before it was destroyed in the fire, is 6 months.

9.8.11. Speedo purchased a new car on May 1 of the current year. Speedo died June 1 of the current year. The personal representative of the estate distributed the property to Speedo's son, Rollo, on July 1. Rollo sold the car 4 months later on October 31. What is Rollo's holding period for the property?

   A. 4 months.

   B. 5 months.

   C. 12 months.

   D. More than 12 months.

Answer (D) is correct. *(Publisher, adapted)*
REQUIRED: The beneficiary's holding period for property acquired from a decedent and sold within 1 year of the decedent's death.
DISCUSSION: Section 1223(11) provides that a person who acquires property from a decedent and sells such property within 12 months after the decedent's death is considered to have held the property for more than 12 months. Rollo acquired the car from a decedent since it was distributed from Speedo's estate, and he sold it within 12 months of Speedo's death. Therefore, Rollo is considered to have held the car for more than 12 months regardless of actual holding period.
Answer (A) is incorrect. The amount of time from distribution to sale is 4 months. Answer (B) is incorrect. The amount of time from death to sale is 5 months. Answer (C) is incorrect. Rollo's holding period is not 12 months.

9.8.12. Which of the following statements concerning the holding period of assets is true?

   A. In the case of stocks and bonds, the holding period begins on the day after the trading date.

   B. In the case of nontaxable exchanges, the holding period begins 45 days after the date you transfer the property.

   C. In the case of a gift, the holding period begins on the date you receive the gift.

   D. In the case of inherited property, there is no holding period.

Answer (A) is correct. *(Publisher, adapted)*
REQUIRED: The day the holding period of assets begins.
DISCUSSION: For a security that is purchased and sold on a registered security exchange, the holding period begins on the day after the taxpayer purchases the security.
Answer (B) is incorrect. In the case of nontaxable exchanges, the holding period does not begin 45 days after the date the property is transferred. Answer (C) is incorrect. In the case of a gift, the holding period does not begin on the date the gift is received. Answer (D) is incorrect. In the case of inherited property, there is a holding period.

9.8.13. For purposes of determining the holding period for property, the holding period begins on the day you acquired the property and ends on the day before the sale of the property.

   A. True.

   B. False.

Answer (B) is correct. *(SEE, adapted)*
DISCUSSION: The general rule for the holding period of property is that the date the property was acquired is excluded and the date of disposition is included. For properties acquired on the last day of a month, the holding period is determined by using calendar months (Rev. Rul. 66-5).

9.8.14. If you receive a gift of property acquired by the donor in 1976 and your basis is determined by the donor's basis, the first day of your holding period is the date you received the gift.

   A. True.

   B. False.

Answer (B) is correct. *(SEE, adapted)*
DISCUSSION: The holding period begins on the same date the appropriate basis valuation arises. If the donor's basis is used (carryover basis), the holding period includes the donor's holding period [Sec. 1223(2)].

9.8.15. If you receive a nontaxable stock dividend, your holding period includes the holding period of the stock on which the dividend was distributed.

   A. True.

   B. False.

Answer (A) is correct. *(Publisher, adapted)*
DISCUSSION: Under Sec. 1223(5), the holding period for stock, the basis of which is determined under Sec. 307, includes the period the taxpayer held the stock in the distributing corporation before the distribution. The basis of stock is determined under Sec. 307 when a shareholder receives a nontaxable stock dividend from the corporation.

STUDY UNIT TEN
DEPRECIATION, AMORTIZATION, AND DEPLETION

10.1 Depreciable Assets and Recovery Property

10.1.1. Which of the following assets are depreciable or amortizable for federal income tax purposes?

1. Land
2. Personal residence
3. Rental residence
4. Inventory
5. Acquired goodwill
6. Business automobile

A. 3, 5, and 6.

B. 1, 2, and 3.

C. 1 and 4.

D. 3, 4, and 6.

Answer (A) is correct. *(SEE, adapted)*
REQUIRED: The assets that may be depreciated for income tax purposes.
DISCUSSION: Section 167(a) provides a depreciation deduction with respect to property used in a trade or business or held for the production of income. A rental residence and a business automobile are both used in a trade or business or for the production of income. Therefore, they are depreciable. Goodwill that is acquired (as contrasted to internally created amounts) is amortizable under Sec. 197. Land, a personal residence, and inventory are not depreciable. Land is generally not subject to a decrease in value due to wear and tear, so it may not be depreciated. A personal residence may not be depreciated because it is not used in a trade or business or for the production of income. Inventory may not be depreciated because it is not used in a business; instead, it is sold.
Answer (B) is incorrect. Land, a personal residence, and inventory are not depreciable. Land is generally not subject to a decrease in value due to wear and tear, so it may not be depreciated. A personal residence may not be depreciated because it is not used in a trade or business or for the production of income. Answer (C) is incorrect. Land and inventory are not depreciable. Land is generally not subject to a decrease in value due to wear and tear, so it may not be depreciated. Inventory may not be depreciated because it is not used in a business; instead, it is sold. Answer (D) is incorrect. Inventory is not depreciable. Inventory may not be depreciated because it is not used in a business; instead, it is sold.

10.1.2. Which of the following is not depreciable under MACRS?

A. Customer list, acquired in a purchase transaction, with an established acquisition cost and an expected life in excess of 1 year.

B. Low-income housing.

C. Technical books with a 5-year useful life.

D. A business automobile driven by the business owner.

Answer (A) is correct. *(Publisher, adapted)*
REQUIRED: The asset that is not depreciable under MACRS.
DISCUSSION: From 1981 to 1987, Sec. 168(c) defined recovery property for the ACRS rules as tangible property of a character subject to depreciation that is used in a trade or business or held for the production of income. The 1986 Tax Act revised Sec. 168 and does not use the term "recovery property" for the MACRS rules. Instead, Sec. 168 now applies to tangible property depreciable under Sec. 167. In effect, however, the same property is included, so the term "recovery property" is still useful. A customer list is not tangible property, so it is not depreciable under MACRS. It is, however, intangible property, which is amortizable over 15 years under Sec. 197 [Sec. 197(d)(1)].
Answer (B) is incorrect. Low-income housing is tangible property used in a trade or business and qualifies as recovery property. Answer (C) is incorrect. Technical books with a 5-year useful life are tangible property used in a trade or business and qualify as recovery property. Answer (D) is incorrect. A business automobile driven by the business owner is tangible property used in a trade or business and qualifies as recovery property.

10.1.3. Which of the following placed in service in the current year is not a class of recovery property?

A. 3-year property.

B. 7-year property.

C. 15-year property.

D. Low-income housing.

Answer (D) is correct. *(Publisher, adapted)*
REQUIRED: The item that is not a class of recovery property.
DISCUSSION: Section 168(e) defines for MACRS purposes the classes of recovery property as 3-year, 5-year, 7-year, 10-year, 15-year, 20-year, residential rental, and nonresidential real property. Low-income housing does not have a separate class and is generally residential rental property depreciable using the straight-line method over 27.5 years.
Answer (A) is incorrect. Three-year property is a class of recovery property under Sec. 168(e). Answer (B) is incorrect. Seven-year property is a class of recovery property under Sec. 168(e). Answer (C) is incorrect. Fifteen-year property is a class of recovery property under Sec. 168(e).

10.1.4. Intangible property may be depreciated (or amortized) if its use in the business or in producing income is definitely limited in duration. Which one of the following may not be depreciated (or amortized)?

A. Patent.

B. Baseball contract.

C. Interest in a partnership.

D. Leasehold.

Answer (C) is correct. *(D.B. Bradley)*
REQUIRED: The intangible asset that may not be depreciated for income tax purposes.
DISCUSSION: Section 167(a) provides a depreciation deduction with respect to property used in a trade or business or held for the production of income. The deduction is not allowed if an asset lacks a determinable useful life. Since the usefulness of an interest in a partnership is considered to be of indefinite duration, it may not be depreciated under Sec. 167. An interest in a partnership is specifically excluded from the definition of a Sec. 197 intangible that is amortizable [Sec. 197(e)(1)].
Answer (A) is incorrect. A patent has a definite useful life and may be depreciated or amortized. Answer (B) is incorrect. A baseball contract has a definite useful life and may be depreciated or amortized. Answer (D) is incorrect. A leasehold has a definite useful life and may be depreciated or amortized.

10.1.5. Which of the following assets qualifies for MACRS treatment?

A. Tangible personal property purchased and placed in service in 1985 as 20-year property.

B. Real property acquired in 1992 from a related party who had acquired the property in 1986.

C. A truck purchased in 1999 used entirely for trade or business purposes.

D. Real property purchased in 1996 and leased back to its previous owner who had acquired it in 1986.

Answer (C) is correct. *(SEE, adapted)*
REQUIRED: The asset(s) qualifying for MACRS treatment.
DISCUSSION: To be eligible for MACRS treatment, an asset must be tangible property used in a trade or business or held for the production of income and not excluded by Sec. 168(f). Section 168(f) excludes property acquired by the taxpayer after 1986 if the property was owned by a related person at any time during 1986. It also excludes property acquired after 1986 and leased to any person who owned the property at any time during 1986. The new rules also generally do not apply to property placed in service before 1987 (with some exceptions and transitional rules).
Answer (A) is incorrect. Tangible personal property purchased and placed in service in 1985 as 20-year property is an example of property excluded by Sec. 168(f) and is thus ineligible for MACRS treatment. Answer (B) is incorrect. Real property acquired in 1992 from a related party who had acquired the property in 1986 is an example of property excluded by Sec. 168(f) and is thus ineligible for MACRS treatment. Answer (D) is incorrect. Real property purchased in 1996 and leased back to its previous owner who had acquired it in 1986 is an example of property excluded by Sec. 168(f) and is thus ineligible for MACRS treatment.

10.1.6. Which of the following characteristics helps in assigning recovery property to a particular class?

A. Business use.

B. Tangible or intangible.

C. Asset Depreciation Range midpoint.

D. Listed property or not.

Answer (C) is correct. *(Publisher, adapted)*
REQUIRED: The characteristic that is helpful in classifying recovery property.
DISCUSSION: The assignment of recovery property to classes is determined on the basis of the property's Asset Depreciation Range (ADR) midpoint. Each recovery class has a midpoint range into which the property must fall.
Answer (A) is incorrect. Only property used in a trade or business or held for the production of income is depreciable. Whether it is used in a business or held for production of income does not affect its classification. Answer (B) is incorrect. Only tangible property is treated as recovery property (intangible property must be depreciated or amortized under Secs. 167 or 197), but it does not affect the assignment to a particular class. Answer (D) is incorrect. Whether the property is classified as listed property or not under Sec. 280F(d)(4) has no effect on the recovery class to which the property is assigned.

10.1.7. Recovery property is tangible property of a character that is subject to the allowance for depreciation. It is used in a trade or business or held for the production of income and must have been placed in service after 1980.

A. True.

B. False.

Answer (A) is correct. *(SEE, adapted)*
DISCUSSION: In general, recovery property is tangible property of a character subject to the allowance for depreciation and used in a trade or business or held for the production of income [Secs. 168(a) and 167(a)]. The property must have been placed in service after 1980 and before 1987. (Although not called recovery property, the MACRS rules use asset categories similar to the recovery classes of the ACRS rules.)

10.1.8. In the current year, Marty purchased assets to be used in his business. One of the assets purchased was a copyright. The copyright is considered to be property subject to the allowance for depreciation under MACRS.

A. True.

B. False.

Answer (B) is correct. *(SEE, adapted)*
DISCUSSION: Property depreciable under the MACRS rules is tangible property of a character subject to the allowance for depreciation. Since a copyright is not tangible property, it is not subject to the allowance for depreciation under the MACRS rules. However, it is generally amortizable using the straight-line method over its life under Sec. 197 [Sec. 197(d)(1)(c)(iii)].

10.1.9. Ms. Bird moved to a new residence in September of the current year. In October of the current year, she began renting out her former residence that she had purchased in 1980. Ms. Bird is required to compute depreciation on the rental property under the MACRS method of depreciation.

A. True.

B. False.

Answer (B) is correct. *(SEE, adapted)*
DISCUSSION: Although Ms. Bird converted the property to business use after 1980, she owned the property in 1980. Section 168(f) excludes real property from ACRS or MACRS treatment if owned by the taxpayer in 1980. Depreciation will be calculated using the pre-ACRS rules.

10.1.10. Mr. Parker's lease agreement for equipment used in his business is intended to be a conditional sales contract rather than a lease. Mr. Parker should capitalize the lease payments and depreciate them over the recovery period for the asset.

A. True.

B. False.

Answer (A) is correct. *(SEE, adapted)*
DISCUSSION: Since the equipment will be used in Mr. Parker's business and is intended to be a conditional sale, the asset should be capitalized. The capitalized lease payments should be depreciated over the asset's recovery period.

10.2 Depreciable Basis

NOTE: (Also see Study Unit 9, "Basis," for additional questions.)

10.2.1. Dorothy purchased a car in the current year to be used three-fourths of the time in her business and one-fourth of the time for personal purposes. The car cost $8,000 and is 5-year recovery property. No Sec. 179 expense deduction is taken. The car's basis for MACRS depreciation is

A. $1,600

B. $2,000

C. $6,000

D. $8,000

Answer (C) is correct. *(Publisher, adapted)*
REQUIRED: The depreciable basis of an asset used for business and personal purposes.
DISCUSSION: The basis of property for depreciation is determined under the general basis rules. Under Sec. 1012, the basis for an asset is generally its cost. The cost of the car is $8,000, which must be allocated between business and personal use. Since she uses the car three-fourths for business, the basis for depreciation is $6,000 ($8,000 × 75%). Since no Sec. 179 expense deduction was taken, there are no other reductions to basis.
Answer (A) is incorrect. The amount of $1,600 is the cost divided by the recovery period. Answer (B) is incorrect. The personal portion of the basis is $2,000. Answer (D) is incorrect. The basis must be apportioned between personal and business use.

10.2.2. Mrs. Howser converted her personal residence (originally acquired in 1981) to rental property in the current year. At the time of the change in use, the property had an adjusted basis of $45,000, of which $5,000 was for the land and $40,000 for the house. The fair market value at the time of the change was $50,000, of which $11,000 was for land and $39,000 for the house. What is Mrs. Howser's basis for determining depreciation?

A. $39,000

B. $40,000

C. $45,000

D. $50,000

Answer (A) is correct. *(SEE, adapted)*
REQUIRED: The depreciable basis of a personal residence converted to rental property.
DISCUSSION: If personal use assets are converted to business or income-producing use, the basis for ACRS and MACRS depreciation is the lower of the adjusted basis or the fair market value when converted [Prop. Reg. 1.168-2(j)(6)]. Only the basis of the house is considered because the land is not depreciable.
Since the fair market value of the house on the date of conversion ($39,000) is less than the adjusted basis ($40,000), the depreciable basis of Mrs. Howser's rental property is $39,000.
The anti-churning rules of Sec. 168(f)(5) do not apply to residential rental property or nonresidential real property [Sec. 168(f)(5)(B)(i)]. Therefore, even though the property was acquired in a pre-MACRS tax year, the MACRS depreciation rules will be used to depreciate the property.
Answer (B) is incorrect. The fair market value of the house is less than the adjusted basis of the house. Answer (C) is incorrect. The adjusted basis of the house and the land is $45,000. Answer (D) is incorrect. The fair market value of the house and the land is $50,000.

10.2.3. In 1988, Brian Todd built his home for $50,000 on a lot that cost $8,000. Before he converted the property to rental use in the current year, he had added $10,000 of permanent improvements and claimed a $3,000 deduction for a casualty loss to the house. Mr. Todd also paid $20,000 in real estate taxes from 1988 to the present. On the date of use change, Todd's property had a fair market value of $72,000, of which $9,000 was for the land and $63,000 for the house. What is Mr. Todd's basis in the house for depreciation purposes?

A. $50,000

B. $57,000

C. $63,000

D. $77,000

Answer (B) is correct. *(SEE, adapted)*
REQUIRED: The depreciable basis of a personal residence converted to rental property.
DISCUSSION: Regulation 1.167(g)-1 and Prop. Reg. 1.168-2(j)(6) state that if personal use assets are converted to business or income-producing use, the basis for depreciation is the lower of the adjusted basis or the fair market value when the property is converted. The adjusted basis of the property is its cost under Sec. 1012 plus adjustments under Sec. 1016 for capital expenditures and losses. Since the basis of the house is $57,000 (computed below) and the fair market value is $63,000, Todd's basis for depreciation is $57,000.

Cost	$50,000
Improvements	10,000
Less: casualty loss	(3,000)
Depreciable basis	$57,000

Answer (A) is incorrect. The cost of the house is $50,000. Answer (C) is incorrect. The fair market value of the house is $63,000. Answer (D) is incorrect. Basis in the house does not include real estate taxes paid.

10.2.4. In March 2017, Jesse traded in a 2014 van for a new 2017 model. He used both the old van and the new van 75% for business. Jesse has claimed actual expenses for the business use of the old van since 2014. He did not claim a Sec. 179 deduction of the old or new van. Jesse paid $12,800 for the old van in June 2014. Depreciation claimed on the 2014 van was $7,388, which included one half-year for 2017. Jesse paid $9,800 cash in addition to a trade-in allowance of $2,200 to acquire the new van. What is Jesse's depreciable basis in the new van?

A. $11,409

B. $9,562

C. $9,009

D. $9,000

Answer (B) is correct. *(SEE, adapted)*
REQUIRED: The depreciable basis for the new van.
DISCUSSION: The basis for figuring depreciation for the new van is (1) the adjusted basis of the old van ($5,412), determined by subtracting the depreciation taken ($7,388) from the cost of the old van ($12,800), plus (2) any additional amount paid for the new van ($9,800), totaling $15,212, minus (3) the excess, if any, of the total amount of depreciation that would have been allowable before the trade if the old van had been used 100% for business ($9,850), over the total amounts actually allowable as depreciation during those years ($7,388), totaling $2,462. The total depreciation basis for the new van ($12,750) must be reduced by the amount of personal use (25%) to determine the depreciation basis for the new van ($9,562).
Answer (A) is incorrect. The depreciable basis does not equal $11,409. Answer (C) is incorrect. The depreciable basis does not equal $9,009. Answer (D) is incorrect. The depreciable basis does not equal $9,000.

10.3 Election to Expense

10.3.1. Mr. Anderson, a sole proprietor, purchased $12,000 worth of office equipment and furniture in 2017 for use in his business. He elected to take the maximum Sec. 179 deduction. What is Mr. Anderson's basis for the MACRS computation?

A. $12,000

B. $7,000

C. $2,000

D. $0

Answer (D) is correct. *(SEE, adapted)*
REQUIRED: The depreciable basis for MACRS after taking the full Sec. 179 deduction in 2017.
DISCUSSION: The original cost of an asset must be reduced for any Sec. 179 expense up to $510,000 in 2017. Since Mr. Anderson took the Sec. 179 expense deduction of $12,000 in 2017, he must reduce the cost of his property. Mr. Anderson's depreciable basis is

Original cost	$12,000
Less: Sec. 179 deduction	(12,000)
Depreciable basis	$ 0

Answer (A) is incorrect. The amount of $12,000 (the cost of the property) is less than the Sec. 179 deduction for 2017. Answer (B) is incorrect. The 2017 Sec. 179 deduction is greater than $5,000. Answer (C) is incorrect. The 2017 Sec. 179 deduction is greater than $10,000.

10.3.2. All of the following statements regarding the Sec. 179 deduction for 2017 are true except

A. The amount that is not deductible due to the taxable income limitation can be carried forward.

B. The amount expensed cannot exceed the taxable income derived from any trade or business during the tax year.

C. The maximum deductible amount is reduced if property placed in service during the tax year exceeds $2.03 million.

D. The maximum cost that is deductible for tax year 2017 is $25,000.

Answer (D) is correct. *(SEE, adapted)*
REQUIRED: The false statement concerning Sec. 179 expense.
DISCUSSION: There are several limitations on the deduction allowed by Sec. 179. One limitation is taxable income and to the extent that causes an amount to be nondeductible, such amount may be carried forward to be deducted in future years. This carryover is subject to all the limitations as if it was an expense of the current year. The maximum cost that is deductible for tax year 2017 is $510,000. This amount is reduced if the Sec. 179 property placed in service during the year exceeds $2.03 million.
Answer (A) is incorrect. The amount that is not deductible due to the taxable income limitation can be carried forward. Answer (B) is incorrect. The amount expensed cannot exceed the taxable income derived from any trade or business during the tax year. Answer (C) is incorrect. The maximum deductible amount is reduced if property placed in service during the tax year exceeds $2.03 million.

10.3.3. On July 1, 2017, Ms. K, who is single and owns and operates a specialty shop, paid $30,000 for a new automobile that she uses 60% of the time for business purposes. She purchased no other business assets in 2017. The taxable income of the business before the Sec. 179 deduction is $20,000. What is the maximum allowable Sec. 179 deduction that Ms. K may elect to take in 2017?

A. $3,160

B. $1,896

C. $18,000

D. $30,000

Answer (B) is correct. *(SEE, adapted)*
REQUIRED: The Sec. 179 expense deduction in 2017.
DISCUSSION: In 2017, Sec. 179 allows a taxpayer to treat up to $510,000 of the cost of Sec. 179 property acquired as an expense. However, only the 60% portion of the automobile used for business will qualify. Therefore, the Sec. 179 expense would normally be $18,000 ($30,000 × 60%).
But Sec. 280F limits the first-year capital recovery deduction for automobiles to $3,160 for 2017. The capital recovery deductions include the amount expensed under Sec. 179 and depreciation. This amount must be reduced by personal use for the automobile during the year. The redetermined amount is the limit times the percentage of business/investment use during the year ($1,896 = $3,160 × 60%).
Answer (A) is incorrect. The amount of $3,160 is the limit for the first year capital recovery deduction for an automobile. This amount must be reduced by the amount for personal use of the automobile. Answer (C) is incorrect. The amount of $18,000 is the Sec. 179 expense without considering the $3,160 Sec. 280F limitation for the first-year capital recovery deduction for an automobile for personal usage. Answer (D) is incorrect. The amount of $30,000 is the cost of the automobile, which is not fully deductible in the first year.

10.3.4. Ellwood and Elmo were equal partners in a used guitar store. In 2017, they bought a used amplifier for use in the store to demonstrate guitars. The amplifier cost $25,000. The taxable income of the business before the Sec. 179 deduction is $18,000. How much Sec. 179 expense can Ellwood and Elmo each deduct in 2017 if neither has any other Sec. 179 deductions?

A. $0

B. $9,000

C. $12,000

D. $12,500

Answer (B) is correct. *(Publisher, adapted)*
REQUIRED: The cost of used property that partners can expense in the year of acquisition.
DISCUSSION: Section 179 allows a taxpayer to elect to treat all or part of the cost of Sec. 179 property as an expense. Section 179 property is any tangible property, subject to depreciation, that is Sec. 1245 property and was acquired by purchase for use in a trade or business. It does not matter that the property is used. The maximum amount that may be taken into account for this election is $510,000 in 2017, but it is limited to the taxable income of the partnership before the Sec. 179 deduction. Hence, the total amount that the partnership can deduct is $18,000, or $9,000 each for Ellwood and Elmo. The additional first-year depreciation does not apply to used equipment.
Answer (A) is incorrect. An amount may be deducted by each partner based on taxable income. Answer (C) is incorrect. The total Sec. 179 deduction allowed is $18,000, which is allocated to each partner. Answer (D) is incorrect. The amount of $12,500 is half of the cost of the amplifier.

10.3.5. Juliet bought and placed in service computer equipment in 2017. She paid $10,000 and received a $2,000 trade-in allowance for her old computer equipment. She had an adjusted basis of $3,000 in the old computer equipment. Juliet used both the old and new equipment 90% for business and 10% for personal purposes. Her allowable Sec. 179 expense deduction is

A. $12,000

B. $10,800

C. $10,000

D. $9,000

Answer (D) is correct. *(SEE, adapted)*
REQUIRED: The allowable Sec. 179 expense deduction.
DISCUSSION: In 2017, Sec. 179 allows a taxpayer to treat up to $510,000 of the cost of Sec. 179 property acquired as an expense rather than as a capital expenditure. However, the cost of Sec. 179 property does not include the basis determined by reference to other property held by the taxpayer [Sec. 179(d)(3)]. The basis of the new computer is $13,000 ($3,000 basis of old computer + $10,000 purchase price). Since Sec. 179 does not apply to any portion of the basis that references an asset that was previously held by the taxpayer, only $10,000 of basis is eligible for Sec. 179 [Reg. 1.179-4(d)]. Only the 90% portion of the computer used for business will qualify, however. Therefore, the Sec. 179 expense is $9,000 ($10,000 cost × 90%).
Answer (A) is incorrect. The Sec. 179 expense is not equal to the amount paid for the new computer plus the amount received for the old computer. Answer (B) is incorrect. Section 179 does not apply to any portion of the basis that references an asset that was previously held by the taxpayer. Answer (C) is incorrect. The Sec. 179 expense applies only to the business portion of the asset.

10.3.6. In 2017, Walt Sheen purchased and placed in service a packaging machine at a cost of $2,045,000. He had $37,000 taxable income from his business before considering the deduction allowed under Sec. 179. What is Walt's allowable Sec. 179 deduction for 2017?

    A. $510,000

    B. $495,000

    C. $37,000

    D. $0

Answer (C) is correct. *(SEE, adapted)*
    REQUIRED: The Sec. 179 expense deduction for 2017.
    DISCUSSION: Section 179 allows a taxpayer to treat up to $510,000 of the cost of Sec. 179 property acquired in 2017 as an expense rather than as a capital expenditure. There are certain limitations that can reduce the allowable deduction. One limitation is that the amount deductible under Sec. 179 must be reduced by the amount by which the cost of Sec. 179 property placed in service during the year exceeds $2.03 million. Walt's deduction is reduced from $510,000 to $495,000 by this limitation. Another limitation is that the total cost that can be deducted is limited to the taxable income from the active conduct of any trade or business during the tax year. Walt had only $37,000 of taxable income. Because this amount is smaller than either the general rule or the limitation based on property placed in service, his deduction is limited to $37,000. The remaining $458,000 ($495,000 – $37,000) may be carried forward to 2018.
    Answer (A) is incorrect. The entire maximum Sec. 179 deduction is not available. Answer (B) is incorrect. The deduction is further limited by the amount of taxable income. Answer (D) is incorrect. A limited Sec. 179 deduction is available.

10.3.7. Raccoon Tails, Ltd., processes exotic pet food. Raccoon purchased a kibble machine in 2017 for $25,000. It is 5-year recovery property. Raccoon claimed the maximum expense under Sec. 179. The kibble machine was its only asset acquisition for 2017. Raccoon Tails reports taxable income of $60,000 excluding depreciation for 2017. What is Raccoon's basis for MACRS depreciation?

    A. $0

    B. $1,000

    C. $15,000

    D. $25,000

Answer (A) is correct. *(Publisher, adapted)*
    REQUIRED: The basis for depreciation of property on which an election to use the Sec. 179 expensing has been made.
    DISCUSSION: The basis for computing the MACRS depreciation is reduced by the $25,000 election to expense part of the asset's cost under Sec. 179. Thus, the depreciable basis is $0 ($25,000 cost – $25,000 Sec. 179 expense).
    Answer (B) is incorrect. Basis is cost less the allowable Sec. 179 deduction. Answer (C) is incorrect. The cost is less than the allowable Sec. 179 deduction. Answer (D) is incorrect. The amount of $25,000 is the cost, not the basis.

10.3.8. In 2017, Johnson Corporation purchased an electric passenger vehicle built by an original equipment manufacturer for $14,000. Johnson's taxable income before any Sec. 179 deduction is $12,000. What is Johnson's allowable deduction under Sec. 179?

    A. $0

    B. $11,160

    C. $12,000

    D. $14,000

Answer (B) is correct. *(Publisher, adapted)*
    REQUIRED: The Sec. 179 deduction for a special passenger vehicle in 2017.
    DISCUSSION: Section 280F places limits on the amount of depreciation allowed on certain vehicles. The limit in the first recovery year is $11,160.
    Answer (A) is incorrect. Johnson has an allowable, yet limited, deduction. Answer (C) is incorrect. Johnson's taxable income before any Sec. 179 deduction is $12,000. Answer (D) is incorrect. The cost of the vehicle is $14,000.

10.3.9. The Sec. 179 deduction can be claimed on tangible personal property that is held for the production of income.

    A. True.

    B. False.

Answer (B) is correct. *(SEE, adapted)*
    DISCUSSION: Section 179 property is any tangible property that is Sec. 1245 property and is purchased for use in the active conduct of a trade or business [Sec. 179(d)(1)]. Property held merely for investment purposes (production of income) is not Sec. 179 property.

10.4 Depreciation (Assets Acquired 1981-86)

10.4.1. Mike Wright bought a marina in Florida on September 15, 1984. The purchase price was allocated among the land, buildings, and other personal property. The part of the price allocated to the buildings was $225,000. What is Wright's maximum depreciation deduction on the buildings in 2017?

A. $0

B. $12,500

C. $15,000

D. $6,750

Answer (A) is correct. *(Publisher, adapted)*
REQUIRED: The maximum amount of 2017 cost recovery (depreciation) under ACRS for real property acquired in 1984.
DISCUSSION: For real property placed in service after June 22, 1984, and before May 9, 1985, unadjusted basis is recovered over a period of 18 years. Under ACRS, components of Sec. 1250 class property may not be depreciated separately. The asset will have been fully depreciated before 2017, so no depreciation deduction can be taken.
Answer (B) is incorrect. The annual depreciation for 18-year property under the straight-line method is $12,500. Answer (C) is incorrect. The amount of $15,000 is 6.7% of the building's cost. Answer (D) is incorrect. The amount of $6,750 is the 3% deduction for the last year before full depreciation.

10.4.2. Which of the following is a true statement concerning the Accelerated Cost Recovery System (ACRS) for assets placed in service after 1980 but before 1987?

A. Either ACRS or depreciation under IRC Sec. 167 can be elected.

B. Depreciation under IRC Sec. 167 is no longer used.

C. ACRS uses the half-year convention for properties other than real property.

D. A taxpayer may change from Sec. 167 depreciation to ACRS.

Answer (C) is correct. *(SEE, adapted)*
REQUIRED: The true statement concerning the ACRS.
DISCUSSION: ACRS applies to all tangible property subject to depreciation (with limited exceptions) that is placed in service after 1980 and before 1987. For other than real property, ACRS is applied by the use of tables that have the 150%-declining-balance method and the half-year convention built into them. The asset is treated as if placed in service at mid-year. No cost recovery (depreciation) is allowed in the year of disposition.
Answer (A) is incorrect. ACRS is mandatory for depreciable, tangible property placed in service after 1980. Answer (B) is incorrect. Depreciation under Sec. 167 still applies to property placed in service prior to 1981 and to intangible property. (Depreciation of intangibles is sometimes called amortization.) Answer (D) is incorrect. A taxpayer may not use ACRS for property placed in service prior to 1981, and no change is allowed.

10.4.3. For real property (that is not low-income housing) with a class life greater than 12.5 years and acquired after May 8, 1985, but before January 1, 1987, what is the statutory recovery period?

A. 18 years.

B. 19 years.

C. 35 years.

D. 45 years.

Answer (B) is correct. *(Publisher, adapted)*
REQUIRED: The recovery period for real property acquired between May 8, 1985, and December 31, 1986.
DISCUSSION: Prior to the 1986 TRA, Sec. 168(c)(2)(D) defined the recovery period for real property that has a class life greater than 12.5 years and is not low-income housing. For property acquired from January 1, 1981, through March 15, 1984, the recovery period was 15 years. From March 16, 1984, through June 22, 1984, it was 18 years. From June 23, 1984, through May 8, 1985, it was 18 years with a mid-month convention. From May 9, 1985, through December 31, 1986, it was 19 years.
Answer (A) is incorrect. The recovery period for property acquired from March 16, 1984, through May 8, 1985, is 18 years. Answer (C) is incorrect. The statutory recovery period for 18- or 19-year real property under Alternate ACRS is 35 years. Answer (D) is incorrect. The statutory recovery period for 18- or 19-year real property under Alternate ACRS is not 45 years.

10.5 Depreciation (Assets Acquired after 1986)

10.5.1. Under MACRS, the cost of depreciable property is recovered using

- A. The applicable depreciation method.
- B. The applicable recovery period.
- C. The applicable convention.
- D. All of the answers are correct.

Answer (D) is correct. *(SEE, adapted)*
REQUIRED: The true statement regarding the cost of depreciable property recovered under MACRS.
DISCUSSION: Under MACRS, useful lives for assets are termed recovery periods and are prescribed by statute. Each asset is deemed to have a particular useful life of 3, 5, 7, 10, 15, 20, 27.5, or 39 years. Also, salvage value is unimportant.
Answer (A) is incorrect. Under MACRS, the cost of depreciable property is recovered by also using the applicable convention and the applicable recovery period. Answer (B) is incorrect. Under MACRS, the cost of depreciable property is recovered by also using the applicable depreciation method and the applicable convention. Answer (C) is incorrect. Under MACRS, the cost of depreciable property is recovered by also using the applicable depreciation method and the applicable recovery period.

10.5.2. Which of the following is a true statement concerning MACRS for assets acquired after 1986?

- A. The 200%-declining-balance method is used for all property except 27.5-year, 31.5-year, and 39-year real property.
- B. An election to use the straight-line method may be made on an annual basis but only for an entire recovery class of assets.
- C. The alternative depreciation system allows a choice of recovery periods for each recovery class of assets.
- D. For 3-year through 10-year property, only 200%-declining-balance and straight-line methods are available.

Answer (B) is correct. *(Publisher, adapted)*
REQUIRED: The true statement about MACRS after the 1986 Tax Act.
DISCUSSION: Generally, for personal property acquired after 1986, MACRS uses the 200%-declining-balance method over a prescribed recovery period. Straight-line depreciation may be elected in any year for one or more classes of property in lieu of the accelerated method. This election is irrevocable once made and must be made for all assets acquired that year in a particular class of property, not on an asset-by-asset basis.
Answer (A) is incorrect. The 200%-declining-balance method is used for 3-year through 10-year property; the 150%-declining-balance method is used for 15-year and 20-year property; and the straight-line method is used for 27.5-year, 31.5-year, and 39-year property. Answer (C) is incorrect. The alternative depreciation system (used for property predominantly used outside the U.S., tax-exempt use property, etc.) uses different (longer) recovery periods than MACRS, but there is only one for each class of property. Answer (D) is incorrect. A taxpayer may use (for regular tax purposes) the alternative depreciation system used in computing the alternative minimum tax and that uses the 150%-declining-balance method.

10.5.3. All of the following statements regarding the alternative MACRS depreciation system are true except

- A. The election to use the alternative MACRS system can be revoked.
- B. The election must be made by the due date, including extensions, for the tax return of the year in which the property was placed in service.
- C. The alternative MACRS depreciation system is figured using straight-line method, no salvage value, and the class life of the asset or 12 years if no class life is assigned.
- D. Excluding nonresidential real and residential rental property, the election of the alternative MACRS depreciation system for a recovery class of property applies to all property in that recovery class that is placed in service during the tax year of the election.

Answer (A) is correct. *(SEE, adapted)*
REQUIRED: The false statement regarding the alternative MACRS depreciation system.
DISCUSSION: For personal property acquired after 1986, MACRS uses the 200%-declining-balance method or the 150%-declining-balance method over a prescribed recovery period. The alternative MACRS depreciation system of Sec. 168(g) may be elected in any year for one or more recovery classes of property in lieu of the regular method or the straight-line method of Sec. 168(b)(5). The alternative depreciation system uses the straight-line method over a recovery period established in Sec. 168(g)(2) that is generally longer than that used under regular MACRS. However, this election is irrevocable once made [Sec. 168(g)(7)(B)] and must be made for all assets acquired that year in a particular recovery class of property. Nonresidential real property and residential rental property elections are made on a property-by-property basis.
Answer (B) is incorrect. Regarding the alternative MACRS depreciation system, the election must be made by the due date, including extensions, for the tax return of the year in which the property was placed in service. Answer (C) is incorrect. The alternative MACRS depreciation system is figured using straight-line method, no salvage value, and the class life of the asset or 12 years if no class life is assigned. Answer (D) is incorrect. Excluding nonresidential real and residential rental property, the election of the alternative MACRS depreciation system for a recovery class of property applies to all property in that recovery class that is placed in service during the tax year of the election.

10.5.4. Under the MACRS depreciation rules for property placed in service after 1986,

A. Used tangible depreciable property is excluded from the computation.

B. Salvage value is ignored for purposes of computing the MACRS deduction.

C. No type of straight-line depreciation is allowable.

D. The recovery period for residential rental property is 39 years.

Answer (B) is correct. *(CPA, adapted)*
   REQUIRED: The true statement regarding MACRS.
   DISCUSSION: Under the MACRS rules, salvage value is not included in the computation of the depreciation amount. This leads to fewer disputes with the IRS over the proper salvage value to be used.
   Answer (A) is incorrect. Used tangible depreciable property is included in the computation. Answer (C) is incorrect. Straight-line depreciation is allowable for tangible personal property and real property. Answer (D) is incorrect. The recovery period for residential rental property is 27.5 years, and the recovery period for nonresidential real property is 39 years (31.5 years for MACRS property placed in service before May 13, 1993).

10.5.5. During the current year, Danny, a calendar-year taxpayer, acquired and placed in service the following business assets:

January: Delivery trucks	$ 50,000
March: Warehouse building	150,000
June: Computer system	30,000
September: Automobile	30,000
November: Office equipment	90,000

Which convention(s) is(are) used to figure Danny's depreciation for the current year?

A. Mid-quarter for all assets except the warehouse building, which uses mid-month.

B. Half-year for all of the assets.

C. Mid-quarter for all of the assets.

D. Half-year for all assets except the warehouse building, which uses mid-month; half-year for the automobile and the office equipment.

Answer (A) is correct. *(SEE, adapted)*
   REQUIRED: The convention(s) to be used in calculating depreciation.
   DISCUSSION: Under the MACRS rules, the mid-quarter convention must be used for all personal property placed in service during the year if substantial property was placed in service during the last 3 months of the year [Sec. 168(d)(3)]. Substantial property is defined as greater than 40% of the aggregate bases of property placed in service during the year. The $90,000 office equipment constitutes 45% ($90,000 ÷ $200,000) of all personal property placed in service, so the mid-quarter convention must be used. A mid-month convention is used in the year of acquisition for real property. Therefore, the mid-month convention is used for the warehouse building.
   Answer (B) is incorrect. The mid-quarter convention must be used for the personal property, whereas the mid-month convention must be used for the warehouse. Answer (C) is incorrect. The mid-month convention must be used for the warehouse. Answer (D) is incorrect. The mid-quarter convention must be used for the personal property.

10.5.6. With regard to depreciation computations made under the general MACRS method, the half-year convention provides that

A. One-half of the first year's depreciation is allowed in the year in which the property is placed in service, regardless of when the property is placed in service during the year, and a half-year's depreciation is allowed for the year in which the property is disposed of.

B. The deduction will be based on the number of months the property was in service, so that one-half month's depreciation is allowed for the month in which the property is placed in service and for the month in which it is disposed of.

C. Depreciation will be allowed in the first year of acquisition of the property only if the property is placed in service no later than June 30 for calendar-year corporations.

D. Depreciation will be allowed in the last year of the property's economic life only if the property is disposed of after June 30 of the year of disposition for calendar-year corporations.

Answer (A) is correct. *(CPA, adapted)*
   REQUIRED: The correct meaning of the half-year convention.
   DISCUSSION: The half-year convention applies to all property placed in service after 1986 except for residential rental property and nonresidential real property (to which the mid-month convention applies) and except when the mid-quarter convention applies. Under the half-year convention, all property to which it applies is treated as placed in service or disposed of at the midpoint of the year. Therefore, only one-half of the first year's depreciation and one-half of the disposal year's depreciation is allowed.
   Answer (B) is incorrect. With the mid-month convention, the deduction will be based on the number of months the property was in service, so that one-half month's depreciation is allowed for the month in which the property is placed in service and for the month in which it is disposed of. Answer (C) is incorrect. With the modified half-year convention, depreciation will be allowed in the first year of acquisition of the property only if the property is placed in service no later than June 30 for calendar-year corporations. This convention is no longer used for tax purposes. Answer (D) is incorrect. With the modified half-year convention, depreciation will be allowed in the last year of the property's economic life only if the property is disposed of after June 30 of the year of disposition for calendar-year corporations. This convention is no longer used for tax purposes.

10.5.7. A business auto that is purchased and placed in service in the current year is classified under MACRS as

A. 3-year property/with annual limitations.

B. 3-year property/without annual limitations.

C. 5-year property/with annual limitations.

D. 5-year property/without annual limitations.

Answer (C) is correct. *(SEE, adapted)*
REQUIRED: The correct classification of an automobile used in business.
DISCUSSION: Section 168(e)(3)(B) specifically provides that an automobile is 5-year property. Section 280F(a)(1) provides annual limitations on the amount of depreciation and Sec. 179 expense each year for automobiles.
Answer (A) is incorrect. Automobiles are not 3-year property. Answer (B) is incorrect. Automobiles are not 3-year property without annual limitations. Answer (D) is incorrect. There are annual limitations on the depreciation.

10.5.8. Which of the following is a true statement concerning depreciation of automobiles placed in service in 2017, ignoring bonus depreciation?

A. The amount of depreciation and Sec. 179 expense is limited to $11,160 per year.

B. The amount of depreciation is limited to $3,160 in the first year.

C. If the automobile is used 50% or less for business use, no depreciation is allowed.

D. If the use of an automobile for business decreases to 50% or less after the first year, only the current and subsequent years' depreciation will be affected.

Answer (B) is correct. *(Publisher, adapted)*
REQUIRED: The true statement concerning depreciation of automobiles placed in service in 2017.
DISCUSSION: Section 280F limits the depreciation deduction for automobiles placed in service in 2017 to a maximum of $3,160. The Sec. 179 expense amount is treated as depreciation for this purpose, limited to $3,160 in the first year. This amount is reduced if business use is less than 100%.
Answer (A) is incorrect. The amount of $11,160 included bonus depreciation. Answer (C) is incorrect. Depreciation for an automobile used 50% or less in business is computed by the alternative depreciation system. Answer (D) is incorrect. If an automobile's use decreases to 50% or less in subsequent years, any depreciation in prior years in excess of the alternative depreciation system is included in gross income for the years in which the business use decreased to 50% or less.

10.5.9. In 2017, Master Corporation provided each one of its salespeople with a new automobile costing $25,000. The automobiles are used 100% of the time in the business. Assuming Master elected a half-year convention in 2017, the maximum 2018 depreciation deduction the corporation may take for any one car is

A. $7,800

B. $5,100

C. $11,160

D. $3,050

Answer (B) is correct. *(CMA, adapted)*
REQUIRED: The maximum second-year depreciation deduction for an automobile placed in service in 2017.
DISCUSSION: Section 280F(a) limits the depreciation deduction for an automobile placed in service in 2017 to $11,160 for the first year, $5,100 for the second year, $3,050 for the third year, and $1,875 for each succeeding year.
Answer (A) is incorrect. It is the actual second-year MACRS depreciation for property placed in service in 2017, which cannot be claimed because it exceeds the Sec. 280F limitation. Answer (C) is incorrect. It is first-year depreciation for property placed in service in 2017. Answer (D) is incorrect. It is third-year depreciation for property placed in service in 2017.

10.5.10. Sam files a calendar-year return. In February 2015, he purchased and placed in service for 100% use in his business a light-duty truck (5-year property) for a cost of $10,000. He used the half-year convention and figured his MACRS deductions for the truck were $2,000 in 2015 and $3,200 in 2016. He did not take the Sec. 179 deduction on it. He sold the truck in May 2017 for $7,000. The MACRS deduction in 2017, the year of sale, is $960 (1/2 of $1,920). How much of the gain will be treated as ordinary income in 2017?

A. $3,160

B. $2,200

C. $3,840

D. None of the answers are correct.

Answer (A) is correct. *(SEE, adapted)*
REQUIRED: The amount of gain treated as ordinary income.
DISCUSSION: Sam purchased the truck for $10,000 and took $6,160 in depreciation, leaving a basis of $3,840. The gain on the sale is $3,160. Under Sec. 1245, if the gain is less than the depreciation taken, the entire gain is reported as ordinary income.
Answer (B) is incorrect. Sam is allowed to decrease his basis in the truck by the MACRS deduction he took in 2017 ($960). Answer (C) is incorrect. This amount represents the basis, not the amount treated as ordinary income. Answer (D) is incorrect. Sam purchased the truck for $10,000 and took $6,160 in depreciation, leaving a basis of $3,840. The gain on the sale is $3,160. Under Sec. 1245, if the gain is less than the depreciation taken, the entire gain is reported as ordinary income.

10.5.11. On March 15, 2017, Mr. Driver, a calendar-year taxpayer, purchased and placed in service a light truck to be used in his business. The truck has an ADR midpoint of 8 years. The truck costs $30,000, and the salvage value is estimated to be 10% of cost. What is the MACRS deduction for the current year?

A. $11,160

B. $15,000

C. $0

D. $30,000

Answer (A) is correct. *(SEE, adapted)*
 REQUIRED: The 2017 MACRS depreciation deduction.
 DISCUSSION: Light duty trucks are 5-year property subject to the 200%-declining-balance method. Salvage value is zero and the half-year convention applies in the year of acquisition. Driver's depreciation is limited to $3,160 for 2017 by the luxury auto limits. Bonus depreciation for 2017 of $8,000 is allowed for a total of $11,160.
 Answer (B) is incorrect. The amount of $15,000 is greater than the luxury auto limit. Answer (C) is incorrect. Light duty trucks qualify for the luxury limits of Sec. 179. Answer (D) is incorrect. The luxury auto rule limits the Sec. 179 deduction.

10.5.12. Cub Corporation purchased an automated tube bender for $500,000 in 2016. The tube bender, used to manufacture folding chairs, has an estimated life of 10 years and an estimated salvage value of $60,000. It is 5-year property under the MACRS rules. Cub's taxable income for 2017 before the depreciation deduction is $120,000. The maximum depreciation for tax purposes in 2017 is (ignore Sec. 179 election and bonus depreciation)

A. $100,000

B. $117,600

C. $120,000

D. $160,000

Answer (D) is correct. *(CMA, adapted)*
 REQUIRED: The maximum depreciation in the second year of use for property acquired in 2016.
 DISCUSSION: The depreciation on property under MACRS is computed by applying the applicable method for the class of property to the unadjusted basis of the property ($500,000).
 The applicable depreciation method for 5-year property is the 200%-declining-balance method. As an alternative to computing the depreciation each year on the adjusted basis, then subtracting the depreciation, and the next year recomputing depreciation on the remaining basis, the IRS has developed tables of percentages to apply to the original unadjusted basis. These percentages in effect compute the depreciation at the 200%-declining-balance method. The percentage for 5-year property in the second year is 32%. Therefore, Cub's maximum amount of deductible depreciation for 2017 is $160,000 ($500,000 × 32%).
 Answer (A) is incorrect. The amount of $100,000 is 20% of the unadjusted basis. Twenty percent is the MACRS depreciation for the first year, not the second year. Answer (B) is incorrect. The maximum depreciation is $160,000. Answer (C) is incorrect. The taxable income is $120,000.

10.5.13. On April 1, 2015, Mr. C purchased office furniture costing $10,000. The furniture has an ADR midpoint life of 10 years and is 7-year property under the MACRS rules. Mr. C purchased no other assets during 2015 and did not elect a Sec. 179 deduction or bonus depreciation. What is C's maximum amount of depreciation deduction for 2017?

A. $1,429

B. $1,440

C. $1,676

D. $1,749

Answer (D) is correct. *(SEE, adapted)*
 REQUIRED: The maximum depreciation in the third year of use for property acquired in 2015.
 DISCUSSION: The depreciation on property under MACRS is computed by applying the applicable method for the class of property to the unadjusted basis of the property. The applicable method for 7-year property is the 200%-declining-balance method. Using the IRS table for the 200%-declining-balance method and the half-year convention, the percentage in the third year is 17.49%. Therefore, C's maximum amount of deductible depreciation for 2017 is $1,749 ($10,000 × 17.49%).
 Answer (A) is incorrect. The amount of $1,429 results from using the rate for the first year. Answer (B) is incorrect. The amount of $1,440 results from using the rate for 10-year property. Answer (C) is incorrect. The amount of $1,676 results from using the rate for the mid-quarter convention for the third year.

10.5.14. On January 1, 2017, Mr. Long purchased and placed in service a passenger automobile that cost $10,000 and qualified as a 100% business vehicle. Long did not elect a Sec. 179 deduction but did make the election to use the alternative MACRS depreciation system. What is Mr. Long's allowable MACRS deduction for 2017?

A. $1,000

B. $2,000

C. $3,160

D. $3,334

Answer (A) is correct. *(SEE, adapted)*
 REQUIRED: The depreciation deduction for 2017 using the alternative depreciation system.
 DISCUSSION: Section 168(g)(7) allows a taxpayer to elect the alternative depreciation system. The half-year convention still applies, and the election applies for all items in that class of property placed in service during the tax year. The straight-line method is used, and the recovery period for automobiles is 5 years [Sec. 168(g)(3)(D)]. Long's $1,000 [($10,000 ÷ 5 years) × 1/2] of depreciation deduction for 2017 can be determined from the MACRS tables.
 Answer (B) is incorrect. The half-year convention applies in the year of acquisition. Answer (C) is incorrect. The taxpayer elected to use the alternative depreciation system. Answer (D) is incorrect. The result of using the MACRS rate for 3-year property is $3,334.

10.5.15. On January 2 of the current year, Mr. Quick, a sole proprietor, purchased a new van to be used in his business. He traded in a used van with an adjusted basis of $2,500 and paid $7,500 cash. He did not elect a Sec. 179 deduction or bonus depreciation for the van. Assuming the van is a 5-year asset, what is the amount that will be depreciable over that life?

A. $10,000

B. $7,500

C. $2,500

D. $0

Answer (B) is correct. *(SEE, adapted)*
REQUIRED: The allowable depreciation deduction for an asset acquired through a nontaxable exchange.
DISCUSSION: Taxpayers who exchange modified accelerated cost recovery system (MACRS) through either a Sec. 1031 like-kind exchange or a Sec. 1033 involuntary conversion are required to treat the excess basis of the acquired MACRS property as newly purchased. According to Notice 2000-4, the new asset will now be treated as two separate properties for depreciation purposes. The $7,500 will be depreciated as a newly acquired asset, and the $2,500 basis of the former asset will continue to be depreciated under the former depreciation schedule.
Answer (A) is incorrect. Although the basis is $10,000, only the part of the basis attributable to the new truck is depreciated over its 5-year life. Answer (C) is incorrect. This amount is the basis of the former asset that will continue to be depreciated under the former depreciation schedule. Answer (D) is incorrect. The new asset has a depreciable amount associated with it.

10.5.16. Mainstream Company purchased depreciable equipment in 2016 for $119,000 and claimed a Sec. 179 deduction of $112,000 but no bonus depreciation. The equipment qualified as 5-year property under MACRS. Mainstream sold all of this equipment on June 30, 2017. What is the amount of Mainstream's MACRS deduction for 2017?

A. $0

B. $1,120

C. $2,240

D. $4,480

Answer (B) is correct. *(SEE, adapted)*
REQUIRED: The amount of MACRS depreciation in the year of disposition of property acquired after 1986.
DISCUSSION: The deduction for MACRS depreciation is calculated using the 200%-declining-balance method for 5-year property. The basis is reduced by $112,000 (the Sec. 179 deduction). The half-year convention allows a one-half year depreciation deduction in the year of acquisition and a one-half year depreciation deduction in the year of disposition. Therefore, Mainstream's 2017 MACRS depreciation is $1,120.

Cost of equipment	$119,000
Less: Sec. 179 deduction	(112,000)
Depreciable basis	$ 7,000
Times: MACRS percentage (5-year property, second year)	× .32
	$ 2,240
Times: one-half (half-year convention)	× .50
2017 depreciation	$ 1,120

Answer (A) is incorrect. Some depreciation can be claimed. Answer (C) is incorrect. Only a one-half year depreciation deduction is taken in the year of sale. Answer (D) is incorrect. The depreciable basis is $7,000, the MACRS percentage is 32%, and the half-year convention is used.

10.5.17. On July 20 of the current year, the rock group Redhead bought a studio for $900,000 exclusive of land (located in California) to record their albums. The studio has a useful life of 50 years. What is Redhead's maximum depreciation deduction in the current year?

A. $0

B. $10,593

C. $13,095

D. $15,000

Answer (B) is correct. *(Publisher, adapted)*
REQUIRED: The maximum depreciation under MACRS on nonresidential real property acquired in the current year.
DISCUSSION: Under Sec. 168, tangible property is depreciable under the recovery period assigned, regardless of actual useful life. Nonresidential real property is depreciated on the straight-line method over 39 years using the assumption that all property is placed in service at mid-month. For nonresidential real property placed in service in July, Redhead's depreciation deduction according to the MACRS table is $10,593.
Answer (A) is incorrect. Some depreciation can be claimed. Answer (C) is incorrect. This amount of depreciation pertains to a recovery period of 31.5 years. Answer (D) is incorrect. This amount of depreciation pertains to a recovery period of 27.5 years.

10.5.18. Ichabod Crane purchased a mechanical horse on January 1, 2016, to use at his riding academy. He paid $5,000 cash and signed a promissory note for $15,000. The horse was 5-year recovery property, and Ichabod elected to use the straight-line method over 5 years to depreciate it. What is Ichabod's basis in the horse at the end of 2017, assuming he did not take Sec. 179 or bonus depreciation?

    A. $3,000

    B. $9,000

    C. $14,000

    D. $16,000

Answer (C) is correct. *(Publisher, adapted)*
    REQUIRED: The basis of property acquired by becoming personally liable on a debt.
    DISCUSSION: The original basis of property is its cost (Sec. 1012), which is reduced by depreciation allowable [Sec. 1016(a)(2)]. The cost of property includes debt on which the purchaser is personally liable, since (s)he will be legally obligated to pay this amount. Accordingly, the original basis of the mechanical horse was $20,000 ($5,000 cash + $15,000 debt).
    Under Section 168, 5-year recovery property may be depreciated on the straight-line method over 5 years. Ichabod's annual depreciation is $4,000 ($20,000 ÷ 5 years). Because the property is treated as having been acquired at midyear in the year of acquisition [Sec. 168(d)(1)], Ichabod's total depreciation at the end of the second year will be $6,000 ($2,000 in the first year + $4,000 in the second year). The basis of the property will be $14,000 ($20,000 cost – $6,000 depreciation).
    Answer (A) is incorrect. The amount of $3,000 is the adjusted basis if only the $5,000 cash acquisition price is depreciated using the straight-line method for all of 2016 and 2017. Answer (B) is incorrect. The $6,000 of depreciation is subtracted from the total purchase price, not just from the portion that is financed. Answer (D) is incorrect. A 10-year recovery period was used with a full year of depreciation for 2016 and 2017 being taken.

10.5.19. Residential rental property that was placed in service during the current year using MACRS is depreciated over how many years, using which depreciation method and convention?

    A. 15 years, 150%-declining-balance method, half-year convention.

    B. 27.5 years, straight-line method, mid-month convention.

    C. 39 years, straight-line method, mid-month convention.

    D. 40 years, 200%-declining-balance method, half-year convention.

Answer (B) is correct. *(SEE, adapted)*
    REQUIRED: The proper recovery period and method for residential rental property.
    DISCUSSION: Section 168(c) provides that the recovery period for residential rental property is 27.5 years. Section 168(b)(3) provides that the straight-line method shall be used for residential rental property. Section 168(d)(2) provides that the mid-month convention shall be used for residential rental property.
    Answer (A) is incorrect. The recovery period is not 15 years, the 150%-declining-balance method is not used, and the half-year convention does not apply. Answer (C) is incorrect. The 39-year recovery period is for nonresidential property. Answer (D) is incorrect. The recovery period is not 40 years, the 200%-declining-balance method is not used, and the half-year convention does not apply.

10.5.20. Canada Films produced the film *Greatest Heroes in Hockey* at a cost of $20 million. Canada Films uses the income-forecast method to compute depreciation of property. First-year income is $10 million, and total estimated income without regard to future video revenue is $25 million. Estimated video revenue is $15 million. What is the first-year depreciation deduction for the cost of the film?

    A. $5,000,000

    B. $8,000,000

    C. $10,000,000

    D. $15,000,000

Answer (A) is correct. *(Publisher, adapted)*
    REQUIRED: The depreciation deduction allowed using the income-forecast depreciation method.
    DISCUSSION: Under Sec. 167(g), the income-forecast method may be used to determine depreciation of property that cannot be depreciated under either MACRS rules or the Sec. 197 intangible amortization provisions. This includes property such as films, videotapes, television films, master sound recordings, and video game machines. Under the income-forecast method, depreciation is determined by multiplying the cost of the property (less estimated salvage value) by a fraction, with the numerator being the income generated by the property during the year and the denominator being equal to the total estimated income to be derived from the property during its useful life (usually up to 11 tax years).
    Answer (B) is incorrect. The 1996 Small Business Act specifically disallows the exclusion of estimated video revenues when using the income-forecast method. Answer (C) is incorrect. The amount of $10 million is the first-year income used to calculate the fraction of cost to be deducted the first year, under the income-forecast method. Answer (D) is incorrect. The amount of $15 million is the estimated video revenue included in the denominator for calculating the fraction of cost to be deducted the first year, under the income-forecast method.

10.5.21. The Bearcat Corporation purchased an apartment building in October of the current year. The cost of the building was $4,000,000 and its estimated life was 40 years. Corporate management wants to know the alternative methods of deducting the cost of the building for tax purposes. The company may use the straight-line method over 27.5 years or can elect to use the

A. Straight-line method over a recovery period of 35 or 45 years.

B. Straight-line method over a recovery period of any length between 27.5 and 45 years.

C. Straight-line method over a recovery period of 40 years.

D. Declining-balance method at 125% of the straight-line rate using a recovery period of 27.5 or 40 years.

Answer (C) is correct. *(CMA, adapted)*
REQUIRED: The alternative method(s) of depreciating a building acquired in the current year.
DISCUSSION: Apartment buildings acquired after 1986 are classified as residential rental property and are normally depreciated in accordance with the straight-line method over 27.5 years. A taxpayer may elect to use the straight-line method over 40 years for real property under the alternative depreciation system.
Answer (A) is incorrect. Recovery periods of 35 and 45 years are not permissible. Answer (B) is incorrect. A recovery period cannot be an arbitrary length between 27.5 and 45 years. Answer (D) is incorrect. The declining-balance method at 125% of straight-line is not permissible.

10.5.22. Which of the following assets may be depreciated using the income-forecast method?

A. Copyrights.

B. Sound recordings.

C. Film.

D. All of the answers are correct.

Answer (D) is correct. *(Publisher, adapted)*
REQUIRED: The property that may be depreciated using the income-forecast method.
DISCUSSION: Under the Taxpayer Relief Act of 1997, the use of the income forecast is limited to film, videotape, sound recordings, copyrights, books, patents, and other property that is specified by regulations.
Answer (A) is incorrect. Sound recordings and film may also be depreciated using the income-forecast method. Answer (B) is incorrect. Copyrights and film may also be depreciated using the income-forecast method. Answer (C) is incorrect. Copyrights and sound recordings may also be depreciated using the income-forecast method.

10.5.23. The alternative depreciation system for computing depreciation under MACRS uses a recovery percentage based on a modified straight-line method that allows the use of any recovery period, provided it exceeds the regular recovery period under MACRS.

A. True.

B. False.

Answer (B) is correct. *(SEE, adapted)*
DISCUSSION: The alternative depreciation system uses the straight-line method over a specific recovery period, which generally depends on the ADR midpoint for the property. The ADR midpoint is considered to be 12 years, if the property has no ADR midpoint, and 40 years for residential rental and nonresidential real property.

10.6 Amortization

10.6.1. Alice leased an office building on January 1, 2016, for 15 years with no option to renew. On July 1, 2017, Alice paid $10,000 for a new roof for the building. What is Alice's allowable amortization deduction for 2017?

A. $118

B. $327

C. $236

D. $654

Answer (A) is correct. *(SEE, adapted)*
REQUIRED: The taxpayer's allowable amortization deduction for capital improvements on leased property.
DISCUSSION: Section 168(i)(8) provides that improvements made on leased property are recovered as a MACRS deduction. A new roof on an office building is considered nonresidential real property and is depreciated over a 39-year period. The mid-month convention applies. Alice's allowable deduction in 2017 is $118 [($10,000 ÷ 39 years) × (5.5 ÷ 12)].
Answer (B) is incorrect. The amount of $327 uses the remaining 14 years of the lease. Answer (C) is incorrect. The amount of $236 uses a 200% declining balance. Answer (D) is incorrect. The amount of $654 uses a 200% declining balance and only the remaining 14 years of the lease.

10.6.2. The cost of a building or improvements constructed after 1986 on leased land is recovered

A. Over a 60-month amortization period.

B. As a MACRS deduction.

C. Over the lease term.

D. Over the lesser of the remaining period of the lease or the MACRS recovery period for the type of improvements.

Answer (B) is correct. *(Publisher, adapted)*
REQUIRED: The period of time over which a lessee may deduct the cost of improvements constructed on leased land.
DISCUSSION: Section 168(i)(8) provides that any building erected (or improvements made) on leased property after 1986 is recovered as a MACRS deduction. This means the recovery period is determined by the type of property the improvements consist of regardless of the remaining term of the lease.
Answer (A) is incorrect. The cost of a building or building improvements placed in service after 1986 is not recovered over a 60-month amortization period. Answer (C) is incorrect. The cost of a building or building improvements placed in service after 1986 is not recovered over the lease term. Answer (D) is incorrect. The cost of a building or building improvements placed in service after 1986 is not recovered over the lesser of the remaining period of the lease or the MACRS recovery period for the type of improvements.

10.6.3. Construction period interest on self-constructed property that is not inventory is generally

A. Capitalized and recovered as depreciation deductions over the recovery period of the asset.

B. Capitalized and amortized over a 10-year period.

C. Expensed in the year incurred.

D. Capitalized and deducted when the property is sold.

Answer (A) is correct. *(Publisher, adapted)*
REQUIRED: The proper treatment of construction period interest.
DISCUSSION: The 1986 Tax Act added Sec. 263A(f), which provides that interest is capitalized on self-constructed property used in a business and recovered as depreciation deductions over the useful life of the asset. The interest must have been incurred during the production period and the property must have a long useful life, an estimated production period of over 2 years, or an estimated production period over 1 year with a cost of over $1 million.
Answer (B) is incorrect. Section 189, which provided for such treatment, has been repealed. Answer (C) is incorrect. Section 263A requires production costs (direct and indirect) to be capitalized. Answer (D) is incorrect. Such treatment applies to production costs of inventory.

10.6.4. All of the following statements in respect to the amortization of start-up costs are true, except

A. If your attempt to go into business is not successful, the costs you had as a result of a preliminary investigation of a business may be deducted in full in year of abandonment.

B. Start-up costs include salaries and wages for employees who are being trained and for their instructors.

C. If you have both start-up and organizational costs, you may elect a period for start-up costs that is different from the period you elect for organizational costs, as long as both are 180 months or more.

D. To be amortizable, a start-up cost must be a cost that would be deductible if it were paid or incurred to operate an existing trade or business and it must be paid or incurred by you before you actually begin business operations.

Answer (A) is correct. *(SEE, adapted)*
REQUIRED: The false statement in respect to the amortization of start-up costs.
DISCUSSION: Section 195 disallows a full deduction for start-up expenditures. Instead, the expenditures may be amortized over a period of not less than 180 months. Up to $5,000 of start-up expenditures may be expensed immediately. Start-up expenditures include any amount paid in connection with investigating the creation or acquisition of an active trade or business. Investigation costs are start-up expenditures regardless of whether the business attempt was successful or not. Therefore, the investigation costs are not deductible in full in the year of abandonment.
Answer (B) is incorrect. The cost of training employees is a start-up cost. Answer (C) is incorrect. Start-up costs and organizational costs do not have to have the same recovery period, although both must be amortized over a period not less than 180 months. Answer (D) is incorrect. A start-up cost must be a cost that would be deductible if paid or incurred in connection with an existing trade or business, and it must be paid before the day business actually begins.

10.6.5. In 2016, Mr. D incurred the following expenses in connection with starting a manufacturing business to begin January 1, 2017. All of the expenses are start-up costs that must be capitalized and then amortized except

    A. Salaries and wages for employees who are being trained.

    B. Advertisements for the opening of the manufacturing plant.

    C. Travel expense to secure prospective distributors.

    D. Mr. D's share of real estate taxes on a factory building that he purchased.

Answer (D) is correct. *(SEE, adapted)*
    REQUIRED: The expense that is not a start-up cost amortizable under Sec. 195.
    DISCUSSION: Section 195 allows a taxpayer to elect to amortize start-up expenditures over a period of not less than 180 months (beginning with the month in which the business begins). Start-up expenditures are those paid or incurred in connection with investigating the creation or acquisition of an active trade or business, or with creating an active trade or business, and that, if paid or incurred in connection with the expansion of an existing business, would be allowable as a deduction in the year paid or incurred. The kinds of expenditures include those for research of a product and the market for it. But real estate taxes are deductible under Sec. 164 regardless of whether incurred in a trade or business, so they do not need to be amortized. Up to $5,000 of start-up expenses may be expensed immediately.

10.6.6. Allen purchased Miller Manufacturing on January 1 of the current year for $1 million. Included in the purchase price was a 5-year noncompete covenant valued at $75,000. What is Allen's allowable amortization deduction attributable to the noncompete covenant?

    A. $15,000

    B. $5,000

    C. $1,875

    D. $0

Answer (B) is correct. *(Publisher, adapted)*
    REQUIRED: The allowable amortization deduction for the current year.
    DISCUSSION: Under Sec. 197, the cost of acquiring any intangible assets, including noncompete covenants, is amortizable over a 15-year period, beginning in the month of acquisition. The actual useful life of the covenant is ignored. Allen's deduction for the current year is $5,000 ($75,000 ÷ 15). A noncompete covenant acquired outside the purchase of a business is amortizable over the covenant period.
    Answer (A) is incorrect. The useful life of 5 years is ignored. Answer (C) is incorrect. The amount of $1,875 equals the deduction taken over a 40-year period. Answer (D) is incorrect. Allen may take a deduction.

10.6.7. Joseph purchased a business on May 1 of the current year. Of the purchase price, $45,000 was attributable to the acquisition of existing employment contracts. The contracts are deemed to have a useful life of 12 years. What is Joseph's allowable amortization deduction for the current year?

    A. $0

    B. $2,000

    C. $2,500

    D. $3,000

Answer (B) is correct. *(Publisher, adapted)*
    REQUIRED: The allowable amortization deduction for the current year.
    DISCUSSION: Under Sec. 197, the cost of acquiring existing employment contracts is amortizable over a 15-year period beginning in the month of acquisition. Actual useful life is ignored. Joseph's deduction for the current year is $2,000 [($45,000 ÷ 15) × 8/12 months].
    Answer (A) is incorrect. Joseph may take an amortization deduction of $2,000. Answer (C) is incorrect. The useful life of 12 years is ignored for amortization purposes. Answer (D) is incorrect. Joseph can take a deduction only for the period from May through December.

10.6.8. All of the following are Sec. 197 intangible assets except

    A. Trademark.

    B. Liquor license.

    C. Covenant not to compete acquired in the purchase of the assets of a business.

    D. Any interest in a corporation, partnership, trust, or estate.

Answer (D) is correct. *(Publisher, adapted)*
    REQUIRED: The asset that is not a Sec. 197 intangible.
    DISCUSSION: Section 197(e)(1) specifically excludes from the definition of a Sec. 197 intangible any interest in a corporation, partnership, trust, or estate.
    Answer (A) is incorrect. Trademarks are Sec. 197 intangible assets [Sec. 197(d)(1)]. Answer (B) is incorrect. Liquor licenses are Sec. 197 intangible assets [Sec. 197(d)(1)]. Answer (C) is incorrect. Covenants not to compete are Sec. 197 intangible assets [Sec. 197(d)(1)].

10.6.9. On July 1 of the current year, Leigh opened a business supply store. Prior to opening the business, she incurred the following costs:

Purchase of fixtures	$ 600
Accounting fees related to creating the business	1,000
Interest expense for funds borrowed prior to opening the store	300
Conducted a market survey	500
Costs to hire and train employees	2,000
Travel expenses to secure prospective suppliers	2,500

What amount of the start-up expenditures may Leigh amortize for the current year if she elects to use the shortest amortization period allowed?

A. $0

B. $33

C. $43

D. $600

Answer (B) is correct. *(SEE, adapted)*
REQUIRED: The amortization in the first year of business for start-up expenditures.
DISCUSSION: Section 195 allows a taxpayer to elect to amortize start-up expenditures over a period of not less than 180 months (beginning with the month in which the business begins). Start-up expenditures are those paid or incurred in connection with investigating the creation or acquisition of an active trade or business, or with creating an active trade or business, and that, if paid or incurred in connection with the expansion of an existing business, would be allowable as a deduction in the year paid or incurred. The kinds of expenditures include those for research of one's product and the market for it, accounting fees, the training of employees, and the securing of suppliers. Interest expense and the cost of fixtures do not qualify as start-up expenditures. Leigh is entitled to 6 months of amortization (from when she began business) in the current year. Up to $5,000 of start-up expenses may be expensed immediately.

Accounting fees	$1,000
Market survey	500
Hiring and training	2,000
Travel expenses	2,500
Total start-up expenditures	$6,000
Less: Immediate expensing	(5,000)
Available for amortization	$1,000
Current-year amortization ($1,000 × 6/180 months)	$ 33

Answer (A) is incorrect. The travel expenses of $2,500 should be treated as a start-up expenditure. Answer (C) is incorrect. The interest expense is not a start-up expenditure. Answer (D) is incorrect. The $600 excludes the $5,000 immediate deduction and applies a 60-month amortization period.

10.6.10. All of the following statements are true regarding Sec. 197 intangible assets except

A. The costs of Sec. 197 intangibles are amortized over a 15-year period beginning in the month of acquisition.

B. Section 197 intangible assets do not include interests in a corporation or partnership.

C. The 15-year amortization period applies to Sec. 197 intangibles unless the actual useful life of the asset is less than 15 years.

D. Section 197 intangible assets include the portion of an acquired business attributable to the existence of a customer base.

Answer (C) is correct. *(Publisher, adapted)*
REQUIRED: The false statement regarding Sec. 197 intangibles.
DISCUSSION: Under Sec. 197, the capitalized costs of Sec. 197 intangibles are amortized over a 15-year period beginning in the month of acquisition. This 15-year period applies regardless of actual useful life.
Answer (A) is incorrect. The costs of Sec. 197 intangibles are amortized over a 15-year period beginning in the month of acquisition. Answer (B) is incorrect. Section 197 intangible assets do not include interests in a corporation or partnership. Answer (D) is incorrect. Section 197 intangible assets include the portion of an acquired business attributable to the existence of a customer base.

10.6.11. The costs of acquiring a lease or leasehold for business purposes may be recovered by amortizing the costs over the term of the lease.

A. True.

B. False.

Answer (A) is correct. *(SEE, adapted)*
DISCUSSION: The cost of acquiring a lease is a capital expenditure that may be amortized over the term of the lease under Sec. 167. A lease is an intangible asset, so the Sec. 168 MACRS rules do not apply. Leases are excluded from Sec. 197 intangibles under Sec. 197(e)(5).

10.6.12. On January 2 of the current year, Mr. Q, a calendar-year taxpayer, acquired an existing lease on property to be used in his business. Mr. Q paid $25,000 to the previous lessee. In addition, Mr. Q paid a commission of $5,000 to his broker as a finder's fee. The lease had a remaining life of 10 years with an option to renew for 5 years. If the cost of acquiring the lease for the base period is less than 75% of the total cost to acquire the lease, Mr. Q's amortization deduction for the current year will be $2,000.

A. True.

B. False.

Answer (A) is correct. *(SEE, adapted)*
DISCUSSION: The $25,000 paid to the previous lessee and the $5,000 commission are costs of acquiring a lease that may be amortized over the term of the lease. Under Sec. 178, the term of the lease includes any period for which the lease may be renewed if less than 75% of the cost of acquiring the lease is attributable to the portion of the lease excluding the option period. The cost is allocated over both periods since it is not specified otherwise. Therefore, two-thirds (10/15ths, which is less than 75%) of the cost applies to the initial term. The $30,000 cost is thus allocated over 15 years at $2,000 per year.

10.6.13. Skypipes, Inc., installed certified pollution control equipment to prevent certain toxic fumes from being discharged into the air. It was certified by the proper state and federal authorities. The equipment neither eliminated the visible exhaust nor increased the company's output or the useful life of the plant. Skypipes may amortize the equipment over 60 months.

A. True.

B. False.

Answer (A) is correct. *(Publisher, adapted)*
DISCUSSION: Section 169 allows a taxpayer to amortize the cost of a certified pollution control facility over a period of 60 months. A certified pollution control facility is a new, identifiable treatment facility used in connection with a plant or property in operation prior to 1976. The facility must abate or control water or atmospheric pollution or contamination and be certified by both the relevant state and federal authorities. Furthermore, it must not significantly increase the output or capacity, extend the useful life, or reduce the total operating costs of such plant or property, or alter the nature of the manufacturing or production process or facility. It need not eliminate any visible exhaust as long as it does remove pollutants.

10.6.14. A commission paid by the borrower to find and obtain a mortgage for business or income-producing property is a capital expenditure. The commission may not be added to the basis of the property but may be amortized over the life of the mortgage.

A. True.

B. False.

Answer (A) is correct. *(SEE, adapted)*
DISCUSSION: Capitalized expenditures are not deductible in the current year, but must be amortized over the useful life of the asset to which they relate. Since the commission that was paid to obtain the mortgage fits into this category, it must be amortized over the life of the mortgage.
A commission paid by the borrower to locate a mortgage for businesses or income producing property is a capital expenditure. These outlays are amortized over the life of the loan and deducted accordingly (Rev. Rul. 70-360). Those related to a business property are deductible under Sec. 162, and those related to income producing property are deductible under Sec. 212. The commission is not added to the cost of the asset because it would instead be recovered through depreciation.

10.6.15. The cost of acquiring a governmental license to be held in connection with a trade or business can be amortized over a 15-year period.

A. True.

B. False.

Answer (A) is correct. *(Publisher, adapted)*
DISCUSSION: The cost of acquiring a license, permit, or other right from a governmental unit is amortizable under Sec. 197. Section 197 intangible assets are amortized over a 15-year period beginning in the month of acquisition. The 15-year period applies even if the actual useful life of the intangible is less or more than 15 years.

10.7 Depletion

10.7.1. For a taxpayer to claim a deduction for depletion, (s)he must possess an "economic interest" in the natural resource. For an economic interest to be considered present, the taxpayer is only required to

A. Possess an ownership interest in the land containing the mineral in place prior to extraction.

B. Have acquired by investment any interest in the mineral in place.

C. Look solely to the extraction and sale of the mineral for a return of capital.

D. Have acquired by investment any interest in the mineral in place, and look solely to the extraction and sale of the mineral for a return of capital.

Answer (D) is correct. *(E.D. Fenton, Jr.)*
REQUIRED: The definition of economic interest for depletion purposes.
DISCUSSION: Regulation 1.611-1(b)(1) states that a taxpayer possesses an economic interest when (s)he has acquired by investment any interest in the mineral in place and secures income derived from the extraction of the mineral to which (s)he must look for a return of capital. The courts have said that an actual cash investment in the property is not necessary. The investment can be in the form of land in a controlling position over the natural resource or in nonmovable equipment used for the extraction and production of the mineral.
Answer (A) is incorrect. Ownership of the land is different from ownership of the mineral rights and is not required. Answer (B) is incorrect. Having acquired by investment any interest in the mineral in place is not the only requirement that must be met. Answer (C) is incorrect. Looking solely to the extraction and sale of the mineral for a return of capital is not the only requirement that must be met.

10.7.2. Wendy Flower has an adjusted basis of $20,000 in mineral property. It is estimated that there are 40,000 tons of recoverable coal on the property. Wendy produced and sold 10,000 tons during the current year. What is her cost depletion deduction for the current year?

A. $1,000

B. $5,000

C. $10,000

D. $15,000

Answer (B) is correct. *(SEE, adapted)*
REQUIRED: The taxpayer's cost depletion deduction for mineral property.
DISCUSSION: Section 611(a) states that a deduction is allowed for reasonable depletion of mines, oil and gas wells, other natural deposits, and timber. Cost depletion for any year is the adjusted basis of the mineral property, divided by the number of units of mineral estimated as of the beginning of the taxable year, times the number of units of mineral sold within the taxable year.

Adjusted basis	$ 20,000
Divided by units of mineral	÷ 40,000
Depletion per unit	$ .50
Times units sold in the current year	× 10,000
Cost depletion deduction	$ 5,000

Answer (A) is incorrect. Cost depletion is not $.05 per ton. Answer (C) is incorrect. Cost depletion is not $1.00 per ton. Answer (D) is incorrect. Cost depletion is not $1.50 per ton.

10.7.3. Donny owns and leases a coal mine to Brian. The lease agreement states that Brian will pay Donny $4 per ton royalty on coal mined. What is Brian's percentage depletion deduction for the current year from the information given below?

Gross income from coal	$250,000
Income from trucking coal	20,000
Royalty paid Donny	30,000
Taxable income on coal (excluding depletion)	40,000
Coal depletion rate	10%

A. $20,000

B. $22,000

C. $24,000

D. $25,000

Answer (A) is correct. *(SEE, adapted)*
REQUIRED: The taxpayer's percentage depletion deduction on a coal mine.
DISCUSSION: Section 611(a) authorizes a reasonable allowance for depletion of mines, oil and gas wells, other natural deposits, and timber. Percentage depletion (for other than oil and gas wells) is provided in Sec. 613 as the specified percentage (10% for coal) of the gross income from the property (excluding any rents or royalties paid or incurred by the taxpayer with respect to the property). This depletion allowance may not exceed 50% of the taxpayer's taxable income from the property computed before the allowance for depletion. Percentage depletion is the lesser of

1) 10% of gross income, i.e.,
   ($250,000 – $30,000 royalty) × 10% = $22,000; or
2) 50% of taxable income, i.e., $40,000 × 50% = $20,000.

Brian's percentage depletion deduction is thus limited to $20,000 (50% of his taxable income).
Answer (B) is incorrect. The amount of $22,000 is 10% of gross income. Answer (C) is incorrect. The amount of $24,000 is 60% of taxable income. Answer (D) is incorrect. The amount of $25,000 is 10% of gross income before reduction for royalties and does not take into account the taxable income ceiling.

STUDY UNIT ELEVEN
CAPITAL GAINS AND LOSSES

11.1 Capital Assets Identified

11.1.1. Joe Hall owns a limousine for use in his personal service business of transporting passengers to airports. The limousine's adjusted basis is $40,000. In addition, Hall owns his personal residence and furnishings, that together cost him $280,000. Hall's capital assets amount to

A. $320,000

B. $280,000

C. $40,000

D. $0

Answer (B) is correct. *(CPA, adapted)*
REQUIRED: The amount of capital assets owned by an individual.
DISCUSSION: Capital assets are any property held by the taxpayer (whether or not they are connected with his or her business), but not inventory, depreciable business property, real property used in a trade or business, copyrights and artistic compositions created by the owner, accounts and notes receivable, and certain U.S. government publications acquired at reduced cost (Sec. 1221). Personal-use property, such as the personal residence and furnishings ($280,000), are capital assets. The limousine is depreciable business property and not a capital asset.
Answer (A) is incorrect. The limousine is depreciable business property, and not a capital asset. Answer (C) is incorrect. The limousine is depreciable business property and not a capital asset, but the personal residence and furnishings are capital assets. Answer (D) is incorrect. Hall has capital assets.

11.1.2. Estie Tate is in the real estate business. She purchased a vacant office building for the purpose of reselling it. Estie's sister, not a real estate dealer, owns a large tract of residential land she purchased 7 years ago as an investment. Winfield Nestar is a tax lawyer. He converted an apartment building into condominiums and is trying to sell them. He also owns a tract of land that is zoned for business use and was received in payment for his fees last year. Nestar subdivided this land and is selling it as an office park. Which of the following will produce capital gain or loss?

A. Estie's sister's subdivision of the residential land into five lots and sale to five purchasers.

B. Estie's sale of the office building.

C. Nestar's sale of the condominiums to the residents.

D. Nestar's sale of the office park lots.

Answer (A) is correct. *(Publisher, adapted)*
REQUIRED: The land transaction that will produce capital gain or loss.
DISCUSSION: Generally, the subdivision of land into parcels converts the parcels into property held primarily for sale to customers, so the property is not a capital asset and the gain therefrom is ordinary income. Nevertheless, Sec. 1237 provides that land held by a taxpayer other than a corporation is not deemed to be held primarily for sale to customers solely because the taxpayer subdivided the land for purposes of sale. The land will be considered a capital asset only if the following requirements are met: The taxpayer must not have previously held the land for sale to customers; in the same year in which the sale occurs, the taxpayer must not hold any other real property for sale to customers; no substantial improvements may have been made on the land while held by the taxpayer; and the land must have been held by the taxpayer for at least 5 years. Since Estie's sister meets all of the requirements, her subdivision and sale will produce capital gain or loss.
Answer (B) is incorrect. Estie purchased the office building with the purpose of reselling it to a customer in the ordinary course of her trade or business. Therefore, it is not a capital asset under Sec. 1221(1). Answer (C) is incorrect. The subdivision of a building into condominiums converts the property to that held primarily for sale to customers, i.e., the equivalent of inventory. Answer (D) is incorrect. The subdivision of land converts the property to that held primarily for sale to customers, i.e., the equivalent of inventory.

11.1.3. Halbert Zweistein is a renowned physicist and Nobel Prize winner who holds numerous patents. Halbert owns the copyrights to the 75 books he wrote in a long career. He has also collected his voluminous correspondence, notes, journals, and other papers that he plans to sell to a library in a major eastern city. Which of the following will result in capital gain or capital loss?

A. The sale of the patents.

B. The lease of the patents.

C. The sale of the copyrights.

D. The sale of the papers.

Answer (A) is correct. *(Publisher, adapted)*
   REQUIRED: The asset and transaction that will result in a capital gain or loss.
   DISCUSSION: A capital gain or loss results from a sale or exchange of a capital asset. Patents are capital assets since they are not excluded from being capital assets by Sec. 1221.
   Answer (B) is incorrect. Although patents are capital assets, the lease of a patent will result in royalty income, rather than capital gain or loss, since a lease is not a sale or exchange. If the lease had transferred all substantial rights to a patent, then the income therefrom might produce a capital gain or loss under Sec. 1235. Answer (C) is incorrect. Copyrights held by the taxpayer whose personal efforts created them are not capital assets under Sec. 1221(3). Answer (D) is incorrect. Letters held by the taxpayer whose personal efforts created them are not capital assets under Sec. 1221(3).

11.1.4. Mr. E, a sole proprietor, is in the process of selling his retail store. Based on the following list of assets used in his business, what is the total amount of E's capital assets?

Accounts receivable	$20,000
Merchandise inventories	30,000
Buildings	40,000
Copyrights created by E	20,000
Goodwill acquired in 1990	30,000
Land	40,000
Furniture and fixtures	20,000

The goodwill is not being amortized.

A. $30,000

B. $0

C. $80,000

D. $200,000

Answer (A) is correct. *(SEE, adapted)*
   REQUIRED: The total amount of a sole proprietor's capital assets.
   DISCUSSION: Under Sec. 1221, a capital asset is defined as any property held by the taxpayer (whether or not it is connected with his or her trade or business) that is not specifically excluded by Sec. 1221. Land used in a business, accounts receivable, inventories, and copyrights created by the owner are specifically excluded. Buildings and furniture and fixtures are excluded as depreciable property used in a business. E's only capital asset is the goodwill ($30,000) acquired in 1990. This goodwill is not eligible to be amortized under Sec. 197, since it was acquired before July 25, 1991 (the earliest date that Sec. 197 applies to goodwill).
   Answer (B) is incorrect. Accounts receivable are not capital assets. Answer (C) is incorrect. The land and furniture are not capital assets per Sec. 1221. Answer (D) is incorrect. Not all of the items listed are capital assets.

11.1.5. "Bear" Wall is a dealer in stocks. She sells them to customers in the ordinary course of business. "Bull" Street is in the business of trading stocks for his own benefit. He buys and sells stocks as his sole means of support and business activity. Which of the following statements is true?

A. Stocks held by "Bear" are capital assets, but stocks held by "Bull" are not capital assets.

B. Stocks held by "Bear" are not capital assets, but stocks held by "Bull" are capital assets.

C. Stocks held by both "Bull" and "Bear" are capital assets.

D. Stocks held by neither "Bull" nor "Bear" are capital assets.

Answer (B) is correct. *(Publisher, adapted)*
   REQUIRED: The true statement regarding whether stocks held by a trader and/or a dealer are capital assets.
   DISCUSSION: Capital assets are defined as all property held by a taxpayer which is not excluded by Sec. 1221. One exclusion is the stock in trade of a taxpayer properly included in inventory, or property held primarily for sale to customers in the ordinary course of a trade or business. A dealer in stock does hold the stock primarily for sale to customers in the ordinary course of business (unless the dealer "identifies" the stock as an investment by the close of the business day of acquisition). Accordingly, the stocks held by "Bear" are not capital assets.
   Cases have held that a person who trades stocks for his or her own account is entitled to capital gain or loss on the transactions. The stocks of a trader are not considered held for sale to customers, so stocks held by "Bull" are capital assets.
   Answer (A) is incorrect. Stocks held by "Bear" are not capital assets, and the stocks held by "Bull" are capital assets. Answer (C) is incorrect. Stocks held by both "Bull" and "Bear" are not capital assets. Answer (D) is incorrect. One of these people does hold capital assets.

11.1.6. Helen Chambers owns and manages an apartment building. She also paints seascapes that she exhibits and sells, and she published several volumes of art criticism for which she owns the copyrights. With the profits from the books, she acquired stock in a local art supply company. If Helen sold any of the foregoing property, which would give rise to capital gains or losses?

   A. The apartment building.

   B. The paintings.

   C. The copyrights.

   D. The stock in the art supply company.

Answer (D) is correct. *(Publisher, adapted)*
   REQUIRED: The property that is a capital asset.
   DISCUSSION: Capital gains and losses result from the sale or exchange of capital assets. Capital assets are defined as all property held by a taxpayer which are not excluded by Sec. 1221. Shares of stock are not specified in Sec. 1221, so stock is a capital asset as long as it is not held by a dealer for sale to customers in the taxpayer's trade or business.
   Answer (A) is incorrect. An apartment building is depreciable real property used in a trade or business and is excluded from being a capital asset by Sec. 1221(2). Answer (B) is incorrect. Artistic compositions held by the taxpayer who created them are excluded from the definition of a capital asset by Sec. 1221(3). Answer (C) is incorrect. Copyrights held by the taxpayer who created them are excluded from the definition of a capital asset by Sec. 1221(3).

11.1.7. Which of the following is a capital asset?

   A. Inventory held primarily for sale to customers.

   B. Accounts receivable.

   C. A computer system used by the taxpayer in a personal accounting business.

   D. Land held as an investment.

Answer (D) is correct. *(CPA, adapted)*
   REQUIRED: The property classified as a capital asset.
   DISCUSSION: All property is classified as a capital asset unless specifically excluded. Accounts receivable, inventory, and depreciable property or real estate used in a business are not capital assets. Land held as an investment, however, is a capital asset unless it is held by a dealer (the general rule and not an exception is being tested).
   Answer (A) is incorrect. Inventory held primarily for sale to customers is not included in the capital assets classification. Answer (B) is incorrect. Accounts receivable are specifically excluded as capital assets. Answer (C) is incorrect. A computer system is amortized over its useful life (i.e., depreciable property used in a trade or business) and is not considered a capital asset.

11.1.8. Fully depreciated property used in your trade or business is a capital asset.

   A. True.

   B. False.

Answer (B) is correct. *(SEE, adapted)*
   DISCUSSION: Property used in a trade or business, which is subject to the allowance for depreciation, is specifically excluded from capital asset characterization under Sec. 1221(2). It does not matter whether the property is partially or fully depreciated.

11.1.9. Capital assets may be given preferential tax treatment. Some examples of capital assets are stocks and bonds held in a personal account, a personal residence, and household furnishings.

   A. True.

   B. False.

Answer (A) is correct. *(SEE, adapted)*
   DISCUSSION: To determine the tax treatment of a capital asset transaction, the holding period of the asset must first be known. Capital transactions are treated as long-term if held for more than 1 year, while capital assets held for 1 year or less are considered short-term and are subject to the ordinary income rates. For tax years beginning after December 31, 2012, the capital gains rate for individuals is 20% if the taxpayer is in the 39.6% income tax bracket, 15% if in the 25%, 28%, 33%, or 35% tax bracket, and 0% if in the 10% or 15% tax bracket. For all years, the capital gains tax rate is 25% for unrecaptured Sec. 1250 gains, and 28% for collectibles and gain on qualified small business stock. An individual's investment securities and personal-use property are capital assets because they are not excluded under Sec. 1221.

11.1.10. Mr. N transferred all substantial rights to a trade secret to an unrelated third party for $25,000. Mr. N must report the entire proceeds as ordinary income.

   A. True.

   B. False.

Answer (B) is correct. *(SEE, adapted)*
   DISCUSSION: A trade secret qualifies as a capital asset. It is property (intangible) and not excluded in Sec. 1221. If all substantial rights are transferred, the transaction will be treated as a sale and not a licensing agreement (Sec. 1235). The gain will be capital and short- or long-term depending on the asset's holding period.

11.2 Capital Gains from Sale of Stock

11.2.1. Mr. L purchased stock in Corporation O in Year 1 for $500. In Year 2, Mr. L received a distribution of $200 at a time when Corporation O had no current or accumulated earnings and profits, so it was a nontaxable return of capital. Mr. L sold his Corporation O stock in Year 3 for $700. What is the amount of gain to be reported by Mr. L?

A. $0

B. $200

C. $400

D. $700

Answer (C) is correct. *(SEE, adapted)*
REQUIRED: The amount and character of the gain or loss on the sale of the stock in Year 3.
DISCUSSION: L's gain will be the amount realized ($700) less the adjusted basis of the stock. The adjusted basis is L's original basis of $500 reduced by the return of capital ($200), or $300 [Sec. 1016(a)(4)]. The $400 gain ($700 – $300) is long-term because the stock had been held for more than 1 year.
Answer (A) is incorrect. Mr. L has a long-term capital gain. Answer (B) is incorrect. The basis of the stock is reduced by the return of capital distribution. Answer (D) is incorrect. The proceeds of the sale is $700, which should be reduced by the adjusted basis of the stock.

11.2.2. During Year 1, Mr. F acquired 100 shares of stock in ABC Corporation for $500. During Year 3, he sold the stock for $1,000. His adjusted basis in the stock at the time of sale was $500, and he had no other capital gains or losses during the year. What is the amount and character of income to be reported on F's income tax return for Year 3?

A. $500 long-term capital gain.

B. $500 short-term capital gain.

C. $500 ordinary income.

D. $500 tax-exempt income.

Answer (A) is correct. *(SEE, adapted)*
REQUIRED: The amount and character of the gain or loss on the sale of stock.
DISCUSSION: F's gain is the amount realized less the adjusted basis of the stock. The amount realized is the $1,000 selling price. The adjusted basis is the original $500 purchase price. Therefore, his gain is $500 ($1,000 – $500).
Stock acquired as an investment or by a trader is a capital asset. The character of the gain is long-term capital gain. Under Sec. 1222(3), long-term capital gain is gain from the sale or exchange of a capital asset held for more than 1 year.
Answer (B) is incorrect. Stock acquired as an investment is a long-term capital asset if held for more than 1 year. Answer (C) is incorrect. The stock is a capital asset and was held for more than 1 year. Answer (D) is incorrect. A long-term capital gain realized from the sale of stock is not tax-free income.

11.2.3. During 2017, Abby sold several shares of stock held for investment. The following is a summary of her capital transactions for the year:

Acquired	Sold	Selling Price	Cost
02/15/17	07/15/17	$2,100	$1,400
06/25/15	08/02/17	3,500	2,300
09/25/17	12/15/17	800	1,000
12/28/14	06/15/17	600	900

What is the amount of Abby's capital gain (loss) for 2017?

	Long-Term	Short-Term
A.	$(900)	$(500)
B.	$900	$500
C.	$1,200	$1,000
D.	$1,500	$900

Answer (B) is correct. *(SEE, adapted)*
REQUIRED: The amount of net long-term and short-term capital gain or loss for 2017.
DISCUSSION: For property acquired after 1987, long-term capital gain or loss is the gain or loss from the sale or exchange of a capital asset held for more than 1 year (Sec. 1222). If the capital gain or loss is not long-term, it is short-term.
A net long-term capital gain is the excess of long-term capital gains over long-term capital losses. The two long-term transactions (the sales in June and August) resulted in a net long-term capital gain of $900.
A net short-term capital gain is the excess of short-term capital gains over short-term capital losses. There were two short-term transactions: the sales in July and December, resulting in a net short-term capital gain of $500.

Date of Sale	Long-Term	Short-Term
07/15/17		$700
08/02/17	$1,200	
12/15/17		(200)
06/15/17	(300)	
	$ 900	$500

Answer (A) is incorrect. The two long-term transactions result in a $900 gain, not loss, and the two short-term transactions result in a $500 gain, not loss. Answer (C) is incorrect. The long-term capital loss of $(300) was added to the short-term capital gain. The short-term capital loss of $(200) was not included. Answer (D) is incorrect. The long-term and short-term capital losses of $(300) and $(200) were added to the long-term and short-term capital gains.

11.2.4. On July 1, Year 1, Lila Perl paid $90,000 for 450 shares of Janis Corporation common stock. Lila received a nontaxable stock dividend of 50 new common shares in November of Year 4. On December 20, Year 5, Lila sold the 50 new shares for $11,000. How much should Lila report in her Year 5 return as long-term capital gain?

A. $0

B. $1,000

C. $2,000

D. $11,000

Answer (C) is correct. *(CPA, adapted)*
REQUIRED: The amount of gain that should be reported.
DISCUSSION: When a shareholder receives a nontaxable stock dividend, the basis of the new stock must be determined by allocating to it part of the adjusted basis of the old stock (Sec. 307). The new shares (50) represented 10% of the total shares owned (500) after the stock dividend. Therefore, the basis of the new shares is $9,000 ($90,000 × 10%). The holding period of the new shares includes the holding period of the old shares, i.e., from July 1, Year 1 [Sec. 1223(5)]. This results in a $2,000 long-term capital gain as computed below.

Sale proceeds	$11,000
Less: allocated basis	(9,000)
Realized and recognized gain	$ 2,000

Answer (A) is incorrect. A long-term capital gain is reported. Answer (B) is incorrect. If no basis allocation is made when the stock dividend is received, $1,000 is the long-term capital gain that results. Answer (D) is incorrect. The proceeds from the sale of stock is $11,000, which must be reduced by the basis of the shares sold.

11.2.5. On June 1 of the current year, Ben Rork sold 500 shares of Kul Corporation stock. Rork had received this stock on May 1 of the same year as a bequest from the estate of his uncle, who died on March 1 of the current year. Rork's basis was determined by reference to the stock's fair market value on March 1. Rork's holding period for this stock was

A. Short-term.

B. Long-term.

C. Short-term if sold at a gain; long-term if sold at a loss.

D. Long-term if sold at a gain; short-term if sold at a loss.

Answer (B) is correct. *(CPA, adapted)*
REQUIRED: The holding period for stock received from a decedent.
DISCUSSION: Under Sec. 1223(11), if property acquired from a decedent is sold or otherwise disposed of by the recipient within 12 months of the decedent's death, then the property is considered to have been held for more than 12 months.
Answer (A) is incorrect. The holding period for this stock is not short-term. Answer (C) is incorrect. The holding period for this stock is not short-term if sold at a gain, and long-term if sold at a loss. Answer (D) is incorrect. The holding period for this stock is not long-term if sold at a gain, and short-term if sold at a loss.

11.2.6. On March 10, 2017, James Rogers sold 300 shares of Red Company common stock for $4,200. Rogers acquired the stock in 2012 at a cost of $5,000. On April 4, 2017, he repurchased 300 shares of Red Company common stock for $3,600 and held them until July 18, 2017, when he sold them for $6,000. How should Rogers report the above transactions for 2017?

A. A long-term capital loss of $800.

B. A long-term capital gain of $1,000.

C. A long-term capital gain of $1,600.

D. A long-term capital loss of $800 and a short-term capital gain of $2,400.

Answer (C) is correct. *(CPA, adapted)*
REQUIRED: The amount and character of capital gain after identical stocks are sold and repurchased within 30 days.
DISCUSSION: The sale of stock on March 10 was a wash sale under Sec. 1091 because identical stock was repurchased within 30 days (on April 4). No deduction is allowable for any loss that occurs in a wash sale. The $800 realized loss ($4,200 – $5,000) that occurred in March will not be recognized for tax purposes. The disallowed loss is added to the basis of the stock that is subsequently purchased in April. The basis in the stock purchased in April is $4,400 ($3,600 cost + $800 disallowed loss), and a gain of $1,600 is recognized when the stock is sold for $6,000 on July 18. The holding period of stock acquired in a wash sale includes the holding period of the originally purchased stock, so the gain is long-term.
Answer (A) is incorrect. The loss may not be recognized in a wash sale. Instead, the $800 should be added to the new stock's basis, and then used to determine the subsequent gain. Answer (B) is incorrect. The amount of $1,000 uses the $5,000 basis for the first block of stock as the basis in the second block of stock purchased. This basis should be the purchase price of $3,600 plus the $800 disallowed loss from the wash sale. Answer (D) is incorrect. This would be the answer if the first sale had not been a wash sale.

11.2.7. Iam Broke frequently traded on the stock market. On November 1, Year 1, when stock prices were very high, Broke sold short (sold without owning any stock by borrowing from the broker) 100 shares of Ducko, Inc., at $80 per share. On July 1, Year 2, Broke purchased 100 shares of Ducko for $50 per share and delivered them on December 1, Year 2. Broke also purchased 100 shares of High Tech, Inc., on February 1, Year 1, for $60 per share. He sold 100 shares of High Tech short on December 1, Year 1, at $100 per share. Broke delivered these 100 shares on September 1, Year 2. Broke is in the 35% income tax bracket. What is Broke's gain on the sales?

A. $4,000 short-term capital gain in Year 1, and $3,000 short-term capital gain in Year 2.

B. $3,000 long-term capital gain in Year 1, and $4,000 short-term capital gain in Year 2.

C. $7,000 long-term capital gain in Year 1.

D. $7,000 short-term capital gain in Year 2.

Answer (A) is correct. *(Publisher, adapted)*
REQUIRED: The time of recognition and character of gain from short sales of stock.
DISCUSSION: Under Sec. 1259, certain hedging transactions are treated as constructive sales. A taxpayer is considered to have made a constructive sale of an appreciated position if the taxpayer enters into a short sale. In a short sale, a taxpayer who owns appreciated shares of stock borrows identical shares from a third party (e.g., a broker) and sells them. The proceeds of the sale are held by the broker until the taxpayer closes the transaction by delivering the borrowed shares. The borrowed shares can be securities originally held by the taxpayer or newly purchased shares.
Since the Ducko stock is not held by Broke at the end of Year 1, the gain (loss) from the short sale is not reasonably known. Accordingly, the gain from this transaction will not be recognized until Year 2, when the gain can be sufficiently determined. The shares of Ducko used to close the first short sale were purchased after the short sale and prior to the closing, so the gain is a short-term capital gain.
Conversely, the short-term capital gain from the short sale of High Tech stock is recognized in Year 1. Immediately after the short sale, Broke's gain is effectively locked in at $4,000. Regardless of the change in the price of High Tech stock, Broke's gain will remain $4,000 because he holds the requisite number of shares when the transaction is initiated. The assets were held for less than 12 months, and Broke's gain on the sale of High Tech stock is "locked in" in Year 1.
Answer (B) is incorrect. Broke does not have a $3,000 long-term capital gain in Year 1 and a $4,000 short-term capital gain in Year 2. Answer (C) is incorrect. The assets were held for less than 12 months, and Broke's gain on the sale of High Tech stock was "locked in" in Year 1. Answer (D) is incorrect. Broke does not have a $7,000 short-term capital gain in Year 2.

11.2.8. Stanley Garret purchased 1,000 shares of Pat Corporation common stock at $5 per share in Year 1. On September 19, Year 3, he received 1,000 stock rights entitling him to buy 250 additional shares of Pat Corporation common stock at $10 per share. On the day that the rights were issued, the fair market value of the stock was $12 per share ex-rights and that of the rights was $1 each. Garret did not exercise the rights; he let them expire on November 28, Year 3. What should be the loss that Garret can report for Year 3?

A. No gain or loss.

B. A short-term capital loss of $250.

C. A long-term capital loss of $2,500.

D. A short-term capital loss of $1,000.

Answer (A) is correct. *(CPA, adapted)*
REQUIRED: The amount of loss that Garret can report for Year 3.
DISCUSSION: When a taxpayer receives nontaxable stock rights, the cost basis of the rights under Sec. 307 is determined by allocating part of the basis of the stock on which the distribution was made. If the fair market value of the rights at the time of the distribution is less than 15% of the fair market value of the stock held at that time, the allocation is elective, but no allocation is made unless the stock rights are sold or exercised. If stock rights are allowed to expire, no allocation is made and no loss is recognized [Reg. 1.307-1(a)].
Answer (B) is incorrect. Garret should not report a short-term capital loss of $250. Answer (C) is incorrect. Garret should not report a long-term capital loss of $2,500. Answer (D) is incorrect. Garret should not report a short-term capital loss of $1,000.

11.2.9. Mr. and Mrs. Able are investors in a mutual fund that is not part of a qualified retirement plan. For the current year, the fund notified them that it had allocated a $9,500 long-term capital gain to their account. Of this total, only $4,500 was distributed in the current year. In addition, the fund paid $500 in federal income taxes on their behalf. What is the amount of long-term capital gain that the Ables should report on their current-year tax return?

A. $10,000

B. $9,500

C. $5,000

D. $4,500

Answer (B) is correct. *(SEE, adapted)*
REQUIRED: The amount of long-term capital gain to be included in gross income.
DISCUSSION: A mutual fund is a regulated investment company, the taxation of which is determined by Sec. 852. Dividends paid by the mutual fund to shareholders are taxed. Undistributed capital gains must be included in income by shareholders, but a credit is allowed for their proportionate share of any tax on the capital gain paid by the mutual fund. Therefore, the Ables must report the full $9,500 as a long-term capital gain.
Answer (A) is incorrect. The $500 of federal income taxes paid is not reported as capital gain but is taken by the Ables as a credit. Answer (C) is incorrect. Both the distributed and the undistributed amounts of capital gain must be reported as income. Answer (D) is incorrect. The actual amount of the gain, not only the amount distributed, must be reported.

11.2.10. In January of Year 1, Kirk Kelly bought 100 shares of a listed stock for $8,000. In March of Year 2, when the fair market value was $6,000, Kirk gave this stock to his cousin, Clara. No gift tax was paid. Clara sold this stock in June of Year 3 for $7,000. How much is Clara's reportable gain or loss in Year 3 on the sale of this stock?

A. $0

B. $1,000 loss.

C. $1,000 gain.

D. $7,000 gain.

Answer (A) is correct. *(CPA, adapted)*
REQUIRED: The amount of reportable gain or loss from the sale of stock received as a gift.
DISCUSSION: The basis of property received by gift is the donor's basis (transferred or carryover basis). If the fair market value of the property at the time of the gift is lower, however, the basis for purposes of determining loss is the fair market value (Sec. 1015). Clara's basis for gain is $8,000, and her basis for loss is $6,000. Therefore, neither gain nor loss is recognized [Reg. 1.1015-1(a)(2)].

	Gain	Loss
Sales price	$7,000	$7,000
Less basis	(8,000)	(6,000)
Gain (loss)	No gain	No loss

Answer (B) is incorrect. The purchase price is not used to determine loss at sale of property gifted in a nontaxable transaction. Answer (C) is incorrect. The FMV at time of sale is not used to determine gain of property gifted in a nontaxable transaction. Answer (D) is incorrect. The gain or loss are affected by values at time of purchase and gift.

11.2.11. On April 5, Year 3, Mr. Jeffries sold all his shares of C Corporation stock for $50,000. He originally purchased the shares on January 30, Year 1, for $10,000. On June 1, Year 3, Mr. Jeffries purchased stock in a specialized small business investment company for $30,000. How much gain must Mr. Jeffries currently recognize on the sale of his C Corporation stock?

A. $0

B. $10,000

C. $20,000

D. $50,000

Answer (C) is correct. *(Publisher, adapted)*
REQUIRED: The amount of gain to be recognized when small business investment company stock is subsequently purchased.
DISCUSSION: If an individual realizes a capital gain on the sale of publicly traded stock and uses the proceeds from the sale within 60 days to purchase stock in a specialized small business investment company (SBIC), the individual may elect to defer recognition of the gain (Sec. 1044). Gain must be recognized currently to the extent the sales proceeds exceed the cost of the new stock. Mr. Jeffries must recognize $20,000 of the $40,000 ($50,000 – $10,000 adjusted basis) realized gain ($50,000 proceeds – $30,000 cost of SBIC stock = $20,000 recognized). Individuals can exclude the lesser of the realized gain, the amount of the proceeds that were not reinvested, an annual ceiling of $50,000, or a lifetime ceiling of $500,000 minus the excluded gain for prior tax years, of exclusion in any tax year. Thus, he must currently recognize only $20,000 of capital gain.
Answer (A) is incorrect. There is a gain recognized on the sale of the C corporation stock. Answer (B) is incorrect. Gain is recognized to the extent the sales proceeds exceed the cost of the new stock. Answer (D) is incorrect. The amount realized equals $50,000.

11.2.12. On September 30 of the current year, Peter sold 100 shares of Solid Corporation stock for $16,000. Peter inherited the stock from his uncle who died on May 15 of the same year. It was included in the uncle's federal estate tax return at its May 15 fair market value of $18,000. Peter has a long-term capital loss of $2,000 from this transaction.

A. True.

B. False.

Answer (A) is correct. *(SEE, adapted)*
DISCUSSION: Peter acquired the stock from a decedent. He takes the stock's fair market value at the date of the decedent's death as his basis. There is a $2,000 loss ($16,000 – $18,000) on the sale. The character is long-term. Under Sec. 1223(11), when property is acquired from a decedent and a sale subsequently occurs within 12 months of the decedent's death, the property is considered to have been held long-term.

11.2.13. Mr. W purchased two shares of XYZ Corporation common stock. He paid $90 for the first share and $60 for the second share. XYZ declared a stock dividend that gave stockholders two new shares of common stock for each share they held. After the distribution, Mr. W had six shares of stock with an adjusted basis of $25 each.

A. True.

B. False.

Answer (B) is correct. *(SEE, adapted)*
DISCUSSION: A taxpayer cannot average the basis for shares of stock in a corporation. The basis for each share is its cost, subject to allocation for stock dividends under Sec. 307. Two new shares are attributable to the $90 share, so each is assigned a basis of $30 ($90 ÷ 3 shares). Two new shares are attributable to the $60 share, so each is assigned a basis of $20 ($60 ÷ 3 shares). After the distribution Mr. W has six shares of stock, three shares with a basis of $30, and three shares with a basis of $20.

11.2.14. Mrs. D, a calendar-year, cash-basis taxpayer, sold stock through the stock exchange for $25,000 on December 30, Year 1. She had purchased the stock on May 28, Year 1, for $20,000. The cash was received and the sale closed by delivery of the stock on January 9, Year 2, in accordance with the rules of the stock exchange. Mrs. D has a short-term capital gain of $5,000 on her Year 2 return.

A. True.

B. False.

Answer (B) is correct. *(SEE, adapted)*
   DISCUSSION: Both cash and accrual taxpayers must report, in the year of sale, gain or loss from sales of stocks or securities which are traded on an established securities market [Sec. 453(k)(2)]. Mrs. D has a $5,000 gain which occurred on December 30, Year 1, and is reported as a short-term capital gain on her Year 1 return.

11.2.15. Mary is one of 37 individuals who acquired stock of DiscLap Corp. on its formation in Year 1 in exchange for a contribution to capital of $100,000 cash. DiscLap, a C corporation, immediately commenced operations of a mail-order laptop computer business. All of its revenues are from computer sales-related activities. Computers are advertised by catalog at discount prices, based on anticipation of high volume, low overhead, and the terms of sale. DiscLap offers no financing or leasing arrangements. Payment by cash or credit card must be received in full prior to shipment. DiscLap is operating a qualified trade or business for purposes of the Sec. 1202 exclusion of gain on the sale of stock.

A. True.

B. False.

Answer (A) is correct. *(Publisher, adapted)*
   DISCUSSION: Section 1202(a) allows a noncorporate taxpayer to exclude from gross income 50% of any gain from the sale or exchange of qualified small business stock held for more than 5 years. A noncorporate taxpayer is also allowed to roll over the gain on the sale of qualified small business stock (if held for more than 6 months) if the proceeds are used to purchase other qualified small business stock within 60 days of the sale. Stock is not treated as qualified small business stock unless the corporation meets active business requirements [Sec. 1202(c)(2)]. One requirement is that at least 80% (by value) of the corporation's assets are used in the active conduct of one or more qualified trades or businesses [Sec. 1202(e)(1)(A)]. Any business is "qualified" unless it is of one of the types listed in Sec. 1202(e)(3). Generally, the nonqualified types are in the business of (1) professional services, (2) banking or finance, (3) farming, (4) mining, or (5) the hotel or restaurant business. Thus, DiscLap's operation is a qualified trade or business.

11.2.16. Jim owns five shares of stock in X Corporation. The corporation declared a 5% stock dividend. It also set up a plan wherein fractional shares were sold and the cash proceeds distributed to the stockholders. Jim should treat the amount he received for the fractional share stock dividend as an ordinary taxable dividend.

A. True.

B. False.

Answer (B) is correct. *(SEE, adapted)*
   DISCUSSION: When a corporation declares a stock dividend, it is not uncommon for some shareholders to be entitled to fractional shares. If cash is distributed in lieu of fractional shares to avoid dealing in fractional shares, the cash received by shareholders is treated as though the fractional shares were distributed as part of the stock dividend and then redeemed by the distributing corporation under Sec. 302 [Reg. 1.305-3(c)]. If the corporation issues and sells the fractional shares and then distributes the proceeds as part of a plan, however, the transaction is treated as if the shareholders had received the fractional shares and then sold them. Jim should treat the amount received as part capital gain and part reduction of basis of his other stock (to the extent basis would have been allocated if the fractional shares had been received).

11.3 Gains from Sale of Other Capital Assets

11.3.1. In December of the current year, Emily sold an antique rug for $4,100. She bought the rug 5 years ago for $1,100. What is her taxable gain and at what maximum rate will it be taxed?

A. $3,000 long-term capital gain, taxed at a regular rate.

B. $3,000 long-term capital gain, taxed at 28% rate.

C. $1,500 long-term capital gain, taxed at a regular rate.

D. $1,500 long-term capital gain, taxed at 28% rate.

Answer (B) is correct. *(SEE, adapted)*
   REQUIRED: The taxable gain and maximum rate for the sale of a collectible item.
   DISCUSSION: The sale of the antique rug qualifies as a sale of a collectible item. For individuals, capital transactions involving long-term holding periods are grouped by tax rates. A 28% rate is applied to gains or losses from the sale of collectible items. The amount of the gain is $3,000 ($4,100 FMV – $1,100 basis).
   Answer (A) is incorrect. Capital gains on collectible items are not taxed at a regular rate. Answer (C) is incorrect. That is only half of the gain. Also, capital gains on collectible items are not taxed at a regular rate. Answer (D) is incorrect. The amount of $1,500 is only half of the gain.

11.3.2. Mr. J bought an asset on June 19, 2016. What is the earliest date on which Mr. J could have sold that asset and qualified for long-term capital gain or loss treatment?

A. December 19, 2016.

B. December 20, 2016.

C. June 19, 2017.

D. June 20, 2017.

Answer (D) is correct. *(SEE, adapted)*
REQUIRED: The date on which a long-term holding period begins.
DISCUSSION: For assets acquired after 1987, long-term capital gain or loss treatment is provided if the asset is held for more than 1 year. The general rule is that the date the property is acquired is excluded and the date that the property is disposed of is included in this computation of the holding period. Since Mr. J bought the asset on June 19, 2016, his holding period is treated as beginning June 20, 2016. Exactly 1 year is considered to have expired on June 19, 2017. Therefore, on June 20, 2017, more than 1 year has passed, which would satisfy the long-term holding period requirement.
Answer (A) is incorrect. December 19, 2016, is not the earliest date to qualify for long-term capital gain or loss treatment. Answer (B) is incorrect. December 20, 2016, is not the earliest date to qualify for long-term capital gain or loss treatment. Answer (C) is incorrect. June 19, 2017, is not the earliest date to qualify for long-term capital gain or loss treatment.

11.3.3. Jack had the following items of income and loss in Year 7:

Wages	$122,500
Nonbusiness bad debt	1,400
Gain on stock held since Year 5	2,600
Flood loss to his personal residence owned since Year 1	4,100
Loss on stock held since Year 4	300
Gain on stock held for 4 months	2,050

What is his total taxable capital gain or total deductible capital loss for Year 7?

A. $1,150 loss.

B. $2,300 gain.

C. $2,950 gain.

D. $4,350 gain.

Answer (C) is correct. *(SEE, adapted)*
REQUIRED: The taxable capital gain or deductible capital loss from all the transactions.
DISCUSSION: Jack had a net long-term capital gain of $2,300 resulting from the $2,600 gain on the sale of stock and the $300 loss on the sale of some other stock. Jack had a net short-term capital gain of $650 resulting from the sale of stock held for 4 months and the $1,400 nonbusiness bad debt. Nonbusiness bad debts are treated as short-term capital losses under Sec. 166. The flood loss is an itemized deduction, not a capital loss.

Net long-term capital gain ($2,600 – $300)	$2,300
Net short-term capital gain ($2,050 – $1,400)	650
Total taxable capital gain	$2,950

Answer (A) is incorrect. The flood loss is not a capital loss. Answer (B) is incorrect. The short-term capital gain on the sale of the stock held 4 months and the short-term capital loss on the nonbusiness bad debt need to be included in this amount. Answer (D) is incorrect. The nonbusiness bad debt is a short-term capital loss and should be included in this amount.

11.3.4. On July 1 of the current year, Mr. A, a cash-method taxpayer, sold a painting for which he received $50,000 in cash and a note with a face value of $50,000 and a fair market value of $35,000. He paid a commission of $5,000 on the sale. Mr. A had acquired the painting 15 years ago, and his basis was $5,000. What is A's recognized gain for the current year?

A. $95,000

B. $90,000

C. $75,000

D. $50,000

Answer (C) is correct. *(SEE, adapted)*
REQUIRED: The recognized gain on the sale of the painting.
DISCUSSION: The amount realized under Sec. 1001 includes money received plus the fair market value of other property. Mr. A realized $85,000 ($50,000 cash + $35,000 note). Commissions reduce the amount realized under Reg. 1.263(a)-2. Consequently, Mr. A recognized a gain of $75,000.

Amount realized	$85,000
Less: commission	(5,000)
Net proceeds	$80,000
Less: adjusted basis	(5,000)
Recognized gain	$75,000

Answer (A) is incorrect. The note should be valued at its FMV, and not its face amount, when determining the amount realized. The commission should also reduce the amount realized. Answer (B) is incorrect. The note should be valued at its FMV, not its face amount. Answer (D) is incorrect. The amount of cash received is $50,000.

11.3.5. Kerry Orange owned a 20% interest for 20 years in the T & T Partnership, which owns no unrealized receivables or inventory items. In the current year, he sold his interest for $30,000 and was relieved of his share of partnership liabilities of $2,200. At the date of sale, Orange's total basis in his partnership interest was $24,000. What gain or loss should Orange report?

A. $3,800 ordinary income.

B. $6,000 capital gain.

C. $8,200 capital gain.

D. $8,200 ordinary income.

11.3.6. Mr. Patel sold a piece of land he had purchased for $40,000. The buyer paid cash of $50,000 and transferred to Mr. Patel a piece of farm equipment having a fair market value of $30,000. The buyer also assumed Mr. Patel's $10,000 loan on the land. Mr. Patel paid selling expenses of $5,000. What is Mr. Patel's recognized gain on this sale?

A. $25,000

B. $45,000

C. $50,000

D. $90,000

11.3.7. On September 1, Year 1, Sam purchased for $9,200 cash a $10,000 bond with 10% annual interest that matures in Year 11. Sam did not elect to accrue market discount currently as interest income. On September 2, Year 2, Sam sold the bond for $9,400. The amount and character of gain Sam must recognize in Year 2 from this transaction is

A. $600 long-term capital loss.

B. $200 short-term capital gain.

C. $80 ordinary income; $120 short-term capital gain.

D. $80 ordinary income; $120 long-term capital gain.

Answer (C) is correct. *(SEE, adapted)*
REQUIRED: The amount and character of gain from the sale of the partnership interest.
DISCUSSION: Gain or loss on the sale of a partnership interest is capital gain or loss under Sec. 741. Liabilities assumed by the purchaser are part of the amount realized on the sale. Therefore, Orange is considered to have received $32,200 for his partnership interest ($30,000 + $2,200). His capital gain is $8,200 ($32,200 – $24,000).
Answer (A) is incorrect. A partner's release from a share of a partnership liability is added to the cash proceeds (not subtracted), and the gain's character is capital. Answer (B) is incorrect. A partner's release from a share of a partnership liability is added to the cash proceeds. Answer (D) is incorrect. Orange will not report $8,200 ordinary income from the transaction.

Answer (B) is correct. *(SEE, adapted)*
REQUIRED: The gain when property is given, liabilities assumed, and selling expenses incurred.
DISCUSSION: The amount realized under Sec. 1001 includes money received, fair market value of other property received, and any liabilities of which the seller is relieved. Mr. Patel realized $90,000 ($50,000 cash + $30,000 fair market value equipment + $10,000 liability relieved). Under Reg. 1.263(a)-2, commissions reduce the amount realized. Section 1001(a) provides that the gain from the sale of property is the excess of the amount realized over the adjusted basis. Therefore, Mr. Patel recognized a gain of $45,000.

Amount realized	$90,000
Less: commissions paid	(5,000)
Net proceeds	$85,000
Less: adjusted basis	(40,000)
Realized and recognized gain	$45,000

Answer (A) is incorrect. The $10,000 liability increases the amount realized. It does not reduce the amount realized. Answer (C) is incorrect. The $5,000 of selling expenses reduces the amount realized. Answer (D) is incorrect. The amount realized is $90,000, not the recognized gain.

Answer (D) is correct. *(Publisher, adapted)*
REQUIRED: The amount and the character of gain that must be recognized on the sale of a bond purchased at a market discount.
DISCUSSION: Section 1276(a)(1) requires that gain on the disposition of any market discount bond be treated as ordinary income to the extent that the market discount could have been accrued as interest. In this case, the market discount was $800 ($10,000 – $9,200). The accrued market discount is the amount bearing the same ratio to the market discount as the number of days the taxpayer held the bond bears to the number of days from acquisition to maturity. The accrued market discount is $80 [$800 × (1 year ÷ 10 years)]. The total gain was $200 ($9,400 – $9,200), so the gain consists of $80 ordinary income and $120 long-term capital gain.
Answer (A) is incorrect. Sam does not have a $600 long-term capital loss from this transaction. Answer (B) is incorrect. Sam does not have a short-term capital gain from this transaction, and he does have ordinary income to recognize. Answer (C) is incorrect. The gain on the transaction is not short-term.

11.3.8. Soft Cream sells franchises to independent operators. In the current year, it sold a franchise to Edward Trent, charging an initial fee of $20,000 and a monthly fee of 2% of sales. Soft Cream retains the right to control such matters as employee and management training, quality control and promotion, and the purchase of ingredients. Mr. Trent's current-year sales amounted to $200,000. From the transactions with Trent, Soft Cream, an accrual-basis taxpayer, would include in its computation of current-year taxable income

A. Long-term capital gain of $24,000.

B. Long-term capital gain of $20,000, ordinary income of $4,000.

C. Long-term capital gain of $4,000, ordinary income of $20,000.

D. Ordinary income of $24,000.

Answer (D) is correct. *(CPA, adapted)*
REQUIRED: The amount and character of income from the sale of the franchise.
DISCUSSION: The transfer of a franchise is not treated as a sale or exchange of a capital asset if the transferor retains significant power, rights, or continuing interest with respect to the franchise (Sec. 1253). The right to control employee and management training, quality control and promotion, and the purchase of ingredients constitutes significant power, rights, and continuing interest. Therefore, the transfer is not a sale but merely a licensing agreement, and all the income ($20,000 initial fee and $4,000 monthly fee) is ordinary income.
Answer (A) is incorrect. Soft Cream does not have a long-term capital gain of $24,000 from the transactions. Answer (B) is incorrect. Soft Cream does not have a long-term capital gain of $20,000 and ordinary income of $4,000 from the transactions. Answer (C) is incorrect. Soft Cream does not have a long-term capital gain of $4,000 and ordinary income of $20,000 from the transactions.

11.3.9. On September 1, Year 1, Leslie purchased a 10-year, $10,000 bond with 7% annual interest that matures September 1, Year 6. Leslie borrowed $8,000 to help finance the $9,100 purchase price of the bond. For Year 1, Leslie's interest expense for the borrowed funds is $321, and the interest income from the bonds is $234. What is the total deduction resulting from this transaction in Year 1?

A. $321

B. $261

C. $234

D. $27

Answer (B) is correct. *(Publisher, adapted)*
REQUIRED: The total deduction allowed for interest paid on funds borrowed to purchase a market discount bond.
DISCUSSION: Section 1277 provides that the net direct interest expense with respect to a market discount bond is deductible only to the extent that it exceeds the market discount allocable to the days during the year the bond was held by the taxpayer. The term "net direct interest expense" means the excess of the interest expense on indebtedness over total interest (including original issue discount) includible in gross income for the taxable year with respect to the bond. The market discount allocable to the taxable year is based on the number of days the bond was held during the taxable year. Interest expense, to the extent of the interest income from the bond, is also deductible.

Interest paid or accrued on debt	$321
Interest from the bond includible in gross income	(234)
Net direct interest expense	$ 87
Market discount allocable to Year 1 {[($10,000 − $9,100) ÷ 5 years] × (122 days ÷ 365 days)}	(60)
Net direct interest expense deduction	$ 27
Interest deductible to extent of income	234
Total interest deduction	$261

Answer (A) is incorrect. The amount of interest expense paid is $321, which must be adjusted. Answer (C) is incorrect. The cash interest income that was received is $234. Answer (D) is incorrect. The $27 is the net direct interest expense deduction but does not include interest expense that is deductible to the extent of income earned.

11.3.10. On March 1 of the current year, Barry Beech received a gift of income-producing real estate having a donor's adjusted basis of $50,000 at the date of the gift. Fair market value of the property at the date of the gift was $40,000. Beech sold the property for $46,000 on August 1 of the current year. How much gain or loss should Beech report for the year?

A. No gain or loss.

B. $6,000 short-term capital gain.

C. $4,000 short-term capital loss.

D. $10,000 ordinary loss.

Answer (A) is correct. *(CPA, adapted)*
REQUIRED: The amount of gain or loss on the sale of property acquired by gift.
DISCUSSION: For the purpose of computing gain, a donee's basis is the same as the donor's basis. For computing loss, the donee takes the lower of the donor's basis or the fair market value of the property (Sec. 1015). Beech has no gain or loss, as shown below.

	Gain	Loss
Amount realized	$46,000	$46,000
Less: basis	(50,000)	(40,000)
Gain/loss	No gain	No loss

Answer (B) is incorrect. The difference between the sales price and the FMV of the gift is $6,000. Answer (C) is incorrect. The difference between the adjusted basis and the sales price is $4,000. Answer (D) is incorrect. The basis for computing the loss is the FMV at the date of the gift.

11.3.11. On January 3, 2017, Mrs. Y acquired a patent for her invention. On September 30, 2017, she sold all her substantial rights to this patent. Mrs. Y is entitled to long-term capital gain treatment.

    A. True.

    B. False.

Answer (A) is correct. *(SEE, adapted)*
    DISCUSSION: Under Sec. 1235, the transfer by the inventor of property that consists of all substantial rights to a patent shall be considered the sale or exchange of a capital asset that has been held for the long-term gain (loss) holding period and is subject to the maximum preferential rate. The gain on sale of this patent will be considered long-term capital gain in the 15% basket, even though it had been held for less than 12 months.

11.3.12. Mr. B, a car dealer, assigns cars from his new inventory to be used as demonstrators. In June, he sold one demonstrator for $12,000. It cost $10,000 and no depreciation had been deducted. Mr. B should report a $2,000 capital gain.

    A. True.

    B. False.

Answer (B) is correct. *(SEE, adapted)*
    DISCUSSION: Demonstrators are stock in trade (inventory), and are specifically excluded from the capital asset definition of Sec. 1221. The gain on the sale of inventory is ordinary gain to the taxpayer. However, it could be argued that the demonstrators are Sec. 1231 property if held and depreciated for more than 1 year (but the depreciation would be recaptured under Sec. 1245).

11.3.13. On May 5, 2015, Mr. E purchased a rare gem as an investment. On April 25, 2017, he exchanged it for another rare gem in a nontaxable exchange. On December 31, 2017, he sold it for cash. Any gain or loss on the sale is a long-term capital gain or loss in the 28% basket.

    A. True.

    B. False.

Answer (A) is correct. *(SEE, adapted)*
    DISCUSSION: Property held for investment is a capital asset. The holding period for property received in an exchange includes the period of the property exchanged if the property received is a capital or Sec. 1231 asset and it has the same basis in whole or in part as the property exchanged [Sec. 1223(1)]. Under Sec. 1031, the exchange of the gems is a like-kind exchange, and the basis of the gem received is the same as the basis of the gem exchanged. Therefore, the gain or loss on the subsequent sale is a long-term capital gain or loss because the holding period exceeded 1 year. Even though the holding period exceeded 1 year, the sale or exchange of collectibles is specifically classified as long-term capital gain or loss in the 28% basket.

11.3.14. In Year 1, Mr. C, who is not a dealer in real estate, purchased a tract of land and divided it into four lots. Mr. C substantially increased the value of the lots by installing gas, electricity, sewer, and water, and sold the lots at a gain in Year 7. Mr. C is entitled to capital gain treatment on the sale of the lots.

    A. True.

    B. False.

Answer (B) is correct. *(SEE, adapted)*
    DISCUSSION: The subdivision of land is generally considered to convert investment property to property held for sale in a trade or business, i.e., inventory that produces ordinary income. Section 1237 does not allow capital gain in this case because Mr. C made substantial improvements. Installing utilities is not considered substantial improvements only if the property is held by the taxpayer for 10 years or more.

11.3.15. Ashby held a tract of land for 3 years during which time he made no substantial improvements. Ashby made a gift of the land to his son Hank, who held the land for 3 additional years. Hank subdivided the tract without improving it and sold four lots at a gain. Neither Mr. Ashby or Hank are real estate dealers. Hank has a long-term capital gain from the sale of the four lots.

    A. True.

    B. False.

Answer (A) is correct. *(SEE, adapted)*
    DISCUSSION: The gift of the land by Ashby to his son, Hank, allows for Hank to include Ashby's 3-year holding period. At the time of the sale, Hank has a holding period of 6 years. This satisfies one of three requirements under Sec. 1237. The other two requirements are that (1) such tract, or any lot or parcel thereof, had not previously been held by such taxpayer primarily for sale to customers in the ordinary course of a trade or business and (2) no substantial improvement that substantially enhances the value of the lot or parcel sold is made by the taxpayer on such tract while held by the taxpayer. These two requirements are met in this transaction. Section 1237(b)(1) further limits the benefit of capital gains status by allowing no more than five lots or parcels contained in the same tract to qualify for capital gain treatment. In this transaction, there are four lots sold. So all lots qualify for long-term capital gain treatment. The portion of Sec. 1237 that requires ordinary income to be recognized equal to 5% of the selling price when more than five lots are sold does not apply here since only four lots have been sold by the end of the current year.

11.3.16. Mr. D is a sole proprietor using the cash method of accounting. In May, he retired and sold his trade accounts receivable totaling $30,000 for $20,000. The result of the sale of the accounts receivable is an ordinary gain of $20,000.

A. True.

B. False.

Answer (A) is correct. *(SEE, adapted)*
DISCUSSION: Capital assets are defined in Sec. 1221. Accounts receivable are explicitly excluded from the definition of a capital asset. Therefore, the sale of accounts receivable results in ordinary income. Since he was a cash-method taxpayer, his basis in the receivables was zero and the entire proceeds were ordinary income.

11.3.17. Mr. Wills, a cash-basis farmer, sold a calf born on his farm in March. The sales price was $150 and the cost of raising the calf was $90, which Mr. Wills deducted. The gain from this sale is a capital gain of $60.

A. True.

B. False.

Answer (B) is correct. *(SEE, adapted)*
DISCUSSION: Capital assets are defined in Sec. 1221. Section 1221 specifically excludes from the definition of a capital asset any property held by the taxpayer primarily for sale to customers in the ordinary course of business. The sale of a calf is considered to be in the ordinary course of Mr. Wills' business. Therefore, the sale results in ordinary income of $60.

11.4 Net Capital Gain Computations

NOTE: Also see Study Unit 12 for long-term capital gains under Sec. 1231 and Subunit 11.9 for tax calculations for capital gains transactions.

11.4.1. The maximum tax rate on net capital gains for individuals for 2017 is

A. 20%

B. 28%

C. 25%

D. 15%

Answer (B) is correct. *(SEE, adapted)*
REQUIRED: The maximum tax rate on net capital gains.
DISCUSSION: For tax years beginning after December 31, 2012, the capital gains rate for individuals is 20% if the taxpayer is in the 39.6% income tax bracket; 15% if in the 25%, 28%, 33%, or 35% income tax bracket; and 0% if in the 10% or 15% income tax bracket. For all tax years, the capital gains tax rate is 25% for unrecaptured Sec. 1250 gain and 28% for collectibles and gain on qualified small business stock.
Answer (A) is incorrect. The maximum tax rate on net capital gains for individuals is not 20%. Answer (C) is incorrect. The maximum tax rate on net capital gains for individuals is not 25%. Answer (D) is incorrect. The maximum tax rate on net capital gains for individuals is not 15%.

11.4.2. During the year, Mr. G had the following capital transactions:

	Short-Term	Long-Term (28% Basket)	Long-Term (15% Basket)
Gains	$ 9,000	$15,000	$ 8,000
Losses	10,000	10,000	12,000

Determine the overall result of the transactions.

A. $1,000 short-term capital loss.

B. $0 long-term capital gain.

C. $4,000 long-term capital gain.

D. $5,000 long-term capital gain.

Answer (B) is correct. *(Publisher, adapted)*
REQUIRED: The result of the transactions.
DISCUSSION: Net capital gains and losses are computed separately for each basket. This step leaves a $5,000 long-term gain in the 28% basket and a $4,000 long-term loss in the 15% basket. The 28% basket contains collectible gains and losses and gains from Sec. 1202 (certain small business stock). The 28% basket also includes any net short-term capital loss for the tax year and long-term capital loss carryovers from other years. Therefore, the $1,000 short-term loss reduces the net gain in the 28% basket to $4,000. A net loss in the 15% basket is used first to reduce net gain from the 28% basket, then to reduce gain from the 25% basket. Accordingly, the $4,000 net loss from the 15% basket is applied against the $4,000 net gain in the 28% basket, resulting in a complete offset of gains and losses.
Answer (A) is incorrect. A loss of $1,000 is only the net short-term capital loss. Answer (C) is incorrect. The long-term capital loss in the 15% basket is $4,000. Answer (D) is incorrect. The long-term capital gain in the 28% basket is $5,000.

11.4.3. Taxpayer G had the following items of income and loss in 2017:

Wages	$28,000
Nonbusiness bad debt	1,000
Gain on commodity futures held 14 months	1,000
Loss on stock purchased in 2000	800
Flood loss on personal residence owned since 2002	4,500
Gain on stock held 13 months	4,500

Determine the overall result of the transactions.

A. $200 long-term capital gain.

B. $800 long-term capital loss.

C. $3,700 long-term capital gain.

D. $4,700 long-term capital gain.

Answer (C) is correct. *(SEE, adapted)*
REQUIRED: The amount of capital gain or loss to be included in taxable income.
DISCUSSION: Nonbusiness bad debts are treated as short-term capital losses. The nonbusiness bad debt is the only short-term transaction. The long-term transactions are the $800 loss on stock, the $4,500 gain on stock, and the $1,000 gain on commodity futures. The flood loss is an itemized deduction, not a deductible capital loss.

Net short-term gain or loss:		
Nonbusiness bad debt		$(1,000)
Net long-term gain or loss:		
2000 stock loss	$ (800)	
13-month stock gain	4,500	
Commodity futures gain	1,000	4,700
Net capital gain		$ 3,700

The net capital gain is included in taxable income and is taxed as a long-term gain.
Answer (A) is incorrect. The nonbusiness bad debt should be subtracted, and the 13-month stock gain should be added. Answer (B) is incorrect. The flood loss is not a capital loss; it is a casualty loss that is an itemized deduction. Answer (D) is incorrect. The nonbusiness bad debt is a short-term capital loss, which should be subtracted from the net long-term capital gain.

11.4.4. For 2017, Mr. Opal had the following capital gains and losses:

Short-term gains	$ 4,300
Short-term loss from a partnership	(3,000)
Short-term gain from an S corporation	22,500
Short-term carryover loss from 2016	(5,700)
Long-term gains (15% basket)	7,500
Long-term losses (28% basket)	(11,000)

Determine the overall result of the transactions.

A. $14,600 short-term capital gain.

B. $17,600 short-term capital gain.

C. $18,100 short-term capital gain.

D. $20,300 short-term capital gain.

Answer (A) is correct. *(SEE, adapted)*
REQUIRED: The amount of capital gain or loss.
DISCUSSION: A taxpayer's distributive shares of capital gains and losses from a partnership or an S corporation must be combined with the taxpayer's personal capital gains and losses. Mr. Opal has a net short-term capital gain of $18,100 ($4,300 + $22,500 – $3,000 – $5,700). Mr. Opal has long-term gains of $7,500 in the 15% rate basket and long-term losses of $11,000 in the 28% rate basket. The net loss in the 28% basket is used to reduce the net gain in the 15% basket. Therefore, the $11,000 of losses first offsets the $7,500 of gains in the 15% basket. The remaining long-term capital loss of $3,500 is then applied against the short-term capital gain of $18,100. The remaining $14,600 of capital gain is included in taxable income and is taxed as a short-term capital gain.
Answer (B) is incorrect. The partnership's short-term loss of $3,000 is not accounted for. Answer (C) is incorrect. The net long-term capital loss of $3,500 is not accounted for. Answer (D) is incorrect. The carryover loss of $5,700 is used to offset the net short-term capital gain.

11.4.5. Billy Luker made several stock sales during 2017. Determine the overall result of the following transactions:

Date Purchased	Cost	Date Sold	Sales Price
1-1-17	$ 4,000	6-2-17	$ 6,000
7-6-16	10,000	7-7-17	14,000
7-6-16	20,000	7-6-17	17,000
4-3-16	5,000	6-2-17	4,000

A. $2,000 net short-term capital gain.

B. $3,000 net long-term capital gain and $1,000 net short-term capital loss.

C. $2,000 net long-term capital gain.

D. $4,000 net long-term capital gain and $2,000 net short-term capital loss.

Answer (B) is correct. *(SEE, adapted)*
REQUIRED: The capital gain/loss resulting from several stock sales.
DISCUSSION: The term "net long-term capital gain" means the excess of long-term capital gains for the taxable year over the long-term capital losses for such year (IRC Sec. 1222). Section 1222 states that gains and losses resulting from the sale or exchange of capital assets held 1 year or less are characterized as short-term. All other gains are characterized as long-term. The first and third stock sales are short-term and equal a net $1,000 loss. The second and fourth stock sales are long-term and equal a net $3,000 gain.
Answer (A) is incorrect. Section 1222 states that gains and losses resulting from the sale or exchange of capital assets less than 1 year are characterized as short-term. All other gains are characterized as long-term. Answer (C) is incorrect. Net short-term capital gain does not offset net long-term capital gain. Answer (D) is incorrect. The fourth transaction is a long-term capital transaction.

11.4.6. David sells depreciable real property held for more than 12 months in 2017. It is his only capital transaction for the year, and he has no capital loss carryovers to 2017. He has a net capital gain of $100,000 from the sale, $80,000 of which is attributed to prior depreciation deductions not recaptured as ordinary income. David is in the 35% income tax bracket. What is(are) the appropriate basket(s) for the net capital gain in 2017?

A. $100,000 – 15% basket.

B. $80,000 – 25% basket, $20,000 – 28% basket.

C. $80,000 – 25% basket, $20,000 – 15% basket.

D. $100,000 – 25% basket.

Answer (C) is correct. *(Publisher, adapted)*
REQUIRED: The net capital gain basket(s) from the sale of depreciable real property held over 12 months.
DISCUSSION: For tax years beginning after December 31, 2012, the capital gains rate for individuals is 20% if the taxpayer is in the 39.6% income tax bracket; 15% if in the 25%, 28%, 33%, or 35% income tax bracket; and 0% if in the 10% or 15% income tax bracket. For all tax years, the capital gains tax rate is 25% for unrecaptured Sec. 1250 gain and 28% for collectibles and gain on qualified small business stock. The 25% rate basket consists of unrecaptured Sec. 1250 gain. (There are no losses in this basket.) Unrecaptured Sec. 1250 gain is long-term capital gain, not otherwise recaptured as ordinary income, attributed to prior depreciation of real property and is from property held for more than 12 months. Accordingly, the $80,000 gain due to prior depreciation deductions is properly contained in the 25% rate basket. Since David is in the 35% income tax bracket and the property was held over 12 months, the remaining $20,000 gain belongs in the 15% rate basket.
Answer (A) is incorrect. The unrecaptured Sec. 1250 gain is taxed at a 25% rate, while the remaining gain is taxed at a 15% tax rate. Answer (B) is incorrect. The 28% tax rate is not correct. Answer (D) is incorrect. The total $100,000 is not taxed at the 25% tax rate.

11.4.7. For the current year, Diana Clark had salary income of $38,000. In addition, she had the following capital transactions during the year:

Long-term capital gain (15% basket)	$14,000
Short-term capital gain	6,000
Long-term capital loss (28% basket)	(4,000)
Short-term capital loss	(8,000)

There were no other items includible in her gross income. What is her adjusted gross income for the current year?

A. $38,000

B. $41,200

C. $46,000

D. $48,000

Answer (C) is correct. *(CPA, adapted)*
REQUIRED: The amount of adjusted gross income given various capital transactions.
DISCUSSION: Long-term gains and losses are offset against each other first, then the short-term loss offsets the long-term gains. The long-term capital loss of $4,000 in the 28% basket is used to reduce the $14,000 gain in the 15% basket, leaving a $10,000 gain in the 15% basket. The net short-term loss of $2,000 then reduces the $10,000 gain in the 15% basket to $8,000. The $8,000 net capital gain is subject to a maximum capital gains rate of 15%.

Wages	$38,000
Net capital gain	8,000
Adjusted gross income	$46,000

Answer (A) is incorrect. The amount of $38,000 does not include the net capital gain. Answer (B) is incorrect. Adjusted gross income is $46,000. Answer (D) is incorrect. There is a $2,000 net short-term capital loss, not gain.

11.4.8. Alan Kupper had the following transactions during 2017:

● Gain of $7,000 on sale of common stock purchased on January 15, 2016 and sold on April 15, 2017.

● Gain of $5,000 on sale of common stock purchased on October 15, 2016, and sold on March 25, 2017.

● Receipt of a $10,000 installment payment on an installment contract created in 2009, when Kupper sold for $100,000 (exclusive of 6% interest on installments) land acquired in 1999 for $20,000. The contract provides for 10 equal annual principal payments of $10,000 beginning on July 1, 2009, and ending on July 1, 2018.

Determine the result of the transactions.

A. $15,000 long-term capital gain.

B. $8,000 long-term capital gain.

C. $7,500 long-term capital gain.

D. $6,000 long-term capital gain.

Answer (A) is correct. *(CPA, adapted)*
REQUIRED: The amount of capital gain included in taxable income.
DISCUSSION: The sale of stock in April resulted in a long-term capital gain. The sale of stock in March resulted in a short-term capital gain because the stock was held less than 1 year. The sale of land in 2009 resulted in a long-term capital gain because it had been held more than 1 year. Therefore, Kupper's installment receipt in 2017 is considered long-term, and $8,000 of it represents gain under the installment method.

Long-term gains:	
Sale of stock in April 2017	$ 7,000
Installment payment	
[($10,000 ÷ $100,000) × $80,000]	8,000
Net capital gain	$15,000

Note that a net capital gain is the excess of net long-term capital gains over net short-term capital losses. Kupper's net short-term capital gain is not included in the net capital gain. However, the net short-term capital gain is included in taxable income (but is not given any special treatment).
Answer (B) is incorrect. The amount of $8,000 omits the gain from the sale of stock in April. Answer (C) is incorrect. That is 50% of Kupper's net capital gain. Answer (D) is incorrect. That is 40% of Kupper's net capital gain.

11.5 Nonbusiness Bad Debts

11.5.1. In 2015, Susan lent Pat $2,000 as a gesture of their friendship, and the loan had not been repaid in 2017 at the time when Pat died insolvent. For 2017, Susan should account for nonpayment of the loan as a(n)

- A. Long-term capital loss.
- B. Short-term capital loss.
- C. Ordinary loss.
- D. Itemized deduction.

Answer (B) is correct. *(SEE, adapted)*
   REQUIRED: The treatment of the nonpayment of a personal loan.
   DISCUSSION: A nonbusiness debt is defined under Sec. 166 as a debt other than one which is created or acquired in connection with a taxpayer's trade or business. Assuming that the loan creates a bona fide debtor-creditor relationship, a loan to a friend is a nonbusiness debt. When any nonbusiness debt becomes worthless, the loss is treated as a short-term capital loss. Note that a short-term capital loss is a deduction for adjusted gross income (above the line), but is limited to a total deduction of $3,000 per year for all capital losses in excess of capital gains.
   Answer (A) is incorrect. A worthless nonbusiness bad debt is not treated as a long-term capital loss. Answer (C) is incorrect. A worthless nonbusiness bad debt is not treated as an ordinary loss. Answer (D) is incorrect. A worthless nonbusiness bad debt is not treated as an itemized deduction.

11.5.2. Earl Cook, who worked as a machinist for Precision Corporation, lent Precision $1,000 in 2013. Cook did not own any of Precision's stock, and the loan was not a condition of employment. In 2017, Precision declared bankruptcy, and Cook's note receivable from Precision became worthless. What loss can Cook claim on his 2017 income tax return?

- A. $0
- B. $500 long-term capital loss.
- C. $1,000 short-term capital loss.
- D. $1,000 business bad debt.

Answer (C) is correct. *(CPA, adapted)*
   REQUIRED: The treatment of an uncollectible loan made by an employee to the employer.
   DISCUSSION: When a nonbusiness bad debt becomes worthless, the loss that results is treated as a short-term capital loss under Sec. 166. A nonbusiness bad debt is one that is created or acquired other than in connection with a trade or business of the taxpayer. Loans made to employers are not considered business loans unless made as a condition of employment or in order to keep employment. Earl's loss is from a nonbusiness bad debt and is treated as a short-term capital loss in the amount of $1,000.
   Answer (A) is incorrect. Cook can claim a loss. Answer (B) is incorrect. The entire loan became worthless, and nonbusiness bad debts are treated as short-term. Answer (D) is incorrect. Losses from nonbusiness bad debt are short-term capital losses.

11.5.3. Mr. Richards made a personal loan of $6,000 to Mr. Henry on January 30, 2015, so that he could meet personal obligations. The loan was evidenced by a promise to pay and was to bear interest at the prevailing rate. Mr. Henry repaid $1,000 of the loan in 2016. On June 30, 2017, Mr. Henry filed for bankruptcy, and settlement was made with his creditors. Under the bankruptcy plan, Mr. Richards received $1,000 in settlement of his claim in 2017. This is the only gain or loss incurred by Mr. Richards in 2017. On his 2017 income tax return, Mr. Richards can deduct

- A. $4,000 as a long-term capital loss.
- B. $4,000 as a short-term capital loss.
- C. $3,000 as a short-term capital loss.
- D. $4,000 as an ordinary loss.

Answer (C) is correct. *(SEE, adapted)*
   REQUIRED: The proper treatment of an uncollectible nonbusiness loan.
   DISCUSSION: A taxpayer is entitled to a deduction when a debt becomes worthless during the tax year. The loss by an individual is considered a short-term capital loss if the debt was a nonbusiness debt. A nonbusiness debt is one not created or acquired in connection with the creditor's trade or business. Assuming Mr. Richards was not in the business of lending money, the debt was a nonbusiness bad debt, and the loss is treated as a short-term capital loss. The amount of the loss equals the $6,000 originally lent less the $2,000 principal collected in 2016 and 2017. Of this $4,000 loss, only $3,000 may be deducted in 2017 (the annual limit).
   Answer (A) is incorrect. The amount of $4,000 exceeds the annual limit, and nonbusiness bad debts are not treated as long-term. Answer (B) is incorrect. The amount of $4,000 exceeds Mr. Richards' annual limit. Answer (D) is incorrect. The loss is not an ordinary loss, and Mr. Richards cannot deduct $4,000.

11.5.4. In 2017, Mr. K had totally worthless nonbusiness bad debts of $10,000 and business bad debts of $5,000. His taxable income (figured without either of these losses) was $50,000, all of which originated from salary and interest income. Mr. K had no other gains or losses. What is the maximum amount Mr. K can deduct with respect to his bad debts in 2017?

A. $5,000

B. $8,000

C. $10,000

D. $13,000

Answer (B) is correct. *(SEE, adapted)*
REQUIRED: The maximum amount deductible given both business and nonbusiness bad debts.
DISCUSSION: Under Sec. 166, a bad debt is deductible as an ordinary loss in the year the debt becomes partially or totally worthless as long as it is not a nonbusiness bad debt. Mr. K can deduct the full amount of his business bad debt ($5,000). Nonbusiness bad debts are treated as short-term capital losses. Capital losses are deductible up to the lesser of taxable income or $3,000 in any year. Mr. K can deduct $3,000 of his nonbusiness bad debt in 2017 and the balance in subsequent years. His 2017 deduction is thus $8,000 ($5,000 + $3,000).
Answer (A) is incorrect. The annual capital loss ceiling of the nonbusiness bad debts may also be deducted. Answer (C) is incorrect. Mr. K's total amount of nonbusiness bad debts is $10,000, which cannot all be deducted. However, he is allowed to deduct business bad debt without any annual limitation. Answer (D) is incorrect. The nonbusiness bad debt deduction is limited to the lesser of the annual capital loss ceiling or taxable income. The full amount of the business bad debt is deductible.

11.5.5. Mr. B lent his sister, Mrs. M, $2,000 in 2010 to assist her in completing her education. Mrs. M did not sign a note, no terms for repayment were established, and B made no efforts to collect the $2,000. Mrs. M filed for bankruptcy in 2017. Mr. B may take a nonbusiness bad debt deduction in 2017.

A. True.

B. False.

Answer (B) is correct. *(SEE, adapted)*
DISCUSSION: Under Reg. 1.166-1(c), only a bona fide debt qualifies for deduction as a bad debt. A bona fide debt is one that arises from a debtor-creditor relationship based on a valid and enforceable obligation to pay a sum of money. Since there was no note, no terms for repayment, and no effort by B to collect the $2,000 for 7 years, the debt is not considered a bona fide debt and is not deductible.

11.5.6. Nonbusiness bad debts are deductible only as short-term capital losses on Form 8949.

A. True.

B. False.

Answer (A) is correct. *(SEE, adapted)*
DISCUSSION: Under Sec. 166, a nonbusiness bad debt is treated as a short-term capital loss. Under Sec. 166, when a nonbusiness bad debt becomes worthless, the resulting loss is treated as a short-term capital loss. Individual taxpayers report short-term capital losses on Form 8949.

11.5.7. Mr. B contracted with Ace Home Builders to build his personal residence at a cost of $50,000 and advanced Ace $10,000 prior to the start of construction. Due to insolvency, Ace was unable to start construction and B had to hire another contractor. Since B was unable to collect the $10,000 from Ace, he can take a nonbusiness bad debt deduction of $10,000, which is treated as a short-term capital loss subject to the capital loss limitation.

A. True.

B. False.

Answer (A) is correct. *(SEE, adapted)*
DISCUSSION: When the contractor could not perform or return the money, the advance became a bad debt for Mr. B. The debt is nonbusiness because it relates to a personal residence. Nonbusiness bad debts are deductible as short-term capital losses under Sec. 166.

11.5.8. In order to protect his investment, Mr. C, an officer and shareholder of Corporation Z, guaranteed payment of a bank loan received by the Corporation. Z defaulted on the loan and Mr. C was required to pay off the balance. Mr. C was unable to collect from Z. Mr. C has a deductible nonbusiness bad debt.

A. True.

B. False.

Answer (A) is correct. *(SEE, adapted)*
DISCUSSION: A nonbusiness bad debt is a debt other than one incurred or acquired in connection with the trade or business of the taxpayer. The investment is not considered a trade or business, and a shareholder who makes a loan to a corporation to protect his or her investment is not considered to have made a business loan. Therefore, Mr. C has a nonbusiness bad debt. It is deductible as a short-term capital loss.

11.6 Small Business Stock

11.6.1. Which of the following is not a requirement for stock to be qualified as "small business stock" (Sec. 1244)?

- A. The corporation was qualified as a small business corporation.
- B. The stock is not convertible into other securities of the corporation.
- C. The stock was issued for money or property other than stock or securities.
- D. The stock must be voting common stock.

Answer (D) is correct. *(SEE, adapted)*
    REQUIRED: The item that is not required for stock to qualify as Sec. 1244 stock.
    DISCUSSION: A loss on Sec. 1244 stock (limited to $50,000, or $100,000 on a joint return) is treated as an ordinary loss instead of a capital loss. Such stock may be common stock or preferred stock, whether voting or nonvoting.
    Answer (A) is incorrect. The corporation must be a "small business corporation," which means its paid-in capital does not exceed $1 million. Answer (B) is incorrect. The stock may be common stock or preferred stock but not convertible into other securities [Reg. 1.1244(c)-1]. Answer (C) is incorrect. The stock must be issued for money or other property, not including stock or securities.

11.6.2. During the current year, Mrs. Venture sold her interests in two small business corporations (Sec. 1244). Her loss on Corporation X stock was $120,000, and her loss on Corporation Y stock was $20,000. Mrs. Venture files jointly with her husband. What are the amount and the character of Mrs. Venture's loss to be reported on their joint return for the current year?

- A. $140,000 ordinary; $0 capital.
- B. $100,000 ordinary; $40,000 capital.
- C. $40,000 ordinary; $100,000 capital.
- D. $0 ordinary; $140,000 capital.

Answer (B) is correct. *(SEE, adapted)*
    REQUIRED: The amount and the character of loss to be reported from Sec. 1244 stock.
    DISCUSSION: Unlike losses on most capital assets held long-term, part of the loss from the sale or exchange of Sec. 1244 stock is treated as ordinary loss. Under Sec. 1244(b), the aggregate amount treated by the taxpayer by reason of Sec. 1244 as an ordinary loss shall not exceed $100,000 in the case of a husband and wife filing a joint return. The aggregate Sec. 1244 loss, in this case, is $140,000 ($120,000 from Corporation X + $20,000 from Corporation Y). Subject to the Sec. 1244(b) limitation, $100,000 is allowed as ordinary loss; the remaining $40,000 is treated as a capital loss.
    Answer (A) is incorrect. The ordinary loss is limited. The remaining amount is a capital loss. Answer (C) is incorrect. The ordinary loss, not the capital loss, is $100,000. Answer (D) is incorrect. The loss is ordinary up to the limit, with the excess reported as capital loss.

11.6.3. During 2015, Martha was issued 100 shares of qualifying small business stock (Section 1244 stock) for $40,000. On June 30, 2016, Martha purchased an additional 100 shares of Section 1244 stock from a retiring shareholder for $60,000. Her 200 shares had a total basis of $100,000. On June 30, 2017, she learned that her entire investment had become worthless. Martha filed a joint income tax return with her husband for 2017. How much could she claim as an ordinary loss or a capital loss for 2017?

- A. $50,000 ordinary loss and $50,000 capital loss.
- B. $40,000 ordinary loss and $60,000 capital loss.
- C. $60,000 ordinary loss and $40,000 capital loss.
- D. $100,000 ordinary loss and $0 capital loss.

Answer (B) is correct. *(SEE, adapted)*
    REQUIRED: The amount and the character of loss to be reported from Sec. 1244 stock.
    DISCUSSION: An individual taxpayer is entitled to recognize the loss on Sec. 1244 stock as an ordinary loss, subject to a maximum amount of $50,000 per year ($100,000 per year for a husband and wife filing a joint return). To qualify for Sec. 1244 treatment, the stock must have been issued directly from the corporation. Therefore, the $60,000 of stock which Martha purchased from a shareholder is not subject to Sec. 1244 treatment. The $40,000 loss on the original shares is an ordinary loss under Sec. 1244. The remaining $60,000 loss is treated as a capital loss.
    Answer (A) is incorrect. The $50,000 ordinary loss exceeds the limit based on qualifying stock purchase. Answer (C) is incorrect. The $60,000 ordinary loss exceeds the limit based on qualifying stock purchase. Answer (D) is incorrect. The $100,000 ordinary loss exceeds the limit based on qualifying stock purchase.

11.6.4. In December 2017, Angela sold 20 shares of Neely Co. stock for $8,000 (Sec. 1202). This was qualified small business stock that she had bought in September 2009. Her basis is $2,000. What is her taxable gain?

- A. $0
- B. $6,000
- C. $1,500
- D. $4,500

Answer (C) is correct. *(SEE, adapted)*
    REQUIRED: The taxable gain from the sale of qualified small business stock.
    DISCUSSION: Under Sec. 1202(a), an individual may exclude from gross income 50% of any gain from the sale or exchange of qualified small business stock held for more than 5 years. The exclusion is 75% if purchased between February 27, 2009, and September 28, 2010. Angela has met all of the requirements of Sec. 1202(a). Therefore, of the $6,000 ($8,000 − $2,000) gain, only $1,500 ($6,000 × .25) is taxable.
    Answer (A) is incorrect. Angela must recognize a taxable gain. Answer (B) is incorrect. Only 25% of the gain realized on the sale of qualified small business stock must be recognized. Answer (D) is incorrect. The amount of gain that can be excluded is 75%, not 25%.

11.6.5. Mr. F transferred property with an adjusted basis of $1,000 and a fair market value of $250 to a qualifying corporation for its small business stock (Sec. 1244). He later sold the stock for $200. What are the amount and the character of F's loss?

A. $250 ordinary and $750 capital.

B. $200 ordinary and $750 capital.

C. $50 ordinary and $750 capital.

D. $0 ordinary and $750 capital.

Answer (C) is correct. *(SEE, adapted)*
REQUIRED: The amount and the character of loss when property having basis in excess of FMV is exchanged for Sec. 1244 stock and the stock is later sold for a loss.
DISCUSSION: Under Sec. 1244(d)(1)(A), when property having a basis in excess of its value is exchanged for Sec. 1244 stock, the basis taken in the stock is the basis of the property exchanged. When there is a loss on the sale of the Sec. 1244 stock, however, the basis is reduced by the difference between the basis and the fair market value at the time of the original exchange. In this case, the difference was $750 ($1,000 – $250). This $750 is a capital loss. The new basis is $250 [$1,000 basis – ($1,000 – $250)]. So, the ordinary loss is $50 ($200 sales price – $250 basis).
Answer (A) is incorrect. The total loss was only $800.
Answer (B) is incorrect. The sale price of the stock is $200.
Answer (D) is incorrect. There is an ordinary loss allowed.

11.6.6. Doug formed and invested $100,000 in Noah Corporation, a manufacturer of sports equipment, on September 20, 2012. Noah is a qualified small business under Sec. 1202. On September 5, 2017, Doug sold his Noah stock for $550,000. On September 26, 2017, he purchased stock in the newly formed Thomas Corporation, a manufacturer of sports equipment components, for $500,000. Thomas is also a qualified small business. What amount of gain is recognized by Doug on the sale of Noah stock in 2017 if the appropriate election is made?

A. $0

B. $50,000

C. $400,000

D. $450,000

Answer (B) is correct. *(Publisher, adapted)*
REQUIRED: The amount of gain recognized from the sale of qualified small business stock.
DISCUSSION: A noncorporate taxpayer may elect to roll over the capital gain from the sale of qualified small business stock held for more than 6 months if other small business stock is purchased by the individual during the 60-day period beginning on the date of the sale. Gain on the sale is recognized only to the extent that the sales price exceeds the cost of the stock purchased (less any portion of the cost previously taken into account under this rule). Any gain not recognized reduces the basis of the stock purchased. The holding period of the stock purchased generally includes the holding period of the stock sold, except for purposes of determining whether the 6-month holding period is met.
Therefore, Doug recognizes a $50,000 gain on the sale of Noah stock. His basis in the Thomas stock is $100,000. The holding period of his Noah stock is tacked onto the holding period of his Thomas stock for all purposes except determining whether Thomas Corporation stock meets the 6-month holding period. For applying the 100% exclusion of Sec. 1202 and other purposes, the holding period for the Thomas stock began on September 20, 2012.
A gain must be recognized to the extent the cost of the newly purchased stock does not exceed the sales price of the previously held stock.
Answer (A) is incorrect. A gain must be recognized to the extent the cost of the newly purchased stock does not exceed the sales price of the previously held stock. Answer (C) is incorrect. The amount of $400,000 neglects the full effect of the September 26, 2017, purchase. Answer (D) is incorrect. Recognized gain is affected by purchase of new stock within 60 days.

11.6.7. Maria Mordant acquired all of the original stock of The Diamond, Inc., a Section 1244 small business, on January 10, 2013, for $10,000. She contributed another $9,000 to capital before selling all of her stock on June 30, 2017, for $10,000. How much loss should Maria report on her 2017 return, and is the loss capital or ordinary?

A. Deduct $4,737 as ordinary loss and $4,263 as capital loss subject to limitations.

B. Deduct $3,000 of her loss on Schedule D as a capital loss and carry over the remainder.

C. Deduct her $9,000 loss as an ordinary loss.

D. None of the answers are correct.

Answer (A) is correct. *(SEE, adapted)*
REQUIRED: The amount and character of loss reported by a taxpayer.
DISCUSSION: If an owner of Sec. 1244 stock invests additional capital but is not issued additional shares of stock, the amount of the additional investment is added to the basis of the originally issued stock, but this subsequent increase to the basis of the originally issued stock does not qualify for ordinary loss treatment. Any resulting loss must then be apportioned between the qualifying Sec. 1244 stock and the nonqualifying additional capital interest (Sec. 1244). Since the additional capital interest of $9,000 is 9/19 of the total basis of $19,000, the $9,000 loss is apportioned as follows: $4,263 of capital loss (9/19 of $9,000) and $4,737 of qualifying ordinary loss.
Answer (B) is incorrect. Any resulting loss must be apportioned between the qualifying Sec. 1244 stock and the nonqualifying additional capital interest. Answer (C) is incorrect. Only a fraction of Maria's loss is ordinary. Answer (D) is incorrect. Only 9/19 of the loss is capital, and the rest is ordinary.

11.6.8. Which of the following statements is true about the deferral of gain on the sale of publicly traded securities where the proceeds are reinvested in a specialized small business investment company?

A. The exclusion is only available for individual taxpayers.

B. Publicly traded securities include only stock traded on a major stock exchange.

C. A specialized small business investment company includes any partnership or corporation licensed by the Small Business Administration under Sec. 301(d) of the Small Business Investment Act of 1958.

D. Eligible reinvestments include common and preferred stock or partnership interests in a specialized small business company.

Answer (C) is correct. *(Publisher, adapted)*
REQUIRED: The true statement concerning qualifying for deferral of gain on the sale of publicly traded securities.
DISCUSSION: A partnership and a corporation licensed under Sec. 301(d) are the two types of entities into which a qualifying specialized small business investment company investment can be made [Sec. 1044(c)(3)].
Answer (A) is incorrect. The exclusion is available to individuals and C corporations. The exclusion is not available for investments made by estates, trusts, partnerships, or S corporations. Answer (B) is incorrect. Investments in any securities traded on an established securities market can be sold in a qualifying sale. Answer (D) is incorrect. Eligible reinvestments include only common stock or partnership interests [Sec. 1044(c)(3)].

11.6.9. Qualified small business stock under Section 1202, for purposes of applying rollover and exclusion rules, is stock that meets all the following tests except

A. Stock in a C corporation.

B. Originally issued after August 10, 1993.

C. Acquired by original issue in exchange for money or other property or as pay for services.

D. Total gross assets of $100 million or less at all times after August 10, 1993, and before it issued the stock.

Answer (D) is correct. *(SEE, adapted)*
REQUIRED: The item that is not a test for qualified small business stock.
DISCUSSION: Stock qualifies as Section 1202 stock if it is received after August 10, 1993, the corporation is a domestic C corporation, the seller is the original owner of the stock, and the corporation's gross assets do not exceed $50 million at the time the stock was issued. Additional requirements do exist. However, the total gross assets requirement is $50 million, not $100 million.
Answer (A) is incorrect. Qualified small business stock must be stock in a C corporation. Answer (B) is incorrect. Qualified small business stock must be stock originally issued after August 10, 1993. Answer (C) is incorrect. Qualified small business stock must be stock acquired by original issue in exchange for money or other property or as payment for services.

11.6.10. On July 8, 2012, Mr. Cole purchased 100 shares of qualified small business (Sec. 1202) stock for $50,000. If Mr. Cole sells the shares for $130,000 on August 22, 2017, how much gain must he recognize?

A. $0

B. $20,000

C. $80,000

D. $130,000

Answer (A) is correct. *(Publisher, adapted)*
REQUIRED: The amount of gain to be recognized from the sale of qualified small business stock.
DISCUSSION: If a noncorporate investor purchases qualified small business stock and holds it for more than 5 years, up to 50% of the gain realized on the disposition of such stock may be excluded from gross income. The exclusion is 100% if purchased after September 27, 2010. The gain eligible for exclusion is limited to the greater of $10 million (reduced by the aggregate amount of eligible gain excluded by the taxpayer with respect to investments in the corporation whose stock is being sold during all prior tax years) or 10 times the aggregate adjusted bases of qualified small business stock issued by such corporation and disposed of by the taxpayer during the tax year (Sec. 1202). Since Mr. Cole held the stock for more than 5 years, he may exclude all $80,000 from his gross income ($80,000 realized gain × 100%). Alternatively, Mr. Cole can roll over the gain on the sale of his qualified small business stock if the proceeds are used to purchase other qualified small business stock within 60 days of the sale.
Answer (B) is incorrect. The exclusion is equal to 100% of the realized gain if purchased after Sept. 27, 2010. Answer (C) is incorrect. None of the $80,000 gain must be recognized. Answer (D) is incorrect. Mr. Cole does not recognize any of the amount realized.

11.6.11. Corporation H was incorporated in the current year and received $750,000 as a contribution to capital and $300,000 as paid-in surplus in exchange for its stock. Corporation H qualifies as a small business corporation under Sec. 1244 of the Internal Revenue Code.

A. True.

B. False.

Answer (B) is correct. *(SEE, adapted)*
   DISCUSSION: To qualify under Sec. 1244, the corporation must be a small business corporation. To be classified as a small business corporation, the aggregate amount of money and other property received by the corporation for stock, as a contribution to capital and as paid-in surplus, cannot exceed $1,000,000. Even though the paid-in capital exceeds $1,000,000, part of the stock (up to $1,000,000) will be designated by the corporation as qualifying for Sec. 1244 ordinary loss treatment.

11.6.12. The AB Partnership acquired $500,000 in qualifying Sec. 1244 stock in Corporation X as an investment in 2010. Corporation X went bankrupt in 2017. Partners A and B have been 50/50 owners since the partnership's inception. Partners A and B are entitled to individually claim $250,000 of ordinary loss with respect to the worthless stock of Corporation X in 2017.

A. True.

B. False.

Answer (B) is correct. *(SEE, adapted)*
   DISCUSSION: An individual taxpayer is entitled to recognize the loss on Sec. 1244 stock as an ordinary loss, subject to a maximum amount of $50,000 per year ($100,000 per year for a husband and wife filing a joint return). If a partnership owns the stock, individual partners are entitled to the Sec. 1244 ordinary loss. Each partner may claim only a $50,000 ($100,000 if filing jointly with a spouse) ordinary loss with respect to the worthless stock of Corporation X in 2017. Any remaining loss is a capital loss.

11.6.13. The ordinary loss provisions on small business stock (Sec. 1244) are available only to the original owner of the stock.

A. True.

B. False.

Answer (A) is correct. *(SEE, adapted)*
   DISCUSSION: Section 1244(a) provides that an individual is entitled to an ordinary loss on a sale of Sec. 1244 stock which was issued to such individual. Regulation 1.1244(a)-1(b) provides that to claim the deduction under Sec. 1244, the individual must have continuously held the stock from the date of issuance. For example, the ordinary loss treatment would not apply to an individual who acquires the stock by gift or inheritance.

11.7 Capital Loss Limitations and Carryovers

11.7.1. Capital losses incurred by a married couple filing a joint return

A. Will be allowed only to the extent of capital gains.

B. Will be allowed to the extent of capital gains, plus up to $3,000 of ordinary income.

C. May be carried forward up to a maximum of 5 years.

D. Are not allowable losses.

Answer (B) is correct. *(CPA, adapted)*
   REQUIRED: The true statement concerning deductibility of capital losses incurred by a married couple filing jointly.
   DISCUSSION: The amount of capital losses that can be deducted is the lesser of the excess of capital losses over capital gains or $3,000 [Sec. 1211(b)]. The maximum amount in excess of capital gains allowed as a deduction is $3,000 ($1,500 for married taxpayers filing separately).
   Answer (A) is incorrect. Capital losses are deductible in excess of capital gains, but this excess is limited. Answer (C) is incorrect. Capital losses that are not deductible in the current year may be carried forward indefinitely. The capital losses disappear at death. Answer (D) is incorrect. Capital losses are allowable losses, subject to limitations.

11.7.2. Bob and Gloria sold securities during the current year. The sales resulted in a capital loss of $7,000. They had no other capital transactions. Their taxable income was $26,000. How much can they deduct on their joint return?

A. $7,000

B. $3,000

C. $4,000

D. $0

Answer (B) is correct. *(SEE, adapted)*
   REQUIRED: The amount of capital loss deductible on a joint return.
   DISCUSSION: Individuals and other noncorporate taxpayers may deduct up to $3,000 of a capital loss against ordinary income. Any excess capital loss may be carried over for an unlimited time period until the loss is exhausted.
   Answer (A) is incorrect. The total capital loss for the year is $7,000. The loss is subject to limitation. Answer (C) is incorrect. The amount of $4,000 exceeds the capital loss deduction limit. Answer (D) is incorrect. Bob and Gloria have a capital loss deduction, subject to limitation.

11.7.3. Bob sold securities in 2017. The sales resulted in a capital loss of $7,000. He had no other capital transactions. He and his wife Gloria decide to file separate returns for 2017. His taxable income was $26,000. What amount of capital loss can he deduct on his 2017 return and what amount can he carry over to 2018?

A. $7,000 in 2017 and $0 carry over to 2018.

B. $3,000 in 2017 and $4,000 carry over to 2018.

C. $4,000 in 2017 and $3,000 carry over to 2018.

D. $1,500 in 2017 and $5,500 carry over to 2018.

Answer (D) is correct. *(SEE, adapted)*
REQUIRED: The amount of capital loss a taxpayer filing separately may deduct in the current year and the amount (s)he may carry over.
DISCUSSION: If loss deductions exceed taxable income for the tax year, the excess is taken into account as negative taxable income for up to $3,000 ($1,500 if married filing a separate return). Thus, Bob will deduct $1,500 in 2017 and carry over $5,500 to 2018.
Answer (A) is incorrect. Bob cannot deduct the entire $7,000 capital loss in 2017, so he also has a loss carryover. Answer (B) is incorrect. A $3,000 deduction in 2017 exceeds the limit. Answer (C) is incorrect. A $4,000 deduction in 2017 exceeds the limit.

11.7.4. Mr. J, who has $15,000 of salary income, sold land that he had purchased for investment purposes 10 years ago to Ms. P for $5,000 cash and her assumption of an existing mortgage of $2,000 and delinquent back taxes of $1,500. Mr. J's adjusted basis in the land was $10,000, and he paid $600 in selling costs. What is Mr. J's deductible loss, assuming he had no other capital asset transactions?

A. $0

B. $(1,500)

C. $(2,100)

D. $(2,400)

Answer (C) is correct. *(SEE, adapted)*
REQUIRED: The deductible loss from the sale of investment property on which the buyer assumes a mortgage and pays back taxes.
DISCUSSION: The gain or loss from the sale of property is the amount realized less the adjusted basis (Sec. 1001). Mr. J realized $5,000 in cash, relief of a mortgage liability of $2,000, and relief of back taxes of $1,500. This gross amount realized totals $8,500. However, selling costs decrease the amount realized, so Mr. J's net amount realized is $7,900 ($8,500 – $600). Mr. J's recognized loss is $2,100 ($7,900 realized – $10,000 basis). This is a long-term capital loss since property held for investment is a capital asset and such property has been held for more than 1 year. It is all deductible since it does not exceed the $3,000 annual limitation of Sec. 1211.
Answer (A) is incorrect. Some loss is deductible. Answer (B) is incorrect. The $600 in selling costs must be subtracted from the $8,500 amount realized before determining the deductible loss. Answer (D) is incorrect. The amount realized includes the release from the delinquent tax liability, but does not include the selling costs that were included as part of the amount realized.

11.7.5. During 2017, Mr. H, who is married filing separately, made the following sales of stock:

100 shares of ABC Company on 6/1/17 Purchased 2/1/17 for $2,000	$1,000
100 shares of XYZ Company on 9/1/17 Purchased 4/1/17 for $1,500	750
100 shares of EFG Company on 11/1/17 Purchased 9/15/15 for $3,000	1,000

Mr. H is in the 31% marginal tax bracket. What is the amount of H's deductible capital loss for 2017?

A. $0

B. $1,500

C. $3,000

D. $3,750

Answer (B) is correct. *(SEE, adapted)*
REQUIRED: The deductible capital loss for a married taxpayer filing separately.
DISCUSSION: Mr. H has a net short-term capital loss of $1,750 ($1,000 from the stock sold in June and $750 from the stock sold in September). He has net long-term capital loss in the 15% basket of $2,000 from the stock sold in November. His total capital loss is therefore $3,750 ($1,000 + $750 + $2,000).
Under Section 1211(b), a noncorporate taxpayer is allowed a deduction for capital losses in excess of capital gains limited to the lesser of the excess of capital losses over capital gains, or $3,000. But this $3,000 limitation is $1,500 for a taxpayer who is married filing separately. Therefore, H's deductible capital loss is $1,500. Short-term losses are deducted first.
Answer (A) is incorrect. Mr. H has a limited deductible capital loss based on filing status. Answer (C) is incorrect. The amount of $3,000 is the deductible limit for married taxpayers filing jointly. Answer (D) is incorrect. The amount of $3,750 is the total capital loss.

11.7.6. For 2017, Mr. G has a short-term capital loss of $4,000, a short-term capital gain of $1,900, a short-term capital loss carryover from 2015 of $700, a long-term capital gain of $800 from property held for 3 years, and a long-term capital loss of $1,500 from property held for 4 years. Mr. G is in the 35% marginal tax bracket. What is Mr. G's deductible loss in 2017?

A. $0

B. $2,800

C. $3,000

D. $3,500

11.7.7. For the current year, Michael King reported salary and taxable interest income of $40,000. His capital asset transactions during the year were as follows:

Long-term capital gains (15% basket)	$2,000
Long-term capital losses (28% basket)	(8,000)
Short-term capital gains	1,000

For the current year, King should report adjusted gross income of

A. $35,000

B. $37,000

C. $38,500

D. $39,000

11.7.8. On February 16, Year 1, Fred Samson purchased 100 shares of Oscar Corporation stock at $40 per share. On July 28, Year 5, he sold the 100 shares at $25 per share. On August 10, Year 5, his wife purchased 50 shares of Oscar Corporation at $30 per share. These are the only capital asset transactions by the Samsons during Year 5. In computing his taxable income for Year 5, Fred may deduct, from his ordinary income of $15,000, a capital loss in the amount of

A. $375

B. $750

C. $1,000

D. $1,500

Answer (C) is correct. *(SEE, adapted)*
REQUIRED: The amount of deductible capital loss.
DISCUSSION: Short-term capital gains and losses and long-term capital gains and losses are first netted to determine the capital loss deduction. The carryover from 2015 retains its character as a short-term capital loss and is netted with the other short-term transactions.

Short-term: ($1,900 – $4,000 – $700)	$(2,800)
Long-term (15% basket): ($800 – $1,500)	(700)
Capital loss	$(3,500)

Since the loss computed above exceeds $3,000, the amount deductible is limited to the lesser of $3,000 or taxable income (Sec. 1211). Long-term capital losses of $500 are carried forward to the 28% basket.
Answer (A) is incorrect. Some capital losses may be deducted. Answer (B) is incorrect. The total capital loss without considering the two carryovers is $2,800. Answer (D) is incorrect. The total capital loss is $3,500.

Answer (B) is correct. *(CPA, adapted)*
REQUIRED: The taxpayer's adjusted gross income.
DISCUSSION: Under Sec. 1211, a taxpayer may deduct the excess of the net long-term capital loss over net short-term capital gain, provided that such amount does not exceed $3,000. The long-term capital loss in the 28% basket is first offset against the long-term capital gain in the 15% basket. After the gain in the 15% basket is exhausted, the remaining net capital loss of $6,000 ($2,000 – $8,000) is applied against the net short-term capital gain of $1,000. King's excess of net long-term capital loss over net short-term capital gain is $5,000 ($6,000 – $1,000). Therefore, the $3,000 limit applies.

Salary and interest income	$40,000
Less: capital loss deduction	(3,000)
Adjusted gross income	$37,000

Answer (A) is incorrect. The total net capital losses of $5,000 are limited in how much may be deducted. Answer (C) is incorrect. The capital loss deduction is limited to $3,000 for a single taxpayer, not to $1,500 for a married taxpayer filing separately. Answer (D) is incorrect. The amount of $2,000 of long-term loss is deductible in addition to the $1,000 of short-term capital loss.

Answer (B) is correct. *(CPA, adapted)*
REQUIRED: The amount of capital loss that the taxpayer may deduct from ordinary income.
DISCUSSION: Fred sold 100 shares of stock on July 28, and his wife subsequently purchased 50 shares of the same corporation's stock on August 10. Consequently, 50 of the shares Fred sold are not eligible for the capital loss deduction because this would be considered a wash sale (spouses are treated as the same taxpayer for this purpose). Under Sec. 1091, a wash sale occurs when substantially the same securities are purchased within 30 days of being sold for a loss. A capital loss deduction is available for the other 50 shares. The sale of 50 shares resulted in a $750 loss. The full amount of the loss is deductible.

Sales price (50 × $25)	$ 1,250
Less: adjusted basis (50 × $40)	(2,000)
Long-term capital loss	$ (750)

Answer (A) is incorrect. Fifty shares, not 25 shares, of stock qualify for a loss deduction. The other 50 shares are sold in a wash sale in which the loss is disallowed. Answer (C) is incorrect. Only 50 shares of stock qualify for the capital loss deduction since the other 50 shares of the stock constitute a wash sale. Answer (D) is incorrect. Fifty shares of stock are sold in a wash sale in which the loss is disallowed.

11.7.9. The income tax treatment of individual and corporate taxpayers agrees in which of the following respects?

A. Excess capital losses may be carried forward 5 years, and losses may not be carried back.

B. Excess capital losses may be offset against income from other sources but only to a limited extent.

C. Excess capital losses retain their identity as either long-term or short-term losses in the year to which they are carried.

D. None of the answers are correct.

Answer (D) is correct. *(CPA, adapted)*
REQUIRED: The true statement regarding similarity of capital loss treatment for corporate and individual taxpayers.
DISCUSSION: None of the statements are true (Secs. 1211 and 1212). The only similarity between the corporate and individual treatment of capital losses is that the capital loss definition is the same. Corporate capital gains do not have the multiple long-term baskets like individual capital gains do.
Answer (A) is incorrect. Individuals can carry excess losses forward indefinitely, while corporations may carry them forward for only 5 years. Also, excess capital losses are not carried back by individuals but are carried back 3 years by corporations. Answer (B) is incorrect. Excess capital losses may be offset against ordinary income to a limited extent by individual taxpayers, but corporations may offset capital losses only with capital gains. Answer (C) is incorrect. Carryovers retain their identity as long- or short-term for individuals, but all corporate losses are carried over as short-term capital losses.

11.7.10. On March 1, Year 1, Roland Doe bought 200 shares of Gummit stock at $40 per share. On April 1, Year 2, Roland sold short (sold without delivering) 100 shares of Gummit stock for $50 per share. On December 1, Year 2, Roland bought 100 shares of Gummit stock for $60 per share and closed the short sale by delivering this stock. What is the tax result to Roland Doe?

A. $1,000 short-term capital loss.

B. $1,000 short-term capital gain.

C. $1,000 long-term capital loss.

D. $1,000 long-term capital gain.

Answer (D) is correct. *(Publisher, adapted)*
REQUIRED: The gain or loss from a short sale when substantially identical stock has been held long-term.
DISCUSSION: Section 1259 provides that there is a constructive sale of an appreciated financial position when the taxpayer sells short stock that is substantially identical to stock held. The taxpayer must recognize gain as if the position were sold, assigned, or otherwise terminated at its fair market value as of the date of the constructive sale. Since the stock was held long term, Roland Doe has a $1,000 long-term capital gain. The stock purchased to cover the short sale will have a basis equal to its purchase price.
Answer (A) is incorrect. A $1,000 short-term capital loss results from having held a short position for less than 1 year, then buying the stock to settle for more than the short sale price and no previous stock was purchased. Answer (B) is incorrect. The gain would be long-term, as the stock held at the time of the short-sell was held for more than 1 year. Answer (C) is incorrect. A $1,000 long-term capital loss results from having held a long position for more than 1 year when entering into the short sale.

11.7.11. In the current year, Mr. K decided to go into a new business. He incurred the following costs:

Travel to look over various business alternatives	$1,000
Travel to look for possible business locations	500
Market surveys for various businesses	1,500
Legal fees to set up the new business	2,000
Advertising to promote the new business	2,500
Expenses to train employees	2,000

Despite K's efforts, circumstances beyond his control prevented him from actually starting business operations, and he abandoned the project late in the year. How should Mr. K handle these costs in his current-year tax return?

	Ordinary Loss or Schedule C Loss	Capital Loss
A.	$0	$0
B.	$0	$6,500
C.	$6,500	$0
D.	$6,500	$3,000

Answer (B) is correct. *(SEE, adapted)*
REQUIRED: The amount of ordinary loss and capital loss for business start-up costs when the business was abandoned.
DISCUSSION: Business start-up expenditures in excess of $5,000 are normally amortizable under Sec. 195 and not otherwise deductible. However, when the business is disposed of prior to full amortization, the unamortized balance is deductible as a loss [Sec. 195(b)(2)]. The legal fees, advertising, and expenses to train employees are start-up expenditures under Sec. 195. These expenditures total $6,500. The travel and market surveys are not Sec. 195 start-up expenditures and are not deductible at all because they do not relate to the organization of a specific business. Rather, they are merely general investigatory expenditures.
The $6,500 loss is a capital loss because the capitalizable start-up expenditures are deemed to be capital assets since they do not fall within an exclusion specified in Sec. 1221.
Answer (A) is incorrect. Mr. K has a capital loss in the current year. Answer (C) is incorrect. The legal fees, advertising, and training expenses are start-up costs totaling $6,500, which is a capital loss when the business is discontinued. Answer (D) is incorrect. Travel and market surveys are not qualified start-up costs. In addition, qualified expenses are a capital loss.

Questions 11.7.12 and 11.7.13 are based on the following information. During 2017, Stacy, who is single and has no dependents, sold the following shares of stock:

Stock	Date Purchased	Adjusted Basis	Date Sold	Sales Proceeds
Alpha Corp.	12/2/15	$3,500	6/29/17	$1,100
Beta Corp.	7/11/15	2,000	4/15/17	100
Delta Corp.	5/27/16	3,000	5/26/17	1,500
Gamma Corp.	1/22/17	1,500	7/28/17	200

Stacy's taxable income for 2017 is $500 before the personal exemption and capital loss deductions. Stacy is in the 10% marginal tax bracket.

11.7.12. What is the amount of Stacy's allowable capital loss deduction in 2017?

A. $0

B. $500

C. $1,500

D. $3,000

Answer (B) is correct. *(SEE, adapted)*
REQUIRED: The capital loss deduction for a single taxpayer in 2017.
DISCUSSION: The capital losses from the four transactions are categorized as follows:

	Gain or Loss	
Stock	Short-term	Long-term
Alpha		$(2,400)
Beta		(1,900)
Delta	$(1,500)	
Gamma	(1,300)	
Total	$(2,800)	$(4,300)

The loss on the Delta stock is short-term since the stock has been held for only 1 year. Normally, Sec. 1211 limits the capital loss deduction to $3,000 and $4,100 of excess losses would be carried over to 2018.

However, Stacy's taxable income (before the capital loss and personal exemption deductions) of $500 is less than the $3,000 capital loss deduction, and she will obtain a tax benefit from only part of the capital loss deduction. The carryover to 2018 is instead computed as if her capital loss deduction was limited to the $500 of taxable income. Thus, Stacy's carryover to 2018 is $6,600.

Answer (A) is incorrect. There is a capital loss deduction because a capital loss cannot create a NOL. Answer (C) is incorrect. The amount of $1,500 is the limit for married taxpayers filing separately, and it also exceeds taxable income. Answer (D) is incorrect. Capital losses are limited to the lesser of $3,000 or taxable income.

11.7.13. What are the amount and the character of Stacy's capital loss carryover to 2018?

A. $0 short-term; $6,600 long-term.

B. $2,800 short-term; $1,300 long-term (28% basket).

C. $2,300 short-term; $1,900 long-term (28% basket); $2,400 long-term.

D. $2,300 short-term; $4,300 long-term (28% basket).

Answer (D) is correct. *(SEE, adapted)*
REQUIRED: The amount and the character of the capital loss carryover to 2018.
DISCUSSION: Stacy reported $7,100 ($2,800 + $4,300) of capital losses, of which $500 were deductible in 2017; $6,600 ($7,100 – $500) of these losses can be carried over to 2018. For 2017's deduction, short-term losses were used first. Because only $500 of losses provided a tax benefit, $2,300 ($2,800 – $500) of the short-term losses are carried over to 2018. The short-term loss carryover is first applied against any short-term gains in the current year. A net short-term loss is then applied to reduce any net long-term gain from the 28% rate basket, then to reduce gain from the 25% rate basket, and finally to reduce net gain from the 15% rate basket. The $4,300 loss in the 15% basket is carried over to the long-term 28% basket in 2018.

Answer (A) is incorrect. The short-term loss will retain its character in 2018. Answer (B) is incorrect. The $500 capital loss deduction in 2017 is first applied against short-term loss, not long-term loss. Answer (C) is incorrect. Long-term loss carryovers belong in the 28% basket, regardless of its basket in the prior year, to give the taxpayer the optimal loss offset.

11.7.14. During the current year, Nancy had the following transactions:

Short-term capital loss	($2,400)
Short-term capital gain	2,000
Short-term capital loss carryover from 2 years ago	(1,400)
Long-term capital gain (15% basket)	3,800
Long-term capital loss (28% basket)	(8,000)

Nancy is in the 35% marginal tax bracket for the current year. What is the amount of her capital loss deduction in the current year, and what is the amount and character of her capital loss carryover?

	Deduction	Carryover
A.	$0	$6,000 long-term (28% basket)
B.	$3,000	$3,000 long-term (28% basket)
C.	$6,000	$0
D.	$3,000	$3,000 short-term

Answer (B) is correct. *(SEE, adapted)*
REQUIRED: The taxpayer's current capital loss deduction and carryover.
DISCUSSION: The deduction for any capital loss is the excess of capital losses over capital gains (Sec. 1211). The capital loss deduction, however, is limited to $3,000 in any year. Unused capital losses may be carried forward indefinitely. Short-term capital losses are considered first to determine the character of the carryover. In this case, there is an $1,800 short-term capital loss ($400 current-year net loss + $1,400 carryover from 2 years ago). Since there is a long-term loss in the 28% basket, both losses must be completely applied against the long-term gain in the 15% basket. The $1,800 short-term loss is applied first, leaving $2,000 of long-term gain in the 15% basket to offset $8,000 the long-term loss in the 28% basket. The $8,000 long-term loss in the 28% basket is offset by the $2,000 gain in the 15% basket, and $3,000 of the remaining $6,000 loss is taken as a deduction in the current year. The remaining $3,000 is a long-term loss carryover to the 28% basket.

Long-term capital gain (15% basket)	$ 3,800
Short-term capital loss	(1,800)
Gain to be offset by long-term capital loss (28% basket)	$ 2,000
Long-term capital loss (28% basket)	(8,000)
	$(6,000)
Capital loss deduction for the current year	3,000
Capital loss carryover (28% basket)	$(3,000)

Answer (A) is incorrect. Some of the losses may be deducted. Also, $6,000 carryover fails to account for current year deduction. Answer (C) is incorrect. The deductible losses are limited, and the remaining amount is carried over as a long-term loss. Answer (D) is incorrect. The remaining carryover is a long-term loss.

11.7.15. For 2017, Mr. H had taxable income of $120,000, excluding exemptions and capital transactions. In 2017, H's capital transactions were as follows:

	Short-Term	Long-Term (28% Basket)	Long-Term (15% Basket)
Gains	$10,000	$20,000	$ 2,000
Losses	(13,000)	(24,000)	(0)

In addition, Mr. H had a $2,200 short-term capital loss carryover and a $1,000 long-term capital loss carryover, both from 2016. Mr. H is not in the 10% or 15% income tax brackets. What is the amount of H's capital loss deduction in 2017 and capital loss carryover to 2018?

		Carryover		
	Deduction	Short-Term	Long-Term (28% Basket)	Long-Term (15% Basket)
A.	$0	$5,200	$5,000	$0
B.	$3,000	$200	$5,000	$0
C.	$3,000	$200	$0	$5,000
D.	$3,000	$2,200	$3,000	$0

Answer (D) is correct. *(Publisher, adapted)*
REQUIRED: The capital loss deduction in 2017 and the capital loss carryover to 2018.
DISCUSSION: A net loss of $5,000 is contained in the 28% basket ($20,000 gain – $24,000 loss – $1,000 long-term loss carryover). The long-term loss carryover of $1,000 belongs in the 28% basket, regardless of its basket in the prior year. The net loss in the 28% basket is first applied to the long-term gain in the 15% basket. The netting reduces the 15% basket to zero and a net loss of $3,000 remains in the 28% basket. The $2,200 short-term capital loss carryover is included in the short-term calculation for the current year. The net short-term capital loss for 2017 is $5,200 ($10,000 gain – $13,000 loss – $2,200 carryover). The short-term capital loss is applied against ordinary income up to a limit of $3,000 and a $2,200 net short-term capital loss then remains.
Answer (A) is incorrect. A deduction of $3,000 can be applied to the short-term capital loss and the net loss in the 28% basket can be applied to the gain in the 15% basket. Answer (B) is incorrect. The long-term capital loss in the 28% basket, not the net short-term capital loss, is first applied toward the gain in the 15% basket. Answer (C) is incorrect. The short-term capital loss is not reduced by the gain in the 15% long-term basket and the loss in the 28% basket does not flow to the 28% basket.

11.7.16. Mr. D's capital losses for the current year exceeded the $3,000 capital loss limitation. He may elect to carry the unused capital loss back to an earlier year.

A. True.

B. False.

Answer (B) is correct. *(SEE, adapted)*
DISCUSSION: An individual taxpayer may only carry an unused capital loss forward (Sec. 1212). Only corporations are entitled to carry back excess capital losses (for 3 years).

11.7.17. If an individual has capital losses from 2 or more years and they are carried to the same year, the loss from the earliest year is deducted first. When that loss is completely used up, the loss from the next earliest year is deducted, and so on.

A. True.

B. False.

Answer (B) is correct. *(SEE, adapted)*
   DISCUSSION: An individual's capital losses are carried forward indefinitely [Sec. 1212(b)(1)]. The net short-term loss or net long-term capital loss carryover that is not offset against capital gains or deducted in the carryover year is treated as a short-term loss or long-term loss, as the case may be, that is incurred in the succeeding year. These carryovers are offset against capital gains in the succeeding year using the regular combining rules for capital gains and losses. Carryovers that are not offset against capital gains can be deducted starting with the short-term losses first and then the long-term losses. Therefore, the earliest incurred loss is not always deducted first.

11.8 Sales to Related Parties

11.8.1. Among which of the following relatives are losses from sales and exchanges recognized for tax purposes?

A. Grandfather and granddaughter.

B. Father-in-law and son-in-law.

C. Brother and sister.

D. Lineal descendants.

Answer (B) is correct. *(Publisher, adapted)*
   REQUIRED: The related parties who would recognize losses from sales and exchanges.
   DISCUSSION: Under Sec. 267, losses are not allowed on sales or exchanges of property between related parties. A father-in-law and a son-in-law are not considered related parties for purposes of Sec. 267, so losses between the two may be recognized.
   Answer (A) is incorrect. A grandfather and a granddaughter are related parties under Sec. 267. Answer (C) is incorrect. A brother and a sister are related parties under Sec. 267. Answer (D) is incorrect. Lineal descendants are related parties under Sec. 267.

11.8.2. Larry sold stock with a cost basis of $10,500 to his son for $8,500. Larry cannot deduct the $2,000 loss. His son sold the same stock to an unrelated party for $15,000, realizing a gain. What is his son's reportable gain?

A. $6,500

B. $4,500

C. $2,000

D. No gain.

Answer (B) is correct. *(SEE, adapted)*
   REQUIRED: The amount of gain recognized when property is sold after acquisition from a related party in a lost transaction.
   DISCUSSION: Under Sec. 267(a)(1), losses are not allowed on sales or exchanges of property between related parties. Related parties include a father and a son. Larry realized a $2,000 loss on the sale but may not deduct it. On the subsequent sale, his son realized a $6,500 gain. However, he recognizes only a $4,500 reportable gain. The disallowed loss is used to offset the subsequent gain on the sale of the property ($6,500 realized gain – $2,000 disallowed loss).
   Answer (A) is incorrect. The gain must be offset by the disallowed loss. Answer (C) is incorrect. The amount by which the gain will be offset is $2,000. Answer (D) is incorrect. A gain must be reported.

11.8.3. Allen sold stock, a capital asset, he had purchased for $40,000 to his sister Alice for $30,000. Later, Alice sold the stock to an unrelated party for $45,000. What is the amount of Alice's recognized gain?

A. $5,000

B. $10,000

C. $15,000

D. $0

Answer (A) is correct. *(SEE, adapted)*
   REQUIRED: The amount of recognized gain when stock is sold after acquisition from a related party in a loss transaction.
   DISCUSSION: Under Sec. 267, losses are not allowed on sales or exchanges of property between related parties. Allen realized a $10,000 ($40,000 – $30,000) loss on the sale but may not deduct it. On the subsequent sale, Alice realized a $15,000 gain ($45,000 sales price – $30,000 basis). However, she recognizes only a $5,000 capital gain [Sec. 267(d)]. The disallowed loss is used to offset the subsequent gain on the sale of the property ($15,000 realized gain – $10,000 disallowed loss).
   Answer (B) is incorrect. The amount of $10,000 is the unrecognized loss to a related party. Answer (C) is incorrect. The $10,000 of disallowed loss offsets Alice's realized gain of $15,000. Answer (D) is incorrect. Alice must recognize a gain on the sale.

11.8.4. S. Lumlord owns the large, two-story home in which his mother lives. It is situated in a neighborhood adjacent to a large university. S. Lumlord purchased the property several years ago for $60,000. The property has recently been rezoned to permit apartment buildings. S. Lumlord owns 60% of the Gainsburg Student Living Co., and the remainder is owned by a local city commissioner. S. Lumlord sells the personal residence, subject to a first mortgage of $40,000, to the Gainsburg Student Living Co. for $30,000 cash and a promissory note secured by a second mortgage for $30,000. The Gainsburg Student Living Co. will rent the rooms in the building to students. How is the gain taxed to S. Lumlord?

A. $0

B. $30,000 long-term capital gain.

C. $40,000 long-term capital gain.

D. $40,000 ordinary income.

Answer (D) is correct. *(Publisher, adapted)*
REQUIRED: The treatment of the gain on the sale of depreciable property to a more-than-50%-owned entity.
DISCUSSION: S. Lumlord's gain is $40,000. Lumlord realized $30,000 cash, was relieved of a mortgage of $40,000, and received a note for $30,000. These total $100,000 and, after deducting the basis of $60,000, result in a gain of $40,000.

The gain on the sale of investment property is normally capital gain, but Sec. 1239 provides that the gain on sale of property between related persons will be treated as ordinary income if the property is depreciable in the hands of the transferee. Related persons include a taxpayer and a more-than-50%-owned entity. Since S. Lumlord owns 60% of the Gainsburg Student Living Co. and the property is depreciable in the hands of the Gainsburg Student Living Co. (because it is being rented), the $40,000 gain will be treated as ordinary income.

Answer (A) is incorrect. There is a gain. Answer (B) is incorrect. There is not a $30,000 long-term capital gain on the sale. Answer (C) is incorrect. A sale of personal property that will be depreciated to a related party is considered ordinary income under Sec. 1239.

11.8.5. James Webb directly owns 85% of the outstanding stock of Webb Corporation. If Webb Corporation sells property to Mr. Webb and incurs a loss, it would not be allowed to deduct the loss.

A. True.

B. False.

Answer (A) is correct. *(SEE, adapted)*
DISCUSSION: Under Sec. 267(a)(1), losses are not allowed on sales or exchanges of property between related parties. Related parties include an individual and a corporation in which the individual owns more than 50% of the outstanding stock. James Webb and Webb Corporation are therefore treated as related parties.

11.9 Capital Gains Tax Calculations

11.9.1. Alex and Mary, both under 65, file a joint tax return for 2017. Their adjusted gross income is $55,100. This total includes $4,000 of long-term capital gain from stock that had been held 3 years and 2 months prior to its sale in July. Alex and Mary claim the standard deduction and two personal exemptions. Their total income tax liability for 2017 is

A. $3,613

B. $3,813

C. $4,213

D. $4,413

Answer (A) is correct. *(Publisher, adapted)*
REQUIRED: The income tax liability in 2017 for a married couple filing jointly.
DISCUSSION: The adjusted gross income is reduced by the standard deduction ($12,700) and two personal exemptions ($8,100).

AGI	$55,100
Standard deduction	(12,700)
Personal exemptions	(8,100)
Taxable income	$34,300

For capital gain income on property held over 12 months, if the taxable income (as reduced by net capital gains) is greater than the amount of taxable income in the 15% bracket ($75,900), the income tax due is the sum of (1) the regular tax on taxable income minus net capital gain plus (2) 15% of the net capital gain included in the 15% basket. The 2017 tax liability is calculated below. Since income does not exceed the 15% bracket, the maximum tax rate for the capital gain income from property held over 12 months is 0%.

Taxable income	$34,400
Less: net capital gain	(4,000)
Ordinary taxable income	$30,400
Tax on ordinary income	$ 3,613

Answer (B) is incorrect. The amount of $3,813 includes a 5% capital gains tax. Answer (C) is incorrect. Capital gains are taxed at 0% for taxpayers in the 15% marginal tax bracket. Answer (D) is incorrect. The capital gain is taxed at 0%, not 20%.

11.9.2. Calvin and Alice Heston, both under 65, file a joint return for 2017. Their adjusted gross income is $205,700. Included in this total is $30,000 of taxable net long-term capital gains from the sale of collectible assets. Calvin and Alice claim the standard deduction and two personal exemptions. The Hestons' income tax liability for 2017 is

A. $30,257

B. $34,757

C. $37,757

D. $38,657

Answer (D) is correct. *(Publisher, adapted)*
REQUIRED: The income tax liability in 2017 for a married couple filing jointly.
DISCUSSION: The adjusted gross income is reduced by the standard deduction ($12,700) and two personal exemptions ($8,100).

AGI	$205,700
Standard deduction	(12,700)
Personal exemptions	(8,100)
Taxable income	$184,900

For taxable capital gain income on collectible assets, if the taxable income (as reduced by net capital gains) is greater than the amount of taxable income in the 25% bracket ($153,100), the income tax due is the sum of (1) the regular tax on taxable income minus net capital gain plus (2) 28% of the net capital gain included in the 28% basket. The 2017 tax liability is calculated below. In this case, the taxable income minus net capital gain exceeds the 15% bracket ceiling.

Taxable income	$184,900
Less net capital gain	(30,000)
Ordinary taxable income	$154,900
First $153,100 (rounded to the nearest dollar)	$ 29,753
Excess over $153,100 [($154,900 − $153,100) × 28%]	504
Capital gain ($30,000 × 28%)	8,400
Total tax liability	$ 38,657

Answer (A) is incorrect. The amount of $30,257 does not include the capital gains tax. Answer (B) is incorrect. The capital gains rate is 28%, not 15%. Answer (C) is incorrect. The capital gains rate is 28%, not 25%.

11.9.3. Warren, age 26, is single. Warren's son lives with the child's mother, who has waived her right to claim the child. Warren's adjusted gross income for 2017 is $34,050. Included in this total is $5,000 of long-term capital gain from the sale of an asset held over 12 months and $1,000 of taxable long-term capital gain from the sale of a collectible. Warren claims the standard deduction and two personal exemptions. Warren's income tax liability for 2017 is

A. $1,719

B. $2,469

C. $3,069

D. $3,249

Answer (A) is correct. *(Publisher, adapted)*
REQUIRED: The income tax liability in 2017 for a single taxpayer in the 15% marginal tax bracket.
DISCUSSION: The taxpayer's adjusted gross income is reduced by his standard deduction ($6,350) and two personal exemptions ($8,100).

AGI	$34,050
Standard deduction	(6,350)
Personal exemptions	(8,100)
Taxable income	$19,600

In 2017, the marginal tax rate for income not over $37,950 is 15%. For capital gain income on property held over 12 months when the taxpayer is in the 15% income tax bracket, the applicable tax rate is 0%. For a collectible taxable gain, the maximum rate is 28%. However, this gain is taxed at 15% because the ordinary rate does not meet or exceed 28%. The 2017 tax liability is calculated below:

Taxable income	$19,600
Less net capital gain taxed at preferential rate	(6,000)
Ordinary taxable income	$13,600
Ordinary income tax liability	$ 1,574
$1,000 capital gain at 15%	150
Total tax liability	$ 1,724

Answer (B) is incorrect. The $5,000 long-term capital gain from the property held over 12 months is not taxed at the 15% rate. Answer (C) is incorrect. The $5,000 long-term capital gain from the property held over 12 months and the collectible are not taxed at 25%. Answer (D) is incorrect. The $5,000 long-term capital gain from the property held over 12 months and the collectible are not taxed at 28%.

11.9.4. Judy Tower, age 34, is single. Her adjusted gross income for 2017 is $212,050. Included in this total is $5,000 of net long-term capital gains from assets held over 12 months. Judy claims the standard deduction and one personal exemption. Judy's income tax liability for 2017 is

A. $46,644

B. $48,294

C. $49,044

D. $49,944

Answer (C) is correct. *(Publisher, adapted)*
REQUIRED: The income tax liability in 2017 for a single taxpayer in the 33% marginal tax bracket.
DISCUSSION: The taxpayer's adjusted gross income is reduced by her standard deduction ($6,350) and one personal exemption ($4,050).

AGI	$212,050
Standard deduction	(6,350)
Personal exemption	(4,050)
Taxable income	$201,650

For capital gain income on property held over 12 months, if the taxable income (as reduced by net capital gains) is greater than the amount of taxable income in the 15% bracket ($37,650), the income tax due is the sum of (1) the regular tax on taxable income minus net capital gain plus (2) 15% of the net capital gain included in the 15% basket. If the taxpayer was in the 15% income tax bracket, the gain on the property held over 12 months would be 0%. The 2016 tax liability is calculated below. In this case, the taxable income minus net capital gain exceeds the 15% bracket ceiling.

Taxable income	$201,650
Less net capital gain	(5,000)
Ordinary taxable income	$196,650
First $191,650	$ 46,644
Excess over $191,650	
[($196,650 – $191,650) × 33%]	1,650
Capital gain ($5,000 × 15%)	750
Total tax liability	$ 49,044

Answer (A) is incorrect. The amount of $46,644 is the tax on the first $191,650. Answer (B) is incorrect. The capital gain is taxed at 15%. Answer (D) is incorrect. The capital gain is taxed at 15%, not the ordinary rate.

11.9.5. Long-term capital gains and losses may include gains taxed at both the 28% and 15% rate.

A. True.

B. False.

Answer (A) is correct. *(SEE, adapted)*
DISCUSSION: For tax years beginning after December 31, 2012, the capital gains rate for individuals is 20% if the taxpayer is in the 39.6% income tax bracket; 15% if in the 25%, 28%, 33%, or 35% income tax bracket; and 0% if in the 10% or 15% income tax bracket. For all tax years, the capital gains tax rate is 25% for unrecaptured Sec. 1250 gain and 28% for collectibles and gain on qualified small business stock.

STUDY UNIT TWELVE
SALE OF BUSINESS PROPERTY

12.1 Section 1231 Property

12.1.1. The following property is all used in a trade or business and has been held in excess of 1 year. Which property will not qualify for gains or losses from Sec. 1231 property upon its disposition by sale or exchange?

A. Property held for production of rent and royalties.

B. Business property condemned for public use.

C. Depreciable property used in a trade or business.

D. Property includible in inventory.

Answer (D) is correct. *(SEE, adapted)*
REQUIRED: The property that does not meet the definition of Sec. 1231 property.
DISCUSSION: Gains and losses receive special treatment under Sec. 1231. Property that qualifies under Sec. 1231 generally must have been held for more than 1 year and either have been used in a trade or business or be an involuntarily converted nonpersonal capital asset. Inventory is specifically excluded.
Answer (A) is incorrect. The property is used in a trade or business. Answer (B) is incorrect. Condemnation of business property is specifically included as a Sec. 1231 transaction. Answer (C) is incorrect. Depreciable property used in a trade or business is a primary example of Sec. 1231 property.

12.1.2. Which of the following assets will not qualify for gain or loss treatment under Sec. 1231?

A. Factory machine, acquired March 1, Year 1, sold August 1, Year 2.

B. Land used as a parking lot, acquired August 1, Year 1, sold September 1, Year 2.

C. Sculpture acquired August 1, Year 1, by an investor for the purpose of making a profit on it, which was destroyed in a fire on September 1, Year 2.

D. Personal automobile, acquired August 1, Year 1, destroyed in a collision on September 1, Year 2.

Answer (D) is correct. *(Publisher, adapted)*
REQUIRED: The asset that is not Sec. 1231 property.
DISCUSSION: Section 1231 property is depreciable or real property used in a trade or business and held for more than 1 year, or an involuntarily converted nonpersonal capital asset (i.e., held in connection with a trade or business or a transaction entered into for profit) held for more than 1 year. The personal automobile is a personal use capital asset and does not qualify for treatment under Sec. 1231.
Answer (A) is incorrect. The factory machine is depreciable business property and was held for more than a year. Answer (B) is incorrect. Land used as a parking lot, acquired August 1, Year 1, sold September 1, Year 2, is an example of Sec. 1231 property. Answer (C) is incorrect. A sculpture acquired August 1, Year 1, by an investor for the purpose of making a profit on it, which was destroyed in a fire on September 1, Year 2, is an example of Sec. 1231 property.

12.1.3. Trudy Holiday has been selling greeting cards for several years as a sole proprietor. In May of Year 3, she purchased land and a building to use in the greeting card business. In October of Year 3, she sold the entire business, including inventory held since Year 1 and the land and building. Trudy's automobile, used exclusively in her business and purchased in Year 1, was swallowed by a sinkhole before the sale in Year 3. Which of the following is a Sec. 1231 asset?

A. The inventory acquired in Year 1.

B. The building.

C. The land.

D. The automobile.

Answer (D) is correct. *(Publisher, adapted)*
REQUIRED: The asset that is Sec. 1231 property.
DISCUSSION: Section 1231 property is depreciable or real property used in a trade or business and held for more than 1 year, and nonpersonal capital assets, held more than 1 year, which are involuntarily converted. Trudy's business automobile is Sec. 1231 property because it was held long term and was involuntarily converted.
Answer (A) is incorrect. Inventory is not real or depreciable property used in a trade or business. Answer (B) is incorrect. The building was not held for more than 1 year, so it is not Sec. 1231 property even though it was used in a trade or business. Answer (C) is incorrect. The land was not held for more than 1 year, so it is not Sec. 1231 property even though it was used in a trade or business.

12.1.4. John owned a printing business and sold the following assets in 2017:

Printing press:
Sales price	$25,000
Original cost	20,000
Allowed or allowable depreciation	8,000

Computer equipment:
Sales price	$30,000
Original cost	28,000
Allowed or allowable depreciation	14,000

John had a net Sec. 1231 loss of $6,000 in 2016. What is the amount and character of John's gain for 2017?

A. $14,000 ordinary income; $15,000 capital gain.

B. $22,000 ordinary income; $7,000 capital gain.

C. $28,000 ordinary income; $1,000 capital gain.

D. $0 ordinary income; $29,000 capital gain.

12.1.5. Ms. C sold a building used in her business. Her records reflect the following information:

Cost of building	$ 90,000
Cost of new roof	15,000
Straight-line depreciation deducted	35,000
Cash received on sale	145,000
Taxes assumed by buyer	7,000
Mortgage assumed by buyer	25,000
Selling expenses	6,000

What is the amount of Ms. C's recognized gain on the sale?

A. $101,000

B. $90,000

C. $66,000

D. $30,000

Answer (C) is correct. *(SEE, adapted)*
REQUIRED: The amount and character of gain on the sale of assets used in a business.
DISCUSSION: Section 1231 property is depreciable or real property used in a trade or business and held for more than 1 year or an involuntarily converted nonpersonal capital asset (i.e., held in connection with a trade or business or a transaction entered into for profit) held for more than 1 year. A taxpayer who has a net Sec. 1231 gain (i.e., excess of Sec. 1231 gains over Sec. 1231 losses) for the tax year must review the 5 most recent preceding tax years for possible recapture of net Sec. 1231 losses for such years. If there were any net Sec. 1231 losses during such period, the taxpayer must treat the current year's net Sec. 1231 gain as ordinary income to the extent of the amount of unrecaptured net Sec. 1231 losses for that past period [Sec. 1231(c)]. The losses are to be recaptured on a first-in, first-out (FIFO) basis. John realizes a total gain of $29,000. Since the assets also qualify as Sec. 1245 property, this Sec. 1231 gain is recharacterized as ordinary income to the extent of depreciation recaptured ($22,000) and to the extent of any unaccounted for Sec. 1231 loss ($6,000). The remaining $1,000 is recognized as a Sec. 1231 gain.
Answer (A) is incorrect. John has both ordinary income and a capital gain affected by recapture and Sec. 1231 losses. Answer (B) is incorrect. Gains on the sale of Sec. 1231 assets can be recharacterized as ordinary to the extent of any unaccounted for prior Sec. 1231 losses. Answer (D) is incorrect. Depreciation recapture and Sec. 1231 losses recharacterize gains as ordinary.

Answer (A) is correct. *(SEE, adapted)*
REQUIRED: The amount of recognized gain on the sale of a building used in a business.
DISCUSSION: Under Sec. 1001, the gain on the sale or other disposition of property is the excess of the amount realized over the adjusted basis. Any capital repairs, such as a new roof, are added to the adjusted basis. The amount realized is the sum of any money received plus the fair market value of the nonmoney property received. The amount realized includes relief from liabilities and, in this case, the assumption of the mortgage and real estate taxes by the buyer. The full amount of the realized gain is recognized unless all or some portion thereof is specifically excluded by another statute. Ms. C's recognized gain is calculated as follows:

Cash received	$145,000
Plus: Real estate taxes assumed	7,000
Mortgage assumed	25,000
Amount realized	$177,000
Minus: Adjusted basis of building	(70,000)
Selling expenses	(6,000)
Realized and recognized gain	$101,000

Answer (B) is incorrect. The cost of the building is $90,000. Answer (C) is incorrect. The recognized gain is the amount realized less the building's adjusted basis and selling expenses. The depreciation claimed needs to reduce the building's adjusted basis. Answer (D) is incorrect. (1) The amount realized includes not only the cash received but also the real estate tax liability assumed and the mortgage (which now reduces the amount realized), (2) the selling expenses must reduce the amount realized, and (3) the adjusted basis of the building needs to be increased by the cost of the new roof and reduced by the depreciation claimed.

12.1.6. Mary Brown purchased an apartment building 6 years ago for $275,000. The building was depreciated using the straight-line method. The building was sold for $285,000 when the asset basis net of accumulated depreciation was $215,000. On her current-year tax return, Brown should report

A. Section 1231 gain of $70,000.

B. Ordinary income of $70,000.

C. Section 1231 gain of $60,000 and ordinary income of $10,000.

D. Section 1231 gain of $10,000 and ordinary income of $60,000.

Answer (A) is correct. *(CPA, adapted)*
REQUIRED: The amount and character of gain that must be recognized.
DISCUSSION: When depreciable property used in a trade or business is sold by a noncorporate owner at a gain, first Sec. 1245 and Sec. 1250 are applied, then the balance of the gain not recaptured as ordinary income is Sec. 1231 gain. In this case, Sec. 1245 does not apply (the building was not acquired before 1987), and Sec. 1250 recapture is limited to the excess of accelerated depreciation taken by the taxpayer over straight-line depreciation. Since the building was depreciated on the straight-line method, the entire $70,000 gain ($285,000 − $215,000) is Sec. 1231 gain.
Answer (B) is incorrect. Brown should not report ordinary income of $70,000. Answer (C) is incorrect. Brown cannot report Sec. 1231 gain of $60,000 and ordinary income of $10,000. Answer (D) is incorrect. Brown cannot report Sec. 1231 gain of $10,000 and ordinary income of $60,000.

12.1.7. Mr. Investor sold a parcel of land realizing a $50,000 gain. Investor has used this parcel for a parking lot during the 120 months that he has owned the land. The amount and tax classification of the gain recognized by Investor on this sale is

A. Ordinary income of $50,000.

B. A $50,000 Sec. 1231 gain.

C. A $50,000 Sec. 1245 gain.

D. A $50,000 Sec. 1250 gain.

Answer (B) is correct. *(SEE, adapted)*
REQUIRED: The amount and type of gain recognized on the sale of a parking lot.
DISCUSSION: Section 1231 property includes real property used in a trade or business that is held for more than 1 year. Therefore, the entire gain is Sec. 1231 gain.
Answer (A) is incorrect. The amount and tax classification of the gain recognized by Investor on this sale is not ordinary income of $50,000. Answer (C) is incorrect. Section 1245 generally applies to depreciable property other than real property. Answer (D) is incorrect. Section 1250 only applies to depreciable real property.

12.1.8. The sale of which of the following types of business property should be reported as Sec. 1231 (Property Used in the Trade or Business and Involuntary Conversions) property?

A. Inventory held for resale.

B. Machinery held for 6 months.

C. Cattle held for 6 months.

D. Land held for 18 months.

Answer (D) is correct. *(CPA, adapted)*
REQUIRED: The Section 1231 property.
DISCUSSION: Real property used in a trade or business held for longer than 1 year is considered Sec. 1231 property.
Answer (A) is incorrect. Inventory is specifically excluded from the definition of Sec. 1231 property. Answer (B) is incorrect. Tangible personal property used in a trade or business is typically included in Sec. 1231 property. However, the property must be held for longer than 1 year to be treated as Sec. 1231 property. Answer (C) is incorrect. Tangible personal property used in a trade or business is typically included in Sec. 1231 property. However, the property must be held for longer than 1 year to be treated as Sec. 1231 property.

12.1.9. If held long-term, all of the following are considered to be Sec. 1231 transactions:

● Sale of depreciable personal property
● Sale of leasehold used in a business
● Sale of rental real property
● Net casualty gains on business property
● Business or investment property condemned for public use

A. True.

B. False.

Answer (A) is correct. *(SEE, adapted)*
DISCUSSION: The sale or exchange of property used in a trade or business [as defined in Sec. 1231(b)] is a Sec. 1231 transaction, whether a gain or loss results. Property used in a trade or business includes real property and depreciable property held for more than 1 year. Net casualty gains and gains or losses from condemnation of either business property or capital assets, held for more than 1 year and in connection with a trade or business or a transaction entered into for profit, are also considered Sec. 1231 transactions.

12.2 Section 1245 Property

12.2.1. Which of the following buildings is Sec. 1245 property? An office building acquired and placed in service in

A. 1980 and depreciated using an accelerated method.

B. 1984 and depreciated using regular ACRS percentages.

C. 1985 and depreciated using the straight-line method.

D. 1998 and depreciated using the regular MACRS method.

Answer (B) is correct. *(Publisher, adapted)*
   REQUIRED: The asset that is Sec. 1245 property.
   DISCUSSION: Nonresidential buildings placed in service after 1980 and before 1987 are Sec. 1245 property unless the straight-line method of depreciation is elected.
   Answer (A) is incorrect. Buildings placed in service prior to 1981 (prior to ACRS) are Sec. 1250 property, regardless of the method of depreciation used and regardless of whether used for residential or commercial purposes. Answer (C) is incorrect. Nonresidential buildings placed in service from 1981 through 1986 are Sec. 1250 property if the straight-line method of depreciation is elected. Answer (D) is incorrect. Both residential and commercial buildings placed in service after 1986 are Sec. 1250 property. The straight-line method of depreciation is required.

12.2.2. A gain on the disposition of Sec. 1245 property is treated as ordinary income to the extent of

A. Depreciation allowed or allowable.

B. Excess of the accelerated depreciation allowed or allowable over the depreciation figured for the same period using the straight-line method.

C. Excess of the appreciated value over depreciation allowed or allowable using the straight-line method.

D. The difference between the amount realized over the cost of the property.

Answer (A) is correct. *(SEE, adapted)*
   REQUIRED: The maximum amount of gain that can be characterized as ordinary income.
   DISCUSSION: A gain on the disposition of Sec. 1245 property is treated as ordinary income to the extent of the total amount of depreciation allowed or allowable. The recaptured gain cannot exceed the amount of the realized gain.
   Answer (B) is incorrect. The method of depreciation used makes no difference in the calculation of ordinary income. Answer (C) is incorrect. The excess of the appreciated value over depreciation allowed under any method receives Sec. 1231 treatment. Answer (D) is incorrect. The amount realized in excess of the asset's original cost is Sec. 1231 gain.

12.2.3. Which of the following is not Sec. 1245 property?

A. Computer.

B. Office building.

C. Display shelving.

D. Covenant not to compete.

Answer (B) is correct. *(SEE, adapted)*
   REQUIRED: The item that is not Sec. 1245 property.
   DISCUSSION: Section 1245 property generally is depreciable personal property. It is tangible or intangible depreciable personal property, recovery property including specified real property, and tax benefit property. Other tangible property (excluding a building or its structural components) includes property used as an integral part of a trade or business, e.g., manufacturing or production equipment used in a trade or business. Intangible amortizable personal Sec. 1245 property examples include

1. Leaseholds of Sec. 1245 property

2. Professional athletic contracts, e.g., baseball

3. Patents

4. Goodwill acquired in connection with the acquisition of a trade or business

5. Livestock

6. Covenant not to compete

   Answer (A) is incorrect. A computer is an example of Sec. 1245 property. Answer (C) is incorrect. Display shelving is an example of Sec. 1245 property. Answer (D) is incorrect. A covenant not to compete is an example of Sec. 1245 property.

12.2.4. Mr. Boyette built and occupied a manufacturing plant for use in his business. All of the following assets located in the building are Sec. 1245 property except

A. Large mainframe computer system used by Boyette's research department.

B. Elevators and escalators.

C. Office furniture.

D. Packaging machine in the shipping department.

Answer (B) is correct. *(SEE, adapted)*
REQUIRED: The asset that is not Sec. 1245 property.
DISCUSSION: Section 1245 property is property depreciable under Sec. 167 or 168 that is either personal property, specified real property, or most recovery property under Sec. 168. Whether a building is Sec. 1245 property depends on the year it is placed in service, whether it is commercial or residential, and the method of its depreciation. Elevators and escalators placed in service after 1986 are not Sec. 1245 property and are treated as part of the building, which is Sec. 1250 property.
Answer (A) is incorrect. A large mainframe computer system used by Boyette's research department is an example of Sec. 1245 property. Answer (C) is incorrect. Office and furniture are examples of Sec. 1245 property. Answer (D) is incorrect. A packaging machine in the shipping department is an example of Sec. 1245 property.

12.2.5. All of the following statements with respect to the disposition of Sec. 1245 property are true except

A. Gain is treated as ordinary income to the extent of the excess depreciation allowed or allowable over the depreciation that would have been available under the straight line method.

B. Section 1245 property includes a building placed in service in 1984 and depreciated using the regular ACRS method.

C. In figuring the deductions affecting the recomputed basis of Sec. 1245 property, it is necessary to include any basis adjustment that was made for the investment credit (e.g., the energy credit).

D. Amounts deducted under Sec. 179 are recovered as ordinary income to the extent of any gain on a sale or disposition.

Answer (A) is correct. *(SEE, adapted)*
REQUIRED: The incorrect application of Sec. 1245.
DISCUSSION: The method of depreciation makes no difference in the calculation of ordinary income. Any depreciation taken must be recaptured as ordinary income.
Answer (B) is incorrect. Nonresidential real estate property that was placed in service after 1980 and before 1987 and also qualifies as recovery property under the ACRS rules is Sec. 1245 property. Answer (C) is incorrect. Section 50(c)(4) requires the amount of the basis reduction for the investment credit that is not recaptured under Sec. 50(a) to be included in the depreciation claimed with respect to the property for Secs. 1245 and 1250 purposes. Answer (D) is incorrect. Section 1245(a)(2)(C) requires deductions claimed under Sec. 179 to be recaptured as ordinary income.

12.2.6. If the fair market value of Sec. 1245 property is greater than its basis, which of the following transactions will give rise to Sec. 1245 income?

A. Disposition at death.

B. Disposition by gift.

C. A like-kind exchange in which boot is received.

D. A Sec. 351 exchange with a newly formed corporation for all of its stock.

Answer (C) is correct. *(Publisher, adapted)*
REQUIRED: The transaction to which Sec. 1245 applies.
DISCUSSION: The general rule of Sec. 1245(a) is that it applies notwithstanding any other section of the Code. However, Sec. 1245(b) provides certain exceptions and limitations for its application. In a like-kind exchange, Sec. 1245 applies to the amount of gain recognized plus the fair market value of non-Sec. 1245 property received that is not already taken into account in calculating the recognized gain. Under Sec. 1031, the amount of gain recognized is the smaller of the gain realized or boot received.
Answer (A) is incorrect. Section 1245(b) provides that it will not apply to dispositions by death. Answer (B) is incorrect. Section 1245(b) provides that it will not apply to dispositions by gift. Answer (D) is incorrect. Section 1245(b) provides that depreciation will only be recaptured on a Sec. 351 exchange to the extent that gain is recognized under Sec. 351. Generally, no gain is recognized upon the transfer of assets to a new corporation solely for stock.

12.2.7. In July, Tommy Trimball sold a printing press used in his business that originally cost him $10,000 for $10,000. His adjusted basis at the time of the sale was $1,000, and Tommy paid $1,000 in selling expenses. What is the amount of the gain that would be ordinary income under Sec. 1245?

A. $0

B. $8,000

C. $9,000

D. $10,000

Answer (B) is correct. *(SEE, adapted)*
REQUIRED: The amount of gain classified as ordinary income under Sec. 1245.
DISCUSSION: Under Sec. 1001, the gain realized and recognized on the sale of property is the excess of the amount realized over its adjusted basis. Selling expenses also reduce the gain recognized. Thus, Tommy recognizes

Money received	$10,000
Less: Adjusted basis of printing press	(1,000)
Selling expenses	(1,000)
Realized and recognized gain	$ 8,000

Section 1245 requires the recapture of ordinary income up to the amount of depreciation taken. Thus, the full $8,000 recognized gain must be recaptured as ordinary income since $9,000 of depreciation expense was incurred ($10,000 original basis – $1,000 ending basis).
Answer (A) is incorrect. Some gain is recaptured as ordinary income. Answer (C) is incorrect. The amount of depreciation recapture potential under Sec. 1245 is $9,000, but it is limited. Answer (D) is incorrect. The amount received is $10,000.

12.2.8. Mr. Adamson changed jobs and sold his car that he had used 60% for business. Mr. Adamson had purchased the car for $12,000 and sold it for $10,000. He had claimed $2,000 depreciation on the car. What is the taxable gain or deductible loss on the sale, assuming no replacement vehicle was acquired?

A. $0

B. $800 gain.

C. $800 loss.

D. $2,000 gain.

Answer (B) is correct. *(SEE, adapted)*
REQUIRED: The gain or loss recognized upon sale of a car used for both business and personal purposes.
DISCUSSION: Since the taxpayer used the car for both business and personal reasons, the business and personal portions must be computed separately. The adjusted basis of the car for personal use was 40% of the original cost of $12,000, or $4,800. The adjusted basis of the business portion of the car was $5,200 [($12,000 cost × 60%) – $2,000 depreciation]. There was a realized loss of $800 on the personal portion of the car and a realized gain of $800 on the business portion of the car. A loss on the sale of personal use property is not deductible (Sec. 165), so there is a recognized gain on the sale of $800.

	Personal (40%)	Business (60%)
Sales proceeds	$ 4,000	$ 6,000
Less: Adjusted basis	(4,800)	(5,200)
Realized gain (loss)	$ (800)	$ 800
Recognized gain (loss)	$ 0	$ 800

Answer (A) is incorrect. There is a gain on the sale of the business portion of the vehicle. Answer (C) is incorrect. The $800 loss is on the personal portion of the vehicle. The loss is not deductible. Answer (D) is incorrect. The vehicle costs must be allocated between personal and business use portions, and the depreciation claimed must reduce the property's adjusted basis.

12.2.9. Mr. X acquired a machine for use in his business on January 5, Year 4, for $30,000. Depreciation was taken on the asset using the MACRS rules in the following amounts:

Year 4	$6,000
Year 5	$4,800

Mr. X sold the machine on January 26, Year 6, for $32,000. What is the amount and character of X's gain on the disposition of the asset?

	Sec. 1231 Gain	Sec. 1245 Gain
A.	$0	$12,800
B.	$2,000	$10,800
C.	$10,800	$2,000
D.	$12,800	$0

Answer (B) is correct. *(SEE, adapted)*
REQUIRED: The amount and character of the gain on the sale of property given depreciation recapture.
DISCUSSION: The realized gain from the sale of the machine is $12,800 [$32,000 – ($30,000 – $10,800)]. Since the machine is Sec. 1245 property, the recognized gain is characterized as ordinary to the extent of any depreciation that has been taken. Thus, $10,800 will be classified as ordinary income due to depreciation recapture, and the remaining gain of $2,000 will be classified as Sec. 1231 gain.
Answer (A) is incorrect. Section 1245 gain is recognized only up to the amount of depreciation claimed. Answer (C) is incorrect. The amount of depreciation taken is the Sec. 1245 gain; the remaining gain is the Sec. 1231 gain. Answer (D) is incorrect. The Sec. 1231 gain is the remaining gain after the Sec. 1245 gain has been determined.

12.2.10. Mr. Monopoly sold equipment used in his business for $11,000. The equipment cost $10,000, and Monopoly had properly claimed MACRS deductions totaling $4,000. Straight-line depreciation, if it had been used, would have been $2,500. What is the amount of gain that should be reported under Secs. 1231 and 1245?

	Sec. 1231	Sec. 1245
A.	$5,000	$0
B.	$3,500	$1,500
C.	$1,000	$4,000
D.	$0	$5,000

Answer (C) is correct. *(SEE, adapted)*
   REQUIRED: The amount of the gain recognized under Secs. 1245 and 1231 on the sale of property depreciated using MACRS.
   DISCUSSION: The sale resulted in a $5,000 realized gain as computed below. Since the property was Sec. 1245 property, the realized gain must be recognized as ordinary income to the extent of depreciation taken. Therefore, $4,000 must be recognized as Sec. 1245 ordinary income. The remaining $1,000 ($5,000 gain – $4,000 ordinary income) is recognized as Sec. 1231 gain.

Original cost	$10,000
Less: depreciation	(4,000)
Adjusted basis	$ 6,000
Sales proceeds	$11,000
Less: adjusted basis	(6,000)
Realized and recognized gain	$ 5,000

   Answer (A) is incorrect. The Sec. 1231 gain equals the remaining gain after the Sec. 1245 gain has been determined. Answer (B) is incorrect. The Sec. 1245 gain equals the actual depreciation taken, not the excess of the actual depreciation over the straight-line depreciation. Answer (D) is incorrect. The Sec. 1245 gain equals only the amount of depreciation taken.

12.2.11. On January 2, Year 1, Rob, a sole proprietor, purchased a business truck for $10,000. On January 2, Year 3, Rob gave the truck to his son, Scott, who also used it in his business. At the time of the gift, the truck had an adjusted basis to Rob of $5,000 and a fair market value of $3,000. The truck had a remaining useful life of 5 years and no salvage value. Scott elected straight-line depreciation. On January 2, Year 5, Scott sold the truck for $6,000. What are the amount and the character of Scott's gain?

	Sec. 1231 Gain	Sec. 1245 Gain
A.	$0	$3,000
B.	$0	$4,200
C.	$1,000	$2,000
D.	$3,000	$1,200

Answer (A) is correct. *(SEE, adapted)*
   REQUIRED: The amount and the character of the gain on the sale of the truck.
   DISCUSSION: Since this property is depreciable business property personal in nature, under Sec. 1245, any realized gain must be recognized as ordinary income to the extent of any depreciation previously taken. Since the truck was acquired by gift from his father, Scott must recapture any depreciation previously taken, including that taken by his father. Scott's initial basis is $5,000 for gain purposes and $3,000 for loss purposes. The total depreciation ($5,000 by Rob + $2,000 by Scott) exceeds the realized gain, and therefore the entire gain will be ordinary income.

Sales proceeds		$6,000
Less: adjusted basis:		
Carryover basis	$5,000	
Minus depreciation*	(2,000)	(3,000)
Realized and recognized gain		$3,000

*1/2 year in Year 3 and Year 5 and a full year in Year 4 ($5,000 ÷ 5) × 2 = $2,000.

   Answer (B) is incorrect. The amount of $4,200 is based on a gain resulting from Scott's using the property's FMV as the depreciable basis. Answer (C) is incorrect. The depreciation recapture potential includes both Rob's and Scott's depreciation, which makes the total depreciation more than the recognized gain. Answer (D) is incorrect. Scott does not have a Sec. 1231 gain.

12.2.12. Allen purchased a trademark on January 1 of last year for $150,000. On January 1 of this year, Allen sold the trademark for $200,000. How much of Allen's gain on the sale of the trademark is Sec. 1245 gain?

A. $5,000

B. $10,000

C. $50,000

D. $60,000

Answer (B) is correct. *(Publisher, adapted)*
   REQUIRED: The amount of Sec. 1245 gain.
   DISCUSSION: Under Sec. 197, a trademark is an intangible asset that is amortizable over a 15-year period, beginning in the month of acquisition. Total amortization for the period January 1 of last year through January 1 of this year equals $10,000 ($150,000 ÷ 15). Allen's realized gain is $60,000 [$200,000 sales price – ($150,000 cost – $10,000 amortization)]. Section 1245 requires the gain to be recognized as ordinary income to the extent of the amortization taken. Therefore, $10,000 of the $60,000 gain is Sec. 1245 gain [Sec. 1245(a)(3)].
   Answer (A) is incorrect. Half a year's amortization is $5,000. Answer (C) is incorrect. The realized gain calculated without regard for the amortization basis adjustment is $50,000. Answer (D) is incorrect. The realized gain is $60,000.

12.2.13. John Burtt sold his small office building for $290,000 in 2017. Burtt acquired the building in January 1986 for $270,000 and made improvements costing $15,000 at that time. John used accelerated depreciation under ACRS, and the asset was fully depreciated. For tax purposes, Burtt should treat the gain as

A. $241,550 Sec. 1231 gain.

B. $5,000 Sec. 1231 gain; $225,000 ordinary income.

C. $5,000 Sec. 1231 gain; $285,000 ordinary income.

D. $16,550 Sec. 1231 gain; $225,000 ordinary income.

Answer (C) is correct. *(D.L. Crumbley)*
REQUIRED: The amount of gain on the sale of an office building subject to depreciation recapture.
DISCUSSION: The office building is 19-year real property under the pre-1987 ACRS system. It is also Sec. 1245 recovery property since it does not fall within any of the exceptions (such as residential rental property, low-income housing, or property on which an election to use the straight-line method is made). Under Sec. 1245, all the depreciation is recaptured as ordinary income up to the amount of the gain on the sale.
Basis was $0. The gain on the sale was $290,000 ($290,000 sales price – $0 basis). The amount of the gain subject to depreciation recapture is $285,000, the total depreciation taken.
Answer (A) is incorrect. The gain is not $241,550 Sec. 1231 gain. Answer (B) is incorrect. The depreciation under the straight-line method would have been $225,000. Answer (D) is incorrect. The correct amount of Sec. 1231 gain is not $16,550, and $225,000 would have been the depreciation under the straight-line method.

12.2.14. Belle purchased a new freezer case for her grocery store at a cost of $60,000 on July 1 of last year. Belle elected to expense $10,000 of the cost last year and depreciated the remaining $50,000 basis using MACRS. Depreciation taken totaled $18,000 prior to the sale of the equipment on December 1 of this year. Straight-line depreciation would have been $9,000. The sales price on December 1 of this year was $52,000. Gain on the sale was

A. $28,000 Sec. 1231 gain.

B. $20,000 Sec. 1231 gain.

C. $18,000 ordinary income, $2,000 Sec. 1231 gain.

D. $20,000 ordinary income.

Answer (D) is correct. *(Publisher, adapted)*
REQUIRED: The amount and character of gain on the sale when Sec. 179 expense was claimed.
DISCUSSION: The realized gain of $20,000 is subject to recapture under Sec. 1245 because the freezer is depreciated under Sec. 168 and is not excepted by Sec. 1245. Thus, any realized gain is recognized as ordinary income to the extent of any depreciation taken. The $10,000 that was expensed under Sec. 179 counts as depreciation expense in determining the character of the gain. Therefore, all the recognized gain is ordinary income.

Original cost	$60,000
Sec. 179 expense	(10,000)
Depreciation	(18,000)
Adjusted basis	$32,000
Sales proceeds	$52,000
Adjusted basis	(32,000)
Realized and recognized gain	$20,000

Answer (A) is incorrect. The amount of $28,000 is the depreciation of $18,000 taken prior to the sale of the freezer case and added to the $10,000 of depreciation expensed under Sec. 179. Answer (B) is incorrect. The correct amount of Sec. 1231 gain is not $20,000. Answer (C) is incorrect. Ordinary income should be recaptured to the extent of the depreciation taken. Depreciation taken includes the $10,000 expensed under Sec. 179.

12.2.15. Mike Verdisco owns the Buffalo Pit Bulls of the Universal Football League. The team purchased a weight machine in December of last year for $11,000, and $10,000 of the purchase price was expensed under Sec. 179. MACRS depreciation claimed was $143 last year and $122 this year. In December of this year, when the weight machine had a fair market value of $8,000, the team exchanged it for a whirlpool bath that had a fair market value of $7,000. The team also received $1,000 in cash. What is the gain or loss of the Buffalo Pit Bulls?

A. No gain or loss.

B. $265 of Sec. 1245 gain and $735 of Sec. 1231 gain.

C. $1,000 of Sec. 1245 gain.

D. $7,265 of Sec. 1245 gain.

Answer (C) is correct. *(Publisher, adapted)*
REQUIRED: The amount and character of gain from a like-kind exchange of Sec. 1245 property.
DISCUSSION: Under Sec. 1031, the exchange of the weight machine for the whirlpool bath qualifies as a like-kind exchange, and the gain recognized is limited to the boot received of $1,000. Under Sec. 1245(b)(4), the amount of recapture in a like-kind exchange is limited to the amount of gain recognized plus the fair market value of property acquired that is not Sec. 1245 property not already included in calculating the gain recognized. The whirlpool bath is Sec. 1245 property. Under Sec. 1245(a)(2), the amount of Sec. 1245 recapture includes both depreciation claimed and the expense deducted under Sec. 179. Consequently, the entire $1,000 gain is recaptured as ordinary income.
Answer (A) is incorrect. There is a gain or loss on this transaction. Answer (B) is incorrect. There is no Sec. 1231 gain on this transaction. Answer (D) is incorrect. This is a Sec. 1031 like-kind exchange. The recognized gain is limited to the boot received.

12.2.16. Gary Lary owns the Boston Maulers of the Universal Basketball League as a sole proprietor. The assets include a device for suspending a player from the ceiling to stretch his or her back to increase height. The machine cost $20,000 when purchased several years ago and $10,000 of straight-line depreciation had been claimed when Gary died on December 31 of the current year. Gary willed all of the team assets to Hondo Hadacheck. The device had a fair market value of $15,000 on Gary's death, and a short time later, Hondo sold it for $18,000. How much Sec. 1245 recapture is recognized, and when?

    A. None.

    B. $5,000 on Gary's death.

    C. $3,000 when Hondo sells it.

    D. $8,000 when Hondo sells it.

Answer (A) is correct. *(Publisher, adapted)*
    REQUIRED: The amount and timing of depreciation recapture on Sec. 1245 property that is transferred at death and later sold.
    DISCUSSION: Under Sec. 1245(b)(2), there is no recapture on disposition by death. When Gary died, the basis of the device was stepped up to its fair market value on the date of death [Sec. 1014(a)]. Therefore, when Hondo sold it for $18,000, he recognized a $3,000 gain ($18,000 − $15,000 basis). Regulation 1.1245-2(c)(3) states that depreciation recapture potential exists following a transfer at death to the extent of the depreciation deductions allowed the transferee before the decedent's death that reduce the transferee's basis in the property under Sec. 1014(b)(9). Generally, such a reduction occurs when property is acquired from a decedent prior to death (e.g., creation of a joint interest involving the decedent and the transferee). Since the property was acquired from Gary Lary at death and no subsequent depreciation was claimed, no basis reduction occurs under Sec. 1014(b)(9). Therefore, none of the $3,000 recognized gain is depreciation recapture under Sec. 1245.
    Answer (B) is incorrect. There is no recapture at the time of death. Answer (C) is incorrect. The correct amount of Sec. 1245 recapture when Hondo sells the device is not $3,000. Answer (D) is incorrect. The correct amount of Sec. 1245 recapture when Hondo sells the device is not $8,000.

12.2.17. If you dispose of both depreciable personal property and other property in one transaction and realize a gain, in the absence of an agreement between the buyer and seller, an allocation of the amount realized between the two types of property disposed of in proportion to their fair market values must occur to figure the part of the gain to be reported as ordinary income due to depreciation recapture.

    A. True.

    B. False.

Answer (A) is correct. *(SEE, adapted)*
    DISCUSSION: When different types of property are disposed of in one transaction, an allocation must be made between the different properties. This is especially true when part of the property is depreciable, to account for the depreciation recapture under Sec. 1245. The allocation is generally made on the basis of the relative fair market values of each property or portion of a property. Normally, if the allocation is made in an agreement between the buyer and the seller, the agreement will be used (Sec. 1060). Not only must the amount realized be allocated, but if it is property that has several uses (e.g., business and personal), then the basis of the property also must be allocated in order to determine a gain on the disposition of each.

12.2.18. Section 1245 property includes tangible as well as intangible personal property that is or has been amortized under Sec. 197.

    A. True.

    B. False.

Answer (A) is correct. *(SEE, adapted)*
    DISCUSSION: Section 1245 property means any property that is or has been property of a character subject to the allowance for depreciation or amortization and is either personal (tangible or intangible) property or other property (not including a building or its structural components). Examples of intangible property that are considered Sec. 1245 property include goodwill, leaseholds of Sec. 1245 property, baseball and football players' contracts, and patents [Sec. 197(f)(7)].

12.2.19. Oil and gas storage tanks, grain storage bins, silos, blast furnaces, coke ovens, and coal tipples are special-purpose structures or storage facilities that qualify as Sec. 1245 property.

    A. True.

    B. False.

Answer (A) is correct. *(SEE, adapted)*
    DISCUSSION: The properties described in this question are specifically deemed to be Sec. 1245 property under Sec. 1245(a)(3).

12.2.20. On January 2, Year 1, Charles bought office furniture for $3,000. He deducted $600 in depreciation under MACRS. On January 3, Year 2, a fire destroyed the furniture for which he was reimbursed $2,800 by his insurance company. Charles replaced the furniture at a cost of $2,600. Charles has ordinary income of $200.

A. True.

B. False.

Answer (A) is correct. *(SEE, adapted)*
   DISCUSSION: Under Sec. 1033, if property is involuntarily converted into property similar or related in service or use, no gain shall be recognized unless the money received exceeds the adjusted basis of the similar property purchased; then the gain shall be recognized to the extent of excess money received. For this example, the adjusted basis at the time of the involuntary conversion was $2,400 ($3,000 − $600 depreciation). The following calculation will be made to determine the gain recognized:

Insurance reimbursement	$2,800
Less: adjusted basis	(2,400)
Gain realized	$ 400

Under Sec. 1033, only $200 of this gain needs to be recognized since the $2,800 insurance reimbursement less the $2,600 cost of replacement furniture equals $200. The entire $200 is ordinary income because the furniture is Sec. 1245 property, and $600 of depreciation had been claimed.

12.2.21. The deduction for the cost of removal of barriers for the handicapped must be considered similar to depreciation when considering the treatment of gain from a sale of the property.

A. True.

B. False.

Answer (A) is correct. *(SEE, adapted)*
   DISCUSSION: Under Sec. 190, the cost of the removal of barriers for the handicapped is deductible. Under Sec. 1245(a)(3)(C), property that has an adjusted basis that reflects adjustments under Sec. 190 is deemed to be Sec. 1245 property. This deduction must be considered as an adjustment to basis similar to depreciation to prevent the taxpayer from receiving a double tax benefit.

12.3 Section 1250 Property

12.3.1. Which of the following dispositions of depreciable property would trigger recapture?

A. Installment sale.

B. Gift.

C. Transfer at death.

D. Tax-free exchange where no money or unlike property is received.

Answer (A) is correct. *(SEE, adapted)*
   REQUIRED: The disposition of depreciable property that would trigger recapture.
   DISCUSSION: Neither Sec. 1245 nor Sec. 1250 applies to a gift disposition, or a disposition by bequest, devise, or intestate succession. Like-kind exchanges also do not involve the recapture of depreciable property. In an installment sale, any ordinary income because of the depreciation recapture rules must be recognized upon the sale. Only capital gain is allowed to be reported on the installment method.
   Answer (B) is incorrect. Neither Sec. 1245 nor Sec. 1250 applies to a gift disposition. Answer (C) is incorrect. Neither Sec. 1245 nor Sec. 1250 applies to a disposition by bequest, devise, or intestate succession. Answer (D) is incorrect. Like-kind exchanges do not involve the recapture of depreciable property.

12.3.2. HICO, Inc., controls various income-producing real properties. Included among its assets are a shopping mall built in 1980 and depreciated by an accelerated method; an apartment building purchased in 1981 and depreciated by the regular ACRS method; and an office building purchased in 1982, which is depreciated under the straight-line ACRS method. Which of the following is not Sec. 1250 property?

A. The shopping mall.

B. The apartment building.

C. The land on which the apartment building is built.

D. The office building.

Answer (C) is correct. *(Publisher, adapted)*
   REQUIRED: The asset that is not Sec. 1250 property.
   DISCUSSION: Section 1250 property is depreciable real property that is not Sec. 1245 property. Since land is not depreciable, it is not Sec. 1250 property (nor Sec. 1245 property).
   Answer (A) is incorrect. Real property put into service prior to 1981 is Sec. 1250 property unless it is an item specified in Sec. 1245. Answer (B) is incorrect. Buildings used for residential rental purposes are Sec. 1250 property regardless of when placed in service. Answer (D) is incorrect. Nonresidential real property placed in service from 1981 through 1986 is Sec. 1250 property if the straight-line method of depreciation is used.

12.3.3. Which of the following assets placed in service from 1981 through 1986 is Sec. 1250 property?

A. Low-income housing depreciated by the regular ACRS method.

B. A warehouse depreciated by the regular ACRS method.

C. An elevator depreciated by the straight-line ACRS method.

D. A farmer's silo depreciated by the straight-line ACRS method.

Answer (A) is correct. *(Publisher, adapted)*
REQUIRED: The asset that is Sec. 1250 property.
DISCUSSION: Section 1250 property is depreciable real property that is not Sec. 1245 property. Low-income housing is not Sec. 1245 property regardless of when placed in service; therefore, it is Sec. 1250 property.
Answer (B) is incorrect. Commercial (nonresidential) buildings placed in service from 1981 through 1986 are Sec. 1245 property unless the straight-line method of depreciation is elected. Answer (C) is incorrect. Elevators were specifically listed in Sec. 1245(a)(3)(C) as Sec. 1245 property prior to 1987. Answer (D) is incorrect. A facility used for the bulk storage of fungible commodities is specifically listed in Sec. 1245(a)(3)(B).

12.3.4. General Company purchased a building on January 2, 1979, for $1.2 million, electing to depreciate it over an estimated useful life of 40 years. On December 31, 2017, General sold the building for $1.3 million. At the time the building was sold, it had an adjusted basis of $0. General Company must report a gain of

A. $1,300,000 ordinary income.

B. $1,300,000 Sec. 1231 income.

C. $100,000 Sec. 1231 income and $1,200,000 ordinary income.

D. $1,060,000 Sec. 1231 income and $240,000 ordinary income.

Answer (D) is correct. *(CMA, adapted)*
REQUIRED: The amount and character of income to be recognized by a corporation in 2017.
DISCUSSION: This transaction resulted in a realized gain of $1,300,000 after reducing the acquisition cost for the $1,200,000 of depreciation claimed. Depreciable real property acquired prior to 1981 is Sec. 1250 property. Under Sec. 1250, realized gain is recognized as ordinary income to the extent the depreciation taken exceeds depreciation under the straight-line method. However, the building has been fully straight-line depreciated over the 40 year useful life General has used the building. Section 291(a) requires that a corporation treat 20% of the excess from Sec. 1245 gain (i.e., $1,200,000) over regular Sec. 1250 gain ($0) as if it were Sec. 1250 gain. The remainder of General's realized gain is recognized as Sec. 1231 gain.

Sales proceeds	$1,300,000
Less: adjusted basis	(0)
Realized and recognized gain	$1,300,000

Sec. 1250 gain:		
Sec. 291 gain:		
$1,200,000 × 20%	=	240,000

Sec. 1231 gain:		
$1,300,000 − $240,000	=	$1,060,000

Answer (A) is incorrect. The entire gain is not ordinary income. Answer (B) is incorrect. The entire gain is not Sec. 1231 income. Answer (C) is incorrect. The ordinary income recaptured is only $240,000. The $1,300,000 realized gain must be reduced by the Sec. 1250 gain/Sec. 291 gain to find the Sec. 1231 gain.

12.3.5. Mario sold an office building on July 1, 2017, for $180,000. He had purchased the building in 1980 for $150,000 and had properly deducted $108,000 of depreciation, which included $15,500 in additional depreciation. What amount may Mario report as Sec. 1231 gain?

A. $15,500

B. $42,000

C. $122,500

D. $138,000

Answer (C) is correct. *(SEE, adapted)*
REQUIRED: The amount of Sec. 1231 gain recognized on the sale of a Sec. 1250 asset.
DISCUSSION: The amount of Sec. 1250 recapture is the lesser of the gain realized or the amount of additional depreciation (accelerated depreciation claimed in excess of straight-line depreciation). The amount of additional depreciation is $15,500 as given in the question. The property's adjusted basis is $42,000 ($150,000 − $108,000). The realized gain on the transaction is $138,000 ($180,000 selling price − $42,000 basis). The amount of Sec. 1231 gain is limited to $122,500 because the $15,500 additional depreciation must be recaptured as ordinary income.
Answer (A) is incorrect. Additional depreciation is $15,500 and is recaptured as ordinary income by Sec. 1250. Answer (B) is incorrect. The difference between the purchase price and the depreciation taken is $42,000. Answer (D) is incorrect. The realized gain is $138,000, which contains both Sec. 1231 and Sec. 1250 gains.

12.3.6. In 1985, TapKeg Corporation purchased an apartment building for a total purchase price of $3,500,000. The property was placed in service on July 1, 1985. TapKeg depreciated the building using the ACRS rules and the building was fully depreciated before selling the building. TapKeg sold the building on December 31, 2017, for $4,000,000. Gain on the sale will be reported as a

A. Section 1231 gain of $4,000,000.

B. Section 1245 gain of $3,500,000 and Sec. 1231 gain of $500,000.

C. Section 1250 gain of $700,000 and Sec. 1231 gain of $3,300,000.

D. Section 1245 gain of $700,000 and Sec. 1231 gain of $3,300,000.

Answer (C) is correct. *(Publisher, adapted)*
REQUIRED: The amount and character of gain recognized on the sale of the apartment building.
DISCUSSION: The sale of the apartment building resulted in a realized gain of $4,000,000. The building is Sec. 1250 residential real property since it is excluded from Sec. 1245 property by Sec. 1245(a)(3) as in effect prior to the 1986 Tax Act. The realized gain is recognized as ordinary income to the extent the depreciation taken exceeded depreciation under the straight-line method. Since the building was fully depreciated, there is no excess depreciation. In addition, Sec. 291(a) requires a corporation to treat as additional Sec. 1250 gain 20% of the excess of Sec. 1245 gain (as if the property had been Sec. 1245 property) over the regular Sec. 1250 gain. The remaining portion of the realized gain is recognized as Sec. 1231 gain.

Sales proceeds	$4,000,000
Less: adjusted basis ($3,500,000 – $3,500,000)	0
Realized and recognized gain	$4,000,000

Sec. 1250 gain:			
$3,500,000 – $3,500,000	=	$	0
Sec. 291 gain:			
$3,500,000 × 20%	=		700,000
Total Sec. 1250 gain:		$	700,000

Sec. 1231 gain:			
$4,000,000 – $700,000	=		$3,300,000

Answer (A) is incorrect. There is some ordinary income gain. Answer (B) is incorrect. The building is not Sec. 1245 property under the ACRS rules. Answer (D) is incorrect. The building is not Sec. 1245 property under ACRS rules.

12.3.7. A.K. Rabbits bought an office building 13 years ago for $2 million. Rabbits spent an additional $1 million to renovate the plumbing and heating systems in the building before renting it. Rabbits chose to use straight-line depreciation and claimed a total of $896,875 in depreciation. In the current year, the office building had a fair market value of $3.3 million. Rabbits exchanged the office building for an apartment house owned by Fox Corporation with a fair market value of $2.8 million and basis to Fox of $2 million. In the exchange, Fox assumed a $500,000 liability on the office building. Gain or loss on the exchange will be reported

A. $500,000 Sec. 1231 gain.

B. $500,000 Sec. 1250 gain.

C. $300,000 Sec. 1231 gain; $896,875 Sec. 1245 gain.

D. $1,196,875 Sec. 1231 gain.

Answer (A) is correct. *(Publisher, adapted)*
REQUIRED: The amount and character of gain or loss recognized on the exchange of the office building.
DISCUSSION: The realized gain on this exchange was $1,196,875. Since both properties are real property held for use in a trade or business or for investment, the transaction is a like-kind exchange under Sec. 1031. Gain is recognized to the extent of boot received (relief from a liability) of $500,000.
Since the office building was depreciated on a straight-line basis, it is considered Sec. 1250 property. Section 1250 recapture is limited to depreciation taken in excess of straight-line depreciation. There is no excess depreciation, so Sec. 1250 does not apply and all the recognized gain is Sec. 1231 gain.

Original cost of office building	$2,000,000
Renovation	1,000,000
Depreciation	(896,875)
Adjusted basis of office building	$2,103,125

FMV of property received	$2,800,000
Liability assumed by Fox	500,000
Amount realized	$3,300,000
Adjusted basis of office building	(2,103,125)
Realized gain	$1,196,875
Recognized as Sec. 1231 gain	$ 500,000

Answer (B) is incorrect. There is not a Sec. 1250 gain resulting from this exchange. Answer (C) is incorrect. There is not a Sec. 1245 gain resulting from this exchange. Answer (D) is incorrect. The total realized gain on the exchange is $1,196,875.

12.3.8. Karey bought a small shopping mall on July 15, Year 1, for a total price of $2,340,000. Karey used straight-line depreciation and deducted $565,000 before the mall was sold for $2.5 million on December 31, Year 10. The gain on the sale should be reported as

    A. $565,000 ordinary income and $160,000 Sec. 1231 gain.

    B. $160,000 capital gain.

    C. $725,000 Sec. 1231 gain.

    D. $725,000 ordinary income.

Answer (C) is correct. *(Publisher, adapted)*
    REQUIRED: The amount and character of gain recognized on the sale of the shopping mall.
    DISCUSSION: All real property purchased after 1986 is classified as Sec. 1250 property. Under Sec. 1250, only depreciation in excess of straight-line is recaptured. Since real property placed in service after 1986 must be depreciated under the straight-line method according to the MACRS rules, no Sec. 1250 recapture is required for post-1986 real property held for more than 1 year.

Original cost	$2,340,000
Less: depreciation	(565,000)
Adjusted basis	$1,775,000
Sales proceeds	$2,500,000
Less: adjusted basis	(1,775,000)
Realized and recognized gain	$ 725,000

    Answer (A) is incorrect. There is no Sec. 1250 gain since the straight-line depreciation method was used. Answer (B) is incorrect. The adjusted basis of the building must be reduced by the depreciation claimed to determine the recognized gain. Answer (D) is incorrect. Ordinary income is not $725,000.

12.3.9. If depreciable real property is held for 1 year or less, any depreciation that has been deducted is treated as additional depreciation for purposes of figuring the part of any gain to be reported as ordinary income.

    A. True.

    B. False.

Answer (A) is correct. *(SEE, adapted)*
    DISCUSSION: In addition to accelerated depreciation in excess of straight-line, all depreciation is subject to recapture if the Sec. 1250 property has not been held more than 1 year [Sec. 1250(b)(1)].

12.3.10. In computing Sec. 1250 recapture on qualified low-income housing for periods after 1975, the applicable percentage is 100%, minus 1% for each full month the property was held in excess of 100 full months.

    A. True.

    B. False.

Answer (A) is correct. *(SEE, adapted)*
    DISCUSSION: Generally, Sec. 1250 requires that excess depreciation be recaptured in full for property acquired after 1975. However, after 1986, real property is depreciated using the straight-line method, thereby eliminating Sec. 1250 recapture.

12.4 Sale of a Business

12.4.1. Sonny Shapiro was the sole proprietor of a high-volume drug store that he owned for 15 years before he sold it to Dale Drug Stores, Inc., in the current year. Besides the $900,000 selling price for the store's tangible assets and goodwill, Sonny received a lump sum of $30,000 in the current year for his agreement not to operate a competing enterprise within 10 miles of the store's location for a period of 6 years. The $30,000 will be taxed to Sonny as

    A. $30,000 ordinary income in the current year.

    B. $30,000 short-term capital gain in the current year.

    C. $30,000 long-term capital gain in the current year.

    D. Ordinary income of $5,000 a year for 6 years.

Answer (A) is correct. *(CPA, adapted)*
    REQUIRED: The proper treatment of a payment received for an agreement not to compete.
    DISCUSSION: The sale of a business often includes a covenant not to compete. Cases and rulings have held that income from the covenant is ordinary income because it is similar to payments for services; it is simply a payment for not performing services.
    Answer (B) is incorrect. The covenant is not a capital asset. Answer (C) is incorrect. The $30,000 will not be taxed to Sonny as a long-term capital gain in the current year, as the covenant is not a capital asset. Answer (D) is incorrect. The income must all be recognized in the year received.

Questions 12.4.2 through 12.4.4 are based on the following information. Mr. Rabbit sold his retail business consisting of the following assets, all held long-term except for the noncompetition agreement:

1. Goodwill
2. Noncompetition agreement that can be severed from goodwill
3. Exclusive franchise
4. Accounting records

5. Trade accounts receivable
6. Business realty
7. Furniture and equipment
8. Inventory

12.4.2. Which of Rabbit's assets are capital assets?

A. 1, 5, and 8.
B. 1 and 4.
C. 3, 6, and 7.
D. 2 and 4.

Answer (B) is correct. *(SEE, adapted)*
REQUIRED: The items listed that are capital assets.
DISCUSSION: Section 1221 defines capital assets as property held by the taxpayer and not excluded by its subsections. Goodwill generated internally by Mr. Rabbit through his business operations and accounting records are capital assets because they are not inventory, depreciable, or otherwise excluded. Goodwill that is acquired in an acquisition (e.g., a customer list) and an exclusive franchise are generally considered purchased intangibles under Sec. 197 and are not capital assets since they are amortizable over 15 years.
Answer (A) is incorrect. Trade accounts receivable and inventory are excluded from being capital assets by Sec. 1221. Answer (C) is incorrect. An exclusive franchise, business realty, and furniture and equipment are excluded from being capital assets by Sec. 1221. Answer (D) is incorrect. A noncompetition agreement represents ordinary income under cases and rulings. Accounting records are excluded from being capital assets by Sec. 1221.

12.4.3. Which are real or depreciable property used in a trade or business?

A. 2, 3, and 4.
B. 2 and 6.
C. 6 and 7.
D. 6, 7, and 8.

Answer (C) is correct. *(SEE, adapted)*
REQUIRED: The items listed that are real or depreciable property used in a trade or business.
DISCUSSION: Business realty is real property used in a trade or business. Furniture and equipment are depreciated under Sec. 167 before 1981 and under Sec. 168 after 1980.
Goodwill and accounting records generally do not have a fixed or determinable life so they are not depreciable. Accounts receivable and inventory are not used in a trade or business (accounts receivable are collected and inventory is sold) so they are not depreciable. Goodwill acquired in an acquisition (e.g., a customer list) and an exclusive franchise are generally considered purchased intangibles under Sec. 197 and are amortizable over 15 years rather than being depreciated. A noncompetition agreement is generally considered amortizable rather than depreciable.
Answer (A) is incorrect. A noncompetition agreement, an exclusive franchise, and accounting records are not considered real or depreciable property used in a trade or business. Answer (B) is incorrect. A noncompetition agreement is not considered real or depreciable property used in a trade or business. Answer (D) is incorrect. Inventory is not considered real or depreciable property used in a trade or business.

12.4.4. Which are other properties generating ordinary income?

A. 1, 2, and 8.

B. 3, 6, and 7.

C. 1, 5, and 8.

D. 2, 5, and 8.

Answer (D) is correct. *(SEE, adapted)*
REQUIRED: The items listed that generate ordinary income.
DISCUSSION: The noncompetition agreement generates ordinary income because the seller receives payment for not performing services. Courts have held such payments similar to income from services. Accounts receivable and inventory are not capital assets under Sec. 1221 nor are they Sec. 1231 property; therefore, they produce ordinary income.

Internally generated goodwill and accounting records are capital assets. Business realty and furniture and equipment are Sec. 1231 property but can produce ordinary income under Secs. 291, 1245, or 1250 when sold or exchanged. Similarly, purchased goodwill and exclusive franchises can produce ordinary income under Sec. 1245 when they have been amortized and then are sold or exchanged.

Answer (A) is incorrect. Goodwill is a capital asset.
Answer (B) is incorrect. An exclusive franchise, business realty, and furniture and equipment do not generate ordinary income.
Answer (C) is incorrect. Goodwill does not generate ordinary income.

12.4.5. Mr. Mac, a sole proprietor on the accrual basis, prepared the following balance sheet for his business on December 15, 2017:

Assets		
Accounts receivable		$ 8,000
Inventory		14,000
Equipment (purchased in 2005)	$40,000	
Accumulated depreciation	(30,000)	10,000
Goodwill (tax basis)		15,000
		$47,000

Capital	
Mac, Capital	$47,000

The goodwill was acquired in 1992 and has not been amortized. On December 15, 2017, Mr. Mac sold this business. The allocation of the selling price of $63,000 was stipulated in the sales agreement as follows:

Accounts receivable	$ 8,000
Inventory	17,000
Equipment	16,000
Goodwill	22,000
Total selling price	$63,000

How should this sale be reported in Mr. Mac's 2017 individual tax return?

A. Zero ordinary income and $16,000 long-term capital gain.

B. $3,000 ordinary income and $13,000 long-term capital gain.

C. $9,000 ordinary income and $7,000 long-term capital gain.

D. $16,000 ordinary income and zero long-term capital gain.

Answer (C) is correct. *(CPA, adapted)*
REQUIRED: The amount and character of gain recognized on the sale of the business.
DISCUSSION: The sale of the business resulted in a realized gain of $16,000. The accounts receivable had a tax basis of $8,000 because they were already recognized as income under the accrual method of accounting. The $3,000 gain on inventory is ordinary income because inventory is not a capital asset under Sec. 1221 nor is it Sec. 1231 property. The realized gain of $6,000 on the equipment must be recognized as ordinary income under the recapture provisions of Sec. 1245 because $30,000 in depreciation had previously been taken on the equipment. Goodwill acquired before 1995 is a capital asset, so the $7,000 realized gain is a capital gain since the asset is not a Sec. 197 intangible.

Asset	Sales Price	Basis	Gain
Accounts receivable	$ 8,000	$ 8,000	$ 0
Inventory	17,000	14,000	3,000
Equipment	16,000	10,000	6,000
Goodwill	22,000	15,000	7,000
Realized gain			$16,000
Ordinary income: Inventory			$ 3,000
Sec. 1245			6,000
Total			$ 9,000
Capital gain: Goodwill			$ 7,000

Answer (A) is incorrect. There is ordinary income from this sale. Answer (B) is incorrect. Inventory and Sec. 1245 gain produce ordinary income, and goodwill produces a long-term capital gain. Answer (D) is incorrect. There is a long-term capital gain from this sale.

12.4.6. Needle Taylor, a sole proprietor, sold his small clothing business for $50,000 in the current year. The sales agreement does not allocate the sales price among the assets, which include accounts receivable, inventory, equipment, and goodwill. How should the $50,000 price be allocated among the assets?

A. Based on the relative adjusted bases of the assets.

B. Based on the relative fair market values of the assets except for goodwill.

C. In any manner so long as it is consistent between the purchaser and seller.

D. In accordance with an IRS determination since the buyer and seller did not agree.

Answer (B) is correct. *(Publisher, adapted)*
REQUIRED: The proper method for allocating the purchase price among assets when the parties did not agree.
DISCUSSION: When a sole proprietorship is sold (or purchased), the price must be allocated among the assets because the transaction is essentially a sale of each individual asset. The difference between the purchase price and the sum of the fair market values of the tangible and identifiable intangible assets is allocated to goodwill (Sec. 1060). The rest of the allocation is based on the relative fair market values of the assets. Section 1060(a) provides that, if a transferee and a transferor agree in writing as to the allocation of any consideration, or as to the fair market values of any of the assets, in an applicable asset transfer [defined under Sec. 1060(c)], then such agreement is binding on both the transferor or transferee unless the IRS determines that the allocation is not appropriate.
Answer (A) is incorrect. When the parties have not agreed, the allocation is based on the relative fair market values, not the adjusted bases of the assets. Answer (C) is incorrect. Agreements between the purchaser and seller as to the allocation of consideration or as to fair market values are permitted unless the IRS determines that the allocation or valuation is not appropriate. Answer (D) is incorrect. The IRS has no authority to make a determination other than one based on the relative fair market values of the assets.

12.5 Sales to Related Parties

12.5.1. Christina and Anne are equal partners in the capital and profits of Agee & Nolan but are otherwise unrelated. The following information pertains to 300 shares of Mast Corporation stock purchased by Anne 12 years ago and sold this year to Agee & Nolan.

Basis (cost)	$9,000
Sales price (equal to fair market value)	$4,000

The amount of long-term capital loss that Anne recognized in the current year on the sale of this stock was

A. $5,000

B. $3,000

C. $2,500

D. $0

Answer (A) is correct. *(CPA, adapted)*
REQUIRED: The long-term capital loss that Anne recognized on the sale of stock to a partnership that she equally shared in the capital and profits with another partner.
DISCUSSION: Under Sec. 1001, Anne would realize and recognize a $5,000 long-term capital loss on the sale of stock to the partnership, since she held the stock for more than a year. If Anne had owned greater than a 50% interest in the capital or profits of Agee & Nolan, Anne would not be able to report her loss on the sale [Sec. 707(b)(1)(A)].
Answer (B) is incorrect. The correct amount of capital loss Anne can recognize is not $3,000. Answer (C) is incorrect. The correct amount of capital loss Anne can recognize is not $2,500. Answer (D) is incorrect. Anne can recognize a loss.

12.5.2. Doug Outt, a former baseball coach, decided to open a sporting goods store. He formed a corporation and sold a building for $80,000 to the corporation. The building originally cost Doug $75,000, and $25,000 of straight-line depreciation had been claimed prior to the sale during a period when Doug leased it to a tavern. The corporation will use the building as the location of the sporting goods store. What is Doug's gain on the sale of the building?

A. $0

B. $5,000 capital gain.

C. $30,000 ordinary income.

D. $25,000 ordinary income and $5,000 capital gain.

Answer (C) is correct. *(Publisher, adapted)*
REQUIRED: The gain recognized on the sale of depreciated property by a shareholder to a 100%-owned corporation.
DISCUSSION: Doug realized a gain of $30,000 ($80,000 realized – $50,000 adjusted basis). There is no depreciation recapture since the straight-line method was used (Sec. 1250). The property is Sec. 1231 property, and the gain would normally be long-term capital gain if Doug had no other Sec. 1231 transactions. However, Sec. 1239(a) provides that any gain recognized on the sale of property between related persons is ordinary income if the property is depreciable in the hands of the transferee. Related persons include a taxpayer and a more than 50%-owned entity. Doug's entire $30,000 gain is therefore ordinary income.
Answer (A) is incorrect. Doug has a gain on the sale of the building. Answer (B) is incorrect. The basis of the building must be reduced by the depreciation claimed. Answer (D) is incorrect. There is no capital gain resulting from the sale of the building.

12.5.3. Justin Justice owns 55% of the outstanding stock of Rego Corporation. During the current year, Rego sold a trailer to Justin for $10,000. The trailer had an adjusted tax basis of $12,000 and had been owned by Rego for 3 years. In its current year income tax return, what is the allowable loss that Rego can claim on the sale of this trailer?

A. $0

B. $2,000 ordinary loss.

C. $2,000 Sec. 1231 loss.

D. $2,000 Sec. 1245 loss.

Answer (A) is correct. *(CPA, adapted)*
REQUIRED: The amount and character of loss on the sale of property by a corporation to a 55% shareholder.
DISCUSSION: Rego realized a $2,000 loss ($10,000 realized – $12,000 adjusted basis). Section 267(a) provides that a loss from the sale or exchange of property between related parties is not deductible. Related parties include a corporation and an individual who owns more than 50% of the stock. Since Justin owns more than 50% of the Rego stock, the loss is not deductible.
Answer (B) is incorrect. The allowable loss is not an ordinary loss. Answer (C) is incorrect. The allowable loss is not a Sec. 1231 loss. Answer (D) is incorrect. The allowable loss is not a Sec. 1245 loss.

12.5.4. Senior sold Junior (his son) a rental residence with an adjusted basis of $60,000 for $40,000. Junior rented the house to an unrelated tenant for 2 years, properly claiming $8,000 in depreciation on the house. He then sold it for $42,000. As a result of the sale, Junior will

A. Report no gain or loss.

B. Report a $10,000 loss.

C. Report a $10,000 gain.

D. Have his father report a $10,000 loss.

Answer (A) is correct. *(J.M. Ruble)*
REQUIRED: The gain or loss upon the sale of property acquired from a related party.
DISCUSSION: Under Sec. 267(a), Senior's $20,000 loss incurred on the sale or exchange of property to Junior is not deductible. Section 267(d) provides that, if a loss has previously been disallowed because of the related party rules, any subsequent gain on the sale of such property is recognized only to the extent that the gain exceeds the previously disallowed loss. Thus, the $10,000 gain realized by Junior on the sale of the house is not recognized because it does not exceed the loss disallowed to Senior.

Sales proceeds		$42,000
Less: adjusted basis		
Cost	$40,000	
Depreciation	(8,000)	(32,000)
Realized gain		$10,000

Answer (B) is incorrect. Junior will not report a $10,000 loss. Answer (C) is incorrect. Junior will not report a $10,000 gain. Answer (D) is incorrect. Junior's father will not report a $10,000 loss.

12.5.5. If a husband sells depreciable property to a trust in which his wife is the sole beneficiary, the gain on the sale will be treated as ordinary income.

A. True.

B. False.

Answer (A) is correct. *(SEE, adapted)*
DISCUSSION: Under Sec. 1239, gain recognized on a sale of property between related persons is ordinary income if the property is depreciable in the hands of the transferee. Related persons include a taxpayer and a trust in which the taxpayer or spouse is the sole beneficiary.

12.6 Effect on Taxable Income

12.6.1. During the current year, a corporation retired obsolete equipment purchased 10 years ago having an adjusted basis of $30,000 and sold it as scrap for $1,000. The corporation also had $50,000 taxable income from operations. The taxable income of the corporation was

A. $21,000

B. $47,000 with a capital loss carryover of $26,000.

C. $50,000 with a Sec. 1231 loss carryover of $29,000.

D. $50,000 with a capital loss carryover of $29,000.

Answer (A) is correct. *(CPA, adapted)*
REQUIRED: The taxable income of the corporation after retiring obsolete equipment.
DISCUSSION: The corporation realized a loss of $29,000 ($1,000 realized – $30,000 adjusted basis) on the sale of the retired equipment for scrap. This is a Sec. 1231 loss. Since there are no other Sec. 1231 gains or losses to net, it is treated as an ordinary loss. Taxable income is

Taxable income from operations	$50,000
Less: loss on equipment	(29,000)
Taxable income	$21,000

Answer (B) is incorrect. The loss is not limited to $3,000. Answer (C) is incorrect. The Sec. 1231 loss is deductible in the current year as an ordinary loss. Answer (D) is incorrect. The loss is not a capital loss.

12.6.2. Ben Green operates a parking lot that yielded net income of $13,000 during the current year. The only other transactions that Mr. Green had during the year were a gain of $16,000 on the sale of some Westinghouse Corporation stock that he bought 2 years ago, a loss of $10,000 on the sale of 1 acre of the land used in his parking lot business, and a gain of $4,000 on the sale of 1/2 acre of the land used in his parking lot business. All of the land used in his parking lot operations was purchased 7 years ago. Mr. Green's net capital gain from sale or exchange of capital assets for the current year is

A. $20,000

B. $16,000

C. $10,000

D. $0

Answer (B) is correct. *(CPA, adapted)*

REQUIRED: The net capital gain from the sale of capital assets.

DISCUSSION: Section 1222(11) defines "net capital gain" as the excess of the net long-term capital gain for the taxable year over the net short-term capital loss for the year. Mr. Green had two Sec. 1231 transactions: the $10,000 loss and the $4,000 gain. Real property (land) used in a trade or business is a Sec. 1231 asset, and land is neither Sec. 1245 nor Sec. 1250 property. These result in a net Sec. 1231 loss of $6,000, so both are treated as ordinary gains and losses. The sale of the Westinghouse stock resulted in a $16,000 long-term capital gain. Green's net capital gain is $16,000.

Answer (A) is incorrect. The sale of the land used in a business results in a net $6,000 Sec. 1231 loss. This amount is not subtracted from the net capital gain. Answer (C) is incorrect. Long-term capital gains are no longer eligible for a special 60% capital gains deduction. Answer (D) is incorrect. There is net capital gain.

12.6.3. Steve Bullman sold his business in the current year for $120,000. The sales contract allocated $40,000 to inventory and $80,000 to real property. The adjusted basis of the inventory was $38,000. The real property, held more than 1 year, had a cost of $40,000 and depreciation claimed on a straight-line basis was $20,000. In the current year, Steve received a down payment of $60,000, of which $40,000 was payment for the inventory. Steve had no other Sec. 1231 transactions. What is the amount and nature of the gain that Steve should report using the installment method?

	Ordinary Income	Capital Gain
A.	$2,000	$15,000
B.	$2,000	$40,000
C.	$2,000	$60,000
D.	$40,000	$80,000

Answer (A) is correct. *(SEE, adapted)*

REQUIRED: The amount and nature of the gain under the installment method.

DISCUSSION: The sale of the business is essentially a sale of each of the separate assets. The inventory was sold at a gain of $2,000, which is ordinary income because inventory is neither a capital asset nor Sec. 1231 property.

The real property was sold at a gain of $60,000. Since this is a Sec. 1231 gain and Steve has no other Sec. 1231 transactions, the entire amount will be considered long-term capital gain. Steve's gross profit percentage on the real property is 75% ($60,000 gain ÷ $80,000 contract price). Under the installment sale rules of Sec. 453, Mr. B must recognize $15,000 of the Sec. 1231 (capital) gain (received in the current year $20,000 × 75%).

	Inventory	Real Property
Sales proceeds	$40,000	$80,000
Less: adjusted basis	(38,000)	(20,000)
Realized gain	$ 2,000	$60,000

Answer (B) is incorrect. The correct capital gain is not $40,000. Answer (C) is incorrect. The correct capital gain is not $60,000. Answer (D) is incorrect. The correct ordinary income is not $40,000, and $80,000 is not the correct capital gain.

12.6.4. The results of Digimatic Corporation's first 3 years of operations are presented below:

Year	Results of Operations
Year 1	Sec. 1231 losses of $10,000
Year 2	Sec. 1231 losses of $15,000
Year 3	Sec. 1231 gain of $75,000

Digimatic Corporation's Year 3 Sec. 1231 gain can best be characterized as

A. A net long-term capital gain of $75,000.

B. A net long-term capital gain of $50,000.

C. A net long-term capital gain of $50,000 and ordinary income of $25,000.

D. A net long-term capital gain of $25,000 and ordinary income of $50,000.

Answer (C) is correct. *(CMA, adapted)*

REQUIRED: The characterization of Sec. 1231 gain given prior-year Sec. 1231 transactions.

DISCUSSION: The net Sec. 1231 gain for any taxable year is treated as ordinary income to the extent that the gain does not exceed the nonrecaptured net Sec. 1231 losses. The nonrecaptured net Sec. 1231 loss is the excess of all Sec. 1231 losses for the 5 most recent taxable years over the portion of such losses already recaptured [Sec. 1231(c)].

For Digimatic Corporation in Year 3, the nonrecaptured net Sec. 1231 loss is $25,000 ($10,000 in Year 1 + $15,000 in Year 2). Therefore, the $75,000 net Sec. 1231 gain in Year 3 must be treated as $25,000 of ordinary income (recapture of the previous Sec. 1231 losses of $25,000) and $50,000 of long-term capital gain.

Answer (A) is incorrect. The Year 3 Sec. 1231 gain is not best characterized as a net long-term capital gain of $75,000. Answer (B) is incorrect. The Year 3 Sec. 1231 gain is not best characterized as a net long-term capital gain of $50,000. Answer (D) is incorrect. Digimatic does not have a net long-term capital gain of $25,000 and ordinary income of $50,000.

12.6.5. Hoss Cartwrong has owned a cattle ranch in Florida for 10 years. In the current year, he had the following gains and losses:

Gain when 10 acres of his spread were condemned	$3,000
Loss when breeding cattle were stolen that he had owned for 1 1/2 years	2,000
Gain on the sale of 5 acres used for pasturage	5,000
Loss when the bunkhouse burned	7,000
Insurance reimbursement for the bunkhouse	6,000

Hoss has $30,000 of taxable income from the ranch, not including the above occurrences. What is Hoss's taxable income?

A. $38,000

B. $37,000

C. $35,000

D. $32,000

Answer (C) is correct. *(Publisher, adapted)*

REQUIRED: The taxable income for the current year of a person who has several Sec. 1231 transactions.

DISCUSSION: All the property qualifies as Sec. 1231 property except the stolen cattle because Sec. 1231(b)(3) requires breeding cattle to be held 24 months or more to constitute Sec. 1231 property. Therefore, the theft loss is an ordinary loss outside of Sec. 1231.

The computation under Sec. 1231 must be made in two steps. First, gains and losses from casualties and thefts are netted (the "subnet"). Since casualty and theft losses exceed gains, all are considered ordinary gains and losses and are not included in further Sec. 1231 computations. Second, net gains from the "subnet" and all other Sec. 1231 gains and losses are netted (the "major net"). The subnet is not part of the major net for Hoss since its losses exceeded its gains. Since gains in the major net exceed losses, all these gains and losses are long-term capital gains and losses. Note that the condemnation is in the "major net" because it is similar to an actual sale rather than a casualty.

Subnet	
Loss on bunkhouse	$ (7,000)
Reduced by insurance	6,000
Net loss in subnet	$ (1,000)

Major Net	
Gain on condemnation	$ 3,000
Gain on sale	5,000
Net gain in major net	$ 8,000

Taxable Income	
Tentative taxable income	$30,000
Loss on theft of cattle	(2,000)
Net loss in subnet	(1,000)
Net gain in major net	8,000
Taxable income	$35,000

Answer (A) is incorrect. (1) The insurance proceeds are used to offset the bunkhouse casualty loss and are not a separate gross income item, and (2) the $8,000 gain from the major net is no longer eligible for the special 60% long-term capital gains deduction. Answer (B) is incorrect. The cattle theft loss is deductible. Answer (D) is incorrect. The gain on the land condemnation is included in gross income and not able to be deferred.

☑≡
☐≡ Use **Gleim Test Prep** for interactive study and easy-to-use detailed analytics!
☐≡

STUDY UNIT THIRTEEN
NONTAXABLE PROPERTY TRANSACTIONS

13.1 Introduction

13.1.1. A property transaction (e.g., sale, exchange, casualty) may give rise to a realized gain or loss that is not recognized. Such a transaction is often referred to as a nontaxable or tax-free transaction. Which of the following is a true generalization concerning gain which is not recognized in such a transaction?

A. The gain is a tax deferral included in taxable income in the year subsequent to the transaction.

B. When gain is not recognized, a permanent tax savings is effected.

C. The effect of not recognizing gain is generally to cause a deferral of taxation for an indefinite time until the property is again sold, exchanged, or disposed of.

D. The tax on the deferred gain is computed at the rates in effect when the gain was realized.

13.1.2. The deferral of taxation on unrecognized gains from a nontaxable property transaction

A. Is generally accomplished by adjustments to the basis of the new or acquired property.

B. Becomes a permanent tax savings if the property is held for the statutory period following the transaction.

C. Generally has no effect on the basis of the property.

D. Results in a reduction of the basis of the acquired property by the amount of tax paid in a subsequent transfer of the property.

Answer (C) is correct. *(Publisher, adapted)*
REQUIRED: The true statement concerning deferral of gain in a nontaxable transaction.
DISCUSSION: In most cases, a nontaxable transaction results only in deferral of gain. The basis of the new or acquired property is either the same as the basis in the old property or the cost of the new property less any gain not recognized. With a low basis in the new or acquired property, the deferred gain is generally recognized when the property is again disposed of in a taxable transaction. One major exception is the exclusion of gain on the sale of a personal residence for which there is a permanent tax savings for part or all of the realized gain. A second exception occurs when the property is held until death and a step-up in basis occurs.
Answer (A) is incorrect. The gain is deferred until a taxable transaction occurs. Answer (B) is incorrect. Generally, there is a tax deferral and not a permanent tax savings. Answer (D) is incorrect. Tax on the deferred gain is computed at the rates in effect when the subsequent taxable transaction occurs, not when the deferred gain was realized.

Answer (A) is correct. *(Publisher, adapted)*
REQUIRED: The true statement concerning deferral of taxation on unrecognized gains from nontaxable transactions.
DISCUSSION: A nontaxable property transaction generally results in the deferral of gain rather than a permanent tax savings. This is usually accomplished by transferring the basis of the old property to the new or by determining the basis of the new or acquired property at its cost less the unrecognized gain. One major exception is the exclusion of gain on the sale of a personal residence for which there is a permanent tax savings.
Answer (B) is incorrect. There is no statutory period after which deferred gain becomes a permanent tax savings. Answer (C) is incorrect. The deferred gain is usually reflected in a lower basis for the new or acquired property. Answer (D) is incorrect. When a subsequent taxable transaction takes place and the gain is recognized, the tax does not alter the basis of the property.

13.1.3. On June 1, Year 1, Mr. Smart purchased investment land. On January 31, Year 2, Mr. Smart traded the land plus cash for some other investment land in a nontaxable exchange. On August 15, Year 3, he sold the land received in the nontaxable exchange for a gain. What is the character of Mr. Smart's gain for Year 3?

A. Short-term capital gain.

B. Long-term capital gain.

C. Part short-term capital gain and part long-term capital gain.

D. Ordinary income.

Answer (B) is correct. *(SEE, adapted)*
REQUIRED: The character of gain from the sale of land received in a nontaxable exchange.
DISCUSSION: If property received in an exchange has the same basis in whole or in part as that of the property given (and if the property given is a capital asset or a Sec. 1231 asset), the holding period of the property received includes the period for which the property given was held [Sec. 1223(1)]. Thus, when the property is sold, the holding period includes the holding period of the property exchanged. And, under Sec. 1222, capital assets held more than 1 year are treated as long-term.
Answer (A) is incorrect. Nontaxable transactions normally give rise to a carryover of basis. Answer (C) is incorrect. Gain from sale of property received in a nontaxable transaction is not allocated based on the date of the nontaxable transfer. Answer (D) is incorrect. The asset is a capital asset. Thus, the gain is characterized as a capital gain.

13.1.4. A gain is recognized in a nontaxable exchange to the extent that you receive property or cash.

A. True.

B. False.

Answer (B) is correct. *(Publisher, adapted)*
DISCUSSION: A gain is recognized in a nontaxable exchange (e.g., a Sec. 1031 like-kind exchange) to the extent of the lesser of the taxpayer's realized gain or the amount of boot (i.e., cash plus fair market value of noncash property) that is received. Thus, when the realized gain is less than the boot received, the recognized gain is less than the amount of property or cash that is received.

13.1.5. A loss is recognized in a nontaxable exchange to the extent you receive nonqualifying property or cash.

A. True.

B. False.

Answer (B) is correct. *(SEE, adapted)*
DISCUSSION: A loss is fully recognized on an involuntary conversion (Sec. 1033). A loss cannot be recognized in a like-kind exchange (Sec. 1031) even if nonlike-kind property or cash is received.

13.2 Like-Kind Exchanges

13.2.1. All of the following statements regarding tax-free, like-kind exchanges are true except

A. The property must be held for productive use in a trade or business, or it must be investment property.

B. The property must be tangible property.

C. The exchange of personal property for similar personal property may qualify for a tax-free exchange.

D. If you pay money in addition to giving up like property in a like-kind exchange, you may have a taxable gain or deductible loss.

Answer (D) is correct. *(SEE, adapted)*
REQUIRED: The false statement concerning tax-free like-kind exchanges.
DISCUSSION: Section 1031(a)(1) requires that property qualifying for tax-free treatment must be held for productive use in a trade or business or investment. Section 1031(a)(2) exempts intangible property such as stocks, bonds, and partnership interests from tax-free exchange treatment. Section 1031(a) requires that property exchanged tax-free must be of like kind. Regulation 1.1031(a)-1(b) states that "like kind" refers to the nature or character of the property, i.e., a class of property such as real or personal property. Hence, personal property exchanged for similar personal property would qualify for tax-free treatment.
Although Sec. 1031(b) requires that gain be recognized to the extent of boot received, there is no requirement that gain or loss be recognized to the extent of boot given. Thus, the statement "If you pay money in addition to giving up like property in a like-kind exchange, you may have a taxable gain or deductible loss" is false.
Answer (A) is incorrect. Regarding tax-free, like-kind exchanges, the property must be held for productive use in a trade or business, or it must be investment property. Answer (B) is incorrect. Regarding tax-free, like-kind exchanges, the property must be tangible property. Answer (C) is incorrect. The exchange of personal property for similar personal property may qualify for a tax-free exchange.

13.2.2. In a like-kind exchange of an investment asset for a similar asset that will also be held as an investment, no taxable gain or loss will be recognized on the transaction if both assets consist of

A. Convertible debentures.

B. Convertible preferred stock.

C. Partnership interests.

D. Rental real estate located in different states.

Answer (D) is correct. *(CPA, adapted)*
REQUIRED: The true use of like-kind exchanges.
DISCUSSION: Section 1031(a) outlines several exceptions to which like-kind exchanges do not apply. These include stocks, evidences of indebtedness, and partnership interests. Regulation 1.1031(a)-1 indicates that the term "like kind" refers to the nature or character of property, i.e., a class of property, such as real or personal property. Therefore, an exchange of rental real estate located in two different states qualifies as a like-kind exchange.
Answer (A) is incorrect. If both assets consist of convertible debentures, it is an exception to tax-free, like-kind exchanges. Answer (B) is incorrect. If both assets consist of convertible preferred stock, it is an exception to tax-free, like-kind exchanges. Answer (C) is incorrect. If both assets consist of partnership interests, it is an exception to tax-free, like-kind exchanges.

13.2.3. For purposes of determining like-kind property for nontaxable exchanges, which of the following exchanges of property held for business or investment purposes does not involve like-kind property?

A. Real estate for real estate.

B. Personal computer for a printer.

C. Real estate for personal property.

D. Personal property for personal property.

Answer (C) is correct. *(SEE, adapted)*
REQUIRED: The exchange of property that does not qualify as a like-kind exchange.
DISCUSSION: The term "like kind" refers to the nature or character of the property, i.e., a class of property such as real or personal property [Reg. 1.1031(a)-1]. An exchange of real estate for real estate qualifies as a like-kind exchange even if the properties are as different as a rental office building and a parking lot. An exchange of personal property for personal property also qualifies as a like-kind exchange. However, an exchange of real estate for personal property does not qualify as a like-kind exchange.
Answer (A) is incorrect. Real estate for real estate is an exchange of property within the same class and qualifies for like-kind treatment when held for business or investment purposes. Answer (B) is incorrect. A personal computer for a printer is an exchange of property within the same class and qualifies for like-kind treatment when held for business or investment purposes. Answer (D) is incorrect. Personal property for personal property is an exchange of property within the same class and qualifies for like-kind treatment when held for business or investment purposes.

13.2.4. Assuming all items are held for use in a business or for investment, which of the following does not qualify as a nontaxable like-kind exchange?

A. The trade of an apartment house for a store building that is subsequently rented out.

B. The exchange of a vacant city lot for unimproved farm land.

C. The exchange of real estate you own for a real estate lease that runs 30 years or more.

D. The exchange of stock of one corporation held for investment for stock of another corporation to be held for investment.

Answer (D) is correct. *(SEE, adapted)*
REQUIRED: The exchange of property that does not qualify for like-kind treatment.
DISCUSSION: Section 1031(a) specifically excludes stocks (and other securities and debt instruments) from qualifying for like-kind exchange treatment. Therefore, even though the exchange of stock is for property within the same class, such an exchange does not qualify for like-kind treatment.
Answer (A) is incorrect. An apartment house and a store building are both real property and qualify as like-kind property even though the buildings are used for different purposes. Answer (B) is incorrect. A vacant city lot and unimproved farm land are both real property, even if one of the properties was improved. Answer (C) is incorrect. A real estate lease that runs 30 years is treated as real property, and the exchange of it for other real estate qualifies under Sec. 1031 as long as the parties to the exchange are not dealers in real estate.

13.2.5. Which of the following statements with respect to the exchange of like-kind property is true?

A. If there is an exchange of like-kind property in which you also receive cash and the exchange results in a loss to you, you are allowed to deduct the loss to the extent of cash received.

B. If there is an exchange of like-kind property in which you also give cash and the exchange results in a loss to you, you cannot deduct the loss.

C. If there is an exchange of like-kind property in which you also receive cash and the exchange results in a gain to you, you do not report the gain.

D. If there is an exchange of like-kind property in which you also give cash and the exchange results in a gain to you, you must report the gain to the extent of the cash given.

Answer (B) is correct. *(SEE, adapted)*
REQUIRED: The true statement with respect to a like-kind exchange.
DISCUSSION: Loss is not recognized on a like-kind exchange, even when cash is given in addition to the property.
Answer (A) is incorrect. Loss is not recognized on a like-kind exchange. Answer (C) is incorrect. Gain must be recognized to the extent of cash (boot) received. Answer (D) is incorrect. Gain is recognized when boot is received, not given.

13.2.6. If there is a like-kind exchange of property between related parties, how long do they have to wait to dispose of the property received in order not to recognize any gain on the exchange?

A. No waiting period.

B. 6 months.

C. 1 year.

D. 2 years.

Answer (D) is correct. *(SEE, adapted)*
REQUIRED: The waiting period to dispose of the property in a like-kind exchange between related parties.
DISCUSSION: Section 1031(f) outlines special rules for like-kind exchanges between related parties. In order not to recognize any gain on the initial exchange, the taxpayer cannot dispose of the property within 2 years after the date of the last transfer that was part of the exchange.
Answer (A) is incorrect. There is a waiting period for a related party to dispose of property in order not to recognize gain. Answer (B) is incorrect. Six months is not the correct waiting period according to Sec. 1031(f). Answer (C) is incorrect. One year is not the correct waiting period according to Sec. 1031(f).

13.2.7. Alex is a general partner in the XYZ Partnership. The basis of his partnership interest is $50,000 and the fair market value is $100,000. Bill is a limited partner in the ABC Partnership. The basis of his partnership interest is $30,000, and the fair market value is $100,000. Alex and Bill exchange their partnership interests. No other consideration is involved in the exchange. Which of the following is the best answer?

A. Neither party must recognize gain.

B. Alex must recognize a gain of $50,000. The receipt of a limited partnership interest for a general partnership interest is not a like-kind exchange.

C. Bill must recognize a gain of $70,000. The receipt of a general partnership interest for a limited partnership interest is not a like-kind exchange.

D. Alex must recognize a gain of $50,000, and Bill must recognize a gain of $70,000. The receipt of a limited partnership interest for a general partnership interest is not a like-kind exchange, and the receipt of a general partnership interest for a limited partnership interest is not a like-kind exchange.

Answer (D) is correct. *(Publisher, adapted)*
REQUIRED: The proper treatment of an exchange of partnership interests.
DISCUSSION: Section 1031(a)(2)(D) excludes the transfer of partnership interests in different partnerships from the like-kind exchange provisions. Therefore, each participant in the exchange should recognize gain equal to the excess of the amount realized over his basis. Alex must recognize a gain of $50,000 ($100,000 FMV – $50,000 basis), and Bill must recognize a gain of $70,000 ($100,000 FMV – $30,000 basis). However, tax-free exchanges of interests in the same partnership (e.g., a general interest for a limited interest) are permitted.
Note that it is not possible to exchange a general partnership interest for a general partnership interest under Sec. 1031. Under pre-1984 law, such an exchange fell within Sec. 1031 provided the property held by the partnerships was of like kind. Currently partnership interests will not qualify as tax-free exchanges.
Answer (A) is incorrect. Both Alex and Bill must recognize gains. Answer (B) is incorrect. Bill must also recognize a gain. Answer (C) is incorrect. Alex must also recognize a gain.

13.2.8. Mr. Monty owned an office building that he had purchased at a cost of $600,000 and that now had an adjusted basis of $400,000. In the current year, he traded it to a person who was not related to him for an apartment house having a fair market value of $500,000. The apartment house has 50 units and rents to individuals. The office building has 25 units and rents to Monty's businesses. What is Mr. Monty's recognized gain or loss on this exchange?

A. $100,000 long-term capital gain.

B. $100,000 long-term capital loss.

C. $100,000 ordinary gain.

D. $0

Answer (D) is correct. *(SEE, adapted)*
REQUIRED: The recognized gain on the exchange of an office building for an apartment building.
DISCUSSION: Section 1031(a) provides for the nonrecognition of gain or loss on the exchange of like-kind property held for productive use in a trade or business for investment. "Like kind" refers to the nature or character of property (here, real property) and not to its grade or quality [Reg. 1.1031(a)-1(b)]. The parcels of real property are like-kind property regardless of whether they are improved, unimproved, or used for different purposes.
Mr. Monty has a realized gain of $100,000 ($500,000 amount realized − $400,000 adjusted basis). However, none of this gain is recognized under Sec. 1031.
Answer (A) is incorrect. Section 1031 provides for nonrecognition of the $100,000 gain. Answer (B) is incorrect. Section 1031 allows for nonrecognition of this like-kind exchange. Answer (C) is incorrect. Section 1031 allows for nonrecognition of a realized gain or loss on a like-kind exchange.

13.2.9. Bolo Corporation exchanged a machine used in its business and $26,000 cash for an updated version of the same machine. Its old machine had an adjusted basis of $27,000 and a fair market value of $32,000 at the date of the exchange. The new machine had a fair market value of $58,000. What is Bolo's recognized gain on the exchange and Bolo's tax basis of the new machine?

	Bolo's Recognized Gain	Bolo's Tax Basis of the New Machine
A.	$0	$27,000
B.	$0	$53,000
C.	$5,000	$32,000
D.	$31,000	$58,000

Answer (B) is correct. *(CMA, adapted)*
REQUIRED: The amount of recognized gain or loss and the new basis of property acquired in a like-kind exchange.
DISCUSSION: The transaction would qualify for like-kind treatment under Sec. 1031 since Bolo is exchanging personal property used in its business for personal property to be used in the business. Gain is recognized in a like-kind exchange only to the extent nonlike-kind property is received. The property received was solely of like kind and therefore no gain or loss would be recognized on this transaction. The basis of the new machine is equal to the adjusted basis of the machine surrendered, increased by the amount of cash given [Sec. 1031(d)].

Adjusted basis of old machine	$27,000
Additional cash given	26,000
Basis of new machine	$53,000

Alternatively, the basis of the new machine is the fair market value of the new machine less any unrecognized gain, or $53,000 [$58,000 FMV − ($32,000 FMV − $27,000 basis)].
Answer (A) is incorrect. The tax basis of the new machine includes the additional cash given. Answer (C) is incorrect. The figure of $5,000 is not the correct amount of Bob's recognized gain from the exchange. Answer (D) is incorrect. The figure of $31,000 is not the correct amount of Bob's recognized gain from the exchange.

13.2.10. Python Corporation wants to obtain commercial property located in Mainstreet. Paul, one of its customers, owns the property and uses it in his business. Python offers to give Paul the land it owns next to its business and inventory items worth $70,000 in exchange for his Mainstreet property. Paul's basis in the Mainstreet property is $160,000, and its fair market value is $350,000. The land owned by Python has an adjusted basis to Python of $100,000 and a fair market value of $280,000. Paul will hold the land he receives from Python for investment purposes. What is the amount of Paul's recognized gain if he accepts the offer?

A. $0

B. $70,000

C. $120,000

D. $190,000

Answer (B) is correct. *(SEE, adapted)*
REQUIRED: The recognized gain on the exchange of real property for real property and personal property.
DISCUSSION: The transaction would qualify for like-kind treatment under Sec. 1031 since Paul is exchanging real property used in his trade or business for real property held for investment purposes. Section 1031(b) requires that a gain be recognized in a like-kind exchange only to the extent that nonlike-kind property is received. Since the inventory items received by Paul are personal property, they are considered nonlike-kind (boot) property. Inventory is also excluded from being like-kind property by Sec. 1031(a)(2)(A).
Paul realizes a gain of $190,000 ($280,000 FMV of new property + $70,000 FMV of inventory − $160,000 basis of old property). The gain recognized is the lesser of the boot received ($70,000) or the realized gain ($190,000).
Answer (A) is incorrect. Paul has a gain if he accepts the offer. Answer (C) is incorrect. The amount of $120,000 is the difference between Paul's basis in the Mainstreet property and the FMV of the Python land. Answer (D) is incorrect. The amount of $190,000 is the realized gain.

13.2.11. Mr. A exchanged stock and real estate that he held for investment for other real estate he intends to hold for investment. The stock at the time of the exchange had a fair market value of $30,000 and an adjusted basis to A of $27,000. A's old real estate had a fair market value of $150,000 and an adjusted basis to him of $90,000. The real estate acquired by Mr. A had a fair market value of $180,000 at the time of the exchange. What is the amount of A's recognized gain (or loss) on the exchange?

A. $(30,000)

B. $0

C. $3,000

D. $30,000

Answer (C) is correct. *(SEE, adapted)*
REQUIRED: The recognized gain or loss on an exchange of like-kind property when appreciated boot is given.
DISCUSSION: Neither gain nor loss is recognized on an exchange of like-kind property held for productive use in a trade or business or for investment [Sec. 1031(a)]. In addition, recognition of gain or loss is not triggered when boot is given. However, when boot is given, there is no provision preventing recognition of gain or loss on the boot itself.
The stock Mr. A exchanged with the real estate is boot. Hence, Mr. A realizes and recognizes a $3,000 gain on the stock ($30,000 fair market value – $27,000 adjusted basis). There is no other gain or loss on the exchange because the old and new real estate exchange qualifies under Sec. 1031.
Answer (A) is incorrect. The stock is considered boot that is transferred. Answer (B) is incorrect. There is a gain or loss on the exchange. Answer (D) is incorrect. The amount of $30,000 is the difference between the FMV of the new real estate and the FMV of the old real estate.

13.2.12. Katrina transferred an apartment building held for investment to Mona in exchange for an office building. The apartment building was subject to a liability of $10,000, which Mona assumed for legitimate business purposes. The office building had an adjusted basis of $20,000 and a fair market value of $35,000. The apartment building had a fair market value of $50,000 and an adjusted basis of $30,000. Katrina received $5,000 cash in addition to receiving the office building. What is Katrina's recognized gain on this exchange?

A. $0

B. $5,000

C. $15,000

D. $20,000

Answer (C) is correct. *(SEE, adapted)*
REQUIRED: The recognized gain or loss on an exchange of like-kind property when boot is received and a liability is assumed.
DISCUSSION: Since the transaction qualifies as a like-kind exchange, Sec. 1031(b) requires gain to be recognized only to the extent of boot received. Regulation 1.1031(d)-2 provides that liabilities assumed by the other party are to be treated as money received by the taxpayer. Thus, the total boot received by Katrina is $15,000 ($5,000 cash received + $10,000 of liabilities transferred).
Katrina realizes a gain of $20,000 ($35,000 FMV of property received + $10,000 of liabilities transferred + $5,000 cash – $30,000 adjusted basis of property transferred). The gain recognized is the lesser of total boot received ($15,000) or the realized gain ($20,000).
Answer (A) is incorrect. Katrina has a gain from this exchange. Answer (B) is incorrect. The liability assumed by Mona is also considered boot to Katrina. Answer (D) is incorrect. The amount of $20,000 is the realized, not the recognized, gain.

13.2.13. On October 1 of the current year, Donald Anderson exchanged an apartment building, having an adjusted basis of $375,000 and subject to a mortgage of $100,000, for $25,000 cash and another apartment building with a fair market value of $550,000 and subject to a mortgage of $125,000. The property transfers were made subject to the outstanding mortgages. What amount of gain should Anderson recognize in his tax return for the year?

A. $0

B. $25,000

C. $125,000

D. $175,000

Answer (B) is correct. *(CPA, adapted)*
REQUIRED: The recognized gain in a like-kind exchange of properties subject to mortgages.
DISCUSSION: Anderson's realized gain is computed as follows:

Fair market value of building received		$550,000
Mortgage on old building		100,000
Cash received		25,000
Total amount realized		$675,000
Less: Basis of old building	$375,000	
Mortgage on new building	125,000	(500,000)
Realized gain		$175,000

Under Reg. 1.1031(d)-2, the mortgages are netted so that Anderson is considered to have given $25,000 boot by taking the larger mortgage. The cash boot received by Anderson cannot be netted with the mortgages. Accordingly, Anderson recognizes gain to the extent of the $25,000 cash received.
Answer (A) is incorrect. Anderson must recognize a gain. Answer (C) is incorrect. The mortgage on the old building is not considered as boot. Answer (D) is incorrect. The amount of $175,000 is the realized gain.

13.2.14. Mr. Cline exchanged a 30-ton press used in his business for the assets listed below. The press had an adjusted basis to Cline of $78,000.

One used, 20-ton press for use in his business, fair market value of	$40,000
An automobile for his personal use, fair market value of	9,500
Cash	10,000

What is the amount of Mr. Cline's basis in the 20-ton press he received?

- A. $40,000
- B. $49,500
- C. $58,500
- D. $78,000

Answer (C) is correct. *(SEE, adapted)*
REQUIRED: The basis of property acquired in a like-kind exchange when boot is received.
DISCUSSION: The exchange qualifies for like-kind treatment under Sec. 1031 since personal property used in Mr. Cline's business is exchanged for other personal property to be used in the business. The realized loss is $18,500 [($40,000 press + $10,000 cash + $9,500 fair market value of automobile) – $78,000 basis], which cannot be recognized under Sec. 1031(c). The basis of the property received is $58,500 ($78,000 adjusted basis of the property surrendered – $10,000 cash received – $9,500 fair market value of automobile).
Answer (A) is incorrect. The amount of $40,000 is the FMV of the new press. Answer (B) is incorrect. The amount of $49,500 is the FMV of the press plus the FMV of the automobile. Answer (D) is incorrect. The amount of $78,000 is the adjusted basis of the old press, which should be decreased by boot received, the cash, and the FMV of the automobile that were received.

13.2.15. Ms. M exchanged an auto used in her business that had an adjusted basis to her of $12,000, with an outstanding liability of $2,000, for a new auto to be used in her business, with a fair market value of $11,000 and $1,000 in cash. Ms. M's liability was assumed by the other party. What is Ms. M's basis in the new auto?

- A. $9,000
- B. $10,000
- C. $11,000
- D. $12,000

Answer (C) is correct. *(SEE, adapted)*
REQUIRED: The basis of property acquired in a like-kind exchange when boot is received.
DISCUSSION: Ms. M recognized a $2,000 gain on the exchange. She received $14,000 ($11,000 FMV of auto + $2,000 debt relieved of + $1,000 cash) and she relinquished an auto with a basis of $12,000. Ms. M's realized gain is $2,000 ($14,000 amount realized – $12,000 adjusted basis). The recognized gain is the lesser of the $3,000 boot received or the $2,000 realized gain, or $2,000. Her basis in the new automobile is $11,000 ($12,000 basis of the old car – $3,000 boot received + $2,000 gain recognized).
Answer (A) is incorrect. The amount of $9,000 neglects the recognized gain and only subtracts the boot received from the adjusted basis of the auto. Answer (B) is incorrect. Subtracting the outstanding liability from the auto's adjusted basis is not the accepted method of determining the new basis from an exchange. Answer (D) is incorrect. The amount of $12,000 is the adjusted basis of the old auto.

13.2.16. In April, Year 1, Nathan, a Schedule C business owner, transferred office equipment used in his business to Crown Corporation of which Nathan is a 60% shareholder. The equipment had an adjusted basis of $28,000 to Nathan and a fair market value of $34,000. In exchange for Nathan's equipment, Crown transferred office equipment to Nathan having an adjusted basis to Crown of $37,000 and a fair market value of $32,000. In February, Year 3, Nathan sold the equipment to Carl, an unrelated party, for $33,000. What is the amount of Nathan's recognized gain for Year 3?

- A. $0
- B. $1,000
- C. $2,000
- D. $5,000

Answer (D) is correct. *(SEE, adapted)*
REQUIRED: The amount of gain recognized in a like-kind exchange.
DISCUSSION: This is a like-kind transaction not involving the transfer of boot, and accordingly, the basis of the assets received is the basis of the assets transferred. The fact that the exchange took place between related parties is irrelevant. Therefore, Nathan had a realized and recognized gain of $5,000 in Year 3.

Amount realized	$33,000
Adjusted basis	(28,000)
Gain recognized	$ 5,000

Answer (A) is incorrect. Nathan must recognize a gain in Year 3. Answer (B) is incorrect. The figure of $1,000 is the amount realized over the fair market value of the equipment. Answer (C) is incorrect. The figure of $2,000 is the difference between fair market values.

13.2.17. All of the following statements with respect to the identification requirement of like-kind property for a nonsimultaneous exchange of like-kind properties are true except

A. You can identify more than one replacement property.

B. Money or unlike property received in full payment for property transferred will still qualify as a nontaxable exchange as long as you receive replacement property within 180 days.

C. The property to be received must be identified on or before the day that is 45 days after the date you transfer the property given up in the exchange.

D. You must clearly describe the replacement property in a signed written document and deliver it to the other person involved in the exchange.

Answer (B) is correct. *(SEE, adapted)*
REQUIRED: The false statement regarding like-kind property.
DISCUSSION: For purposes of Sec. 1031, a deferred exchange is defined as an exchange in which, pursuant to an agreement, the taxpayer transfers property held for productive use in a trade or business or for investment (the relinquished property) and subsequently receives property to be held either for productive use in a trade or business or for investment (the replacement property). Failure to satisfy one or more of the requirements for a deferred exchange results in part or all of the replacement property received being treated as property that is not of a like kind to the property relinquished [Reg. 1.1031(k)-1(a)]. In a like-kind exchange, any unlike property or money received results in part or all of the realized gain being recognized. This result does not change merely because a deferred exchange is taking place since money and unlike property are not qualifying replacement properties [Reg. 1.1031(k)-1(f)].
Answer (A) is incorrect. Regulation 1.1031(k)-1(c)(4) permits the identification of multiple replacement properties. Answer (C) is incorrect. One of the requirements of a deferred exchange under Sec. 1031(a)(3)(A) is the property to be received must be identified on or before the day that is 45 days after the date you transfer the property given up in the exchange. Answer (D) is incorrect. Regulation 1.1031(k)-1(c) requires the replacement to be unambiguously described in a written document or agreement, which is delivered to the other party.

13.2.18. Timbertoppers, Inc., is in the forestry business. It wanted to acquire a parcel of property owned by Woodsy, who held the property for investment. Woodsy would not sell but agreed to exchange the property if Timbertoppers could find other suitable property. Timbertoppers could not locate suitable property immediately, so the parties entered into an agreement by which Timbertoppers took title to Woodsy's property (which had a fair market value of $400,000 and a basis of $50,000) on August 1, Year 1, and an escrow arrangement was set up in which Timbertoppers placed certificates of deposit as security until real property could be found to suit Woodsy. If one parcel valued at $300,000 is identified on September 1, Year 1, and transferred to Woodsy on January 10, Year 2, and a second parcel valued at $100,000 is identified on October 1, Year 1, and transferred to Woodsy on December 20, Year 1, what is Woodsy's gain?

A. $0

B. $100,000 in Year 1; $0 in Year 2.

C. $300,000 in Year 1; $50,000 in Year 2.

D. $0 in Year 1; $100,000 in Year 2.

Answer (B) is correct. *(Publisher, adapted)*
REQUIRED: The amount of gain on a nonsimultaneous exchange of like-kind properties.
DISCUSSION: Woodsy will realize a gain of $350,000 ($400,000 realized – $50,000 basis). Provided the escrow is arranged so that the certificates of deposit in escrow are clearly the property of Timbertoppers pending performance and Woodsy has no right in such escrow except upon the failure of Timbertoppers to perform, a nonsimultaneous exchange will also qualify for nonrecognition of gain under the case of *Starker* (602 F.2d 1341, 9th cir., 1979).
However, Sec. 1031(a)(3), enacted following the *Starker* decision, requires, for transfers after July 18, 1984, that the property to be received be identified as such within 45 days after transferring the old property being exchanged and that the new property actually be received within 180 days or by the due date of the taxpayer's tax return if sooner. If these requirements are not met, the property received will be treated as boot. These requirements were met for the parcel received on January 10, Year 2, but not for the parcel received on December 20, Year 1, so Woodsy must recognize $100,000 (the amount of the boot) in Year 1.
Answer (A) is incorrect. Woodsy has a gain. Answer (C) is incorrect. Woodsy does not have a gain in Year 2. Answer (D) is incorrect. Woodsy has a gain in Year 1, but not in Year 2, due to the failure to identify the second parcel in a timely manner, causing it to be boot property.

Questions 13.2.19 and 13.2.20 are based on the following information. Seminole Airways is a small passenger airline operating in Florida. This year, due to heavy losses, it decided to get out of the airline business and into real estate investment. As part of its disposition of assets, Seminole traded a hangar (with a fair market value of $100,000 and a basis of $50,000) and an airplane (with a fair market value of $300,000 and a basis of $100,000) for an apartment building acquired by the seller during the current year with a fair market value of $400,000. The difference between the fair market value and basis of Seminole's assets was entirely due to MACRS depreciation.

13.2.19. What is Seminole's recognized gain on this transaction?

A. $0

B. $200,000 ordinary income.

C. $250,000 ordinary income.

D. $200,000 ordinary income and $50,000 Sec. 1231 gain.

Answer (B) is correct. *(Publisher, adapted)*
REQUIRED: The amount and character of gain recognized on the exchange of real property and personal property solely for real property.
DISCUSSION: Seminole Airways has a realized gain of $250,000 ($400,000 amount realized – $50,000 basis in hangar – $100,000 basis in airplane). The hangar and the apartment building are like-kind properties because they are both real property. No gain is recognized on this part of the exchange. The airplane is not like-kind property with respect to the apartment building. Therefore, gain of $200,000 ($300,000 FMV received – $100,000 basis) is recognized. This gain is ordinary income under Sec. 1245 as MACRS depreciation recapture.
Answer (A) is incorrect. Some ordinary income should be recognized due to depreciation recapture on the airplane. Answer (C) is incorrect. The hangar and the apartment building are a like-kind exchange, so the $50,000 remaining gain is not recognized. Answer (D) is incorrect. The $50,000 remaining gain is not recognized, since the hangar and the apartment building are a like-kind exchange.

13.2.20. If the apartment building had a basis of $300,000 and MACRS depreciation of $100,000, what is the prior owner's gain?

A. $0

B. $50,000 ordinary income and $50,000 Sec. 1231 gain.

C. $100,000 ordinary income.

D. $100,000 Sec. 1231 gain.

Answer (D) is correct. *(Publisher, adapted)*
REQUIRED: The amount and character of gain when real property and personal property are received in exchange for real property.
DISCUSSION: The exchange of the apartment building for the hangar qualifies as a like-kind exchange; however, the receipt of the airplane is boot because it is not like-kind property. Under Sec. 1031(b), gain is recognized to the extent of the fair market value of boot received. The prior owner of the apartment building had a realized gain of $100,000 ($400,000 realized – $300,000 adjusted basis). This entire gain is recognized because boot with a value of $300,000 was received.
The apartment building is Sec. 1250 property because it is real property that was depreciated under the MACRS rules. Under Sec. 1250(a), the amount of recapture is the lesser of gain recognized or the additional depreciation (depreciation subject to recapture). Because the MACRS rules for real property require straight-line depreciation to be used, there is no additional depreciation. The non-Sec. 1250 property that was received will trigger the recognition of the entire $100,000 realized gain. The gain that is recognized is Sec. 1231 gain.
Answer (A) is incorrect. There is gain resulting from this transaction. Answer (B) is incorrect. The sum of these two is Sec. 1231 gain. Answer (C) is incorrect. The amount of $100,000 should be considered something other than ordinary income.

13.2.21. In the current year, Mr. Brown traded an old truck, which had been used in his business, for a new personal automobile. Mr. Brown paid an additional $4,000 for the new automobile. This exchange is a nontaxable exchange.

A. True.

B. False.

Answer (B) is correct. *(SEE, adapted)*
DISCUSSION: The property given and the property received in an exchange must be held for productive use in a trade or business or for investment for the transaction to qualify as a nontaxable, like-kind exchange (Sec. 1031). Since Mr. Brown traded a truck used in his business for a personal automobile, the exchange is not a nontaxable, like-kind exchange.

13.2.22. Mr. O, a real estate broker and dealer in real property, exchanges a 100-acre tract of farm land held for sale (fair market value $100,000, adjusted basis $50,000) for a one-block-square parking lot located in a large metropolitan area (fair market value $200,000). In the transaction, Mr. O assumes a $100,000 mortgage. Mr. O must report a $50,000 gain on the exchange.

A. True.

B. False.

Answer (A) is correct. *(SEE, adapted)*
DISCUSSION: The exchange of property held primarily for sale does not qualify as a nontaxable like-kind exchange because the property is not held for productive use in a trade or business or for investment. Mr. O must recognize the entire gain on the transaction. The amount realized is $100,000 ($200,000 FMV received – $100,000 mortgage assumed). Thus, the gain is $50,000 ($100,000 realized – $50,000 basis).

13.2.23. Mr. Knot wants to get a new truck for his business. His old truck has an adjusted basis of $2,600 and a fair market trade-in value of $3,100. The new truck has a sales price of $8,000. The dealer will take Mr. Knot's truck plus $4,900 cash. Mr. Knot's basis in the new truck would be $7,500. However, he wants a higher basis for depreciation, so he agrees to pay the dealer $8,000 cash for the new truck, and the dealer agrees to pay him $3,100 cash for the old truck. This transaction is treated as a nontaxable exchange, and Mr. Knot's basis in the new truck would still be $7,500, which is the same as if he had traded his old truck.

A. True.

B. False.

Answer (A) is correct. *(SEE, adapted)*
DISCUSSION: The basis of property acquired in a like-kind exchange is equal to the adjusted basis of property surrendered, decreased by any boot received and increased by any gain recognized or boot given [Sec. 1031(d)]. Thus, Mr. Knot's basis in the new truck would be $7,500 ($2,600 basis of old truck + $4,900 of boot given).
However, the taxpayer attempts to increase his depreciable basis to $8,000 by buying the new truck from the dealer for $8,000 in return for the dealer's promise to pay him $3,100 for his old truck. This attempt would fail since Rev. Rul. 61-119 indicates that a nontaxable exchange exists when a taxpayer sells property to a dealer and then purchases like-kind property from the same dealer. Hence, the property's basis shall be determined under the like-kind exchange rules.

13.2.24. No gain or loss is recognized on the exchange of an annuity contract for another annuity contract.

A. True.

B. False.

Answer (A) is correct. *(Publisher, adapted)*
DISCUSSION: Section 1035 allows tax-free exchanges among certain exchanges of life insurance, endowment, and annuity contracts. Under Sec. 1035(a)(3), no gain or loss is recognized on the exchange of an annuity contract for another annuity contract.

13.3 Involuntary Conversions

13.3.1. Bennet Hanover purchased a tract of land for $20,000 in Year 1 when he heard that a new highway was going to be constructed through the property and that the land would soon be worth $200,000. Highway engineers surveyed the property and indicated that he would probably get $175,000. The highway project was abandoned in Year 3, and the value of the land fell to $15,000. Hanover can claim a loss in Year 3 of

A. $0

B. $5,000

C. $160,000

D. $180,000

Answer (A) is correct. *(CPA, adapted)*
REQUIRED: The amount of loss recognized from the decrease in value of land held for investment.
DISCUSSION: Section 1033 does not apply to losses. Section 165 allows a deduction for uncompensated losses sustained during the taxable year. Since Hanover has not sold, exchanged, or otherwise disposed of the land, he has not realized a loss. Therefore, he cannot claim any loss in Year 3. When the land is sold or exchanged, his realized loss or gain will be equal to the amount realized minus his adjusted basis.
Answer (B) is incorrect. The amount of $5,000 is the difference between the price Hanover paid for the land and its value in Year 3, after the highway project was abandoned. Answer (C) is incorrect. The amount of $160,000 is the difference between the estimated price indicated by the highway engineers and the value of the land in Year 3, after the highway project was abandoned. Answer (D) is incorrect. The amount of $180,000 is the difference between the estimated worth of the land after the highway construction and the price for which Hanover purchased the land.

13.3.2. Which of the following does not constitute an involuntary conversion?

- A. Factory building destroyed by fire.
- B. Embezzlement of funds by a teller working in a bank.
- C. Diamond necklace mislaid or lost by the owner.
- D. Condemnation of land held for investment by a state highway department.

Answer (C) is correct. *(SEE, adapted)*
REQUIRED: The occurrence that does not constitute an involuntary conversion.
DISCUSSION: An involuntary conversion results from the destruction, theft, seizure, requisition or condemnation, or the disposition under threat or imminence of requisition or condemnation of the taxpayer's property [Sec. 1033(a)]. Losing or mislaying property does not fall under the definition of an involuntary conversion.
Answer (A) is incorrect. It results from destruction and does constitute involuntary conversion. Answer (B) is incorrect. It results from theft and does constitute involuntary conversion. Answer (D) is incorrect. It results from condemnation and does constitute involuntary conversion.

13.3.3. If the taxpayer owns an office building that (s)he does not personally manage and the office building is involuntarily converted, which of the following will qualify as replacement property with nonrecognition of gain?

- A. A hotel that the taxpayer will personally manage.
- B. An interest in a gold mine.
- C. An apartment building which the taxpayer will not personally manage.
- D. A retail sole proprietorship.

Answer (C) is correct. *(Publisher, adapted)*
REQUIRED: The property that will qualify as replacement property for an involuntary conversion.
DISCUSSION: Section 1033(a) provides for the nonrecognition of gain if property is involuntarily converted and replaced with property similar or related in service or use. "Similar or related in service or use" has been interpreted to mean, for an investor, that the property must have a similar service or use with respect to the taxpayer-owner. Since both the office building and the apartment building are operated as passive leasing investments, the latter will qualify as replacement property.
Answer (A) is incorrect. The active management of a hotel is a different use of property from the passive investment in an office building. Answer (B) is incorrect. An interest in a gold mine is a speculative venture quite different from the passive investment in real property. Answer (D) is incorrect. A sole proprietorship requires an active management role, which is different from the passive renting of a building.

13.3.4. One of Matthew Corporation's warehouses, on which it had taken straight-line depreciation, was completely destroyed by fire during 2016. The warehouse had an adjusted basis of $75,000 and a market value of $120,000 on the day of the fire. The warehouse was insured for $100,000, and settlement in that amount was received on August 1. On February 16, 2017, Matthew purchased from an unrelated individual all of the outstanding stock of Warehouse, Inc., a corporation that owned a warehouse equal in size to the destroyed warehouse. Purchase price of the stock was $95,000. How would these events have been reported on Matthew's federal income tax returns for 2016 and 2017 in order to minimize its tax liability?

- A. $20,000 loss in 2016; no effect on the 2017 returns.
- B. $25,000 gain in 2016; $20,000 deduction in 2017.
- C. $5,000 gain in 2016; no effect in 2017.
- D. No effect in 2016; $5,000 gain in 2017.

Answer (C) is correct. *(CMA, adapted)*
REQUIRED: The amount and timing of a gain recognized on the involuntary conversion of a warehouse.
DISCUSSION: Matthew received insurance proceeds of $100,000 on a destroyed warehouse with an adjusted basis of $75,000, thereby realizing a gain of $25,000. Matthew can elect nonrecognition of the gain by purchasing other similar or related property or by purchasing 80% or more of the stock of a corporation owning similar property [Sec. 1033(a)(2)]. The purchase of the stock qualifies as replacement property, and the gain will be recognized under Sec. 1033 only to the extent that the amount realized on the involuntary conversion ($100,000) exceeds the cost of the replacement property ($95,000), or $5,000. The $5,000 gain is realized and must be recognized in the year in which the conversion occurred, not in the year in which reinvestment occurred. An amended 2016 income tax return may be required for Matthew.
For involuntary conversions occurring after August 20, 1997, the basis of the corporate stock that was acquired, as well as the basis of the corporation's assets, must be reduced by the gain deferred under the involuntary conversion rules. The basis of the corporate assets, however, is not reduced below the basis for the corporate stock.
Answer (A) is incorrect. Matthew did not have a $20,000 loss in 2016. Answer (B) is incorrect. Matthew did not have a $25,000 gain in 2016 or a $20,000 deduction in 2017. Answer (D) is incorrect. There is a tax effect in 2016, but not in 2017.

13.3.5. During the current year, Mr. G had property that had an adjusted basis of $78,000, condemned by the state. The state paid G $93,000 for the property. Mr. G immediately purchased similar new property for $87,000. G properly reported a $6,000 gain on his current-year federal income tax return. What is the amount of Mr. G's basis in the new property?

A. $72,000

B. $78,000

C. $87,000

D. $93,000

Answer (B) is correct. *(SEE, adapted)*
REQUIRED: The basis of replacement property received as a result of an involuntary conversion.
DISCUSSION: Section 1033(a)(2) provides for a taxpayer to elect nonrecognition of gain as a result of an involuntary conversion when money is received and used to replace the converted property within 2 years of the conversion. Section 1033(a)(2), however, requires recognition of gain to the extent the amount realized on conversion exceeds the cost of replacement property.
Mr. G realizes a $15,000 gain ($93,000 condemnation proceeds – $78,000 basis of converted property) but is only required to recognize $6,000 ($93,000 condemnation proceeds – $87,000 cost of replacement property). Under Sec. 1033(b), the basis of replacement property is its purchase price less any realized gain not recognized. Therefore, Mr. G's basis in the replacement property is $78,000 ($87,000 cost of replacement property – $9,000 realized gain not recognized).
Answer (A) is incorrect. The amount of $72,000 is the adjusted basis of the condemned property reduced by the $6,000 recognized gain. Answer (C) is incorrect. The amount of $87,000 is the cost of the new property. Answer (D) is incorrect. The amount of the award is $93,000.

13.3.6. Ms. N's business building was destroyed by a hurricane. The building had an adjusted basis to Ms. N of $200,000 and a fair market value immediately before the hurricane of $300,000. Ms. N received a reimbursement of $270,000 from her insurance company and immediately spent $268,000 for a new business building. What amount must Ms. N include in her gross income?

A. $32,000 loss.

B. $30,000 loss.

C. $2,000 gain.

D. $70,000 gain.

Answer (C) is correct. *(SEE, adapted)*
REQUIRED: The gross income resulting from the involuntary conversion of insured property.
DISCUSSION: Ms. N received insurance proceeds of $270,000 on destroyed property with an adjusted basis of $200,000 and thereby realized a gain of $70,000. Since the replacement property was similar, under Sec. 1033(a)(2), Ms. N may elect to recognize the gain only to the extent that the amount realized ($270,000) exceeds the cost of the replacement property ($268,000), or $2,000.
Answer (A) is incorrect. The amount of $32,000 is the difference between the property's FMV before the hurricane and the cost of the new building. Answer (B) is incorrect. The amount of $30,000 is the difference between the FMV before the hurricane and the insurance reimbursement. Answer (D) is incorrect. The amount of $70,000 is the realized gain.

13.3.7. Mercury owned a racetrack, including the land and improvements (track, stands, and buildings). The property was condemned when Mercury's basis in the land was $30,000 and his basis in the improvements was $40,000. Mercury received new land worth $100,000 and cash of $200,000, which he immediately used to build a track, stands, and buildings to operate a new racetrack. Mercury elected to defer as much gain as possible. What is Mercury's basis in the new racetrack?

A. $30,000 in the land and $40,000 in the improvements.

B. $30,000 in the land and $200,000 in the improvements.

C. $100,000 in the land and $40,000 in the improvements.

D. $100,000 in the land and $200,000 in the improvements.

Answer (A) is correct. *(Publisher, adapted)*
REQUIRED: The basis of replacement property received as a result of an involuntary conversion.
DISCUSSION: Under Sec. 1033(a)(1), no gain is recognized on an involuntary conversion when the converted property is replaced with similar property. Under Sec. 1033(b), the basis of the replacement property is the same as the basis in the converted property. Mercury's basis in the land is therefore $30,000.
Section 1033(a)(2) also provides for a taxpayer to elect nonrecognition of gain as a result of an involuntary conversion when money is received and used to replace the converted property within 2 years of the conversion. Under Sec. 1033(b), the basis of such replacement property is its purchase price less any gain not recognized. The realized gain is $160,000 ($200,000 cash received – $40,000 basis). Thus, Mercury's basis in the improvements is $40,000 ($200,000 – $160,000 gain not recognized).
Answer (B) is incorrect. The improvements' basis is the property's acquisition cost less the gain not recognized. Answer (C) is incorrect. The land's basis is the same as that of the condemned land. Answer (D) is incorrect. The land's basis is the same as that of the condemned land, and the improvements' basis is the property's acquisition cost less the gain not recognized.

Questions 13.3.8 and 13.3.9 are based on the following information. Michael owned a building with an adjusted basis of $80,000 and land with an adjusted basis of $20,000. A tornado leveled the building. Michael used an insurance settlement of $140,000 plus $25,000 from a mortgage to construct a new building on the same land within 1 year.

13.3.8. Assuming Michael elects any possible gain deferral, his recognized gain from the insurance settlement will be

A. $0
B. $40,000
C. $60,000
D. $85,000

Answer (A) is correct. *(Publisher, adapted)*
REQUIRED: The recognized gain from an insurance settlement when the proceeds are invested in a similar business.
DISCUSSION: This situation qualifies as an involuntary conversion. Section 1033(a) provides that, if the property is converted into money or other property not similar or related in service or use to the converted property, as in the case of insurance proceeds, the taxpayer may elect to defer gain by investing an amount equal to or greater than that of the proceeds received in the conversion. Since Michael reinvested an amount greater than the insurance proceeds in similar property, he will not be required to recognize any gain.
Answer (B) is incorrect. The figure of $40,000 is not the correct amount of recognized gain from the insurance settlement. Answer (C) is incorrect. The amount of $60,000 is the difference between the insurance settlement and the building's adjusted basis. Answer (D) is incorrect. Michael is not required to recognize any gain.

13.3.9. Assume Michael used only $80,000 of the insurance proceeds and incurred a mortgage liability of $85,000 to construct the new building. His recognized gain from the insurance settlement will be

A. $0
B. $40,000
C. $60,000
D. $85,000

Answer (A) is correct. *(Publisher, adapted)*
REQUIRED: The amount of gain recognized from the receipt of insurance proceeds.
DISCUSSION: As long as a taxpayer reinvests an amount equal to or greater than the proceeds received upon the involuntary conversion, (s)he may elect to defer all of the gain realized. The source of the funds for reinvestment (i.e., insurance proceeds or loan) is immaterial. Michael reinvested $165,000, which is greater than the $140,000 of insurance proceeds, so he will not recognize any gain [Sec. 1033(a)(2)].
Answer (B) is incorrect. Michael is not required to recognize any gain. Answer (C) is incorrect. The amount of $60,000 is the difference between the insurance settlement and the building's adjusted basis. Answer (D) is incorrect. The amount of $85,000 is the mortgage liability incurred to construct the new building.

13.3.10. You are a calendar-year taxpayer. You were notified by the city council on December 1, Year 1, of its intention to acquire your real property used in your business by negotiation or by condemnation. On June 1, Year 2, when the property had an adjusted basis of $40,000 to you, the city converted the property and paid you $50,000. When does your replacement period end?

A. June 1, Year 4.
B. December 1, Year 4.
C. June 1, Year 5.
D. December 31, Year 5.

Answer (D) is correct. *(SEE, adapted)*
REQUIRED: The last date to acquire qualified replacement property for nonrecognition of gain on an involuntary conversion.
DISCUSSION: Section 1033(g)(4) provides that in the case of the condemnation of real property held for productive use in a trade or business or for investment, the replacement period ends 3 years after the close of the taxable year in which the gain is realized. Since the gain was realized in Year 2, the replacement period ends December 31, Year 5.
Answer (A) is incorrect. The replacement period ends later than June 1, Year 4. Answer (B) is incorrect. Section 1033(g)(4) provides for a different replacement period. Answer (C) is incorrect. The replacement period ends 3 years after the close of the taxable year.

Questions 13.3.11 and 13.3.12 are based on the following information. Two transactions for a sole proprietorship were made during the current year. These were the only sales or exchanges of capital assets or Sec. 1231 assets (there were no unrecaptured Sec. 1231 losses from the previous year).

A machine used in the business was sold for $40,000. It cost $33,000 when purchased 3 years ago, and its adjusted tax basis when sold was $21,000. Depreciation had been recorded on an accelerated basis; straight-line depreciation would have been $9,900.

A $50,000 insurance recovery on a small warehouse destroyed by fire was received. It was used in the business and depreciated using the straight-line method. Its adjusted tax basis at the date of the fire was $52,400. A new warehouse was rebuilt at a cost of $60,000.

13.3.11. What is the net tax effect of these two transactions?

A. $7,000 long-term capital gain and $9,600 ordinary income.

B. $4,600 long-term capital gain and $12,000 ordinary income.

C. $19,000 long-term capital gain and $2,400 ordinary loss.

D. $7,000 long-term capital gain; $12,000 ordinary income; and $2,400 ordinary loss.

Answer (A) is correct. *(CPA, adapted)*
REQUIRED: The net tax effect of the sale of depreciable business property and the involuntary conversion of business property.
DISCUSSION: The sale of the machine resulted in a realized gain of $19,000 ($40,000 amount realized – $21,000 adjusted basis). A portion of the gain equal to the depreciation already taken is recaptured as ordinary income under Sec. 1245. Thus, $12,000 of the gain on the sale of the machine is ordinary income. The remaining $7,000 of gain is characterized under Sec. 1231. The involuntary conversion results in a realized loss of $2,400 ($50,000 amount realized – $52,400 adjusted basis). Realized losses on involuntary conversions are fully recognized.
Under Sec. 1231(a), if losses on business property from involuntary conversions by casualty or theft exceed such gains, they are not netted with other 1231 gains and losses. The $2,400 loss will be treated as ordinary loss and netted with the $12,000 of Sec. 1245 ordinary income for a total of $9,600. The $7,000 of Sec. 1231 gain will be treated as long-term capital gain.
Answer (B) is incorrect. The $2,400 loss from the warehouse casualty is treated as an ordinary loss and netted with the Sec. 1245 income, not the Sec. 1231 gain from the machine sale. Answer (C) is incorrect. There is not an ordinary loss resulting from the two transactions. Answer (D) is incorrect. The ordinary income and ordinary loss must be netted.

13.3.12. What is the basis of the new warehouse?

A. $52,400

B. $57,600

C. $60,000

D. $62,400

Answer (C) is correct. *(CPA, adapted)*
REQUIRED: The basis of a warehouse acquired as a result of an involuntary conversion.
DISCUSSION: Section 1033 applies only to gains arising from involuntary conversions, and this was a loss. The realized loss was fully recognized, so the basis of the new warehouse is its cost of $60,000 (Sec. 1012).
Answer (A) is incorrect. The amount of $52,400 is the adjusted basis of the old warehouse. Answer (B) is incorrect. The amount of $57,600 is the insurance recovery minus the recognized loss. Answer (D) is incorrect. The amount of $62,400 is the adjusted basis of the old warehouse plus the $10,000 excess of the cost of the new warehouse over the insurance recovery.

13.3.13. Mr. C has a personal residence with an adjusted basis of $50,000 and a fair market value of $60,000. Mr. C's property was condemned by the state for a highway project. If Mr. C receives $35,000 compensation, what is his gain or deductible loss?

A. $0

B. $15,000 gain.

C. $15,000 loss.

D. $25,000 loss.

Answer (A) is correct. *(SEE, adapted)*
REQUIRED: The gain or deductible loss arising from the condemnation of a personal residence.
DISCUSSION: If Mr. C receives $35,000 for the condemnation of a personal residence with an adjusted basis of $50,000, he will have realized a loss of $15,000. Under Sec. 165(c), however, losses incurred by individuals on personal use assets can be recognized only if they arise from fire, storm, shipwreck, other casualty, or theft. Loss from the condemnation of a personal use asset is never recognized. Furthermore, Sec. 1033 does not apply to losses.
Answer (B) is incorrect. The proceeds are less than the adjusted basis, so no gain is recognized on the condemnation. Answer (C) is incorrect. Under Sec. 165(c), Mr. C will not suffer a loss due to condemnation. Answer (D) is incorrect. Loss from condemnation of a personal use asset is never recognized.

13.3.14. In the current year, ABC Corporation owned a warehouse building that was completely destroyed by a flood. The flooded region is one of the special areas designated by the President of the United States to be eligible for federal government assistance under the Disaster Relief and Emergency Assistance Act. The building had an FMV of $350,000 and an adjusted basis of $200,000 at the time of the flood. Six months later, ABC received an insurance check in the amount of $300,000. ABC used these proceeds to update its computer system to move into a new line of business. What is ABC's recognized gain on this transaction?

A. $0

B. $100,000

C. $150,000

D. $300,000

Answer (A) is correct. *(Publisher, adapted)*
REQUIRED: The amount of gain recognized on an involuntary conversion due to a Presidentially designated disaster area.
DISCUSSION: For purposes of gain recognition, the Small Business Act of 1997 provides that any replacement property purchased as a result of a Presidentially designated disaster will be treated as similar or related in service or use. Therefore, no gain will be recognized as a result of the involuntary conversion.
Answer (B) is incorrect. The amount of $100,000 is the difference between the FMV of the building and its adjusted basis at the time of the flood. Answer (C) is incorrect. The figure of $150,000 is the difference between the FMV of the building at the time of the flood and the amount of the insurance check ABC received. Answer (D) is incorrect. The figure of $300,000 is the amount of the insurance check ABC received.

13.3.15. On October 2, Year 1, Pamela's freezers in her grocery store went off due to a tornado, causing her to lose $5,000 of frozen foods. Her insurance company reimbursed her $4,000 on January 7, Year 2. Pamela had a beginning inventory of $10,000, purchases of $8,000, and an ending inventory of $3,000. Which of the following is a proper method to account for this event?

A. Do nothing for Year 1; adjust ending inventory by $5,000 and report the $4,000 as additional gross receipts for Year 2.

B. Do nothing to inventory for Year 1; report the $4,000 as additional gross receipts in Year 2.

C. Reduce beginning inventory by $5,000 for Year 1, and deduct a $1,000 loss on her Year 2 return.

D. Reduce purchases by $5,000 for Year 1, and deduct a $1,000 loss on her Year 2 tax return.

Answer (B) is correct. *(SEE, adapted)*
REQUIRED: The proper accounting treatment for an involuntary conversion.
DISCUSSION: If property is involuntarily converted into money or other property not similar to the converted property, such as insurance proceeds, the taxpayer must report the realized amount as gain in the year the money or other property is received.
Answer (A) is incorrect. Pamela should do nothing to inventory in Year 1 and only report the additional gross receipts for Year 2. Answer (C) is incorrect. Pamela should not reduce beginning inventory for Year 1 or deduct a $1,000 loss on her Year 2 return. Answer (D) is incorrect. Pamela should not reduce purchases for Year 1 or deduct a $1,000 loss on her Year 2 tax return.

13.3.16. Mr. M read in the newspaper that the state highway department had decided to take his real estate held for investment purposes for public use. Mr. M verified the news by phoning an official of the highway department who is involved in the project acquiring this property. This is a threat of condemnation.

A. True.

B. False.

Answer (A) is correct. *(SEE, adapted)*
DISCUSSION: A threat of condemnation under Sec. 1033 requires the taxpayer to obtain confirmation that there has been a decision to acquire property for public use and to have reasonable grounds to believe the property will be taken (Rev. Rul. 63-221). Mr. M's reading about the condemnation in the newspaper and his confirming it by phone with a public official give him reasonable grounds to believe the property will be taken by condemnation unless a voluntary sale can be arranged. A threat of condemnation sufficient to constitute an involuntary conversion therefore exists.

13.3.17. Mr. K is considered to be under threat or imminence of condemnation if he has received a health department notice that a building he owns is unfit and will be condemned if necessary improvements are not made.

A. True.

B. False.

Answer (B) is correct. *(SEE, adapted)*
DISCUSSION: Involuntary conversions under Sec. 1033 include a condemnation for public use. But a notice that a building will be condemned because it is in need of improvements is not a condemnation for pubic use. A notice is not an actual condemnation, and a taxpayer's failure to repair property cannot be turned into an involuntary conversion. Therefore, the nonrecognition of gain under Sec. 1033 does not apply.

13.3.18. Mr. L owns a rental building with an adjusted basis of $75,000 and a fair market value of $70,000. During the current year, the state condemned the property for a highway project and paid him $70,000, which he immediately reinvested in a similar rental property. Mr. L may recognize a loss.

    A. True.

    B. False.

Answer (A) is correct. *(SEE, adapted)*
    DISCUSSION: Mr. L received a $70,000 condemnation award for investment property with an adjusted basis of $75,000, thereby realizing a loss of $5,000. Section 165 allows a deduction for any loss on business property sustained during the taxable year that is not compensated. Accordingly, Mr. L may recognize this loss. Note that Sec. 1033 applies only to realized gains.

13.3.19. Advance payment to a contractor, within the qualified replacement period, for construction of replacement property does not qualify as being the purchase of replacement property if construction is not completed within the replacement time period.

    A. True.

    B. False.

Answer (A) is correct. *(SEE, adapted)*
    DISCUSSION: A person who makes an advance payment to a contractor may receive a right to receive the replacement property at a stated time. The purchase of this right is not the same as the purchase of replacement property (for the purpose of nonrecognition of gain), and it would not satisfy the tests to determine whether the replacement property qualifies. The actual replacement property must be acquired within the time limit (Rev. Rul. 56-543).

13.3.20. Baylor Corporation, a C corporation, is 100%-owned by Don Smith. Baylor's manufacturing building was involuntarily converted in Year 1. A qualifying replacement property was acquired from Don Smith in November, Year 2. Smith had been leasing the building to an unrelated tenant. When the lease expired in Year 2, Baylor used its insurance proceeds to purchase the building from Don Smith. Baylor can defer recognition of gain on the involuntarily converted building by purchasing a replacement building from its sole shareholder.

    A. True.

    B. False.

Answer (B) is correct. *(Publisher, adapted)*
    DISCUSSION: Taxpayers are not permitted to use the gain deferral provisions of Sec. 1033(a) when a replacement property or qualifying stock is acquired from a related person [Sec. 1033(i)]. A related person is defined under the rules of Secs. 267(b) or 707(b)(1). Don Smith is considered a related person under Sec. 267(b). An exception is provided, however, when the related person acquired the building during the 2-year or longer replacement period allowed when property is converted into money. Individuals are allowed to defer the gain if it is $100,000 or less.

13.3.21. Mr. P's dairy herd developed a disease that required him to sell the cows for less than the going market rate. This is considered an involuntary conversion.

    A. True.

    B. False.

Answer (A) is correct. *(SEE, adapted)*
    DISCUSSION: Livestock that are sold or exchanged because they are diseased or have been exposed to disease and that would not otherwise have been sold or exchanged at that particular time are treated as involuntarily converted [Sec. 1033(d)]. Therefore, Mr. P's selling of the cows is an involuntary conversion.

13.3.22. Mr. L planned to build a warehouse for use in his business on unimproved property he owned. The property had an adjusted basis to him of $100,000. In March, before he could build the warehouse, the state condemned the property and reimbursed Mr. L $125,000. In October of the same year, Mr. L bought improved real property for $150,000 that had buildings on it that he could use as rentals. The improved real estate qualifies as replacement property, and Mr. L may postpone the tax on the gain from the condemnation.

    A. True.

    B. False.

Answer (A) is correct. *(SEE, adapted)*
    DISCUSSION: Under Sec. 1033(a)(2), a taxpayer may elect nonrecognition of gain resulting from an involuntary conversion if money is received and used to replace the converted property within 2 years of the close of the first tax year in which any part of the gain is realized. Generally, the replacement must be similar or related in service or use to the converted property. The unimproved property is not similar in service or use to property with rental buildings. However, for real property used in a trade or business or held for investment that is condemned, the replacement property need only be of like kind as under Sec. 1031 [Reg. 1.1033(g)-1]. Both the unimproved and improved property are of like kind under Sec. 1031, so the gain may be deferred under Sec. 1033.

13.4 Sale of a Principal Residence

13.4.1. Richard Rich owns a houseboat in Florida, a condominium in Colorado, a house in California, and stock in a housing cooperative in New York City. For the last 4 years, Richard Rich and his family have spent 3 months in the winter on the Florida houseboat, 1 month in the Colorado condominium, and the rest of the year in the New York City apartment. Prior to the last 4 years, Richard Rich and his family lived in the California house year-round. It is now vacant. Richard just put his stock in the New York City cooperative up for sale. Which property qualifies as a principal residence under Sec. 121?

A. The Florida houseboat.

B. The Colorado condominium.

C. The California house.

D. The stock in the New York City cooperative.

Answer (D) is correct. *(Publisher, adapted)*
REQUIRED: The property that qualifies as a principal residence under Sec. 121.
DISCUSSION: Sec. 121 requires the property to have been used as a principal residence by the taxpayer for 2 or more years out of the 5-year period ending on the date of sale. A principal residence may include houseboats, condominiums, and stock in a cooperative housing corporation [Reg. 1.1034-1(c)(3)]. The stock in the New York City cooperative qualifies as a principal residence. The proposed Regs. under Sec. 121 state that if a taxpayer alternates between two properties, using each as a residence for successive periods of time, the property that the taxpayer uses a majority of the time during the year will ordinarily be considered the taxpayer's principal residence.
Answer (A) is incorrect. The Florida houseboat is not a principal residence since it was used for only 12 months in the past 5 years. Answer (B) is incorrect. The Colorado condominium also has not been used for a sufficient amount of time or with the intent to be a principal residence. Answer (C) is incorrect. Although the California house was a principal residence 4 years ago, it has not been used as a principal residence for 2 years of the preceding 5-year period.

13.4.2. Which of the following statements about the frequency with which the $500,000 exclusion of gain that is available on the sale of a principal residence (Sec. 121) may be used is true?

A. There is no limit on the use of the exclusion.

B. The exclusion may be used once per year.

C. The exclusion may be used once every 2 years.

D. The exclusion may be used once in a lifetime.

Answer (C) is correct. *(Publisher, adapted)*
REQUIRED: The frequency with which the exclusion of gain on the sale of a principal residence is allowed.
DISCUSSION: The exclusion of gain on the sale of a principal residence applies to one exchange every 2 years.
Answer (A) is incorrect. There is a limit on the exclusion. Answer (B) is incorrect. The exclusion may not be used once per year. Answer (D) is incorrect. The exclusion may be used more than once in a lifetime.

13.4.3. Which of the following situations would disqualify a married couple from using the $500,000 exclusion of gain realized on the sale of a principal residence?

A. Only one spouse meets the ownership requirement.

B. Only one spouse meets the use test.

C. Both spouses used the exclusion 5 years ago.

D. None of the answers are correct.

Answer (B) is correct. *(Publisher, adapted)*
REQUIRED: The situation that would disqualify a married couple from using the $500,000 exclusion of gain on the sale of a principal residence.
DISCUSSION: Married individuals are eligible for a $500,000 exclusion if (1) either spouse meets the ownership test, (2) both spouses meet the use test, and (3) neither spouse is ineligible due to use of the exclusion in the past 2 years. However, if only one spouse meets the use test, they may be eligible for a prorated exclusion.
Answer (A) is incorrect. Only one spouse meeting the ownership requirement will not disqualify the married individuals from using the entire exclusion. Answer (C) is incorrect. Both spouses using the exclusion 5 years ago will not disqualify married individuals from using the entire exclusion. Answer (D) is incorrect. There is a correct answer.

13.4.4. Mr. and Mrs. Smith sold their principal residence for $750,000. They had lived in their home for 20 years, and it had an adjusted basis of $210,000. The Smiths have decided not to purchase a new home and will instead rent a condominium on the beach. What amount of gain must they recognize on this transaction?

A. $0

B. $40,000

C. $540,000

D. $750,000

Answer (B) is correct. *(Publisher, adapted)*
REQUIRED: The amount of gain recognized on the sale of a principal residence.
DISCUSSION: Mr. and Mrs. Smith will realize a gain of $540,000 ($750,000 sales price – $210,000 adjusted basis) on the sale of the residence. Section 121 allows an exclusion of up to $500,000 for married taxpayers filing jointly on the sale of a principal residence. Therefore, the Smiths' recognized gain is $40,000 ($540,000 realized gain – $500,000 exclusion).
Answer (A) is incorrect. The exclusion is limited to $500,000. Answer (C) is incorrect. The amount of $540,000 is the realized gain. Answer (D) is incorrect. The amount of $750,000 is the sales price.

13.4.5. Which of the following statements is true regarding exclusion of the gain on the sale of a principal residence?

A. An individual may exclude $250,000 of gain on the sale of a residence (s)he purchased 10 years ago.

B. A married couple may exclude $500,000 of gain on the sale of a residence they purchased jointly 5 years ago.

C. The exclusion amount is proportioned and becomes the maximum exclusion when due to a change in job location.

D. All of the answers are correct.

Answer (D) is correct. *(Publisher, adapted)*
REQUIRED: The true statement regarding exclusion of the gain on the sale of a principal residence.
DISCUSSION: An individual may exclude $250,000 ($500,000 for married individuals filing jointly) on the sale of a principal residence provided (s)he lived there for at least 2 years. Additionally, a pro rata exclusion is available if the sale occurred prior to 2 years if the sale was as a result of a change in job locations or other unforeseen circumstances.
Answer (A) is incorrect. In addition to an individual excluding $250,000 of gain on the sale of a residence (s)he purchased 10 years ago, a married couple may also exclude $500,000 of gain on the sale of a residence they purchased jointly 5 years ago. Also, the exclusion amount is proportioned and becomes the maximum exclusion when due to a change in job location. Answer (B) is incorrect. In addition to a married couple excluding $500,000 of gain on the sale of a residence they purchased jointly 5 years ago, an individual may exclude $250,000 of gain on the sale of a residence (s)he purchased 10 years ago. Also, the exclusion amount is proportioned and becomes the maximum exclusion when due to a change in job location. Answer (C) is incorrect. In addition to the exclusion amount being proportioned and becoming the maximum exclusion when due to a change in job location, an individual may exclude $250,000 of gain on the sale of a residence (s)he purchased 10 years ago, and a married couple may also exclude $500,000 of gain on the sale of a residence they purchased jointly 5 years ago.

13.4.6. On December 1, 2016, Joe Jackson purchased a home for $90,000. On June 1, 2017, Joe received a job offer that would require him to move across the country. On August 1, 2017, Joe sold his house for $100,000 and moved to his new location. Upon relocating, Joe purchased a new home for $95,000. What is his recognized gain on the sale of his first house?

A. $0

B. $3,333

C. $6,667

D. $10,000

Answer (A) is correct. *(Publisher, adapted)*
REQUIRED: The amount of gain recognized upon the sale of a principal residence when the ownership requirements are not met.
DISCUSSION: In order to use the $250,000 exclusion provided by Sec. 121, use and ownership requirements must be met. The taxpayer must have used and owned the home as a principal residence for 2 of the 5 previous years. In situations in which the taxpayer sells his or her house due to changes in employment or health, a pro rata portion of the $250,000 exclusion may be used. Since Joe lived in and owned the house for 8 months, he may exclude up to $83,333 ($250,000 exclusion ÷ 24 × 8). Therefore, Joe can exclude the entire realized gain.
Answer (B) is incorrect. The amount of $3,333 results from prorating the $10,000 gain rather than the $250,000 exclusion. Answer (C) is incorrect. The amount of $6,667 results from prorating the $10,000 gain rather than the $250,000 exclusion, and over the course of 12 months rather than 24 months. Answer (D) is incorrect. Joe may exclude the entire realized gain of $10,000.

13.4.7. On December 10, 2016, Ms. Poor, a single taxpayer, signed a contract to sell her home, which had been used as a principal residence for the last 12 years. Her home had an adjusted basis of $124,000. On January 20, 2017, she sold her house for $200,000. On March 1, 2017, she purchased a new home for $175,000. What is her recognized gain and the adjusted basis of the new home?

	Recognized Gain	Adjusted Basis
A.	$0	$175,000
B.	$0	$99,000
C.	$76,000	$175,000
D.	$76,000	$99,000

Answer (A) is correct. *(Publisher, adapted)*
REQUIRED: The recognized gain from the sale of a taxpayer's principal residence and the adjusted basis of the replacement residence.
DISCUSSION: Ms. Poor realized a $76,000 gain on the sale of her house ($200,000 sales price – $124,000 basis of old residence). A taxpayer may exclude up to $250,000 of gain ($500,000 for taxpayers filing jointly) on the sale of a principal residence. A taxpayer may use this exclusion once in a 2-year period. Since this is an exclusion and not a deferral, there is no adjustment to the basis of a new residence. Therefore, the adjusted basis of the new house is its cost.
Answer (B) is incorrect. There are no adjustments to the basis of the new residence. Answer (C) is incorrect. There is an exclusion of gain of up to $250,000. Answer (D) is incorrect. There is an exclusion of gain of up to $250,000, and there are no adjustments to the basis of the new residence.

13.4.8. Joe and Mary, each 35 years old, purchased their residence 10 years ago for $150,000. On October 28 of the current year, they had a loan outstanding on the home in the amount of $120,000 when the bank foreclosed. They did not purchase another home. The net proceeds from the foreclosure sale were $175,000, of which Joe and Mary received $55,000. What are the amount and the character of the taxable gain Joe and Mary should include in their income?

A. $0 gain.

B. $25,000 long-term capital gain.

C. $55,000 ordinary gain.

D. $55,000 long-term capital gain.

Answer (A) is correct. *(SEE, adapted)*
REQUIRED: The amount and the character of the gain on the foreclosure.
DISCUSSION: Joe and Mary's realized gain on the foreclosure is $25,000 [($120,000 release from mortgage + $55,000 cash) − $150,000 adjusted basis for residence]. Section 121 provides for an exclusion of gain on the sale of a principal residence of up to $500,000 for married taxpayers filing jointly. Therefore, Joe and Mary have no taxable gain on this transaction.
Answer (B) is incorrect. The Taxpayer Relief Act of 1997 provides for an advance gain on the sale of a principal residence. Answer (C) is incorrect. The amount of $55,000 neglects the implications of Sec. 121 for a married couple. Answer (D) is incorrect. Joe and Mary should not include any gain on a sale of their principal residence.

13.4.9. Wynn, a 60-year old single individual, sold his personal residence for $450,000. Wynn had owned his residence, which had a basis of $250,000, for 6 years. Within 8 months of the sale, Wynn purchased a new residence for $400,000. What is Wynn's recognized gain from the sale of his personal residence?

A. $0

B. $50,000

C. $75,000

D. $200,000

Answer (A) is correct. *(CPA, adapted)*
REQUIRED: The amount of recognized gain from sale of a personal residence.
DISCUSSION: Wynn will realize a $200,000 ($450,000 sales price − $250,000 adjusted basis) gain on the sale of the residence. Section 121, as amended by the Taxpayer Relief Act of 2000, allows an exclusion of up to $250,000 for single taxpayers on the sale of a principal residence. Therefore, Wynn's recognized gain is $0 ($200,000 realized gain − up to $250,000 exclusion).
Answer (B) is incorrect. The purchase price of the new residence does not calculate into the gain of the old residence. Answer (C) is incorrect. The amount of gain to be recognized is equal to the realized gain on the sale of the residence, $200,000, less the exclusion amount of up to $250,000. Answer (D) is incorrect. The amount of $200,000 is the realized gain on the sale of Wynn's principal residence. The exclusion amount of up to $250,000 from Sec. 121 offsets this amount so that the recognized gain is $0.

13.4.10. Amanda Jones buys a property on January 1, 2016, for $400,000 and uses it as rental property for 2 years, claiming $20,000 of depreciation deductions. On January 1, 2018, Amanda converts the property to her principal residence. On January 1, 2020, Amanda moves out and sells the property for $700,000 on January 1, 2021. What is the amount of gain excludable from Amanda's income?

A. $320,000

B. $250,000

C. $120,000

D. $180,000

Answer (D) is correct. *(Publisher, adapted)*
REQUIRED: The maximum exclusion allowed for gain on the sale of a principal residence.
DISCUSSION: Gain from the sale of a principal residence will no longer be excluded from gross income under Sec. 121 for the period that the home was not used as the principal residence. This new income inclusion rule applies to home sales after December 31, 2008. Under a transition rule, the inclusion is based only on nonqualified use periods that begin on or after January 1, 2009.
Periods of temporary absence from the taxpayer's principal residence that do not exceed 2 years in total because of a change of employment, health conditions, or other unforeseen circumstances are not considered nonqualifying use.
Any portion of the 5-year period ending on the date the property is sold that is after the last date that the property is used as the principal residence of the taxpayer or the taxpayer's spouse is not considered a period of nonqualified use.
Depreciation allowed or allowable after May 6, 1997, is not excluded from income and is not included when calculating the amount of gain allocated to nonqualified use.
As under present law, $20,000 gain attributable to the depreciation deductions is included in income. Of the remaining $300,000 gain, 40% of the gain (2 years divided by 5 years), or $120,000, is allocated to nonqualified use and is not eligible for the exclusion. Since the remaining gain of $180,000 is less than the maximum gain of $250,000 that may be excluded, gain of $180,000 is excluded from gross income.
Answer (A) is incorrect. The exclusion is not allowed for depreciation or the time the home was rental property. Answer (B) is incorrect. The allowable exclusion is less than the maximum exclusion available. Answer (C) is incorrect. The amount disallowed for the exclusion is $120,000.

STUDY UNIT FOURTEEN
PARTNERSHIPS: FORMATION AND OPERATION

14.1 Partnerships Defined

14.1.1. For federal income tax purposes, a partnership other than a publicly traded partnership is

A. Required to pay a tax upon its profits, which in turn must be assumed by its partners.

B. Considered to be a nontaxable entity but must file an information return.

C. A taxable entity similar to a trust or estate.

D. Treated the same as an association for tax purposes.

Answer (B) is correct. *(SEE, adapted)*
REQUIRED: The true statement concerning the nature of a partnership for tax purposes.
DISCUSSION: Section 701 states that the partners, not the partnership, are subject to federal income tax. The partnership is required to file an information return (Form 1065) under Sec. 6031. For the purpose of reporting income, a partnership is a conduit which distributes the income to the partners.
Answer (A) is incorrect. Only the partners are liable for income taxes on partnership profits. Answer (C) is incorrect. A partnership is not a taxable entity but an aggregation of partners for the purpose of payment of tax. Answer (D) is incorrect. An association is a taxable entity subject to the corporate income tax, while a partnership is not subject to income tax. However, some partnerships classified as publicly traded partnerships are taxed as corporations.

14.1.2. Which of the following organizations formed after 1996 cannot be classified as a partnership?

A. An insurance company.

B. A tax-exempt organization.

C. A real estate investment trust.

D. All of the answers are correct.

Answer (D) is correct. *(SEE, adapted)*
REQUIRED: The organization formed after 1996 that cannot be classified as a partnership.
DISCUSSION: A partnership is defined under Sec. 761(a) as including a syndicate, group, pool, joint venture, or other unincorporated organization that carries on a business and is not a corporation, a trust, or an estate. Partnerships include organizations that carry on a business, financial operation, or venture with a profit motive. Also, under Reg. 301.7701-2(b), an insurance company is a corporation.
Answer (A) is incorrect. Certain entities are considered per se corporations and must be classified as corporations for federal tax purposes. Under Reg. 301.7701-2(b), an insurance company is a corporation. Answer (B) is incorrect. Partnerships include organizations that carry on business, financial operation, or venture with a profit motive. Answer (C) is incorrect. A partnership is defined under Sec. 761(a) as including a syndicate, group, pool, joint venture, or other unincorporated organization that carries on a business and is not a corporation, a trust, or an estate.

14.1.3. Which one of the following is least important when reviewing the partnership agreement for income tax purposes?

A. Income and expense allocation.

B. Modifications of the agreement.

C. Economic effect of allocations to partners.

D. The form of the agreement.

Answer (D) is correct. *(SEE, adapted)*
  REQUIRED: The least important item when reviewing the partnership agreement for income tax purposes.
  DISCUSSION: For income tax purposes, there are no formal requirements regarding the partnership agreement. A partnership agreement or modifications thereof may be oral or written [Reg. 1.761-1(c)].
  Answer (A) is incorrect. Income and expense allocation is important in determining each partner's taxable income. Answer (B) is incorrect. The partnership agreement includes any modifications made prior to the date prescribed for filing the partnership return. Answer (C) is incorrect. The economic effect of allocations to partners is considered in determining whether the allocation will be allowed for tax purposes.

14.1.4. For federal income tax purposes, all of the following statements regarding partnerships are true except

A. The term partnership includes a syndicate, group, pool, joint venture, or other unincorporated organization that is carrying on a business and that may not be classified as a trust, estate, or corporation.

B. A partnership is the relationship between two or more persons who join together to carry on a trade or business.

C. Co-ownership of property that is maintained and leased or rented is considered a partnership if the co-owners provide no services to the tenants.

D. The term "person" when used to describe a partner means an individual, a corporation, a trust, an estate, or another partnership.

Answer (C) is correct. *(SEE, adapted)*
  REQUIRED: The false statement regarding partnerships for federal income tax purposes.
  DISCUSSION: Under Reg. 301.7701-1(a), mere co-ownership, maintenance, repair, and rental of property does not constitute a partnership. The co-owners are partners only if, in addition to renting the property, they provide additional services to the occupants and share the profits.
  Answer (A) is incorrect. It is the definition of a partnership under Sec. 761. Answer (B) is incorrect. A partnership is characterized by two or more persons carrying on a trade or business. Answer (D) is incorrect. It is the definition of a person under Sec. 7701(a)(1).

14.1.5. Which of the following statements is false with respect to partnership agreements?

A. Modifications to the partnership agreement must be agreed to by all the partners or adopted in any other manner provided by the partnership agreement.

B. The partnership agreement or modifications can be oral or written.

C. The partnership agreement can be modified for a particular tax year after the close of the year, but not later than the date for filing the partnership return for that year, including extensions.

D. A partner's share of income, gains, losses, deductions, or credits is usually determined by the partnership agreement.

Answer (C) is correct. *(SEE, adapted)*
  REQUIRED: The statement about partnership agreements that is false.
  DISCUSSION: A partnership agreement may be modified with respect to a particular tax year after the close of the year, but not later than the date for filing the partnership return for that year, not including any extensions [Reg. 1.761-1(c)].
  Answer (A) is incorrect. A partnership agreement includes the original agreement and any modifications agreed to by all the partners or adopted in any other manner provided by the partnership agreement. Answer (B) is incorrect. A partnership agreement and/or modifications to it can be oral or written. Answer (D) is incorrect. Allocations of partnership items of income, loss, etc., in the partnership agreement are generally respected for federal income tax purposes.

14.1.6. Mr. Diaz and Mr. Garcia are both dentists who maintain separate practices, but they share the same office space. They equally divide the expenses, such as receptionist salary, rent, and utilities. This arrangement is a partnership for federal income tax purposes.

A. True.

B. False.

Answer (B) is correct. *(SEE, adapted)*
  DISCUSSION: Partnerships include organizations that carry on a business, financial operation, or venture with a profit motive. A joint undertaking merely to share expenses is not a partnership [Reg. 301.7701-1(a)]. Mr. Diaz and Mr. Garcia do not have a partnership for federal income tax purposes.

14.1.7. Certain investing or operating agreement partnerships may be completely excluded from being treated as a partnership for federal income tax purposes. All of the members must choose to be excluded and the partnership has to file a partnership return, Form 1065, by the due date of the return, including extensions, for the first year it wishes to be excluded.

A. True.

B. False.

Answer (A) is correct. *(SEE, adapted)*
DISCUSSION: Section 761(a) allows a partnership that is essentially an operating agreement or that exists for investment purposes only and not for the active conduct of a business to be excluded from treatment as a partnership (under Subchapter K only) if all of the members so elect. Each member must separately include his or her share of the income and deductions.

14.1.8. Subchapter K rules apply both to general partnerships and to limited partnerships.

A. True.

B. False.

Answer (A) is correct. *(Publisher, adapted)*
DISCUSSION: Subchapter K is the part of the Code containing most of the tax rules that apply to partnerships. A partnership is defined under Sec. 761(a) as including a syndicate, group, pool, joint venture, or other unincorporated organization that carries on a business and is not a corporation, trust, or estate. Both limited and general partnerships fall within this definition.

14.2 Classification of Business Entity

14.2.1. All of the following are available tax classifications for a single-member entity under the check-the-box regulations except

A. Association taxed as a C corporation.

B. Sole proprietorship.

C. Association taxed as an S corporation.

D. Limited liability company.

Answer (D) is correct. *(Publisher, adapted)*
REQUIRED: The tax classifications available to a single-member entity under the check-the-box regulations.
DISCUSSION: For a single-member entity formed after the institution of the check-the-box regulations, the default classification is for the entity to be disregarded as a separate entity from the taxpayer (i.e., a sole proprietorship). However, an election can be made by the entity to be treated as an association taxed as a corporation. Electing to be treated as an association, the entity is able to choose to be taxed as either an S corporation or a C corporation. To be an S corporation, it must make an S election plus the election under the check-the-box regulations to be treated as an association. A limited liability company is an entity for legal purposes but is not recognized as a distinct tax classification.
Answer (A) is incorrect. An association taxed as a C corporation is an available tax classification for a single-member entity under the check-the-box regulations. Answer (B) is incorrect. A sole proprietorship is an available tax classification for a single-member entity under the check-the-box regulations. Answer (C) is incorrect. An association taxed as an S corporation is an available tax classification for a single-member entity under the check-the-box regulations.

14.2.2. A group of six individuals organizes an LLC to conduct a software publishing business in Florida. No individual is specifically authorized to make the election. What individual(s) is(are) required to make the election?

A. President.

B. Every member of the entity.

C. Any officer.

D. Any manager or officer.

Answer (B) is correct. *(Publisher, adapted)*
REQUIRED: The required member(s) needed to elect an entity's classification.
DISCUSSION: An eligible entity may elect its classification on Form 8832. The election must be signed by every member of the entity, or any officer, manager, or member of the entity who is authorized to make the election. Since no member is authorized to make the election, every member must sign the election for it to be effective. The election must include all required information and the entity's taxpayer identification number. A copy of Form 8832 must be attached to the entity's tax return for the election year.
Answer (A) is incorrect. The president is not exclusively authorized to make the election. Answer (C) is incorrect. Any officer is not exclusively authorized to make the election. Answer (D) is incorrect. Any manager or officer is not exclusively authorized to make the election.

14.2.3. All of the following are available tax classifications for a two-member entity under the check-the-box regulations except

A. Association taxed as a C corporation.

B. An entity disregarded as a separate entity from the taxpayers.

C. Association taxed as an S corporation.

D. Partnership.

Answer (B) is correct. *(Publisher, adapted)*
REQUIRED: The tax classifications available to a two-member entity under the check-the-box regulations.
DISCUSSION: For an entity with more than one member formed after the institution of the check-the-box regulations, the default classification is for the entity to be taxed as a partnership. However, an election can be made by the eligible entity to be treated as an association taxed as a corporation. Electing to be taxed as an association, the entity may be able to choose its treatment as either an S corporation or a C corporation. To be an S corporation, it must make an S election, plus the election under the check-the-box regulations to be treated as an association. For a two-member entity, an election to be disregarded as a separate entity from the taxpayer (i.e., a sole proprietorship) is not available.
Answer (A) is incorrect. An association taxed as a C corporation is an available tax classification for a two-member entity under the check-the-box regulations. Answer (C) is incorrect. An association taxed as an S corporation is an available tax classification for a single-member entity under the check-the-box regulations. Answer (D) is incorrect. A partnership is an available tax classification for a two-member entity under the check-the-box regulations.

14.2.4. KLM, a domestic limited liability company (LLC), is formed in March of the current year. The entity has two members and does not disregard its default classification for tax purposes. What is the default classification of KLM for tax purposes?

A. Association taxed as a corporation.

B. Partnership.

C. Limited liability company.

D. Sole proprietorship.

Answer (B) is correct. *(Publisher, adapted)*
REQUIRED: The classification of an entity under the check-the-box regulations.
DISCUSSION: The check-the-box regulations adopt a default for domestic entities other than corporations, under which a newly formed LLC (or other eligible entity) is classified as a partnership if it has at least two members. The classification is automatic and is granted without any action on the part of the LLC. However, an election can be made to have the entity treated as an association and, accordingly, taxed as a corporation. Electing to be taxed as an association, the entity may be able to choose to be treated as either an S corporation or a C corporation. For foreign entities, the determination is more complex.
Answer (A) is incorrect. The default classification for a domestic entity other than a corporation with at least two members is a partnership. Answer (C) is incorrect. An LLC is not itself a classification for tax purposes. Answer (D) is incorrect. Treatment as a sole proprietorship is the election that is permissible for an entity other than a corporation having only one member.

14.2.5. EJH Partnership was organized in the current year with three partners: E, J, and H. The three individuals elected to use the default classification when filing the entity's federal income tax return. The partnership wants to change its tax classification from being a partnership to being an association taxed as a C corporation. How long after changing to C corporation status must the EJH Partnership wait before it can make another change in classification by election?

A. The change in election can be made at any time.

B. 12 months.

C. 24 months.

D. 60 months.

Answer (D) is correct. *(Publisher, adapted)*
REQUIRED: The amount of time an entity must wait before making another classification election.
DISCUSSION: If an entity makes an election to change its classification, it cannot reelect its classification by election during the 60 months following the effective date of the election. The taxpayer must specify the effective date of the election. The effective date cannot be more than 75 days before or 12 months after the date the election was filed.
Answer (A) is incorrect. A subsequent election change cannot be made within a certain statutory period of time. Answer (B) is incorrect. Twelve months is within the disallowed period of time to make a subsequent election. Answer (C) is incorrect. Twenty-four months is within the disallowed period of time to make a subsequent election.

14.2.6. Sunshine LLC is formed in the current year with six members. Which of the following is a false statement about Sunshine's possible tax status under the check-the-box regulations?

A. Sunshine does not have to make a special election to be taxed as a partnership.

B. If Sunshine elects to be taxed as a C corporation, the LLC is treated as having undergone a corporate formation transaction.

C. Sunshine must wait 2 years after an election is filed before it can be taxed as a C corporation.

D. The election must be signed by every member of Sunshine or by any officer, manager, or member of Sunshine who is authorized to make the election.

Answer (C) is correct. *(Publisher, adapted)*

REQUIRED: The false statement regarding an LLC's election under the check-the-box regulations.

DISCUSSION: An eligible entity may elect its classification on Form 8832. If no election is made, the default classification for an eligible entity with two or more members is a partnership. If the LLC does not wish to be taxed as a partnership, every member of the entity, or an officer, manager, or member of the LLC who is authorized to make the election, must sign an election to be taxed as an association taxed as a corporation. If an entity makes an election to change its classification, the taxpayer must specify the effective date of the election. The effective date cannot be more than 75 days before or 12 months after the date the election was filed. Therefore, Sunshine LLC does not have to wait 2 years before it will be taxed as a C corporation. When Sunshine elects to be taxed as a C corporation, it is treated as having undergone a corporate formation transaction that is generally tax-free under Sec. 351.

Answer (A) is incorrect. Sunshine does not have to make a special election to be taxed as a partnership under the check-the-box regulations. Answer (B) is incorrect. If Sunshine elects to be taxed as a C corporation, the LLC is treated as having undergone a corporate formation transaction under the check-the-box regulations. Answer (D) is incorrect. The election must be signed by every member of Sunshine or by any officer, manager, or member of Sunshine who is authorized to make the election under the check-the-box regulations.

14.2.7. Most unincorporated businesses formed after 1996 can choose whether to be taxed as a partnership or a corporation. The regulations provide for a default rule if no election is made. If an election is not made and the default rules apply, which of the following is true?

A. Any new domestic eligible entity having at least two or more members is classified as a partnership.

B. Any new domestic eligible entity with a single member is disregarded as an entity separate from its owner.

C. If all members of a new foreign entity have limited liability, the entity is classified as an association.

D. All of the answers are correct.

Answer (D) is correct. *(SEE, adapted)*

REQUIRED: The true statement regarding the default rules for the taxation of business if no election is made.

DISCUSSION: Under a "check-the-box" system, certain business entities are automatically treated as corporations for federal tax purposes, while others may elect to be treated as corporations for federal tax purposes. If an entity has one owner and is not automatically considered a corporation, it may nevertheless elect to be treated as a corporation or, by default, it will be treated as a sole proprietorship. Similarly, if an entity has two or more owners and is not automatically considered a corporation, it can elect to be taxed as a corporation for federal tax purposes; otherwise, it will be taxed as a partnership. Further, if all members of a new foreign entity have limited liability, the entity is classified as a corporation. One type of a corporation as defined in the Internal Revenue Code is an association.

Answer (A) is incorrect. Also, any new domestic entity with a single member is disregarded as an entity separate from its owner. In addition, if all members of a new foreign entity have limited liability, the entity is classified as an association. Answer (B) is incorrect. Also, any new domestic entity having at least two or more members is classified as a partnership. In addition, if all members of a new foreign entity have limited liability, the entity is classified as an association. Answer (C) is incorrect. Also, any new domestic entity having at least two or more members is classified as a partnership. In addition, any new domestic entity with a single member is disregarded as an entity separate from its owner.

14.2.8. All of the following businesses, formed after 1996, are automatically classified as corporations except

   A. An insurance company.

   B. A partnership that possesses at least three of the following characteristics: limited liability, centralized management, free transferability of interest, and continuity of life.

   C. Certain foreign businesses.

   D. A business wholly owned by a state or local government.

Answer (B) is correct. *(SEE, adapted)*
REQUIRED: The business formed after 1996 that is not automatically classified as a corporation.
DISCUSSION: After 1996, the corporate characteristics are not determinative of corporate status. Only certain entities are required to be corporations. Other entities, such as limited liability companies, can choose partnership taxation even though the entity may possess all four of the corporate characteristics of (1) continuity of life, (2) centralization of management, (3) limited liability, and (4) free transferability of interests.
Answer (A) is incorrect. Insurance companies must be taxed as corporations if they are formed after 1996. Answer (C) is incorrect. Certain foreign businesses must be taxed as corporations if they are formed after 1996. Answer (D) is incorrect. A business wholly owned by a state or local government must be taxed as a corporation if it is formed after 1996.

14.2.9. To be classified as a corporation for federal income tax purposes, a professional service organization must be both organized under a State Professional Association Act and operated as a corporation.

   A. True.

   B. False.

Answer (B) is correct. *(SEE, adapted)*
DISCUSSION: Generally, if a professional service organization is organized under a State Professional Association Act and operated as a corporation, the IRS will recognize the corporate form. In the case of an individual who incorporates to provide his or her professional services, the IRS would require organization under a State Professional Association Act. The IRS's answer to this question was "True."
However, an organization may qualify as a corporation even if it fails to qualify under a recognized state statute if it satisfies the Sec. 7704 criteria or if it is an LLC that elects association status.

14.2.10. For federal tax purposes, certain business entities formed after 1996 are automatically classified as corporations. Other business entities with at least two members can choose to be classified as either an association taxable as a corporation or a partnership. A business entity with a single member can choose either to be classified as an association taxable as a corporation or to be disregarded as an entity separate from its owner.

   A. True.

   B. False.

Answer (A) is correct. *(SEE, adapted)*
DISCUSSION: Under a "check-the-box" system, certain business entities are automatically treated as corporations for federal tax purposes, while others may elect to be treated as corporations for federal tax purposes. If an entity has one owner and is not automatically considered a corporation, it may nevertheless elect to be treated as a corporation or, by default, it will be treated as a sole proprietorship. Similarly, if an entity has two or more owners and is not automatically considered a corporation, it can elect to be taxed as a corporation for federal tax purposes; otherwise, it will be taxed as a partnership.

14.2.11. A corporation, for federal income tax purposes, includes associations, joint stock companies, and insurance companies.

   A. True.

   B. False.

Answer (A) is correct. *(SEE, adapted)*
DISCUSSION: The term "corporation" under federal tax law includes associations, joint stock companies, and life insurance companies [Sec. 7701(a)(3)].

14.3 Formation of a Partnership

14.3.1. Which of the following statements with respect to property contributed to a partnership is false?

A. Usually, neither the partners nor the partnership recognizes a gain or loss when property is contributed to the partnership in exchange for a partnership interest.

B. For property contributed to a partnership after June 8, 1997, the contributing partner must recognize gain or loss on a distribution of the property to another partner within 7 years of the contribution.

C. Exchanges of partnership interests generally qualify for nontaxable treatment as exchanges of like-kind property.

D. If a partner contributed appreciated property in exchange for his or her partnership interest, some or all remaining precontribution gain will be recognized if the fair market value of distributed property exceeds his or her adjusted basis in his or her partnership interest and the distribution occurs within 7 years of the property contribution.

Answer (C) is correct. *(SEE, adapted)*
REQUIRED: The false statement with respect to property contributed to a partnership.
DISCUSSION: Section 1031 provides for nonrecognition on exchange of like-kind properties under certain circumstances. It does not apply to any exchange of interests in a partnership [Sec. 1031(a)(2)(D)].
Answer (A) is incorrect. Section 721(a) generally provides for nonrecognition when property is contributed to a partnership in exchange for a partnership interest. Answer (B) is incorrect. If the partnership distributes property to a partner other than the contributing partner within 7 years of its contribution, the contributing partner must recognize any gain or loss realized but not recognized on contribution [Sec. 704(c)(1)(B)]. Answer (D) is incorrect. Remaining precontribution gain (or the difference, if smaller) must be recognized if the fair market value of distributed property exceeds the adjusted basis in the partnership [Sec. 737(a)].

14.3.2. In return for a 20% partnership interest, Kathy contributed land having a $60,000 fair market value and a $30,000 basis to the partnership. The partnership assumes Kathy's $15,000 liability arising from her purchase of the land. The partnership's liabilities arising from its purchases of assets is $4,000 immediately prior to the contribution. What is Kathy's basis in her partnership interest?

A. $18,800

B. $30,000

C. $15,000

D. $15,800

Answer (A) is correct. *(SEE, adapted)*
REQUIRED: The partner's basis in his or her partnership interest.
DISCUSSION: Under Sec. 722, the basis of a partnership interest acquired by the contribution of property is the adjusted basis of the property to the contributing partner. Under Sec. 752(b), the assumption by a partnership of a partner's individual liabilities is treated as a distribution of money to the partner, which reduces the basis of the partner's interest (Sec. 733). Moreover, the basis of a partner's interest in a partnership is increased by his or her percentage of ownership of the partnership's liabilities. Kathy's basis in her partnership interest will be the $30,000 basis of the land to the partnership, decreased by the $12,000 ($15,000 × 80%) liability assumed by the partnership, and increased by her $800 ($4,000 × 20%) share of partnership liabilities. Therefore, Kathy's basis is $18,800 ($30,000 – $12,000 + $800).
Answer (B) is incorrect. The amount of $30,000 accounts for neither the partnership's nor Kathy's assumption of liabilities. Answer (C) is incorrect. Kathy is only relieved from 80% of her mortgage liability, and she must also add 20% of the partnership's liabilities to her basis. Answer (D) is incorrect. Kathy is only relieved from 80% of her mortgage liability.

14.3.3. On May 1 of the current year, Mr. Good contributed 500 shares of stock in Candid Corporation to the partnership of Murphy & Wooster for a 25% interest in the partnership's capital and profits. The stock, which he purchased 10 years ago for $20,000, had a fair market value on May 1 of $100,000. On May 1 of the current year, the fair market value of the partnership's net assets, after Good's contribution, was $400,000. What is the amount of Good's recognized gain in the current year on the exchange?

A. $0

B. $80,000 ordinary income.

C. $80,000 long-term capital gain.

D. $80,000 Sec. 1231 gain.

Answer (A) is correct. *(SEE, adapted)*
REQUIRED: The gain recognized by a partner on the exchange of stock for a partnership interest.
DISCUSSION: Under Sec. 721, no gain or loss is recognized by a partnership or its partners when property is contributed to the partnership in exchange for a partnership interest. Good has a realized gain of $80,000 (25% of the $400,000 value of the partnership minus his $20,000 basis in his contribution). This gain is not recognized under Sec. 721. For assets contributed after March 31, 1984, the precontribution gain on the asset is allocated to the contributing partner when the partnership later sells the asset.
Note that stock does constitute property under Sec. 721. But if the partnership would be an investment company if it were incorporated, the gain will be recognized. For this purpose, an investment company is one in which the partner has diversified his or her interest in stocks and securities and in which 80% or more of the partnership's assets are marketable stocks or securities.
Answer (B) is incorrect. Ordinary income would only be recognized, under Sec. 1245 or 1250 recapture, if the partnership assumed liabilities on the contribution in excess of Good's aggregate adjusted basis in the property. Answer (C) is incorrect. The realized gain is not recognized but is allocated to Good when the partnership later sells the asset. Answer (D) is incorrect. Stock is not Sec. 1231 property, and no gain is recognized.

14.3.4. On June 1 of the current year, Kelly received a 10% interest in Rock Co., a partnership, for services contributed to the partnership. Rock's net assets at that date had a basis of $70,000 and a fair market value of $100,000. In Kelly's current-year income tax return, what amount must Kelly include as income from the transfer of the partnership interest?

A. $7,000 ordinary income.

B. $7,000 capital gain.

C. $10,000 ordinary income.

D. $10,000 capital gain.

Answer (C) is correct. *(CPA, adapted)*
REQUIRED: The income recognized when a partnership interest is received for services.
DISCUSSION: An individual must recognize compensation income when a partnership interest is received in exchange for services (whether current or past) rendered [Reg. 1.721-1(b)(1)]. The receipt of a capital interest in a partnership for services must be included in the year of receipt under Sec. 83. The income that should be recognized is the $10,000 ($100,000 × 10%) fair market value of the partnership interest received unless the interest is nontransferable or subject to a substantial risk of forfeiture. The income is ordinary because it is compensation for services.
Answer (A) is incorrect. The amount of $7,000 is based on the adjusted basis of the partnership's net assets. Answer (B) is incorrect. The amount of $7,000 is based on the adjusted basis of the partnership's net assets, and the amount recognized should be characterized as ordinary income since it is compensation for services. Answer (D) is incorrect. Compensation for services is not characterized as a capital gain.

14.3.5. The following information pertains to Carr's admission to the Smith & Jones partnership on July 1 of the current year:

Carr's contribution of capital: 800 shares of Ed Corporation stock bought 10 years ago for $30,000; fair market value $150,000 on July 1 of the current year.
Carr's interest in capital and profits of Smith & Jones: 25%.
Fair market value of net assets of Smith & Jones on July 1 of the current year after Carr's admission: $600,000.

Carr's recognized gain in the current year on the exchange of the Ed stock for Carr's partnership interest was

A. $0

B. $120,000 ordinary income.

C. $120,000 long-term capital gain.

D. $120,000 Section 1231 gain.

14.3.6. Ben Krug, sole proprietor of Krug Dairy, hired Jan Karl in Year 1 for an agreed salary and the promise of a 10% partnership capital interest if Karl continued in Krug's employ until the end of Year 4. On January 1, Year 5, when the net worth of the business was $300,000, the partnership was formed as agreed. On what amount will Karl have to pay tax in Year 5 for the partnership capital interest received by him?

A. $0

B. $12,000

C. $18,000

D. $30,000

14.3.7. Jeffrey, the sole proprietor of a hardware business, hired Eastwood on January 1, Year 1, for an agreed salary and a promise to give him a 25% ownership interest if he were still employed at the end of 3 years, and an additional 25% interest if he continued in the business for a second 3-year period. On January 1, Year 4, a partnership was formed and Eastwood received a 25% interest in the capital and profits of the business. On that date, the net worth of the partnership was $60,000. The partnership has no liabilities. What is Eastwood's tax basis of his partnership interest at January 1, Year 4, and what amount should be added to his gross income for Year 4?

	Basis for Partnership Interest	Addition to Gross Income
A.	$0	$0
B.	$15,000	$15,000
C.	$30,000	$15,000
D.	$30,000	$30,000

Answer (A) is correct. *(CPA, adapted)*
REQUIRED: The recognized gain to a partner on the exchange of stock for a partnership interest.
DISCUSSION: Under Sec. 721, no gain or loss is recognized by a partnership or its partners when property is contributed to the partnership in exchange for a partnership interest. Carr has a realized gain of $120,000 (25% of the $600,000 value of the partnership minus his $30,000 basis in his contribution). This gain is not recognized under Sec. 721. For assets contributed after March 31, 1984, the precontribution gain on the asset is allocated to the contributing partner when the partnership later sells the asset or distributes it to another partner within 7 years.
Note that stock does constitute property under Sec. 721. But if the partnership would be an investment company if it were incorporated, the gain will be recognized. For this purpose, an investment company is one in which the partner has diversified his or her interest in stocks and securities and in which 80% or more of the partnership's assets are marketable stocks or securities.
Answer (B) is incorrect. Ordinary income would only be recognized, under Sec. 1245 recapture, if the partnership assumed liabilities on the contribution in excess of the partner's aggregate adjusted basis of the property. Answer (C) is incorrect. The realized gain is not recognized but allocated to the contributing partner when the partnership later sells the asset. Answer (D) is incorrect. Stock is not Sec. 1231 property, and no gain is recognized.

Answer (D) is correct. *(CPA, adapted)*
REQUIRED: The effect of receipt of interest in a partnership for services to a sole proprietor.
DISCUSSION: Ordinary income is recognized if services are rendered in return for property. The transaction is treated as if Jan received an undivided 10% interest in each of the enterprise's assets and then contributed them to the partnership.
The partnership's basis in the assets deemed contributed by Jan will be their FMV. Jan should recognize income of 10% of the $300,000 net worth of the enterprise, or $30,000.
Answer (A) is incorrect. Karl will have to pay tax in Year 5 on an amount for the partnership capital interest received by him. Answer (B) is incorrect. The amount of $12,000 is only 4% of the partnership's net worth at January 1, Year 5. Answer (C) is incorrect. The amount of $18,000 is only 6% of the partnership's net worth at January 1, Year 5.

Answer (B) is correct. *(CPA, adapted)*
REQUIRED: The basis of a partnership interest and the amount of gross income when a partner receives the interest in exchange for services.
DISCUSSION: When a partnership interest is received in exchange for services performed, income equal to the fair market value of the partnership interest must be recognized by the partner [Reg. 1.721-1(b)(1)]. A partner's basis in his or her partnership interest received for services rendered is equal to the income recognized (Reg. 1.722-1). Eastwood must recognize gross income of $15,000 (25% of $60,000), which is the value of the partnership interest received for services rendered. Eastwood's basis in the partnership is $15,000, the amount of income recognized.
Answer (A) is incorrect. Eastwood has a tax basis and an addition to gross income from the partnership interest. Answer (C) is incorrect. The basis of this partnership interest is the same as the gross income amount since the partnership has no liabilities. Answer (D) is incorrect. Eastwood received only a 25% partnership interest, not a 50% interest.

14.3.8. Eng contributed the following assets to a partnership in exchange for a 50% interest in the partnership's capital and profits:

Cash	$50,000
Equipment:	
Fair market value	35,000
Adjusted basis	25,000

The partnership has no liabilities. The basis for Eng's interest in the partnership is

   A. $37,500

   B. $42,500

   C. $75,000

   D. $85,000

Answer (C) is correct. *(CPA, adapted)*
REQUIRED: The partner's basis in a partnership interest received in exchange for cash and property.
DISCUSSION: The basis of a partner's interest acquired by contribution of property and money is the amount of money contributed plus the adjusted basis of property contributed (Sec. 722). Eng's basis in the partnership interest is

Money contributed	$50,000
Adjusted basis of equipment	25,000
Basis	$75,000

Answer (A) is incorrect. The amount of $37,500 is only 50% of the cash and 50% of the adjusted basis of the equipment. Answer (B) is incorrect. The amount of $42,500 is 50% of the cash and 50% of the FMV of the equipment. Answer (D) is incorrect. The interest in the partnership is based on the adjusted basis of the equipment, not its FMV.

14.3.9. Ralph Elin contributed land to the partnership of Anduz & Elin. Elin's adjusted basis in this land was $50,000, and its fair market value was $75,000. Under the partnership agreement, Elin's capital account was credited with the full fair market value of the land. Anduz made a $75,000 cash contribution to the partnership. Thus, each partner's capital account was credited for $75,000. Elin and Anduz share profits and losses equally. The partnership has no liabilities. What is the adjusted basis of Elin's partnership interest?

   A. $25,000

   B. $37,500

   C. $50,000

   D. $75,000

Answer (C) is correct. *(CPA, adapted)*
REQUIRED: The adjusted basis of a partner's interest acquired by contributing property.
DISCUSSION: The adjusted basis of a partner's interest is the amount of money contributed plus the adjusted basis of property contributed (Sec. 722). Elin's adjusted basis in the partnership interest is $50,000 (adjusted basis of the land contributed). Stated capital account values and contributions by other partners (except liabilities) have no effect on a partner's basis for tax purposes.
Answer (A) is incorrect. The amount of $25,000 is one-half of the adjusted basis of the land. Answer (B) is incorrect. The amount of $37,500 is one-half of the FMV of the land contributed. Answer (D) is incorrect. The amount of $75,000 is the FMV of the land contributed.

14.3.10. Earl acquired a 20% interest in a partnership by contributing property that had an adjusted basis to him of $8,000 and that was subject to a mortgage of $12,000. Which of the following results is correct?

	Capital Gain Recognized	Basis of Partnership Interest
A.	$1,600	$1,600
B.	$0	$(1,600)
C.	$4,000	$8,000
D.	$1,600	$0

Answer (D) is correct. *(SEE, adapted)*
REQUIRED: The amount of capital gain recognized and the basis of a partnership interest to a partner.
DISCUSSION: Under Sec. 722, the basis of a partnership interest acquired by the contribution of property is the adjusted basis of the property to the contributing partner. Under Sec. 752(b), the assumption by a partnership of a partner's individual liabilities is treated as a distribution of money to the partner, which reduces the basis of the partner's interest (Sec. 733). If the amount of liabilities assumed by the partnership exceeds the contributing partner's basis in the partnership, the excess is treated as a capital gain. Earl's basis is the $8,000 adjusted basis of the property contributed less the relieved individual liability ($12,000 × 80% = $9,600). However, since basis can never be negative, Earl will have $0 basis in his partnership interest, and the $1,600 excess of the liability assumed over the adjusted basis of the contributed property will be treated as a capital gain.
Answer (A) is incorrect. Earl will not have any basis in his partnership interest. Answer (B) is incorrect. Earl will have to recognize a capital gain. Further, basis is never a negative amount. Answer (C) is incorrect. Earl will only recognize a capital gain to the extent of income recognized on the transaction. Also, Earl does not have any basis in his partnership interest.

14.3.11. The following information pertains to land contributed by Pink for a 50% interest in a new partnership:

Adjusted basis to Pink	$100,000
Fair market value	300,000
Mortgage assumed by partnership	30,000

The partnership has no other liabilities. The basis for Pink's partnership interest is

A. $70,000

B. $85,000

C. $100,000

D. $300,000

Answer (B) is correct. *(CPA, adapted)*

REQUIRED: The partner's basis in a partnership interest acquired by contributing property subject to a mortgage.

DISCUSSION: Under Sec. 722, the basis of a partner's interest in a partnership is the partner's adjusted basis in the contributed property. When the partnership assumes a mortgage or takes the property subject to a mortgage, the contributing partner is deemed to have received a distribution of cash to the extent of the relieved liability [Sec. 752(b)]. This deemed distribution reduces the partner's basis.

Adjusted basis of land contributed	$100,000
Less: share of mortgage assumed by the other partners ($30,000 × 50%)	(15,000)
Basis	$ 85,000

Answer (A) is incorrect. Only one-half of the mortgage assumed by the partnership reduces Pink's basis. Answer (C) is incorrect. The adjusted basis of the land must be reduced by one-half of the mortgage assumed by the partnership. Answer (D) is incorrect. The amount of $300,000 is the FMV of the land, and no adjustment is made for the mortgage.

14.3.12. Mr. McRich is a limited partner with a 60% loss interest and a 30% profit interest in the XYZ Partnership. Mr. McRich contributed $10,000 cash for his partnership interest. At the time of his contribution, the partnership had recourse liabilities of $100,000 and nonrecourse liabilities of $70,000. There is no minimum gain related to the nonrecourse debt. For the recourse debt, economic risk of loss is shared by the partners based on each partner's loss interest. Mr. McRich's basis in his partnership interest is

A. $10,000

B. $31,000

C. $61,000

D. $91,000

Answer (B) is correct. *(Publisher, adapted)*

REQUIRED: The limited partner's basis in a partnership that has both recourse and nonrecourse liabilities.

DISCUSSION: A partner receives a basis in a partnership equal to the basis of the property contributed to the partnership (Sec. 722). Under Sec. 752(a), an increase in a partner's share of liabilities is treated as a contribution of money by such partner, which increases the partner's basis. Partners share recourse liabilities based on their share of economic losses [Reg. 1.752-2(a)]. In the absence of guarantees and special arrangements, this is usually limited to the amount of additional contributions the limited partner must make. All partners, including limited partners, share true nonrecourse debts first as the minimum gain is shared with the excess shared in the same proportion as profits.

Mr. McRich's basis in the partnership includes the $10,000 cash contributed plus his share of nonrecourse liabilities based on his profit interest. His total basis in the partnership is $31,000 [$10,000 + $21,000 ($70,000 × 30%) of nonrecourse liabilities].

Answer (A) is incorrect. Mr. McRich's basis in his partnership interest also includes a 30% share of the nonrecourse liabilities. Answer (C) is incorrect. Only nonrecourse debt increases a limited partner's basis. Answer (D) is incorrect. A 60% loss interest of the recourse liabilities is not included in a limited partner's basis.

14.3.13. Bill and Ted form a partnership with cash contributions of $40,000 each. Bill is a limited partner. Under the partnership agreement, Bill and Ted share all partnership profits and losses equally. The partnership borrows $100,000 from a local bank to purchase depreciable equipment to be used in the partnership's business. Ted is required under the partnership agreement to pay the creditor if the partnership defaults. Based upon these facts, what are Bill's and Ted's bases in the partnership?

	Ted	Bill
A.	$40,000	$40,000
B.	$90,000	$90,000
C.	$140,000	$40,000
D.	$140,000	$140,000

Answer (C) is correct. *(SEE, adapted)*

REQUIRED: The general and the limited partners' bases in a partnership that has nonrecourse liabilities.

DISCUSSION: An increase in a partner's share of liabilities is treated as a contribution of money by such partner, which increases the partner's basis. Partners share recourse liabilities based on their ratio for sharing economic losses [Reg. 1.752-2(a)]. In the absence of guarantees and special arrangements, the limited partner's economic loss is usually limited to the amount of additional contributions the partner must make.

Ted's basis in the partnership includes the full $100,000 liability because he would be liable for the $100,000 under the partnership agreement.

Answer (A) is incorrect. Ted's basis is increased for the liability owed to the bank, as he alone must pay the debt in default. Answer (B) is incorrect. The liability is not shared because Bill would not be responsible for paying in default. Answer (D) is incorrect. Both Bill and Ted are not jointly responsible for the full amount of the loan.

14.3.14. Dave Burr acquired a 20% interest in a partnership by contributing a parcel of land. At the time of Burr's contribution, the land had a fair market value of $35,000, an adjusted basis to Burr of $8,000, and was subject to a mortgage of $12,000. Payment of the mortgage was assumed by the partnership. The partners share economic risk of loss according to their loss interest. The partnership has no other liabilities. Burr's basis for his interest in the partnership is

A. $0

B. $5,600

C. $8,000

D. $23,000

Answer (A) is correct. *(CPA, adapted)*
REQUIRED: The partner's basis in a partnership to which he contributed property with a liability in excess of basis.
DISCUSSION: Under Sec. 722, the basis of an interest in a partnership acquired by the contribution of property is the adjusted basis of such property to the contributing partner. Section 752(b) treats a decrease in a partner's individual liabilities by reason of the assumption by the partnership of such liabilities as a distribution of money to the partner, which reduces the basis of the partner's interest under Sec. 733 (but not below zero).
When Burr became a 20% partner, he was relieved of 80% of his $12,000 mortgage, or $9,600. Burr's basis in his partnership interest is the $8,000 basis in the property contributed minus the $9,600 relief of liability. However, his basis may not be less than zero. Note that he also has a gain of $1,600.
Answer (B) is incorrect. The amount of $5,600 is adjusted basis reduced by only 20% of the liabilities. Answer (C) is incorrect. The adjusted basis of the property must be reduced by 80% of the liabilities assumed by the partnership, but not below zero, to arrive at Burr's basis in the partnership. Answer (D) is incorrect. The amount of $23,000 is the FMV of the land reduced by the full amount of the liabilities. This difference cannot be used as the partner's basis.

14.3.15. Elton received a 25% capital interest in Z Associates, a partnership, in return for services rendered plus a contribution of assets with a basis to Elton of $25,000 and a fair market value of $40,000. The fair market value of Elton's 25% interest was $50,000. The partnership has no liabilities. How much is Elton's basis for his interest in Z?

A. $25,000

B. $35,000

C. $40,000

D. $50,000

Answer (B) is correct. *(CPA, adapted)*
REQUIRED: The basis of a partner's interest when property and services are contributed.
DISCUSSION: A partner's basis in a partnership is his or her adjusted basis in the property contributed (Sec. 722) plus income recognized by the partner for receiving the interest in exchange for services (Reg. 1.722-1). Regulation 1.721-1(b)(1) states that the value of a partnership interest received as compensation for services is income to the partner (FMV of the interest received). The fair market value of Elton's services is $10,000 ($50,000 FMV of the interest – $40,000 FMV of assets contributed).

Adjusted basis of assets contributed	$25,000
Income recognized for services rendered	10,000
Elton's partnership basis	$35,000

Answer (A) is incorrect. The amount of $25,000 fails to take into account the service contribution made by Elton. Answer (C) is incorrect. The amount of $40,000 uses the FMV of the asset contribution and fails to take into account the service contribution. Answer (D) is incorrect. The basis of the interest is not its FMV.

14.3.16. A and B formed a partnership by transferring the following assets to the partnership: A transferred $25,000 in cash and equipment, which cost $27,000, had an adjusted basis of $19,800, and had a fair market value of $30,000; B transferred cash of $50,000. The partnership's basis in equipment transferred to the partnership by A is

A. $19,800

B. $27,000

C. $30,000

D. $44,800

Answer (A) is correct. *(P.J. Markou)*
REQUIRED: The partnership's basis in contributed property.
DISCUSSION: Under Sec. 723, the partnership's basis for contributed property is the adjusted basis of such property to the contributing partner at the time of contribution, provided it is not an investment partnership. A's basis in the equipment was $19,800, so the partnership's basis in the equipment is $19,800.
Answer (B) is incorrect. The amount of $27,000 is the original cost of the equipment. Answer (C) is incorrect. The amount of $30,000 is the FMV of the equipment. Answer (D) is incorrect. The adjusted basis of the equipment does not include the cash contributed to the partnership.

14.3.17. ABC Partnership was formed on March 1 of the current year by three individuals. A contributed $20,000 cash for a 25% interest. B contributed property with an adjusted basis of $28,000 and fair market value of $32,000, subject to a $12,000 mortgage. C contributed property with an adjusted basis of $20,000 and fair market value of $64,000, subject to a $24,000 liability. B and C received 25% and 50% partnership interests, respectively. The partnership assumed both partners' liabilities. The partnership has no other liabilities. On March 1 of the current year, B's gain recognized on contribution and basis in partnership interest are

   A. $0 gain, $19,000 basis.

   B. $9,000 gain, $25,000 basis.

   C. $0 gain, $25,000 basis.

   D. $9,000 gain, $19,000 basis.

Answer (C) is correct. *(C.K. Craig)*
   REQUIRED: The calculation of both gain recognized from partnership contributions and basis in the partnership interest.
   DISCUSSION: In general, under Sec. 721, no gain or loss shall be recognized by a partnership or any of its partners when contributing property to the partnership in exchange for a partnership interest.
   Under Section 722, the basis of an interest in a partnership acquired by a contribution of property, including money, to the partnership is the adjusted basis of such property to the contributing partner. Section 752 requires that increases in a partner's share of partnership liabilities be treated as contributions of money and decreases in such liabilities be treated as distributions of money.
   As of March 1 of the current year, B's basis in the partnership interest is as follows:

Basis in property contributed	$28,000
Less: liabilities assumed by partnership ($12,000 × 75%)	(9,000)
Plus: liabilities assumed by B ($24,000 × 25%)	6,000
Basis in partnership interest to B	$25,000

   Answer (A) is incorrect. B's basis also includes 25% of C's liabilities assumed by the partnership. Answer (B) is incorrect. No gain is recognized on a contribution of property to the partnership by a partner in exchange for partnership interest. Answer (D) is incorrect. No gain is recognized and because B's basis also includes 25% of C's liabilities assumed by the partnership.

14.3.18. A, B, and C formed a calendar-year partnership. Profits and losses are to be shared equally. A contributed a building to be used in the business that had an adjusted basis to A of $100,000 and a fair market value of $130,000. The partnership also assumed A's $60,000 mortgage on the building. B and C each contributed $40,000 in cash to the partnership's capital. What is the partnership's basis for determining depreciation on the building?

   A. $0

   B. $40,000

   C. $100,000

   D. $130,000

Answer (C) is correct. *(SEE, adapted)*
   REQUIRED: The partnership's basis in contributed property.
   DISCUSSION: Under Sec. 723, the partnership's basis in property is the contributing partner's basis at the time of contribution. Therefore, the partnership's basis in the building is A's adjusted basis of $100,000. No adjustment in basis of the building is made for the mortgage.
   Answer (A) is incorrect. The partnership has basis in the building for determining the building's depreciation. Answer (B) is incorrect. The adjusted basis should not be reduced by the mortgage on the building to determine the partnership's basis. Answer (D) is incorrect. The amount of $130,000 is the FMV of the building.

14.3.19. Last year, Jim Cash, one of two equal partners, contributed land with a basis to him of $15,000 and a fair market value of $10,000 to the partnership of which he was a member. His capital account was credited for $10,000. The land was later sold for $8,000. As a result of this sale, Cash must report on his personal income tax return a

   A. $1,000 loss.

   B. $3,500 loss.

   C. $5,000 loss.

   D. $6,000 loss.

Answer (D) is correct. *(CPA, adapted)*
   REQUIRED: The tax effect to a partner when property contributed is sold subsequent to formation of the partnership.
   DISCUSSION: Under Sec. 721, neither the partnership nor any partner generally recognizes gain or loss when property is contributed in exchange for a partnership interest. Under Sec. 723, the partnership's basis in the property is $15,000 (the contributing partner's basis at the time of contribution). The sale of the property by the partnership resulted in a $7,000 loss ($8,000 proceeds less $15,000 adjusted basis). Under Sec. 704(c), precontribution loss must be allocated to the contributing partner. Accordingly, Cash must recognize a precontribution loss of $5,000 ($15,000 basis – $10,000 FMV contribution) plus his $1,000 share of post-contribution loss [($10,000 FMV of contribution – $8,000 sales price) × 1/2].
   Answer (A) is incorrect. Cash must also recognize the precontribution loss of $5,000 for the difference between his AB and FMV. Answer (B) is incorrect. The precontribution loss has not been allocated exclusively to Cash. Answer (C) is incorrect. Cash must also recognize his share of the $2,000 post-contribution loss.

14.3.20. The holding period of property acquired by a partnership as a contribution to the contributing partner's capital account

A. Begins with the date of contribution to the partnership.

B. Includes the period during which the property was held by the contributing partner.

C. Is equal to the contributing partner's holding period prior to contribution to the partnership.

D. Depends on the character of the property transferred.

Answer (B) is correct. *(CPA, adapted)*
REQUIRED: The holding period of contributed property.
DISCUSSION: The partnership's holding period for contributed property includes the period of time the property was held by the contributing partner [Sec. 1223(2)]. The holding period of the partner "tacks on" because the partnership receives a carryover basis in the contributed property. This is true even if the contributing partner recognizes a gain or loss.
Answer (A) is incorrect. The holding period does not begin with the date of contribution to the partnership. Answer (C) is incorrect. The holding period does not equal the contributing partner's holding period prior to contribution to the partnership. Answer (D) is incorrect. The holding period does not depend on the character of property transferred.

14.3.21. A and B formed a calendar-year partnership on April 1 of the current year. Certain costs were incurred before beginning business September 1 of the current year:

Legal fees in drawing up agreement	$ 900
Cost of placing notice required by local law in newspapers	600
Commissions paid to sell limited partners' interests	5,400
Costs of filing with the state	300

What is the allowable deduction for organizational costs in the current year?

A. $20

B. $40

C. $90

D. $1,800

Answer (D) is correct. *(SEE, adapted)*
REQUIRED: The partnership's allowable deduction for organizational costs.
DISCUSSION: Section 709(b) allows a partnership to amortize organizational expenses over a period of 180 months, beginning with the month in which the partnership begins business. If the organization costs are less than $50,000, the first $5,000 is deductible. The organizational expenses that may be amortized are those incident to the creation of the partnership and chargeable to the capital account.

Legal fees	$ 900
Cost of notices required by law	600
Costs of filing with the state	300
Total deductible costs	$1,800

The partnership formed by A and B may deduct the full $1,800. The commissions paid are syndication expenses, which must be capitalized and cannot be amortized [Reg. 1.709-2(b)].
Answer (A) is incorrect. Legal fees, notice costs, and filing fees are all deductible as organizational costs. Answer (B) is incorrect. Commissions to sell limited interests in the partnership are syndication expenses, which cannot be amortized. Answer (C) is incorrect. The amortization begins with the month in which the partnership begins business, not at the time the partnership is formed.

14.3.22. In August of Year 1, Jacob contributed land (held as an investment) to the Fastbuck Real Estate partnership for a 20% interest. Jacob had a $75,000 basis in the land, and its fair market value at the date of the contribution was $35,000. Fastbuck developed the land into building lots at a total cost of $20,000. During Year 3, Fastbuck sold all the lots for a total of $60,000. What are the amount and the character of the partnership's gain or loss?

A. $35,000 ordinary loss.

B. $35,000 capital loss.

C. $5,000 ordinary loss.

D. $5,000 capital gain.

Answer (B) is correct. *(Publisher, adapted)*
REQUIRED: The amount and the character of a partnership's gain or loss on the sale of contributed capital gain property.
DISCUSSION: Under Sec. 723, the partnership's basis in the land is $75,000 (the contributing partner's basis at the time of contribution). The partnership increased its basis in the property to $95,000 by the $20,000 development costs. The sale of the property by the partnership resulted in a $35,000 loss ($60,000 proceeds – $95,000 basis). For capital assets contributed to a partnership after March 31, 1984, Sec. 724(c) requires any loss to be treated as a capital loss to the extent of the loss inherent in the property at the time of contribution (basis in excess of FMV). This applies even if the property is not a capital asset in the hands of the partnership. Since Jacob had an inherent capital loss of $40,000 in the property when he contributed it ($75,000 basis – $35,000 FMV), the partnership's $35,000 loss is a capital loss.
Answer (A) is incorrect. The sale does not result in an ordinary loss. Answer (C) is incorrect. The sale does not result in a $5,000 ordinary loss, as the inherent loss on the property at contribution was not ordinary. Furthermore, the wrong basis is used to calculate the partnership's loss. Answer (D) is incorrect. There is not a capital gain from the sale. The partnership's basis will equal that of the contributing partner's at contribution.

14.3.23. Sam and Terry formed the ST Partnership as equal partners on July 15 of the current year. As part of the formation, Sam contributed land with a basis to him of $70,000 and a fair market value of $200,000, and Terry contributed property with a basis equal to its $100,000 fair market value. On July 16 of the current year, the partnership mortgaged the land for $150,000 and distributed $100,000 cash to Sam. How much gain (loss) should Sam recognize from these transactions?

- A. $0
- B. $30,000
- C. $65,000
- D. $130,000

Answer (C) is correct. *(Publisher, adapted)*
REQUIRED: The gain (loss) a partner should recognize when (s)he contributes property to a partnership and receives an immediate distribution.
DISCUSSION: Section 707(a)(2) will treat such a transaction as a sale of the property by Sam (when the transaction is essentially a sale) with respect to the portion of the property given up to the other partner(s).
Therefore, Sam will be treated as having sold one-half of the property for $100,000 and contributed the other half to the partnership. His gain on the "sale" is $65,000 [$100,000 − ($70,000 × 50%)]. He has no gain on his contribution of the remaining one-half of the land.
Answer (A) is incorrect. Sam must recognize a gain based on partnership apportionment. Answer (B) is incorrect. The distribution rules do not apply to the transaction. Instead, Sam will treat the transaction as a sale of one-half the land. Answer (D) is incorrect. The amount of $130,000 is the difference between Sam's basis in the land and the land's FMV.

14.3.24. Mr. D and Mr. E formed a calendar-year partnership. Mr. D contributed land that had a basis to him of $5,000 and a fair market value of $10,000. The land was contributed subject to a mortgage of $3,000. Mr. E is to manage the partnership's business for which he will receive a one-half interest in the profits, losses, and capital of the partnership. Neither of the partners nor the partnership is required to recognize gain or loss on the formation of the partnership.

- A. True.
- B. False.

Answer (B) is correct. *(SEE, adapted)*
DISCUSSION: In general, no gain or loss is recognized by the partnership or the partners when property is contributed to the partnership in exchange for a partnership interest [Sec. 721(a)]. However, Sec. 721 does not prevent a partner from recognizing compensation income when a partnership interest is received in exchange for services. Mr. E must recognize the fair market value of the partnership interest he received as ordinary income. The partners other than E will recognize gain with respect to the portion of the partnership assets transferred to E as compensation.

14.3.25. The rule that neither the partner nor the partnership recognizes a gain or loss when property is contributed to the partnership in exchange for a partnership interest applies only at the time the partnership is being formed.

- A. True.
- B. False.

Answer (B) is correct. *(SEE, adapted)*
DISCUSSION: In general, under Sec. 721, no gain or loss shall be recognized by a partnership or any of its partners when contributing property to the partnership in exchange for a partnership interest.

14.3.26. A contribution of property by Partner N to her partnership may be treated as a transaction in which gain or loss is recognized if, after a short period of time, either before or after the contribution, the partnership distributes other property to N and the property contributed by N is retained by the partnership.

- A. True.
- B. False.

Answer (A) is correct. *(SEE, adapted)*
DISCUSSION: Section 721(a) states that no gain or loss shall be recognized by a partnership or by any of its partners in the case of a contribution of property to the partnership in exchange for an interest in the partnership. Section 707(a)(2)(B) states that, if there is a direct or indirect transfer of money or other property by a partner to the partnership and there is a related direct or indirect transfer of money or other property by the partnership to such partners, then the two transfers, when viewed together, are to be characterized as a sale of the property. Because the two transfers take place in a short period of time, gain or loss will be recognized by Partner N.

14.3.27. The adjusted basis of the partnership interest is determined without considering any amount shown in the partnership books as a capital, equity, or a similar account.

- A. True.
- B. False.

Answer (A) is correct. *(SEE, adapted)*
DISCUSSION: The original basis of a partner's interest acquired in exchange for contributions of property is the sum of the money contributed, the adjusted basis of property contributed, and the amount of any recognized gain by the partner on the contribution. The assumption of liabilities by the partner is treated as a contribution of money to the partnership and increases basis. The amount of liabilities assumed by the partnership is treated as a distribution to the contributing partner and reduces basis.

14.3.28. Partner N contributed property with an adjusted basis of $400 and a fair market value of $1,000 to Partnership B. Partner L contributed $1,000 cash. The partnership has no liabilities. Under the partnership agreement, each partner will have a capital account reflected in the partnership books of $1,000, but the adjusted basis of Partner N's interest is only $400.

A. True.

B. False.

Answer (A) is correct. *(SEE, adapted)*
DISCUSSION: The basis of a partnership interest acquired by a contribution of property is the adjusted basis of the property contributed (Sec. 722). Although the partners will have equal capital account balances, the adjusted bases of their interests will not be equal.

14.3.29. Mr. Snow and Ms. White formed a partnership. Snow contributed $20,000 in cash, and White contributed equipment having a fair market value of $20,000 and an adjusted basis to her of $16,000. The partnership's basis in the equipment is $20,000.

A. True.

B. False.

Answer (B) is correct. *(SEE, adapted)*
DISCUSSION: Under Sec. 723, the partnership's basis in property is the contributing partner's basis at the time of the contribution. Therefore, the partnership's basis in the equipment is Ms. White's adjusted basis of $16,000.

14.3.30. On March 10, Year 1, Daniel contributed land in exchange for a partnership interest in Parr Company. The fair market value of the land at that time was $40,000, and Daniel's adjusted basis was $25,000. On December 2, Year 2, Parr distributed that land to another partner. The fair market value at that time was $40,000. These transactions would not require a gain to be recognized by Daniel.

A. True.

B. False.

Answer (B) is correct. *(SEE, adapted)*
DISCUSSION: Under Sec. 737, precontribution gain must be recognized if the contributed property is distributed to another partner within 7 years of the contribution. Accordingly, Daniel must recognize all of the precontribution gain of $15,000 ($40,000 FMV contribution – $25,000 basis).

14.3.31. Syndication fees, which are costs connected with the issuing and marketing of interests in a partnership, such as commissions, professional fees, and printing costs, must be capitalized and amortized over a period of 180 months.

A. True.

B. False.

Answer (B) is correct. *(SEE, adapted)*
DISCUSSION: Syndication fees must be capitalized and cannot be amortized. However, Sec. 709(b) allows a partnership to amortize organizational expenses over a period of 180 months.

14.4 Partnership's Tax Year

14.4.1. When a partner in a six-partner partnership dies, the partnership tax year must close

A. On a date selected by the remaining partners.

B. At a date determined by the executor/executrix of the estate.

C. At the date of death for the surviving partners.

D. At the end of the regular partnership year for the surviving partners.

Answer (D) is correct. *(SEE, adapted)*
REQUIRED: The date the partnership tax year closes when a partner dies.
DISCUSSION: For tax years beginning after December 31, 1997, the taxable year of a partnership, with respect to a partner who dies, closes at the date of death [Sec. 706(c)(2)(A)(ii)]. The partnership tax year does not close, however, with respect to the five surviving partners.

Answer (A) is incorrect. The partnership tax year does not close on a date selected by the remaining partners when a partner dies. Answer (B) is incorrect. When a partner dies, the partnership tax year does not close at a date determined by the executor/executrix of the estate. Answer (C) is incorrect. When a partner dies, the partnership tax year does not close at the date of death for the surviving partners.

14.4.2. With respect to a partner who sells or exchanges his entire interest in a partnership, the closing of the partnership year occurs

    A. At the end of the partnership year.

    B. On a date selected by the above partner.

    C. On the date of the sale or exchange.

    D. On a date agreed upon by all partners.

Answer (C) is correct. *(P.J. Markou)*
    REQUIRED: The date a partnership year closes with respect to a partner who sells or exchanges his partnership interest.
    DISCUSSION: Under Sec. 706(c)(2)(A), the taxable year closes with respect to a partner on the date he sells or exchanges his entire interest.
    Answer (A) is incorrect. With respect to a partner selling or exchanging his entire interest in a partnership, the closing of the partnership year does not occur at the end of the partnership year. Answer (B) is incorrect. With respect to a partner selling or exchanging his entire interest in a partnership, the closing of the partnership year does not occur on a date selected by the selling/exchanging partner. Answer (D) is incorrect. With respect to a partner selling or exchanging his entire interest in a partnership, the closing of the partnership year does not occur on a date agreed upon by all partners.

14.4.3. Which taxable year may a newly formed partnership not adopt without obtaining prior approval from the IRS?

    A. A taxable year that is the same as that of its majority partners.

    B. The least aggregate deferral year if majority partners and principal partners have varied year ends.

    C. A January 31 year end if it is a retail enterprise with a natural business year ending January 31 and all of its majority and principal partners are on a calendar year.

    D. The taxable year of all its principal partners if its majority partners do not have a common tax year end.

Answer (C) is correct. *(CPA, adapted)*
    REQUIRED: The taxable year a new partnership may not adopt without IRS approval.
    DISCUSSION: A partnership's required taxable year is that of the partner(s) owning more than 50% of partnership capital and profits if they held the same tax year on the first day of the partnership tax year. If the majority partner(s) do not have the same taxable year or have not kept their same tax year for the required period, the taxable year of all principal (5%) partners must be adopted. If all principal partners do not have the same taxable year, a partner's tax year that results in the least aggregate deferral to the partners must be used [Reg. 1.706-1(b)(2)(i)(c)].
    Although Section 444 permits a partnership to elect a fiscal year, a newly formed partnership may not elect a fiscal year with more than a 3-month deferral period (i.e., the number of months between the beginning of the tax year selected and the end of the required tax year). A January 31 year end has an 11-month deferral period. Another fiscal year may be chosen only with the consent of the IRS and only if a business purpose (e.g., natural business year) is established.
    Answer (A) is incorrect. A taxable year that is the same as that of its majority partners is a permitted tax year that can be adopted without the prior approval of the IRS. Answer (B) is incorrect. The least aggregate deferral year if majority partners and principal partners have varied year ends is a permitted tax year that can be adopted without the prior approval of the IRS. Answer (D) is incorrect. The taxable year of all its principal partners if its majority partners do not have a common tax year end is a permitted tax year that can be adopted without the prior approval of the IRS.

14.4.4. Which one of the following statements regarding a partnership's tax year is true?

    A. A partnership formed on July 1 is required to adopt a tax year ending on June 30.

    B. A partnership may elect to have a tax year other than the generally required tax year if the deferral period for the tax year elected does not exceed 3 months.

    C. A "valid business purpose" can no longer be claimed as a reason for adoption of a tax year other than the generally required tax year.

    D. Within 30 days after a partnership has established a tax year, a form must be filed with the IRS as notification of the tax year adopted.

Answer (B) is correct. *(CPA, adapted)*
    REQUIRED: The true statement regarding a partnership tax year.
    DISCUSSION: Section 444 permits a partnership to elect a fiscal year with no more than a 3-month deferral period, i.e., the number of months between the beginning of the tax year selected and the end of the required tax year.
    Answer (A) is incorrect. A partnership may elect any taxable year as long as it corresponds to that of its majority partner(s), all its principal partners, any taxable year given that its principal partners change to the same tax year, or a partner's tax year that results in the least aggregate deferral of income to the partners. Answer (C) is incorrect. Any fiscal year may be chosen if a business purpose is established and the IRS gives its consent. Answer (D) is incorrect. The partnership elects its tax year on its first return, which must be filed by the 15th day of the third month following the end of its tax year.

14.4.5. Rose and Irene each have a 50% interest in a partnership that started business on July 1. Rose uses a calendar year, while Irene has a fiscal year ending November 30. Which of the following is true?

A. The partnership may also use the calendar year because at least 50% is owned by a calendar-year taxpayer.

B. The partnership must use the fiscal year ending November 30 because it results in a deferral of 11 months.

C. The partnership must use the fiscal year ending November 30 because it results in a deferral of 1 month.

D. The partnership may use either the calendar year or fiscal year ending November 30 because each partner owns an equal percentage.

Answer (C) is correct. *(SEE, adapted)*
REQUIRED: The tax year the partnership must use.
DISCUSSION: A partner reports his or her distributive share of partnership items, including guaranteed payments, in that tax year of the partner within (or with) which the partnership's tax year ended. Unless an exception applies, the partnership must use a required tax year. The required tax year is the first of 1., 2., or 3., following, that applies. The partners, not the partnership, are obligated to make any estimated tax payments.

1. Majority interest tax year is the tax year of partners owning more than 50% of partnership capital and profits if they held the same tax year on the first day of the partnership tax year.

2. Principal partners' tax year is the same tax year of all principal partners, i.e., partners owning 5% of more in capital and profits.

3. Least aggregate deferral tax year is determined by multiplying each partner's ownership percentage by the number of months of income deferral for each possible partnership tax year and then selecting the tax year that produces the smallest total tax deferral.

12/31 Year End	Year End	Interest in Partnership	Months of Deferral for 12/31 Year End	Interest × Deferral
Rose	12/31	.5	0	0
Irene	11/30	.5	11	5.5
			Total deferral	5.5

11/30 Year End	Year End	Interest in Partnership	Months of Deferral for 11/30 Year End	Interest × Deferral
Rose	12/31	.5	1	.5
Irene	11/30	.5	0	0
			Total deferral	.5

Answer (A) is incorrect. Each partner has a 50% interest. Therefore, no majority ownership exists. Answer (B) is incorrect. A fiscal year ending November 30 results in a 1-month deferral. Answer (D) is incorrect. Unless an exception applies, the partnership must use a required tax year that is prescribed in the Code.

14.4.6. Alpha Partnership is on a fiscal year ending March 31. Partner Alf reports income on the fiscal year ending March 31, and Partner Omega reports income on the fiscal year ending September 30. Both partners have a 50% interest in partnership profits. Assume the partnership does not make a Sec. 444 election and does not establish a business purpose for a different period. The tax year that the partnership must use to file its tax return ends on

A. Any month end.

B. March 31.

C. September 30.

D. December 31.

Answer (B) is correct. *(SEE, adapted)*
REQUIRED: The tax year the partnership must use to file its tax return.
DISCUSSION: A partnership's required tax year is that of the partner(s) owning more than 50% of partnership capital and profits. If the majority partner(s) do not have the same year, the tax year of all principal (5%) partners must be adopted. If all principal partners do not have the same taxable year, under Reg. 1.706-1(b), the partnership must adopt the tax year of the partner that results in the least aggregate deferral of income to the partners. Aggregate deferral is the sum of the products of deferral for each partner and each partner's interest in partnership profits. Using Alpha's tax year results in aggregate deferral of 3.0 [(0 × 50%) + (6 × 50%)]. Using Omega's tax year would result in aggregate deferral of 3.0 [(6 × 50%) + (0 + 50%)]. Regulation 1.706-1(b) further provides that if 1 of more than 1 qualifying tax years is also the partnership's existing tax year, the partnership must maintain its existing tax year.
Answer (A) is incorrect. Regulation 1.706-1(b) requires that the partnership adopt a tax year that results in the least aggregate deferral of income to the partners. Answer (C) is incorrect. If one of more than one qualifying tax years (of the partners) is also the partnership's existing tax year, the partnership must maintain its existing tax year. Answer (D) is incorrect. December 31 is not the correct date for the end of the partnership's tax year.

14.4.7. Which of the following is a true statement with respect to a partnership electing, under Sec. 444, a fiscal year that is not normally required and for which a business purpose does not exist?

A. The election requires the partners to pay an additional tax on their income from the partnership.

B. The election requires a payment to approximate the tax the partners would have paid if the partnership switched to its required year.

C. The election requires minimum distributions to be made to the partners.

D. Any fiscal year may be selected if the required payment is made.

Answer (B) is correct. *(SEE, adapted)*
REQUIRED: The true statement concerning a partnership's election of a fiscal year under Sec. 444.
DISCUSSION: A partnership may elect, under Sec. 444, a fiscal year other than normally required and for which a business purpose does not exist. However, for the election to be effective, Sec. 7519 requires a payment intended to approximate the tax the partners would have paid if the entity had switched to its required year.
Answer (A) is incorrect. The partnership makes the additional payment (similar to a deposit), not the partners. Answer (C) is incorrect. Minimum distributions are required of a personal service corporation to elect a fiscal year, not a partnership. Answer (D) is incorrect. The fiscal year may not result in more than a 3-month deferral, unless the partnership existed in 1986 and is retaining the fiscal year it had at that time.

14.4.8. Maggie and Simon each have a 50% interest in a partnership that started business October 1. Maggie uses a calendar year while Simon has a fiscal year ending November 30. Which of the following is true?

A. The partnership must use the fiscal year ending September 30 provided a Sec. 444 election and payment are made.

B. The partnership must use the fiscal year ending November 30 as that results in the least deferral.

C. The partnership must use the calendar year.

D. The partnership may use the fiscal year ending September 30 provided a Sec. 444 election and payment are made, AND the partnership may use the fiscal year ending November 30 as that results in the least deferral.

Answer (D) is correct. *(SEE, adapted)*
REQUIRED: The tax year the partnership must use.
DISCUSSION: A partner reports his or her distributive share of partnership items, including guaranteed payments, in that tax year of the partner within (or with) which the partnership's tax year ended. Unless an exception applies, the partnership must use a required tax year. The required tax year is the first of 1., 2., or 3., following, that applies. The partners, not the partnership, are obligated to make any estimated tax payments.

1. Majority interest tax year is the tax year of partners owning more than 50% of partnership capital and profits if they held the same tax year on the first day of the partnership tax year.

2. Principal partners' tax year is the same tax year of all principal partners, i.e., partners owning 5% or more in capital and profits.

3. Least aggregate deferral tax year is determined by multiplying each partner's ownership percentage by the number of months of income deferral for each possible partnership tax year and then selecting the tax year that produces the smallest total tax deferral.

Under Sec. 444, a partnership may elect a tax year that is neither the required year nor a natural business year. The year elected may result in no more than 3 months' deferral (between the beginning of a tax year elected and the required tax year). The partnership must also pay an amount approximating the amount of additional tax that would have resulted had the election not been made.
Answer (A) is incorrect. It is also true that the partnership may use the fiscal year ending November 30, as it results in the least deferral. Answer (B) is incorrect. It is also true that the partnership may use the fiscal year ending September 30 provided a Sec. 444 election and payment are made. Answer (C) is incorrect. The calendar year would result in a longer deferral than a November 30 tax year.

14.4.9. ABCD Partnership was formed on January 1. Mr. A, Mr. B, and Mr. C are all calendar-year taxpayers. D is a corporation and uses the fiscal year ending June 30 for reporting its taxable income. Each partner owns a 25% interest in the partnership. The partnership is required to use the calendar year as its tax year.

A. True.

B. False.

Answer (A) is correct. *(SEE, adapted)*
DISCUSSION: A partnership's required taxable year is that of the partners owning more than 50% of partnership capital and profits, if they held the same tax year on the first day of the partnership tax year. Here, three partners own 75% of the capital and profits and they are all calendar-year taxpayers. Therefore, the partnership must use the calendar year.

14.4.10. A principal partner is one who owns more than half of the partnership's capital interests.

A. True.

B. False.

14.4.11. A newly formed partnership may not adopt a calendar year without the consent of the Commissioner of Internal Revenue if both partners report their income on a fiscal year basis ending June 30.

A. True.

B. False.

14.4.12. Each of Partnership MNO's three equal partners has a different tax year. All three change their tax years at different times in the current year so that they have the same tax year. The partnership must also change to the same year if no business purpose exists for a fiscal year, and prior approval of the IRS is not required.

A. True.

B. False.

14.4.13. WMW Partnership began operations on September 11, Year 1, and is qualified to make a Sec. 444 election to use a November 30 year end for its tax year beginning September 11, Year 1. WMW must file Form 8716, *Election to Have a Tax Year Other Than a Required Tax Year*, by February 15, Year 2, which is the due date of the partnership's tax return for the period September 11, Year 1, to November 30, Year 1.

A. True.

B. False.

14.4.14. As a general rule, a partnership tax year is closed by the death of a partner even though the partnership is not terminated.

A. True.

B. False.

14.4.15. Under Sec. 444, certain partnerships may elect to use a tax year that is different from their required tax year. A newly formed partnership that begins operations on December 1 and is owned by calendar-year partners may make a Sec. 444 election to adopt a September 30 tax year, assuming they meet the other requirements.

A. True.

B. False.

Answer (B) is correct. *(Publisher, adapted)*
DISCUSSION: A principal partner is defined in Sec. 706(b)(3) as one having an interest of 5% or more in partnership profits or capital.

Answer (A) is correct. *(SEE, adapted)*
DISCUSSION: Under Sec. 706(b)(1), a partnership may not adopt a taxable year other than that of the partners owning more than 50% of partnership profits and capital if the partners had the same tax year on the first day of the partnership tax year. Only with IRS approval could the partnership use some other taxable year for which it establishes a business purpose.

Answer (B) is correct. *(SEE, adapted)*
DISCUSSION: Under Sec. 706(b)(1), a partnership must adopt the taxable year of partners owning more than 50% of partnership profits and capital if the partners had the same tax year on the first day of the partnership tax year. Because the time period requirement of the majority partner rule is not met in this question, MNO escapes the majority rule. Each of the partners is a principal partner, and the partnership would be required to adopt the taxable year of all principal partners. However, a fiscal year election may be made under Sec. 444, provided there is no more than a 3-month deferral period from the otherwise required year end.

Answer (A) is correct. *(SEE, adapted)*
DISCUSSION: A Sec. 444 election is made by filing a properly prepared Form 8716, *Election to Have a Tax Year Other Than a Required Tax Year*. Under Temp. Reg. 1.444-3T(b), the Form 8716 must be filed by the earlier of (1) the 15th day of the fifth month following the month that includes the first day of the taxable year for which the election will first be effective or (2) the due date (without regard for extension) of the income tax return resulting from the Sec. 444 election. Under (1), the date would be February 15 (15th day of the fifth month beginning after September), and under (2), the date would be February 15 (15th day of the third month beginning after November 30). Since both dates are the same, the Form 8716 must be filed by February 15, Year 2.

Answer (B) is correct. *(SEE, adapted)*
DISCUSSION: For tax years beginning after December 31, 1997, Sec. 706(c) provides the general rule that the tax year of a partnership closes with respect to the deceased partner when a partner dies. The partnership tax year does not close, however, with respect to the other partners until the close of the partnership's regular tax year.

Answer (A) is correct. *(SEE, adapted)*
DISCUSSION: Section 444 permits the election of a tax year other than that required by Sec. 706. However, it may not have more than a 3-month deferral period (i.e., the number of months between the beginning of the tax year selected and the end of the required tax year). There is a 3-month deferral period here, which is acceptable.

14.5 Partnership Ordinary Income

14.5.1. In the computation of the ordinary income of a partnership, a deduction is allowed for

A. Contributions to qualified charities.

B. The net operating loss deduction.

C. Guaranteed payments to partners.

D. Short-term and long-term capital losses.

Answer (C) is correct. *(CPA, adapted)*
REQUIRED: The deduction allowed in computing the ordinary income of a partnership.
DISCUSSION: The ordinary income of a partnership is the balance of the taxable income excluding all items required to be separately stated under Sec. 702(a). Guaranteed payments to partners are deductible under Sec. 707(c), provided they meet the requirements of Sec. 162(a), i.e., if they are ordinary and necessary business expenses.
Answer (A) is incorrect. Contributions to qualified charities are not deductible but must be separately stated. Answer (B) is incorrect. The partnership does not have a net operating loss deduction. Answer (D) is incorrect. Short-term and long-term capital losses are not deductible but must be separately stated.

14.5.2. Partnership M, a law partnership, had the following items for the current year:

Income from clients	$200,000
Repairs	1,000
Depreciation	2,000
Dividends on capital stock	500
Other operating expenses	125,000
Charitable contributions	1,500
Sec. 1231 gain on sale of office furniture	1,200
Sec. 1245 gain on sale of office furniture	1,000

What is Partnership M's ordinary income?

A. $70,500

B. $72,700

C. $73,000

D. $73,500

Answer (C) is correct. *(SEE, adapted)*
REQUIRED: The amount of ordinary income of the partnership.
DISCUSSION: Partnership ordinary income is the portion of partnership taxable income that is not required to be separately stated under Sec. 702(a). Charitable contributions are not deductible by a partnership but must be separately stated. Dividends must be separately stated because they are portfolio income and must be separated from active and passive income. Section 1231 gain must be separately stated. Note that Sec. 1245 gain does not have to be separately stated since it is always taxed as ordinary income. Partnership M's ordinary income is

Income from clients	$200,000
Repairs	(1,000)
Depreciation	(2,000)
Operating expenses	(125,000)
Sec. 1245 gain	1,000
Ordinary income	$ 73,000

Answer (A) is incorrect. Section 1245 gains are included in ordinary income, and charitable contributions are not. Answer (B) is incorrect. Section 1231 gains and charitable contributions are not included in ordinary income. Answer (D) is incorrect. Dividends are not included in ordinary income.

14.5.3. During the current year, the EEE Partnership paid insurance premiums for the following coverage:

Life insurance on the lives of all the partners in order to get or protect a business loan	$ 700
Group term life on the lives of all the partners with the partnership designated as the beneficiary	300
Workers' compensation on behalf of all the partners who render services and the premiums are determined without regard to partnership income	600
Use and occupancy and business interruptions due to fire or other causes	900
Public liability that covers the partnership's liability for bodily injury suffered by persons who are not employees of the partnership and for property damage to others	1,000

What is the amount of the partnership's deductible insurance expense for the current year?

A. $3,500

B. $2,800

C. $2,500

D. $1,900

Answer (C) is correct. *(SEE, adapted)*
REQUIRED: The premiums paid on insurance policies taken out by a partnership that are deductible.
DISCUSSION: Section 264(a) denies a deduction for premiums paid on any life insurance policy concerning the life of any officer, employee, or person financially interested in any trade or business carried on by taxpayer, when the taxpayer is directly or indirectly a beneficiary under the policy. The premium paid on life insurance on the lives of all the partners in order to get or protect a business loan is nondeductible (*Yarnall*, 9 T.C. 616). The premium paid on the group term life insurance on the partners with the partnership being the beneficiary is also nondeductible under Sec. 264(a) since the partners can be considered "financially interested" individuals. Premiums paid on workers' compensation for the partners are guaranteed payments under Sec. 707(c) if the premiums are paid for services rendered in the capacity of a partner and to the extent the premiums are determined without regard to partnership income. As guaranteed payments, the premiums are deductible under Sec. 162. The premiums on the business interruption insurance and public liability insurance are trade or business expenses deductible under Sec. 162.
Answer (A) is incorrect. The premiums paid for the life insurance taken out to obtain a business loan, group term life insurance, and workers' compensation are not deductible. Answer (B) is incorrect. The premiums paid for the group term life insurance and workers' compensation are not deductible. Answer (D) is incorrect. The premiums paid for the group term life insurance are not deductible.

14.5.4. Dunn and Shaw are partners who share profits and losses equally. In the computation of the partnership's current-year book income of $100,000, guaranteed payments to partners totaling $60,000 and charitable contributions totaling $1,000 were treated as expenses. What amount should be reported as ordinary income on the partnership's current-year tax return?

A. $100,000

B. $101,000

C. $160,000

D. $161,000

Answer (B) is correct. *(CPA, adapted)*
REQUIRED: The amount of the partnership's ordinary income for tax purposes.
DISCUSSION: A partnership's ordinary income consists of the balance of the taxable income of a partnership, which is not required to be separately stated [Sec. 702(a)(8)].
Deductible guaranteed payments do enter into the calculation. Charitable contributions are not deductible in computing a partnership's taxable income. The $1,000 of charitable contributions that were deducted must be added back.

Operating income	$100,000
Plus: charitable contributions	1,000
Partnership ordinary income	$101,000

Answer (A) is incorrect. Charitable contributions should be added back to book income to determine ordinary income. Answer (C) is incorrect. The guaranteed payments should not be added back to book income; however, the charitable contributions should be added back to determine ordinary income. Answer (D) is incorrect. The guaranteed payments should not be added back to book income when determining ordinary income.

14.5.5. The partnership (rather than the partner) must make elections as to the tax treatment of all the following items except

A. Partnership accounting methods.

B. Inventory method.

C. Reinvestment of proceeds from an involuntary conversion pursuant to Sec. 1033.

D. Deduction or credit of foreign taxes paid.

Answer (D) is correct. *(Publisher, adapted)*
REQUIRED: The election that is made by individual partners rather than the partnership.
DISCUSSION: Under Sec. 703(b), almost all elections affecting the computation of taxable income derived from a partnership are made by the partnership. However, there are five elections that are made by the individual partners rather than the partnership. One of these is the election under Sec. 901 to claim a credit for foreign taxes rather than a deduction.
Answer (A) is incorrect. Determining partnership accounting methods is an election that falls under the general rule of Sec. 703(b) and is made by the partnership rather than the partners. Answer (B) is incorrect. Choosing the most appropriate inventory method is an election that falls under the general rule of Sec. 703(b) and is made by the partnership rather than the partners. Answer (C) is incorrect. Deciding whether to reinvest the proceeds from an involuntary conversion pursuant to Sec. 1033 is an election made by the partnership rather than the partners.

14.5.6. All of the following items are taken into account in figuring the ordinary income or loss of a partnership except

A. Depletion allowance with respect to partnership oil and gas properties.

B. Rent expense for the building where a partnership conducts business.

C. Business bad debts.

D. Guaranteed payments to partners.

Answer (A) is correct. *(SEE, adapted)*
REQUIRED: The deduction not allowed in computing the ordinary income of a partnership.
DISCUSSION: A partnership's ordinary income consists of the balance of the taxable income of a partnership that is not required to be separately stated [Sec. 702(a)(8)]. In computing partnership ordinary income, Sec. 703(a)(2)(F) specifically disallows depletion deductions with respect to oil and gas wells.
Answer (B) is incorrect. Rent expense for the building where a partnership conducts business is deductible in computing partnership ordinary income or loss. Answer (C) is incorrect. Business bad debts are deductible in computing partnership ordinary income or loss. Answer (D) is incorrect. Guaranteed payments to partners are deductible in computing partnership ordinary income or loss.

14.5.7. The partnership of Truman, Inc., and Bill Hanover realized the following items of income during the current year:

Net income from sales	$62,000
Dividends from domestic corporations	4,000
Interest on corporate bonds	3,000
Net long-term capital gains	5,000
Net short-term capital gains	1,000
Net rental income	7,000

The total income that should be reported as ordinary income of the partnership for the current year is

A. $62,000

B. $69,000

C. $72,000

D. $76,000

Answer (A) is correct. *(CPA, adapted)*
REQUIRED: The amount of ordinary income of the partnership.
DISCUSSION: The ordinary income of a partnership consists of the balance of taxable income, which does not have to be separately stated [Sec. 702(a)(8)].
Capital gains must be separately stated to allow the appropriate netting at the partner level. Dividends must also be separately stated because of the availability of a dividends-received deduction to corporate partners. Interest on corporate bonds and dividends are portfolio income and must be separated from active or passive income. Rental income is passive income and must be separately stated. Since these items are separately stated, they do not enter into the partnership's ordinary income computation.
Answer (B) is incorrect. Dividends and interest (or net rental income) are separately stated items and are not included in ordinary income. Answer (C) is incorrect. Dividends, net long-term capital gains, and net short-term capital gains are not included in ordinary income. Answer (D) is incorrect. Dividends, interest, and net rental income are separately stated items which are not included in ordinary income.

14.5.8. For the current calendar year, the partnership of Bicent and Tennial reported ordinary income of $260,000, which included the following items of expenses and losses:

Salaries paid (other than to partners)	$70,000
Real estate taxes for partnership office	8,000
Charitable contributions	2,000
Repairs	1,000
Foreign income taxes	5,000
Loss on sale of machinery held 7 years	12,000

As a result of the above items, the partnership should adjust its ordinary income and report what amount separately on its tax return?

A. $19,000

B. $23,000

C. $27,000

D. $72,000

Answer (A) is correct. *(CPA, adapted)*
REQUIRED: The amount that must be reported separately by the partnership.
DISCUSSION: Partnerships compute taxable income in the same way as individuals except that certain items must be separately stated [Sec. 703(a)]. Partnership ordinary income is the balance of taxable income not required to be separately stated. The sum of the items that the partnership included in its ordinary income computation but that should have been separately stated is

Contributions [Sec. 702(a)(4)]	$ 2,000
Foreign income taxes [Sec. 702(a)(6)]	5,000
Loss on sale of machinery (Sec. 1231 loss) [Sec. 702(a)(3)]	12,000
Total	$19,000

Answer (B) is incorrect. Real estate taxes and repairs are included in ordinary income, but foreign income taxes are not. Answer (C) is incorrect. Real estate taxes are included in ordinary income. Answer (D) is incorrect. Salaries paid are included in ordinary income, but foreign income taxes and the loss on the sale of machinery are not.

14.5.9. Section 179 expensing of assets is deducted on Form 1065 in computing partnership ordinary income.

A. True.

B. False.

Answer (B) is correct. *(SEE, adapted)*
DISCUSSION: Each partner must take into account separately his or her share of any item that could result in a different tax liability if it were separately taken into account [Reg. 1.702-1(a)(8)(ii)]. Since there is a limit on Sec. 179 expensing of assets at the partner level (as well as at the partnership level), it must be taken into account separately by the partners and not deducted in computing partnership ordinary income.

14.6 Partners' Distributive Shares of Income and Gain

NOTE: The rules discussed in this subunit do not apply to electing large partnerships. The rules for electing large partnerships are discussed in Study Unit 15, Subunit 7.

14.6.1. For the current year, the Gil and Bill Partnership had book income of $37,000, which included the following:

Dividend income	$1,000
Short-term capital loss	(4,000)
Sec. 1231 gain	7,000
Sec. 1245 gain	1,500
Interest income	750

The partners share profits and losses equally. What amount of partnership income (excluding all partnership items that must be reported separately) should each partner report on his individual income tax return for the current year?

A. $19,625

B. $18,500

C. $16,125

D. $7,313

Answer (C) is correct. *(SEE, adapted)*
    REQUIRED: The amount of each partner's share of partnership ordinary income.
    DISCUSSION: The ordinary income of a partnership is the portion of taxable income which is not required to be separately stated [Sec. 702(a)(8)]. Note that Sec. 1245 recapture income is not required to be separately stated since it will always be ordinary income. Book income must be adjusted to exclude the effects of all separately stated items.

Book income	$37,000
Add back: Short-term capital loss	4,000
Subtract:	
Sec. 1231 gain	(7,000)
Dividends	(1,000)
Interest	(750)
Partnership ordinary income	$32,250

Since Gil and Bill share profits and losses equally, each partner's share of partnership ordinary income is 50% of $32,250, or $16,125.
    Answer (A) is incorrect. Section 1231 gain should also be subtracted. Answer (B) is incorrect. The short-term capital loss should be added back and the Sec. 1231 gains, dividends, and interest should be subtracted. Answer (D) is incorrect. The short-term capital loss should be added back, the Sec. 1231 gain should be subtracted, and a 50% interest (instead of a 25% interest) should be allocated to each partner.

14.6.2. The Rainy Day Partnership reported a Sec. 1231 gain of $30,000, a long-term capital loss of $33,000, a $400 charitable contribution, and ordinary income of $40,000 for the current year. Mr. Umbrella, a single taxpayer with no dependents, owned a 40% profit and loss interest in the partnership. Umbrella had a $2,000 long-term capital gain and $30,000 ordinary income but no Sec. 1231 transactions, charitable contributions, or short-term capital gains or losses before considering the partnership results. Umbrella had itemized deductions from AGI of $7,000 without considering partnership results. He has no dependents. Umbrella's taxable income for the current year was

A. $30,000

B. $35,590

C. $39,640

D. $46,640

Answer (B) is correct. *(Publisher, adapted)*
    REQUIRED: The partner's taxable income including his share of partnership items.
    DISCUSSION: Under Sec. 702(a), each partner separately takes into account his or her distributive share of the partnership's long-term capital gains and losses, Sec. 1231 gains and losses, charitable contributions, and ordinary income of the partnership. Mr. Umbrella's share of each of these items is 40%.

His own ordinary income		$30,000
Partnership ordinary income ($40,000 × 40%)		16,000
Capital gain:		
Partnership 1231 gain		
($30,000 × 40%)	$12,000	
His own LTCG	2,000	
Partnership LTCL ($33,000 × 40%)	(13,200)	800
Adjusted gross income		$46,800
Itemized deductions:		
His own	$ 7,000	
Partnership charitable contributions		
($400 × 40%)	160	(7,160)
Personal exemption		(4,050)
Taxable income		$35,590

Answer (A) is incorrect. Mr. Umbrella must include his share of the partnership ordinary income and separately stated items in determining taxable income, along with his own itemized deductions and personal exemption. Answer (C) is incorrect. Mr. Umbrella's personal exemption must also reduce taxable income. Answer (D) is incorrect. Mr. Umbrella's own itemized deductions and personal exemption must also reduce taxable income.

14.6.3. For the current year, the Murray and Parker Partnership had book income of $100,000, which included the following:

Long-term capital gain	$ 7,000
Sec. 1231 loss	(3,000)
Dividends	200
Interest paid to partners for use of capital	12,000

The partners share profits and losses equally. What amount of partnership income (excluding all partnership items which must be reported separately) should each partner report in his or her individual income tax return for the current year?

    A. $47,900

    B. $48,000

    C. $50,000

    D. $53,900

Answer (A) is correct. *(CPA, adapted)*
    REQUIRED: The amount of partnership ordinary income that should be reported by each partner.
    DISCUSSION: A partnership's ordinary income is the portion of taxable income not required to be stated separately [Sec. 702(a)(8)]. The interest paid to partners is a guaranteed payment which results in an ordinary deduction. Book income may be adjusted to ordinary income by excluding all items of income and adding back all deduction and loss items, which must be separately stated. The partnership's ordinary income is

Book income	$100,000
Add back: Sec. 1231 loss	3,000
Subtract:	
Long-term capital gain	(7,000)
Dividends	(200)
Partnership ordinary income	$ 95,800

Because the partners share profits and losses equally, each partner's share of partnership income is $47,900 ($95,800 × 50%).
    Answer (B) is incorrect. The dividends must be subtracted to arrive at partnership ordinary income. Answer (C) is incorrect. The book income must be adjusted to arrive at partnership ordinary income. Answer (D) is incorrect. The partnership ordinary income does not equal $100,800.

14.6.4. Charles Jordan files his income tax return on a calendar-year basis. He is a 3% partner of a partnership reporting on a June 30 fiscal-year basis. Jordan's share of the partnership's ordinary income was $24,000 for the fiscal year ended June 30, Year 1, and $72,000 for the fiscal year ended June 30, Year 2. How much should Jordan report on his Year 1 return as his share of taxable income from the partnership?

    A. $24,000

    B. $36,000

    C. $60,000

    D. $72,000

Answer (A) is correct. *(CPA, adapted)*
    REQUIRED: The amount of partnership income that a partner should report when the partnership has a different tax year.
    DISCUSSION: When computing taxable income, a partner is required to include his or her share of partnership income and separately stated items for any partnership year that ends within his or her taxable year [Sec. 706(a)]. Since the partnership's fiscal year ending June 30, Year 1, ended within Jordan's Year 1 calendar-year reporting period, Jordan must report $24,000 (his share of the partnership's income for the fiscal year ending June 30, Year 1).
    Answer (B) is incorrect. The amount of $36,000 is half of the partnership's Year 2 ordinary income. Jordan needs only to report ordinary income from the partnership year that ends during his tax year. Answer (C) is incorrect. Jordan does not allocate the 6 months of the partnership's ordinary income for fiscal Year 2, even though it occurs during his calendar-year tax period. Answer (D) is incorrect. The amount of $72,000 is Jordan's share of ordinary income from the partnership for the fiscal year ended June 30, Year 2, which will fall within his Year 2 calendar-year return.

14.6.5. A partner's taxable income arising from the partner's interest in a partnership includes

    A. Only the partner's share of partnership income actually distributed to the partner during the year.

    B. The partner's share of partnership income, whether or not distributed to the partner during the year.

    C. Only the partner's salary actually paid to the partner during the year.

    D. Only the partner's salary and interest paid to the partner during the year and deducted by the partnership during that year.

Answer (B) is correct. *(CPA, adapted)*
    REQUIRED: The amount of partnership income to be reported by the partner.
    DISCUSSION: Distributive shares of partnership income are reported by partners for their taxable year during which the end of the partnership tax year occurs. The partner will be taxed on the partnership income whether it is distributed or not.
    Answer (A) is incorrect. A partner's taxable income arising from the partner's interest in a partnership is not limited to the partner's share of partnership income actually distributed to the partner during the year. Answer (C) is incorrect. A partner's taxable income arising from the partner's interest in a partnership is not limited to the partner's salary actually paid to the partner during the year. Answer (D) is incorrect. A partner's taxable income arising from the partner's interest in a partnership is not limited to the partner's salary and interest paid to the partner during the year, and it need not be deducted by the partnership during that year for it to be included.

14.6.6. Mojo is a calendar-year, accrual-basis partnership. At the beginning of the current year, the partnership had three partners: Mark, Roger, and Monica. Under the partnership agreement, profits and losses are to be shared in proportion to their contributions. As of January 1 of this year, this was 40% for Mark, 40% for Roger, and 20% for Monica. On November 1 of this year, Monica withdrew from the partnership. The new profit and loss ratios, as of November 1, were 50% for Mark and 50% for Roger. For its tax year ended December 31 of the current year, Mojo had net income of $90,000, which was earned in substantially equal amounts over the course of the year. What is the amount of partnership income that Mark should include on his current-year individual federal income tax return?

A. $30,000

B. $36,000

C. $37,500

D. $45,000

Answer (C) is correct. *(SEE, adapted)*
REQUIRED: The income of a partner when interests vary during the year.
DISCUSSION: Under Sec. 706(a), a partner includes his or her share of partnership income for a partnership taxable year that ends within the partner's tax year. Under Sec. 706(d), if there is a change in a partners' interest during the year, each partner's distributive share must take into account the varying interests of the partners. Accordingly, the shares of partnership income must be prorated. Mark's share is computed as follows based on the length of time of ownership.

$90,000 ×	40% ×	10/12 months =	$30,000
$90,000 ×	50% ×	2/12 months =	7,500
Mark's distributive share (total)			$37,500

Answer (A) is incorrect. A 50% allocation of the last 2 months of partnership income must also be included. Answer (B) is incorrect. The amount of $36,000 is 40% of the income. The partnership income must be allocated by the number of months that Mark was a 40% and a 50% partner. Answer (D) is incorrect. The amount of $45,000 is 50% of partnership income.

14.6.7. At June 30, Year 1, Burns and Cooper were equal partners in a partnership with net assets having a tax basis and fair market value of $100,000. On July 1, Year 1, Todd contributed securities with a fair market value of $50,000 (purchased 10 years ago at a cost of $35,000) to become an equal partner in the new firm of Burns, Cooper, and Todd. The securities were sold on December 15, Year 2, for $65,000. How much of the partnership's capital gain from the sale of these securities should be allocated to Todd?

A. $5,000

B. $10,000

C. $15,000

D. $20,000

Answer (D) is correct. *(CPA, adapted)*
REQUIRED: The amount of partnership capital gain on contributed property to be allocated to the contributing partner.
DISCUSSION: Section 704(c) requires a special allocation for the difference between fair market value at the time of contribution and basis of contributed property. The gain attributable to the precontribution appreciation in the securities must be allocated entirely to Todd, and the gain attributable to post-contribution appreciation should be shared equally by Burns, Cooper, and Todd. Todd's share is

Precontribution appreciation	
($50,000 FMV – $35,000 basis)	$15,000
Plus: 1/3 of post-contribution appreciation	
($65,000 proceeds – $50,000 7/1/Year 1 FMV)	5,000
Todd's share of the capital gain	$20,000

Answer (A) is incorrect. In addition to the one-third post-contribution appreciation, Todd should also be allocated the precontribution appreciation. Answer (B) is incorrect. Todd is allocated the entire precontribution appreciation and also his equal share of the post-contribution appreciation. Answer (C) is incorrect. In addition to the precontribution appreciation, Todd is also allocated his equal share of the post-contribution appreciation.

14.6.8. David and Robert form an equal partnership. David contributed $10,000 cash to the partnership and Robert contributed depreciable property with a fair market value of $10,000 and an adjusted basis of $4,000. What is the partnership's basis for depreciation of the property, and how is the depreciation deduction allocated to the partners (assuming the depreciation rate is 10% per year)?

	Partnership's Basis for Depreciation	Annual Depreciation Deduction	
		David's Share	Robert's Share
A.	$4,000	$200	$200
B.	$4,000	$400	$0
C.	$4,000	$0	$400
D.	$10,000	$500	$500

Answer (B) is correct. *(SEE, adapted)*
REQUIRED: The partnership's basis for depreciation of property and the amount of depreciation allocated to the partners.
DISCUSSION: Under the traditional method [704(b)], depreciation on contributed property will first be allocated to the noncontributing partner. The basis of the asset to the partnership is $4,000. Thus, the depreciation for the year is $400 ($4,000 over 10 years). David's share of the depreciation would normally be $500 ($10,000 FMV × 50% × 1/10); however, his share of the depreciation is limited to $400 because that is the maximum allowed the partnership.
Answer (A) is incorrect. Robert's share of the deduction is not $200 because he did not contribute the property. Answer (C) is incorrect. David has a share of the deduction. Answer (D) is incorrect. The depreciation is calculated on the basis of the property to the partnership, which was the adjusted basis to the contributing partner.

14.6.9. On January 1 of the current year, Dan and Lee formed a partnership to manufacture furniture. Dan has been a developer and land dealer. He contributed land from the inventory of his other business that had a $25,000 basis and a fair market value at the time of the transfer of $30,000. Lee contributed $25,000 in cash. Both partners and the partnership use the calendar year and cash method. On October 31 of the current year, the partnership sold the land contributed by Dan for $35,000. Which of the following statements is true?

A. For the current year, Dan reports ordinary income of $10,000 and the basis of his partnership interest is $35,000.

B. The partnership reports a capital gain of $10,000.

C. The partnership reports ordinary income of $10,000.

D. The partnership reports capital gain of $30,000 and ordinary income of $5,000.

Answer (C) is correct. *(SEE, adapted)*
REQUIRED: The true statement concerning the contribution of inventory to a partnership and its subsequent sale.
DISCUSSION: Under Sec. 724(b), the characterization of the gain or loss on contributed inventory property is carried over from the contributing partner. No gain or loss is recognized by the partner or partnership on the contribution of the land held as inventory. The basis of the land to Dan was $25,000. The land is considered inventory by Dan so when it is sold, it is considered ordinary income unless held by the partnership for more than 5 years. Here, the land is sold within 1 year so it retains ordinary income character. There is a $10,000 gain recognized by the partnership on the sale of the land ($35,000 sales price – $25,000 basis). The gain is all ordinary income. The first $5,000 of gain ($30,000 contribution – $25,000 basis) is precontribution gain and allocated to Dan. The remaining $5,000 gain is reported by the partnership as ordinary income and allocated to the partners according to their profits interests.
Answer (A) is incorrect. Dan's gain will equal his precontribution gain plus his allocated share of the partnership gain on the sale. Answer (B) is incorrect. The partnership does not report a capital gain. The land was characterized as inventory for the contributing partner. Answer (D) is incorrect. The partnership does not report a capital gain of $30,000 and ordinary income of $5,000.

14.6.10. Which one of the following statements is false?

A. Each individual partner's distributive share of partnership income or loss must be reported on his or her Form 1040.

B. Generally, a partner's distributive share of income or loss is determined by the partnership agreement.

C. Distributions by the partnership are generally not taxable to the partners unless the distributions are treated as a liquidation or sale or exchange of their capital interests.

D. The partnership is required to file a declaration of estimated tax in any year it anticipates a profit.

Answer (D) is correct. *(SEE, adapted)*
REQUIRED: The false statement concerning a partnership.
DISCUSSION: A partnership is not required to file an estimated tax declaration because it is not liable for such tax (Sec. 701). The partnership tax return is only an informational return.
Answer (A) is incorrect. Each partner is required to report his or her share of partnership income [Sec. 702(a)] although, if a partner is not an individual, it would be reported on a different return. Answer (B) is incorrect. Under Sec. 704(a), a partner's distributive share is determined by the agreement unless the allocation does not have substantial economic effect. Answer (C) is incorrect. Distributions are generally not taxed to partners since they are taxed as the partnership earns the income whether or not it is distributed.

14.6.11. CDH Partnership, a fiscal-year partnership, is equally owned by C, D, and H. The partnership reported net income of $120,000 for the tax year ending October 31, Year 1. Partner C, a calendar-year taxpayer, withdrew $25,000 from his capital account during the fiscal year. The partnership reported net income of $90,000 for the tax year ending October 31, Year 2. What is the amount of partnership income C must report on his Year 1 income tax return?

A. $25,000

B. $30,000

C. $40,000

D. $65,000

Answer (C) is correct. *(SEE, adapted)*
REQUIRED: The amount of partnership income that a partner should report when the partnership has a different tax year and a partner has draws.
DISCUSSION: When computing taxable income, a partner is required to include his or her share of partnership income and separately stated items for any partnership tax year that ends within his or her tax year [Sec. 706(a)]. Here, CDH Partnership's fiscal year ending October 31, Year 1, ended within C's calendar-year return for Year 1. C must report $40,000 (his 1/3 share of the $120,000 partnership income for the fiscal year ending October 31, Year 1). The withdrawal from C's capital account is merely a reduction in his basis.
Answer (A) is incorrect. The amount of money withdrawn from the partnership is $25,000. Answer (B) is incorrect. C's income for Year 2 is $30,000. Answer (D) is incorrect. The amount of $65,000 is the $40,000 of income in Year 1 plus the $25,000 cash withdrawal in Year 1.

402 SU 14: Partnerships: Formation and Operation

14.6.12. In each of the following situations, assume that capital accounts are maintained in accordance with the Sec. 704 regulations, the allocation is reflected in the capital account, and liquidation is in accordance with capital accounts with deficit balances to be restored on liquidation. Which of these special allocations has substantial economic effect?

A. Partner A is allocated $10,000 of Sec. 1231 loss and all other partners are allocated $10,000 of depreciation deductions.

B. Partner A is allocated 10% of all foreign source income of the partnership and all other partners receive the same dollar amount of U.S. source income.

C. Partner A is allocated all income (but not gain or loss) from $100,000 face amount 10% municipal bonds and Partner B is allocated all dividends (but not gain or loss) from $100,000 fair market value of G.M. stock. The interest and dividends are likely to be close to the same amount.

D. Partner A receives all depreciation deductions. Gains and losses from the sale of depreciable assets are allocated pro rata among the partners.

Answer (D) is correct. *(Publisher, adapted)*
REQUIRED: The special allocation that has substantial economic effect.
DISCUSSION: A partner's distributive share of income, gain, loss, deduction, or credit may be determined by special allocation in the partnership agreement provided it has substantial economic effect (Sec. 704). Otherwise, the distributive share will be determined in accordance with the partner's interest in the partnership. Under case law and Reg. 1.704-1(b)(2), substantial economic effect exists if the allocation may substantially affect the dollar amount of the partners' shares of the total partnership income or loss independent of tax consequences. The answer that states "Partner A receives all depreciation deductions. Gains and losses from the sale of depreciable assets are allocated pro rata among the partners" has substantial economic effect since Partner A's receipt of funds upon liquidation will be reduced according to the depreciation taken and charged to his or her capital account.
Answer (A) is incorrect. Partner A being allocated $10,000 of Sec. 1231 loss and all other partners being allocated $10,000 of depreciation deductions does not have a substantial economic effect. Answer (B) is incorrect. Partner A being allocated 10% of all foreign source income of the partnership and all other partners receiving the same dollar amount of U.S. source income does not have a substantial economic effect. Answer (C) is incorrect. Such an allocation to Partner A and to Partner B does not have a substantial economic effect.

14.6.13. Irving Aster, Dennis Brill, and Robert Clark were partners who shared profits and losses equally. On February 28 of the current year, Aster sold his interest to Phil Dexter. On March 31 of the same year, Brill died, and his estate held his interest for the remainder of the year. The partnership continued to operate and for the fiscal year ending June 30 of the current year had a profit of $45,000. Assuming that partnership income was earned on a pro rata monthly basis and that all partners were calendar-year taxpayers, the distributive shares to be included in current-year gross income should be

A. Aster $10,000, Brill $0, Estate of Brill $15,000, Clark $15,000, and Dexter $5,000.

B. Aster $10,000, Brill $11,250, Estate of Brill $3,750, Clark $15,000, and Dexter $5,000.

C. Aster $0, Brill $11,250, Estate of Brill $3,750, Clark $15,000, and Dexter $15,000.

D. Aster $0, Brill $0, Estate of Brill $15,000, Clark $15,000, and Dexter $15,000.

Answer (B) is correct. *(CPA, adapted)*
REQUIRED: The correct statement concerning the distributive shares of each partner to be included in gross income.
DISCUSSION: Under Sec. 706(a), a partner includes his or her share of partnership income for a partnership taxable year that ends within the partner's tax year. Section 706(d) requires each partner to include only his or her share of partnership income for the period of time (s)he owned the partnership interest; i.e., the partnership tax year closes with respect to a partner who sells his or her entire interest [Sec. 706(c)]. Accordingly, Aster and Dexter must prorate their share of partnership income based on the length of time of ownership. For tax years beginning after December 31, 1997, the tax year of a partnership, with respect to a partner who dies, closes at the date of death [Reg. 1.706-1(c)(3)].

Profit of $45,000 ÷ 3 partners ÷ 12 months = $1,250 monthly income per partner

Aster:	$1,250 × 8 months = $10,000
Brill:	$1,250 × 9 months = $11,250
Estate of Brill:	$1,250 × 3 months = $3,750
Clark:	$1,250 × 12 months = $15,000
Dexter:	$1,250 × 4 months = $5,000

Answer (A) is incorrect. Brill receives a share of the partnership income. Also, the Estate of Brill does not receive 12 months of partnership income, as Brill was alive during the fiscal year. Answer (C) is incorrect. Aster receives his share of the partnership income up until the date he sold his interest, and Dexter only receives a share for the months he owned his interest during the fiscal year. Answer (D) is incorrect. Aster and Brill both receive a share of the partnership income. Also, the Estate of Brill and Dexter only receive prorated shares for the months they owned their respective partnership interests during the fiscal year.

14.6.14. When the AQR partnership was formed, partner Acre contributed land with a fair market value of $100,000 and a tax basis of $60,000 in exchange for a one-third interest in the partnership. The AQR partnership agreement specifies that each partner will share equally in the partnership's profits and losses. During its first year of operation, AQR sold the land to an unrelated third party for $160,000. What is the proper tax treatment of the sale?

A. Each partner reports a capital gain of $33,333.

B. The entire gain of $100,000 must be specifically allocated to Acre.

C. The first $40,000 of gain is allocated to Acre, and the remaining gain of $60,000 is shared equally by the other two partners.

D. The first $40,000 of gain is allocated to Acre, and the remaining gain of $60,000 is shared equally by all the partners in the partnership.

Answer (D) is correct. *(CPA, adapted)*
REQUIRED: The proper tax treatment of the sale of partnership property with precontribution gain.
DISCUSSION: When determining the gain or loss allocable to each partner, you must first allocate any precontribution gain or loss (gain or loss that existed in the asset at the time it was contributed to the partnership but went unrecognized) to the contributing partner, followed by their proportionate share of the gain or loss. In this case, Acre contributed land with a built-in $40,000 gain ($100,000 FMV − $60,000 adjusted basis). Upon disposition, the partnership realizes a gain of $100,000 ($160,000 amount realized − $60,000 carryover basis). Of this gain, $40,000 is allocated to Acre as precontribution gain. The remaining gain of $60,000 is shared equally among the partners per the partnership agreement. Thus, Acre reports a total gain of $60,000 [$40,000 precontribution gain + ($60,000 remaining gain ÷ 3)] and the other two partners each report a gain of $20,000 ($60,000 remaining gain ÷ 3).
Answer (A) is incorrect. Each partner does not recognize a pro rata share of the entire $100,000 gain. Answer (B) is incorrect. Not all of the gain is allocated to Acre. Answer (C) is incorrect. All of the partners, not just the remaining two partners, share in the remaining gain.

14.6.15. Ms. M, a cash-basis, calendar-year taxpayer, became a partner in Partnership C on July 1, Year 1, by purchasing her partnership interest for $10,000. C files its return for a fiscal year ending June 30. On December 31, Year 1, C made a cash distribution to Ms. M of $5,000. Ms. M's share of C's partnership income for the year ending June 30, Year 2, was $10,000. Ms. M does not have to report any income from the partnership on her Year 1 return.

A. True.

B. False.

Answer (A) is correct. *(SEE, adapted)*
DISCUSSION: Section 706(a) provides that, when a partner computes taxable income, (s)he must include his or her distributive share of partnership income for any partnership tax year that ends within his or her tax year. Ms. M will report her $10,000 share of partnership income for the year ending June 30, Year 2, on her Year 2 return. The $5,000 cash distribution reduces Ms. M's basis, but it is not income to her since it is not in excess of her basis.

14.6.16. The character of a partner's distributive share of a partnership item of income, gain, loss, credit, or deduction that the partner must take into account separately is determined as if the partner had realized it directly from the same source or incurred it in the same manner as it was realized or incurred by the partnership.

A. True.

B. False.

Answer (A) is correct. *(SEE, adapted)*
DISCUSSION: The question restates Sec. 702(b), under which a partner's share of the partnership income (and other tax items) retains the same character to the partner that it had to the partnership.

14.6.17. For federal income tax purposes, the specific allocations of income, credits, and deductions to the partners will be controlled by the partnership agreement even though it cannot be demonstrated that the allocations have substantial economic effect.

A. True.

B. False.

Answer (B) is correct. *(SEE, adapted)*
DISCUSSION: A partner's distributive share of income, gain, loss, deduction, or credit may be determined by special allocation provided it has substantial economic effect [Sec. 704(b)]. Otherwise, the distributive share will be determined in accordance with the partner's interest in the partnership.

14.6.18. A partnership does not pay a minimum tax. Each partner must separately take into account his or her distributive share of the partnership's tax preference items.

A. True.

B. False.

Answer (A) is correct. *(SEE, adapted)*
DISCUSSION: Partnerships are not taxpaying entities. Partners report their share of partnership taxable income or loss and other items on their individual returns. Partners are subject to the alternative minimum tax on their share of partnership tax preference items.

14.6.19. Mr. Y, a calendar-year taxpayer, died on September 1 of the current year. He was a partner in a March 31 fiscal-year partnership. Under applicable state law, the partnership terminated with the death of Mr. Y. Mr. Y's final return will include his share of the partnership items only from the partnership year ending March 31 of the current year, but not the period ending with his death.

A. True.

B. False.

Answer (B) is correct. *(SEE, adapted)*
DISCUSSION: Section 706(a) requires a partner to include his or her share of partnership income for a partnership tax year ending within the partner's tax year. For tax years beginning after December 31, 1997, the tax year of a partnership with respect to a partner who dies closes at the date of death. Therefore, the decedent's distributive share of partnership income includes income up to the date of Mr. Y's death, or a total of 18 months of income.

14.6.20. Kelly Green's distributive share of income from the Shamrock Partnership was $22,000 in Year 2. Kelly Green received a distribution of $15,000 of Shamrock Partnership's Year 1 earnings on December 15, Year 2. She should report $15,000 as ordinary income from Shamrock Partnership, a calendar-year partnership, on her Year 2 individual return, Form 1040.

A. True.

B. False.

Answer (B) is correct. *(SEE, adapted)*
DISCUSSION: A partner must report his or her distributive share of partnership income [Sec. 702(a)]. This is because the partner is taxed on the partnership income whether it is distributed or not. Green should thus report $22,000 as income from the partnership.

14.7 Partnership Losses

14.7.1. J&D Partnership's books and records reflected the following for the current tax year:

Gross receipts	$90,000
Operating expenses	95,000
Sec. 1231 gain	21,000
Charitable contributions	2,000
Guaranteed payments to partners	40,000
Depletion on oil and gas properties	3,000

What is the amount of the partnership's ordinary loss?

A. $5,000

B. $45,000

C. $47,000

D. $50,000

Answer (B) is correct. *(SEE, adapted)*
REQUIRED: The amount of a partnership's ordinary loss.
DISCUSSION: A partnership's ordinary income or loss is the balance of the taxable income (loss) excluding all items required to be separately stated under Sec. 702(a) and disallowed deductions under Sec. 703. The partnership's loss equals $45,000 ($90,000 – $95,000 – $40,000). The Sec. 1231 gain and charitable contributions are items to be separately stated and do not enter into the computation. The depletion deduction with respect to oil and gas properties is disallowed to the partnership by Sec. 703.
Answer (A) is incorrect. Guaranteed payments are included in the determination of the ordinary loss. Answer (C) is incorrect. Charitable contributions are separately stated items and are not included in the determination of the ordinary loss. Answer (D) is incorrect. The charitable contributions and depletion on gas properties are separately stated items and are not included in the determination of the ordinary loss.

14.7.2. Partnership Y reported a $50,000 ordinary loss for its first year of operation. Partner Alex, who materially participates, had invested $10,000 cash in exchange for a 60% interest in partnership profits. The partnership agreement stated that Alex was liable for all of the partnership's debts. The only partnership debt at year end was a $10,000 loan from a local bank. Alex and the general partner had a separate agreement that Alex's liability to the bank would not exceed $5,000. What is the amount of Alex's deductible loss?

A. $30,000

B. $20,000

C. $15,000

D. $10,000

Answer (C) is correct. *(SEE, adapted)*
REQUIRED: The amount of a partner's deductible loss.
DISCUSSION: The amount of loss that may be deducted is limited to the partner's adjusted basis in the partnership interest [Sec. 704(d)]. Under Sec. 752 regulations, Alex's basis includes recourse debt only in the amount that is his potential economic loss after considering all agreements among the partners. Alex's basis is, accordingly, $15,000 ($10,000 contribution + $5,000 share of liabilities), and this is his deductible loss.
Answer (A) is incorrect. The amount of $30,000 is 60% of the ordinary loss, but it is only deductible to the extent of A's basis in the partnership. Answer (B) is incorrect. The basis is limited to an increase of $5,000 for the liability. Answer (D) is incorrect. The amount of $10,000 is the basis before adjustment for A's share of the partnership's liabilities.

14.7.3. Tony has a 40% interest in a partnership, and he materially participates in the partnership's business. Tony's adjusted basis in the partnership was $30,000 at the beginning of the current year. There were no distributions to Tony during the year. During the current year, the partnership borrowed $200,000 from a local bank for the following reasons:

Purchase equipment needed for business	$120,000
Pay balance of existing note in full	80,000

All of the partners are personally liable for all partnership debts. The partnership incurred a $400,000 loss in the current year. What amount can Tony claim as a loss from the partnership on his current-year individual tax return?

A. $30,000

B. $78,000

C. $110,000

D. $160,000

Answer (B) is correct. *(SEE, adapted)*
REQUIRED: The partner's deduction for a partnership loss.
DISCUSSION: In determining his or her income tax, a partner must separately take into account his or her distributive share of the partnership's income, gain, loss, deduction, or credit [Sec. 702(a)]. A partner's distributive share of partnership loss is allowed only to the extent of the adjusted basis of such partner's interest in the partnership [Sec. 704(d)]. The partnership's debt increased by $120,000 ($200,000 new debt – $80,000 old debt) during the year. Tony's basis increased by $48,000 ($120,000 × 40%).
Tony should deduct a $78,000 ordinary loss [the adjusted basis of his partnership interest at year end ($30,000 + $48,000)]. The remainder of his share of partnership loss [($400,000 × 40%) – $78,000 = $82,000] may be deducted in a subsequent year when his basis in the partnership is increased.
Answer (A) is incorrect. The amount of $30,000 is Tony's adjusted basis in the partnership before adjustment for the additional $120,000 debt. Answer (C) is incorrect. Tony's basis is not increased by 40% of the new debt of $200,000. Answer (D) is incorrect. The amount of $160,000 is the total loss available, but it is only deductible to the extent of Tony's $78,000 basis in the partnership.

14.7.4. Linda and Mark each have a 50% interest in the LM Partnership. The partnership and the individuals file on a calendar-year basis. For its Year 1 tax year, LM Partnership had a $30,000 loss. Linda's adjusted basis in her partnership interest on January 1, Year 1, was $8,000. Linda materially participates in the partnership. The partnership has no nonrecourse debt. In Year 2, LM Partnership had a profit of $28,000. Assuming there were no other adjustments to Linda's basis in the partnership in Year 1 and Year 2, what amount of partnership income (loss) would Linda show on her Year 1 and Year 2 individual income tax returns?

	Year 1	Year 2
A.	$(8,000)	$0
B.	$(8,000)	$7,000
C.	$(15,000)	$7,000
D.	$(15,000)	$14,000

Answer (B) is correct. *(SEE, adapted)*
REQUIRED: The share of a partnership loss that may be deducted by a partner.
DISCUSSION: A partner's distributive share of partnership loss is allowed only to the extent of the adjusted basis of such partner's interest in the partnership at the end of the partnership's tax year [Sec. 704(d)]. Any remaining loss that cannot be deducted in the current year may be deducted in a subsequent year when the partner's partnership basis is increased.
In Year 1, Linda should report an $8,000 loss. There is a $15,000 ($30,000 × 50%) loss but her basis limits the loss to $8,000. The remaining $7,000 ($15,000 loss – $8,000 reported loss) loss may be deducted when her partnership basis is increased. In Year 2, Linda's partnership basis is increased by $14,000 ($28,000 × 50%) profit, so she is entitled to report the remaining $7,000 loss from Year 1. In Year 2, Linda reports $7,000 ($14,000 income – $7,000 loss) of income.
Answer (A) is incorrect. Linda has a greater than zero share of income on her Year 2 tax return. Answer (C) is incorrect. Linda is limited in recognizing loss to her adjusted basis in her partnership interest on her Year 1 tax return. Answer (D) is incorrect. Linda is limited in recognizing loss to her adjusted basis in her partnership interest on her Year 1 tax return. Also, she can use her nonrecognized loss from Year 1 on her Year 2 tax return.

14.7.5. ABC is a calendar-year partnership with three partners: Alan, Bob, and Cathy. The profits and losses are shared in proportion to each partner's contributions. On January 1, the ratio was 90% for Alan, 5% for Bob, and 5% for Cathy. On December 1, Bob and Cathy each contributed additional amounts, and the new profit and loss sharing ratios were 30% for Alan, 35% for Bob, and 35% for Cathy. For its tax year ending December 31, the partnership had a loss of $1,200. This loss occurred equally over the partnership's tax year. How is the loss allocated?

A. Alan $720, Bob $240, Cathy $240.

B. Alan $360, Bob $420, Cathy $420.

C. Alan $1,020, Bob $90, Cathy $90.

D. Alan $1,080, Bob $60, Cathy $60.

Answer (C) is correct. *(SEE, adapted)*
REQUIRED: The pro rata share of a partnership loss among its partners.
DISCUSSION: In determining his or her income tax, a partner must separately consider his or her distributive share of the partnership's income, gain, loss, deduction, or credit. If the loss occurred equally throughout the year, the partnership had a loss of $100 per month, which is allocated to the partners based on their contributions throughout the year. Alan is allocated $90 per month for 11 months and $30 for December, for a total of $1,020. Bob and Cathy are allocated $5 per month for 11 months and $35 for December, for a total of $90 each.
Answer (A) is incorrect. The additional capital contributions occurred in December, not June. The new profit/loss ratios do not take effect until December. Answer (B) is incorrect. The new profit (loss) ratios do not take effect until December when the additional capital contributions were made. Answer (D) is incorrect. The partners made additional capital contributions during the year that affect the profit/loss ratios.

14.7.6. The partners Martin, Cynthia, and Libby share profits and losses in a ratio of 4:3:3, respectively. All three materially participate in the partnership's business. The tax basis of each partner as of December 31 of the current year was as follows:

Martin	$7,200
Cynthia	6,000
Libby	2,500

The partnership has no nonrecourse liabilities. During the year, the partnership incurred an operating loss of $15,000. The loss is not reflected in the tax basis figures shown above. As a result of this loss, Martin, Cynthia, and Libby should deduct, respectively, on their current-year individual returns

A. $6,000, $4,500, and $2,500.

B. $6,000, $4,500, and $4,500.

C. $7,000, $5,500, and $2,500.

D. $7,100, $5,400, and $2,500.

Answer (A) is correct. *(CPA, adapted)*
REQUIRED: The amount of each partner's deductible share of the partnership loss.
DISCUSSION: A partner may deduct his or her distributive share of loss as provided in the partnership agreement for a partnership in which (s)he actively participates. The amount of loss that may be deducted is limited, however, to the partner's adjusted basis in the partnership interest [Sec. 704(d)]. The deductible loss of each partner is

Martin:	$15,000 × 40% =$6,000
Cynthia:	$15,000 × 30% =$4,500
Libby:	$15,000 × 30% =$4,500, but limited to adjusted basis of $2,500

Libby will be able to deduct her remaining $2,000 loss at the end of a subsequent year in which her adjusted basis in the partnership is increased.
Answer (B) is incorrect. Libby's loss deduction is limited to her basis of $2,500. Answer (C) is incorrect. Libby's $2,000 nonrecognized loss deduction is not allocated evenly to the other partners. Answer (D) is incorrect. Libby's $2,000 nonrecognized loss deduction is not allocated by tax basis to the other partners.

14.7.7. The XYZ Partnership was formed on January 1 of the current year and incurred a $48,000 loss for the year ending December 31 of the same year. Each of the three partners share profits and losses equally. Mr. Y is a passive investor in the partnership. On January 1 of the current year, Y contributed $6,000. Mr. Y contributed $10,000 more during the year and had draws of $2,500. The partnership has no portfolio income and no partnership liabilities. What is Y's deductible loss from XYZ for the year if he had $9,500 in income from other passive investments?

A. $9,500

B. $13,500

C. $16,000

D. $23,500

Answer (A) is correct. *(SEE, adapted)*
REQUIRED: The partner's deductible loss from a passive partnership investment.
DISCUSSION: A partner may deduct his or her distributive share of partnership loss only to the extent of his or her adjusted basis in the partnership at the end of the year in which the loss occurs [Sec. 704(d)]. Further, loss from a passive investment can offset income from passive investments only (Sec. 469). Y's adjusted basis at year end is

Adjusted basis January 1	$ 6,000
Contributions during the year	10,000
Distributions during the year	(2,500)
Adjusted basis December 31 before loss	$13,500

Y's distributable share of the loss is $16,000 ($48,000 × 1/3). Y's allowable loss for the year is limited to his December 31 adjusted basis of $13,500. It is further limited to income from other passive investments of $9,500.
Answer (B) is incorrect. The amount of $13,500 is Y's adjusted basis in the partnership; however, passive income is used to limit deductible losses of passive investors. Answer (C) is incorrect. The amount of $16,000 is Y's distributable share of the loss, which is limited as to recognition. Answer (D) is incorrect. The distributable loss allocation is only $16,000, and it is limited to the amount of passive investment income.

14.7.8. In February of Year 1, Mary contributed cash of $50,000 and Kay contributed land with an adjusted basis of $70,000 and a fair market value of $50,000 to form a partnership. In Year 3, the land was sold for $36,000. Kay's share of the loss from the sale of land is

A. $34,000

B. $27,000

C. $17,000

D. $7,000

Answer (B) is correct. *(Publisher, adapted)*
REQUIRED: The contributing partner's share of loss from the sale of property with a precontribution loss.
DISCUSSION: Gain or loss with respect to property contributed to the partnership must be allocated to take into account the variation between the basis of the property to the partnership and its fair market value at the time of contribution. Mary and Kay did this by allocating the $20,000 ($50,000 FMV − $70,000 basis) of precontribution decline in value. Upon the sale for $36,000, Kay's share of the loss is

Precontribution loss	$20,000
Postcontribution loss [($50,000 − $36,000) × 50%]	7,000
Total share of the loss	$27,000

Answer (A) is incorrect. The amount of $34,000 is the total loss from the sale of the land. Answer (C) is incorrect. The entire precontribution loss should be included in Kay's share of the loss. Answer (D) is incorrect. The precontribution loss is also part of Kay's share of the loss.

14.7.9. In February of Year 1, Alberta, Bert, and Chad started a partnership to purchase and lease a commercial office building. Alberta actively participates in the partnership's business, but Bert and Chad are not involved. Income and losses are shared equally. Economic risk of loss is also shared equally. Each partner invested $100,000 cash, and the partnership borrowed $700,000 from the bank on a recourse basis, using the building as security, in Year 1. For Years 1 through 5, the partnership had losses that totaled $210,000. For Year 6, a loss of $180,000 was incurred. What amount may Bert claim as a loss from the partnership on his Year 6 income tax return, assuming he has no passive income?

- A. $0
- B. $12,000
- C. $60,000
- D. $64,000

Answer (A) is correct. *(SEE, adapted)*
REQUIRED: The amount of deductible loss from a passive activity given adjusted basis and recourse debt.
DISCUSSION: Each partner's basis in his or her partnership interest includes his or her cash investment plus his or her allocable share of recourse liabilities or $333,333 [$100,000 + ($700,000 × 1/3)]. In Years 1 through 5, each partner's deductible loss was limited only by his or her basis (which is also his or her at-risk basis), so each partner could claim $70,000 in losses and had a $263,333 ($333,333 – $70,000) basis at the beginning of Year 6. The passive loss rules generally limit deduction of passive losses to the amount of passive income [Sec. 469(a)]. For rental real estate activities in which a partner actively participates, up to $25,000 in loss may also be allowed under the passive loss rules. However, Bert does not actively participate in the partnership, so the $25,000 allowance is not available to him. He can deduct none of his allowable share of partnership losses.

Answer (B) is incorrect. Bert may not claim $12,000 as a loss from the partnership on his Year 6 tax return, as he has no passive income or active participation. Answer (C) is incorrect. Bert may not claim $60,000 as a loss from the partnership on his Year 6 tax return, as he has no passive income or active participation. Answer (D) is incorrect. Bert may not claim $64,000 as a loss from the partnership on his Year 6 tax return, as he has no passive income or active participation.

14.7.10. L, M, and N formed an equal general partnership in January of the current year, each contributing $1,000 cash and each actively participating in the business. Although the partnership is engaged in real estate rental activities, it does not qualify as a real property trade or business. The partnership uses the cash method of accounting. The partnership purchased real property for $100,000, paying $3,000 in cash and giving a $97,000 nonrecourse note for which none of the partners is personally liable and which is not qualified real estate nonrecourse financing. The partnership incurred an operating loss of $15,000 for the year. Each partner has adjusted gross income from other activities of approximately $75,000 and no other passive losses. What is each partner's deductible share of the loss?

- A. $0
- B. $1,000
- C. $4,000
- D. $5,000

Answer (B) is correct. *(SEE, adapted)*
REQUIRED: The deductible share of loss attributed to each partner from a real estate rental activity, the assets for which were purchased with a nonrecourse note.
DISCUSSION: Under Sec. 465, each partner may deduct a loss only to the extent that (s)he is at risk with respect to the activity. Since the $97,000 note is nonrecourse, none of the partners has any risk with respect to it. Each partner is at risk with respect to only $1,000. Note that Sec. 465 applies at the partner level rather than at the partnership level.

Further, rental activity is generally passive. Passive losses must be netted at the partner level with other passive income and losses. Net passive losses from rental real estate activities may offset up to $25,000 of active or portfolio income for partners who actively participate in the rental activity as long as their modified AGI does not exceed $150,000. The maximum $25,000 offset is reduced by 50% of the amount that the taxpayer's modified AGI exceeds $100,000. Therefore, each partner can deduct his or her $1,000 passive loss from the rental real estate activity. Note that passive activity loss rules do not apply to certain taxpayers involved in a real property trade or business.

Answer (A) is incorrect. Each partner may deduct a loss to the extent they are at risk. Answer (C) is incorrect. The amount of $4,000 is each partner's loss that is carried over to subsequent tax years. Answer (D) is incorrect. The amount of $5,000 is one-third of the operating loss, which each partner cannot fully deduct.

14.7.11. On January 1, Year 1, Thomas contributed real estate he held for investment to Fog Partnership, a dealer in real estate. The real estate had an adjusted basis to Thomas of $50,000 and a fair market value at the time of the transfer of $43,000. On June 1, Year 3, Fog sold the real estate for $40,000. What are the amount and the character of the partnership's loss?

   A. $3,000 capital loss; $7,000 ordinary loss.

   B. $7,000 capital loss, $3,000 ordinary loss.

   C. $10,000 ordinary loss; $0 capital loss.

   D. $10,000 capital loss; $0 ordinary loss.

Answer (B) is correct. *(SEE, adapted)*
   REQUIRED: The amount and the character of the partnership's loss on the sale of contributed property.
   DISCUSSION: The partnership's basis in the property was $50,000 under Sec. 723. The loss realized and recognized on its sale was $10,000 (Sec. 1001). If property is contributed that would have generated a capital loss if sold by the partner, a loss on the disposition of the property within 7 years of its contribution (5 years for property contributed before June 9, 1997) is a capital loss [Sec. 724(c)]. The amount of the loss characterized as capital is the amount of capital loss the contributing partner would have recognized if (s)he had sold the property on the contribution date ($50,000 – $43,000 = $7,000). The remaining loss has the character it would have to the partnership.
   Answer (A) is incorrect. The amount of the loss characterized as capital is the amount of capital loss the contributing partner would have recognized if (s)he had sold the property on the contribution date. Answer (C) is incorrect. When property is contributed that would have generated a capital loss if sold by the partner, a loss on the disposition of the property within 7 years of its contribution is a capital loss to the extent of the loss that would have occurred at contribution. Answer (D) is incorrect. The partnership has an ordinary loss from this sale attributable to the portion of the loss that would not have been allocated to the contributing partner. This portion is ordinary because the partnership ordinarily deals in real estate.

14.7.12. The XYZ Partnership is a cash-basis, calendar-year entity. During the current year, the partnership incurred $12,000 in interest expense evenly throughout the year, but the total interest expense was not paid until December 31 of the current year. Otherwise, revenues equaled expenses, and XYZ reported a $12,000 loss for the tax year. Zorro became a 40% partner by making a $10,000 cash contribution on December 1 of the current year. How much of the partnership loss can be allocated to him for the year?

   A. $0

   B. $400

   C. $4,800

   D. $10,000

Answer (B) is correct. *(Publisher, adapted)*
   REQUIRED: The partnership loss that can be allocated to a partner who enters a cash-basis partnership.
   DISCUSSION: Under Sec. 706(d)(1), a partner's distributive share of any item of income, loss, deduction, or credit must take into account the varying interests of the partners during the year. Section 706(d)(2) requires cash-basis partnerships to allocate items such as interest to the days of the year to which they are applicable and to the partners based on their ownership interest each day. However, the allocation to partners may be done using a monthly convention for administrative ease.
   Since Zorro is a 40% partner, he may be allocated 40% of the loss attributed to the period while a partner. Therefore, Zorro's distributive share of the partnership loss is $400 ($12,000 × 40% × 1/12).
   Answer (A) is incorrect. Part of the partnership loss can be allocated to Zorro. Answer (C) is incorrect. Zorro was only a partner for 1 month. Answer (D) is incorrect. The amount of $10,000 is Zorro's basis in the partnership.

14.7.13. Your distributive share of partnership loss in the tax year in which the loss occurred is limited to the adjusted basis, before reduction by the current year's loss, of your partnership interest at the beginning of the partnership's tax year in which the loss occurred.

   A. True.

   B. False.

Answer (B) is correct. *(SEE, adapted)*
   DISCUSSION: A partner's distributive share of partnership loss is allowed only to the extent of the adjusted basis of such partner's interest in the partnership at the end (not beginning) of the partnership's tax year but before reduction for any losses of the current year [Sec. 704(d)].

14.7.14. A partner in a partnership that invests exclusively in real estate is allowed to use his or her allocable share of qualified nonrecourse financing as part of his or her basis for purposes of determining his or her at-risk loss limitation.

   A. True.

   B. False.

Answer (A) is correct. *(SEE, adapted)*
   DISCUSSION: An increase in a partner's share of partnership liabilities is considered a contribution of money by the partner to the partnership [Sec. 752(a)]. Therefore, a partner's basis for determining his or her loss limitation is also increased by his or her share of a nonrecourse loan. Section 465 "at-risk" limitations do apply to real estate activities, but an investor is considered at risk for his share of qualified nonrecourse financing incurred to hold real property and secured by real property [Sec. 465(b)(6)].

14.8 Guaranteed Payments

14.8.1. Which of the following is most likely to qualify as a guaranteed payment under Sec. 707(c)?

A. A, B, and C decide to form a partnership to build an apartment building. A, an architect, draws up the plans for the building. The partnership pays A his usual fee.

B. A and B contribute cash to their partnership as a capital contribution and agree that the partnership will pay them an 8% annual payment for the use of their capital. The partnership pays the annual amount.

C. A, a partner in the AB Partnership, lends $10,000 to the partnership on a 10% 1-year secured note. Regular payments of interest are made.

D. B, a stockholder and a 30% partner, sells stock to the ABC Partnership. The stock is sold for its fair market value.

14.8.2. Nash and Ford are partners who share profits and losses equally. For the year ended December 31, the partnership had book income of $80,000, which included the following deductions:

Guaranteed salaries to partners:
Nash	$35,000
Ford	25,000
Charitable contributions	5,000

What amount should be reported as ordinary income on the partnership return for the year?

A. $75,000
B. $85,000
C. $140,000
D. $145,000

14.8.3. Partnership K uses a fiscal year ending October 31 as its tax year and pays all guaranteed payments when they are deducted. J, a calendar-year partner, received guaranteed payments of $5,000 on November 30, Year 1, $15,000 on October 28, Year 2, and $15,000 on November 30, Year 2. J's distributive share of partnership income for the year ended October 31 of Year 2 was $75,000. How much income from the partnership must be included on J's Year 2 income tax return?

A. $75,000
B. $95,000
C. $105,000
D. $110,000

Answer (B) is correct. *(Publisher, adapted)*
REQUIRED: The transaction that qualifies as a guaranteed payment.
DISCUSSION: Under Sec. 707(c), guaranteed payments are payments to a partner for services or for the use of capital that are determined without regard to the income of the partnership. If the transaction is other than in the partner's capacity as a member of the partnership, however, it will be treated under Sec. 707(a) and not as a guaranteed payment. The payment of 8% for the use of the partners' capital is a guaranteed payment under Sec. 707(c) and does not fall under Sec. 707(a).
Answer (A) is incorrect. The architectural services rendered for an investment partnership would probably be performance by the partner other than in his or her capacity as a member of the partnership and would fall under Sec. 707(a) rather than Sec. 707(c). Answer (C) is incorrect. A bona fide loan is a transaction under Sec. 707(a) and is treated as occurring between a partnership and one who is not a partner. Answer (D) is incorrect. The sale of property between a partnership and a partner also falls under Sec. 707(a).

Answer (B) is correct. *(CPA, adapted)*
REQUIRED: The amount of the partnership's ordinary income.
DISCUSSION: If a payment is made to a partner for services rendered in his or her capacity as a partner, the payment is deductible under Sec. 707(c) as a guaranteed payment provided the amount of the payment is not determined with regard to the income of the partnership. The question states that the payments to the partners are guaranteed payments under Sec. 707(c), and they are therefore deductible. Charitable contributions are not deductible by a partnership [Sec. 703(a)]. The partnership's ordinary income is computed by adding back the charitable contribution deduction to book income.

Book income	$80,000
Plus: charitable contributions	5,000
Ordinary income	$85,000

Answer (A) is incorrect. Charitable contributions should be added back to, not subtracted from, book income. Answer (C) is incorrect. Charitable contributions should be added back to book income, and guaranteed payments should not be added back to book income. Answer (D) is incorrect. Guaranteed payments should not be added back to book income.

Answer (B) is correct. *(SEE, adapted)*
REQUIRED: The amount of a partner's income from a partnership given guaranteed payments.
DISCUSSION: Guaranteed payments are considered as made to a nonpartner, so they are deductible by the partnership [Sec. 707(c)]. The $75,000 of partnership income is therefore net of the guaranteed payments. A partner's share of partnership income is included in his or her tax year in which the partnership tax year ends. Guaranteed payments are included as income in the recipient's tax year, which includes the end of the partnership tax year in which they were deducted. Therefore, the amount of partnership income included on J's return equals $95,000 ($5,000 + $15,000 + $75,000).
Answer (A) is incorrect. Any guaranteed payments made during the partnership's tax year that ends within the partner's tax year must also be included in J's income. Answer (C) is incorrect. Year 1 income includes only the payments made during the partnership's tax year that ends within the partner's tax year. Answer (D) is incorrect. The guaranteed payment made on November 30, Year 2, is not included until next year.

14.8.4. G and H each contributed $25,000 to a newly formed partnership. The partnership agreement provides that G is entitled to a fixed annual salary of $10,000 without regard to the income of the partnership for managing the business. Any profit or loss after the deduction of G's salary is to be shared equally between the two partners. The first year's operation resulted in a loss of $15,000 after G's salary was deducted. What amount of net income or loss from the partnership should G report on his individual income tax return assuming he is a material participant in the partnership's business?

A. $10,000 income.

B. $2,500 income.

C. $2,500 loss.

D. $7,500 loss.

Answer (B) is correct. *(SEE, adapted)*
REQUIRED: The net income of a partner from a guaranteed payment and a partnership loss.
DISCUSSION: A fixed salary paid to a partner for managing the business that is determined without regard to the income of the partnership is a guaranteed payment under Sec. 707(c). The recipient partner includes the guaranteed payment as ordinary income. G's share of the partnership loss is $7,500 ($15,000 × 50%). The $10,000 guaranteed payment income minus the $7,500 loss produces net income for G of $2,500. Since G is a material participant in the partnership's business, the passive loss rules do not apply. Note that both the guaranteed payment and the partnership loss should be separately reported, not netted.
Answer (A) is incorrect. G's income also includes his share of the operating loss. Answer (C) is incorrect. The $2,500 net amount is income. Answer (D) is incorrect. His net income also includes the $10,000 guaranteed payment.

14.8.5. Gilroy, a calendar-year taxpayer, is a long-time partner in the firm of Adams and Company, which has a fiscal year ending June 30. The partnership agreement provides for Gilroy to receive 25% of the ordinary income of the partnership. Gilroy also receives a guaranteed payment of $1,000 monthly, which is deductible by the partnership. The partnership reported ordinary income of $88,000 for the year ended June 30, Year 2, and $132,000 for the year ended June 30, Year 3. How much should Gilroy report on his Year 2 return as total income from the partnership?

A. $25,000

B. $30,500

C. $34,000

D. $39,500

Answer (C) is correct. *(CPA, adapted)*
REQUIRED: The partner's income from a partnership including guaranteed payments.
DISCUSSION: In determining his or her income, each partner must take into account his or her distributive share of the partnership's income for the tax year of the partnership that ends within the partner's tax year [Sec. 706(a)]. This means Gilroy must include his share of the $88,000 income for the year ended June 30, Year 2, on his Year 2 return. A partner includes guaranteed payments in income in his or her tax year, which includes the end of the partnership tax year in which the guaranteed payments were deducted [Reg. 1.707-1(c)]; i.e., Gilroy includes the guaranteed payments made July, Year 1, through June, Year 2, in his Year 2 income.

Distributive share of ordinary income ($88,000 × 25%)	$22,000
Guaranteed payments ($1,000 × 12 months)	12,000
Total Year 2 income	$34,000

Answer (A) is incorrect. Gilroy receives 100% of his guaranteed monthly payments, which are not subject to the 25% sharing agreement. Answer (B) is incorrect. The amount of $30,500 is not the correct amount of income from the partnership that Gilroy should report on his Year 2 return. Answer (D) is incorrect. Gilroy does not use a prorated share of the partnership's income that falls during his calendar tax year.

14.8.6. Arthur is to receive 30% of partnership income, but not less than $5,000. The partnership has net income of $10,000 before any allocation. How much income should the partners report?

	Arthur's Guaranteed Payment	Other Distributive Share	Total Distributive Share
A.	$5,000	$1,500	$3,500
B.	$5,000	$3,000	$2,000
C.	$0	$3,000	$7,000
D.	$2,000	$3,000	$5,000

Answer (D) is correct. *(SEE, adapted)*
REQUIRED: The amount of income the partners should report.
DISCUSSION: Most guaranteed payments are in the form of a specific amount (e.g., a stated salary amount). Some guaranteed payments are in the form of a guaranteed minimum; that is, the partner is guaranteed a minimum amount from the partnership each year. In such a situation, the guaranteed payment is the excess of the partner's guaranteed minimum over the partner's distributive share. Arthur's guaranteed payment is $2,000 [$5,000 guaranteed minimum – ($10,000 × 30%)] and is deductible by the partnership. Arthur's 30% distributive share of partnership income before the guaranteed payment is $3,000. Arthur reports it on his individual tax return [Sec. 702(a)]. The guaranteed payment of $2,000 is also reported as ordinary income on his individual tax return. Therefore, Arthur's total distributive share of income is $5,000.
Answer (A) is incorrect. The total distributive share is not less than $5,000. Answer (B) is incorrect. The total distributive share will equal the sum of the guaranteed payment and the other distributive share. Answer (C) is incorrect. Arthur has a guaranteed payment.

14.8.7. Den and Carr are partners in the Den-Carr Partnership. Under the terms of the partnership agreement, Den is to receive 25% of all partnership income or loss plus a guaranteed payment of $80,000 per year. In the current tax year, Den-Carr had $72,000 of ordinary income before the deduction for Den's payment. What will Carr report as her income (loss) from the partnership assuming she materially participates in the partnership business?

A. $0

B. $54,000 ordinary income.

C. $10,000 ordinary income.

D. $6,000 ordinary loss.

Answer (D) is correct. *(Publisher, adapted)*
REQUIRED: The partner's income (loss) when a guaranteed payment to another partner causes a partnership loss.
DISCUSSION: The $80,000 payment to Den is treated as a guaranteed payment, and it will cause an $8,000 loss to the partnership ($72,000 – $80,000). Since Den is to receive 25% of the partnership income, Carr must receive 75% of the income or loss. This results in a $6,000 ordinary loss ($8,000 × 75%).
Answer (A) is incorrect. Carr will report income(loss) from the partnership. Answer (B) is incorrect. The amount of $54,000 is 75% of the ordinary income before deducting the guaranteed payment. Answer (C) is incorrect. Carr will not report $10,000 in ordinary income.

14.8.8. Under a partnership agreement, Sybil is to receive 40% of the partnership's income, but not less than $15,000 a year. The partnership's net income for the year was $30,000 before considering the guaranteed amount. What amount can the partnership deduct, and what amount of income is Sybil required to report on her individual tax return?

	Partnership	Sybil
A.	$3,000	$15,000
B.	$15,000	$15,000
C.	$3,000	$27,000
D.	$15,000	$27,000

Answer (A) is correct. *(SEE, adapted)*
REQUIRED: The amount the partnership can deduct and the amount the partner reports on his or her individual tax return.
DISCUSSION: Most guaranteed payments are in the form of a specific amount (e.g., a stated salary amount). Some guaranteed payments are in the form of a guaranteed minimum; that is, the partner is guaranteed a minimum amount from the partnership each year. In such a situation, the guaranteed payment is the excess of the partner's guaranteed minimum over the partner's distributive share. Sybil's guaranteed payment is $3,000 [$15,000 guaranteed minimum – ($30,000 × 40%)] and is deductible by the partnership. Sybil's 40% distributive share of partnership income before the guaranteed payment ($30,000) is $12,000. She reports it on her individual tax return [Sec. 702(a)]. The guaranteed payment of $3,000 is also reported as ordinary income on her individual tax return.
Answer (B) is incorrect. The partnership can only deduct the guaranteed payment. Answer (C) is incorrect. Sybil will not receive both a guaranteed minimum payment amount and her distributive share amount. Answer (D) is incorrect. The partnership can only deduct the guaranteed payment and because Sybil will not receive both a guaranteed minimum payment amount and her distributive share amount.

14.8.9. Doug sold 50% of his business to his son, Ben. The resulting partnership had a profit of $60,000. Capital is a material income-producing factor. Doug performed services worth $24,000, which is reasonable compensation, and Ben performed no services. What is the maximum amount of profit that Ben can report from the partnership for the tax year?

A. $30,000

B. $36,000

C. $12,000

D. $18,000

Answer (D) is correct. *(SEE, adapted)*
REQUIRED: The maximum amount of profit a partner can report in the tax year in which he sold an interest to his son.
DISCUSSION: Under Sec. 707(c), guaranteed payments are payments to a partner for services or for the use of capital that are determined without regard to the income of the partnership. Guaranteed payments are deductible by the partnership. After deducting the payment, the partnership's remaining income is $36,000. This income is split between the partners on a 50% basis. Thus, Ben will report his share, which is $18,000.
Answer (A) is incorrect. The amount of $30,000 does not account for the guaranteed payment. Answer (B) is incorrect. Doug is still entitled to his share of the profits after the guaranteed payment has been made. Answer (C) is incorrect. The amount of $12,000 is 50% of Doug's guaranteed payment, not the partnership's distributive income.

14.8.10. Guaranteed payments made to a cash-basis partner for organizing the partnership are deductible by the partnership in the year paid.

A. True.

B. False.

Answer (B) is correct. *(SEE, adapted)*
DISCUSSION: Guaranteed payments are deductible under Sec. 707(c), provided the payment is for services that would have been deductible if performed by an outsider. Section 709(b) provides for capitalization of expenses to organize a partnership and amortization over a period of not less than 180 months.

14.8.11. Guaranteed payments made by a partnership to a partner for services or for the use of capital, to the extent they are figured without regard to the income of the partnership, are treated by the partnership in the same way as payments made to a person who is not a partner. This treatment applies only for the purposes of determining gross income and deductible business expenses.

A. True.

B. False.

Answer (A) is correct. *(SEE, adapted)*
   DISCUSSION: Guaranteed payments under Sec. 707(c) are treated as if they were payments to an outsider for purposes of determining gross income and business expenses. They generate ordinary income to the recipient and represent either a deduction from ordinary income or a capitalized item to the partnership.

14.8.12. Helen, a calendar-year taxpayer, is a partner in a partnership that is on a fiscal year that ends January 31. Starting on February 1, Year 1, Helen is entitled to a fixed monthly payment of $1,000 without regard to the income of the partnership. Helen should report the guaranteed payments of $11,000 on her Year 1 individual income tax return.

A. True.

B. False.

Answer (B) is correct. *(SEE, adapted)*
   DISCUSSION: Under Sec. 706(a), a partner must include guaranteed payments deducted in a partnership's taxable year ending within his or her taxable year. The $11,000 in guaranteed payments will be deducted by the partnership in its fiscal year ending January 31, Year 2. Thus, Helen will include the payments on her Year 2 individual income tax return.

14.8.13. Under the terms of a partnership agreement, Tom is entitled to a fixed annual payment of $10,000 without regard to the income of the partnership. Tom's distributive share of the partnership is 20%. The partnership has a $40,000 loss after deducting Tom's guaranteed payment. Tom must report the full amount of the guaranteed payment and separately take into account his share of the partnership loss.

A. True.

B. False.

Answer (A) is correct. *(SEE, adapted)*
   DISCUSSION: When computing taxable income, a partner must include his or her distributive share of partnership items for any partnership tax year ending within his or her tax year [Sec. 706(a)]. A partner must also include guaranteed payments deducted in a partnership's tax year ending within his or her tax year. Guaranteed payments are deductible by the partnership [Sec. 707(c)].

14.9 Adjustments to Basis in Partnership Interest

14.9.1. Mr. G and Mr. H do business as a partnership. They file partnership and individual returns on a calendar-year basis. The partnership had a loss of $12,000 in Year 1 and a profit of $10,000 in Year 2. Mr. G's distributive share of the loss in Year 1 was $6,000 and his share of the profit in Year 2 is $5,000. The adjusted basis of his partnership interest before the Year 1 loss was $3,000. What is Mr. G's adjusted basis of his partnership interest at the end of Year 2?

A. $0

B. $2,000

C. $3,000

D. $5,000

Answer (B) is correct. *(SEE, adapted)*
   REQUIRED: The adjusted basis in partnership interest.
   DISCUSSION: Under Sec. 705(a), the adjusted basis of a partner's interest in a partnership is increased or decreased by his or her distributive share of partnership income or losses, respectively. In Year 1, Mr. G can deduct only $3,000 of his $6,000 share of the partnership loss because of the basis limitation. After deducting this loss, Mr. G's adjusted basis is zero. In Year 2, Mr. G's adjusted basis is increased by his $5,000 share of partnership income. He may also deduct the remaining $3,000 share of the Year 1 partnership loss, leaving him with an adjusted basis of $2,000 ($0 + $5,000 − $3,000).
   Whether the passive loss rules apply has no effect on basis. Basis is decreased by losses even if the losses are not currently deductible under the passive loss rules.
   Answer (A) is incorrect. Mr. G has a basis in his partnership interest at the end of Year 2. Answer (C) is incorrect. The amount of $3,000 is G's adjusted basis before adjusting it for his share of partnership gains and losses. Answer (D) is incorrect. The zero basis at the beginning of Year 2 is increased by the partnership profit allocable to G in Year 2 and is reduced by the loss carryover from Year 1.

14.9.2. Ted and Jane form a cash-basis general partnership with cash contributions of $20,000 each. They share all partnership profits and losses equally. They borrow $60,000 and purchase depreciable business equipment. Jane, however, is required to pay the creditor if the partnership defaults. Which of the following is true?

A. Ted and Jane each have a basis of $80,000 in the partnership.

B. Ted has a basis of $50,000 and Jane has a basis of $80,000.

C. Ted and Jane each have a basis of $50,000 in the partnership.

D. Ted has a basis of $20,000 and Jane has a basis of $80,000 in the partnership.

Answer (D) is correct. *(SEE, adapted)*
REQUIRED: The partners' bases in the partnership.
DISCUSSION: A partner receives a basis in a partnership equal to the basis of the property contributed to the partnership (Sec. 722). Under Sec. 752(a), an increase in a partner's share of liabilities is treated as a contribution of money by such partner, which increases the partner's basis. Jane's basis increases by $60,000, the amount of the liabilities, because she is the guarantor of the loan and her share of liabilities has increased.
Answer (A) is incorrect. Only Jane's basis will be increased by the liability. Answer (B) is incorrect. Ted's basis is unaffected by Jane's guarantee of the loan. Answer (C) is incorrect. Ted's basis is unaffected by Jane's guarantee of the loan. Further, Jane's basis will be increased by the entire amount of the liability.

14.9.3. Hall and Haig are equal partners in the firm of Arosa Associates. On January 1, each partner's adjusted basis in Arosa was $40,000. During the year, Arosa borrowed $60,000 for which Hall and Haig are personally liable. Arosa sustained an operating loss of $10,000 for the year ended December 31. The basis of each partner's interest in Arosa at December 31 is

A. $35,000

B. $40,000

C. $65,000

D. $70,000

Answer (C) is correct. *(CPA, adapted)*
REQUIRED: The adjusted basis of a partner's partnership interest.
DISCUSSION: The adjusted basis of a partner's interest is the original basis of such interest, increased by the partner's distributive share of the partnership's income and allocable portion of liabilities, and decreased by the partner's distributive share of the partnership's loss (Secs. 705 and 752). The bases of Hall's and Haig's interests would each be the same:

Basis on January 1	$40,000
Increase in liabilities ($60,000 × 50%)	30,000
Share of partnership loss ($10,000 × 50%)	(5,000)
Basis on December 31	$65,000

Answer (A) is incorrect. Each partner's basis increases by his or her share of the additional liability. Answer (B) is incorrect. Each partner's basis is $40,000 before adjusting it for his or her share of the additional liability and the operating loss. Answer (D) is incorrect. Each partner's adjusted basis must be reduced by his or her share of the operating loss.

14.9.4. In January of the current year, Martin and Louis formed a partnership with each contributing $75,000 cash. The partnership agreement provided that Martin would receive a guaranteed salary of $20,000 and that partnership profits and losses (computed after deducting Martin's salary) would be shared equally. For the first year ending December 31, the partnership's operations resulted in a loss of $18,000 after payment of Martin's salary. The partnership had no outstanding liabilities as of December 31. What is the amount of Martin's partnership basis as of December 31 of the current year?

A. $46,000

B. $66,000

C. $76,000

D. $86,000

Answer (B) is correct. *(CPA, adapted)*
REQUIRED: The adjusted basis of a partner's partnership interest.
DISCUSSION: Section 705(a) provides that the adjusted basis of a partner's interest is the original basis of such interest, increased by the partner's distributive share of partnership income, and decreased by the partner's share of partnership loss. Section 707(c) provides that guaranteed payments (determined without regard to partnership income) are considered as if made to a nonpartner for purposes of computing gross income and business expenses. This means the guaranteed salary paid to Martin is not considered a distribution and does not affect Martin's partnership basis. Martin's partnership basis is

Original basis	$75,000
Share of partnership loss ($18,000 × 50%)	(9,000)
Year-end basis	$66,000

Answer (A) is incorrect. The guaranteed payment does not decrease Martin's basis. Answer (C) is incorrect. One-half of the guaranteed payment does not increase Martin's basis. Answer (D) is incorrect. The entire guaranteed payment does not increase Martin's basis.

14.9.5. Clark and Kent share profits and losses of 60% and 40%, respectively. The tax basis of each partner's interest in the partnership as of December 31, Year 1, was as follows:

Clark	$24,000
Kent	18,000

During Year 2, the partnership had ordinary income of $50,000 and a long-term capital loss of $10,000 from the sale of securities. There were no distributions to the partners during Year 2. What is the amount of Kent's tax basis as of December 31, Year 2?

A. $33,000

B. $34,000

C. $38,000

D. $42,000

Answer (B) is correct. *(CPA, adapted)*
REQUIRED: The tax basis of a partner's interest after a year of operation.
DISCUSSION: Sections 705(a) and 733 provide that the adjusted basis of a partner's interest is the original basis, increased by the partner's distributive share of income of the partnership, and decreased by the partner's distributive share of losses and distributions received from the partnership. Kent's tax basis is

Kent's tax basis on 1/1/Year 2	$18,000
Share of income ($50,000 × 40%)	20,000
Share of loss ($10,000 × 40%)	(4,000)
Kent's tax basis on 12/31/Year 2	$34,000

Answer (A) is incorrect. The tax basis is adjusted for Kent's share of income and loss for the year. Answer (C) is incorrect. The tax basis is also adjusted for the loss. Answer (D) is incorrect. The share of the loss is subtracted from the basis, not added.

14.9.6. Arnold Money invested $20,000 for a one-third interest in capital and profits of a partnership. Subsequent to his investment, the partnership had taxable income of $30,000 and nontaxable income of $6,000, and Money withdrew $9,000. After this series of events, the tax basis of Money's interest in the partnership is

A. $11,000

B. $20,000

C. $21,000

D. $23,000

Answer (D) is correct. *(CPA, adapted)*
REQUIRED: The tax basis of a partner's partnership interest.
DISCUSSION: Sections 705(a) and 733 provide that a partner's adjusted basis is the original basis of the interest, increased by the partner's distributive share of partnership income (both taxable and nontaxable) and decreased by distributions from the partnership. Money's basis in the partnership is

Original basis (amount invested)	$20,000
Share of:	
Taxable income ($30,000 × 1/3)	10,000
Nontaxable income ($6,000 × 1/3)	2,000
Distributions	(9,000)
Tax basis after events	$23,000

Answer (A) is incorrect. Taxable and nontaxable income should be added to the original basis. Answer (B) is incorrect. The original basis should be adjusted for Money's share of the partnership's taxable and nontaxable income and distributions. Answer (C) is incorrect. One-third of the nontaxable income also increases Money's basis.

14.9.7. On January 1 of the current year, the Hack Partnership was formed. Bill acquired a 20% interest in the partnership by contributing a computer system that had an adjusted basis to him of $15,000 and was subject to a $5,000 liability. During the year, the partnership paid off the entire $5,000 liability. The partnership reported ordinary income of $75,000 on its first partnership return. What is the amount of Bill's basis in the partnership on December 31 of the current year?

A. $35,000

B. $30,000

C. $25,000

D. $20,000

Answer (C) is correct. *(SEE, adapted)*
REQUIRED: The basis of a partner's partnership interest.
DISCUSSION: Under Sec. 722, the basis of an interest in a partnership acquired by a contribution of property, including money, to the partnership is the adjusted basis of such property to the contributing partner. Under Sec. 752, increases in a partner's share of liabilities are treated as contributions, and decreases in such liabilities are treated as distributions. Therefore, Bill's basis is

Original basis (adjusted basis)	$15,000
Liabilities assumed by partnership ($5,000 × 80%)	(4,000)
Decrease in liabilities ($5,000 × 20%)	(1,000)
Ordinary income ($75,000 × 20%)	15,000
Year-end basis	$25,000

Answer (A) is incorrect. The basis must be reduced, not increased, by the portion of Bill's liability assumed by Bill's other partners and the repayment of Bill's share of the liability. Answer (B) is incorrect. The basis must be reduced by the portion of Bill's liability assumed by Bill's other partners and the repayment of Bill's share of the liability. Answer (D) is incorrect. The basis must be reduced, not increased, by the portion of Bill's liability assumed by Bill's other partners and the repayment of Bill's share of the liability. Also, Bill's share of ordinary income should increase his basis.

14.9.8. On January 1 of the current year, the Pizza Partnership was formed. Tony acquired a 25% share in the partnership by contributing both an oven that had an adjusted basis to him of $10,000 and $5,000 in cash. The oven was subject to a $2,000 liability. During the year, the partnership also incurred a $20,000 nonrecourse loan and paid off the entire $2,000 liability attached to the oven. There are no guarantees or loss limitation agreements associated with the nonrecourse loan. Operations for the current year resulted in a $2,000 ordinary loss. What is Tony's basis in the partnership at the end of the current year?

A. $14,500

B. $17,500

C. $19,000

D. $19,500

Answer (B) is correct. *(Publisher, adapted)*
REQUIRED: The basis of a partner's partnership interest.
DISCUSSION: Under Sec. 722, the basis of an interest in a partnership acquired by a contribution of property, including money, to the partnership is the adjusted basis of such property to the contributing partner. Under Sec. 752, increases in a partner's share of liabilities are treated as contributions, and decreases in such liabilities are treated as distributions. Accordingly, Tony's basis in the partnership interest at the end of the current year is

Original basis (adjusted basis):		
Cash	$ 5,000	
Oven	10,000	$15,000
Liabilities assumed by partnership:		
Oven ($2,000 × 75%)	$ (1,500)	
Nonrecourse loan ($20,000 × 25%)	5,000	3,500
Decrease in liabilities:		
Oven ($2,000 × 25%)		(500)
Ordinary loss ($2,000 × 25%)		(500)
Year-end basis		$17,500

Answer (A) is incorrect. The basis must be adjusted for the increase and decrease of liabilities. Answer (C) is incorrect. The basis must be adjusted for the oven liability assumed by the partnership. Answer (D) is incorrect. The basis must be adjusted for the oven liability assumed by the partnership and the decrease in liabilities.

14.9.9. The Salt and Pepper Partnership was formed in January of the current year when Salt and Pepper each contributed $10,000 cash and together began to operate a business as equal partners. Both work full-time in the partnership. The partnership borrowed $40,000 on a nonrecourse basis during the year. There are no guarantees or loss limitation agreements. Operations in the year resulted in a $5,000 ordinary loss, $2,000 tax-exempt income, and an $800 charitable contribution. What is Salt's basis at the end of the current year?

A. $8,100

B. $27,500

C. $28,100

D. $28,500

Answer (C) is correct. *(Publisher, adapted)*
REQUIRED: The general partner's basis in a partnership after a year of operations.
DISCUSSION: A contributing partner receives an original basis in a partnership equal to the amount of money contributed. This basis is increased by the partner's share of nonrecourse partnership debt under Sec. 752 because debt is treated as a contribution of money by the partner. The basis of a partner's interest is further increased by both taxable and tax-exempt income under Sec. 705(a)(1), and decreased by partnership losses and nondeductible expenditures (such as charitable contributions) under Sec. 705(a)(2).

Original contribution	$10,000
Partnership liability ($40,000 × 50%)	20,000
Tax-exempt income ($2,000 × 50%)	1,000
Ordinary loss ($5,000 × 50%)	(2,500)
Charitable contribution ($800 × 50%)	(400)
Year-end basis	$28,100

Answer (A) is incorrect. Salt's share of the partnership liability increases basis. Answer (B) is incorrect. Fifty percent of the separately stated items (e.g., tax-exempt income and charitable contributions) should be added or subtracted from basis. Answer (D) is incorrect. One-half of the charitable contribution decreases Salt's basis.

14.9.10. Partnership LIFE's profits and losses are shared equally among the four partners. The adjusted basis of Partner E's interest in the partnership on December 31, Year 1, was $25,000. On January 2, Year 2, Partner E withdrew $10,000 cash. The partnership reported $200,000 as ordinary income on its Year 2 partnership return. In addition, $5,000 for qualified travel, meals, and entertainment was shown on a separate attachment to E's Schedule K-1 of Form 1065. Due to the limitation, $2,500 of the $5,000 is unallowable as a deduction. What is the amount of E's basis in the partnership on December 31, Year 2?

- A. $60,000
- B. $61,000
- C. $65,000
- D. $71,000

Answer (A) is correct. *(SEE, adapted)*
REQUIRED: The adjusted basis of a partner's partnership interest.
DISCUSSION: The adjusted basis of a partner's interest is the original basis of such interest, increased by the partner's distributive share of the partnership's income and allocable portion of liabilities, and decreased by the partner's distributive share of partnership loss and distributions (Secs. 705, 733, and 752). Partnership basis is also reduced by nondeductible expenses.

Beginning basis	$25,000
Ordinary income ($200,000 × 25%)	50,000
Cash distribution	(10,000)
Travel, meals, entertainment expense	(5,000)
Year-end basis	$60,000

Answer (B) is incorrect. The nondeductible portion of a separately stated expense also reduces partnership basis. Answer (C) is incorrect. The $5,000 for travel, meals, and entertainment expense should be deducted from the partnership basis since it is a separately stated item. Answer (D) is incorrect. Both the cash distribution and the nondeductible portion of the separately stated expense decrease basis.

14.9.11. A partnership has three general and two limited partners. Each of the limited partners contributed $5,000. The partnership liabilities are

Accounts payable	$20,000
Accrued expenses	25,000
Mortgage payable (nonrecourse -- secured only by a partnership building with a basis of $150,000)	75,000
Nonrecourse notes payable (personally guaranteed by general partners)	40,000

If all partners have equal shares of partnership income, loss, and minimum gain, what is each limited partner's share of the liabilities?

- A. $5,000
- B. $9,000
- C. $10,000
- D. $15,000

Answer (D) is correct. *(SEE, adapted)*
REQUIRED: The amount of each limited partner's share of liabilities.
DISCUSSION: A limited partner's share of liabilities may not exceed his or her obligation for additional contributions to the partnership, unless no partners have personal liability for a partnership liability. Then all partners (including limited) share the liability based first on their share of minimum gain, then their share of any Sec. 704(c) minimum gain, with the remainder shared based on their profit-sharing ratio [Reg. 1.752-3(a)]. But limited partners cannot share in nonrecourse debt guaranteed by a general partner. In this question, there is no minimum gain. Therefore, each limited partner's share of liabilities is limited to 20% of the nonrecourse mortgage ($75,000 × 20% = $15,000).

Answer (A) is incorrect. The amount of $5,000 is the amount of money contributed by each of the limited partners. It does not set a ceiling on a partner's share of liabilities. Answer (B) is incorrect. The limited partners do not receive a share of the accounts payable and accrued expenses but do receive a share of the mortgage payable. Answer (C) is incorrect. Each limited partner's share of the liabilities is not reduced by his or her basis.

14.9.12. A partner's share of partnership liabilities will be determined in accordance with the partner's ratio for sharing profits under the partnership agreement.

- A. True.
- B. False.

Answer (B) is correct. *(SEE, adapted)*
DISCUSSION: Partners share recourse liabilities based on their potential for economic loss. Only nonrecourse liabilities in excess of minimum gain are shared based on the profit-sharing ratio.

14.9.13. A partner's adjusted basis for an interest in a partnership can be less than zero.

- A. True.
- B. False.

Answer (B) is correct. *(SEE, adapted)*
DISCUSSION: A partner's basis may not be decreased below zero [Sec. 705(a)(2)].

14.9.14. A partner's basis in a partnership interest is increased by the partner's share of tax-exempt receipts of the partnership.

A. True.

B. False.

Answer (A) is correct. *(SEE, adapted)*
   DISCUSSION: Section 705(a) provides the adjustments to a partner's basis for partnership operations. A partner's basis in a partnership interest is increased by the partner's share of tax-exempt income.

14.9.15. The amount shown in the partnership books as a partner's capital account is the same as the basis of a partner's interest in the partnership.

A. True.

B. False.

Answer (B) is correct. *(SEE, adapted)*
   DISCUSSION: The basis of a partner's interest in a partnership reflects the money and adjusted basis of any property contributed and includes the partner's share of liabilities. A partner's capital account, however, usually reflects the money and fair market value of property contributed and does not include liabilities. There is no requirement that the capital account and basis relate to each other.

14.10 Transactions between the Partnership and a Partner

14.10.1. In determining the ownership rules of partnerships, which one of the following combinations would not total at least 50% ownership of The Desk Company for Joe?

A.	Joe	40%
	Wife	5%
	Joe's son	2%
	Joe's sister	53%
B.	Joe	40%
	His cousin's trust	60%
C.	Joe	30%
	Wife	5%
	Joe's C corporation	65%
D.	Joe	30%
	Wife	10%
	His dad's estate, which Joe will receive someday	60%

Answer (B) is correct. *(SEE, adapted)*
   REQUIRED: The combination that would not total at least 50% ownership of the partnership.
   DISCUSSION: The constructive ownership rules of Sec. 267(c) other than paragraph (3) determine constructive ownership. Under Sec. 267(c)(1), each beneficiary is treated as owning a proportion of the interest owned by a trust. But an interest owned by a cousin is not treated as owned by the other cousin. Therefore, in this combination, Joe is treated as owning only 40% of The Desk Company.
   Answer (A) is incorrect. Under Sec. 267(c)(2) and (4), Joe is treated as owning the interests actually owned by his spouse, his lineal descendants, his siblings, and even his ancestors. Answer (C) is incorrect. Under Sec. 267(c)(1), Joe is treated as owning the stock owned by his corporation. Answer (D) is incorrect. Under Sec. 267(c)(1), Joe is treated as owning the stock of an estate in proportion to his beneficial interest in it.

14.10.2. Sara Loy is a member of a four-person equal partnership. Sara is unrelated to the other partners. In the current year, Sara sold 100 shares of a listed stock to the partnership for the stock's fair market value of $20,000. Sara's basis for this stock, which was purchased 15 years ago, was $14,000. Sara's recognized gain on the sale of this stock was

A. $0

B. $1,500

C. $4,500

D. $6,000

Answer (D) is correct. *(CPA, adapted)*
   REQUIRED: The partner's recognized gain on the sale of stock to the partnership.
   DISCUSSION: When a partner engages in a transaction with the partnership not in his or her capacity as a partner, the transaction is considered to occur between the partnership and a nonpartner [Sec. 707(a)]. Therefore, Sara may recognize a $6,000 long-term capital gain ($20,000 proceeds less $14,000 adjusted basis). Note that if Sara had owned more than 50% of the capital or profit interest of the partnership, a gain could still have been recognized, but a loss on a sale to the partnership could not be recognized [Sec. 707(b)(1)].
   Answer (A) is incorrect. A gain is recognized. Sara did not receive additional partnership interest. Answer (B) is incorrect. The gain is not limited to her profit sharing ratio in the partnership. Answer (C) is incorrect. The amount of $4,500 is less than the gain recognized.

14.10.3. Dianne owns 10% interest in DJJ Partnership and 20% of the outstanding stock of PAD Corporation. Her son, Nick, owns 60% of the outstanding shares of PAD Corporation. The PAD Corporation owns 50% interest in the DJJ Partnership. Dianne's sister, Dolores, owns 40% interest in the DJJ Partnership. Using the constructive ownership rules for partnerships, Dianne is considered to own how much of DJJ Partnership?

A. 80%

B. 50%

C. 90%

D. 20%

Answer (C) is correct. *(SEE, adapted)*
REQUIRED: The total interest a partner owns under the constructive ownership rules.
DISCUSSION: An individual is treated as owning the stock owned by his or her spouse, children, grandchildren, siblings, and parents. If 50% or more in value of the stock in a corporation is owned, directly or indirectly, by or for any person, that person is considered to own the stock, directly or indirectly, by or for his or her corporation in the proportion that the value of the stock (s)he owns bears to the value of all the stock in the corporation. Dianne is considered to own 90% of the partnership: 10% direct ownership, plus 80% indirect ownership (made up of her 20% ownership of the corporation plus her son's 60% ownership of the corporation times the 50% corporate ownership of the partnership plus her sister's 40% ownership).
Answer (A) is incorrect. Dianne's indirect ownership through the corporation must be included (20% × 50%). Answer (B) is incorrect. The stock Dianne's sister owns must be included. Answer (D) is incorrect. Twenty percent is the percentage of stock that Dianne owns in PAD Corporation.

14.10.4. On December 1 of the current year, Alan Younger, a member of a three-man equal partnership, bought securities from the partnership for $27,000, their market value. The securities had been acquired by the partnership for $15,000 on August 1 of that same year. By what amount will this transaction increase Younger's taxable income for the year?

A. $0

B. $1,600

C. $4,000

D. $12,000

Answer (C) is correct. *(CPA, adapted)*
REQUIRED: The amount by which a sale by a partnership to a partner will increase the partner's taxable income.
DISCUSSION: The general rule under Sec. 707(a) is that, when a partner engages in a transaction with the partnership other than in his or her capacity as a partner, the transaction is considered to occur between the partnership and a nonpartner. This means that the partnership would recognize a gain of $12,000 ($27,000 proceeds – $15,000 basis). The increase in Younger's taxable income as a result of his share of partnership income is $4,000 ($12,000 × 1/3).
Answer (A) is incorrect. Taxable income will increase. Answer (B) is incorrect. Each partner recognizes a one-third share of the gain. Answer (D) is incorrect. The $12,000 gain increases each partner's taxable income by his or her distributive share.

14.10.5. Kay Shea owns a 55% interest in the capital and profits of Admor Antiques, a partnership. In the current year, Kay sold an oriental lamp to Admor for $5,000. Kay bought this lamp 16 years ago for her personal use at a cost of $1,000 and used it continuously in her home until she sold it to Admor. Admor purchased the lamp as inventory for sale to customers in the ordinary course of business. What is Kay's reportable gain in the current year on the sale of the lamp to Admor?

A. $4,000 ordinary income.

B. $4,000 long-term capital gain.

C. $2,200 ordinary income.

D. $2,200 long-term capital gain.

Answer (A) is correct. *(CPA, adapted)*
REQUIRED: The partner's reportable gain from a sale of capital gain property to the partnership.
DISCUSSION: Under Sec. 707(b)(2), gains recognized on sales to or from a person who directly or indirectly owns more than a 50% interest in the partnership are treated as ordinary income if the property is not a capital asset in the hands of the buyer. Since the lamp will be sold as inventory by the partnership, Kay's reportable gain is $4,000 ordinary income ($5,000 proceeds – $1,000 basis).
Answer (B) is incorrect. The gain is not a long-term capital gain. Answer (C) is incorrect. Kay's reported ordinary income is not limited to her partnership interest share. Answer (D) is incorrect. Kay's income will be characterized as ordinary because the lamp will be used as inventory by the partnership. Moreover, the entire gain will be recognized.

14.10.6. Carmen has a 55% capital interest and 40% interest in the profits and losses of CCD Partnership. She also owns 60% interest in the profits and losses of Dream Partnership. On September 25 of the current year, CCD Partnership sold a piece of real estate to Dream for $20,000. CCD's adjusted basis at the time of the sale was $26,000. What is the amount of loss that CCD Partnership can recognize in the current year?

A. $6,000

B. $3,300

C. $2,400

D. $0

Answer (D) is correct. *(SEE, adapted)*
REQUIRED: The amount of loss a partnership can recognize on the sale of property to related partnership.
DISCUSSION: CCD realized a $6,000 loss on the sale. However, Sec. 707(b)(1) provides that losses from sales or exchanges of property between two partnerships in which the same person or persons own more than 50% of the capital or profit interest are not deductible. When the property is subsequently sold, any realized gain is recognized only to the extent that it exceeds the unrecognized loss.
Answer (A) is incorrect. The amount of $6,000 is the realized loss. Answer (B) is incorrect. The amount of $3,300 is a 55% share of the realized loss, which cannot be currently recognized. Answer (C) is incorrect. The amount of $2,400 is a 40% share of the realized loss, which cannot be currently recognized.

14.10.7. Walter owned a 30% general partnership interest in the ABC Partnership and a 60% general partnership interest in the WXY Partnership. Under the terms of the partnership agreement, Walter receives 60% of the profits from each partnership. On April 15 of the current year, ABC sold a building to WXY for $200,000. ABC's adjusted basis in the building at the time of the sale was $250,000. ABC will not be allowed to recognize any loss on the sale of the building to WXY.

A. True.

B. False.

Answer (A) is correct. *(SEE, adapted)*
DISCUSSION: Section 707(b)(1) provides that losses are not deductible on sales or exchanges of property between a partnership and a partner owning more than a 50% interest in the capital or profits, or two partnerships in which the same person or persons own more than 50% of the capital or profits interests. Walter owns more than a 50% profits interest in both partnerships, so the partnership may not deduct the loss on the sale between the two partnerships.

14.10.8. A&B is a partnership that rents commercial office buildings. A and B are brothers. A buys one of the partnership buildings at fair market value and continues renting it. If the partnership has a gain on the sale, the gain is treated as ordinary income.

A. True.

B. False.

Answer (A) is correct. *(SEE, adapted)*
DISCUSSION: When sale or exchange of property occurs between a partnership and a partner owning more than 50% of the capital or profit interest, and the property transferred is not a capital asset to the transferee, the gain is ordinary [Sec. 707(b)(2)]. Under the rules of constructive ownership, A owns 100% (A's 50% + B's 50%) of the partnership.

14.10.9. Mr. White, a 50% partner in the Red and White Partnership, lent the partnership $10,000 on a secured basis with a market interest rate. The partnership can deduct only 50% of the interest paid to Mr. White.

A. True.

B. False.

Answer (B) is correct. *(Publisher, adapted)*
DISCUSSION: A bona fide loan from a partner to a partnership is treated as occurring between a partnership and one who is not a partner under Sec. 707(a). All the interest paid to a partner on borrowed funds is deductible.

14.10.10. Nilla Wayfer, an accountant, was paid $100 each month to prepare the books for the Wayfer-Water Partnership in which Nilla held a 30% interest. The partnership will treat Nilla's $100 payment as a deductible expense.

A. True.

B. False.

Answer (A) is correct. *(Publisher, adapted)*
DISCUSSION: Payments to a partner for services rendered to the partnership are generally deductible. The payment is treated as an ordinary expense under Sec. 707(a) and considered to occur between a partnership and a nonpartner if the services are not generally those performed by a partner.

STUDY UNIT FIFTEEN
PARTNERSHIPS: DISTRIBUTIONS, SALES, AND EXCHANGES

15.1 Current Distributions

15.1.1. The adjusted basis of Stan's partnership interest is $15,000. He receives a distribution of cash of $6,000 and property with an adjusted basis to the partnership of $11,000. (This was not a distribution in liquidation.) What is the basis of the distributed property in Stan's hands?

A. $9,000

B. $11,000

C. $5,000

D. $17,000

Answer (A) is correct. *(SEE, adapted)*
REQUIRED: The basis of distributive property in the partnership.
DISCUSSION: Section 732(a) provides that the basis of property distributed to a partner is the property's adjusted basis to the partnership immediately before such distribution. This basis, however, cannot exceed the adjusted basis of the partner's interest in the partnership less any money received in the same distribution [Sec. 732(a)(2)]. Stan's basis in the property distributed is

Basis of partnership interest	$15,000
Less: cash received	(6,000)
Basis in distributed property	$ 9,000

Answer (B) is incorrect. The basis of the distributed property cannot exceed the adjusted basis of the partner's interest in the partnership. Answer (C) is incorrect. The basis will not be equal to the difference between the amount of cash received and the partnership's basis in the property. Answer (D) is incorrect. The amount of $17,000 exceeds Stan's adjusted basis of his interest in the partnership.

15.1.2. Marvel has an adjusted basis in a partnership interest of $25,000 before receiving a current distribution of $4,000 cash, inventory with an adjusted basis of $6,000 and a fair market value of $9,000, and land with a fair market value of $7,000 and an adjusted basis of $8,000. Section 751 does not apply. What is Marvel's basis in the partnership interest after the distribution?

A. $25,000

B. $8,000

C. $7,000

D. $5,000

Answer (C) is correct. *(Publisher, adapted)*
REQUIRED: The partner's basis in the partnership after receiving a current distribution.
DISCUSSION: A partner's basis in a partnership is reduced by the amount of money and the basis to the partner of distributed property in a nonliquidating distribution (Sec. 733). Marvel's basis in the partnership after the distribution is

Beginning basis	$25,000
Less: Cash	(4,000)
Inventory	(6,000)
Land	(8,000)
Ending basis	$ 7,000

Answer (A) is incorrect. The partnership interest must be reduced by the three current distributions. Answer (B) is incorrect. The land reduces the basis of the partnership interest by its adjusted basis and not its FMV. Answer (D) is incorrect. The inventory and the land reduce the partnership basis by their bases, not by their FMV.

15.1.3. Mondy had an adjusted basis in her partnership interest of $39,000 before receiving a current distribution. In the current distribution (to which Sec. 751 does not apply), she received the following:

	Basis	Fair Market Value
Cash	$ 3,000	$ 3,000
Inventory	15,000	17,000
Land 1	10,000	15,000
Land 2	20,000	25,000

What is her basis in each of the items received?

A. $3,000 cash; $15,000 inventory; $10,000 land 1; $20,000 land 2.

B. $3,000 cash; $12,000 inventory; $12,000 land 1; $12,000 land 2.

C. $3,000 cash; $15,000 inventory; $10,500 land 1; $10,500 land 2.

D. $3,000 cash; $15,000 inventory; $7,000 land 1; $14,000 land 2.

Answer (D) is correct. *(Publisher, adapted)*
REQUIRED: The partner's basis in property.
DISCUSSION: A partner's basis in a nonliquidating distribution is determined under Sec. 732(a) as the property's adjusted basis to the partnership immediately before the distribution. This transferred basis is not to exceed the adjusted basis of the partner's interest in the partnership reduced by any money distributed in the same transaction. If this limitation applies, Sec. 732(c) provides that the basis is allocated first to unrealized receivables and inventory items. Under new law as promulgated by the Taxpayer Relief Act of 1998, any excess basis is next allocated, first, to the extent of each distributed property's adjusted basis to the partnership. Then, the allocation of any remaining basis depends on whether the adjusted bases of the distributed properties exceed the partner's remaining basis in the partnership interest or not. If the partnership's bases in the distributed properties do exceed the partner's remaining basis in the partnership, a decrease is allocated among the properties with unrealized depreciation, in proportion to their respective amounts of unrealized depreciation (to the extent of each property's depreciation), and then in proportion to the properties' respective adjusted bases (considering the adjustments already made). Alternatively, if the partner's remaining basis in the partnership exceeds the adjusted bases of the distributed properties, then an increase is allocated among the properties with unrealized appreciation, in proportion to their respective amounts of unrealized appreciation (to the extent of each property's appreciation), and then in proportion to the properties' fair market values.

In this case, Mondy will have a $3,000 basis in the cash and a $15,000 basis in the inventory. This leaves $21,000 of basis to allocate to the two parcels of land ($39,000 beginning basis − $3,000 cash − $15,000 inventory). The first step, however, is to assign each parcel of land its carryover basis from the partnership ($10,000 for land 1 and $20,000 for land 2). Since the total adjusted bases of the distributed properties exceed the partner's remaining basis in the partnership, a $9,000 decrease must be allocated next ($30,000 total adjusted bases of land − $21,000 remaining basis in partnership interest = $9,000 decrease to allocate). The $9,000 decrease is allocated in proportion to the respective adjusted bases of the land at this point in the calculation ($10,000 land 1, and $20,000 land 2) [($3,000) to land 1 and ($6,000) to land 2]. The calculation of the allocation of basis to land is shown below:

	Land 1	Land 2
Carryover basis	$10,000	$20,000
Allocated decrease (1/3 to land 1 and 2/3 to land 2)	(3,000)	(6,000)
Basis	$ 7,000	$14,000

Answer (A) is incorrect. The transferred basis is not to exceed the adjusted basis of the partner's interest in the partnership reduced by any money distributed in the same transaction. Answer (B) is incorrect. Section 732(c) provides that the basis is allocated first to unrealized receivables and inventory, after the partnership interest is reduced by the cash received. The remaining distribution receives a prorated basis up to the remaining partnership interest. Answer (C) is incorrect. The $9,000 decrease must be allocated in proportion to the respective adjusted bases of land.

15.1.4. Betty contributed land with a $6,000 basis and a $10,000 FMV to the ABC Partnership in Year 1. In Year 2, the land was distributed to Sally, another partner in the partnership. At the time of the distribution, the land had a $12,000 fair market value, and Sally had a $30,000 basis for her partnership interest. What gain is recognized by Betty on the distribution? What is Sally's basis for the distributed land?

	Gain Recognized	Basis for Land
A.	$0	$6,000
B.	$4,000	$6,000
C.	$4,000	$10,000
D.	$6,000	$12,000

Answer (C) is correct. *(Publisher, adapted)*
REQUIRED: The distributee partner's basis in, and the contributing partnership's gain recognized on a distribution.
DISCUSSION: For property contributed to a partnership after June 8, 1998, that had a deferred precontribution gain or loss, the contributing partner must recognize the precontribution gain or loss when the property is distributed to any other partner within 7 years of its contribution [Sec. 704(c)(1)(B)]. The precontribution gain or loss that is recognized equals the remaining precontribution gain or loss that would have been allocated to the contributing partner if the property had instead been sold for its fair market value on the distribution date. Betty recognizes a $4,000 gain ($10,000 FMV at contribution date – $6,000 adjusted basis). The partnership's $6,000 basis in the land is increased by the $4,000 gain. Sally takes a $10,000 basis for the land and reduces the basis of her partnership interest by a corresponding amount.
Answer (A) is incorrect. Betty recognizes her precontribution gain and Sally takes the partnership's basis in the land that is increased by the precontribution gain recognized. Answer (B) is incorrect. Sally takes the partnership's basis in the land that is increased by the precontribution gain recognized. Answer (D) is incorrect. Betty does not recognize a $6,000 gain and Sally does not take a $12,000 basis for the land.

15.1.5. On March 10, Year 1, Daniel contributed land in exchange for a 25% partnership interest in Parr Company. The fair market value of the land at that time was $40,000, and Daniel's adjusted basis was $25,000. On December 2, Year 3, Parr distributed that land to Daniel. The fair market value at that time was $50,000. What is the amount of Daniel's recognized gain from this transaction?

A. $0
B. $10,000
C. $15,000
D. $25,000

Answer (A) is correct. *(SEE, adapted)*
REQUIRED: The amount of gain recognized by a partner when property (s)he contributed is distributed to him or her.
DISCUSSION: Generally, no gain is recognized on a distribution of property from a partnership. Remaining precontribution gain may be recognized under Secs. 704 or 737 if property is distributed, but neither rule applies if a partner receives the property he contributed. Accordingly, Daniel recognizes no gain on the receipt of the land that he had contributed to the partnership.
Answer (B) is incorrect. This figure is not the correct amount of Daniel's recognized gain. Answer (C) is incorrect. This figure is not the correct amount of Daniel's recognized gain. Answer (D) is incorrect. This figure is not the correct amount of Daniel's recognized gain.

15.1.6. In Year 1, Bob contributed investment land with basis of $14,000 and FMV of $20,000 in exchange for a 20% capital and profits interest in the ABC Partnership. Bob recognized no gain on the contribution. In Year 3, when Bob had a basis in his partnership interest of $35,000, he received a current distribution of machinery with a basis of $34,000 and fair market value of $37,000. Bob has not recognized any of his precontribution gain prior to the distribution. On the distribution, Bob must recognize

A. No gain or loss.
B. $1,000 capital gain.
C. $2,000 capital gain.
D. $6,000 capital gain.

Answer (C) is correct. *(Publisher, adapted)*
REQUIRED: The partner's recognized gain if a current distribution is made when precontribution gain has not previously been recognized.
DISCUSSION: Property distributions made to a partner may cause a partner to recognize any remaining precontribution gain if the FMV of the distributed property exceeds the partner's basis in his partnership interest prior to the distribution. The gain recognized under Sec. 737 is the lesser of (1) the remaining precontribution gain or (2) the excess of the FMV of the distributed property over the adjusted basis of the partnership interest immediately before the property distribution (but after any reduction for any money distributed at the same time). The Sec. 737 gain is in addition to any gain otherwise recognized under Sec. 731.
The partnership distribution rules would require Bob to recognize no gain since the adjusted basis of the distributed property ($34,000) is less than Bob's basis in his partnership interest ($35,000). However, under Sec. 737, Bob recognizes a $2,000 capital gain, the lesser of the $6,000 remaining precontribution gain, or the excess of the property's $37,000 fair market value over Bob's $35,000 basis in the partnership interest.
Answer (A) is incorrect. A gain or loss is recognized on the distribution. Answer (B) is incorrect. The gain is not calculated as the basis in the partnership interest less the basis of the machinery received. Answer (D) is incorrect. This figure is not the correct amount of capital gain Bob must recognize.

15.1.7. At a time when Nedra's basis in her partnership interest was $5,000, she received a current distribution of $6,000 cash, and land with an adjusted basis of $2,000 and a fair market value of $3,000. The partnership had no unrealized receivables or substantially appreciated inventory. What is the result of this distribution to Nedra?

A. $0 gain or loss, $0 basis in land, $(1,000) basis in partnership interest.

B. $3,000 capital gain, $2,000 basis in land, $0 basis in partnership interest.

C. $1,000 ordinary income, $2,000 basis in land, $0 basis in partnership interest.

D. $1,000 capital gain, $0 basis in land, $0 basis in partnership interest.

Answer (D) is correct. *(Publisher, adapted)*
REQUIRED: The tax result of a current distribution to a partner.
DISCUSSION: Gain is not recognized to a partner on a distribution except to the extent that money distributed exceeds the partner's adjusted basis in the partnership interest. Since Nedra received $6,000 when she had a $5,000 basis in the partnership interest, she will recognize a $1,000 gain which is a capital gain under Sec. 741. The basis in the land is zero under Sec. 732(a)(2) since the basis of property received in a distribution may not exceed the partner's basis in the partnership interest less any money received in the distribution. Nedra's basis in the partnership interest after the distribution is zero because her basis was reduced by the money distributed to her (Sec. 733).
Answer (A) is incorrect. Capital gain is recognized, and Nedra's basis in her partnership interest after the distribution cannot go below zero. Answer (B) is incorrect. Nedra does not have a $3,000 capital gain and a $2,000 basis in land resulting from the distribution. Answer (C) is incorrect. Nedra does not have $1,000 in ordinary income and a $2,000 basis in land resulting from the distribution.

15.1.8. Dale's distributive share of income from the calendar-year partnership of Dale & Eck was $50,000 in Year 1. On December 15, Year 1, Dale, who is a cash-basis taxpayer, received a $27,000 distribution of the partnership's Year 1 income, with the $23,000 balance paid to Dale in May of Year 2. In addition, Dale received a $10,000 interest-free loan from the partnership in Year 1. This $10,000 is to be offset against Dale's share of Year 2 partnership income. What total amount of partnership income is taxable to Dale in Year 1?

A. $27,000

B. $37,000

C. $50,000

D. $60,000

Answer (C) is correct. *(CPA, adapted)*
REQUIRED: The total amount of partnership income taxable to a partner within his or her tax year.
DISCUSSION: Section 706(a) provides that the last day of the partnership's taxable year is the date used by the partners to report their distributive shares of the partnership's items of income, gain, loss, deduction, or credit and the guaranteed payment of salary or interest on capital received from the partnership. The $50,000 should be reported by Dale for Year 1. The $10,000 interest-free loan is not considered income to the partner. It will be considered a distribution next year. The two distributions are tax-free since Dale has sufficient basis to cover the distributions.
Answer (A) is incorrect. The $23,000 that was not distributed is also income in Year 1. Answer (B) is incorrect. The loan is not income in Year 1, but the $23,000 balance that was not distributed is income in Year 1. Answer (D) is incorrect. The loan is not income to the partner; it is a distribution in the next year.

15.1.9. The adjusted basis of Mr. E's partnership interest was $65,000. In a partial liquidation, Mr. E exchanged one-half of his interest for the following properties:

	Adjusted Basis	Fair Market Value
Cash	$60,000	$60,000
Inventory	15,000	20,000
Land	15,000	5,000
	$90,000	$85,000

The inventory was not substantially appreciated, nor did the partnership have any unrealized receivables. As a result of the partial liquidation, Mr. E's proportionate share of partnership liabilities also declined by one-half, or $10,000. The partnership had no other liabilities. What is Mr. E's total recognized gain or loss on the disposition?

	Capital Gain	Ordinary Income
A.	$30,000	$5,000
B.	$10,000	$0
C.	$5,000	$0
D.	$0	$0

Answer (C) is correct. *(SEE, adapted)*
REQUIRED: The recognized gain or loss on a distribution with no Sec. 751 assets.
DISCUSSION: Gain is recognized by a partner on a distribution only to the extent that money distributed exceeds the partner's adjusted basis in the partnership interest immediately before the distribution [Sec. 731(a)(1)]. The decrease of a partner's proportionate share of partnership liabilities is treated as a cash distribution. The result of the distribution is as follows:

Actual cash received	$60,000
Deemed cash (decrease in liability)	10,000
	$70,000
Less: adjusted basis of partnership interest before the distribution	(65,000)
Recognized gain	$ 5,000

This gain is capital gain under Sec. 741. Note that all the remaining assets distributed will have a zero basis and Mr. E's remaining basis in the partnership interest is zero.
Answer (A) is incorrect. Mr. E does not have a capital gain of $30,000 and ordinary income of $5,000 on the disposition. Answer (B) is incorrect. Mr. E does not have a capital gain of $10,000 on the disposition. Answer (D) is incorrect. Mr. E has a capital gain on the disposition.

15.1.10. The M and M Partnership made a current distribution to Mac, a partner owning 50% of the partnership, of land with a fair market value of $6,000 (adjusted basis of $4,000) and a building with a fair market value of $100,000 (adjusted basis $40,000). This distribution was proportionate with respect to unrealized receivables and substantially appreciated inventory. The building had Sec. 1250 recapture potential of $55,000. What is the tax effect of this distribution on M and M?

A. No gain or loss.

B. $7,000 capital; $55,000 ordinary income.

C. $2,000 capital; $60,000 ordinary income.

D. $62,000 capital gain.

Answer (A) is correct. *(Publisher, adapted)*
REQUIRED: The tax effect to the partnership of a distribution of property with potential recapture.
DISCUSSION: A partnership recognizes no gain on a distribution to a partner of property [Sec. 731(b)] when there is not a disproportionate distribution of unrealized receivables or substantially appreciated inventory. The potential recapture is also not recognized under Sec. 1250(d)(3) when no gain is recognized in a Sec. 731 distribution.
Answer (B) is incorrect. The tax effect on M and M of this distribution is not a $7,000 capital gain and $55,000 in ordinary income. Answer (C) is incorrect. The tax effect on M and M of this distribution is not a $2,000 capital gain and $60,000 in ordinary income. Answer (D) is incorrect. The tax effect on M and M of this distribution is not a $62,000 capital gain.

15.1.11. Ms. A's adjusted basis in AB Partnership on December 31 of the current year, just prior to a nonliquidating distribution, is $10,000. If $11,000 in cash is distributed to A on December 31 of the current year in a nonliquidating distribution, A must include $1,000 in income on her current-year tax return.

A. True.

B. False.

Answer (A) is correct. *(SEE, adapted)*
DISCUSSION: Section 731(a) provides that in a current distribution by a partnership to a partner, gain is recognized only to the extent that any money distributed exceeds the adjusted basis of the partner's interest in the partnership. Because the $11,000 cash distributed to A exceeded A's adjusted basis in the partnership interest by $1,000, A must include this amount in income in the current year.

15.1.12. When various kinds of property are distributed by a partnership to a partner in a nonliquidating distribution, the basis of the partner's interest in the partnership must first be allocated to depreciable property, then to unrealized receivables. Any remaining basis is then allocated to any other property distributed.

A. True.

B. False.

Answer (B) is correct. *(SEE, adapted)*
DISCUSSION: Section 732(c) states that the basis of the partner's interest in the partnership is allocated first to any unrealized receivables (and inventory items), and then, to the extent of any remaining basis, to any other distributed properties in proportion to a factor related to both adjusted basis and fair market value. There is no special allocation to depreciable property.

15.2 Liquidating Distributions and Retirement of Partners

15.2.1. The basis to a partner of property distributed "in kind" in complete liquidation of the partner's interest is the

A. Adjusted basis of the partner's interest increased by any cash distributed to the partner in the same transaction.

B. Adjusted basis of the partner's interest reduced by any cash distributed to the partner in the same transaction.

C. Adjusted basis of the property to the partnership.

D. Fair market value of the property.

Answer (B) is correct. *(CPA, adapted)*
REQUIRED: The basis of property distributed "in kind" in complete liquidation of a partnership interest.
DISCUSSION: In a liquidating distribution, a partner's basis for his or her partnership interest is reduced by the amount of money received [Sec. 732(b)]. Any remaining basis is then allocated to other property received.
Answer (A) is incorrect. A cash distribution reduces the partnership interest. Answer (C) is incorrect. The basis to a partner of property distributed "in kind" in complete liquidation of the partner's interest is not the adjusted basis of the property to the partnership. Answer (D) is incorrect. The basis to a partner of property distributed "in kind" in complete liquidation of the partner's interest is not the fair market value of the property.

15.2.2. Which of the following statements about payments made to a retiring partner or successor in interest of a deceased partner that are not made in exchange for an interest in the partnership property is true?

A. Payments made within 5 years of the partner's retirement or death are always treated as made in exchange for an interest in the partnership property.

B. Payments made within 5 years of the partner's retirement or death are always treated as distributive shares of partnership income.

C. If the amount of the payment is based on partnership income, the payment is taxable as a distributive share of partnership income.

D. If the amount of the payment is based on partnership income, the payment is treated as a guaranteed payment.

Answer (C) is correct. *(SEE, adapted)*
REQUIRED: The true statement regarding payments that are not made in exchange for an interest in the partnership property.
DISCUSSION: Payments made to a retiring partner or successor in interest of a deceased partner that are not made in exchange for an interest in the partnership property are treated as either (1) a distributive share of partnership income or (2) a guaranteed payment. Payments that are made based on partnership income are taxable as a distributive share of partnership income. However, if the payment is not based on partnership income, it is a guaranteed payment.
Answer (A) is incorrect. Payments made within 5 years of the partner's retirement or death are not always treated as made in exchange for an interest in the partnership property. Answer (B) is incorrect. Payments made within 5 years of the partner's retirement or death are not always treated as distributive shares of partnership property. Answer (D) is incorrect. The payment must not be based on partnership income to be treated as a guaranteed payment.

15.2.3. The adjusted basis of Vance's partnership interest in Lex Associates was $180,000 immediately before receiving the following distribution in complete liquidation of Lex:

	Basis to Lex	Fair Market Value
Cash	$100,000	$100,000
Real Estate	70,000	96,000

What is Vance's basis in the real estate?

A. $96,000

B. $83,000

C. $80,000

D. $70,000

Answer (C) is correct. *(CPA, adapted)*
REQUIRED: The basis of property received in liquidation of a partnership interest.
DISCUSSION: In a liquidating distribution, a partner's basis for his or her partnership interest is reduced by the amount of money received [Sec. 732(b)]. Any remaining basis is then allocated to other property received. Vance's partnership interest basis of $180,000 is reduced by the $100,000 cash distributed. Accordingly, Vance's basis in the real estate distributed is the remaining $80,000.
Answer (A) is incorrect. The amount of $96,000 is the real estate's FMV. Answer (B) is incorrect. Vance's basis in the real estate is the remaining partnership interest basis after deducting the cash distribution. Answer (D) is incorrect. The amount of $70,000 is the partnership's basis for the real estate.

15.2.4. Ms. A's interest in Partnership D had an adjusted basis of $40,000. In complete liquidation of D, Ms. A received $20,000 cash, inventory items with a basis to D of $10,000, and land used in the partnership more than 1 year with an adjusted basis to D of $15,000 and a fair market value of $18,000. What is A's basis in the land received?

A. $8,000

B. $10,000

C. $15,000

D. $18,000

Answer (B) is correct. *(SEE, adapted)*
REQUIRED: The partner's basis in property received in liquidation.
DISCUSSION: Under Sec. 732(b), the basis of property received by a partner in liquidation of his or her interest in the partnership is the adjusted basis of the partner's interest less any money received in the same distribution. The basis of distributed property is allocated first to inventory items and unrealized receivables up to the amount of the partnership's adjusted basis in these items, then to other distributed properties in proportion to their adjusted bases to the partnership [Sec. 732(c)].

A's adjusted basis in partnership interest	$40,000
Less: cash received	(20,000)
Basis to be allocated	$20,000
Less: basis allocated to inventory	(10,000)
Basis to be allocated to land	$10,000

Answer (A) is incorrect. The land's basis is the remaining basis in the partnership interest after reduction for the cash distribution and the inventory distribution. Answer (C) is incorrect. The amount of $15,000 is the land's adjusted basis before the liquidation, which is limited to Ms. A's remaining basis in the partnership interest. Answer (D) is incorrect. The amount of $18,000 is the FMV of the land.

15.2.5. Mike's interest in Sun Partnership has an adjusted basis of $150,000. In a complete liquidation of his interest, he received the following:

	Adjusted Basis	Fair Market Value
Cash	$70,000	$70,000
Building	80,000	90,000
Computer	20,000	10,000
Inventory	30,000	30,000

Assume no depreciation on either the computer or the building. What is Mike's basis in the building and computer, respectively?

	Building	Computer
A.	$67,500	$7,500
B.	$45,000	$5,000
C.	$44,444	$5,556
D.	$40,000	$10,000

Answer (C) is correct. *(SEE, adapted)*
REQUIRED: The basis in properties received in liquidation of the partnership interest.
DISCUSSION: Section 732(b) provides that the basis of properties distributed by a partnership in a liquidating distribution to a partner is the adjusted basis of the partner's interest in the partnership less any money received in the same distribution. The basis of distributed property is allocated first to inventory items and unrealized receivables up to the amount of the partnership's adjusted basis in these items, then to other property to the extent of each distributed property's adjusted basis to the partnership. The remaining basis increase or decrease is allocated depending on whether the adjusted bases of the distributed properties exceed the partner's remaining basis in the partnership interest or not. Since the partnership's bases in the distributed properties exceed the partner's remaining basis in the partnership, a decrease must be allocated among the properties with unrealized depreciation, in proportion to their respective amounts of unrealized depreciation (to the extent of cash property's depreciation), and then in proportion to the properties' respective adjusted bases (considering the adjustments already made). In this case, a $50,000 decrease (reduced by $10,000 because of the decrease in the computer's value to fair market value) is allocated based on the properties' respective adjusted bases as follows:

	Building	Equipment
Carryover basis	$80,000	$20,000
Allocated decline		(10,000)
	$80,000	$10,000
Allocated decrease (8/9 to building and 1/9 to equipment)	(35,556)	(4,444)
Basis	$44,444	$ 5,556

Answer (A) is incorrect. The bases of the building and the computer are allocated based on their relative adjusted bases, not their FMV. Answer (B) is incorrect. The bases of the building and computer are not $45,000 and $5,000, respectively. Answer (D) is incorrect. The bases of the building and computer are not $40,000 and $10,000, respectively.

15.2.6. Mr. K owned a 50% interest in K&L Partnership. It reports income on the accrual basis. On April 1 of the current year, the partnership was dissolved and it distributed to K one-half of all partnership assets. The partnership had no liabilities. The following assets were distributed to K:

	Basis	Fair Market Value
Cash	$ 5,000	$ 5,000
Accounts receivable	10,000	10,000
Inventory	8,000	10,000
Land	20,000	25,000

K's basis in the partnership interest was $43,000. As of December 31 of the current year, K had sold the inventory for $10,000 and collected all accounts receivable. What gain will K report in the year?

A. $2,000 capital gain.

B. $2,000 ordinary income.

C. $32,000 capital gain.

D. $32,000 ordinary income.

Answer (B) is correct. *(SEE, adapted)*
REQUIRED: The gain recognized by a partner from partnership assets distributed in liquidation and later sold.
DISCUSSION: Under Sec. 731(a), a partner recognizes no gain when property is distributed by the partnership except to the extent that money distributed exceeds the partner's adjusted basis in the partnership. Since the cash received ($5,000) did not exceed K's basis in the partnership ($43,000), K recognizes no gain under Sec. 731(a).
Under Sec. 732, the basis of property distributed is the partner's adjusted basis in the partnership interest less any money distributed ($43,000 – $5,000 = $38,000). This basis is first allocated to unrealized receivables and inventory items in an amount not to exceed the adjusted basis of such property to the partnership. K's basis in the inventory is $8,000, and he has a $2,000 gain when it is sold. This gain is ordinary under Sec. 735(a)(2) since the inventory was sold within 5 years of the distribution. K recognizes no gain on collection of $10,000 in accounts receivable since his basis in them is also $10,000. K still holds land with a basis of $20,000 at year end.
Answer (A) is incorrect. K will not report a $2,000 capital gain from the sale of the inventory. Answer (C) is incorrect. K will not report a $32,000 capital gain from the sale of the inventory. Answer (D) is incorrect. K will not report $32,000 in ordinary income from the sale of the inventory.

15.2.7. On December 31, Year 1, Fred's interest in Partnership C had an adjusted basis of $20,000, which included his $25,000 share of partnership liabilities for which neither Fred, the other partners, nor the partnership had assumed any personal liability. C had no other liabilities, no unrealized receivables, or substantially appreciated inventory items. On January 2, Year 2, Fred withdrew from the partnership and was relieved of his share of the partnership's liabilities. What are the amount and the character of Fred's gain or (loss)?

A. $5,000 capital gain.

B. $5,000 ordinary gain.

C. $0

D. $(20,000) capital loss.

15.2.8. K&C, a boat dealership, distributed a cabin cruiser from its inventory (basis $35,000, fair market value $40,000) to Mr. C in complete liquidation of his partnership interest (adjusted basis $50,000). Mr. C used the cabin cruiser personally for 6 years, then sold it for $55,000. K&C's inventory is not substantially appreciated and it has no unrealized receivables. Which of the following is true?

A. In the year of liquidation, Mr. C did not recognize a loss but was entitled to a $50,000 adjusted basis in the cabin cruiser.

B. In the year of liquidation, Mr. C recognized a capital loss of $10,000.

C. In the year of liquidation, K&C partnership recognized ordinary income of $5,000.

D. In the year Mr. C sold his cabin cruiser, he recognized a capital gain of $20,000.

15.2.9. David Beck and Walter Crocker were equal partners in the calendar-year partnership of Beck & Crocker. On July 1, Year 1, Beck died. Beck's estate became the successor in interest and continued to share in Beck & Crocker's profits until Beck's entire partnership interest was liquidated on April 30, Year 2. At what date was the partnership considered terminated for tax purposes?

A. April 30, Year 2.

B. December 31, Year 1.

C. July 31, Year 1.

D. July 1, Year 1.

Answer (A) is correct. *(SEE, adapted)*
REQUIRED: The amount and the character of gain of a withdrawing partner whose share of partnership liabilities exceeds his basis.
DISCUSSION: Under Sec. 731(a), a partner does not recognize gain except to the extent that money distributed exceeds the partner's adjusted basis in the partnership. Fred's basis in his partnership interest before withdrawal was $20,000. The relief from $25,000 of partnership liabilities is treated as a distribution of money under Sec. 752(b), so Fred recognizes $5,000 of gain. The gain is capital under Secs. 731(a) and 741.
Answer (B) is incorrect. Fred does not have a $5,000 ordinary gain. Answer (C) is incorrect. Fred has a gain or loss. Answer (D) is incorrect. A decrease in a partner's share of partnership liabilities is considered a distribution of money to the partner [Sec. 752(b)].

Answer (D) is correct. *(SEE, adapted)*
REQUIRED: The true statement about a partnership distribution of inventory in complete liquidation of a partner's interest.
DISCUSSION: Under Sec. 731(a)(2), a partner recognizes loss on a liquidation distribution if (s)he receives no assets other than cash, unrealized receivables, and inventory and if the basis of the assets received is less than his or her basis in the partnership. Therefore, C recognizes a loss of $15,000 ($50,000 – $35,000 basis in boat) on the liquidating distribution. Under Sec. 732, the basis of inventory distributed is the partnership's adjusted basis in the property. Therefore, Mr. C has a $35,000 adjusted basis in the cruiser and a gain of $20,000 on the sale ($55,000 – $35,000). Since the cruiser was sold more than 5 years after the distribution, the gain is capital gain [Sec. 735(a)(2)].
Answer (A) is incorrect. Mr. C recognized a loss, and was not entitled to a $50,000 adjusted basis in the cabin cruiser. Answer (B) is incorrect. Mr. C did not recognize a capital loss of $10,000 in the year of liquidation. Answer (C) is incorrect. The boat is not substantially appreciated inventory, so Sec. 751 does not apply.

Answer (A) is correct. *(CPA, adapted)*
REQUIRED: The date the partnership is considered terminated for tax purposes following a partner's death.
DISCUSSION: A partnership generally does not terminate for tax purposes on the death of a partner since the deceased partner's estate or successor in interest continues to share in partnership profits and losses (Sec. 708). The Beck & Crocker partnership terminated on April 30, Year 2, because, when Beck's entire partnership interest was liquidated, the business ceased to be operated as a partnership.
Answer (B) is incorrect. December 31, Year 1, is not the date the partnership was considered terminated for tax purposes. Answer (C) is incorrect. July 31, Year 1, is not the date the partnership was considered terminated for tax purposes. Answer (D) is incorrect. July 1, Year 1, is the date Beck died.

Questions 15.2.10 and 15.2.11 are based on the following information. Mr. Bonet, a one-third partner, had a $12,000 basis in his partnership interest. Mr. Bonet withdrew from the ABC Partnership on January 1 of the current year when the partnership had the following balance sheet:

Assets	Basis	FMV		Equities		
Cash	$12,000	$12,000		Accounts payable	$ 9,000	$ 9,000
Accounts receivable	0	30,000		Abbot, capital	9,000	20,000
Land	24,000	27,000		Bonet, capital	9,000	20,000
	$36,000	$69,000		Costell, capital	9,000	20,000
					$36,000	$69,000

15.2.10. If Mr. Bonet received $20,000 cash in a liquidating distribution, what will he report as his gain or loss?

A. No gain or loss.

B. $8,000 capital gain.

C. $11,000 capital gain.

D. $10,000 ordinary income; $1,000 capital gain.

Answer (D) is correct. *(Publisher, adapted)*
REQUIRED: The gain or loss from a liquidating distribution.
DISCUSSION: Payments made in liquidation of a retiring partner are considered a distribution under Sec. 736(b) to the extent the payments are made in exchange for the interest of the partner in the partnership property. The payment made for the unrealized receivables of $10,000 ($30,000 × 1/3) is ordinary income to Mr. Bonet under Sec. 751.
Mr. Bonet is considered to have received a distribution of $10,000 cash plus $3,000 relief of liabilities (share of accounts payable). Under Sec. 731(a), he will have a capital gain of $1,000 ($13,000 remaining proceeds – $12,000 basis).
Answer (A) is incorrect. Mr. Bonet will report a gain or loss. Answer (B) is incorrect. The amount of $8,000 is the difference between the cash received and Bonet's basis in the partnership interest. Answer (C) is incorrect. This figure is not the correct amount of capital gain reported by Bonet.

15.2.11. What gain or loss will the ABC Partnership recognize if Bonet receives $5,000 cash and accounts receivable with a fair market value of $15,000 in a liquidating distribution?

A. No gain or loss.

B. $5,000 ordinary income.

C. $556 capital gain.

D. $15,000 ordinary income.

Answer (B) is correct. *(Publisher, adapted)*
REQUIRED: The gain or loss to the partnership.
DISCUSSION: Under Sec. 751(b), when more unrealized receivables are distributed to a partner than his or her share, the partnership is treated as having sold the amount of unrealized receivables in excess of the partner's share. The gain or loss on such a constructive sale is ordinary. Mr. Bonet's share of accounts receivable was $10,000 ($30,000 × 1/3). Therefore, he received $5,000 excess accounts receivable. These are treated as having been sold to Mr. Bonet in exchange for other partnership property of which he did not receive his share. Since the accounts receivable had a zero basis, the partnership will have $5,000 ordinary income.
Answer (A) is incorrect. ABC Partnership will recognize a gain or loss. Answer (C) is incorrect. ABC Partnership will not recognize a $556 capital gain. Answer (D) is incorrect. ABC Partnership will not recognize $15,000 in ordinary income.

15.2.12. For tax purposes, a retiring partner who receives retirement payments ceases to be regarded as a partner

A. On the last day of the taxable year in which the partner retires.

B. On the last day of the particular month in which the partner retires.

C. On the day that the partner retires.

D. Only after the partner's entire interest in the partnership is liquidated.

Answer (D) is correct. *(CPA, adapted)*
REQUIRED: The date a retiring partner ceases to be recognized as a partner.
DISCUSSION: Section 736(b)(1) states that payments made in liquidation of the interest of a retiring partner are to be considered a distribution by the partnership. Accordingly, Sec. 706(c)(2)(A) provides that the taxable year of a partnership shall close with respect to a partner whose interest is liquidated. Therefore, a retiring partner remains a partner until his interest has been completely liquidated by partnership distributions.
Answer (A) is incorrect. For tax purposes, a retiring partner who receives retirement payments does not cease to be regarded as a partner on the last day of the taxable year in which the partner retires. Answer (B) is incorrect. For tax purposes, a retiring partner who receives retirement payments does not cease to be regarded as a partner on the last day of the particular month in which the partner retires. Answer (C) is incorrect. For tax purposes, a retiring partner who receives retirement payments does not cease to be regarded as a partner on the day that the partner retires.

15.2.13. On June 30, Year 1, Berk retired from his partnership. At that time, his basis was $80,000, including his share of the partnership's liabilities of $30,000. Berk's retirement payments consisted of being relieved of his share of the partnership liabilities and receipt of cash payments of $5,000 per month for 18 months, commencing July 1, Year 1. Assuming Berk makes no election with regard to the recognition of gain from the retirement payments, he should report income of

	Year 1	Year 2
A.	$13,333	$26,667
B.	$20,000	$20,000
C.	$40,000	$0
D.	$0	$40,000

Answer (D) is correct. *(CPA, adapted)*
REQUIRED: The amounts of income to be reported for retirement payments received.
DISCUSSION: A retiring partner who receives payments from the partnership is considered to be a partner until the last payment is received [Sec. 706(c)(2)(A)]. Payments made in complete liquidation of a partnership interest are considered distributions by the partnership to the extent made in exchange for the interest of the partner in partnership property [Sec. 736(b)(1)]. Gain on a distribution is recognized only to the extent money distributed exceeds the partner's basis in the interest [Sec. 731(a)]. Thus, gain is recognized after basis is used up, that is, on the payments Berk receives last.
Answer (A) is incorrect. Berk will not report income of $13,333 in Year 1 and $26,667 in Year 2. Answer (B) is incorrect. Berk will not report income of $20,000 in either Year 1 or Year 2. Answer (C) is incorrect. Berk will not report income of $40,000 in Year 1, and will report some amount of income in Year 2.

15.2.14. Mr. W, a calendar-year taxpayer, was a 10% partner in Partnership Z. Z uses a fiscal year ending June 30. Mr. W died on October 1, Year 1. Z's taxable income for the fiscal years ending June 30, Year 1, and June 30, Year 2, was $60,000 and $120,000, respectively. Income is earned evenly over each period. What is the amount of partnership income and self-employment income that must be reported on W's final return?

	Partnership Income	Self-Employment Income
A.	$6,000	$9,000
B.	$6,000	$10,000
C.	$9,000	$10,000
D.	$9,000	$9,000

Answer (C) is correct. *(SEE, adapted)*
REQUIRED: The amount of partnership and self-employment income that must be reported in the year of a partner's death.
DISCUSSION: A partner's income includes his or her distributive share of partnership income for any taxable year of the partnership ending within or with the taxable year of the partner [Sec. 706(a)]. For partnership tax years beginning after 1998, the taxable year of a partnership will close with respect to a partner whose entire interest in the partnership terminates by reason of death. The partnership is not considered to have terminated with respect to the surviving partners. Accordingly, Mr. W's final return will include his share of income for the tax year ending June 30, Year 1, or $6,000 ($60,000 × 10%), and his share of Year 2 income up to the date of his death, or $3,000 ($120,000 × 10% × 3/12).
For purposes of computing self-employment income (for the self-employment FICA tax), the deceased partner's share of the partnership's ordinary income attributable to the period ending on the first day of the month following the partner's death must also be included. For this calculation, the partnership's income is treated as realized ratably over the partnership taxable year [Sec. 1402(f)]. Accordingly, Mr. W's final return must include self-employment income of $10,000 [$6,000 from the year ending June 30, Year 1, plus $4,000 ($120,000 × 10% × 4/12) from the year ended June 30, Year 2].
Answer (A) is incorrect. These figures are not the correct amounts reported on W's final return. Answer (B) is incorrect. The amount of $6,000 in partnership income is not the correct amount reported on W's final return. Answer (D) is incorrect. The amount of $9,000 in self-employment is not the correct amount reported on W's final return.

15.2.15. Sunshine Partnership is owned equally by partners Buddy, Jeb, and Bob. Sunshine owns an intangible asset with a basis of $0 and a fair market value of $800, a printing machine with a basis of $300 and a fair market value of $2,000, and a collating machine with a basis of $150 and a fair market value of $200. Bob has a basis of $400 in his partnership interest. The intangible asset and the other collating machine are distributed to Bob in liquidation of his interest. What are Bob's bases in his intangible asset and collating machine?

	Machine	Intangible
A.	$400	$0
B.	$150	$0
C.	$165	$235
D.	$200	$200

Answer (C) is correct. *(Publisher, adapted)*
REQUIRED: The basis in distributed assets.
DISCUSSION: The Taxpayer Relief Act of 1998 modified the allocation of basis to distributed property. Under the new law, the distributee partner's basis in his or her partnership interest is first allocated to unrealized receivables and inventory. If the distributee partner's allocable basis exceeds the basis the partnership had in the distributed unrealized receivables and inventory, that remaining basis is allocated among any other assets to the extent of the partnership's basis in the other distributed assets. To the extent allocable basis exceeds the partnership's basis in the other distributed assets, it is allocated in relation to the unrealized appreciation in those assets. Finally, any remaining basis is allocated among those assets based on the relative fair market value of those assets.

Therefore, Bob must first allocate basis to the production machine ($150) since the intangible asset has no basis. Next, the remaining basis is allocated among the two assets based on the unrealized appreciation in those assets. The intangible asset would be allocated a basis of $235 [($800 ÷ $850) × $250], and the collating machine would receive basis of $15 [($50 ÷ $850) × $250]. The total bases allocated to the collating machine and the intangible asset are $165 and $235, respectively.

Answer (A) is incorrect. These are the allocated bases amounts under prior law. Answer (B) is incorrect. The remaining basis is allocated to the unrealized appreciation of the assets. Answer (D) is incorrect. The amount of $200 is not the correct basis for either the machine or the intangible asset.

15.2.16. On January 1 of the current year, Ruth had a basis in her partnership interest of $55,000. Thereafter, in liquidation of her entire interest, she received an apartment house and an office building. The apartment house has an adjusted basis to the partnership of $5,000 and a fair market value of $40,000. The office building has an adjusted basis to the partnership of $10,000 and a fair market value of $10,000. What is Ruth's basis in each property after the distribution?

A. Apartment house, $40,000; office building, $15,000.

B. Apartment house, $44,000; office building, $11,000.

C. Apartment house, $25,000; office building, $30,000.

D. Apartment house, $45,000; office building, $10,000.

Answer (B) is correct. *(SEE, adapted)*
REQUIRED: The partner's basis in property after a distribution in liquidation.
DISCUSSION: If a partner's interest is liquidated solely through a distribution of partnership property other than money, no gain is recognized. If the partnership distributes property other than money, the partner's basis in the partnership must be transferred to the distributed assets. When a liquidation occurs and the partner's basis in the partnership exceeds the partnership's basis in the distributed assets, the excess of the partner's basis in the partnership must also be allocated among the distributed assets. Any basis increase required is allocated first to properties with unrealized appreciation in proportion to the respective amounts of unrealized appreciation inherent in each property (but only to the extent of each properties unrealized appreciation). Any remaining increase is then allocated in proportion to the property's fair market values. The apartment house is first assigned its basis of $5,000 and the office building is assigned $10,000. Another $40,000 ($55,000 partnership basis – $15,000 assigned to properties) must be allocated to the two properties. The apartment house is allocated $35,000 [($35,000 increase in FMV ÷ $35,000 total increase in FMV) × $35,000]. Accordingly, $5,000 still remains to be allocated. It is allocated based on the FMVs of the properties. The apartment house will be allocated $4,000 [$40,000 FMV ÷ ($40,000 FMV of the apartment + $10,000 FMV of the building) × $5,000 remaining increase], and the building will be allocated the remaining $1,000. Thus, the basis in the apartment house will be $44,000 ($5,000 + $35,000 + $4,000), and the basis in the office building will be $11,000 ($10,000 + $1,000).

Answer (A) is incorrect. The bases in the properties will not be based solely on the FMV of the apartment house. Answer (C) is incorrect. The excess of the FMV over the adjusted bases of the properties is not divided equally among the assets. Answer (D) is incorrect. After the initial appreciation, any remaining increase is then allocated in proportion to the properties' fair market values.

15.2.17. A partner's adjusted basis in his partnership is $40,000. In complete liquidation of his interest he receives $15,000 in cash, inventory items having a basis to the partnership of $22,000, and a company automobile having an adjusted basis to the partnership of $6,000. The automobile also has a $6,000 basis in the hands of the partner.

A. True.

B. False.

Answer (B) is correct. *(SEE, adapted)*
   DISCUSSION: The basis of property received in a liquidating distribution is determined under Sec. 732(b). The partner's adjusted basis in the partnership is first reduced by cash received, then allocated to inventory and unrealized receivables. Any remaining basis is allocated to other assets received. The basis of the automobile is

Adjusted basis in partnership	$40,000
Less: cash received	(15,000)
Less: basis allocated to inventory	(22,000)
Basis of automobile	$ 3,000

15.2.18. If the basis of a partner's partnership interest is more than the adjusted basis to the partnership of the unrealized receivables and inventory items distributed, and if no other property is distributed to which (s)he can apply his or her remaining basis, (s)he has an ordinary loss to the extent of the remaining basis of his or her partnership interest.

A. True.

B. False.

Answer (B) is correct. *(SEE, adapted)*
   DISCUSSION: A loss is only recognized under Sec. 731(a)(2) in a liquidation of a partner's interest when the money and basis of unrealized receivables and inventory are less than the partner's partnership basis. Assuming this is a liquidating distribution, the loss is treated as coming from the sale of a capital asset.

15.2.19. Mr. W, a partner in a business consulting firm, received $25,000 as his share of accounts receivable in the firm's dissolution. The partnership used the cash method. If the accounts receivable are later collected, or if Mr. W sells them, the amount he receives will be ordinary income to him.

A. True.

B. False.

Answer (A) is correct. *(SEE, adapted)*
   DISCUSSION: Gain on the sale of accounts receivable distributed by a partnership is treated as ordinary income [Sec. 735(a)]. The character of the income is unchanged by the character of the accounts receivable in the hands of the partner regardless of the length of time he holds them.

15.2.20. On June 15 of the current year, Mr. Pill received, in complete liquidation of his partnership interest, land with a fair market value of $20,000 and an adjusted basis to the PK Partnership of $16,000. PK purchased the land 17 years ago. Mr. Pill acquired his partnership interest 10 years ago. Mr. Pill's holding period for the land begins on June 15 of the current year.

A. True.

B. False.

Answer (B) is correct. *(Publisher, adapted)*
   DISCUSSION: Under Sec. 735(b), a partner's holding period for property received in a distribution includes the partnership's holding period for the property. Since PK's holding period began 17 years ago, Mr. Pill's holding period is treated as beginning on that date.

15.2.21. If a partnership terminates its existence and the partners, as individuals, continue to make guaranteed installment payments to a previously retired partner, they are entitled to a capital loss in the year of payment in the amount of the total payments made by each.

A. True.

B. False.

Answer (B) is correct. *(SEE, adapted)*
   DISCUSSION: Payments made in liquidation of a retiring partner's interest are considered guaranteed payments if determined without regard to the partnership income and are not paid for partnership property. As guaranteed payments, they are generally deductible by the partnership as ordinary business expenses [Sec. 707(c)]. If the partnership terminates and the former remaining partners continue to make guaranteed payments to the retired partner, they may deduct the payments under Sec. 162 (Rev. Rul. 75-154).

15.2.22. Payments to a retiring partner, in liquidation of an interest, that are treated as distributive shares of partnership income or as guaranteed payments are subject to self-employment tax.

A. True.

B. False.

Answer (A) is correct. *(SEE, adapted)*
DISCUSSION: General partners are treated as self-employed taxpayers. Each partner must report his or her share of partnership net earnings from self-employment. Net earnings from self-employment are the sum of the partner's distributive share of partnership income and guaranteed payments received by the partner from the partnership.

15.3 Sale of a Partnership Interest

15.3.1. All of the following statements with respect to a partner's sale or exchange of a partnership's interest are true, except

A. The sale or exchange of a partner's interest in a partnership usually results in a capital gain or loss.

B. Gain or loss recognized by the selling partner is the difference between the amount realized and the adjusted basis of the partner's interest in the partnership.

C. The selling partner must include, as part of the amount realized, any partnership liability (s)he is relieved of.

D. The installment method cannot be used by the partner who sells a partnership interest at a gain.

Answer (D) is correct. *(SEE, adapted)*
REQUIRED: The false statement with respect to a partner's sale or exchange of a partnership's interest.
DISCUSSION: Section 741 provides the general rule that capital gain or loss is recognized on the sale of a partnership interest. A selling partner's relief of liabilities is included in the amount realized [Sec. 752(d)]. Gain or loss recognized by the selling partner is the difference between the amount realized and the adjusted basis of the partner's interest in the partnership [Reg. Sec. 1.741-1(a)]. The installment method is available when at least one payment is received after the tax year in which the sale occurs [Sec. 453(a)]. No exception is provided that prevents the use of the installment method for the sale of a partnership interest.
Answer (A) is incorrect. Generally, capital gain or loss is recognized on the sale of a partnership interest. Answer (B) is incorrect. Gain or loss recognized is computed under Sec. 1001. Answer (C) is incorrect. Relief from liabilities is included in the amount realized [Sec. 752(d)].

15.3.2. Which of the following statements about the effect of a sale or exchange of a partner's interest in a partnership is true?

A. The entire transaction is always treated as the sale of a capital asset.

B. The partnership may make an election for an optional adjustment to the basis of partnership assets in the year the interest is transferred.

C. The exchange of a partnership interest generally qualifies for like-kind exchange treatment.

D. The gain on the sale of a partnership interest may not be reported on the installment basis.

Answer (B) is correct. *(SEE, adapted)*
REQUIRED: The true statement regarding the effect of a sale or exchange of a partner's interest in a partnership.
DISCUSSION: In the event of a sale or exchange of a partner's interest in a partnership, the partnership may elect under Sec. 754 to adjust the basis of the partnership's assets by the amount of the difference between the transferee partner's basis for the partnership interest and the proportionate share of the basis of all partnership property.
Answer (A) is incorrect. Any gain realized on the sale of a partnership interest is a capital gain or loss except to the extent of unrealized receivables and inventory. The latter amounts are ordinary income. Answer (C) is incorrect. Partnership interests in different partnerships do not qualify for treatment under the like-kind exchange provisions of Sec. 1031. Answer (D) is incorrect. The installment method is an appropriate method on which the gain on the sale of a partnership may be reported.

15.3.3. Cobb, Danver, and Evans each owned a one-third interest in the capital and profits of their calendar-year partnership. On September 18, Year 1, Cobb and Danver sold their partnership interests to Frank and immediately withdrew from all participation in the partnership. On March 15, Year 2, Cobb and Danver received full payment from Frank for the sale of their partnership interests. For tax purposes, the partnership

A. Terminated on September 18, Year 1.

B. Terminated on December 31, Year 1.

C. Terminated on March 15, Year 2.

D. Did not terminate.

Answer (A) is correct. *(CPA, adapted)*
REQUIRED: The date a partnership terminated for tax purposes.
DISCUSSION: Under Sec. 708, a partnership terminates if more than a 50% capital or profits interest is sold or exchanged within a 12-month period. The termination occurs on the date Cobb and Danver sell 66.66% of the partnership to Frank.
Answer (B) is incorrect. The partnership did not terminate on December 31, Year 1. Answer (C) is incorrect. The partnership did not terminate on March 15, Year 2. Answer (D) is incorrect. The partnership did terminate.

15.3.4. Mr. Y sold his 30% interest in XYZ Partnership in the current year. The partnership was formed 10 years ago, and it reports income on the cash basis. Mr. Y's adjusted basis in his partnership interest was $32,700, and the partnership had no liabilities at the date of sale. The partnership had the following assets at the time Mr. Y sold his interest:

	Adjusted Basis	Fair Market Value
Cash	$ 20,000	$ 20,000
Accounts receivable of $10,000 less bad debt reserve of $1,000	0	9,000
Inventory	6,000	10,000
Machinery and equipment	12,000	6,000
Less accumulated depreciation	(9,000)	0
Land	80,000	100,000
	$109,000	$145,000

Mr. Y sold his interest for $43,500. What is his gain or loss to be reported in the current year?

	Ordinary Income	Capital Gain
A.	$1,200	$9,600
B.	$3,600	$7,200
C.	$0	$10,800
D.	$4,800	$6,000

15.3.5. On January 2, Year 1, Harvey contributed $12,000 cash to Partnership K, a calendar-year partnership, for a one-fifth interest. On February 1, Year 1, the partnership borrowed $50,000 from a local bank. Neither Harvey, the other partners, nor the partnership has assumed personal liability for the debt. There is no minimum gain and the partners have no loss limitation agreements. The partnership has no other liabilities and has no unrealized receivables or inventory items. On November 1, Year 1, Harvey received a $15,000 cash distribution from the partnership. For Year 1, K reported ordinary income of $60,000 and the partners reported their distributive shares on their individual income tax returns. On January 2, Year 2, Harvey sold his interest in K for $20,000 cash. What is the amount of Harvey's capital gain or (loss)?

A. $(1,000)

B. $1,000

C. $8,000

D. $11,000

Answer (D) is correct. (SEE, adapted)
REQUIRED: The amount and character of gain on the sale of a partnership interest including Sec. 751 items.
DISCUSSION: Section 741 provides that gain or loss on the sale or exchange of a partnership interest is capital gain or loss. Under Sec. 751(a), gain attributable to unrealized receivables or inventory is ordinary income. The Taxpayer Relief Act of 1998 deletes the requirement that inventory be substantially appreciated, but only when a partnership interest is sold or exchanged. Therefore, when a partnership interest is sold or exchanged, a portion of any amount realized will be treated as ordinary income to the seller even if the partnership's inventory is not substantially appreciated. There are three assets included in the definition of inventory under Sec. 751(d)(2) whose basis and FMV are as follows:

	Basis	FMV
Receivables	$ 0	$ 9,000
Inventory	6,000	10,000
Recapture	0	3,000
	$6,000	$22,000

Y's payment for Sec. 751 assets totals 30% of the FMV, or $6,600, and his basis for these assets is the basis he would have had if his 30% interest in each asset had been distributed to him, or $1,800. He will recognize ordinary income of $4,800 ($6,600 – $1,800). The $36,900 ($43,500 – $6,600) remainder of his amount realized and the $30,900 ($32,700 – $1,800) remainder of his basis determine his $6,000 capital gain amount.
Answer (A) is incorrect. Ordinary income also includes Y's ratable share of the receivables and depreciation recapture. Answer (B) is incorrect. Ordinary income also includes Y's ratable share of the appreciation on the inventory since it is a Sec. 751 asset. Answer (C) is incorrect. Ordinary income includes Y's ratable share of the gain on the receivables, inventory, and recapture.

Answer (D) is correct. (SEE, adapted)
REQUIRED: The capital gain or (loss) recognized on the sale of a partnership interest.
DISCUSSION: A partner's adjusted basis is increased by his or her distributive share of partnership income and decreased by cash distributions from the partnership. The nonrecourse liability is shared according to the profit ratio since there is no minimum gain. Harvey's adjusted basis at the time of sale is $19,000.

Adjusted basis at contribution of cash	$12,000
Plus: 20% of the partnership liabilities	10,000
Less: cash distribution	(15,000)
Plus: distributive income share ($60,000 × 20%)	12,000
Adjusted basis 1/2/Yr 2	$19,000

The capital gain is $11,000 and is calculated as follows:

Cash proceeds	$20,000
Liabilities assumed by the purchaser	10,000
Amount realized	$30,000
Less: adjusted basis	(19,000)
Capital gain	$11,000

Answer (A) is incorrect. Harvey does not have a capital loss. Answer (B) is incorrect. The assumption of the liabilities must also be considered in calculating the amount realized. Answer (C) is incorrect. The adjusted basis of the partnership interest includes the partner's distributive share of income and distributions for Year 1.

15.3.6. On August 1 of the current year, George Hart, Jr., acquired a 25% interest in the Wilson, Hart, and Company partnership by gift from his father. The partnership interest had been acquired by a $50,000 cash investment by Hart, Sr., 20 years ago. The basis of Hart, Sr.'s partnership interest was $60,000 at the time of the gift. No gift tax was paid. Hart, Jr., sold the 25% partnership interest for $85,000 on December 17 of this year. What type and amount of gain should Hart, Jr., report on his current-year tax return?

A. A long-term capital gain of $25,000.

B. A short-term capital gain of $25,000.

C. A long-term capital gain of $35,000.

D. A short-term capital gain of $35,000.

Answer (A) is correct. *(CPA, adapted)*
REQUIRED: The amount and type of gain on the sale of a partnership interest acquired by gift.
DISCUSSION: Under Sec. 1015, the basis of property acquired by gift is the same as the adjusted basis of the donor plus gift tax paid by the donor on the property's appreciation. Hart, Jr.'s basis was therefore $60,000. Section 741 provides that the gain on the sale of a partnership interest is capital gain. Hart, Jr.'s gain is long-term since Sec. 1223(2) provides that if property has the same basis as it did in the hands of the previous owner, the holding period of the present owner includes the holding period of the previous owner. Note that this problem assumes there is no change in basis between August 1 and December 17, which would be unlikely. Under this assumption, Hart, Jr.'s gain is

Proceeds	$85,000
Less: adjusted basis	(60,000)
Long-term capital gain	$25,000

Answer (B) is incorrect. Hart, Jr.'s holding period includes that of Hart, Sr. Answer (C) is incorrect. The long-term capital gain is based on AB. Answer (D) is incorrect. Hart, Jr., does not have a short-term capital gain nor is it $35,000.

15.3.7. A partnership that is not an electing large partnership is terminated for tax purposes

A. Only when it has terminated under applicable local partnership law.

B. When at least 50% of the total interest in partnership capital and profits changes hands by sale or exchange within 12 consecutive months.

C. When the sale of partnership assets is made only to an outsider, and not to an existing partner.

D. When the partnership return of income (Form 1065) ceases to be filed by the partnership.

Answer (B) is correct. *(CPA, adapted)*
REQUIRED: The condition that terminates a partnership that is not an electing large partnership for tax purposes.
DISCUSSION: Under Sec. 708(b)(1), a partnership terminates for tax purposes only if (1) no part of any business, financial operation, or venture of the partnership continues to be carried on by its partners in a partnership or (2) within a 12-month period there is a sale or exchange of 50% or more of the total interest in partnership capital and profits.
Answer (A) is incorrect. Local law terminations result in tax terminations only if one of the two conditions above is met. Answer (C) is incorrect. A sale of 50% or more of the partnership's capital and profits to an existing partner will terminate the partnership for all partnerships that are not electing large partnerships. Answer (D) is incorrect. Ceasing to file a return does not terminate a partnership.

15.3.8. Tracy has a one-fourth interest in the TANY Partnership. The adjusted basis of his interest at the end of the current year is $30,000. He sells his interest in the TANY Partnership to Roy for $50,000 cash. There was no agreement between Tracy and Roy for any allocation of the sales price. The basis and fair market value of the partnership's assets (there are no liabilities) are as follows:

Assets	Basis	Fair Market Value
Cash	$ 40,000	$ 40,000
Unrealized receivables	0	36,000
Inventory	40,000	92,000
Land	40,000	32,000
	$120,000	$200,000

What is the amount and character of Tracy's gain or loss?

A. $0 ordinary income, $0 capital gain.

B. $20,000 ordinary income, $0 capital gain.

C. $10,000 ordinary income, $10,000 capital gain.

D. $22,000 ordinary income, $2,000 capital loss.

Answer (D) is correct. *(SEE, adapted)*
REQUIRED: The amount and character of a partner's gain (loss) when selling his or her partnership interest.
DISCUSSION: The gain or loss on the sale of the partnership interest is a capital gain or loss, subject to long- or short-term treatment, depending upon the length of time the selling partner owned the interest in the partnership. An exception to this rule applies when the partnership owns unrealized receivables or inventory. In this case, the selling partner must allocate a portion of the sale proceeds to the unrealized receivables and to the inventory and, to that extent, will realize ordinary income. The unrealized receivables and the inventory are Sec. 751 assets, meaning $22,000 [($52,000 gain from inventory + $36,000 gain from unrealized receivables) × 1/4] is ordinary income. But the gain is only $20,000; thus there is a $2,000 capital loss.
Answer (A) is incorrect. Tracy has ordinary income. Answer (B) is incorrect. Under Sec. 751(a), gain attributable to unrealized receivables or inventory is ordinary income. Answer (C) is incorrect. These figures are not correct for ordinary income or capital gain.

Questions 15.3.9 and 15.3.10 are based on the following information. The personal service partnership of Allen, Baker, & Carr had the following cash-basis balance sheet on December 31, Year 1:

Assets

	Adjusted Basis per Books	Market Value
Cash	$102,000	$102,000
Unrealized accounts receivable	--	420,000
Totals	$102,000	$522,000

Liability and Capital

Note payable	$ 60,000	$ 60,000
Capital accounts:		
Allen	14,000	154,000
Baker	14,000	154,000
Carr	14,000	154,000
Totals	$102,000	$522,000

Carr, an equal partner, sold his partnership interest to Dole, an outsider, for $154,000 cash on January 1, Year 2, when Carr's basis in the partnership was $34,000. In addition, Dole assumed Carr's share of the partnership's liability.

15.3.9. What was the total amount realized by Carr on the sale of his partnership interest?

A. $174,000

B. $154,000

C. $140,000

D. $134,000

Answer (A) is correct. *(CPA, adapted)*
    REQUIRED: The amount realized on the sale of a partnership interest.
    DISCUSSION: Cash received by the selling partner is included in the amount realized. Also, a selling partner's amount realized includes liabilities assumed by the buyer [Sec. 752(d)]. Therefore, Carr's amount realized is

Cash	$154,000
Liabilities assumed by the buyer ($60,000 × 1/3)	20,000
Amount realized	$174,000

    Answer (B) is incorrect. The amount realized is increased by the liabilities assumed by the purchaser. Answer (C) is incorrect. The amount of $140,000 is the ordinary income Carr reports from the sale. Answer (D) is incorrect. The cash received is not decreased by the liabilities assumed by the purchaser.

15.3.10. What amount of ordinary income should Carr report in his Year 2 income tax return on the sale of his partnership interest?

A. $0

B. $20,000

C. $34,000

D. $140,000

Answer (D) is correct. *(CPA, adapted)*
    REQUIRED: The amount of ordinary income to report on the sale of a partnership interest including Sec. 751 items.
    DISCUSSION: Section 741 provides that a sale or exchange of an interest in a partnership results in capital gain or loss, except as otherwise provided by Sec. 751. Section 751 requires the amount of money attributable to unrealized receivables of the partnership to be treated as an amount realized from other than the sale of a capital asset.
    Carr's ordinary income is $140,000 ($420,000 FMV of unrealized receivables × 1/3) for his share of unrealized receivables. His basis in the unrealized receivables is the carryover basis he would have in the receivables if he had received them as a distribution from the partnership ($0). Accordingly, his ordinary income is $140,000.
    Answer (A) is incorrect. Ordinary income includes gain attributable to URs. Answer (B) is incorrect. This figure is the amount of the liabilities assumed by Dole. Answer (C) is incorrect. The amount of $34,000 is the adjusted basis in the partnership interest on January 1, Year 2.

15.3.11. On December 31 of the current year, the basis of Partner D's interest in BRBQ Partnership was $30,000, which included his $20,000 share of partnership liabilities. There were no unrealized receivables or inventory items. D sold his interest in BRBQ for $20,000 cash, and the purchaser assumed D's partnership liabilities. D's basis had already been adjusted for his share of BRBQ's income for the year. What is the amount of D's gain or (loss)?

A. $20,000

B. $10,000

C. $(10,000)

D. $(20,000)

Answer (B) is correct. *(SEE, adapted)*
REQUIRED: The amount of gain or loss on the sale of a partnership interest.
DISCUSSION: Because there were no unrealized receivables or inventory, the sale of the interest in the partnership results in capital gain or loss (Sec. 741). The relief from partnership liabilities is treated as an amount realized on the sale [Sec. 752(d)]. Partner D's gain is

Proceeds ($20,000 cash + $20,000 liabilities assumed by purchaser)	$40,000
Less: adjusted basis	(30,000)
Capital gain	$10,000

Answer (A) is incorrect. D's gain is reduced by his AB. Answer (C) is incorrect. The purchaser assumed D's share of partnership liabilities. Answer (D) is incorrect. The amount of D's loss is not $20,000.

15.4 Section 754 Basis Adjustment

15.4.1. Which of the following statements regarding a Sec. 754 optional basis adjustment election is false?

A. The new partner elects to adjust the basis of its assets.

B. The basis adjustment election may be revoked by the partnership subject to certain limitations.

C. The application for revocation of the election must be made not later than 30 days after the close of the tax year of the partnership with respect to which the revocation is intended to take effect.

D. An automatic 12-month extension of time to make the election is available.

Answer (A) is correct. *(Publisher, adapted)*
REQUIRED: The false statement regarding a Sec. 754 optional basis adjustment election.
DISCUSSION: A partnership generally does not adjust the basis of partnership assets to reflect the distribution of property or the transfer of a partnership interest to a new partner. However, Sec. 754 allows a partnership to elect to adjust the basis of the assets of the partnership with respect to a partner that acquires an interest in the partnership from another partner by sale or exchange or by inheritance and to reflect alterations in value. Note that the partnership, not the new partner, makes the election to adjust the basis of its assets.
Answer (B) is incorrect. The Sec. 754 optional basis adjustment election may be revoked by the partnership subject to certain limitations. Answer (C) is incorrect. Regarding the Sec. 754 optional basis adjustment, the application for revocation of the election must be made not later than 30 days after the close of the tax year of the partnership with respect to which the revocation is intended to take effect. Answer (D) is incorrect. Regarding the Sec. 754 optional basis adjustment, an automatic 12-month extension of time to make the election is available.

15.4.2. Mr. Gorda, in liquidation of his interest, receives Property #1. Mr. Gorda has a basis of $10,000 for his one-third interest in a partnership. The partnership assets are cash of $4,000, Property #1 with a basis of $11,000 and fair market value of $11,000, and Property #2 with a basis of $15,000 and fair market value of $18,000. The distributed property takes Mr. Gorda's basis of $10,000 in his hands. If the partnership elects Sec. 754 optional basis adjustment, what is the basis of Property #2 retained by the partnership?

A. $14,000

B. $15,000

C. $16,000

D. $19,000

Answer (C) is correct. *(Publisher, adapted)*
REQUIRED: The basis of retained partnership property when a partnership elects Sec. 754 optional basis adjustment.
DISCUSSION: Although the partnership usually does not adjust its basis for its retained property when it distributes other property to a partner, under Sec. 754, the partnership may elect to increase basis if the basis to the partnership of the distributed property exceeds the basis at which the distributee may take that property. In this case, the $1,000 that is "unused" in the basis of the distributed property may be added to the basis of Property #2 retained by the partnership. Thus, the basis of Property #2 is $16,000.
Answer (A) is incorrect. The $1,000 is added to, not subtracted from, the basis of Property #2. Answer (B) is incorrect. The $1,000 is added to the basis of Property #2. Answer (D) is incorrect. The $1,000 is added to basis, not fair market value.

15.4.3. Marwick sold his 30% interest in the PM Partnership to Moses for $90,000 when PM had the following balance sheet:

Assets	Basis	FMV
Cash	$ 50,000	$ 50,000
Inventory	105,000	110,000
Land	70,000	140,000
	$225,000	$300,000

Equities		
Marwick, capital	$ 67,500	$ 90,000
Plum, capital	$157,500	$210,000
	$225,000	$300,000

PM had a Sec. 754 election in effect at the time of sale. Moses' share of the partnership's basis in its assets is

	Cash	Inventory	Land
A.	$15,000	$31,500	$21,000
B.	$15,000	$31,500	$42,000
C.	$15,000	$33,000	$21,000
D.	$15,000	$33,000	$42,000

15.4.4. T. Palms has a basis of $20,000 for her one-third interest in a partnership. The partnership has no liabilities, cash of $22,000, and property with a partnership basis of $38,000 and fair market value of $44,000. For her one-third interest, Palms receives the cash of $22,000. If the partnership elects Sec. 754 optional basis adjustment, what is the basis of the retained partnership property?

A. $36,000

B. $38,000

C. $39,000

D. $40,000

15.4.5. An election under Sec. 754 to adjust the basis of partnership assets requires adjustments both for transfers of partnership interests and for distributions by the partnership.

A. True.

B. False.

15.4.6. Once a Sec. 754 election is made, a partnership can revoke the election with the consent of all partners.

A. True.

B. False.

Answer (D) is correct. *(Publisher, adapted)*

REQUIRED: The basis of partnership assets with respect to a purchasing partner when a Sec. 754 election is in effect.

DISCUSSION: The basis of partnership property is not adjusted as the result of a transfer of a partnership interest unless the election under Sec. 754 is in effect. When the Sec. 754 election is in effect, a partnership increases the adjusted basis of the partnership property by the excess of the basis to the transferee partner of his or her interest in the partnership over his or her proportionate share of the adjusted basis of the partnership property, but the increase belongs only to the purchasing partner [Sec. 743(b)].

PM's increase in basis is the difference between $90,000 and $67,500 ($225,000 × 30%), or $22,500. This is allocated under Sec. 755 to assets on the basis of relative appreciation. As shown below, the adjustment to inventory is $1,500, which increases its basis from $31,500 to $33,000. The increase in the land is $21,000, which increases its basis to $42,000 from $21,000.

Sec. 755 allocation:
| Inventory [($5,000 ÷ $75,000) × $22,500] | $ 1,500 |
| Land [($70,000 ÷ $75,000) × $22,500] | $21,000 |

Answer (A) is incorrect. The increase in basis is allocated based on the relative appreciation of the assets. Answer (B) is incorrect. The correct amount of basis in the inventory is not $31,500. Answer (C) is incorrect. The correct amount of basis in the land is not $21,000.

Answer (D) is correct. *(Publisher, adapted)*

REQUIRED: The basis of partnership property when a partnership elects a Sec. 754 optional basis adjustment.

DISCUSSION: The partnership generally does not adjust its basis for its retained property when it distributes other property to a partner. However, if any gain is recognized by the distributee partner, the partnership may elect under Sec. 754 to increase its basis in its retained property by the amount of that recognized gain. Here, Palms recognized a $2,000 gain on the receipt of cash. The partnership can increase its property's basis by the recognized gain of $2,000 to $40,000.

Answer (A) is incorrect. The recognized gain is added to the partnership basis, not subtracted. Answer (B) is incorrect. The recognized gain is added to the partnership basis. Answer (C) is incorrect. The recognized gain is $2,000.

Answer (A) is correct. *(Publisher, adapted)*

DISCUSSION: If an election is in effect under Sec. 754, the basis of assets is required to be adjusted for both transfers of partnership interests under Sec. 743(b) and for distributions by the partnership under Sec. 734(b).

Answer (B) is correct. *(Publisher, adapted)*

DISCUSSION: A Sec. 754 election may only be revoked with the approval of the district director for the Internal Revenue district in which the partnership return is required to be filed [Reg. 1.754-1(c)].

15.5 Family Partnerships

15.5.1. A family partnership is one in which the members are closely related through blood or marriage. For family partnerships, family members include all the following except

- A. Ancestors.
- B. Spouses and lineal descendants.
- C. Trusts for their benefit.
- D. Brothers and sisters.

Answer (D) is correct. *(SEE, adapted)*
REQUIRED: The relationship in a family partnership that is not considered a family member.
DISCUSSION: Under Sec. 704(e)(3), "the family of any individual shall include only his spouse, ancestors, and lineal descendants, and any trusts for the primary benefit of such persons." Brothers and sisters do not qualify under this definition.
Answer (A) is incorrect. Ancestors are considered family members when determining a family partnership. Answer (B) is incorrect. Spouses and lineal descendants are considered family members when determining a family partnership. Answer (C) is incorrect. Trusts for the benefit of the family are considered family members when determining a family partnership.

15.5.2. Howard Harper has conducted his hardware store business as a sole proprietorship for 25 years. In May, he gave a one-fourth interest in this business to his son, Lanny. After the transfer of this one-fourth interest, under what circumstances would the business be considered a partnership for federal income tax purposes?

- A. Under no circumstances.
- B. Only if the son is a bona fide owner of the interest which was said to have been transferred to him.
- C. Only if the son gives his father a promissory note for the value of the interest transferred to him.
- D. Only if the son works in the hardware store.

Answer (B) is correct. *(CPA, adapted)*
REQUIRED: The circumstances under which a person who receives an interest in a business is recognized as a partner.
DISCUSSION: Section 704(e)(1) provides that a person is recognized as a partner for tax purposes, whether or not his or her interest was a gift from any other person, as long as (s)he owns a capital interest in a partnership in which capital is a material income-producing factor. If the son is a bona fide owner of the interest, he will be recognized as a partner and the business will be considered a partnership.
Answer (A) is incorrect. The recipient of a gift of a business interest will be recognized as a partner as long as (s)he is a bona fide owner. Answer (C) is incorrect. A partnership interest can be created by gift. Answer (D) is incorrect. A recipient of a partnership interest by gift is a partner if he owns a capital interest in a partnership in which capital is a material income-producing factor.

15.5.3. Andrew gave his children, Tom and Theresa, each a 20% interest in his manufacturing company. Tom, age 17, is still a minor but has worked in the business since he was 12 and has developed significant management skills. Theresa, age 22, attends college in another state and is not interested in the business. Andrew gave her 20% of the interest in the partnership but, under the terms of the gift, Theresa cannot sell or pledge her interest without her father's written approval. Which of the children, if any, is in partnership with Andrew?

- A. Neither child is a partner.
- B. Only Theresa is a partner because Tom, as a minor, cannot be a partner.
- C. Only Tom is a partner because Theresa has a restricted right to dispose of her interest.
- D. Both Tom and Theresa are partners.

Answer (C) is correct. *(Publisher, adapted)*
REQUIRED: The child who will be recognized as a partner after receiving the gift of interest in a manufacturing concern.
DISCUSSION: Section 704(e)(1) provides that a person will be recognized as a partner if (s)he owns a capital interest in a partnership in which capital is a material income-producing factor, whether or not such interest was derived by purchase or gift from any other person. Regulation 1.704-1(e) discusses factors that are to be considered in determining whether the donee of a gift has actually acquired ownership of a capital interest in a partnership.
A minor child is generally not recognized as a partner if the interest is not held in trust, except when the child is shown to be competent to manage his or her own property and participate in the partnership activities. Tom should therefore be recognized as a partner. Retained control by the donor of the interest that (s)he has purported to transfer causes the donor to be treated as the continuing owner of the interest. Consequently, Andrew is considered as remaining the substantial owner of Theresa's interest.
Answer (A) is incorrect. One of the children is a partner. Answer (B) is incorrect. Theresa has a restrictive right. Answer (D) is incorrect. Both children are not partners.

440 *SU 15: Partnerships: Distributions, Sales, and Exchanges*

15.5.4. On January 2 of the current year, Mrs. W sold 50% of her business to her daughter Leigh. The resulting partnership had a profit of $100,000 for the tax year, and capital is a material income-producing factor. Mrs. W performed services for which $40,000 was reasonable compensation. Leigh performed no services. What is the maximum amount of income Leigh can report from the partnership for the year?

A. $20,000

B. $30,000

C. $40,000

D. $50,000

Answer (B) is correct. *(SEE, adapted)*
REQUIRED: The distributive share of partnership income of a family member who purchased his interest.
DISCUSSION: Section 704(e)(2) requires that the distributive share of partnership income of a donee must take into account a reasonable allowance for services rendered by the donor. For this purpose, an interest purchased by a family member from another is considered a gift from the seller [Sec. 704(e)(3)]. Therefore, the value of the mother's services must be taken into account in computing the distributive shares as if the mother had given the daughter her interest. The balance of partnership income must be allocated according to their capital interests. Leigh's share is

Partnership income	$100,000
Less: value of mother's services	(40,000)
Income to be allocated according to capital interests	$ 60,000
	× .50
Leigh's share of partnership income	$ 30,000

Answer (A) is incorrect. The amount of $20,000 is one-half of the value of the mother's services. Answer (C) is incorrect. The amount of $40,000 is the value of the mother's services. Answer (D) is incorrect. The amount of $50,000 is one-half of the partnership profits.

15.5.5. Elizabeth Moore owned a 50% interest in a partnership in which capital is a material income-producing factor. Effective January 1 of the current year, pursuant to a model custodian act, she gave 10% of her interest to her minor nephew and 20% of her interest to her minor niece. The custodian is Mrs. Moore's brother, who is the father of the children. The nephew's distributive share of income is used to satisfy part of his father's support obligation, while the niece's share is deposited in her own savings account. Assuming the partnership income for the year is $10,000, Mrs. Moore's original 50% distributive share should be included in the respective gross incomes of

A. Mrs. Moore as $4,000 and her niece as $1,000.

B. Mrs. Moore as $3,500 and her brother as $1,500.

C. Mrs. Moore as $3,500, her niece as $1,000, and her brother as $500.

D. Mrs. Moore as $3,500, her niece as $1,000, and her nephew as $500.

Answer (C) is correct. *(CPA, adapted)*
REQUIRED: The amount of partnership income that should be included in each person's gross income.
DISCUSSION: A person is recognized as a partner for income tax purposes if (s)he owns a capital interest in a partnership in which capital is a material income-producing factor, whether such interest was derived by purchase or gift [Sec. 704(e)(1)]. The niece and nephew are considered partners since a gift to a minor under a model custodian act generally makes the minor a bona fide owner. However, when the income of a trust is used to satisfy the trustee's obligation of support (the custodian is a trustee), the income so used is taxed to the trustee [Sec. 678(c)]. Since the nephew's distributive share was used to satisfy the support obligation of his father (who is the custodian), it is included in his father's gross income. The amounts to be included in each person's gross income are

Mrs. Moore ($10,000 × 35%)	$3,500
Niece ($10,000 × 10%)	1,000
Mrs. Moore's brother ($10,000 × 5%)	500

Answer (A) is incorrect. Mrs. Moore does not have gross income of $4,000. Answer (B) is incorrect. Mrs. Moore's brother does not have gross income of $1,500. Answer (D) is incorrect. Mrs. Moore and her niece recognize their respective shares of 35% and 10%. The nephew's share is recognized by Mrs. Moore's brother since he uses part of the money to satisfy a support obligation for the nephew.

15.5.6. Andrew is a 40% partner in the ABC Partnership, in which capital is a material income-producing factor. He gives one-half of his interest to his brother, John. During the current year, Andrew performs services for the partnership for which reasonable compensation is $65,000 but for which he accepts no pay. Andrew and John are each credited with a $100,000 distributive share of the partnership's ordinary income. How much should Andrew report?

A. $132,500

B. $100,000

C. $67,500

D. $105,000

Answer (A) is correct. *(SEE, adapted)*
REQUIRED: The maximum amount of profit a partner can report in the tax year in which he gave an interest to his son.
DISCUSSION: The partnership agreement is disregarded to the extent a partner receives less than reasonable compensation for services. Of ABC's $200,000 gross income credited to Andrew and John, $65,000 must be allocated to Andrew for his services. The remaining $135,000 is split between the two. Thus, Andrew should report $132,500 [($65,000 + ($135,000 × 1/2)].
Answer (B) is incorrect. Of ABC's $200,000 gross income credited to Andrew and John, $65,000 must be allocated to Andrew for his services. The remaining $135,000 is split between the two. Answer (C) is incorrect. There must also be $65,000 for services allocated to Andrew. Answer (D) is incorrect. The partnership agreement is disregarded to the extent a partner receives less than reasonable compensation for services. Of ABC's $200,000 gross income credited to Andrew and John, $65,000 must be allocated to Andrew for his services. The remaining $135,000 is split between the two.

15.5.7. Partnership G is a family partnership, with Mr. and Mrs. G each owning 30% and their four children each owning 10%. Capital is a material income-producing factor in the partnership, and both Mr. and Mrs. G are active in the business. The children, who are full-time students, acquired their interests in a bona fide gift transaction by Mr. and Mrs. G. There are no limits on the amount that may be allocated to the children as their distributive share of partnership income.

A. True.

B. False.

Answer (B) is correct. *(SEE, adapted)*
DISCUSSION: A person is recognized as a partner for tax purposes if (s)he owns a capital interest in a partnership in which capital is a material income-producing factor, whether such interest was derived by purchase or gift [Sec. 704(e)(1)]. Section 704(e)(2), however, requires that the distributive share of partnership income of a donee take into account a reasonable allowance for services rendered by the donor.

15.5.8. Spouses who carry on a business together and share in the profits and losses, but do not have a formal partnership agreement, may report income or loss from the business either on a *U.S. Partnership Return of Income* (Form 1065) or on separate Schedules C (Form 1040) in the name of each spouse.

A. True.

B. False.

Answer (B) is correct. *(SEE, adapted)*
DISCUSSION: If spouses carry on a business together and share in the profits and losses, they may in fact be partners whether or not they have a formal partnership agreement. In this case, income or loss should be reported on Form 1065 rather than on Schedule C of 1040. By reporting in this manner, each spouse will be credited with his or her pro rata share of self-employment tax.

15.5.9. Members of a family who work together will be recognized as partners only if their invested capital is a material income-producing factor.

A. True.

B. False.

Answer (B) is correct. *(SEE, adapted)*
DISCUSSION: In a family partnership where the material income-producing factor is not a capital asset, the family member must provide substantial or vital services to the partnership to be considered a partner for federal tax purposes.

15.6 Filing Requirements and Tax Audit Procedures

15.6.1. The ABC Partnership, consisting of 20 partners, timely filed its 2017 partnership return on March 15, 2018, but failed to include all the necessary information on the return. On September 8, 2018, it provided the required information but was unable to show reasonable cause for the omission. What is the amount of the penalty to be assessed against the partnership?

A. $200

B. $20,000

C. $1,200

D. $24,000

Answer (D) is correct. *(SEE, adapted)*
REQUIRED: The amount of penalty for failure to provide necessary information on a partnership return.
DISCUSSION: The penalty for failing to file a complete partnership return is $200 per month (or part of a month) that the partnership return is late or incomplete, up to a maximum of 12 months, times the number of persons who were partners at any time during the tax year. The penalty in this case is $24,000 (20 partners × $200 per month × 6 months).
Answer (A) is incorrect. The penalty per month for one partner is $200. Answer (B) is incorrect. The penalty for only 5 months is $20,000. Answer (C) is incorrect. The total penalty for one partner is $1,200. However, the penalty is assessed based on the total number of partners in the partnership.

15.6.2. A fiscal-year partnership must file its partnership return on or before the 15th day of the third month following the close of the fiscal year, except when that day is a Saturday, Sunday, or legal holiday.

A. True.

B. False.

Answer (A) is correct. *(SEE, adapted)*
DISCUSSION: Section 6072 provides that a partnership must file its return on or before the 15th day of the third month following the close of the partnership's taxable year. When that day is a Saturday, Sunday, or legal holiday, Sec. 7503 provides that the time for performance is extended to the next succeeding day that is not a Saturday, Sunday, or legal holiday.

15.6.3. All partners are required to sign a partnership return.

A. True.

B. False.

Answer (B) is correct. *(SEE, adapted)*
DISCUSSION: Section 6063 provides that a partnership return may be signed by any one of the partners. The signature of a partner on the return is considered evidence that such partner is authorized to sign the return.

15.6.4. D, N, and S formed a partnership on December 1 of the current year. The partnership is on a calendar-year basis. The agreement calls for each of the partners to put up one-third of the capital required to buy a business by January 15 of next year. No other expenses are incurred. No partnership return is required for the current year.

A. True.

B. False.

Answer (A) is correct. *(SEE, adapted)*
DISCUSSION: For purposes of filing a partnership return, an unincorporated organization will not be considered, within the meaning of Sec. 761(a), to carry on a business, financial operation, or venture as a partnership before the first tax year in which such organization receives income or incurs any expenditures treated as deductions for federal income tax purposes [Reg. 1.6031-1(a)(1)].

15.6.5. Each partner is required either to treat items on his or her return consistently with the treatment on the partnership return or to file a statement with his or her return identifying the inconsistency.

A. True.

B. False.

Answer (A) is correct. *(Publisher, adapted)*
DISCUSSION: Under Sec. 6222, a partner is required to treat a partnership item on his or her own return in a manner consistent with the partnership return. This requirement does not apply if the partner files a statement identifying the inconsistency. Section 6222 does not apply to partnerships with 10 or fewer partners, each of whom is a natural person (other than a nonresident alien) or estate [Sec. 6231(a)(1)(B)].

15.6.6. A "tax matters partner" (TMP) has the authority to reach a settlement with the IRS on behalf of any partner who has not clearly stated that (s)he will not be bound by the TMP's settlement.

A. True.

B. False.

Answer (A) is correct. *(Publisher, adapted)*
DISCUSSION: Under Sec. 6224 in an administrative proceeding, a partner who has not filed a statement that the "tax matters partner" will not have authority to enter into a settlement agreement on behalf of such partner is bound by a settlement reached by the tax matters partner. This does not apply to partnerships with 10 or fewer partners, each of whom is a natural person or estate.

15.6.7. The IRS must offer every partner in a partnership settlement terms consistent with those offered any one partner in the partnership.

A. True.

B. False.

Answer (A) is correct. *(Publisher, adapted)*
DISCUSSION: Section 6224(c)(2) requires the IRS, when it has entered into a settlement agreement with any partner with respect to partnership items, to offer consistent settlement terms to every other partner who so requests. This does not apply to partnerships with 10 or fewer partners, each of whom is a natural person or estate.

15.6.8. Z owns a partnership interest in XYZ Partnership. XYZ Partnership timely filed its fiscal-Year 1 Form 1065 on March 1, Year 2. On the return, the partnership reported a loss. Z filed her Year 1 individual tax return on April 15, Year 2, and claimed her pro rata share of the loss. In April Year 5, the IRS assesses a deficiency on Z due to a misstatement attributable to the Year 1 XYZ Partnership loss. Because more than 3 years have elapsed from the time the partnership filed its Form 1065, the IRS is barred from assessing a deficiency against Z.

A. True.

B. False.

Answer (B) is correct. *(Publisher, adapted)*
DISCUSSION: The 3-year statute of limitations on assessments begins at the time a pass-through entity's shareholder or partner files an individual income tax return. The date the pass-through entity files its information return has no bearing on the statute of limitations [Sec. 6501(c)].

15.7 Electing Large Partnerships

15.7.1. A partnership is able to elect large-partnership status if it has at least how many partners in the preceding tax year?

A. 15

B. 25

C. 50

D. 100

Answer (D) is correct. *(Publisher, adapted)*
REQUIRED: The number of partnership members needed to elect large-partnership status.
DISCUSSION: Large partnerships with 100 or more partners (not counting service partners) in the preceding tax year may elect large-partnership status for tax years beginning after December 31, 1998 [Sec. 775(a)]. An electing large partnership combines most items of partnership income, deduction, credit, and loss at the partnership level and passes through net amounts to the partners.

15.7.2. All of the following items are separately reportable items for electing large partnerships except

A. Tax-exempt interest.

B. Taxable income or loss from passive loss limitation activities.

C. Section 1231 gains and losses.

D. Net capital gain or loss.

Answer (C) is correct. *(Publisher, adapted)*
REQUIRED: The item that is not separately stated for electing large partnerships.
DISCUSSION: For tax years beginning after December 31, 1998, to simplify reporting of partnership income, the new provision reduces the number of items that must be separately reported to partners by an electing large partnership. The taxable income of an electing large partnership considers Sec. 1231 gains and losses. Net Sec. 1231 gain is considered long-term capital gain, while net Sec. 1231 loss is considered ordinary and is consolidated with other partnership ordinary income.
Answer (A) is incorrect. Tax exempt interest is separately stated for electing large partnerships. Answer (B) is incorrect. Taxable income or loss from passive loss limitation activities are separately stated for electing large partnerships. Answer (D) is incorrect. Net capital gain or loss is separately stated for electing large partnerships.

15.7.3. Partnership Q, an electing large partnership, reported the following items in the current year:

Income from sales	$300,000
Tax-exempt interest	500
Charitable contributions	1,500
Depreciation	2,500
Sec. 1231 loss on sale of equipment	1,250
Other business expenses	150,000

What is Partnership Q's ordinary income?

A. $144,750

B. $145,250

C. $146,250

D. $147,500

Answer (A) is correct. *(Publisher, adapted)*
REQUIRED: The ordinary income of an electing large partnership.
DISCUSSION: For an electing large partnership, the law reduces the number of items that must be separately reported to the partners. While tax-exempt interest must be separately stated, all the other items are considered in the determination of ordinary income. For charitable contributions, the deduction is calculated similarly to the method for corporate donors, with the deduction limited to 10% of the taxable income of the partnership. Since the $1,500 is below the 10% threshold, the entire amount qualifies for a deduction. Therefore, the total amount of ordinary income equals $144,750.
Answer (B) is incorrect. Tax-exempt interest is required to be separately stated. Answer (C) is incorrect. Charitable contributions are not separately stated but reduce ordinary income up to a 10% ceiling. Answer (D) is incorrect. Charitable contributions and the Sec. 1231 loss are not separately stated.

15.7.4. Atlantic Partnership, an electing large partnership, had the following items for the current year:

Income from sales	$500,000
Dividends on capital stock	2,000
Tax-exempt interest	500
Net rental income	5,000
Net long-term capital gain (28% basket)	4,000
Net short-term capital loss	1,000
Other business expenses	250,000

What are Atlantic Partnership's ordinary income and capital item(s) for the current year?

A. $257,500 ordinary income; $3,000 long-term capital gain.

B. $255,000 ordinary income; $3,000 long-term capital gain.

C. $250,000 ordinary income; $3,000 long-term capital gain.

D. $250,000 ordinary income; $4,000 long-term capital gain; $1,000 short-term capital loss.

Answer (C) is correct. *(Publisher, adapted)*
REQUIRED: The income of an electing large partnership.
DISCUSSION: An electing large partnership simplifies the reporting of partnership income and loss. However, portfolio income (i.e., dividends), tax-exempt interest, and passive income (rental income) all remain separately stated items, even for electing large partnerships. The net long-term capital gain and the net short-term capital loss are offset at the partnership level, leaving a net long-term capital gain of $3,000. The total income of the partnership includes $250,000 of ordinary income ($500,000 – $250,000) and $3,000 of long-term capital gain.
Answer (A) is incorrect. Portfolio income, tax-exempt interest, and passive income are separately stated. Answer (B) is incorrect. Passive income is separately stated. Answer (D) is incorrect. Net capital gains and losses are reflected at the partnership level.

15.7.5. For an electing large partnership, miscellaneous itemized deductions are considered at the partnership level by

A. Applying the 2% floor to each of the miscellaneous itemized deduction items in determining partnership taxable income.

B. Combining the items and disallowing 70% of the deductions in determining partnership taxable income.

C. Disallowing all miscellaneous itemized deductions at the partnership level in determining partnership taxable income.

D. Allowing all miscellaneous itemized deductions to reduce partnership taxable income at the partnership level without limitation.

Answer (B) is correct. *(Publisher, adapted)*
REQUIRED: The treatment of miscellaneous itemized deductions in an electing large partnership.
DISCUSSION: Miscellaneous itemized deductions are generally combined at the partnership level. Instead of applying the 2% floor to each deduction, 70% of the total of these deductions are disallowed at the partnership level [Sec. 773(b)(3)].
Answer (A) is incorrect. For an electing large partnership, miscellaneous itemized deductions are not considered at the partnership level by applying the 2% floor to each of the items in determining taxable income. Answer (C) is incorrect. For an electing large partnership, miscellaneous itemized deductions are not disallowed at the partnership level in determining taxable income. Answer (D) is incorrect. For an electing large partnership, miscellaneous itemized deductions are not allowed to reduce partnership taxable income at the partnership level without limitation.

15.7.6. For an electing large partnership, charitable contributions are

A. Separately reported to the partners.

B. Allowed as a deduction at the partnership level without limitation.

C. Allowed as a deduction at the partnership level, subject to a 10%-of-partnership-taxable-income limitation.

D. Allowed as a deduction at the partnership level, subject to a 50%-of-partnership-taxable-income limitation.

Answer (C) is correct. *(Publisher, adapted)*
REQUIRED: The treatment of charitable contribution deductions in electing large partnerships.
DISCUSSION: An electing large partnership does not separately state its charitable contributions to its partners. Instead, the Sec. 170 charitable contribution deduction is allowed at the partnership level in determining partnership taxable income, subject to a 10%-of-taxable-income limitation, similar to the limitation applicable to corporate donors [Sec. 773(b)(2)].
Answer (A) is incorrect. The electing large partnership does not separately state its charitable contributions. Answer (B) is incorrect. The electing large partnership is not allowed charitable contributions as deductions at the partnership level, without limitation. Answer (D) is incorrect. The electing large partnership is not allowed charitable contributions as deductions at the partnership level, subject to a 50%-of-partnership-taxable-income limitation.

15.7.7. For electing large partnerships, combining capital gains and losses occurs

A. Completely at the partner level.

B. Completely at the partnership level.

C. At the partnership level, except net capital gain or loss for passive activity and portfolio items are each separately stated.

D. At the partnership level with passive activity and portfolio items being reported together, and all other capital gains and losses being separately stated.

Answer (D) is correct. *(Publisher, adapted)*
REQUIRED: The treatment of capital gains and losses in electing large partnerships.
DISCUSSION: For electing large partnerships, netting of capital gains and losses occurs at the partnership level. Each partner separately takes into account the partner's distributive shares of net capital gain or loss for each passive activity and for portfolio and active business items. Net capital gain or loss that is taken into account by a partner is treated as long-term capital gain or long-term capital loss [Sec. 772(c)(4)]. Any excess net short-term capital gain over net long-term capital loss will be consolidated with the partnership's other taxable income and will not be separately reported.
Answer (A) is incorrect. For electing large partnerships, combining capital gains and losses does not occur completely at the partnership level. Answer (B) is incorrect. For electing large partnerships, combining capital gains and losses does not occur completely at the partnership level. Answer (C) is incorrect. For electing large partnerships, combining capital gains and losses occurs at the partnership level, but passive activity and portfolio items are not separately stated.

15.7.8. For electing large partnerships, the foreign tax credit is

A. Not allowed as a credit to a partner of an electing large partnership.

B. Not allowed as a credit to a partner of an electing large partnership but, instead, the partner may deduct the foreign taxes.

C. Allowed as a credit to a partner of an electing large partnership or, instead, the partner may deduct the foreign taxes.

D. Allowed as the only means of considering foreign taxes paid.

Answer (C) is correct. *(Publisher, adapted)*
REQUIRED: The availability of the foreign tax credit to partners of electing large partnerships.
DISCUSSION: Instead of claiming the foreign tax credit, a partner may instead choose to deduct the foreign taxes [Sec. 772(d)(6)]. Consequently, the electing large partnership must continue to separately report to its partners creditable foreign taxes and the source of any income, gain, loss, or deduction taken into account by the partnership. In addition, all elections, computations, and limitations relating to foreign tax credits continue to be made by the partner.
Answer (A) is incorrect. For electing large partnerships, the foreign tax credit is allowed as a credit to a partner. Answer (B) is incorrect. For electing large partnerships, the foreign tax credit is allowed as a credit to a partner or, instead, the partner may deduct the foreign taxes. Answer (D) is incorrect. For electing large partnerships, the foreign tax credit is not the only means of considering foreign taxes paid.

15.7.9. All of the following are characteristics of electing large partnerships except

A. Once an election of large partnership status is made, it is irrevocable without the consent of the IRS.

B. A partnership may cease to be treated as an electing large partnership if the number of partners falls below 100 (excluding service partners) during any partnership tax year.

C. An electing large partnership combines most items of partnership income, deduction, credit, and loss at the partnership level and passes through net amounts to the partners.

D. An electing large partnership will terminate for tax purposes when 50% or more of its interests are sold or exchanged within a 12-month period.

Answer (D) is correct. *(Publisher, adapted)*
REQUIRED: The statement that does not describe a characteristic of an electing large partnership.
DISCUSSION: An electing large partnership will not terminate for tax purposes when 50% or more of its interests are sold or exchanged within a 12-month period. The constructive termination rules of Sec. 708(b)(1)(B) do not apply to an electing large partnership because the IRS recognized that large partnerships need to have readily transferable interests [Sec. 774(c)].
Answer (A) is incorrect. Once an election of large partnership status is made, it is irrevocable without the consent of the IRS. Answer (B) is incorrect. A partnership may cease to be treated as an electing large partnership if the number of partners falls below 100 (excluding service partners) during any partnership tax year. Answer (C) is incorrect. An electing large partnership combines most items of partnership income, deduction, credit, and loss at the partnership level and passes through net amounts to the partners.

15.7.10. All of the following are characteristics of the simplified audit procedures for electing large partnerships except

A. Partnership adjustments generally will flow through to the partners for the year to which the adjustment relates.

B. The partnership can forgo flowing partnership adjustments through to its partners by electing to pay an "imputed underpayment" at the partnership level.

C. The partnership, not the individual partners, will be liable for any interest or penalties that result from a partnership adjustment.

D. The IRS is not required to provide notice to partners of either the commencement of an administrative proceeding or a final adjustment.

Answer (A) is correct. *(Publisher, adapted)*
REQUIRED: The statement that does not describe a characteristic of the simplified audit procedures for electing large partnerships.
DISCUSSION: Under the new IRS auditing procedures for electing large partnerships, partnership adjustments generally will flow through to the partners for the tax year in which the adjustment takes effect, not the tax year to which the adjustment relates. The adjustments will generally not affect prior-year returns of any partners (except in the case of changes to any partner's distributive share).
Answer (B) is incorrect. Concerning the simplified audit procedures of electing large partnerships, the partnership can forgo flowing through partnership adjustments to its partners by electing to pay an "imputed underpayment" at the partnership level. Answer (C) is incorrect. Concerning the simplified audit procedures of electing large partnerships, the partnership (not the individual partners) will be liable for any interest or penalties that result from a partnership adjustment. Answer (D) is incorrect. Concerning the simplified audit procedures of electing large partnerships, the IRS is not required to provide notice to partners of either the commencement of an administrative proceeding or a final adjustment.

15.7.11. A partnership cannot make the election to be taxed as a large partnership if substantially all the partners of the partnership are (1) individuals performing substantial services in connection with the activities of the partnership or (2) personal service corporations with owner-employees who perform the substantial services.

A. True.

B. False.

Answer (A) is correct. *(Publisher, adapted)*
DISCUSSION: A service partnership cannot elect to be taxed as a large partnership. In addition to the individuals performing the services, retired members who had performed services and spouses of partners who are performing the services cannot be considered in determining whether there are 100 partners or more and therefore whether the partnership is eligible to elect large-partnership status.

15.7.12. An electing large partnership, like other partnerships, must appoint a representative to handle matters with the IRS. The representative must be a partner of the partnership.

A. True.

B. False.

Answer (B) is correct. *(Publisher, adapted)*
DISCUSSION: An electing large partnership must appoint a representative to handle matters with the IRS. However, unlike other partnerships, the representative does not need to be a partner [Sec. 6255(b)].

15.8 Publicly Traded Partnerships

15.8.1. Which characteristic of a publicly traded partnership is most likely to cause it to be taxed as a corporation in the current year?

A. The partnership was formed after 1987.

B. 90% of the partnership's gross income consists of interest, dividends, and real property rents.

C. A market for the partnership interests is created by brokers and dealers.

D. The partnership has been in existence and publicly traded since 1986 and elects to pay the 3.5% tax to retain partnership status.

Answer (A) is correct. *(Publisher, adapted)*
REQUIRED: The characteristic of a publicly traded partnership that is most likely to be taxed as a corporation.
DISCUSSION: Section 7704 requires certain publicly traded partnerships to be taxed as corporations after 1987. For existing partnerships that were publicly traded on December 17, 1987, the provision does not apply until after 1998. Therefore, if a partnership is formed after 1987, it is likely to be required to be taxed as a corporation.
Answer (B) is incorrect. If 90% of the partnership's gross income is qualifying income (e.g., interest, dividends, or property rents, etc.), it will not be taxed as a corporation unless it adds a significant new line of business. Answer (C) is incorrect. If brokers or dealers create a market for the partnership interests, the partnership will be considered publicly traded. Answer (D) is incorrect. A partnership that was in existence and publicly traded on December 17, 1987, is "grandfathered" and will not be taxed as a corporation until after 1998 unless it adds a substantial new line of business. This "electing 1987 partnership" can avoid being treated as a corporation for tax purposes after 1998 by paying a 3.5% tax on gross income from the active conduct of a trade or business.

15.8.2. Which of the following describes the tax treatment of an electing 1987 partnership?

A. A 3.5% tax is imposed on the partnership's gross income from the active conduct of a trade or business.

B. The partnership is taxed as a corporation.

C. A 3.5% tax is imposed on the partnership's taxable income.

D. A 3.5% tax is imposed on the partnership's gross income from qualifying passive income sources.

Answer (A) is correct. *(Publisher, adapted)*
REQUIRED: The tax treatment of an electing 1987 partnership.
DISCUSSION: A partnership that was publicly traded on December 17, 1987, will be treated as a corporation for tax purposes in tax years beginning after December 31, 1998 (Treas. Reg. 1.7704-2). However, after 1998, an electing 1987 partnership will not be taxed as a corporation if it elects to be taxed at a 3.5% rate on the partnership's gross income from the active conduct of a trade or business. The partnership's gross income must include its share of gross trade or business income of any higher- or lower-tier partnerships. The tax imposed under this provision cannot be offset by tax credits.
Answer (B) is incorrect. The partnership being taxed as a corporation does not describe the tax treatment of an electing 1987 partnership. Answer (C) is incorrect. A 3.5% tax being imposed on the partnership's taxable income does not describe the tax treatment of an electing 1987 partnership. Answer (D) is incorrect. A 3.5% tax being imposed on the partnership's gross income from qualifying passive income sources does not describe the tax treatment of an electing 1987 partnership.

15.8.3. All of the following are requirements for a publicly traded partnership to be an electing 1987 partnership except

A. The partnership was in existence on December 31, 1987.

B. The rule treating a publicly traded partnership as a corporation has not applied (and without regard to the passive-type income exception for PTPs would not have applied) to the partnership for all prior tax years beginning after December 31, 1987, and before January 1, 1999.

C. The partnership consents to the application of the 3.5% gross income tax for its first tax year beginning after December 31, 1998.

D. The partnership adds a substantial new line of business before January 1, 1999.

Answer (D) is correct. *(Publisher, adapted)*
REQUIRED: The statement that is not a requirement to be an electing 1987 partnership.
DISCUSSION: An electing 1987 partnership is an existing partnership. Existing partnerships include partnerships that (1) were publicly traded on December 17, 1987; (2) filed a registration statement with the Securities and Exchange Commission on or before December 17, 1987, indicating that the partnership was to be a publicly traded partnership (PTP); and (3) filed an application with a state regulatory commission on or before December 17, 1987, seeking permission to restructure a portion of a corporation as a PTP [Treas. Reg. 1.7704-2(b)]. A partnership will not qualify as an existing partnership and will be taxed as a corporation after a substantial new line of business is added.
Answer (A) is incorrect. An electing 1987 partnership is in existence on December 31, 1987. Answer (B) is incorrect. The partnership must not have been treated as a corporation for any prior tax years beginning after 12/31/87 and before 1/1/98. Answer (C) is incorrect. The electing 1987 partnership must elect to have the new rules apply and consent to the 3.5% gross income tax.

15.8.4. All of the following are characteristics of a partnership that was publicly traded on December 17, 1987, except

A. Prior to 1999, the entity was taxed as a partnership.

B. For tax years beginning after December 31, 1998, the entity is treated as a corporation unless an election is made to continue to be taxed as a partnership and pay a special tax.

C. It is taxed as a partnership and must have added a substantial new line of business since December 17, 1987.

D. It has partnership interests that are traded on an established securities market or are readily traded on a secondary market (or its substantial equivalent).

Answer (C) is correct. *(Publisher, adapted)*
REQUIRED: The statement that does not describe a characteristic of a publicly traded partnership (PTP) in existence on December 17, 1987.
DISCUSSION: A PTP is a partnership with interests traded on an established securities market or readily tradable on a secondary market (or its substantial equivalent). Partnerships that were in existence on December 17, 1987, and have not added a substantial new line of business since that date are grandfathered and treated as partnerships for tax purposes.
    These grandfathered partnerships will be treated as corporations under the PTP rules for tax years beginning after December 31, 1998, unless they make a special election and pay a 3.5% annual tax on gross income. Alternatively, they can become "private" partnerships, which do not have their interests publicly traded.
    Answer (A) is incorrect. A characteristic of a partnership that was publicly traded on December 17, 1987, is that prior to 1999, the entity was taxed as a partnership. Answer (B) is incorrect. A characteristic of a partnership that was publicly traded on December 17, 1987, is that for tax years beginning after December 31, 1998, the entity is treated as a corporation unless an election is made to continue to be taxed as a partnership and pay a special tax. Answer (D) is incorrect. A characteristic of a publicly traded partnership (PTP) in existence on December 17, 1987, is that it has partnership interests that are traded on an established securities market or are readily traded on a secondary market (or its substantial equivalent).

15.8.5. In which of the following situations will a publicly traded partnership be taxed as a corporation in the current year?

A. It has been publicly traded since January 1, 1987, and has no new line of business. Its income is solely from a merchandising business, and it elects to pay a 3.5% tax on gross income from the active conduct of its trade or business.

B. It was newly formed in the current year. Its income is solely from a merchandising business.

C. It was newly formed in the current year. Its income is 90% from real property rents and 10% from a merchandising business.

D. It has been publicly traded since December 1986 and has no new line of business. It would qualify as a regulated investment company if it were a domestic corporation. It elects to pay a 3.5% tax on gross income from its active conduct of a trade or business.

Answer (B) is correct. *(Publisher, adapted)*
REQUIRED: The determination of whether a publicly traded partnership will be treated as a partnership or a corporation.
DISCUSSION: Section 7704 generally requires publicly traded partnerships (PTPs) to be taxed as corporations. A publicly traded partnership is any partnership that is traded on a secondary market (or the equivalent thereof). Partnerships that were not publicly traded prior to 1988 are generally subject to these rules.
    Answer (A) is incorrect. After December 31, 1998, if a grandfathered PTP elects to be subject to a 3.5% tax on gross income from the active conduct of a trade or business, it may continue to be treated as a partnership. In addition, a publicly traded partnership will not be taxed as a corporation if 90% or more of its gross income consists of "qualifying income" for the current tax year and each succeeding tax year beginning after 1987 during which the partnership was in existence. Qualifying income includes real property rents. Answer (C) is incorrect. A publicly traded partnership will not be taxed as a corporation if 90% or more of its gross income consists of "qualifying income" for the current tax year and each succeeding tax year beginning after 1987 during which the partnership was in existence. Qualifying income includes real property rents. Answer (D) is incorrect. This publicly traded partnership will not be taxed as a corporation, as it is a grandfathered PTP.

15.8.6. An electing 1987 partnership that wants to revoke its election to be taxed as a partnership may do so without IRS consent. However, once an election is revoked, it may not be reinstated for 60 months.

A. True.

B. False.

Answer (B) is correct. *(Publisher, adapted)*
DISCUSSION: The election and consent of an electing 1987 partnership applies to the tax year for which it is made (generally the first post-December 31, 1998, tax year) and all later tax years unless revoked by the partnership. An electing 1987 partnership may revoke its election without IRS consent, but it is not permitted to reinstate the election at a later date [Sec. 7704(g)(4)].

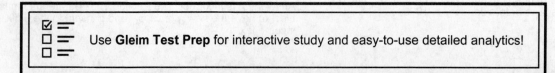

Use **Gleim Test Prep** for interactive study and easy-to-use detailed analytics!

STUDY UNIT SIXTEEN
CORPORATE FORMATIONS AND OPERATIONS

16.1 Corporate Formations

16.1.1. Donna exchanges property having an $18,000 adjusted basis and a $35,000 fair market value for 70 shares of the newly created Table Corporation stock. Evelyn exchanges legal services worth $15,000 for the remaining 30 shares of Table's stock. Which of the following is true?

A. Evelyn recognizes no income, and the exchange is nontaxable.

B. Evelyn must recognize $15,000 of income, but Donna's transfer of property qualifies under IRC Sec. 351 as nontaxable.

C. Evelyn must recognize $15,000 of income, and Donna must recognize $17,000 gain on the exchange.

D. The exchange qualifies as a nontaxable exchange under IRC Sec. 351.

Answer (C) is correct. *(SEE, adapted)*
 REQUIRED: The amount of income and gain recognized on the exchange of property and services for stock in a corporation.
 DISCUSSION: Section 351(a) provides that no gain or loss is recognized if one or more persons transfer property to a corporation solely in exchange for stock in such corporation and if immediately after the exchange such person or persons are in control of the corporation. "Control" is defined in Sec. 368(c) as the ownership of stock possessing at least 80% of the total combined voting power of all classes of voting stock and at least 80% of the total number of shares of all other classes of stock. However, a tax-free transfer to a controlled corporation applies only to a transfer of property. A transfer of services in exchange for stock is fully taxable. Accordingly, Evelyn must recognize $15,000 of income for the legal services provided. Donna must recognize $17,000 ($35,000 – $18,000) of gain because she is not in control of the corporation for purposes of nonrecognition under Sec. 351. Since Evelyn provided only services, her shares are not counted when determining control.
 Answer (A) is incorrect. A tax-free transfer to a controlled corporation applies only to a transfer of property and a transfer in exchange for stock is fully taxable. Answer (B) is incorrect. Donna must recognize $17,000 of gain because she is not in control of the corporation for purposes of nonrecognition under Sec. 351. Answer (D) is incorrect. Evelyn must recognize income for the services provided. Donna must recognize income because she did not attain 80% ownership through her exchange of property for stock.

16.1.2. Jones incorporated a sole proprietorship by exchanging all the proprietorship's assets for the stock of Nu Co., a new corporation. To qualify for tax-free incorporation, Jones must be in control of Nu immediately after the exchange. What percentage of Nu's stock must Jones own to qualify as "control" for this purpose?

A. 50.00%

B. 51.00%

C. 66.67%

D. 80.00%

Answer (D) is correct. *(CPA, adapted)*
 REQUIRED: The minimum stock ownership constituting "control" for purposes of a tax-free incorporation.
 DISCUSSION: Section 351 provides the rules for a tax-free incorporation. It refers to Sec. 368(c) for the definition of "control." Section 368(c) defines "control" as the ownership of stock possessing at least 80% of the total combined voting power of all classes of stock entitled to vote and at least 80% of the total number of shares of all other classes of stock of the corporation.

16.1.3. Aaron transferred property worth $75,000 and services worth $25,000 to the BJ Corporation. In exchange, he received stock in BJ valued at $100,000. Immediately after the exchange, Aaron owned 80% of the only class of outstanding stock. Which of the following is true with regard to Aaron's treatment of this transaction?

A. Short-term capital gain of $100,000.

B. Short-term capital gain of $25,000.

C. Ordinary income of $25,000.

D. No income until the stock is sold.

Answer (C) is correct. *(SEE, adapted)*
REQUIRED: The true statement regarding the transfer of property and the treatment of services performed for a corporation in exchange for stock.
DISCUSSION: The general rule of Sec. 351 is that no gain or loss is recognized if one or more persons transfer property to a corporation solely for stock and if immediately after the exchange such person or persons are in control of the corporation (i.e., own at least 80% of the stock). Section 351(d) states, however, that stock issued for services is not issued in return for property. Stock issued for services falls outside the general rule, and income must be recognized on such a transfer. The fair market value of stock received for services ($25,000) must be included in Aaron's income. All other stock received was in exchange for property, and no gain or loss is recognized on its transfer.
Answer (A) is incorrect. The general rule of Sec. 351 is that no gain or loss is recognized if one or more persons transfer property to a corporation solely for stock and if immediately after the exchange such person or persons are in control of the corporation (i.e., own at least 80% of the stock). Answer (B) is incorrect. The $25,000 is considered ordinary income. Answer (D) is incorrect. Income must be recognized on stock issued for services.

16.1.4. You transfer property with an adjusted basis of $20,000 and a fair market value of $31,000 in exchange for 100% of the stock in a new corporation. You receive 100 shares of stock having a fair market value of $16,000 and $10,000 in cash. The corporation also assumes a $5,000 mortgage on the property. Which of the following is true?

A. $11,000 gain realized; $0 recognized.

B. $15,000 gain realized; $11,000 recognized.

C. $11,000 gain realized; $10,000 recognized.

D. $10,000 gain realized; $5,000 recognized.

Answer (C) is correct. *(SEE, adapted)*
REQUIRED: The amount of gain realized and recognized regarding the exchange of property for stock in a corporation.
DISCUSSION: The gain realized on this transaction is $11,000 [($16,000 FMV of stock + $10,000 cash + $5,000 assumption of liability) – $20,000 adjusted basis of transferred property]. However, the transaction qualifies under Sec. 351 for nonrecognition. Transfer of mortgaged property to a controlled corporation does not require the recognition of gain unless the liabilities transferred or assumed are greater than the basis of all the property transferred. Accordingly, the only gain that must be recognized is the gain attributable to the amount of boot property received. The $10,000 cash received is boot property.
Answer (A) is incorrect. The gain that must be recognized is the gain attributable to the amount of boot received. Answer (B) is incorrect. The gain realized is not equal to the sum of the liabilities and cash, and the $11,000 is not the amount of gain recognized. Answer (D) is incorrect. The amount of the boot is not the realized gain and the recognized gain is not equal to the mortgage.

16.1.5. Which of the following is not taken into account when determining if a gain or loss should be recognized on the transfer of property to a corporation in exchange for a controlling interest in stock of the corporation?

A. Ownership of at least 80% of the total combined voting power of all stock entitled to vote.

B. Ownership of at least 80% of the total number of shares of all other classes of stock.

C. Receipt of money in addition to stock.

D. Fair market value of property transferred.

Answer (D) is correct. *(SEE, adapted)*
REQUIRED: The item not taken into account when determining if gain or loss is recognized on the transfer of property to a corporation.
DISCUSSION: Section 351(a) provides that no gain or loss is recognized if one or more persons transfer property to a corporation solely in exchange for stock in such corporation, and immediately after the exchange such person(s) are in control of the corporation. Control is defined in Sec. 368(c) as the ownership of stock possessing at least 80% of the total combined voting power of all classes of voting stock and at least 80% of the total number of shares of all other classes of stock. In a Sec. 351 exchange, the FMV of property transferred is not taken into account when determining the amount of the recognized gain or loss.
Answer (A) is incorrect. When determining if the corporation is controlled by the transferors, ownership of at least 80% of the total combined voting power of all stock entitled to vote must be considered. Answer (B) is incorrect. When determining if the corporation is controlled by the transferors, ownership of at least 80% of the total number of shares of all other classes of stock must be considered. Answer (C) is incorrect. Section 351(b) provides that gain is recognized when other property or money is received in addition to the stock.

16.1.6. Paul, Randy, and Steve form North Corporation by transferring the following properties:

Transferor	Asset	Transferor's Adjusted Basis	FMV	Consideration Received
Paul	Machinery	$10,000	$12,500	25 shares North stock
Randy	Land	$18,000	$25,000	40 shares North stock and $5,000 North note
Steve	Cash	$17,500	$17,500	35 shares North stock

(The 100 shares represent all of the outstanding stock of North Corporation.)

Using the rules for IRC Sec. 351, which of the following is true?

A. The exchange does not qualify for IRC Sec. 351 nontaxable treatment.

B. The exchange qualifies for IRC Sec. 351 and is nontaxable except that Randy must recognize $7,000 of capital gain.

C. The exchange qualifies for IRC Sec. 351 and is nontaxable except that Randy must recognize $5,000 of capital gain.

D. The exchange qualifies for IRC Sec. 351 and is nontaxable except that Randy must recognize $5,000 of ordinary income.

Answer (C) is correct. *(SEE, adapted)*
REQUIRED: The true statement regarding the exchange of property for stock in a corporation and the recognition of the associated gain.
DISCUSSION: Section 351 states that no gain or loss is recognized when property is transferred to a corporation in exchange for the corporation's stock if the person or persons transferring the property are in control of the corporation immediately after the transfer. "Control" is defined by the Code as at least 80% ownership of the corporation's voting and nonvoting stock. Paul, Randy, and Steve meet the requirements under Sec. 351. However, if other property or money is received in addition to the stock, any gain realized by the recipient is recognized but not in excess of the sum of the money plus the fair market value of other property received. The sum of the boot property received is $5,000 (the note received by Randy). Therefore, Randy must recognize the $5,000. The gain is a capital gain because the land given up is a capital asset.
Answer (A) is incorrect. Paul, Randy, and Steve meet the requirements under Sec. 351. Answer (B) is incorrect. The sum of the boot property received is $5,000; therefore, Randy must recognize $5,000 of capital gain. Answer (D) is incorrect. The gain is a capital gain because the note is a capital asset.

16.1.7. Taxpayer C acquired sufficient stock of Corporation Y in an exchange to meet the nonrecognition of gain or loss requirements. Stock was acquired as follows (stock listed at fair market value):

Received $30,000 in stock for cash of $20,000

Received $100,000 in stock for property with adjusted basis of $50,000

Received $15,000 in stock for services rendered

Received $25,000 in stock for bonds of Corporation Y (basis of $18,000) per conversion privilege

What is the total amount includible in Taxpayer C's income?

A. $10,000

B. $15,000

C. $25,000

D. $32,000

Answer (B) is correct. *(SEE, adapted)*
REQUIRED: The amount included in income from an exchange of property and services for stock.
DISCUSSION: The general rule of Sec. 351 is that no gain or loss is recognized if property is transferred to a corporation by one or more persons solely for stock, and immediately after the exchange such person or persons are in control of the corporation (i.e., own at least 80% of the stock). Section 351(d) states, however, that stock issued for services are not issued in return for property. Stock issued for services falls outside the general rule, and income must be recognized on such a transfer. The fair market value of stock received for services ($15,000) must be included in C's income. All other stock received was in exchange for property and no gain or loss is recognized on its transfer.
Note that the discrepancy in the amount of stock received for cash does not affect the Sec. 351 transaction as long as it was a bona fide exchange; e.g., the stock may have been overvalued. However, if the excess $10,000 of stock were additional compensation for services, it too would be included in C's income.
Answer (A) is incorrect. The excess of the value of stock received over the cash paid is not included in C's income. Answer (C) is incorrect. Only the value of the stock received for services is included in C's gross income. The excess of the value of stock received over the cash paid is not included in C's gross income. Answer (D) is incorrect. The excess of the value of stock received over the cash paid, the excess of the value of the stock received over the property's basis, and the excess of the value of the stock received over the bonds surrendered are not included in C's gross income.

16.1.8. Anna transferred land with an adjusted basis to her of $20,000 and a fair market value of $56,000 to Elm Corporation in exchange for 100% of Elm Corporation's only class of stock. The land was subject to a liability of $26,000, which Elm assumed for legitimate business purposes. The fair market value of Elm's stock at the time of the transfer was $30,000. What is the amount of Anna's recognized gain?

A. $0

B. $6,000

C. $10,000

D. $36,000

Answer (B) is correct. *(SEE, adapted)*
REQUIRED: The gain recognized on an exchange of property with a liability in excess of basis.
DISCUSSION: The general rule of Sec. 351 is that no gain is recognized if a shareholder transfers property in exchange for stock of a corporation as long as the shareholder(s) involved in the transaction control the corporation immediately after the exchange. Control is defined in Sec. 368(c) as 80% of the voting power and 80% of all classes of nonvoting stock. Anna received 100% of Elm Corporation's stock and therefore has control immediately after the exchange. But Sec. 357(c) provides that gain must be recognized by the shareholder to the extent that liabilities assumed, or taken subject to, by the corporation exceed the adjusted basis of all property transferred. The liability on the land exceeded the adjusted basis of the land Anna transferred by $6,000 ($26,000 liability assumed – $20,000 adjusted basis). Thus, Anna must recognize a gain of $6,000.
Answer (A) is incorrect. A gain is recognized by the transferor if the liability assumed by the transferee exceeds the adjusted basis of the property transferred. Answer (C) is incorrect. The fair market value of the stock received less Anna's adjusted basis in the land is $10,000. Answer (D) is incorrect. The fair market value of the stock received plus the excess of the liability assumed over Anna's adjusted basis is $36,000.

16.1.9. Stone, a cash-basis taxpayer, incorporated her CPA practice. No liabilities were transferred. The following assets were transferred to the corporation:

Cash (checking account)	$ 500
Computer equipment	
Adjusted basis	30,000
Fair market value	34,000
Cost	40,000

Immediately after the transfer, Stone owned 100% of the corporation's stock. The corporation's total basis for the transferred assets is

A. $30,000

B. $30,500

C. $34,500

D. $40,500

Answer (B) is correct. *(CPA, adapted)*
REQUIRED: The corporation's basis in assets received in exchange for stock.
DISCUSSION: Section 362(a) provides that the basis of property acquired by a corporation in connection with a Sec. 351 transaction is the same as the basis in the hands of the transferor (shareholder), increased by the amount of gain recognized by the transferor on such transfer. Since Stone did not receive any boot, she did not recognize any gain. Thus, the corporation's total basis in the transferred assets is the same as that in Stone's hands, or $30,500 ($500 cash + $30,000 adjusted basis).
Answer (A) is incorrect. The amount of $30,000 excludes the cash transferred. Answer (C) is incorrect. The fair market value of the property transferred is $34,500. Answer (D) is incorrect. The cost of the property transferred is $40,500.

16.1.10. Jack Carson transferred a building that had an adjusted basis of $75,000 and a fair market value of $130,000 to Corporation R in exchange for 80% of R's only class of stock and a car with an adjusted basis to R of $25,000. The fair market value of the stock at the time of the transfer was $100,000, and the car's fair market value was $30,000. What is the amount of R's basis in the building?

A. $130,000

B. $105,000

C. $100,000

D. $75,000

Answer (B) is correct. *(SEE, adapted)*
REQUIRED: The corporation's basis in transferred property when property other than stock is received by the shareholder.
DISCUSSION: Section 362(a) provides that the basis to a corporation of property acquired in a Sec. 351 transaction is the same as the basis in the hands of the transferor, increased by the gain recognized by the transferor. Here, the transfer qualifies as a Sec. 351 transaction since greater than 80% of all stock was held by the shareholder after the exchange.
Jack received a car with a $30,000 fair market value in addition to the stock. Jack realizes a gain of $55,000 ($100,000 FMV of stock + $30,000 FMV car – $75,000 adjusted basis in the building). Jack recognizes a gain of $30,000, which is the FMV of the property other than the stock received. Thus, R's basis in the building is $105,000 ($75,000 Jack's adjusted basis + $30,000 gain recognized).
Answer (A) is incorrect. The amount of $130,000 is the FMV of the property received by the shareholder. Answer (C) is incorrect. The amount of $100,000 is the FMV of the stock. Answer (D) is incorrect. The amount of $75,000 is the adjusted basis of the building.

16.1.11. Mr. Wind transferred property subject to a $35,000 liability to Corporation X in exchange for 90% of X's only class of outstanding stock. Mr. Wind's adjusted basis in the property transferred was $40,000. The fair market value of the stock at the time of the transfer was $60,000. What is Corporation X's basis in the property received and what is Mr. Wind's basis in the stock received?

	Corporation X	Mr. Wind
A.	$35,000	$5,000
B.	$40,000	$5,000
C.	$60,000	$40,000
D.	$75,000	$75,000

Answer (B) is correct. *(SEE, adapted)*
REQUIRED: The basis of the stock and property exchanged in a Sec. 351 transfer.
DISCUSSION: Section 358(a)(1) provides that, in a Sec. 351 exchange, the basis of the stock received by the transferors (shareholders) is the basis of the property transferred decreased by the fair market value of other property received, the amount of any money received, and the amount of loss that was recognized by the taxpayer. The basis is increased by the amount of gain recognized by the taxpayer. Section 357(a) exempts the taxpayer from recognizing gain on the transfer due to assumption of the liability. Under Sec. 358(d), the assumption of a liability by the transferee corporation is treated as money received by the taxpayer in the exchange. Thus, Mr. Wind's basis in the stock received is $5,000 ($40,000 basis of property transferred – $35,000 liability).
The basis to Corporation X for the assets received is determined by Sec. 362(a) as the same as that of the transferor ($40,000) plus the gain recognized by the transferor ($0), or $40,000.
Answer (A) is incorrect. Corporation X's basis in the property received is not equal to the value of the liability assumed in the exchange. Answer (C) is incorrect. Corporation X's basis in the property received is not equal to the fair value of the stock transferred, and Mr. Wind's basis in the stock received is not equal to the adjusted basis of the property transferred. Answer (D) is incorrect. Both Corporation X's and Mr. Wind's basis in the property received is not equal to the sum of the liability and the adjusted basis of the property transferred.

16.1.12. On June 10 of last year, Celeste purchased a computer for $6,000 that she uses in her sole proprietorship. The computer is 5-year property under the MACRS rules. Depreciation in the amount of $1,200 was claimed last year by Celeste on the computer. On February 1 of this year, Celeste transferred the computer and the other assets of her proprietorship to C Corporation in exchange for all of C's stock. No gain or loss was recognized on the exchange. What amount of depreciation is claimed by Celeste and C Corporation on the computer in the current year?

	Celeste	C Corporation
A.	$0	$1,920
B.	$0	$1,200
C.	$160	$1,760
D.	$960	$960

Answer (C) is correct. *(Publisher, adapted)*
REQUIRED: The amount of depreciation claimed on a transfer of an asset for stock.
DISCUSSION: Under Sec. 362, when property is transferred to a corporation in exchange for its stock in a transaction in which no gain or loss is recognized, the corporation's basis in the property will be the same as the property's basis in the hands of the transferor. Under Sec. 168, 5-year property is depreciated at a rate of 32% in its second year. Since the asset was transferred, the current-year depreciation must be apportioned between Celeste and C Corporation. The depreciation is apportioned based on the number of complete months each taxpayer owned the property. Under the MACRS rules, the transferee corporation is presumed to have held the property for the entire month in which the property is transferred. Celeste's deduction is $160 ($6,000 × 32% × 1/12). Therefore, the computer will have a $4,640 ($6,000 – $1,200 – $160) adjusted basis to the corporation. C Corporation's current-year depreciation deduction is $1,760 ($6,000 × 32% × 11/12).
Answer (A) is incorrect. Celeste owned the computer for part of the current year; therefore, the depreciation must be apportioned between Celeste and C Corporation. Answer (B) is incorrect. Celeste owned the computer for part of the current year; therefore, the depreciation must be apportioned between Celeste and C Corporation. In addition, the ratio for the current year from the MACRS table must be used to calculate the amount of depreciation that may be deducted in the current year. Answer (D) is incorrect. Celeste and the corporation do not split the depreciation equally. It is based on the number of months each held the computer.

16.1.13. On August 15 of last year, the ABC Partnership purchased telephone equipment for $10,000. The equipment is 5-year property under the MACRS rules. Depreciation in the amount of $2,000 was claimed by ABC on the equipment last year. On April 1 of the current year, ABC Partnership was incorporated with its assets being exchanged for King Corporation stock and notes. Gain of $1,000 was recognized on the transfer of the equipment that was purchased last year. What amount of depreciation is claimed by ABC and King on the equipment in the current year?

	ABC	King
A.	$800	$2,400
B.	$800	$2,600
C.	$1,600	$1,600
D.	$880	$2,640

Answer (B) is correct. *(Publisher, adapted)*
REQUIRED: The amount of depreciation claimed by the transferor of property and the recipient of the property.
DISCUSSION: Under Sec. 1012, the basis of property is generally the cost of the property. ABC's basis in the telephone equipment is therefore initially $10,000. Section 362 provides that, when property is transferred to a corporation in a transaction to which Sec. 351 applies, the corporation's basis in the property is the same as the transferor's basis, increased in the amount of any gain recognized by the transferor on the transfer. Therefore, King's basis in the property is $9,000 ($8,000 transferor's adjusted basis + $1,000 gain recognized by ABC on the transfer).
Because the property was transferred during the second year of its life, the depreciation must be apportioned between ABC and King. The depreciation is apportioned based on the number of complete months the property was owned. The step-up in basis of $1,000 is treated as a second property whose depreciation commences on April 1 of the current year. Under IRS depreciation tables, depreciation rates of 20% and 32% are applied to 5-year property in its first and second years, respectively. ABC's depreciation deduction is $800 ($10,000 basis × 32% × 3/12). King Corporation's depreciation deduction is $2,600 [($10,000 basis × 32% × 9/12) + ($1,000 basis × 20%)].
Answer (A) is incorrect. The depreciation is apportioned between ABC and King based on the number of months that each party owned the property. The $1,000 step-up in basis is treated as a separate property. Answer (C) is incorrect. The depreciation is not split equally between ABC and King. Answer (D) is incorrect. ABC does not have depreciation of $880, and King does not have depreciation of $2,640.

16.1.14. The selection of an accounting method for tax purposes by a newly incorporated C corporation

A. Is made on the initial tax return by using the chosen method.
B. Is made by filing a request for a private letter ruling from the IRS.
C. Must first be approved by the company's board of directors.
D. Must be disclosed in the company's organizing documents.

Answer (A) is correct. *(CPA, adapted)*
REQUIRED: The manner in which a C corporation selects an accounting method for tax purposes.
DISCUSSION: A newly incorporated C corporation makes its initial accounting method selection simply by using the chosen method on their initial return. This is a form of an election.
Answer (B) is incorrect. No private letter ruling is required from the IRS. Answer (C) is incorrect. It is likely that the management of the corporation must approve the accounting method, but this is not an absolute requirement under tax law. Answer (D) is incorrect. The accounting method need not be disclosed in the company's organizing documents.

16.1.15. John Smith transferred money and property to Corporation X solely in exchange for stock in X. Immediately after the exchange, John owned 80% of the total combined voting power of all classes of stock entitled to vote and 51% of all other classes of stock. No gain or loss will be recognized by John or X.

A. True.
B. False.

Answer (B) is correct. *(SEE, adapted)*
DISCUSSION: Section 351 provides the rules for a tax-free incorporation. It refers to Sec. 368(c) for the definition of "control." Section 368(c) defines "control" as the ownership of stock possessing at least 80% of the total combined voting power of all classes of stock entitled to vote and at least 80% of the total number of shares of all other classes of stock of the corporation. Since John owns only 51% of all other classes of stock, he must recognize gain or loss on the transaction.

16.1.16. Mr. Z transfers the business assets of his sole proprietorship to Z Corporation in a nontaxable exchange on September 1 of the current year. The holding period for all of Mr. Z's stock in Z Corporation commences on September 1 of the current year.

A. True.
B. False.

Answer (B) is correct. *(Publisher, adapted)*
DISCUSSION: The holding period of stock received in a tax-free exchange under Sec. 351 is determined under Sec. 1223(1). The holding period includes that for transferred property, provided it was either a capital asset or Sec. 1231 property, i.e., real or personal property used in a trade or business. When a sole proprietorship is incorporated, each share of stock has a split holding period under Rev. Rul. 85-164 when either capital asset or Sec. 1231 property is transferred along with ordinary income property.

16.2 Assets Acquired for Stock

16.2.1. In an exchange transaction, Jesse transferred land worth $50,000 to his 80%-controlled corporation in exchange for additional stock of the corporation worth $20,000 and cash of $20,000. The basis of the property to him was $15,000 and was subject to a $10,000 mortgage, which the corporation assumed. Jesse must report a gain of

A. $10,000

B. $20,000

C. $30,000

D. $35,000

Answer (B) is correct. *(CPA, adapted)*
REQUIRED: The gain recognized by a transferor who exchanges land for stock and cash.
DISCUSSION: Section 351(a) provides nonrecognition of gain or loss if property is transferred to a corporation by a person solely in exchange for stock in the corporation and, immediately after the exchange, such person is in control of the corporation (i.e., owns at least 80% of the stock). Under Sec. 351(b), if other property or money is received in addition to the stock, any gain realized by the recipient is recognized to the extent of the amount of money plus the fair market value of other property received. Section 351 will apply to Jesse's transaction since its conditions are met even though this is not a corporate formation. Jesse's reportable gain is

Amount realized ($20,000 stock + $20,000 cash + $10,000 liabilities assumed by the corporation)	$50,000
Less: adjusted basis of land transferred	(15,000)
Realized gain	$35,000
Gain recognized (limited to cash received)	$20,000

Note that, under Sec. 357(a), liabilities assumed by the corporation (that have a business purpose and are not in excess of basis) are not considered property or money for the purpose of recognizing gain.
Answer (A) is incorrect. The amount of the mortgage is $10,000. The cash is treated as boot property, but the mortgage is not. Answer (C) is incorrect. The cash received plus the mortgage is $30,000. The mortgage is not boot property. Answer (D) is incorrect. The gain realized is $35,000.

16.2.2. Ms. D transferred the following assets to Corporation E:

	Adjusted Basis	Fair Market Value
Cash	$1,000	$1,000
Equipment	2,000	1,500
Land	4,500	6,000

In exchange, Ms. D received 51% of E's only class of outstanding stock. The stock had no established value. What is Corporation E's total basis in all the assets received, assuming that Ms. D recognized the correct amount of gain on the exchange?

A. $6,000

B. $7,000

C. $7,500

D. $8,500

Answer (D) is correct. *(SEE, adapted)*
REQUIRED: The corporation's basis in assets acquired in exchange for its stock.
DISCUSSION: Because less than 80% of E's stock was exchanged for the assets, this transfer does not qualify for nonrecognition under Sec. 351. Since this is a taxable transaction, Ms. D must recognize all realized gains on this transaction. However, the Sec. 267 related party rules will disallow her loss on the equipment. Her gain (loss) is computed as follows:

Equipment:
Amount realized	$1,500
Adjusted basis	(2,000)
Realized loss	(500)
Recognized loss (Sec. 267)	$ 0

Land:
Amount realized	$6,000
Adjusted basis	(4,500)
Realized and recognized gain	$1,500

Additionally, since this is a taxable transaction, E's basis in the transferred property will be equal to its cost.

Cash	$1,000
Equipment	1,500
Land	6,000
Total basis	$8,500

Answer (A) is incorrect. The amount of $6,000 is the FMV of only the land. Answer (B) is incorrect. The amount of $7,000 is the total of the FMV of the equipment, the adjusted basis of the land, and the cash transferred. Answer (C) is incorrect. The amount of $7,500 is the total basis of the assets transferred instead of their FMV.

16.2.3. Mr. A owned 75% of the voting stock and 85% of the nonvoting stock of Corporation Y. Mr. A transferred property with a fair market value of $90,000 and an adjusted basis of $70,000 to Y for an additional 5% of the voting stock and 5% of the nonvoting stock. What is the amount of gain to be recognized by Mr. A?

A. $0

B. $8,000

C. $10,000

D. $20,000

Answer (A) is correct. *(SEE, adapted)*
REQUIRED: The gain recognized on transfer of assets to a corporation by an existing shareholder in exchange for additional stock.
DISCUSSION: If the requirements of Sec. 351(a) are met, no gain or loss is recognized when property is transferred to a corporation. The requirements are that the transfer be made by one or more persons, solely in exchange for stock, and the transferor(s) must be in control of the corporation immediately after the exchange. Section 368(c) defines control as the ownership of at least 80% of both the voting and nonvoting stock. After the transaction, Mr. A owns 80% (75% + 5%) of the voting stock and 90% (85% + 5%) of the nonvoting stock. He therefore meets the criteria and qualifies under Sec. 351(a). No gain or loss is recognized.
Answer (B) is incorrect. The correct amount of gain to be recognized by Mr. A is not 10% of the average of FMV and adjusted basis. Answer (C) is incorrect. The correct amount of gain to be recognized by Mr. A is not 50% of the difference between FMV and adjusted basis. Answer (D) is incorrect. The difference between the FMV and the adjusted basis of the property Mr. A transferred to Corporation Y equals $20,000.

16.2.4. Sam owns 100% of M Corporation's single class of stock. Sam transfers land and a building having a $30,000 and $100,000 adjusted basis, respectively, to M Corporation in exchange for additional M Corporation common stock worth $200,000 and IBM stock worth $20,000. The IBM stock had a $5,000 basis on M Corporation's books. Peter transfers $50,000 in cash for 15% of the M Corporation common stock. What amount of gain or loss is recognized by Sam and M Corporation on the exchange?

	Sam	M Corporation
A.	$0	$0
B.	$0	$15,000
C.	$20,000	$0
D.	$20,000	$15,000

Answer (D) is correct. *(Publisher, adapted)*
REQUIRED: The gain or loss recognized on the exchange.
DISCUSSION: Section 351 states that no gain or loss is recognized when property is transferred to a corporation in exchange for the corporation's stock if the person or persons transferring the property are in control of the corporation immediately after the transfer. "Control" is defined by the Code as at least 80% ownership of the corporation's voting and nonvoting stock. Because Sam meets the control test, he recognizes no gain on the receipt of the M Corporation stock. However, he does recognize a $20,000 gain on the receipt of the IBM stock. Section 351(b)(1) states that, if other property is received by the transferor, the transferor must recognize gain equal to the fair market value of the property. Therefore, Sam must recognize a $20,000 gain.
M Corporation recognizes no gain or loss on the receipt of the land and building in exchange for its own stock (Sec. 1032). However, M Corporation does recognize a gain on the transfer of the IBM stock. Under Sec. 311(b)(1), if a corporation distributes appreciated property, the corporation will recognize gain to the extent that the property's fair market value exceeds its adjusted basis. Therefore, M Corporation must recognize a $15,000 gain ($20,000 fair market value − $5,000 basis) on the transfer of the IBM stock to Sam.
Answer (A) is incorrect. Both Sam and M Corporation will recognize a gain or loss on the exchange. Answer (B) is incorrect. Sam will recognize a gain or loss on the exchange. Answer (C) is incorrect. M Corporation will recognize a gain or loss on the exchange.

16.2.5. Edward purchased an office building on January 1, 2008. He exchanged the building for 80% of the stock in Payroll Corporation on January 1, 2017, in a qualifying Sec. 351 transfer. Payroll Corporation's holding period for the office building begins on January 2, 2017.

A. True.

B. False.

Answer (B) is correct. *(SEE, adapted)*
DISCUSSION: A transferee corporation's holding period generally includes the transferor's holding period if the transferor transferred the property in a nontaxable exchange for stock. Therefore, Payroll's holding period for the office building begins on January 2, 2008.

16.2.6. If a shareholder of a controlled or solely owned corporation receives no additional shares for a contribution of property to the corporation, the basis of the property received by the corporation is the same as it was to the shareholder.

A. True.

B. False.

Answer (A) is correct. *(SEE, adapted)*
DISCUSSION: The basis of property acquired by a corporation as a contribution to capital is the transferor's basis increased by the amount of gain recognized by the transferor [Sec. 362(a)]. No gain will be recognized on the contribution of property to an 80%-or-more-owned corporation.

16.2.7. A corporation's holding period for an asset received in a nontaxable capital contribution includes the time the asset was held by the transferor.

A. True.

B. False.

Answer (A) is correct. *(SEE, adapted)*
DISCUSSION: Section 1223(2) provides that, in determining a taxpayer's holding period, the period for which property was held by any other person will be included if the property has the same basis as it had in the hands of such other person. Under Sec. 362(a), the corporation's basis in a Sec. 351 transaction or capital contribution where no gain is recognized is the same as the basis in the hands of the transferor (shareholder), so Sec. 1223(2) will apply. The corporation's holding period will include the time the transferor owned the assets.

16.3 Gifts to Corporations

16.3.1. The City of Cleveland transferred land worth $250,000 to Monitor Corporation as part of an inducement to locate a new plant in the city. The land had been acquired by the city several years ago at a cost of $100,000. The income that Monitor must recognize as a result of the transfer and the basis of the land to Monitor are

A. $250,000 of income, $250,000 of basis.

B. $100,000 of income, $100,000 of basis.

C. $0 of income, $100,000 of basis.

D. $0 of income, $0 of basis.

Answer (D) is correct. *(CMA, adapted)*
REQUIRED: The income and basis recognized on a contribution of property by a nonshareholder.
DISCUSSION: The general rule of Sec. 118(a) is that gross income does not include any contribution to the capital of a corporation. Monitor Corporation should not include any income with respect to the land contributed.
Section 362(c) provides that, if property other than money is acquired by a corporation through a contribution from a nonshareholder, the tax basis of such property is zero.
Answer (A) is incorrect. The correct amount of income or of basis of the land to Monitor is not $250,000. Answer (B) is incorrect. The correct amount of income or of basis of the land to Monitor is not $100,000. Answer (C) is incorrect. The correct amount of basis of the land to Monitor is not $100,000.

16.3.2. On January 2 of the current year, City M gave the A Corporation $200,000 cash to purchase a building within the city limits. The building was purchased on June 1 of the same year for $150,000. What is the correct method of handling the excess money received?

A. Long-term capital gain.

B. Short-term capital gain.

C. Reduction of basis in other assets.

D. Nontaxable contribution to capital with $50,000 that is not spent being added to the basis of the building that was purchased.

Answer (C) is correct. *(SEE, adapted)*
REQUIRED: The correct tax treatment of the excess money received as a contribution from a nonshareholder.
DISCUSSION: Section 362(c) states that, if money is received by a corporation as a contribution from a nonshareholder, the basis of any property acquired with the money must be reduced by the amount of the contribution. Any excess is to be applied to the reduction of the basis of any other property held by the taxpayer. The reduction of basis is applied first to all depreciable property, then to all amortizable property, and finally to all remaining property [Reg. 1.362-2(b)].
Answer (A) is incorrect. Under Sec. 118, contributions to capital are not included in gross income. Answer (B) is incorrect. The excess money received would not be treated as a short-term capital gain. Answer (D) is incorrect. Section 362(c) requires a reduction in basis.

16.4 Pre-Operating Expenses

16.4.1. All of the following items can be amortized as a qualified organizational expense except

A. Fee paid to a state for incorporation.

B. Expense of organizational meeting of directors.

C. Expense for issuance or sale of stock.

D. Organizational meetings of shareholders.

Answer (C) is correct. *(SEE, adapted)*
REQUIRED: The item that is not considered an organizational expense.
DISCUSSION: An organizational expense must be capitalized unless an election is made under Sec. 248 to amortize it over 180 months. An organizational expenditure is one incurred in the creation of the corporation. Regulation 1.248-1(b)(3) specifically excludes expenditures connected with issuing or selling stock such as commissions, professional fees, and printing costs. These expenditures represent a reduction in the proceeds from the issuance of the stock and are not amortizable.
Answer (A) is incorrect. A fee paid to a state for incorporation is an expenditure that will qualify for amortization over 180 months under Sec. 248. Answer (B) is incorrect. The expense of an organizational meeting of directors is an expenditure that will qualify for amortization over 180 months under Sec. 248. Answer (D) is incorrect. Expenses for organizational meetings of shareholders are expenditures that will qualify for amortization over 180 months under Sec. 248.

16.4.2. Which of the following are organizational costs?

A. Expenses of temporary directors; a survey of potential markets.

B. Advertisements for the opening of business; state incorporation fees.

C. Deductible research and experimental costs; set-up accounting services.

D. Legal services for drafting the charter; cost of organizational meetings.

Answer (D) is correct. *(SEE, adapted)*
REQUIRED: The items that are classified as organizational costs.
DISCUSSION: Organizational expenditures include those that are incidental to the creation of a corporation, chargeable to a capital account, and amortizable over a limited life if they are expended incident to the creation of a corporation with such a life. Examples of organizational expenditures include expenses to obtain the corporate charter, fees paid to the state of incorporation, and expenses of temporary directors. Organizational costs must be distinguished from start-up and investigation costs.
Answer (A) is incorrect. The costs associated with surveying potential markets are start-up expenses. Answer (B) is incorrect. Advertisements for the opening of business are start-up expenses. Answer (C) is incorrect. Deductible research and experimental costs and set-up of accounting services are not organizational costs.

16.4.3. Dale Corporation's book income before federal income taxes was $520,000 for the current year ended December 31. Dale was organized this year. Organization costs of $360,000 are being written off over a 20-year period for financial statement purposes. For tax purposes, these costs are being written off over the minimum allowable period. For the current year ended December 31, taxable income is

A. $794,000

B. $514,000

C. $520,000

D. $546,000

Answer (B) is correct. *(CPA, adapted)*
REQUIRED: The taxable income of a corporation whose organization costs are treated differently for tax and financial accounting purposes.
DISCUSSION: Under Sec. 248, a corporation may elect to amortize its organizational expenditures over 180 months, beginning with the month in which the corporation begins business. Dale's taxable income is computed by adding back to book income the book amortization costs of $18,000 ($360,000 ÷ 20 years) and then deducting the maximum tax amortization amount of $24,000 [$360,000 × (12 ÷ 180 months)]. Taxable income is $514,000 ($520,000 + $18,000 − $24,000).
Answer (A) is incorrect. The book amortization costs of $26,000 are added back to book income. Answer (C) is incorrect. The amount of $520,000 is equal to the book value income. Answer (D) is incorrect. The amount of $546,000 is equal to the book value and the book amortization costs summed.

16.4.4. Corporation R was organized and began active business on January 4 of the current year. R incurred the following expenses in connection with creating the business:

Professional fees for issuance of stock	$ 4,000
State incorporation fees	2,000
Printing cost for stock certificates	1,500
Broker's commissions on sale of stock	7,000
Legal fees for drafting the charter	5,000
Expense for temporary directors	7,000
Total	$26,500

The maximum amount of organizational expense that may be deducted by Corporation R on its current-year income tax return is

A. $5,600

B. $5,300

C. $14,000

D. $26,500

Answer (A) is correct. *(SEE, adapted)*
REQUIRED: The maximum amount of organizational expenses a corporation may deduct on its first tax return.
DISCUSSION: Section 248 allows a corporation to elect to amortize its organizational expenses over 180 months starting with the month in which it begins business. Organizational expenditures are those (1) incurred incidental to the creation of the corporation, (2) charged to the corporation's capital account, and (3) amortized over a limited life if expended incidental to the creation of a corporation having a limited life [(Sec. 248(B), Reg. 1.248-1(B)]. Regulation 1.248-1(b)(3) specifically excludes expenditures connected with issuing or selling stock and with transferring assets to the corporation. The corporation may deduct the first $5,000 of organizations reduced by any amounts exceeding $50,000. The remainder of such organizational expenditures shall be allowed as a deduction over a 180-month period. Corporation R's current-year amortization deduction (assuming it is a calendar-year corporation) is

State incorporation fees	$ 2,000
Legal fees for drafting the charter	5,000
Expense for temporary directors	7,000
Total allowable expenses	$14,000
Current-year amortization [$5,000 + ($9,000 × 12 ÷ 180 months)]	$ 5,600

Answer (B) is incorrect. The cost of printing stock certificates is not an eligible organizational expenditure, and 12 months of amortization cannot be claimed in the current year. Answer (C) is incorrect. The 12 months of amortization cannot be claimed in the current year. Answer (D) is incorrect. The cost of printing stock certificates is not an eligible organizational expenditure.

16.4.5. When determining the proper treatment of a corporation's organizational and start-up costs, which of the following is true?

A. The election must be made on the tax return for the first tax year you are in business, even if the return is not timely filed.

B. The period of amortization may be 60 months or more.

C. Costs associated with the transfer of assets to the corporation are amortizable organization costs.

D. Amortization of organization and start-up costs start with the month business operations begin.

Answer (D) is correct. *(SEE, adapted)*
REQUIRED: The true statement regarding the proper treatment of a corporation's organizational and start-up costs.
DISCUSSION: Section 248 allows a corporation to elect to amortize its organizational expenditures over 180 months, and Sec. 195 allows a corporation to amortize its start-up costs over 180 months, beginning with the month in which the corporation starts business.
Answer (A) is incorrect. The election must be made on the corporation's first return, and the return must be timely filed. Answer (B) is incorrect. Sixty months or more was the law prior to October 23, 2005. Answer (C) is incorrect. Costs associated with the transfer of assets to the corporation are added to the bases of the assets.

16.4.6. If a corporation does not make an election to amortize qualifying organizational expenditures for the first tax year, the corporation must capitalize these expenses and not deduct them until the year in which the corporation is liquidated.

A. True.

B. False.

Answer (A) is correct. *(SEE, adapted)*
DISCUSSION: Organizational expenditures must be capitalized over 180 months. If an election is not made under Sec. 248 to amortize them, they may be deducted only on dissolution of the corporation.

16.4.7. Advertising expenses for the opening of a business of a corporation that has not yet begun its business operations must be considered a start-up expense.

A. True.

B. False.

Answer (A) is correct. *(SEE, adapted)*
DISCUSSION: Pre-opening advertising costs are deemed start-up expenses and generally must be amortized.

16.4.8. A corporation incurs an additional expense in setting up its accounting system after the close of the tax year but before the due date of its initial return. This is an organizational expense and may be amortized.

A. True.

B. False.

Answer (B) is correct. *(SEE, adapted)*

DISCUSSION: Under Sec. 248, a corporation may elect to amortize its organizational expenditures over 180 months, beginning with the month in which it begins business. Regulation 1.248-1(a)(2) provides that this election only applies to expenses incurred before the end of the taxable year in which the corporation begins business. Even though the expense of setting up an accounting system may be considered an organizational expenditure, it cannot be amortized since it was incurred after the end of the corporation's first taxable year.

16.4.9. Corporation X, a calendar-year taxpayer, began business on January 1 of last year. X deducted $10,000 in organizational expenses on its first tax return, which was filed on August 15 of this year. X had properly obtained an extension. On September 1 of this year (ignoring Saturdays, Sundays, and holidays), after realizing its error, Corporation X filed an amended return electing to amortize its organizational expenses over 180 months. X made a proper election by choosing to amortize its organizational expenses.

A. True.

B. False.

Answer (A) is correct. *(SEE, adapted)*

DISCUSSION: Regulation 1.248-1(c) states that the election to deduct an amortized portion of organizational expenditures be made in a statement attached to the taxpayer's return for the taxable year in which it begins business. The return and statement must be filed not later than the date prescribed by law for filing the return (including any extensions of time) for the taxable year in which the taxpayer begins business. The extended due date in this case is September 15. Since the amended tax return was filed after the August 15 initial filing date and before the September 15 extended due date, the election to amortize the organizational expenditures is considered to have been made in a timely manner.

16.5 Business Deductions

NOTE: See Study Unit 3 for additional questions on business expenses and Study Unit 10 for questions on depreciation, amortization, and depletion.

16.5.1. Expenses that may be deducted for federal income tax purposes entirely in the year incurred by the corporation are

A. Research and experimental expenses.

B. Organizational expenditures.

C. Internally developed computer software costs.

D. Research and experimental expenses and internally developed computer software costs.

Answer (D) is correct. *(CMA, adapted)*

REQUIRED: The expenses that may be deducted entirely in the year incurred.

DISCUSSION: Research and experimental expenditures either may be deducted in the year they are paid or incurred or may be deferred and amortized (Sec. 174). Regulation 1.174-2(a) defines research and experimental expenditures as generally including all costs incidental to the development of a model, process, or similar property. Therefore, research and experimental expenses and internally developed computer software costs would both be deductible in the year incurred (Rev. Proc. 69-21). Note that there are certain requirements or qualifications for internal development of computer software to qualify as research and experimental expenditures.

Answer (A) is incorrect. Although research and experimental expenses may be deducted in the year incurred, "Research and experimental expenses and internally developed computer software costs" is a more complete choice. Answer (B) is incorrect. Section 248 provides that organizational expenditures may be amortized over 180 months or capitalized but not expensed. Answer (C) is incorrect. Although internally developed computer software costs may be deducted in the year incurred, "Research and experimental expenses and internally developed computer software costs" is a more complete choice.

16.5.2. Which one of the following items would not be fully deductible by a corporation?

- A. Group term life insurance premiums where the average policy had a face value of $80,000.
- B. Entertainment of employees at a Christmas party on the employer's premises.
- C. Depreciation on luxury cars used entirely for business purposes.
- D. Parking fines.

Answer (D) is correct. *(CMA, adapted)*
REQUIRED: The item that is not deductible for federal income tax purposes.
DISCUSSION: Fines and penalties paid to a governmental unit or agency are not deductible [Sec. 162(f)]. If fines were deductible, the effect of the punishment would be reduced and businesses would be less inclined to adhere to the law.
Answer (A) is incorrect. Premiums paid for life insurance are generally deductible as long as the corporation is not the beneficiary. Answer (B) is incorrect. Entertaining employees is an ordinary and necessary business expense [Sec. 274(e)(4)]. It is not subject to the 50% disallowance rule [Sec. 274(n)(2)]. Answer (C) is incorrect. The automobile is used entirely (100%) for business purposes. The fact that the automobile is a luxury vehicle only spreads out the depreciation deduction over more years.

16.5.3. Able Corporation is owned entirely by Mr. A. Able pays Mr. A $300,000 in salary for the current year. As a result of an IRS audit, reasonable compensation for Mr. A is determined to be $180,000. Which one of the following statements regarding Mr. A's compensation is false?

- A. The $120,000 of unreasonable compensation is a dividend to Mr. A.
- B. The $120,000 of unreasonable compensation cannot be deducted by Able.
- C. The $120,000, if repaid by Mr. A as part of a repayment agreement, can be deducted by Mr. A in the year in which the repayment occurs.
- D. The $120,000, if not repaid by Mr. A, is treated as a capital contribution made by Mr. A to Able.

Answer (D) is correct. *(Publisher, adapted)*
REQUIRED: The false statement regarding unreasonable compensation to a shareholder.
DISCUSSION: Section 162(a) provides that a corporation can deduct a reasonable allowance for salaries or compensation. The unreasonable compensation is normally treated as a constructive dividend to the shareholder (not a capital contribution by the shareholder) under Sec. 301, assuming that the corporation has sufficient earnings and profits.
Answer (A) is incorrect. The $120,000 of unreasonable compensation is a dividend to Mr. A. Answer (B) is incorrect. Section 162(a)(1) only allows a deduction for reasonable salaries. Answer (C) is incorrect. A repayment under an agreement is deductible as a trade or business expense by the employee in the year in which it occurs.

16.5.4. Mr. B is the nonshareholder president of Corporation M. He paid $50 a share for 100 shares of M stock that has a par value of $60 and a fair market value of $100. The stock was subject to a substantial risk of forfeiture at the time of purchase on January 28, Year 1. Mr. B sold this stock to his wife on February 1, Year 1, for $10 a share. On February 28, Year 2, the stock was no longer subject to a substantial risk of forfeiture and had a fair market value of $120 a share. Assume that M withholds any necessary amount on the portion of the income considered compensation to Mr. B. How much can Corporation M deduct on this transaction for Year 2?

- A. $0
- B. $1,000
- C. $5,000
- D. $6,000

Answer (D) is correct. *(SEE, adapted)*
REQUIRED: The corporation's deduction when a substantial risk of forfeiture lapses on stock sold to an employee below fair market value.
DISCUSSION: Under Sec. 83(a), an employee includes in income the excess of fair market value of property received for services over the amount paid for such property only when the property is no longer subject to a substantial risk of forfeiture. The employer is allowed a deduction for the amount the employee must include in income when the employee includes it in income [Sec. 83(h)].
Mr. B's stock was no longer subject to a substantial risk of forfeiture on February 28, Year 2. At that time, the fair market value was $120 per share, so his income was $120 minus the $50 he paid for each share. Under Reg. 1.83-1(c), however, Mr. B was required to recognize as income the $10 per share realized from the sale to his wife since it was not an arm's-length sale. This is considered an increase in the amount paid for the stock. Consequently, Mr. B must include $6,000 in income and Corporation M can deduct $6,000 in Year 2 [100 shares × ($120 − $60)].
Answer (A) is incorrect. Corporation M has a deduction for this transaction in Year 2. Answer (B) is incorrect. The $1,000 on the sale to his wife is recognized in Year 1. Answer (C) is incorrect. The income for Year 2 is calculated as the fair market value of the shares less the amount paid for the stock increased by the income recognized in Year 1.

16.5.5. Corporation H, a calendar-year, accrual-basis taxpayer, distributed shares of Corporation B stock to H's employees in lieu of salaries. The salary expense would have been deductible as compensation if paid in cash. On the date of the payment, H's adjusted basis in Corporation B stock was $15,000 and the stock's fair market value was $85,000. What is the tax effect to Corporation H?

A. $85,000 deduction.

B. $15,000 deduction.

C. $85,000 deduction and a $70,000 recognized gain.

D. $15,000 deduction and a $70,000 recognized gain.

Answer (C) is correct. *(SEE, adapted)*
REQUIRED: The tax effect to Corporation H of satisfying a salary liability with appreciated property.
DISCUSSION: Under Sec. 83(a), the employee includes in income the fair value of property received for services. Under Sec. 83(h), the employer is allowed a deduction for the amount the employee must include in income when the employee includes it in income. However, when property other than cash is distributed in exchange for services, the employer must recognize a gain on the deemed sale. Since the employees will include the $85,000 FMV of shares in income, Corporation H may deduct the $85,000. However, Corporation H must also recognize a $70,000 gain ($85,000 FMV – $15,000 adjusted basis) on the deemed sale.
Answer (A) is incorrect. A $70,000 gain is recognized as if the shares were sold to a third party. Answer (B) is incorrect. The employer may deduct the FMV of property relinquished. However, a gain must also be recognized as if the shares were sold to a third party. Answer (D) is incorrect. The amount of $15,000 is H's adjusted basis in the stock, not the FMV of the property given up.

16.5.6. Lynch Corporation is a publicly traded corporation whose top executives are subject to the $1 million limitation on their compensation. David Lynch, the corporation's chief executive officer, receives $1.8 million of salary for the current year. How does the executive and corporation report the compensation that is paid?

A. David Lynch reports $1 million of earned income and $800,000 of dividend income, and the corporation deducts $1 million.

B. David Lynch reports $1.8 million of earned income, and the corporation deducts $1 million of compensation.

C. David Lynch reports $1 million of earned income, and the corporation deducts $1 million of compensation.

D. None of the answers are correct.

Answer (B) is correct. *(Publisher, adapted)*
REQUIRED: The tax treatment of the $1.8 million salary paid to the CEO of a publicly held corporation.
DISCUSSION: Section 162(m) disallows a deduction to a publicly held corporation for compensation in excess of $1 million paid to the chief executive officer in any tax year. The $1 million is deductible by the corporation as compensation expense under Sec. 162 and is included by the CEO as ordinary income under Sec. 61(a). The disallowance of the compensation deduction under Sec. 162(m) does not automatically require reporting of the nondeductible portion of the payment as a dividend. Therefore, one could suspect that the payment would be called compensation provided that it is reasonable in amount under Sec. 162(a) even though it is not deductible under Sec. 162(m).
Answer (A) is incorrect. David Lynch does not report dividend income of $800,000. Answer (C) is incorrect. This figure is not the correct amount of earned income David Lynch must report. Answer (D) is incorrect. There is a correct answer.

16.5.7. A $1 million limitation has been placed on the compensation that is deductible by employers. Which one of the following statements is false?

A. The limitation applies for both the regular (income) tax and the alternative minimum tax calculations.

B. The limitation applies only to publicly held companies.

C. The limitation applies to all compensation earned by any employee of the corporation.

D. The limitation does not change the reporting of the disallowed compensation amount by the employee.

Answer (C) is correct. *(Publisher, adapted)*
REQUIRED: The false statement about the $1 million limitation on deductible employee compensation.
DISCUSSION: Section 162(m) disallows deduction of compensation exceeding $1 million per tax year paid to certain employees. The limitation applies to any publicly held corporations, and its application is not restricted to the regular income tax. Several forms of remuneration are excepted, including income from pensions, benefits that are tax-free under the Code, and compensation based on performance goals. The limit only applies to compensation paid to the CEO and the four other highest compensated officers whose compensation must be reported to shareholders under the Securities Exchange Act of 1934. The disallowance of the deduction for the compensation payment does not change the employee's reporting of the compensation for income tax purposes. Section 162(m) does not require that the salary, bonus, or other payment be treated as a dividend. Dividend reporting for part of the compensation may be required if part or all of the compensation is not reasonable in amount under Sec. 162(a).
Answer (A) is incorrect. The Sec. 162(m) limitation on deductible compensation applies for both the regular (income) tax and the alternative minimum tax calculations. Answer (B) is incorrect. The Sec. 162(m) limitation on deductible compensation applies only to publicly held companies. Answer (D) is incorrect. The Sec. 162(m) limitation on deductible compensation does not change the reporting of the disallowed compensation amount by the employee.

16.5.8. Phantom Corporation, a cash-method corporation, paid the following educational expenses for its employees:

Tuition	$15,000
Textbooks	5,000
Travel	3,000
Laboratory fees	1,000

The education was not required of the employees to maintain or improve their skills in their present positions. Phantom can claim a deduction for these expenses of

A. $0

B. $15,000

C. $21,000

D. $24,000

Answer (D) is correct. *(SEE, adapted)*
REQUIRED: The amount that a corporation may deduct for educational expenses paid for employees.
DISCUSSION: Section 162(a) states that a deduction is allowed for the ordinary and necessary expenses paid or incurred during the year in any trade or business. Although an individual may not be entitled to deduct educational expenses not required to maintain or improve skills in the employee's present position [Reg. 1.162-5(a)], an employer can deduct such amounts as compensation paid to or for its employees. As long as the expenses are treated as compensation, even the travel need not be documented as travel and entertainment [Sec. 274(e)].
Answer (A) is incorrect. Phantom can claim a deduction. Answer (B) is incorrect. The textbooks, travel, and laboratory fees are also deductible as compensation. Answer (C) is incorrect. The travel is also deductible as compensation.

16.5.9. Included in Kell Corporation's operating expenses were the following life insurance premiums:

Term life insurance premiums paid on the life of Kell's controller, with Kell as owner and beneficiary of the policy	$ 2,000
Group-term life insurance premiums paid on employees' lives, with the employees' dependents as owners and beneficiaries of the policies	18,000

In its income tax return, what amount should Kell deduct for life insurance premiums?

A. $20,000

B. $18,000

C. $2,000

D. $0

Answer (B) is correct. *(CPA, adapted)*
REQUIRED: The amount that a corporation may deduct for payment of life insurance premiums.
DISCUSSION: Kell Corporation may deduct the premiums paid for the employees' group-term life insurance under Sec. 162. However, according to Sec. 264, no deduction is allowed for premiums paid for life insurance for which the corporation is the beneficiary. Thus, only the $18,000 paid for its employees' group-term life insurance is deductible by Kell.
Answer (A) is incorrect. The term life insurance premiums are not deductible since the corporation is the beneficiary. Answer (C) is incorrect. The term life insurance premiums are not deductible, but the group-term life insurance premiums are deductible. Answer (D) is incorrect. Kell has a deduction for life insurance premiums.

16.5.10. Kelso Corporation is a publicly held corporation whose securities are traded on a national exchange and are registered under Sec. 12 of the Securities Exchange Act of 1934. The CEO's compensation package is approved annually by an outside compensation committee and the corporation's shareholders. The following compensation is paid to its CEO during the year:

I. Salary

II. Bonus that is paid based upon the attainment of certain profit performance minimums

III. Fringe benefits that are nontaxable to the employee

IV. Incentive stock options that are awarded annually upon the attainment of certain profit performance minimums

Which of the following types of compensation are included in determining whether the CEO's compensation exceeds the $1 million executive compensation limitation?

A. I only.

B. I and II.

C. I, II, and III.

D. I, II, III, and IV.

Answer (A) is correct. *(Publisher, adapted)*
REQUIRED: The types of compensation subject to the $1 million executive compensation limitation.
DISCUSSION: Section 162(m) disallows a deduction to a publicly held corporation for remuneration over $1 million paid to the chief executive officer. But several types of compensation are not included in computing the $1 million [Sec. 162(m)(4)]. Each of the following is a form of compensation deductible without regard to the limit of Sec. 162(m): (1) income from pension plans, annuity plans, and specified employer trusts; (2) benefits that are tax-free under the Code; (3) commissions based on income generated by the individual performance of the employee; (4) compensation based on performance goals; and (5) income payable under a pre-February 17, 1994, contract.
Answer (B) is incorrect. Item II is not included in determining whether the CEO's compensation exceeds the $1 million limitation of Sec. 162(m). Answer (C) is incorrect. Items II and III are not included in determining whether the CEO's compensation exceeds the $1 million limitation of Sec. 162(m). Answer (D) is incorrect. Items II, III, and IV are not included in determining whether the CEO's compensation exceeds the $1 million limitation of Sec. 162(m).

16.5.11. On December 31, Year 1, ABC Corporation, an accrual-basis personal service corporation (PSC), accrued a $25,000 bonus to Mrs. Adams, an employee-owner. She owns 15% of the outstanding stock of the corporation. Mrs. Adams is a cash-basis taxpayer and received the bonus on April 15, Year 2. ABC Corporation, a calendar-year taxpayer, may take a deduction on its Year 1 return of which of the following amounts?

A. $25,000

B. $21,250

C. $3,750

D. $0

Answer (D) is correct. *(SEE, adapted)*
REQUIRED: The deduction for a PSC when the bonus is distributed the following year to a cash-basis taxpayer.
DISCUSSION: Under Sec. 162(a), a reasonable allowance for salaries or other compensation for personal services actually rendered is deductible by the corporation if paid or incurred during the tax year. ABC Corporation is denied the deduction for the accrual in Year 1 under the related party rules. A corporation that uses an accrual method of accounting cannot deduct business expenses owed to a related person who uses the cash method of accounting until the corporation makes the payment and the corresponding amount is includible in the related person's gross income. For the purposes of this rule, a related person is any employee-owner if the corporation is a PSC, regardless of the amount of stock owned by the employee-owner.
Authors' note: Even if the related party rules did not deny the deduction in Year 1, it still would have been denied because it was not paid by March 15.
Answer (A) is incorrect. The amount of $25,000 is the accrued bonus to Mrs. Adams. Answer (B) is incorrect. The amount of $21,250 is the accrued bonus to Mrs. Adams less 15% of that bonus. Answer (C) is incorrect. The amount of $3,750 is 15% of the accrued bonus to Mrs. Adams.

16.5.12. Daynite Corporation, a domestic corporation, acquired a 90% interest in KDN Corporation 5 years ago for $50,000. During the current year, the stock of KDN was declared worthless. KDN's income for all taxable years was from sources other than passive or portfolio income. What are the character and the amount of the deduction Daynite should take in the current year?

A. Long-term capital loss of $50,000.

B. Ordinary loss of $50,000.

C. Long-term capital loss of $3,000.

D. No loss is permitted.

Answer (B) is correct. *(SEE, adapted)*
REQUIRED: The character and the amount of the deduction of worthless securities.
DISCUSSION: Section 165(g)(1) states that, if a security becomes worthless during the taxable year, the resulting loss will be treated as a loss from the sale or exchange of the security. However, Sec. 165(g)(3) provides an exception to this rule in the case of affiliated corporations. Under this exception, if a domestic corporation owns at least 80% of the voting and nonvoting stock of a corporation that derives at least 90% of its income from sources other than passive income, the stock is not treated as a capital asset. Therefore, any loss will be treated as an ordinary loss. Daynite will claim an ordinary loss of $50,000 on the KDN stock.
Answer (A) is incorrect. The loss is not a long-term capital loss. Answer (C) is incorrect. The domestic corporation owns at least 80% of the voting and nonvoting stock of a corporation that derives at least 90% of its income from sources other than passive income. Answer (D) is incorrect. A loss is permitted.

16.5.13. In the case of a corporation that is not a financial institution, which of the following statements is true with regard to the deduction for bad debts?

A. Either the reserve method or the direct charge-off method may be used, if the election is made in the corporation's first taxable year.

B. On approval from the IRS, a corporation may change its method from direct charge-off to reserve.

C. If the reserve method was consistently used in prior years, the corporation may take a deduction for a reasonable addition to the reserve for bad debts.

D. A corporation is required to use the direct charge-off method rather than the reserve method.

Answer (D) is correct. *(CPA, adapted)*
REQUIRED: The method for recognizing a corporation's bad debt expense.
DISCUSSION: Under Sec. 166, for tax years beginning after 1986, the reserve method is no longer allowed (except for certain financial institutions). Corporations that are not financial institutions must use the direct charge-off method or the nonaccrual-experience method.
Answer (A) is incorrect. The reserve method may not be used. Answer (B) is incorrect. A corporation may not change its method from direct charge-off to reserve, even with IRS approval. Answer (C) is incorrect. Even if the reserve method was consistently used in prior years, it may not be used (except for certain financial institutions) after 1986.

16.5.14. Carey Corporation, a calendar-year taxpayer, employs the allowance method for its bad debts for financial reporting purposes. The credit balance in the allowance account was $100,000 on December 31 of last year. On December 31 of the current year, Carey determined that a reasonable allowance would be $87,500. Carey wrote off $75,000 against the allowance account during this year. Carey's current-year deduction for bad debt expense on its federal income tax return is

A. $100,000
B. $87,500
C. $75,000
D. $62,500

Answer (C) is correct. *(CMA, adapted)*
REQUIRED: The corporation's bad debt expense in Year 2.
DISCUSSION: Under Sec. 166 for tax years beginning after 1986, the reserve method of computing the bad debt deduction is no longer allowed (except for certain financial institutions). The direct charge-off method must be used. Therefore, Carey's current-year bad debt deduction is $75,000, the actual bad debts written off during the year.
Answer (A) is incorrect. The balance in the allowance account at the beginning of the year is $100,000. Answer (B) is incorrect. The ending balance in the allowance account is $87,500. Answer (D) is incorrect. The current-year financial accounting bad debt expense account is $62,500 ($75,000 reduced by the difference between $100,000 and $87,500).

16.5.15. Finway Corporation has paid the following ordinary and necessary business expenses with regard to its sales force in the current year:

Daily auto rental	$2,000
Meals at restaurants while traveling	2,500
Meals furnished on business premises that are excluded from the employees' gross income	500
Cabs and limousines	1,000
Reimbursements for auto expenses of employees using the IRS standard mileage rate	2,250

The total amount that Finway may deduct for tax purposes in the current year is

A. $8,250
B. $7,000
C. $6,750
D. $6,500

Answer (B) is correct. *(CMA, adapted)*
REQUIRED: The deductible amount of business expenses.
DISCUSSION: Travel expenses are deductible under Reg. 1.162-2(a). Meals are generally limited to a deduction of 50% of the cost of the meal provided. Expenditures for food and beverages furnished on the taxpayer's business premises primarily for employees are not subject to the 50% limitation on deductions for food and beverage provided the expenditure is a de minimis fringe benefit (Sec. 132) or the meals are excludable under Sec. 119 [Reg. 1.274-2(f)(2)(ii)]. The first case apparently applies here. In *Boyd Gaming Corp. v. Commissioner*, 106 T.C. 343 (1997), the Tax Court ruled that, if meals provided on the business premises qualify as a de minimis fringe benefit, they will qualify for a 100% deduction. At issue in this case was whether the meals provided to employees met the requirements for a de minimis fringe benefit. Finway's allowable deduction is computed as follows:

Auto rental	$2,000
Meals (50% deductible)	1,250
Meals furnished on business premises	500
Cabs and limousines	1,000
Reimbursements for auto expenses	2,250
Total	$7,000

Answer (A) is incorrect. Only 50% of the meals furnished on the business premises and purchased while traveling is deductible in the current year. Answer (C) is incorrect. Only 50% of the meals furnished on business premises is deductible. Answer (D) is incorrect. Deductible expenses also include 50% of the meals furnished on business premises.

16.5.16. Kara Corp. incurred the following expenditures in connection with the repurchase of its stock from shareholders to avert a hostile takeover:

Interest on borrowings used to repurchase stock	$100,000
Legal and accounting fees in connection with the repurchase	400,000

The total of the above expenditures deductible is

A. $0
B. $100,000
C. $400,000
D. $500,000

Answer (B) is correct. *(CPA, adapted)*
REQUIRED: The amount that a corporation may deduct for expenses related to the repurchase of its stock.
DISCUSSION: Under Sec. 163, the interest expense incurred on business borrowings is deductible in the period in which it is paid or accrued. However, other expenses related to a stock repurchase or reorganization are generally not deductible. The 1997 tax act amended Sec. 162(k), which specifically prohibits deductions for amounts paid or incurred in connection with a stock redemption. Thus, only $100,000 interest is deductible, and the $400,000 must be capitalized and amortized.
Answer (A) is incorrect. Some of the interest expense is deductible. Answer (C) is incorrect. Legal and accounting fees are not deductible; however, the interest expense on borrowings is deductible. Answer (D) is incorrect. The legal and accounting fees are not deductible.

16.5.17. Corporation R gave a real estate agency 100 shares of its stock for its advice when the corporation purchased a new office building. If the par value and the fair market value are both $10 a share, the corporation can deduct $1,000 as a current expense.

A. True.

B. False.

Answer (B) is correct. *(SEE, adapted)*
    DISCUSSION: Under Reg. 1.162-1(a), no item may be included in business expenses to the extent it is used by the taxpayer in computing the cost of property included in its inventory or used in determining the gain or loss basis of plant, equipment, or other property. The cost of advice of the real estate agency must be capitalized under Reg. 1.263(a)-2(a) and included as part of the building's basis. Accordingly, Corporation R may not deduct the amount as a current expense.

16.5.18. If a corporation grants a transferable nonstatutory stock option in return for noncapital services and the option has an ascertainable fair market value, the corporation can take a current deduction.

A. True.

B. False.

Answer (A) is correct. *(SEE, adapted)*
    DISCUSSION: Under Regs. 1.61-15 and 1.83-7, a nonstatutory stock option is included in the income of the employee when granted if the stock option has an ascertainable fair market value. At the same time, the employer is allowed a deduction in a corresponding amount. It must be for noncapital services so that the amount can be expensed rather than capitalized.

16.5.19. Todd, an individual, is the holder and owner of an interest-bearing note of Madison corporation. All of Madison's stock was owned by Todd on December 31, Year 1. Todd and Madison are both calendar-year taxpayers. Madison uses an accrual method of accounting. Todd uses a combination of accounting methods; he uses the cash receipts and disbursements method in respect to items of gross income. Madison does not pay any interest on the note to Todd during the calendar year, nor does Madison credit any interest to Todd's account in such a manner that it is subject to Todd's demand. Madison Corporation can claim a deduction for Year 1 for the interest accruing on the note in Year 1.

A. True.

B. False.

Answer (B) is correct. *(SEE, adapted)*
    DISCUSSION: An accrual-basis corporation cannot deduct any expenses paid to a related cash-basis person until the payment is made and the amount is includible in the gross income of the person paid.

16.5.20. Service, Inc., operates a cafeteria on its business premises where its employees may purchase lunch at one-half its cost. Guests are occasionally served in the cafeteria. The cost to Service of providing the meals, including the cost of operating the facility but after reduction for amounts the employees paid for lunches, was $100,000. Considering Sec. 274, which generally limits deductibility of entertainment, meals, and travel as ordinary and necessary business expense, Service may deduct 50% of the $100,000 expense.

A. True.

B. False.

Answer (A) is correct. *(Publisher, adapted)*
    DISCUSSION: Section 274 restricts what may be deducted as ordinary and necessary business expense under Sec. 162 for meals and entertainment. Section 274(n) further limits the amount of otherwise deductible expense for meals and entertainment to 50%. Section 274(e)(1) specifically exempts expenses for food and beverages (and facilities used in connection therewith) furnished on the business premises of the taxpayer primarily for his or her employees. Under Reg. 1.274-2(d)(1)(ii), this exception applies not only to expenditures for food or beverages furnished in a typical company cafeteria or an executive dining room, but also to expenditures with respect to the operation of such facilities, and the exception applies even though guests are occasionally served in the cafeteria or dining room. Although Sec. 274(e)(1) specifically exempts the meals expense from Sec. 274(a), it is not exempt from the 50% rule of Sec. 274(n)(1). Note that Sec. 119 provides an exclusion from gross income of employees for the value of meals furnished on the business premises of the employer (if they are furnished for the convenience of the employer).

16.6 Bonds and Other Debt Obligations

16.6.1. All of the following are true except

A. An original issue discount must be included in income as it accrues over the term of the debt instrument, whether or not any payments are received from the issuer.

B. The original issue discount rules do not apply to U.S. savings bonds.

C. The amount of original issue discount is the difference between the stated redemption price at maturity and the par value.

D. An original issue discount can be treated as zero if it is less than one-fourth of 1% (.0025) of the stated redemption price at maturity multiplied by the number of years from the date of issue to maturity.

Answer (C) is correct. *(SEE, adapted)*
REQUIRED: The false statement regarding original issue discount (OID).
DISCUSSION: An original issue discount (OID) is equal to the difference between the issue price and the stated redemption price at maturity. OID exists only if the discount exceeds 1/4 of 1% of the stated redemption price times the number of years to maturity [Sec. 1273(a)(3)].
Answer (A) is incorrect. An original issue discount must be included in income as it accrues over the term of the debt instrument, whether or not any payments are received from the issuer. Answer (B) is incorrect. The original issue discount rules do not apply to U.S. savings bonds. Answer (D) is incorrect. An original issue discount can be treated as zero if it is less than one-fourth of 1% (.0025) of the stated redemption price at maturity multiplied by the number of years from the date of issue to maturity.

16.6.2. On August 1 of this year, Corporation A, which is a calendar-year taxpayer, issued original issue discount bonds with a face value of $500,000 and carrying an 11% coupon rate. The bonds had a 4-year maturity and an issue price of $456,300. What is A's original issue discount deduction for the current year assuming a current market yield of 14%?

A. $10,925

B. $8,882

C. $4,579

D. $3,723

Answer (D) is correct. *(SEE, adapted)*
REQUIRED: The corporation's deduction for original issue discount under the effective yield method.
DISCUSSION: For original issue discount bonds issued after July 1, 1982, Sec. 163(e) provides that the deduction for original issue discount is the aggregate of the daily portions of the original issue discount for the number of days in the year. The daily portions are determined under Sec. 1272(a) as the ratable portion of the excess of the product of the bond's yield to maturity and its adjusted issue price over the interest payable for the bond year. The adjusted issue price is the original issue price adjusted for original issue discount previously taken into income.

Yield times adjusted issue price ($456,300 × 14%)	$ 63,882
Less: interest payable ($500,000 × 11%)	(55,000)
Annual discount amortization	$ 8,882
Ratable portion [$8,882 × (153 days left in year divided by 365 days)]*	$ 3,723

*August 1 through December 31

Answer (A) is incorrect. The amount of $10,925 is the difference between the face value and the issue price amortized annually using the straight-line method over 4 years. Answer (B) is incorrect. The amount of $8,882 is the annual discount amortization. Answer (C) is incorrect. The amount of $4,579 represents the ratable portion of the annual discount that would be deductible if the straight-line method were permitted to be used.

16.6.3. Delve Co., Inc., issued $1 million of 40-year convertible bonds on October 1, 1981, for $892,000. The amount of bond discount deductible on Delve's income tax return for the year ended March 31, 2017, is

A. $0

B. $2,700

C. $10,800

D. $108,000

Answer (B) is correct. *(CPA, adapted)*
REQUIRED: The amount of bond discount that is deductible by a corporation.
DISCUSSION: Regulation 1.163-4 provides for the corporation issuing bonds at a discount before July 2, 1982, to accrue and deduct a ratable portion of the original issue discount each year. Delve's deduction for bond discount is

Par value	$1,000,000
Less: proceeds	(892,000)
Original issue discount	$ 108,000
Monthly portion ($108,000 ÷ 480 months)	$ 225
Months outstanding in tax year ending 3/31/17	× 12
Bond discount deductible	$ 2,700

Answer (A) is incorrect. A corporation may deduct a ratable portion of a bond discount. Answer (C) is incorrect. The deduction is limited to the ratable portion. Answer (D) is incorrect. Delve may not deduct the entire discount in one period.

16.6.4. Shaney Corporation repurchased its own outstanding bonds in the open market for $258,000 on May 31 of the current year. The bonds were originally issued on May 5, 3 years ago, at face value of $250,000. For its tax year ending December 31 of the current year, Shaney should report

    A. Neither income nor a deduction.

    B. A capital gain of $8,000.

    C. A capital loss of $8,000.

    D. An ordinary deduction of $8,000.

Answer (D) is correct. *(CPA, adapted)*
    REQUIRED: The tax effect a corporation must report as a result of repurchasing its own bonds.
    DISCUSSION: Under Reg. 1.163-4(c), if bonds are issued and subsequently repurchased by the corporation at a price in excess of the issue price, the excess of the purchase price over the issue price is deductible as interest expense for that taxable year. Shaney should therefore report a deduction of $8,000 (repurchase price of $258,000 less issue price of $250,000).
    Answer (A) is incorrect. Shaney has either an income or a deduction. Answer (B) is incorrect. Shaney does not have a capital gain of $8,000. Answer (C) is incorrect. Shaney does not have a capital loss of $8,000.

16.6.5. On May 15, Corporation A issued callable 20-year convertible bonds at a face value of $200,000 bearing interest at 5% per year. Under the terms of the bonds, the call price before May 15 of next year is $210,000. On July 1 of the current year, A calls the bonds for $210,000. What amount of the premium can A deduct on its current-year income tax return?

    A. $0

    B. $5,000

    C. $10,000

    D. $150,000

Answer (C) is correct. *(SEE, adapted)*
    REQUIRED: The amount of premium a corporation may deduct as a result of calling its convertible bonds.
    DISCUSSION: Regulation 1.163-4(c) provides that, if bonds are issued and subsequently repurchased by the corporation at a price greater than the issue price, the excess of the purchase price over the issue price is deductible as interest expense for the taxable year. Corporation A can deduct $10,000 (redemption price of $210,000 less issue price of $200,000) in the current year.
    Section 249 limits the deduction to the amount of the normal call premium on convertible debt. Excess amounts can be deducted only if the taxpayer can show that the excess is not attributable to the conversion feature. Regulation 1.249-1(d)(1) holds that a normal call premium on a convertible obligation is an amount equal to the normal call premium (in dollars) on a nonconvertible obligation that is comparable to the convertible obligation. Since the call premium does not exceed one year's interest, it is considered under the safe harbor rule of Reg. 1.249-1(d)(2) to be a normal call premium and can be deducted in full.
    Answer (A) is incorrect. The call premium may be deducted by the corporation. Answer (B) is incorrect. The excess of the purchase price over the issue price is deductible as interest expense for the taxable year. Answer (D) is incorrect. The correct amount Corporation A can deduct is not $150,000.

16.6.6. On December 31, 1982, Homer Corporation issued $2 million of 50-year bonds for $2.6 million. On December 31, 2017, Homer issued new bonds with a face value of $3 million for which it received $3.4 million and used part of the proceeds to repurchase for $2,176,000 the bonds issued in 1982. No elections were made to adjust the basis of any property. What is the taxable income to Homer on the repurchase of the 1982 bonds?

    A. $0

    B. $4,000

    C. $180,000

    D. $424,000

Answer (B) is correct. *(CPA, adapted)*
    REQUIRED: The amount of taxable income to a corporation on the repurchase of its bonds.
    DISCUSSION: Under Reg. 1.61-12(c)(3), if bonds are issued by a corporation and are subsequently repurchased at a price less than the issue price minus any amount of premium already recognized as income, the difference is included in income for the taxable year. Prior to 1987, a corporation could elect under Sec. 108 to exclude the income and reduce the basis of property, but this election is available in post-1986 years only in cases of bankruptcy or insolvency. The amount of income taxable to Homer is

Original issue price	$ 2,600,000
Less: Face value	(2,000,000)
Total premium	$ 600,000
Issue price	$ 2,600,000
Less: Premium already recognized as income [($600,000 ÷ 50 years) × 35 years]	(420,000)
Issue price less premium already included in income	$ 2,180,000
Less: Repurchase price	(2,176,000)
Amount included in 2017 income	$ 4,000

    Answer (A) is incorrect. Homer has taxable income on the repurchase of the bonds. Answer (C) is incorrect. The repurchase price is used to calculate the amount included in income, not the face value. Answer (D) is incorrect. The difference between the original issue price and the repurchase price is $424,000.

16.6.7. Andi Corp. issued $1 million face amount of bonds 5 years ago and established a sinking fund to pay the debt at maturity. The bondholders appointed an independent trustee to invest the sinking fund contributions and to administer the trust. In the current year, the fund earned $60,000 in interest on bank deposits and $8,000 in net long-term capital gains. All of the trust income is accumulated with Andi's periodic contributions so that the aggregate amount will be sufficient to pay the bonds when they mature. What amount of trust income was taxable to Andi in the current year?

A. $0

B. $8,000

C. $60,000

D. $68,000

Answer (D) is correct. *(CPA, adapted)*
REQUIRED: The amount of income from a sinking fund that is taxable to the corporation.
DISCUSSION: Regulation 1.61-13(b) provides that, if a corporation establishes a sinking fund under the control of a trustee for the payment of its debt, any gain arising from the fund must be included in income of the corporation. Therefore, Andi must include both the interest and the net long-term capital gains in its taxable income, or $68,000 ($60,000 + $8,000).
Answer (A) is incorrect. Both the interest and net long-term capital gains are included. Answer (B) is incorrect. The amount of $8,000 excludes the $60,000 interest. Answer (C) is incorrect. The amount of $60,000 excludes the $8,000 net long-term capital gains.

16.6.8. Sanders Corporation issued a $1 million 10-year debenture for $1.2 million on January 1, Year 1. In Year 7, how much income must Sanders report on its Year 7 income tax return from issuance of this bond?

A. $240,000

B. $200,000

C. $20,000

D. $0

Answer (C) is correct. *(SEE, adapted)*
REQUIRED: The income reported from the issuance.
DISCUSSION: Under Reg. 1.61-12(c)(2), in the case of a bond, the amount of amortizable bond premium for the taxable year is included in income. Thus, Sanders must report $20,000 [($1,200,000 − $1,000,000) ÷ 10].
Answer (A) is incorrect. The amount of $240,000 incorrectly amortizes the issue price over 5 years. Answer (B) is incorrect. The total premium is $200,000. Answer (D) is incorrect. The premium may be amortized over the life of the bond.

16.6.9. Scott Corporation transferred stock with a fair market value of $20,000 to its creditor in satisfaction of indebtedness of $30,000. The stock's book value was $15,000. How much income from this transaction should Scott include in its income tax return?

A. $0

B. $5,000

C. $10,000

D. $15,000

Answer (C) is correct. *(SEE, adapted)*
REQUIRED: The amount of income included from the transfer of stock used to satisfy a debt.
DISCUSSION: Under Sec. 61(a)(12), taxpayers, including corporations, must recognize gain from the discharge of indebtedness. If a corporation transfers stock to its creditors in satisfaction of indebtedness, it will have income from the discharge of the indebtedness to the extent that the amount or adjusted issue price of the debt satisfied exceeds the value of the distributed stock. The exception that existed under Sec. 108(a), whereby a corporation would not have income from the discharge of indebtedness if it is insolvent or is involved in bankruptcy, was repealed by OBRA 93 for stock transferred (1) after December 31, 1995, or (2) in connection with Title II or similar cases filed before January 1, 1995. Therefore, the amount of gain included on Scott's return is $10,000.
Answer (A) is incorrect. Scott has income from this transaction. Answer (B) is incorrect. The amount of $5,000 is the difference between the stock's FMV and its book value. Answer (D) is incorrect. The correct amount of gain from this transaction is not $15,000.

16.6.10. If a corporation issues its own bonds at a discount, it has in effect paid additional interest that is deductible over the life of the bonds.

A. True.

B. False.

Answer (A) is correct. *(SEE, adapted)*
DISCUSSION: For bonds issued prior to July 2, 1982, Reg. 1.163-4 permits the deduction of the original issue discount (as interest) over the life of the bond on a ratable basis. For bonds issued after July 1, 1982, Sec. 163(e)(1) allows the deduction of original issue discount over the life of the bond based on the "yield" method of amortizing the discount.

16.6.11. Corporation P repurchased at a premium convertible bonds it had issued. The amount of the premium that P may deduct as interest may not be in excess of a normal call premium for comparable nonconvertible corporate indebtedness.

A. True.

B. False.

Answer (B) is correct. *(SEE, adapted)*
DISCUSSION: Section 249 provides the general rule that no deduction is allowed to an issuing corporation for any repurchase premium that exceeds a normal call premium. But a repurchase premium that exceeds a normal call premium may be deducted to the extent that the corporation demonstrates to the commissioner that such repurchase price is not attributable to the conversion feature. Consequently, under certain circumstances the premium which P may deduct may exceed a normal call premium [Reg. 1.249-1(e)].

16.7 Dividends-Received Deduction

16.7.1. Which of the following qualifies for the dividends-received deduction?

A. Dividends received from a foreign corporation that earned all of its income from sources outside the United States.

B. Dividends on deposits in a mutual savings bank.

C. Dividends paid from a real estate investment trust ordinary income.

D. Dividends from a taxable domestic corporation.

Answer (D) is correct. *(SEE, adapted)*
REQUIRED: The dividends that qualify for the dividends-received deduction.
DISCUSSION: Section 243 permits a corporation to deduct 70% of dividends received from a domestic taxable corporation of which it owns less than 20% of the stock, 80% of dividends received if the stock is 20% or more owned, and 100% of dividends received if the stock is 80% or more owned.
Answer (A) is incorrect. A dividends-received deduction is allowed only to the extent of dividends paid from U.S.-source income. Answer (B) is incorrect. Section 243(d) provides that amounts received as dividends from mutual savings banks are not eligible. Answer (C) is incorrect. Section 243(d) provides that amounts received as dividends from real estate investment trusts are not eligible.

16.7.2. Corporations cannot take a deduction for dividends received from any of the following entities except

A. A regulated investment company.

B. A real estate investment trust.

C. A corporation whose stock has been held less than 46 days during the 90-day period beginning 45 days before the stock becomes ex-dividend with respect to the dividend.

D. Any corporation under an obligation (pursuant to a short sale or otherwise) to make related payments for positions in substantially similar or related property.

Answer (A) is correct. *(SEE, adapted)*
REQUIRED: The entity from which a corporation can take a dividends-received deduction.
DISCUSSION: A corporation may take a deduction for dividends received from a regulated investment company. However, in determining the deduction, dividends received from a regulated investment company shall be subject to the regulations provided in Sec. 854.
Answer (B) is incorrect. A corporation cannot take a deduction for dividends received from a real estate investment trust. Answer (C) is incorrect. A corporation cannot take a deduction for dividends received from a corporation whose stock has been held less than 46 days during the 90-day period beginning 45 days before the stock becomes ex-dividend with respect to the dividend. Answer (D) is incorrect. A corporation cannot take a deduction if it holds a short position in substantially similar or related property.

16.7.3. The dividends-received deduction for a corporation allows a(n)

A. 80% deduction for all dividends received from nonaffiliated corporations.

B. 70% deduction for all dividends received from nonaffiliated corporations.

C. 70% deduction for dividends received from a corporation when ownership is less than 20%, an 80% deduction for dividends received from nonaffiliated corporations when ownership is 20% or more (but less than 80%), and a 100% deduction for dividends received from affiliated corporations when ownership is 80% or more.

D. 70% deduction for dividends received from a corporation when ownership is less than 20% and an 80% deduction for dividends received from nonaffiliated corporations when ownership is 20% or more.

Answer (C) is correct. *(CMA, adapted)*
REQUIRED: The percentage of dividends received that qualifies for the dividends-received deduction.
DISCUSSION: Section 243 permits a corporation to deduct 70% of dividends received from a domestic taxable corporation of which it owns less than 20% of the stock, 80% of dividends received if the stock is 20% or more (but less than 80%) owned, and 100% of dividends received if the stock is 80% or more owned.
Answer (A) is incorrect. The dividends-received deduction for a corporation does not allow an 80% deduction for all dividends received from nonaffiliated corporations. Answer (B) is incorrect. The dividends-received deduction for a corporation does not allow a 70% deduction for all dividends received from nonaffiliated corporations. Answer (D) is incorrect. Depending on the stock ownership percentage of the distributee corporation, 70%, 80%, and 100% dividends-received deductions are allowed.

16.7.4. For a domestic corporation to deduct a percentage of the dividends it receives from a foreign corporation, certain tests must be met. Which of the following conditions need not be present?

- A. The domestic corporation owns at least 10% of the foreign corporation.
- B. The foreign corporation has income effectively connected with a trade or business in the U.S.
- C. The corporation is not a foreign personal holding company.
- D. The foreign corporation has derived income effectively connected with its U.S. business amounting to at least 50% of its gross income from all sources for a 36-month period.

Answer (D) is correct. *(SEE, adapted)*
REQUIRED: The condition that need not be met for a domestic corporation to deduct a percentage of dividends received from a foreign corporation.
DISCUSSION: Section 245 lists requirements that must be met for the dividends of a foreign corporation to qualify for the dividends-received deduction. These requirements include that the foreign corporation (1) not be a foreign personal holding company, (2) be subject to U.S. federal income taxation, (3) be 10% or more owned by the domestic corporation, and (4) have income from effectively connected business sources within the United States. For dividends received before 1987, prior law required the foreign corporation to have derived 50% or more of its gross income from effectively connected business sources within the U.S.
Answer (A) is incorrect. For a domestic corporation to deduct a percentage of the dividends it receives from a foreign corporation, the domestic corporation owns at least 10% of the foreign corporation. Answer (B) is incorrect. For a domestic corporation to deduct a percentage of the dividends it receives from a foreign corporation, the foreign corporation has income effectively connected with a trade or business in the U.S. Answer (C) is incorrect. For a domestic corporation to deduct a percentage of the dividends it receives from a foreign corporation, the corporation is not a foreign personal holding company.

16.7.5. For this year, Pine Corporation had losses of $20,000 from operations. It received $180,000 in dividends from a 25%-owned domestic corporation. Pine's taxable income is $160,000 before the dividends-received deduction. What is the amount of Pine's dividend-received deduction?

- A. $0
- B. $144,000
- C. $128,000
- D. $180,000

Answer (C) is correct. *(SEE, adapted)*
REQUIRED: The dividends-received deduction of a corporation.
DISCUSSION: A corporate deduction for dividends received from domestic taxable corporations is allowed. Pine Corporation may deduct 80% of dividends received from a domestic corporation in which Pine owned between 20% and 80% of the stock. This dividends-received deduction is limited to 80% of taxable income. Without regard to the limitation, Pine could deduct $144,000 ($180,000 × 80%). Pine, however, is limited to a $128,000 deduction ($160,000 taxable income × 80%). Thus, Pine's dividends-received deduction is $128,000.
Answer (A) is incorrect. Pine is entitled to a dividends-received deduction. Answer (B) is incorrect. Pine's dividends-received deduction is limited to 80% of taxable income. Answer (D) is incorrect. Pine may not deduct all of the dividends received.

16.7.6. Alpha is a U.S. corporation that owns 21% of the stock of Omega, a foreign corporation that is not a foreign personal holding company. Forty percent of Omega's post-1986 undistributed income is from effectively connected business sources in the U.S. Alpha's dividend from Omega is $20,000 in the current year. Alpha has no debt related to its stockholdings. What is Alpha's dividends-received deduction?

- A. $0
- B. $1,280
- C. $6,400
- D. $16,000

Answer (C) is correct. *(Publisher, adapted)*
REQUIRED: The dividends-received deduction for dividends from a foreign corporation.
DISCUSSION: A portion of dividends from a foreign corporation 10% or more of which is owned by a U.S. corporation qualifies for the dividends-received deduction. The portion of the dividends that qualify is the U.S. source portion of the dividends [Sec. 245(a)]. The U.S. source portion is the portion of undistributed earnings earned after 1986 attributable to income effectively connected with the conduct of a business in the U.S. and subject to U.S. tax. The dividends-received deduction is 80% for dividends received from corporations in which the recipient owns 20% or more of the stock.
Therefore, Alpha's dividends-received deduction is $6,400 ($20,000 dividend × 40% effectively connected income × 80%).
Answer (A) is incorrect. Alpha has an available dividends-received deduction. Answer (B) is incorrect. The dividends-received deduction is 40% of the generally available 80% dividends-received deduction. The deduction is only allowed for the portion of Omega's income that is effectively connected with the conduct of a U.S. trade or business. This amount is not multiplied by the 20% stock ownership. Answer (D) is incorrect. The amount of $16,000 is 80% of the dividends Alpha received from Omega.

16.7.7. Britney, Inc., has gross income for the current year of $150,000 excluding dividends of $100,000 received from nonaffiliated, domestic, taxpaying corporations in which Britney owns a 5% interest. The dividends were not from debt-financed portfolio stock. The company's operating expenses for the year are $160,000. Britney's allowable dividends-received deduction is

A. $63,000

B. $70,000

C. $72,000

D. $80,000

Answer (A) is correct. *(CMA, adapted)*
REQUIRED: The corporation's allowable deduction for dividends received in the current year.
DISCUSSION: Section 243 allows a corporation to deduct 70% of dividends received from a domestic corporation of which it owns less than 20% of the stock. Section 246(b), however, limits the dividends-received deduction to 70% of the corporation's taxable income, computed without regard to the dividends-received deduction, dividends-paid deduction, net operating loss deduction, capital loss carryback, and certain adjustments for extraordinary dividends. Britney's taxable income before the dividends-received deduction is $90,000 ($150,000 gross profit − $160,000 expenses + $100,000 dividends). Britney's allowable deduction for dividends received is limited to $63,000 ($90,000 taxable income × 70%) instead of the entire $70,000 ($100,000 dividends × 70%) otherwise available.
Answer (B) is incorrect. The amount of $70,000 is the dividends-received deduction, which must be limited to 70% of taxable income. Answer (C) is incorrect. The dividends-received deduction must be limited to 70% of taxable income, not 80% of taxable income. Answer (D) is incorrect. An 80% dividends-received deduction is for ownership of 20% or more of the distributing corporation's stock.

16.7.8. Andron Corporation owns 30% of the stock of Blackbird Corporation, 10% of the stock of Connie Corporation, and 80% of the stock of Dannin Corporation. Blackbird and Connie are both U.S. corporations, and Dannin is a foreign (non-U.S.) corporation doing 100% of its business in South America. Andron has taxable income before the dividends-received deduction of $200,000 and has received the following dividends:

Blackbird	$ 5,000
Connie	10,000
Dannin	20,000

The dividends-received deduction for Andron Corporation would be

A. $10,500

B. $11,000

C. $12,000

D. $31,500

Answer (B) is correct. *(CMA, adapted)*
REQUIRED: The dividends-received deduction (DRD).
DISCUSSION: Under Sec. 243, a corporation is entitled to a special deduction from gross income for dividends received from a taxable domestic corporation. The amount of the deduction is based upon the value and the percentage of the voting stock of the distributing corporation owned by the recipient. The deduction is 70% of dividends received from corporations owned less than 20% by the recipient corporation or 80% of dividends received from a corporation 20% or more owned. The DRD is 100% if the recipient owns 80% or more of the distributing corporation and they are members of the same affiliated group. The total DRD is limited to 70% (80% in the case of a 20%-owned corporation) of the recipient corporation's taxable income without regard to any NOL deduction, DRD, capital loss carryback, or adjustments for nontaxed portions of extraordinary dividends received.
Under Sec. 245, a dividends-received deduction is available for dividends received from a foreign corporation if owned 10% or more by a domestic corporation. However, it is available only on the portion of the dividend distribution attributable to income that is effectively connected with the conduct of a U.S. trade or business. Since Dannin Corporation has no effectively connected income, Andron Corporation receives no dividends-received deduction for dividends received from Dannin Corporation. The DRD is $11,000 as computed below.

Corporation	Deduction %	Dividend	DRD
Connie	70%	$10,000	$ 7,000
Blackbird	80%	5,000	4,000
Total			$11,000

Andron may be able to claim a deemed paid foreign tax credit (Sec. 902) with respect to the dividend from Dannin.
Answer (A) is incorrect. The deduction for dividends from Blackbird is 80%, not 70%. Answer (C) is incorrect. The deduction for dividends from Connie is 70%, not 80%. Answer (D) is incorrect. The deduction for dividends from Blackbird is 80%, not 70%; the deduction for dividends from Connie is 70%, not 80%; and no deduction is allowed for dividends from Dannin since it is a foreign corporation that earns all of its income outside the United States.

16.7.9. Snow Corporation owns a 20% interest in Hail Corporation, a domestic corporation. For the current year, Snow had gross receipts of $390,000, operating expenses of $400,000, and dividend income of $120,000 from Hail. The dividends were not from debt-financed portfolio stock. What is Snow's dividends-received deduction for the current year?

A. $24,000

B. $84,000

C. $88,000

D. $96,000

Answer (C) is correct. *(SEE, adapted)*
REQUIRED: The corporation's dividends-received deduction when a 20% interest is owned.
DISCUSSION: Under Sec. 243(a) and (c), a corporation is allowed a deduction for 80% of dividends received from unaffiliated domestic corporations of which it owns at least 20% of the stock. Section 246(b) limits the dividends-received deduction to 80% of taxable income before inclusion of the dividends-received deduction, dividends-paid deduction, net operating loss deduction, capital loss carrybacks, and certain adjustments for extraordinary dividends. (Note this deduction is 70% of taxable income for dividends from less than 20%-owned corporations.) Eighty percent of Snow's dividend income is $96,000. However, 80% of the taxable income before the dividends-received deduction is $88,000. This limit restricts the dividends-received deduction that can be claimed.

Gross business income	$ 390,000
Dividend income	120,000
Gross income	$ 510,000
Less: operating expenses	(400,000)
Taxable income without dividends-received deduction	$ 110,000
Deduction is lesser of:	
80% of dividend income, or	$ 96,000
80% of taxable income without dividend deduction	$ 88,000

Answer (A) is incorrect. The amount of $24,000 is 20% of the dividend income. Answer (B) is incorrect. The amount of $84,000 is 70% of the dividend income and Snow owns a 20% interest in Hail. Answer (D) is incorrect. Section 246(b) limits deduction to 80% of taxable income before the dividends-received deduction.

16.7.10. Pugsley Corporation purchased 20% of Mantle Corporation's common stock in August of the current year and paid for the purchase with $100,000 cash and $100,000 borrowed from its bank. During the current year, Pugsley received $30,000 in dividends from Mantle and paid $10,000 in interest expense on the bank loan. Pugsley did not make any principal payments on the loan during the year. If Pugsley had taxable income of $50,000 before special deductions, what is its dividends-received deduction for the year?

A. $0

B. $12,000

C. $14,000

D. $24,000

Answer (C) is correct. *(Publisher, adapted)*
REQUIRED: The corporate dividends-received deduction when stock is debt financed.
DISCUSSION: Section 246A restricts the dividends-received deduction when portfolio stock is debt financed. Debt-financed portfolio stock is any stock of a corporation if the taxpayer does not own at least 50% of the stock of such corporation and if, at some time during the base period, portfolio indebtedness exists with respect to the stock. The dividends-received deduction (when the recipient owns 20% or more of the payor corporation) is limited to a percentage equal to 80% times 100% minus the average indebtedness percentage. This percentage is the average amount of portfolio indebtedness divided by the average amount of adjusted basis of the stock during the period. However, the reduction in the dividends-received deduction cannot be more than the interest deducted for the portfolio indebtedness.
Pugsley's average indebtedness percentage is 50% ($100,000 ÷ $200,000), so the allowable deduction is 40% [80% × (100% – 50%)], giving a dividends-received deduction of $12,000 ($30,000 × 40%). The full deduction would have been $24,000 ($30,000 × 80%). The total reduction in the dividends-received deduction ($24,000 – $12,000 = $12,000) is greater than the interest-expense deduction for the period ($10,000), so the reduction is limited by Sec. 246A(e) to the $10,000 of interest expense. Pugsley's dividends-received deduction is thus $14,000 [($30,000 × 80%) – $10,000].
Answer (A) is incorrect. Pugsley is entitled to a dividends-received deduction. Answer (B) is incorrect. The amount of $12,000 is the portion of the 80% dividends-received deduction that is allowed under the debt financing rules; however, the disallowed dividends-received deduction is reduced because it cannot be greater than the interest expense. Answer (D) is incorrect. The amount of $24,000 is the full dividends-received deduction, which is limited under the debt financing rules.

16.7.11. Universal Corporation had the following items of income and expenses in the current year:

Gross income	$1,000,000
Deductible expenses	1,200,000
Dividends received from domestic corporations (20%-owned)	20,000

Universal had no debt related to its stock ownership. Universal is entitled to a dividends-received deduction in the current year of

A. $0

B. $14,000

C. $16,000

D. $20,000

Answer (C) is correct. *(CMA, adapted)*
REQUIRED: The dividends-received deduction for a corporation with a net operating loss.
DISCUSSION: Section 243(a) allows a corporation to deduct 80% of the dividends received from domestic corporations where the taxpayer owns 20% or more of the distributing corporation. Section 246(b) limits this deduction to 80% of the corporation's taxable income computed without the dividends-received deduction and certain other deductions and losses. This limit, however, does not apply for any taxable year in which the dividends-received deduction creates or increases a net operating loss.
Since Universal has a net operating loss of $180,000 ($1,000,000 income + $20,000 dividends – $1,200,000 expenses), the 80% of income limitation does not apply and the dividends-received deduction will be 80% of dividends received from domestic corporations, which is $16,000 ($20,000 × 80%).
Answer (A) is incorrect. Universal is entitled to a dividends-received deduction. Answer (B) is incorrect. The deduction is not 70%. Answer (D) is incorrect. The entire $20,000 dividend is deductible if the ownership of the corporation is 80% or more.

16.7.12. The dividends-received deduction

A. Must exceed the applicable percentage of the recipient shareholder's taxable income.

B. Is affected by a requirement that the investor corporation must own the investee's stock for a specified minimum holding period.

C. Is unaffected by the percentage of the investee's stock owned by the investor corporation.

D. May be claimed by S corporations.

Answer (B) is correct. *(CPA, adapted)*
REQUIRED: The true statement regarding the dividends-received deduction.
DISCUSSION: Section 246(c) requires that a corporate shareholder must hold the stock for 46 days during the 90-day period that begins on the date that is 45 days before the date that the stock becomes ex-dividend. To claim a dividends-received deduction with respect to a distribution on a share of preferred stock, a corporate shareholder must hold the stock for 91 days during the 180-day period that begins 90 days before the date that the stock becomes ex-dividend.
Answer (A) is incorrect. Under Sec. 246(b), the deduction may be limited to the applicable percentage of taxable income before the deduction. Answer (C) is incorrect. Under Sec. 243(a), the deduction is 80% of the dividends received unless the investor owns less than 20% of the stock, in which case the deduction is 70%. Answer (D) is incorrect. The deduction is not available to S corporations.

16.7.13. Dividends on deposits or withdrawable accounts in mutual savings banks qualify for the dividends-received deduction when received by a corporation.

A. True.

B. False.

Answer (B) is correct. *(SEE, adapted)*
DISCUSSION: Section 243(d) provides that dividends paid by mutual savings banks are not considered dividends (they are more like interest) for the purpose of the dividends-received deduction. Therefore, dividends from mutual savings banks do not qualify for the dividends-received deduction.

16.7.14. Small business investment companies may deduct 100% of the dividends received from a taxable domestic corporation.

A. True.

B. False.

Answer (A) is correct. *(SEE, adapted)*
DISCUSSION: Under Sec. 243(a), a small business investment company operating under the Small Business Investment Act of 1958 may deduct 100% of the dividends received from a domestic taxable corporation.

16.7.15. Alba Corporation owns 100% of the stock of Hutchinson Corporation. The two corporations have always filed separate tax returns. During this year, Hutchinson pays Alba a $250,000 dividend. Alba can take a maximum 80% dividends-received deduction with respect to the dividend.

A. True.

B. False.

Answer (B) is correct. *(Publisher, adapted)*
DISCUSSION: Section 243(a)(3) permits a corporation to claim a 100% dividends-received deduction with respect to dividends received from affiliated corporations. The needed affiliation exists when the distributee owns at least 80% of the total combined voting power and 80% of each other class of stock (other than certain nonvoting preferred stock issues) of the distributing corporation [Sec. 243(b)(1)]. The dividend also needs to be paid from a tax year in which the distributing corporation and distributee were members of the same affiliated group for each day of the year.

16.8 Charitable Contributions Deduction

16.8.1. Which of the following contributions made by Natvale Corporation, a domestic corporation, is not deductible for federal income tax purposes?

A. 100 shares of Natvale's preferred stock to Soo Valley Community College; the stock has been held in the treasury ($60 per share FMV on the date of gift).

B. $2,500 to the local humane society.

C. $7,500 to the American Red Cross.

D. $2,000 to Chilean Adoptions, a private foundation in Chile that operates orphanages.

Answer (D) is correct. *(CMA, adapted)*
REQUIRED: The contribution not deductible for federal income tax purposes.
DISCUSSION: Section 170(c) defines charitable contributions to include any contribution to an organization operated exclusively for religious, charitable, scientific, literary, or educational purposes. However, the organization must have been created or organized in the United States or selected foreign countries with which the U.S. has a tax treaty. Chilean Adoptions does not qualify since the foundation is organized in Chile, and the U.S. does not have a tax treaty with Chile.
Answer (A) is incorrect. The 100 shares of Natvale's preferred stock contributed to Soo Valley Community College is deductible because the college qualifies as an organization under Sec. 170(c). Answer (B) is incorrect. The $2,500 contribution to the local humane society is deductible because the humane society qualifies as an organization under Sec. 170(c). Answer (C) is incorrect. The American Red Cross qualifies as an organization under Sec. 170(c), so the contribution is deductible.

16.8.2. In the current year, Rock Corporation made contributions totaling $20,000 to qualified charitable organizations. Due to the 10% limit, it could only deduct $15,000 of the contributions on its return. Which of the following statements is true regarding the excess contributions of $5,000?

A. Charitable contributions in excess of the limit may, subject to limitations, be carried back to each of the 3 prior years.

B. A contribution carryover, subject to limitations, is used before the deduction of contributions for the carryover year.

C. Charitable contributions in excess of the limit may, subject to limitations, be carried over to each of the following 5 years.

D. Charitable contributions in excess of the limit may, subject to limitations, be carried over to each of the following 20 years.

Answer (C) is correct. *(SEE, adapted)*
REQUIRED: The true statement regarding charitable contributions made by a corporation.
DISCUSSION: Section 170(d) provides that excess charitable contributions may be carried over to each of the succeeding 5 years, subject to certain limitations. Under Sec. 170(b)(2), the total deductions for charitable contributions of a corporation may not exceed 10% of the taxable income computed before special deductions.
Answer (A) is incorrect. Charitable contributions may not be carried back. Answer (B) is incorrect. The current-year contributions are used before the carryovers. Answer (D) is incorrect. The carryover is allowed for only 5 years.

16.8.3. During the current year, a corporation contributed three computers (that were for sale as inventory) to the New Roads Elementary School. The computers had a fair market value of $700 each and a basis of $500 each. What is the corporation's charitable contribution with regard to the computers?

A. $2,100

B. $1,800

C. $1,500

D. $500

Answer (C) is correct. *(SEE, adapted)*
REQUIRED: The allowable charitable contribution deduction for a corporation.
DISCUSSION: A corporation may deduct the AB of ordinary income property contributed.
Answer (A) is incorrect. The FMV of the contributed computers is $2,100. The deduction is limited to the AB. Answer (B) is incorrect. The deduction for a contribution is generally limited to its basis by Sec. 170(e)(1). However, the enhanced deduction expired in 2011. Answer (D) is incorrect. The correct amount of the corporation's charitable contribution for the computers is $500 for each of the three computers.

16.8.4. Brave, Inc., made cash donations of $30,000 to various qualified charities during the current year. The following data for this year are also available:

Revenue from operations	$800,000
Interest income from various corporate bonds	150,000
Business expenses (not including the charitable contribution deduction)	700,000

Brave had no dividend income or carryovers of any type for the year. Brave's allowable charitable deduction for the year is

A. $5,000

B. $12,500

C. $25,000

D. $30,000

Answer (C) is correct. *(CMA, adapted)*

REQUIRED: The corporation's deduction for charitable contributions for the current year.

DISCUSSION: Under Sec. 170(b)(2), a corporation may deduct charitable contributions of up to 10% of the corporate taxable income computed without taking into consideration the charitable contributions and other special deductions. Brave's charitable contribution deduction is

Revenue from operations	$800,000
Interest income	150,000
Less: business expenses	(700,000)
Taxable income before charitable contribution deduction	$250,000
Times: Limit percentage	× .10
Charitable contribution deduction limit	$ 25,000

The $5,000 of excess charitable contributions may be carried forward 5 years and deducted.

Answer (A) is incorrect. The amount of $5,000 is the excess deduction that is carried over to next year. Answer (B) is incorrect. The amount of $12,500 is one-half of the allowable deduction. Answer (D) is incorrect. The amount of $30,000 is the total current year donations, which are limited to 10% of corporate taxable income. Any excess contributions are carried forward 5 years.

16.8.5. During the current year, Corporation G received $30,000 in dividends from a 60%-owned taxable domestic corporation. G received no other dividends. G's charitable contributions for the year totaled $15,000. G's taxable income for the year was $70,000 after the dividends-received deduction but before the deduction for charitable contributions. What is the amount of Corporation G's charitable contribution deduction for the year?

A. $7,000

B. $9,400

C. $10,000

D. $15,000

Answer (B) is correct. *(SEE, adapted)*

REQUIRED: The charitable contribution deduction for a corporation.

DISCUSSION: Section 170(b)(2) provides that the charitable contribution deduction for a corporation may not exceed 10% of the corporation's taxable income computed before the charitable contribution deduction, net operating loss carryback, capital loss carryback, and the dividends-received deduction. G's charitable contribution is limited to $9,400 as computed below. The excess of $5,600 ($15,000 − $9,400) may be carried over for 5 years.

G's taxable income before deduction for charitable contributions	$70,000
Add back: Dividends-received deduction ($30,000 × 80%)	24,000
Adjusted taxable income	$94,000
Times: Limit percentage	× .10
10% limit on contribution deduction	$ 9,400

Answer (A) is incorrect. The dividends-received deduction needs to be added back before determining the charitable contribution deduction limit. Answer (C) is incorrect. A $10,000 deduction is achieved by adding back the total dividends received (instead of the dividends-received deduction) before the 10% limit is applied. Answer (D) is incorrect. The deduction is limited to 10% of the corporation's taxable income before special deductions.

16.8.6. During the year, Sweetheart Corporation had the following income and expenses:

Gross receipts	$1,200,000
Salaries and wages	600,000
Contribution to qualified charities	90,000
Capital gains	30,000
Depreciation expense	70,000
Dividend income from a 20%-owned domestic corporation	120,000
Dividends-received deduction	96,000

What is the amount of Sweetheart's charitable contribution deduction for the year?

A. $90,000

B. $68,000

C. $52,000

D. $43,000

Answer (B) is correct. *(SEE, adapted)*
REQUIRED: The allowable charitable contribution deduction for a corporation.
DISCUSSION: Under Sec. 170, charitable contributions made to qualified organizations and paid within the taxable year may be deducted from taxable income. A corporation's charitable deduction is limited to 10% of taxable income computed before the charitable contribution deduction, net operating loss carryback, capital loss carryback, and the dividends-received deduction. Sweetheart's charitable contribution deduction for the year is $68,000, as computed below.

Gross receipts	$1,200,000
Capital gains	30,000
Dividend income	120,000
Less: Salaries	(600,000)
Less: Depreciation expense	(70,000)
Taxable income before special deductions	$ 680,000
Times: Limit percentage	× .10
Charitable contribution deduction	$ 68,000

Answer (A) is incorrect. The amount of the actual charitable contribution made during the year is $90,000. Answer (C) is incorrect. The charitable contribution deduction is limited to 10% of the taxable income computed for the purposes of such deduction. Answer (D) is incorrect. The correct amount of Sweetheart's charitable contribution deduction for the year is not $43,000.

16.8.7. Norwood Corporation is an accrual-basis taxpayer. For the year ended December 31, Year 1, it had book income before tax of $450,000 after deducting a charitable contribution of $50,000. The contribution was authorized by the board of directors in December, Year 1, but was not actually paid until March 1, Year 2. How should Norwood treat this charitable contribution for tax purposes to minimize its Year 1 taxable income?

A. It cannot claim a deduction in Year 1 but must apply the payment against Year 2 income.

B. Make an election claiming a deduction for Year 1 of $50,000 with no carryover.

C. Make an election claiming a deduction for Year 1 of $45,000 with no carryover.

D. Make an election carrying the deduction back 3 years.

Answer (B) is correct. *(CPA, adapted)*
REQUIRED: The corporation's maximum charitable contribution deduction.
DISCUSSION: Section 170(a)(2) allows an accrual-basis corporation to deduct a charitable contribution if authorized during the taxable year and paid within 2 1/2 months after year-end. Since the contribution was paid by March 15, Year 2, it is deductible in Year 1. Section 170(b)(2) provides that the charitable contribution deduction may not exceed 10% of a corporation's taxable income computed before certain special deductions and the charitable contribution deduction. Norwood's maximum deduction is $50,000, which is within the limit as shown below.

Taxable income after contribution	$450,000
Add: Charitable contributions made	50,000
Taxable income before contribution	$500,000
Times: Limit percentage	× .10
contribution deduction limit	$ 50,000

Answer (A) is incorrect. Norwood can claim a deduction in Year 1. Answer (C) is incorrect. The deduction can be claimed in Year 1 with no carryover. Answer (D) is incorrect. Norwood cannot make an election carrying the charitable contribution deduction back 3 years.

16.8.8. In Year 2, Green Corporation had a net operating loss and has a net operating loss carryback of $4,400 available to Year 1. Green had the following income and expenses for Year 1 when it was originally reported:

Gross profit	$205,000
Other deductions (including $1,700 of charitable contributions)	194,200

What is Green's deduction for contributions when the Year 1 taxable income is recomputed?

A. $640

B. $810

C. $1,080

D. $1,250

Answer (D) is correct. *(SEE, adapted)*
REQUIRED: The corporation's contribution deduction when there are NOL carrybacks.
DISCUSSION: Section 170(b)(2) limits a corporation's charitable deduction to 10% of the corporation's taxable income computed before the charitable contribution deduction, net operating loss carryback, capital loss carryback, and dividends-received deduction. Green's contribution deduction is $1,250 because the 10% limit is less than actual contributions. This limitation does not change because of Year 2's NOL carryback.

Gross profit	$205,000
Less: deductions	(194,200)
Add: charitable contributions made	1,700
Taxable income before special deductions	$ 12,500
Times: Limitation percentage	× .10
Contribution deduction limitation	$ 1,250

Answer (A) is incorrect. The contributions must be added back before determining the limit, and the NOL carryback should not be subtracted from income when determining the limit. Answer (B) is incorrect. The NOL carryback should not be subtracted from Year 1 income when determining the contribution deduction limitation. Answer (C) is incorrect. The contributions must be added back before determining the contribution deduction limitation.

16.8.9. For Year 2, a corporation had taxable income of $70,000 without regard to the contribution deduction. Contributions made in Year 2 totaled $5,000, and a $4,000 carryover of excess contributions from Year 1 is available to apply to Year 2. What is the amount of contribution carryover available for Year 3 and what is its source?

A. $0

B. $2,000 from Year 2.

C. $2,000 from Year 1.

D. $3,000 from Year 1.

Answer (C) is correct. *(SEE, adapted)*
REQUIRED: The corporation's excess contribution carryover.
DISCUSSION: Section 170(b)(2) limits the charitable contribution deduction to 10% of the corporation's taxable income computed before the charitable contribution deduction and certain special deductions. Section 170(d)(2) allows a corporation to carry excess contributions forward for 5 years. The total charitable contribution deduction including contribution carryovers, however, may not exceed the 10% limit. The current contributions are deducted first so that the Year 3 carryover consists of $2,000 from Year 1.

Contributions made in Year 2	$5,000
Carryover from Year 1	4,000
Total charitable contributions	$9,000
Year 2 deduction limited to $70,000 × 10%	(7,000)
Carryover to Year 3 from Year 1	$2,000

Answer (A) is incorrect. Contributions may be carried over and deducted in later years. Answer (B) is incorrect. Current-year contributions are deducted first. Answer (D) is incorrect. The amount of contribution carryover available for Year 3 is not $3,000 from Year 1.

16.8.10. Corporation D donated meat products inventory with a cost of $8,500 and a fair market value of $10,000 to a public charity. The conditions regarding the special rule on appreciation have been met (i.e., the charity used the inventory for the care of the needy). D's taxable income before the contribution deduction is $95,000. What is D's allowable contribution deduction?

A. $750

B. $8,500

C. $9,250

D. $9,500

Answer (C) is correct. *(SEE, adapted)*
REQUIRED: The corporation's allowable deduction for charitable contributions of inventory.
DISCUSSION: Normally, the deduction for a contribution of inventory is limited to its basis by Sec. 170(e)(1). However, Sec. 170(e)(3) provides that, when a corporation contributes inventory to be used by the donee for the care of the needy, the qualified contribution is reduced by only one-half the amount of potential ordinary income if the property had instead been sold at its fair market value. Corporation D's allowable contribution deduction is $9,250 and is not limited since it does not exceed $9,500 ($95,000 adjusted taxable income × 10%).

Contributions	$10,000
Less: potential ordinary income if sold [($10,000 FMV – $8,500 basis) × 50%]	(750)
Contribution deduction	$ 9,250

Answer (A) is incorrect. A deduction is allowed for the FMV less one-half of ordinary income potential. Answer (B) is incorrect. One-half of ordinary income potential may also be deducted. Answer (D) is incorrect. The deduction is limited to one-half of potential income plus basis.

16.8.11. In Year 1 at its December board meeting, Corporation A, an accrual-method taxpayer, authorized a contribution to Charitable Organization Y. Corporation A's Year 1 calendar-year tax return was filed on June 13, Year 2. The payment to Y was made on May 1, Year 2. Corporation A can deduct the charitable contribution made to Y on its Year 1 tax return.

A. True.

B. False.

Answer (B) is correct. *(SEE, adapted)*
DISCUSSION: A corporation that reports income on the accrual basis may elect to treat a contribution as paid (and therefore deductible) during the taxable year if the board of directors authorizes the contribution during such year and the contribution is paid within 2 1/2 months following the close of the taxable year [Sec. 170(a)(2)]. For Corporation A to deduct the contribution on its Year 1 tax return, it would have had to pay the contribution by March 15, Year 2.

16.9 C Corporation Net Operating Losses

16.9.1. For the current year, Lakeside Corporation had the following results:

Gross income from operations	$200,000
Dividends from a 25%-owned domestic corporation for which an 80% deduction is allowed	50,000
Operating expenses	340,000
Charitable contributions	20,000
NOL carryforward	30,000

What is the amount of Lakeside's net operating loss for the current year before NOL carryforward?

A. $110,000 ($250,000 – $360,000)

B. $90,000 ($250,000 – $340,000)

C. $80,000 ($50,000 + $30,000)

D. $130,000

Answer (D) is correct. *(SEE, adapted)*
REQUIRED: The net operating loss for the current year before NOL carryforward.
DISCUSSION: Section 172(c) defines a net operating loss as the excess of deductions over gross income, with certain modifications. Lakeside may not deduct any of the charitable contributions. One modification is that the dividends-received deduction is computed without regard to the 80% of taxable income limitation in Sec. 246(b). Thus, Lakeside's NOL is $130,000, as computed below.

Gross income from operations	$ 200,000
Dividend income	50,000
Less: Operating expenses	(340,000)
Gross income	$ (90,000)
Less: Dividends-received deduction ($50,000 × 80%)	(40,000)
Net operating loss	$(130,000)

Answer (A) is incorrect. Charitable contributions may not be deducted, but Lakeside is entitled to a dividends-received deduction. Answer (B) is incorrect. Lakeside is entitled to a dividends-received deduction. Answer (C) is incorrect. Gross income from operations, operating expenses, and the dividends-received deduction should be considered.

16.9.2. Based on the following information, what is the amount of Corporation X's net operating loss for the current year?

Gross income from business operations	$500,000
Dividends from 20%-owned taxable domestic corporations	150,000
Business expenses	625,000
Last year's net operating loss (available for carryover to the current year)	100,000

A. $0

B. $5,000

C. $75,000

D. $95,000

Answer (D) is correct. *(SEE, adapted)*
   REQUIRED: The corporation's net operating loss when there is dividend income and a NOL carryover.
   DISCUSSION: Section 172(c) defines a net operating loss as the excess of deductions over gross income, with certain modifications. One modification is that the dividends-received deduction is computed without regard to the Sec. 246(b) limitation of 80% of taxable income. Also, a deduction for a net operating loss carryover is not allowed in computing a current NOL. Consequently, Corporation X's NOL is computed as follows:

Gross income from business operations	$ 500,000
Dividends received	150,000
Gross income	$ 650,000
Less: Business expenses	(625,000)
Dividends received deduction ($150,000 × 80%)	(120,000)
Net operating loss	$ (95,000)

   Answer (A) is incorrect. Corporation X has a NOL. Answer (B) is incorrect. The income if the dividends-received deduction is limited to 80% of adjusted taxable income is $5,000. This limit does not apply since an NOL is created when the full dividends-received deduction is claimed. Answer (C) is incorrect. The amount of $75,000 is the result of deducting last year's NOL and not taking the dividends-received deduction.

16.9.3. How much of Corporation A's Year 1 net operating loss of $100,000 may be deducted in Year 2 based on the following information pertaining to A's Year 2 return?

Taxable income before the net operating loss deduction	$81,000
Charitable contribution deduction	9,000
Total charitable contributions for Year 2	12,000

A. $69,000

B. $81,000

C. $90,000

D. $93,000

Answer (B) is correct. *(SEE, adapted)*
   REQUIRED: The corporation's utilization of a prior year's net operating loss.
   DISCUSSION: The amount of Year 1 NOL carryover that may be deducted on the Year 2 return is the Year 2 taxable income as adjusted under Sec. 172. In the absence of a NOL, the charitable contribution limitation is $9,000 [($81,000 + $9,000) × 10%], and a $3,000 contribution carryover to Year 3 would occur. Taking into account the NOL carryover, the corporation is allowed no charitable contributions deduction, taxable income is zero, a NOL carryover of $10,000 is available, and a contribution carryover of $12,000 is available. Under Reg. 1.170A-11(c)(2), the NOL carryover to Year 3 is determined by claiming $9,000 of charitable contribution deduction and $81,000 of NOL carryover. Thus, a $19,000 NOL ($100,000 – $81,000) to Year 3 remains. In addition, a $3,000 ($12,000 – $9,000) charitable contribution carryover to Year 3 remains.
   Answer (A) is incorrect. The amount of $69,000 is the taxable income after deducting all Year 2 charitable contributions. Answer (C) is incorrect. The amount of $90,000 is the pre-NOL taxable income plus the $9,000 charitable contribution deduction. Answer (D) is incorrect. The amount of $93,000 is the pre-NOL taxable income plus the total charitable contributions.

16.9.4. Items that pertain to Ward Corporation for the year are presented below.

Taxable loss before capital transactions	$(15,000)
Short-term capital gains	10,000
Long-term capital losses	(30,000)

For the year, Ward Corporation has a net operating loss of

A. $35,000

B. $15,000 and a capital loss deduction of $3,000.

C. $5,000 and a long-term capital loss of $30,000.

D. $15,000 and a long-term capital loss of $20,000.

Answer (D) is correct. *(CMA, adapted)*
   REQUIRED: The corporation's net operating loss and net capital loss.
   DISCUSSION: Under Sec. 172, a corporation may carry back or carry forward a net operating loss. However, a net capital loss may only offset capital gains and may not be combined with a net operating loss. Therefore, Ward has a $15,000 net operating loss and a separate $20,000 ($30,000 – $10,000) long-term capital loss. Corporations carry their capital losses back 3 years and forward 5 years as short-term losses [Sec. 1212(a)].
   Answer (A) is incorrect. The corporation's capital loss is not combined with its net operating loss. Answer (B) is incorrect. The corporation is not entitled to treat $3,000 of the capital loss as an operating loss. Answer (C) is incorrect. The $30,000 long-term capital loss is first offset against the $10,000 short-term capital gain.

16.9.5. Yuma Corporation had a net operating loss in the current year. The net operating loss

A. Can only be carried back to each of the 3 years before the current year and not carried forward.

B. May be carried back to each of the 3 years before the current year and then carried forward to each of the 5 years after the current year.

C. Must be carried back to each of the 3 years before the current year and then carried forward to each of the 7 years after the current year.

D. May be carried back to each of the 2 years before the current year and then carried forward to each of the 20 years after the current year.

Answer (D) is correct. *(CMA, adapted)*
REQUIRED: The years to which a corporation may carry a net operating loss.
DISCUSSION: For tax years beginning after August 5, 1998, a net operating loss may be carried back to each of the 2 preceding taxable years and carried forward to each of the 20 succeeding taxable years [Sec. 172(b)]. However, the 3-year carryback period is retained for the portion of the NOL that relates to casualty and theft losses of individual taxpayers and to NOLs that are attributable to Presidentially declared disaster areas and are incurred by taxpayers engaged in farming or a small business. An election can be made to forgo the 2-year carryback and only carry the loss forward 20 years [Sec. 172(b)(3)]. In either case, the loss must be carried first to the earliest allowed year. There was special carryback of up to 5 years for 2009 and 2010.
Answer (A) is incorrect. The net operating loss may not be carried back to each of the 3 years before the current year and not carried forward. Answer (B) is incorrect. The net operating loss may not be carried back to each of the 3 years before the current year and then carried forward to each of the 5 years after the current year. Answer (C) is incorrect. The net operating loss may not be carried back to each of the 3 years before the current year and then carried forward to each of the 7 years after the current year.

16.9.6. In its first year of operations, which began on March 12 of the current year, KAN Corporation had a loss from operations of $30,000 and short-term capital gains of $10,000. Included in the loss from operations was a net fire loss of $5,000. What is the amount of KAN's net operating loss carryover from the current year?

A. $15,000

B. $20,000

C. $25,000

D. $30,000

Answer (B) is correct. *(SEE, adapted)*
REQUIRED: The net operating loss carryover from first-year operations.
DISCUSSION: Under Sec. 172, a net operating loss incurred in a tax year beginning after August 5, 1998, may be carried back 2 years and forward 20 years. The net operating loss must be carried to the earliest taxable year to which such loss may be carried. Since the current year is KAN's first year of operation, the net operating loss will be carried forward 20 succeeding taxable years or until used up. The amount of the net operating loss carryover is the excess of deductions over gross income. The fire loss (included in the $30,000 loss) may be fully deducted since KAN is a corporation (Sec. 165). KAN's net operating loss carryover is

Short-term capital gains	$ 10,000
Loss from operations	(30,000)
Net operating loss carryover	$(20,000)

There was special carryback of up to 5 years for 2009 and 2010.
Answer (A) is incorrect. The net fire loss may be fully deducted. Answer (C) is incorrect. The net fire loss is included in the $30,000 loss from operations. Answer (D) is incorrect. The short-term capital gains are first applied against the loss from operations.

16.9.7. Which one of the following statements about a current-year corporate net operating loss (NOL) is true?

A. The carryback period may be forgone and the carryforward period increased to 22 years.

B. A dividends-received deduction may not create, nor may it add to, an NOL.

C. A corporation does not make adjustments to its NOL for nonbusiness deductions.

D. If the corporation elects to carry back the current-year loss, the immediately prior taxable year would be the first year to which the loss would be carried.

Answer (C) is correct. *(CMA, adapted)*
REQUIRED: The true statement about net operating losses.
DISCUSSION: A corporation does not have any nonbusiness deductions and therefore does not make any adjustments to its NOL for them.
Answer (A) is incorrect. Section 172(b)(3) allows a corporation to elect to forgo the entire carryback period and only carry the loss forward, but it does not extend the carryforward period. Answer (B) is incorrect. Section 172(d)(5) provides that the dividends-received deduction may create or increase a NOL. Answer (D) is incorrect. Section 172(b) provides that a net operating loss incurred in a tax year must be carried back to each of the 2 preceding taxable years and carried forward to each of the 20 succeeding taxable years. The net operating loss must be carried to the earliest of the taxable years to which such loss may be carried.

16.9.8. For tax year 2017, Windy Corporation had taxable income of $80,000 before using any of its net operating loss from 2016. Windy never elected to forgo the carryback of any of its losses since its incorporation in 2012. Windy's books and records reflect the following income (losses) since its incorporation:

2012	$ 20,000
2013	(55,000)
2014	30,000
2015	35,000
2016	(50,000)

What is the amount of taxable income Windy Corporation should report on its 2017 tax return?

A. $50,000

B. $60,000

C. $70,000

D. $80,000

Answer (B) is correct. *(SEE, adapted)*
REQUIRED: The taxable income reported by Windy Corporation.
DISCUSSION: Under Sec. 172, a net operating loss incurred in a tax year beginning after August 5, 1997, may be carried back 2 years and forward 20 years. The net operating loss must be carried to the earliest taxable year to which the loss may be carried. The $55,000 NOL in 2013 is first carried back to offset the $20,000 income in 2012. The $35,000 NOL carryover is then used to offset the $30,000 income from 2014, leaving a $5,000 NOL carryover. The $5,000 carryover is used to reduce the 2015 income to $30,000. The 2016 NOL of $50,000 is first carried back to offset the remaining $30,000 of 2015 income. This leaves a $20,000 NOL carryover, which is carried forward to reduce 2017's $80,000 taxable income to $60,000.
Answer (A) is incorrect. The amount of $50,000 is the NOL for 2016. Answer (C) is incorrect. The amount of $70,000 incorrectly uses a $10,000 NOL carryforward. Answer (D) is incorrect. The amount of $80,000 is the 2017 taxable income before using any of the 2016 NOL carryover.

16.9.9. Geyer, Inc., a calendar-year corporation, had net income per books of $80,000 for 2017. For each of the years 2013-2016, Geyer's net income (loss) per books was as follows:

2013	$ 5,000
2014	15,000
2015	10,000
2016	(60,000)

Included in Geyer's gross revenues for 2016 were taxable dividends of $20,000 received from an unrelated 20%-owned domestic corporation. When filing its tax return for 2016 on March 10, 2017, Geyer elected to give up the 2-year carryback of the loss for 2016. Geyer should report a net operating loss carryforward on its tax return for 2017 of

A. $30,000

B. $46,000

C. $60,000

D. $76,000

Answer (D) is correct. *(CPA, adapted)*
REQUIRED: The net operating loss carryforward to 2017.
DISCUSSION: Under Sec. 172(b)(1), a net operating loss incurred in a tax year beginning after August 5, 1997, may be carried back to each of the 2 preceding taxable years and forward to the 20 succeeding taxable years. The net operating loss must be carried to the earliest possible year, unless an election is made to give up the carryback [Sec. 172(b)(3)]. Since Geyer made this election, the 2016 net operating loss is a carryforward to 2017. In computing the net operating loss, the dividends-received deduction that is claimed is computed without regard to the 80% of taxable income limitation. Geyer's net operating loss carryforward from 2016 to 2017 is

Net loss per books	$(60,000)
Dividends-received deduction ($20,000 × 80%)	(16,000)
Net operating loss carryforward	$(76,000)

Answer (A) is incorrect. The amount of $30,000 is the total NOL carryback incorrectly computed for the 3 preceding years under the previous election time frames. Answer (B) is incorrect. The amount of $46,000 is the NOL carryforward if $30,000 is carried back to the 3 preceding years under the previous election time frames. Answer (C) is incorrect. The $16,000 dividends-received deduction is included in the NOL carryforward.

16.9.10. Corporation X sustained a $10,000 net operating loss reflected on its 2017 calendar-year tax return. Corporation X carried this loss back to its 2015 calendar-year tax return. In 2015, Corporation X had $5,000 of gross income and $3,100 in total expenses of which $100 was a charitable contribution. What is the amount of Corporation X's NOL carryback to 2016?

A. $0

B. $8,000

C. $8,100

D. $10,000

Answer (C) is correct. *(SEE, adapted)*
REQUIRED: The net operating loss carryback to 2016.
DISCUSSION: Under Sec. 172(b)(1), a net operating loss incurred in a tax year beginning after August 5, 1997, may be carried back to each of the 2 preceding taxable years and forward to the 20 succeeding taxable years. Unless an election to give up the carryback is made under Sec. 172(b)(3), the loss must be carried back to the earliest possible year. Note that the charitable contribution is still deductible in 2015 because the limit is 10% of taxable income before a net operating loss carryback. Corporation X's net operating loss carryback to 2016 is

2017 net operating loss	$10,000
Carried to 2015	(1,900)
Carryback to 2016	$ 8,100

Answer (A) is incorrect. Corporation X has a NOL carryback. Answer (B) is incorrect. The charitable contribution deduction is still deductible. Answer (D) is incorrect. A NOL must be used to offset income from the earliest year first.

16.9.11. Corporation R incurred a net operating loss of $96,000 in 2017 and carried it back to 2015. In 2015, R had gross income of $470,000 and business expenses of $390,000, including charitable contributions of $1,000. A net operating loss of $70,000 from 2016 had also been carried back to 2015. How much of R's 2017 net operating loss can be deducted against 2015 income?

A. $0

B. $10,000

C. $11,000

D. $80,000

Answer (B) is correct. *(SEE, adapted)*
REQUIRED: The amount of the 2017 NOL that may be carried back to 2015.
DISCUSSION: Under Sec. 172(b)(1), a net operating loss incurred in a tax year beginning after August 5, 1997, may be carried back to each of the 2 preceding taxable years and forward to the 20 succeeding taxable years. Unless an election to forgo the carryback is made, the loss must be carried back to the earliest possible year. The charitable contribution is still deductible in 2015 because the limitation is on taxable income before a net operating loss carryback [Sec. 170(b)(2)(C)]. For 2015, Corporation R had gross income of $470,000 and business expenses of $390,000, producing taxable income of $80,000. Since a $70,000 NOL from 2016 was carried back to 2015, $10,000 of income remains for that year to which the 2017 NOL may be applied.
Answer (A) is incorrect. A portion of the NOL can be deducted against 2015 income. Answer (C) is incorrect. The $1,000 charitable contribution is still deductible when determining 2015 taxable income. Answer (D) is incorrect. The $80,000 of taxable income must first be reduced by the 2016 carryback, and the remaining income is used to offset a 2017 NOL.

16.9.12. Which of the following statements concerning net operating losses is false?

A. There are no limitations on the use of net operating losses.

B. Section 382 generally limits the "pre-change in ownership" NOLs absorbed in any "post-change in ownership" taxable year.

C. Section 382 limits the use of NOLs to the product of the fair market value of the loss corporation's stock times the "long-term tax-exempt rate."

D. The Sec. 382 limitation is triggered by a more than 50-percentage-point change in ownership.

Answer (A) is correct. *(Publisher, adapted)*
REQUIRED: The false statement about net operating losses.
DISCUSSION: Section 382 provides that, when a corporation has a more than 50-percentage-point change in ownership, special rules shall apply to limit the use of NOL carryovers incurred prior to the change in ownership and used after the change in ownership. The carryovers are limited by formula, but in concept they are limited to the amount that would be realized each year had the firm sold its assets and invested the proceeds in high-grade, tax-exempt securities.
Answer (B) is incorrect. Section 382 generally limits the "pre-change in ownership" NOLs absorbed in any "post-change in ownership" taxable year. Answer (C) is incorrect. Section 382 limits the use of NOLs to the product of the fair market value of the loss corporation's stock times the "long-term tax-exempt rate." Answer (D) is incorrect. The Sec. 382 limitation is triggered by a more than 50-percentage-point change in ownership.

16.9.13. C Corporation P, a calendar-year taxpayer, sustained a net operating loss in Year 1. The Year 1 tax return was filed on April 1, Year 2. P uses Form 1120X to carry back the net operating loss. What is the latest date Corporation P can file Form 1120X (ignoring holidays and weekends)?

A. December 31, Year 2.

B. April 1, Year 3.

C. April 15, Year 3.

D. April 15, Year 5.

Answer (D) is correct. *(SEE, adapted)*
REQUIRED: The latest date a corporation may file to carry back a net operating loss.
DISCUSSION: Form 1120X, *Amended Corporate Income Tax Return*, must be filed within the time set by law for a refund to be allowed [Sec. 6511(b)]. A claim for refund generally must be filed within 3 years of the time the return was filed or 2 years from the time the tax was paid, whichever expires later [Sec. 6511(b)]. However, if the return is filed before the due date, the 3-year period starts to run from the date the return was due [Sec. 6513(a)]. C corporations on the calendar year must file income tax returns by April 15 (ignoring holidays and weekends). The latest date Corporation P may file Form 1120X is April 15, Year 5 (3 years from the due date of the return).
Answer (A) is incorrect. December 31, Year 2, is not the latest date a C corporation may file to carry back a net operating loss. Answer (B) is incorrect. April 1, Year 3, is not the latest date a C corporation may file to carry back a net operating loss. Answer (C) is incorrect. April 15, Year 3, is not the latest date a C corporation may file to carry back a net operating loss.

16.9.14. KAD, Inc., a calendar-year corporation incorporated in January 2012, had a net operating loss of $75,000 in 2016. For each of the years 2012-2015, KAD reported taxable income (loss) before net operating loss deduction as follows:

2012	$ 15,000
2013	(20,000)
2014	10,000
2015	30,000

When filing its tax returns for both 2013 and 2016, KAD did not elect to give up the carryback of its losses. KAD's taxable income before the net operating loss deduction for 2017 was $80,000. What is the amount of net operating loss KAD should report on its tax return for 2017?

- A. $30,000
- B. $35,000
- C. $40,000
- D. $55,000

Answer (C) is correct. *(SEE, adapted)*
REQUIRED: The net operating loss deduction for 2017.
DISCUSSION: Section 172(b) provides that a net operating loss incurred in a tax year beginning after August 5, 1997, may be carried back to each of the 2 preceding taxable years and forward to the succeeding 20 taxable years. Unless an election is made under Sec. 172(b)(3)(c) to forgo the carryback, the loss must be carried to the earliest possible taxable year. The amount of loss that may be carried to any tax year is equal to the taxable income after any earlier net operating losses. KAD's 2017 net operating loss deduction is

2013 net operating loss	$20,000
Carried back to 2012	(15,000)
Carried forward to 2014	(5,000)
Remaining net operating loss	$ 0
2016 net operating loss	$75,000
Carried back to 2014	
($10,000 – $5,000 2014	
net operating loss used)	(5,000)
Carried back to 2015	(30,000)
Carryover to 2017	$40,000

Answer (A) is incorrect. The amount of $30,000 is the NOL carryback used in 2015. Answer (B) is incorrect. The amount of $35,000 is the total NOL carryback used from the 2016 NOL. Answer (D) is incorrect. KAD did not elect to forgo the carryback in 2013.

16.9.15. C Corporation L incurred a net operating loss for the year ended June 30, Year 3. L was granted an automatic 7-month extension and filed its tax return on December 15, Year 3. If Corporation L wishes to use Form 1139 to carry back the net operating loss, it must do so on or before which of the following dates? (Assume none of the dates falls on a Saturday, Sunday, or legal holiday.)

- A. September 15, Year 3.
- B. December 31, Year 3.
- C. April 15, Year 4.
- D. June 30, Year 4.

Answer (D) is correct. *(SEE, adapted)*
REQUIRED: The date on or before which the form for obtaining a quick refund must be filed.
DISCUSSION: Section 6411 provides a procedure that allows a taxpayer to obtain a quick refund for certain loss and credit carrybacks, including a net operating loss carryback. The corporate application for such a refund is Form 1139. Application for a quick refund may not be filed sooner than the date for filing the return for the year of the loss, nor later than 12 months from the end of such tax year. Therefore, Corporation L must file Form 1139 on or before June 30, Year 4.

Answer (A) is incorrect. Form 1139 does not have to be filed on or before September 15, Year 3. Answer (B) is incorrect. Form 1139 does not have to be filed on or before December 31, Year 3. Answer (C) is incorrect. Form 1139 does not have to be filed on or before April 15, Year 4.

16.9.16. Stone Corporation, a calendar-year taxpayer, began operation in 2014 and had modified taxable income in 2014 and 2015. In 2016, Stone incurred a net operating loss and elected to forgo the carryback period. Stone incurred another net operating loss in 2017. Since Stone elected to forgo the carryback period for 2016, it cannot carry the 2017 net operating loss back to 2015.

- A. True.
- B. False.

Answer (B) is correct. *(SEE, adapted)*
DISCUSSION: Under Sec. 172(b)(3), a taxpayer may elect to relinquish the entire carryback period with respect to a particular net operating loss. This election, however, only applies to the net operating loss of the taxable year for which the election is made. The election made by Stone applies only to the 2015 net operating loss. Stone may carry the 2017 net operating loss back to 2015.

16.9.17. A corporation must deduct as much of its net operating loss as possible. Any of the NOL that is left over after modified taxable income is reduced to zero can be carried over to the next year.

- A. True.
- B. False.

Answer (A) is correct. *(SEE, adapted)*
DISCUSSION: Section 172 provides that net operating losses must be used to their fullest extent in each year to which they are carried. Therefore, the taxpayer cannot pick and choose which years to take the net operating loss, except to elect to forgo the net operating loss carryback under Sec. 172(b)(3).

16.10 Capital Gains and Losses

16.10.1. Wonder, Inc., had taxable income of $200,000 exclusive of the following:

Gain on sale of land used in business	$25,000
Loss on sale of machinery used in business	(13,000)
Loss on sale of securities held 3 years	(4,000)
Loss on sale of securities held 3 months	(3,000)

On what amount of taxable income should Wonder compute tax?

- A. $200,000
- B. $202,500
- C. $205,000
- D. $212,000

Answer (C) is correct. *(CPA, adapted)*

REQUIRED: The corporation's taxable income with both capital and Sec. 1231 gains and losses.

DISCUSSION: The sale of the land and machinery used in the business are Sec. 1231 transactions, assuming the assets were held more than 1 year. Since the Sec. 1231 gain and loss net to a gain, they are considered a long-term capital gain and loss. The securities are capital assets so the losses are capital losses. Under Sec. 1211, a corporation may only deduct capital losses to the extent of capital gains. In this case, the capital losses are fully deductible because they do not exceed the $12,000 net Sec. 1231 gain.

Taxable income before capital gains/losses		$200,000
Capital gains/losses:		
Gain on sale of land	$25,000	
Loss on sale of machinery	(13,000)	
Loss on sale of securities (held 3 years)	(4,000)	
Loss on sale of securities (held 3 months)	(3,000)	
Net capital gain		5,000
Taxable income		$205,000

Answer (A) is incorrect. The $5,000 net capital gain should be added to this amount. Answer (B) is incorrect. The entire capital gain should be added to taxable income. Answer (D) is incorrect. The $7,000 in capital losses must be deducted from the $12,000 net Sec. 1231 gain before adding to taxable income.

16.10.2. With regard to the treatment of capital losses by a corporation other than an S corporation, which of the following statements is false?

- A. If a corporation has a net capital loss, it cannot deduct the loss in the current year.
- B. When a corporation carries a long-term net capital loss to another year, it is treated as a short-term loss.
- C. A corporation may not carry a capital loss from, or to, a year during which it is an S corporation.
- D. When figuring a current-year net capital loss, you must include any capital loss carried from another year.

Answer (D) is correct. *(SEE, adapted)*

REQUIRED: The false statement regarding the treatment of capital losses by a corporation other than an S corporation.

DISCUSSION: A corporation's capital losses are deductible only to the extent of capital gains, whether they are short- or long-term. A net capital loss is not deductible against OI in the tax year incurred. It cannot produce or increase a NOL. Net capital loss (NCL) = CLs (ST + LT) – CG (ST + LT). When figuring a current-year net capital loss, capital losses carried from other years are not included.

Answer (A) is incorrect. Capital losses can be used only to offset capital gains (Sec. 1211). Answer (B) is incorrect. A capital loss carried to another year is treated as a short-term loss. Answer (C) is incorrect. A capital loss cannot be carried from, or to, any year during which the corporation was classified as an S corporation.

16.10.3. In the current year, Little Company sold land that had been held strictly for investment purposes for $70,000. The original cost of the land when purchased 2 years ago was $80,000. During the year, Little also had a capital gain of $6,000 and received dividends from investments of $3,000. The amount of the loss that is deductible by Little in the current year from the sale of the land is

- A. $0
- B. $3,000
- C. $6,000
- D. $9,000

Answer (C) is correct. *(CMA, adapted)*

REQUIRED: The amount of capital losses allowed as an offset against other taxable income.

DISCUSSION: Section 1211 provides that a corporation may deduct capital losses only to the extent of capital gains (without regard to whether they are short- or long-term). Therefore, Little can only deduct $6,000 of its net long-term capital loss in the current year. The remaining $4,000 long-term capital loss will be carried back 3 years or carried over to the next year.

Note that a corporation's capital loss must be treated as a short-term capital loss when carried back or forward.

Answer (A) is incorrect. Little has loss that is deductible. Answer (B) is incorrect. Capital losses are offset against capital gains but not against dividend income. Answer (D) is incorrect. The dividends do not offset capital losses.

16.10.4. In its first year of operations, Rowley Corporation, not a dealer in securities, realized taxable income of $128,000 from the operation of its business. In addition to its regular business operations, it realized the following gains and losses from the sale of marketable securities:

Short-term capital gain	$ 10,000
Short-term capital loss	(4,000)
Long-term capital gain	12,000
Long-term capital loss	(32,000)

What is Rowley's total taxable income?

- A. $114,000
- B. $124,000
- C. $128,000
- D. $134,000

Answer (C) is correct. *(CPA, adapted)*
REQUIRED: The corporation's total taxable income including capital gains and losses.
DISCUSSION: Section 1211 provides that a corporation may only deduct capital losses to the extent of capital gains (without regard to whether they are short- or long-term). Therefore, Rowley may only deduct $22,000 of its capital losses since capital gains are $22,000 ($10,000 short-term and $12,000 long-term). The $14,000 balance of the capital losses may be carried forward 5 years. Rowley's total taxable income is

Income from operations	$128,000
Capital gains	22,000
Capital losses	(22,000)
Taxable income	$128,000

Note that a corporation's capital loss must be treated as a short-term capital loss when carried back or forward.
Answer (A) is incorrect. Capital losses may be deducted only to the extent of Rowley's capital gains. Answer (B) is incorrect. The correct amount of Rowley's taxable income is not $124,000. Answer (D) is incorrect. The correct amount of Rowley's taxable income is not $134,000.

16.10.5. General Corporation, a calendar-year taxpayer, reported taxable income of $100,000, all ordinary, on its corporate income tax return. The company has discovered that it inadvertently omitted a long-term capital gain of $15,000 from the return. General's income tax liability should have been larger by

- A. $4,200
- B. $5,100
- C. $5,250
- D. $5,850

Answer (D) is correct. *(CMA, adapted)*
REQUIRED: The effect of a long-term capital gain on a corporation's tax liability.
DISCUSSION: Long-term capital gain is included in a corporation's taxable income. The tax rate is 39%, which is the corporate rate of 34% plus the 5% surtax for income in excess of $100,000 (but not in excess of $335,000). The 35% corporate alternative tax rate for long-term capital gains under Sec. 1201 is not applicable at current tax rates. Thus, General Corporation's tax liability will be increased by $5,850 ($15,000 × 39%).
Answer (A) is incorrect. The amount of $4,200 is a 28% rate applied to the capital gain. The 28% capital gains rate is available only to individuals. The corporation's tax rate of 39% should also be used with the capital gain. Answer (B) is incorrect. The amount of $5,100 is 34% of $15,000. The corporation's tax rate of 39% should also be used with the capital gain. Answer (C) is incorrect. The amount of $5,250 is 35% of $15,000. The corporation's tax rate of 39% should also be used with the capital gain.

16.10.6. Which one of the following statements is applicable to corporate capital gains for the current tax year?

- A. Long-term capital gains are eligible for an alternative tax rate of 20%.
- B. If capital losses exceed capital gains, only $3,000 of the excess is currently deductible.
- C. Capital gains are excluded in computing the 10%-of-income limitation for charitable contribution purposes.
- D. Whether carried forward or backward, excess long-term capital losses are treated as short-term capital losses for the year to which they are carried.

Answer (D) is correct. *(CMA, adapted)*
REQUIRED: The true statement about corporate capital gains.
DISCUSSION: Section 1212(a)(1) provides that, if a corporation has a net capital loss, the capital loss may be carried back to each of the 3 preceding taxable years and forward to each of the 5 succeeding taxable years. The carryback or carryforward is treated as a short-term capital loss in each such taxable year.
Answer (A) is incorrect. Long-term capital gains being eligible for an alternative tax rate of 20% applies to individuals, not corporations. Answer (B) is incorrect. If capital losses exceed capital gains for individuals, only $3,000 of the excess is currently deductible. Answer (C) is incorrect. Section 170(b)(2) defines taxable income for charitable contribution purposes to include corporate capital gains.

16.10.7. In 2017, Capital Corporation reported gross profits of $150,000, deductible expenses of $28,000, and a net capital loss of $10,000. Capital reported the following net capital gains during 2014-2016:

Year	Net Capital Gains
2014	$5,000
2015	1,000
2016	3,000

What is the amount of Capital's capital loss carryover to 2018?

  A. $10,000

  B. $7,000

  C. $5,000

  D. $1,000

Answer (D) is correct. *(SEE, adapted)*
  REQUIRED: The capital loss carryover of a corporation.
  DISCUSSION: The net capital loss for the corporation may be carried back 3 years and forward 5 years. The current year's net capital loss will be carried back first to 2014, where it will offset $5,000 in net capital gain, then to 2015, where it will offset $1,000 of net capital gain, and then to 2016, where it will offset $3,000 of net capital gain. The remaining net capital loss of $1,000 will be carried over to 2018.
  Answer (A) is incorrect. The net capital loss carried over to 2018 is reduced by the capital loss carryback for the past 3 years. Answer (B) is incorrect. The capital loss carryback is for 3 years, not 1 year. Answer (C) is incorrect. The capital loss carryback for 3 years includes all years in between, not just the amount for the gain of the third year from the current year.

16.10.8. In Year 1, Corporation E had a net short-term capital gain of $15,000, a net long-term capital gain of $8,000, and an $11,000 short-term capital loss carryback from Year 3. In Year 1, what is E's net long-term capital gain after the carryback?

  A. $0

  B. $4,000

  C. $6,000

  D. $8,000

Answer (D) is correct. *(SEE, adapted)*
  REQUIRED: The corporation's net long-term capital gain after a capital loss carryback.
  DISCUSSION: Section 1212(a)(1) provides that, if a corporation has a net capital loss, the capital loss may be carried back to each of the 3 preceding taxable years and forward to each of the 5 succeeding taxable years. The carryback or carryforward is treated as a short-term capital loss in each such taxable year. Corporation E's net long-term capital gain is $8,000 since the capital loss carryback is treated as a short-term capital loss. In addition, E has a net short-term capital gain of $4,000 ($15,000 − $11,000).
  Answer (A) is incorrect. Corporation E has a net long-term capital gain. Answer (B) is incorrect. The net short-term capital gain is $4,000. Answer (C) is incorrect. The net long-term capital gain is not affected by the short-term capital loss carryback since the short-term capital gain exceeds the short-term capital loss.

16.10.9. Corporation Z's net long-term capital loss exceeded its net short-term capital gain by $5,000 in Year 6. To what taxable year is the net capital loss first carried?

  A. Year 1.

  B. Year 3.

  C. Year 5.

  D. Year 7.

Answer (B) is correct. *(SEE, adapted)*
  REQUIRED: The taxable year to which a net capital loss is first carried.
  DISCUSSION: A corporation's net capital loss is the excess of short- and long-term capital losses over short- and long-term capital gains. Under Sec. 1212(a)(1), a corporation that has a net capital loss may carry the capital loss back to each of the 3 preceding taxable years and forward to each of the 5 succeeding taxable years. The entire amount of the net capital loss must be carried to the earliest of the allowable taxable years. Corporation Z's net capital loss must first be carried back 3 years to Year 3. Unlike the net operating loss provisions, there is not an election to forgo the carryback.
  Answer (A) is incorrect. The net capital loss is not first carried back to Year 1. Answer (C) is incorrect. The net capital loss is not first carried back to Year 5. Answer (D) is incorrect. The net capital loss is not first carried forward to Year 7.

16.10.10. Smyth Corp. has both a capital loss and a net operating loss for the current year. The capital loss

  A. Cannot be deducted currently but can be carried forward for 5 years.

  B. Is included in the net operating loss.

  C. Cannot be deducted currently but can be carried back 3 years, then carried forward 5 years.

  D. Is treated as an ordinary loss.

Answer (C) is correct. *(CMA, adapted)*
  REQUIRED: The proper treatment of a net capital loss.
  DISCUSSION: A corporation's losses from the sale or exchange of capital assets are allowed only to the extent of the net gain from such sales or exchanges [Sec. 1211(a)]. The net capital loss (excess of capital losses over capital gains) may be carried back to each of the 3 preceding years and forward to each of the 5 succeeding taxable years (Sec. 1212).
  Answer (A) is incorrect. There is also a 3-year carryback. Answer (B) is incorrect. A net operating loss is defined as not including capital losses. Answer (D) is incorrect. There is no provision allowing capital losses to be treated as ordinary losses.

16.10.11. Ryan Corporation had the following gains and losses during the current year:

Long-term capital gain	$5,000
Long-term capital loss	8,000
Short-term capital gain	3,000
Short-term capital loss	7,000
Sec. 1245 gain from depreciation recapture	6,000

The nature and amount of Ryan's current-year capital loss carryback/carryforward is a

A. $1,000 short-term capital loss.

B. $1,000 long-term capital loss.

C. $7,000 short-term capital loss.

D. $3,000 long-term capital loss and a $4,000 short-term capital loss.

Answer (C) is correct. *(CMA, adapted)*
REQUIRED: The nature and amount of the capital loss carryback/carryforward.
DISCUSSION: The Sec. 1245 gain from depreciation recapture is treated as ordinary income and does not enter into the capital loss computation. The capital losses for each year are allowed only to the extent of capital gains (Sec. 1211). Thus, only the excess of the capital losses over the capital gains may be carried back or forward. The carryback/carryforward must be treated as a short-term capital loss in each year to which it is carried.

	Short-Term	Long-Term
Capital gains	$ 3,000	$ 5,000
Capital losses	(7,000)	(8,000)
Net capital loss	$(4,000)	$(3,000)

Answer (A) is incorrect. The loss carryback (carryforward) is not a $1,000 short-term capital loss. Answer (B) is incorrect. The loss carryback (carryforward) is not a $1,000 long-term capital loss. Answer (D) is incorrect. The $7,000 carryback (carryforward) must be treated as a short-term capital loss in each year to which it is carried.

16.10.12. Corporation X is a calendar-year taxpayer which began operations in Year 1. It incurred the following during the years indicated:

	Net Long-Term Capital Gain (Loss)	Net Short-Term Capital Gain (Loss)
Year 1	$(1,000)	0
Year 2	0	$(2,000)
Year 3	$2,000	0
Year 4	0	$(3,000)
Year 5	$1,000	0
Year 6	0	$(1,000)

What is the total carryover to Year 7 identified as to year and amount?

A. $(1,000); Year 3 – $2,000, Year 4 – $(3,000).

B. $(2,000); Year 4 – $(3,000), Year 5 – $1,000.

C. $(4,000); Year 1 – $(1,000), Year 4 – $(3,000).

D. $(4,000); Year 4 – $(3,000), Year 6 – $(1,000).

Answer (D) is correct. *(SEE, adapted)*
REQUIRED: The amount and the year of origination of a capital loss carryover.
DISCUSSION: Section 1211 provides that corporations may deduct capital losses only to the extent of capital gains. Under Sec. 1212, if a corporation has a net capital loss, it may be carried back to each of the 3 preceding taxable years and carried forward to each of the 5 succeeding taxable years. Oldest net capital losses are used first against capital gains. The year and the amount of Corporation X's capital loss carryover to Year 7 are

Year	Net Capital Gain (Loss)	Year Used and Amount	Remaining
1	$(1,000)	Year 3 – $1,000	0
2	$(2,000)	Year 3 – $1,000	0
		Year 5 – $1,000	
4	$(3,000)	0	$(3,000)
6	$(1,000)	0	$(1,000)
Capital loss carryover			$(4,000)

Answer (A) is incorrect. The correct amount of the loss carryover is not $1,000. Answer (B) is incorrect. The correct amount of the loss carryover is not $2,000. Answer (C) is incorrect. The loss is not carried over to Year 1.

16.10.13. The following information was taken from Wolverine Corporation's current-year federal income tax return:

Gross income	$700,000
Dividends-received deduction	60,000
Other business deductions	750,000
Net short-term capital loss	5,000
Net long-term capital loss	10,000

Which one of the following most accurately reflects Wolverine's federal income tax position for the current year?

A. Net operating loss of $50,000; the dividends-received deduction and the capital losses are separate carryback and carryover items.

B. Net operating loss of $50,000; only the capital losses are separate carryback and carryover items.

C. Net operating loss of $65,000; the dividends-received deduction is not allowed and cannot be carried over.

D. Net operating loss of $110,000; the capital losses are separate carryback and carryover items.

Answer (D) is correct. *(CMA, adapted)*
 REQUIRED: The most accurate reflection of a corporation's federal income tax position.
 DISCUSSION: Section 1211(a) provides that a corporation may deduct capital losses only to the extent of capital gains. Any net capital loss may be carried back 3 years and forward 5 years. Therefore, the capital losses are separate carryback and carryover items (not included in Wolverine's net operating loss).
 The dividends-received deduction limitation based on taxable income does not apply when the taxpayer has a net operating loss. Since Wolverine has a net operating loss, it may take the full deduction. Wolverine's net operating loss is

Gross income	$ 700,000
Less:	
Business deductions	(750,000)
Dividends-received deduction	(60,000)
Net operating loss	$(110,000)

Answer (A) is incorrect. The dividends-received deduction is taken when determining the amount of NOL, but the capital losses are separate carryback/carryforward items. Answer (B) is incorrect. Wolverine Corporation does not have a $50,000 net operating loss. Answer (C) is incorrect. Wolverine Corporation does not have a $65,000 net operating loss. Also, the dividends-received deduction is taken when determining the amount of NOL.

16.10.14. During its first year of operations, Laser Corporation incurred an operating loss of $50,000 and a long-term capital loss of $8,000. In Year 2, the corporation had ordinary taxable income totaling $125,000, a net short-term capital gain of $10,000, and a net long-term capital gain of $15,000. Laser's taxable income, classified by type of tax treatment, for Year 2 is

A. $67,000 ordinary income and $25,000 long-term capital gain.

B. $75,000 ordinary income and $17,000 long-term capital gain.

C. $75,000 ordinary income, $2,000 short-term gain, and $15,000 long-term capital gain.

D. $85,000 ordinary income and $7,000 long-term capital gain.

Answer (C) is correct. *(CMA, adapted)*
 REQUIRED: The amount and classification of a corporation's taxable income.
 DISCUSSION: Section 172 allows a net operating loss to be carried back 2 years and forward 20 years. Since Laser incurred a $50,000 operating loss during its first year of operations, it may only carry this loss forward. Under Sec. 1211(a), a corporation may deduct capital losses only to the extent of capital gains. A net capital loss may be carried back 3 years and forward 5 years and is treated as a short-term capital loss in each such year. Since the net capital loss of $8,000 occurred during Laser's first year of operations, it must be carried forward 5 years. The $8,000 loss is considered short term and offsets the $10,000 of short-term gain in Year 2. Laser's income is

Year 2 ordinary income	$125,000
Year 1 NOL carryover	(50,000)
Year 2 ordinary income	$ 75,000
Year 2 net short-term capital gain	
($10,000 – $8,000 carryover)	$ 2,000
Year 2 long-term capital gain	$ 15,000

Answer (A) is incorrect. Laser does not have $67,000 of ordinary income and a $25,000 long-term capital gain. Answer (B) is incorrect. The Year 2 net short-term capital gain and the Year 1 NOL carryover are included in the determination of ordinary income. Answer (D) is incorrect. Laser does not have $85,000 in ordinary income and a $7,000 long-term capital gain.

16.10.15. If a corporation's capital losses from 2 or more years are carried to the same year, the loss from the earliest year is deducted first. When that loss is completely used up, the loss from the next earliest year is deducted, and so on.

A. True.

B. False.

Answer (A) is correct. *(SEE, adapted)*
 DISCUSSION: If a corporation has two or more capital loss carrybacks to the same year, the earliest such loss must be applied first [Sec. 1212(a)]. This rule is to the corporation's advantage since the loss from the latest year can be carried forward longer.

16.11 Treasury Stock

16.11.1. During the current year, Webster Corporation repurchased 2,000 shares of its $1 par common stock in the open market for $5,000. Webster later resold 1,000 of these treasury shares to new shareholders when the stock was selling for $4 per share. Webster will report a gain (loss) on its current-year tax return of

A. $0

B. $(1,000)

C. $1,500

D. $3,000

Answer (A) is correct. *(CMA, adapted)*
REQUIRED: The amount of gain that a corporation recognizes on the purchase and sale of its treasury stock.
DISCUSSION: Under Sec. 1032(a), a corporation recognizes no gain or loss on the receipt of money or other property in exchange for its own stock, including treasury stock. Therefore, Webster should not report any gain.
Answer (B) is incorrect. The difference in total transaction amounts is $(1,000). Answer (C) is incorrect. The excess amount the 1,000 shares sold for is $1,500. Answer (D) is incorrect. The excess amount that all 2,000 shares would have sold for is $3,000.

16.11.2. The following information pertains to treasury stock sold by Lee Corporation to an unrelated broker in the current year:

Proceeds received	$50,000
Cost	30,000
Par value	9,000

What amount of capital gain should Lee recognize in the current year on the sale of this treasury stock?

A. $0

B. $41,000

C. $20,000

D. $21,000

Answer (A) is correct. *(CPA, adapted)*
REQUIRED: The gain a corporation should report as a result of the purchase and sale of treasury stock.
DISCUSSION: Under Sec. 1032(a), a corporation does not recognize gain or loss on the receipt of money or other property in exchange for its stock, including treasury stock. Therefore, no gain or loss is recognized by Lee as a result of the treasury stock transactions.
Answer (B) is incorrect. The amount of $41,000 is the difference between the proceeds received and the par value. Answer (C) is incorrect. The amount of $20,000 is the difference between the proceeds received and the cost. Answer (D) is incorrect. The amount of $21,000 is the difference between the cost and the par value.

16.12 Taxable Income and Tax Calculations

16.12.1. All of the following statements about the current corporate tax rates are true except

A. Corporate taxable income is subject to tax under an eight-bracket graduated rate system.

B. The tax rate is 15% of the first $50,000 of taxable income.

C. The tax rate is 30% if taxable income is over $1,000,000 but not over $10,000,000.

D. The largest U.S. corporations pay a 35% marginal tax rate.

Answer (C) is correct. *(SEE, adapted)*
REQUIRED: The statement that does not describe the current corporate tax system.
DISCUSSION: The current corporate tax system under Sec. 11 is based on an eight-bracket graduated rate system as follows:

Taxable Income		Marginal
Is at Least	But Not Over	Tax Rate
0 –	50,000	15%
50,000 –	75,000	25%
75,000 –	100,000	34%
100,000 –	335,000	39%
335,000 –	10,000,000	34%
10,000,000 –	15,000,000	35%
15,000,000 –	18,333,333	38%
Over	18,333,333	35%

Two rate brackets include surtaxes. A surtax of 5% is charged on income between $100,000 and $335,000, which eliminates the tax savings on the first $100,000 of taxable income. A 3% surtax is charged on income between $15,000,000 and $18,333,333, which recaptures the $100,000 tax savings from $335,000 to $10,000,000.
Answer (A) is incorrect. Corporate taxable income is subject to tax under an eight-bracket graduated rate system. Answer (B) is incorrect. The corporate tax rate is 15% of the first $50,000 of taxable income. Answer (D) is incorrect. The largest U.S. corporations pay a 35% marginal tax rate.

16.12.2. The following information is available for Briner Corporation for the current tax year ended December 31:

Revenues from sales	$ 8,000,000
Cost of goods sold	(4,000,000)
Operating expenses	(2,000,000)
Taxable income	$ 2,000,000

The tax liability for Briner's current tax year ended December 31 is

A. $670,000

B. $680,000

C. $690,000

D. $691,250

Answer (B) is correct. *(Publisher, adapted)*
REQUIRED: The corporation's income tax liability when income exceeds $335,000.
DISCUSSION: Section 11 imposes a tax on the increments that make up the first $100,000 of taxable income of 15%, 25%, and 34%, respectively. Thereafter, the rate is 34%. However, an additional 5% surtax is added to the $100,000 to $335,000 range to cause taxpayers with income in excess of $335,000 (but not over $10,000,000) to pay a flat 34%. Briner's tax is therefore $680,000 ($2,000,000 × 34%).
Answer (A) is incorrect. The amount of $670,000 is reduced by 5% of taxable income. Answer (C) is incorrect. The amount of $690,000 is increased by 5% of taxable income. Answer (D) is incorrect. The amount of $691,250 adds $11,250.

16.12.3. Tina, Inc., a calendar-year corporation, has taxable income of $150,000 for the current year with no capital gains. Tina's tax liability before credits for the current year is

A. $39,250

B. $41,750

C. $48,000

D. $50,500

Answer (B) is correct. *(E.D. Fenton, Jr.)*
REQUIRED: The corporation's tax liability before credits when income exceeds $100,000.
DISCUSSION: Corporations with taxable income in excess of $100,000 must increase the tax liability computed under the graduated rates by the lesser of (1) 5% of such excess or (2) $11,250. Corporations with taxable income of $335,000 or more will realize no benefits from the graduated rates of Sec. 11.

15% of $50,000	$ 7,500
25% of $25,000	6,250
34% of $75,000	25,500
Tax per graduated rates	$39,250
Add: $50,000 excess × 5%	2,500
Tax liability	$41,750

Answer (A) is incorrect. Corporations with taxable income in excess of $100,000 must increase the tax liability. Answer (C) is incorrect. The amount of $48,000 adds the 25% portion of the tax twice. Answer (D) is incorrect. The amount of $50,500 includes the $11,250, not 5% of the excess.

16.12.4. Net income per books of Pat Jordan's psychology clinic was $140,825 for the year ended September 30, 2017. Select from the following account information those items that would be necessary to reconcile book income to the income to be reported on the return, and compute taxable income per return.

Capital gains	$ 3,600
Capital losses	8,200
Entertainment expenses (before limitation)	10,850
Federal income tax expense	62,225
Tax-exempt interest income	5,000
Net income	140,825
Cash distribution to shareholders	20,000

A. $203,050

B. $208,075

C. $202,225

D. $207,650

Answer (B) is correct. *(SEE, adapted)*
REQUIRED: The taxable income per return computed from the items necessary to reconcile book income to the income to be reported.
DISCUSSION: Schedule M-1 reconciles income or loss per books with income or loss per tax return.

Net income per books	$140,825
Add back:	
Federal income taxes	62,225
Excess net capital losses	4,600
Excess entertainment	5,425
	$213,075
Subtract:	
Tax-exempt interest	(5,000)
Taxable income	$208,075

Answer (A) is incorrect. The net income per books plus the federal income tax expense equals $203,050. Answer (C) is incorrect. The sum of the net income per books, the federal income tax expense, and the excess net capital loss, less the excess entertainment deduction equals $202,225. Answer (D) is incorrect. The sum of the net income per books, the federal income tax expense, and the excess net capital losses equals $207,650.

16.12.5. For the current year, Sun Corporation had operating income of $80,000, exclusive of the following capital gains and losses:

Long-term capital gain	$14,000
Short-term capital gain	6,000
Long-term capital loss	(2,000)
Short-term capital loss	(8,000)

What is Sun's income tax liability for the current year?

- A. $15,450
- B. $18,250
- C. $18,850
- D. $22,250

Answer (C) is correct. *(SEE, adapted)*
REQUIRED: The current-year income tax liability of a calendar-year corporation.
DISCUSSION: Section 11 imposes a tax on the taxable income of every corporation. Sun Corporation's taxable income includes $80,000 of operating income and a net long-term capital gain of $10,000 [($14,000 – $2,000) + ($6,000 – $8,000)], or $90,000. The current-year tax liability of Sun Corporation is

$50,000 × 15%	$ 7,500
$25,000 × 25%	6,250
$15,000 × 34%	5,100
Total	$18,850

Answer (A) is incorrect. The $10,000 of net long-term capital gain is included in arriving at taxable income of $90,000. Answer (B) is incorrect. The 28% maximum tax rate on long-term capital gains applies only to individual taxpayers. Answer (D) is incorrect. Capital losses of $10,000 are deductible in arriving at taxable income of $90,000.

16.12.6. Sappington Corporation is a C corporation that has a $1 million net operating loss carryover from last year. Sappington's taxable income (before deducting the loss carryover) for the current year is $12 million. What is its income tax liability?

- A. $3,740,000
- B. $3,750,000
- C. $4,080,000
- D. $4,100,000

Answer (B) is correct. *(Publisher, adapted)*
REQUIRED: The current-year income tax liability of a corporation with taxable income of $12 million before deducting a $1 million NOL.
DISCUSSION: The net operating loss may be carried forward under Sec. 172(b) to reduce current-year taxable income to $11 million. Section 11 imposes a tax on the increments that make up the first $100,000 of taxable income of 15%, 25%, and 34%, respectively. An additional 5% surtax is added in the $100,000 to $335,000 range to cause taxpayers with taxable income between $335,000 and $10,000,000 to pay a flat 34%. Taxpayers with taxable income between $10,000,000 and $15,000,000 pay a 35% marginal tax rate. Therefore, the corporation's income tax liability, is $3,750,000 [$3,400,000 + ($1,000,000 × 35%)].
Answer (A) is incorrect. The rate that is applied to the $1,000,000 of taxable income in excess of $10,000,000 is not 34%. Answer (C) is incorrect. The tax rate is not a flat 34%, and taxable income is not $12,000,000. Answer (D) is incorrect. The NOL carryover should be deducted from the $12,000,000 before determining the tax liability.

16.12.7. Caddo Corporation is owned by three engineers, all of whom are employed by the corporation. It primarily performs civil engineering activities with respect to construction projects. During the current year, Caddo Corporation earned $150,000 of taxable income. Caddo has not elected to be taxed under Subchapter S. What is Caddo's current-year regular tax liability?

- A. $39,250
- B. $41,750
- C. $51,000
- D. $52,500

Answer (D) is correct. *(Publisher, adapted)*
REQUIRED: The corporate tax liability for the current year.
DISCUSSION: Caddo Corporation is a personal service corporation. Section 448(d)(2) defines a personal service corporation as a corporation substantially all of the activities of which involve the performance of services in the field of health, law, engineering, architecture, accounting, actuarial science, performing arts, or consulting, and whose stock is owned by employees who perform the services. Under Sec. 11(b)(2), the taxable income of a personal service corporation is taxed at a flat rate of 35%. Therefore, Caddo Corporation's current-year tax liability is $52,500 ($150,000 × 35%).
Answer (A) is incorrect. The amount of $39,250 is the result of applying the graduated corporate rates to the taxable income and not applying the additional 5% surtax to the last $50,000 of taxable income. A flat 35% rate should have been used for the personal service corporation. Answer (B) is incorrect. The amount of $41,750 is the result of applying the 15-39% graduated corporate tax rates to the taxable income. Answer (C) is incorrect. The amount of $51,000 is the result of applying a flat rate of 34% to the $150,000 of taxable income.

16.12.8. For the current year, Corporation Z had $60,000 of taxable income from operations. It also sold depreciable assets to its 100% shareholder as follows:

Sale Date	Property	Sales Price	Cost	Total Depreciation Claimed
Jan. 30	A	$ 4,000	$ 8,000	$3,000
June 10	B	7,000	8,000	4,000
Dec. 10	C	15,000	15,000	3,000

What is Z's corporate income tax for the current year?

A. $9,750

B. $11,250

C. $11,500

D. $14,000

Answer (C) is correct. *(SEE, adapted)*
REQUIRED: The corporation's income tax liability given sales of assets to its sole shareholder.
DISCUSSION: Under Sec. 267, losses on sales or exchanges between certain related parties are not recognized. A corporation and its 100% shareholder are related, so the loss on property A is not recognized. The gains of $3,000 each on property B and property C are treated as ordinary income (if not already taxed as ordinary income under one of the recapture provisions) because gains on the sale of depreciable property between certain related parties are ordinary under Sec. 1239. For this purpose also, the corporation and its 100% shareholder are related parties. Accordingly, total income is $66,000 ($60,000 + $3,000 + $3,000), which is taxed as follows:

$50,000 × 15%	$ 7,500
$16,000 × 25%	4,000
Tax liability	$11,500

Answer (A) is incorrect. The loss on property A's sale should not be subtracted from taxable income from operations; however, the two gains should be added to taxable income from operations. Answer (B) is incorrect. The loss from property A's sale to a related party does not reduce taxable income from operations. Answer (D) is incorrect. The gains on the three property sales were determined by reducing the sales price by the amount of depreciation claimed.

16.12.9. Which one of the following statements about the taxation of personal service corporations is false for tax years beginning after December 31, 1993?

A. Personal service corporations are subject to the "flat" 35% tax rate only if more than 75% of their gross income is earned income.

B. Taxable income of a qualified personal service corporation is taxed at a 35% rate without benefit of the 15% and 25% reduced rates.

C. Substantially all of the stock of the corporation must be owned by current or retired employees (or their estates or heirs) that are employed performing services for the corporation in connection with activities in certain professional fields.

D. The fields covered by the personal service corporation rules are health, law, engineering, architecture, accounting, actuarial science, performing arts, or consulting.

Answer (A) is correct. *(Publisher, adapted)*
REQUIRED: The false statement about the taxation of personal service corporations.
DISCUSSION: Under Sec. 448(d)(2), a personal service corporation has two main characteristics: (1) Substantially all of its activities must involve the performance of services in the field of health, law, engineering, architecture, accounting, actuarial science, performing arts, or consulting, and (2) substantially all of its stock must be owned by employees who perform the services. Section 11(b)(2) provides that the taxable income of a personal service corporation is taxed at a flat rate of 35% for tax years beginning after December 31, 1993. There is no requirement that more than 75% of the gross income be earned income for the flat 35% tax rate.
Answer (B) is incorrect. Taxable income of a qualified personal service corporation is taxed at a 35% rate without benefit of the 15% and 25% reduced rates. Answer (C) is incorrect. Substantially all of the stock of a personal service corporation must be owned by current or retired employees (or their estates or heirs) that are employed performing services for the corporation in connection with activities in certain professional fields. Answer (D) is incorrect. The fields covered by the personal service corporation rules are health, law, engineering, architecture, accounting, actuarial science, performing arts, or consulting.

16.12.10. Which of the following determinations made in corporate financial accounting may need adjustment to conform with tax accounting requirements?

A. Dividend revenue from other domestic corporations.

B. Charitable contribution expense.

C. Insurance expense.

D. All of the answers are correct.

Answer (D) is correct. *(S. Byrd)*
REQUIRED: The difference(s) between financial and tax accounting for corporations.
DISCUSSION: For tax purposes, dividend revenue from domestic corporations may be eligible for the dividends-received deduction; charitable contributions are limited to 10% of the taxable income after adjustments; and insurance expense may be reduced by the amount paid for life insurance when the corporation is a beneficiary. These deductions and limitations do not apply for financial accounting purposes.
Answer (A) is incorrect. Dividend revenue from other domestic corporations may need adjustment to conform with tax accounting requirements. Answer (B) is incorrect. Charitable contribution expense may need adjustment to conform with tax accounting requirements. Answer (C) is incorrect. Insurance expense may need adjustment to conform with tax accounting requirements.

16.12.11. The Tinkers, Evers, and Chance Corporations have taxable income, all resulting from regular operations, of $100,000, $300,000, and $450,000, respectively. None is a member of a controlled group. The tax liabilities before credits in the current year are

	Tinkers	Evers	Chance
A.	$22,250	$90,250	$141,250
B.	$22,250	$100,250	$153,000
C.	$22,250	$117,000	$153,000
D.	$34,000	$102,000	$153,000

Answer (B) is correct. *(C.J. Skender)*
REQUIRED: The current-year income tax liabilities of three corporations.
DISCUSSION: Section 11 imposes a tax on the taxable income of every corporation. The amounts are determined by using the graduated rates below. Graduated tax rates are phased out by imposing an additional 5% tax on income between $100,000 and $335,000, which effectively offsets the graduated rates on the initial $75,000.

	Tinkers	Evers	Chance
$50,000 × 15%	$ 7,500	$ 7,500	$ 7,500
$25,000 × 25%	6,250	6,250	6,250
Taxable income in excess of $75,000 × 34%	8,500	76,500	127,500
Taxable income (limited to $335,000 − $100,000) × 5%	0	10,000	11,750
Tax liability	$22,250	$100,250	$153,000

Corporations with taxable income between $335,000 and $10,000,000 are taxed at a flat 34% rate ($450,000 taxable income of Chance × 34% = $153,000).
Answer (A) is incorrect. The 5% surcharge is applied incorrectly to Evers and Chance Corporations. Answer (C) is incorrect. The graduated rates were not applied correctly to Evers Corporation. Answer (D) is incorrect. A flat 34% rate is not applied to each corporation's taxable income.

16.12.12. The Sunra Corporation had the following data available for the current year:

Gross profit on sales	$40,000
Dividend income from nonaffiliated domestic corporations (not debt financed – 20%-owned)	2,000
Operating expenses (exclusive of charitable contributions)	28,000
Charitable contributions	1,500

Sunra's taxable income for the current year is

A. $10,600
B. $10,900
C. $11,000
D. $12,400

Answer (C) is correct. *(CPA, adapted)*
REQUIRED: The corporation's taxable income given deductions and expenses.
DISCUSSION: Section 63(a) defines taxable income as gross income less deductions allowed. Section 162 allows a deduction for ordinary and necessary business expenses. Section 170 allows a deduction for contributions made to qualified charitable organizations, limited to 10% of taxable income computed before the charitable contribution deduction and the dividends-received deduction. In this case, the limit applies because taxable income before special deductions is $14,000 ($40,000 + $2,000 − $28,000), and the $1,400 limit is less than actual contributions. Section 243 allows a deduction for dividends received from 20% or more owned domestic corporations of 80% of the dividends received, which is $1,600 ($2,000 × 80%). Sunra's taxable income is

Gross profit	$40,000
Dividend income	2,000
Gross income	$42,000
Less:	
Operating expenses	(28,000)
Charitable contributions	(1,400)
Dividends-received deduction	(1,600)
Taxable income	$11,000

Answer (A) is incorrect. The dividends-received deduction is not $2,000. Answer (B) is incorrect. The charitable deduction is not $1,500. Answer (D) is incorrect. The charitable contribution deduction was not deducted.

16.12.13. In the reconciliation of income per books with income per return,

A. Only temporary differences are considered.

B. Only permanent differences are considered.

C. Both temporary and permanent differences are considered.

D. Neither temporary nor permanent differences is considered.

Answer (C) is correct. *(CPA, adapted)*
  REQUIRED: The differences included in the reconciliation of income per books with income per return.
  DISCUSSION: Reconciling income per books with income per return considers both temporary differences (i.e., differences expected to be eliminated in the future, such as an accelerated method of depreciation for tax purposes and a straight-line method for financial reporting purposes) and permanent differences (i.e., differences not expected to be eliminated in the future, such as that caused by the deduction of federal income taxes for financial reporting purposes).
  Answer (A) is incorrect. Not only temporary differences are considered. Answer (B) is incorrect. Not only permanent differences are considered. Answer (D) is incorrect. Both temporary and permanent differences are considered when reconciling income per books with income per return.

16.12.14. Wright Corporation reported $100,000 of book income before income taxes for the current year. The income statement disclosed the following information:

Christmas gifts to 40 customers at $100 each.

Dividends of $20,000 received from Morley, Ltd., a 20%-owned corporation that is not subject to United States income tax.

Insurance premiums of $15,000 on a policy insuring the life of the president of the corporation, under which Wright Corporation is the beneficiary.

What should Wright report as its taxable income for the current year?

A. $98,000

B. $103,000

C. $115,000

D. $118,000

Answer (D) is correct. *(CPA, adapted)*
  REQUIRED: The amount of a corporation's taxable income.
  DISCUSSION: Under Sec. 274(b), business gifts are limited to $25 for each gift. Under Sec. 245, dividends received from foreign corporations are eligible for the dividends-received deduction only if the corporation is subject to U.S. income tax. Under Sec. 264, no deduction is allowed for life insurance premiums on a policy covering the life of an officer if the corporation is directly or indirectly a beneficiary. Wright's taxable income is

Pretax income per books	$100,000
Add back:	
Christmas gifts (40 × $75)	3,000
Insurance premiums	15,000
Taxable income	$118,000

Note that the portion of Christmas gifts added back is the excess deduction taken in computing book income. Also, the dividends were included in book income, but no dividends-received deduction is allowed since the dividend is from a foreign corporation having no U.S. trade or business income.
  Answer (A) is incorrect. Wright should not subtract the $20,000 dividend from pretax income per books. Answer (B) is incorrect. Wright must also add back the insurance premium. Answer (C) is incorrect. Wright must also add back the nondeductible portion of the gifts.

16.12.15. For the current year, Maple Corporation's book income before federal income tax was $100,000. Included in this $100,000 were the following:

Provision for state income tax	$1,000
Interest earned on U.S. Treasury bonds	6,000
Interest expense on bank loan to purchase U.S. Treasury bonds	2,000

Maple's taxable income for the current year was

A. $96,000

B. $97,000

C. $100,000

D. $101,000

Answer (C) is correct. *(CPA, adapted)*
  REQUIRED: The corporation's taxable income given book income and some of its components.
  DISCUSSION: State income taxes are deductible, unlike federal income taxes. There is no exclusion for interest income on U.S. obligations. Relatedly, the interest on debt to carry the U.S. obligations is deductible. Therefore, book income and taxable income are the same, $100,000.
  Answer (A) is incorrect. The interest earned on U.S. Treasury bonds is included in income, and the interest expense on the bank loan is deductible. Answer (B) is incorrect. The interest expense on the bank loan and the state income taxes are deductible in determining financial accounting income and should not be deducted a second time in arriving at taxable income. Answer (D) is incorrect. The state income tax is deductible when determining taxable income.

16.12.16. Grady Corporation's book income before income taxes was $300,000 for the current year. Organization costs of $150,000 incurred at the organization date 2 years earlier were written off when incurred for financial reporting purposes and over the minimum period for income tax purposes. Assuming there were no other reconciling items, what is Grady's taxable income for the current year?

A. $270,000

B. $290,000

C. $300,000

D. $310,000

Answer (B) is correct. *(CPA, adapted)*
   REQUIRED: The amount of a corporation's taxable income.
   DISCUSSION: Section 248 provides that a corporation may elect to amortize organizational expenditures over a period of 15 years. The amortization for tax purposes is $10,000 ($150,000 divided by 15 years). Consequently, an additional $10,000 is deductible in the current year. Grady's taxable income for the year is

Book income	$300,000
Less: Additional amortization	(10,000)
Taxable income	$290,000

   Answer (A) is incorrect. The organizational costs are amortized over 15 years, not 5 years. Answer (C) is incorrect. The amount of $300,000 must be adjusted for the amortization claimed for tax purposes. Answer (D) is incorrect. The amortization reduces (instead of increasing) taxable income.

16.12.17. For the current year, accrual-basis Corp. A's books and records reflected the following:

Net income per books	$104,000
Accrued federal income tax	35,000
Net capital loss	4,000
Tax-exempt interest	5,000
Book depreciation in excess of allowable tax depreciation	2,000

Based on the above facts, what is the amount of A's taxable income?

A. $69,000

B. $70,000

C. $140,000

D. $150,000

Answer (C) is correct. *(SEE, adapted)*
   REQUIRED: The corporation's taxable income for the current year.
   DISCUSSION: Federal income tax, excess capital losses, and book depreciation in excess of tax depreciation are not deductible. These amounts must be added back to book income. Tax-exempt interest is not taxable and must be subtracted from book income. These adjustments are done on Schedule M-1 of the corporation tax return.

Net income per books	$104,000
Add back:	
Federal income tax	35,000
Net capital loss	4,000
Excess book depreciation	2,000
	$145,000
Subtract: Tax-exempt interest	(5,000)
Taxable income	$140,000

   Answer (A) is incorrect. Federal income tax is added to, not subtracted from, book net income. Also, the net capital loss and excess book depreciation must be added back, and tax-exempt interest income must be subtracted. Answer (B) is incorrect. Federal income taxes are not subtracted; they are added back to book net income. Answer (D) is incorrect. The tax-exempt interest is not added back; it is subtracted from book net income.

16.12.18. In the current year, Acorn, Inc., had the following items of income and expense:

Sales	$500,000
Cost of sales	250,000
Dividends received	25,000

The dividends were received from a corporation of which Acorn owns 30%. In Acorn's current-year income tax return, what amount should be reported as income before special deductions?

A. $525,000

B. $505,000

C. $275,000

D. $250,000

Answer (C) is correct. *(CPA, adapted)*
   REQUIRED: The income before special deductions.
   DISCUSSION: Income before special deductions accounts for all items except for NOL carrybacks, capital loss carrybacks, and dividends-received deduction. Thus, income before special deductions is $275,000 ($500,000 + $25,000 – $250,000).
   Answer (A) is incorrect. The amount of $525,000 fails to deduct the cost of sales. Answer (B) is incorrect. The amount of $505,000 incorrectly takes the dividends-received deduction, and it fails to deduct cost of sales. Answer (D) is incorrect. The amount of $250,000 fails to include the dividends received as income.

16.12.19. In the current year, Sting Corporation had net income per books of $65,000, tax-exempt interest of $1,500, excess contributions of $3,000, excess tax depreciation over book depreciation of $4,500, premiums paid on term life insurance on corporate officers of $10,000 (Sting is the beneficiary), and accrued federal income tax of $9,700. Based on this information, what is Sting Corporation's taxable income as would be shown on Schedule M-1 of its corporate tax return?

A. $58,700

B. $61,700

C. $81,700

D. $93,700

Answer (C) is correct. *(SEE, adapted)*
REQUIRED: The taxable income for Sting Corporation.
DISCUSSION: Schedule M-1 reconciles income or loss per books with income or loss per tax return.

Net income per books	$65,000
Add back:	
Federal income taxes	9,700
Excess contributions	3,000
Life insurance premiums	10,000
	$87,700
Subtract:	
Tax-exempt interest	(1,500)
Excess depreciation	(4,500)
Taxable income	$81,700

Answer (A) is incorrect. Tax-exempt interest income and excess tax depreciation are not subtracted; they are added back to taxable income. Answer (B) is incorrect. Federal income taxes must also be subtracted from taxable income. Answer (D) is incorrect. Tax-exempt interest income and excess tax depreciation are added to, not subtracted from, taxable income. Federal income taxes and the net capital loss are subtracted from, not added to, taxable income.

16.12.20. Barbaro Corporation's retained earnings balance at January 1 of the current year was $600,000. During the year, Barbaro paid cash dividends of $150,000 and received a federal income tax refund of $26,000 (which was not included in book income) as a result of an IRS audit of Barbaro's tax return from 3 years ago. Barbaro's net income per books for the current year ended December 31 was $274,900 after deducting federal income tax of $133,300. How much should be shown in the reconciliation Schedule M-2 of Form 1120 as Barbaro's retained earnings at December 31?

A. $600,900

B. $724,900

C. $750,900

D. $900,900

Answer (C) is correct. *(CPA, adapted)*
REQUIRED: The amount of unappropriated retained earnings on Schedule M-2 of Form 1120.
DISCUSSION: Schedule M-2 in the corporation's tax return is used to compute unappropriated retained earnings, which equals the balance at the beginning of the year plus book net income less distributions of cash, stock, or property. Other adjustments may be made as necessary. The federal income tax refund requires a positive adjustment. The balance of retained earnings at year end is

Balance, January 1	$600,000
Plus: Net income for year	274,900
Federal income tax refund	26,000
Less: Cash dividends	(150,000)
Balance, December 31	$750,900

Answer (A) is incorrect. The cash dividends were subtracted from net income for the year and from the beginning retained earnings balance. Answer (B) is incorrect. The federal income tax refund was not added to the beginning retained earnings balance. Answer (D) is incorrect. The cash dividends must be subtracted from the beginning retained earnings balance.

16.12.21. Dantor Corporation, a domestic corporation, has $250,000 of taxable income from business conducted solely in the U.S. Dantor also operates two foreign branch offices. The Hamburg branch has $50,000 of taxable income related to business conducted solely in Germany. The Rome branch has $150,000 of taxable income, of which 50% is related to business conducted solely in Italy and 50% is related to business conducted solely in the U.S. Dantor's income subject to taxation in the U.S. is

A. $250,000

B. $325,000

C. $400,000

D. $450,000

Answer (D) is correct. *(CMA, adapted)*
REQUIRED: The amount of income subject to taxation in the U.S.
DISCUSSION: Regulation 1.11-1 states that, as a general rule, a domestic corporation will be taxed on its worldwide income with no distinction between income from sources inside or outside the U.S. Therefore, the entire $450,000 of income earned by Dantor is subject to taxation in the U.S.

Answer (A) is incorrect. Dantor is also taxed on the German and Italian income. Answer (B) is incorrect. Dantor is taxed on all worldwide income, not just the 50% of the Italian income that is due to the U.S. business. Answer (C) is incorrect. Dantor is also taxed on the German income.

16.12.22. Corporation T's records reflect the following information:

Net income per books	$50,000
Federal income tax	8,500
Refund of prior year's income tax	1,000
Contributions carryover from prior year	300
Increase in reserve for contingencies	1,200
Unappropriated retained earnings at beginning of year	40,000
Cash dividends paid	2,000
Stock dividends paid	1,500
Tax-exempt interest	3,500

Based on this information and using generally accepted accounting principles, what is T's unappropriated retained earnings balance at the end of the year?

- A. $74,000
- B. $77,800
- C. $85,300
- D. $86,300

Answer (C) is correct. *(SEE, adapted)*
REQUIRED: The corporation's unappropriated retained earnings balance.
DISCUSSION: A corporation's unappropriated retained earnings balance is computed on Schedule M-2 of Form 1120. The balance at the end of the year is the beginning balance, plus net income per books, less distributions of cash, property, or stock. Other adjustments may be made as necessary. T's unappropriated retained earnings balance is

Beginning balance	$40,000
Add:	
Net income per books	50,000
Less:	
Reserve for contingencies	(1,200)
Cash dividends paid	(2,000)
Stock dividends paid	(1,500)
Unappropriated retained earnings	$85,300

The refund of prior year's income tax is not added back because it was included in this year's book income. The reserve for contingencies is subtracted because it represents an amount that is appropriated. The other items in the facts not used in the answer only represent differences between book and taxable income, which do not affect retained earnings.
Answer (A) is incorrect. Contribution carryovers, tax-exempt interest, and federal income taxes do not reduce unappropriated retained earnings, and the refund on prior year's income tax is not added to unappropriated retained earnings. Answer (B) is incorrect. Federal income taxes do not reduce unappropriated retained earnings, and the refund on prior year's income tax is not added to unappropriated retained earnings. Answer (D) is incorrect. The refund on prior year's income tax is not added to unappropriated retained earnings.

16.12.23. Which one of the following statements about corporate tax rates for the current year is true?

- A. The marginal tax rate is 34% if taxable income is over $50,000 but not over $75,000.
- B. A 5% surtax is charged on taxable income between $100,000 and $335,000, and a 3% surtax is charged on taxable income between $15,000,000 and $18,333,333.
- C. Corporate taxable income is subject to a top marginal tax rate of 39.6%.
- D. The marginal tax rate is 25% on the first $50,000 of taxable income.

Answer (B) is correct. *(Publisher, adapted)*
REQUIRED: The statement that describes the current corporate tax rates.
DISCUSSION: The current corporate tax system under Sec. 11 is based on an eight-bracket graduated rate system as follows:

Taxable Income		Marginal
Is at Least	But Not Over	Tax Rate
$ 0 – $ 50,000		15%
$ 50,000 – 75,000		25%
75,000 – 100,000		34%
100,000 – 335,000		39%
335,000 – 10,000,000		34%
10,000,000 – 15,000,000		35%
15,000,000 – 18,333,333		38%
18,333,333		35%

Two rate brackets include surtaxes. A surtax of 5% is charged on income between $100,000 and $335,000, which eliminates the tax savings on the first $100,000 of taxable income. A 3% surtax is charged on income between $15,000,000 and $18,333,333, which recaptures the $100,000 tax savings from $335,000 to $10,000,000.
Answer (A) is incorrect. The marginal tax rate is 25% if taxable income is between $50,000 and $75,000. Answer (C) is incorrect. The highest marginal tax rate for corporations is 39% (i.e., if taxable income is between $100,000 and $335,000). Answer (D) is incorrect. The marginal tax rate is 15% on the first $50,000 of taxable income.

16.12.24. If a corporation issues a shareholder or an employee a below-market loan, the corporation will have to report additional income.

A. True.

B. False.

Answer (A) is correct. *(SEE, adapted)*
DISCUSSION: Under Sec. 7872(a)(1), the forgone interest on any below-market loan is treated as a transfer from the lender to the borrower and as a retransfer by the borrower to the lender as interest. Thus, the corporation, not the employee, will have to report the additional income.

16.13 Alternative Minimum Tax

16.13.1. The corporate alternative minimum tax for taxable years is

A. The excess of (1) a tentative minimum tax of 20% of alternative minimum taxable income reduced by an exemption amount over (2) the regular tax.

B. 20% of alternative minimum taxable income reduced by an exemption amount.

C. 20% of taxable income adjusted for tax preferences.

D. 15% of the excess of (1) the sum of tax preferences over (2) the greater of $10,000 or the regular tax.

Answer (A) is correct. *(Publisher, adapted)*
REQUIRED: The calculation of the alternative minimum tax for corporations.
DISCUSSION: The alternative minimum tax is imposed by Sec. 55 for both individuals and corporations. The term "alternative" is a misnomer because the tax as defined by Sec. 55 is imposed only to the extent that it exceeds the regular tax. It is really an add-on tax. The tax is a tentative tax of 20% of the excess of alternative minimum taxable income over an exemption amount, reduced by the regular tax.
Answer (B) is incorrect. The amount computed increases the tax liability only to the extent it exceeds the regular tax. Answer (C) is incorrect. It does not take into account adjustments to taxable income other than tax preferences or the exemption amount. Answer (D) is incorrect. It describes the corporate minimum tax in effect before 1987.

16.13.2. If a corporation's tentative minimum tax exceeds the regular tax, the excess amount is

A. Carried back to the first preceding taxable year.

B. Carried back to the third preceding taxable year.

C. Payable in addition to the regular tax.

D. Subtracted from the regular tax.

Answer (C) is correct. *(CPA, adapted)*
REQUIRED: The correct application of the alternative minimum tax.
DISCUSSION: Section 55(a) provides that the excess of the tentative minimum tax over the regular tax is payable in addition to the regular tax. This excess is called the alternative minimum tax and is due on the same date as the regular tax.
Answer (A) is incorrect. Carrybacks are used for NOLs and capital losses. Answer (B) is incorrect. Carrybacks are not used when a corporation's tentative minimum tax exceeds the regular tax. Answer (D) is incorrect. A corporation's tax payable is the amount of its tentative minimum tax minus the regular tax amount.

16.13.3. For property placed in service after 1999, which of the following is a true statement of the depreciation adjustment required to compute alternative minimum taxable income?

A. The alternative depreciation system of Sec. 168(g) is used in its entirety.

B. The alternative depreciation system of Sec. 168(g) is used with the 150%-declining-balance method (switching to straight-line when larger) for personal property.

C. There is no adjustment for depreciation on real property.

D. It is the same as for property placed in service prior to 1987.

Answer (B) is correct. *(Publisher, adapted)*
REQUIRED: The true statement concerning the adjustment for depreciation on property placed in service after 1986.
DISCUSSION: The deduction allowed for depreciation of any tangible property (personal and real) placed in service after 1986 is generally determined under the alternative depreciation system of Sec. 168(g). However, for personal property, the 150%-declining-balance method is used and switches to a straight-line method in the first year the straight-line method yields a larger deduction. For nonresidential real and residential rental property, the straight-line method is used over a 40-year recovery period [Sec. 56(a)(1)]. However, for Sec. 1250 property placed in service after 1999, the adjustment is based on the property's regular MACRS recovery period, which eliminates the adjustment.
Answer (A) is incorrect. The 150%-declining-balance method is used for personal property. Answer (C) is incorrect. Real property must generally be depreciated over 40 years for alternative minimum taxable income purposes instead of the shorter 27.5- to 39-year recovery period that is used for regular tax purposes. For Sec. 1250 property placed in service after 1999, however, the adjustment is based on the property's regular MACRS recovery period, which eliminates the adjustment. Answer (D) is incorrect. For property placed in service prior to 1987, accelerated depreciation over straight-line is a tax preference item. This generally only applies to real property.

16.13.4. Alternative minimum taxable income is

A. Taxable income increased by tax preferences and increased or decreased by adjustments and other statutory modifications.

B. The sum of all tax preferences.

C. Computed the same for individuals and corporations.

D. Taxable income adjusted by tax preferences and reduced by an exemption amount.

Answer (A) is correct. *(SEE, adapted)*
REQUIRED: The definition of alternative minimum taxable income.
DISCUSSION: Taxable income is adjusted by positive and negative adjustments and various other statutory items to arrive at alternative minimum taxable income. There are numerous adjustments to items taken into account in determining taxable income as well as some additional adjustments. Tax preference items are also added to taxable income to arrive at alternative minimum taxable income.
Answer (B) is incorrect. The sum of all tax preferences is only one adjustment to taxable income to arrive at alternative minimum taxable income. Answer (C) is incorrect. Some of the adjustments differ for individuals and corporations, although many are the same. Answer (D) is incorrect. The exemption amount is subtracted from alternative minimum taxable income to arrive at a tax base before the tax rate is applied.

16.13.5. Rona Corp.'s current-year alternative minimum taxable income was $200,000. Assuming that Rona is not a small corporation, the exempt portion of Rona's alternative minimum taxable income was

A. $0

B. $12,500

C. $27,500

D. $52,500

Answer (C) is correct. *(CPA, adapted)*
REQUIRED: The corporation's exemption amount for the alternative minimum tax.
DISCUSSION: Under Sec. 55(d), the basic exemption amount for corporations is $40,000. However, this is reduced by 25% of the excess of alternative minimum taxable income over $150,000. Therefore, Rona's exemption amount is $27,500 [$40,000 − 25% × ($200,000 − $150,000)].
Answer (A) is incorrect. The exemption is not completely phased out until the alternative minimum taxable income reaches $310,000. Answer (B) is incorrect. The amount by which the exemption is reduced is $12,500. Answer (D) is incorrect. The amount of $52,500 incorrectly adds the phased-out portion of the exemption to the $40,000 exemption.

16.13.6. Which of the following is a false statement regarding the adjusted current earnings adjustment to alternative minimum taxable income?

A. It is an increase by 75% of the excess of adjusted current earnings over alternative minimum taxable income (excluding the adjusted current earnings adjustment and the alternative minimum tax NOL deduction).

B. It is a decrease by 75% of the excess of alternative minimum taxable income (excluding the adjusted current earnings adjustment and the alternative minimum tax NOL deduction) over adjusted current earnings.

C. It applies to personal holding companies.

D. The negative adjusted current earnings adjustment can be made without limitation.

Answer (D) is correct. *(Publisher, adapted)*
REQUIRED: The false statement concerning the adjusted current earnings adjustment to alternative minimum taxable income.
DISCUSSION: The adjusted current earnings adjustment applies only for taxable years beginning after 1989. The negative adjustment is limited to 75% of the excess of AMTI over ACE. Additionally, the negative adjustment may not exceed cumulative prior-year positive and negative adjustments. This adjustment may not be carried forward.
Answer (A) is incorrect. The adjusted current earnings adjustment to alternative minimum taxable income is an increase by 75% of the excess of adjusted current earnings over alternative minimum taxable income (excluding the adjusted current earnings adjustment and the alternative minimum tax NOL deduction). Answer (B) is incorrect. The adjusted current earnings adjustment to alternative minimum taxable income is a decrease by 75% of the excess of alternative minimum taxable income (excluding the adjusted current earnings adjustment and the alternative minimum tax NOL deduction) over adjusted current earnings. Answer (C) is incorrect. The adjusted current earnings adjustment to alternative minimum taxable income applies to personal holding companies.

16.13.7. Which of the following is not an adjustment to taxable income in order to compute alternative minimum taxable income?

A. The percentage-of-completion method must be used for long-term contracts.

B. The alternative tax net operating loss is used instead of the regular tax net operating loss deduction.

C. The installment method is not allowed for sales of inventory and items held for sale to customers by dealers.

D. The bad debt deduction is reduced by the excess of the reserve method over actual write-offs.

Answer (D) is correct. *(Publisher, adapted)*
REQUIRED: The item that is not an adjustment in computing alternative minimum taxable income.
DISCUSSION: Since the reserve method is not allowed for bad debts, there is no adjustment related to bad debts in computing alternative minimum taxable income.
Answer (A) is incorrect. It is a required adjustment in computing alternative minimum taxable income as provided by Sec. 56(a)(3). Answer (B) is incorrect. It is a required adjustment in computing alternative minimum taxable income as provided by Sec. 56(a)(4). Answer (C) is incorrect. It is a required adjustment in computing alternative minimum taxable income as provided by Sec. 56(a)(6).

16.13.8. Which one of the following is a tax preference item in figuring a corporation's alternative minimum taxable income?

A. Excess intangible drilling costs on an oil and gas property accruing to an independent producer.

B. Excess percentage depletion on an oil and gas property accruing to an independent producer.

C. Net operating losses.

D. Tax-exempt interest from private activity bonds.

Answer (D) is correct. *(SEE, adapted)*
REQUIRED: The item that is a tax preference item for purposes of calculating the alternative minimum tax.
DISCUSSION: Tax-exempt interest from private activity bonds issued after August 7, 1986, is a tax preference item. Other forms of tax-exempt interest may be an adjustment to alternative minimum taxable income under the ACE rules.
Answer (A) is incorrect. Excess intangible drilling costs on an oil and gas property accruing to an independent producer is no longer a tax preference item after 1993. Answer (B) is incorrect. Excess percentage depletion on an oil and gas property accruing to an independent producer is no longer a tax preference item after 1993. Answer (C) is incorrect. Net operating losses are an adjustment for alternative minimum tax purposes. The alternative tax net operating loss deduction is used to calculate alternative minimum taxable income.

16.13.9. January Corporation was liable for alternative minimum tax for tax year 2014 of $85,000. For tax year 2015, it had a total tax liability of $80,000, including $75,000 tentative minimum tax. For tax years 2016 and 2017, it had losses and no tentative minimum tax nor regular corporate tax liability. The tax year 2018 tax liability is undetermined. January Corporation is not exempt from alternative minimum tax. Which of the following is correct regarding the prior-year alternative minimum tax credit?

A. 2015: Use AMT credit of $5,000; carry over $80,000 to 2016 (unused); carry over $80,000 to 2017 (unused); carry over $0 to 2018 (carryover period expired).

B. 2015: Use AMT credit of $80,000; carry over $5,000 to 2016 (unused); carry over $5,000 to 2017 (unused); carry over $5,000 to 2018 (available).

C. 2015: Use AMT credit of $75,000; carry over $10,000 to 2016 (unused); carry over $10,000 to 2017 (unused); carry over $10,000 to 2018 (available).

D. 2015: Use AMT credit of $5,000; carry over $80,000 to 2016 (unused); carry over $80,000 to 2017 (unused); carry over $80,000 to 2018 (available).

Answer (D) is correct. *(SEE, adapted)*
REQUIRED: The prior-year alternative minimum tax credit of a corporation.
DISCUSSION: Corporations are allowed a credit for the full amount of AMT paid in a tax year against regular tax liability in one or more subsequent tax years. Any minimum tax credit amount is carried forward indefinitely.
Answer (A) is incorrect. The minimum tax credit amount is carried forward indefinitely. Answer (B) is incorrect. January Corporation cannot use an AMT credit of $80,000 in 2015. Answer (C) is incorrect. The credit amount in 2015 cannot exceed the regular tax liability.

16.13.10. Tiger Corporation reports adjusted current earnings (ACE) of $600,000 for the current year. Its alternative minimum taxable income (excluding the alternative tax NOL deduction and the ACE adjustment) is $250,000. The company is not a small corporation under the AMT rules. Its alternative minimum taxable income for the year is

A. $250,000

B. $375,000

C. $512,500

D. $600,000

Answer (C) is correct. *(Publisher, adapted)*

REQUIRED: The correct alternative minimum taxable income for the current year.

DISCUSSION: After 1989, the adjusted current earnings of corporations are treated as an adjustment. Section 56(g) states that the alternative minimum taxable income of a corporation must be increased by 75% of the amount by which the adjusted current earnings exceed the alternative minimum taxable income (determined without regard to the adjusted current earnings and the alternative tax net operating loss deduction). Therefore, Tiger Corporation's alternative minimum taxable income for the year is $512,500 [$250,000 + 75% × ($600,000 – $250,000)].

Answer (A) is incorrect. The amount of $250,000 is the alternative minimum taxable income excluding the ACE adjustment. Answer (B) is incorrect. The ACE adjustment is $262,500, which is added to the $250,000 preadjustment AMTI. Answer (D) is incorrect. The amount of $600,000 is the ACE.

16.13.11. Bear Corporation, which was organized in Year 1, reports the following adjusted current earnings (ACE) and alternative minimum taxable income (AMTI) amounts (excluding the ACE adjustment and alternative tax NOL deduction) for the period Year 1 through Year 3.

	Year 1	Year 2	Year 3
ACE	$200	$200	$200
AMTI	100	200	400

What is Bear Corporation's ACE adjustment for Year 3?

A. $75

B. $(75)

C. $150

D. $(150)

Answer (B) is correct. *(Publisher, adapted)*

REQUIRED: The ACE adjustment for Year 3.

DISCUSSION: Section 56(g) provides that the ACE adjustment shall be 75% of the difference between ACE and AMTI (excluding the ACE adjustment and the alternative tax NOL deduction). However, in a tax year in which AMTI exceeds ACE, the negative adjustment is limited to the aggregate positive adjustments for prior years over the aggregate negative adjustments for prior years. Bear's AMTI exceeds its ACE by $200 in Year 3, 75% of which equals $150. However, this negative adjustment amount is limited to the $75 positive adjustment made in Year 1 [($200 ACE – $100 AMTI) × 75% = $75].

Answer (A) is incorrect. A negative adjustment is required since AMTI exceeds ACE. Answer (C) is incorrect. The correct amount of Bear Corporation's ACE adjustment for Year 3 is not $150. Answer (D) is incorrect. The negative ACE adjustment is limited to the positive adjustment made in Year 1.

16.13.12. Which one of the following items properly reported by the corporation in determining alternative minimum taxable income is not adjusted in order to determine adjusted current earnings?

A. Life insurance policy proceeds received by the corporation on the death of a corporate officer.

B. Organizational expenditures that were amortized under Sec. 248.

C. Tax-exempt interest from a local government bond that is not a private activity bond.

D. Long-term capital gains.

Answer (D) is correct. *(Publisher, adapted)*

REQUIRED: The item not adjusted in order to determine adjusted current earnings.

DISCUSSION: Section 56(g) lists adjustments that apply in determining adjusted current earnings. These adjustments include life insurance proceeds received by the corporation on the death of a corporate officer, organizational expenditures that were amortized under Sec. 248, and tax-exempt interest from a local government bond that is not a private activity bond. Long-term capital gains are not included as an adjustment in determining adjusted current earnings. If the interest were earned from a private activity bond, it would be included in alternative minimum taxable income as a tax preference item and no adjustment would be needed.

Answer (A) is incorrect. Life insurance policy proceeds received by the corporation on the death of a corporate officer is an item that is adjusted in order to determine ACE. Answer (B) is incorrect. Organizational expenditures that were amortized under Sec. 248 is an item that is adjusted in order to determine ACE. Answer (C) is incorrect. Tax-exempt interest from a local government bond that is not a private activity bond is an item that is adjusted in order to determine ACE.

16.13.13. Corporation X had $100,000 of taxable income in the current year on which its regular tax is $22,250. Depreciation on machinery placed in service after 1986 and before January 1 of the current year amounted to $100,000 (it would be $70,000 using the 150%-declining-balance method of the alternative depreciation system). Depreciation on real estate placed in service in 1986 amounted to $15,000 (it would be $10,000 using the straight-line method). Charitable contributions for the current year were $10,000, consisting of T Corporation stock with a basis of $3,000. The full $10,000 was deducted in determining taxable income. Adjusted current earnings amounted to $182,000. The current-year alternative minimum tax (AMT) for Corporation X is

A. $0

B. $4,813

C. $5,250

D. $11,800

Answer (B) is correct. *(Publisher, adapted)*
REQUIRED: The alternative minimum tax for a corporation.
DISCUSSION: Section 55 imposes an alternative minimum tax on corporations. First, a tentative minimum tax of 20% is computed on the excess of the alternative minimum taxable income (AMTI) over an exemption amount. The alternative minimum tax is the excess of the tentative minimum tax over the regular tax. Depreciation on personal property placed in service after 1986 is computed using 150%-declining-balance method. Depreciation on real property placed in service prior to 1987 is generally depreciated using the straight-line method. For property placed in service after 1999, however, the adjustment on Sec. 1250 property is eliminated. The untaxed appreciation allowed as a regular tax deduction for charitable contributions is no longer added back as a tax preference item for contributions made after December 31, 1993. Alternative minimum taxable income must also be increased by 75% of the amount by which the adjusted current earnings exceeds the alternative minimum taxable income.

Regular taxable income		$100,000
Adjustments for AMTI:		
Depreciation on equipment		
($100,000 – $70,000)		30,000
Tax preference items:		
Excess depreciation on real estate		5,000
Tentative AMTI		$135,000
Adjusted current earnings	$ 182,000	
Tentative AMTI	(135,000)	
ACE/AMTI tax difference	$ 47,000	
Times: Percentage	× .75	
ACE/AMTI adjustment		$ 35,250
AMTI		$170,250
Less: exemption*		(34,937)
AMT tax base		$135,313
Times: AMT rate		× .20
Tentative minimum tax		$ 27,063
Less: regular tax		(22,250)
AMT		$ 4,813

*The exemption amount is reduced as follows:

Base exemption		$ 40,000
Less: Excess of AMTI	$170,250	
over $150,000	(150,000)	
	$ 20,250	
Times: Percentage	× .25	$ 5,063
Exemption		$ 34,937

Answer (A) is incorrect. There is an AMT. Answer (C) is incorrect. The charitable contribution tax preference item only applies to contributions of capital gain property made before January 1 of the current year. Answer (D) is incorrect. The calculation fails to take into account the $34,938 exemption that reduces AMTI.

16.13.14. Zak Corporation has an alternative minimum tax credit available as a result of alternative minimum tax paid for the current year. Which of the following is true regarding how the minimum tax credit may be carried?

A. Carry back 5 years, then forward 5 years.

B. Carry back 5 years, then forward 20 years.

C. Carry forward 20 years.

D. Carry forward indefinitely.

Answer (D) is correct. *(SEE, adapted)*
REQUIRED: The true statement regarding the minimum tax credit.
DISCUSSION: Under Sec. 53, the minimum tax credit can be carried forward indefinitely. It may be used to offset regular tax liabilities in future years to the extent the regular tax liability exceeds the corporation's tentative minimum tax in the carryforward year.
Answer (A) is incorrect. This applies to capital losses. Answer (B) is incorrect. This applies to NOLs. Answer (C) is incorrect. This applies to NOLs if the election is made to relinquish the carryback period.

16.13.15. Which of the following statements is false concerning the calculation of adjusted current earnings (ACE)?

A. The starting point for the ACE calculation is the taxpayer corporation's alternative minimum taxable income (excluding the ACE adjustment and the alternative minimum tax NOL deduction).

B. Build-ups in life insurance contracts are included in ACE.

C. Amortization of organizational expenditures is not deductible when determining ACE.

D. The excess of depreciation claimed on property placed in service after December 31, 1994, for alternative minimum taxable income purposes over the depreciation claimed for adjusted current earnings purposes is added back to preadjustment AMTI to arrive at ACE.

16.13.16. What is the alternative minimum tax for a corporation whose tax return reflects the following?

Alternative minimum taxable income	$107,500
Foreign tax credits	1,375
Regular tax	6,890

A. $5,235

B. $6,610

C. $12,125

D. $13,500

16.13.17. A corporation is permitted to claim the entire amount of the excess of its tentative minimum tax liability over its regular tax liability as a minimum tax credit.

A. True.

B. False.

Answer (D) is correct. *(Publisher, adapted)*
REQUIRED: The false statement concerning the calculation of adjusted current earnings.
DISCUSSION: The adjusted current earnings (ACE) adjustment for depreciation has been repealed for property placed in service after December 31, 1994. The same depreciation is now used for ACE and alternative minimum taxable income purposes.
Answer (A) is incorrect. The starting point for the ACE calculation is the taxpayer corporation's alternative minimum taxable income (excluding the ACE adjustment and the alternative minimum tax NOL deduction). Answer (B) is incorrect. Build-ups in life insurance contracts are included in the calculation of adjusted current earnings. Answer (C) is incorrect. Amortization of organizational expenditures is not deductible when determining ACE.

Answer (A) is correct. *(SEE, adapted)*
REQUIRED: The corporation's alternative minimum tax.
DISCUSSION: Section 55 imposes a minimum tax on corporations. First, a tentative tax of 20% is computed on the excess of the alternative minimum taxable income over an exemption amount. The exemption amount is $40,000, provided the alternative minimum taxable income does not exceed $150,000. The minimum tax is the excess of this tentative minimum tax over the regular tax.
The corporation's alternative minimum taxable income of $107,500 is reduced by the exemption amount of $40,000. The tentative minimum tax before foreign tax credits is $13,500 ($67,500 × 20%). The minimum tax is $5,235.

Tentative minimum tax	$13,500
Less: foreign tax credit	(1,375)
Tentative minimum tax	$12,125
Less: regular tax	(6,890)
Alternative minimum tax	$ 5,235

The alternative minimum tax can be reduced by a foreign tax credit, which is limited to 90% of the tentative minimum tax. This limit does not restrict the ability to claim the foreign tax credit.
Answer (B) is incorrect. The amount of $6,610 is the tentative minimum tax. Answer (C) is incorrect. The amount of $12,125 is the alternative minimum taxable income less the foreign tax credits. Answer (D) is incorrect. The amount of $13,500 is the tentative tax.

Answer (A) is correct. *(Publisher, adapted)*
DISCUSSION: A corporation that pays an alternative minimum tax liability in one year may use the tax as a credit in later years to offset the regular tax liability in the carryover year. The maximum minimum tax credit that can be used in the carryover year equals the regular tax liability minus all available tax credits against such tax over the tentative minimum tax for the year.
The credit is now available for deferral and exclusion adjustments and preferences. Previously, the credit was only available for deferral items. The corporation minimum tax credit rules are different from those applying to individual taxpayers [Sec. 53(d)(1)(B)(iv)].

16.13.18. For tax years beginning after 1998, the alternative minimum tax does not apply to small corporations with gross profits of not more than $5 million.

A. True.

B. False.

Answer (B) is correct. *(SEE, adapted)*
  DISCUSSION: Corporations having an average of $5 million or less in annual gross receipts (not gross profits) for the previous 3-year period are exempt from the AMT. Once a corporation is recognized as a small corporation, it will continue to be exempt from the AMT for as long as its average gross receipts for the prior 3-year period do not exceed $7.5 million. Corporations not in existence for the entire 3-year period will apply the $5 million test for the period during which they are in existence.

16.13.19. Dividends-received deductions are not allowed in determining adjusted current earnings.

A. True.

B. False.

Answer (B) is correct. *(Publisher, adapted)*
  DISCUSSION: The 100% and 80% dividends-received deductions are permitted in determining the adjusted current earnings adjustment. However, the 70% dividends-received deduction is not permitted.

16.13.20. A corporation may have to pay the alternative minimum tax if taxable income for regular income tax purposes, when combined with certain adjustments and preference items that apply in computing the alternative minimum tax, totals more than $40,000.

A. True.

B. False.

Answer (A) is correct. *(SEE, adapted)*
  DISCUSSION: Under Sec. 55, the alternative minimum tax must be considered if taxable income plus tax preferences and adjustments exceeds the $40,000 exemption. The corporation must pay the alternative minimum tax if the tentative minimum tax exceeds its regular tax.
  Note: The 1998 tax act provides that small corporations are exempt from the AMT. To qualify as a small corporation, a corporation must have average gross receipts of $5,000,000 or less for the 3 tax years that ended with the first tax year beginning after December 31, 1997.

16.13.21. Corporation X carries its net operating loss for the current year back to the second preceding year for which X incurred an alternative minimum tax liability. Corporation X must recompute its alternative minimum tax liability for the second preceding year.

A. True.

B. False.

Answer (A) is correct. *(SEE, adapted)*
  DISCUSSION: When the taxable income of a corporation is adjusted in any tax year, the alternative minimum tax must be recomputed as well as the regular tax.

16.14 Return Filing and Payment Requirements

16.14.1. Under which of the following circumstances would a corporation be required to file a federal income tax return?

A. The corporation has disposed of all of its assets except for a small sum of cash retained to pay state taxes to preserve its corporate charter.

B. A corporation with no assets stops doing business and dissolves and is treated as a corporation under state law for limited purposes connected with winding up its affairs.

C. The corporation has dissolved and is in bankruptcy.

D. Last year, Corporation M ceased doing business and disposed of all of its assets. However, during all of the current year, M was in the process of suing Corporation B.

Answer (A) is correct. *(SEE, adapted)*
  REQUIRED: The corporation that is required to file a federal income tax return.
  DISCUSSION: Section 6012(a)(2) requires every corporation subject to taxation under subtitle A of the Code to file a federal income tax return.
  Answer (B) is incorrect. A corporation with no assets that stops doing business and dissolves and is treated as a corporation under state law for limited purposes connected with winding up its affairs does not have to file a federal income tax return. Answer (C) is incorrect. A corporation that has dissolved and is in bankruptcy does not have to file a federal income tax return. Answer (D) is incorrect. Corporation M has ceased business and dissolved; therefore, it does not have to file a federal income tax return.

16.14.2. ABC Corporation, a C corporation, ends its tax year on October 30. When must ABC's income tax return be filed for the year ending October 30, Year 1?

A. February 15, Year 2.

B. April 15, Year 2.

C. January 15, Year 2.

D. March 15, Year 2.

Answer (A) is correct. *(SEE, adapted)*
REQUIRED: The proper income tax return due date for a fiscal-year corporation.
DISCUSSION: Section 6072(b) provides that a C corporation must file its return on or before the 15th day of the fourth month following the close of the tax year. For a fiscal-year corporation with a year-end of 10/30/Yr 1, the return must be filed by 2/15/Yr 2.

16.14.3. Martin, a C corporation's bookkeeper, told the owner that she could not have all the tax information ready for the accountant immediately after the tax year end of June 30. She was having surgery and asked if the tax return could be postponed. The accountant's answer should be:

A. No, the return must be filed by September 15.

B. Yes, we can request an extension until October 15.

C. Yes, we can request an extension until the following April 15.

D. No, the return must be filed by October 15.

Answer (C) is correct. *(SEE, adapted)*
REQUIRED: The allowable extension for a corporation to file its income tax return.
DISCUSSION: Regulation 1.6081-3(a) allows a C corporation with a June 30 fiscal year end an automatic extension of 7 months for filing its income tax return if the corporation files the appropriate form (7004) and pays its estimated unpaid tax liability on or before the due date of the return. The IRS may revoke the extension at any time. Martin's tax return is normally due by September 15 but will be due April 15 after the extension.
Answer (A) is incorrect. An extension can be requested. Answer (B) is incorrect. The extension is for 7 months. Answer (D) is incorrect. An automatic extension of 7 months can be requested.

16.14.4. In each of the following situations, a Form 7004, *Application for Automatic Extension of Time to File Certain Business Income Tax, Information, and Other Returns*, was properly and timely filed for a C corporation. Which one of the following tax returns was filed late?

	Tax Year Ended	Date Filed
A.	November 30, Year 1	September 15, Year 2
B.	August 31, Year 1	June 2, Year 2
C.	July 31, Year 1	May 30, Year 2
D.	December 31, Year 1	September 15, Year 2

Answer (C) is correct. *(SEE, adapted)*
REQUIRED: The 1120 return that is filed later than required by the Code.
DISCUSSION: Section 6072(b) requires calendar-year C corporate taxpayers to file a return by April 15 of the following year. Fiscal-year corporate taxpayers must file by the 15th day of the fourth month following the close of the fiscal year. Under Sec. 6081(a), in a timely filing of Form 7004, the corporation will receive an automatic 6-month extension for filing the tax return. If a corporation's tax year ended on July 31, Year 1, and a timely extension was filed, the return is due on May 15, Year 2.
Answer (A) is incorrect. The return is due on September 15, Year 2. Answer (B) is incorrect. The return is due on June 15, Year 2. Answer (D) is incorrect. The return is due on September 15, Year 2.

16.14.5. P Corporation, a C corporation, filed a federal tax return and appropriately paid $1,150,000 for its federal tax liability incurred in Year 1, which was a full 12-month calendar-year tax year. Early in Year 2, P estimated its Year 2 tax liability and paid a total of $1.2 million in equal installments on appropriate due dates. On February 12, Year 3, the corporation's Year 2 return was completed. The return indicated an actual liability of $1.3 million. The corporation desires to defer the payment of the balance of tax due as long as possible, while paying the least amount. What are the amount and the due date(s) in Year 3 of the corporation's minimum obligation (not considering weekends and holidays)?

A. $50,000 on April 15 and September 15.

B. $50,000 on April 15 and June 15.

C. $100,000 on April 15.

D. $100,000 on September 15.

Answer (C) is correct. *(SEE, adapted)*
REQUIRED: The amount and due date(s) of a corporation's smallest tax payment(s).
DISCUSSION: A C corporation's entire tax liability is due on the same date as the return. Under Sec. 6072(b), a calendar-year C corporation must file its income tax return on or before the 15th day of April following the close of the calendar year. P Corporation must therefore pay $100,000 of tax on April 15. An extension of time to file the tax return does not provide an extension of time to pay the tax liability without incurring interest and/or penalty.
Answer (A) is incorrect. The $50,000 payment may not be extended to September 15. Answer (B) is incorrect. The $50,000 payment may not be extended to June 15. Answer (D) is incorrect. The corporation must file its tax return on or before the 15th day of April following the close of the calendar year.

16.14.6. A calendar-year S corporation filed its Year 1 return on April 30, Year 2, without securing an extension of time to file. It could not show reasonable cause. If the tax due was $5,000 and no payments had been made prior to filing, the failure to file and failure to pay penalties would equal

A. $250

B. $500

C. $750

D. $1,000

Answer (B) is correct. *(SEE, adapted)*
REQUIRED: The delinquency penalty for failure to file a return and pay taxes by the due date.

DISCUSSION: A delinquency penalty is imposed by Sec. 6651(a) for failure to file a tax return or to pay tax. The penalty for failure to file is 5% of the amount of unpaid tax for each month or fraction of a month that the failure to file a return continues. The penalty for failure to pay is 0.5% of the amount of unpaid tax for each month or fraction of a month that the failure to pay continues. If the taxpayer fails to file the tax return and to pay the tax, the 5% failure to file penalty is reduced by the 0.5% failure to pay penalty. The corporation's combined delinquency penalty for failure to file its return and pay its taxes is

Tax due	$5,000
Total penalty percentage	× .05
Monthly penalty	$ 250
Months outstanding	× 2
Failure to file and failure to pay penalty	$ 500

If calculated separately, the failure to pay penalty is $50 ($5,000 × .005 × 2 months), and the failure to file penalty is $450 [($5,000 × .05 × 2) − $50].
Answer (A) is incorrect. The monthly penalty is $250. Answer (C) is incorrect. The penalty is not assessed for 3 months. Answer (D) is incorrect. The penalty is not assessed for 4 months.

16.14.7. The results of an examination of PKP Corporation's tax return from 3 years ago in the current year reflected an additional tax liability of $10,000, which was caused by the negligent actions of the corporate officers. Excluding interest on the underpayment, PKP owes the IRS

A. $10,000

B. $10,500

C. $11,000

D. $12,000

Answer (D) is correct. *(M. Yates)*
REQUIRED: The penalty for underpayment of tax due to negligence.

DISCUSSION: Section 6662(b)(1) provides that an accuracy-related penalty shall be assessed against any underpayment of tax liability that is attributable to negligence or intentional disregard of rules and regulations. The amount of the penalty is 20% of the underpayment that is attributable to the negligent item(s), determined as follows:

Additional tax liability	$10,000
Times: Penalty rate	× .20
Negligence penalty	$ 2,000
Additional tax liability	$10,000
Negligence penalty	2,000
Total owed the IRS	$12,000

In addition to these two amounts that are owed, PKP will also owe interest on the unpaid tax liability.
Answer (A) is incorrect. A 20% penalty will also be due. Answer (B) is incorrect. The penalty is not 5%. Answer (C) is incorrect. The penalty is not 10%.

16.14.8. Corporation Z, a calendar-year taxpayer, submitted a timely application for automatic extension of time for filing its Year 1 federal income tax return. At the time of filing the application, Z determined its tax liability to be $20,000. During Year 1, Z had made estimated tax payments totaling $10,000. On August 15, Year 2, Z filed its return and paid the balance due of $10,000. Z is not subject to the failure to pay penalty.

A. True.

B. False.

Answer (B) is correct. *(SEE, adapted)*
DISCUSSION: Section 6151(a) requires the tax to be paid when the return is due. Section 6651 imposes a penalty of 0.5% per month (or part of a month) for failure to pay tax when due.

16.14.9. Interest is charged by the IRS at the applicable annual rate on the difference between the tentative tax reported on a request for extension of time for filing and the actual tax a corporation must pay when it files its Form 1120.

A. True.

B. False.

Answer (A) is correct. *(SEE, adapted)*
   DISCUSSION: Under Sec. 6601(a), interest is imposed on the underpayment of tax. Interest is charged on the difference between the tentative tax and the actual tax a corporation must pay when filing its Form 1120. The tentative tax must be timely paid to obtain the extension. The underpayment is the additional actual tax.

16.14.10. Corporation D, a U.S. corporation, made payments to a nonresident alien individual. Corporation D is required to file Form 1042, *Annual Withholding Tax Return for U.S. Source Income of Foreign Persons*, even though no income tax was withheld and deducted because of a specific exemption.

A. True.

B. False.

Answer (A) is correct. *(SEE, adapted)*
   DISCUSSION: Every withholding agent is required to file an annual return, Form 1042, of the tax required to be withheld on payments made to nonresident aliens and foreign corporations. This form, which is due on or before March 15, must be filed even though no tax was withheld [Reg. 1.1461-2(b)].

16.15 Estimated Tax Payments

16.15.1. For Year 2, Corporation N, a calendar-year taxpayer, had a tax liability of $100,000, consisting of $45,000 in regular taxes and $55,000 in alternative minimum taxes. N's Year 1 tax liability was $200,000. What is the amount N must have paid for each quarter for Year 2 to avoid any penalty or interest for underpayment of estimated tax?

A. $11,250

B. $22,250

C. $25,000

D. $50,000

Answer (C) is correct. *(SEE, adapted)*
   REQUIRED: The corporation's estimated tax payments given a liability for both the regular tax and the alternative minimum tax.
   DISCUSSION: Section 6655(d) provides that a corporation will not be considered to have underpaid its income tax if it pays the lesser of (1) 100% of the tax shown on the return for the tax year or (2) 100% of the tax shown on the return for the preceding year. The definition of tax for this purpose is found in Sec. 6655(g). This definition includes the alternative minimum tax.
   Corporation N has a total tax liability of $100,000 for Year 2. It must pay 100% of this amount in estimated taxes in order to avoid any penalties or interest. The quarterly payment is $25,000 ($100,000 ÷ 4).
   Answer (A) is incorrect. The correct amount of estimated tax N must have paid for each quarter for Year 2 is not $11,250. Answer (B) is incorrect. The definition of tax for estimated tax purposes includes the alternative minimum tax. Answer (D) is incorrect. These payments assume Year 2 taxes will be equal to Year 1.

16.15.2. Finbury Corporation's taxable income for the year ended December 31, Year 2, was $2 million. Finbury's Year 1 income tax liability was $600,000. For Finbury to escape the estimated tax underpayment penalty for the year ending December 31, Year 2, its total Year 2 estimated tax payments must equal at least

A. 100% of its Year 1 tax liability.

B. 90% of its Year 2 tax liability.

C. 97% of its Year 2 tax liability.

D. 100% of its Year 2 tax liability.

Answer (D) is correct. *(CPA, adapted)*
   REQUIRED: The minimum amount of estimated tax payments to avoid the underpayment penalty for Year 2.
   DISCUSSION: Section 6655(d)(2) provides that a large corporation will not be considered to have underpaid its income tax if it pays 100% of the tax shown on the return for the tax year. A large corporation is defined by Sec. 6655(g)(2) as a corporation having $1 million or more taxable income during any of its 3 preceding tax years. Large corporations are not able to avoid underpaying their taxes by relying on the 100% of the tax shown on the return for the preceding year exception.
   Answer (A) is incorrect. The Year 1 tax liability cannot be used to determine the total Year 2 required payments for a large corporation. Answer (B) is incorrect. A large corporation must pay 100% of the current-year tax liability by making estimated tax payments. The first installment can be based on the prior-year tax liability, with a catch-up adjustment required for the second installment. Answer (C) is incorrect. A large corporation cannot only pay 97% of the Year 2 tax liability by making estimated tax payments.

16.15.3. On March 31, Govan, a calendar-year corporation, determined its estimated tax liability of the previous year to be $12,000. It should have made estimated tax payments of

A. $4,000 no later than the 15th day of the fourth, sixth, and ninth months.

B. $3,000 no later than the 15th day of the fourth, seventh, and 10th months of the current year and first month of the following year.

C. $3,000 no later than the 15th day of the third, sixth, ninth, and 12th months.

D. $3,000 no later than the 15th day of the fourth, sixth, ninth, and 12th months.

Answer (D) is correct. *(SEE, adapted)*
REQUIRED: The due dates of a calendar-year corporation's estimated tax payments.
DISCUSSION: A corporation is required to pay 1/4 of its estimated taxes each quarter. However, the first payment is not due until April 15. Therefore, Govan must pay $3,000 ($12,000 × 25%) on the 15th day of the fourth, sixth, ninth, and 12th months of the year.
Answer (A) is incorrect. The correct amount of the estimated tax payments is not $4,000. Answer (B) is incorrect. The corporation is required to pay 1/4 of its estimated taxes each quarter. Answer (C) is incorrect. The corporation does not have to pay the first $3,000 on the 15th day of the third month.

16.15.4. In order for Corporation X, a calendar-year taxpayer, to be required to make estimated tax payments in the current year, its expected tax liability would have to be

A. $500 or more.

B. $600 or more.

C. $1,000 or more.

D. $2,000 or more.

Answer (A) is correct. *(SEE, adapted)*
REQUIRED: The amount of estimated tax liability that requires a corporation to make estimated tax payments.
DISCUSSION: All corporations must make estimated tax payments, except those with an estimated tax liability of less than $500 [Sec. 6655(f)].
Answer (B) is incorrect. The corporation may still be required to make estimated tax payments if its expected liability is less than $600. Answer (C) is incorrect. The corporation may still be required to make estimated tax payments if its expected liability is less than $1,000. Answer (D) is incorrect. The corporation may still be required to make estimated tax payments if its expected liability is less than $2,000.

16.15.5. The Snow Corporation, a calendar-year taxpayer, estimates at the end of March, Year 1 that its federal income tax for Year 1 will be $800,000. It pays $200,000 of estimated tax by April 15, Year 1, and pays another $200,000 on June 15, Year 1. At the end of August, a recalculation shows that its tax is expected to be $900,000. Which of the following is true?

A. Payment due September 15 – $200,000; payment due December 15 – $300,000.

B. Payment due September 15 – $250,000; payment due December 15 – $250,000.

C. Payment due September 15 – $200,000; payment due December 15 – $200,000; payment due March 15, Year 2 – $100,000.

D. Payment due September 15 – $275,000; payment due December 15 – $225,000.

Answer (D) is correct. *(SEE, adapted)*
REQUIRED: The estimated tax payments of a calendar-year taxpayer.
DISCUSSION: Section 6655(e) requires that the estimated payment in the subsequent quarter be large enough so that 100% of the shortfall is paid in. A corporate taxpayer who continues to use the annualization exception for making its estimated tax payments will, in later quarters, have paid in 100% of the tax due on the new annualized income. If this amount is paid in when income is increasing, 100% of the shortfall will be paid in as is required by Sec. 6655(e). Although Snow correctly estimated its first two tax payments, the amount of estimated tax for the year increased to $900,000. Since Snow should have made quarterly payments of $225,000 ($900,000 ÷ 4), it must adjust the next quarterly payment by the amount of the shortfall. Therefore, the payment due September 15 is $275,000 ($225,000 quarterly payment + $50,000 shortfall), and the payment due December 15 is $225,000.
Answer (A) is incorrect. The payment due on September 15 is not $200,000, and the payment due on December 15 is not $300,000. Answer (B) is incorrect. The payments due on September 15 and December 15 are not $250,000. Answer (C) is incorrect. One of the payments cannot be due on March 15, Year 2.

16.15.6. A corporation may apply for a refund of an overpayment of estimated tax before the close of its tax year if its overpayment is at least 10% of the expected tax liability and amounts to at least $500.

A. True.

B. False.

Answer (B) is correct. *(SEE, adapted)*
DISCUSSION: Section 6425 provides that a corporation that makes an overpayment of estimated income tax may file an application (Form 4466) after, not before, the close of the tax year and before the 15th day of the third month after year end for an adjustment. The adjustment will be allowed only if it is (1) at least 10% of the amount that the corporation estimates as its income tax liability for the taxable year and (2) at least $500.

16.15.7. Corporation T had a credit of $1,400 from its Year 1 calendar-year return to be applied to its Year 2 estimated tax. Its Year 1 tax was $1,800. T accurately estimates its tax for Year 2 to be $1,600. T will be assessed a penalty if it makes no additional estimated tax payments.

A. True.

B. False.

Answer (A) is correct. *(SEE, adapted)*
    DISCUSSION: Under Sec. 6655, a corporation is subject to a penalty for underpayment of its estimated tax. Although a penalty will not be assessed if the tax is less than $500, Corporation T's Year 2 tax is $1,600. T must make total estimated payments equal to $1,600 ($1,600 × 100%) to avoid the penalty. The $1,400 credit from its Year 1 return reduces the remaining estimated payments to $200.

16.15.8. A corporation's required estimated tax payments must be deposited with an authorized commercial bank, trust company, domestic building and loan association, credit union, or Federal Reserve bank. Each deposit must be accompanied by Form 8109-B.

A. True.

B. False.

Answer (A) is correct. *(SEE, adapted)*
    DISCUSSION: Regulation 31.6302-1 states that a corporation must deposit estimated tax payments with a Federal Reserve bank or with an authorized financial institution. Form 8109-B must accompany each remittance of tax.

16.15.9. A corporation has the option of annualizing income and paying its estimated taxes accordingly. If later during the current year a corporation's income increased so that an earlier estimated tax payment was inadequate, the corporation has to pay enough in the subsequent quarter's installment to have paid 100% of the tax due on the new annualized income.

A. True.

B. False.

Answer (A) is correct. *(Publisher, adapted)*
    DISCUSSION: Section 6655(e) requires that the estimated payment in the subsequent quarter be large enough so that 100% of the shortfall is paid in. A corporate taxpayer who continues to use the annualization exception for making its estimated tax payments will in later quarters have paid in 100% of the tax due on the new annualized income. If this amount is paid in when income is increasing, 100% of the shortfall will be paid in as is required by Sec. 6655(e).

Use **Gleim Test Prep** for interactive study and easy-to-use detailed analytics!

STUDY UNIT SEVENTEEN
ADVANCED CORPORATE TOPICS

17.1 Earnings and Profits

17.1.1. Which of the following items is not an adjustment to taxable income when determining a corporation's current earnings and profits amount?

A. Life insurance proceeds.

B. Municipal bond interest income.

C. Charitable contributions made in excess of the 10%-of-adjusted-taxable-income limitation.

D. Capital contributions.

Answer (D) is correct. *(Publisher, adapted)*

REQUIRED: The item that is not an adjustment to taxable income when determining current earnings and profits.

DISCUSSION: Section 312 provides a partial definition of earnings and profits. Capital contributions are excluded from the corporation's gross income under Sec. 118. They are also excluded from earnings and profits since they do not represent an increase in corporate earnings that are available to be paid out in the form of a dividend. As a result, no adjustment to taxable income is made for capital contributions.

Answer (A) is incorrect. Life insurance proceeds are an item that is not part of the taxable income calculation and must be included in calculating current earnings and profits under Sec. 312 and the related regulations. The proceeds represent an increase in the corporation's assets. Answer (B) is incorrect. Municipal bond interest income is not part of the taxable income calculation and must be included in calculating current earnings and profits under Sec. 312 and the related regulations. This interest income represents an increase in the corporation's assets. Answer (C) is incorrect. Charitable contributions made in excess of the 10%-of-adjusted-taxable-income limitation are an item that is not part of the taxable income calculation and must be included in calculating current earnings and profits under Sec. 312 and the related regulations. These contributions represent a decrease in the corporation's assets.

17.1.2. Ben has owned all 100 outstanding shares of N and M Corporation's stock for the past 10 years. Ben's basis for the stock is $50,000. N and M have earnings and profits of $100,000. The corporation redeemed 25 shares of Ben's stock for $75,000 in the current year. How will Ben report this?

A. $75,000 gain.

B. $75,000 dividend.

C. $50,000 gain.

D. None of the answers are correct.

Answer (B) is correct. *(SEE, adapted)*
REQUIRED: The treatment of a distribution to a shareholder owning 100% of the corporation when the distribution is less than E&P.
DISCUSSION: Because Ben owns 100% of the stock before and after the redemption, the transaction is a dividend to the extent that N and M Corporation has E&P. Because the distribution ($75,000) is less than earnings and profits ($100,000), the entire amount is taxable as a dividend.
Answer (A) is incorrect. Ben owns 100% of the stock before and after the redemption. Ben will not report the $75,000 as a gain. Answer (C) is incorrect. The distribution is less than earnings and profits. Answer (D) is incorrect. There is a correct answer.

17.1.3. Rose Corporation, a calendar-year corporation, had accumulated earnings and profits of $40,000 as of January 1, Year 1. However, for the first 6 months of Year 1, Rose Corporation had an operating loss of $36,000 and finished the year with a total net operating loss for tax Year 1 of $55,000. Rose Corporation distributed $15,000 to its shareholders on July 1, Year 1. Which of the following is true?

A. The entire distribution of $15,000 is taxable.

B. The entire distribution is not taxable.

C. The part of the distribution that is taxable is $12,500.

D. The part of the distribution that is taxable is $14,000.

Answer (C) is correct. *(SEE, adapted)*
REQUIRED: The amount of a distribution that is taxable when it exceeds a corporation's current and accumulated E&P.
DISCUSSION: When a distribution is made during the course of the year, the E&P must be prorated to reflect the accumulated E&P balance on the date of the distribution. Because the distribution occurred on July 1, the accumulated E&P were $12,500 {$40,000 − [$55,000 × (6 months ÷ 12 months)]}. A corporate distribution is a "dividend" that must be included in the recipient's gross income under Sec. 301(c)(1) to the extent it comes from current or accumulated E&P of a corporation. To the extent the distribution exceeds current and accumulated E&P, it is treated as a return of capital to the shareholder. Once the basis of the stock has been reduced to zero, any distributions received are treated as a gain from the sale of the stock. Therefore, each shareholder will recognize $12,500 of ordinary income.
Answer (A) is incorrect. When a distribution is made during the course of the year, the E&P must be prorated to reflect the accumulated E&P balance on the date of the distribution. Answer (B) is incorrect. Part of the distribution is taxable. Answer (D) is incorrect. The correct amount of the distribution that is taxable is not $14,000.

17.1.4. Corporation W, which uses the accrual method of accounting, had earnings and profits of $95,000 on December 31, Year 1. Based on the following information, compute earnings and profits as of December 31, Year 2:

Taxable income per return	$185,000
Contributions in excess of 10% limitation	1,500
Interest paid for tax-exempt bonds	1,000
Tax-exempt interest received	3,000
Federal income taxes	55,400
MACRS depreciation from post-1986 property acquisitions on return in excess of straight-line alternative depreciation system	1,500

A. $220,600

B. $226,600

C. $228,600

D. $282,000

Answer (B) is correct. *(SPE, adapted)*
REQUIRED: The earnings and profits balance as of December 31, Year 2.
DISCUSSION: Calculation of earnings and profits begins with taxable income according to the tax return. Tax-exempt income is added to the taxable income, and nondeductible expenditures are subtracted, e.g., federal income taxes, charitable contributions in excess of the 10% limitation, and interest paid for tax-exempt bonds. Also, earnings and profits are calculated based upon straight-line depreciation using the alternative depreciation system, so excess MACRS depreciation must be added back for property acquired after 1986.

E&P at December 31, Year 1	$ 95,000
Taxable income for Year 2	185,000
Add: Tax-exempt interest	3,000
Excess depreciation	1,500
Deduct: Excess contributions	(1,500)
Interest paid on tax-exempt bonds	(1,000)
Federal income taxes	(55,400)
E&P at December 31, Year 2	$226,600

Answer (A) is incorrect. The $3,000 of tax-exempt interest is added to, not subtracted from, taxable income. Answer (C) is incorrect. Interest paid for tax-exempt bonds should be subtracted from, not added to, taxable income. Answer (D) is incorrect. Federal income taxes should be subtracted from taxable income.

17.1.5. Francis Corporation had taxable income of $260,000 for its initial taxable year. A review of company records revealed the following information:

1. The current-year tax depreciation expense on furniture and fixtures, the only asset owned by Francis Corporation, was $10,000. If Francis had used the alternative depreciation system (straight-line method), depreciation expense deducted would have been $5,000.

2. Francis had tax-exempt interest income of $22,000 that has not been included in taxable income.

3. Francis paid dividends of $16,000 that were not deducted.

4. Francis had $20,000 of returns and allowances that were deducted on the return.

5. Francis reported a $20,000 gain on an installment sale of a noninventory item. The total gain on the sale was $100,000.

Earnings and profits for Francis Corporation at the close of the current year were

A. $351,000

B. $346,000

C. $271,000

D. $266,000

Answer (A) is correct. *(CMA, adapted)*
REQUIRED: The earnings and profits in the current year.
DISCUSSION: In computing earnings and profits of a corporation, all income that is nontaxable or exempt from tax is added to taxable income. The earnings and profits are reduced by any expenditures or expenses of the corporation that are not deductible for tax purposes. Depreciation is usually determined under the alternative depreciation system (straight-line method). If depreciation reported for tax purposes exceeds straight-line depreciation, the difference is added back to taxable income. A corporation that sells property on the installment basis is treated for earnings and profits purposes as if it had not used the installment method. No adjustment is required for returns and allowances since deducting returns and allowances is an acceptable tax accounting procedure for computing taxable income and earnings and profits. The computation of earnings and profits for Francis Corporation in the current year is as follows:

Taxable income	$260,000
Depreciation ($10,000 – $5,000)	5,000
Tax-exempt interest income	22,000
Installment sale gain not reported for tax purposes ($100,000 – $20,000)	80,000
Current earnings and profits	$367,000
Less: Dividends paid out of current earnings and profits	(16,000)
Earnings and profits balance	$351,000

Answer (B) is incorrect. A $5,000 depreciation adjustment should be added back to taxable income to determine E&P. Answer (C) is incorrect. The $80,000 of deferred installment gain should be added back to taxable income. Answer (D) is incorrect. A deferred installment gain of $80,000 and a $5,000 depreciation adjustment should be added back to taxable income.

17.1.6. Orville Company had earnings and profits of $82,000 for the current year before distribution of dividends. On December 31 of the current year, the company distributed inventory with a fair market value of $16,000 and an adjusted basis of $12,000 as a dividend to its sole individual shareholder, Orville. The company values its inventory by the first-in, first-out method. Assume the corporate tax rate is 35%. What is the earnings and profits balance at the end of the current year?

A. $66,000

B. $68,600

C. $70,000

D. $82,000

Answer (B) is correct. *(Publisher, adapted)*
REQUIRED: The earnings and profits of a corporation after distributing a dividend of inventory.
DISCUSSION: The general rule under Sec. 311(a) is that a corporation recognizes no gain or loss on the distribution of property with respect to its stock. An exception to this nonrecognition principle is the distribution of property with an FMV in excess of its basis. A gain is recognized to the extent of such excess. Thus, Orville Company must recognize a $4,000 gain ($16,000 – $12,000) and pay $1,400 ($4,000 × .35) in taxes on the gain [Sec. 311(b)].
Section 312(b) provides that, when appreciated assets are distributed, earnings and profits are increased by the excess of fair market value over the adjusted basis of the assets and decreased by the fair market value.

E&P before distribution	$ 82,000
Increase by gain recognized ($16,000 – $12,000)	4,000
Decrease by FMV	(16,000)
Decrease by federal income taxes paid	(1,400)
E&P after distribution	$ 68,600

Answer (A) is incorrect. E&P must also be increased by the gain recognized, or the difference between the market value and the adjusted basis of the inventory, and decreased by the taxes imposed on the gain recognized. Answer (C) is incorrect. E&P must also be decreased by the taxes paid. Answer (D) is incorrect. The amount of $82,000 is E&P before taking into account the inventory distribution.

17.1.7. T, a calendar-year corporation that began doing business 10 years ago, had $35,000 in accumulated earnings and profits on January 1 of this year. T had an operating loss of $60,000 for the first 6 months of this year but had $10,000 in earnings and profits for the entire year. T made a distribution of $25,000 cash to its shareholders on April 1 this year. What is the amount of T's accumulated earnings and profits at the close of business on December 31?

A. $0

B. $10,000

C. $20,000

D. $45,000

17.1.8. During the current year, Fiddle Corporation made the following distribution to an individual shareholder who owns 40% of Fiddle's only class of stock:

Cash	$20,000
Real estate:	
Adjusted basis to Fiddle	75,000
Fair market value	85,000
Subject to a mortgage of	15,000

The shareholder assumed the $15,000 mortgage on the property. Fiddle had earnings and profits of $70,000 prior to the distribution. The real estate is Sec. 1245 property to Fiddle. Assume a 35% corporate tax rate. What is the "net" adjustment to be made to the earnings and profits account due to this distribution?

A. $10,000 increase.

B. $60,000 decrease.

C. $70,000 decrease.

D. $76,500 decrease.

17.1.9. Corporation Z had accumulated earnings and profits (E&P) of $75,000 as of January 1 of the current year. On April 1 of the same year, Z distributed $80,000 in cash to Ms. Jones, Corporation Z's sole shareholder. Corporation Z had a current E&P deficit of $76,000 for the year. Ms. Jones had an adjusted basis of $65,000 in her stock before the distribution. What is the amount of Corporation Z's current E&P on December 31 of the current year?

A. $(81,000)

B. $(76,000)

C. $(57,000)

D. $0

Answer (C) is correct. *(SPE, adapted)*
REQUIRED: The effect of a cash distribution to shareholders upon the corporations earnings and profits (E&P).
DISCUSSION: Determination must first be made as to whether or not the cash distribution is a dividend. Section 316 defines a dividend as a distribution of earnings and profits. Regulation 1.316-1(a)(1)(ii) states that current E&P is to be computed at the end of the tax year without regard to distributions during the year. At December 31 of this year, T has a current E&P of $10,000 and accumulated E&P of $35,000. The cash distribution comes first from current E&P ($10,000 – $10,000 = $0), with the balance from accumulated E&P, thereby leaving a $20,000 balance ($35,000 – $15,000).
Answer (A) is incorrect. There is an amount of E&P. Answer (B) is incorrect. The amount of $10,000 is the current E&P for last year. Answer (D) is incorrect. A distribution of $10,000 comes out of current E&P, and the remaining $15,000 of the distribution decreases the accumulated E&P.

Answer (C) is correct. *(SPE, adapted)*
REQUIRED: The reduction in a corporation's earnings and profits (E&P) due to a distribution.
DISCUSSION: Upon the distribution, Fiddle Corporation recognizes a $10,000 increase in earnings and profits for the gain recognized under Sec. 311(b) ($85,000 fair market value – $75,000 adjusted basis) and a $3,500 decrease in earnings and profits for federal income taxes on the gain ($10,000 gain × .35). This provides a predistribution earnings and profits balance of $76,500 ($70,000 + $10,000 – $3,500). The real estate distribution produces a $70,000 reduction in earnings and profits ($85,000 fair market value of real estate – $15,000 liability attaching to real estate). In addition, a cash distribution of $20,000 is made, which results in a total reduction of $90,000 ($70,000 + $20,000). This total exceeds the available E&P of $76,500. Because a distribution cannot create an E&P deficit, the E&P balance is reduced to zero. The "net" adjustment is thus $70,000.
Answer (A) is incorrect. E&P is also decreased by the taxes imposed on the gain and the lesser of the available E&P or the sum of the FMV of the real estate distributed (after reduction for the mortgage) plus the cash distributed. Answer (B) is incorrect. A $60,000 decrease ignores the taxes imposed on the gain and the cash distributed and incorrectly calculates the amount of the real estate distribution. Answer (D) is incorrect. The E&P available before the distribution is only $70,000.

Answer (C) is correct. *(SPE, adapted)*
REQUIRED: The E&P of a corporation after distributing a dividend, with a current-year E&P deficit.
DISCUSSION: Section 312(a) provides that E&P of a corporation shall be decreased by the amount of money distributed. This decrease is limited to the amount of E&P of the corporation. The current-year E&P deficit is assumed to occur ratably during the year. Assuming that each month has 30 days, the E&P deficit through March 31 of $19,000 ($76,000 × 3/12) reduces accumulated E&P to $56,000. The first $56,000 of the distribution comes out of accumulated E&P. The remaining $24,000 of the distribution is a return of capital. The $57,000 of current E&P deficit ($76,000 – $19,000) from April 1 through December 31 is the current E&P deficit at year end.
Answer (A) is incorrect. This amount incorrectly reduces the accumulated E&P by the cash distribution and the current E&P deficit. Answer (B) is incorrect. This amount is the current E&P deficit for the year. Answer (D) is incorrect. An accumulated E&P deficit exists.

17.1.10. In determining the amount of corporate earnings and profits, depreciation for tangible property placed in service after 1986 must be calculated using the "Alternative Depreciation System" rather than the MACRS rules.

A. True.

B. False.

Answer (A) is correct. *(SPE, adapted)*
DISCUSSION: Earnings and profits must be computed using the alternative depreciation system of Sec. 168(g) [Sec. 312(k)(3)]. The alternative depreciation system uses the straight-line depreciation method over longer recovery periods, rather than accelerated methods over shorter recovery periods, as is used under MACRS.

17.1.11. Corporation X elected to expense the cost of certain property under Sec. 179. In computing earnings and profits, the Sec. 179 deduction is deducted ratably over a 5-year period that begins in the month the cost is deductible.

A. True.

B. False.

Answer (A) is correct. *(SPE, adapted)*
DISCUSSION: Section 312(k)(3)(B) provides that any amount deductible under Sec. 179 shall be allowed as a deduction ratably over 5 years in computing the earnings and profits of a corporation.

17.1.12. Corporation C makes a cash distribution to its shareholders. C's earnings and profits should be reduced by this cash distribution, but not below zero.

A. True.

B. False.

Answer (A) is correct. *(SPE, adapted)*
DISCUSSION: Section 312(a) provides that earnings and profits of a corporation shall be decreased by the amount of money distributed. This decrease is limited to the amount of earnings and profits of the corporation.

17.1.13. For a distribution of an obligation of the distributing corporation, decrease the earnings and profits by the principal amount of that obligation, which may result in negative earnings and profits.

A. True.

B. False.

Answer (B) is correct. *(SEE, adapted)*
DISCUSSION: A distribution cannot produce a deficit in (i.e., reduce below zero) E&P. If current E&P are exhausted, the balance reduces prior-year E&P. The reductions do not produce or increase a deficit accumulated E&P. Any distributions in excess of E&P reduces paid-in capital.

17.1.14. Before distribution of appreciated property (other than the corporation's obligations), earnings and profits must be increased by the excess of the fair market value over the adjusted basis of the appreciated property.

A. True.

B. False.

Answer (A) is correct. *(SEE, adapted)*
DISCUSSION: If a corporation distributes property, other than its own obligations, to a shareholder and the property's FMV exceeds the corporation's adjusted basis, the property is treated as sold at the time of distribution. The corporation recognizes gain on the excess of the FMV over the adjusted basis of the property.

17.2 Dividend Distributions to Shareholders

NOTE: See Study Unit 9 for additional questions on stock dividends and stock rights. See Study Unit 11 for additional questions on sales of corporate stock.

17.2.1. In figuring the amount of a distribution by a corporation to its shareholders, the term "property" includes all of the following except

A. Money.

B. Securities.

C. Indebtedness of the distributing corporation.

D. Stock of the distributing corporation.

Answer (D) is correct. *(SPE, adapted)*
REQUIRED: The item not considered property for distribution purposes.
DISCUSSION: Under Sec. 317(a), "property" is defined as money, securities, and any other property except stock or stock rights of the distributing corporation.
Answer (A) is incorrect. Money is specifically defined as property under Sec. 317(a). Answer (B) is incorrect. Securities are specifically defined as property under Sec. 317(a). Answer (C) is incorrect. Indebtedness of the distributing corporation is specifically defined as property under Sec. 317(a).

17.2.2. A distribution of taxable stock rights or dividends generally is treated the same as

A. Any other property distribution, and the holding period begins on the day after the distribution date.

B. The distribution of an obligation of the distributing corporation.

C. A cash distribution.

D. Any other property distribution, but the holding period begins on the day of the issue of the underlying stock.

Answer (A) is correct. *(SEE, adapted)*
   REQUIRED: The proper treatment of a distribution of taxable stock rights or dividends.
   DISCUSSION: If a distribution of a stock dividend or stock right is taxable when received, the basis is the fair market value on the date of distribution. When the dividend is taxable, there is no tacking of the holding period for the underlying stock. The holding period begins the day following the acquisition date.
   Answer (B) is incorrect. A distribution of taxable stock rights or dividends is not treated the same as the distribution of an obligation of the distributing corporation. Answer (C) is incorrect. A distribution of taxable rights or dividends is not treated the same as a cash distribution. Answer (D) is incorrect. The holding period of the stock begins on the day following the acquisition date.

17.2.3. A distribution of stock or rights to acquire stock in the distributing corporation is excluded from the recipient's gross income unless

A. It is not a distribution instead of money or other property.

B. It is not a disproportionate distribution.

C. The distribution of stock or rights is greater than 15% of the value of the stock or rights with respect to which the rights were distributed.

D. It is either a disproportionate distribution, or a distribution instead of money or other property.

Answer (D) is correct. *(SEE, adapted)*
   REQUIRED: The situation in which a distribution of stock, or rights to acquire stock in the distributing corporation, is included in the recipient's gross income.
   DISCUSSION: Usually, a shareholder does not include a distribution of stock or rights to acquire stock in gross income unless it is (1) a distribution in lieu of money, (2) a disproportionate distribution, (3) a distribution on preferred stock, (4) a distribution of convertible preferred stock, or (5) a distribution of common and preferred stock resulting in receipt of preferred stock by some shareholders and common stock by other shareholders.
   Answer (A) is incorrect. Distribution of stock or rights to acquire stock in the distributing corporation is included in the recipient's income if it is a distribution instead of money or other property. Answer (B) is incorrect. A distribution of stock or rights to acquire stock in the distributing corporation is included in the recipient's income if it is a disproportionate distribution. Answer (C) is incorrect. It is not a requirement for inclusion in the recipient's gross income.

17.2.4. Margaret Corporation, which had one shareholder, had suffered losses in its earlier years up through Year 11 but was profitable in Year 12. Margaret Corporation has current earnings and profits for the Year 12 tax year of $15,000 and accumulated earnings and profits for prior years of $(14,000). An IRS audit of Year 12 determined that the shareholder benefited from constructive dividends from personal use of corporate vehicles and equipment. The amount agreed on for the constructive dividend was $12,000. There were no other dividends or distributions. Which of the following is true?

A. The constructive dividend is not taxable because it does not exceed the prior-year accumulated earnings and profits.

B. The taxable portion of the constructive dividend is $1,000.

C. The constructive dividend is fully taxable.

D. The taxable portion of the constructive dividend is $11,000.

Answer (C) is correct. *(SEE, adapted)*
   REQUIRED: The true statement regarding the constructive dividend.
   DISCUSSION: A corporate distribution is a "dividend" that must be included in the recipient's gross income under Sec. 301(c)(1) to the extent it comes from current or accumulated earnings and profits of a corporation. Distributions that must be included in gross income include constructive dividends. To the extent the distribution exceeds current and accumulated earnings and profits, it is treated as a return of capital to the shareholder. Once the basis of the stock has been reduced to zero, any distributions received are treated as a gain from the sale of the stock. Since Margaret Corporation has current earnings and profits of $27,000 ($15,000 + $12,000), the dividend of $12,000 is fully taxable. Remember that the disallowance of the expense increases current earnings and profits by $12,000.
   Answer (A) is incorrect. The dividend is fully taxable. Margaret Corporation has sufficient current earnings and profits. Answer (B) is incorrect. It is the amount of accumulated earnings and profits at year end without regard to the dividend. Answer (D) is incorrect. The full amount of the distribution is taxable.

17.2.5. A distribution of stock or stock rights is generally considered a dividend unless it is which of the following?

   A. Distribution in lieu of money.

   B. Proportionate distribution.

   C. Distribution with respect to preferred stock.

   D. Distribution of convertible preferred stock.

Answer (B) is correct. *(SPE, adapted)*
   REQUIRED: The distribution of stock or stock rights that would not be considered a dividend.
   DISCUSSION: A proportionate distribution of stock or stock rights would not be considered a dividend under Sec. 305(a) and would not be included in the gross income of the distributee.
   Answer (A) is incorrect. A distribution in lieu of money is an exception under Sec. 305(b) to the general rule, and such a distribution would receive dividend treatment. Answer (C) is incorrect. A distribution with respect to preferred stock is an exception under Sec. 305(b) to the general rule, and such a distribution would receive dividend treatment. Answer (D) is incorrect. A distribution of convertible preferred stock is an exception under Sec. 305(b) to the general rule, and such a distribution would receive dividend treatment.

17.2.6. XYZ, a calendar-year corporation, had accumulated earnings and profits of $5,000 as of January 1 of the current year. XYZ's earnings and profits for the year were $8,000. During the year, XYZ distributed one stock right for each of the 10,000 outstanding shares of its only class of stock. The fair market value of each stock right was $15. The corporation gave shareholders the option of receiving the stock rights or cash. No other dividends were paid during the year. Ms. Y is a 10% shareholder and elects to receive the stock rights. What is the amount of the distribution that is includible in Ms. Y's current-year gross income?

   A. $0

   B. $1,300

   C. $13,000

   D. $15,000

Answer (B) is correct. *(SPE, adapted)*
   REQUIRED: The amount includible in gross income from a distribution of stock rights.
   DISCUSSION: When a shareholder has the option of receiving either stock rights or cash, the entire amount of the distribution received by the shareholder will be treated as a taxable dividend under Sec. 305(b)(1). Section 316(a) defines a dividend as a distribution made from current and accumulated earnings and profits. The amount by which the distribution exceeds current and accumulated earnings and profits shall be treated as a return of capital and will reduce the shareholder's basis in the stock. XYZ's total distribution is $150,000 (10,000 × $15). The amount considered a dividend would be $13,000 ($8,000 + $5,000), and the remaining $137,000 would be a return of capital. The total amount taxable to Ms. Y would be $1,300 ($13,000 × 10%). Accordingly, Ms. Y would reduce the basis in her 1,000 shares of stock by $13,700 ($137,000 × 10%).
   Answer (A) is incorrect. The shareholder has the option of receiving either stock rights or cash. Answer (C) is incorrect. The total amount of the XYZ distribution considered as a dividend is $13,000. Answer (D) is incorrect. The total distribution of $15,000 is not entirely treated as a dividend.

17.2.7. Mr. P owned 100 shares of Corporation C common stock. During the current year, Mr. P received $300 in cash dividends, 50 additional shares of C's common stock, and the right to purchase 50 more shares. The fair market values of the stock and stock rights were $200 and $100, respectively. The distributions were not disproportionate, and the shareholders were not given an option to receive cash instead of the stock or stock rights. What amount of the distributions is includible in Mr. P's income for the current year?

   A. $300

   B. $400

   C. $500

   D. $600

Answer (A) is correct. *(SPE, adapted)*
   REQUIRED: The amount of income a shareholder must report from dividends of cash, stock, and stock rights.
   DISCUSSION: The $300 in cash dividends are included in taxable income under the general rule of Sec. 61(a)(7). Cash dividends from taxable domestic corporations are included in income provided they are paid out of earnings and profits (which is assumed unless information is given otherwise in the question). However, under Sec. 305(a), gross income generally does not include a proportionate stock dividend when the shareholder did not have the right to receive cash. Rights to purchase stock are also treated as a stock dividend for this purpose. There are exceptions under Sec. 305(b), but the usual stock dividend paid on common stock falls within the general rule and is not included in the shareholder's income. Therefore, Mr. P will not include any gross income from the stock dividend or distribution of stock rights.
   Mr. P's total taxable income from these distributions is the $300 of cash dividends. Note that, under Sec. 307(a), Mr. P will be required to allocate some of the basis of his original shares of common stock to the stock and stock rights received as distributions.
   Answer (B) is incorrect. The stock rights are a nontaxable distribution. Answer (C) is incorrect. The additional stock is a nontaxable distribution. Answer (D) is incorrect. Both the stock rights and the additional stock are nontaxable distributions.

Questions 17.2.8 and 17.2.9 are based on the following information. In January of the current year, Joan Hill bought one share of Orban Corporation stock for $300. On March 1 of this year, Orban distributed one share of a new class of preferred stock for each share of common stock held. This distribution was nontaxable. On March 1 of this year, Joan's one share of common stock had a fair market value of $450, while the preferred stock had a fair market value of $150.

17.2.8. After the distribution of the preferred stock, Joan's bases for her Orban stocks are

	Common	Preferred
A.	$300	$0
B.	$225	$75
C.	$200	$100
D.	$150	$150

Answer (B) is correct. *(CPA, adapted)*
REQUIRED: The allocation of basis after stock is received as a stock dividend.
DISCUSSION: Section 307(a) provides that if a shareholder receives a nontaxable stock dividend, the basis of the old stock must be allocated between the old and the new stock based on their relative fair market values. The basis allocation is computed as follows:

Common basis: $\dfrac{\$450}{\$450 + \$150} \times \$300 = \$225$

Preferred basis: $\dfrac{\$150}{\$450 + \$150} \times \$300 = \$75$

Answer (A) is incorrect. The basis of the common stock must be allocated between the common and the preferred stock based on their relative fair market values. Answer (C) is incorrect. The basis is not allocated as one-fourth to the preferred stock and three-fourths to common stock. Answer (D) is incorrect. The basis is divided equally between the common and the preferred stock. The basis of the common stock before the distribution must be allocated between the common and the preferred stock based on their relative fair market values.

17.2.9. The holding period for the preferred stock starts in

A. January of the current year.

B. March of the current year.

C. December of the current year.

D. None of the answers are correct.

Answer (A) is correct. *(CPA, adapted)*
REQUIRED: The holding period for preferred stock distributed in a nontaxable transaction.
DISCUSSION: Section 1223(5) requires that stock with a basis determined by reference to the basis of other stock (Sec. 307) shall include in its holding period the holding period of the referenced stock.
Answer (B) is incorrect. The holding period for the preferred stock does not start in March of the current year. Answer (C) is incorrect. The holding period for the preferred stock does not start in December of the current year. Answer (D) is incorrect. One of the answers is correct.

17.2.10. Corporation T, with earnings and profits of $60,000, distributed cash of $20,000 and property with a fair market value of $25,000 and an adjusted basis of $30,000 to its corporate shareholders. What is the amount of the distribution received by the shareholders?

A. $20,000

B. $30,000

C. $45,000

D. $50,000

Answer (C) is correct. *(SPE, adapted)*
REQUIRED: The amount of a distribution received by corporate shareholders.
DISCUSSION: Section 301(b) provides that the amount distributed to a shareholder (corporate or noncorporate) is equal to the amount of money received, plus the fair market value of other property received. Corporation T distributed cash of $20,000 plus property with a fair market value of $25,000. Hence, the corporate shareholders will recognize a distribution of $45,000.
Answer (A) is incorrect. The distribution also includes the FMV of the property. Answer (B) is incorrect. The distribution includes both the FMV of the property and the amount of cash distributed. Answer (D) is incorrect. The distribution includes the FMV of the property, not the adjusted basis.

17.2.11. Core Corporation reported current earnings and profits of $250,000. It distributed a building with an adjusted basis to Core of $170,000 and a fair market value of $230,000, to its sole shareholder. The building had a mortgage of $90,000, which the shareholder will assume. What is the amount of the dividend received by the shareholder?

A. $80,000

B. $140,000

C. $230,000

D. $250,000

Answer (B) is correct. *(SPE, adapted)*
REQUIRED: The amount of a dividend received by a shareholder.
DISCUSSION: Section 301(b)(1) provides that the distribution to a shareholder is equal to the fair market value of the property distributed. Under Sec. 301(b)(2)(A), this amount must be decreased by any liabilities assumed by the shareholder or to which the property is subject. The distribution to the shareholder is $140,000 ($230,000 FMV – $90,000 liability).
Under Sec. 316, a distribution is a dividend to the extent that it comes from earnings and profits. The earnings and profits would be increased by the gain (net of tax) on the distribution. Gain is recognized to the extent the FMV of the building exceeds the adjusted basis [Sec. 311(b)], or $60,000. In any event, the corporation has at least $250,000 of earnings and profits. Therefore, the entire $140,000 is a dividend.
Answer (A) is incorrect. The amount of $80,000 is not the correct amount of the dividend received by the shareholder. Answer (C) is incorrect. The amount of $230,000 is the FMV of the building, which has not been reduced by the mortgage assumed. Answer (D) is incorrect. The amount of $250,000 is the E&P balance, which exceeds the amount of the distribution.

17.2.12. Dahl Corporation was organized and commenced operations 75 years ago. At December 31 of the current year, Dahl had accumulated earnings and profits of $9,000 before a dividend declaration and distribution. On December 31, Dahl distributed cash of $9,000 and a vacant parcel of land to Mr. Green, Dahl's only shareholder. At the date of distribution, the land had a basis of $5,000 and a fair market value of $40,000. What was Mr. Green's taxable dividend income in the current year from these distributions assuming a 35% corporate tax rate?

A. $9,000

B. $31,750

C. $44,000

D. $49,000

Answer (B) is correct. *(CPA, adapted)*
REQUIRED: The amount of a corporation's dividend distribution made to a sole shareholder.
DISCUSSION: Under Sec. 301(b)(1), the amount of a distribution to a distributee equals the amount of money received plus the fair market value of nonmoney property received. Section 311(b) requires Dahl Corporation to recognize gain on the distribution of appreciated property of $35,000 ($40,000 FMV – $5,000 adjusted basis). The total amount of Dahl's distribution is

Cash	$ 9,000
Basis of property plus gain (equal to FMV)	40,000
Total distribution	$49,000

Section 316 provides that a distribution is a dividend to the extent it comes from earnings and profits. Dahl's $9,000 E&P must be increased by the gain on the distribution and decreased by the taxes on the gain. This calculation is as follows:

E&P – December 31	$ 9,000
Gain on land distribution	35,000
Less: taxes on gain ($35,000 × 35%)	(12,250)
E&P after Sec. 311(b) adjustment	$ 31,750

Thus, only $31,750 of the total $49,000 paid is considered a dividend distribution. The remaining $17,250 is either a return of capital or a capital gain, depending on Mr. Green's stock basis [Sec. 301(c)(2) and (3)].
Answer (A) is incorrect. The amount of $9,000 is only the cash portion of the distribution. Answer (C) is incorrect. The amount of $44,000 is the cash distribution plus the gain recognized on the land. Answer (D) is incorrect. The amount of $49,000 is the FMV of the distributed property.

17.2.13. Corporation P distributed depreciable personal property having a fair market value of $7,500 to its shareholders. The property had an adjusted basis of $4,000 to the corporation. P had properly deducted $2,000 in depreciation on the property. What amount must Corporation P include in ordinary income under Sec. 1245 as a result of the distribution?

A. $0
B. $2,000
C. $3,500
D. $7,500

Answer (B) is correct. *(SPE, adapted)*
REQUIRED: The corporation's ordinary income upon the distribution of depreciable property.
DISCUSSION: Section 311(b) requires that gain on the distribution of appreciated property be recognized as if the property had been sold. Therefore, Corporation P will recognize $3,500 ($7,500 fair market value – $4,000 basis) of total gain. As a result of Sec. 1245 depreciation recapture, $2,000 of this gain will be ordinary income.
Answer (A) is incorrect. Corporation P must recognize ordinary income as a result of the distribution. Answer (C) is incorrect. The amount of $3,500 is the total gain. Answer (D) is incorrect. The amount of $7,500 is the FMV of the property.

17.2.14. Corporation K distributed a parcel of real estate to a shareholder that had an adjusted basis to the corporation of $50,000 and a fair market value of $75,000. The property was subject to a mortgage of $80,000, which was assumed by the shareholder. What is Corporation K's recognized gain (or loss) on the distribution to the shareholder?

A. $(5,000)
B. $0
C. $25,000
D. $30,000

Answer (D) is correct. *(SPE, adapted)*
REQUIRED: The corporation's recognized gain (or loss) on the distribution of property with a mortgage in excess of basis.
DISCUSSION: Section 311(b) requires a corporation to recognize gain to the extent the FMV of property distributed exceeds the adjusted basis of such property. If liabilities exceed basis, FMV is treated as not less than the liabilities assumed or acquired by the shareholder [Sec. 311(b)(2)]. Therefore, the FMV is treated as $80,000.

FMV of property distributed	$ 80,000
Less: adjusted basis	(50,000)
Gain recognized under Sec. 311(b)	$ 30,000

Answer (A) is incorrect. The gain or loss on the distribution is not determined by comparing the FMV of the property with the amount of the liability discharged. Answer (B) is incorrect. A gain or loss is recognized. Answer (C) is incorrect. The amount of $50,000 is the adjusted basis of the property to the corporation.

17.2.15. Seven years ago, Mr. X purchased stock in Corporation Y for $5,000. Five years ago, he received a distribution of $1,200, when Corporation Y had no current or accumulated earnings and profits. This year, Mr. X received a $400 dividend, when Corporation Y had earnings and profits in excess of its dividend distribution. There has been no other distribution activity on this stock. What is Mr. X's basis in his stock of Corporation Y as of December 31 of this year?

A. $3,400
B. $3,800
C. $4,600
D. $5,000

Answer (B) is correct. *(SPE, adapted)*
REQUIRED: The calculation of a shareholder's remaining basis when a distribution represents both dividend and return of capital.
DISCUSSION: A corporate distribution is taxable to the recipient to the extent it comes from accumulated or current earnings and profits [Sec. 301(c)(1) and Sec. 316(a)]. Any remaining distribution is treated as a return of capital. Since there were not any current or accumulated E&P when the first distribution was made 5 years ago, Mr. X's basis was reduced by the amount of the $1,200 distribution. Since this year's E&P was in excess of the $400 distribution, the $400 is a taxable dividend to Mr. X. Thus, Mr. X's adjusted basis in his stock of Y Corporation at year end is $3,800 ($5,000 – $1,200).
Answer (A) is incorrect. The $400 distribution in the current year is ordinary income because there was sufficient E&P. Answer (C) is incorrect. The amount of $4,600 incorrectly deducted the $400 current-year distribution and failed to deduct the $1,200 distribution made 5 years ago. Answer (D) is incorrect. The $1,200 distribution made 5 years ago was a return of capital because there were no current or accumulated E&P.

17.2.16. Ten years ago, Mr. P purchased stock for $1,000. Last year, he received a return of capital of $800 and reduced the basis of his stock by that amount. This year, he received another return of capital that amounted to $300, which reduced the basis of his stock to zero. At no time did the corporation have earnings and profits. He would report the $100 that was in excess of his basis as

A. An additional basis reduction that reduces the stock basis to a negative $100.

B. Long-term capital gain.

C. Dividend.

D. Short-term capital gain.

Answer (B) is correct. *(SPE, adapted)*
REQUIRED: The portion of a distribution to be treated as a gain from a sale or exchange of property by an individual shareholder.
DISCUSSION: A corporate distribution is a "dividend" that must be included in the recipient's gross income under Sec. 301(c)(1) to the extent it comes from current or accumulated earnings and profits of a corporation. To the extent the distribution exceeds current and accumulated earnings and profits, it is treated as a return of capital to the shareholder. Once the basis of the stock has been reduced to zero, any distributions received are treated as a gain from the sale of the stock. Mr. P's capital gain is long-term because he held the stock for more than 1 year.
Answer (A) is incorrect. Once the basis of the stock has been reduced to zero, any distributions received are treated as a gain from the sale of the stock. Answer (C) is incorrect. A corporate distribution is a "dividend" that must be included in the recipient's gross income to the extent it comes from current or accumulated earnings and profits of a corporation. Answer (D) is incorrect. The stock was held for more than 1 year, making it a long-term gain.

17.2.17. On April 1 of the current year, Stan Corporation bought 1,000 shares (30%) of Lee Corporation common stock for $40,000. On August 1 of the same year, Stan received a $7,000 cash distribution that was a dividend on these shares. The fair market value of the shares on the ex-dividend date was $30,000. Stan claimed the full 80% dividends-received deduction. On November 1 of the same year, Stan sold the Lee stock to an unrelated third party for $50,000. What is Stan's gain on the sale?

A. $10,000

B. $15,600

C. $17,000

D. $50,000

Answer (B) is correct. *(Publisher, adapted)*
REQUIRED: The corporate shareholder's gain on sale of stock after an extraordinary dividend.
DISCUSSION: A corporation's basis in stock is reduced by the nontaxed portion of an extraordinary dividend if the stock has been held for 2 years or less (Sec. 1059). An extraordinary dividend is a dividend paid after March 1, 1984, that exceeds 10% of the shareholder's basis in the stock (or if the taxpayer can establish it, the stock's fair market value for dividends declared after July 18, 1986, in taxable years ending after such date). The nontaxable portion is the amount of the dividends-received deduction.
Stan held the Lee stock for less than 2 years, and the dividend was greater than 10% of its basis or ex-dividend fair market value, so Stan must reduce its basis in the Lee stock by the nontaxable portion of the dividend, or $5,600 ($7,000 × 80%). Thus, Stan's gain is $15,600 [$50,000 – ($40,000 – $5,600)]. If the nontaxed portion had exceeded the basis in the Lee stock, Stan would have been required to recognize a gain immediately.
Answer (A) is incorrect. The basis of the stock must be reduced for the nontaxable portion of an extraordinary dividend. Answer (C) is incorrect. The basis of the stock is not reduced by the entire cash distribution; only the nontaxable portion reduces basis. Answer (D) is incorrect. The amount realized for the stock is $50,000.

17.2.18. Corporation T, a domestic corporation, distributes the following dividends to its shareholders in the current year:

$1,000 to Shareholder A, an unrelated foreign corporation
$1,200 to Shareholder B, a foreign partnership
$1,300 to Shareholder C, a resident alien
$1,400 to Shareholder D, a nonresident alien, with an address in care of another person in the U.S.

All income of Corporation T was from sources within the United States. Assume no tax treaties to which the U.S. is a party are involved. On what amount of dividends must T withhold tax?

A. $0

B. $1,000

C. $2,200

D. $3,600

Answer (D) is correct. *(SPE, adapted)*
REQUIRED: The amount of dividends on which the distributor must withhold tax.
DISCUSSION: Section 1441 requires the corporation paying dividends to a foreign partnership and a nonresident alien to withhold tax on such amounts. Section 1442 requires the same withholding on dividends paid to foreign corporations. There is no special withholding requirement for resident aliens.
Therefore, the withholding by Corporation T is required for Shareholders A, B, and D. Their dividends total $3,600.
Answer (A) is incorrect. T must withhold tax on the dividends. Answer (B) is incorrect. Tax must also be withheld on dividends paid to Shareholders B and D. Answer (C) is incorrect. Tax must also be withheld on dividends paid to Shareholder D.

17.2.19. Net Corporation has owned 70% of Cable Corporation's single class of stock since April 1 of last year. Net Corporation's basis is $50,000 for the Cable stock. On December 31 of the current year, Net received a $100,000 cash distribution from Cable Corporation. The Net stock was worth $400,000 on the distribution date. In the current year, what amount of gain must Net Corporation recognize from receiving the distribution?

A. $0

B. $30,000

C. $50,000

D. $100,000

Answer (B) is correct. *(Publisher, adapted)*
REQUIRED: The gain required to be recognized when an extraordinary dividend has been received by a corporate shareholder.
DISCUSSION: A corporate shareholder that receives an extraordinary dividend must reduce the basis of the stock with respect to which the dividend was received by the untaxed portion of the dividend unless the stock was held for more than 2 years before the dividend was declared [Sec. 1059(a)]. For common stock, an extraordinary dividend is a dividend that generally exceeds 10% of (1) the taxpayer's adjusted basis in the stock or (2) the fair market value of the stock just before the ex-dividend date (Sec. 1059). Untaxed dividends may arise because the corporate shareholder can deduct a certain percentage of the payment through the use of the dividends-received deduction. When making a basis reduction due to the extraordinary dividend, the untaxed portion of the dividend cannot reduce basis in the stock below zero. Prior to the Taxpayer Relief Act of 1997, the portion of the dividend received in excess of the stock basis was not taxed as a gain until a later sale of the stock. Now a gain must be recognized immediately in the tax year in which the extraordinary dividend is received to the extent the nontaxed portion exceeds the basis of the stock. Therefore, since Net owns 70% of the stock of Cable, 80% of the $100,000 is untaxed. Accordingly, Net must reduce its basis in Cable by the untaxed amount received ($80,000), and a gain of $30,000 ($80,000 untaxed amount less $50,000 basis) must be recognized in the current year.
Answer (A) is incorrect. A gain must be recognized. Answer (C) is incorrect. Only 80% of the dividend is untaxable, not 100%. Answer (D) is incorrect. The untaxed distribution must first be applied against basis.

17.2.20. Corporation A sold equipment used in its business to its sole shareholder Mr. B for $13,000. On the date of the sale, the fair market value of the equipment was $16,000, and A's adjusted basis was $11,000. Corporation A also canceled a $4,000 debt of Mr. B. What is the amount of the dividend received by Mr. B, assuming Corporation A has a large amount of earnings and profits?

A. $20,000

B. $15,000

C. $7,000

D. $3,000

Answer (C) is correct. *(SPE, adapted)*
REQUIRED: The amount of dividend income to a shareholder from a bargain purchase.
DISCUSSION: A constructive distribution will be treated as a dividend for tax purposes if sufficient E&P is available. A bargain purchase of corporate property by shareholders is such a transaction [Reg. 1.301-1(j)]. Under Sec. 301(b)(1), the amount of a distribution to a distributee is the fair market value of the property distributed. The difference between the fair market value and the amount paid by the shareholder is treated as a constructive distribution. Cancelation of debt is also a constructive dividend.

FMV of equipment	$ 16,000
Less: Amount paid	(13,000)
Plus: Cancelation of debt	4,000
Distribution	$ 7,000

To the extent the distribution comes from earnings and profits, it is treated as a dividend [Sec. 316(a)]. Since Corporation A had sufficient E&P, the entire $7,000 distribution is considered a dividend.
Answer (A) is incorrect. The amount of $20,000 fails to deduct the $13,000 consideration paid by the shareholder. Answer (B) is incorrect. The amount of $15,000 is the corporation's adjusted basis in the property plus the $4,000 canceled debt. Answer (D) is incorrect. The $4,000 cancelation of debt is also a constructive dividend.

17.2.21. Two years ago, Mr. P bought 100 shares of stock in Corporation X for $20 per share. Last year, Mr. P bought 100 shares of Corporation X stock for $28 per share. This year, X declared a 2-for-1 stock split. The fair market value of the stock at the time of the split was $50 per share. What is Mr. P's basis in Corporation X stock?

    A. 200 shares at $10 per share and 200 shares at $14 per share.

    B. 400 shares at $12 per share.

    C. 400 shares at $50 per share.

    D. 100 shares at $20 per share, 100 shares at $28 per share, and 200 shares at $50 per share.

Answer (A) is correct. *(SPE, adapted)*
    REQUIRED: The basis of stock to the shareholder after a stock split.
    DISCUSSION: Section 307 requires a shareholder to allocate the basis of the old shares to the new shares. Mr. P's total basis is apportioned among the new shares as follows:

1st purchase: $\dfrac{100 \text{ shares} \times \$20}{200 \text{ shares}}$ = 200 shares × $10

2nd purchase: $\dfrac{100 \text{ shares} \times \$28}{200 \text{ shares}}$ = 200 shares × $14

    Answer (B) is incorrect. The total basis for each block of stock is apportioned among the old and new shares. Answer (C) is incorrect. Mr. P's basis in Corporation X stock is not 400 shares at $50 per share. Answer (D) is incorrect. Mr. P's basis in Corporation X stock is not 100 shares at $20 per share, 100 shares at $28 per share, and 200 shares at $50 per share.

17.2.22. With regard to the filing of Form 1099-DIV, all of the following are true except

    A. Corporate payers file this form to report dividends and other distributions of stock of $10 or more.

    B. Corporate payers file this form for every person for whom any federal income taxes were withheld under the backup withholding rules.

    C. Corporate payers file this form for each person to whom payments of $600 or more were made as a part of a liquidation.

    D. This form is filed by payers for royalties paid to authors.

Answer (D) is correct. *(SEE, adapted)*
    REQUIRED: The false statement regarding the filing of Form 1099-DIV.
    DISCUSSION: A corporation is required to file a 1099-DIV if (1) distributions in excess of $10 were made as dividends, capital gains, or nontaxable distributions; (2) tax was withheld under the backup withholding rules; or (3) a liquidating payment of $600 was distributed. Royalties are reported on Form 1099-MISC.
    Answer (A) is incorrect. A corporation is required to file Form 1099-DIV if distributions in excess of $10 were made as dividends, capital gains, or nontaxable distributions. Answer (B) is incorrect. A corporation is required to file Form 1099-DIV if tax was withheld under the backup withholding rules. Answer (C) is incorrect. A corporation is required to file Form 1099-DIV if a liquidating payment of $600 was distributed.

17.2.23. If the common shareholders of a corporation receive a pro rata distribution of preferred stock and have the option to immediately redeem the preferred stock for money, the distribution is considered to be in lieu of money and is included in the gross income of the shareholders.

    A. True.

    B. False.

Answer (A) is correct. *(SPE, adapted)*
    DISCUSSION: Under Sec. 305, a stock dividend is not generally taxable. However, Sec. 305(b) provides exceptions to this general rule. One is for distributions payable in either stock or property. The option of immediate redemption of preferred stock for money effectively makes the distribution payable in either stock or property (money), so it is taxable.

17.2.24. If common shareholders of a corporation receive a distribution of common and preferred stock resulting in a receipt of preferred by some and common by others, the distribution is taxable as a dividend provided there is sufficient earnings and profits.

    A. True.

    B. False.

Answer (A) is correct. *(SPE, adapted)*
    DISCUSSION: Section 305(b)(3) states that if a distribution results in the receipt of common stock by some shareholders and preferred stock by other shareholders, the general rule of Sec. 305(a) shall not apply, and the distribution will be taxed as a dividend under Sec. 301.

17.2.25. A corporation distributes property with a fair market value of $18,000 and an adjusted basis of $21,000 to a shareholder. The property's basis in the shareholder's hands is $21,000.

    A. True.

    B. False.

Answer (B) is correct. *(Publisher, adapted)*
    DISCUSSION: Under Sec. 301(d), the basis of property received by a distributee in a dividend distribution is the fair market value of such property. The distributee will have a basis in the property of $18,000, even though the corporation's basis was higher.

17.2.26. A corporation distributes property with a fair market value of $30,000 and an adjusted basis of $24,000 to a shareholder. The distributee's holding period includes the holding period of the distributing corporation.

A. True.

B. False.

Answer (B) is correct. *(Publisher, adapted)*
DISCUSSION: Under Sec. 301(d), the basis of property received by a distributee in a dividend distribution is the fair market value of the property. Since the basis for the property does not carry over from the distributing corporation, the carryover holding period provided in Sec. 1223 will not apply. The holding period will commence on the day after the distribution date.

17.3 Stock Redemptions

17.3.1. With respect to the redemption of stock, each of the following tests establishes that the redemption can be treated as an exchange of stock rather than as a dividend except

A. The redemption is substantially disproportionate with respect to the shareholder's constructive holdings.

B. The redemption is not substantially equivalent to a dividend.

C. The redemption terminates the shareholder's entire interest in the corporation.

D. The redemption is of stock held by a corporate shareholder and is made in partial liquidation of the redeeming corporation.

Answer (D) is correct. *(SPE, adapted)*
REQUIRED: The test that does not establish that the redemption can be treated as an exchange of stock rather than a dividend.
DISCUSSION: A redemption qualifies for sale or exchange treatment if (1) the redemption is substantially disproportionate, (2) the redemption is a complete termination of the shareholder's interest, (3) the redemption is not essentially equivalent to a dividend, (4) the redemption is a partial liquidation of the distributing corporation in redemption of part or all of a noncorporate shareholder's stock, or (5) the redemption is made in order to pay death taxes. A redemption of stock held by a noncorporate shareholder in a partial liquidation will receive sale or exchange treatment, but not a redemption of stock held by a corporate shareholder.
Answer (A) is incorrect. A test to establish sale or exchange treatment for a redemption is the redemption being substantially disproportionate with respect to the shareholder's constructive holdings. Answer (B) is incorrect. The redemption not being substantially equivalent to a dividend can establish sale or exchange treatment for a redemption. Answer (C) is incorrect. The redemption terminating the shareholder's entire interest in the corporation can establish sale or exchange treatment for a redemption.

17.3.2. Mr. X owned 40% of Corporation B's only class of stock outstanding. The remaining 60% of B's stock was owned by Mr. Y (not related to Mr. X). Corporation B redeemed all of X's stock for $75,000 and one-half of Y's stock for $50,000. Mr. X's and Mr. Y's bases in their stock of Corporation B were $30,000 and $25,000, respectively. B's earnings and profits were $200,000. Assuming that no partial liquidation occurred, what are the amount and the character of X's and Y's recognized gains?

	Mr. X	Mr. Y
A.	$45,000 capital gain	$25,000 dividend
B.	$75,000 dividend	$50,000 dividend
C.	$45,000 capital gain	$25,000 capital gain
D.	$45,000 capital gain	$50,000 dividend

Answer (D) is correct. *(SPE, adapted)*
REQUIRED: The amount and character of gain resulting from a corporate distribution.
DISCUSSION: Under Sec. 302(b)(3), if a corporation redeems all of its stock owned by a shareholder, the shareholder is treated as having sold his stock to the corporation and will report a capital gain to the extent that the distribution exceeds his basis in the stock. Therefore, Mr. X has a capital gain of $45,000 ($75,000 distribution − $30,000 basis).
If the distribution is not a redemption of all the shareholder's stock, Sec. 302(b)(2) must be applied to determine whether the distribution will be treated as a payment in exchange for the stock or as a dividend. One of the requirements of Sec. 302(b)(2) is that the shareholder must own less than 50% of the total combined voting power of all classes of stock immediately after the redemption. Alternatively, the distribution must not be essentially equivalent to a dividend under Sec. 302(b)(1). This alternative requires a meaningful reduction in the shareholder's interest in the distributing corporation.
Since all of Mr. X's stock was redeemed, Mr. Y owns 100% of the voting stock. Therefore, the requirements of Secs. 302(b)(2) or 302(b)(1) are not met, and the $50,000 distribution is treated as a dividend since it is less than B Corporation's earnings and profits.
Answer (A) is incorrect. Mr. Y's dividend is the amount distributed, and not the redeemed stock's adjusted basis. Answer (B) is incorrect. Mr. X's redemption is eligible for capital gain treatment. Answer (C) is incorrect. Mr. Y's redemption is not a capital gain.

17.3.3. All of the following statements regarding stock redemptions are true except

A. A redemption occurs when a corporation reacquires its stock in exchange for property.

B. The term property includes money, securities, and any other property except stock or stock rights in the distributing corporation.

C. The stock that is redeemed by a corporation may not be held as treasury stock.

D. Redemptions that are not complete or partial liquidations can be distributions in part or full payment for the stock surrendered.

Answer (C) is correct. *(SPE, adapted)*
   REQUIRED: The statement regarding stock redemptions that is false.
   DISCUSSION: Section 317(b) states that stock is treated as redeemed by a corporation if the corporation acquires its stock from a shareholder in exchange for property, whether or not the acquired stock is canceled, retired, or held as treasury stock.
   Answer (A) is incorrect. Section 317(b) provides that stock is treated as redeemed when a corporation acquires its own stock from a shareholder in exchange for property. Answer (B) is incorrect. Property, as defined by Sec. 317(a), includes anything distributed by a corporation except its own stock or rights to acquire its own stock. Answer (D) is incorrect. Under Sec. 302, several types of redemptions are treated as part or full payment for the stock even though there is no partial or complete liquidation of the corporation.

17.3.4. Rambo Corporation owns, as an investment, 10% of the stock of Duntulum Corporation with a basis of $8,000 and a fair market value of $50,000. Rambo uses the Duntulum stock to redeem approximately 1%, or $10,000 par value, of its own outstanding stock from unrelated, noncorporate shareholders. As a result of this transaction, Rambo must report

A. No gain or loss.

B. $40,000 gain.

C. $42,000 gain.

D. $50,000 gain.

Answer (C) is correct. *(CPA, adapted)*
   REQUIRED: The amount of gain recognized by the distributing corporation on a redemption using appreciated property.
   DISCUSSION: The general rule under Sec. 311(a) is that a corporation does not recognize gain or loss on the distribution of property with respect to its stock. However, Sec. 311(b) requires a corporation that distributes appreciated property to recognize gain equal to the excess of the fair market value of the property over its adjusted basis, as if the stock were sold to the distributee immediately before the exchange. Thus, Rambo's gain is determined as follows:

FMV of stock distributed	$50,000
Less: adjusted basis	(8,000)
Recognized gain	$42,000

   Answer (A) is incorrect. A gain is reported. Answer (B) is incorrect. The par value of the stock is not used when determining the recognized gain. Answer (D) is incorrect. The FMV of the Duntulum stock is $50,000.

17.3.5. Corporation H has 1,000 shares of stock outstanding. Mr. K, the founder, owns 40% of the stock, his wife owns 10%, his son owns 20%, and the balance is owned by unrelated parties. Under the constructive ownership rules of the stock redemption provisions, what percentage of stock is Mr. K considered to own?

A. 50%

B. 60%

C. 70%

D. 100%

Answer (C) is correct. *(SPE, adapted)*
   REQUIRED: The percentage of stock a taxpayer is considered to own under the constructive ownership rules for a stock redemption.
   DISCUSSION: The stock redemption provisions found in Sec. 302 use the constructive ownership (attribution) rules of Sec. 318. Under the Sec. 318(a)(1) rules, an individual is considered to own the stock owned by members of his or her family including his or her spouse, children, grandchildren, and parents. Therefore, Mr. K owns 40% of the stock directly, and he indirectly owns the stock owned by his wife and son. Mr. K has direct and indirect ownership of 70% (40% + 20% + 10%) of Corporation H. For that matter, so do his wife and son.
   Answer (A) is incorrect. The amount of 50% omits Mr. K's constructive ownership of his son's stock. Answer (B) is incorrect. The amount of 60% omits Mr. K's constructive ownership of his wife's stock. Answer (D) is incorrect. Mr. K does not constructively own the stock of the unrelated parties.

17.3.6. Danny owns 35% of Batch Corporation's only class of stock outstanding. His daughter Ann and son-in-law Tony each own 20%. Ann is legally separated from Tony. Danny's father owns 25% of Batch's outstanding stock. What is Ann's percentage of stock ownership under the attribution rules for stock redemption?

A. 55%

B. 75%

C. 80%

D. 100%

Answer (A) is correct. *(SPE, adapted)*
REQUIRED: The number of shares of stock constructively owned by a shareholder in a family corporation.
DISCUSSION: Under Sec. 318, a shareholder is considered to constructively own stock that is in fact owned by another shareholder. Section 318(a)(1)(A) states that a shareholder is considered to own the stock owned by the shareholder's spouse, children, grandchildren, and parents. However, Sec. 318(a)(1)(A) excludes a spouse who is legally separated from the shareholder. Therefore, Ann constructively owns 55% of the stock (Ann's 20% and her father's 35%).
Answer (B) is incorrect. The amount of 75% includes Tony's percentage of stock, but he is excluded because he and Ann are separated. Answer (C) is incorrect. The amount of 80% includes Danny's father's (Ann's grandfather) percentage of stock. Answer (D) is incorrect. The amount of 100% includes Tony and Danny's father's percentage of stock.

17.3.7. The Z Corporation's common stock is owned by the following individuals and corporations:

	Number of Shares
Mr. B	20
Mrs. B	20
T Corporation	30
X Corporation	30
Total	100

The B family does not own any of T or X Corporation's stock. Mr. B would like to redeem some of his shares and have the redemption treated as an exchange. The minimum number of Mr. B's shares that Z Corporation must redeem in order for the redemption to qualify for exchange treatment under the substantially disproportionate rules of Sec. 302(b)(2) is (rounded to the nearest share)

A. 20

B. 8

C. 28

D. 12

Answer (D) is correct. *(Publisher, adapted)*
REQUIRED: The minimum number of shares redeemed to qualify under the substantially disproportionate rules of Sec. 302(b)(2).
DISCUSSION: Under Sec. 302(b)(2), a stock redemption will be considered substantially disproportionate and will receive exchange treatment if the following two requirements are met: (1) The shareholder's stock ownership percentage is less than 50% after the redemption, and (2) the shareholder's stock ownership percentage after the redemption is less than 80% of his or her stock ownership percentage before the redemption.
When computing the ownership percentages, the stock attribution rules of Sec. 318 must be applied. Mr. B is deemed to own not only his stock but also the stock of his wife, or a total of 40 shares of Z stock.
The minimum number of shares that must be redeemed may be determined algebraically.

$$\frac{40 - x}{100 - x} < y$$

Where: x is the minimum number of shares needed to be redeemed, and
y is 80% of the shareholder's stock interest immediately before the redemption.

Note that, when calculating the ownership percentage after the redemption, both the numerator and denominator must be reduced by the shares redeemed. B owned 40% (40/100) before the redemption, and 80% of 40% is 32% (80% × 40%). Solving the equation for when $y < .32$ produces an x value of 12, or 12 shares of Z stock that must be redeemed. Immediately after the redemption, Mr. and Mrs. B will own 28 (8 for Mr. B + 20 for Mrs. B) of the 88 (or 31.81818%) outstanding shares.
Answer (A) is incorrect. The number of shares Mrs. B will have after the redemption is 20. Answer (B) is incorrect. The number of shares Mr. B will have after the redemption is 8. Answer (C) is incorrect. The combined number of shares Mr. and Mrs. B will own after the redemption is 28.

17.3.8. Corporation Z has 100 shares of stock issued and outstanding, owned by the following:

Shares	Shareholder
10	R
10	R's wife
10	R's son
10	R's mother
10	R's brother
10	R's uncle
10	Partnership X (R is a 10% partner)
10	Corporation A (R is a 40% shareholder)
10	Corporation B (R is a 50% shareholder)
10	Corporation C (R is an 80% shareholder)
100	

Neither R's relatives nor the partnership or corporations are partners in X or shareholders in A, B, or C. Under constructive ownership rules for Sec. 302 stock redemptions, what percentage of stock is R considered to own?

A. 54%

B. 58%

C. 64%

D. 74%

Answer (A) is correct. *(SPE, adapted)*
REQUIRED: The percentage of stock a taxpayer is considered to own under the constructive ownership rules.
DISCUSSION: Section 318 contains the constructive ownership rules for stock redemptions. An individual is considered to own the stock owned by his or her spouse, children, grandchildren, and parents, but not by brothers, sisters, aunts, or uncles. If a shareholder owns 50% or more in value of the stock of a corporation, (s)he is considered to own the stock the corporation owns in proportion to the value of the stock that (s)he owns in the corporation. Stock owned directly or indirectly by a partnership is considered to be owned proportionately by the partners, even if the partner owns less than 50% of the partnership.

	Shares Owned
R owns personally	10
From R's wife	10
From R's son	10
From R's mother	10
From Partnership X (10 shares × 10%)	1
From Corporation B (10 shares × 50%)	5
From Corporation C (10 shares × 80%)	8
Shares actually and constructively owned under Sec. 318	54

Answer (B) is incorrect. R is not considered to own four shares through Corporation A since he does not own 50% or more of Corporation A. Answer (C) is incorrect. R does not constructively own either his brother's or his uncle's shares of Z. Answer (D) is incorrect. R does not constructively own either his brother's or his uncle's stock.

17.3.9. Mr. Fox owns 500 shares of stock in Ocean Corporation, which represents 52% of Ocean's only class of stock issued and outstanding. Mr. Fox's basis in the stock is $50,000 ($100 per share). Ocean redeems 250 shares of Mr. Fox's stock for $40,000. The redemption is properly treated as a distribution of cash in exchange for the stock. What is Mr. Fox's basis in his remaining shares of stock?

A. $50,000

B. $40,000

C. $35,000

D. $25,000

Answer (D) is correct. *(SPE, adapted)*
REQUIRED: The shareholder's basis in his remaining stock following a partial redemption.
DISCUSSION: The shareholder's basis in his remaining stock depends on the treatment of the distribution. If the distribution is essentially equivalent to a dividend, the shareholder's basis in the remaining stock will be increased by the basis of the stock that is redeemed [Reg. 1.302-2(c)]. If the distribution is treated as payment in exchange for the shareholder's redeemed stock, the basis of the redeemed stock offsets the amount received by the shareholder and the basis of the remaining shares is unchanged. Section 302 governs the determination of the distribution's character. Since Fox still owns Ocean stock after the redemption, a complete termination under Sec. 302(b)(3) did not occur. The best choice from the remaining alternatives is the substantially disproportionate redemption test of Sec. 302(b)(2), which requires that immediately after the redemption the shareholder own less than 50% of the total combined voting power of all classes of voting stock. Since approximately 961 shares are outstanding before redemption (500 ÷ .52 = 961.5), 35% of the Ocean stock is owned by Fox after the redemption [(500 – 250) ÷ (961 – 250) = .35]. A second requirement for Sec. 302(b)(2) treatment is that the percentage of stock ownership after the redemption be less than 80% of the percentage ownership immediately before the redemption (.8 × .52 = .416; .35 < .416). Therefore, the redemption is substantially disproportionate and is considered a sale. Hence, the basis is $25,000 (250 remaining shares × $100 per share).
Answer (A) is incorrect. The amount of $50,000 would be the basis if the redemption was considered equivalent to a dividend. Answer (B) is incorrect. The amount received for the redeemed stock is $40,000. Answer (C) is incorrect. The 250 remaining shares have a $100 basis per share.

17.3.10. T, an individual shareholder, owned 25% of the Towne Corporation stock. Pursuant to a series of stock redemptions, Towne redeemed 10% of the shares of stock T owned in exchange for land having a fair market value of $30,000 and an adjusted basis of $10,000. T's basis for all of his Towne stock was $200,000. T reported the redemption transaction as if it were a dividend. T's basis in the land and his Towne stock (immediately after the redemption) is

A.   Land, $30,000; stock, $200,000.

B.   Land, $10,000; stock, $180,000.

C.   Land, $30,000; stock, $180,000.

D.   Land, $10,000; stock, $200,000.

Answer (A) is correct. *(Publisher, adapted)*
REQUIRED: The basis in land received in a redemption of stock treated as a dividend, and the basis in the stock after the redemption.
DISCUSSION: Under Sec. 302, if a redemption of shares does not qualify as a sale or exchange, it is treated as a dividend under Sec. 301. Section 301(b)(1) provides that the amount of a dividend distribution is the amount of money received plus the fair market value of the property received, so T has a $30,000 dividend. Section 301(d) provides that the basis of property received in a distribution will be the fair market value of such property. Therefore, T's basis in the land is $30,000. A dividend distribution does not affect the basis in a shareholder's stock, so the basis in the stock T holds after the redemption is $200,000 [Reg. 1.302-2(c)].
Answer (B) is incorrect. T's basis in the land is not $10,000, and T's basis in the stock is not $180,000. Answer (C) is incorrect. The distribution is considered to be a dividend, and the basis of the dividend property received is its FMV. The basis of the stock is not affected. Answer (D) is incorrect. T's basis in the land is not $10,000.

17.3.11. Select the answer that best describes what happens when shareholders receive a series of distributions, not part of an installment obligation, covering 2 or more consecutive tax years in redemption of all of the stock of a corporation pursuant to a plan intended to result in the complete liquidation of the corporation.

A.   The shareholders will be allowed to recover their respective basis in the stock before recognizing any gains.

B.   The shareholders will treat the distributions as dividends to the extent of the corporation's earnings and profits.

C.   The shareholders will recognize a pro rata portion of the gain in each of the years that distributions are received.

D.   No losses from the transactions will be deductible.

Answer (A) is correct. *(SPE, adapted)*
REQUIRED: The tax treatment of a series of distributions in the course of a complete liquidation.
DISCUSSION: If a corporation makes a series of distributions in the course of a complete liquidation, each shareholder is entitled to recover the entire basis in his or her shares before recognizing gain.
Answer (B) is incorrect. The distributions are made in complete liquidation of the corporation. Answer (C) is incorrect. No gain is recognized until basis is fully recovered. Answer (D) is incorrect. Losses could be deductible.

17.3.12. The two equal shareholders of a C corporation are thinking of filing an election to have the company treated as an S corporation. Which of the following consequences is an advantage of this election?

A.   The corporation's net operating loss carryovers from prior years are immediately deductible by the shareholders.

B.   The corporation's tax-free fringe benefits for the shareholders will be deductible by the corporation.

C.   The shareholders of the S corporation will be taxed only on distributions from the corporation.

D.   The corporation's capital losses can be claimed on the tax returns of the shareholders.

Answer (D) is correct. *(CPA, adapted)*
REQUIRED: The benefits of S corporation election for owners.
DISCUSSION: Capital losses of the corporation will flow-through to the shareholders, who may use them to offset any of their own capital gains.
Answer (A) is incorrect. Though carryovers, such as NOLs, between C and S corporations are permitted, NOLs do not become immediately deductible. Answer (B) is incorrect. Employee fringe benefits must be included in gross income of all persons who own more than 2% of the stock of an S corporation. Thus, two 50% owners would not benefit. Answer (C) is incorrect. Shareholders of the S corporation are taxed on their share of S corporation income. However, distributions will be tax-free to the extent of their basis in the S corporation.

17.3.13. Mr. G actually and constructively owned 90% of Corporation V's only stock issued and outstanding as of March 1 of the current year. On March 2, V redeemed some of Mr. G's stock for property. After the redemption, Mr. G actually and constructively owned 60% of V's stock. This exchange is considered a substantially disproportionate redemption.

A. True.

B. False.

Answer (B) is correct. *(SPE, adapted)*
DISCUSSION: For the redemption to be considered substantially disproportionate, Mr. G's ownership after the redemption would have to be less than 50% of the voting power of all classes of outstanding stock entitled to vote (he does not meet this requirement). Also, his percentage of the total of outstanding voting stock after the redemption would have to be less than 80% of his percentage ownership of the stock immediately before the redemption. This requirement is met since Mr. G's 60% ownership interest is less than 80% of his prior interest (.9 × .80 = 72%). Since Mr. G meets only one of the two requirements, this exchange is not considered substantially disproportionate.

17.3.14. Under the constructive ownership rules that apply to a stock redemption, a waiver of family attribution may qualify a redemption for exchange treatment.

A. True.

B. False.

Answer (A) is correct. *(SPE, adapted)*
DISCUSSION: Under Sec. 302(b)(3), a complete termination of a shareholder's interest is treated as a distribution in part or full payment in exchange for his or her stock. For purposes of determining whether a complete termination has occurred, the family stock attribution rules of Sec. 318 do not apply if, immediately after the distribution, the former stockholder has no interest in the corporation other than an interest as a creditor, does not acquire any such interest within 10 years from the date of the distribution, and files an agreement to notify the IRS of any acquisition of stock in the corporation within 10 years from the date of the redemption [Sec. 302(c)(2)].

17.3.15. Corporation Z has 500 shares of its only class of stock outstanding. A and B each own 200 shares and C owns 100 shares. None of the parties are related. During the current year, Z redeemed 100 shares from both A and B and 50 shares from C. This redemption is considered to be a distribution equivalent to a dividend.

A. True.

B. False.

Answer (A) is correct. *(SPE, adapted)*
DISCUSSION: Section 302 determines whether a redemption is considered a distribution equivalent to a dividend or payment for the stock eligible for capital gain or loss treatment. Under Sec. 302(b)(2), a substantially disproportionate redemption qualifies for capital gain or loss treatment. For a redemption to be substantially disproportionate, the shareholder must own less than 50% of all outstanding voting stock immediately after the redemption, and his or her total percentage of ownership must be less than 80% of his or her ownership percentage immediately before the redemption.

Each of the three shareholders owns less than 50% of all outstanding voting stock immediately after the redemption, so the first test is met. However, the percentage of stock owned by each shareholder has not changed as a result of the redemption. Therefore, the second test is not met and the redemption is not substantially disproportionate. The redemption is considered to be equivalent to a dividend since a meaningful reduction in the shareholders' ownership interests did not occur [Sec. 302(b)(1)].

17.3.16. Mr. Y holds 30% of the common stock of T-Bone Corporation and 250 shares of T-Bone's preferred stock (Sec. 306 stock). Mr. Y also has a basis of $100,000 in his common stock and $15,000 in his preferred stock. However, T-Bone redeemed all of Mr. Y's preferred stock for $25,000 at a date when T-Bone had only $15,000 of earnings and profits. T-Bone had $100,000 of earnings and profits when Mr. Y originally received the preferred stock. Mr. Y has dividend income of $15,000, and the basis in his common stock is increased to $105,000.

A. True.

B. False.

Answer (A) is correct. *(Publisher, adapted)*
DISCUSSION: When Sec. 306 stock is redeemed, the full amount received by the shareholder is treated as a Sec. 301 distribution. Mr. Y has a $15,000 dividend since there is only $15,000 of earnings and profits at the time of the redemption. Unlike a sale of Sec. 306 stock, the earnings and profits at the time of redemption are important rather than the earnings and profits at the time the preferred stock was distributed. Mr. Y's basis in the preferred stock is reduced by the additional $10,000 received in the redemption that is not a dividend. The remaining $5,000 basis of the preferred stock is assigned to the common stock, which increases its basis to $105,000.

17.3.17. Corporation Z has only one class of stock outstanding, composed of 300 shares that are owned by three unrelated parties. Mr. K and Mrs. Y each own 125 shares, and Mrs. P owns 50 shares. If Z makes a cash redemption of 75 shares from both Mr. K and Mrs. Y and 25 shares from Mrs. P, the proceeds will qualify for capital gain or loss treatment by the shareholders as a substantially disproportionate distribution.

A. True.

B. False.

Answer (B) is correct. *(SPE, adapted)*
DISCUSSION: For the redemption to be considered substantially disproportionate under Sec. 302(b)(2), each shareholder's ownership percentage before and after the redemption is tested. The shareholder must own less than 50% of the voting power of all classes of outstanding voting stock after the redemption, and his or her total percentage ownership after the redemption must be less than 80% of his or her percentage ownership immediately before the redemption.

	Percentage Ownership	
	Before	After
Mr. K	41.67%	40%
Mrs. Y	41.67%	40%
Mrs. P	16.66%	20%
	100.00%	100%

None of the shareholders meet the 80% test since 40% is more than 33.4% (41.7% × 80%) and 20% is more than 13.4% (16.7% × 80%). Therefore, the redemption distribution is likely to be taxed as a dividend to all three shareholders to the extent of Corporation Z's earnings and profits. For K and Y, it is possible that capital gain treatment may be available if their ownership reduction is considered "meaningful" and the distribution is considered not equivalent to a dividend under Sec. 302(b)(1).

17.3.18. Corporation W has 2,000 shares of its only class of stock outstanding. Mr. D owns 1,500 shares and his son, Randy, owns 500 shares. W redeemed all 1,500 shares from Mr. D for $45,000. Mr. D kept his position in W as an officer and director. This redemption qualifies for capital gain treatment by Mr. D since all of his ownership in W has been terminated.

A. True.

B. False.

Answer (B) is correct. *(SPE, adapted)*
DISCUSSION: Under Sec. 302(b)(3), a redemption qualifies for capital gain treatment if it is a complete redemption of all the shareholder's stock. The redemption must completely terminate the shareholder's interest in the corporation. The distributee cannot retain an interest in the corporation as an officer, director, or employee, but can retain a creditor interest [Sec. 302(c)(2)(A)(i)]. If the distributee retains such an interest, the attribution rules of Sec. 318(a)(1) will apply. Since Mr. D retains an interest in the corporation other than a creditor interest, Sec. 318(a)(1) will attribute his son's stock ownership to him and he will be considered to own 100% of the corporation's stock after the redemption. The distribution will not qualify for capital gain treatment and will be treated as a dividend.

17.3.19. Tiger Corporation has 1,000 shares of stock outstanding. Three hundred of the shares are owned by individual K, who died on March 12 of last year. K's cost basis for his Tiger stock is $100,000. The stock was valued at $600,000 for estate tax purposes. K's gross estate was $1,000,000. Debts of his estate were $100,000. Funeral expenses of $90,000 and death taxes of $60,000 were incurred by the estate. An amount of $100,000 of the Tiger stock was redeemed by the estate on April 5 of this year in order to provide liquidity to the estate. The $100,000 proceeds are taxed as a dividend to the estate.

A. True.

B. False.

Answer (B) is correct. *(Publisher, adapted)*
DISCUSSION: Under Sec. 303, an estate may treat a stock redemption as a sale or exchange of property. In order to obtain this favorable treatment, the value of the stock that is being redeemed must be greater than 35% of the value of the gross estate after taking the deductions allowed under Sec. 2053 (funeral expenses, administration expenses, claims against the estate, and unpaid mortgages) and Sec. 2054 (casualty and theft losses). The stock being redeemed is valued at its value for estate tax purposes.

After deducting the allowable expenses, K's adjusted gross estate is valued at $810,000 ($1,000,000 gross estate − $100,000 debts and $90,000 funeral expenses). The value of the total Tiger stockholdings is 74% of the value of the gross estate after taking the allowable deductions ($600,000 ÷ $810,000). Death taxes are a claim against the estate, but they do not reduce the estate under Sec. 2053 [Sec. 2053(c)(1)(B)]. The requirement of Sec. 303 is met, and the redemption is treated as a sale or exchange of the stock, not as a dividend.

17.4 Partial Liquidations

17.4.1. All of the following are requirements for a distribution to be treated as a partial liquidation of a corporation except

- A. The distribution is not essentially equivalent to a dividend that is determined at the shareholder level rather than at the corporate level.
- B. The distribution is attributable to the distributing corporation's ceasing to conduct a qualifying trade or business that was actively conducted throughout the 5-year period ending on the date of the redemption.
- C. The distribution is pursuant to a plan and occurs within the taxable year in which the plan is adopted or within the succeeding taxable year.
- D. All of the answers would be treated as a distribution in partial liquidation of a corporation.

Answer (A) is correct. *(SPE, adapted)*
REQUIRED: The statement that is not a requirement for a distribution to be treated as a partial liquidation of a corporation.
DISCUSSION: The determination of whether a distribution is not essentially equivalent to a dividend is made at the corporate level. The distribution must be the result of a bona fide contraction of the corporation's business. A distribution satisfies the "not essentially equivalent to a dividend" standard if it meets the safe harbor rule under Sec. 302(e)(2).
Answer (B) is incorrect. A requirement for a distribution to be treated as a partial liquidation of a corporation is that the distribution be attributable to the distributing corporation's ceasing to conduct a qualifying trade or business that was actively conducted throughout the 5-year period ending on the date of the redemption. Answer (C) is incorrect. A requirement for a distribution to be treated as a partial liquidation of a corporation is that the distribution be pursuant to a plan and occur within the taxable year in which the plan is adopted or within the succeeding taxable year. Answer (D) is incorrect. Not all of the answers describe requirements for a distribution to be treated as a partial liquidation of a corporation.

17.4.2. Zebra Corporation distributed property in proportionate redemption of its stock in a partial liquidation. Zebra had earnings and profits exceeding the amount of the distribution. A distribution was made to Tiger Corporation, a 25% shareholder. The distributed property had a $75,000 fair market value and a $40,000 adjusted basis to Zebra. Tiger had an adjusted basis of $25,000 in the stock redeemed by Zebra. What is the tax effect to Tiger?

- A. $25,000 capital gain.
- B. $35,000 dividend.
- C. $75,000 capital gain.
- D. $75,000 dividend.

Answer (D) is correct. *(SPE, adapted)*
REQUIRED: The tax effect of a partial liquidation.
DISCUSSION: Section 302(b)(4) allows shareholders who receive redemptions in partial liquidation to treat the distribution as payment for their stock. Any gain on the redemption is eligible for capital gain treatment. The provisions of Sec. 302(b)(4) apply only to noncorporate shareholders. Therefore, a corporation that receives a redemption in partial liquidation must treat the distribution as a dividend to the extent of earnings and profits of the distributing corporation, unless the distribution is eligible for capital gain treatment under one of the three other exchange exceptions of Sec. 302(b) (i.e., a complete termination, substantially disproportionate, or not essentially equivalent to a dividend). None of these exceptions applies here. Therefore, Tiger has received a $75,000 dividend.
Answer (A) is incorrect. The amount of $25,000 is the adjusted basis of the stock redeemed, not the fair market value of the property distributed, and the transaction should be treated as a dividend. Answer (B) is incorrect. The amount of $35,000 is the difference between the distributing corporation's adjusted basis and the property's fair market value. Answer (C) is incorrect. Only distributions to noncorporate shareholders qualify for capital gain treatment under Sec. 302(b)(4).

17.4.3. How does a noncorporate shareholder treat the gain on a redemption of stock that qualifies as a partial liquidation of the distributing corporation?

- A. Entirely as capital gain.
- B. Entirely as a dividend.
- C. Partly as capital gain and partly as a dividend.
- D. As a tax-free transaction.

Answer (A) is correct. *(CPA, adapted)*
REQUIRED: The proper treatment accorded a partially liquidating distribution received by a noncorporate shareholder.
DISCUSSION: Section 302(b)(4) states that a noncorporate shareholder who receives a distribution in redemption of stock in a partial liquidation treats the distribution as payment in exchange for the stock. Any gain or loss on the exchange will be treated as capital in nature.
Answer (B) is incorrect. A noncorporate shareholder will not treat the redemption entirely as a dividend. Answer (C) is incorrect. The partial liquidation treats the distribution as a payment in exchange for stock. Answer (D) is incorrect. A noncorporate shareholder will not treat the redemption as a tax-free transaction.

17.4.4. Turbo Corporation distributed land to shareholder Lea in partial liquidation of her interest. At the time of the distribution, the land had an adjusted basis of $80,000 and a fair market value of $125,000. Lea exchanged 90 of 100 shares of Turbo stock for the land. At the time of the partial liquidation, Lea's adjusted basis in the 90 shares was $60,000. Other unrelated shareholders of Turbo own a combined 150 shares outstanding. Just prior to the distribution, Turbo had earnings and profits of $150,000. What are the amounts and the character of income that Turbo Corporation and Lea must recognize on the partial liquidation?

	Turbo	Lea
A.	$0	$65,000 capital gain
B.	$0	$65,000 dividend
C.	$45,000 capital gain	$65,000 capital gain
D.	$45,000 capital gain	$125,000 dividend

Answer (C) is correct. *(SPE, adapted)*
REQUIRED: The amount and the character of income recognized from a partial liquidation.
DISCUSSION: A redemption distribution is substantially disproportionate with respect to a shareholder (and qualifies for capital gains treatment) if, after the redemption, (s)he owns less than 50% of the total combined voting power of all classes of voting stock and his or her percentage of voting stock and ownership percentage of common stock after the redemption are less than 80% of that immediately before the redemption. Lea meets these criteria and has $65,000 of capital gain ($125,000 land value – $60,000 stock basis). Turbo has capital gain of $45,000 because a corporation that makes an in-kind distribution of property whose fair market value ($125,000) exceeds its basis ($80,000) recognizes gain as if it had sold the property to the shareholder at its fair market value.
Answer (A) is incorrect. Turbo Corporation must recognize a capital gain. Answer (B) is incorrect. Both Turbo Corporation and Lea must recognize a capital gain. Answer (D) is incorrect. Lea does not have a $125,000 dividend resulting from the partial liquidation.

17.4.5. Shale Corporation made two liquidating distributions of $1,000, on January 9, Year 1, and February 13, Year 1, to shareholder Patricia. Shale must file Form 1099-DIV, *Dividends and Distributions*, with the Internal Revenue Service by

A. December 31, Year 1.

B. January 31, Year 2.

C. February 28, Year 2.

D. March 15, Year 2.

Answer (C) is correct. *(SPE, adapted)*
REQUIRED: The date on which Form 1099-DIV must be filed.
DISCUSSION: A corporation making any distribution in complete or partial liquidation must file a Form 1099-DIV in each calendar year of the liquidation for each shareholder to whom it makes a distribution of $600 or more. These forms must be sent to the shareholders by January 31 of the year following the calendar year in which the liquidating distribution is made [Sec. 6042(c)] and filed with the IRS by the end of February [Reg. 1.6043-2(a)].
Answer (A) is incorrect. December 31, Year 1, is the end of the tax year and not the date by which the 1099-DIV must be sent to the shareholders or the date by which they must be filed with the IRS. Answer (B) is incorrect. January 31, Year 2, is the date when the 1099-DIV forms must be sent to the shareholders. Answer (D) is incorrect. S corporation tax returns must be filed by March 15, Year 2.

17.4.6. Corporation B has been in business for 18 years. On January 1 of the current year, a fire destroyed some of the assets of the corporation, causing a cessation of part of its activities. As a result, B's president decided on a permanent contraction of the business. On May 31 of the current year, the corporation distributed unused insurance proceeds, recovered as a result of the fire, in exchange for some of its outstanding stock. The distribution consisted of $25,000 in cash. B had earnings and profits of $50,000 prior to the distribution. This distribution will qualify as a partial liquidation.

A. True.

B. False.

Answer (A) is correct. *(SPE, adapted)*
DISCUSSION: Section 302(e) provides that a distribution can qualify as a partial liquidation if it is not essentially equivalent to a dividend. A distribution meets this requirement if it is attributable to the termination of one of the corporation's businesses, i.e., a bona fide contraction of the corporate business. The distribution of unused insurance proceeds recovered as a result of a fire that destroyed part of a business qualifies as a partial liquidation [Reg. 1.346-1(a)(2)]. Note that only noncorporate shareholders are eligible to treat the redemption as a sale or exchange under Sec. 302(b)(4). Corporate shareholders may apply one of the other exceptions of Sec. 302(b).

17.5 Complete Liquidations

17.5.1. Ann owned two blocks of Lou Corporation stock, which had the following characteristics:

Block	Shares	Acquired	Basis
1	200	1/1/Year 1	$20,000
2	50	7/2/Year 2	12,500

Ann's two blocks of stock combined represented 10% of Lou Corporation's outstanding stock. Pursuant to Lou's complete liquidation, Ann received a $50,000 cash distribution on December 1, Year 2, in exchange for her 250 shares. Lou's earnings and profits balance immediately before any liquidating distributions was $50,000. What are the amount and the character of Ann's gain or loss?

A. $50,000 dividend income.

B. $17,500 long-term capital gain.

C. $20,000 long-term capital gain and $2,500 short-term capital loss.

D. No gain or loss.

17.5.2. Mr. L owned 100 shares of stock in Willow Corporation. During the current year, Willow completely liquidated and distributed the following to L:

Cash	$ 25,000
Land: Fair market value	450,000
Subject to a mortgage of	200,000

Mr. L's adjusted basis in Willow's stock was $50,000 and he will assume the mortgage on the land. What is L's basis in the land received?

A. $50,000

B. $75,000

C. $250,000

D. $450,000

17.5.3. Krol Corporation distributed marketable securities in redemption of its stock in a complete liquidation. On the date of distribution, these securities had a basis of $100,000 and a fair market value of $150,000. What gain does Krol have as a result of the distribution?

A. $0

B. $50,000 capital gain.

C. $50,000 Sec. 1231 gain.

D. $50,000 ordinary gain.

Answer (C) is correct. *(SPE, adapted)*
REQUIRED: The amount and the character of gain or loss to be reported as a result of a complete liquidation.
DISCUSSION: Section 331 provides capital gain or loss treatment for distributions received by a shareholder in complete liquidation of a corporation. The gain or loss will be long-term or short-term, depending on the length of time the stock has been held (Sec. 1222).
The shareholder's gain or loss is the difference between the amount realized and the basis in the stock. The amount realized by Ann is $200 per share ($50,000 distribution ÷ 250 shares owned). The sale of Block 1 produces a gain of $20,000 [200 shares × ($200 selling price – $100 per share basis)]. The gain is long-term because the stock was held for more than 1 year. The sale of Block 2 produces a loss of $2,500 [50 shares × ($250 per share basis – $200 per share selling price)]. The loss is short-term because the stock was held less than 1 year.
Answer (A) is incorrect. The amount of the distribution, not the amount of the gain/loss, is $50,000. Answer (B) is incorrect. The gain and loss should be allocated to the different blocks of stock. The amounts should not be aggregated ($50,000 – $32,500 total basis). Answer (D) is incorrect. A gain and a loss are recognized because the transaction is treated as a sale.

Answer (D) is correct. *(SPE, adapted)*
REQUIRED: The basis of land received in a complete liquidation.
DISCUSSION: Section 334(a) states that, if property is received in complete liquidation, and if gain or loss is recognized on receipt of such property, the basis of the property in the distributee's hands will be the fair market value of the property at the time of the distribution.
Mr. L will recognize a gain of $225,000 on the receipt of the cash and land [($450,000 fair market value of land + $25,000 cash – $200,000 liability) – his $50,000 basis in the stock]. Since he recognizes a gain, the provisions of Sec. 334(a) apply and his basis in the land received is its fair market value at the time of distribution.
Answer (A) is incorrect. The amount of $50,000 is the adjusted basis of the stock. Answer (B) is incorrect. The amount of $75,000 is the adjusted basis of the stock plus the cash distributed. Answer (C) is incorrect. The amount of $250,000 is the FMV of the land less the mortgage. A shareholder's basis is not reduced by the assumption of a corporate liability.

Answer (B) is correct. *(CPA, adapted)*
REQUIRED: The gain to a corporation on the distribution of property in redemption of its stock in a complete liquidation.
DISCUSSION: Section 336 provides that gain or loss is recognized when a corporation distributes property as part of a complete liquidation. Therefore, Krol Corporation will recognize a $50,000 ($150,000 – $100,000) gain. It is a capital gain because the marketable securities are a capital asset.
Answer (A) is incorrect. Krol has a gain as a result of the distribution. Answer (C) is incorrect. Krol does not have a Sec. 1231 gain. Answer (D) is incorrect. Krol does not have an ordinary gain.

17.5.4. Under a plan of complete liquidation, Len Corporation distributed land, having an adjusted basis to Len of $26,000, to its sole shareholder. The land was subject to a liability of $38,000, which the shareholder assumed for legitimate business purposes. The fair market value of the land on the date of distribution was $35,000. What is the amount of Len Corporation's recognized gain or (loss)?

A. $(29,000)

B. $(3,000)

C. $9,000

D. $12,000

Answer (D) is correct. *(SPE, adapted)*
REQUIRED: The amount of gain (loss) recognized by the distributing corporation when a liability exists during a complete liquidation.
DISCUSSION: Section 336(a) provides that a corporation should treat a complete liquidation as a sale using the fair market value. However, Sec. 336(b) requires that the fair market value used should not be less than any liability accepted by the distributee. Since Len is transferring property with a liability of $38,000, which is higher than the $35,000 FMV, the $38,000 is used as the new FMV. Therefore, Len Corporation recognizes a $12,000 gain ($38,000 new FMV – $26,000 adjusted basis).
Answer (A) is incorrect. The amount of $(29,000) includes the adjusted basis, the liability, and the fair market value [$35,000 – ($26,000 + $38,000)]. Answer (B) is incorrect. The amount of $(3,000) is the difference between the $35,000 market value and $38,000 liability; the adjusted basis was never considered. Answer (C) is incorrect. The amount of $9,000 excludes the effects of the liability on the transaction.

17.5.5. A corporation was completely liquidated and dissolved during the current year. The filing fees, professional fees, and other expenditures incurred in connection with the liquidation and dissolution are

A. Deductible in full by the dissolved corporation.

B. Deductible by the shareholders and not by the corporation.

C. Treated as capital losses by the corporation.

D. Not deductible by either the corporation or the shareholders.

Answer (A) is correct. *(CPA, adapted)*
REQUIRED: The tax treatment for expenses incurred in connection with a corporate liquidation.
DISCUSSION: The filing fees, professional fees, and other liquidation-related expenses are deductible in the final tax return of the corporation under Sec. 162(a).
Answer (B) is incorrect. The expense is not incurred by the shareholders. Therefore, the shareholders cannot deduct them. Answer (C) is incorrect. The expenses are not treated as capital losses by the corporation. Answer (D) is incorrect. The expenses are deductible as trade or business expenses under Sec. 162(a) by the corporation.

17.5.6. Individual Z contributed property with an adjusted basis of $1,000 and a fair market value of $100 to Alpha Corporation. Z owned 10% of Alpha. Individual T, who owned the remaining 90% of the Alpha stock, contributed $900 cash at the same time. The primary purpose of the contributions was to permit Z and Alpha to recognize losses during Alpha's pending liquidation. The following year, Alpha adopted a plan of complete liquidation. In computing the loss on making the liquidation distribution, Alpha's basis will be

A. $0

B. $100

C. $900

D. $1,000

Answer (B) is correct. *(Publisher, adapted)*
REQUIRED: The corporation's basis for computing loss on depreciated property.
DISCUSSION: Normally gain or loss is recognized by a corporation on a liquidating distribution of its assets [Sec. 336(a)]. But if property is contributed to a corporation less than 2 years before a plan of liquidation is adopted and the principal purpose of the contribution is to recognize loss upon sale or distribution of the property, the basis for determining loss on such property acquired by the corporation in a Sec. 351 transaction, or as a contribution to capital, will be reduced (but not below zero) by the excess of the basis of the property on the date of contribution over its fair market value on such date [Sec. 336(d)(2)]. The tax avoidance presumption, however, can be avoided by using the property in the corporation's trade or business.
If these requirements are met by Individual Z and Alpha Corporation with respect to the property contributed, Alpha's basis for determining loss will be $100 ($1,000 – $900 excess of basis over fair market value at the time of contribution). If the fair market value is less than $100 at the time of liquidation, Alpha will still be able to recognize a loss with respect to that difference. On the other hand, if the fair market value has increased to greater than $1,000, then Alpha could recognize a gain using $1,000 as the basis for determining gain.
Answer (A) is incorrect. Alpha has basis in the property. Answer (C) is incorrect. Alpha's basis will not be $900 in computing the loss on making the liquidation distribution. Answer (D) is incorrect. Alpha's gain basis for the property is $1,000.

17.5.7. Individual Y owns 55% of Beta Corporation. Five years ago, Y contributed property with an adjusted basis of $20,000 and a fair market value of $8,000 to Beta in a transaction qualifying under Sec. 351. In the current year, Beta adopted a plan of complete liquidation and distributed this same property to Y. At this time, the property had an adjusted basis of $18,000 and a fair market value of $5,000. How much loss will Beta recognize on the distribution?

A. $0

B. $3,000

C. $12,000

D. $13,000

Answer (A) is correct. *(Publisher, adapted)*
REQUIRED: The loss recognized in a liquidation on the distribution of recently contributed property to a related shareholder.
DISCUSSION: Normally gain or loss is recognized on a liquidating distribution of assets [Sec. 336(a)]. However, under Sec. 336(d)(1), a loss is not recognized in a liquidation on the distribution of property to a related person (which includes a greater-than-50% shareholder) unless the property is distributed to all shareholders on a pro rata basis and the property was not acquired in a Sec. 351 transaction or contribution to capital during the 5 preceding years (also known as disqualified property). Since the distribution was of property acquired in a Sec. 351 transaction within the 5 preceding years, no loss is recognized on the distribution of the disqualified property to the related person. The fact that the distribution was not pro rata does not affect the ability to recognize the loss.
Answer (B) is incorrect. The amount of $3,000 is the difference between the FMV 5 years ago and the current FMV. Answer (C) is incorrect. The amount of $12,000 is the difference between the adjusted basis and FMV 5 years ago. Answer (D) is incorrect. The amount of $13,000 is the difference between the adjusted basis of the property and its fair market value at the time of liquidation.

17.5.8. Corporation T is deemed to be a collapsible corporation under the provisions of Sec. 341. Individual A owned 15 of T's 100 outstanding shares of common stock since its formation. A's basis for these shares is $15,000. T Corporation is liquidated on December 7 of the current year after being in business for 2 years. Pursuant to the liquidation, A receives cash and property worth $22,500. As a result of the liquidation, A reports a $7,500 long-term capital gain.

A. True.

B. False.

Answer (A) is correct. *(Publisher, adapted)*
DISCUSSION: Under the general rules of Sec. 331(a), amounts received in a distribution in complete liquidation of a corporation are normally treated as payments in exchange for the stock, which will result in recognition of a capital gain. Since Sec. 336(a) requires the recognition of gain by T when making a liquidating distribution, the Sec. 341(b)(1)(A) substantial realization of income test has likely been met and the corporation will not be deemed to have been formed with an intent towards collapsing the corporation. If this requirement has been met, the shareholder will have capital gain instead of ordinary income.

17.5.9. Corporation Z is a cash-basis taxpayer. Z distributed $50,000 of its accounts receivable to an individual shareholder, Able, pursuant to its complete liquidation. Corporation Z does not need to recognize income as a result of the distribution, and Able takes a zero basis for the accounts receivable.

A. True.

B. False.

Answer (B) is correct. *(Publisher, adapted)*
DISCUSSION: Section 336 provides that gain or loss is recognized when a corporation distributes property as part of a complete liquidation. Therefore, Corporation Z will recognize $50,000 ($50,000 – $0 basis) of income. It will be ordinary income because collection of the accounts receivable would have resulted in ordinary income being reported. Able's basis in the accounts receivable will be their $50,000 fair market value [Sec. 334(a)].

17.5.10. Corporation G, in complete liquidation, distributed to Shareholder Y cash of $5,000 and $8,000 during last year and this year, respectively. The corporation is not required to file Form 1099-DIV until this year, the year of the final distribution.

A. True.

B. False.

Answer (B) is correct. *(SPE, adapted)*
DISCUSSION: In a complete liquidation that is to be accomplished by a series of partial distributions, a corporation is required to file Form 1099-DIV each calendar year in which it distributes a partial payment of $600 or more [Reg. 1.6043-2(a)]. Therefore, Form 1099-DIV should be filed in each of the 2 years.

17.5.11. A corporation may request an advance ruling from the Internal Revenue Service before entering into transactions such as liquidations and stock redemptions.

A. True.

B. False.

Answer (A) is correct. *(SPE, adapted)*
DISCUSSION: Corporations may request advance rulings from the IRS before entering into transactions such as liquidations and stock redemptions. However, there are limitations; e.g., the IRS will not ordinarily issue an advance ruling for a partial liquidation unless it results in at least a 20% reduction in (1) gross revenue, (2) net fair market value of assets, and (3) employees (Rev. Proc. 97-3).

17.5.12. Within 30 days after the adoption of a resolution or plan (including any amendment or supplements to it) for the dissolution of a corporation or its complete or partial liquidation, the corporation must file an information return (Form 966, *Corporate Dissolution or Liquidation*) with the Internal Revenue Service Center with which the corporation is required to file its income tax returns.

    A. True.

    B. False.

Answer (A) is correct. *(SPE, adapted)*
    DISCUSSION: A corporation must report the adoption of a plan of liquidation to the IRS within 30 days by filing Form 966, an information return [Sec. 6043(a)].

17.5.13. Corporation M dissolved on December 31 of last year and disposed of all its assets by that date. After filing M's final return on March 15 of the current year, the trustee in liquidation filed a written request for a prompt assessment. The assessment must be made within 18 months after the receipt of the written request or 3 years from the date the return was filed, whichever is earlier.

    A. True.

    B. False.

Answer (A) is correct. *(SPE, adapted)*
    DISCUSSION: Section 6501(d) permits a request for prompt assessment to be made by a corporation. The effect of such a request is to notify the IRS that the corporation contemplates dissolution at or before the expiration of 18 months from the date of the request. The request limits the time in which a tax assessment may be made, or a court proceeding begun, to 18 months from the date the request was filed. The request, however, does not extend the assessment period beyond 3 years from the date the return was filed.

17.6 Liquidations of Subsidiary Corporations

17.6.1. Which one of the following statements is true regarding the complete liquidation of a subsidiary corporation under Sec. 332?

    A. Gain is recognized on the liquidation only to the extent of the parent corporation's ratable share of the subsidiary's earnings and profits.

    B. The tax attributes of the subsidiary corporation carry over to the parent.

    C. The liquidated corporation recognizes no gain or loss on the liquidation except for depreciation recapture under Sec. 1245 and Sec. 1250.

    D. The minority shareholders must, like the parent corporation, recognize no gain or loss on the liquidation.

Answer (B) is correct. *(Publisher, adapted)*
    REQUIRED: The true statement of a complete liquidation of a subsidiary under Sec. 332.
    DISCUSSION: When a subsidiary corporation is liquidated into the parent corporation in a Sec. 332 transaction, no gain or loss is recognized by either corporation on the liquidation. The tax attributes of the subsidiary corporation carry over to the parent corporation under Sec. 381.
    Answer (A) is incorrect. No gain is recognized on the liquidation of a subsidiary corporation under Sec. 332. Answer (C) is incorrect. Section 1245 and 1250 recapture is not recognized; it carries over to the new owner of the property [Secs. 1245(b)(3) and 1250(d)(3)]. Answer (D) is incorrect. Section 332 applies only to the parent corporation. Minority shareholders report the liquidating distribution under Sec. 331.

17.6.2. On January 1 of the current year, Pearl Corporation owned 90% of the outstanding stock of Seso Corporation. Both companies were domestic corporations. Pursuant to a plan of liquidation adopted by Seso in March of the same year, Seso distributed all of its property in September in complete redemption of all its stock. Seso's accumulated earnings were $18,000 on the distribution date. Seso had never been insolvent. Pursuant to the liquidation, Seso transferred to Pearl a parcel of land with a basis of $10,000 and a fair market value of $40,000 in redemption of its stock. How much gain must Seso recognize in the current year on the transfer of this land to Pearl?

    A. $0

    B. $18,000

    C. $27,000

    D. $30,000

Answer (A) is correct. *(CPA, adapted)*
    REQUIRED: The amount of gain that must be recognized by a solvent subsidiary on the distribution of appreciated property to its parent in a complete liquidation.
    DISCUSSION: Section 337 generally requires that a controlled corporation recognize no gain or loss upon making a liquidating distribution of property to its parent corporation. This exception to the general rule of Sec. 336 applies only if the control requirement is met. The control requirement is that the parent corporation must own at least 80% of the voting power and 80% of the total value of the stock of the corporation being liquidated.
    Under this rule, Seso will recognize no gain on the transfer of the land to Pearl.
    Answer (B) is incorrect. The amount of $18,000 is Seso's accumulated earnings at the distribution date. Answer (C) is incorrect. The amount of $27,000 is 90% of the difference between the fair market value of the land and Seso's basis in it. Answer (D) is incorrect. The amount of $30,000 is the difference between the fair market value of the land and Seso's basis in it.

17.7 Corporate Divisions and Reorganizations

17.7.1. On July 1 of the current year, in connection with a recapitalization of Yorktown Corporation, Robert Moore exchanged 1,000 shares of stock, that cost him $95,000, for 1,000 shares of new stock worth $108,000 and bonds in the principal amount of $10,000 with a fair market value of $10,500. What is the amount of Moore's recognized gain during the year?

A. $0

B. $10,000

C. $10,500

D. $23,500

Answer (C) is correct. *(CPA, adapted)*
REQUIRED: The amount of gain recognized by a shareholder receiving stock and bonds for stock in a recapitalization.
DISCUSSION: A recapitalization is a Type E reorganization under Sec. 368(a)(1)(E). Section 354(a)(1) provides that no gain or loss is recognized if stock or securities in a corporation are exchanged solely for stock or securities in the same or another corporation pursuant to a plan of reorganization. Therefore, the exchange of the stock for stock qualifies as a tax-free exchange. The bonds are generally considered securities and would qualify except that Sec. 354(a)(2) denies tax-free treatment when securities (bonds) are received but none are surrendered. Under Sec. 356, the gain recognized is the lesser of the realized gain or the fair market value of the nonqualifying property received (in this case, the bonds).
The realized gain is the total amount realized of $118,500 ($108,000 stock + $10,500 bonds) less basis of $95,000 in the stock given up, or $23,500. The recognized gain is limited to $10,500 (the FMV of the bonds received).
Answer (A) is incorrect. Moore has a recognized gain in the current year. Answer (B) is incorrect. The principal amount of the bonds is $10,000. Answer (D) is incorrect. A gain is not recognized on the stock-for-stock exchange.

17.7.2. Which one of the following is not a corporate reorganization as defined in the Internal Revenue Code?

A. Stock redemption.

B. Recapitalization.

C. Mere change in identity.

D. Statutory merger.

Answer (A) is correct. *(CPA, adapted)*
REQUIRED: The transaction that does not constitute a corporate reorganization.
DISCUSSION: A stock redemption is normally a taxable transaction to the shareholder(s). It is not a taxable transaction to the corporation unless appreciated property is used to make the redemption. However, stock redemptions do not fall under the corporate reorganization rules defined in Sec. 368(a)(1).
Answer (B) is incorrect. A recapitalization is a Type E reorganization [Sec. 368(a)(1)(E)]. Answer (C) is incorrect. A mere change in identity is a Type F reorganization [Sec. 368(a)(1)(F)]. Answer (D) is incorrect. A statutory merger is a Type A reorganization [Sec. 368(a)(1)(A)].

17.7.3. Pursuant to a plan of reorganization adopted in the current year, Eagle Corporation exchanged property with an adjusted basis of $100,000 for 10,000 of the shares of the Hawkeye Corporation. The shares of Hawkeye had a fair market value of $120,000 on the date of the exchange. Eagle Corporation was liquidated shortly after the exchange, with its sole shareholder A receiving the Hawkeye shares. The sole shareholder A had a $110,000 basis in the Eagle shares surrendered. As a result of this exchange, A's recognized gain and her basis in the Hawkeye stock are as follows:

	Recognized Gain	Stock Basis
A.	$0	$100,000
B.	$0	$110,000
C.	$0	$120,000
D.	$20,000	$120,000

Answer (B) is correct. *(Publisher, adapted)*
REQUIRED: The gain recognized on receipt of stock for property under a plan of reorganization and the basis in the acquired stock.
DISCUSSION: The asset-for-stock exchange entered into by Eagle and Hawkeye Corporations is a Type C reorganization [Sec. 368(a)(1)(C)]. Section 354(a) provides that no gain or loss is recognized on a Type C reorganization if a shareholder exchanges stock or securities pursuant to a plan of reorganization solely for stock or securities in another corporation. Thus, A will recognize no gain.
The basis of the stock received by the shareholder is determined under Sec. 358(a) and is the same as the basis of the stock exchanged. The shareholder's basis in the Eagle stock exchanged was $110,000, so her basis in the Hawkeye stock received will also be $110,000.
Answer (A) is incorrect. The amount of $100,000 is the adjusted basis for Eagle Corporation's property. Answer (C) is incorrect. The amount of $120,000 is the FMV of Hawkeye Corporation's stock. Answer (D) is incorrect. No gain is recognized if stock is exchanged for stock in a Type C reorganization. Also, $120,000 is not the correct basis for the stock.

17.7.4. With regard to corporate reorganizations, which one of the following statements is true?

A. A mere change in identity, form, or place of organization of one corporation does not qualify as a reorganization.

B. The reorganization provisions cannot be used to provide tax-free treatment for corporate transactions.

C. Securities in corporations not parties to a reorganization are always "boot."

D. A "party to the reorganization" does not include the consolidated company.

Answer (C) is correct. *(CPA, adapted)*
REQUIRED: The true statement regarding reorganizations.
DISCUSSION: Under Sec. 354(a), a corporation must be a party to a reorganization, as defined in Sec. 368(b), in order for its property, stock, or securities to be exchanged tax free. Securities in corporations not parties to a reorganization are boot.
Answer (A) is incorrect. This is a Type F reorganization under Sec. 368(a)(1)(F). Answer (B) is incorrect. Sections 354 and 368 provide for tax-free treatment of corporate reorganizations. Answer (D) is incorrect. Section 368(b) includes the new corporation, the consolidated corporation in a Type A reorganization which is a consolidation, as a party to the reorganization.

17.7.5. Pursuant to a plan of corporate reorganization adopted in the current year, Myra Eber exchanged 1,000 shares of Faro Corporation common stock, which she had purchased for $75,000, for 1,800 shares of Judd Corporation common stock having a fair market value of $86,000. As a result of this exchange, Eber's recognized gain and her basis in the Judd stock should be

	Recognized Gain	Basis
A.	$11,000	$86,000
B.	$11,000	$75,000
C.	$0	$86,000
D.	$0	$75,000

Answer (D) is correct. *(CPA, adapted)*
REQUIRED: The gain recognized on an exchange of stock in a Type B reorganization and the basis in the new stock.
DISCUSSION: Under Sec. 354(a)(1), a shareholder does not recognize any gain or loss in a reorganization on an exchange of stock or securities in a corporation solely for stock or securities in the same or another corporation that is a party to the reorganization. Since, pursuant to a reorganization, Eber exchanged shares of Faro stock solely for shares of Judd stock, Eber will recognize no gain.
Under Sec. 358, when a Sec. 354 exchange takes place with no recognition of gain or loss, the property received in the transaction has the same basis as the property exchanged. Thus, Eber's basis in the new stock will be the same as her $75,000 basis in the stock exchanged.
Answer (A) is incorrect. No gain or loss is recognized when stock is exchanged for stock in a Type B reorganization. Also, $86,000 is not the correct basis for the stock. Answer (B) is incorrect. No gain or loss is recognized when stock is exchanged for stock in a Type B reorganization. Answer (C) is incorrect. The correct basis for the stock is not $86,000.

17.7.6. Meal Corporation distributes all of the stock of its wholly owned subsidiary, Big Sub Corporation, to its shareholders in Year 1. Meal Corporation has a $50,000 basis in Big Sub. Big Sub's value on the distribution date is $100,000. In Year 2, Detroit Corporation, an unrelated corporation, purchases 51% of Big Sub stock from Meal Corporation's shareholders for cash. What amount of gain must Meal Corporation recognize on the distribution of the stock in Year 1?

A. $0

B. $50,000

C. $51,000

D. $100,000

Answer (B) is correct. *(Publisher, adapted)*
REQUIRED: The amount of gain recognized on distributions of a controlled corporation's stock.
DISCUSSION: Section 355 provides an exception to the general rule of gain recognition to both the shareholder and the distributing corporation when appreciated property is distributed to shareholders with respect to their stock. Nevertheless, gain is recognized by the distributing corporation, as of the date of the distribution, if one or more persons who are not the distributee shareholders acquire 50% or more of the stock (measured by either voting power or value) of either the distributing corporation (parent) or the company whose stock is distributed (controlled corporation), pursuant to a plan or arrangement that was in place at the time of distribution. There is a presumption that any acquisition, occurring within the 4-year period beginning 2 years before the distribution, occurred pursuant to a plan or arrangement. However, taxpayers may rebut the presumption by proving the acquisition was unrelated to the distribution. Since the acquisition occurred within the 4-year period and according to a plan, a gain must be recognized by Meal on the distribution date. Hence, a $50,000 gain ($100,000 value – $50,000 basis) is recognized by Meal Corporation in Year 1.
Answer (A) is incorrect. A gain must be recognized on the date of distribution (Year 1). Answer (C) is incorrect. The amount of $51,000 is 51% of the $100,000 value of Big Sub. Answer (D) is incorrect. The gain is computed as if the stock was sold or exchanged at its fair market value.

17.7.7. Pursuant to a tax-free reorganization in the current year, Sandra Peel exchanged 100 shares of Lorna Corporation stock for 100 shares of Wood Corporation stock and, in addition, received $1,000 cash, which was not in excess of Peel's ratable share of Lorna's undistributed earnings and profits. Peel paid $20,000 for the Lorna stock 18 years ago. The Wood stock had a fair market value of $24,000 on the date of the exchange and represented a 5% interest in the outstanding Wood stock. What is the recognized gain to be reported by Peel in the current year?

A. $0

B. $1,000 dividend.

C. $1,000 long-term capital gain.

D. $5,000 long-term capital gain.

Answer (C) is correct. *(CPA, adapted)*

REQUIRED: The amount and character of gain recognized upon the tax-free reorganization.

DISCUSSION: Section 354 provides that no gain or loss is recognized in a reorganization if stock or securities are exchanged solely for stock or securities in the same or another corporation. When property other than stock or securities is received, Sec. 356(a)(1) requires gain to be recognized to the extent of the lesser of the realized gain or the other property (boot) received. Realized gain is $5,000 (stock of $24,000 + cash of $1,000 – basis of $20,000), but the gain recognized is limited to the $1,000 of cash received.

Under Sec. 356(a)(2), this gain is treated as a dividend if the exchange has the effect of a dividend distribution and there are earnings and profits. Because Peel received equivalent stock and her ratable share of earnings and profits exceeds the recognized gain, the $1,000 gain would ordinarily be a dividend.

Note that, in determining dividend equivalency, the Sec. 302(b) redemption rules are applied to the stock of the acquiring company. In applying the Sec. 302 rules, Peel is considered to have received all stock in the transaction and then redeemed a portion of the stock for cash [Rev. Rul. 93-61]. Section 302 is tested against Peel's stock ownership in the acquiring corporation. Peel's receipt of cash likely will qualify under Sec. 302(b)(1) as being not essentially equivalent to a dividend since she owned a minority position in Wood before the hypothetical redemption and had a meaningful reduction in her interest in Wood as a result of the hypothetical redemption. This permits a capital gain to be recognized.

Answer (A) is incorrect. Peel has a recognized gain in the current year. Answer (B) is incorrect. The recognized gain is not a dividend under the Sec. 302(b)(2) redemption rules. Answer (D) is incorrect. The recognized gain is limited to the cash received.

17.7.8. Single Corporation, which is owned equally by four individual shareholders, owns all of the stock of Double Corporation. The Double Corporation stock was acquired 8 years ago. It has a fair market value of $80,000 and an adjusted basis of $20,000. Single distributes the Double stock equally to the four shareholders as part of a spinoff transaction at the time that it has $120,000 of earnings and profits. What amount and type of income does each of Single's shareholders report as a result of the distribution?

A. $20,000 dividend income.

B. $20,000 capital gain.

C. $15,000 capital gain.

D. $0

Answer (D) is correct. *(Publisher, adapted)*

REQUIRED: The income recognized by shareholders in a spinoff distribution.

DISCUSSION: Section 355 provides that a corporation may transfer to its shareholders tax-free the stock of a controlled corporation, provided certain conditions are met. The distributing corporation must have at least 80% control of the distributed corporation before the spinoff occurs. After the distribution, both the distributing corporation and the controlled corporation must be engaged in the active conduct of a trade or business. In addition, the trade or business must have been conducted throughout the 5-year period ending on the date of distribution, must not have been acquired in a taxable transaction within the preceding 5-year period, and must not have been conducted by another corporation whose control was acquired in a taxable transaction during this 5-year period. The distributing corporation must transfer control to the shareholders in the spinoff. If one or more persons, who are not the shareholders that received the distributed stock, acquire 50% or more of the stock (measured by either vote or value) of either the distributing corporation or the corporation whose stock is distributed (i.e., controlled corporation) in a prearranged plan or agreement, then gain must be recognized by the distributing corporation. A plan or agreement is presumed if an acquisition occurs within the 4-year period beginning 2 years before the distribution occurred. Single Corporation meets all of these requirements, so the distribution of the Double stock to Single's shareholders results in the recognition of no income or gain.

Answer (A) is incorrect. Single's shareholders do not have $20,000 dividend income as a result of this distribution. Answer (B) is incorrect. Single's shareholders do not have a $20,000 capital gain as a result of this distribution. Answer (C) is incorrect. Single's shareholders do not have a $15,000 capital gain as a result of this distribution.

17.7.9. Pursuant to a plan of reorganization adopted in the current year, Summit Corporation exchanged 1,000 shares of its common stock and paid $40,000 cash for Hansen Corporation's assets with an adjusted basis of $200,000 (fair market value of $300,000). Hansen Corporation was liquidated shortly after the exchange, with its shareholders receiving the Summit stock and cash. The 1,000 shares of Summit common stock had a fair market value of $260,000 on the date of the exchange. What is the basis to Summit of the assets acquired in the exchange?

A. $200,000

B. $240,000

C. $260,000

D. $300,000

Answer (A) is correct. *(CPA, adapted)*
REQUIRED: The basis to the acquiring corporation of assets received in a Type C reorganization.
DISCUSSION: Summit Corporation's exchange of 1,000 shares of common stock and $40,000 cash for the assets of Hansen Corporation will qualify as a Type C reorganization, assuming that all or substantially all of Hansen's assets are acquired [Sec. 368(a)]. As a result of a Type C reorganization, Hansen, the transferor corporation, will have a realized gain of $100,000 ($300,000 received – $200,000 adjusted basis). Section 361, however, provides that, in a qualifying reorganization, the transferor corporation recognizes no gain if the assets other than stock or securities received are distributed immediately to its shareholders or creditors.
The basis of the assets to Summit, determined under Sec. 362(b), equals the transferor's adjusted basis in the assets ($200,000) increased by any gain recognized by the transferor ($0) or $200,000.
Answer (B) is incorrect. The acquiring corporation's basis for the assets is equal to the transferor corporation's adjusted basis. Answer (C) is incorrect. The amount of $260,000 is the FMV of the Summit common stock received. Answer (D) is incorrect. The amount of $300,000 is the FMV of the assets transferred.

17.7.10. Parent transfers the assets of one of its manufacturing divisions to its wholly owned corporation, Subsidiary, immediately before Parent distributes the Subsidiary stock to Parent's shareholders. Subsidiary may engage in a public offering of 49% of its stock as part of the plan of distribution without causing Parent's transfer and distribution to be taxable to Parent or its shareholders.

A. True.

B. False.

Answer (A) is correct. *(Publisher, adapted)*
DISCUSSION: When the distributing corporation (Parent) transfers property to the controlled corporation (Subsidiary) immediately prior to a distribution of stock of the controlled corporation, the transfer will continue to be treated as a tax-free transfer if the shareholders receiving stock in the controlled corporation (Subsidiary) hold stock representing at least a 50% interest in the vote and value of the controlled corporation after the distribution [Sec. 355(e)].

17.7.11. Changing the state in which a corporation is incorporated represents a Type F reorganization.

A. True.

B. False.

Answer (A) is correct. *(Publisher, adapted)*
DISCUSSION: A Type F reorganization is defined by Sec. 368(a)(1)(F) as a mere change in identity, form, or place of organization of a single corporation. Under Rev. Rul. 57-276, reincorporation in another state qualifies as a Type F reorganization.

17.7.12. A transfer of an operating division of an existing corporation to a newly created subsidiary corporation, followed by the distribution of all of the subsidiary corporation's stock by the transferor corporation, can be accomplished tax-free under the Type D reorganization rules.

A. True.

B. False.

Answer (A) is correct. *(Publisher, adapted)*
DISCUSSION: A Type D reorganization is defined by Sec. 368(a)(1)(D) as a transfer by a corporation of all or part of its assets to another corporation that is controlled immediately after the transfer by the transferor corporation or its shareholders. The stock or securities of the controlled corporation must also be distributed by the transferor corporation in a transaction that qualifies under Sec. 354, 355, or 356. The distribution in the question would be covered by Sec. 355, and the entire transaction can be accomplished tax-free as a Type D reorganization.

17.8 Consolidated Tax Returns

17.8.1. Which of the following corporations is considered to be an "includible corporation" in an affiliated group of corporations?

A. Holding company.

B. Domestic international sales corporation (DISC).

C. Real estate investment trust (REIT).

D. Regulated investment company.

Answer (A) is correct. *(CPA, adapted)*
REQUIRED: The organization that is considered an "includible corporation."
DISCUSSION: An "includible corporation" means any corporation except those corporations listed in Sec. 1504(b). A holding company is not listed as an exception. A holding company is generally one that conducts little or no active business and only holds stock in other corporations. The significance of includible corporations is that they may be part of an affiliated group that may file a consolidated tax return.
Answer (B) is incorrect. DISCs (domestic international sales corporations) are specifically excluded under the definition of includible corporations in Sec. 1504(b). Answer (C) is incorrect. REITs (real estate investment trusts) are specifically excluded under the definition of includible corporations in Sec. 1504(b). Answer (D) is incorrect. Regulated investment companies are specifically excluded under the definition of includible corporations in Sec. 1504(b).

17.8.2. All of the following are true with respect to the filing of consolidated tax returns except that

A. Each corporation that has been a member of a parent-subsidiary affiliated group during any part of the taxable year for which the first consolidated return is to be filed must consent to the initial filing.

B. Once a consolidated return is filed, the affiliated group must continue to file consolidated returns unless it obtains permission from the IRS to do otherwise.

C. The filing of consolidated returns is available to brother-sister corporations.

D. By filing a consolidated return, the corporations in the group can defer intercompany profits and losses.

Answer (C) is correct. *(CMA, adapted)*
REQUIRED: The false statement concerning the filing of consolidated tax returns.
DISCUSSION: Corporations must be members of an affiliated group to file a consolidated tax return. An affiliated group consists of one or more chains of includible corporations that are connected through stock ownership with a common parent corporation [Sec. 1504(a)]. Eighty percent of voting power and 80% of value ownership are required. Only parent-subsidiary affiliated groups will meet this requirement of having a common parent corporation. Brother-sister corporations do not have a common parent and therefore cannot file a consolidated tax return.
Answer (A) is incorrect. Each corporation that has been a member of a parent-subsidiary affiliated group during any part of the taxable year for which the first consolidated return is to be filed must consent to the initial filing. Answer (B) is incorrect. Once a consolidated return is filed, the affiliated group must continue to file consolidated returns unless it obtains permission from the IRS to do otherwise. Answer (D) is incorrect. By filing a consolidated return, the corporations in the group can defer intercompany profits and losses.

17.8.3. Dana Corporation owns stock in Seco Corporation. For Dana and Seco to qualify for the filing of consolidated returns, at least what percentage of Seco's total voting power and total value of stock must be directly owned by Dana?

	Total Voting Power	Total Value of Stock
A.	51%	51%
B.	51%	80%
C.	80%	51%
D.	80%	80%

Answer (D) is correct. *(CPA, adapted)*
REQUIRED: The percentage of total voting power and total value of stock that must be owned in order to file a consolidated tax return.
DISCUSSION: Under Secs. 1501 and 1504(a)(2), a corporation must own 80% of the total voting power and 80% of the total value of the stock (excluding certain preferred stock issues) in order to file a consolidated return.
Answer (A) is incorrect. At least 51% of total voting power and 51% of the total value of Seco's stock are not the correct amounts Dana must own to file a consolidated return. Answer (B) is incorrect. At least 51% of total voting power is not the correct amount Dana must own to file a consolidated return. Answer (C) is incorrect. At least 51% of the total value of Seco's stock is not the correct amount Dana must own to file a consolidated return.

17.8.4. A group of corporations (A, B, C, D, and E) all having only one class of stock have the following ownership and classification:

Corp. A -- Domestic corporation that owns 85% of B, 20% of C, and 100% of E's outstanding stock
Corp. B -- Domestic corporation that owns 70% of C and 100% of D's outstanding stock
Corp. C -- Domestic corporation that owns 10% of A's stock
Corp. D -- B's Foreign Sales Corporation (FSC)
Corp. E -- Foreign corporation that owns 10% of C and 5% of B's stock

Which are members of an affiliated group?

A. A and B.
B. B, C, and D.
C. A, B, C, D, and E.
D. A, B, and C.

Answer (D) is correct. *(SPE, adapted)*
REQUIRED: The corporations that are members of an affiliated group.
DISCUSSION: Under Sec. 1504(a), an affiliated group means one or more chains of includible corporations connected through stock ownership with a common parent corporation if at least 80% of the total voting power and value is owned directly by one or more of the other corporations, and if the common parent corporation owns directly at least 80% of the total voting power and value of at least one of the other corporations. Although Corporations D and E are wholly owned, they are not members of the affiliated group because foreign corporations (which include FSCs) are excluded from the definition of includible corporations by Sec. 1504(b).
Corporation A is the common parent because it owns 85% of Corporation B directly, and Corporation A combined with Corporation B owns 90% of Corporation C. Thus, Corporations A, B, and C are members of an affiliated group.
Answer (A) is incorrect. A and B are not the only members of the affiliated group. Answer (B) is incorrect. D cannot be a member of the affiliated group since it is a foreign corporation. Also, A is a member of the affiliated group. Answer (C) is incorrect. D and E cannot be members of the affiliated group since they are foreign corporations.

17.8.5. When a consolidated return is filed by an affiliated group of includible corporations connected from inception through the requisite stock ownership with a common parent,

A. Intercompany dividends are excludable to the extent of 80%.
B. Operating losses of one member of the group offset operating profits of other members of the group.
C. The parent's basis in the stock of its subsidiaries is unaffected by the earnings and profits of its subsidiaries.
D. Each of the subsidiaries is entitled to an accumulated earnings tax credit.

Answer (B) is correct. *(CPA, adapted)*
REQUIRED: The true statement concerning a consolidated return filed by an affiliated group of includible corporations.
DISCUSSION: Operating losses of one group member must be used to offset current-year operating profits of other group members before a net operating loss carryback or carryover can occur (Reg. 1.1502-21).
Answer (A) is incorrect. Intercompany dividends are excluded entirely (100%). Answer (C) is incorrect. The parent's basis in the stock of its subsidiaries is adjusted for the subsidiaries, earnings and losses, distributions, loss carryovers, etc. The positive basis adjustment for the subsidiaries' current-year profits and distributions is based on the subsidiaries' modified taxable income. Answer (D) is incorrect. Only one accumulated earnings tax credit is allowed for consolidated returns.

17.8.6. Able Corporation and Baker Corporation file a consolidated return on a calendar-year basis. Last year, Able sold land to Baker for its fair market value of $50,000. At the date of sale, Able had an adjusted basis in the land of $35,000 and had held the land for several years as an investment. Baker held the land primarily for sale to its customers in the ordinary course of its business and sold it to a customer early this year for $60,000.
As a result of the sale of the land this year, the corporations should report on their consolidated return

A. $10,000 ordinary income.
B. $25,000 ordinary income.
C. $25,000 long-term capital gain.
D. $15,000 long-term capital gain and $10,000 ordinary income.

Answer (B) is correct. *(CPA, adapted)*
REQUIRED: The amount and character of gain to be reported on the consolidated return.
DISCUSSION: Under Reg. 1.1502.13, a sale or an exchange of property between members of an affiliated group that files a consolidated tax return is an intercompany transaction. In the case of nondepreciable property (e.g., land) not sold on the installment basis, the seller's intercompany item (Able's gain) is reported when the buyer's corresponding item occurs. Thus, the $15,000 gain reported by Able last year is deferred. The corresponding item in this case is Baker's sale of the property outside the group in the current year. Under Reg. 1.1502-13 that was issued in 1995, the character of the gain is determined as if the property was transferred between divisions of a single corporation. The total gain that is reported by the affiliated group in the current year is $25,000 ($60,000 sale price to third party – $35,000 basis on Able's books). The entire gain from the two transactions is ordinary income even though Able held the land as a capital asset [Reg. 1.1502-13(c)(7)(ii)(j), Ex. (2)].
Answer (A) is incorrect. The corporations should not use FMV for the basis of the land. Answer (C) is incorrect. The corporations should not report $25,000 as a long-term capital gain on their consolidated returns. Answer (D) is incorrect. The corporations should not split the amount between a long-term capital gain and ordinary income on their consolidated returns.

17.8.7. In the consolidated income tax return of a corporation and its wholly owned subsidiary, what percentage of cash dividends paid by the subsidiary to the parent is tax-free?

A. 0%

B. 70%

C. 80%

D. 100%

Answer (D) is correct. *(CPA, adapted)*
REQUIRED: The percentage of cash dividends paid by a subsidiary corporation that is tax-free to its parent corporation.
DISCUSSION: Dividends received by group members are treated differently depending on whether they come from corporations inside or outside the affiliated group. A dividend paid from one group member to another group member is an intercompany transaction [Reg. 1.1502-13(f)(7), Ex. (1)]. An intercompany distribution paid by the distributing member is not included in the gross income of the distributee member if the distribution (1) would otherwise be taxable under Sec. 301 and (2) produces a corresponding negative adjustment to the basis of the distributing corporation's stock. Stock basis is generally decreased for intercompany distributions, whether paid from preaffiliation or post-affiliation earnings. Distributions from outside the affiliated group are eligible for the 70%, 80%, or 100% dividends-received deductions that are available to corporations that do not make a consolidated tax return election.
Answer (A) is incorrect. A percentage of cash dividends paid by the subsidiary to the parent is tax free. Answer (B) is incorrect. If percentage of ownership in the distributing corporation is less than 20%, only 70% of the dividends received is deductible by the recipient corporation. Answer (C) is incorrect. Corporations may only deduct 80% of dividends received if the percentage of ownership in the distributing corporation is between 20% and 80%.

17.8.8. A consolidated tax return must be filed by all members of an affiliated group once they have made the appropriate election.

A. True.

B. False.

Answer (A) is correct. *(Publisher, adapted)*
DISCUSSION: The election to file a consolidated tax return must be made with the consent of every includible corporation in an affiliated group (Sec. 1501). Once the election is filed, all members must continue to file the consolidated return unless permission is obtained from the IRS to file separately [Reg. 1.1502-75(a)(2)].

17.9 Multiple Corporations

17.9.1. Which one of the following statements about a controlled group of corporations is false?

A. Any controlled group may elect to file consolidated federal income tax returns.

B. A parent corporation and its 80%-owned subsidiary make up a controlled group.

C. All members of a controlled group need not use the parent's tax year.

D. Members of a controlled group are entitled to only one accumulated earnings tax credit.

Answer (A) is correct. *(CMA, adapted)*
REQUIRED: The false statement concerning a controlled group of corporations.
DISCUSSION: Under Sec. 1563(a), a controlled group of corporations may be a parent-subsidiary controlled group, a brother-sister controlled group, or a combined group. Either a parent-subsidiary controlled group or the parent-subsidiary portion of a combined group may file a consolidated tax return because there is a common parent corporation and the includible corporations are all 80%-owned. However, a brother-sister controlled group exists when two or more corporations are owned by five or fewer persons who own at least 80% of the voting stock or 80% of the value of the outstanding stock. There is no common parent corporation, so a consolidated tax return could not be filed. The affiliated group definition requires ownership of 80% of the voting stock and 80% of the value of the controlled corporation. The controlled group definition is an "or" test, and some controlled groups may meet one, but not both, of the tests and not be able to file a consolidated return.
Answer (B) is incorrect. It describes a parent-subsidiary controlled group. Answer (C) is incorrect. There is no requirement that members of a controlled group use the parent's tax year. However, the members of the parent-subsidiary controlled group must use the parent's tax year once a consolidated tax return election has been made. Answer (D) is incorrect. One of the purposes of ascertaining whether a controlled group exists is to allocate to the group various tax benefits that can be claimed once by the group and not by each of the individual members. These benefits include the accumulated earnings tax credit, the $40,000 alternative minimum tax exemption, the graduated rates, etc.

17.9.2. The only class of outstanding stock of Corporations L, M, N, O, and P is owned by the following unrelated individuals:

Individual	Corporations/Percent of Stock Owned				
	L	M	N	O	P
G	30%	40%	50%	50%	5%
H	10%	5%	10%	20%	5%
I	30%	40%	30%	10%	5%
J	30%	15%	10%	20%	5%
K	-0-	-0-	-0-	-0-	5%

Which of the following corporations are members of a brother-sister controlled group?

A. Only L, M, N, and O.

B. Only M, N, O, and P.

C. Only L, M, O, and P.

D. Only L, M, and N.

Answer (A) is correct. *(SPE, adapted)*
REQUIRED: The corporations that are members of a brother-sister controlled group.
DISCUSSION: The significance of a controlled group is that members are not allowed many of the benefits of separate corporations; e.g., all members must share the graduated tax rates, Accumulated Earnings Credit, 100% General Business Tax Credit offset, etc., as one corporation. Under Sec. 1563(a), a brother-sister controlled group means two or more corporations of which five or fewer persons who are individuals, estates, or trusts own at least 80% of the voting power or value of each corporation, and more than 50% of the voting power or value of the stock of each corporation counting only identical ownership interests (i.e., the smallest amount owned by each person in any of the corporations is all that is counted in the other corporations for the 50% test). Individual K's ownership is not counted because (s)he does not own stock in each corporation. Corporation P does not pass the 80% test and so is not included in the 50% test. The 50% test is met for L, M, N, and O.

Total Percent of Each Corporation Owned by G, H, I, and J		Identical Percent Owned in Each of L, M, N, O	
Corporation L	100%	Individual G	30%
Corporation M	100%	Individual H	5%
Corporation N	100%	Individual I	10%
Corporation O	100%	Individual J	10%
Corporation P	20%	Total	55%

Answer (B) is incorrect. L is a member of a brother-sister controlled group, while P is not. Answer (C) is incorrect. N is a member of a brother-sister controlled group. P is not a member because only 20% of P's stock is owned by G, H, I, and J, and the 50% common ownership requirement is also not met. Answer (D) is incorrect. O is also a member of a brother-sister controlled group.

17.9.3. Corporations X, Y, and Z are component members of a controlled group of corporations on December 31 of the current year. For the current year, they allocate the taxable income brackets under an apportionment plan as follows:

Corporation X	1/4 of each tax bracket
Corporation Y	1/2 of each tax bracket
Corporation Z	1/4 of each tax bracket

Corporation Y has taxable income of $80,000 for the current year. What is Corporation Y's income tax liability if the controlled group's total taxable income is $97,000?

A. $12,000

B. $15,450

C. $18,680

D. $21,325

Answer (D) is correct. *(SPE, adapted)*
REQUIRED: The income tax liability of a member of a controlled group.
DISCUSSION: Under Sec. 1561(a)(1), component members of a controlled group of corporations are limited to using the taxable income brackets in Sec. 11 as if they were one corporation. Unless the members agree otherwise, the tax brackets are allocated equally. Under the apportionment plan, Y is entitled to 50% of each tax bracket. Y's income tax is

Tax Brackets	50%	Tax
1st $50,000	$25,000 × 15%	$ 3,750
Next $25,000	12,500 × 25%	3,125
Remainder	42,500 × 34%	14,450
Total		$21,325

Note that, although each tax bracket is allocated in the same manner here, different allocations are permitted. Since the total taxable income of the controlled group is less than $100,000, no recapture of the tax savings resulting from the 15% and 25% marginal tax brackets occurs. The additional 5% tax will not apply unless the total taxable income of the controlled group exceeds $100,000. The allocation selected by the group is less than optimal since the full amount of the 15% and 25% tax bracket benefits are not used when taxable income is $97,000. The group should consider revising its allocation for the current year.
Answer (A) is incorrect. The tax liability was calculated using a flat 15% rate. Answer (B) is incorrect. The amount of $15,450 is the tax liability under the normal rate schedule without apportioning the tax brackets among the members. Answer (C) is incorrect. The amount of $18,680 reflects $33,000 taxed at the 15% bracket, $25,000 at the 25% bracket, and $22,000 at the 34% bracket. This is the lowest tax liability for Y Corporation if a special apportionment plan is elected.

17.9.4. A controlled group of corporations that has filed an apportionment plan to divide the taxable income brackets

A. Must divide them equally.

B. Must divide them in accordance with the taxable income of each corporation.

C. May have more than one apportionable $50,000 amount in their lowest taxable income bracket.

D. May adopt an unequal apportionment plan.

Answer (D) is correct. *(SPE, adapted)*
REQUIRED: The true statement about the apportionment of the taxable income brackets.
DISCUSSION: Under Sec. 1561(a), component members of a controlled group of corporations must use the taxable income brackets of Sec. 11 as if they were one corporation. The tax brackets are allocated equally unless the members agree otherwise. The members may adopt an unequal apportionment plan.
Answer (A) is incorrect. The group does not have to divide the taxable income brackets equally. Answer (B) is incorrect. The group does not have to divide the taxable income brackets in accordance with the taxable income of each corporation. Answer (C) is incorrect. The tax brackets are allocated equally unless the members agree otherwise.

17.9.5. For a domestic corporation, the general business tax credit is limited to the lesser of (1) its net income tax, with certain adjustments for other credits, over the greater of its tentative minimum tax for the year or (2) 25% of its net regular tax liability for the year that exceeds $25,000. How does a controlled group of corporations treat the $25,000?

A. Each corporation is allowed $25,000.

B. The $25,000 is divided equally among the corporations.

C. The $25,000 is divided among the corporations in any manner they choose.

D. The $25,000 is divided according to each corporation's tax liability.

Answer (C) is correct. *(SPE, adapted)*
REQUIRED: The correct method of apportionment of the $25,000 amount in determining the general business tax credit with respect to a controlled group.
DISCUSSION: Section 38(c)(3)(B) provides that, for members of a controlled group, the $25,000 amount must be apportioned among the members as the regulations provide. The regulations allow the members to apportion the $25,000 amount in any manner they choose [Reg. 1.46-1(p)(2)]. They need to agree on an apportionment plan.
Answer (A) is incorrect. Each corporation is not allowed $25,000. Answer (B) is incorrect. The members do not necessarily have to divide the $25,000 equally among the corporations. Answer (D) is incorrect. The $25,000 is not necessarily divided according to each corporation's tax liability.

17.9.6. Which one of the following methods is not acceptable to determine an arm's-length price on the sale of tangible property among a group of controlled entities (Sec. 482)?

A. Comparable uncontrolled price method.

B. Resale price method.

C. Direct costing method.

D. Cost-plus method.

Answer (C) is correct. *(Publisher, adapted)*
REQUIRED: The unacceptable method to determine an arm's-length price on the sale of tangible property among a group of controlled entities.
DISCUSSION: When one member of a group of controlled entities sells tangible property to another member of the group at other than an arm's-length price, an allocation must be made between the buyer and the seller to reflect an arm's-length price for such sale. An arm's-length price is the price that an unrelated party would have paid for the property under the same circumstances. Regulation 1.482-3 lists five methods of determining an arm's-length price and the standards for applying each method. These methods are the comparable uncontrolled price method, the resale price method, the cost-plus method, the comparable profits method, and other methods acceptable to the IRS.
Answer (A) is incorrect. The comparable uncontrolled price method is an allowable method for determining an arm's-length price. Answer (B) is incorrect. The resale price method is an allowable method for determining an arm's-length price. Answer (D) is incorrect. The cost-plus method is an allowable method for determining an arm's-length price.

17.9.7. Mr. T owns 100% of the single classes of outstanding stock of Corporations A and B. Corporation A owns 90% of the single class of outstanding voting stock of Corporation Z. Corporations A, B, and Z are members of a controlled group of corporations.

A. True.

B. False.

Answer (A) is correct. *(SPE, adapted)*
DISCUSSION: Under Sec. 1563(a), Corporations A, B, and Z are a combined group because A and B are a brother-sister controlled group, and A and Z are a parent-subsidiary controlled group. Mr. T's 100% ownership of A and B satisfies the 80% and 50% common ownership tests for a brother-sister controlled group. A's 90% ownership satisfies the 80% required ownership for a parent-subsidiary controlled group.

17.9.8. Corporation D owns 80% of Corporation H's single class of stock. Corporations D and H are brother-sister corporations.

A. True.

B. False.

Answer (B) is correct. *(SPE, adapted)*
DISCUSSION: Under Sec. 1563(a)(1), Corporations D and H are members of a parent-subsidiary controlled group, not a brother-sister controlled group.

17.9.9. Members of a controlled group of corporations must divide the $40,000 exemption allowed for the alternative minimum tax among themselves in proportion to their respective regular tax amounts.

A. True.

B. False.

Answer (B) is correct. *(SPE, adapted)*
DISCUSSION: Under Sec. 1561(a), the members of a controlled group may divide the $40,000 alternative minimum tax exemption among themselves in any manner they choose. If they do not so agree, it is divided equally.

17.10 Accumulated Earnings Tax

17.10.1. The accumulated earnings tax

A. Can be avoided by sufficient dividend distributions.

B. Is 50% of accumulated taxable income.

C. Applies to both corporations and partnerships.

D. Applies only to controlled and affiliated corporate groups.

Answer (A) is correct. *(Publisher, adapted)*
REQUIRED: The true statement concerning the accumulated earnings tax.
DISCUSSION: The accumulated earnings tax is imposed by Sec. 531 on unreasonably large accumulations of earnings in a corporation. If the corporation pays out sufficient dividends, it will not have unreasonably large accumulations of earnings and will not be subject to the tax.
Answer (B) is incorrect. The tax is 15% of the accumulated taxable income. Answer (C) is incorrect. The accumulated earnings tax applies only to corporations, not to partnerships. Answer (D) is incorrect. The accumulated earnings tax can apply to any corporation (not subject to the personal holding company tax) that has unreasonably large accumulated earnings.

17.10.2. The accumulated earnings tax does not apply to

A. Corporations that have more than 100 shareholders.

B. Personal holding companies.

C. Corporations filing consolidated returns.

D. Corporations that have more than one class of stock.

Answer (B) is correct. *(CPA, adapted)*
REQUIRED: The type of corporation to which the accumulated earnings tax is not applicable.
DISCUSSION: The accumulated earnings tax is imposed by Sec. 531 on unreasonably large accumulations of earnings in a corporation. The purpose of the tax is to require the shareholders to include the earnings in their income, usually as dividends. Under Sec. 532, the accumulated earnings tax does not apply to personal holding companies since they are already subject to a penalty tax on undistributed income.
Answer (A) is incorrect. The accumulated earnings tax applies to corporations that have more than 100 shareholders. Answer (C) is incorrect. The accumulated earnings tax applies to corporations filing consolidated returns. Answer (D) is incorrect. The accumulated earnings tax applies to corporations that have more than one class of stock.

17.10.3. An item not subtracted in determining accumulated taxable income for the accumulated earnings tax is

A. Dividends paid within 2 1/2 months after the end of the corporate tax year.

B. Net capital losses.

C. Net long-term capital gains reduced by the attributable taxes.

D. A net operating loss deduction from a prior year.

Answer (D) is correct. *(CMA, adapted)*
REQUIRED: The item that does not reduce accumulated taxable income.
DISCUSSION: The accumulated earnings tax is applied to the accumulated taxable income, defined in Sec. 535(a) as taxable income, subject to certain adjustments. The net operating loss deduction is not allowed.
Answer (A) is incorrect. Dividends paid, including those declared and then paid within 2 1/2 months of year end, reduce adjusted taxable income to compute accumulated taxable income. Answer (B) is incorrect. Net capital losses are deductible in full for the accumulated earnings tax. Answer (C) is incorrect. There is allowed as a deduction the net long-term capital gain reduced by taxes attributable to such net capital gain.

17.10.4. In determining whether a corporation is subject to the accumulated earnings tax, which of the following items is not a subtraction in arriving at accumulated taxable income?

A. Federal income tax.

B. Capital loss carryback.

C. Dividends-paid deduction.

D. Accumulated Earnings Credit.

Answer (B) is correct. *(CPA, adapted)*
REQUIRED: The item that does not reduce accumulated taxable income.
DISCUSSION: The accumulated earnings tax is applied to accumulated taxable income, defined in Sec. 535(a) as taxable income, subject to certain adjustments. Capital loss carrybacks and carryovers are not allowed. Instead, capital losses are deductible in full in the year incurred but must be reduced by prior net capital gain deductions.
Answer (A) is incorrect. Federal income taxes are deducted as an adjustment to taxable income. Answer (C) is incorrect. The dividends-paid deduction is subtracted from adjusted taxable income. Answer (D) is incorrect. The Accumulated Earnings Credit is subtracted from adjusted taxable income.

17.10.5. The minimum Accumulated Earnings Credit is

A. $150,000 for all corporations.

B. $150,000 for nonservice corporations only.

C. $250,000 for all corporations.

D. $250,000 for nonservice corporations only.

Answer (D) is correct. *(CPA, adapted)*
REQUIRED: The amount of the minimum Accumulated Earnings Credit.
DISCUSSION: The Accumulated Earnings Credit is defined as the increase in the reasonable needs of a business during the tax year. Without showing a reason for the accumulation, the minimum Accumulated Earnings Credit is $250,000 for nonservice corporations [Sec. 535(c)(2)]. The credit is $150,000 for certain service corporations such as those in the fields of health, law, engineering, architecture, accounting, actuarial science, performing arts, or consulting.
Answer (A) is incorrect. The minimum Accumulated Earnings Credit is not $150,000 for all corporations. Answer (B) is incorrect. The minimum Accumulated Earnings Credit is not $150,000 for nonservice corporations only. Answer (C) is incorrect. The minimum Accumulated Earnings Credit is not $250,000 for all corporations.

17.10.6. Which of the following would not be considered reasonable needs of a business in determining the accumulated earnings tax?

A. Specific plans to update factory machinery.

B. Definite long-range commitment to purchase raw materials.

C. A feasible long-range plan to expand factory production.

D. Specific and feasible plan to declare a stock dividend to all shareholders.

Answer (D) is correct. *(SPE, adapted)*
REQUIRED: The item not considered as meeting the reasonable needs of a business with regard to the accumulated earnings tax.
DISCUSSION: For a corporation to justify its accumulation of earnings, there must be evidence that the future needs of the business will require such an accumulation and that the corporation has specific and feasible plans for the use of the accumulation [Reg. 1.537-1(b)]. A specific plan to declare a stock dividend to all shareholders will not qualify as the reasonable needs of a business since such dividends usually do not involve a use of funds. The accumulated earnings tax was imposed to prevent corporations from accumulating excess earnings and not distributing them as taxable dividends.
Answer (A) is incorrect. Specific plans to update factory machinery are considered reasonably necessary to meet the needs of the business. Answer (B) is incorrect. Definite long-range commitment to purchase raw materials is considered reasonably necessary to meet the needs of the business. Answer (C) is incorrect. A feasible long-range plan to expand factory production is considered reasonably necessary to meet the needs of the business.

17.10.7. Daystar Corp., which is not a mere holding or investment company, derives its income from retail sales. Daystar had accumulated earnings and profits of $145,000 at December 31 of last year. For the current year, it had earnings and profits of $115,000 and a dividends-paid deduction of $15,000 for a dividend paid in June. No throwback distributions have been made. It has been determined that $20,000 of the current and accumulated earnings and profits for this year is required for the reasonable needs of the business. How much is the allowable Accumulated Earnings Credit at December 31 of the current year?

A. $105,000

B. $125,000

C. $150,000

D. $250,000

Answer (A) is correct. *(CPA, adapted)*
REQUIRED: The allowable Accumulated Earnings Credit.
DISCUSSION: The Accumulated Earnings Credit of Sec. 535(c) is the greater of (1) the difference between $250,000 and the accumulated earnings and profits at the end of the prior year or (2) the current earnings and profits retained for the reasonable needs of the business minus the long-term capital gain adjustments of the current year. The dividends-paid deduction is used to compute the accumulated taxable income but not the Accumulated Earnings Credit.
The difference between $250,000 and Daystar's accumulated earnings and profits at the end of the prior year ($145,000) is $105,000. Since this is greater than the $20,000 of reasonable needs of the business, the available Accumulated Earnings Credit is $105,000. Of the available credit, $100,000 ($115,000 current E&P – $15,000 dividends-paid deduction) will be used in the current year, and $5,000 will be available in following years.
Answer (B) is incorrect. The Accumulated Earnings Credit is not the prior year's E&P less the earnings required for the reasonable needs of the business. Answer (C) is incorrect. The minimum Accumulated Earnings Credit for service corporations is $150,000. Answer (D) is incorrect. The minimum Accumulated Earnings Credit for nonservice corporations is $250,000.

17.10.8. The accumulated earnings tax rate is 20% for 2017.

A. True.

B. False.

Answer (A) is correct. *(Publisher, adapted)*
DISCUSSION: The accumulated earnings tax rate is equal to 20% in 2017.

17.10.9. Azure Corporation is a law firm with accumulated retained earnings of $240,000. Azure has determined that it has no plans for expansion and that the current level of working capital is satisfactory. Azure may be subject to the accumulated earnings tax.

A. True.

B. False.

Answer (A) is correct. *(SPE, adapted)*
DISCUSSION: Under Sec. 535(c)(2)(B), certain service corporations are limited to a $150,000 minimum Accumulated Earnings Credit. The practice of law is one of the functions specifically listed in this provision. Since the law firm has accumulated earnings in excess of its minimum credit with no business plans for the funds, it may be subject to the tax.

17.10.10. The Bardahl formula determines the amount of earnings that satisfies working capital needs by estimating a corporation's future expenses using estimated future data.

A. True.

B. False.

Answer (B) is correct. *(Publisher, adapted)*
DISCUSSION: The Bardahl formula is one method used to determine the reasonable accumulation of earnings to satisfy working capital needs based on historical data. The formula uses the average operating cycle from historical data to estimate how much working capital is necessary to operate on the average in the future [*Bardahl International Corporation*, 25 TCM 935 (1966)].

17.11 Personal Holding Company Tax

17.11.1. The personal holding company tax

A. Qualifies as a tax credit that may be used by partners or shareholders to reduce their individual income taxes.

B. May be imposed on both corporations and partnerships.

C. Should be self-assessed by filing a separate schedule with the regular tax return.

D. May be imposed regardless of the number of equal shareholders in a corporation.

Answer (C) is correct. *(CPA, adapted)*
REQUIRED: The true statement regarding the personal holding company tax.
DISCUSSION: The personal holding company tax should be self-assessed by a corporation by filing Schedule PH along with its regular Form 1120 tax return.
Answer (A) is incorrect. The personal holding company tax does not apply to partnerships and no credit is available for personal holding company taxes paid. Answer (B) is incorrect. The personal holding company tax does not apply to partnerships. Answer (D) is incorrect. The personal holding company tax may be imposed only if more than 50% of the value of a corporation's stock is owned by five or fewer individuals.

17.11.2. When passive investment income is involved, the personal holding company tax may be imposed

    A. On both partnerships and corporations.

    B. On companies whose gross income arises solely from rentals, if the lessors render no services to the lessees.

    C. If more than 50% of the company is owned by five or fewer individuals.

    D. On small business investment companies licensed by the Small Business Administration.

Answer (C) is correct. *(CPA, adapted)*
    REQUIRED: The true statement about the personal holding company tax.
    DISCUSSION: The personal holding company tax is imposed by Sec. 541 on undistributed income of a personal holding company. A personal holding company is a corporation that is more than 50% owned by five or fewer shareholders any time during the last half of the year and that has 60% of its income as personal holding company income (generally passive income).
    Answer (A) is incorrect. The personal holding company tax applies only to corporations. Answer (B) is incorrect. Rents are excluded from personal holding company income if they constitute more than 50% of the corporation's adjusted ordinary gross income and there is only a limited amount of other personal holding company income. Answer (D) is incorrect. Small business investment companies are specifically excluded by Sec. 542(c) from being personal holding companies.

17.11.3. Benson, a singer, owns 100% of the outstanding capital stock of Lund Corporation. Lund contracted with Benson, specifying that Benson was to perform personal services for Magda Productions, Inc., in consideration of which Benson was to receive $50,000 a year from Lund. Lund contracted with Magda, specifying that Benson was to perform personal services for Magda, in consideration of which Magda was to pay Lund $1 million a year. Personal holding company income will be attributable to

    A. Benson only.

    B. Lund only.

    C. Magda only.

    D. All three contracting parties.

Answer (B) is correct. *(CPA, adapted)*
    REQUIRED: The corporation the personal holding company income will be attributed to.
    DISCUSSION: Section 543(a)(7) includes amounts received by corporations under personal service contracts involving a 25%-or-more shareholder as personal service company income if the contract designates specifically that the shareholder will provide the services. As such, Lund has personal service income of $1 million a year.
    Answer (A) is incorrect. Benson is an individual, and personal holding company income only applies to corporations. Answer (C) is incorrect. Magda is paying the income, not receiving it. Answer (D) is incorrect. Personal holding company income will not be attributed to Benson and Magda.

17.11.4. Which of the following types of income is not generally considered personal holding company income?

    A. Dividends.

    B. Interest.

    C. Royalties.

    D. Personal services income.

Answer (D) is correct. *(SPE, adapted)*
    REQUIRED: The type of income that is not personal holding company income.
    DISCUSSION: The personal holding company tax is imposed by Sec. 541 on undistributed income of a personal holding company. A personal holding company is a corporation that is more than 50% owned by five or fewer shareholders any time during the last half of the tax year and that has at least 60% of its income as personal holding company income. Under Sec. 543(a), personal holding company income is generally passive income such as dividends, interest, and royalties. Personal services income is generally not included in the definition of personal holding company income.
    Note that personal services income is included in the personal holding company income definition only if earned by a 25%-or-more shareholder from a personal service contract and either some person other than the corporation has the right to designate the individual who is to perform the services or the individual who is to perform the services is designated by name or description in the contract.
    Answer (A) is incorrect. Personal holding company income is generally passive income such as dividends. Answer (B) is incorrect. Personal holding company income is generally passive income such as interest. Answer (C) is incorrect. Personal holding company income is generally passive income such as royalties.

17.11.5. Acme Corp. has two shareholders who own all of its common stock. Acme derives all of its income from investments in stocks and securities, and it regularly distributes 51% of its after-tax income as dividends to its shareholders. Acme is a

A. Corporation subject to tax only on income not distributed to shareholders.

B. Corporation subject to the accumulated earnings tax.

C. Regulated investment company.

D. Personal holding company.

Answer (D) is correct. *(CPA, adapted)*
REQUIRED: The correct term for a corporation having only two shareholders and deriving its income solely from investments in stock and securities.
DISCUSSION: Under Sec. 542, a corporation is a personal holding company if at least 60% of its adjusted gross income for the year is "personal holding company income" and at any time during the last half of the taxable year more than 50% of the value of its outstanding stock is owned by not more than five individuals. "Personal holding company income," under Sec. 543, includes income received from stocks and securities.
Answer (A) is incorrect. A personal holding company is subject to the regular tax on corporate income as well as a 20% tax on its undistributed personal holding company income. Answer (B) is incorrect. Personal holding companies are not subject to the accumulated earnings tax. Answer (C) is incorrect. A regulated investment company must be registered under the Investment Company Act of 1940 or file an election to be a regulated investment company.

17.11.6. The following information pertains to Hull, Inc., a personal holding company, for the current year ended December 31:

Undistributed personal holding company income	$100,000
Dividends paid during May	20,000
Consent dividends reported in the current-year individual income tax returns of the holders of Hull's common stock but not paid in cash by Hull to its shareholders	10,000

In computing its current-year personal holding company tax, what amount should Hull deduct for dividends paid?

A. $0

B. $10,000

C. $20,000

D. $30,000

Answer (D) is correct. *(CPA, adapted)*
REQUIRED: The deduction for dividends paid by a personal holding company.
DISCUSSION: Under Sec. 561(a), the deduction for dividends paid is equal to the sum of the dividends of cash and property paid during the year, consent dividends for the year, throwback dividends, and the dividend carryover for personal holding companies. The consent dividend of Hull would be considered a dividend if it were paid in cash to its shareholders. Therefore, Hull has a dividends-paid deduction of $30,000 ($20,000 dividends paid + $10,000 consent dividends).
Answer (A) is incorrect. There is a dividends-paid deduction. Answer (B) is incorrect. The amount of $10,000 does not include the cash dividends paid during the year. Answer (C) is incorrect. The amount of $20,000 does not include the consent dividends.

17.11.7. Which of the following rates is used to compute the personal holding company tax for 2017?

A. 20%

B. 25%

C. 28%

D. 35%

Answer (A) is correct. *(SPE, adapted)*
REQUIRED: The personal holding company tax rate for 2017.
DISCUSSION: Under Sec. 541, the personal holding company tax for 2017 is equal to 20% of the undistributed personal holding company income. The application of the tax is straightforward. The difficulties arise in determining whether a corporation is a personal holding company and the amount of undistributed personal holding company income.
Answer (B) is incorrect. The correct rate to compute the personal holding company tax is not 25%. Answer (C) is incorrect. The correct rate used to compute the personal holding company tax is not 28%. Answer (D) is incorrect. The correct rate used to compute the personal holding company tax is not 33%.

17.11.8. Alpha Properties is owned by three shareholders. During the current year, Alpha reported the following:

Rental income	$200,000
Dividend income	20,000
Depreciation expense	40,000
Property taxes	10,000
Interest expense on mortgage on rental property	50,000

Alpha's adjusted ordinary gross income (AOGI) and personal holding company income (PHCI) are

A. AOGI, $120,000; PHCI, $20,000.

B. AOGI, $220,000; PHCI, $120,000.

C. AOGI, $120,000; PHCI, $120,000.

D. AOGI, $220,000; PHCI, $220,000.

Answer (A) is correct. *(Publisher, adapted)*
REQUIRED: The adjusted ordinary gross income and personal holding company income.
DISCUSSION: Section 543(b) defines ordinary gross income as gross income less capital gains and Sec. 1231 gains. Ordinary gross income is further reduced by a number of items, including depreciation, property taxes, and interest allocable to rental property, to arrive at adjusted ordinary gross income. Alpha has ordinary gross income of $220,000. Adjusted ordinary gross income is $120,000 ($220,000 ordinary gross income − $100,000 rental expenses).
Personal holding company income (PHCI) includes dividends, interest, annuities, royalties, rents, and similar passive income [Sec. 543(a)]. Rents are excluded, however, if they constitute more than 50% of the corporation's adjusted ordinary gross income and if PHCI other than rents (reduced by dividend distributions) is not in excess of 10% of ordinary gross income. For this purpose, rents are rental income minus depreciation, property taxes, and allocable interest. Alpha's PHC rent is $100,000 ($200,000 rental income − $100,000 depreciation, property taxes, and interest). Since the rent is more than 50% of adjusted ordinary gross income ($120,000) and the other PHCI ($20,000) is less than 10% of ordinary gross income ($220,000 × 10% = $22,000), the rent will not be included as PHCI. Therefore, only dividend income of $20,000 is PHCI, and Alpha is not a personal holding company.
Answer (B) is incorrect. AOGI includes a reduction for depreciation expense, property taxes, and interest expense. PHCI is only the dividend income, because the adjusted income from rents passes both tests for exclusion from PHCI. Answer (C) is incorrect. PHCI is not $120,000. Answer (D) is incorrect. AOGI and PHCI are not each $220,000.

17.12 S Corporation Election

17.12.1. What is the maximum number of shareholders allowable for eligibility as an S corporation in the current year?

A. 15

B. 25

C. 75

D. 100

Answer (D) is correct. *(CPA, adapted)*
REQUIRED: The maximum number of shareholders allowable for eligibility as an S corporation.
DISCUSSION: Under Sec. 1361(b), one of the requirements of an S corporation is that it have no more than 100 shareholders.
Note: All members of a family (up to six generations from the common ancestors of lineal descendants) are counted as a single shareholder for purposes of Sec. 1361(b) so, in effect, 1,000 individuals composing 100 families constitutes 100 shareholders.
Answer (A) is incorrect. Fifteen is not the maximum number of shareholders to be eligible for an S corporation election. Answer (B) is incorrect. Twenty-five is not the maximum number of shareholders to be eligible for an S corporation election. Answer (C) is incorrect. Seventy-five is not the maximum number of shareholders to be eligible for an S corporation election.

17.12.2. Which one of the following conditions would prevent a corporation from qualifying as an S corporation in the current year?

A. A corporation that has an estate as a shareholder.

B. A corporation that is not a member of an affiliated group.

C. A corporation that has only one class of stock.

D. A corporation that has nonresident aliens as shareholders.

Answer (D) is correct. *(SPE, adapted)*
REQUIRED: The condition that prevents a corporation from qualifying as an S corporation.
DISCUSSION: A small business corporation (S corporation) is defined in Sec. 1361. Section 1361(b)(1)(C) states that a corporation is eligible for the S corporation election and status only if all its shareholders are U.S. citizens or resident aliens. Thus, a corporation having a nonresident alien as a shareholder would be ineligible for S corporation status.
Answer (A) is incorrect. An estate can be a shareholder in an S corporation. Answer (B) is incorrect. A corporation that is not a member of an affiliated group can be an S corporation. However, after 1996 an S corporation is allowed to own 80% or more of the stock of a C corporation. Answer (C) is incorrect. An S corporation can have only one class of stock.

17.12.3. What qualifications are necessary for an electing small business trust to be eligible to hold stock in an S corporation?

A. All beneficiaries of the trust must be individuals, and a specific election to be treated as an electing trust must be filed by all beneficiaries.

B. All beneficiaries of the trust must be individuals, and the trust must not have any interest acquired in a purchase transaction.

C. All beneficiaries of the trust must be individuals, estates, or charitable organizations that are eligible to be S corporation shareholders, and the trust must have an interest acquired by purchase.

D. All beneficiaries of the trust must be individuals, estates, or charitable organizations that are eligible to be S corporation shareholders, and the trust must not have an interest acquired by purchase. A specific election to be treated as an electing small business trust must be filed by the trustee.

Answer (D) is correct. *(Publisher, adapted)*
REQUIRED: The necessary requirements for an electing small business trust to be an S corporation shareholder.
DISCUSSION: An electing trust is one that does not have as a beneficiary any person other than (1) an individual, (2) an estate, or (3) an organization eligible to accept charitable contributions under Sec. 170. Also, an electing small business trust cannot have any interest acquired by purchase, and a specific election to be treated as an electing trust must be filed by the trustee.
Answer (A) is incorrect. Beneficiaries may be estates or charitable organizations. Answer (B) is incorrect. All beneficiaries of the trust do not have to be individuals. Answer (C) is incorrect. A small business trust cannot have any interest acquired by purchase.

17.12.4. Which of the following entities is ineligible to be an S corporation shareholder?

A. Charitable remainder annuity trust.

B. Employee stock option plan (ESOP).

C. Electing small business trust.

D. Qualified retirement plan trust.

Answer (A) is correct. *(Publisher, adapted)*
REQUIRED: The entity ineligible to be an S corporation shareholder.
DISCUSSION: Charitable remainder unitrusts (CRUTs) and charitable remainder annuity trusts (CRATs) cannot qualify as electing small business trusts. All beneficiaries of an electing small business trust must be individuals or estates eligible to be S corporation shareholders. While CRUTs and CRATs provide income to individuals, they must also provide a remainder interest to a charitable organization.
Answer (B) is incorrect. An employee stock option plan (ESOP) is eligible to be an S corporation shareholder. Answer (C) is incorrect. An electing small business trust is eligible to be an S corporation shareholder. Answer (D) is incorrect. A qualified retirement plan trust is eligible to be an S corporation shareholder.

17.12.5. All of the following entities are allowed to elect S status except a

A. Domestic international sales corporation (DISC).

B. Domestic building and loan association.

C. Mutual savings bank.

D. Cooperative bank without capital stock organized and operated for mutual purposes and without profit.

Answer (A) is correct. *(Publisher, adapted)*
REQUIRED: The entity that cannot elect S status.
DISCUSSION: Certain entities cannot elect S status. These include some insurance companies, possession corporations, DISCs and former DISCs, and some institutions using the reserve method of accounting for bad debts. However, domestic building and loan associations, mutual savings banks, and a cooperative bank--without capital stock organized and operated for mutual purposes and without profit--are all able to elect S status.
Answer (B) is incorrect. A domestic building and loan association may elect S corporation status. Answer (C) is incorrect. A mutual savings bank may elect S corporation status. Answer (D) is incorrect. A cooperative bank without capital stock organized and operated for mutual purposes and without profit may elect S corporation status.

17.12.6. Which one of the following is not a requirement to make an S corporation election?

    A.   The corporation must have no trusts as shareholders.

    B.   Shareholder consent must be unanimous.

    C.   Only one class of stock can be outstanding.

    D.   The entity must be a domestic entity that elects corporation treatment under the check-the-box regulations.

Answer (A) is correct. *(CMA, adapted)*
    REQUIRED: The item not required to make an S corporation election.
    DISCUSSION: Certain trusts qualify as shareholders of an S corporation.
    Answer (B) is incorrect. All shareholders must consent to S corporation status. Answer (C) is incorrect. An S corporation may have only one class of stock. Answer (D) is incorrect. An S corporation no longer has to be a domestic corporation, but only has to be a domestic entity that elects to be taxed as a corporation under the check-the-box regulations.

17.12.7. Which of the following will prevent a corporation from qualifying as an S corporation in the current year?

    A.   Deriving more than 40% of its gross receipts from passive income sources.

    B.   Having a partnership as a shareholder.

    C.   Owning more than 80% of the stock of a domestic corporation.

    D.   Having 100 shareholders.

Answer (B) is correct. *(SPE, adapted)*
    REQUIRED: The action that will prevent a current-year S corporation election.
    DISCUSSION: An S corporation may not have more than 100 shareholders; shareholders who are not individuals, estates, or certain kinds of trusts and exempt organizations; a nonresident alien as a shareholder; or more than one class of stock [Sec. 1361(b)]. Having a partnership as a shareholder will prevent a corporation from making an S corporation election.
    Answer (A) is incorrect. Earning passive income will not prevent a corporation from electing S corporation treatment if it has no Subchapter C earnings and profits. Further, the termination of S corporation status will not occur unless the S corporation had Subchapter C earnings and profits at the end of each of 3 consecutive years and, for each of those years, had passive income in excess of 25% of gross receipts. Answer (C) is incorrect. Since 1996, the Small Business Act allows an S corporation to own 80% or more of the stock of a C corporation. Answer (D) is incorrect. Having up to 100 shareholders is permissible for an S corporation.

17.12.8. Which of the following tax years may an S corporation use for its taxable year beginning after 1986 (assuming no business purpose exists for another year and assuming an election is not made under Sec. 444)?

    A.   A calendar year.

    B.   A fiscal year ending in the last quarter of the calendar year.

    C.   The same year as is used by any of its shareholders.

    D.   Any tax year that it wants to use.

Answer (A) is correct. *(SPE, adapted)*
    REQUIRED: The correct taxable year for an S corporation after 1986.
    DISCUSSION: For taxable years beginning after 1986, an S corporation is required to use a calendar year unless it establishes a business purpose for using another year and the IRS consents [Sec. 1378(a)]. Otherwise, a fiscal year can be elected under Sec. 444 if a required payment is made.
    Answer (B) is incorrect. An S corporation may not use a fiscal year ending in the last quarter of the calendar year as its taxable year unless a business purpose is established or an election is made under Sec. 444. Answer (C) is incorrect. An S corporation may not use for its taxable year the same year as is used by any of its shareholders unless a business purpose is established or an election is made under Sec. 444. Answer (D) is incorrect. An S corporation may not use any tax year that it wants to use as its taxable year.

17.12.9. Lindal Corporation, organized in the current year, immediately filed an election for S corporation status under the Subchapter S rules. What is the maximum amount of passive investment income that Lindal will be allowed to earn and still qualify as an S corporation?

A. 80% of gross receipts.

B. 50% of gross receipts.

C. 20% of gross receipts.

D. No limit on passive investment income.

Answer (D) is correct. *(CPA, adapted)*
REQUIRED: The maximum amount of passive investment income allowable to an S corporation.
DISCUSSION: There is no limit on the amount of passive investment income that a corporation can earn and still qualify as an S corporation. S corporation status can be terminated if the corporation has had passive investment income in excess of 25% of gross receipts for 3 consecutive taxable years and has accumulated earnings and profits at the end of each of these taxable years (Sec. 1362). Before the 1996 Tax Act, a corporation was required to have Subchapter C earnings and profits to be disqualified as an S corporation.
Answer (A) is incorrect. Eighty percent of gross receipts is not the correct limit on passive investment income for an S corporation to earn and still qualify as an S corporation. Answer (B) is incorrect. Fifty percent of gross receipts is not the correct limit on passive investment income for an S corporation to earn and still qualify as an S corporation. Answer (C) is incorrect. Twenty percent of gross receipts is not the correct limit on passive investment income for an S corporation to earn and still qualify as an S corporation.

17.12.10. Mary and Paul are plumbers. They went into business together and decided that the corporation structure would be in their best interest. On January 1, Year 1, they formed the M & P Corp. They did not file a Form 2553. Mary and Paul filed an 1120S return at the end of the year and paid self-employment tax on their respective shares of the income. All of the following statements are true except

A. They are not permitted to file an 1120S return because they have not made a valid election.

B. The income distributed by a corporation is not subject to self-employment tax.

C. Mary and Paul have until March 15, Year 2, to make a valid election for Year 2.

D. Both Mary and Paul must sign Form 2553 to make a valid election.

Answer (C) is correct. *(SEE, adapted)*
REQUIRED: The false statement regarding the business structure.
DISCUSSION: The election to be taxed under Subchapter S is made on Form 2553 (election by small business corporation to tax corporate income directly to shareholders). This form may be filed during the previous tax year or within 2 1/2 months of the beginning of the current tax year to qualify for S corporation status for the current tax year [Sec. 1362(b)]. In the case of a calendar-year S corporation, this would mean filing before March 15 of the current year. Under Sec. 1362(b)(5), the IRS may treat a late-filed election as timely filed if reasonable cause existed (for tax years beginning after 12/31/82). Each person who is a shareholder at the time of election must consent by signing Form 2553. In addition, each person who was a shareholder at any time during the part of the tax year before the election is made must also consent. If any former shareholders do not consent, the election is considered made for the following year. Accordingly, Mary and Paul have not made a valid S election for Year 1.
Answer (A) is incorrect. A valid election made through Form 2553 must be completed before an 1120S return can be filed. Answer (B) is incorrect. S corporation distributions are not considered self-employment income (Rev. Rul. 59-221). Answer (D) is incorrect. Each person who is a shareholder at the time of election must consent by signing Form 2553. In addition, each person who was a shareholder at any time during the part of the tax year before the election is made must also consent. If any former shareholders do not consent, the election is considered made for the following year.

17.12.11. Tau Corporation, which has been operating for 15 years, has an October 31 year end, which coincides with its natural business year. On May 15 of this year, Tau filed the required form to elect S corporation status. All of Tau's shareholders consented to the election, and all other requirements were met. The earliest date that Tau can be recognized as an S corporation is

A. November 1 of last year.

B. May 15 of this year.

C. November 1 of this year.

D. November 1 of next year.

Answer (C) is correct. *(CPA, adapted)*
REQUIRED: The earliest date an S corporation election will be effective.
DISCUSSION: Section 1362(b) allows a corporation to make a proper election within the first 2 1/2 months of the year and be effective the first day of that tax year. An election made after the first 2 1/2 months of the year is effective as of the next year. Since Tau filed its election outside the 2 1/2-month period, the election will be effective for the first day of the next tax year beginning November 1 of this year. Under Sec. 1362(b)(5), the IRS may treat a late-filed election as timely filed if reasonable cause existed.
Note that an S corporation may have a fiscal year that coincides with its natural business year (with IRS consent).
Answer (A) is incorrect. November 1 of last year is not the earliest date Tau can be recognized as an S corporation. Answer (B) is incorrect. May 15 of this year is not the earliest date Tau can be recognized as an S corporation. Answer (D) is incorrect. November 1 of next year is not the earliest date Tau can be recognized as an S corporation.

17.12.12. Charitable remainder unitrusts (CRUTs) and charitable remainder annuity trusts (CRATs) cannot qualify as electing small business trusts.

A. True.

B. False.

Answer (A) is correct. *(Publisher, adapted)*
DISCUSSION: CRUTs and CRATs cannot qualify as electing small business trusts. All beneficiaries of an electing small business trust must be individuals or estates eligible to be S corporation shareholders. While CRUTs and CRATs provide income to individuals, they must also provide a remainder interest to a charitable organization.

17.12.13. Corporation X began operations on January 1 of this year and met all of the requirements to qualify as an S corporation. On March 15 of this year, X filed a valid Form 2553 to elect S corporation status. X cannot be treated as an S corporation until next year.

A. True.

B. False.

Answer (B) is correct. *(SPE, adapted)*
DISCUSSION: The election to be taxed under Subchapter S is made on Form 2553 (election by small business corporation to tax corporate income directly to shareholders). Under Sec. 1362(b), the election becomes effective at the beginning of the current tax year if the form is filed during the previous tax year or during 2 1/2 months of the beginning of the current tax year.

17.12.14. Mr. P, Mr. W, and Mrs. S are the only shareholders in a domestic corporation. At a board of directors meeting on February 15 of the current year, W and S voted to elect S corporation status for the current year. Mr. P was available but would not sign the consent. W and S filed the election form, Form 2553, the next day. This constitutes a valid election for S corporation status.

A. True.

B. False.

Answer (B) is correct. *(SPE, adapted)*
DISCUSSION: Section 1362(a)(2) states that an election for S corporation status is valid only if all persons who are shareholders consent to the election. Thus, if Mr. P does not consent to the election, it will not be valid. Under Sec. 1362(b)(5), the IRS has the ability to waive the effect of an invalid election caused by Mr. P failing to sign the consent form in a timely manner. Mr. P does have to file the consent for the election to be valid.

17.12.15. Corporation T wishes to elect S corporation status for the current calendar year. T has 26 shareholders including a qualified Subchapter S trust with seven beneficiaries, only one of which is an income beneficiary. In addition, T has common stock outstanding with differences in voting rights, although the dividend rights and liquidation preferences for each share are equal. Corporation T can elect S corporation status.

A. True.

B. False.

Answer (A) is correct. *(SPE, adapted)*
DISCUSSION: An S corporation can have no more than 100 shareholders and can have only one class of stock. Only individuals, estates, certain types of trusts, and exempt organizations may be shareholders. Under Sec. 1361(c)(2)(A)(i), a qualified subchapter S trust (QSST) may be a shareholder in an S corporation. The deemed owner of the trust is treated as the shareholder. Under Sec. 1361(c)(4), differences in common stock voting rights are disregarded. A corporation will not be treated as having more than one class of stock solely because there are differences in voting rights among the shares of common stock.

17.12.16. Best Bank, a mutual savings bank, uses the reserve method of accounting for bad debts. Best Bank is ineligible to elect S corporation status.

A. True.

B. False.

Answer (B) is correct. *(Publisher, adapted)*
DISCUSSION: The 1996 Tax Act reduces the types of financial institutions that are ineligible to elect S corporation status. The following financial institutions are eligible to elect S corporation status: (1) domestic building and loan associations, (2) any mutual savings bank, and (3) any cooperative bank without capital stock organized and operated for mutual purposes and without profit.

17.12.17. The IRS may waive the effect of an inadvertent termination caused by an entity's failure to obtain required shareholder consents.

A. True.

B. False.

Answer (A) is correct. *(Publisher, adapted)*
DISCUSSION: The IRS has authority to waive the effect of an invalid election caused by an entity's inadvertent failure to obtain the required shareholder consents [Sec. 1362(f)]. This provision is effective with respect to elections for tax years beginning after 1982. The entity has the burden of establishing that, under the relevant facts and circumstances, the IRS should determine that the termination was inadvertent.

17.12.18. A new corporation electing to be an S corporation for a tax year beginning in the current year may make a Sec. 444 election to adopt a fiscal tax year only if the months between the beginning of the tax year elected and the close of the first required tax year is 3 months or less.

A. True.

B. False.

Answer (A) is correct. *(SPE, adapted)*
DISCUSSION: Section 444 allows an S corporation to elect a taxable year other than the calendar year. Section 444(b)(1) states that the election may be made only if the period between the beginning of the tax year elected and the close of the first required tax year (known as the deferral period) is 3 months or less.

17.13 S Corporation Income

17.13.1. Which of the following items is not a separately stated item for Form 1120S shareholders?

A. Charitable contributions made by the corporation.

B. Section 179 deduction.

C. Depreciation.

D. Tax-exempt interest.

Answer (C) is correct. *(SEE, adapted)*
REQUIRED: The item that is not a separately stated item for Form 1120S shareholders.
DISCUSSION: An S corporation passes a pro rata share of its total income (loss) through to the individual shareholders, except for items that require separate treatment by the shareholder. Charitable contributions made by the corporation, Sec. 179 deduction, and tax-exempt interest must be separately stated. Depreciation, however, is combined with other nonseparately stated income or loss.
Answer (A) is incorrect. Charitable contributions made by the corporation are separately stated for Form 1120S shareholders. Answer (B) is incorrect. A Section 179 deduction is a separately stated item for Form 1120S shareholders. Answer (D) is incorrect. Tax-exempt interest is a separately stated item for Form 1120S shareholders.

17.13.2. An S corporation may deduct

A. Charitable contributions within the percentage of income limitation applicable to corporations.

B. Net operating loss carryovers.

C. Foreign income taxes.

D. Compensation of officers.

Answer (D) is correct. *(CPA, adapted)*
REQUIRED: The item an S corporation may deduct.
DISCUSSION: Section 1363(b) provides that the taxable income of an S corporation shall be computed in the same manner as that of an individual, except as otherwise provided. Compensation of officers will be treated as an ordinary and necessary business expense and will result in a reduction of nonseparately stated income. Section 1363(b)(2) states that the deductions referred to in Sec. 703(a)(2) are not allowed to an S corporation. Charitable contributions are referred to in Sec. 703(a)(2).
Answer (A) is incorrect. Section 1363(b)(2) states that the deductions referred to in Sec. 703(a)(2) are not allowed to an S corporation. Charitable contributions are referred to in Sec. 703(a)(2). Answer (B) is incorrect. An S corporation may not deduct net operating loss carryovers. Answer (C) is incorrect. An S corporation may not deduct foreign income taxes.

17.13.3. In computing the nonseparately stated income or loss of an S corporation, which of the following items can be deducted by the corporation?

A. Charitable contributions.

B. Intangible drilling and development costs the corporation elects to expense.

C. Interest expense on investments.

D. Corporate organizational costs.

Answer (D) is correct. *(SPE, adapted)*
REQUIRED: The item that can be deducted by an S corporation in computing nonseparately stated (ordinary) income or loss.
DISCUSSION: The computation of an S corporation's nonseparately stated (ordinary) income or loss is governed by Sec. 1363(b). That section states that Sec. 248 applies to S corporations. Section 248 allows corporate organizational costs to be amortized over a period of not less than 180 months.
Answer (A) is incorrect. Section 1363(b)(2), with reference to Sec. 703(a)(2), does not allow an S corporation to deduct charitable contributions. Answer (B) is incorrect. Items that are separately stated are not allowed as deductions to the S corporation. Intangible drilling and development costs the corporation elects to expense are not included in nonseparately stated (ordinary) income or loss but are separately stated and pass through directly to the shareholders. Answer (C) is incorrect. Items that are separately stated are not allowed as deductions to the S corporation.

17.13.4. Towne Corporation was owned entirely by individual T from January 1 of the current year until September 30 of the same year, at which time she sold her entire stockholdings to individual A. During the year, Towne reported ordinary income of $146,000. It made a $30,000 cash distribution to T on July 1 of the current year. How much income should be reported by individuals T and A in the current year as a result of Towne Corporation's activities (assume a valid S corporation election has been in effect at all times since its inception and ignore leap years)?

A. T, $30,000; A, $116,000.

B. T, $0; A, $146,000.

C. T, $139,200; A, $6,800.

D. T, $109,200; A, $36,800.

Answer (D) is correct. *(Publisher, adapted)*
REQUIRED: The shareholders' income from an S corporation when the shares are transferred during the year.
DISCUSSION: Section 1366(a) provides that each shareholder shall include his or her pro rata share of the corporation's income. Section 1377(a) defines pro rata share as the taxpayer's share of the corporation's income determined on a per-day basis. Individual T owned the shares for 273 days, while individual A owned the shares for 92 days. (The income for the day of transfer is reported by the transferor.) Towne Corporation reported ordinary income of $146,000 for the full year, which is $400 per day ($146,000 ÷ 365 days). Therefore, T must report income of $109,200 ($400 × 273 days), and A must report income of $36,800 ($400 × 92 days). The cash distribution to T is not in excess of her basis for the stock and does not result in any further taxation to T (Sec. 1368), except that it reduced her basis so that she incurred a larger gain on the sale of the stock.
Answer (A) is incorrect. The cash distribution of $30,000 to T does not result in any gross income. Answer (B) is incorrect. T must report a portion of the ordinary income. Answer (C) is incorrect. T and A should each report his or her share of ordinary income based on the number of days each owned stock in the corporation.

17.13.5. What is the nonseparately stated income amount of an accrual-basis, calendar-year S corporation with the following items?

Gross receipts	$200,000
Interest income	12,000
Rental income	25,000
Cost of goods sold and commissions	127,000
Net long-term capital gain	17,000
Compensation paid to shareholder	10,000

A. $63,000

B. $73,000

C. $117,000

D. $127,000

Answer (A) is correct. *(SPE, adapted)*
REQUIRED: The amount of nonseparately stated income for an S corporation.
DISCUSSION: Items of income, gain, expense, loss, and credit must be separately stated if those items are specially treated for tax purposes at the shareholder level. These items include interest income, rental income, and net long-term capital gains.
Answer (B) is incorrect. Compensation paid to a shareholder is not separately stated. Answer (C) is incorrect. The rental income, interest income, and capital gain are not included. Answer (D) is incorrect. The rental income, interest income, and capital gain are not included. However, the compensation to shareholders is included.

17.13.6. At the beginning of the current year, W, an S corporation, was owned equally by two individual shareholders, D and K. During the year, W had ordinary income of $183,000, a net long-term capital gain of $91,500, and charitable contributions of $27,450. What is the amount of ordinary income, capital gain, and charitable contribution from W's activities that D and K must each report in the current year?

	Ordinary Income	Capital Gain	Charitable Contribution
A.	$54,500	$0	$0
B.	$118,950	$45,750	$13,725
C.	$64,050	$45,750	$13,725
D.	$91,500	$45,750	$13,725

Answer (D) is correct. *(SPE, adapted)*
    REQUIRED: The amount of ordinary income, capital gains, and charitable contributions that must be reported by equal shareholders of an S corporation.
    DISCUSSION: Each shareholder of an S corporation must report his or her share of the corporation's ordinary income. Accordingly, D and K will each report $91,500 ($183,000 × .50) of ordinary income from W. The capital gains are also passed through to D and K. Under Sec. 1366(b), the capital gains will retain their character in the shareholders' hands. The charitable contributions cannot be deducted by the S corporation. They will be passed through to D and K and will retain their character. Because D and K are equal shareholders, they will each report $45,750 ($91,500 × .50) of capital gains and $13,725 ($27,450 × .50) of charitable contributions resulting from W's activities.
    Answer (A) is incorrect. D and K must also report a portion of the capital gain and a portion of the charitable contribution. Answer (B) is incorrect. The capital gain plus the charitable contribution is $118,950. Answer (C) is incorrect. The capital gain less the charitable contribution is $64,050.

17.13.7. Mr. Star has a $100,000 basis in the stock of an S corporation. Which of the following items would not decrease his basis in the stock?

A. The amount of the deduction for depletion that is more than the basis of the property being depleted.

B. Distributions by the S corporation that are a return of capital.

C. Any expense of the S corporation that is not deductible in figuring its income and not properly chargeable to the capital account.

D. All loss and deduction items of the S corporation that are separately stated and passed through to the shareholder.

Answer (A) is correct. *(SPE, adapted)*
    REQUIRED: The item that would not decrease an S corporation shareholder's stock basis.
    DISCUSSION: Section 1367(a)(2) provides guidelines covering decreases in the basis of S corporation stock. Decreases in basis are caused by distributions, losses and deductions not included in nonseparately stated (ordinary) income, any nonseparately stated (ordinary) loss, and any expense of the corporation that is not deductible in computing its taxable income and not properly chargeable to the capital account. Basis is also decreased by the amount of the deduction for depletion that does not exceed the basis of the property being depleted. The amount of any deduction for depletion that exceeds the property's basis does not decrease the shareholder's basis in the S corporation stock.
    Answer (B) is incorrect. Distributions by the S corporation that are a return of capital decrease a shareholder's basis in the S corporation stock. Answer (C) is incorrect. Any expense of the S corporation that is not deductible in figuring its income and not properly chargeable to the capital account decreases a shareholder's basis in the S corporation stock. Answer (D) is incorrect. All loss and deduction items of the S corporation that are separately stated and passed through to the shareholder decrease a shareholder's basis in the S corporation stock.

17.13.8. Krista acquires stock in an S corporation by reason of inheritance. The value of the stock acquired is $100,000, and $25,000 represents the share of income accrued to the previous owner. The basis of the stock in the previous owner's hands was $50,000. What is Krista's basis in the stock upon inheritance, and what is Krista's IRD amount?

	Basis	IRD
A.	$100,000	$0
B.	$100,000	$25,000
C.	$75,000	$25,000
D.	$75,000	$50,000

Answer (C) is correct. *(Publisher, adapted)*
    REQUIRED: The adjustment to basis and IRD from inherited S corporation stock.
    DISCUSSION: A person who acquires stock in an S corporation by reason of a bequest, devise, or inheritance must treat as income in respect to a decedent (IRD) the pro rata share of income of the corporation that would have been IRD if the income had been acquired directly from the decedent. The stepped-up basis of the stock acquired from a decedent is reduced by the amount to which the value of the stock is attributable to items of IRD. A deduction under Sec. 691(c) is allowed for the estate tax attributable to IRD. Therefore, Krista receives the S corporation stock with a basis of $75,000 ($100,000 value – $25,000 IRD), and the amount attributable to the S corporation income ($25,000) that is considered IRD.
    Answer (A) is incorrect. Krista has an IRD amount. Answer (B) is incorrect. The stepped-up basis of the stock acquired from a decedent is reduced by the amount to which the value of the stock is attributable to items of IRD. Answer (D) is incorrect. The amount of IRD is the share of income accrued to the previous owner.

17.13.9. Milam, Inc., is an S corporation with ordinary income of $60,000. Bob Milam owns all of the stock in the corporation. The following data are also available for the current tax year ended December 31:

Milam's January 1 stock basis	$ 3,000
Cash distribution to Milam	27,000
Tax-exempt interest	2,000
Section 1250 gain	28,000
Long-term capital loss	4,000
Short-term capital loss	6,000

Milam's stock basis at the end of the current year is

A. $38,000

B. $35,000

C. $28,000

D. $26,000

Answer (C) is correct. *(Publisher, adapted)*
  REQUIRED: The basis of the shareholder's stock in an S corporation after adjustments.
  DISCUSSION: Section 1367 provides guidelines for adjustments to the basis of a shareholder's S corporation stock. The increases include items of income (including tax-exempt income) that are passed through to the shareholder, nonseparately stated (ordinary) income, and the excess of deductions for depletion over the basis of the property subject to depletion. The basis of Milam's stock is decreased for any distributions made by the corporation not includible in income, nonseparately stated loss, and separately stated loss and deduction items, expenses of the corporation not deductible in computing its taxable income, and the amount of the shareholder's deduction for depletion for any oil and gas property held by the S corporation. The Sec. 1250 gain is not added to basis because it is already included in Milam's ordinary income.

Milam's basis at January 1	$ 3,000
Ordinary income of S corporation	60,000
Tax-exempt interest	2,000
Distribution to Milam	(27,000)
Long-term capital loss	(4,000)
Short-term capital loss	(6,000)
Milam's basis at December 31	$28,000

  Answer (A) is incorrect. The long- and short-term capital losses decrease basis. Answer (B) is incorrect. The long- and short-term capital losses decrease basis and the beginning basis should be included. Answer (D) is incorrect. Tax-exempt interest increases basis.

17.13.10. Which of the following is a characteristic of a Qualified Subchapter S Subsidiary (QSub)?

A. A QSub is an entity that would qualify for S corporation status and is at least 80% owned by the subsidiary's parent corporation.

B. The QSub is either a domestic or a foreign entity.

C. All assets, liabilities, and items of income, deduction, and credit are treated as if they belong to the S corporation's parent corporation.

D. If the subsidiary's QSub election terminates, it is not eligible, without IRS consent, to make another QSub election before the second tax year beginning after the first tax year for which the termination was effective.

Answer (C) is correct. *(Publisher, adapted)*
  REQUIRED: The characteristics of a Qualified Subchapter S Subsidiary (QSub).
  DISCUSSION: The QSub is not treated as a separate corporation. Accordingly, all assets, liabilities, and items of income, deduction, and credits of a QSub are treated as belonging to the parent S corporation.
  Answer (A) is incorrect. To qualify as a QSub, the subsidiary must be 100%-owned by the S corporation's parent corporation. Answer (B) is incorrect. Only a domestic entity qualifies as a QSub. Answer (D) is incorrect. A QSub that has terminated cannot reelect to be treated as a QSub within 5 years.

17.13.11. Both separately stated items and the nonseparately stated income or loss are passed through to the shareholders of an S corporation in proportion to their shareholdings.

A. True.

B. False.

Answer (A) is correct. *(SPE, adapted)*
  DISCUSSION: Each shareholder of an S corporation separately accounts for his or her pro rata share of both separately stated and nonseparately stated corporate items in his or her tax year in which the corporation's tax year ends [Sec. 1366(a)]. Items must be separately stated whenever they could affect the shareholder's individual tax liability.

17.13.12. The portion of a small business trust that consists of stock in one or more S corporations is treated as a separate trust for purposes of computing the income tax attributable to the S corporation stock held by the trust, and this portion of the trust's income is taxed at the highest tax rate imposed on estates and trusts.

A. True.

B. False.

Answer (A) is correct. *(Publisher, adapted)*
DISCUSSION: The portion of the small business trust related to the S corporation stock is subject to the highest tax rate imposed on estates and trusts (39.6% for 2017). The taxable income attributable to this portion includes (1) the items of income, loss, or deduction allocated to the trust as an S corporation shareholder under the rules of Subchapter S, (2) gain or loss from the sale of the S corporation stock, and (3) any state or local income taxes and administrative expenses of the trust properly allocable to the S corporation stock. Otherwise, allowable capital losses are only allowed to the extent of capital gains.

17.13.13. For the current year, the books and records of Clover, Inc., a cash-basis S corporation, reflected the following:

Salary to Dad Clover, president and 50% shareholder	$22,000
Salary to Son Clover, janitor and 50% shareholder	60,000
Loans to Dad Clover during the year, no repayments	30,000

Dad Clover worked 40-hour weeks for the entire year but said that the business could not afford to pay him a salary of more than the $22,000. The IRS could reclassify the $30,000 in loans and/or part of the son's salary to Dad Clover and assess income tax withholding as well as employment taxes on those amounts.

A. True.

B. False.

Answer (A) is correct. *(SPE, adapted)*
DISCUSSION: Section 1371(a) provides that Subchapter C rules apply to an S corporation and its shareholders except as otherwise provided or when inconsistent with Subchapter S. The IRC authorizes reallocation of gross income between a corporation and its shareholders (see Sec. 482). Reallocation and recharacterization have also been approved by case law. If reclassification of the loan as salary were upheld, assessment of liability for withholding and employment taxes could follow.

17.14 S Corporation Losses

17.14.1. Corporation D, a calendar-year S corporation, was formed January 1, Year 1. Mr. Homer owns 50% of D's stock, which had a basis to him of $125,000 on January 1, Year 1. On February 1, Year 1, Corporation D borrowed $20,000 from its bank and $25,000 from Mr. Homer for use in its business. Homer materially participates in the company. D had losses from operations of $120,000 in Year 1 and $210,000 in Year 2. D has not repaid any of the loan from Mr. Homer. What amount of Mr. Homer's share of D's Year 2 loss is deductible on his Year 2 individual return?

A. $90,000

B. $100,000

C. $105,000

D. $210,000

Answer (A) is correct. *(SPE, adapted)*
REQUIRED: The amount of loss deductible by an S corporation shareholder in the current year.
DISCUSSION: Under Sec. 1366(d)(1), a taxpayer may deduct losses in the amount of the sum of (1) his or her adjusted basis in the stock, plus (2) the adjusted basis of any corporate indebtedness to him or her. For Year 1, Homer may deduct his entire 50% share of losses since his $150,000 limit ($125,000 basis + $25,000 debt) is greater than his share of losses of $60,000 ($120,000 × 50%). The limit for Year 2 is $90,000 ($125,000 basis – $60,000 Year 1 loss + $25,000 debt). Since the allocable share of the loss of $105,000 ($210,000 × 50%) is greater than the limit, Homer only may deduct $90,000 in Year 2. The remaining $15,000 in losses may be carried over indefinitely. Since Homer materially participates, the passive loss limitation rules do not apply. The corporation's debt to the bank does not affect Homer's basis or loss limitation.
Answer (B) is incorrect. The shareholder's basis does not include Mr. Homer's ratable share of the S Corporation's bank borrowing as would be the case with a partnership. Answer (C) is incorrect. The amount of $105,000 is 50% of the ordinary loss incurred in Year 2. Answer (D) is incorrect. The amount of $210,000 is the total ordinary loss incurred in Year 2, which should be allocated based on Homer's ownership percentage.

17.14.2. Jen and Jerry were shareholders of Water Ice, Inc., an S corporation. On January 1, Year 1, Jen owned 40 shares and Jerry owned 60 shares. Jen sold her shares to Joe for $10,000 on March 30, Year 1. The corporation reported a $50,000 loss at the end of Year 1. How much of the loss is allocated to Joe, assuming a non-leap year?

A. $20,000

B. $15,123

C. $12,500

D. $10,000

Answer (B) is correct. *(SEE, adapted)*
REQUIRED: The loss allocated to an S corporation shareholder owning 40% of the company.
DISCUSSION: An S corporation shareholder includes his or her pro rata share of loss from the S corporation [Sec. 1366(a)]. Section 1377(a) defines pro rata share as the taxpayer's share of loss determined on a per-day and then a per-share basis. Since Joe bought Jen's shares on March 31, Year 1, his per-day basis is 276. The loss must be allocated based on the number of days Joe was a shareholder. The transferor is the owner of the stock on the day transferred. Therefore, the loss allocated to Joe is $15,123 ($50,000 × 40% × 276/365).
Answer (A) is incorrect. The allocation also is done by the amount of time held for the year. Answer (C) is incorrect. The amount of the loss must be allocated as determined by the taxpayer's pro rata share [Sec. 1377(a)]. Answer (D) is incorrect. The amount Joe paid Jen for Jen's shares in Water Ice is $10,000.

17.14.3. Maui Corporation (an S corporation) reported a $72,000 ordinary loss during Year 1. At the beginning of Year 1, Elvis and Frank owned equally all of Maui's stock. On June 30, Year 1, Frank gave one-fourth of his stock to his son, George. What amount of the Year 1 loss is allocated to George, assuming it is not a leap year?

A. $0

B. $4,537

C. $9,000

D. $18,000

Answer (B) is correct. *(SEE, adapted)*
REQUIRED: The loss allocated to an S corporation shareholder who acquired his or her stock in mid-year.
DISCUSSION: An S corporation shareholder includes his or her pro rata share of loss from the S corporation [Sec. 1366(a)]. Section 1377(a) defines pro rata share as the taxpayer's share of loss determined on a per-day and then a per-share basis. Therefore, the amount of loss allocated to George is $4,537 ($72,000 × 12.5% × 184/365).
Answer (A) is incorrect. A part of the loss is allocable to George. Answer (C) is incorrect. The loss is allocated based on a per-day basis. Answer (D) is incorrect. The loss is allocated based on a per-day basis, and George only owns 12.5% of the total stock outstanding.

17.14.4. With regard to S corporations and their shareholders, the "at-risk" rules applicable to losses

A. Depend on the type of income reported by the S corporation.

B. Are subject to the elections made by the S corporation's shareholders.

C. Take into consideration the S corporation's ratio of debt to equity.

D. Apply at the shareholder level rather than at the corporate level.

Answer (D) is correct. *(CPA, adapted)*
REQUIRED: The correct application of the at-risk rules to S corporations and shareholders.
DISCUSSION: The at-risk rules of Sec. 465 do not apply directly to S corporations. They do apply to individuals as shareholders of S corporations. The at-risk rules are incorporated into Sec. 1366(d) to limit a shareholder's deduction for losses and other deductions from an S corporation to the total of (1) the adjusted basis of the shareholder's stock in the S corporation and (2) the shareholder's adjusted basis of any debt owed by the S corporation to the shareholder.
Answer (A) is incorrect. The type of income reported by the S corporation does not have any effect on the at-risk rules. Answer (B) is incorrect. The at-risk rules are not subject to the elections made by the S corporation's shareholders. Answer (C) is incorrect. Taking into consideration the S corporation's ratio of debt to equity does not have any effect on the at-risk rules.

17.14.5. Bill and Ken own Tax, Inc. (an S corporation), equally. In Year 1, the corporation reported a $130,000 ordinary loss. Tax, Inc.'s liabilities at the end of Year 1 included $100,000 of accounts payable, $150,000 of mortgage payable, and a $20,000 note owed to Bill. Each owner had a $40,000 adjusted basis for his stock on January 1, Year 1. Compute the loss reportable by Bill.

A. $65,000

B. $60,000

C. $40,000

D. None of the answers are correct.

Answer (B) is correct. *(SEE, adapted)*
    REQUIRED: The loss of an S corporation shareholder.
    DISCUSSION: Generally, if a shareholder purchases stock, the shareholder's original basis in the stock is its cost. If a shareholder receives stock in exchange for property, the basis is the same as the property's basis. If a shareholder lends money to the S corporation, the basis is usually the amount of the loan. If a shareholder guarantees a third-party loan to an S corporation, the loan does not increase the shareholder's basis. If, however, the shareholder makes payments on the loan, the payments increase the shareholder's basis. The amount of losses and deductions an S corporation shareholder can claim is limited to the adjusted basis of the shareholder's stock. Since Bill lent $20,000 to Tax, Inc., he must increase his basis by the amount of the loan. Therefore, Bill's basis is $60,000, and the amount of losses and deductions an S corporation shareholder can claim is limited to the adjusted basis of the shareholder's stock.
    Answer (A) is incorrect. The amount of $65,000 is one-half of the loss reported by the corporation. Answer (C) is incorrect. The amount of $40,000 is the adjusted basis of Bill's stock. Answer (D) is incorrect. There is a correct answer.

17.14.6. Sunnie owns 50% of the shares of Corporation H, a calendar-year S corporation, having a basis of $7,000. She also guaranteed a corporate loan of $6,000. For the current year, H had an operating loss of $22,000. What is the amount of H's loss that Sunnie can deduct on her individual income tax return for the current year?

A. $11,000

B. $10,000

C. $7,000

D. $0

Answer (C) is correct. *(SPE, adapted)*
    REQUIRED: The amount of loss deductible by an S corporation shareholder in the current year.
    DISCUSSION: A shareholder in an S corporation includes his or her pro rata share of all items of income, loss, deduction, and credit from the S corporation [Sec. 1366(a)]. Sunnie is a 50% shareholder and is allocated 50% of the $22,000 ordinary loss for the current year, or $11,000. However, Sec. 1366(d) limits the losses taken into account by a shareholder to the sum of the shareholder's basis in the stock and his or her basis in any debt of the S corporation to that shareholder. Sunnie's guarantee does not increase her basis in the stock. Sunnie's limit for deduction of losses is the $7,000 basis in her stock. The remaining loss of $4,000 can be carried forward indefinitely until Sunnie has sufficient basis.
    Answer (A) is incorrect. The amount of $11,000 is Sunnie's allocable share of the loss. Answer (B) is incorrect. The amount of $10,000 is not the correct amount of H's loss that Sunnie can deduct on her tax return. Answer (D) is incorrect. Sunnie can deduct a loss.

17.14.7. Jasper owns 50% of Blaster, Inc., an S corporation, filing returns on a calendar year basis. For the Year 1 tax year, the corporation has an operating loss of $13,000 and separately stated tax-exempt income of $10,000. Jasper's basis on January 1, Year 1, is $2,000. What is his basis at the end of the Year 1 tax year?

A. $0

B. $(1,000)

C. $500

D. None of the answers are correct.

Answer (C) is correct. *(SEE, adapted)*
    REQUIRED: The S corporation shareholder's basis in stock at year end.
    DISCUSSION: Section 1367 provides guidelines for adjustments to the basis of a shareholder's S corporation stock. The increases include items of income (including tax-exempt income) that are passed through to the shareholder, nonseparately stated (ordinary) income, and the excess of deductions for depletion over the basis of the property subject to depletion. The basis of Jasper's stock is decreased by the amount of loss allocable to him; however, it cannot reduce his basis below zero.

Basis at January 1	$ 2,000
Tax-exempt income ($10,000 × 50%)	5,000
Ordinary loss of S corporation ($13,000 × 50%)	(6,500)
Basis at December 31	$ 500

    Answer (A) is incorrect. Half of the ordinary loss and half of the tax-exempt income are allocated to basis. Answer (B) is incorrect. Basis is never negative. Answer (D) is incorrect. There is a correct answer.

Questions 17.14.8 and 17.14.9 are based on the following information. Day Corporation, an S corporation, reported a $73,000 ordinary loss for Year 1 (a non-leap year). Day uses the calendar year as its taxable year, as do all of its shareholders. Individual B owns 25% of the Day stock at all times during Year 1. B's basis in his Day Corporation stock at the beginning of Year 1 was $10,000. B materially participates in Day's business. At the end of Year 1, Day is liable for the following:

Third-party creditors	$15,000
Individual B	3,000
Other shareholders	9,000

17.14.8. What amount of Day's losses may be deducted by B in Year 1, and what amount of Day's losses can be carried over by B to Year 2?

- A. Deducted, $18,250; carryover, $0.
- B. Deducted, $13,000; carryover, $0.
- C. Deducted, $13,000; carryover, $5,250.
- D. Deducted, $18,000; carryover, $250.

Answer (C) is correct. *(Publisher, adapted)*

REQUIRED: The amount of loss deductible by an S corporation shareholder in the current year and the amount carried over to future years.

DISCUSSION: A shareholder in an S corporation includes his or her pro rata share of all items of income, loss, deduction, and credit from the S corporation [Sec. 1366(a)]. B is a 25% shareholder and is allocated 25% of the $73,000 ordinary loss for Year 1, or $18,250. However, Sec. 1366(d) limits the losses taken into account by a shareholder to the sum of the shareholder's basis in the stock and his or her basis in any debt of the S corporation to that shareholder. Individual B's limit for deduction of losses is $13,000 ($10,000 basis in stock + $3,000 basis in loan to Day). The remaining loss of $5,250, which cannot be deducted in the current year, can be carried forward indefinitely until B has sufficient basis. Since B materially participates, the passive loss rules do not apply.

Answer (A) is incorrect. B's deductible loss is limited, and any remaining loss carried over to the subsequent year. Answer (B) is incorrect. B has a carryover. Answer (D) is incorrect. B's deductible loss is limited.

17.14.9. What is B's basis in his Day Corporation stock and his basis in the indebtedness he is owed by Day Corporation at the end of Year 1?

- A. Stock, $0; indebtedness, $3,000.
- B. Stock, $0; indebtedness, $0.
- C. Stock, $15,000; indebtedness, $3,000.
- D. None of the answers are correct.

Answer (B) is correct. *(Publisher, adapted)*

REQUIRED: The shareholder's basis in S corporation stock and in the debt owed to the shareholder after deducting losses.

DISCUSSION: When a shareholder deducts losses of an S corporation, his or her basis in the stock is decreased (but not below zero) by the amount of the deduction [Sec. 1367(a)]. When a loss is deducted in excess of the S corporation shareholder's basis in the stock, the basis in debt owed to the shareholder is reduced (but not below zero). Accordingly, B has a zero basis in both the stock and the debt. Future earnings of the corporation will be used first to restore the basis in the debt, and then to increase the basis in the stock [Sec. 1367(b)(2)].

Answer (A) is incorrect. The amount of $3,000 is not the correct amount B is owed by the S corporation. Answer (C) is incorrect. B's stock basis is not $15,000, and the amount owed to B is not $3,000. Answer (D) is incorrect. One of the answers is correct.

17.14.10. A loss on the sale or exchange of property is not deductible if the transaction is directly or indirectly between two S corporations and the same persons own more than 50% in value of the outstanding stock of each corporation.

- A. True.
- B. False.

Answer (A) is correct. *(SPE, adapted)*

DISCUSSION: Loss is not recognized in transactions between related parties. Two S corporations are treated as related if the same persons own more than 50% in value of the outstanding stock in each corporation (Sec. 267).

17.15   Distributions from S Corporations

17.15.1. Mr. Sharp received a distribution from an S corporation that was in excess of the basis of his stock in the corporation. The S corporation had no accumulated earnings and profits. Mr. Sharp should treat the distribution in excess of his basis as

A.   A return of capital.

B.   A capital gain.

C.   Previously taxed income.

D.   A reduction in the basis of his stock.

Answer (B) is correct. *(SPE, adapted)*
REQUIRED: The treatment of a distribution in excess of a shareholder's basis when the corporation has no earnings and profits.
DISCUSSION: Section 1368(b) provides that distributions made by an S corporation having no accumulated earnings and profits reduce the stock's basis. Any distribution in excess of the adjusted basis of the stock shall be treated as gain from the sale or exchange of property. Since Mr. Sharp's S corporation stock is considered a capital asset, the gain is capital gain.
Answer (A) is incorrect. Mr. Sharp should not treat the distribution in excess of his basis as a return of capital. Answer (C) is incorrect. Mr. Sharp should not treat the distribution in excess of his basis as previously taxed income. Answer (D) is incorrect. Mr. Sharp should not treat the distribution in excess of his basis as a reduction in the basis of his stock.

17.15.2. Wiggins is the sole shareholder of the Tamale Corporation, a calendar-year S corporation. Tamale is indebted to Wiggins in the amount of $5,000. For the current year, Tamale earned $25,000 of ordinary income and distributed $10,000 as a dividend to Wiggins. How much income should Wiggins report from Tamale Corporation for the current year?

A. $0

B. $10,000

C. $25,000

D. $35,000

Answer (C) is correct. *(Publisher, adapted)*
REQUIRED: The amount of income a shareholder should recognize from an S corporation.
DISCUSSION: Although shareholders of C corporations report income only as it is distributed to them (usually as dividends), shareholders of S corporations are treated differently. All of an S corporation's income is taxed to the shareholders each year whether distributed or not (Sec. 1366). This increases the shareholder's basis. Distributions in general then reduce the shareholder's basis. Wiggins must report the entire $25,000 of ordinary income of the S corporation in his or her own return. The debt of Tamale to Wiggins does not affect this income computation. The distribution to Wiggins is a tax-free return of capital and does not result in the recognition of income.
Answer (A) is incorrect. Wiggins has income to report from Tamale Corporation. Answer (B) is incorrect. The amount of $10,000 was distributed to Wiggins. The distribution is not taxable to Wiggins. Answer (D) is incorrect. The income earned by Tamale plus the distribution to Wiggins is $35,000. The distribution is not taxable to Wiggins.

17.15.3. The books and records of F, a calendar-year S corporation since 1983, reflect the following information for the current year:

Accumulated adjustments account --	
January 1	$ 30,000
Accumulated earnings and profits --	
January 1	75,000
Ordinary income for the current year	102,000

F has only one shareholder, T, whose basis in F's stock was $50,000 on January 1. During the current year, F distributed $150,000 to T. What is the amount of this distribution that should be treated as a capital gain by T?

A. $0

B. $20,000

C. $130,000

D. $150,000

Answer (A) is correct. *(SPE, adapted)*
REQUIRED: The capital gain recognized by a shareholder on a distribution by an S corporation.
DISCUSSION: Distributions by S corporations with accumulated earnings and profits are governed by Sec. 1368(c). The portion of the distribution that does not exceed the accumulated adjustments account balance reduces the shareholder's basis. The remaining distribution is treated as a dividend to the extent of accumulated earnings and profits. Any remaining distribution is treated as a recovery of the shareholder's remaining basis in the S corporation stock, and a capital gain to the extent it exceeds such basis.
At the end of the year, F's accumulated adjustments account will be $132,000 ($30,000 + $102,000) because of F's current year income. T's basis in the stock will be $152,000 ($50,000 beginning basis and $102,000 ordinary income from the current year). The first $132,000 of the distribution is from the accumulated adjustments account and will reduce T's stock basis to $20,000. The remaining $18,000 of the distribution will reduce T's remaining stock basis. Because T still has a $20,000 basis for his stock, no capital gain results.
Answer (B) is incorrect. T's basis in the stock is $20,000. Answer (C) is incorrect. The amount of $130,000 is not the correct amount of capital gain resulting from the distribution. Answer (D) is incorrect. The distribution F made to T is $150,000.

17.15.4. JLK Corporation was formed in 1981 and elected a calendar tax year. It elected S corporation status in 1982. On December 31 of the current year, JLK made a $50,000 distribution to its founder and sole shareholder, John. JLK had a previously taxed income account of $9,000 and $1,000 of accumulated earnings and profits at the time of the distribution. The accumulated E&P was earned in 1980 while a C corporation. The accumulated adjustments account balance on January 1 of the current year was zero. During the year, JLK earned $12,000 of ordinary income. John's basis in his JLK stock on January 1 of the current year was $10,000. How much income will John report from this S corporation investment in the current year, and what is its character?

	Ordinary Income	Capital Gain
A.	$12,000	$0
B.	$13,000	$0
C.	$50,000	$10,000
D.	$13,000	$27,000

Answer (D) is correct. *(Publisher, adapted)*
REQUIRED: The amount and the character of income reported by a shareholder of an S corporation.
DISCUSSION: Distributions by S corporations with accumulated earnings and profits (E&P) are governed by Sec. 1368(c). The portion of the distribution not in excess of the accumulated adjustments account reduces the shareholder's basis. Money distributions then come from previously taxed income after the accumulated adjustments account has been exhausted. These distributions reduce the shareholder's basis. Distributions next come out of accumulated E&P and are taxable as dividends. Any remaining distribution is treated as a capital gain to the extent it exceeds the shareholder's remaining stock basis.
At the end of the year, JLK's accumulated adjustments account balance is $12,000. John's basis in the stock will be $22,000. The first $12,000 of the distribution comes out of the accumulated adjustments account and reduces the stock basis to $10,000. The next $9,000 comes out of previously taxed income and reduces the stock basis to $1,000. The next $1,000 comes out of accumulated E&P and is taxable as a dividend (thereby resulting in $13,000 of ordinary income). The next $1,000 reduces the stock basis to zero and causes the last $27,000 of the distribution to be a capital gain.
Authors' note: All pre-1983 earnings and profits earned while an S corporation are eliminated for post-1996 tax years.
Answer (A) is incorrect. The amount of $12,000 is not the correct amount of ordinary income from this investment, and there also is a capital gain. Answer (B) is incorrect. John has a capital gain from this investment. Answer (C) is incorrect. The amount of $50,000 is the distribution to John by the corporation. Also, $10,000 is not the correct capital gain John has from this investment.

17.15.5. Naples Corporation, an S corporation, made a $10,000 cash distribution to its sole shareholder, Jimmy, in the current year. Jimmy's basis in the Naples stock at the beginning of the year was $50,000. In the current year, Naples incurred a $60,000 loss. What amount of the cash distribution is taxable to Jimmy in the current year?

A. $20,000

B. $10,000

C. $2,500

D. $0

Answer (D) is correct. *(Publisher, adapted)*
REQUIRED: The basis adjustment for distributions when losses are incurred.
DISCUSSION: Basis adjustments for distributions made by an S corporation during the year are taken into account before applying the loss limitation for the year. Accordingly, distributions reduce the adjusted basis for determining the allowable loss for the year, but the loss does not reduce the adjusted basis for purposes of determining the tax status of the distributions. Jimmy must first reduce his basis by the amount of the distribution. As a result, the distribution is a tax-free return of capital, and he has a basis of $40,000 for purposes of the loss limitation. Of the $60,000 loss in the current year, only $40,000 (the amount of the shareholder's basis) is allowed as a deduction in the current year.
Answer (A) is incorrect. Naples Corporation did not make a cash distribution of $20,000 to Jimmy in the current year. Answer (B) is incorrect. The amount of the cash distribution Naples Corporation made to Jimmy is $10,000. Answer (C) is incorrect. The distribution is first applied against adjusted basis.

17.15.6. Jenny Corporation (an S corporation) is owned entirely by Craig. At the beginning of Year 1, Craig's adjusted basis in his Jenny Corporation stock was $20,000. Jenny reported ordinary income of $5,000 and a capital loss of $10,000. Craig received a cash distribution of $35,000 in November Year 1. What is Craig's gain from the distribution?

A. $0

B. $10,000

C. $20,000

D. $35,000

Answer (B) is correct. *(SEE, adapted)*
REQUIRED: The sole shareholder's gain from the distribution of an S corporation.
DISCUSSION: The basis is increased by the ordinary income to $25,000. The $35,000 distribution is taken next and since it exceeds the basis, there is a $10,000 gain. The capital loss is nondeductible because there is no basis and is carried over.
Answer (A) is incorrect. If the distribution is greater than the basis, the excess is taxable as a sale or an exchange of property (a taxable capital gain). Answer (C) is incorrect. The distribution is taken before the deduction for the capital loss. Answer (D) is incorrect. The entire distribution is not taxable, only the difference between the distribution and the basis.

17.15.7. Pages, Inc. (an S corporation), is owned by Martin and Steve. They share in the income and loss of the corporation on a 50/50 basis. In Year 1, the corporation reported $90,000 in ordinary income and $12,000 of tax-exempt income. Each owner's basis in his stock is $25,000. The corporation was previously a C corporation, and $30,000 in E&P remained on the books at the beginning of the year. Martin and Steve each received an $80,000 distribution from the corporation on December 15, Year 1. What is the character of the distribution to Martin [assume the accumulated adjustment account (AAA) and other adjustments account (OAA) are zero on January 1, Year 1]?

A. $45,000 AAA, $31,000 return of capital, $4,000 dividend, zero capital gains.

B. $45,000 AAA, $15,000 dividend, $20,000 return of capital, zero capital gains.

C. $45,000 AAA, $25,000 return of capital, $10,000 dividend, zero capital gains.

D. $45,000 AAA, $25,000 return of capital, $10,000 capital gains, zero dividends.

Answer (B) is correct. *(SEE, adapted)*
REQUIRED: The character of a distribution to an S corporation shareholder.
DISCUSSION: The ordinary income will increase Martin's share of the AAA to $45,000 and also increase his stock basis to $70,000. The tax-exempt income will increase Martin's share of OAA to $6,000 and increase his stock basis to $76,000. The first $45,000 distributed to Martin comes from AAA, reducing AAA to $0 and his basis to $31,000. The next $15,000 distributed to Martin comes from E&P and is dividend income; Martin's stock basis is not reduced. The next $6,000 distributed to Martin comes from OAA, is tax free, and reduces his basis to $25,000. The remaining $14,000 comes from stock basis, is tax free, and reduces his basis to $11,000.
Answer (A) is incorrect. Distributions from E&P come before return of capital. Answer (C) is incorrect. The distribution order is not correct. Answer (D) is incorrect. Distributions from E&P come before distributions from OAA and return of capital.

17.15.8. XYZ Corporation (S Corporation) had the following items of income and deductions for Year 1. Charles and Diane are equal shareholders in the corporation. They each had an adjusted stock basis of $30,000 on January 1, Year 1.

Gross receipts from sales	$100,000
Cost of goods sold	50,000
Depreciation	10,000
Charitable contributions	10,000
Interest income	5,000
Tax-exempt interest	3,000
Other operating costs	63,000

Diane received a distribution of $15,000 on June 1, Year 1. Her basis on January 1, Year 2, is

A. $15,000

B. $3,500

C. $2,500

D. $0

Answer (C) is correct. *(SEE, adapted)*
REQUIRED: The basis of an S corporation shareholder's stock after a distribution.
DISCUSSION: A shareholder's stock basis is affected by the operations of the corporation. All of the items will affect Diane's stock basis, which will be $2,500 in January Year 2. Only half of the items are allocated to Diane, except for the distribution.

Adjusted stock basis, 1/1/Yr 1	$ 30,000
Gross receipts	50,000
Cost of goods sold	(25,000)
Depreciation	(5,000)
Charitable contributions	(5,000)
Interest income	2,500
Tax-exempt interest	1,500
Operating costs	(31,500)
Distribution	(15,000)
Adjusted stock basis, 1/1/Yr 2	$ 2,500

Answer (A) is incorrect. Diane's basis must be adjusted for her share of the loss, charitable contribution, interest income, and tax-exempt interest. Answer (B) is incorrect. The basis must be adjusted for the charitable contribution, interest income, and tax-exempt interest. Answer (D) is incorrect. The distribution did not eliminate stock basis.

17.15.9. Rap, Inc., was organized in January Year 1 and immediately made an S election. Rap's stock is entirely owned by Howard, who contributed $40,000 to start the business. Rap reported the following results for Year 1:

Ordinary income	$36,000
Short-term capital loss	4,000
Charitable contributions	1,000
Tax-exempt income	1,000
Section 179 deduction	10,000

On April 12, Year 1, Howard received a $30,000 cash distribution from the corporation. What is the adjusted basis of his stock on January 1, Year 2?

A. $41,000

B. $32,000

C. $31,000

D. $10,000

Answer (B) is correct. *(SEE, adapted)*
REQUIRED: The basis of an S corporation shareholder's stock after a distribution.
DISCUSSION: The adjusted basis of the shareholder's stock is figured at year end with increases for the shareholder's pro rata share of all income items, including tax-exempt income, that are separately stated and any nonseparately stated income. Also, all separately and nonseparately stated losses and deduction items decrease the basis of the shareholder's stock on a pro rata basis. Howard's stock basis on January 1, Year 2, is $32,000.

Original basis	$ 40,000
Ordinary income	36,000
Tax-exempt income	1,000
Short-term capital loss	(4,000)
Charitable contributions	(1,000)
Section 179 deduction	(10,000)
Cash distribution	(30,000)
Adjusted basis	$ 32,000

Answer (A) is incorrect. The Sec. 179 deduction and charitable contributions reduce the basis. Answer (C) is incorrect. The charitable contributions reduce the basis. Answer (D) is incorrect. Other factors besides the cash distribution are considered.

17.15.10. Distributions made by an S corporation result in the recognition of gross income only when made out of accumulated earnings and profits, or when the sum of the amount of cash and the fair market value of the property distributed to a shareholder exceeds the basis of his or her stock investment in the corporation.

A. True.

B. False.

Answer (A) is correct. *(Publisher, adapted)*
DISCUSSION: Distributions made by an S corporation are generally a distribution of income that has already been taxed to the shareholder and, accordingly, are made without recognition of additional income (Sec. 1368). If the corporation has no accumulated earnings and profits, all distributions will reduce the basis of the stock until the basis reaches zero, and further distributions will be treated as gain from the sale or exchange of the stock. If the corporation has accumulated earnings and profits, distributions are first made from the accumulated adjustments account, then from accumulated earnings and profits (dividends), and lastly are treated as gain from the sale or exchange of property to the extent they are in excess of the shareholder's remaining basis for the stock.

17.15.11. In the current year, an S corporation distributed property to a shareholder that had a fair market value in excess of its adjusted basis to the S corporation. The shareholder must use the fair market value of the property in determining the amount of the distribution as opposed to the basis of the property in the hands of the S corporation.

A. True.

B. False.

Answer (A) is correct. *(SPE, adapted)*
DISCUSSION: When an S corporation distributes as a nonliquidating distribution property that has a FMV in excess of basis, then the S corporation must recognize gain as if it sold the property at its FMV [Sec. 311(b)]. The FMV of the property then reduces the shareholder's basis for the stock.

17.15.12. For any tax year, an S corporation can elect its distributions as coming first from its C corporation accumulated earnings and profits if all shareholders who receive a distribution during the tax year consent to the election. This election remains in effect for all tax years thereafter.

A. True.

B. False.

Answer (B) is correct. *(SPE, adapted)*
DISCUSSION: Section 1368(e)(3) provides that an S corporation can elect its distributions as coming first from earnings and profits if all affected shareholders consent. An affected shareholder is one to whom the corporation makes a distribution during the tax year. The election is effective only for the tax year for which the election is made.

17.16 Taxes Levied on the S Corporation

17.16.1. In which of the following instances involving the current year will an S corporation be subject to tax?

A. ABL had passive investment income equal to 10% of its gross receipts. ABL has always been an S corporation.

B. XYZ sold an asset at a gain that had a value in excess of its basis when contributed to XYZ. XYZ elected S corporation status 5 years ago for its first year of existence.

C. PQR sold an asset at a gain. The asset had a value in excess of basis when PQR elected S corporation status 4 years ago. PQR began operations 5 years ago.

D. XYZ had a capital gain on the sale of an asset acquired last year. XYZ elected S corporation status 2 years ago after 2 years of operations. XYZ had only a minimal amount of passive income.

Answer (C) is correct. *(Publisher, adapted)*
REQUIRED: The instance in which an S corporation will be subject to tax.
DISCUSSION: If a C corporation makes an S corporation election after 1986, a corporate-level tax is imposed on any gain that arose prior to the conversion if the gain is recognized by the S corporation through sale, collection, exchange, or distribution within 10 years after the date on which the S election took effect. Since PQR had a built-in gain when it elected S corporation status in this answer, this portion of the gain will be recognized by PQR and taxed under Sec. 1374 when it sells the asset.
Answer (A) is incorrect. An S corporation is only taxed on excess net passive income when passive investment income exceeds 25% of gross receipts and there are Subchapter C earnings and profits (i.e., earnings and profits accumulated while a C corporation). Answer (B) is incorrect. The taxation on built-in gains of an S corporation does not apply when a corporation has always been an S corporation unless some of its assets were acquired from a C corporation in a tax-free transaction. Answer (D) is incorrect. An S corporation does not have built-in gains if the asset was acquired after S corporation status was in effect.

17.16.2. If an S corporation recognizes a built-in gain and pays tax on it, the shareholders

A. Report only gain from the transaction that is in excess of the built-in gain, i.e., on appreciation accruing after the first day of the first taxable year for which the corporation was an S corporation.

B. Report no gain from the transaction.

C. Report their share of the entire gain in their own taxable income and obtain a credit for their share of taxes paid by the S corporation.

D. Report their share of the individual gains reduced by the taxes paid by the S corporation that are attributable to such gains.

Answer (D) is correct. *(Publisher, adapted)*
REQUIRED: The effect on shareholders when an S corporation recognizes a built-in gain.
DISCUSSION: The built-in gain of an S corporation is only the excess of the fair market value over the basis that existed on the first day of the first taxable year for which the corporation was an S corporation. Any additional appreciation after the effective date of the S election is not a built-in gain but is treated as ordinary or capital gain of the S corporation. Shareholders must include in their own gross income their share of these gains of the corporation. In addition, a shareholder must include his or her share of the built-in gain, but the amount of built-in gain is reduced by any taxes paid by the S corporation [Sec. 1366(f)(2)].
Answer (A) is incorrect. If an S corporation recognizes a built-in gain and pays tax on it, the shareholders will not report only gain from the transaction that is in excess of the built-in gain. Answer (B) is incorrect. If an S corporation recognizes a built-in gain and pays tax on it, the shareholders will report gain from the transaction. Answer (C) is incorrect. If an S corporation recognizes a built-in gain and pays tax on it, the shareholders will not report their share of the entire gain in their own taxable income and obtain a credit for their share of taxes paid by the S corporation.

17.16.3. Which of the following corporations may be subject to the built-in capital gains tax?

A. K-corp., established in 1964 as a C corporation, elected to be an S corporation on May 13, 1984.

B. G-corp., established in 2010 as a C corporation, elected to be an S corporation on April 15, 2017.

C. J-corp., established in 1986 as an S corporation, terminated its S corporation election on January 1, 2017.

D. All of the answers are correct.

Answer (B) is correct. *(SEE, adapted)*
REQUIRED: The corporation that may be subject to the built-in capital gains tax.
DISCUSSION: An S corporation that, upon conversion from C to S status after 1986, had net appreciation inherent in its assets is subject to tax of 35% on net gain recognized (up to the amount of built-in gain on conversion) during the recognition period. The recognition period is the 10-year (7-year for 2009 and 2010, 5-year for after 2010) period beginning on the date the S election became effective. The tax liability is passed through, as a loss, pro rata to its shareholders.
Answer (A) is incorrect. The conversion from C to S status must occur after 1986. Answer (C) is incorrect. A conversion from C to S status must take place. Answer (D) is incorrect. Not all of the answers are correct.

17.16.4. Prail Corporation is a C corporation that, on February 1 of the current year, elected to be taxed as a calendar-year S corporation. On June 15 of the current year, Prail sold land with a basis of $100,000 for $200,000 cash. The fair market value of the land on January 1 of the current year was $150,000. Prail had no other income or loss for the year and no carryovers from prior years. What is Prail's tax?

A. $7,500

B. $17,500

C. $22,250

D. $35,000

Answer (B) is correct. *(Publisher, adapted)*
REQUIRED: The S corporation's tax when it sells property with a built-in gain.
DISCUSSION: The corporate level tax is imposed on an S corporation on any gain that arose prior to the conversion (S election) if the gain is recognized by the S corporation through sale, collection, exchange, or distribution within 10 years after the first day of the first taxable year for which the corporation is an S corporation. Prail's built-in gain is $50,000 ($150,000 fair market value − $100,000 basis). The tax is imposed by the highest rate of tax in Sec. 11(b) on the lesser of the net recognized built-in gain or the amount that would be the taxable income as defined in Sec. 1375(b)(1)(B) if the corporation was not an S corporation without regard to the dividends-received deduction, the dividends-paid deduction, or the NOL deduction. These two amounts are equal for Prail in the current year, so the tax is $17,500 ($50,000 × 35%).
Prail's shareholders will report their share of the $82,500 gain ($100,000 gain − $17,500 tax paid) and will pay tax on that gain at their individual tax rates.
Answer (A) is incorrect. The tax is not determined by the lowest tax rate (15%). Answer (C) is incorrect. The 35% corporate tax rate is applied to the $50,000 built-in gain. Answer (D) is incorrect. The 35% corporate tax rate is not applied to the entire recognized gain.

17.16.5. Bligh, Inc., is a calendar-year C corporation that, on December 15, Year 1, elected to be taxed as an S corporation commencing with Year 2. On January 1, Year 2, it had land with a basis of $50,000 and a fair market value of $125,000. Bligh sold the land on September 20, Year 4, for $150,000 (its basis was still $50,000). Bligh had a net loss from other operations for Year 4 of $15,000 and a net operating loss carryover from Year 1 of $10,000. What is Bligh's tax?

A. $11,250

B. $22,750

C. $26,250

D. $29,750

Answer (B) is correct. *(Publisher, adapted)*
REQUIRED: The S corporation's tax on built-in gain when it also has current ordinary losses and NOL carryover.
DISCUSSION: The built-in gain of an S corporation is the excess of fair market value over basis of an asset that existed on the first day of the first taxable year for which the corporation was an S corporation. This built-in gain is recognized when the asset is sold within 10 years (7 years for corporations converting to an S corporation in 2009 and 2010, 5 years after 2010) thereafter. Bligh's recognized built-in gain is $75,000 ($125,000 − $50,000). The tax on the built-in gain is 35% [the highest rate specified in Sec. 11(b)] on the lesser of the net recognized built-in gain or the amount that would be the taxable income if the corporation was not an S corporation without regard to the dividends-received deduction, the dividends-paid deduction, or the NOL deduction. Net operating loss carryovers and capital loss carryovers from the C corporation tax-year reduce the recognized built-in gain, but not taxable income. Therefore, Bligh's tax is computed on the lesser of $65,000 ($75,000 built-in gain − $10,000 NOL carryover) or taxable income of $85,000 ($100,000 gain − $15,000 loss from other operations). Bligh's tax is $22,750 ($65,000 × 35%).
Answer (A) is incorrect. The built-in gains tax rate is 35% (not 15%). This rate is applied to the built-in gain after reduction for the NOL carryover. Answer (C) is incorrect. The $75,000 built-in gain should be reduced by the $10,000 NOL carryover before applying the 35% tax rate. Answer (D) is incorrect. The 35% tax rate is applied to the lesser of the built-in gain ($75,000) or the taxable income if the corporation was not an S corporation ($85,000). The built-in gain is further reduced by the NOL carryover.

17.16.6. T, an S corporation, is liable for the tax on its excess net passive income for the current year of $10,000. What is the amount of the tax?

A. $1,500

B. $3,400

C. $3,500

D. $4,000

Answer (C) is correct. *(SPE, adapted)*
REQUIRED: The amount of the tax on excess net passive income of an S corporation.
DISCUSSION: Section 1375(a) provides that the tax on the excess net passive income of an S corporation is the excess net passive income times the highest corporate tax rate (35%). Thus, the tax is $3,500 ($10,000 × 35%).
Answer (A) is incorrect. The lowest tax rate is not applied. Answer (B) is incorrect. The amount of 35%, not 34%, is the highest corporate tax rate. Answer (D) is incorrect. The amount of 35%, not 40%, is the highest corporate tax rate.

17.16.7. All of the following factors serve to determine whether an S corporation may be subject to the tax on excess net passive income except

A. The S corporation has Subchapter C earnings and profits at the end of the tax year.

B. Passive investment income is more than 25% of its gross receipts.

C. More than 50% of loans payable are not at-risk.

D. The S corporation has been an S corporation from the date of its incorporation.

Answer (C) is correct. *(SPE, adapted)*
REQUIRED: The factor not considered when determining if the excess net passive income tax applies.
DISCUSSION: Under Sec. 1375, the excess net passive income tax applies when the S corporation was previously a C corporation, has accumulated earnings and profits (also known as Subchapter C earnings and profits), and has gross receipts of which more than 25% is passive investment income.
Answer (A) is incorrect. A consideration in determining applicability of the excess net passive income tax is the S corporation having Subchapter C earnings and profits at the end of the tax year. Answer (B) is incorrect. A consideration in determining applicability of the excess net passive income tax is passive investment income being more than 25% of its gross receipts. Answer (D) is incorrect. A consideration in determining applicability of the excess net passive income tax is the S corporation having been an S corporation from the date of its incorporation.

17.16.8. Real Corporation, an S corporation, had gross receipts of $100,000, including passive investment income of $75,000. Real also had Subchapter C earnings and profits at the end of the tax year. Real incurred $50,000 in expenses directly related to the earning of the passive investment income. Taxable income for the S corporation is $40,000. The tax on the excess net passive income is

A. $5,667
B. $5,833
C. $14,000
D. $17,500

Answer (B) is correct. *(SPE, adapted)*
REQUIRED: The tax on the excess net passive income of an S corporation.
DISCUSSION: The excess net passive income is an amount bearing the same ratio to net passive income (passive investment income less directly connected expenses) as the excess of passive investment income over 25% of gross receipts bears to the passive investment income. The tax is imposed at the highest rate in Sec. 11(b), which is 35%.

$$x = \text{Excess net passive income}$$
$$x = (\$75,000 - \$50,000) \times \frac{[\$75,000 - (\$100,000 \times 25\%)]}{\$75,000}$$
$$x = \$16,667$$
$$\text{Tax} = \$16,667 \times 35\% = \$5,833 \text{ (rounded)}$$

Answer (A) is incorrect. The highest corporate tax rate is 35%, not 34%. Answer (C) is incorrect. The 35% tax rate is not applied to taxable income. Answer (D) is incorrect. The 35% tax rate is not applied to the $100,000 gross receipts minus the $50,000 of direct expenses.

17.16.9. Tango Corporation, a calendar-year corporation, elected to be taxed as an S corporation on December 1 of last year. The election was effective for the current tax year. During the current year, Tango sold land and marketable securities that resulted in the recognition of a $60,000 gain and a $40,000 loss, respectively. The land was used as a parking lot in its business and had a $90,000 fair market value and a $30,000 basis on January 1 of the current year. The marketable securities had a $50,000 fair market value and a $90,000 adjusted basis on January 1 of the current year. The $40,000 built-in loss can be used to offset the $60,000 built-in gain recognized in the current year in calculating the built-in gains tax.

A. True.
B. False.

Answer (A) is correct. *(Publisher, adapted)*
DISCUSSION: Section 1374 imposes a tax on the built-in gains of a corporation that elects S corporation status after 1986. Built-in gain is defined as the gain accruing on an asset during the period prior to the S corporation election and recognized by the S corporation during a 10-year (7-year for 2009 and 2010, 5-year after 2010) period beginning with the first day of the S corporation's first election year. The tax is applied to the S corporation's net recognized built-in gain, which is defined by Sec. 1374(d)(2) as the lesser of (1) the net of the S corporation's built-in gains and losses or (2) the corporation's taxable income if it were taxed as a C corporation without regard to the dividends-received or dividends-paid deduction or the NOL deduction. The net of the built-in gains and losses is obtained by offsetting built-in losses against built-in gains. Therefore, the $40,000 loss from the sale of the marketable securities can be used to offset the $60,000 gain from the sale of the parking lot in calculating the built-in gains tax.

17.16.10. The tax on built-in gains generally does not apply to any corporation if an election to be an S corporation was in effect for each of its tax years.

A. True.
B. False.

Answer (A) is correct. *(SEE, adapted)*
DISCUSSION: For a former C corporation electing S corporation status after 1986, Sec. 1374 imposes a tax on any gain accruing prior to the conversion that is recognized by the S corporation within a 10-year (7-year for 2009 and 2010, 5-year after 2010) period beginning with the first day of the first taxable year for which the corporation was an S corporation. Section 1374(c) states that this tax is not imposed on a corporation that has always been an S corporation.

17.16.11. If an S corporation is subject to the tax on excess net passive income, it must reduce the items of passive income passed through to shareholders.

A. True.

B. False.

Answer (A) is correct. *(SEE, adapted)*
DISCUSSION: Each item of an S corporation's passive investment income is reduced by a pro rata share of any tax on excess net passive income.

17.16.12. Giant Corporation, a cash-basis, calendar-year corporation, elected to be taxed as an S corporation on February 1 of the current year. The election was effective for the current tax year. On January 1, Giant had uncollected accounts receivable of $175,000 and unpaid accounts payable (all of which are deductible) of $115,000. During this year, all receivables were collected and all payables were paid. Assuming no other transactions or events, Giant Corporation's built-in gains tax base is $175,000.

A. True.

B. False.

Answer (B) is correct. *(Publisher, adapted)*
DISCUSSION: Section 1374(d)(5)(A) states that an item of income attributable to the period before the S corporation election took effect is treated as a recognized built-in gain if it is taken into account during the 10-year (7-year for 2009 and 2010, 5-year after 2010) recognition period (the 10-year period beginning with the first day of the S corporation's first election year). Section 1374(d)(5)(B) states that any amount allowed as a deduction during the recognition period that was attributable to the period before the S corporation election took effect is treated as a recognized built-in loss. Therefore, Giant Corporation has a recognized built-in gain of $175,000 and a recognized built-in loss of $115,000.
The built-in gains tax base is the net recognized built-in gain, which is defined by Sec. 1374(d)(2) as the lesser of (1) the net of the S corporation's built-in gains and losses or (2) taxable income if it were taxed as a C corporation without regard to the dividends-received or dividends-paid deduction or NOL deduction. Since there were no other transactions or events, the built-in gains tax base is the same under either formula. Giant Corporation's built-in gains tax base is $60,000 ($175,000 − $115,000).

17.16.13. Panda, an S corporation since the date of its incorporation, has passive income for the current year in excess of 25% of its gross receipts. It is subject to a tax at the rate of 35% on excess net passive income.

A. True.

B. False.

Answer (B) is correct. *(SPE, adapted)*
DISCUSSION: Under Sec. 1375(a), an S corporation that has passive income in excess of 25% of its gross receipts is subject to a tax at the rate of 35% in the current year on its excess net passive income, but only if it has Subchapter C earnings and profits at the close of the taxable year. A corporation that has been an S corporation since the date of its incorporation generally would not have any Subchapter C earnings and profits and would not be subject to the tax.

17.16.14. King Corporation is a C corporation that elected on December 15 of the current year to be taxed as an S corporation commencing with the following tax year. King Corporation has used the LIFO inventory method for the last 5 of the 8 years it has been in existence. King Corporation must include the excess of the inventory's value on December 31 of the current year using a FIFO cost flow assumption over its value using a LIFO cost flow assumption in its current-year gross income. The tax payable as a result of the income that is recognized is payable in four installments.

A. True.

B. False.

Answer (A) is correct. *(Publisher, adapted)*
DISCUSSION: Section 1363(d)(1) states that a C corporation that inventories its goods under the LIFO method for its last taxable year before an S corporation election becomes effective must include in its gross income a LIFO recapture amount. Section 1363(d)(3) defines LIFO recapture amount as the amount by which the value of the inventory assets under the FIFO method exceeds the value of the inventory assets under the LIFO method. The tax payable as a result of the income that is recognized is payable in four installments [Sec. 1363(d)(2)(A)].

17.17　S Corporation Filing and Estimated Tax Requirements

17.17.1. Which of the following is not information required to be included in an S corporation income tax return?

A. Items of gross income and allowable deductions.

B. Names and addresses of all persons owning stock in the corporation at any time during the tax year.

C. Each shareholder's adjusted basis in the corporation's stock.

D. Number of shares owned by each shareholder at all times during the tax year.

Answer (C) is correct. *(SPE, adapted)*
REQUIRED: The item not required as information on an S corporation income tax return.
DISCUSSION: Section 6037 prescribes the requirements for information to be included in an S corporation tax return. There is no requirement that each shareholder's adjusted basis in the corporation's stock be included.
Answer (A) is incorrect. Items of gross income and allowable deductions are specifically required in Sec. 6037 to be included in an S corporation tax return. Answer (B) is incorrect. Names and addresses of all persons owning stock in the corporation at any time during the tax year are specifically required in Sec. 6037 to be included in an S corporation tax return. Answer (D) is incorrect. The number of shares owned by each shareholder at all times during the tax year is specifically required in Sec. 6037 to be included in an S corporation tax return.

17.17.2. For the current year, an S corporation does not have to make estimated tax payments with respect to which one of the following taxes?

A. Built-in gains tax.

B. Alternative minimum tax.

C. Excess passive investment income tax.

D. Investment tax credits that are recaptured.

Answer (B) is correct. *(Publisher, adapted)*
REQUIRED: The tax for which an S corporation does not have to make estimated tax payments.
DISCUSSION: Section 6655(g)(4) states that S corporations must make estimated tax payments with respect to the built-in gains tax, the excess passive investment income tax, and the investment credits that are recaptured. No alternative minimum tax is imposed on an S corporation.
Answer (A) is incorrect. Estimated tax payments are required for the built-in gains tax. Answer (C) is incorrect. Estimated tax payments are required for the excess passive investment income tax. Answer (D) is incorrect. Estimated tax payments are required for investment tax credits that are recaptured.

17.17.3. The Form 1120S return must be filed by the 15th day of the third month following the end of the corporate year and must include the names and addresses of all shareholders during the year.

A. True.

B. False.

Answer (A) is correct. *(SPE, adapted)*
DISCUSSION: Form 1120S is the form used by an S corporation. It, unlike a regular C corporation return, must be filed by the 15th day of the third month following the end of the corporate year [Sec. 6072(b)]. The names and addresses of all shareholders must be included on the return under Sec. 6037.

17.17.4. An S corporation does not have to make estimated tax payments unless the tax amount owed is at least $500.

A. True.

B. False.

Answer (A) is correct. *(Publisher, adapted)*
DISCUSSION: Section 6655(f) states that a corporation, including an S corporation, does not have to make estimated tax payments if the tax owed is less than $500.

17.17.5. Abe Snake owns 50% of the stock of Delta Corporation, an electing calendar-year S corporation. During the current year, Delta made estimated tax payments on its $30,000 built-in gains tax liability. Abe's ratable share of Delta's ordinary income is $80,000. In addition, long-term capital gains of $30,000 are separately passed through to Abe. Because Delta made $30,000 in estimated tax payments, Abe does not have to include his share of Delta's income in calculating his quarterly estimated tax payments.

A. True.

B. False.

Answer (B) is correct. *(Publisher, adapted)*
DISCUSSION: Section 1366(f)(2) states that the built-in gains tax imposed on an S corporation is treated as a loss sustained by the S corporation. The character of the loss is determined by allocating it proportionately among the recognized built-in gains that gave rise to the tax. Section 1366(a)(1) states that a shareholder must take into account his or her share of the S corporation's items of income, loss, deduction, or credit that are passed through directly to the shareholder, and the S corporation's nonseparately computed income or loss. The estimated tax Delta paid on its built-in gains will affect the amount that passes through to Abe. It does not relieve him of the requirement that he include his share of Delta's income in calculating his quarterly estimated tax payments.

17.17.6. S corporations owing $500 or more in estimated taxes can avoid an underpayment penalty by paying in the lesser of 90% of the tax shown on the current year's tax return or 90% of the tax shown on the prior year's tax return provided both returns are for a 12-month period.

    A. True.

    B. False.

Answer (B) is correct. *(Publisher, adapted)*
    DISCUSSION: Under Sec. 6655(g)(4)(C), an S corporation owing $500 or more in estimated taxes can avoid an underpayment penalty by paying in the lesser of (1) 100% of the tax shown on the current year's tax return or (2) 100% of the built-in gains tax, recaptured investment tax credit for the current year, and 100% of the excess passive investment income tax reported for the preceding taxable year. These requirements are applicable only if both returns are for a 12-month period.

17.18 Termination of S Corporation Status

17.18.1. All of the following events will cause the termination of an S Corporation's S election except

    A. Transaction that results in over 100 shareholders.

    B. Donation of stock to a tax-exempt organization under 501(c)(4).

    C. Sale of stock to a resident alien.

    D. Failing the passive income test for 3 consecutive years.

Answer (C) is correct. *(SEE, adapted)*
    REQUIRED: The event that will not cause the termination of an S corporation's S election.
    DISCUSSION: Upon the occurrence of a terminating event, an S corporation becomes a C corporation. The IRS may waive termination that is a result of the corporation's ceasing to be a small business corporation or failing the passive income test for 3 consecutive years when it has Subchapter C earnings and profits (E&P) if the terminating event is found to be inadvertent and is corrected within a reasonable time after it is discovered. An S corporation election is terminated by any of the following: (1) an effective revocation, which requires the consent of a majority of the shareholders (voting and nonvoting); (2) any eligibility requirement not being satisfied on any day; or (3) passive investment income (PII) termination. One eligibility requirement is that shareholders be individuals who are citizens or resident aliens of the United States. Therefore, sale of stock to a resident alien does not terminate the election.
    Answer (A) is incorrect. An S corporation cannot have over 100 shareholders. Answer (B) is incorrect. Only charitable organizations under Sec. 501(c)(3), not civic leagues under Sec. 501(c)(4), are eligible shareholders. Answer (D) is incorrect. The election is terminated if the corporation has passive investment income exceeding 25% of its gross receipts for 3 consecutive years.

17.18.2. All of the following will result in the termination of a corporation's S corporation status in the current year except

    A. Transferring stock to a partnership.

    B. Acquiring 80% of an operating subsidiary.

    C. Having passive investment income of more than 25% of gross receipts and Subchapter C earnings and profits when the passive income test has been failed for 3 consecutive years.

    D. Creating a second class of nonvoting preferred stock in its initial year.

Answer (B) is correct. *(SPE, adapted)*
    REQUIRED: The event that will not terminate a corporation's S corporation status.
    DISCUSSION: In post-1996 tax years, S corporations can have qualified subsidiaries. Unlike its C corporation subsidiaries, however, an S corporation cannot elect to file a consolidated return with its affiliated C corporations. Dividends received by the S corporation from the C corporation are not considered passive investment income to the extent the dividends are related to the earnings and profits of the C corporation derived from the active conduct of a trade or business.
    Answer (A) is incorrect. An S corporation may not have a partnership as a shareholder. Answer (C) is incorrect. Failing the passive income test will terminate S corporation status if the corporation has Subchapter C earnings and profits and if the test is failed for 3 consecutive years. Answer (D) is incorrect. An S corporation may have only one class of stock unless the only difference is with respect to voting rights.

17.18.3. Which of the following events could cause an S corporation to cease to qualify as an S corporation in the current year?

A. The corporation transfers its stock to a partnership.

B. A shareholder has zero basis in his stock.

C. A 25% shareholder sells his shares to an individual who wants to revoke the corporation's S election.

D. The corporation is liable for tax on excess net passive investment income for 2 consecutive years.

Answer (A) is correct. *(SPE, adapted)*
REQUIRED: The event that could cause an S corporation to cease to qualify as an S corporation.
DISCUSSION: An S corporation is a small business corporation whose shareholders have made an election under Sec. 1362(a). S corporation status may be terminated by the action of a majority of the shareholders. It may also be terminated if the corporation ceases to meet the requirements of a small business corporation. One of those requirements is that the corporation have as shareholders only individuals, estates, certain trusts, and certain exempt organizations. Therefore, transferring its stock to a partnership may cause an S corporation to cease to qualify as an S corporation.
Answer (B) is incorrect. A shareholder's stock basis has no effect on an S corporation's status. Answer (C) is incorrect. An election may be revoked only if shareholders holding more than one-half of the shares of stock consent to the revocation. Answer (D) is incorrect. The corporation must have passive investment income that exceeds 25% of gross receipts for 3 consecutive years (and must also have Subchapter C earnings and profits at the end of each of the 3 years) for the election to be terminated.

17.18.4. Which of the following statements about the termination or revocation of an election to be taxed as an S corporation is true?

A. Once an election is revoked, a new election cannot be made for 3 years.

B. The occurrence of an event that terminates an S election causes the election to be revoked as of the first day of the taxable year.

C. The termination of an S election causes all prior-year losses that have not been deducted by the shareholders to be lost.

D. Having passive investment income of more than 25% of gross receipts in its initial year will not result in the termination of a corporation's status as an S corporation.

Answer (D) is correct. *(SPE, adapted)*
REQUIRED: The true statement concerning the termination or revocation of an S election.
DISCUSSION: An S election may be revoked by shareholders holding more than one-half of the shares of stock. It may also be terminated if the corporation ceases to be a small business corporation as defined by Sec. 1361(b)(1) or if the corporation's passive investment income exceeds 25% of gross receipts for 3 consecutive taxable years (and the corporation has Subchapter C earnings and profits at the end of each year). Having passive investment income of more than 25% of gross receipts in its initial year will not result in the termination of a corporation's status as an S corporation because of the requirement that the passive investment income must exceed 25% of gross receipts for 3 consecutive years, and the corporation must have Subchapter C earnings and profits.
Answer (A) is incorrect. Under Sec. 1362(g), a new election cannot be made for 5 years. Answer (B) is incorrect. The occurrence of an event that terminates an S election causes the election to be terminated on the day preceding the date on which the event occurs. Answer (C) is incorrect. Shareholders may continue to deduct losses that were not deducted in prior years during the post-termination period, which is usually 1 year from the date of the termination [Sec. 1366(d)(3)].

17.18.5. The S corporation status can be revoked only if the shareholders who collectively own more than what percentage of the outstanding shares in the S corporation's stock consent to its revocation?

A. 50%

B. 66 2/3%

C. 75%

D. 80%

Answer (A) is correct. *(SPE, adapted)*
REQUIRED: The percentage of shares required to revoke S corporation status.
DISCUSSION: Section 1362(d)(1) provides that an S corporation's status may be revoked by an election of the shareholders holding more than half of the shares of a corporation.
Answer (B) is incorrect. The amount of 66 2/3% is not the correct percentage of the outstanding shares that must consent to revoke an S corporation's status. Answer (C) is incorrect. The amount of 75% is not the correct percentage of the outstanding shares that must consent to revoke an S corporation's status. Answer (D) is incorrect. The amount of 80% is not the correct percentage of the outstanding shares that must consent to revoke an S corporation's status.

17.18.6. The S corporation status would terminate at the end of 2017 for which of the following?

A. Incorporated in 2005. First year of S status was 2013. Passive investment income equaled 29% of gross receipts in 2015, 27% in 2016, and 25% in 2017. Subchapter C earnings and profits were $10,000 at the end of each year.

B. Incorporated in 2005. First year of S status was 2013. Earnings and profits from C corporation tax years were $10,000. In 2015, passive investment income equaled 35% of gross receipts. The corporation had no passive investment income in prior or later years.

C. Incorporated in 2009. First year of S status was 2014. Passive investment income equaled 27% of gross receipts in 2015, 26% in 2016, and 44% in 2017. Subchapter C earnings and profits were $10,000 at the end of each year.

D. Incorporated in 2009. First year of S status was 2010. Passive investment income equaled 19% of gross receipts in 2015, 34% in 2016, and 35% in 2017.

Answer (C) is correct. *(SEE, adapted)*
REQUIRED: The condition that would terminate S corporation status.
DISCUSSION: Section 1362(d)(3) provides that S corporation status will be terminated when passive investment income exceeds 25% of gross receipts for 3 consecutive taxable years and the corporation has Subchapter C earnings and profits at the end of each year. This answer is the only one that meets both requirements.
Answer (A) is incorrect. In 2017, passive investment income equaled but did not exceed 25% of gross receipts. Passive investment income must exceed 25% of gross receipts for 3 consecutive taxable years. Answer (B) is incorrect. The corporation had passive investment income in only 1 year. Therefore, the condition that passive investment income exceed 25% of gross receipts for 3 consecutive taxable years is not met. Answer (D) is incorrect. In 2015, passive investment income was only 19% of gross receipts.

17.18.7. All of the following are characteristics of the S corporation post-termination transition period except

A. The post-termination transition period ends 1 year after the last day of the corporation's last tax year as an S corporation, or the due date (including extensions) for the tax return for the last year.

B. Distributions made by a former S corporation during a post-termination transition period are treated as if made by a C corporation.

C. The post-termination transition period includes the 120-day period beginning on the date of a determination by a tax court opinion that the corporation's S election had terminated for a previous tax year.

D. The post-termination transition period includes the 120 days beginning on the date of a determination arising out of an audit that follows the S corporation's termination and adjusts a Subchapter S item of income, loss, or deduction claimed by the former S corporation.

Answer (B) is correct. *(Publisher, adapted)*
REQUIRED: The statement that is not a characteristic of the S corporation post-termination transition period.
DISCUSSION: Distributions made by a former S corporation during a post-termination transition period are treated as if they were made by an S corporation. Distributions made outside a post-termination transition period are treated generally as if they were made by a C corporation.
Answer (A) is incorrect. The S corporation post-termination transition period ends 1 year after the last day of the corporation's last tax year as an S corporation, or the due date (including extensions) for the tax return for the last year. Answer (C) is incorrect. The S corporation post-termination transition period includes the 120-day period beginning on the date of a determination by a tax court opinion that the corporation's S election had terminated for a previous tax year. Answer (D) is incorrect. The S corporation post-termination transition period includes the 120 days beginning on the date of a determination arising out of an audit that follows the S corporation's termination and adjusts a Subchapter S item of income, loss, or deduction claimed by the former S corporation.

17.18.8. Corporation B, an S corporation, terminated its status as an S corporation during the current year. Generally, how many tax years must it wait before it can become an S corporation again?

A. 1

B. 3

C. 5

D. 10

Answer (C) is correct. *(SPE, adapted)*
REQUIRED: The number of tax years a corporation must wait to become an S corporation again after terminating such status.
DISCUSSION: According to Sec. 1362(g), a corporation that was an S corporation and terminated such status must wait 5 tax years before electing S corporation status again unless early IRS approval is given.
Answer (A) is incorrect. One year is not the correct amount of time a corporation that terminates its S corporation status must wait before becoming an S corporation again. Answer (B) is incorrect. Three years is not the correct amount of time a corporation that terminates its S corporation status must wait before becoming an S corporation again. Answer (D) is incorrect. Ten years is not the correct amount of time a corporation that terminates its S corporation status must wait before becoming an S corporation again.

17.18.9. Krazy Me, Inc., is equally owned by George, Jerry, Kramer, and Myra. On September 15 of the current year, Myra married Felipe (a nonresident alien) and moved to Brazil (a community-property country). She did not give up her ownership in Krazy Me. Myra's marriage to Felipe and her moving to Brazil caused an inadvertent termination of the corporation's S election.

    A. True.

    B. False.

Answer (A) is correct. *(SEE, adapted)*
    DISCUSSION: A nonresident alien (NRA) may not own any shares. Felipe, through his marriage with Myra, is considered a shareholder. Because Felipe is a nonresident alien, the corporation's S election is terminated.

17.18.10. Mark, Larry, and Steve owned DMV, Inc. Steve owned 60%; Mark and Larry owned 20% each. Steve decided that he would retire and gave his shares to his nephew, Robert, who became the president of the corporation. The transfer of the shares to Robert terminated the S election.

    A. True.

    B. False.

Answer (B) is correct. *(SEE, adapted)*
    DISCUSSION: S corporation status is automatically terminated if any event occurs that would prohibit the corporation from making the election in the first place. Here, no act occurred that would have made S corporation status unavailable.

17.18.11. Carla and Virginia were equal shareholders of CV Corp. (an S corporation). On May 13 of the current year, Carla sold her shares to Virginia who became the sole owner of all the shares of CV Corp. The sale of the shares to Virginia caused the S election to be terminated.

    A. True.

    B. False.

Answer (B) is correct. *(SEE, adapted)*
    DISCUSSION: Eligibility depends on the nature of the corporation, its shareholders, and its stock. An S corporation must have only one class of stock. The number of shareholders may not exceed 100. The corporation must be domestic and not an ineligible corporation. An eligible corporation must make the election for S corporation status. The sale of the shares to Virginia did not cause the S election to be terminated, as long as all of the shareholders (just Virginia in this case) were eligible shareholders.

Use **Gleim Test Prep** for interactive study and easy-to-use detailed analytics!

STUDY UNIT EIGHTEEN
INCOME TAXATION OF ESTATES, TRUSTS, AND TAX-EXEMPT ORGANIZATIONS

18.1 Income and Deductions of Estates and Trusts

NOTE: See Study Unit 1, "Gross Income," for income and deductions included on a decedent's final return.

18.1.1. The taxable income of estates and trusts is generally computed in the same manner as that of which type of taxpayer?

A. Association.

B. Corporation.

C. Individual.

D. Partnership.

Answer (C) is correct. *(Publisher, adapted)*
REQUIRED: The taxpayer whose computation of taxable income is most similar to that of estates and trusts.
DISCUSSION: Except as otherwise provided, the taxable income of an estate or trust is computed in the same manner as that of individuals [Sec. 641(b)]. Most of the variations from the computation of an individual are contained in Sec. 642. Another difference is that an estate or trust is entitled to a deduction for distributions of income to beneficiaries.
Answer (A) is incorrect. An association is taxed as a corporation. Answer (B) is incorrect. The taxation of a corporation is very different from an estate or trust. Answer (D) is incorrect. A partnership has a unique method of taxation that does not apply to an estate or trust.

18.1.2. Dexter, a calendar-year, cash-basis taxpayer who died in June of the current year, was entitled to receive a $10,000 accounting fee that had not been collected before the date of death. The executor of Dexter's estate collected the full $10,000 in July of the current year. This $10,000 should appear in

A. Only the decedent's final individual income tax return.

B. Only the estate's fiduciary income tax return.

C. Only the decedent's estate tax return.

D. Both the fiduciary income tax return and the estate tax return.

Answer (D) is correct. *(CPA, adapted)*
REQUIRED: The correct treatment of income earned before death but not received until after death.
DISCUSSION: Income that a decedent had a right to receive prior to death but which was not includible on his or her final income tax return is income in respect of a decedent (IRD) (IRD is further covered in Subunit 18.6). The $10,000 is properly includible in the estate's (fiduciary) income tax return because Dexter was a cash-basis taxpayer and would not properly include income not yet received at the time of death in his final return. Since the money was owed to Dexter (he has a right to receive it), it is an asset of the estate and must be included on the estate tax return also.
Answer (A) is incorrect. Dexter was a cash-basis taxpayer and would not properly include income not received at the time of death. Answer (B) is incorrect. The $10,000 is an asset of the estate and must also be included on the estate tax return. Answer (C) is incorrect. The $10,000 is income to the estate and must also be included on its income tax return.

18.1.3. With regard to a trust, all of the following statements are true except

A. A trust is a separate taxable entity.

B. Generally, the trust is taxed on the income currently distributed and on the portion it has accumulated.

C. If income is required to be distributed currently or is properly distributed to a beneficiary, the trust is regarded as a conduit with respect to that income.

D. The income allocated to a beneficiary retains the same character in his or her hands as it had in the hands of the trust.

Answer (B) is correct. *(SEE, adapted)*
    REQUIRED: The false statement regarding trusts.
    DISCUSSION: A trust is allowed a distribution deduction for amounts required to be distributed currently and any other amounts properly paid, credited, or required to be distributed.
    Answer (A) is incorrect. A trust is a separate taxable entity. Answer (C) is incorrect. If income is required to be distributed currently or is properly distributed to a beneficiary, the trust is regarded as a conduit with respect to that income. Answer (D) is incorrect. The income allocated to a beneficiary retains the same character in his or her hands as it had in the hands of the trust.

18.1.4. John Smith died on May 15 of the current year. After his death, his estate received interest of $500, dividends of $700, salary of $4,000, and life insurance proceeds of $35,000. How much should Mr. Smith's estate include in income on its current-year income tax return?

A. $1,200

B. $5,200

C. $36,200

D. $40,200

Answer (B) is correct. *(SEE, adapted)*
    REQUIRED: The amount to include in income on the estate's income tax return.
    DISCUSSION: Except as otherwise provided, the taxable income of an estate is computed in the same manner as that of individuals. The salary, interest, and dividends are income to the estate if earned, but not collected, by the decedent before death. Life insurance proceeds are excluded from gross income, unless the policy was transferred for valuable consideration [Sec. 101(a)]. The income taxable to the estate is $5,200 ($4,000 + $500 + $700).
    Answer (A) is incorrect. Salary earned but not collected by the decedent before death is gross income for the estate. Answer (C) is incorrect. Salary earned but not collected by the decedent before death is gross income for the estate. Also, life insurance proceeds are generally excluded from gross income by Sec. 101(a). Answer (D) is incorrect. Life insurance proceeds are generally excluded from gross income by Sec. 101(a).

18.1.5. Which of the following expenses may be deducted in computing the taxable income of an estate (Form 1041)?

1. Funeral expenses of decedent

2. Medical and dental expenses of decedent paid by estate

3. Alimony payments paid out of estate income

4. Decedent's prior-year net operating loss carryover

5. Estate net accounting income distributed to beneficiaries

A. 1 and 3.

B. 2 only.

C. 3 and 5.

D. 4 and 5.

Answer (C) is correct. *(SEE, adapted)*
    REQUIRED: The expense that may be deducted on the income tax return of an estate.
    DISCUSSION: Since the taxable income of an estate is generally computed in the same manner as that of an individual, the alimony is deductible by the estate. Sections 651 and 661 provide a deduction for estate income that is distributed to beneficiaries.
    Answer (A) is incorrect. Funeral expenses may be deducted only for estate tax purposes. Answer (B) is incorrect. Medical and dental expenses of the decedent must be deducted on either the decedent's final income tax return or on the estate tax return [Sec. 213(c)]. Answer (D) is incorrect. Net operating losses of an individual do not carry over to his or her estate but end upon death.

18.1.6. The trust agreement creating Trust X provides for all income of the trust to be distributed to the beneficiaries and requires a reserve equal to tax depreciation to be charged to income. If the trust has gross income of $30,000, expenses charged to income of $28,000, and depreciation of $3,000, how much depreciation can Trust X deduct?

A. $0

B. $300

C. $2,000

D. $3,000

Answer (D) is correct. *(Publisher, adapted)*
   REQUIRED: The amount of depreciation the trust can deduct.
   DISCUSSION: Section 642(e) allows an estate or trust a deduction for depreciation to the extent it is not allowable to beneficiaries. Under Sec. 167(d) and Reg. 1.167(h)-1(b), in the absence of provisions in the trust instrument apportioning the deduction, the deduction is apportioned between the trust and its beneficiaries based on the income allocable to each. Since a reserve is required under the trust instrument, the depreciation deduction is allocated to the trust to the extent income is set aside for a depreciation reserve and actually remains in the trust. The entire $3,000 of depreciation is allocated to and deductible by the trust.
   If no reserve were required under the trust instrument or local law, the beneficiaries would be entitled to the depreciation deduction, since the trust must distribute all of its income currently.
   Answer (A) is incorrect. Trust X can deduct an amount of depreciation. Answer (B) is incorrect. The amount of $300 is the exemption of a simple trust. Answer (C) is incorrect. The amount of $2,000 is the difference between the gross income and the expenses.

18.1.7. The amount of the personal exemption allowed to an estate and a simple trust is

	Estate	Simple Trust
A.	$1,000	$1,000
B.	$600	$300
C.	$600	$100
D.	$300	$100

Answer (B) is correct. *(Publisher, adapted)*
   REQUIRED: The personal exemption deductible by an estate and a simple trust.
   DISCUSSION: Section 642(b) provides a $600 personal exemption for an estate. A simple trust is one that is required to distribute all of its income currently and is entitled to an exemption of $300. A complex trust is one that is not required to distribute all of its income currently and is only entitled to a personal exemption of $100.
   Answer (A) is incorrect. The amount of $1,000 is the sum of personal exemptions allowed to an estate, a simple trust, and a complex trust. Answer (C) is incorrect. The amount of $100 is the personal exemption allowed to a complex trust, not a simple trust. Answer (D) is incorrect. The personal exemption allowed to a simple trust is $300, and the personal exemption allowed to a complex trust is $100.

18.1.8. The charitable contribution deduction on an estate's fiduciary income tax return is allowable

A. If the decedent died intestate.

B. To the extent of the same adjusted gross income limitation as that on an individual income tax return.

C. Only if the decedent's will specifically provides for the contribution.

D. Subject to the 2% threshold on miscellaneous itemized deductions.

Answer (C) is correct. *(CPA, adapted)*
   REQUIRED: The true statement concerning the deduction for a charitable contribution on an income tax return of an estate.
   DISCUSSION: An unlimited estate income tax deduction is allowed for transfers to charitable organizations [Sec. 642(c)]. Although the taxable income of an estate is generally computed in the same manner as in the case of an individual, Sec. 642(c) provides that a deduction for a charitable contribution is only available if paid pursuant to the terms of the will of the decedent.
   Answer (A) is incorrect. An estate is allowed a deduction for a charitable contribution only if the decedent's will specifically provides for the contribution. Answer (B) is incorrect. Section 642(c) allows an unlimited deduction for charitable contributions paid if pursuant to a provision in the will of a decedent. Answer (D) is incorrect. An estate is allowed a charitable contribution deduction that is not subject to the 2% threshold on miscellaneous itemized deductions.

18.1.9. Trust X invests solely in stocks and bonds. During the year it received

Interest from corporate bonds	$6,000
Interest from tax-exempt municipal bonds	2,000
Taxable dividends	2,000

Trust X also paid its trustee $1,000 for earning all of the above investment income. What is Trust X's taxable income before the exemption?

A. $7,000

B. $7,200

C. $9,000

D. $9,800

Answer (B) is correct. *(Publisher, adapted)*
REQUIRED: The taxable income of a trust, before its exemption, given both taxable and tax-exempt income and a trustee fee.
DISCUSSION: Taxable income of a trust (or estate) is computed similarly to that of an individual [Sec. 641(b)]. Interest from the corporate bonds and the taxable dividends must be included in income. Interest from municipal bonds is not included in income (Sec. 103).
The trustee fee is generally deductible, except for the portion relating to the municipal bonds (Sec. 265). The fee must be allocated between the taxable and the tax-exempt income. Since the interest from municipal bonds is 20% of the total accounting income ($2,000 ÷ $10,000), 20% of the fee will not be deductible. Any expenses directly connected with the tax-exempt interest also would have been entirely nondeductible. The trustee's fees are not subject to the 2% nondeductible floor for miscellaneous itemized deductions [William J. O'Neill, Jr., *Irrevocable Trust*, 994 F.2d 302 (6th Cir., 1994)].

Interest from corporate bonds	$6,000
Dividends	2,000
Trustee fee ($1,000 − $200)	(800)
Taxable income before exemption	$7,200

Answer (A) is incorrect. The proportionate share of the trust fees related to the municipal bond interest is not deductible. Answer (C) is incorrect. The municipal bond income is not included in interest, and the entire trustee fees are not deductible. Answer (D) is incorrect. The municipal bond interest is not included in income, and the nondeductible portion of the trustee fee is $200.

18.1.10. Estate D has gross income of $80,000 of which $20,000 is allocated to corpus and $60,000 to the beneficiaries after expenses. Depreciation for the year is $8,000. The decedent's will does not provide a reserve for depreciation. What is the amount of depreciation that Estate D can deduct?

A. $0

B. $2,000

C. $6,000

D. $8,000

Answer (B) is correct. *(SEE, adapted)*
REQUIRED: The amount of depreciation deductible by the estate.
DISCUSSION: Section 642(e) allows an estate to deduct depreciation only to the extent not allowable to beneficiaries. Under Sec. 167(d), in the absence of provisions in the estate instrument apportioning the deduction, the deduction is apportioned between the estate and the beneficiaries on the basis of the income allocable to each. Therefore, the depreciation deduction allowed to the estate is $2,000.

$$\left(\frac{\$20,000}{\$80,000} \times \$8,000 \right)$$

Answer (A) is incorrect. An amount of the depreciation is deductible by the estate. Answer (C) is incorrect. The amount of $6,000 is the beneficiaries' portion of the depreciation. Answer (D) is incorrect. The depreciation must be allocated between the beneficiaries and the trust based on income allocable to each since there is no other method specified in the estate instrument.

18.1.11. Which of the following is a true statement concerning net operating losses (NOLs) of trusts and estates?

A. NOLs are not deductible by either trusts or estates.

B. NOLs are deductible by trusts, but not by estates.

C. NOLs of trusts and estates are deductible each year by the beneficiaries.

D. NOL carryovers of trusts and estates are passed through to the beneficiaries in the last year of the estate or trust.

Answer (D) is correct. *(SEE, adapted)*
REQUIRED: The true statement concerning net operating losses of trusts and estates.
DISCUSSION: Under Sec. 642(h), if on termination an estate or trust has a net operating loss carryover, such carryover is allowed as a deduction to the beneficiaries. In effect, the net operating loss carryover is passed through to the beneficiaries in the last year of the estate or trust.
Answer (A) is incorrect. Net operating losses are deductible by both estates and trusts under Sec. 642(d). Answer (B) is incorrect. Net operating losses are deductible by estates under Sec. 642(d). Answer (C) is incorrect. Beneficiaries are entitled to net operating losses of trusts or estates only if there are net operating loss carryovers in the year of termination.

18.1.12. Charmaine, who was single, died on September 15 of the current year. She had purchased land in February of the same year for $10,000. When she died, the land had a fair market value of $10,500. The alternative valuation date was not elected. Her estate, the legal owner, sold the land in December for $12,000. Her estate also received the following:

Salary owed Charmaine	$3,000
Interest from banks	1,000
Dividends	800

What is the taxable income of Charmaine's estate before the personal exemption if no distributions were made to beneficiaries during the current year?

A. $3,800

B. $4,800

C. $6,300

D. $6,800

Answer (C) is correct. *(SEE, adapted)*
REQUIRED: The taxable income of an estate before deducting the personal exemption.
DISCUSSION: Except as otherwise provided, the taxable income of an estate is computed in the same manner as that of individuals. The salary, interest, and dividends are income to the estate if earned, but not collected, by the decedent before death. The income earned by the decedent but taxable to the estate is $4,800 ($3,000 + $1,000 + $800).
The estate's basis in the land is its fair market value at the date of death [Sec. 1014(a)]. The sale of the land produces a capital gain of $1,500 ($12,000 selling price – $10,500 basis). Therefore, the total taxable income of the estate before deducting the personal exemption is $6,300.
Answer (A) is incorrect. The bank interest and the gain on the sale of the land are also included in taxable income. Answer (B) is incorrect. The gain on the sale of the land is also included in taxable income. Answer (D) is incorrect. The estate's basis in the land is the $10,500 FMV on the date of death.

18.1.13. Estate Z paid the following expenses (which did not relate to the income tax return) in its final taxable year:

Attorney fees	$ 6,000
Accountant fees	3,000
Executor fees	10,000
Miscellaneous administration expenses	4,000

How much can Estate Z deduct on its income tax return without waiving the deduction of these expenses for estate tax purposes?

A. $0

B. $4,000

C. $19,000

D. $23,000

Answer (A) is correct. *(Publisher, adapted)*
REQUIRED: The deduction for administration expenses without waiving the deduction for estate taxes.
DISCUSSION: Attorney fees, accountant fees, and executor fees are all administration expenses deductible for estate tax purposes under Sec. 2053. They may be deducted on the income tax return only if there is a statement filed that such amounts have not been allowed as deductions under Sec. 2053 and the right to deduct such amounts under Sec. 2053 is waived. Therefore, Estate Z can deduct none of these items without filing a waiver.
Answer (B) is incorrect. The miscellaneous administration expenses are not deductible without filing a waiver. Answer (C) is incorrect. Attorney, accountant, and executor fees are not deductible if a waiver is not filed. Answer (D) is incorrect. Attorney, accountant, and executor fees and miscellaneous administration expenses are not deductible if a waiver is not filed.

18.1.14. Which of the following statements is true regarding estate income tax returns filed on Form 1041?

A. Form 1041 has its own tax rate schedule.

B. Estates are never liable for the alternative minimum tax.

C. All estates are subject to the same estimated tax rules that apply to Form 1040.

D. None of the answers are correct.

Answer (A) is correct. *(SEE, adapted)*
REQUIRED: The true statement regarding estate income tax returns filed on Form 1041.
DISCUSSION: Form 1041 is subject to a tax rate schedule that reaches the 39.6% tax bracket for taxable incomes exceeding $12,500 for 2017.
Answer (B) is incorrect. Estates may be subject to the alternative minimum tax. Answer (C) is incorrect. Estates may be subject to estimated payments after 2 years. Answer (D) is incorrect. One of the answers is correct.

18.1.15. The adjusted total income of the estate of Saphira Simon, after the income distribution deduction and all other deductions other than the trust's personal exemption, was $109,500 for its 2017 tax year. Assuming no alternative minimum tax is due and no credits apply, what is the estate's income tax liability for 2017?

A. $25,721

B. $38,174

C. $41,407

D. $41,645

Answer (C) is correct. *(Publisher, adapted)*
REQUIRED: The estate's income tax liability.
DISCUSSION: An estate is entitled to a personal exemption of $600. Taxable income is therefore $108,900. The highest estate and trust tax rate effective for 2017 is $3,233 plus 39.6% of taxable income over $12,500. Thus, the 2017 income tax liability of the estate is $41,407 [$3,233 + ($96,400 × .396)].
Answer (A) is incorrect. Corporate income tax brackets and rates are not used to compute the fiduciary liability. Answer (B) is incorrect. The $3,233 imposed on the first $12,500 of taxable income must be added to the 39.6% of the excess. Answer (D) is incorrect. The estate's $600 personal exemption must be subtracted to derive taxable income.

18.1.16. An estate is a taxable entity that comes into being with the death of an individual. The estate's income must be reported annually, and the personal representative must continue to report the estate's income using the same accounting period used by the decedent.

A. True.

B. False.

Answer (B) is correct. *(SEE, adapted)*
DISCUSSION: An estate is a new taxable entity and may choose a taxable year ending within 12 months after the date of the decedent's death [Reg. 1.441-1T(b)(2)].

18.1.17. An executor or administrator of a decedent's estate must report the estate's income using the same method of accounting used by the decedent.

A. True.

B. False.

Answer (B) is correct. *(SEE, adapted)*
DISCUSSION: An estate is a new taxable entity. Under Reg. 1.446-1(e)(1), a taxpayer filing its first return may adopt any permissible method of accounting. Therefore, the estate may use the accrual method regardless of the method used by the decedent.

18.1.18. Only items of income accrued or received before the decedent's death are accounted for in computing gross income to be included in Form 1041, *U.S. Income Tax Return for Estates and Trusts*.

A. True.

B. False.

Answer (B) is correct. *(SEE, adapted)*
DISCUSSION: Items of income that are accrued (if the decedent is an accrual-method taxpayer) or received (if the decedent is a cash-method taxpayer) before the decedent's death must be included in the decedent's final income tax return. All other items of income received or accrued by the estate are included in Form 1041.

18.1.19. If a decedent was using the cash method of accounting, all income earned, even though not received before death, is included in the decedent's final income tax return.

A. True.

B. False.

Answer (B) is correct. *(SEE, adapted)*
DISCUSSION: For a cash-method taxpayer, income is generally only included when received. Therefore, if a cash-method decedent does not receive income prior to death, it is not included in his or her final income tax return. Instead it will be included in the tax return of the decedent's estate.

18.1.20. An estate, or other recipient, that acquires property from a decedent and sells or otherwise disposes of the property within 12 months of the decedent's death is considered to have held the property for the required long-term holding period of more than 12 months.

A. True.

B. False.

Answer (A) is correct. *(SEE, adapted)*
DISCUSSION: Section 1223(11) provides that a person who acquires property from a decedent will be treated as having held the property for more than 12 months if it is disposed of by such person within 12 months. In other words, the recipient of property from a decedent is treated as holding the property for the long-term holding period and thus is allowed the lower long-term capital gains rates.

18.1.21. The expenses of administering an estate can be deducted either from the gross estate in figuring the federal estate tax or from the estate's gross income in figuring the estate's tax, but not both.

A. True.

B. False.

Answer (A) is correct. *(SEE, adapted)*
DISCUSSION: The expenses of administering an estate are deductible for estate tax purposes under Sec. 2053. They may be deducted on the estate's income tax return (Form 1041) only if there is a statement filed that such amounts have not been allowed as deductions under Sec. 2053 and the right to deduct such amounts under Sec. 2053 is waived [Sec. 642(g)].

18.1.22. Carryover losses resulting from net operating losses or capital losses sustained by the decedent prior to death may be taken as a deduction on the estate's income tax return (Form 1041).

A. True.

B. False.

Answer (B) is correct. *(SEE, adapted)*
DISCUSSION: An estate is a new taxable entity. There is no provision allowing either operating losses or capital losses of an individual to be carried over to an estate after death. Carryover losses of an individual end with the decedent's final return.

18.1.23. If appreciated property is sold by a trust within 2 years of the trust receiving the property, the gain is taxed to the contributor of the property.

A. True.

B. False.

Answer (B) is correct. *(Publisher, adapted)*
    DISCUSSION: Prior to the Taxpayer Relief Act of 1997, the gain would have been taxed to the contributor of the property. However, Sec. 644 was repealed and the gain will be taxed to the trust.

18.2 Distributable Net Income (DNI)

18.2.1. All of the following statements about trusts are true except

A. The income distributed to the beneficiary retains the same character as that earned by the trust.

B. The net distributable income of a simple trust excludes capital gains distributions that are allocable to corpus under the terms of the governing instrument and applicable local law.

C. The income distribution deduction is the greater of distributable net income or net accounting income.

D. All of the taxable income that is not taxed to the beneficiaries is taxed to the trust.

Answer (C) is correct. *(SEE, adapted)*
    REQUIRED: The false statement regarding trusts.
    DISCUSSION: The deduction for distributions allocates taxable income of a trust or an estate (gross of distributions) between the fiduciary and its beneficiaries. The deduction is the lesser of the amount of the distributions (required) or distributable net income (DNI). DNI, generally, is current net accounting income of the fiduciary reduced by any amounts allocated to principal.
    Answer (A) is incorrect. A distribution made to the beneficiary contains a pro rata share of each type of distributable income received by the trust. Answer (B) is incorrect. Tax is imposed on taxable incomes of trusts, not on items treated as fiduciary principal (corpus). Answer (D) is incorrect. Taxable income remaining in the fiduciary after the distributions to beneficiaries is made is taxed to the fiduciary.

18.2.2. Which of the following is not a modification of taxable income used to determine distributable net income?

A. The personal exemption is added back.

B. Capital gains are subtracted to the extent allocated to corpus and not distributed or set aside for a beneficiary.

C. Tax-exempt interest is added.

D. The net operating loss deduction is added back.

Answer (D) is correct. *(Publisher, adapted)*
    REQUIRED: The item that is not a modification of taxable income to determine DNI.
    DISCUSSION: Distributable net income (DNI) is an important concept because it is essentially the limit on both the deduction for distributions to beneficiaries and the amount of income the beneficiaries must recognize from distributions. DNI is defined in Sec. 643(a) as taxable income with certain modifications. These modifications do not include adding back the net operating loss deduction.
    Answer (A) is incorrect. Adding back the personal exemption is a modification listed in Sec. 643(a) in computing DNI. Answer (B) is incorrect. Subtracting capital gains to the extent allocated to corpus and not distributed or set aside for a beneficiary is a modification listed in Sec. 643(a) in computing DNI. Answer (C) is incorrect. Adding tax-exempt interest is a modification listed in Sec. 643(a) in computing DNI.

18.2.3. An estate has $8,000 of dividends from domestic corporations and $6,000 of tax-exempt interest. Its only expense is $1,000 of interest incurred to carry the tax-exempt bonds. What is the estate's distributable net income?

A. $7,400

B. $8,000

C. $12,400

D. $13,000

Answer (D) is correct. *(Publisher, adapted)*
    REQUIRED: The estate's distributable net income.
    DISCUSSION: Under Sec. 643(a), distributable net income includes dividends and tax-exempt interest less expenses allocable to it. The personal exemption is not allowed. Here, the estate's taxable income is $7,400 ($8,000 dividends – $600 personal exemption). The estate's distributable net income is

Taxable income	$ 7,400
Add back: personal exemption	600
Add: tax-exempt interest (net $1,000 of nondeductible interest)	5,000
Distributable net income	$13,000

    Answer (A) is incorrect. The amount of $7,400 is the estate's taxable income. Answer (B) is incorrect. Distributable net income includes tax-exempt interest less the interest expense allocable to it. Answer (C) is incorrect. The personal exemption is not allowed in calculating distributable net income.

18.2.4. Under the terms of the trust agreement, the income of the W Trust is required to be currently distributed to Ryan during his life. Capital gains are allocable to corpus, and all expenses are charged against income. During the taxable year, the trust had the following items of income and expenses:

Dividends	$30,000
Taxable interest	20,000
Nontaxable interest	10,000
Long-term capital gains	15,000
Commissions and miscellaneous expenses allocable to corpus	6,000

The trust's distributable net income is

A. $50,000

B. $54,000

C. $69,000

D. $75,000

Answer (B) is correct. *(SEE, adapted)*
REQUIRED: The trust's distributable net income.
DISCUSSION: Distributable net income of an estate or trust generally consists of the same items that make up the gross income of an estate or trust. However, there are additional adjustments made when determining distributable net income.

1. No deduction is allowed for distributions to beneficiaries.

2. Personal exemption is disallowed.

3. Tax-exempt interest from state and government bonds is excluded.

4. Capital gains allocable to corpus are excluded.

Therefore, the trust's taxable income is $58,700 ($30,000 dividends + $20,000 taxable interest + $15,000 long-term capital gains – $6,000 commissions and expenses allocable to corpus – $300 personal exemption). The trust's distributable net income is

Taxable income	$ 58,700
Add back: personal exemption	300
Add: tax-exempt interest	10,000
Less: capital gains allocable to corpus	(15,000)
Distributable net income	$ 54,000

Answer (A) is incorrect. The amount of $50,000 does not take into account the nontaxable interest of $10,000, the long-term capital gains of $15,000, or the expenses of $6,000. Answer (C) is incorrect. The amount of $69,000 does not take into account the long-term capital gain of $15,000. Answer (D) is incorrect. The amount of $75,000 does not take into account the long-term capital gain of $15,000 or the expenses of $6,000.

18.2.5. Under the terms of a simple trust, all of the income is to be distributed equally to beneficiaries A and B and capital gains are to be allocated to corpus. The trust and both beneficiaries file returns on a calendar-year basis. No provision is made in the governing instrument with respect to depreciation. During the year, the trust had the following items of income and expenses:

Rents	$25,000
Dividend of domestic corporations	50,000
Tax-exempt interest on municipal bonds	25,000
Long-term capital gains	15,000
Taxes and expenses directly attributable to rents	5,000
Trustee's commission allocable to income account	2,600
Trustee's commission allocable to principal account	1,300
Depreciation	5,000

Compute the distributable net income of the trust.

A. $92,400

B. $91,100

C. $67,075

D. None of the answers are correct.

Answer (B) is correct. *(SEE, adapted)*
REQUIRED: The amount of distributable net income of a trust.
DISCUSSION: Under Sec. 643(a), distributable net income is taxable income with tax-exempt interest added and no personal exemption allowed. No deduction is allowed for expenses attributable to the production of tax-exempt income. Also, since the capital gains are not included in the computation of distributable net income, no expenses are allocated to capital gains. This trust is not allowed a depreciation deduction because there is no reserve and all the income is distributable to the beneficiaries [Reg. 1.167(h)-1(b)]. Capital gains are not considered as income for depreciation purposes if they are properly allocable to corpus. The income beneficiaries will be entitled to the depreciation deduction in addition to their income from the trust. The trust's taxable income and distributable income are

Dividends	$ 50,000
Rent	25,000
LTCG	15,000
Less:	
Rent expense	(5,000)
Commission allocable to income	(1,950)
Commission allocable to principal	(975)
Personal exemption	(300)
Taxable income	$ 81,775

Taxable income	$ 81,775
Add back: personal exemption	300
Add: tax-exempt interest	24,025
Subtract: LTCG	(15,000)
Distributable net income	$ 91,100

Answer (A) is incorrect. The long-term capital gain, not the tax exempt interest, is included in the calculation of taxable income. Answer (C) is incorrect. The distributable net income is adjusted for tax-exempt income. Answer (D) is incorrect. A correct answer choice is provided.

18.2.6. A simple trust has tax-exempt interest income of $10,000 and rental income of $15,000. There are fiduciary fees of $5,000 entirely allocable to the rental income. There is $2,000 of depreciation, but the trust is not required to set up a reserve. All the income is distributable to the beneficiaries. What is the trust's distributable net income?

A. $8,000

B. $10,000

C. $18,000

D. $20,000

Answer (D) is correct. *(Publisher, adapted)*
REQUIRED: The simple trust's distributable net income.
DISCUSSION: Under Sec. 643(a), distributable net income is taxable income with tax-exempt interest added and no personal exemption allowed. This trust is not allowed a depreciation deduction because there is no reserve and all the income is distributable to the beneficiaries [Reg. 1.167(h)-1(b)]. The income beneficiaries will be entitled to the depreciation deduction in addition to their income from the trust. The trust's taxable income is $9,700 (rental income $15,000 – fiduciary fees $5,000 – personal exemption $300). The trust's distributable net income is

Taxable income	$ 9,700
Add back: personal exemption	300
Add: tax-exempt interest	10,000
Distributable net income	$20,000

Answer (A) is incorrect. Distributable net income includes the rental income less fiduciary fees, and no depreciation deduction is allowed. Also included is the tax-exempt interest income. Answer (B) is incorrect. Distributable net income includes the rental income less fiduciary fees and also includes the tax-exempt interest income. Answer (C) is incorrect. The depreciation deduction is not allowed. Depreciation may be deducted by the simple trust only when a reserve for depreciation is required.

18.2.7. Gloria is the beneficiary of her sister's estate. The estate is required to distribute all of its income currently. Gloria must report her share of the distributable net income of the estate whether she actually receives it or not.

A. True.

B. False.

Answer (A) is correct. *(SEE, adapted)*
DISCUSSION: Under Sec. 662, a beneficiary of an estate (or complex trust) must include in gross income the amounts required to be distributed currently and any additional amounts actually distributed, but both amounts are limited to distributable net income (DNI). Therefore, if all income is taxable and required to be distributed currently, the beneficiary must include all DNI in income even if it is not actually received.

18.3 Distributions from Estates and Trusts

18.3.1. Which of the following should be allocated entirely to corpus of an estate or trust if the will or trust agreement does not provide otherwise?

A. Royalties for the extraction of natural resources.

B. Gain on the sale of estate or trust property.

C. Tax-exempt interest income.

D. Insurance proceeds for lost profits under strike insurance for a baseball team.

Answer (B) is correct. *(Publisher, adapted)*
REQUIRED: The receipt allocated to corpus rather than fiduciary income.
DISCUSSION: The allocation between corpus (principal) and fiduciary income is generally provided under local law. Most states follow the Revised Uniform Principal and Income Act, which allows the allocation to be modified by the will or trust agreement. However, the general treatment is that gain on the sale of estate or trust property, and any replacement of estate or trust property, is allocated to corpus.
Answer (A) is incorrect. Royalties from natural resources are an income receipt. The Uniform Principal and Income Act does allocate royalties between income (72 1/2%) and corpus (27 1/2%). Answer (C) is incorrect. Most interest receipts are allocated to income whether taxable or tax-exempt. Answer (D) is incorrect. Insurance proceeds for lost profits is the replacement of income.

18.3.2. Which of the following receipts should be allocated by a trustee exclusively to income?

A. A stock dividend.

B. A very large year-end cash dividend.

C. A liquidating dividend whether in complete or partial liquidation.

D. A stock split.

Answer (B) is correct. *(CPA, adapted)*
REQUIRED: The receipts that should be allocated exclusively to income.
DISCUSSION: Cash dividends are exclusively allocable to income. Cash dividends are not a change in the form of the principal, rather they represent earnings from the principal (corpus). For simple trusts (i.e., trusts that must distribute all of their income currently), extraordinary dividends (whether paid in cash or property) or taxable stock dividends can be excluded from "income" if they are not distributed or credited to a beneficiary because the fiduciary in good faith determines that the governing instrument and local law allocate such amounts to corpus [Sec. 643(a)(4)].
Answer (A) is incorrect. Stock dividends are allocated exclusively to principal. Answer (C) is incorrect. Liquidating dividends are allocated exclusively to principal. Answer (D) is incorrect. Stock splits are allocated exclusively to principal.

18.3.3. Shepard created an inter vivos trust for the benefit of his children with the remainder to his grandchildren upon the death of his last surviving child. The trust consists of both real and personal property. One of the assets is an apartment building. In administering the trust and allocating the receipts and disbursements, which of the following would be improper?

A. The allocation of forfeited rental security deposits to income.

B. The allocation to principal of the annual service fee of the rental collection agency.

C. The allocation to income of the interest on the mortgage on the apartment building.

D. The allocation to income of the payment of the insurance premiums on the apartment building.

Answer (B) is correct. *(CPA, adapted)*
REQUIRED: The improper allocation of receipts and disbursements between principal and income.
DISCUSSION: The annual service fee of a rent collection agency represents an ordinary operating expense of the trust. Since it is an expense incurred in the production of income, it is properly chargeable to income.
Answer (A) is incorrect. The allocation is proper. A rent security deposit secures the payment of rent, and provides coverage for minor damages requiring repairs. Since the rent is allocated to income and the repairs are chargeable to income, it follows that the deposits should also be allocated to income. Answer (C) is incorrect. Interest expense is properly charged to income. Answer (D) is incorrect. Insurance premiums represent an ordinary operating expense properly chargeable to income.

18.3.4. Trust W, a simple trust, has taxable interest of $5,000, tax-exempt interest of $10,000, and a short-term capital gain of $20,000. There are two equal beneficiaries. How much gross income does each beneficiary have from Trust W?

A. $2,500

B. $5,000

C. $12,500

D. $15,000

Answer (A) is correct. *(SEE, adapted)*
REQUIRED: The amount of gross income each beneficiary has from a simple trust.
DISCUSSION: Section 652(a) requires a beneficiary of a simple trust to include in gross income the amount of fiduciary income (whether or not distributed) but not to exceed the amount of distributable net income. The character of the income in the hands of the beneficiary is the same as in the hands of the trust [Sec. 652(b)].
The beneficiaries of Trust W are to receive $15,000 of fiduciary income. Since distributable net income is also $15,000, that amount must be included by the beneficiaries. However, $10,000 is tax-exempt interest, which is excluded from the beneficiaries' gross incomes since it retains its character in the hands of the beneficiaries. The beneficiaries must include $5,000 in total in their gross incomes, and each beneficiary must include $2,500 as his or her share.
Answer (B) is incorrect. The figure $5,000 is the combined amount of gross income for the beneficiaries. Answer (C) is incorrect. The capital gains are not included in DNI. Answer (D) is incorrect. Capital gains are not included in DNI, and tax-exempt interest is not included in gross income.

18.3.5. Which of the following receipts or disbursements by a trustee should be credited to or charged against income?

A. Principal payment on real property subject to a mortgage.

B. Capital gain distributions received from a mutual fund.

C. Stock rights received from the distributing corporation.

D. The discount portion received on redemption of treasury bills.

Answer (D) is correct. *(CPA, adapted)*
REQUIRED: The receipts or disbursements credited to or charged against income.
DISCUSSION: The discount portion received on redemption of treasury bills is credited to income. The discount represents a return on investment (earnings) of trust assets, and therefore is the equivalent of interest, which is allocable to income.
Answer (A) is incorrect. The payment of the principal of a mortgage is allocable to principal of the trust. The payment or receipt of the noninterest portion of a mortgage is a mere change in the form of trust assets. Answer (B) is incorrect. A capital gain is credited to principal. Capital gains (and capital losses) represent mere changes in the form of trust assets. Answer (C) is incorrect. Stock rights from the distributing corporations are allocated to principal in the same manner as stock dividends.

Questions 18.3.6 and 18.3.7 are based on the following information. Trust M, a simple trust, has dividends of $4,000 and rent receipts of $8,000. It paid fiduciary fees of $1,000. There is depreciation of $2,000, but no reserve for depreciation is required. The only beneficiary is single.

18.3.6. What is Trust M's distribution deduction?

A. $9,000

B. $10,000

C. $11,000

D. $12,000

Answer (C) is correct. *(Publisher, adapted)*
REQUIRED: The amount of a simple trust's distribution deduction.
DISCUSSION: Section 651 provides the deduction for the distribution of fiduciary income from a simple trust. Fiduciary income is the accounting income determined under the trust agreement or will, and local law. The deduction is the amount of fiduciary income required to be distributed, but limited to the amount of distributable net income (DNI). For this purpose, DNI does not include items of fiduciary income that are not included in gross income.
The fiduciary income of Trust M is $11,000 (dividends $4,000 + rent $8,000 – fiduciary fees $1,000). Since there is no reserve, depreciation is not charged to income. DNI is also $11,000, as is the distribution deduction.
Answer (A) is incorrect. The distribution deduction equals the dividends plus the rent receipts less the fiduciary fees. No depreciation deduction is allowed in determining DNI when a reserve for depreciation is not required. Answer (B) is incorrect. A depreciation deduction is not allowed in determining DNI, but the fiduciary fees are deductible. Answer (D) is incorrect. The fiduciary fees reduce the DNI and distribution deduction.

18.3.7. What is the beneficiary's increase in taxable income from the trust?

A. $0

B. $9,000

C. $10,000

D. $11,000

Answer (B) is correct. *(Publisher, adapted)*
REQUIRED: The increase in a beneficiary's taxable income from a simple trust.
DISCUSSION: Section 652 provides that the fiduciary income of a simple trust is included in the gross income of the beneficiaries (whether or not distributed), but limited to DNI of the trust. Under Sec. 652(b), the income retains the same character in the hands of the beneficiary as in the hands of the trust.
Trust M had $11,000 of fiduciary income, so this amount, limited to DNI (which is also $11,000), is included in the beneficiary's gross income. Also, the depreciation is deductible by the beneficiary since it was not deductible by the trust. Therefore, the beneficiary's increase in taxable income is $9,000 ($11,000 fiduciary income – $2,000 depreciation pass through).
Answer (A) is incorrect. The beneficiary has an increase in taxable income from the fiduciary income less deductions. Answer (C) is incorrect. The amount of $10,000 excludes the fiduciary fees' effect on fiduciary income. Answer (D) is incorrect. The amount of $11,000 is only the fiduciary income.

18.3.8. With respect to simple trusts, all the following statements are true except

A. The trust instrument requires that all the income must be distributed currently.

B. The trust instrument provides that amounts set aside for charitable purposes are deductible only to the trust.

C. The trust does not distribute amounts allocable to the corpus of the trust.

D. The exemption amount for a simple trust is $300.

Answer (B) is correct. *(SEE, adapted)*
REQUIRED: The false statement with respect to simple trusts.
DISCUSSION: A simple trust is formed under an instrument that (1) requires current distribution of all its income, (2) requires no distribution of the res (i.e., principal), and (3) provides for no charitable contributions by the trust.
Answer (A) is incorrect. A simple trust is formed under an instrument requiring current distribution of all its income. Answer (C) is incorrect. A simple trust does not distribute corpus during the taxable year. Answer (D) is incorrect. A deduction is allowable for a personal exemption that is $300 for a simple trust.

18.3.9. Trust N, a simple trust, has taxable interest of $5,000, tax-exempt interest of $10,000, and short-term capital gain of $20,000. What is Trust N's distribution deduction?

A. $5,000

B. $15,000

C. $25,000

D. $35,000

Answer (A) is correct. *(Publisher, adapted)*
REQUIRED: The distribution deduction of a simple trust.
DISCUSSION: Section 651 allows a distribution deduction for a simple trust equal to the fiduciary income of the trust but limited to the distributable net income (DNI). DNI does not include any items of income that are not included in gross income of the trust.
Trust N's fiduciary income is $15,000 ($5,000 taxable interest + $10,000 tax-exempt interest). Capital gains are allocated to corpus, not income. Therefore, Trust N's DNI is $5,000. DNI does not include tax-exempt interest and thus is limited to the $5,000.
The reason the distribution deduction is limited is that the tax-exempt interest was not included in the trust's gross income, so no deduction should be allowed for the tax-exempt interest.
Answer (B) is incorrect. The tax-exempt interest is not included in DNI when calculating the distribution deduction. Answer (C) is incorrect. Capital gains are allocated to corpus and are not included in DNI. Answer (D) is incorrect. Capital gains and tax-exempt interest are not included in DNI when calculating the distribution deduction.

18.3.10. A complex trust is a trust that

A. Must distribute income currently but is prohibited from distributing principal during the taxable year.

B. Invests only in corporate securities and is prohibited from engaging in short-term transactions.

C. Permits accumulation of current income, provides for charitable contributions, or distributes principal during the taxable year.

D. Is exempt from payment of income tax since the tax is paid by the beneficiaries.

Answer (C) is correct. *(SEE, adapted)*
REQUIRED: The characteristics of a complex trust.
DISCUSSION: A complex trust is one that can accumulate income, provide for charitable contributions, or distribute amounts other than income [Reg. 1.661(a)-1]. These characteristics distinguish a complex trust from a simple trust.
Answer (A) is incorrect. A complex trust may distribute principal. Answer (B) is incorrect. A complex trust is not required to invest only in corporate securities and is not prohibited from engaging in short-term transactions. Answer (D) is incorrect. A complex trust, like a simple trust, is taxed on income not distributed to beneficiaries.

18.3.11. Phillip died last year, leaving all his property to his three children. This year, Phillip's estate had $25,000 in distributable net income. The executor of Phillip's estate, who has full discretion as to when income is to be distributed, made a cash payment of $10,000 to each of the children. What is the amount of the estate's distribution deduction?

A. $30,000

B. $25,000

C. $20,000

D. $10,000

Answer (B) is correct. *(SEE, adapted)*
REQUIRED: The amount of a complex trust's distribution deduction.
DISCUSSION: The distribution deduction for complex trusts and estates is determined under Sec. 661. The deduction is the sum of the fiduciary income required to be distributed and any other amounts properly distributed, but limited to distributable net income (DNI).
Since $30,000 was distributed (three children × $10,000), the deduction is $30,000 limited to the amount of DNI. The DNI is $25,000, which is less than the amount distributed. Therefore, the estate's distribution deduction is limited to $25,000.
Answer (A) is incorrect. The total amount distributed is $30,000. Answer (C) is incorrect. The amount of $20,000 is the payments to two of the children and is less than the DNI. Answer (D) is incorrect. The amount of $10,000 is the payment to one child and is less than the DNI.

18.3.12. Bob Jones is sole beneficiary of a trust that requires that all income, but no corpus, be distributed currently. The trust's distributable net income for last year was $20,000, of which $4,000 is a long-term capital gain allocated to income and $2,500 is interest on tax-exempt municipal bonds. Jones received a $15,000 distribution on December 20 of last year and the remaining $5,000 on January 10 of this year. Assuming Jones has no other income, his adjusted gross income for last year should be

   A. $20,000

   B. $17,500

   C. $15,000

   D. $12,500

Answer (B) is correct. *(CPA, adapted)*
   REQUIRED: The adjusted gross income of the sole beneficiary of a simple trust.
   DISCUSSION: Section 652 requires the beneficiary of a simple trust (one that is required to distribute all income currently) to include in gross income the amount of fiduciary income of the trust (whether distributed or not), but limited to the amount of distributable net income. The amount included in a beneficiary's gross income retains the same character as in the hands of the trust.
   Although Jones received only $15,000 last year, all of the distributable net income (which is the same as fiduciary income in this case) must be included in his gross income last year. Since the income retains the same character in the hands of the beneficiary as in the hands of the trust, Bob is entitled to exclude the $2,500 of interest on municipal bonds. Therefore, Bob's adjusted gross income is $17,500 ($20,000 distributable net income – $2,500 tax-exempt interest).
   Answer (A) is incorrect. The tax-exempt interest is excluded from Bob's gross income. Answer (C) is incorrect. Gross income includes fiduciary income whether or not it is distributed. However, the tax-exempt interest is excluded from gross income. Answer (D) is incorrect. Gross income includes fiduciary income whether or not it is distributed.

18.3.13. Trust A, a complex trust, is not required to distribute any income currently. It has $10,000 of taxable interest. Trust A distributes $5,000 of income and $2,000 of corpus to its beneficiaries. What is Trust A's distribution deduction?

   A. $0

   B. $5,000

   C. $7,000

   D. $10,000

Answer (C) is correct. *(Publisher, adapted)*
   REQUIRED: The amount of a complex trust's distribution deduction.
   DISCUSSION: The distribution deduction for complex trusts and estates is determined under Sec. 661. The deduction is the sum of the fiduciary income required to be distributed and any other amounts properly distributed, but limited to distributable net income (DNI).
   Trust A has fiduciary income of $10,000, and DNI is also $10,000. Since $7,000 was distributed, the deduction is also $7,000. The deduction is allowed for the distribution of any amount (whether current income, accumulated income, or corpus), limited to the amount of the distributable net income. In effect, the distributable net income flows out of the trust with any distribution including that of corpus.
   Answer (A) is incorrect. Trust A has a distribution deduction. Answer (B) is incorrect. The deduction is the lesser of DNI and actual distributions. Answer (D) is incorrect. The amount of $10,000 is the DNI, which is more than the distribution.

18.3.14. Trust A, a complex trust, is not required to distribute any income currently. It has $10,000 of taxable interest. Trust A distributes $5,000 of income and $2,000 of corpus to its beneficiaries. How much must the beneficiaries include in their taxable income from the trust?

   A. $0

   B. $5,000

   C. $7,000

   D. $10,000

Answer (C) is correct. *(Publisher, adapted)*
   REQUIRED: The amount of income from a complex trust that beneficiaries must include in their taxable income.
   DISCUSSION: Under Sec. 662, beneficiaries of a complex trust are required to include in gross income the amounts of fiduciary income required to be distributed and all other amounts that are distributed, but limited to DNI. The amounts included in the beneficiaries' gross income retain the same character as in the hands of the estate or trust and are treated as consisting of the same proportion of each class of item entering into the computation of DNI.
   Since $7,000 was distributed to the beneficiaries (and DNI is not less), the beneficiaries must include $7,000 in gross income.
   Answer (A) is incorrect. An amount must be included in taxable income. Answer (B) is incorrect. The distribution from the corpus is also included in the beneficiaries' taxable income. Answer (D) is incorrect. The amount of $10,000 is more than the actual distribution received by the beneficiaries.

18.3.15. Carolyn died in the current year. The terms of her will require the estate to pay $30,000 from assets of the estate to each of her three children in the year of her death. In addition, $20,000 a year is to be paid to each child out of the estate's income. There were no charitable contributions. In the current year, the estate had income of $45,000 after paying $10,000 in expenses. How much does each child include in gross income?

A. $15,000

B. $18,333

C. $35,000

D. $50,000

Answer (A) is correct. *(SEE, adapted)*
REQUIRED: The amount of income from an estate (and a complex trust) that each beneficiary must include in gross income.
DISCUSSION: Under Sec. 662, beneficiaries of an estate (and a complex trust) are required to include in gross income the amounts of fiduciary income required to be distributed and all other amounts which are distributed, but limited to DNI. The amounts included in the beneficiaries' gross income retain the same character as in the hands of the estate or trust and are treated as consisting of the same proportion of each classified item entering into the computation of DNI.
Since DNI is $45,000, each of the three children must include $15,000 in gross income.
Answer (B) is incorrect. The amount of $18,333 is one-third of the estate's income before expenses. Answer (C) is incorrect. The amount of $35,000 is the estate income of $5,000 less $10,000 in expenses. The expenses were already subtracted in arriving at the $45,000 of income. Answer (D) is incorrect. The figure $50,000 is the amount distributed to each child.

18.3.16. A will provided for $25,000 is to be distributed to beneficiary A, property valued at $30,000 with a basis of $20,000 is to be distributed to beneficiary B, and the residual (valued at $40,000) is to be distributed to beneficiary C. If the estate has $50,000 of distributable net income, how much is included in the gross income of all three beneficiaries of the estate?

A. $40,000

B. $45,000

C. $50,000

D. $95,000

Answer (A) is correct. *(Publisher, adapted)*
REQUIRED: The amount of distributions from an estate that beneficiaries must include in gross income when there are specific bequests.
DISCUSSION: Generally, a beneficiary of an estate must include in gross income the amount distributed from an estate, limited to the DNI of the estate (Sec. 662). Section 663(a)(1), however, provides that a gift or bequest of a specific sum of money or specific property that is paid or credited at one time or in no more than three installments is not included in amounts distributed under Sec. 662. The bequest is excluded from the beneficiaries' gross income by Sec. 102(a).
The $25,000 distributed to beneficiary A and the property valued at $30,000 distributed to beneficiary B are specific bequests and are not included in the beneficiaries' gross incomes. The $40,000 residual is not a specific bequest because it is not a specific sum of money until the taxable estate is computed. The $40,000 is considered a distribution under Sec. 662 and is included in gross income, limited to DNI. Since the $40,000 distributed is less than DNI, the entire $40,000 is included in the gross income of beneficiary C.
Answer (B) is incorrect. The $25,000 distributed to beneficiary A and the property with a $20,000 basis distributed to beneficiary B are specific bequests and are not included in the beneficiaries' gross income. Answer (C) is incorrect. The amount of $50,000 is the distributable net income and is greater than the distribution to beneficiary C, which is not a specific bequest. Answer (D) is incorrect. The amount of $95,000 is the bequest of $25,000 to A plus the $20,000 property to B plus the $50,000 DNI.

18.3.17. Given the following information, compute the distribution deduction for a simple trust:

Interest income	$80,000
Dividend income	30,000
Tax-exempt interest	20,000
Capital gains	25,000
Expenses attributable to all interest income	5,000
Trustee's commissions allocable to all income including capital gains	15,000

A. $125,000

B. $110,000

C. $95,400

D. $85,500

Answer (C) is correct. *(SEE, adapted)*
REQUIRED: The distribution deduction for a simple trust.
DISCUSSION: The $5,000 expense for interest is attributed $4,000 to taxable interest and $1,000 to tax-exempt interest. This reduces taxable interest to $76,000 and tax-exempt interest to $19,000. Add in dividends of $30,000 and capital gain of $25,000 results in income of $150,000, which is used to allocate the trustee commission. An allocation to interest of $7,600 [$15,000 × (76 ÷ 150)] makes taxable interest $68,400. An allocation to dividends of $3,000 [$15,000 × (30 ÷ 150)] makes taxable dividends $27,000. Tax-exempt and capital gains are not included in IDD, resulting in IDD of $68,400 + $27,000 = $95,400.
Answer (A) is incorrect. The commissions and expenses must be allocated to the various forms of income and will reduce the distribution. Answer (B) is incorrect. Tax-exempt interest and capital gains are not included, and the expenses must be allocated to the various forms of income. Answer (D) is incorrect. All of the expenses and commissions reduce the deduction.

18.3.18. Trust C, a complex trust, is not required to distribute any income currently to its two beneficiaries. It has $10,000 of taxable interest and $10,000 of tax-exempt interest for the year. Trust C distributes $8,000 of income to Beneficiary A and $2,000 of corpus to Beneficiary B. What is Trust C's distribution deduction?

A. $1,000

B. $4,000

C. $5,000

D. $10,000

Answer (C) is correct. *(Publisher, adapted)*
REQUIRED: The amount of a complex trust's distribution deduction when it has tax-exempt income.
DISCUSSION: The distribution deduction for complex trusts and estates is determined under Sec. 661. The deduction is the sum of the fiduciary income required to be distributed and any other amounts properly distributed, but limited to distributable net income (DNI). This amount eligible for the deduction is treated as consisting of the same proportion of each type of income included in the DNI. Furthermore, no deduction is allowed for any portion treated as distributed which is not included in gross income of the trust or estate.
Trust C has both fiduciary income and DNI of $20,000. The amount of each portion of DNI that is treated as distributed will be 50% (since half of the DNI is tax-exempt). A total of $10,000 of DNI is distributed, of which $5,000 is treated as tax-exempt income. Thus, the distribution deduction is $5,000. This portion of distributable income flows out of the trust with any distribution including that of corpus.
Answer (A) is incorrect. The figure $1,000 is the taxable amount distributed to Beneficiary B. Answer (B) is incorrect. The figure $4,000 is the taxable amount distributed to Beneficiary A. Answer (D) is incorrect. The figure $10,000 is the amount distributed.

18.3.19. Trust C, a complex trust, is not required to distribute any income currently to its two beneficiaries. It has $10,000 of taxable interest and $10,000 of tax-exempt interest for the year. Trust C distributes $8,000 of income to Beneficiary A and $2,000 of corpus to Beneficiary B. How much must the beneficiaries include in their taxable income from the trust?

	Beneficiary A	Beneficiary B
A.	$8,000	$2,000
B.	$4,000	$1,000
C.	$4,000	$0
D.	$0	$1,000

Answer (B) is correct. *(Publisher, adapted)*
REQUIRED: The amount of income from a complex trust with tax-exempt income that beneficiaries must include in taxable income.
DISCUSSION: Under Sec. 662, beneficiaries of complex trusts are required to include in gross income the amounts of fiduciary income required to be distributed and all other amounts that are distributed, but limited to DNI. The amounts included in the beneficiaries' gross income retain the same character as in the hands of the estate or trust and are treated as consisting of the same proportion of each classified item entering into the computation of DNI.
Since Beneficiary A received a distribution of $8,000, half of which is treated as tax-exempt income, A must include $4,000 in gross income. Since Beneficiary B received a distribution of $2,000, half of which is treated as tax-exempt income, B must include $1,000 in gross income.
Answer (A) is incorrect. The total amounts of income each beneficiary received are $8,000 to Beneficiary A and $2,000 to Beneficiary B. Answer (C) is incorrect. Beneficiary B has taxable income from the trust. Answer (D) is incorrect. Beneficiary A has taxable income from the trust.

18.3.20. Under the terms of the will of Gene White, $6,000 a year is to be paid to his widow and $3,000 a year is to be paid to his daughter out of the estate's income during the period of administration. There are no charitable contributions. For the year, the estate's distributable net income is only $6,000. How much must the widow and the daughter include in their gross income?

	Widow	Daughter
A.	$6,000	$3,000
B.	$4,000	$2,000
C.	$3,000	$3,000
D.	$2,000	$1,000

Answer (B) is correct. *(SEE, adapted)*
REQUIRED: The amount the beneficiaries should include in gross income from an estate.
DISCUSSION: Under Sec. 662, a beneficiary of an estate includes in gross income the amount distributed from an estate, but limited to the distributable net income (DNI) of the estate. If the amount distributed exceeds DNI, each beneficiary includes a proportionate amount of the DNI based on the total amount distributed to all beneficiaries [Sec. 662(a)(1)]. The widow received 2/3 of total distributions to beneficiaries, so she will include $4,000 in her gross income ($6,000 DNI × 2/3). The daughter includes the other 1/3 of the $6,000 of DNI.
Answer (A) is incorrect. The total distributions are $6,000 to Gene's widow and $3,000 to his daughter. Answer (C) is incorrect. The amount of $3,000 each to Gene's widow and daughter is not the correct proportionate share. Answer (D) is incorrect. Each beneficiary should include in gross income a proportionate amount of the DNI based on the total amount distributed.

18.3.21. Estate X has DNI of $10,000. Its sole distribution during the year is property (a capital asset) with a basis of $8,000 and a fair market value of $12,000. This property is not a specific bequest. What is the beneficiary's basis in the property and how much must (s)he include in income?

	Income	Basis
A.	$8,000	$8,000
B.	$10,000	$10,000
C.	$10,000	$12,000
D.	$12,000	$12,000

Answer (A) is correct. *(Publisher, adapted)*
REQUIRED: The beneficiary's income and basis in property distributed from an estate.
DISCUSSION: Under Sec. 662, beneficiaries of an estate must include in gross income the amounts distributed from the estate, but limited to DNI. Section 643(e) provides that the basis of property received by a beneficiary is the adjusted basis of the property in the hands of the estate, adjusted for any gain or loss recognized by the estate on the distribution. The amount of the distribution is the lesser of the basis of the property in the hands of the beneficiary, or the fair market value of the property [Sec. 643(e)].
No gain is recognized on the distribution of the property unless the executor elected to treat it as a sale. Hence, the beneficiary's basis in the property is $8,000 (the adjusted basis in the hands of the estate). The amount of the distribution and the amount of the income to the beneficiary are both $8,000 (the lesser of the basis of the property in the hands of the beneficiary or its fair market value).
Answer (B) is incorrect. The amount of $10,000 is neither the beneficiary's income nor the beneficiary's basis in the property. Answer (C) is incorrect. The basis of the property received by the beneficiary is the adjusted basis of the property in the hands of the estate adjusted for any gain or loss recognized by the estate on the distribution. Answer (D) is incorrect. The amount of $12,000 is neither the beneficiary's income nor the beneficiary's basis in the property.

18.3.22. Trust X has $10,000 of distributable net income each year. The trustee accumulates the income for 3 years and does not distribute any to the sole beneficiary, Lettie, age 30. In Year 4, the trustee distributes $30,000 when Trust X's DNI is only $5,000. Which of the following is true?

A. Lettie will include only $5,000 of income from the trust in Year 4.

B. Lettie will include $30,000 of income from the trust in Year 4.

C. Lettie will be taxed in Year 4 on the $25,000 in excess of current DNI as if it had been distributed in the prior years.

D. The trustee has saved taxes equal to the difference between Lettie's and Trust X's tax rates by planning distributions in years when DNI is low.

Answer (C) is correct. *(Publisher, adapted)*
REQUIRED: The true statement about an accumulation distribution from a trust.
DISCUSSION: Under Sec. 662, a beneficiary of an estate or complex trust includes in gross income the amount distributed, but limited to DNI. However, Sec. 666 requires an accumulation distribution to be taxed to the beneficiary of a trust (but not an estate) as if the distribution had been made in the preceding years. The accumulated distribution is the amount of the current distribution in excess of current DNI.
Answer (A) is incorrect. Lettie will not only include $5,000 of trust income in Year 4, but she will also be taxed on the remainder of the distribution as if it had been made in the previous years. Answer (B) is incorrect. The amount of $25,000 of income will be taxed as if distributed in the prior years, and only $5,000 will actually be included in her Year 4 income. Answer (D) is incorrect. The accumulation distribution rules of Sec. 666 prevent the saving of taxes by accumulating income.

18.3.23. Estate X has DNI of $10,000. Its sole distribution during the year is property (a capital asset) with a basis of $8,000 and a fair market value of $12,000. This property is not a specific bequest. The executor elects to recognize a gain on the distribution. What is the beneficiary's basis in the property and how much must (s)he include in income?

	Income	Basis
A.	$8,000	$8,000
B.	$10,000	$10,000
C.	$10,000	$12,000
D.	$12,000	$12,000

Answer (C) is correct. *(Publisher, adapted)*
REQUIRED: The beneficiary's income and basis in property given an election by the estate to recognize gain.
DISCUSSION: An estate may elect to recognize gain under Sec. 643(e) equal to the fair market value of the property in excess of its basis. In such case, the distribution under Sec. 662 is the fair market value of the property. A capital gain generally does not increase DNI since it is allocable to corpus, so the beneficiary must include $10,000 in gross income (the lesser of the amount of the distribution or the DNI).
The beneficiary's basis in the property is the adjusted basis of the property in the hands of the estate adjusted for any gain or loss recognized by the estate on the distribution. The estate's basis in the property was $8,000, and it had a $4,000 gain. Therefore, the beneficiary's basis is $12,000.
Answer (A) is incorrect. The amount of $8,000 is neither the beneficiary's income nor the beneficiary's basis in the property. Answer (B) is incorrect. The beneficiary's basis in the property is not $10,000. Answer (D) is incorrect. The beneficiary's income is not $12,000.

18.3.24. Estate Z, created under the decedent's will and applicable state law, has two beneficiaries, X and Y. In the current year, the estate has distributable net income (DNI) of $50,000, all from taxable sources. Each beneficiary is designated as having a separate 50% share in the assets and income of the estate. During the current year, the executor distributes $25,000 of income (X's 50% share) and $100,000 of corpus to X. X's distribution of corpus is about 20% of the total corpus of her share of the estate. No distribution of corpus or income is made to Y in the current year. How much must X include in her taxable income from the estate?

A. $0

B. $25,000

C. $50,000

D. $125,000

Answer (B) is correct. *(Publisher, adapted)*
REQUIRED: The amount the beneficiary must include in taxable income from an estate.
DISCUSSION: If a decedent's will and applicable state law create separate economic interests that do not affect other economic interests accruing to other beneficiaries, the separate share rule will apply to the decedent's estate. Under the separate share rule, activity such as distributions in one separate share will not affect application of the tax rules or the tax consequences of activity in other shares, regardless of how many beneficiaries there are of any separate share or whether separate books of account are maintained for the separate shares. In other words, it has the effect of treating the estate as two or more separate estates, each with its own DNI. The "separate" DNI is allocated to the specific beneficiary of each share of the estate. The application of the separate share rule is mandatory.
X and Y represent separate shares of the estate. Under the separate share rule, X's gross income inclusion is limited to her share of DNI, or $25,000. X receives the remaining distribution of principal tax-free.
Answer (A) is incorrect. Under Sec. 662, beneficiaries of an estate must include in gross income the amounts distributed from the trust, but limited to DNI. Answer (C) is incorrect. The amount that would be included in gross income if the separate share rule did not exist is $50,000. Answer (D) is incorrect. The amount included is limited to the estate's DNI.

18.3.25. A decedent's estate may elect to treat distributions up to 80 days after the close of the tax year as if they were made on the last day of the year.

A. True.

B. False.

Answer (B) is correct. *(Publisher, adapted)*
DISCUSSION: The Taxpayer Relief Act of 1997 provides that a decedent's estate may elect to treat distributions or any portion of any distribution to a beneficiary within 65 days after the close of the tax year as if they were made on the last day of the year.

18.3.26. A trust may be a simple trust for one year and a complex trust for another year.

A. True.

B. False.

Answer (A) is correct. *(SEE, adapted)*
DISCUSSION: The rules for classifying trusts are applied on a year-by-year basis. Thus, if trust income is accumulated in one year, the trust is a complex trust for that year, but if in a later year, its income is required to be distributed currently and no other amounts are distributed, the trust qualifies as a simple trust in the later year.

18.3.27. Payments to a widow or dependent for support by estate are nondeductible.

A. True.

B. False.

Answer (B) is correct. *(Publisher, adapted)*
DISCUSSION: Payments to a widow or dependent for support by estate, whether from income or principal, are deductible by estate if paid pursuant to a court order or decree.

18.3.28. A distribution of accumulated income from a domestic trust created in 1986 is subject to the throwback rules and is therefore taxed at the marginal tax rate of the individual receiving the distribution.

A. True.

B. False.

Answer (B) is correct. *(Publisher, adapted)*
DISCUSSION: After the Taxpayer Relief Act of 1997, distributions from a domestic trust are exempt from the throwback rules. The rules required that distributions that were previously accumulated in a trust be included in a trust beneficiary's income if the beneficiary's top average marginal tax rate in the previous 5 years was higher than that of the trust.

18.4 Grantor Trusts

18.4.1. Phil, the grantor, set up two irrevocable trusts: Trust K and Trust J. The income of Trust K is to be accumulated for distribution to Phil's spouse after Phil's death. The income of Trust J is to be accumulated for Phil's children, whom Phil is legally obligated to support, and the trustee has the discretion to use any part of the income for the children's support. Half of the income was so used in the current year. Based on this information, which of the following statements is true?

A. All the income from both trusts is taxed to Phil.

B. None of the income from either trust is taxed to Phil.

C. No income from Trust K is taxed to Phil and half of the income from Trust J is taxed to Phil.

D. All the income from Trust K and half from Trust J is taxed to Phil.

Answer (D) is correct. *(SEE, adapted)*
REQUIRED: The true statement concerning the taxation of trust income to the grantor.
DISCUSSION: Under Sec. 677(a), a grantor is treated as the owner of a trust the income of which may be distributed or accumulated for the grantor's spouse (without the approval or consent of an adverse party). Therefore, all of the income from Trust K is taxed to Phil.
The grantor is also taxed on income from a trust in which the income may be applied for the benefit of the grantor [Sec. 677(a)]. Use of income for the support of a dependent is considered the application of income for the benefit of the grantor. Under Sec. 677(b), however, the income of a trust that may be applied for the support of a dependent is not taxable to the grantor if it is not actually used. Therefore, only half of the income of Trust J (used for the children's support) is taxed to Phil.
Answer (A) is incorrect. Not all the income from Trust J is taxed to Phil. A grantor is treated as the owner of a trust when the income may be distributed or accumulated for the grantor's spouse. A grantor is also taxed on income from a trust when the income may be applied for the benefit of the grantor. Answer (B) is incorrect. Phil will be taxed on an amount of income from both trusts. A grantor is treated as the owner of a trust when the income may be distributed or accumulated for the grantor's spouse. A grantor is also taxed on income from a trust when the income may be applied for the benefit of the grantor. Answer (C) is incorrect. A grantor is treated as the owner of a trust when the income may be distributed or accumulated for the grantor's spouse. A grantor is also taxed on income from a trust when the income may be applied for the benefit of the grantor. Phil is subject to tax on income from Trust K.

18.4.2. Four years ago, John created a simple trust that provides that the income from the trust will be payable to his son Joey (age 16) for 12 years. At the end of the 12 years, the principal will revert back to John. Which of the following statements is false regarding this trust?

A. The income from the trust is taxed to Joey.

B. Any capital gains are taxed to John.

C. The income distribution deduction does not include the capital gains.

D. The income from the trust is exempt from tax.

Answer (A) is correct. *(SEE, adapted)*
REQUIRED: The false statement regarding a simple trust.
DISCUSSION: John's reversionary interest is greater than 5%; thus the trust is a grantor trust. All the income is taxable to John, not Joey.
Answer (B) is incorrect. The trust is considered to have remained under the control of John and he, as the grantor, is liable for all taxes on taxable income. Answer (C) is incorrect. Generally, capital gains realized upon the sale of assets are considered to represent a part of principal (corpus) and are not considered income. The capital gains are taxable but are not included in the income distribution deduction. Answer (D) is incorrect. John, as the grantor, is liable for all taxes on taxable income.

18.4.3. If approval or consent of an adverse party is not required for the exercise of the power, which of the following powers held by the grantor of a trust will not cause the income of the trust to be taxable to the grantor?

A. The power to allocate income of a trust among two noncharitable beneficiaries.

B. The power to borrow trust funds interest-free.

C. The power to revoke the trust.

D. The power to use income of the trust for the support of a dependent (other than the grantor's spouse) if it is not so used.

Answer (D) is correct. *(Publisher, adapted)*
REQUIRED: The power held by a grantor that will not cause the trust income to be taxable to the grantor.
DISCUSSION: Under Sec. 671, the income attributable to that portion of a trust of which a grantor is treated as an owner is taxed to the grantor. Under Sec. 677(b), income of a trust is not considered taxable to the grantor merely because the income may be applied or distributed for the support of a beneficiary (other than the grantor's spouse) whom the grantor is legally obligated to support, unless such income is actually so applied or distributed.
Answer (A) is incorrect. The grantor is treated as the owner of a trust in which (s)he has the power to control the beneficial enjoyment of the corpus or the income [Sec. 674(a)]. Answer (B) is incorrect. The grantor is treated as the owner of a trust in which (s)he has the power to borrow funds without interest or without adequate security [Sec. 675(2)]. Answer (C) is incorrect. The grantor is treated as the owner of a trust in which (s)he has the power to revoke the trust [Sec. 676(a)].

18.4.4. Martin created and funded an irrevocable 20-year trust on January 1, 1986, for the benefit of his minor children. At the end of the 20 years, the principal reverts to Martin. Martin named the Bloom Trust Company as trustee and provided that Bloom would serve without the necessity of posting a bond. In understanding the trust and the rules applicable to it, which of the following is true?

A. If Martin dies 10 years after creation of the trust, it is automatically revoked and the property is distributed to the beneficiaries of his trust upon their attaining age 21.

B. Martin may revoke the trust after 11 years, since he created it, and the principal reverts to him at the expiration of the 20 years.

C. The facts indicate that the trust is a separate legal entity for both tax and nontax purposes.

D. The trust is not a separate legal entity for federal tax purposes.

Answer (C) is correct. *(CPA, adapted)*
REQUIRED: The true statement concerning an irrevocable trust for the benefit of minors.
DISCUSSION: Any trust that is validly created is a separate legal entity for nontax purposes. A trust funded before March 2, 1986, and that is to last longer than 10 years is generally treated as a separate entity for tax purposes provided the grantor holds no disqualifying power(s) under Secs. 671-677. The major requirements are that for at least 10 years the trust must be irrevocable, and the income of the trust must not be used for the benefit of the grantor.
Answer (A) is incorrect. A trust that is irrevocable for a 20-year term is not terminated by the death of the grantor. At the end of the 20-year period, the assets of the trust would revert to the heirs of the deceased grantor (absent a provision otherwise in the trust agreement). Answer (B) is incorrect. A grantor who creates an irrevocable trust may not revoke it during the term of its existence. Answer (D) is incorrect. The trust is generally a separate legal entity for tax purposes.

18.4.5. Mackenzie is the grantor of a trust over which Mackenzie has retained a discretionary power to receive income. Kelly, Mackenzie's child, receives all taxable income from the trust unless Mackenzie exercises the discretionary power. To whom is the income earned by the trust taxable?

A. To the trust to the extent it remains in the trust.

B. To Mackenzie because he has retained a discretionary power.

C. To Kelly as the beneficiary of the trust.

D. To Kelly and Mackenzie in proportion to the distributions paid to them from the trust.

Answer (B) is correct. *(CPA, adapted)*
REQUIRED: To whom the income earned by the trust is taxable.
DISCUSSION: A grantor trust is any trust to the extent the grantor is the effective beneficiary. The grantor is taxed on income from a trust in which the income may be applied for the benefit of the grantor. Since Mackenzie retained a discretionary power to receive income, he will be taxed for the income earned by the trust.
Answer (A) is incorrect. The grantor trust is disregarded for tax purposes. Answer (C) is incorrect. The grantor of a grantor trust is taxed on income from a trust in which the income may be applied for the benefit of the grantor. Answer (D) is incorrect. The grantor of a grantor trust is taxed on income from a trust in which the income may be applied for the benefit of the grantor.

18.5 Tax Years, Return Filing, and Estimated Taxes

18.5.1. For income tax purposes, all estates

A. Must adopt a calendar year, except for existing estates with fiscal years that ended in 1986.

B. May adopt a calendar year or any fiscal year.

C. Must adopt a calendar year regardless of the year the estate was established.

D. Must use the same taxable year as that of its principal beneficiary.

Answer (B) is correct. *(CPA, adapted)*
REQUIRED: The taxable year required of estates.
DISCUSSION: An estate is a new taxable entity and may choose a taxable year ending within 12 months after the date of the decedent's death [Reg. 1.441-1T(b)(2)].
Answer (A) is incorrect. There is no requirement for an estate to adopt the calendar year. Answer (C) is incorrect. An estate is not required to use a calendar year, but this rule would apply to most trusts. Answer (D) is incorrect. There is no provision for an estate to use the taxable year of its principal beneficiary.

18.5.2. All trusts, except tax-exempt trusts,

A. Must adopt a calendar year, except for existing trusts with fiscal years that ended in 1986.

B. May adopt a calendar year or any fiscal year.

C. Must adopt a calendar year regardless of the year the trust was established.

D. Must use the same taxable year as that of its principal beneficiary.

Answer (C) is correct. *(CPA, adapted)*
REQUIRED: The required tax year of a trust.
DISCUSSION: Section 645 requires all trusts, both new and existing (for the first taxable year beginning after December 31, 1986), to adopt the calendar year as their taxable year. Only tax-exempt trusts and wholly charitable trusts are exceptions from this rule.
Answer (A) is incorrect. There is no provision to grandfather existing trusts to a fiscal year. Answer (B) is incorrect. Trusts must adopt a calendar year. Answer (D) is incorrect. There is no provision for a trust to adopt the same tax year as its principal beneficiary.

18.5.3. An executor of a decedent's estate that has only U.S. citizens as beneficiaries is required to file a fiduciary income tax return, if the estate's gross income for the year is at least

A. $400

B. $500

C. $600

D. $1,000

Answer (C) is correct. *(CPA, adapted)*
REQUIRED: The gross income for which an estate must file an income tax return.
DISCUSSION: Under Sec. 6012(a)(3), every estate that has gross income of $600 or more must file a tax return. Form 1041 is used.
Answer (A) is incorrect. The amount of $400 is not equal to the personal exemption of an estate. Answer (B) is incorrect. The amount of $500 is not equal to the personal exemption of an estate. Answer (D) is incorrect. The amount of $1,000 is not equal to the personal exemption of an estate.

18.5.4. Estate J, a calendar-year domestic estate, had gross income of $9,850 for Year 1. Without considering any extensions of time and ignoring Saturdays, Sundays, and holidays, what income tax return must the estate file and by what date?

	Income Tax Return	Date
A.	Form 1040	March 15, Year 2
B.	Form 1040	April 15, Year 2
C.	Form 1041	April 15, Year 2
D.	Form 1041	June 15, Year 2

Answer (C) is correct. *(SEE, adapted)*
REQUIRED: The income tax return required by an estate and the date by which it must be filed.
DISCUSSION: Under Sec. 6012(a)(3), every estate which has gross income of $600 or more must file an income tax return. Under Reg. 1.6012-3, the return to be filed by a fiduciary for an estate or a trust is Form 1041. Section 6072 requires the return for a calendar-year estate to be filed on or before April 15 following the close of the calendar year.
Answer (A) is incorrect. Form 1040 is for filing individual taxes, and March 15 is the due date of S corporation returns. Answer (B) is incorrect. Form 1040 is for filing individual taxes. Answer (D) is incorrect. June 15 is the correct date by which the estate must file Year 2's second installment of estimated tax.

18.5.5. With respect to estimated tax payments,

A. A trust must pay them, but not an estate.

B. A trust must pay 80% of its tax in quarterly payments, or 100% of the prior-year tax if less.

C. A trust or estate (unless otherwise exempt) must pay 90% of its tax in quarterly payments, or 100% of the prior-year tax if less.

D. Neither an estate nor a trust is required to pay them.

Answer (C) is correct. *(Publisher, adapted)*
REQUIRED: The true statement regarding estimated tax payments for estates and trusts.
DISCUSSION: Section 6654(l) requires both trusts and estates to make estimated payments of income tax. Four installments of estimated tax for each taxable year are due on April 15, June 15, September 15, and January 15 of the following taxable year. The total of these four installments of estimated tax must be the lesser of (1) 90% of the final tax due on the trust or estate tax return or (2) 100% of its tax for the prior year. The special exception for high-income individual taxpayers (i.e., those taxpayers with adjusted gross incomes in excess of $150,000) requiring 110% of the prior-year tax liability to be paid applies to estates and trusts. The adjusted gross income equivalent for a trust or estate is defined in Sec. 67(e).
The one exception is that an estate is not required to pay estimated taxes for its first 2 taxable years of its existence. After that, filing is required the same as for a trust.
Answer (A) is incorrect. An estate must make estimated tax payments. Answer (B) is incorrect. The amount of 80% is an insufficient percentage of current year tax due that a trust must pay in estimated tax payments. Answer (D) is incorrect. Both estates and trusts are required to make estimated tax payments.

18.5.6. In what circumstance must an estate make estimated tax payments under the rules similar to those applicable to individuals?

A. None, since estates are not required to make estimated tax payments.

B. The estate has a first tax year that covers 12 months.

C. The estate has gross income in excess of $400 in the tax year.

D. The estate has a tax year ending 2 or more years after the date of the decedent's death.

Answer (D) is correct. *(SEE, adapted)*
REQUIRED: The true statement concerning estimated tax payments for an estate.
DISCUSSION: Section 6654(l) requires an estate to make estimated payments of income tax in all tax years except during its first 2 taxable years of existence. No estimated payments are required during its first 2 taxable years.
Answer (A) is incorrect. Estates are required to make payments of estimated tax after the first 2 years of existence. Answer (B) is incorrect. Estimated tax payments are only required after the estate's first 2 years of existence without regard to the length of the first tax year. Answer (C) is incorrect. An estate need not make estimated tax payments for its first 2 years of existence without regard to the amount of its gross income.

18.5.7. The amount included in a beneficiary's gross income is the income of the trust or estate for the tax year ending within the beneficiary's tax year.

A. True.

B. False.

Answer (A) is correct. *(Publisher, adapted)*
DISCUSSION: If a trust or estate and its beneficiary have different tax years, the amount included in the beneficiary's gross income depends on the trust or estate's income for the tax years ending within the beneficiary's tax year.

18.5.8. Trust W uses a calendar year end. For the year ended December 31, Year 1, Trust W has $500 of gross income and $100 of taxable income. Trust W must file Form 1041 on or before April 15, Year 2, unless an extension of time is obtained.

A. True.

B. False.

Answer (A) is correct. *(Publisher, adapted)*
DISCUSSION: Section 6012 requires every trust that has any taxable income or that has gross income of $600 or more (regardless of the amount of taxable income) to file an income tax return. Although Trust W did not have $600 of gross income, it did have $100 of taxable income, so it must file an income tax return. A trust is required to use Form 1041 under Reg. 1.6012-3. The return is due on or before the 15th day of the fourth month after year end (Sec. 6072).

18.5.9. On the first *U.S. Income Tax Return for Estates and Trusts*, Form 1041, the executor or administrator selects the accounting method to be used to report the income of the estate.

A. True.

B. False.

Answer (A) is correct. *(SEE, adapted)*
DISCUSSION: Under Sec. 6012(b), returns of an estate or trust are made by the fiduciary (the executor or administrator of the estate). An estate is a new taxable entity, and under Reg. 1.446-1(e)(1) a taxpayer filing its first return may adopt any permissible method of accounting to compute taxable income. Accordingly, the executor or administrator of an estate must choose the accounting method.

18.5.10. Ms. Penny died October 15, Year 1. During Year 2, her estate received $5,000 in interest income. In September of Year 2, all of her estate's assets were distributed and the estate terminated. The executor of her estate is required to make estimated tax payments.

A. True.

B. False.

Answer (B) is correct. *(SEE, adapted)*
DISCUSSION: Section 6654(l) requires that estates and trusts make estimated tax payments. However, Sec. 6654(l)(2) exempts an estate from making estimated tax payments with respect to any taxable year ending before the date 2 years after the date of the decedent's death. Since the estate terminates before this 2-year period ends, the executor of the estate is not required to make estimated tax payments.

18.5.11. A trustee may elect to treat a payment of estimated tax made by the trust as a payment made by a beneficiary of the trust.

A. True.

B. False.

Answer (A) is correct. *(Publisher, adapted)*
DISCUSSION: Section 643(g) allows a trustee to elect to treat any portion of a payment of estimated tax made by the trust as a payment made by the beneficiary of the trust. For any amount the trustee so elects, it shall be treated as paid or credited to the beneficiary on the last day of such taxable year, the same as a distribution.

18.6 Income in Respect of a Decedent

18.6.1. Which one of the following statements concerning the consequences of income being classified as "income in respect of a decedent" is true?

A. It receives no step-up in basis upon the decedent's death.

B. It is all treated as ordinary income to recipient.

C. It is all taxable to the decedent's estate.

D. It must be included in the decedent's final return.

Answer (A) is correct. *(SEE, adapted)*
REQUIRED: The true statement of the consequences of income in respect of a decedent.
DISCUSSION: Section 1014(a) provides that the basis of property acquired from a decedent is generally the fair market value of the property on the date of the decedent's death. Section 1014(c) provides that property which constitutes a right to receive income in respect of a decedent does not receive a step-up in basis. Therefore, it has a carryover basis.
Answer (B) is incorrect. Income in respect of a decedent is treated as having the same character it would have had in the hands of the decedent [Sec. 691(a)(3)]. Answer (C) is incorrect. Income in respect of a decedent is included when received (as if on a cash basis) by the person who receives it [Sec. 691(a)(1)]. Answer (D) is incorrect. Income in respect of a decedent is that which is earned by the taxpayer but not received prior to his or her death, nor accrued prior to his or her death if on the accrual method. Thus, it is not included in the decedent's final return.

18.6.2. All of the following might include income in respect of a decedent, except

   A. The estate's return, if the estate receives it.

   B. The beneficiary's return, if the right to the income is passed directly to the beneficiary and the beneficiary receives it.

   C. The decedent's final return.

   D. The return of any person to whom the estate properly distributes the right to receive the income.

Answer (C) is correct. *(SEE, adapted)*
   REQUIRED: The return in which income in respect of a decedent is not reported.
   DISCUSSION: Income in respect of a decedent (IRD) is earned by the taxpayer but not received prior to his or her death or accrued prior to his or her death if on the accrual method, so it is not included on the decedent's final return.
   Answer (A) is incorrect. The estate's return might include IRD, if the estate receives it. Under Sec. 691(a)(1), IRD is included in the recipient's income in the year received. Answer (B) is incorrect. The beneficiary's return might include IRD, if the right to the income is passed directly to the beneficiary and the beneficiary receives it. Under Sec. 691(a)(1), IRD is included in the recipient's income in the year received. Answer (D) is incorrect. The return of any person to whom the estate properly distributes the right to receive the income might include IRD. Under Sec. 691(a)(1), IRD is included in the recipient's income in the year received.

18.6.3. Income in respect of a cash-basis decedent

   A. Covers income earned before the taxpayer's death but not collected until after death.

   B. Receives a stepped-up basis in the decedent's estate.

   C. Must be included in the decedent's final income tax return.

   D. Cannot receive capital gain treatment.

Answer (A) is correct. *(CPA, adapted)*
   REQUIRED: The true statement regarding income in respect of a decedent.
   DISCUSSION: Regulation 1.691(a)-1(b) defines income in respect of a decedent as those amounts to which a decedent was entitled as gross income but which were not includible in computing taxable income on his final return. For cash-basis taxpayers, income in respect of a decedent is income earned by the decedent before death, but not paid until after death. A common example of income in respect of a decedent is salary earned by an employee prior to death, but not paid by the employer until after death.
   Answer (B) is incorrect. Section 1014(c) prevents the decedent's estate from receiving a stepped-up basis for the income in respect of a decedent. Answer (C) is incorrect. Income in respect of a decedent is included in the fiduciary tax return (not the decedent's). Answer (D) is incorrect. Income in respect of a decedent is treated as having the same character it would have had in the hands of the decedent [Sec. 691(a)(3)].

18.6.4. Which of the following is income in respect of a decedent?

   A. Cash received from a grandmother's estate.

   B. Royalties received on the deceased father's published book; the right to receive these royalties was distributed from the father's estate.

   C. Certificate of deposit received as a gift.

   D. Cash received from a grandmother's estate and royalties received on the deceased father's published book; the right to receive these royalties was distributed from the father's estate.

Answer (B) is correct. *(SEE, adapted)*
   REQUIRED: The item considered income in respect of a decedent.
   DISCUSSION: Income in respect of a decedent is the amount that is earned by the taxpayer but not received prior to his or her death nor accrued prior to his or her death if on the accrual method, so it is not included in the decedent's final return. Income in respect of a decedent is included in the recipient's (e.g., the estate's) income in the year received or accrued.
   Answer (A) is incorrect. Cash received from a grandmother's estate is not income in respect of a decedent, as it is not earned by the taxpayer. Answer (C) is incorrect. A certificate of deposit received as a gift is not income in respect of a decedent, as it is not earned by the taxpayer. Answer (D) is incorrect. Income in respect of a decedent is the amount that is earned by the taxpayer. The grandmother's estate disbursement of cash does not qualify.

18.6.5. Mr. A sold a tract of land and reported the sale using the installment method of accounting. The net sale price was $80,000 and the cost basis was $40,000. After A's death, the final $10,000 installment (plus interest) was collected by his personal representative. What amount (other than interest) must be reported as profit on a Form 1041, *U.S. Income Tax Return for Estates and Trusts*, for the year in which the $10,000 was received?

A. $10,000

B. $5,000

C. $2,500

D. $0

Answer (B) is correct. *(SEE, adapted)*

REQUIRED: The amount of the payments received after death that are income in respect of a decedent.

DISCUSSION: Income in respect of a decedent is that which the decedent had a right to receive prior to death but which was not properly includible on his or her final income tax return. It retains its same character to the recipient as it would have been in the hands of the decedent. There is no step-up in basis under Sec. 1014(c), so the same gross profit margin is used on an installment receipt. The gross profit margin was 50% ($40,000 ÷ $80,000), so $5,000 ($10,000 × 50%) is income in respect of a decedent. The remaining $5,000 is merely a return of capital.

The interest on the installment debt is not income in respect of a decedent except for the portion accrued before death. All the interest received must also be reported on Form 1041.

Answer (A) is incorrect. The amount of $10,000 is 100% of the sale proceeds. The reported amount is affected by gross profit margin. Answer (C) is incorrect. The amount of $2,500 assumes that the gross profit margin is 25%. Answer (D) is incorrect. There is a profit to be reported on Form 1041. The reported amount is affected by gross profit margin.

18.6.6. Stan is the personal representative of his brother Bruce, who died June 30, 2017. Stan has obtained an identification number for Bruce's estate and has notified the IRS on Form 56 that he has been appointed executor. He has filed his brother's final return for 2017 and has the following information regarding Bruce's remaining estate. What will be the taxable income of the estate?

Unpaid salary not received by Bruce before he died	$ 6,000
Dividend check on XYZ stock received August 15, 2017	600
Form 1099 interest earned on savings after death	2,000
Sales price of coin collection sold to unrelated person	10,000
Value of the coins at the date of death	9,000
Attorney's fees for administration of the estate	1,000

A. $8,600

B. $17,600

C. $8,000

D. None of the answers are correct.

Answer (C) is correct. *(SEE, adapted)*

REQUIRED: The taxable income of the estate.

DISCUSSION: Administration expenses (and debts of a decedent) are deductible on the estate tax return under Sec. 2053, and some may also qualify as deductions for income tax purposes on the estate's income tax return. Section 642(g), however, disallows a double deduction and requires a waiver of the right to deduct them on Form 706 in order to claim them on Form 1041. Therefore, the attorney's fees for administration of the estate can be deducted on the estate return since it is not stated that a waiver was filed. The income earned by the decedent but taxable to the estate is calculated as follows:

Unpaid salary	$ 6,000
Gain on sale of coins	1,000
Dividend income	600
Interest income	2,000
Less: Administrative expense	(1,000)
Exemption deduction	(600)
Estate's taxable income	$ 8,000

Answer (A) is incorrect. An exemption deduction of $600 is allowed for estates. Answer (B) is incorrect. The sales price of the coins must be reduced by their basis, and an exemption deduction of $600 is allowed. Answer (D) is incorrect. The taxable income of the estate is $8,000.

18.6.7. Income that a decedent would have reported had death not occurred that is received by the administrator or executor of the decedent's estate is exempt from federal income tax.

A. True.

B. False.

Answer (B) is correct. *(SEE, adapted)*

DISCUSSION: Income in respect of a decedent is that which is earned by the taxpayer but not received prior to his or her death, nor accrued prior to his or her death if on the accrual method, so it is not included in the decedent's final return. Income in respect of a decedent is included in the recipient's (e.g., the estate's) income in the year received or accrued.

18.6.8. On March 20 of the current year, Mr. L, a cash-method taxpayer, sold his truck for $10,000 payable on September 20 of the same year. His adjusted basis for the truck was $8,000. Mr. L died June 15 before receiving payment. The gain realized on the sale is not income in respect of a decedent.

A. True.

B. False.

Answer (B) is correct. *(SEE, adapted)*

DISCUSSION: Since Mr. L sold the truck prior to death, he was entitled to receive the gross income prior to death. Since payment was not received until after death and is not properly includible on his final income tax return, the profit is income in respect of a decedent. Under Sec. 691(a)(1), it is included in the recipient's income in the year received.

18.6.9. Mr. A, a single, cash-basis taxpayer, died on October 31 of the current year. A salary check that was received on October 31 but not cashed is not income in respect of a decedent.

    A. True.

    B. False.

Answer (A) is correct. *(SEE, adapted)*
    DISCUSSION: Income in respect of a decedent is all gross income the decedent was entitled to prior to death but was not properly includible in his or her final income tax return. A salary check received on October 31 by someone who died on that date should be included in the final income tax return of the decedent. The check is considered the equivalent of cash and need not be cashed to recognize the income.

18.6.10. When a taxpayer dies, no gain is reported on depreciable personal property or real property that is transferred to his or her estate or beneficiary.

    A. True.

    B. False.

Answer (A) is correct. *(SEE, adapted)*
    DISCUSSION: No gain is reported on the transfer of property from a decedent to his or her estate or beneficiary because there is no sale or other disposition of the property.

18.7 Tax-Exempt Organizations

18.7.1. To qualify as an exempt organization, the applicant

    A. Must fall into one of the specific classes upon which exemption is conferred by the Internal Revenue Code.

    B. Cannot, under any circumstances, be a foreign corporation.

    C. Cannot, under any circumstances, engage in lobbying activities.

    D. Cannot be exclusively a social club.

Answer (A) is correct. *(CPA, adapted)*
    REQUIRED: The requirement to qualify for tax-exempt status.
    DISCUSSION: No organization is exempt from tax unless it is one of the specific types upon which the IRC expressly confers exempt status (Sec. 501). Types are listed and described in Secs. 501(c) and (d).
    Answer (B) is incorrect. A foreign corporation can be exempt. Answer (C) is incorrect. Lobbying activity, in itself, does not disqualify an organization from exempt status. A tax approximating 25% of excessive lobbying expenditure is a cost of maintaining exempt status for certain organizations (Sec. 4911). Answer (D) is incorrect. An exclusively social club may be exempt if none of its earnings inure to the benefit of a private shareholder.

18.7.2. Which of the following statements is true with respect to tax-exempt organizations?

    A. A foundation may qualify for exemption from federal income tax if it is organized for the prevention of cruelty to children.

    B. A partnership may qualify as an organization exempt from federal income tax if it is organized and operated exclusively for one or more of the purposes found in Sec. 501(c)(3).

    C. An individual can qualify as an organization exempt from federal income tax.

    D. In order to qualify as an exempt organization, the organization must be a corporation.

Answer (A) is correct. *(SEE, adapted)*
    REQUIRED: The true statement with respect to tax-exempt organizations.
    DISCUSSION: Exempt status generally depends on the nature and purpose of an organization. Among the types of organizations that may qualify as exempt: corporation, trust, foundation, fund, community funds, etc. A more complete list can be found in Sec. 501(c) along with the permitted stated purposes and requirements.
    Answer (B) is incorrect. A partnership is, by definition, a for-profit association. Also, a partnership is not listed as a type of organization that may qualify for exempt status in Sec. 501(c) or (d). Answer (C) is incorrect. An individual is not an organization described in Sec. 501(c) or (d) that may qualify for exempt status. Answer (D) is incorrect. Other types of organizations listed in Sec. 501(c) or (d) may also qualify.

18.7.3. The private foundation status of an exempt organization will terminate if it

    A. Becomes a public charity.

    B. Is a foreign corporation.

    C. Does not distribute all of its net assets to one or more public charities.

    D. Is governed by a charter that limits the organization's exempt purposes.

Answer (A) is correct. *(CPA, adapted)*
    REQUIRED: The event that will terminate the private foundation status of an exempt organization.
    DISCUSSION: Each domestic or foreign exempt organization is a private foundation unless it receives more than one-third of its support (annually) from its members and the general public, in which case it becomes a public charity.
    Answer (B) is incorrect. The private foundation status of an exempt organization does not terminate if it is a foreign corporation. Answer (C) is incorrect. The private foundation status of an exempt organization does not terminate if it does not distribute all of its net assets to one or more public charities. Answer (D) is incorrect. The private foundation status of an exempt organization does not terminate if it is governed by a charter that limits the organization's exempt purposes.

18.7.4. To qualify as an exempt organization other than an employees' qualified pension or profit-sharing trust, the applicant

    A. Is barred from incorporating and issuing capital stock.

    B. Must file a written application with the Internal Revenue Service.

    C. Cannot operate under the "lodge system" under which payments are made to its members for sick benefits.

    D. Need not be specifically identified as one of the classes on which exemption is conferred by the Internal Revenue Code, provided that the organization's purposes and activities are of a nonprofit nature.

Answer (B) is correct. *(CPA, adapted)*
    REQUIRED: The condition for exempt status.
    DISCUSSION: A requirement to qualify for tax-exempt status is that an organization, other than an employees' qualified pension or profit-sharing trust, must apply in writing to the IRS for a ruling or determination that it is tax-exempt, even if the IRS does not provide specific forms to do so [Reg. 1.501(a)-(1)(a)].
    Answer (A) is incorrect. A corporation may qualify as a tax-exempt organization. Answer (C) is incorrect. Fraternal beneficiary associations operating under the lodge system and providing for payment of life, sick, accident, or other benefits to members and their dependents are of a class qualified for tax-exempt status [Sec. 501(c)(8)]. Answer (D) is incorrect. An organization must be of a class specified by the IRC as qualifying for tax-exempt status.

18.7.5. Which of the following organizations, exempt from federal income tax under Sec. 501(a), must file an annual information return on Form 990 or Form 990-PF?

    A. An organization, other than a private foundation, having gross receipts in each year that normally are not more than $5,000.

    B. A school below college level, affiliated with a church or operated by a religious order, that is not an integrated auxiliary of a church.

    C. A private foundation exempt under Sec. 501(c)(3) of the Internal Revenue Code.

    D. A stock bonus, pension, or profit-sharing trust that qualifies under Sec. 401 of the Internal Revenue Code.

Answer (C) is correct. *(SEE, adapted)*
    REQUIRED: The exempt organization that must file an annual information return on Form 990 or Form 990-PF.
    DISCUSSION: A private foundation must use Form 990-PF as its annual information return.
    Answer (A) is incorrect. Every organization exempt from tax under Sec. 501(a) must file an annual information return (on Form 990) except (1) churches and (2) an organization having gross receipts for each tax year that are normally not more than $5,000 (unless it is a private foundation) [Reg. 1.6033-2(a)(2)(i)]. Answer (B) is incorrect. An educational organization below college level affiliated with a church or operated by a religious order is excluded from the filing requirement by Reg. 1.6033-2(g)(1)(vii). Answer (D) is incorrect. An employee's trust described in Sec. 401(a) must file its annual return on Form 990-P [Reg. 1.6033-2(a)(3)].

18.7.6. Which of the following statements is true with regard to exempt organizations?

    A. An organization is automatically exempt from tax merely by meeting the statutory requirements for exemption.

    B. Exempt organizations that are required to file annual information returns must disclose the identity of all substantial contributors, in addition to the amount of contributions received.

    C. An organization will automatically forfeit its exempt status if any executive or other employee of the organization is paid compensation in excess of $150,000 per year, even if such compensation is reasonable.

    D. Exempt status of an organization may not be retroactively revoked.

Answer (B) is correct. *(CPA, adapted)*
    REQUIRED: The requirements for exempt status and the determination of whether retroactive revocation is permitted.
    DISCUSSION: Certain organizations, such as churches and fraternal benefit associations, with annual gross receipts below $5,000, are excluded from the general requirement of exempt organizations to file annual information returns [Sec. 6033(a)(2)]. The organization reports both the amount of contributions received and identifies all substantial contributions together with all other gross income, receipts, and disbursements.
    Answer (A) is incorrect. Application to the IRS for exempt status is required. Answer (C) is incorrect. Compensation paid must be reasonable, but an absolute cap amount is not mandated. Answer (D) is incorrect. Retroactive revocation by the IRS, on the basis of the organization's character, purposes, or operations, has not been rare.

18.7.7. Which of the following statements is true regarding the unrelated business income of exempt organizations?

A. If an exempt organization has any unrelated business income, it may result in the loss of the organization's exempt status.

B. Unrelated business income relates to the performance of services but not to the sale of goods.

C. An unrelated business does not include any activity where all the work is performed for the organization by unpaid volunteers.

D. Unrelated business income tax will not be imposed if profits from the unrelated business are used to support the exempt organization's charitable activities.

Answer (C) is correct. *(CPA, adapted)*
REQUIRED: The true statement regarding unrelated business income.
DISCUSSION: Unrelated business income (UBI) is income from a trade or business, regularly carried on, that is not substantially related to the charitable, educational, or other purpose constituting the basis for an organization's tax-exempt status (Sec. 513). But income is not subject to tax as UBI if substantially all the work is performed for the organization by unpaid volunteers [Sec. 513(a)(1)].
Answer (A) is incorrect. Unrelated business income is subject to tax, but it does not preclude exempt status of itself. Answer (B) is incorrect. Unrelated business income relates to the performance of services or to the sale of goods. Some exceptions apply [see Sec. 502(b)(3)]. Answer (D) is incorrect. An organization operated for the primary purpose of carrying on a business for a profit is taxable on all its income, even if all its profits are payable to exempt organizations [Sec. 502(a)]. Some exceptions apply [see Reg. 1.502-1(b)].

18.7.8. Which of the following activities regularly conducted by a tax-exempt organization will result in unrelated business income?

I. Selling articles made by handicapped persons as part of their rehabilitation, when the organization is involved exclusively in their rehabilitation

II. Operating a grocery store almost fully staffed by emotionally handicapped persons as part of a therapeutic program

A. I only.

B. II only.

C. Both I and II.

D. Neither I nor II.

Answer (D) is correct. *(CPA, adapted)*
REQUIRED: The activity regularly carried on by an exempt organization that will result in unrelated business income.
DISCUSSION: Unrelated business income (UBI) is income from a trade or business, regularly carried on, that is not substantially related to the charitable, educational, or other purpose constituting the basis for an organization's tax-exempt status. Both situations represent sales of items resulting directly from the conduct of the tax-exempt status, the rehabilitation of persons with handicaps.
Answer (A) is incorrect. Selling articles made by persons with handicaps as part of their rehabilitation program would be considered related to the tax-exempt status of each activity. Answer (B) is incorrect. Operating a grocery store almost fully staffed by emotionally handicapped persons as part of a therapeutic program would be considered related to the tax-exempt status of each activity. Answer (C) is incorrect. Selling of items by or made by persons with handicaps as part of a therapeutic program would be considered related to the tax-exempt status of each activity.

18.7.9. During the current year, Help, Inc., an exempt organization, derived income of $15,000 from conducting bingo games. Conducting bingo games is legal in Help's locality and is confined to exempt organizations in Help's state. Which of the following statements is true regarding this income?

A. The entire $15,000 is subject to tax at a lower rate than the corporate income tax rate.

B. The entire $15,000 is exempt from tax on unrelated business income.

C. Only the first $5,000 is exempt from tax on unrelated business income.

D. Since Help has unrelated business income, Help automatically forfeits its exempt status for the current year.

Answer (B) is correct. *(CPA, adapted)*
REQUIRED: The true statement regarding an exempt organization's income from conducting bingo games.
DISCUSSION: Income derived from bingo games is not treated as unrelated business income if the games are conducted in a state in which bingo games are ordinarily not carried out or conducted on a commercial basis and if the games are not illegal under the state's or locality's law [Sec. 513(f)].
Answer (A) is incorrect. The entire $15,000 would be subject to tax at the corporate income tax rate if it was taxable UBI. Answer (C) is incorrect. The figure $5,000 is only a portion of the amount exempt from tax on UBI because the requirements of Sec. 513(f) were met. Answer (D) is incorrect. UBI does not result in automatic forfeiture of exempt status. In addition, the income meets the requirements of Sec. 513(f) for exemption.

18.7.10. If an exempt organization is a corporation, the tax on unrelated business income is

A. Computed at corporate income tax rates.

B. Computed at rates applicable to trusts.

C. Credited against the tax on recognized capital gains.

D. Abated.

Answer (A) is correct. *(CPA, adapted)*
REQUIRED: The tax treatment of an exempt corporation's unrelated business income.
DISCUSSION: Unrelated business income (UBI) over $1,000 of a tax-exempt corporation is subject to tax at corporate regular income tax rates.
Answer (B) is incorrect. Regular corporate income tax rates apply. Answer (C) is incorrect. No such credit is provided in the Code. Answer (D) is incorrect. Tax-exempt corporations are subject to tax on UBI in excess of $1,000.

18.7.11. An incorporated exempt organization subject to tax on its current-year unrelated business income

A. Must make estimated tax payments if its tax can reasonably be expected to be $100 or more.

B. Must comply with the Code provisions regarding installment payments of estimated income tax by corporations.

C. Must pay at least 70% of the tax due as shown on the return when filed, with the balance of tax payable in the following quarter.

D. May defer payment of tax for up to 9 months following the due date of the return.

Answer (B) is correct. *(CPA, adapted)*
REQUIRED: The timing of payment obligations with respect to UBI tax.
DISCUSSION: Exempt organizations subject to tax on UBI are required to comply with the Code provisions regarding installment payments of estimated income tax by corporations [Sec. 6655(g)(3)].
Answer (A) is incorrect. Like a corporation, quarterly payments of estimated tax are required of an exempt organization that expects estimated tax on UBI to equal or exceed $500 for the tax year. Answer (C) is incorrect. Tax on UBI is due in full when the UBI return and annual information return are due. Answer (D) is incorrect. No deferral of payment of tax exists for an incorporated exempt organization subject to tax on its current-year unrelated business income.

18.7.12. If an exempt organization is a charitable trust, then unrelated business income is

A. Not subject to tax.

B. Taxed at rates applicable to corporations.

C. Subject to tax even if this income is less than $1,000.

D. Subject to tax only for the amount of this income in excess of $1,000.

Answer (D) is correct. *(CPA, adapted)*
REQUIRED: The taxability of UBI of a tax-exempt charitable trust.
DISCUSSION: UBI, net of a $1,000 UBI exemption allowed by Sec. 512(b)(12), of an exempt organization is subject to tax.
Answer (A) is incorrect. Some of the UBI is subject to tax. Answer (B) is incorrect. Rates applicable to trusts are applied to UBI of an exempt organization formed as a charitable trust. Answer (C) is incorrect. The UBI of a charitable trust is subject to tax of income in excess of $1,000.

18.7.13. A tax-exempt organization with a calendar tax year was required to file Form 990, *Return of Organizations Exempt from Income Tax*, for Year 1. Disregarding any extensions, when is the return due (do not consider Saturdays, Sundays, or holidays)?

A. March 15, Year 2.

B. April 15, Year 2.

C. May 15, Year 2.

D. June 15, Year 2.

Answer (C) is correct. *(SEE, adapted)*
REQUIRED: The date the tax-exempt organization's tax return is due.
DISCUSSION: Under Sec. 6072(e), the income tax return of an organization exempt from tax under Sec. 501(a) must be filed on or before the 15th day of the fifth month following the close of the taxable year.
Answer (A) is incorrect. March 15, Year 2, is the correct date by which Form 1120S must be filed for an S corporation. Answer (B) is incorrect. April 15, Year 2, is the correct date by which Form 1040 must be filed by an individual or Form 1120 must be filed by a calendar-year C corporation. Answer (D) is incorrect. A Form 990 filed on June 15, Year 2, would be considered late.

18.7.14. A partnership may qualify as an organization exempt from federal income tax if it is organized and operated exclusively for one or more of the purposes found in Sec. 501(c)(3) of the Internal Revenue Code.

A. True.

B. False.

Answer (B) is correct. *(SEE, adapted)*
DISCUSSION: No organization is exempt from tax unless it is one of the specific types upon which the IRC expressly confers exempt status (Sec. 501). The types listed and described in Secs. 501(c) and (d) do not include partnerships. Furthermore, a partnership, by definition, is an association organized for profit.

18.7.15. An exempt organization with $4,999 gross income from an unrelated business is required to file Form 990-T, *Exempt Organization Business Income Return*.

A. True.

B. False.

Answer (A) is correct. *(SEE, adapted)*
DISCUSSION: An unrelated business income (UBI) tax return (Form 990-T) is required of an exempt organization with at least $1,000 of gross income used in computing the UBI tax for the tax year [Reg. 1.6012-2(e)].

18.7.16. Organizations recognized as tax exempt are not responsible for withholding, depositing, paying, and reporting federal income tax, FICA, and FUTA wages paid to their employees.

A. True.

B. False.

Answer (B) is correct. *(SEE, adapted)*
DISCUSSION: An employer, whatever its nature, is responsible for withholding, depositing, paying, and reporting federal income tax, FICA, and FUTA wages paid to its employees, unless specific exemption is provided under the Code [Sec. 3401(a)]. The term employer includes organizations exempt from income tax. Limited exceptions are provided [see Sec. 3121(a)(16)].

18.7.17. An organization described in IRC Sec. 501(c)(3) must apply for tax-exempt status with its key IRS district director. If approved by the IRS, the organization will be recognized as exempt retroactively to the date it was organized if the application was filed within 15 months from the end of the month it was organized.

A. True.

B. False.

Answer (A) is correct. *(SEE, adapted)*
DISCUSSION: To establish its exemption, an organization must file a written application with the key director for the district in which the principal place of business or principal office of the organization is located. There are specific forms depending on the type of organization applying for the exemption. If filed within the 15-month period, retroactive treatment is available.

Use **Gleim Test Prep** for interactive study and easy-to-use detailed analytics!

STUDY UNIT NINETEEN
ACCOUNTING METHODS

19.1 Cash Method

NOTE: Also see Study Unit 6, "Deductions from AGI," for additional questions covering prepaid interest and discounted notes.

19.1.1. Which of the following is prohibited from using the cash receipts and disbursements method?

A. Individual taxpayers.

B. Small farming businesses.

C. Personal service corporations.

D. Tax shelters.

Answer (D) is correct. *(Publisher, adapted)*
REQUIRED: The type of taxpayer prohibited from using the cash method of accounting.
DISCUSSION: Section 448 limits the use of the cash method by certain business entities; i.e., they are required to use the accrual method. C corporations not meeting the $5 million gross receipts test, partnerships with a C corporation as a partner, and tax shelters are not permitted to use the cash receipts and disbursements method. Tax shelters are defined broadly to include syndicates, enterprises whose interests must be registered as a security, and any arrangement the principal purpose of which is the avoidance of federal income tax.
Answer (A) is incorrect. Individuals may use the cash method of accounting. Answer (B) is incorrect. Farming businesses are only required to use the accrual method if they are tax shelters or operated by a corporation or a partnership with a corporation as a partner [Sec. 447(a)]. This rule does not apply to S corporations, corporations owned 50% or more by the same family with annual gross receipts of $25 million or less, and other corporations with annual gross receipts of $1 million or less [Sec. 447(c)]. Answer (C) is incorrect. Personal service corporations engaged in rendering professional services and owned primarily by the employees who provide the services are not required to use the accrual method.

19.1.2. A cash-basis taxpayer should report gross income

A. Only for the year in which income is actually received in cash.

B. Only for the year in which income is actually received whether in cash or in property.

C. For the year in which income is either actually or constructively received in cash only.

D. For the year in which income is either actually or constructively received, whether in cash or in property.

Answer (D) is correct. *(CPA, adapted)*
REQUIRED: The timing of income of a cash-method taxpayer.
DISCUSSION: A cash-method taxpayer accounts for an item of income when the first of the following occurs: (1) cash is actually received; (2) an equivalent of cash is actually received; (3) constructive receipt of cash or its equivalent occurs. Notice that each answer is better than the previous answer.
Answer (A) is incorrect. A cash-basis taxpayer should also report income constructively received and income received in property. Answer (B) is incorrect. A cash-basis taxpayer should also report income constructively received. Answer (C) is incorrect. A cash-basis taxpayer should also report income received in property.

19.1.3. Which of the following entities may not use the cash method of accounting?

A. A partnership with average annual gross receipts in excess of $5 million.

B. A C corporation whose average annual gross receipts for the preceding 3 taxable years do not exceed $5 million.

C. A C corporation that is substantially owned by its employees and whose business is selling goods with annual gross receipts in excess of $5 million for all tax years since its inception.

D. An S corporation.

Answer (C) is correct. *(Publisher, adapted)*
REQUIRED: The business not allowed to use the cash method of accounting.
DISCUSSION: Certain entities are required by Sec. 448 to use the accrual method of accounting. A C corporation is one such entity unless it is a qualified personal service corporation or its annual gross receipts are small enough. To qualify as a personal service corporation, substantially all of the corporation's activities must involve the performance of services in health, law, engineering, architecture, accounting, actuarial science, performing arts, or consulting. A C corporation's average gross receipts must be $5 million or less for the prior 3 years to qualify for the cash method based on gross receipts.
Answer (A) is incorrect. A partnership may use the cash method unless it has a C corporation as a partner. Answer (B) is incorrect. Section 448(b) allows entities that meet this gross receipts test to use the cash method of accounting. Answer (D) is incorrect. S corporations may also use the cash method (if not a tax shelter).

19.1.4. Dowd, a cash-basis engineering consultant, wanted to defer income to next year. A client who was in Dowd's office on December 31 of the current year offered to pay his $2,000 bill immediately, but Dowd told him to pay in January. A check for $5,000 from another client arrived in the mail on December 29, and Dowd told his office manager not to deposit it until January. Dowd also told his office manager not to send a client a bill for $3,000 for services performed in the current year until January of next year. How much income from these transactions should Dowd report in the current year?

A. $8,000

B. $7,000

C. $5,000

D. $0

Answer (B) is correct. *(SEE, adapted)*
REQUIRED: The income of a cash-basis taxpayer that must be recognized before year end.
DISCUSSION: Although a cash-basis taxpayer generally recognizes income only when cash or the equivalent of cash is received, income is also recognized upon its constructive receipt. Under Reg. 1.451-2, income is constructively received when it is credited to a taxpayer's account, set apart for him or her, or otherwise made available so that (s)he may draw upon it at any time. Dowd must recognize the $2,000 of income from the client who offered to pay the bill. The $5,000 check received on December 29 must also be reported as income in the current year because a check is the equivalent of cash. However, income is not recognized merely upon failure to send out a bill. A taxpayer is not required to aggressively seek payment, but (s)he may not turn his or her back upon it when it is available. Dowd must report $7,000 in the current year.
Answer (A) is incorrect. The client bill that was not sent out is not reported as gross income in the current year, but the $2,000 offer of payment on December 31 is reported in the current year. Answer (C) is incorrect. The $2,000 offer of payment made on December 31 is also reported in the current year. Answer (D) is incorrect. Dowd has gross income from these transactions in the current year.

19.1.5. Mat West, a cash-basis taxpayer, owned interests in several corporations. The Wireless Corporation made a practice of sending dividend checks out to all shareholders on the last day of December, so the shareholders would not receive them until January. West received a $50 dividend check from Wireless on January 3, Year 2. The Palace Hotel, Inc., in which West was an officer, mailed its dividend checks in the same manner as Wireless. However, West's $400 check was placed on his office desk on December 31, Year 1. West owned a controlling interest in Gambling Saloon, Inc., and told the bookkeeper not to write his check, which was to be for $6,000, even though all other shareholders' checks were written and delivered in December, Year 1. How much dividend income does West have in Year 1?

A. $0

B. $450

C. $6,400

D. $6,450

Answer (C) is correct. *(Publisher, adapted)*
REQUIRED: The amount of dividend income to be recognized by a cash-basis taxpayer.
DISCUSSION: Although dividends can be constructively received like any other income, a special rule has developed with respect to dividends. If a dividend is declared payable in December and the corporation follows its usual practice of paying the dividends by checks mailed so that the shareholders do not receive them until January of the following year, the dividends are not considered to have been constructively received in December [Reg. 1.451-2(b)]. However, dividends are constructively received when they are made subject to the demand of the shareholder without qualification.
Therefore, West has constructively received the $400 from Palace Hotel, Inc., which was placed on his desk in Year 1, and the $6,000 from Gambling Saloon, Inc., which he declined to receive. West has $6,400 of dividend income in Year 1.
Answer (A) is incorrect. West has dividend income received in Year 1. Answer (B) is incorrect. In Year 1, the $6,000 is constructively received while the $50 is not. Answer (D) is incorrect. The $50 dividend is not reported until Year 2 when received.

19.1.6. What is the amount of income to be reported by Mr. X in Year 2 under the cash method of accounting for the following items?

- Check for $1,200 received January 4, Year 2, for services rendered in December Year 1.
- Check for $900 received December 26, Year 2, for services rendered in October, Year 2; did not cash until January 5, Year 3.
- Dividend check for $500. Check was dated December 31, Year 2, but it is the practice of the issuing corporation to mail checks so they will not be received until January of the following year.
- Check for $600 received on April 1, Year 2, for interest on corporate bonds held for the period October 1, Year 1, through March 31, Year 2. Interest is paid semi-annually on April 1 and October 1.
- Rental income of $800 for December Year 2 received January 3, Year 3.

    A. $1,800

    B. $2,700

    C. $3,500

    D. $4,000

Answer (B) is correct. *(SEE, adapted)*
    REQUIRED: The amount of income recognized under the cash method of accounting.
    DISCUSSION: A cash-basis taxpayer recognizes income when cash or its equivalent is received and when income is constructively received. Under Reg. 1.451-2, income is constructively received when it is credited to a taxpayer's account, set apart for him or her, or otherwise made available so that (s)he may draw upon it at any time. The $1,200 check for Year 1 services, the $900 check for Year 2 services, and the $600 check for bond interest are cash equivalents received during Year 2. Mr. X's income under the cash method totals $2,700. It does not matter that the $900 check was not cashed until January 5, Year 3, since the money had been received prior to year end by Mr. X and was available for his use.
    The dividends of $500 are not treated as received since it was the usual practice of the corporation to delay them. Since the rent was not received until Year 3, there is no reason to include it in Year 2.
    Answer (A) is incorrect. The $900 check received but not cashed in Year 2 is reported in Year 2. Answer (C) is incorrect. The rental income of $800 is not reported until Year 3. Answer (D) is incorrect. The $500 dividend and the $800 of rental income are not reported until Year 3.

19.1.7. Basil Company, a cash-basis taxpayer, had the following activity during Year 1:

Sales in Year 2, uncollected	$ 40,000
Sales in Year 2, collected	1,000,000
Total sales in Year 2	1,040,000
Collections on Year 1 bad debt	50,000

What is the correct amount of income to be reported for Year 2?

    A. $1,040,000

    B. $1,000,000

    C. $1,050,000

    D. $1,090,000

Answer (C) is correct. *(SEE, adapted)*
    REQUIRED: The correct amount of income to be reported for a cash-basis taxpayer.
    DISCUSSION: Because Basil Company reports income and expenses on the cash basis, cash and checks received are deposited and included in income. Therefore, the $40,000 in uncollected sales has not been included in income. The recovery of the bad debt collections will be included in income. Basil Company will report $1,050,000 of income.
    Answer (A) is incorrect. Basil Company is a cash-basis taxpayer. Answer (B) is incorrect. The amount of $1,000,000 does not account for the recovery of bad debt collected in Year 2. Answer (D) is incorrect. Basil Company is a cash-basis taxpayer; thus, the $40,000 of sales that is not collected in Year 2 is not included in income.

19.1.8. Peter is an auto mechanic. On November 25, Year 1, he made some major auto repairs on Harry's Mercedes. Harry is an attorney. In exchange for the service, Harry is going to draft Peter's will and represent him when he settles on his new house. Harry will perform all of these services in Year 2. The repair bill for the Mercedes came to $1,200. Both Peter and Harry are cash-basis taxpayers. How do they report this income?

    A. Both report $1,200 income in Year 1.

    B. Both report $1,200 income in Year 2.

    C. Harry reports $1,200 in Year 1, and Peter reports $1,200 in Year 2.

    D. Peter reports $1,200 in Year 1, and Harry reports $1,200 in Year 2.

Answer (C) is correct. *(SEE, adapted)*
    REQUIRED: The amount of income reported for parties exchanging services.
    DISCUSSION: Under Sec. 451(a) and Reg. 1.451-1(a), a cash-basis taxpayer generally includes an item in income when it is actually or constructively received. Under Sec. 461(a) and Reg. 1.461-1, a cash-basis taxpayer generally reports income only in the year of actual receipt. Constructive receipt is equivalent to actual receipt. The services performed for Harry were completed in Year 1, and therefore he reports $1,200 of income in Year 1. The services performed for Peter were completed in Year 2, and therefore he reports $1,200 of income in Year 2.
    Answer (A) is incorrect. Peter receives services in Year 2. Answer (B) is incorrect. Harry receives services in Year 1. Answer (D) is incorrect. Harry receives services in Year 1, and Peter receives services in Year 2.

19.1.9. John is a cash-basis taxpayer. He received the following items of income in December Year 2:

1. The loan on his truck was forgiven because he performed accounting work for the dealer. He owed $2,000 at the time.

2. He received a retainer of $500 from a new client to guarantee that his services would be available in February when the client would need help preparing financial statements.

3. He finally received the $800 for work he completed in November of Year 1.

How much of this income must John include on his Year 2 tax return?

 A. $500
 B. $1,300
 C. $2,500
 D. $3,300

19.1.10. In July of Year 1, Mr. Brown, a cash-basis, calendar-year farmer, had his bean crop damaged by a flood. He normally would have reported the income from the crop in Year 2. On November 1, Year 1, he received a $40,000 payment under the Disaster Assistance Act of 1988 due to the damage to his beans. Regarding Mr. Brown's reporting of the $40,000 for federal income tax purposes, which of the following statements is true?

 A. $40,000 must be included in his gross income for Year 1.
 B. The $40,000 is nontaxable income.
 C. He may elect to postpone reporting the $40,000 to Year 2 by attaching a statement to his Year 1 income tax return. The statement must include information required by a specific portion of the Income Tax Regulations.
 D. He may note on his Schedule F, Form 1040, that $40,000 from the Disaster Assistance Act will be reported in Year 2.

19.1.11. M, a cash-basis taxpayer, leased property on June 1 of the current year to P at $325 a month. P paid M $325 as a security deposit, which will be returned at the end of the lease. In addition, P paid $650 in advance rent, which is to be applied as rent to the last 2 months in the lease term, plus seven regular monthly payments of $325 each. The lease is to run for a 2-year period. What is M's rental income for the current year?

 A. $2,275
 B. $2,600
 C. $2,925
 D. $3,250

Answer (D) is correct. *(SEE, adapted)*
 REQUIRED: The amount of income a taxpayer must include on his or her tax return.
 DISCUSSION: Gross income means all income from whatever source derived unless specifically excluded (Sec. 61). A taxpayer who is solvent generally realizes income to the extent that debts are forgiven (Sec. 108). Cash-basis taxpayers must report prepaid income when received.
 Answer (A) is incorrect. The forgiven debt and the retainer are both included as gross income. Answer (B) is incorrect. The forgiven debt is included in gross income. Answer (C) is incorrect. The $800 received is included in Year 2, since it is actually received in Year 2.

Answer (C) is correct. *(SEE, adapted)*
 REQUIRED: The amount to be reported by a cash-basis farmer when his crop is destroyed by a flood and he receives payments under the Disaster Assistance Act of 1988.
 DISCUSSION: Section 451(d) provides that payments from the Disaster Assistance Act of 1988 for crop loss from drought, flood, or any other natural disaster shall be treated as insurance proceeds. These payments (in the form of insurance proceeds) may be included in income in the year of receipt, or the taxpayer may elect to include the proceeds in income in the year following the year of destruction as damage if it can be established that, under current practice, income from such crops would have been reported in the following taxable year. A statement verifying that these requirements have been met must be attached to the Year 1 tax return [Reg. 1.451-6(b)].
 Answer (A) is incorrect. Mr. Brown may elect to postpone reporting the $40,000 disaster payment if he can establish that income from the destroyed crops would have been reported in the following tax year. Answer (B) is incorrect. The $40,000 is taxable income. Answer (D) is incorrect. An election statement is required to be attached to the return. A statement on Schedule F noting the deferral is not sufficient.

Answer (C) is correct. *(SEE, adapted)*
 REQUIRED: The cash-basis taxpayer's income from prepaid rent and a security deposit.
 DISCUSSION: Section 451(a) provides that any item of gross income is included in income in the year of receipt, unless properly accounted for otherwise. Regulation 1.451-1(a) states that, under the cash method of accounting, an amount is includible in gross income when actually or constructively received. Regulation 1.61-8(b) requires advance rent payments to be included in gross income in the year of receipt regardless of the accounting method used. The security deposit is not income since M is obligated to return it and does not have an unrestricted right to it. M's rental income for the current year is

Advance rental payments	$ 650
Current rent ($325 × 7 months)	2,275
Rental income for the current year	$2,925

 Answer (A) is incorrect. The amount of $2,275 is the current rent ($325 × 7 months). Answer (B) is incorrect. The amount of $2,600 is the current rent plus the $325 security deposit. Answer (D) is incorrect. The amount of $3,250 is rent for 10 months.

19.1.12. Paul Charles, a cash-basis taxpayer, owns an apartment house. In computing net rental income for the current year, the following data are obtained:

- An analysis of the current-year bank deposit slips shows rents received in the amount of $15,000.

- In December of the current year, Mr. Charles received a $600 negotiable noninterest-bearing promissory note dated December 1 of the current year as rent for the months of December of the current year and January of the following year (fair market value $550).

- Pursuant to instructions from Mr. Charles, a past-due rent check of $175 was given to the building superintendent on December 29 of the current year. He mailed it to the rental office on the 30th; it was received on January 2 and deposited on January 3 of the following year.

- The lease of the tenant in Apt. 4A expired on December 31 of the current year, and the tenant left improvements valued at $500. The improvements were not in lieu of any rent required to have been paid.

In computing his current-year taxable income, Mr. Charles will report gross rents of

A. $16,275

B. $15,775

C. $15,725

D. $15,500

Answer (C) is correct. *(CPA, adapted)*
REQUIRED: The amount of rental income includible by a cash-basis taxpayer.
DISCUSSION: Under the general rule of Sec. 451(a) and Reg. 1.451-1(a), a taxpayer who uses the cash method of accounting includes an item in gross income when it is actually or constructively received. Regulation 1.451-2(a) provides that an item is constructively received if it is set apart for the taxpayer or could be collected by the taxpayer during that taxable year.

The bank deposits and the promissory note were income actually received. Only the fair market value of the note is included in income in the current year, since that is all Charles could realize on it (cash equivalency). Prepaid rent (January) is included in income when received. Upon collection of the note in the following year, an additional $50 will be recognized. The rent check of $175 was constructively received since Charles's agent received it. Improvements left by a tenant (not in lieu of rent) are excluded from gross income (Sec. 109).

Actually received:	
Bank deposits	$15,000
FMV of note	550
Constructively received:	
Rent check given to building supervisor	175
Gross rents	$15,725

Answer (A) is incorrect. The fair market value of the note is included, but the improvements left by a tenant (not in lieu of rent) are excluded. Answer (B) is incorrect. Only the fair market value of the note is included. Answer (D) is incorrect. The fair market value of the note and the past-due rent check are included, but the improvements left by a tenant (not in lieu of rent) are excluded.

19.1.13. Mr. J, a cash-method taxpayer, operates a business and files his return on a calendar-year basis. In Year 1, Mr. J took out a 3-year fire insurance policy on his building effective November 1. On January 1, Year 2, Mr. J paid a premium of $1,800 for the 3 years. What amount may Mr. J deduct as an insurance expense in Year 2?

A. $100

B. $600

C. $700

D. $1,800

Answer (C) is correct. *(SEE, adapted)*
REQUIRED: The amount a cash-basis taxpayer may deduct as insurance expense.
DISCUSSION: Section 461(a) provides that a deduction must be taken in the taxable year that is proper under the method of accounting used by the taxpayer. Regulation 1.461-1(a)(1) states that a taxpayer who uses the cash method of accounting generally should deduct allowable deductions in the taxable year in which they are paid. An exception to this rule occurs if an expenditure results in the creation of an asset having a useful life that extends substantially beyond the close of the taxable year. In such a case, the asset should be capitalized and the basis should be amortized ratably over its life. Mr. J may deduct the premiums applicable to Year 1 (November and December) and Year 2.

Monthly insurance expense	
($1,800 divided by 36 months)	$ 50
Months deductible in Year 2 (November and	
December of Year 1 + Year 2 calendar year)	× 14
Insurance expense	$700

Answer (A) is incorrect. The amount deductible in Year 2 for the insurance premiums for November and December of Year 1 is $100; however, $600 for Year 2 is also deductible. Answer (B) is incorrect. The $100 amount for insurance premiums for November and December of Year 1 is also deductible in Year 2. Answer (D) is incorrect. The premiums should be amortized over 36 months since the policy has a useful life that extends substantially beyond the close of the taxable year.

19.1.14. For a cash-basis taxpayer, gain or loss on a year-end sale of listed stock arises on the

A. Trade date.

B. Settlement date.

C. Date of receipt of cash proceeds.

D. Date of delivery of stock certificate.

Answer (A) is correct. *(CPA, adapted)*
REQUIRED: The date on which gain or loss is recognized on a year-end stock sale.
DISCUSSION: Both cash- and accrual-method taxpayers realize gain or loss on sale of securities on the day the broker completes the transaction on a stock exchange [Sec. 453(k)(2)].
Answer (B) is incorrect. For a cash-basis taxpayer, gain or loss on a year-end sale of listed stock does not arise on the settlement date. Answer (C) is incorrect. For a cash-basis taxpayer, gain or loss on a year-end sale of listed stock does not arise on the date of receipt of cash proceeds. Answer (D) is incorrect. For a cash-basis taxpayer, gain or loss on a year-end sale of listed stock does not arise on the date of delivery of the stock certificate.

19.1.15. Dave operates a home improvement business as a sole proprietor. On December 31 of the current year, he received a delivery of plasterboard and gave the deliveryman a check for $300. Later that day, he bought paint, brushes, and some power tools for use in his business. He bought the paint and brushes for $125 from the Bright Paint Store and charged them on a bank credit card. He bought the tools for $150 from Power Hardware Company and charged them on his Power Hardware credit card. What is the amount of these expenditures that Dave can deduct as business expense in the current year?

A. $575

B. $425

C. $300

D. $275

Answer (B) is correct. *(SEE, adapted)*
REQUIRED: The cash-basis taxpayer's deduction for payments made by check and charge card.
DISCUSSION: Regulation 1.461-1(a)(1) provides that deductions are allowed under the cash method of accounting in the taxable year when paid. A mere promise to pay is generally not considered payment under the cash method of accounting.
A check is considered the equivalent of cash, and payment is considered made when the check is delivered or sent. A charge on a hardware store credit card is merely a promise to that hardware store to pay and is not considered payment until the charge card bill is paid. On the other hand, use of a bank credit card involves a third party. It is equivalent to obtaining a loan from the bank and paying the hardware store. Therefore, the charge with a bank credit card is payment at the time of the charge. Dave's business expense deductions for the current year are $425 ($300 by check + $125 on the bank credit card).
Answer (A) is incorrect. The charge on the Power Hardware credit card is not deductible until the charge card bill is paid. Answer (C) is incorrect. The charge on the bank credit card is deductible in the current year. Answer (D) is incorrect. The charge on the Power Hardware credit card is not deductible; however, the check is deductible.

19.1.16. Dr. Berger reports on the cash basis. The following items pertain to Dr. Berger's medical practice in Year 2:

Cash received from patients in Year 2	$200,000
Cash received in Year 2 from third-party reimbursers for services provided by Dr. Berger in Year 1	30,000
Salaries paid to employees in Year 2	20,000
Year 2 year-end bonuses paid to employees in Year 3	1,000
Other expenses paid in Year 2	24,000

What is Dr. Berger's net business income for Year 2 from his medical practice?

A. $155,000

B. $156,000

C. $185,000

D. $186,000

Answer (D) is correct. *(CPA, adapted)*
REQUIRED: The net business income of cash-basis taxpayers.
DISCUSSION: Under Sec. 451(a) and Reg. 1.451-1(a), a cash-basis taxpayer generally includes an item in income when it is actually or constructively received. Under Sec. 461(a) and Reg. 1.461-1, a cash-basis taxpayer may generally deduct an expense only in the year of actual payment. Dr. Berger's net income from his business is

Income:	
Cash from customers	$200,000
Cash from third parties	30,000
Expenses:	
Salaries	(20,000)
Other business expenses	(24,000)
Net business income	$186,000

The Year 2 year-end bonuses paid in Year 3 are deductible in Year 3.
Answer (A) is incorrect. Cash from third parties is included in income in Year 2, and year-end bonuses paid to employees are not deductible until paid in Year 3. Answer (B) is incorrect. Cash from third parties is included in income in Year 2. Answer (C) is incorrect. The year-end bonuses are deductible when paid in Year 3.

19.1.17. Which of the following is not considered "constructive receipt" of income?

    A. Ms. K was informed her check for services rendered was available on December 15, Year 1, but she waited until January 15, Year 2, to pick up the check.

    B. Earned income of Mr. D was received by his agent on December 29, Year 1, but not received by D until January 5, Year 2.

    C. Mr. W received a check on December 30, Year 1, for services rendered, but was unable to make a deposit until January 4, Year 2.

    D. A payment on a sale of real property was placed in escrow on December 15, Year 1, but not received by Ms. B until January 10, Year 2, when the transaction was closed.

Answer (D) is correct. *(SEE, adapted)*
    REQUIRED: The payment not considered constructive receipt of income.
    DISCUSSION: The general rule under Sec. 451(a) and Reg. 1.451-1(a) is that an item is included in gross income by a cash-basis taxpayer when it is actually or constructively received. Income is constructively received in the taxable year during which it is credited to the taxpayer's account, set apart for him or her, or otherwise made available so that (s)he could have drawn upon it during the taxable year if notice of intention to withdraw had been given. However, income is not constructively received if its receipt is subject to substantial limitations or restrictions. The payment in escrow is subject to substantial limitations or restrictions on receipt and thus not constructively received.
    Answer (A) is incorrect. The check was available to Ms. K. Answer (B) is incorrect. A payment in the hands of an agent is available to the taxpayer-principal. Answer (C) is incorrect. The receipt of a check is equivalent to the receipt of cash.

19.1.18. L.E. operates an accounting service as a sole proprietorship. For income tax purposes, L.E. reports on the cash and calendar-year bases. During Year 2, L.E. made the following expenditures in connection with his business:

Utility bills for services received in Year 2	$ 4,000
Property taxes applicable to	
Year 2	$ 2,000
Year 3	2,400
	4,400
Business loan interest applicable to	
Year 1	$ 1,500
Year 2	1,500
Year 3	1,500
	4,500
Computer rental applicable to	
Year 2	$12,000
Year 3	3,000
	15,000

If L.E. makes no tax elections applicable to Year 2, what is the allowable amount of his business deductions for Year 2?

    A. $27,900

    B. $26,400

    C. $24,900

    D. $23,400

Answer (D) is correct. *(E. Grams)*
    REQUIRED: The amount of a cash-basis taxpayer's business deductions.
    DISCUSSION: Under Sec. 461(a) and Reg. 1.461-1, expenses may be deducted by a cash-basis taxpayer when actually paid. Exceptions to this rule are that a cash-basis taxpayer is required to capitalize (1) payments that create assets having a useful life extending substantially beyond the end of the taxable year and (2) payments for prepaid interest [Sec. 461(g)]. The utility bills and property taxes are fully deductible in the year paid. The business loan interest is deductible except for that applicable to Year 3, which must be capitalized and deducted in Year 3. The prepayment of computer rental arguably creates an asset that will extend beyond the end of the taxable year. On this basis, the payment applicable to Year 3 must be capitalized and deducted in Year 3, but there is case law to the contrary that would allow the deduction in Year 2 for payments that relate to the next year (12 months).

Utility bills	$ 4,000
Property taxes	4,400
Business loan interest (excluding $1,500 applicable to Year 3)	3,000
Computer rentals (excluding $3,000 applicable to Year 3)	12,000
Total allowable deduction	$23,400

    Answer (A) is incorrect. The business loan interest for Year 3 and the computer rentals for Year 3 are not deductible in Year 2. Answer (B) is incorrect. The computer rental for Year 3 is not deductible in Year 2. Answer (C) is incorrect. The business loan interest for Year 3 is not deductible in Year 2.

19.1.19. Pierre, a headwaiter, received tips totaling $2,000 in December of Year 1. On January 5, Year 2, Pierre reported this tip income to his employer in the required written statement. At what amount, and in which year, should this tip income be included in Pierre's gross income?

    A. $2,000 in Year 1.

    B. $2,000 in Year 2.

    C. $1,000 in Year 1 and $1,000 in Year 2.

    D. $167 in Year 1 and $1,833 in Year 2.

Answer (B) is correct. *(CPA, adapted)*
    REQUIRED: The inclusion of tips in income.
    DISCUSSION: Normally, a cash-basis taxpayer includes income when received. However, tips are specially treated. An employee who receives $20 or more in tips in a month (as a result of working for one employer, and not combined from several jobs) must report the total tips to the employer by the 10th day of the next month [Sec. 6053(a)]. These tips are treated as paid when the report is made to the employer [Sec. 451(c)]. Since Pierre properly reported his December, Year 1, tips to his employer in January of Year 2, the tips are not included in gross income until Year 2.
    Answer (A) is incorrect. The tips should not be treated as gross income in Year 1. Answer (C) is incorrect. The tips should not be split between Year 1 and Year 2. Answer (D) is incorrect. None of the tips are treated as gross income in Year 1.

19.1.20. Farmer John, a cash-basis taxpayer, bought $3,000 of cattle feed in Year 1 for use in Year 2. John's other farming expenses for Year 1 amounted to $2,000. In prior years, he also had prepaid expenses in excess of nonprepaid expenses. How much and when is the cattle feed deductible?

	Year 1	Year 2
A.	$0	$1,000
B.	$0	$3,000
C.	$1,000	$2,000
D.	$3,000	$0

Answer (C) is correct. *(Publisher, adapted)*
REQUIRED: The amount of prepaid feed a farmer may deduct.
DISCUSSION: Regulation 1.162-12 provides that farmers (but not farming syndicates) may deduct prepaid feed when the expenditure is incurred even if it is to be consumed by the livestock in a subsequent year. After 1986, even individual farmers' deduction of prepaid farm supplies is limited by Sec. 464(f) to 50% of other farming expenses incurred during the taxable year. Farmer John's deduction of prepaid cattle feed for Year 1 is thus limited to $1,000 ($2,000 other expenses × 50%).
  If the farmer has a principal residence on a farm or his or her principal occupation is farming and if the aggregate of prepaid farm supplies for the prior 3 taxable years is less than 50% of the aggregate of other deductible farming expenses, the 50% limitation does not apply for the current year.
  Answer (A) is incorrect. John has a deduction for cattle feed in Year 1, and $1,000 is not the correct amount of John's deduction in Year 2. Answer (B) is incorrect. John has a deduction for cattle feed in Year 1, and $3,000 is not the correct amount of John's deduction in Year 2. Answer (D) is incorrect. The deduction for cattle feed in Year 1 is limited to 50% of other farming expenses incurred during the year. The remaining balance of the Year 1 expense is deductible in Year 2.

19.1.21. All of the following items are deductible on a cash-basis decedent's final joint return filed with her spouse except

A. Decedent's net operating loss from business operations.

B. Medical expenses paid after the date of death by the surviving spouse for the care of the decedent.

C. Personal exemption for the decedent.

D. Moving expenses incurred, but not paid before date of death.

Answer (D) is correct. *(SEE, adapted)*
REQUIRED: The expenses that are deductible on a cash-basis decedent's final tax return.
DISCUSSION: When a taxpayer dies, his income tax liability must be determined using his or her regular accounting method for the period of time from the beginning of his or her tax year to the date of death. Under Reg. 1.461-1, a taxpayer who uses the cash method of accounting deducts expenses when they are paid. Deductions of a decedent are not accrued on his or her final return unless his or her established accounting method requires it, but are deductible by the estate or other person who is liable for their payment. In the case of the moving expenses, they would be deducted by the estate in the year that they were paid.
  The decedent's net operating loss can be deducted in his or her final tax return. Medical expenses paid by a surviving spouse within 1 year after the date of death are deductible on a joint return filed with the decedent for the year of death or on his or her separate return. A decedent is allowed a personal exemption in his or her final tax return.
  Answer (A) is incorrect. A decedent's net operating loss from business operations is deductible on a cash-basis decedent's final return. Answer (B) is incorrect. Medical expenses paid after the date of death by the surviving spouse for the care of the decedent are deductible on a cash-basis decedent's final return. Answer (C) is incorrect. The personal exemption for the decedent is deductible on a cash-basis decedent's final return.

19.1.22. Y separately operates a small grocery store and a pick-up and delivery messenger service. Y may use the same accounting method and keep one complete set of books for both businesses.

A. True.

B. False.

Answer (B) is correct. *(SEE, adapted)*
DISCUSSION: Under Reg. 1.446-1(a)(4), a taxpayer is required to maintain accounting records to enable him or her to file a correct tax return. Each business is required to keep a separate set of books, so Y may not keep one set of books for both the grocery store and the messenger service. However, Y may use the same accounting method for both businesses or may use a different method of accounting for each business [Reg. 1.446-1(d)]. The grocery store will be required to use the accrual method of accounting for its inventory purchases and sales if average gross receipts exceed $1 million for the 3 previous years.

19.1.23. A lawyer using the cash method of accounting may deduct uncollectible fees as a bad debt.

A. True.

B. False.

Answer (B) is correct. *(SEE, adapted)*
    DISCUSSION: Under Sec. 165, the deduction for a loss is limited to the adjusted basis of the property. Under the cash method of accounting, fees that have not been collected have not been included in income and, therefore, have no basis. Without any basis, there is no loss to deduct.

19.1.24. Mr. X signed a note for $1,500 on May 31, Year 1, at a 12% interest rate, agreeing to repay it in 12 equal installments beginning on April 1, Year 2. Interest of $180 was subtracted from the face value of the note, and Mr. X received $1,320. Mr. X uses the cash method. He may deduct the $180 interest in Year 1.

A. True.

B. False.

Answer (B) is correct. *(SEE, adapted)*
    DISCUSSION: Under Reg. 1.461-1(a)(1), a taxpayer using the cash method of accounting generally deducts expenses when they are paid. However, a taxpayer who receives a loan at a discount has not paid the discount (interest) until the loan is repaid. A cash-basis taxpayer deducts the discount ratably as the loan is repaid.

19.1.25. Mr. Grey owns a cattle ranch in Texas. This area suffered a severe drought in Year 1 and was designated as eligible for federal assistance. Mr. Grey normally buys cattle, raises them for 2 years, then sells them. As a result of the drought, his cattle had to be sold after holding them only 1 year. Under these conditions, Mr. Grey may elect to postpone reporting the income from the sale in Year 1 to Year 2.

A. True.

B. False.

Answer (A) is correct. *(SEE, adapted)*
    DISCUSSION: Section 451(e)(1) provides an exception to the general rule of cash basis accounting by allowing taxpayers to defer recognition of income from sale or exchange of livestock until the tax year following the year in which the sale or exchange occurred. This exception applies only if the sale or exchange would not have occurred were it not for drought, flood, or other weather-related conditions and such conditions resulted in the area being designated as eligible for federal government assistance.

19.1.26. Mr. C is a cash-basis, calendar-year taxpayer. He owns several shares of stock in a mutual fund. On December 29, Year 1, the fund credits to his account a capital gain distribution of $600. C received the $600 on January 15, Year 2. C must report the $600 capital gain distribution as a capital gain on his Year 1 return.

A. True.

B. False.

Answer (A) is correct. *(SEE, adapted)*
    DISCUSSION: The general rule under Sec. 451(a) and Reg. 1.451-1(a) is that income is included by a cash-basis taxpayer when it is actually or constructively received. Income is deemed to be constructively received if it is credited to the taxpayer's account. Hence, C must report the $600 distribution in Year 1. Section 852(b)(3)(B) requires that a capital gain dividend of a mutual fund be treated as a long-term capital gain.

19.2 Accrual Method

19.2.1. Which of the following statements is false?

A. A cash-method taxpayer must report the increase in redemption value each year on U.S. savings bonds issued on a discount basis.

B. An accrual-method taxpayer must report the increase in redemption value each year on U.S. savings bonds issued on a discount basis.

C. A cash-method taxpayer may defer the reporting of interest on Series E or EE U.S. savings bonds until the bonds are cashed or the year the extended maturity period ends, whichever is earlier.

D. A cash-method taxpayer must report interest when received on U.S. savings bonds issued at face value.

Answer (A) is correct. *(SEE, adapted)*
    REQUIRED: The false statement concerning U.S. savings bonds issued at a discount.
    DISCUSSION: A cash-method taxpayer is required to report interest only when actually or constructively received. On a discount bond, interest is received when the bond is surrendered. Section 454(a) provides that a cash-basis taxpayer may elect to treat the annual increase in redemption value of Series E or EE bonds as income each year.
    Answer (B) is incorrect. A taxpayer must report interest as it accrues under the accrual method of accounting. Answer (C) is incorrect. Series E and EE bonds are noninterest-bearing bonds issued at a discount. The interest is not received until they are cashed or they mature. Answer (D) is incorrect. U.S. savings bonds issued at face value pay interest twice a year, and this interest must be included by a cash-method taxpayer when received.

19.2.2. M, an accrual-method taxpayer using the calendar year, had the following transactions during the current year:

Recovery of an account receivable written off in a prior year but that did not reduce his taxes	$ 5,000
Sales to a customer who is directed to transmit the payment to M's brother	3,500
Amounts received in settlement of a breach of contract suit	22,500

What amount must M include in gross income in the current year?

A. $8,500

B. $26,000

C. $27,500

D. $31,000

Answer (B) is correct. *(SEE, adapted)*
REQUIRED: The amount the taxpayer must include in gross income in the current year.
DISCUSSION: Since the taxpayer's tax was not reduced in the year the account receivable was written off, no income is recognized upon the recovery of the receivable (Sec. 111). The taxpayer must include in his or her gross income the $3,500 from the sale to the customer since income cannot be avoided by assigning the right to collection of the income to another. The amounts received in the settlement of the breach of contract suit represent lost income, so the $22,500 must be included in gross income. Therefore, the taxpayer must include $26,000 ($3,500 sale to customer + $22,500 settlement) in gross income.
Answer (A) is incorrect. Recovery of a write-off made in a prior year that did not reduce taxes is not gross income. However, amounts received from a settlement are included in gross income. Answer (C) is incorrect. Recovery of a write-off made in a prior year that did not reduce taxes is not gross income. However, sales with an assignment of the collection amount are included in gross income. Answer (D) is incorrect. Recovery of a write-off made in a prior year that did not reduce taxes is not gross income.

19.2.3. In the current year, Mr. A started a business that rents, sells, and repairs video recorders. Mr. A uses the accrual method of accounting and the calendar year as his tax year. The current-year business receipts included payments for 1-year service contracts and payments for prepaid rent on video recorders. The video recorders are offered for sale without service contracts in the normal course of business. Which of the following statements regarding Mr. A's reporting of gross income is true?

A. He must include the payments for prepaid rent in gross income for the current year, but may include the payments for 1-year service contracts as he earns them over the periods of the contracts.

B. He may include the payments for prepaid rent and 1-year service contracts in gross income as he earns them over the periods of the contracts.

C. He must include the payments for 1-year service contracts in gross income for the current year, but may include the payments for prepaid rent over the periods of the rental contracts.

D. He must include the payments for prepaid rent and for 1-year service contracts in gross income for the current year.

Answer (A) is correct. *(SEE, adapted)*
REQUIRED: The income an accrual-basis taxpayer reports from prepaid services and rent.
DISCUSSION: An accrual-method taxpayer must report income when all events have occurred that fix the right to receive such income and the amount thereof can be determined with reasonable accuracy [Reg. 1.451-1(a)]. As a general rule, an accrual-method taxpayer must recognize prepaid income when received. This is true for rent, but prepaid income for services may be accrued over the period for which the services are to be performed. The deferral period from gross income inclusion for accrued amounts ends at the conclusion of the following year (Rev. Proc. 2004-34). All of Mr. A's prepaid rent must be recognized when received. The prepaid income for services may be accrued over the period of the service contract, since the service period is for 1 year only.
Answer (B) is incorrect. Mr. A may not include the payments for prepaid rent as he earns them over the periods of the contracts. Answer (C) is incorrect. Mr. A does not have to include the payments for 1-year service contracts in gross income for the current year. They can be reported when earned. In addition, Mr. A may not include the payments for prepaid rent as he earns them over the periods of the contracts. Answer (D) is incorrect. Mr. A does not have to include the payments for 1-year service contracts in gross income for the current year.

19.2.4. Perry Refrigerators, an accrual-basis, calendar-year company for both tax and financial reporting, received a $600 payment from the sale of a $1,000 refrigerator in September of Year 1. The cost of the refrigerator to Perry was $550, and the refrigerator was in stock on December 31, Year 1. The refrigerator was shipped to the customer in March of Year 2 after the remaining $400 was paid. When is Perry required to report income from the sale of the refrigerator?

    A. $600 in Year 1 and $400 in Year 2.

    B. $550 in Year 1 and $450 in Year 2.

    C. $1,000 in Year 1.

    D. $1,000 in Year 2.

Answer (D) is correct. *(R. Fernandez)*
    REQUIRED: The period in which to report payments for goods sold.
    DISCUSSION: As a general rule, an accrual-basis taxpayer reports advance payments for the sale of merchandise when they are earned (e.g., when the goods are shipped). This rule applies only if such payments are reported for tax purposes no later than they are reported for financial accounting purposes. Even when this is true, Reg. 1.451-5(c)(1) limits the time of deferral if the taxpayer has received substantial advance payments (defined as greater than the seller's cost of goods sold) and the goods are on hand or available from normal channels. When these two conditions are met, as in this problem, the advance payments must be reported in the earlier of the year reported for financial purposes (Year 2) or the second taxable year after the tax year in which the advance payments become substantial (Year 1 + 2 = Year 3).
    Answer (A) is incorrect. The payment received by Perry for the refrigerator in Year 1 is $600. However, the payment is not required to be reported as income in Year 1. Answer (B) is incorrect. Income is reported when earned. The advance payment does not exceed the cost of sales, so none of the income is reported in Year 1. Answer (C) is incorrect. Perry is not required to report income from the sale of the refrigerator in Year 1.

19.2.5. Mr. S owns and operates an art studio. On December 1, Year 1, he received an advance payment of $12,000 from Ms. A to give her 12 painting lessons. The agreement stated that one lesson would be given in Year 1 and 11 lessons in Year 2. However, due to Ms. A's health, one lesson scheduled for July Year 2 was not given until January Year 3. S uses the calendar year and the accrual method of accounting. Assuming S elects to defer the advance payments, when must S report the income from painting lessons?

    A. $12,000 in Year 1.

    B. $1,000 in Year 1 and $11,000 in Year 2.

    C. $1,000 in Year 1, $10,000 in Year 2, and $1,000 in Year 3.

    D. $12,000 in Year 2.

Answer (B) is correct. *(SEE, adapted)*
    REQUIRED: The amount an accrual-basis taxpayer includes in income from prepaid services.
    DISCUSSION: Generally, an accrual-basis taxpayer must recognize prepaid income when received. Prepaid income for services may be accrued over the period for which the services are to be performed. The deferment from gross income ends the year following payment. (Rev. Proc. 2004-34 example 3). The first lesson of 12 to be performed is given in December of Year 1, so $1,000 is includible in Year 1. The balance of income must be reported by the end of Year 2, even though one lesson is rescheduled until January of Year 3. Therefore, $11,000 is included in Year 2.
    Answer (A) is incorrect. Only 1 month of lessons was given in Year 1. Prepaid income for services may be accrued over the period of performance. Answer (C) is incorrect. The income must be recognized by the end of the year following the first lesson; therefore, $1,000 cannot be deferred to Year 3. Answer (D) is incorrect. One lesson was given in Year 1, so $1,000 of income should be recognized in Year 1.

19.2.6. Mr. D, a calendar-year taxpayer, uses the accrual method of accounting in his manufacturing business. In Year 1, D's brother, Mr. E, a calendar-year, cash-basis taxpayer, was selected to be the foreman of a project in which E would receive a $10,000 bonus upon completion of the project. Work on the project began in Year 1 and was completed in December Year 2. The bonus was paid to E in January Year 3. When may Mr. D deduct the bonus paid to his brother?

    A. Year 1.

    B. A portion in both Year 1 and Year 2.

    C. Year 2.

    D. Year 3.

Answer (D) is correct. *(SEE, adapted)*
    REQUIRED: The taxable year in which an accrual-basis taxpayer may deduct a bonus paid to a related party cash-basis taxpayer.
    DISCUSSION: Mr. D and Mr. E are related parties under Secs. 267(b)(1) and 267(c)(4). When related parties are involved, Sec. 267(a)(2) requires the matching of the deduction claimed by a payor and the income reported by a payee in the case of expense or interest transaction. In this instance, the payee is a cash-basis taxpayer, and he will include the payment in income in the taxable year received (Year 3). The payor (Mr. D) can then deduct the payment in Year 3.
    Answer (A) is incorrect. Mr. D may not deduct the bonus paid to his brother in Year 1. Answer (B) is incorrect. Mr. D may not deduct a portion of the bonus paid to his brother in both Year 1 and Year 2. Answer (C) is incorrect. An accrual taxpayer cannot deduct an expense until the year in which the income is recognized by the cash-basis taxpayer when the taxpayers are related parties under Sec. 267.

19.2.7. LeDoran Sports Cars, a calendar-year taxpayer using the accrual method, purchased supplies from a new supplier in Year 1. The total invoice was for $12,000, but LeDoran claimed that only one-half of the order was received and paid only $6,000 in Year 1. Both parties honestly disputed the bill and LeDoran refused to pay the contested amount. They went to court and a judgment requiring LeDoran to pay an additional $3,000 was issued in Year 2. How should LeDoran report the expense?

A. $6,000 in Year 1 and $3,000 in Year 2.

B. $9,000 in Year 1.

C. $9,000 in Year 2.

D. $12,000 in Year 1 and $3,000 of income in Year 2.

Answer (A) is correct. *(Publisher, adapted)*
REQUIRED: The correct method for deducting a disputed liability.
DISCUSSION: Under the accrual method of accounting, an expense is deductible for the taxable year in which all events (including economic performance) have occurred which determine the fact of the liability and the amount thereof can be determined with reasonable accuracy [Reg. 1.461-1(a)(2)]. When there is a dispute and the amount of a liability is contested, it cannot be said that all events have occurred to determine the entire amount of the liability or that the amount can be determined with reasonable accuracy. Therefore, any part of a liability that remains unpaid and is honestly disputed may not be deducted.
Since $6,000 of the liability was not disputed, it should be deducted in Year 1 when LeDoran became liable. The remaining $3,000 should be deducted in Year 2. Note that Sec. 461(f) allows the deduction of a contested amount that is paid but remains contested.
Answer (B) is incorrect. LeDoran should not report $9,000 of expense in Year 1. Answer (C) is incorrect. The expense required to be paid as a result of the judgment is deducted in Year 2 when the judgment is issued. Answer (D) is incorrect. The amount of the total invoice is $12,000; it is not the correct amount of expense LeDoran should report in Year 1. Also, LeDoran does not have $3,000 of income in Year 2.

19.2.8. Karla operates a clothing store and paid $24,000 in wages to two employees ($12,000 each). She also provided for child care for their children valued at $3,600 for each employee. The employees also received clothing from the store having a total value of $800 for working 5 extra days. How much is deductible by Karla?

A. $24,000

B. $24,800

C. $31,200

D. $32,000

Answer (D) is correct. *(SEE, adapted)*
REQUIRED: The amount deductible for wages, child care, and inventory received by employees.
DISCUSSION: Section 162(a)(1) allows a deduction for reasonable compensation for personal services actually rendered. Section 83(a) allows the deduction to an employer equal to the fair market value of property given to the employee when the property is transferable or is not subject to a substantial risk of forfeiture. The value of the child care services provided by the employer also constitutes compensation for the employee's services and is deductible by the employer.
Answer (A) is incorrect. The child care and clothing expenses are also deductible by Karla. Answer (B) is incorrect. The child care costs are also deductible by Karla. Answer (C) is incorrect. The clothing expenses are deductible.

19.2.9. Mr. Holiday is a calendar-year, accrual-basis taxpayer. His records concerning vacation pay for his employees reflect the following:

• $20,000 paid January 30, Year 2, for Year 1 vacations earned in Year 1; nothing vested at March 15, Year 2
• $100,000 vacation pay accrued and paid in Year 2
• $14,000 accrued in Year 2 and vested by February 14, Year 3
• $10,000 accrued and not vested by March 15, Year 3

What amount can Mr. Holiday deduct as a business expense for Year 2?

A. $114,000

B. $124,000

C. $134,000

D. $144,000

Answer (C) is correct. *(SEE, adapted)*
REQUIRED: The amount an accrual-basis taxpayer may deduct for employee vacation pay.
DISCUSSION: The employer's deduction for accrued vacation pay is restricted by the Sec. 461(h) economic performance rules. Under these rules, the deduction is allowed in the year economic performance occurs; that is, for employee benefits in the year when the employer makes the payment. Under the Sec. 461(h)(3) recurring item exception, however, a deduction is allowed for an accrual-method taxpayer who pays vacation pay on a regular basis in the year the recurring item requirements are met even though the economic performance test is not yet satisfied. To use this exception, the vacation pay must be paid within 2 1/2 months of the end of the tax year. If the 2 1/2-month requirement is not met, the Sec. 404 deferred compensation rules generally will delay the claiming of the deduction until it is paid. With respect to the $14,000, however, the employee has rendered economic performance with respect to the vested pay, and the liability is fixed.
Answer (A) is incorrect. The $20,000 paid in Year 2 for Year 1 vacations is deductible in Year 2. Answer (B) is incorrect. The $10,000 amount is not deductible until Year 3, but the $20,000 amount is deductible in Year 2. Answer (D) is incorrect. The $10,000 amount is deductible in Year 3.

19.2.10. Shady Deal Corporation agreed to purchase the services of an expert appraiser as a consultant over the next 2 years. Every 6 months, the appraiser will value art works owned by Shady Deal for purposes of determining their resale value. Shady Deal paid the cash-basis appraiser $20,000 on December 31, Year 1, for work to be performed in June and December of both Year 2 and Year 3. Shady, an accrual-basis, calendar-year corporation, may deduct

    A. $20,000 in Year 1.

    B. $10,000 in Year 2; $10,000 in Year 3.

    C. $15,000 in Year 2; $5,000 in Year 3.

    D. $20,000 in Year 3.

Answer (B) is correct. *(Publisher, adapted)*
    REQUIRED: The correct amount and timing of deductions for an accrual-basis taxpayer.
    DISCUSSION: An accrual-basis taxpayer can deduct an expense when (1) all events have occurred that established the existence of the liability and (2) the amount of the liability can be determined with reasonable accuracy (the "all events" test). In addition, Sec. 461(h) provides that the "all events" test will not be satisfied for an accrual-basis taxpayer until economic performance has occurred. Economic performance occurs in the case of payments made to another person for services when such other person actually renders the services. Shady will be allowed to deduct the payment to the appraiser ratably as the appraiser performs the appraisals. Shady may therefore deduct $10,000 in Year 2 and $10,000 in Year 3.
    Answer (A) is incorrect. Shady Deal paid the appraiser $20,000 for 2 years of services. Answer (C) is incorrect. The amount of the deduction is allocated based on proportionate share of work performed each year. Answer (D) is incorrect. Shady Deal deducts the payments ratably as the work is performed.

19.2.11. An accrual-method taxpayer must recognize income from providing services during the current year even if before year end it appears that the purchaser will not be able to pay.

    A. True.

    B. False.

Answer (B) is correct. *(Publisher, adapted)*
    DISCUSSION: Under the accrual method of accounting, income is recognized if all the events have occurred that fix the right to receive the income and the amount can be determined with reasonable accuracy [Reg. 1.451-1(a)]. But amounts to be received for services need not be accrued if on the basis of experience they will not be collected [Sec. 448(d)(5)]. This exception to the accrual method is not available if the taxpayer charges interest or a penalty for late payment.

19.2.12. Under the accrual method of accounting, all items of income are included in gross income when they are earned even though the right to receive the income is contingent upon a future year's event.

    A. True.

    B. False.

Answer (B) is correct. *(SEE, adapted)*
    DISCUSSION: Under the accrual method of accounting, an item is includible in gross income when all the events have occurred that fix the right to receive the income and the amount thereof can be determined with reasonable accuracy [Reg. 1.451-1(a)]. If the right to receive the income is contingent upon a future year's event occurring, it is not includible in gross income until the future point in time that all the events have occurred that fix the right to receive the income.

19.2.13. Ray Johnson operates a retail store using the accrual method of accounting and reporting on Schedule C, "Profit or Loss from Business." He plans to start a lawn-care service to operate only in the summer months. The lawn-care business must use the accrual method of accounting because he has already elected this method for his other business and all businesses operated by one individual must use the same method of accounting.

    A. True.

    B. False.

Answer (B) is correct. *(SEE, adapted)*
    DISCUSSION: When a taxpayer has two or more separate businesses and keeps a complete and separate set of books and records for each, the taxpayer may use a different method of accounting for each business so long as such method clearly reflects the income of that particular enterprise.

19.2.14. When inventories are necessary to clearly show income, you must use the accrual method of accounting for sales, purchases, and all other items of income and expense.

    A. True.

    B. False.

Answer (B) is correct. *(SEE, adapted)*
    DISCUSSION: Section 446(a) provides that taxable income shall be computed under the method of accounting on the basis of which a taxpayer regularly computes income and keeps books. Each taxpayer must choose a method that, in the opinion of the Commissioner, clearly reflects income. However, a taxpayer who maintains inventory must use the accrual method of accounting with regard to purchases and sales [Reg. 1.446-1(c)(2)] but is not required to use the accrual method for other items of income or expense. A combination of the accrual and cash methods of accounting is known as the hybrid method.

19.2.15. A farmer who uses the accrual method of accounting may not make the election to postpone reporting the proceeds from a sale of livestock owing to drought conditions.

A. True.

B. False.

Answer (A) is correct. *(SEE, adapted)*
DISCUSSION: Under Sec. 451(e), the special rule that allows taxpayers to postpone reporting the proceeds of a sale of livestock owing to drought conditions is not available to accrual-method taxpayers or to anyone whose principal trade or business is not farming.

19.2.16. Last year, Ms. P, an accrual-basis, calendar-year taxpayer, under a contract, received an advance payment covering services to be performed ratably through the end of the current year. If for some reason Ms. P cannot perform all the services by the end of the current year, she may postpone including the advance payments in income until she earns them.

A. True.

B. False.

Answer (B) is correct. *(SEE, adapted)*
DISCUSSION: As a general rule, an accrual-method taxpayer must recognize prepaid income when received, if the right to receive such income is fixed and the amount thereof can be determined with reasonable accuracy. However, prepaid income for services may be accrued over the period for which the services are to be performed. The deferment from gross income ends the year following payment (Rev. Proc. 2004-34). Even if for some reason Ms. P cannot perform all the services by the end of the current year, she must include the remaining income in the current year.

19.2.17. Mr. Oak, an accrual-basis, calendar-year taxpayer, sells refrigerators at the retail level. For Year 1, his sales totaled $550,000, which included $50,000 from the sale of 1-year service contracts for the refrigerators. From past experience, Mr. Brown knows that for Year 2 he will have expenses of $20,000 relating to those contracts. Since he is on the accrual basis, Mr. Brown can deduct the $20,000 in Year 1, as a contingent liability.

A. True.

B. False.

Answer (B) is correct. *(SEE, adapted)*
DISCUSSION: Under the accrual method of accounting, an expense is deductible for the taxable year in which all events (including economic performance) have occurred that determine the fact of the liability and the amount thereof can be determined with reasonable accuracy. Here, the events that determine the fact of the liability have not occurred.

19.3 Hybrid Method

19.3.1. Mr. G opened a small grocery store. The sale of inventory is an income-producing factor. Mr. G may select either the cash or accrual method of accounting for his grocery business.

A. True.

B. False.

Answer (B) is correct. *(SEE, adapted)*
DISCUSSION: Regulation 1.446-1(c)(2) states that, if an inventory is used, the accrual method of accounting must be used for purchases and sales. Mr. G must use the accrual method of accounting for his purchases and sales, but he may use the cash method of accounting for noninventory transactions. This combination of methods is commonly referred to as a hybrid method. If average gross receipts are less than $1 million, Mr. G can treat inventions in the same manner as materials and supplies that are not inventory.

19.3.2. A manufacturing business in which inventories are necessary to show income correctly must use the accrual accounting method for purchases and sales.

A. True.

B. False.

Answer (A) is correct. *(SEE, adapted)*
DISCUSSION: Under Reg. 1.446-1(c)(2), if an inventory is necessary to the taxpayer's business, the accrual method of accounting must be used with regard to purchases and sales. The cash method of accounting may be used for other receipts and expenses provided it clearly reflects income [Sec. 446(c)].

19.3.3. A sole proprietorship may use the cash method for reporting gross income and the accrual method for reporting expenses.

A. True.

B. False.

Answer (B) is correct. *(SEE, adapted)*
DISCUSSION: Although hybrid methods of accounting are allowed, a taxpayer who uses the cash method to report gross income must also use the cash method to report expenses. Relatedly, a taxpayer who uses the accrual method to report expenses must also use the accrual method to report income. This is necessary to clearly reflect the income of the business.

19.3.4. Mrs. J owns a boutique that is operated as a sole proprietorship. She may use the accrual method of accounting for purchases and sales and the cash method for figuring all other items of income and expense.

    A. True.

    B. False.

Answer (A) is correct. *(SEE, adapted)*
    DISCUSSION: Regulation 1.446-1(c)(2) states that, if an inventory is used, the accrual method of accounting must be used for purchases and sales. Regulation 1.446-1(c)(1)(iv) provides that any combination of permissible methods will be allowed if such combination clearly reflects income and is consistently used. It specifically states that a taxpayer using the accrual method for purchases and sales may use the cash method for all other items of income and expense.

19.4 Long-Term Contracts

19.4.1. Section 460 requires, with limited exceptions, use of the percentage-of-completion method for long-term contracts. For this purpose, which of the following is not a characteristic of a long-term contract?

    A. A contract for the manufacture, building, installation, or construction of property not completed within the taxable year in which it was entered.

    B. A contract for the manufacture of an item that normally takes more than 12 months to complete, regardless of the contract period.

    C. A contract for the manufacture of a unique item not normally carried in finished goods inventory.

    D. A contract estimated to be completed within 2 years of commencement of construction, and the taxpayer's average annual gross receipts for the prior 3 taxable years are $10 million or less.

Answer (D) is correct. *(Publisher, adapted)*
    REQUIRED: The item not characteristic of a long-term contract.
    DISCUSSION: Section 460(e) provides that a construction contract (other than a home construction contract) is not long-term if it is estimated (when entered into) that it will be completed within 2 years of commencement (when construction costs are first incurred), and the taxpayer's average annual gross receipts for the prior 3 taxable years are $10 million or less. If a contract is not long-term because of these criteria, the taxpayer may use the completed-contract method.
    Answer (A) is incorrect. The general definition of a long-term contract [Sec. 460(f)(1)] is a contract for the manufacture, building, installation, or construction of property not completed within the taxable year in which it was entered. Answer (B) is incorrect. A contract for the manufacture of an item that normally takes more than 12 months to complete, regardless of the contract period, is an alternative requirement for manufacturing contracts to be considered long-term. Answer (C) is incorrect. A contract for manufacture of a unique item not normally carried in finished goods inventory is an alternative requirement for manufacturing contracts to be considered long-term.

19.4.2. X Corporation entered into a long-term contract in January to build an apartment building for $10 million. X Corporation normally uses the completed-contract method to account for long-term contracts. At the end of the first year, X Corporation had incurred $3.6 million of the total estimated $8 million in costs for the contract. The contract was completed in 3 years. Using the percentage-of-completion capitalized-cost method to account for the long-term contract, X Corporation would include in gross income for the first year an amount of

    A. $1.35 million.

    B. $3.15 million.

    C. $4.05 million.

    D. $4.5 million.

Answer (B) is correct. *(Publisher, adapted)*
    REQUIRED: The gross income from a long-term contract under the percentage-of-completion capitalized-cost method.
    DISCUSSION: The contract entered into by X Corporation is a residential construction contract, but not a home construction contract. The percentage-of-completion capitalized-cost method must be used to account for the contract. Under the residential construction contract rules for the percentage-of-completion capitalized-cost method, 70% of the items with respect to the contract are taken into account under the percentage-of-completion method and the remaining 30% of the items are taken into account under the taxpayer's normal method of accounting for contracts entered into on or after July 11, 1989 [Sec. 460(e)(5)]. Based on the cost-comparison method, X Corporation is 45% complete with its contract ($3.6 million ÷ $8 million). Under the percentage-of-completion method, X Corporation would include $4.5 million of the contract price in gross income ($10 million × 45%). Therefore, under the percentage-of-completion capitalized-cost method, X Corporation would include $3.15 million in gross income ($4.5 million × 70%).
    In addition, 70% of the $3.6 million of costs would be deducted. The remaining 30% of the contract can be reported under the completed-contract method; i.e., the rest of the income will be reported when the contract is completed.
    Answer (A) is incorrect. The amount of $1.35 million is the difference between the $3.5 million of revenue under the percentage-of-completion method when using the capitalized-cost method rules and the $4.5 million of revenue under the percentage-of-completion method when using the cost-comparison method rules. Answer (C) is incorrect. Gross income is not $4.05 million. Answer (D) is incorrect. The amount of $4.5 million is the revenue earned under the percentage-of-completion method when using the cost-comparison method rules.

19.4.3. On January 5, Year 1, Mr. D, a calendar-year taxpayer with average annual gross receipts of $4 million, contracted to build a road for X County for $1 million. The road will be completed by December 31, Year 2. Mr. D has elected the completed-contract method to report his income. On December 31, Year 1, the county engineer on the project certified that 65% of the road had been completed. Costs in the amount of $500,000 were incurred during Year 1 with respect to the contract. How much net profit should Mr. D report on this contract in Year 1?

A. $0

B. $50,000

C. $75,000

D. $150,000

Answer (A) is correct. *(SEE, adapted)*
REQUIRED: The net profit on a long-term contract under the completed-contract method of accounting.
DISCUSSION: For long-term contracts entered into after July 11, 1989, Sec. 460 requires with limited exceptions use of the percentage-of-completion method. However, since the contract in the question is estimated to be able to be completed in less than 2 years and the taxpayer's average annual gross receipts are $10 million or less, this is not treated as a long-term contract for purposes of Sec. 460. Therefore, the completed-contract method may be used. Regulation 1.451-3(d) states that, under the completed-contract method, gross income and expenses allocable to the long-term contract are accounted for in the taxable year in which such contract is completed. Since Mr. D's contract is not completed until Year 2, no income or expenses allocated to the contract should be included in income for Year 1. However, business expenses such as interest paid and depreciation on idle equipment that are not related to the contract can be deducted in Year 1.
Answer (B) is incorrect. Mr. D uses the completed-contract method, which does not require recognition of gross income and expenses until the contract is complete. Answer (C) is incorrect. The correct amount of net profit Mr. D should report in Year 1 is not $75,000. Answer (D) is incorrect. The correct amount of net profit Mr. D should report in Year 1 is not $150,000.

19.4.4. Costs that may be allocated to long-term contracts include all of the following except

A. Production period interest.

B. Direct costs of the contract.

C. Marketing, selling, and advertising expenses.

D. All costs incurred by reason of the taxpayer's long-term contract activities.

Answer (C) is correct. *(Publisher, adapted)*
REQUIRED: The costs not allocable to long-term contracts.
DISCUSSION: Marketing, selling, and advertising expenses are not included in the costs of long-term contracts, as well as independent research and development costs and expenses of unsuccessful bids and proposals [Sec. 460(c)(4)].
Answer (A) is incorrect. Section 460(c)(3) provides that interest costs shall be allocated to a long-term contract in the same manner as to property produced by the taxpayer under Sec. 263A(f). The production period is amended slightly for long-term contracts. Answer (B) is incorrect. Direct costs are allocated to long-term contracts. Answer (D) is incorrect. All costs incurred by reason of the taxpayer's long-term contract activities are allocated to long-term contracts.

19.4.5. Which one of the following statements is false regarding the use of the percentage-of-completion method to account for long-term contracts?

A. The percentage-of-completion capitalized-cost method of accounting is generally available for long-term contracts if the taxpayer makes the appropriate election.

B. The percentage-of-completion is determined by comparing costs allocated to the contract and incurred before the end of the taxable year with the estimated total contract costs.

C. In determining the taxable income from the long-term contract under the percentage-of-completion method, a taxpayer may elect not to recognize income or account for costs from the contract for a taxable year if less than 10% of the estimated total contract costs have been incurred by the end of the taxable year.

D. All income from the long-term contract must be included in gross income no later than the taxable year after the taxable year in which the contract was completed.

Answer (A) is correct. *(Publisher, adapted)*
REQUIRED: The item not characteristic of the percentage-of-completion method to account for long-term contracts.
DISCUSSION: After July 11, 1989, the percentage-of-completion capitalized-cost method of accounting is no longer acceptable except for limited exceptions (e.g., residential construction contracts).
Answer (B) is incorrect. It describes the application of the percentage-of-completion method under Sec. 460(b)(1)(A). Answer (C) is incorrect. A taxpayer may elect to use the 10% method under Sec. 460(b)(5). Answer (D) is incorrect. It is required under Sec. 460(b)(1).

19.4.6. Corporation V, a calendar-year corporation, is in the construction business and uses the percentage-of-completion method of accounting for long-term contracts. On March 1, Year 1, V signed a long-term contract to construct a building. It began construction on the same date. The contract provides for a payment of $300,000 and completion by November 1, Year 2. In Year 1, V incurred costs totaling $180,000. On December 31, Year 1, V estimated the total contract costs would be $270,000. Using the cost-comparison method, how much gross income from the contract must V report in Year 1?

A. $180,000

B. $200,000

C. $270,000

D. $300,000

Answer (B) is correct. *(SEE, adapted)*
REQUIRED: The long-term contract income under the percentage-of-completion method.
DISCUSSION: According to Reg. 1.451-3(c), under the percentage-of-completion method, the portion of the gross contract price corresponding to the percentage of the entire contract completed during the taxable year is included in gross income for such taxable year.
Using the cost comparison technique, the percentage of completion (66 2/3%) is determined by comparing the costs incurred ($180,000) with the estimated total costs ($270,000). The gross income includible in Year 1 is $200,000 ($300,000 total contract price × 66 2/3% percentage of completion).
Answer (A) is incorrect. The actual amount of costs incurred in Year 1 is $180,000. Answer (C) is incorrect. The estimated total costs of the project is $270,000. Answer (D) is incorrect. The total contract amount, which must be allocated between Year 1 and subsequent years, is $300,000.

19.4.7. Granite Construction Co. contracted to build a dam for $5.4 million. The construction is to last 1.5 years. Granite elects the completed-contract method. Granite's annual gross receipts are less than $10 million. During the current year, Granite incurred the following costs:

Depreciation on idle equipment	$ 45,000
Salaries for construction workers	390,000
Rent on construction equipment	250,000
Materials on dam	800,000
Interest on corporate debt (not related to this project)	12,000

How much can Granite deduct in the current year?

A. $0

B. $57,000

C. $307,000

D. $1,440,000

Answer (B) is correct. *(Publisher, adapted)*
REQUIRED: The deductible business expenses under the completed-contract method of accounting.
DISCUSSION: Under the completed-contract method of accounting, gross income and expenses allocable to the long-term contract are accounted for in the taxable year in which such contract is completed [Reg. 1.451-3(d)(1)]. All costs that are not incidental to and necessary for the performance of the long-term contract may be deducted in the year paid or accrued. In determining what costs are properly allocable to a long-term contract, a form of the full absorption method of accounting is provided in Reg. 1.451-3(d)(5). Those costs that are directly or indirectly related to the contract are allocated to it and accumulated in an inventory account. Depreciation on idle equipment and interest on general corporate debt can be deducted in the current year ($57,000).
Note that complex cost allocation rules apply for indirect expenses incurred on contracts not completed within 3 years. But small contractors ($25 million or less average annual gross receipts) are exempt from these cost allocations (Reg. 1.451-3).
Answer (A) is incorrect. Granite has a deduction in the current year. Answer (C) is incorrect. Rent on the construction equipment is not deductible until the project is completed. Answer (D) is incorrect. The salaries, equipment rent, and material costs are not deductible until the project is completed. However, the depreciation on the idle equipment and interest on unrelated debt are deductible in the current year.

19.4.8. Upon completion of a long-term contract, interest is computed under the look-back method by applying the Sec. 6621 general overpayment rate to the over- or underpayment of tax for each year. The over- or underpayment is determined by allocating contract income among taxable years prior to the year of contract completion on the basis of

A. The estimated price and estimated costs.

B. The estimated price and actual contract price.

C. The estimated costs and actual costs of construction.

D. The actual contract price and actual costs.

Answer (D) is correct. *(Publisher, adapted)*
REQUIRED: The calculation of over- or underpayment of tax under the look-back method.
DISCUSSION: Interest is computed under the look-back method by (1) allocating income under the contract among taxable years before the year in which the contract is completed, on the basis of the actual contract price and actual costs; (2) determining the over- or underpayment of tax for each year (solely for purposes of computing such interest); and (3) applying the Sec. 6621 general overpayment rate to the over- or underpayment [Sec. 460(b)(2)].
Answer (A) is incorrect. The estimated contract costs and estimated price are not used to allocate income using the lease-back method to determine overpayment or underpayment of tax. Answer (B) is incorrect. The estimated contract price is not used to allocate income using the lease-back method to determine overpayment or underpayment of tax. Answer (C) is incorrect. The estimated contract costs are not used to allocate income using the lease-back method to determine overpayment or underpayment of tax.

19.4.9. Mr. Smart contracted for the construction of a building on July 1, Year 1. The contract provided for a payment of $240,000 for the building to be completed on April 1, Year 2. Smart is a calendar-year taxpayer and has elected the percentage-of-completion method to report his income. On December 31, Year 1, the architect of the project certified that 40% of the project had been completed. Costs of $98,000 were incurred during Year 1 with respect to the contract. How much profit or loss should Smart report on his Year 1 income tax return in connection with the construction project?

A. None.

B. $(2,000)

C. $56,800

D. $96,000

Answer (B) is correct. *(SEE, adapted)*
REQUIRED: The profit or loss on a long-term contract under the percentage-of-completion method of accounting.
DISCUSSION: Regulation 1.451-3(c) states that, under the percentage-of-completion method, the portion of the gross contract price that corresponds to the percentage of the entire contract that has been completed during the taxable year must be included in gross income for such taxable year. Instead of comparing costs, the percentage of completion may be determined by a qualified professional such as an architect. All costs (taking into account beginning and ending inventories of materials) incurred during the taxable year are deducted in that taxable year. Smart's loss is

Includible income (40% of $240,000)	$ 96,000
Less: costs incurred in Year 1	(98,000)
Loss for Year 1	$ (2,000)

Answer (A) is incorrect. Smart will report a gain or loss in connection with the construction project. Answer (C) is incorrect. All of the costs incurred in Year 1 must be deducted in Year 1. Answer (D) is incorrect. The amount of $96,000 is 40% of the contract price, which must be reduced by $98,000 of actual costs incurred in Year 1.

19.4.10. Under the look-back method related to long-term contracts, interest is computed

A. On tax with respect to 100% of a contract entered into after July 11, 1989, if the percentage-of-completion method is used.

B. On the difference in tax if income is calculated under the percentage-of-completion method or completed-contract method.

C. On tax with respect to the portion of income determined under the completed-contract method if the percentage-of-completion capitalized-cost method is used.

D. Using the federal short-term rate for original issue discount bonds.

Answer (A) is correct. *(Publisher, adapted)*
REQUIRED: The correct statement concerning the look-back method of computing interest.
DISCUSSION: The look-back method is used to compute interest on the underpayment or overpayment of tax caused by actual costs varying from estimated costs for each of the contract years [Sec. 460(b)(2)]. Interest must be computed under the look-back method for the entire amount when the percentage-of-completion method is used. The look-back method can be applied to 70% of the amount when the percentage-of-completion capitalized-cost method is used for residential construction contracts. Under the 1997 Tax Act, taxpayers may elect (1) not to apply the look-back method to a long-term contract or (2) not to reapply the look-back method to a long-term contract when such method has already been applied. For the first election to be made, the cumulative taxable income (loss) under the contract in each prior year, as determined using estimated contract price and costs, must be within 10% of the cumulative taxable income (loss) using actual contract price and costs. An election can be made not to reapply the look-back method in years after the contract is completed if the cumulative actual income from the contract does not exceed 10% of the cumulative income determined in the most recent year the look-back method was applied (or would have applied except for the other exception).
Answer (B) is incorrect. The look-back method refers to the difference between the actual and estimated costs on the percentage-of-completion portion of the contract, not the completed-contract portion. Answer (C) is incorrect. Under the look-back method related to long-term contracts, interest is not computed on tax with respect to the portion of income determined under the completed-contract method. Answer (D) is incorrect. The general overpayment rate established by Sec. 6621 is used, compounded daily.

19.4.11. Which one of the following statements is false regarding the use of the percentage-of-completion method to account for long-term contracts?

A. The completed-contract method of accounting can be used for any home construction contract.

B. The percentage-of-completion capitalized-cost method of accounting can be used for residential construction contracts.

C. Under the percentage-of-completion capitalized-cost method, 70% of the items with respect to the contract are taken into account under the percentage-of-completion method, and the remaining 30% of the items are taken into account under the taxpayer's normal method of accounting for residential construction contracts.

D. Taxpayers entering into residential or home construction contracts can elect to use either the percentage-of-completion capitalized-cost or completed-contract methods.

Answer (D) is correct. *(Publisher, adapted)*
REQUIRED: The false statement about the percentage-of-completion capitalized-cost method and long-term contracts.
DISCUSSION: Under Sec. 460(e)(1), home construction contracts are excepted from the long-term contract rules, and therefore can use their regular method of accounting or the completed-contract method. Residential construction contracts (that are not also home construction contracts) fall under the percentage-of-completion capitalized-cost method. This method is required under Sec. 460(e)(5) except that 70% of the items under the contract are taken into account under the percentage-of-completion method and 30% under the taxpayer's regular accounting method instead of the 90% and 10% proportions used under the general percentage-of-completion capitalized-cost method rule. Taxpayers under the residential or home construction contract rules cannot make an election to use either percentage-of-completion, capitalized cost, or completed-contract methods.
Answer (A) is incorrect. The completed-contract method of accounting can be used for any home construction contract. Answer (B) is incorrect. The percentage-of-completion method of accounting can be used for residential construction contracts. Answer (C) is incorrect. Under the percentage-of-completion capitalized-cost method, 70% of the items with respect to the contract are taken into account under the percentage-of-completion method, and the remaining 30% of the items are taken into account under the taxpayer's normal method of accounting for residential construction contracts.

19.4.12. Corporation A uses the calendar-year and the completed contract method to report its income. Corporation A's average annual gross receipts exceed $20 million. On June 1, Year 1, Corporation A contracted to build a condominium complex for $15 million. More than 90% of the total contract costs are estimated to be for dwelling units and related improvements. The completion date was scheduled for June 1, Year 4. On December 31, Year 1, the complex was 20% completed. Corporation A received payments of $3,750,000 and incurred expenses of $2 million during Year 1 on this contract. The amount to be reported as gross receipts for Year 1 is $3,750,000.

A. True.

B. False.

Answer (B) is correct. *(SEE, adapted)*
DISCUSSION: The contract satisfies the residential construction contract of Sec. 460(e)(6)(B) in that 80% of the estimated total contract costs are for dwelling units and related improvements. The percentage-of-completion capitalized-cost method must be used to account for the contract. Seventy percent of the items with respect to the contract are taken into account under the percentage-of-completion method, and the remaining 30% of the items are taken into account under the taxpayer's normal method of accounting for contracts entered into on or after July 11, 1989 [Sec. 460(e)(5)]. Regulation 1.451-3(c) provides that, under the percentage-of-completion method, the portion of the gross contract price corresponding to the percentage of the entire contract completed during the taxable year must be included in gross income for such taxable year. Consequently, Corporation A will report gross receipts of $2,100,000 ($15,000,000 contract price × 70% × 20%).

19.4.13. On September 15, Year 1, Corporation R entered into a contract to build a shopping center at a total estimated contract price of $20 million. The project is scheduled for completion in September of Year 6. Corporation R, whose average annual gross receipts for the 3 prior years were $15 million, may elect to defer reporting any income or loss from the contract until the project is completed.

A. True.

B. False.

Answer (B) is correct. *(SEE, adapted)*
DISCUSSION: A construction contract that is estimated to be completed within 2 years of commencement, when the taxpayer's average annual gross receipts are $10 million or less, may use the completed-contract method rather than the methods prescribed by Sec. 460. Corporation R may not use the completed-contract method of accounting.

19.5 Installment Sales

19.5.1. During the current year, Mr. C sold property that had an adjusted basis to him of $19,000. The buyer assumed C's existing mortgage of $15,000 and agreed to pay an additional $10,000 consisting of a cash down payment of $5,000, and payments of $1,000, plus interest, per year for the next 5 years. Mr. C paid selling expenses totaling $1,000. What is C's gross profit percentage?

A. 20%

B. 40%

C. 50%

D. 80%

Answer (C) is correct. *(SEE, adapted)*
REQUIRED: The gross profit percentage for an installment sale.
DISCUSSION: The gross profit percentage is the proportion of gross profit in relation to total contact price. The gross profit is the selling price reduced by the adjusted basis of the property and any selling expenses. The contract price is the total amount the seller will ultimately collect from the buyer. C's gross profit is $5,000 ($25,000 sales price – $19,000 basis – $1,000 selling expenses). The contract price totals $10,000. Thus, the gross profit percentage is 50% ($5,000 gross profit ÷ $10,000 contract price).
Answer (A) is incorrect. The gross profit divided by the sales price is 20%. Answer (B) is incorrect. C's gross profit percentage is not 40%. Answer (D) is incorrect. C's gross profit percentage is not 80%.

19.5.2. Mr. P purchased property from Mr. A by assuming an existing mortgage of $12,000 and agreeing to pay an additional $6,000, plus interest, over the next 3 years. Mr. A had an adjusted basis of $8,800 in the building and paid selling expenses totaling $1,200. What was the sales price and the contract price in this transaction?

	Sales Price	Contract Price
A.	$6,000	$12,000
B.	$18,000	$10,000
C.	$18,000	$8,000
D.	$18,000	$6,000

Answer (C) is correct. *(SEE, adapted)*
REQUIRED: The sales price and contract price in an installment sale transaction.
DISCUSSION: The sales price includes any cash paid, relief of seller's liability by buyer, and any installment note given by the buyer. Here, the sales price is $18,000 ($12,000 relief of liability + $6,000 installment note). The contract price is the total amount the seller will ultimately collect from the buyer. However, if an existing mortgage assumed by the buyer exceeds the adjusted basis of the property, such excess (reduced by selling expenses) is treated as a payment and must be included both in the contract price and in the first year's payment received. The contract price is $8,000 ($6,000 note + $3,200 mortgage in excess of basis – $1,200 selling expenses).
Answer (A) is incorrect. The sales price includes the mortgage assumed and the installment note, and the contract price includes the installment note plus the amount of the mortgage in excess of the property's basis, less the selling expenses. Answer (B) is incorrect. The contract price includes the installment note plus the amount of the mortgage in excess of the property's basis, less the selling expenses. Answer (D) is incorrect. The contract price is not $6,000 in this transaction.

19.5.3. For the current year, the installment method may not be used for

A. Sales of personal property (except farm property) by dealers who regularly sell this type of personal property on an installment plan.

B. Sales of real property (except farm property and certain sales of residential lots or timeshares) held by a dealer for sale in the ordinary course of business.

C. Sales of personal property (except farm property) by dealers who regularly sell this type of personal property on an installment plan or sales of real property (except farm property and certain sales of residential lots or timeshares) held by a dealer for sale in the ordinary course of business.

D. None of the answers are correct.

Answer (C) is correct. *(Publisher, adapted)*
REQUIRED: The transactions for which the installment method of accounting is disallowed.
DISCUSSION: Under current law, use of the installment method is usually disallowed for dispositions of property by dealers [Sec. 453(b)(2)]. This includes any disposition of (1) personal property, if the person regularly sells such personal property on the installment plan, and (2) real property held by the taxpayer for sale to customers in the ordinary course of his or her trade or business. Exceptions are made for property used or produced in the trade or business of farming, and, if so elected, sales of residential lots or timeshares, subject to interest payments on the deferred tax [Sec. 453(l)].
Answer (A) is incorrect. The installment method may not be used for sales of real property (except farm property and certain sales of residential lots or timeshares) held by a dealer for sale in the ordinary course of business. Answer (B) is incorrect. The installment method may not be used for sales of personal property (except farm property) by dealers who regularly sell this type of personal property on an installment plan. Answer (D) is incorrect. Both scenarios are excluded from use of the installment method.

19.5.4. In an installment sale, if the buyer assumes a mortgage that is greater than the installment sale basis of the property sold,

A. There is never a profit or a loss.

B. The transaction is disqualified as an installment sale.

C. The gross profit percentage is always 100%.

D. The gain is treated as short-term capital gain.

Answer (C) is correct. *(SEE, adapted)*
REQUIRED: The statement that applies when a buyer assumes a mortgage greater than the installment sale basis of the property sold.
DISCUSSION: In an installment sale when the buyer assumes a mortgage that is greater than the basis of the asset, the seller is required to recognize the excess mortgage as a payment in year of sale and also increase the contract price by the amount of the excess. If the contract price were not increased, the gross profit percentage would be greater than 100%. The amount of increase in the contract price will make the contract price equal to the gross profit, thus giving a gross profit percentage of 100%.
Answer (A) is incorrect. The installment sale may give rise to a profit or loss. Answer (B) is incorrect. The presented circumstance does not prevent the sale from qualifying as an installment sale. Answer (D) is incorrect. Any gain realized from a disposal of recaptured property in an installment sale is characterized as ordinary income by Secs. 1245 and 1250.

19.5.5. All of the following statements concerning "unstated interest" are true except

A. If you use the installment method for reporting your gain on a sale, both the selling price and the contract price must be reduced by any unstated interest.

B. If an installment sale with some or all of the payments due more than 1 year after the date of the sale does not provide for interest, a part of each payment due more than 6 months after the date of the sale will be treated as interest.

C. If the unstated interest rules apply, both the buyer and the seller must treat a part of the installment sale price as interest.

D. Unstated interest does not affect the amount of the gain.

Answer (D) is correct. *(SEE, adapted)*
REQUIRED: The statement concerning "unstated interest" that is false.
DISCUSSION: Section 483 indicates how unstated interest is accounted for by a purchaser and a seller. Total unstated interest equals the excess of the sum of the payments due under a contract to which Sec. 483 applies over the sum of the present values of the contract and interest payments due under the contract [Sec. 483(b)]. Regulation 1.483-2(a) requires unstated interest to be excluded from the selling price for the property. Therefore, the amount of the gain realized on the sale is affected by the unstated interest, and this answer choice is false.
Unstated interest affects the contract price and selling price when using the installment method. The Sec. 483 imputed interest rules apply only to payments on account of a sale or exchange of property due more than 6 months after the date of the sale provided some or all of the payments are due more than 1 year after the sale or exchange. The Sec. 483 imputed interest rules apply to buyer and seller alike.
Answer (A) is incorrect. If you use the installment method for reporting your gain on a sale, both the selling price and the contract price must be reduced by an unstated interest. Answer (B) is incorrect. If an installment sale with some or all of the payments due more than 1 year after the date of the sale does not provide for interest, a part of each payment due more than 6 months after the date of the sale will be treated as interest. Answer (C) is incorrect. If the unstated interest rules apply, both the buyer and the seller must treat a part of the installment sale price as interest.

19.5.6. During Year 1, Frank, a cash-basis taxpayer, sold a piece of land that had an adjusted basis to him of $110,000 to Tony for $200,000. Tony paid $50,000 down and agreed to pay $30,000 per year plus interest for the next 5 years beginning in January of Year 2. Frank incurred selling expenses of $10,000. What is the amount of gain to be included in Frank's gross income for Year 1?

A. $18,000

B. $20,000

C. $22,500

D. $32,000

Answer (B) is correct. *(SEE, adapted)*
REQUIRED: The amount of gain in the year of an installment sale.
DISCUSSION: The amount of gain under Sec. 453 is the proportion of the payments received in the year that the gross profit bears to the total contract price. The contract price is the total amount the seller will ultimately collect from the buyer. M's gross profit is $80,000 ($200,000 sales price – $110,000 adjusted basis – $10,000 selling expenses). Since $50,000 was received in the year of sale, the gain is $20,000.

$$\frac{\$80,000 \text{ gross profit}}{\$200,000 \text{ contract price}} \times \$50,000 = \$20,000$$

Answer (A) is incorrect. The gross profit percentage is not 36%. Answer (C) is incorrect. The gross profit is reduced by the selling expenses. Answer (D) is incorrect. The gross profit percentage is not 64%.

19.5.7. Mr. A, a cash-basis taxpayer, sold his business in the current year for $120,000. The contract allocated $40,000 to inventory and $80,000 to real property. The book value of the inventory was $38,000. The real property had a cost of $40,000 and depreciation claimed on a straight-line basis was $20,000. In the current year, Mr. A received a down payment of $60,000 of which $40,000 was payment for the inventory. Mr. A had no other Sec. 1231 transactions. What is the amount and nature of the gain that Mr. A should report in the current year using the installment method?

A. $40,000 ordinary income, $60,000 capital gain.

B. $68,000 ordinary income, $10,000 capital gain.

C. $2,000 ordinary income, $20,000 capital gain.

D. $2,000 ordinary income, $15,000 capital gain.

Answer (D) is correct. *(SEE, adapted)*
REQUIRED: The amount and nature of the gain under the installment method.
DISCUSSION: An installment sale is a disposition of property in which at least one payment is to be received after the close of the taxable year in which the disposition occurs. However, sales of inventory consisting of personal property are not installment sales as a general rule [Sec. 453(b)(2)]. A's sale of inventory produces $2,000 of ordinary income ($40,000 – $38,000).

The sale of the real property was an installment sale. Under the installment method, income recognized for any year from a disposition is that proportion of the payments received in that year that the gross profit bears to the total contract price. A's gross profit is $60,000 ($80,000 selling price – $20,000 adjusted basis). The contract price is the total amount the seller will ultimately collect from the purchaser ($80,000). The gain is Sec. 1231 gain since straight-line depreciation was used. In the current year, Mr. A should report Sec. 1231 gain of $15,000.

$$\frac{\$60,000 \text{ gross profit}}{\$80,000 \text{ contract price}} \times \$20,000 = \$15,000$$

Assuming no other transactions involving Sec. 1231 occurred in the current year, the gain is capital gain and goes in the 25% long-term capital gain basket.
Answer (A) is incorrect. The installment method of accounting cannot be used when reporting the inventory sale but can be used when reporting the real property sale. Answer (B) is incorrect. Mr. A does not have $68,000 of ordinary income and a $10,000 capital gain. Answer (C) is incorrect. Mr. A does not have a $20,000 capital gain.

19.5.8. On August 1 of the current year, Roger Company sold machinery used in its business for a total price of $20,000, payable in four equal annual installments of principal plus interest at 10%. The first payment was due and paid on December 31 of the current year. At the time of the sale, Roger had a $4,000 basis in the machinery and $8,000 Sec. 1245 depreciation recapture potential. There were no other Sec. 1231 transactions, and Roger Company had no unrecaptured Sec. 1231 losses from prior years. Ignoring the interest income, what amount must Roger recognize in the current year?

A. $4,000 ordinary income.

B. $8,000 ordinary income and $4,000 capital gain.

C. $8,000 ordinary income and $2,000 capital gain.

D. $8,000 ordinary income and $8,000 capital gain.

Answer (C) is correct. *(Publisher, adapted)*
REQUIRED: The amount and character of gain that must be recognized under the installment method on the sale of depreciable property.
DISCUSSION: Section 453(i) requires full recognition of depreciation recapture in the year of sale regardless of payments. Any amounts treated as ordinary income by reason of the recapture provisions are added to the basis of the property for determining gain or loss. The total gain is $16,000 ($20,000 selling price – $4,000 basis). Therefore, Roger must recognize the full $8,000 of Sec. 1245 depreciation recapture as ordinary income in the current year.

This amount is added to the basis for determining the remaining installment gain or loss. The revised gain is thus $8,000 ($20,000 selling price – $12,000 adjusted basis). The gross profit percentage is 40% ($8,000 gross profit ÷ $20,000 contract price). This percentage will be applied to each of the four equal annual payments to determine the amount of Sec. 1231 capital gain for each year. For the current year, the capital gain is $2,000 [($20,000 ÷ 4) × 40%]. If Roger Company had any unrecaptured Sec. 1231 losses in the 5 prior years, this gain would be ordinary to the extent of those losses.
Answer (A) is incorrect. It would not be correct for Roger to recognize $4,000 of ordinary income in the current year. Answer (B) is incorrect. Roger does not have a $4,000 capital gain. Answer (D) is incorrect. Roger does not have a capital gain of $8,000.

Questions 19.5.9 and 19.5.10 are based on the following information. L.E. operates an accounting service as a sole proprietorship. For income tax purposes, he reports on the cash and calendar-year bases. During Year 3, L.E. received the following receipts in connection with his business, which was his only source of income:

Cash collected for services:		
Rendered in Year 2	$ 2,000	
Rendered in Year 3	90,000	
To be rendered in Year 4	5,000	$97,000
Cash collection on land contract:		
Principal	$40,000	
Interest (14%)	2,000	$42,000

L.E. acquired the land at a cost of $30,000 in Year 1 for future use as a building site. However, the land was never developed and L.E. sold it on March 18, Year 3, for $60,000, with $20,000 of principal payments deferred until Year 4. The $20,000 deferred payment is evidenced by a negotiable note with a fair market value of $20,000.

19.5.9. If L.E. makes no tax elections applicable to Year 3, what amount of gross income must he report for Year 3?

A. $114,000

B. $119,000

C. $134,000

D. $139,000

Answer (B) is correct. *(E. Grams)*
REQUIRED: The amount of gross income for Year 3.
DISCUSSION: A cash-basis taxpayer generally reports income attributable to services in the taxable year cash is received. The installment method applies to this sale of land because L.E. did not elect otherwise. Income recognized under the installment method is determined by applying the gross profit percentage ($30,000 gross profit ÷ $60,000 contract price = 50%) to the amount of payments received during the taxable year. L.E.'s gross income for Year 3 is

Income from services	$ 97,000
Interest income	2,000
Installment sale income ($40,000 × 50%)	20,000
Gross income	$119,000

Answer (A) is incorrect. The amount of $5,000 cash collected for services to be rendered in Year 4 should be included in gross income. Answer (C) is incorrect. Gross income includes cash collected for services to be rendered in Year 4 and only one-half of the installment sales income. Answer (D) is incorrect. Gross income includes only one-half of the installment sales income.

19.5.10. Assume that on December 31, Year 3, uncollected billings for Year 3 services amounted to $9,000. At that date, no accrued interest was uncollected. What amount of gross income must L.E. report for Year 3 if he is an accrual rather than a cash-basis taxpayer?

A. $112,000

B. $121,000

C. $126,000

D. $139,000

Answer (B) is correct. *(E. Grams)*
REQUIRED: The gross income of an accrual-basis taxpayer.
DISCUSSION: An accrual-basis taxpayer generally reports income in the taxable year the right to receive the income becomes fixed. An accrual-basis taxpayer must generally report advance payments of income in the year received under the "claim of right" doctrine. However, Rev. Proc. 71-21 allows the income from services to be reported when earned if all of the services are required to be performed by the end of the tax year following the year of receipt. Accordingly, the $5,000 for services to be rendered in Year 4 can be reported in Year 4.

L.E. already reported the $2,000 of income for services rendered in Year 2. The Tax Relief Extension Act of 1999 prohibited the use of the installment method by accrual-basis taxpayers. However, the Installment Tax Correction Act of 2000 retroactively repealed the prohibition. Therefore, an accrual-basis taxpayer may use the installment method unless he elects otherwise (which he did not). L.E.'s gross income is

Income accrued for Year 3 services	$ 9,000
Income received for Year 3 services	90,000
Interest income	2,000
Installment sale income ($40,000 × 50%)	20,000
Gross income	$121,000

Answer (A) is incorrect. Gross income includes the income accrued for Year 3 services. Answer (C) is incorrect. The $5,000 for services to be rendered in Year 4 is included in Year 4's gross income. Answer (D) is incorrect. Gross income should include only one-half of the installment sale income and should include $2,000 of interest income earned on the installment sale.

19.5.11. In the current year, Mr. U sold property with an adjusted basis to him of $1,000 for $10,000. The sales agreement called for a down payment of $1,000 and payments of $1,500 in each of the next 6 years to be made from an irrevocable escrow account, established by the buyer, that contains the balance of the purchase price plus interest. What is the amount of gain Mr. U should report on his current-year return?

A. $9,000

B. $1,350

C. $1,000

D. $900

Answer (A) is correct. *(SEE, adapted)*
REQUIRED: The amount of gain to be reported in the year of an installment sale when the remaining payments are escrowed.
DISCUSSION: An installment sale is a disposition of property in which at least one payment has to be received after the close of the tax year in which the disposition occurs. Funds can be escrowed provided they are still the property of the purchaser and can revert to the purchaser. But if the escrow is irrevocable, then the seller really has the right to the funds. Therefore, Mr. U will be treated as having received all $10,000 in the year of sale and must report a gain of $9,000 ($10,000 sales price – $1,000 basis) in the current year.
Answer (B) is incorrect. The amount of $1,350 is the gross profit percentage of 90% multiplied by the payment amounts for future years. Answer (C) is incorrect. The amount of $1,000 is the down payment received. Answer (D) is incorrect. The amount recognized in the year of sale if the escrow was not irrevocable would be $900.

19.5.12. In Year 1, Ray sold land with a basis of $40,000 for $100,000. He received a $20,000 down payment and the buyer's note for $80,000. In Year 2, he received the first of four annual payments of $20,000 each, plus 12% interest. What is the gain to be reported in Year 1?

A. None.

B. $8,000

C. $12,000

D. $20,000

Answer (C) is correct. *(SEE, adapted)*
REQUIRED: The amount of gain reported on an installment sale.
DISCUSSION: The transaction qualifies for treatment as an installment sale. The amount of gain under Sec. 453 is the proportion of the payments received in the year that the gross profit bears to the total contract price. The contract price is the total amount the seller will ultimately collect from the buyer. Ray's gross profit is $60,000 ($100,000 sales price – $40,000 adjusted basis). Since $20,000 was received in Year 1, the gain is $12,000.

$$\frac{\$60,000 \text{ gross profit}}{\$100,000 \text{ contract price}} \times \$20,000 = \$12,000$$

Answer (A) is incorrect. A gain must be reported on the sale. Answer (B) is incorrect. It is the amount of the payment that is considered a return of capital. Answer (D) is incorrect. Only the portion that is not a return of capital must be reported as a gain. This portion is determined by calculating the gross profit percentage.

19.5.13. Jake sold an office building in Year 1 on the installment method for $5.5 million. At the end of Year 2, he is still owed $4.9 million on the debt from the sale. In which situation will Jake have to pay interest on the deferred tax of his Year 2 sales if they are all installment sales with no payments in Year 2?

A. In Year 2 he sells a rental duplex for $160,000.

B. In Year 2 he sells a rental duplex for $150,000 and an apartment complex for $4.9 million.

C. In Year 2 he sells a rental duplex for $160,000 and an apartment complex for $4.9 million.

D. More than one of the answers are correct.

Answer (C) is correct. *(Publisher, adapted)*
REQUIRED: The situation in which interest is required to be paid on the deferred tax on installment sales.
DISCUSSION: Interest is charged under Sec. 453A on the deferred tax of nondealer installment sales of over $150,000 involving any type property. Excluded is personal use property, property produced or used in the trade or business of farming, time shares and residential lots. The interest is only charged if the obligation is outstanding at the end of the year and the taxpayer has nondealer installment receivables totaling over $5 million at the end of the year from sales of property described above that occur during the year. If in Year 2 Jake sells a rental duplex for $160,000 and an apartment complex for $4.9 million, his Year 2 installment sales (in receivables at year end) will exceed $5 million. Therefore, the interest will be charged on the deferred tax.
Answer (A) is incorrect. Jake would not have installment receivables at year end from Year 2 sales in excess of $5 million. The receivable from the property sold in Year 1 does not count toward the $5 million minimum. Answer (B) is incorrect. Sales of property for $150,000 or less are not counted toward the $5 million minimum; therefore, Jake would have receivables from appropriate Year 2 sales of only $4.9 million. Answer (D) is incorrect. Only one answer is correct.

19.5.14. Robert, a calendar-year taxpayer, sells an office building in the current year for $9 million, receiving $1 million cash in the current year and a note for $8 million. Assume Robert's gross profit percentage is 30% and the Sec. 6621 rate for underpayments is 10% in December of the current year. Assume that the highest tax rate for individuals in the current year is 40%. What is the interest on the deferred tax for the current year?

A. $0

B. $36,000

C. $40,500

D. $96,000

Answer (B) is correct. *(Publisher, adapted)*
REQUIRED: The interest on the deferred tax for the current year.
DISCUSSION: Interest is computed each year at the underpayment rate of Sec. 6621 that is in effect for the month in which the tax year ends. The interest is computed on the "applicable percentage" of the deferred tax. The applicable percentage is equal to the total face amount (not the balance) of receivables from the current year outstanding at year end in excess of $5 million divided by the total face amount of receivables outstanding at year end from current year sales. The deferred tax is the amount of gain not recognized as of the end of the year multiplied by the highest tax rate applicable to the taxpayer.
At the end of the current year, Robert's deferred taxes are $960,000 ($8 million × 30% gross profit × 40% tax rate). The applicable percentage is 37.5% ($3 million ÷ $8 million). The interest for the current year is $36,000 ($960,000 × 37.5% × 10% interest rate).
Answer (A) is incorrect. There is interest owed on the deferred tax liability in the current year. Answer (C) is incorrect. Deferred taxes are not calculated using $9 million. Answer (D) is incorrect. The $96,000 interest amount must be multiplied by the applicable percentage.

19.5.15. When property (other than marketable securities) is sold to a related person on the installment method, which of the following will cause the seller to recognize the remainder of the gain on the installment obligation before all payments are received?

A. The seller dies.

B. The buyer dies.

C. The buyer resells the property more than 2 years later.

D. The buyer gives the property away within 2 years of the installment sale.

Answer (D) is correct. *(Publisher, adapted)*
REQUIRED: The event for which income recognition from an installment obligation will be accelerated.
DISCUSSION: To prevent intermediary sales on an installment basis to related parties followed by other dispositions, Sec. 453(e) requires the amount realized on a second disposition of property to be treated as received by the person who made the first installment sale to a related party. This rule also applies to a disposition by gift. When the buyer gives the property away, the FMV of the property is deemed realized by the original seller to accelerate the installment obligation.
Answer (A) is incorrect. The death of the seller generally does not accelerate the installment obligation. Answer (B) is incorrect. The death of the buyer generally does not accelerate the installment obligation. Answer (C) is incorrect. The second disposition rule does not apply to dispositions more than 2 years after the first installment sale, except for marketable securities.

19.5.16. With respect to the disposition of an installment obligation, which of the following is false?

A. No gain or loss is recognized on the transfer of an installment obligation between a husband and wife if incident to a divorce.

B. If the obligation is sold, the gain or loss is the difference between the basis in the obligation and the amount realized.

C. A gift of an installment obligation is considered a disposition.

D. If an installment obligation is canceled, it is not treated as a disposition.

Answer (D) is correct. *(SEE, adapted)*
REQUIRED: The incorrect statement with respect to the disposition of an installment obligation.
DISCUSSION: Section 453B provides that, when an installment obligation is disposed of, gain or loss is recognized to the extent of the difference between the basis of the obligation and the amount realized (or the fair market value of the obligation if disposed of other than by sale or exchange). The main purpose of Sec. 453B is to prevent the shifting of income between taxpayers. Section 453B(a) expressly requires recognition whether the obligation is sold or otherwise disposed of. Cancelation of an installment obligation is a disposition of the obligation.
Answer (A) is incorrect. Section 453B(g) excludes from the definition of a disposition a transfer between husband and wife incident to a divorce. The same tax treatment with respect to the obligation that would have applied to the transferor then applies to the transferee. Answer (B) is incorrect. The gain or loss on sale of an installment obligation is the difference between the amount realized and the basis in the obligation. Answer (C) is incorrect. A gift is a disposition for purposes of Sec. 453B.

19.5.17. Last year, Ricardo sold a piece of unimproved real estate to Cliff for $20,000. Ricardo acquired the property 15 years ago at a cost of $10,000. Last year, Ricardo received $4,000 cash and Cliff's note in the amount of $16,000 for the remainder of the selling price, payable in subsequent years. Ricardo reported the sale using the installment method. This year, before Cliff made any further payments, Ricardo sold the note for $15,000 in cash. What is the amount of gain or (loss) Ricardo should report on this year's tax return?

A. $(1,000)

B. $0

C. $7,000

D. $9,000

Answer (C) is correct. *(SEE, adapted)*
REQUIRED: The income recognized on the disposition of an installment obligation.
DISCUSSION: Section 453B provides that, when an installment obligation is disposed of, gain or loss is recognized to the extent of the difference between the basis of the obligation and the amount realized (or the fair market value of the obligation if disposed of other than by sale or exchange). The adjusted basis of the obligation is equal to the face amount of the obligation reduced by the gross profit that would be realized if the holder collected the face amount [Sec. 453B(b)]. The basis is $8,000 [$16,000 face amount × (100% − 50% gross profit percentage)].
Since Ricardo sold the installment obligation, the excess of the amount realized over Ricardo's basis in the obligation is recognized as income on the transfer. This amount of income is $7,000 ($15,000 amount realized − $8,000 basis). The gain is treated as resulting from the sale or exchange of the property in respect of which the installment obligation was originally held.
Answer (A) is incorrect. Ricardo's basis in the note is $8,000 and not the note's $16,000 face amount. Answer (B) is incorrect. A gain should be reported this year. Answer (D) is incorrect. The gain reported on the collection of the $4,000 of cash was reported last year.

19.5.18. In Year 1, Neptune sold his lakefront lot in which he had a basis of $14,000 on the installment method for $28,000. Neptune received $8,000 in Year 1 and $1,000 in Year 2 before having to repossess the land after payments stopped. What is Neptune's gain on the repossession?

A. $0

B. $5,000

C. $6,000

D. $10,000

Answer (B) is correct. *(Publisher, adapted)*
REQUIRED: The gain on repossession of real property that was sold under the installment method.
DISCUSSION: Section 1038(b) provides that, on the repossession of real property that was sold on the installment method, gain is recognized to the extent the payments received prior to the repossession exceed the gain on the property reported in periods prior to the repossession. This gain is limited to the total gain realized on the sale of the property, less the gain recognized in prior periods.
Neptune's gain on the repossession is $5,000 ($9,000 received prior to repossession − $4,000 recognized gain in Year 1). The limitation is $10,000 ($14,000 gain realized in Year 1 − $4,000 recognized in Year 1), which does not apply because it is greater than the gain computed.
Answer (A) is incorrect. Neptune has a gain on the repossession. Answer (C) is incorrect. The gain recognized in Year 1 was not $3,000. Answer (D) is incorrect. The amount of $10,000 is the limitation, which does not apply to this situation since it exceeds the calculated gain.

19.5.19. Four years ago, Mr. B sold his personal property on contract for $200,000, which resulted in a capital gain of $100,000. Mr. B properly elected to use the installment method of reporting and through last year had collected $40,000 on the contract. At the start of this year, the buyer defaulted on the contract, and Mr. B repossessed the property. At the time of repossession, the property had a fair market value of $160,000. What is the gain or loss to be reported on the repossession?

A. $20,000 capital gain.

B. $60,000 ordinary income.

C. $80,000 capital gain.

D. $100,000 capital gain.

Answer (C) is correct. *(SEE, adapted)*
REQUIRED: The amount and character of gain (loss) on the repossession of personal property by a taxpayer who uses the installment method.
DISCUSSION: Under Sec. 453B(f)(1), a taxpayer recognizes a gain or loss (capital if the asset was capital) on the repossession of property sold on the installment method. The gain or loss is the difference between the fair market value of the repossessed property and basis of the obligations of the purchaser so satisfied.

Fair market value of property		$160,000
Less: Balance of contract due	$160,000	
Unrealized profit (50%)	(80,000)	
Basis of contract		(80,000)
Capital gain on repossession		$ 80,000

Answer (A) is incorrect. The figure $20,000 is not the correct amount of capital gain on the repossession. Answer (B) is incorrect. The amount of $60,000 in ordinary income is not reported on the repossession. Answer (D) is incorrect. The amount of $100,000 is the total capital gain resulting from the personal property sale.

19.5.20. Manufacturers of tangible personal property may use the installment method to report income from sales to their dealers.

A. True.

B. False.

Answer (B) is correct. *(Publisher, adapted)*
DISCUSSION: The Taxpayer Relief Act of 1997 repealed the special provision that allowed manufacturers of tangible personal property to use the installment method to report income from sales to their dealers.

19.5.21. Mrs. L sold a business asset with an adjusted basis of $50,000 encumbered with a $25,000 mortgage. The buyer agreed to pay Mrs. L $100,000 over the next 5 years and in addition assumes the mortgage on the property. The contract price is $100,000.

A. True.

B. False.

Answer (A) is correct. *(SEE, adapted)*
DISCUSSION: Under Sec. 453, the contract price is generally the total amount the seller will ultimately collect from the purchaser. Regulation 15A.453-1(b)(2)(iii) provides that an existing mortgage assumed by the buyer is only included in the contract price to the extent that it exceeds the basis of the property. Since the mortgage assumed by the buyer does not exceed the adjusted basis of the property, the contract price is $100,000.

19.5.22. Last year, Mr. L, a calendar-year taxpayer, sold his motorcycle with an adjusted basis of $500 for $700. He agreed to accept a lump-sum payment payable this year. The gain on this sale qualifies for the installment method of reporting.

A. True.

B. False.

Answer (A) is correct. *(SEE, adapted)*
DISCUSSION: Under Sec. 453(b), an installment sale is a disposition of property where at least one payment is to be received after the close of the taxable year in which the disposition occurs. Since Mr. L will receive one payment this year, this sale qualifies for the installment method. Mr. L must elect to have the installment method not apply.

19.5.23. Y, a dealer regularly engaged in the sale of personal property on a revolving credit plan, may report his income from such sales in the current year on the installment method, regardless of the selling price of the products sold or the amount collected in the year of sale.

A. True.

B. False.

Answer (B) is correct. *(SEE, adapted)*
DISCUSSION: Section 453(k) provides that any disposition of personal property under a revolving credit plan may not be reported under the installment method for tax years beginning after 1986. Section 453(b) excludes dealer dispositions of personal property from using the installment method.

19.5.24. Upon disposition of an installment obligation, any gain or loss recognized will always be ordinary income.

A. True.

B. False.

Answer (B) is correct. *(SEE, adapted)*
DISCUSSION: Section 453B(a) provides that any gain or loss on the disposition of an installment obligation is considered as resulting from the sale or exchange of the property for which the installment obligation was received. The character of the gain (loss) will be determined by the kind of property for which the installment obligation was issued.

19.5.25. The cancelation of an installment obligation resulting from the sale of personal property is treated as a disposition other than by sale or exchange. The gain or loss is the difference between the basis of the obligation and the fair market value of the repossessed property resulting in the cancelation of the indebtedness at the time of the cancelation.

A. True.

B. False.

Answer (A) is correct. *(SEE, adapted)*
DISCUSSION: Under Sec. 453B(f)(1), a vendor who is not a manufacturer recognizes a gain or loss on the repossession of personal property sold on the installment method. The gain or loss is the difference between the fair market value of the repossessed property and the basis of the obligation of the purchaser so satisfied. The repossession of real property comes under a different set of rules that may be found in Sec. 1038.

19.5.26. Mr. B sells to Mrs. B an automobile on which part of his realized gain is Sec. 1245 gain. The property will be used in Mrs. B's sole proprietorship. The installment method of accounting does not apply to the sale.

A. True.

B. False.

Answer (B) is correct. *(Publisher, adapted)*

DISCUSSION: The installment method of accounting applies to the sale in question. The controlled entity sale rules of Sec. 453(g)(1) do not apply since a husband and wife are not related parties under the Sec. 1239(b) related party definition. However, even though the installment method of accounting applies to the sale, the realized gain able to be reported using the installment method is reduced by all recapture income (e.g., Sec. 1245 income) that must be recognized in the year of sale [Sec. 453(i)(1)]. Only gain realized in excess of the recapture income, if any, is reported using the installment method.

19.6 Inventories

19.6.1. Which of the following is the most important principle in valuing inventories?

A. Generally accepted accounting principles.

B. Clear reflection of income.

C. Lower of cost or market.

D. Full absorption costing.

Answer (B) is correct. *(Publisher, adapted)*

REQUIRED: The overriding principle in valuing inventories.

DISCUSSION: Regulation 1.471-2(a) provides that the method of valuing inventory must conform as nearly as possible to the best accounting practice in the trade or business, and it must clearly reflect income. Courts have held that the overriding concern is the clear reflection of income. Conformity to the best accounting practice is considered only a method of achieving a clear reflection of income. The inventory practice should also be consistent from year to year to clearly reflect income.

Answer (A) is incorrect. Generally accepted accounting principles are an important factor in valuing inventories, but the clear reflection of income overrides it. Answer (C) is incorrect. Lower of cost or market is merely a method of valuing inventory, not an overriding principle. Answer (D) is incorrect. Full absorption costing is merely a method of valuing inventory, not an overriding principle.

19.6.2. The uniform capitalization rules apply to all of the following business-related costs except

A. Direct materials costs.

B. Indirect costs.

C. Interest on debt to finance the production of real or tangible personal property with a class life of 20 years or more.

D. Marketing, selling, advertising, and distribution costs.

Answer (D) is correct. *(SEE, adapted)*

REQUIRED: The business-related costs to which the uniform capitalization rules do not apply.

DISCUSSION: For costs incurred after 1986, Sec. 263A establishes a uniform set of rules requiring the capitalization of certain previously deductible production costs. Marketing, selling, advertising, and distribution costs are period costs and are not capitalized.

Answer (A) is incorrect. Direct costs must be capitalized. Answer (B) is incorrect. A proper share of indirect costs (including taxes) allocable to property must be capitalized. Answer (C) is incorrect. Interest is capitalized if it is paid or incurred during the production period and is allocable to property produced by the taxpayer.

19.6.3. Which of the following would not be subject to the uniform capitalization rules?

A. Real property or tangible personal property that an individual produces for sale to customers.

B. Tangible personal property that an individual produces for use in a trade or business or profit-making activity.

C. Personal property acquired for resale if an individual has average annual gross receipts of more than $10 million.

D. Property produced under a long-term contract.

Answer (D) is correct. *(SEE, adapted)*

REQUIRED: The property that would be subject to the uniform capitalization rules.

DISCUSSION: Under Sec. 263A(b)(1), the uniform capitalization rules apply to real or tangible personal property produced by the taxpayer. Property produced for the taxpayer's own use is excepted, unless the use is in a trade or business or an activity conducted for profit [Sec. 263A(c)(1)]. The exception for personal property acquired for resale applies only when average annual gross receipts are $10 million or less [Sec. 263A(b)(2)(B)]. Generally, the percentage-of-completion method applies to long-term contracts. Section 263A does not apply to any property produced pursuant to a long-term contract [Sec. 263A(c)(4)].

Answer (A) is incorrect. It is specifically included under Sec. 263A(b)(1). Answer (B) is incorrect. Tangible personal property is excluded only when it is not used in a trade or business or profit-making activity. Answer (C) is incorrect. The exception for personal property acquired for resale applies only when average annual gross receipts are $10 million or less.

19.6.4. Mr. French developed a widget at a total cost of $5 million to be used in his business. The widget has an estimated production period of 4 years. Mr. French incurred interest on a $3 million loan, the proceeds of which were used to develop the widget. He also incurred interest on $6 million of other business debt. What is the amount of debt on which interest must be capitalized for the development of Mr. French's widget?

A. $6,000,000

B. $5,000,000

C. $3,000,000

D. $0

Answer (B) is correct. *(SEE, adapted)*
REQUIRED: The amount of debt on which interest must be capitalized for the construction of property to be used by the taxpayer.
DISCUSSION: When assets are built for a taxpayer's own use, the taxpayer must capitalize production costs and recover them as depreciation deductions over the useful life of the asset. Interest is capitalized only if it is paid or incurred during the production period and is allocable to property produced by the taxpayer. Such property must have a long useful life, an estimated production period over 2 years, or an estimated production period over 1 year and a cost of over $1 million [Sec. 263A(f)]. This applies to interest directly attributable to production expenditures plus interest on any other indebtedness that could have been avoided if the production expenditure had not been incurred.
The interest on Mr. Jones's $3 million loan plus $2 million of other debt, which could have been paid off, for a total of $5 million, must be capitalized.
Answer (A) is incorrect. The total amount of other business debt is $6,000,000. Answer (C) is incorrect. The amount of $3,000,000 of other debt, which could have been paid off, is also included. Answer (D) is incorrect. There is an amount of debt on which interest must be capitalized.

19.6.5. Which of the following occupations or businesses would generally not be required to use inventories in determining gross profit?

1. Manufacturer of toys
2. Doctors
3. Grocery store
4. Painters
5. Clothing store

A. 1 and 3.

B. 1, 2, and 5.

C. 2 and 4.

D. 4 and 5.

Answer (C) is correct. *(SEE, adapted)*
REQUIRED: The businesses generally not required to use inventories in determining gross profit.
DISCUSSION: Regulation 1.471-1 provides that inventories at the beginning and end of each taxable year are necessary in every case in which the production, purchase, or sale of merchandise is an income-producing factor. The production, purchase, or sale of merchandise is not an income-producing factor for doctors or painters.
Answer (A) is incorrect. A toy manufacturer and a grocery store would generally be required to use inventories in determining gross profit. Answer (B) is incorrect. A toy manufacturer and a clothing store would generally be required to use inventories in determining gross profit. Answer (D) is incorrect. A clothing store would generally be required to use inventories in determining gross profit.

19.6.6. Which of the following items is not included in inventory?

A. Raw material.

B. Goods you received on consignment.

C. Work in process.

D. Finished goods.

Answer (B) is correct. *(SEE, adapted)*
REQUIRED: The item that is not included in inventory.
DISCUSSION: Regulation 1.471-1 provides that inventory should include all finished goods, work in process, and raw materials and supplies that will physically become a part of merchandise intended for sale. Merchandise should be included in inventory only if title thereto is vested in the taxpayer. In the case of goods received by the taxpayer on consignment, the title remains with the consignor and the goods are not included in inventory.
Answer (A) is incorrect. Raw material is included in inventory. Answer (C) is incorrect. Work in process is included in inventory. Answer (D) is incorrect. Finished goods are included in inventory.

19.6.7. Mr. Cheta owns a retail hardware store. Which of the following should be included in his ending inventory?

A. Envelopes and stationery not held for sale.

B. Lawnmower sold but not yet delivered.

C. Shipment of nails purchased f.o.b. supplier but still in transit.

D. Small power tools rented to customers.

Answer (C) is correct. *(SEE, adapted)*
REQUIRED: The item(s) included in a retail hardware store owner's ending inventory.
DISCUSSION: Regulation 1.471-1 provides that inventory should include all merchandise if title thereto is vested in the taxpayer. The title to items shipped f.o.b. supplier transfers to the purchaser as soon as the items leave the supplier. Therefore, Mr. Cheta has title to the shipment of nails.
Answer (A) is incorrect. The envelopes and stationery were not acquired for sale. Answer (B) is incorrect. The title has been transferred to the purchaser. Answer (D) is incorrect. The small power tools are not intended for sale.

19.6.8. Which of the following inventory practices is not acceptable for tax purposes?

A. The LIFO method of identifying inventory.

B. Deducting a reserve for price changes in the value of the inventory.

C. Lower of cost or market method of valuing inventory.

D. Specific cost identification method of inventory valuation.

Answer (B) is correct. *(SEE, adapted)*
    REQUIRED: The inventory practice that is not acceptable for tax purposes.
    DISCUSSION: The method of valuing inventory must conform as nearly as possible to the best accounting practice in the trade or industry, and it must clearly reflect income [Reg. 1.471-2(a)]. Regulation 1.471-2(f) gives examples of unacceptable methods of valuing inventory. One is deducting a reserve for price changes from inventory or estimating shrinkage on the value of inventory. However, the taxpayer may accrue inventory shrinkage if (s)he conducts regular and consistent physical inventory counts at each location where inventory is held and adjusts its shrinkage estimates and estimating methods to reflect the results of physical counts.
    Answer (A) is incorrect. The LIFO method of identifying inventory means "last in, first out" and is acceptable. Answer (C) is incorrect. The two basic methods of valuing inventory are to use cost and the lower of cost and market. Answer (D) is incorrect. The specific cost identification method is acceptable. It refers to actually identifying each item of inventory and the item's cost.

19.6.9. All of the following are acceptable in valuing inventory for federal income tax purposes except

A. Allocating indirect production costs to inventory by means of the manufacturing burden rate method.

B. Identifying direct material costs with particular units or groups of the product.

C. Allocating variable indirect production costs to cost of goods produced while treating fixed indirect production costs as currently deductible period costs.

D. Figuring cost of goods on hand by use of perpetual inventories when the account is charged with cost of goods purchased and credited with value of goods sold.

Answer (C) is correct. *(SEE, adapted)*
    REQUIRED: The method that is not acceptable for valuing inventory.
    DISCUSSION: Regulation 1.471-2(f) gives examples of unacceptable methods for valuing inventory. One is the allocation of only variable costs to cost of goods produced while treating fixed costs as period costs. This approach is commonly referred to as the "direct cost" method.
    Answer (A) is incorrect. Allocating indirect production costs to inventory by means of the manufacturing burden rate method is an acceptable method of valuing inventory. Answer (B) is incorrect. Identifying direct material costs with particular units or groups of the product is an acceptable method of valuing inventory. Answer (D) is incorrect. Figuring cost of goods on hand by use of perpetual inventories when the account is charged with cost of goods purchased and credited with value of goods sold is an acceptable method of valuing inventory.

19.6.10. All of the following costs must be included in valuing inventory using the full-absorption method except

A. Materials that become an integral part of the finished product.

B. Shift differential pay to production workers.

C. Payroll taxes related to production workers.

D. Research and experimentation costs.

Answer (D) is correct. *(SEE, adapted)*
    REQUIRED: The item that is not included in inventory under the full-absorption method.
    DISCUSSION: Under the full-absorption method of inventory costing, both direct and indirect production costs must be taken into account. Research and experimentation costs are not considered production costs [Reg. 1.263A-1(e)(3)(iii)(B)].
    Answer (A) is incorrect. Materials that become an integral part of the finished product is a direct production cost under Reg. 1.263A-1(e)(2)(i). Answer (B) is incorrect. Shift differential pay to production workers is a direct production cost under Reg. 1.263A-1(e)(2)(i). Answer (C) is incorrect. Payroll taxes related to production workers are a direct production cost under Reg. 1.263A-1(e)(2)(i).

19.6.11. For federal tax purposes, all of the following affect the cost of goods sold except

A. Cash discounts taken that are credited to a separate discount account.

B. Trade discounts taken.

C. Purchase returns and allowances.

D. Freight-in on raw materials.

Answer (A) is correct. *(SEE, adapted)*
    REQUIRED: The item that does not affect the cost of goods sold for federal tax purposes.
    DISCUSSION: Under Reg. 1.471-3(b), the cost of merchandise purchased during the taxable year includes the invoice price less trade or other discounts, except for strictly cash discounts that are deducted at the option of the taxpayer.
    Answer (B) is incorrect. Trade discounts do affect the cost of goods sold [Reg. 1.471-3(b)]. Answer (C) is incorrect. Purchase returns decrease the cost of goods on hand (inventory). Answer (D) is incorrect. The cost of raw materials includes transportation or other necessary charges incurred in acquiring possession of goods.

19.6.12. Ms. Zickert, a slot machine manufacturer, paid and incurred the following expenses during the year:

Raw materials	$75,000
Materials and supplies	8,000
Freight-in on raw materials	5,000
Freight on shipment of finished slot machines	6,000
Direct labor	40,000
Indirect labor	22,000
Allocable overhead expenses for production	28,000
Beginning inventory	40,000
Ending inventory	29,000

What was the amount of Ms. Zickert's cost of goods sold for the year?

A. $189,000

B. $195,000

C. $218,000

D. $224,000

Answer (A) is correct. *(Publisher, adapted)*
REQUIRED: The cost of goods sold for the year.
DISCUSSION: The cost of goods sold is calculated as follows:

Beginning inventory	$ 40,000
Add:	
Raw materials	75,000
Materials and supplies	8,000
Freight-in on raw materials	5,000
Direct labor	40,000
Indirect labor	22,000
Allocable overhead expenses for production	28,000
Less:	
Ending inventory	(29,000)
Cost of goods sold	$189,000

    Answer (B) is incorrect. The freight on shipment of finished slot machines is not included in the cost of goods sold calculation. Answer (C) is incorrect. The ending inventory must be subtracted to arrive at cost of goods sold. Answer (D) is incorrect. The freight on shipment of finished slot machines is not included in the cost of goods sold calculation, and the ending inventory must be subtracted to arrive at cost of goods sold.

19.6.13. Mr. B properly uses the lower-of-cost-or-market method of valuing his inventory. B's closing inventory for the current year consisted of the following:

Items	Cost	Market
L	$300	$500
M	200	100
N	650	250

What is the value of B's closing inventory?

A. $350

B. $650

C. $850

D. $1,150

Answer (B) is correct. *(SEE, adapted)*
REQUIRED: The value of inventory using the lower-of-cost-or-market method.
DISCUSSION: The two basic methods of valuing inventory are to use cost and lower of cost or market. When using the lower of cost or market, the cost and market value of each item on hand at the inventory date must be compared. It is not acceptable to value the entire inventory at cost and also at market and then use the lower of these two. The computation is below:

Items	Cost	Market	Lower of Cost or Market
L	$300	$500	$300
M	200	100	100
N	650	250	250
Total			$650

    Answer (A) is incorrect. The amount of $350 does not include the cost of Item L. Answer (C) is incorrect. Item L should be valued at cost. Answer (D) is incorrect. Items M and N should be valued at market value.

19.6.14. Mr. Y, who uses the LIFO method in computing his inventory, had 1,000 units left at the end of the current year. Based on the following information, what is the value of Y's inventory on December 31?

	Units	Cost per Unit	Market Value per Unit
Opening inventory	500	$2.00	$3.00
Current-year purchases			
9/25	1,500	3.00	3.00
11/15	1,000	4.00	5.00

A. $2,500

B. $3,000

C. $4,000

D. $5,000

Answer (A) is correct. *(SEE, adapted)*
REQUIRED: The value of ending inventory using the LIFO method.
DISCUSSION: The LIFO (last in, first out) method is a flow of goods assumption. The cost of goods sold under the LIFO method contains the costs of the most recently purchased units. The cost of the ending inventory contains the costs of the earlier acquired units. The ending inventory is $2,500 given 1,000 units on hand at December 31.

Date Purchased	Units	Price	Total
Opening Inventory	500	$2.00	$1,000
9/25 purchase	500	3.00	1,500
Ending inventory	1,000		$2,500

Note that a taxpayer who uses the LIFO method must value inventory at cost rather than at lower of cost or market.
    Answer (B) is incorrect. Opening inventory should be valued at cost, not market value. Answer (C) is incorrect. The amount of $4,000 would be the ending inventory balance under FIFO. Answer (D) is incorrect. The amount of $5,000 would be the ending inventory value if the inventory were priced at its market value and accounted for using the FIFO method.

19.6.15. For Year 2, Mr. P, who uses the FIFO method of identifying inventory, had a beginning inventory of 3,500 units purchased in Year 1 consisting of the following:

    1,000 purchased 4/20 @ $1.00 per unit
    2,000 purchased 6/24 @ $2.00 per unit
    500 purchased 7/24 @ $3.00 per unit

During Year 2, Mr. P purchased the following units:

    3,000 purchased 9/25 @ $4.00 per unit
    1,000 purchased 12/1 @ $5.00 per unit

During Year 2, P sold 2,300 units. What is the value of P's ending inventory on December 31, Year 2?

A. $13,300

B. $15,600

C. $19,900

D. $22,100

Answer (C) is correct. *(SEE, adapted)*
REQUIRED: The cost of ending inventory using the FIFO method.
DISCUSSION: The FIFO (first in, first out) method is based on a flow of goods assumption. The cost of goods sold under the FIFO method contains the costs of the earlier acquired units. The cost of the ending inventory contains the costs of the more recently acquired items. The ending inventory is $19,900 with a total of 5,200 units on hand (3,500 beginning inventory + 4,000 purchased – 2,300 sold).

Date Purchased	Units	Price	Total
6/24/Year 1	700	$2.00	$ 1,400
7/24/Year 1	500	3.00	1,500
9/25/Year 2	3,000	4.00	12,000
12/1/Year 2	1,000	5.00	5,000
Ending inventory	5,200		$19,900

Answer (A) is incorrect. The amount of $13,300 is the value of ending inventory under the LIFO method. Answer (B) is incorrect. The average cost of $3 was applied to the 5,200 units of ending inventory. Answer (D) is incorrect. The $4.25 average cost of Year 2 purchases was applied to the 5,200 units of ending inventory.

19.6.16. M is a manufacturing company. It uses the same accounting method for financial reports as for tax purposes. In M's financial reports, inventory costs include depreciation of production machinery. Its records reflect the following:

Interest expense on loans to finance production machinery	$10,000
Repairs and maintenance expense on production machinery	20,000
Tax depreciation expense on production machinery	40,000
Tools and equipment exhausted within 1 year	35,000
Research and experimental expenses	55,000
Quality control costs	25,000
Vacation and holiday pay (factory labor)	30,000

What amount must M include in indirect costs in valuing inventory for tax purposes?

A. $80,000

B. $120,000

C. $130,000

D. $150,000

Answer (C) is correct. *(SEE, adapted)*
REQUIRED: The amount that a manufacturer must include in indirect costs in valuing inventory for tax purposes.
DISCUSSION: Under the uniform capitalization rules of Sec. 263A, a manufacturer must use the full-absorption method of inventory costing and include indirect production costs. Regulation 1.263A-1(e) prescribes the basic rules about the direct and indirect costs included in inventory by a manufacturer under the uniform capitalization rules. These rules provide that maintenance and repair expenses, utilities, rent, indirect labor and production wages, indirect materials and supplies, tools and equipment not capitalized, and costs of quality control and inspection must be included in inventory costs regardless of their treatment in a manufacturer's financial reports. Interest on debt incurred to finance any asset used in the production process is included in inventory. Depreciation allowable for tax purposes is included in inventory irrespective of what is done on the financial statements.
Costs not included in inventory include research and experimental expenses, and marketing expenses. Vacation and holiday pay for factory labor is a direct production cost, not an indirect cost. The amount which M must include in indirect costs is

Interest	$ 10,000
Repairs and maintenance	20,000
Depreciation expense	40,000
Tools and equipment used	35,000
Quality control costs	25,000
Indirect costs includible	$130,000

Answer (A) is incorrect. Tax depreciation expense and interest on production machinery are included in the indirect costs. Answer (B) is incorrect. Interest on production machinery must be included in indirect costs. Answer (D) is incorrect. Vacation pay is not included in indirect costs, but interest on production machinery is included.

19.6.17. For the current year, Ms. K's books and records reflect the following information regarding item X:

• Opening inventory purchased last year:
  500 units purchased in July at $1.00 per unit
  300 units purchased in December at $3.00 per unit

• Purchased during the current year:
  500 units in April at $2.00 per unit
  400 units in August at $3.00 per unit

• Sold in the current year:
  1,400 units

What is the cost of goods sold under both the FIFO and LIFO methods of identifying inventory?

	FIFO	LIFO
A.	$2,450	$3,000
B.	$2,700	$3,300
C.	$2,850	$3,075
D.	$1,400	$4,200

Answer (B) is correct. *(SEE, adapted)*
REQUIRED: The value of cost of goods sold determined under the FIFO and the LIFO methods.
DISCUSSION: FIFO (first in, first out) is a flow of goods assumption. The cost of goods sold under the FIFO method consists of the earliest purchased units. LIFO ("last in, first out") is another flow-of-goods assumption in which cost of goods sold consists of the most recently purchased units. The value of X's cost of goods sold is

Date Purchased	FIFO	
July of last year	500 @ $1.00	$ 500
December of last year	300 @ $3.00	900
April of this year	500 @ $2.00	1,000
August of this year	100 @ $3.00	300
Cost of goods sold	1,400 units	$2,700

Date Purchased	LIFO	
July of last year	200 @ $1.00	$ 200
December of last year	300 @ $3.00	900
April of this year	500 @ $2.00	1,000
August of this year	400 @ $3.00	1,200
Cost of goods sold	1,400 units	$3,300

Answer (A) is incorrect. Cost of goods sold under FIFO is not $2,450, nor is the cost of goods sold under LIFO $3,000. Answer (C) is incorrect. Cost of goods sold under FIFO is not $2,850. Additionally, cost of goods sold under LIFO is not $3,075. Answer (D) is incorrect. Cost of goods sold under FIFO of $1,400 is the 1,400 units sold multiplied by $1.00; cost of goods sold under LIFO of $4,200 is the 1,400 units sold multiplied by $3.00.

19.6.18. Inventory data for ABC Retailing Co. at December 31 of the current year are as follows:

	Cost	Retail
Sales		$95,000
Inventory, 1/1	$10,000	24,000
Purchases	40,000	84,000
Additional markups		18,000
Markup cancelations		6,000
Markdowns		9,000
Markdown cancelations		4,000

What is the ending inventory at approximate lower of cost or market under the retail method?

A. $8,334

B. $8,696

C. $20,000

D. None of the answers are correct.

Answer (A) is correct. *(K. McMullen)*
REQUIRED: The ending inventory under the retail method to approximate the lower-of-cost-or-market method.
DISCUSSION: The ending inventory under the retail method to approximate the lower-of-cost-or-market method is calculated as follows:

	Cost	Retail
Inventory, 1/1	$10,000	$ 24,000
Purchases	40,000	84,000
Markups (net)		12,000
	$50,000	$120,000

$50,000 ÷ $120,000 = 41.67%

Markdowns (net)	(5,000)
Sales	(95,000)
Ending inventory at retail	$ 20,000
	× .4167
Ending inventory at LCM	$ 8,334

Under lower of cost or market, it is assumed either that goods marked down are sold at year end or that any decline in profitability of these goods must be recognized if they are still in inventory. With that in mind, net markdowns are treated like sales in calculating percentage of cost versus retail. The lower-of-cost-or-market percentage will always be lower than the cost percentage when markdowns occur.

Answer (B) is incorrect. Net markdowns should be treated like sales and should not enter into the calculation of the cost-retail ratio. Answer (C) is incorrect. The amount of $20,000 is ending inventory at retail value. Answer (D) is incorrect. One of the answers is correct.

19.6.19. XYZ Company adopted dollar-value LIFO for inventory valuation on January 1 of the current year when the price index for its type of goods was 120. Its inventory on that date at average cost was $150,000. At December 31 of the current year, inventory costed at year-end prices was $210,000, when the price index was 144. What is the cost of its December 31 inventory under dollar-value LIFO?

A. $30,000

B. $150,000

C. $180,000

D. $210,000

Answer (C) is correct. *(K. McMullen)*
REQUIRED: The value of ending inventory using dollar-value LIFO.
DISCUSSION: Costing of inventory under dollar-value LIFO entails first determining if a new layer of LIFO inventory has been created during the year. To discover this, the ending inventory taken at current replacement cost must be restated at beginning costs, and then compared to beginning inventory.

Ending inventory at current costs	$210,000
Price index change	×120/144
Ending inventory at beginning costs	$175,000
Beginning inventory	(150,000)
New layer at beginning costs	$ 25,000

The new layer at beginning costs is then restated by applying the price index change to create the new layer at current costs. Then it is added to the base layer to arrive at ending inventory under dollar-value LIFO.

New layer at beginning costs	$ 25,000
Price index change	×144/120
New layer at ending costs	$ 30,000
Original layer	150,000
Ending inventory at dollar-value LIFO	$180,000

Note that Sec. 474 provides an option for eligible small businesses (those with average annual gross receipts for the 3 preceding taxable years of $5 million or less) whereby such small businesses may elect to use a simplified dollar-value LIFO method of pricing inventories.
Answer (A) is incorrect. The amount of $30,000 is the value of the new layer at ending costs. Answer (B) is incorrect. The amount of $150,000 is the value of the original layer (beginning inventory). Answer (D) is incorrect. The $210,000 ending inventory at current costs must be adjusted for the change in the price index and divided into its two components: the beginning inventory and the new layer.

19.6.20. Tammy purchased 2,000 shares of IXB Corp. common stock on the New York Stock Exchange for $10,000 on July 1, Year 1. Tammy, as a dealer in securities, did not acquire the shares as part of her normal inventory, but for sale to customers. She sold 1,000 of the shares on December 31, Year 1, when the fair market value was $7 per share, and when the fair market value dropped to $6.50 per share on September 11, Year 2, she sold the rest. What gain or loss does Tammy, a calendar-year, cash-method taxpayer, recognize on the stock sale in Year 2?

A. $500 ordinary loss.

B. $0

C. $1,500 ordinary income.

D. $1,500 capital gain.

Answer (A) is correct. *(Publisher, adapted)*
REQUIRED: The amount and character of gain or loss reported on the sale of noninventory stock by a dealer in securities.
DISCUSSION: For tax years ending on or after 1993, security dealers are required by Sec. 475 to use the mark-to-market method for valuing noninventory securities. The dealer must recognize gain or loss each year as if the security was sold on the last day of the tax year. In Year 1, Tammy recognizes gain of $2,000 [1,000 × ($7 – $5)] on the 1,000 shares sold. Tammy also recognizes gain of $2,000 on the 1,000 shares she owned on December 31 of Year 1, when she makes the mark-to-market adjustment. Section 475(a) provides for gains or losses on the sale of the security to be adjusted to reflect gains and losses accounted for by marking to market. Thus, Tammy will have $500 [(1,000 × $6.50) – ($5,000 basis + $2,000 previously reported income)] of loss in Year 2. Note that the income in Year 1 and the loss in Year 2 are both ordinary [Sec. 475(d)(3)(A)].
Answer (B) is incorrect. Tammy must recognize a gain or loss on the stock sale in Year 2. Answer (C) is incorrect. A security dealer must treat the securities as if they are sold at FMV at the end of each tax year. Answer (D) is incorrect. Tammy does not have a $1,500 capital gain on the stock sale.

19.6.21. The cost of inventory must be reduced by cash discounts.

A. True.

B. False.

Answer (B) is correct. *(Publisher, adapted)*
DISCUSSION: Under Reg. 1.471-3, cash discounts (those received for paying early) may reduce the cost of inventory or be treated as income, as long as a consistent method is followed. On the other hand, trade discounts (discounts for volume) must be reflected in a lower cost of inventory.

19.6.22. Taxpayers who change to LIFO inventory valuations have 3 years (beginning with the year of change) to take back into income any inventory writedowns from use of lower-of-cost-or-market valuations.

A. True.

B. False.

Answer (A) is correct. *(Publisher, adapted)*
   DISCUSSION: Under Sec. 472(d), the beginning inventory for the first taxable year that LIFO is used must be valued at cost. Any change in the inventory amount resulting from changing the beginning inventory to cost (e.g., from lower of cost or market) must be taken into account ratably for the first 3 years beginning with the adoption of the LIFO method.

19.6.23. Under the LIFO method of identifying inventory, a taxpayer has the option of using the cost method or the lower-of-cost-or-market method in valuing inventory.

A. True.

B. False.

Answer (B) is correct. *(SEE, adapted)*
   DISCUSSION: A taxpayer who uses the LIFO method must value inventory at cost, rather than at the lower of cost or market.

19.6.24. On January 1 of the current year, Mason Corporation took an inventory of all of its goods that were available for sale. No inventories were taken during the year, and Mason did not take a year-end inventory. Mason Corp. is allowed to take a deduction for inventory shrinkage on its current year's return.

A. True.

B. False.

Answer (B) is correct. *(Publisher, adapted)*
   DISCUSSION: A business is generally allowed a reasonable deduction for inventory shrinkage when determining year-end inventory. Under the Taxpayer Relief Act of 1997, a year-end inventory count is not required for this deduction if periodic inventory counts were made throughout the year. Since Mason did not take a year-end count and no periodic inventory counts were made, it is not allowed a deduction for inventory shrinkage.

19.6.25. Kris owns and operates a company that manufactures fans. His gross receipts for Year 1 through Year 4 were as follows:

Year 1	$ 8,000,000
Year 2	9,000,000
Year 3	10,000,000
Year 4	12,000,000

During Year 4, he leased a warehouse for use in his business. The total lease payments in Year 4 were $40,000. Kris may not deduct the entire $40,000 in Year 4 since he is subject to the uniform capitalization rules.

A. True.

B. False.

Answer (A) is correct. *(SEE, adapted)*
   DISCUSSION: Under the uniform capitalization rules of Sec. 263A, a manufacturer must use the full-absorption method of inventory costing and include indirect production costs. Regulation 1.263A-1(e) prescribes the direct and indirect costs to be included in inventory by a manufacturer under the uniform capitalization rules. These rules provide that rent of facilities must be included in inventory costs.
   Also, Reg. 1.263A-1(e)(3)(ii)(H) requires capitalization of storage and warehousing costs incurred with respect to production or resale activities.

19.6.26. When a dealer in securities holds inventory or noninventory stocks and securities at the end of the current tax year, the dealer must generally recognize built-in gains and losses by revaluing the securities at their year-end market value.

A. True.

B. False.

Answer (A) is correct. *(Publisher, adapted)*
   DISCUSSION: Section 475 requires that, for tax years ending on or after December 31, 1993, security dealers value inventory securities or other securities held at year end using the mark-to-market method. The security must be valued at fair market value, and the dealer reports as ordinary income or loss any increase or decrease in the security's value for the tax year. Section 475(b)(1) exempts from the mark-to-market rule any securities held for investment. Although mark-to-market treatment is mandatory for securities dealers, the Taxpayer Relief Act of 1997 also gives the option to make the mark-to-market election to commodities dealers and traders in securities or commodities.

19.6.27. If a taxpayer wants to estimate its inventory shrinkage, the taxpayer will be treated as if it changed its method of accounting.

A.   True.

B.   False.

Answer (A) is correct. *(Publisher, adapted)*
DISCUSSION: Under the Taxpayer Relief Act of 1997, a taxpayer that utilizes the estimate of inventory shrinkage will be treated as if it changed its method of accounting. The taxpayer is not required to secure the permission of the IRS in order to make the change. Any adjustment to income required by Sec. 481 because of this change of method is reported over a 4-year period.

19.7 Change of Accounting Methods

19.7.1. Which of the following items is not a change in the method of accounting requiring the consent of the IRS?

A.   Change from the cash method to the accrual method or vice versa.

B.   Change in the method or basis used to value inventories (except the FIFO method to LIFO method change).

C.   Change in the method of figuring depreciation (except certain changes to the straight-line method).

D.   An adjustment in the useful life of a depreciable asset.

Answer (D) is correct. *(SEE, adapted)*
REQUIRED: The change that does not require the permission of the IRS.
DISCUSSION: To change an accounting method, the taxpayer must generally obtain the permission of the IRS [Sec. 446(e)]. However, the taxpayer is required to notify the Commissioner of a change in the useful life of a depreciable asset only if the taxpayer and the Commissioner had entered into a written agreement specifying the useful life. Note that most assets have fixed periods over which to compute depreciation under ACRS and MACRS.
Answer (A) is incorrect. A change from the cash method to the accrual method or vice versa is a change in the overall plan of accounting for gross income or deductions or a change in the treatment of any material item used in such overall plan, and thus qualifies as a change in accounting method [Reg. 1.446-1(e)(2)]. Answer (B) is incorrect. A change in the method or basis used to value inventories (except the FIFO method to LIFO method change) is a change in accounting method requiring the consent of the IRS. Answer (C) is incorrect. A change in the method of figuring depreciation (except certain changes to the straight-line method) is a change in accounting method requiring the consent of the IRS.

19.7.2. All of the following changes in method of accounting require the consent of the Commissioner of Internal Revenue except

A.   From the cash or accrual method to a long-term contract method.

B.   From the cash method to the accrual method.

C.   Change in the method or basis used to value inventories (except the FIFO method to LIFO method change).

D.   Adoption of a 15-year amortization period for purchased intangible assets that have previously not been amortized.

Answer (D) is correct. *(SEE, adapted)*
REQUIRED: The change in method of accounting not requiring the consent of the IRS.
DISCUSSION: Section 446(e) requires the taxpayer to obtain permission from the IRS to change a method of accounting. Section 197(a) permits intangible property acquired after August 6, 1993, that is held in connection with the conduct of a trade or business or an income-producing activity to be amortized. Previously, such intangibles were able to be amortized only when they were separable from goodwill and had a fixed and determinable useful life. Items that are now amortizable under Sec. 197 include goodwill, going concern value, work force value, business books and records, operating systems, patents, copyrights, and formulas. Amortization occurs over a 15-year period beginning with the month in which such intangible was acquired. A taxpayer's commencing to amortize purchased intangibles is not a change in accounting method.
Answer (A) is incorrect. A change from the cash or accrual method to a long-term contract method requires the permission of the IRS. Answer (B) is incorrect. A change from the cash method of the accrual method requires the permission of the IRS. Answer (C) is incorrect. A change in the method or basis used to value inventories (except the FIFO method to LIFO method change) requires the permission of the IRS.

19.7.3. Which of the following accounting changes do not require the filing of Form 3115 to request a change in accounting method?

A. Correction of a math error.

B. Change from accrual method to cash method.

C. Change in the method inventory is valued.

D. Change from cash method to accrual method.

Answer (A) is correct. *(SEE, adapted)*
REQUIRED: The accounting change that does not require the filing of Form 3115.
DISCUSSION: Section 446(e) requires the taxpayer to obtain permission from the IRS to change a method of accounting. A change from the accrual method to the cash method of accounting, or vice-versa, and the change in the method of inventory valuation are changes in the method of accounting that would require the filing of Form 3115. However, a correction of an error in calculating tax is not a change in accounting method [Reg. 1.446-1(e)(2)(ii)(b)].
Answer (B) is incorrect. A change from the accrual method to the cash method would require the filing of Form 3115. Answer (C) is incorrect. A change in the method of inventory valuation would require the filing of Form 3115. Answer (D) is incorrect. A change from the cash method to the accrual method would require the filing of Form 3115.

19.7.4. When you file your first tax return, you may, without the consent of the IRS, choose any appropriate accounting method. The method you choose must clearly show your income and must be used from year to year, unless you get a consent from the IRS to change your accounting method.

A. True.

B. False.

Answer (A) is correct. *(SEE, adapted)*
DISCUSSION: A taxpayer may choose any appropriate accounting method without the consent of the IRS as long as it clearly reflects income. Under Sec. 446(e), a taxpayer must obtain permission from the IRS in order to change a method of accounting.

19.8 Tax Year

19.8.1. For the first 6 months of 2017, Mr. Heston, who files jointly with his wife, had adjusted gross income of $31,700 and itemized deductions of $6,000. He is entitled to a total of four exemptions. Mr. Heston changed his accounting period and is required to file a short period return for this 6-month period. What is Mr. Heston's annualized income?

A. $51,400

B. $35,200

C. $17,600

D. $9,500

Answer (B) is correct. *(SEE, adapted)*
REQUIRED: The annualized income of a taxpayer who changes accounting periods.
DISCUSSION: Section 443(a)(1) requires a taxpayer who changes accounting periods to file a short period return, in which income must be annualized [Sec. 443(b)]. Income is annualized by multiplying the short period modified taxable income (gross income minus deductions allowed and using a proportionate amount of personal exemptions) by 12, dividing the result by the number of months in the short period. Heston's annualized income is

Adjusted gross income	$31,700
Less: itemized deductions	(6,000)
Less: personal exemptions	
(4 × $4,050 × 6/12 months)	(8,100)
Taxable income for short period	$17,600
	× 12/6
Annualized income	$35,200

Note that Mr. Heston should compute tax on $35,200 and then pay one-half the tax (6/12 months).
Answer (A) is incorrect. The personal exemptions for the short period must reduce short period taxable income before annualization occurs. Answer (C) is incorrect. The amount of $17,600 is the taxable income for the short period. Answer (D) is incorrect. The amount of $9,500 is taxable income for the short period with personal exemptions included for the entire year.

19.8.2. All of the following tax years are acceptable tax years except

- A. 52- to 53-week tax year.
- B. A short tax year that occurred because a business was not in existence for an entire year.
- C. A short tax year that occurred because a business had a change in accounting period.
- D. A fiscal year (other than a 52- to 53-week tax year) that ends on any day of the month other than the last day.

Answer (D) is correct. *(SEE, adapted)*
REQUIRED: The incorrect statement regarding tax years.
DISCUSSION: Under Sec. 441(e), a fiscal year is a period of 12 months ending on the last day of any month other than December.
Answer (A) is incorrect. A 52- to 53-week tax year is allowed under Sec. 441(f). Answer (B) is incorrect. A short tax year is allowed for a business not in existence for an entire year under Sec. 443(a)(2). Answer (C) is incorrect. A short tax year is permitted when an accounting period is changed under Sec. 443(a)(1).

19.8.3. A calendar-year accounting period covers a 12-month period and may end on the last day of any month of the year.

- A. True.
- B. False.

Answer (B) is correct. *(SEE, adapted)*
DISCUSSION: A calendar-year accounting period covers a 12-month period ending on December 31. The taxpayer may choose a fiscal year covering a 12-month period ending on the last day of any month except December.

19.8.4. Mr. P established a calendar tax year when he filed his first individual income tax return. Mr. P in a later year began business as a sole proprietorship and wished to change his tax year to a fiscal year ending in January. P may change his tax year without securing permission from the Commissioner of Internal Revenue.

- A. True.
- B. False.

Answer (B) is correct. *(SEE, adapted)*
DISCUSSION: Section 442 provides that a taxpayer must obtain consent from the IRS before changing his or her annual accounting period. An application to change tax years is made on Form 1128.

19.8.5. Form 1128, *Application to Adopt, Change or Retain a Tax Year*, when used to make a change of a tax period where advance IRS approval is required, will be considered late if not filed by the 15th day of the second calendar month after the close of the short tax year.

- A. True.
- B. False.

Answer (A) is correct. *(SEE, adapted)*
DISCUSSION: Regulation 1.442-1(b) provides that a taxpayer must file an application on Form 1128 to change the tax year on or before the 15th day of the second calendar month following the close of the short period.

19.8.6. Because this is the first year for Mr. Pluto to file a federal income tax return, the 12-month period ending February 15, 2017, can be adopted if the election is timely.

- A. True.
- B. False.

Answer (B) is correct. *(SEE, adapted)*
DISCUSSION: In a taxpayer's first year, any taxable year that meets the requirement in Sec. 441 may be adopted without obtaining prior approval. Section 441, however, allows the adoption of only a calendar or fiscal year as a taxable year. A calendar year is the period of 12 months ending on December 31. A fiscal year is a period of 12 months ending on the last day of any month other than December, or a 52- to 53-week annual accounting period. Because the 12-month period ending February 15 is not a fiscal or calendar year, it is not an allowable tax year.

19.8.7. The date a sole proprietorship begins business determines the tax year on which it must file its returns.

- A. True.
- B. False.

Answer (B) is correct. *(SEE, adapted)*
DISCUSSION: Permission from the IRS is generally not needed to place a taxpayer's first tax year on either a calendar- or a fiscal-year basis. A taxpayer's first tax year is selected on the initial return. However, in order to adopt a fiscal year, the new taxpayer must adopt that year on the books and records before the due date for filing the return for that year (not including extensions). The date a sole proprietorship begins business does not determine the tax year.

19.8.8. A calendar-year C corporation that has been inactive for a number of years can change to a June 30 fiscal year when business is resumed.

A. True.

B. False.

Answer (A) is correct. *(SEE, adapted)*
   DISCUSSION: Under Reg. 1.442-1(c)(2), a corporation may change its accounting period without prior approval if the following conditions are met: (1) The corporation has not changed its accounting period within the preceding 10 calendar years; (2) the short tax year has no net operating loss; (3) the taxable income for the short tax year when annualized is at least 80% of the taxable income from the preceding full tax year; and (4) if the corporation has a special status, it must retain this status. If a corporation has been inactive, these requirements would probably be met. Also, Rev. Rul. 60-51 allows a corporation that has been inactive (in effect not in existence) for several years to adopt a new accounting year without consent.

19.8.9. In order to adopt a 52- to 53-week year, a corporation must file a statement showing

1. The day of the week upon which the tax year will always end;

2. Whether it will end on the last such day of the week occurring in the calendar month or on the date such day of the week occurs nearest the end of the month; and

3. The month in which (or with reference to which) the tax year will end.

A. True.

B. False.

Answer (A) is correct. *(SEE, adapted)*
   DISCUSSION: Regulation 1.441-2T(c)(2) requires a statement to be filed for a taxpayer to adopt a 52- to 53-week year. This statement must include the following information: (1) the calendar month with reference to which the tax year will end, (2) the day of the week on which the tax year will always end, and (3) whether the tax year will end on the last such day of the week occurring in the calendar month or on the date such day of the week occurs nearest the end of the month.

19.8.10. A partnership may elect a fiscal year when the deferral of income to the partners is for not more than a 3-month period.

A. True.

B. False.

Answer (A) is correct. *(Publisher, adapted)*
   DISCUSSION: Under Sec. 706, a business purpose must be established to permit the use of a taxable year other than one determined under the normal rules, e.g., that of the majority partner(s) or the tax year that provides the least aggregate deferral if no single tax year is used by the majority partners. A 3-month deferral of income is not a business purpose. But Sec. 444 allows a partnership to elect a fiscal tax year if a required payment is made. The fiscal year may be the fiscal year the partnership had at the end of 1986 or a fiscal year with no more than a 3-month deferral period. But if the fiscal year at the end of 1986 had less than a 3-month deferral, then a new fiscal year may not have a greater deferral.

19.8.11. A C corporation must always elect to use the calendar year as its tax year.

A. True.

B. False.

Answer (B) is correct. *(SEE, adapted)*
   DISCUSSION: In general, in a corporation's first year, it may choose any taxable year that meets the requirement in Sec. 441 without obtaining prior approval. This is true for a C corporation.

19.8.12. A newly formed S corporation's taxable year is restricted to a calendar year or a fiscal year for which a business purpose can be established.

A. True.

B. False.

Answer (B) is correct. *(Publisher, adapted)*
   DISCUSSION: Section 1378(a) specifies that an S corporation's taxable year is restricted to a permitted year. A permitted year is a calendar year or a fiscal year for which a business purpose is established. But Sec. 444 allows an S corporation to elect a fiscal tax year if a required payment is made. The fiscal year may be the fiscal year the S corporation had at the end of 1986 or a fiscal year with no more than a 3-month deferral period. But if the fiscal year at the end of 1986 had less than a 3-month deferral, then a new fiscal year may not have a greater deferral.

19.8.13. Personal service corporations must use a calendar year as its taxable year unless the IRS consents otherwise.

A. True.

B. False.

Answer (B) is correct. *(Publisher, adapted)*
DISCUSSION: Section 441(i) requires that personal service corporations must use a calendar year unless the IRS consents to some other year based on a business purpose. But Sec. 444 allows a personal service corporation to elect a fiscal tax year if it makes "minimum distributions to its shareholders." The fiscal year may either be the fiscal year the personal service corporation had at the end of 1986 or a fiscal year with no more than a 3-month deferral period. But if the fiscal year at the end of 1986 had less than a 3-month deferral, than a new fiscal year may not have a greater deferral.

19.8.14. Automatic approval of a period change is available for a corporation making an S corporation election.

A. True.

B. False.

Answer (A) is correct. *(Publisher, adapted)*
DISCUSSION: Automatic approval of a period change is available for a corporation making an S corporation election effective for the taxable year immediately following a change in accounting period. The corporation must change to a permitted S corporation taxable year.

19.9 Recordkeeping Requirements

19.9.1. All of the following statements with respect to effective recordkeeping are true, except

A. Records should identify the source of income in order to determine if an income item is taxable or nontaxable.

B. If an individual cannot provide a canceled check to prove payment of an expense item, (s)he may be able to prove it with certain financial account statements.

C. Records that support the basis of property should be kept until the statute of limitations expires for the year that the property was acquired.

D. Records should show how much of an individual's earnings are subject to self-employment tax.

Answer (C) is correct. *(SEE, adapted)*
REQUIRED: The false statement with respect to effective recordkeeping.
DISCUSSION: Section 6001 requires every person liable for any tax imposed by the Internal Revenue Code to keep records sufficient to establish the amount of items required to be shown by such a person in any return of tax or information. Regulation 1.6001-1(a) provides that books of account or records should be sufficient to establish the amount of gross income, deductions, credits, or other matters required to be shown by such persons in any tax or information return.
Regulation 1.6001-1(e) provides that a taxpayer's records must be kept as long as the contents may be material in the administration of any Internal Revenue law. Records relating to the basis of property should be retained as long as they may be material [Reg. 1.6001-1(e)]. The basis of property is material until the statute of limitations expires for the year in which the property is sold.
Answer (A) is incorrect. Records should identify the source of income in order to determine if an income item is taxable or nontaxable. Answer (B) is incorrect. The taxpayer's statement corroborated by financial account statements may suffice [Reg. 1.274-5(c)(3)]. Answer (D) is incorrect. Records should be sufficient to establish the amount of gross income, deductions, credits, or other matters required to be shown in any tax or information return.

19.9.2. Which of the following items represents sufficient documentary evidence to substantiate expenditures for travel, entertainment, or gift expenses?

A. A canceled check written to pay a motel bill on a business trip.

B. A statement from the taxpayer's employer.

C. An account book maintained daily by the taxpayer for her business meals (no meal was over $10).

D. Memos on a desk calendar.

Answer (C) is correct. *(SEE, adapted)*
REQUIRED: The item providing sufficient documentary evidence to substantiate expenditures for travel, entertainment, or gift expenses.
DISCUSSION: Temporary Regulation 1.274-5T outlines rules for substantiation. Substantiation of who, when, where, why, and the amount is generally required. A taxpayer must maintain adequate records or sufficient evidence corroborating the taxpayer's statement. An account book maintained daily by the taxpayer would meet the rules for substantiation. Documentary evidence such as a receipt is not required for meals costing less than $75 [Reg. 1.274-5T(c)(2)(iii)(B)].
Answer (A) is incorrect. The business purpose is not evident from a canceled check. Answer (B) is incorrect. A statement from the taxpayer's employer is not an adequate record. Answer (D) is incorrect. Memos on a desk calendar are usually not made at or near the time of expenditure. The record should be made at or near the time of the expenditure.

19.9.3. All of the following are specific records that are required to be maintained for income tax withholding except

- A. The total amount and date of each wage payment and the period of time the payment covers.
- B. The fair market value and date of each payment of noncash compensation made to a retail commission salesperson, if no income tax was withheld.
- C. Each employee's date of birth.
- D. Any agreement between the employer and the employee for the voluntary withholding of additional amounts of tax.

Answer (C) is correct. *(SEE, adapted)*
REQUIRED: The record that need not be maintained for income tax withholding.
DISCUSSION: Under Reg. 31.6001-5(a), every employer required to withhold income tax on wages must keep records of all remuneration paid to the employees. The list of items required to be shown in such records does not include each employee's date of birth.
Answer (A) is incorrect. The total amount and date of each wage payment and the period of time the payment covers is an item listed in Reg. 31.6001-5(a) as one that must be shown in records required to be maintained for income tax withholding. Answer (B) is incorrect. The fair market value and date of each payment of noncash compensation made to a retail commission salesperson, if no income tax was withheld, is an item listed in Reg. 31.6001-5(a) as one that must be shown in records required to be maintained for income tax withholding. Answer (D) is incorrect. Any agreement between the employer and the employee for the voluntary withholding of additional amounts of tax is an item listed in Reg. 31.6001-5(a) as one that must be shown in records required to be maintained for income tax withholding.

19.9.4. A business operated as a sole proprietorship must use the double-entry accounting method to reflect both income and expenses for computing taxable income.

- A. True.
- B. False.

Answer (B) is correct. *(SEE, adapted)*
DISCUSSION: Under Sec. 446(a), a taxpayer is required to compute taxable income using the method of accounting regularly used in keeping his or her books. There are no specified methods as long as the method used clearly reflects income.

19.9.5. Federal law does not require a taxpayer to maintain any special form of records, but the records must be such that the taxpayer can prepare a complete and accurate income tax return.

- A. True.
- B. False.

Answer (A) is correct. *(SEE, adapted)*
DISCUSSION: Section 6001 requires every person liable for any tax imposed by the Internal Revenue Code to keep records sufficient to establish the amount of items required to be shown by such a person in any return of tax or information. Regulation 31.6001-1(a), however, states that no particular form is required for keeping records.

19.9.6. Adequate records must include sufficient documents (sales slips, invoices, canceled checks, etc.) that clearly establish the income, deductions, and credits shown on the return.

- A. True.
- B. False.

Answer (A) is correct. *(SEE, adapted)*
DISCUSSION: Regulation 1.6001-1(a) provides that books of accounts or records should be sufficient to establish the amount of gross income, deductions, credits, or other matters required to be shown by such persons in any tax or information return.

19.9.7. Microfilm and microfiche reproductions of general books of accounts, such as cash books, journals, voucher registers, and ledgers, are accepted by the Internal Revenue Service for recordkeeping if they comply with applicable revenue procedures.

- A. True.
- B. False.

Answer (A) is correct. *(SEE, adapted)*
DISCUSSION: Revenue Procedure 81-46 sets forth the conditions under which microfilm reproductions will be considered books and records under Sec. 6001. As long as the microfilm and microfiche reproductions satisfy the requirements, they will be accepted by the IRS for recordkeeping.

19.9.8. For federal tax purposes, an automatic data processing record-keeping system must provide an audit trail so that details (invoices and vouchers) may be identified and made available upon request.

- A. True.
- B. False.

Answer (A) is correct. *(SEE, adapted)*
DISCUSSION: Revenue Procedure 91-59 sets forth the guidelines for record requirements in an ADP system. One of the requirements is that an audit trail must be designed so that details underlying the summary accounting data, such as invoices and vouchers, may be identified and made available to the IRS upon request.

19.9.9. If you receive a cash gift from a relative, you should maintain a record to substantiate its receipt in order to prevent it from later being characterized as taxable income.

A. True.

B. False.

Answer (A) is correct. *(SEE, adapted)*
DISCUSSION: If the IRS challenges the treatment of an item, the taxpayer must produce sufficient records to support his or her claim. Therefore, it would be a good idea to record the receipt of a cash gift from a relative.

19.9.10. An accountant should furnish records or information to the Internal Revenue Service on first request, even if (s)he feels the information is privileged.

A. True.

B. False.

Answer (B) is correct. *(SEE, adapted)*
DISCUSSION: If an accountant feels information is privileged, (s)he should not furnish the records or information to the IRS since unauthorized disclosure of information by preparers of returns can constitute a misdemeanor, punishable by fines up to $1,000 and/or imprisonment of up to 1 year [Sec. 7216(a)].

19.9.11. Employers are required to keep records on employment taxes (income tax withholding, Social Security, Medicare, and federal unemployment tax) for at least 4 years after the due date of the return or after the date the tax is paid, whichever is later.

A. True.

B. False.

Answer (A) is correct. *(SEE, adapted)*
DISCUSSION: The general rule of Reg. 31.6001-1(e)(2) is that persons required to keep records concerning a tax must maintain them for at least 4 years after the due date of the return or after the date the tax is paid, whichever is later.

19.9.12. Employers are not required to retain withholding exemption certificates (Form W-4) filed by employees after the date of the current year's returns.

A. True.

B. False.

Answer (B) is correct. *(SEE, adapted)*
DISCUSSION: Under Reg. 31.6001-5(a)(13), employers are required to retain in their records Form W-4 for each employee. These records must be retained for at least 4 years [Reg. 31.6001-1(e)(2)].

19.9.13. Purchasing property with a long life, adopting the LIFO method of inventory, and changing a method of accounting are all examples of business decisions that may require a person to maintain records longer than the general requirement of 3 years after the return was due or filed or 2 years after the date the tax was paid, whichever is later.

A. True.

B. False.

Answer (A) is correct. *(SEE, adapted)*
DISCUSSION: Regulation 1.6001-1(e) provides that a taxpayer's records must be kept as long as the contents may be material in the administration of any Internal Revenue law. Since the IRS generally has 3 years from the date a return was due or filed, or 2 years from the date the tax was paid, whichever is later, to assess tax [Sec. 6501(a)], a taxpayer must retain his or her records at least until the later time.

☑ ☰
☐ ☰   Use **Gleim Test Prep** for interactive study and easy-to-use detailed analytics!
☐ ☰

STUDY UNIT TWENTY
EMPLOYMENT TAXES AND WITHHOLDING

20.1 Social Security Tax Overview

20.1.1. During the examination of the financial statements of Viscount Manufacturing Corporation, the CPAs noted that, although Viscount had 860 full-time and part-time employees, it had completely overlooked its responsibilities under the Federal Insurance Contributions Act (FICA). Under these circumstances, which of the following is true?

A. No liability under the act will attach if the employees voluntarily relinquish their rights under the act in exchange for a cash equivalent paid directly to them.

B. If the union that represents the employees has a vested pension plan covering the employees that is equal to or exceeds the benefits available under the act, Viscount has no liability.

C. Since employers and employees owe FICA taxes and since the employer must withhold the employees' tax from their wages as paid, Viscount must remit to the government a tax equal to the amount assessed directly against the employer and the employee.

D. The act does not apply to the part-time employees.

Answer (C) is correct. *(CPA, adapted)*
REQUIRED: The true statement concerning an employer's responsibility under FICA.
DISCUSSION: Employers and employees are each liable for FICA taxes. Under Sec. 3102(a), an employer is liable for collecting (withholding) the employees' tax from wages. Employers who fail to collect these taxes are responsible for the employees' tax, in addition to their own [Sec. 3111(a)]. Furthermore, Viscount could be subject to a 100% penalty under Sec. 6672 in addition to the taxes, if the failure to withhold or pay is willful.
Answer (A) is incorrect. Coverage under the Social Security Act is mandatory and employees may not give up Social Security rights in exchange for money paid directly or indirectly to them. Answer (B) is incorrect. Coverage under Social Security is mandatory and not replaceable by union benefits or pension plans. Answer (D) is incorrect. The Social Security Act applies to all employees, including part-time employees, unless specifically exempted by the Code.

20.1.2. The Social Security Act provides for the imposition of taxes and the disbursement of benefits. Which of the following is a true statement regarding these taxes and disbursements in the current year?

A. Only those who have contributed to Social Security are eligible for benefits.

B. As between an employer and its employee, the tax rates are the same.

C. A deduction for federal income tax purposes is allowed the employee for Social Security taxes paid.

D. Social Security benefits are fully includible in gross income for federal income tax purposes unless they are disability benefits.

Answer (B) is correct. *(CPA, adapted)*
REQUIRED: The true statement concerning the Social Security tax and benefits.
DISCUSSION: Under the Federal Insurance Contributions Act (FICA), the tax rate for employers and employees is the same (7.65% for 2017). This requirement of shared responsibility has been followed since the Social Security Act was enacted in 1935.
Answer (A) is incorrect. Benefits under Social Security are paid to more than those who have contributed to it. Recipients of Social Security benefits include surviving spouses and children of retired, deceased, or disabled workers. Answer (C) is incorrect. Employment taxes are not deductible by an employee (Sec. 3502). Answer (D) is incorrect. Social Security benefits are included in gross income only to the extent that a recipient's income is in excess of certain statutory amounts.

20.1.3. All of the following items of information are required to be maintained for Social Security tax purposes except

- A. The amount and date of each wage, annuity, or pension payment.
- B. The dates and amounts of tax deposits made.
- C. The names, addresses, Social Security numbers, and occupations of employees and recipients of payments.
- D. Any agreement between the employee and employer for the voluntary withholding of additional amounts of FICA tax.

20.1.4. Bank Z makes annuity payments as an agent for an employees' trust and the trust is the payor. If the trust has withholding taxes due, but no employees with wages subject to FICA taxes, it should file Form 945.

- A. True.
- B. False.

20.1.5. Every employer required to report employment taxes or give tax statements to employees must obtain an employer identification number.

- A. True.
- B. False.

20.1.6. Although an organization is recognized as tax exempt, it is responsible for withholding, depositing, and reporting federal income tax and FICA tax on wages paid to its employees.

- A. True.
- B. False.

20.2 Employee vs. Independent Contractor

20.2.1. Harry hires an opera ensemble to perform indefinitely at his night spot. They perform nightly and are paid by the hour. Harry withholds the players' share of FICA taxes from their wages and pays both this and the employer's share to the government. Both Harry and the ensemble claim income tax deductions for the FICA taxes. Which of the following is a true statement?

- A. Harry should not deduct FICA taxes as a business expense.
- B. The ensemble properly claimed their share of FICA taxes as an income tax deduction.
- C. Harry may deduct his share of FICA taxes but the ensemble may not.
- D. Harry should not withhold FICA taxes from the ensemble's wages.

Answer (D) is correct. *(SEE, adapted)*
REQUIRED: The information not required to be maintained by an employer for Social Security tax purposes.
DISCUSSION: Circular E provides a list of records that should be kept for at least 4 years for employment tax purposes. An employee may have additional amounts of income tax withheld but not Social Security taxes.
Answer (A) is incorrect. The amount and date of each wage, annuity, or pension payment are employer records that should be maintained for 4 years. Answer (B) is incorrect. The dates and amounts of tax deposits made are employer records that should be maintained for 4 years. Answer (C) is incorrect. The names, addresses, Social Security numbers, occupations of employees, and recipients of payments are employer records that should be maintained for 4 years.

Answer (A) is correct. *(SEE, adapted)*
DISCUSSION: Form 941 is used to report withholding and Social Security taxes collected by an employer. If an employer collects withholding taxes, but has no employees with wages subject to Social Security taxes, the proper form for reporting withholding taxes collected is Form 945 (*Annual Return of Withheld Federal Income Tax*).

Answer (A) is correct. *(SEE, adapted)*
DISCUSSION: Any employer who is required to report employment taxes or give tax statements to employees must obtain an identification number in order to facilitate the filing of the information (Sec. 6109).

Answer (A) is correct. *(SEE, adapted)*
DISCUSSION: Employers are required to perform these functions. The term employer includes exempt organizations.

Answer (C) is correct. *(Publisher, adapted)*
REQUIRED: The true statement concerning the deduction of FICA taxes.
DISCUSSION: Section 164(a) lists the taxes that may be deducted by any person. FICA taxes are not listed as deductible. However, Sec. 164(a) does provide that taxes not described, but that are paid or accrued in carrying on a trade or business, may also be deducted. Since Harry is carrying on a trade or business, he may deduct the employer's share of the FICA taxes. The ensemble (employees) is not allowed to deduct FICA taxes.
Answer (A) is incorrect. The employer is allowed to deduct FICA taxes. Answer (B) is incorrect. The employees are not allowed to deduct FICA taxes. Answer (D) is incorrect. An employer is required to withhold the employees' share of FICA taxes from their wages and pay them to the government. Failure to do so can cause the employer to be liable for the full amount of the taxes.

20.2.2. Certain sales agents are classified as independent contractors for purposes of employment taxes. To which of the following does this safe harbor not apply?

- A. Licensed real estate agent.
- B. Seller of consumer goods in the home to a buyer for resale.
- C. Seller of consumer goods in the home, not for resale.
- D. Seller whose remuneration is based on hours worked.

Answer (D) is correct. *(Publisher, adapted)*
REQUIRED: The seller who is not within the safe harbor provisions as an independent contractor.
DISCUSSION: A safe harbor is provided for certain real estate agents and direct sellers to be classified as independent contractors, but the seller's remuneration must be directly related to the sales or output and not be based on hours worked (Sec. 3508).
Answer (A) is incorrect. A licensed real estate agent will not be classified as an employee if substantially all of his or her remuneration is directly related to sales or output rather than to the number of hours worked, and if the services are pursuant to a written contract that provides that the individual will not be treated as an employee with respect to such service for federal tax purposes. Answer (B) is incorrect. A seller of consumer goods in the home rather than in a permanent retail establishment for resale will not be classified as an employee if substantially all of his or her remuneration is directly related to sales or output rather than to the number of hours worked, and if the services are pursuant to a written contract that provides that the individual will not be treated as an employee with respect to such service for federal tax purposes. Answer (C) is incorrect. A seller of consumer goods in the home, not for resale, will not be classified as an employee if substantially all of his or her remuneration is directly related to sales or output rather than to the number of hours worked, and if the services are pursuant to a written contract that provides that the individual will not be treated as an employee with respect to such service for federal tax purposes.

20.2.3. If A has the legal right to control both the method and the result of B's services, B is an employee under common law.

- A. True.
- B. False.

Answer (A) is correct. *(SEE, adapted)*
DISCUSSION: The status of a taxpayer as an employee under common law is important because an employee under common law is an employee for federal employment tax purposes [Sec. 3121(d)]. Under common-law principles, an employee is a person whose performance is subject to the control of the employer. This control extends not only to the result but also to the details and means by which the result is accomplished by the employee. Note that certain persons other than employees under common law are also treated as employees for federal employment tax purposes.

20.2.4. A homeworker, working according to specifications of the person for whom the services are performed, on materials or goods furnished by and required to be returned to that person, is not an employee for Social Security tax purposes.

- A. True.
- B. False.

Answer (B) is correct. *(SEE, adapted)*
DISCUSSION: Under Sec. 3121(d)(3)(C), a homeworker performing work according to the specifications of, and with materials or goods furnished by and required to be returned to, the "employer" is considered an employee for federal employment tax purposes.

20.2.5. A commission-driver who distributes soft drinks for a principal is an employee for Social Security tax purposes.

- A. True.
- B. False.

Answer (A) is correct. *(SEE, adapted)*
DISCUSSION: The definition of an employee includes any person who performs services for remuneration as an agent-driver or commission-driver engaged in distributing meats, vegetables, fruits, beverages, etc., for his or her principal [Sec. 3121(d)(3)(A)].

20.2.6. Drivers for M Trucking Co. often engage laborers to unload their trucks. This is done with the implied consent of M, and the drivers pay the unloaders from funds provided by M. The unloaders are employees of M Trucking Co.

- A. True.
- B. False.

Answer (A) is correct. *(SEE, adapted)*
DISCUSSION: Under common-law principles, an employee is defined as a person whose performance (both method and result) is subject to the control of the employer. Assuming the drivers (employees of M) control the performance of the unloaders, the unloaders are effectively controlled by M, who also consented to their hiring and provides funds for their compensation.

20.2.7. Sue and Bob Johnson have a baby-sitter who was sent to them by a baby-sitting agency. The agency sets the baby-sitter's fee, requires regular reports from the sitter, and exercises control over the sitter relative to dress and rules of conduct. The Johnsons are required to pay employment taxes and file Form 1040, Schedule H (*Household Employment Taxes*), for wages paid to the sitter.

A. True.

B. False.

Answer (B) is correct. *(SEE, adapted)*
    DISCUSSION: When an agency provides a worker, sets the fee, and exercises control over the worker, the agency is the employer of that worker. Therefore, the agency, not the Johnsons, is liable for Social Security taxes and needs to file the appropriate forms. Furthermore, the agency is an independent contractor with respect to the Johnsons.

20.3 FICA for Employees

20.3.1. The federal Social Security Act

A. Does not apply to self-employed persons.

B. Excludes professionals such as accountants, lawyers, and doctors.

C. Provides for a deduction for Social Security taxes paid by the employee that is available against his or her federal income tax.

D. Provides that bonuses and commissions paid as compensation are included as wages in the calculation of employer-employee contributions.

Answer (D) is correct. *(CPA, adapted)*
    REQUIRED: The true statement concerning the federal Social Security Act.
    DISCUSSION: The definition of wages on which contributions are based includes all remuneration for employment [Sec. 3121(a)]. Bonuses and commissions are wages and are used in the calculation of the employer-employee contributions.
    Answer (A) is incorrect. The Social Security Act does apply to self-employed persons, and coverage is mandatory. Answer (B) is incorrect. The Social Security Act does not exclude professionals such as accountants, lawyers, and doctors. Answer (C) is incorrect. An employee may not deduct his or her Social Security tax payments (Sec. 3502).

20.3.2. You are the accountant for Company R, and you are requested to file Form 941, *Employer's Quarterly Federal Tax Return for Federal Income Tax Withheld from Wages and for Federal Insurance Contributions Act Taxes*, for the third quarter of 2017. Given the following information, what is the total FICA tax due for the third quarter (rounded to the nearest dollar)?

Employee	Wages Paid Third Quarter	Wages Paid First Two Quarters
X	$ 5,000	$ 5,000
Y	20,000	108,200
Z	5,000	0

A. $3,596

B. $3,720

C. $4,466

D. $4,590

Answer (C) is correct. *(SEE, adapted)*
    REQUIRED: The amount of FICA tax due during the third quarter of 2017.
    DISCUSSION: The two components of the FICA tax [Social Security (SS) and Medicare] must be reported separately on Form 941. The rate for SS is 6.2% for employers and employees on wages up to $127,200 (in 2017). The rate for Medicare is 1.45% each for employers and employees, with no wage ceiling. With respect to the SS component, the tax is paid until the wage ceiling is reached. Then no SS tax is paid for the rest of the year; i.e., it is not paid ratably over the year. The total wages subject to the SS component in the third quarter of 2017 amount to $29,000 since Y's wages exceed the SS limitation before the end of the quarter. The total FICA tax is 7.65% in 2017. However, the employee and the employer are each required to pay the 7.65%, and the combined percentage of 15.3% is reported on Form 941, separated into its two components.

	Wages		
Employee	Social Security	Medicare	Total
X	$ 5,000	$ 5,000	$ 5,000
Y	19,000	20,000	20,000
Z	5,000	5,000	5,000
Total	$29,000	$30,000	$30,000
Times: Rate	× 0.124	× 0.029	
Tax Liability	$ 3,596	$ 870	$ 4,466

Answer (A) is incorrect. The amount of $3,596 is only the employer and employee share of the SS portion of the FICA tax. Answer (B) is incorrect. The FICA tax on Form 941 includes both the employer and employee share of the tax, which totals 15.3% of gross wages. Answer (D) is incorrect. The amount of $4,590 fails to limit Y's income for SS to $127,200.

20.3.3. The Social Security tax does not apply to which of the following?

A. Medical and hospital reimbursements by the employer that are excluded from gross income.

B. Compensation paid in forms other than cash.

C. Self-employment income of $1,000.

D. Bonuses and vacation time pay.

Answer (A) is correct. *(CPA, adapted)*
REQUIRED: The payment to which the Social Security tax does not apply.
DISCUSSION: The Social Security tax imposed by the Federal Insurance Contribution Act (FICA) applies to virtually all compensation received for employment, including money or other forms of wages, bonuses, commissions, vacation pay, severance allowances, and tips. Reimbursements by one's employers for medical and hospital expenses that are not included in gross income are not subject to FICA [Sec. 3121(a)(2)]. However, sick pay, which is a wage payment paid when unable to work, is subject to FICA.
Answer (B) is incorrect. Compensation paid in forms other than cash is subject to FICA. Answer (C) is incorrect. Self-employment income is taxed for the same Social Security benefits although the tax is imposed by Sec. 1401 rather than Secs. 3101 and 3111. Answer (D) is incorrect. Bonuses and vacation time pay are subject to FICA.

20.3.4. Ernesto was an employee of Med-Tech Corporation for all of 2017. He earned $129,200 in salary. What is the amount of Social Security taxes paid by Med-Tech Corporation with respect to Ernesto?

A. $7,886

B. $9,731

C. $9,759

D. $9,884

Answer (C) is correct. *(Publisher, adapted)*
REQUIRED: The Social Security taxes required to be paid by an employer in 2017.
DISCUSSION: Beginning in 1994, only the OASDI (old-age, survivors, and disability insurance) component of the FICA tax has a wage ceiling. The OASDI rate is 6.20% for employers up to a maximum of $127,200 (in 2017). For the Medicare component, which has no wage ceiling, the rate is 1.45% for employers and employees. The employment taxes paid by Med-Tech with respect to Ernesto in 2017 are as follows:

OASDI	$127,200 × .0620	=	$7,886
Medicare	$129,200 × .0145	=	1,873
Total			$9,759

Answer (A) is incorrect. The amount of $7,886 is only the OASDI portion of the Social Security tax. Answer (B) is incorrect. The Medicare portion of the tax is not limited to $127,200 of wages. Answer (D) is incorrect. The OASDI portion of the Social Security tax is applied only to a maximum of $127,200 of wages. The Medicare portion has no limit.

20.3.5. For the current year, Mr. K, a farmer-employer, will have to pay Social Security taxes on which of the following?

A. $400 cash wages paid to Mr. K's 17-year-old son.

B. $800 cash wages paid to Mr. K's father.

C. $100 cash wages paid to Mr. K's wife. Total cash wages paid to all employees is $1,300.

D. 100 bushels of soybeans with a fair market value of $600 given to an unrelated person by Mr. K in lieu of wages.

Answer (B) is correct. *(SEE, adapted)*
REQUIRED: The item on which a farmer-employer must pay Social Security tax in the current year.
DISCUSSION: The Social Security taxes are imposed by Secs. 3101 and 3111 on wages paid by an employer. Wages are defined in Sec. 3121(a) as all remuneration for employment, not including that paid for agricultural labor unless the cash remuneration in the year is $150 or more to the employee, or the employer pays at least $2,500 during the year for all agricultural labor [Sec. 3121(a)(8)]. Mr. K's father earned more than $150, and his wages therefore qualify under the definition of wages. Employment for FICA purposes includes that of a parent by a child.
Answer (A) is incorrect. Employment for FICA purposes excludes services performed by a child under 18 in the employ of his or her parent. Answer (C) is incorrect. After 1987, an individual in the employ of his or her spouse is no longer automatically exempt from the FICA tax. However, since Mrs. K earned less than $150 and total wages paid to agricultural labor is less than $2,500, her wages are exempt from the FICA tax. Answer (D) is incorrect. Wages subject to FICA tax do not include compensation paid in forms other than cash for agricultural labor.

20.3.6. Mrs. C is employed part-time as a waitress with restaurants A and B. During the month of June, she received tips totaling $15 from her employment at A, and tips totaling $85 from her employment at B. For employment tax purposes, what amount of June tips must Mrs. C report to her employers?

A. $0

B. $65

C. $85

D. $100

Answer (C) is correct. *(SEE, adapted)*
    REQUIRED: The amount of income from tips that the employee must report to her employers.
    DISCUSSION: Under Sec. 3121(a)(12), an employee is required to report tips only if they exceed $20 in 1 month. This $20 applies to each place of employment. Therefore, Mrs. C must report her tips to her employer at restaurant B, but she is not required to report her tips to her employer at restaurant A.
    Answer (A) is incorrect. Mrs. C must report an amount of June tips. Answer (B) is incorrect. All of the tips from employment at B must be reported. Answer (D) is incorrect. Tips are not reported if they are less than $20 per month at a place of employment.

20.3.7. An employee who has had Social Security tax withheld in an amount greater than the maximum for a particular year may claim

A. Such excess as either a credit or an itemized deduction, at the election of the employee, if that excess resulted from correct withholding by two or more employers.

B. Reimbursement of such excess from his employers, if that excess resulted from correct withholding by two or more employers.

C. The excess as a credit against income tax, if that excess resulted from correct withholding by two or more employers.

D. The excess as a credit against income tax, if that excess was withheld by one employer.

Answer (C) is correct. *(CPA, adapted)*
    REQUIRED: The true statement about the result of Social Security tax withheld in excess of the maximum amount.
    DISCUSSION: When an employee overpays the Social Security tax, Sec. 6413(a) provides that proper adjustments shall be made, without interest, pursuant to regulations. If the overpayment cannot be adjusted, the amount shall be refunded pursuant to regulations [Sec. 6413(b)]. If the overpayment resulted from correct withholding by two or more employers, the extra Social Security tax may be used to reduce income taxes.
    Answer (A) is incorrect. The overpayment is not available as a deduction. Answer (B) is incorrect. It is not the employer's responsibility to refund the tax (the employer turned it over to the government). Answer (D) is incorrect. Only when an employee has worked for two or more employers can the extra Social Security tax be used to reduce income taxes.

20.3.8. A waiter works in a restaurant and earns more than $1,000 in tips monthly. His tips are subject to income tax withholding and the employer's portion of Social Security taxes.

A. True.

B. False.

Answer (A) is correct. *(SEE, adapted)*
    DISCUSSION: The Social Security employer tax and income tax withholding applies to wages that are paid by the employer to the employee. Under Sec. 3401(f), tips are considered to be wages. The employer is required to collect employee Social Security tax and income tax on tips reported by an employee. The employer must also pay the employer portion of the Social Security tax on tips reported by an employee. Section 6053(a) requires an employee receiving tips in a calendar month to report the amount of these tips on or before the 10th day of the following month.

20.3.9. The mandatory gratuity charges assessed on members by a country club are not tips but wages subject to withholding for income tax, Social Security tax, and FUTA.

A. True.

B. False.

Answer (A) is correct. *(SEE, adapted)*
    DISCUSSION: Mandatory gratuity charges assessed by the employer are not considered tips since they are under the control and possession of the employer. When the employer distributes part or all of these charges to the employee, this is considered to be a wage paid by the employer and thus is subject to income tax withholding, FICA, and FUTA (Rev. Rul. 66-74). FUTA is the Federal Unemployment Tax.

20.3.10. Mr. A works part-time as a waiter for a restaurant. Mr. A splits all of his tips with the busboy, giving him one-fourth. In January of the current year, Mr. A received tips totaling $100 and gave the busboy $25 for his share. Mr. A is required to report $75 in tips to the employer, but the busboy does not have to report his $25 share.

A. True.

B. False.

Answer (B) is correct. *(SEE, adapted)*
    DISCUSSION: Under Sec. 3121(a)(12), an employee is required to report tips if they are $20 or more in any 1 month. Where employees practice tip-splitting, each employee is required to report only what (s)he receives. Therefore, both Mr. A and the busboy must report tips earned in January of the current year.

20.3.11. If you do not report tips to your employer as required, you may be subject to a penalty equal to 50% of the employee Social Security tax, in addition to the tax that is owed.

A. True.

B. False.

Answer (A) is correct. *(SEE, adapted)*
DISCUSSION: If the failure is the result of willful neglect rather than reasonable cause, the employee must pay the FICA tax on the unreported tips plus 50% of such tax [Sec. 6652(b)].

20.3.12. Subject to the general business credit limitations, a nonrefundable income tax credit is provided to an employer in a food and beverage establishment business for part of the FICA tax liability incurred or paid by the employer on employee tips.

A. True.

B. False.

Answer (A) is correct. *(Publisher, adapted)*
DISCUSSION: Section 45B allows a credit, as a component of the general business credit, when the tipping of employees serving food or beverages is customary for the business. The credit is the 7.65% FICA tax rate times the amount of tips received by an employee during the month that exceed the amount that would be payable at the minimum wage rate under the Fair Labor Standards Act, minus the wages (excluding tips) actually paid by the employer during the month.

20.3.13. Since noncash items are difficult to value, only wages paid in cash are subject to federal employment taxes.

A. True.

B. False.

Answer (B) is correct. *(SEE, adapted)*
DISCUSSION: Under Sec. 3121(a), wages are all forms of compensation paid for employment including the cash value of compensation paid in any medium other than cash. Wages are equal to cash plus the fair market value of any property received for services performed.

20.3.14. Ms. C is a waitress at a restaurant employing over 20 employees and where tipping is customary. The restaurant's food and beverage sales totaled $2 million for the year. Employees reported tips of $80,000, or 4% of total sales. The restaurant will allocate among the employees who receive tips directly from customers the excess of 8% of total sales over the 4% reported. The allocated amount will be reported by the restaurant on C's W-2 separate from wages and reported tips. However, no allocation will be made to C if she reported tips at least equal to her share of 8% of total sales.

A. True.

B. False.

Answer (A) is correct. *(SEE, adapted)*
DISCUSSION: A large food or beverage establishment (one providing food or beverage for consumption on the premises, where tipping is customary, and having more than 10 employees on a typical day in all food or beverage operations) must allocate tips if employees report tips of less than 8% of gross receipts (less carryout sales and sales with a 10% service charge added) [Sec. 6053(c)(3)]. The 8% threshold may be reduced (but not below 2%) by petition of the employer or a majority of the employees.

20.3.15. All of the following employees are subject to the withholding of Social Security taxes:

1. Resident alien, services performed in United States.

2. Son under 18 employed by parent.

3. Parent employed by son in course of his business.

4. Full-time life insurance salesman.

5. Federal employees.

A. True.

B. False.

Answer (B) is correct. *(SEE, adapted)*
DISCUSSION: Under Sec. 3121(b)(3), a child under the age of 18 in the employ of his or her father or mother is not subject to the withholding of Social Security taxes. Federal employees are no longer exempt as they are no longer covered under a separate retirement plan. Aliens who perform services in the U.S., parents of employer children, and insurance salespeople are all subject to FICA.

20.3.16. Mr. and Mrs. Brinson file a joint federal income tax return for the current year. The Brinsons hired a 21-year-old child care provider, who took care of their child Robbie on a part-time basis in their home. In the current year, the wages paid by the Brinsons to the child care provider exceeded $1,000 in three of the four quarters. Wages paid by the Brinsons are subject to FICA tax, federal income tax withholding, and FUTA tax.

A. True.

B. False.

Answer (A) is correct. *(Publisher, adapted)*
    DISCUSSION: Payments to an employee for domestic service are treated as wages for FICA tax purposes if the amount is $2,000 or more in cash in a calendar year [Sec. 3121(a)(7)(B)]. Even amounts paid to a baby-sitter are subject to FICA when this test is met. Since the Brinsons paid their child care provider more than $1,000 in at least one quarter, all wages paid to the child care provider are subject to the FUTA tax. Excluded from the FUTA tax are payments made to a spouse, a child under age 21, or a parent. If the payments made to the child care provider are large enough, they are subject to federal income tax withholding.

20.3.17. Mr. and Mrs. Brinson file a joint federal income tax return for the current year. The Brinsons hired a 21-year-old child care provider, who took care of their child Robbie on a part-time basis in their home. In the current year, the wages paid by the Brinsons to the child care provider exceeded $1,000 in three of the four quarters. The reporting of the FICA tax, FUTA tax, and federal income tax withholding that is owed by the Brinsons is reported on Form 941 *(Employer's Quarterly Federal Tax Return for Federal Income Tax Withheld from Wages and for FICA Taxes)*.

A. True.

B. False.

Answer (B) is correct. *(Publisher, adapted)*
    DISCUSSION: For 1995 and later tax years, the FICA tax, FUTA tax, and federal income tax withholding that is owed is reported by the Brinsons on Schedule H, Form 1040 *(Household Employment Taxes)*. The amount of these taxes are paid with the Form 1040, 1040A, etc., that the Brinsons will file.

20.3.18. Mr. G was employed by B from January to September of the current year and was paid $88,000 in earned wages. On October 15 of the current year, he started a new job with S. If G informs his new employer that he has already met the wage limitation for FICA tax, and provides verification, S is not required to withhold FICA tax from G's wages for the current year.

A. True.

B. False.

Answer (B) is correct. *(SEE, adapted)*
    DISCUSSION: Each employer must withhold a deduction for Social Security taxes from its employee's wages. No provision allows an employer to take into account that an employee has already reached the annual limit while working for another employer. Only when both corporations have a common paymaster can wages be accumulated from different employers to reach the wage limitation.
    NOTE: For 1994 and later years, G has met the Social Security limit for FICA taxes, but there is no salary cap for Medicare.

20.3.19. If you worked for only one employer and more than the maximum Social Security tax was withheld, you may claim the extra amount as a credit to reduce your income tax when you file your return.

A. True.

B. False.

Answer (B) is correct. *(SEE, adapted)*
    DISCUSSION: Section 6413(a) provides that proper adjustments, with respect to both the tax and the amount to be deducted, shall be made, without interest, pursuant to regulations. If the overpayment cannot be adjusted, the amount shall be refunded by the employer pursuant to regulations [Sec. 6413(b)]. Only when you worked for two or more employers can the extra Social Security tax be used to reduce income taxes.

20.3.20. In June of the current year, Corporation Y purchased all of the assets of Corporation Z. Ms. B, who had worked for Z, continued to work for Y. Ms. B had received $35,600 in wages in the current year before the date of the purchase. Corporation Y is subject to the Social Security tax on only the first $82,900 of wages paid to Ms. B during the rest of the current year.

A. True.

B. False.

Answer (A) is correct. *(SEE, adapted)*
    DISCUSSION: The employee and the employer pay the full FICA taxes on the first $118,500 of an employee's wages for calendar year 2015. Wages paid in excess of $118,500 are still subject to the Medicare tax. There is no ceiling on the amount of wages subject to the Medicare tax. The successor employer (one acquiring all or substantially all of the property used in the business of the predecessor) may use the wages paid by the predecessor employer to the employee in calculating the $118,500 Social Security limit.

20.4 FICA for the Self-Employed

20.4.1. Gilda Bach is a cash-basis, self-employed consultant. For the year 2017, she determined that her net income from self-employment was $80,000. In reviewing her books, you determine that the following items were deducted in arriving at the net income of $80,000:

Salary drawn by Gilda Bach	$20,000
Estimated federal income taxes paid	6,000
Malpractice insurance premiums	4,000
Cost of attending professional seminar	1,000

Based upon the above information, what should Gilda Bach report as her net earnings from self-employment for 2017?

A. $89,872

B. $97,891

C. $106,000

D. $110,000

Answer (B) is correct. *(CPA, adapted)*
REQUIRED: The amount of income to be reported as net earnings from self-employment.
DISCUSSION: The net income per books amounted to $80,000. It is necessary to add back the salary that was drawn ($20,000) since an individual may not claim a deduction for salary that is paid to himself or herself. In addition, the estimated federal income taxes paid of $6,000 are not deductible. The malpractice insurance premium and the cost of attending the seminar are deductible business expenses. Bach's tentative net self-employment income is $106,000.

Net income per books	$ 80,000
Items added back	
Salary	20,000
Federal income taxes	6,000
Tentative net earnings from	
self-employment	$106,000

The tentative net earnings from self-employment are reduced by the employer portion (7.65%) of the self-employment tax rate times the taxpayer's tentative net earnings from self-employment. This reduction is calculated as follows:

Tentative net earnings from self-employment	$106,000
Times: Employer rate	× 0.0765
Reduction	$ 8,109

The net earnings from self-employment for Gilda Bach equals $97,891 ($106,000 – $8,109).
Answer (A) is incorrect. The employer rate of 7.65% is deducted from tentative net earnings from self employment. Answer (C) is incorrect. The tentative net earnings from self-employment is $106,000, which must be reduced by 7.65% of this amount. Answer (D) is incorrect. Malpractice insurance premiums are not added back to net income, and a 7.65% tax should be deducted from the tentative net earnings.

20.4.2. Which one of the following statements about the self-employment tax is false for 2017?

A. The maximum self-employment tax that can be owed by a self-employed individual is 15.3% times $127,200, or $19,462.

B. Self-employed individuals may deduct one-half of their self-employment taxes for income tax purposes.

C. In addition to deducting one-half of the self-employment taxes for income tax purposes, self-employment net earnings can be reduced by the product of the net earnings from self-employment times one-half of the self-employment tax rate.

D. The old-age, survivors, and disability insurance (OASDI) portion of the self-employment tax has a $127,200 net earnings ceiling, while the hospital insurance (Medicare) portion of the self-employment tax has no ceiling.

Answer (A) is correct. *(Publisher, adapted)*
REQUIRED: The false statement about the self-employment tax for 2017.
DISCUSSION: The maximum self-employment tax that can be owed by a self-employed individual on the first $127,200 of self-employment income is 15.3%, or $19,462. In addition, the 2.9% Medicare tax component of the self-employment tax can be levied on self-employment income in excess of $127,200. There is no maximum wage base to which the 2.9% rate is applied.
Answer (B) is incorrect. Self-employed individuals may deduct one-half of their self-employment taxes for income tax purposes. Answer (C) is incorrect. In addition to deducting one-half of the self-employment taxes for income tax purposes, self-employment net earnings can be reduced by the product of the net earnings from self-employment times one-half of the self-employment tax rate. Answer (D) is incorrect. The OASDI portion of the self-employment tax has a $127,200 net earnings ceiling, while the Medicare portion of the self-employment tax has no ceiling.

Questions 20.4.3 and 20.4.4 are based on the following information.

Sabrina is a cash-basis self-employed accountant. During 2017, she had the following income and expense items:

Gross receipts	$154,000
Operating expenses	31,000
Guaranteed payments from partnership for service to partnership	6,000
Share of income from general partnership that operates bakery	10,000
Net operating loss carryover	(6,000)
Share of S corporation's ordinary income	7,000
Gain on sale of a computer used in the business	500

20.4.3. What is the amount of earnings Sabrina will have to pay the OASDI portion of the self-employment tax on for 2017?

A. $127,200

B. $128,367

C. $139,000

D. $134,831

Answer (A) is correct. *(SEE, adapted)*
REQUIRED: The amount of earnings on which the Social Security portion of the self-employment tax must be paid in 2017.
DISCUSSION: Section 1401 imposes a tax on an individual's self-employment income. Under Reg. 1.1402(a)-1, net earnings from self-employment includes the net income from a trade or business, guaranteed payments for services from a partnership, and a partner's distributive share of income from a partnership. Gains from the disposition of property, NOL carryovers, and income from S corporations are not included in the computation of net earnings from self-employment.
The self-employment tax is divided into two components: Social Security and Medicare. The maximum net earnings subject to the Social Security portion are $127,200 for 2017. Sabrina's tentative net earnings from self-employment total $139,000 [($154,000 gross receipts less $31,000 operating expenses) plus $6,000 guaranteed payments and $10,000 partnership income]. Section 1402(a)(12) allows a reduction in the tentative net earnings from self-employment equal to the employer portion of the self-employment tax rate times the tentative amount of net earnings from self-employment to arrive at the net earnings from self-employment. This reduces the net earnings to $128,367 [$139,000 − ($139,000 × .0765)]. Since Sabrina's net earnings from self-employment ($128,367) exceed the Social Security ceiling ($127,200), Sabrina will have to pay the Social Security portion of the tax on only $127,200.
Answer (B) is incorrect. The amount of $128,367 exceeds the Social Security ceiling. Answer (C) is incorrect. Sabrina is not taxed on her tentative net earnings from self-employment. Answer (D) is incorrect. The share of the S corporation ordinary income is not included in self-employment income.

20.4.4. What is the amount of earnings on which Sabrina will have to pay the Medicare portion of the self-employment tax for 2017?

A. $127,200

B. $128,367

C. $139,000

D. $134,831

Answer (B) is correct. *(Publisher, adapted)*
REQUIRED: The amount of earnings on which the Medicare portion of the self-employment tax must be paid in 2017.
DISCUSSION: The Medicare portion of the self-employment tax has no ceiling. Thus, Sabrina will pay the hospital insurance portion of the tax on her earnings from self-employment of $128,367.
Answer (A) is incorrect. The maximum net earnings subject to the Social Security portion of the self-employment tax is $127,200. Answer (C) is incorrect. Sabrina's tentative net earnings from self-employment is $139,000, on which she is not taxed. Answer (D) is incorrect. The share of the S corporation ordinary income is not included in self-employment income.

20.4.5. The federal Social Security Act

A. Applies to self-employed persons.

B. Excludes professionals such as accountants, lawyers, and doctors.

C. Provides for a deduction for Social Security taxes paid by the employee against his or her federal income tax.

D. Applies to professionals at their option.

Answer (A) is correct. *(CPA, adapted)*
    REQUIRED: The true statement concerning the federal Social Security Act.
    DISCUSSION: The Social Security Act applies to self-employed persons who must pay a tax on self-employment income (15.3% on the first $127,200 and 2.90% on all other wages in 2017).
    Answer (B) is incorrect. The Social Security Act does not exclude professionals from mandatory coverage. Answer (C) is incorrect. An employee's contribution to Social Security is not deductible for federal income tax purposes. After 1989, one-half of a self-employed person's self-employment tax is deductible for federal income tax purposes [Sec. 164(f)]. Answer (D) is incorrect. The Social Security Act does not exclude professionals from mandatory coverage.

20.4.6. Mr. and Mrs. B file a joint income tax return. Mr. B owns and operates a grocery store that had a net income of $15,000 in 2017. Mrs. B is a self-employed physical therapist, and her net income was $42,900. What is the total amount of self-employment tax Mr. and Mrs. B must report on their joint return for 2017?

A. $4,090

B. $6,630

C. $8,181

D. $8,859

Answer (C) is correct. *(SEE, adapted)*
    REQUIRED: The couple's self-employment tax for 2017.
    DISCUSSION: The tax on self-employment income is imposed by Sec. 1401 on all taxpayers whose net earnings from self-employment exceed $400 [Sec. 1402(b)]. For 2017, the tax is divided into two components: the Social Security and Medicare taxes, which are based on the net earnings from self-employment. The Social Security tax is imposed at a 12.4% rate up to a $127,200 maximum. The Medicare tax is imposed at a 2.9% rate, and there is no maximum. Taxpayers may reduce their tentative net earnings from self-employment by the product of the employer's portion of the self-employment tax rate (7.65%) times the tentative net earnings from self-employment [Sec. 1402(a)(12)]. The self-employment tax is computed separately for each spouse. Their taxes are

	Mr. B	Mrs. B
Net income (tentative net earnings from self-employment)	$15,000	$42,900
Less: Employer's portion of self-employment tax rate times net income	(1,148)	(3,282)
Net earnings from self-employment	$13,852	$39,618
Times: Tax Rate	× 0.153	× 0.153
Self-employment tax	$ 2,119	$ 6,062

The total self-employment tax for Mr. and Mrs. B is $8,181 ($2,119 + $6,062).
    Answer (A) is incorrect. After deducting a 7.65% tax from each income, the net earnings should not be multiplied by 7.65%. Answer (B) is incorrect. The amount of $6,630 only includes the Social Security portion of FICA tax (12.4%) to determine self-employment tax. Answer (D) is incorrect. The amount of $8,859 is the 15.3% tax rate applied to Mr. and Mrs. B's tentative net earnings from self-employment.

20.4.7. All of the following individuals are generally subject to the self-employment tax except

A. Grocery store sole proprietor.

B. Bricklayer – independent contractor.

C. Minister – member of the clergy.

D. Factory worker – paid on piecemeal basis.

Answer (D) is correct. *(SEE, adapted)*
    REQUIRED: The individual not subject to the self-employment tax.
    DISCUSSION: The self-employment tax applies to those individuals who have self-employment income. A factory worker paid on a piecemeal basis is an employee of a factory regardless of the method of payment. Therefore, the factory worker is subject to the FICA tax for employees rather than self-employed persons.
    Answer (A) is incorrect. A grocery store sole proprietor is a self-employed individual with self-employment income. Answer (B) is incorrect. A bricklayer is a self-employed individual with self-employment income. Answer (C) is incorrect. A minister is generally subject to the self-employment tax, although (s)he may make an irrevocable election to be exempt from it.

20.4.8. Mr. Y operates his own tax practice. For 2017, his books and records reflect the following:

Fees received	$65,000
Operating expenses	24,300
Loss on office equipment destroyed by fire	(400)
Gain on sale of computer used in the business	350

Mr. Y also had a part-time job for which he received $22,100 in wages that were subject to Social Security tax. What is the amount of earnings Mr. Y will have to pay self-employment tax on?

A. $40,700

B. $40,650

C. $40,300

D. $37,586

20.4.9. In 2017, Mr. K had $87,900 in wages subject to Social Security tax and $41,300 in net earnings from self-employment. What is the amount of K's self-employment tax for 2017 (rounded to the nearest dollar)?

A. $6,013

B. $6,071

C. $6,319

D. $19,768

Answer (D) is correct. *(SEE, adapted)*
REQUIRED: The amount of earnings subject to self-employment tax.
DISCUSSION: The Social Security component of the self-employment tax is imposed at a 12.4% tax rate on the first $127,200 of net earnings from self-employment in 2017, reduced by any wages that were already subject to the Social Security tax. The ceiling for Mr. Y in 2017 is $105,100 ($127,200 – $22,100). (There is no ceiling for the Medicare component of the FICA tax.)
Mr. Y's tentative net earnings from self-employment for 2017 is $40,700 ($65,000 – $24,300 operating expenses). The casualty loss of business property and the gain on the sale of business property are not included in the calculation of net earnings from self-employment. The tentative amount is reduced by the product of the employer's portion of the self-employment tax rate (7.65%) times the net earnings from self-employment ($40,700) [Sec. 1402(a)(12)]. Net earnings from self-employment for Mr. Y equals $37,586 ($40,700 – $3,114). Taxes will be paid on this amount since it is less than the Social Security ceiling.
Answer (A) is incorrect. Tentative net earnings from self-employment is $40,700, which should be reduced to find net earnings from self-employment. Answer (B) is incorrect. Net earnings does not include a reduction for the casualty loss or an increase for the gain on the sale of the computer. Answer (C) is incorrect. Net earnings does not include a reduction for the loss.

Answer (B) is correct. *(SEE, adapted)*
REQUIRED: The self-employment tax of a person who earned wages as an employee in 2017.
DISCUSSION: For 2017, the self-employment tax is separated into two components: Social Security and Medicare. The Social Security tax is 12.4% of the first $127,200 (2017) of self-employment income. The Medicare tax is 2.9% of all self-employment income (no ceiling applies). In computing the self-employment tax, taxpayers may reduce the tentative earnings from self-employment by the employer's portion of the self-employment tax rate times the tentative net earnings from self-employment (before this adjustment) to arrive at net earnings from self-employment. Such an adjustment has been made in arriving at the $41,300 amount. Mr. K's employment taxes on wages of $87,900 have already been paid through withholding by his employer. Therefore, he must pay the Social Security portion of the self-employment tax on $39,300 ($127,200 – $87,900). He must pay Medicare tax on the full $41,300. Mr. K's self-employment tax is thus $6,071 [($39,300 × 12.4%) + ($41,300 × 2.9%)].
Answer (A) is incorrect. The amount of $6,013 is the 15.3% self-employment tax rate times the $39,300 of net self-employment earnings needed to reach the $127,200 ceiling on the Social Security portion of the self-employment tax. Answer (C) is incorrect. A two-step calculation is applied to determine the tax, instead of the flat 15.3% rate that was used. Answer (D) is incorrect. Mr. K's employment taxes on wages of $87,900 have already been paid through withholding by his employer. The 12.4% Social Security rate applies only to the first $39,300 of net self-employment earnings needed to reach the $127,200 ceiling on the Social Security portion of the self-employment tax, while the 2.9% rate applies to the entire net earnings from self-employment.

20.4.10. For self-employment tax purposes, which of the following is not considered earnings from self-employment?

A. Net profit of a delicatessen operated by a sole proprietor.

B. Salary received by a corporate officer who is also the sole shareholder.

C. Distributive share of income from an operating partnership received by a general partner.

D. Guaranteed payment received from a partnership by a limited partner for services (s)he has performed.

Answer (B) is correct. *(SEE, adapted)*
REQUIRED: The earnings not subject to self-employment taxes.
DISCUSSION: Self-employment income is defined in Sec. 1402 generally as the net income derived by an individual from a trade or business. Wages and salary from a corporation are not self-employment income; they are earnings of an employee regardless of his or her stock ownership.
Answer (A) is incorrect. Net profit of a delicatessen operated by a sole proprietor constitutes income derived from a trade or business and therefore would be considered net earnings from self-employment. Answer (C) is incorrect. Distributive share of income from an operating partnership received by a general partner constitutes income derived from a trade or business and therefore would be considered net earnings from self-employment. Answer (D) is incorrect. A guaranteed payment received from a partnership by a limited partner for services (s)he has performed constitutes income derived from a trade or business and therefore would be considered net earnings from self-employment.

20.4.11. Based on the following information, how much will Cassie have to report as self-employment income?

Salary from her S corporation	$ 3,000
S corporation ordinary income	20,000
Corporate director fees	1,200
Schedule C net profit from sole proprietorship	300
Payment from insurance company for lost income due to cessation of business	11,000
Partnership income (inactive general partner)	5,000
Guaranteed payments from partnership	4,000

Cassie's salary is reasonable for the services she provides the S corporation.

A. $300

B. $10,500

C. $21,500

D. $44,500

Answer (C) is correct. *(SEE, adapted)*
REQUIRED: The amount of self-employment income.
DISCUSSION: Under Sec. 1402(a) and Reg. 1.1402(a)-1, net earnings from self-employment include the net income from a trade or business, guaranteed payments for services from a partnership, and a partner's distributive share of income from a partnership (whether the partner is active or not). Director's fees are self-employment income. Revenue Ruling 91-19 held that payments received for lost earnings were included in net earnings from self-employment. S corporation earnings required to be included in a shareholder's gross income are not self-employment income (Rev. Rul. 59-221). A bona fide salary is income from employment, not self-employment.
Cassie's self-employment income is computed as follows:

Director's fees	$ 1,200
Schedule C net profit	300
Payment for lost earnings	11,000
Distributive share of partnership income	5,000
Guaranteed payments from partnership	4,000
Income from self-employment	$21,500

Answer (A) is incorrect. Payment for lost income, a distributive share of partnership income, partnership guaranteed payments, and director's fees are also considered self-employment income. Answer (B) is incorrect. Payment for lost income is also self-employment income. Answer (D) is incorrect. The salary from the S corporation and the ordinary income from the S corporation are not considered self-employment income.

20.4.12. A general partner must include his or her distributive share of partnership income or loss in computing net earnings from self-employment.

A. True.

B. False.

Answer (A) is correct. *(SEE, adapted)*
DISCUSSION: Under Sec. 1402(a), net earnings from self-employment include the distributive share (whether or not distributed) of ordinary income or loss from any trade or business carried on by a partnership of which the taxpayer is a member. Special rules apply to limited partners in a limited partnership in determining their self-employment income [Sec. 1402(a)(13)].

20.4.13. An inactive general partner's distributive share of his or her partnership income is not considered to be net earnings from self-employment to the partner for self-employment tax purposes.

A. True.

B. False.

Answer (B) is correct. *(SEE, adapted)*
DISCUSSION: Under Sec. 1402(a), net earnings from self-employment include the partner's distributive share of ordinary income or loss whether distributed or not. There is no requirement that the partner be active in the partnership.

20.4.14. Mr. Q owns and operates a hotel that provides housekeeping and maid services for the occupants. The rents received are considered earnings from self-employment.

    A. True.

    B. False.

Answer (A) is correct. *(SEE, adapted)*
    DISCUSSION: Rents received from operating a hotel are considered net earnings from self-employment derived by an individual from conducting a trade or business under Sec. 1402(a).

20.4.15. Dividends on securities received by a dealer in securities are not self-employment income.

    A. True.

    B. False.

Answer (B) is correct. *(SEE, adapted)*
    DISCUSSION: Dividends and interest (generally) on securities is excluded from self-employment income unless received in the course of a trade or business as a dealer in stocks or securities [Sec. 1402(a)(2) and Reg. 1.1402(a)-5(a) and (b)].

20.4.16. The rentals that an individual receives from real estate and from personal property leased with the real estate are earnings from self-employment even though the individual is not engaged in a trade or business of being a real estate dealer.

    A. True.

    B. False.

Answer (B) is correct. *(SEE, adapted)*
    DISCUSSION: Rentals an individual receives from real estate and from personal property leased with the real estate are earnings from self-employment under Sec. 1402 only when the individual is engaged in the trade or business of dealing in real estate. When such rentals are received other than from the conduct of a trade or business, they are not net earnings from self-employment [Sec. 1402(a)(1)].

20.4.17. Mr. T operates an appliance repair shop with a fiscal year ending June 30. On January 1 of this year, the maximum earnings subject to the self-employment tax increased. T must compute the maximum earnings subject to the self-employment tax for the fiscal year ending June 30 of this year based upon a weighted average of the maximums for last year and this year.

    A. True.

    B. False.

Answer (B) is correct. *(SEE, adapted)*
    DISCUSSION: Since Mr. T's business uses a tax year other than a calendar year, he must use the tax rate and the maximum income limit in effect at the beginning of the fiscal year (July 1 of last year) throughout the year. Hence, the change in the income limit on January 1 of this year does not affect his self-employment tax for the fiscal year.

20.4.18. The net operating loss deduction should not be used to reduce net earnings from self-employment when figuring the self-employment tax.

    A. True.

    B. False.

Answer (A) is correct. *(SEE, adapted)*
    DISCUSSION: The net operating loss deduction is not allowed under Sec. 1402(a)(4) in computing the net earnings from self-employment.

20.4.19. H and his spouse, W, file a joint return. H has net earnings from a sole proprietorship of $35,000. H and W may split the $35,000 and file separate Form 1040s (each with the appropriate Schedule SE) in order to provide Social Security coverage for W.

    A. True.

    B. False.

Answer (B) is correct. *(SEE, adapted)*
    DISCUSSION: If one spouse has net earnings from self-employment and the couple elects to file separate tax returns, the spouse who had the net earnings from self-employment will report the entire amount. The spouse who did not have the net earnings from self-employment would report none of the income. Even spouses in community property states are required to report net earnings from self-employment for FICA tax purposes in this manner.

20.4.20. An honorary director of a corporation, who served as an active director for many years but who is no longer required to perform services, does not have to include the fees from the corporation in self-employment income.

    A. True.

    B. False.

Answer (B) is correct. *(SEE, adapted)*
    DISCUSSION: The fees paid to the now inactive director are paid because of his or her prior service, not as a gratuitous gift. Compensation for prior services is gross income under Sec. 61.

20.4.21. An ordained, licensed, or commissioned minister must include the rental value of a home provided him or her as part of his or her pay for duties performed as earnings from self-employment for purposes of the self-employment tax.

A. True.

B. False.

Answer (A) is correct. *(SEE, adapted)*
DISCUSSION: Under Sec. 1402(a)(8), an ordained, licensed, or commissioned minister must include the rental value of a home provided to him or her as part of his or her pay for duties performed as earnings from self-employment for purposes of the self-employment tax. This is true even though the rental value of such a home is not included in gross income for income tax purposes.

20.4.22. You are exempt from the self-employment tax if you are a United States citizen employed in the United States by a foreign government.

A. True.

B. False.

Answer (B) is correct. *(SEE, adapted)*
DISCUSSION: Wages received by a U.S. citizen employed in the U.S. by a foreign government are excluded from the employment taxes of Sec. 3121. Under Sec. 1402, however, these earnings are picked up as net earnings from self-employment (any trade or business) to the extent they are not covered by the employment taxes of Sec. 3121. There is no similar exemption under Sec. 1402 [see Sec. 1402(c)(2)].

20.5 Filing a Social Security Tax Return

20.5.1. During the current year, M paid $40 a week to a 17-year-old child (who is not M's child) to baby-sit and perform domestic services in M's home after school and on weekends while M was working. M files a Form 1040 to report her federal income taxes. Which of the following applies?

A. Form 941 must be filed.

B. Form 943 must be filed.

C. Schedule H must be filed.

D. No form or returns need be filed.

Answer (C) is correct. *(SEE, adapted)*
REQUIRED: The appropriate form to file when reporting wages paid to a domestic employee.
DISCUSSION: A domestic worker in a private home is subject to tax if his or her wages are at least $2,000 in any calendar year. When the domestic worker is subject to taxation, the employer must withhold FICA taxes and file the appropriate forms. Schedule H is a simplified form that may be used by employers of domestic workers in private homes.
Answer (A) is incorrect. Form 941 is the standard employer's quarterly federal tax return, which need not be filed when Schedule H is used. Answer (B) is incorrect. Form 943 is used by employers of agricultural workers. Answer (D) is incorrect. Schedule H is used by employers of household employees who earn more than $2,000 in a calendar year.

20.5.2. Mr. J, a farmer, has seven farm employees. Which one of the following returns is Mr. J required to file for taxes withheld from wages?

A. Form 941.

B. Form 943.

C. Form 945.

D. Schedule H.

Answer (B) is correct. *(SEE, adapted)*
REQUIRED: The appropriate form to file with respect to Social Security taxes withheld from agricultural employees.
DISCUSSION: An employer of agricultural employees is required to withhold both Social Security taxes and income taxes from wages. Form 943 is used by employers of agricultural workers to report the withholding of Social Security taxes.
Answer (A) is incorrect. Form 941 is the standard employer's quarterly federal tax return, which need not be filed when Form 943 is filed. Answer (C) is incorrect. Form 945 is used to report nonpayroll income taxes that are withheld (e.g., withholding on pensions or annuities). Answer (D) is incorrect. Schedule H is used by employers of domestic workers in private homes.

20.5.3. All of the following are characteristics of the Electronic Federal Tax Payment System (EFTPS) except

A. If a taxpayer was required to make deposits by electronic funds transfer and failed to do so, (s)he could be subject to a 10% penalty.

B. Taxpayers who are not required to make electronic deposits may not participate in EFTPS.

C. If a taxpayer's total deposits of Social Security, Medicare, railroad retirement, and withheld income taxes were more than $200,000, (s)he must make electronic deposits for all depository tax liabilities.

D. Penalties are imposed for failure to use EFTPS.

Answer (B) is correct. *(Publisher, adapted)*
REQUIRED: The item that is not a characteristic of EFTPS.
DISCUSSION: The EFTPS must be used to make electronic deposits. Taxpayers who are not required to make electronic deposits may voluntarily participate in EFTPS. If a taxpayer is required to make deposits by electronic funds transfer and fails to do so, (s)he could be subject to a 10% penalty.
Answer (A) is incorrect. A characteristic of EFTPS is if a taxpayer was required to make deposits by electronic funds transfer and failed to do so, (s)he could be subject to a 10% penalty. Answer (C) is incorrect. A characteristic of EFTPS is if a taxpayer's total deposits of Social Security, Medicare, railroad retirement, and withheld income taxes were more than $200,000, (s)he must make electronic deposits for all depository tax liabilities. Answer (D) is incorrect. Penalties are imposed for failure to use EFTPS.

20.5.4. Mr. C, a calendar-year taxpayer, uses the accrual method of accounting. He pays his employees on the third day of each month. As of December 31 of the current year, accrued wages for the month of December were $30,000. Wages paid October 3 totaled $20,000; November 3, $25,000; and December 3, $22,000. Mr. C's fourth-quarter return, Form 941, should show total wages of

A. $45,000

B. $67,000

C. $75,000

D. $97,000

Answer (B) is correct. *(SEE, adapted)*
REQUIRED: The amount of wages that should be reported on an employer's fourth-quarter return of Form 941.
DISCUSSION: Taxable wages and employment taxes are reported only when wages are actually paid. Employment taxes are imposed by a separate part of the Internal Revenue Code and have no relationship to the employer's method of accounting for income tax purposes. Therefore, accrued wages are not included on Form 941; only wages actually paid are included. Mr. C's fourth-quarter return should show total wages of

Paid October 3	$20,000
Paid November 3	25,000
Paid December 3	22,000
Total wages in fourth quarter	$67,000

Answer (A) is incorrect. The December 3 wages paid are included in total wages. Answer (C) is incorrect. The December 3 wages should be included and the accrued December wages should not be included in total wages. Answer (D) is incorrect. The accrued December wages are not included in the fourth-quarter return.

20.5.5. A taxpayer may use private delivery services designated by the IRS to meet the "timely mailing as timely filing/paying" rule for Form 941 and payments.

A. True.

B. False.

Answer (A) is correct. *(Publisher, adapted)*
DISCUSSION: A taxpayer may use certain private delivery services designated by the IRS for tax returns and payments. The IRS publishes a list of the designated private delivery services in September of each year.

20.5.6. If you withhold income tax from wages or are liable for Social Security taxes, you must file a quarterly return on Form 941 unless the wages you pay are for domestic service or agricultural labor.

A. True.

B. False.

Answer (A) is correct. *(SEE, adapted)*
DISCUSSION: If you, as an employer, pay wages and withhold taxes on those wages, you are required to file Form 941 as a collecting agent. If the wages that you pay are for domestic services, you are generally required to file Schedule H for Form 1040 instead. If you are a sole proprietor and file Form 941 for business employees, taxes paid for household employees can be reported on your Form 941. If the wages that you pay are for agricultural labor, you are required to file Form 943.

20.6 Federal Unemployment Tax

20.6.1. Given the following wage information, what are the total gross wages subject to Federal Unemployment Tax for the current year?

Employee	Wages Paid during the Current Year
T	$ 4,200
E	5,800
M	22,900

A. $7,000

B. $12,000

C. $17,000

D. $32,900

Answer (C) is correct. *(SEE, adapted)*
REQUIRED: The amount of gross wages subject to the Federal Unemployment Tax Act for the current year.
DISCUSSION: Under Sec. 3306(b)(1), wages are taxed for federal unemployment taxes up to $7,000 for each employee. Wages earned in excess of $7,000 are not subject to federal unemployment taxes. The full amount of wages paid during the current year to employee T and employee E is taxable. Only $7,000 of the wages paid to M is subject to federal unemployment taxes. Thus, the total amount of wages paid in the current year that is subject to federal unemployment taxes is $17,000.

Employee	Wages Subject to Unemployment Tax
T	$ 4,200
E	5,800
M	7,000
Total	$17,000

Answer (A) is incorrect. The limit of income per person that is subject to federal unemployment taxes is $7,000. Answer (B) is incorrect. Income up to $7,000 per person is subject to federal unemployment taxes. Answer (D) is incorrect. The wages of Employee M subject to federal unemployment taxes are limited to $7,000.

20.6.2. All of the following individuals who perform services for a business are subject to taxes under the Federal Insurance Contributions Act (FICA) and the Federal Unemployment Tax Act (FUTA) except

A. Part-time employee.

B. Officer of a corporation.

C. Office manager.

D. Director of a corporation.

Answer (D) is correct. *(SEE, adapted)*
REQUIRED: The individual who is not subject to FICA and FUTA.
DISCUSSION: Employers are subject to both FICA and FUTA. Self-employed persons are subject to self-employment taxes but not unemployment taxes. The director of a corporation is a self-employed individual, not an employee, so (s)he is not subject to FUTA.
Answer (A) is incorrect. A part-time employee is subject to FICA and FUTA. Answer (B) is incorrect. An officer of a corporation is subject to FICA and FUTA. Answer (C) is incorrect. An office manager is subject to FICA and FUTA.

20.6.3. The theatrical agency of Power & Tyrone employs two people full-time. Which of the following is true with regard to federal unemployment insurance?

A. In terms of industry and number of employees, Power & Tyrone is within the class of employers covered by the Federal Unemployment Tax Act.

B. Service agencies are exempt.

C. Since the number of employees is small, an exemption can be obtained from coverage if a request is filed with the appropriate federal agency.

D. If the employees all reside in one state and do not travel interstate on company business, Power & Tyrone is exempt from compliance with the act.

Answer (A) is correct. *(CPA, adapted)*
REQUIRED: The correct statement regarding federal unemployment insurance.
DISCUSSION: An employer that (1) employs one or more persons covered by the Social Security Act for at least part of a day in each of 20 different calendar weeks in a year or the preceding year or (2) pays wages of $1,500 or more during any calendar quarter in a year or the preceding year must pay a federal unemployment tax on the first $7,000 of each employee's wages [Sec. 3306(a)]. Thus, a theatrical agency employing two persons full-time would fall within the class of employers covered by the federal unemployment tax.
Answer (B) is incorrect. Businesses classified as service agencies are not exempt. Answer (C) is incorrect. No exemption from the tax can be obtained by filing a request with any federal agency. Answer (D) is incorrect. For purposes of Social Security and its various benefits, employment is considered to affect interstate commerce and falls within federal jurisdiction regardless of residence and travel.

20.6.4. C, a sole proprietor, has three employees. His FUTA tax liability for each quarter of Year 1 was as follows:

First Quarter	$250
Second Quarter	225
Third Quarter	325
Fourth Quarter	250

Assuming the due date does not fall on a Saturday, Sunday, or legal holiday, C was required to make his first deposit of FUTA tax by which date?

A. April 30, Year 1.

B. July 31, Year 1.

C. October 31, Year 1.

D. January 31, Year 2.

Answer (C) is correct. *(SEE, adapted)*
REQUIRED: The date the employer is required to deposit FUTA taxes.
DISCUSSION: Form 940 is required to be filed by January 31 each year with respect to FUTA taxes for the prior calendar year. However, quarterly payments must be made as soon as the liability for unpaid taxes exceeds $500. These quarterly payments are due on April 30, July 31, October 31, and January 31.
Since C's FUTA tax liability did not reach $500 until the third quarter, the first deposit of FUTA tax is due by October 31, Year 1.
Answer (A) is incorrect. April 30, Year 1, is not the correct date when C was required to make his first deposit of FUTA tax. Answer (B) is incorrect. July 31, Year 1, is not the correct date when C was required to make his first deposit of FUTA tax. Answer (D) is incorrect. January 31, Year 2, was not the correct date when C was required to make his first deposit of FUTA tax.

20.6.5. In the current year, the services of an individual who works for his or her spouse in a trade or business are covered by Social Security taxes but not by federal unemployment taxes.

A. True.

B. False.

Answer (A) is correct. *(SEE, adapted)*
DISCUSSION: Section 3101 imposes (with limited exceptions) Social Security taxes on the income of every individual. One such exemption is that employment excludes services performed by a child in the employ of his or her father or mother. No Social Security tax exemptions are provided for an individual who works for his or her spouse in a trade or business. Section 3301 imposes federal unemployment taxes on employers. Under Sec. 3306(c)(5), the employer does not have to pay federal unemployment taxes on services performed by the employer's spouse, or by the employer's son or daughter if (s)he is under age 21.

20.7 Withholding

20.7.1. Which of the following statements is false in respect to the penalty assessed against a person who willfully fails to account for and pay over income and employment taxes, or to pay over collected excise taxes?

A. The penalty is equal to 100% of the tax required to be collected and paid over.

B. The penalty is computed based on the withheld income tax and the employee's and employer's employment taxes, or collected excise tax.

C. The penalty may be assessed against any person responsible for "accounting for and paying over income and employment taxes, or paying over collected excise taxes," who willfully fails to do so.

D. If the taxpayer does not agree with the IRS district's recommendation that the penalty be assessed, the taxpayer may request a hearing with the regional appeals office.

Answer (B) is correct. *(SEE, adapted)*
REQUIRED: The false statement about the penalty for willful failure to account for and pay over income and employment taxes, or to pay over collected excise taxes.
DISCUSSION: Under Sec. 6672, any person required to collect, account for, and pay over any Internal Revenue tax and who willfully fails to do so may be liable for a penalty equal to the total amount of the tax not collected and paid over. For not withholding income tax, the employer may, therefore, suffer a 100% penalty. The penalty is based on the tax not collected and paid over. The 100% penalty does not apply to the employer's matching portion of employment taxes. IRS policy has been to assert the penalty against a responsible person, such as the organization's accountant, other than the employer, etc., only when the taxes cannot be collected against the employer, etc. In addition, the employer is liable for the payment of the tax required to be deducted and withheld from employees' wages (Sec. 3403).
Answer (A) is incorrect. The Sec. 6672 penalty is equal to 100% of the tax required to be collected and paid over. Answer (C) is incorrect. The Sec. 6672 penalty may be assessed against any person responsible for "accounting for and paying over income and employment taxes, or paying over collected excise taxes," who willfully fails to do so. Answer (D) is incorrect. If the taxpayer does not agree with the IRS district's recommendation that the Sec. 6672 penalty be assessed, the taxpayer may request a hearing with the regional appeals office.

20.7.2. Which of the following employee benefits is not subject to income tax withholding by an employer?

A. Bonuses only paid at year end.

B. Sick pay.

C. Medical expense reimbursements under a self-insured plan.

D. Employee's personal use of company car.

Answer (C) is correct. *(Publisher, adapted)*
REQUIRED: The employee benefit that is not subject to withholding for income taxes.
DISCUSSION: Section 3402(a) requires every employer who pays wages to withhold from the wages a tax determined in accordance with tables prescribed by the Secretary of the Treasury. These wages are defined in Sec. 3401(a) as all remuneration for services performed by an employee including the cash value of all noncash payments. However, wages do not include medical care reimbursements under a self-insured medical reimbursement plan since these reimbursements are excluded from the employee's income under Sec. 105.
Answer (A) is incorrect. Bonuses are wages subject to withholding whenever they are paid. Answer (B) is incorrect. Sick pay is also subject to withholding since there is no exclusion for it from gross income. Answer (D) is incorrect. An employee's personal use of a company car is noncash remuneration and is subject to withholding.

20.7.3. The penalty for willful failure to collect or pay over to the government the amounts required to be withheld from employees is what percentage of the tax?

A. .5%

B. 5%

C. 50%

D. 100%

Answer (D) is correct. *(Publisher, adapted)*
REQUIRED: The percentage of the tax that may be imposed as a penalty against an employer for willful failure to withhold income tax.
DISCUSSION: Under Sec. 6672, any person who is required to collect, account for, and pay over any Internal Revenue tax and who willfully fails to do so may be liable for a penalty equal to the total amount of the tax not collected and paid over. For not withholding income tax, the employer may, therefore, suffer a 100% penalty. In addition, the employer is liable for the payment of the tax required to be deducted and withheld from employees' wages (Sec. 3403). As a result, the employer who fails to withhold can be required to pay, not just withhold, the tax and still be subject to a 100% penalty.
Answer (A) is incorrect. Half of a percent is not the correct penalty for willful failure to withhold income taxes from employees. Answer (B) is incorrect. Five percent is not the correct penalty for willful failure to withhold income taxes from employees. Answer (C) is incorrect. Fifty percent is not the correct penalty for willful failure to withhold income taxes from employees.

20.7.4. Corporation X, a foreign corporation engaged in the conduct of a U.S. trade or business, received interest income from the following U.S. sources in the current year. All of the income is effectively connected with the conduct of a U.S. trade or business. What amount is subject to withholding tax?

Passbook savings	$2,500
Certificates of deposit	3,000
Deposits with an insurance company	1,500

A. $0

B. $2,500

C. $3,000

D. $7,000

Answer (A) is correct. *(SEE, adapted)*
REQUIRED: The amount of income of a foreign corporation that is subject to withholding tax.
DISCUSSION: Under Reg. 1.1441-4(a), no withholding is required for income received by a foreign corporation if the income is effectively connected with the conduct of a trade or business within the U.S. Under Sec. 864(c)(2), interest income from passbook savings, certificates of deposit, and deposits with an insurance company are all considered income effectively connected with the conduct of a trade or business within the U.S. if the income items satisfy an "asset-use" test or if the trade or business activities were a material factor in the production of the income.
Answer (B) is incorrect. The amount of passbook savings is $2,500. Answer (C) is incorrect. The amount of certificate of deposit is $3,000. Answer (D) is incorrect. This figure is not the correct amount subject to withholding tax.

20.7.5. Corporation R, a domestic corporation, distributed the following dividends to its shareholders in the current year:

$5,000 to Shareholder A, a foreign partnership
$4,000 to Shareholder B, an unrelated foreign corporation
$3,000 to Shareholder C, a resident alien
$2,000 to Shareholder D, a nonresident alien

All of the income of Corporation R was from sources within the United States and is not eligible for special treatment under a tax treaty. On what amount of dividends must R withhold tax?

A. $0

B. $7,000

C. $9,000

D. $11,000

Answer (D) is correct. *(SEE, adapted)*
REQUIRED: The amount of dividends subject to withholding.
DISCUSSION: Under Sec. 1441(a), a corporation paying a dividend from income from sources within the United States to any nonresident alien individual or any foreign partnership is required to deduct and withhold a tax equal to 30% (or a lower rate specified in a tax treaty) of the dividend. Section 1442(a) requires that a tax of 30% (or a lower rate specified in a tax treaty) be withheld on dividends paid to a foreign corporation that are derived from gross income from sources within the United States. The total amount of dividends on which R must withhold tax is $11,000 ($5,000 + $4,000 + $2,000).
Answer (A) is incorrect. Some amount of dividends is subject to withholding. Answer (B) is incorrect. Shareholder B's dividends are also subject to withholding. Answer (C) is incorrect. Shareholder D's dividends are also subject to withholding.

20.7.6. All of the following items of gross income earned by a foreign corporation in the United States are subject to 30% withholding except

A. Rents.

B. Sale of real property.

C. Interest.

D. Dividends.

Answer (B) is correct. *(SEE, adapted)*
REQUIRED: The item of gross income earned by a foreign corporation in the United States that is not subject to 30% withholding.
DISCUSSION: Section 1442(a) states that, in the case of foreign corporations, a tax of 30% is to be withheld on items of income provided in Sec. 1441. Section 1441(b) states that items of income subject to withholding are interest, dividends, rent, salaries, wages, premiums, annuities, compensations, remunerations, emoluments, or other fixed or determinable annual or periodical gains. A sale of real property is not subject to withholding unless it is a U.S. real property interest [as defined under Secs. 897(c) and 1445(a) and Reg. 1.1445-2(a)]. If the real property is a U.S. real property interest, withholding is required at a 10% rate on the amount realized from the sale [Sec. 1445(a)].
Answer (A) is incorrect. Rents are subject to 30% withholding unless reduced by a tax treaty. Answer (C) is incorrect. Interest is subject to 30% withholding unless reduced by a tax treaty. Answer (D) is incorrect. Dividends are subject to 30% withholding unless reduced by a tax treaty.

20.7.7. On which of the following is withholding not required?

A. Payments of dividends or interest of $10 or more to a U.S. payee when the payee has furnished his or her taxpayer identification number.

B. Payments of $600 or more to an independent contractor for services if the taxpayer identification number of the U.S. payee recipient is not provided.

C. Payments of deferred compensation if the recipient has not elected otherwise.

D. Payments to foreign persons for the purchase in the current year of U.S. real property used in a trade or business.

Answer (A) is correct. *(Publisher, adapted)*
REQUIRED: The payments on which the payor is not required to withhold income taxes.
DISCUSSION: The Sec. 3406 backup withholding rules require the payor to withhold 28% of dividend or interest payments of $10 or more. Withholding is not required, however, if the payee furnishes his or her taxpayer identification number to the payor. The payor is then required to report the payment to the IRS.
Answer (B) is incorrect. The payor must withhold 28% of such payments unless the independent contractor gives the taxpayer identification number to the payor. Answer (C) is incorrect. Section 3405(a)(1) requires the payor of periodic payments (such as deferred compensation) to withhold an amount as if it were paid as wages. However, an individual may elect under Sec. 3405(a)(2) against this withholding. Answer (D) is incorrect. Section 1445 requires anyone who purchases U.S. real property from a foreign person to withhold 10% of the amount the foreign person has realized on the sale. The purchase of a personal residence for $300,000 or less is one of several exceptions.

20.7.8. On January 3 of the current year, an employee of Corporation T filed a Form W-4, *Employee's Withholding Allowance Certificate*, claiming 25 withholding allowances. T must notify the employee that this number of withholding allowances is excessive and disregard the Form W-4 for withholding purposes.

A. True.

B. False.

Answer (B) is correct. *(SEE, adapted)*
DISCUSSION: An employee may be directed to send certain Forms W-4 to the IRS for review. This is done at the request of the IRS and not automatically by the employer regardless of the number of withholding allowances claimed. The employer is not required to disregard the Form W-4 for withholding purposes. The IRS will notify the employer as to what action to take. An employee can be liable for penalties and criminal prosecution for fraudulent filings of Form W-4.

20.7.9. If no income tax is withheld, an employer must keep a record of the fair market value and date of each payment of noncash compensation made to a retail commission salesperson.

A. True.

B. False.

Answer (A) is correct. *(SEE, adapted)*
DISCUSSION: Regulation 31.3402(j)-1 allows an employer to disregard wages paid in a medium other than cash for services by a retail commission salesperson if the employer ordinarily pays in cash. In that case, however, the employer must keep a record of the fair market value and date of each payment of noncash compensation.

20.7.10. Agency Corp. has withheld tax on Jewel's regular wages during the current year. In Jewel's last paycheck for the year, Agency included an additional amount of $160. The amount represented the balance of a bonus, which was separately stated, net of tax withheld on the bonus. The $40 amount withheld is sufficient even if the bonus was $200 because Agency made no allowance for exemptions.

A. True.

B. False.

Answer (B) is correct. *(Publisher, adapted)*
DISCUSSION: When tax has been withheld on regular wages and a supplemental amount (such as a bonus) is not paid in a single payment together with regular wages, or is paid with the regular wages but is separately stated, the employer may choose to treat the supplemental wages as wholly separate from the regular wages and withhold at a flat rate on the supplemental wage payment without making any allowance for exemptions [Reg. 31.3402(g)-(2)]. The flat rate is 28% in 1994 and later years. The amount withheld is not sufficient because Agency withheld at only a 20% rate ($200 × 20% = $40).

20.7.11. Corporation F, a foreign corporation, has a store located in the United States that sells cosmetics. Generally, the income derived from selling the cosmetics is effectively connected with the conduct of a business within the United States and is not subject to the withholding tax on foreign corporations.

A. True.

B. False.

Answer (A) is correct. *(SEE, adapted)*
DISCUSSION: Income derived from selling cosmetics through a store located in the United States is treated as income effectively connected with the conduct of a trade or business within the United States. Under Secs. 1441 and 1442, no withholding is required for any income (other than compensation for personal services) that is effectively connected with the conduct of a trade or business within the United States.

20.7.12. Generally, if dividends are paid by a domestic corporation to a foreign corporation or partnership or to a nonresident alien having an address outside of the United States, taxes must be withheld. Even if the foreign corporation, partnership, or nonresident alien gives the domestic corporation a United States address, the domestic corporation must continue to withhold taxes unless the foreign person establishes U.S. residency.

A. True.

B. False.

Answer (A) is correct. *(SEE, adapted)*
DISCUSSION: For dividends, when a payor corporation has no definite knowledge of the status of a shareholder, the tax under Sec. 1441 must be withheld if the shareholder's address is outside the United States. If the shareholder's address is within the United States, it may be assumed that the shareholder is a citizen or resident of the United States or a domestic partnership or a domestic corporation, as the case may be [Reg. 1.1441-3(b)(3)]. But, under Reg. 1.1441-4(b)(2)(iii), if a withholding agent is not able to readily determine the relationship between the agent and a foreign payee or the relationship between a foreign payee and a foreign corporation, the agent is required to withhold 30% of the amount paid.

20.7.13. Corporation N, a foreign corporation, received a dividend payment from Corporation O, a U.S. corporation. Corporation O will compute the withholding on the total amount of the dividend payment less the dividends-received deduction.

A. True.

B. False.

Answer (B) is correct. *(SEE, adapted)*
   DISCUSSION: A dividends-received deduction is only available to a foreign corporation on its dividend income received from a domestic corporation that is effectively connected with the conduct of a U.S. trade or business. Section 1441(c) provides an exemption from the 30% withholding requirement of Sec. 1441(a) for income effectively connected with the conduct of a U.S. trade or business. The U.S. taxes due on such income are paid by the foreign corporation by making estimated tax payments.

20.7.14. Form 1042, *Annual Withholding Tax Return for U.S. Source Income of Foreign Persons*, is due by March 15 of the year following the tax year even if there was no withholding because of a specific withholding exemption.

A. True.

B. False.

Answer (A) is correct. *(SEE, adapted)*
   A U.S. corporation that makes payments to a nonresident alien is required to file Form 1042 each year even if no income tax is withheld because of exemptions to which the nonresident alien was entitled [Reg. 1.1461-2(b)].

20.7.15. Form 1042S, *Foreign Person's U.S. Source Income Subject to Withholding*, is required for each payee (recipient) of income to whom payments were made during the calendar year, regardless of the amount of tax withheld.

A. True.

B. False.

Answer (A) is correct. *(SEE, adapted)*
   DISCUSSION: Regulation 1.1461-2(c) states that every withholding agent is required to file Form 1042S for each payee of income to whom payments were made during the calendar year. The form is required regardless of the amount of tax withheld.

Use **Gleim Test Prep** for interactive study and easy-to-use detailed analytics!

STUDY UNIT TWENTY-ONE
WEALTH TRANSFER TAXES

21.1 Gifts Defined

21.1.1. Which of the following situations does not constitute a transfer that comes within the gift tax statutes?

A. An individual creates a trust under the terms of which a child is to get income for life and a grandchild the remainder at the child's death.

B. An individual, with personal funds, purchases real property and has title conveyed to the individual and the individual's brother as joint tenants.

C. An individual creates a trust giving income for life to his wife and providing that, at her death, the corpus is to be distributed to his son. The individual reserves the right to revoke the transfer at any time without the consent of the other parties.

D. An individual, with his own funds, purchases a U.S. savings bond made payable to himself and his wife. His wife surrenders the bond for cash to be used for her benefit.

Answer (C) is correct. *(SEE, adapted)*
REQUIRED: The transfer that does not come within the gift tax statutes.
DISCUSSION: The gift tax applies to most gratuitous shifting of property or property rights during one's lifetime. The concept of a gift for gift tax purposes is generally broader than (and not well integrated with) the narrow concept of a gift for income tax exclusion purposes. Section 2511(a) provides that the gift tax applies to transfers made in trust, to indirect gifts, and to intangible property in addition to outright and direct transfers of tangible property. However, the gift tax applies only to completed gifts, and Reg. 25.2511-2(c) provides that a gift is incomplete if the donor retains the power to revest the beneficial title to the property in himself or herself. If the transfer is revocable without the consent of the other parties, it is not complete and not taxable.
Answer (A) is incorrect. The gift tax applies to gifts made in trust, to income interests, and to remainder interests. Answer (B) is incorrect. The brother received an ownership interest in the land so that partial interest is taxable. Answer (D) is incorrect. The individual has conferred a benefit upon his wife in the amount of the bond surrendered.

21.1.2. Raff created a joint bank account for himself and his friend's son, Dave. There is a gift to Dave when

A. Raff creates the account.

B. Raff dies.

C. Dave draws on the account for his own benefit.

D. Dave is notified by Raff that the account has been created.

Answer (C) is correct. *(CPA, adapted)*
REQUIRED: The time when a completed gift is made.
DISCUSSION: A gift is complete when the donor has so parted with dominion and control as to leave him or her no power to change its disposition [Reg. 25.2511-2(b)]. Raff made an indirect transfer of the money to Dave by opening the bank account. Only when Dave withdraws the money will Raff lose all dominion and control over the property so that the action will complete the gift [Reg. 25.2511-1(h)(4)].
Answer (A) is incorrect. When Raff creates the account, he can still withdraw the money so that it is not a completed gift. Answer (B) is incorrect. When Raff dies, there may be no transfer to Dave or there may be a devise, but not a gift because a gift only occurs during lifetime. Answer (D) is incorrect. Notice has no effect here since Dave must draw on the account for a completed gift.

21.1.3. Which of the following represents taxable gifts?

I.   Transfer of wealth to a dependent family member that represents support

II. Payment of son's tuition for law school

III. Payment of $14,000 of medical bills for a friend

    A.   None of the choices is a taxable gift.

    B.   Only I is a taxable gift.

    C.   Only II is a taxable gift.

    D.   Both II and III are taxable gifts.

Answer (A) is correct. *(Publisher, adapted)*
    REQUIRED: The taxable gift(s) among the items listed.
    DISCUSSION: Section 2503(e), which defines taxable gifts, specifically excludes bona fide transfers made on behalf of any individual as tuition to an educational organization or as payment to someone who provides medical care for such individual. Accordingly, neither payment of a son's tuition for law school (II) nor payment of $14,000 of medical bills for a friend (III) is a taxable gift.
    Item I is not a taxable gift because transfers that represent support are not considered gifts.
    Answer (B) is incorrect. The transfer is excluded from the definition of a taxable gift by Sec. 2503(e). Answer (C) is incorrect. Payment of the son's tuition for law school is not a taxable gift. Answer (D) is incorrect. The two transfers are both excluded from the definition of a taxable gift by Sec. 2503(e).

21.1.4. During the current year, Mr. and Mrs. X made joint gifts to their son of the following items:

● A painting with an adjusted basis of $16,000 and a fair market value of $45,000.

● Stock with an adjusted basis of $27,000 and a fair market value of $30,000.

● An auto with an adjusted basis of $16,000 and a fair market value of $18,000.

● An interest-free loan of $8,000 for a boat (for the son's personal use) on January 1 of the current year, which was repaid by their son on December 31 of the current year. Assume the applicable federal rate was 11% per annum.

What is the gross amount of gifts includible in Mr. and Mrs. X's gift tax return?

    A. $93,880

    B. $93,000

    C. $59,880

    D. $59,000

Answer (B) is correct. *(SEE, adapted)*
    REQUIRED: The gross amount of gifts including an interest-free loan.
    DISCUSSION: The amount of a gift made in property is the fair market value of the property on the date of the gift [Sec. 2512(a)]. The auto, painting, and stock have a combined fair market value of $93,000.
    In general, an interest-free loan results in deemed transfers of interest between the borrower and lender. When the two parties are related, the lender is deemed to have made a gift of the interest amount to the borrower [Sec. 7872(a)(1)]. However, Sec. 7872(c)(2) excludes gift loans between individuals from this provision if the aggregate outstanding principal does not exceed $10,000. Accordingly, the $8,000 interest-free loan does not result in a gift.
    Answer (A) is incorrect. The amount of $93,880 includes $880 worth of interest from the loan. Answer (C) is incorrect. The amount of $59,880 includes $880 worth of interest, and the properties are valued at their adjusted-basis amounts. Answer (D) is incorrect. The amount of $59,000 values the properties at their adjusted-basis amounts.

21.1.5. All of the following statements relating to qualified transfers for gift tax purposes are true except

    A.   The exclusion for a qualified transfer is in addition to the annual exclusion.

    B.   A qualified transfer is allowed without regard to the relationship between the donor and donee.

    C.   Only that part of a payment to a qualified educational institution that applies to direct tuition costs is a qualified transfer.

    D.   A payment made directly to an individual to reimburse him for his medical expenses is a qualified transfer.

Answer (D) is correct. *(SEE, adapted)*
    REQUIRED: The false statement about qualified transfers for gift tax purposes.
    DISCUSSION: Section 2503(e) provides an exclusion from the gift tax for transfers made to pay tuition at an educational institution or to pay medical bills. "A payment made directly to an individual to reimburse him for his medical expenses is a qualified transfer" is a false statement because the qualified transfer must be made directly to the provider of medical care.
    Answer (A) is incorrect. The exclusion for a qualified transfer is in addition to the annual exclusion. Answer (B) is incorrect. A qualified transfer is allowed without regard to the relationship between the donor and donee. Answer (C) is incorrect. Only that part of a payment to a qualified educational institution that applies to direct tuition costs is a qualified transfer.

21.1.6. In which of the following circumstances would a gift tax return be due?

A. Check for $26,000 to son.

B. Transfer of stock valued at $30,000 to spouse.

C. Payment of a friend's $16,000 tuition expense.

D. None of the answers are correct.

Answer (A) is correct. *(SEE, adapted)*
REQUIRED: The circumstance in which a gift tax return is required to be filed.
DISCUSSION: A donor is required to file a gift tax return, Form 709, for any gift(s), unless all gifts are excluded under the annual $14,000 exclusion, the exclusion for medical or tuition payments, and the deduction for qualified transfers to the donor's spouse. These exclusions apply for gifts of present interests only. Any gift of a future interest requires the filing of Form 709. Gift-splitting does not excuse the donor from the requirement to file. A check for $26,000 exceeds the amount of the exclusion.
Answer (B) is incorrect. The deduction for qualified transfers to the donor's spouse is permitted. Answer (C) is incorrect. An exclusion exists for payment of tuition. Answer (D) is incorrect. A check for $26,000 to a son does not qualify for an exclusion.

21.1.7. A gift is complete if a donor has parted with dominion and control over the transferred property or property interest and if the donor is left without the power to change its disposition whether for the benefit of the donor or for the benefit of others.

A. True.

B. False.

Answer (A) is correct. *(SEE, adapted)*
DISCUSSION: Regulation 25.2511-2 discusses the effect of the donor's dominion and control over transferred property. If the donor has so parted with dominion and control over the property as to leave him or her no power to change its disposition, whether for his or her own benefit or for the benefit of another, the gift is complete.

21.1.8. A sale is completed in the ordinary course of Mr. Toad's business and the sales price is less than the fair market value of the property. The difference between the fair market value and the sales price is not a gift.

A. True.

B. False.

Answer (A) is correct. *(Publisher, adapted)*
DISCUSSION: Section 2512(b) provides that, when property is transferred for less than an adequate and full consideration in money or money's worth, the amount by which the value of the property exceeds the value of the consideration is deemed a gift. However, a sale, exchange, or other transfer of property made in the ordinary course of business (in a transaction that is bona fide, at arm's length, and free from any donative intent) is made for adequate and full consideration in money or money's worth (Reg. 25.2512-8).

21.1.9. Donative intent must be present before a gift tax can be levied.

A. True.

B. False.

Answer (B) is correct. *(Publisher, adapted)*
DISCUSSION: Donative intent on the part of the transferor is not an essential element in application of the gift tax to the transfer. Application of the gift tax is based on objective facts of the transfer and circumstances under which it is made rather than on subjective motives of the donor [Reg. 25.2511-1(g)(1)].

21.2 Valuation of Gifts

21.2.1. On December 1 of last year, Sam gave his son, Stan, a taxable gift of land with a fair market value of $15,000 on the date of the gift. Sam paid gift tax of $4,200. Sam had purchased the land 7 years ago for $10,000, which was his adjusted basis on the date of the gift. On January 1 of this year, Stan sold the land for $14,000. What was the value of the land for gift tax purposes, and what was Stan's basis?

	Gift Tax Value	Stan's Basis
A.	$14,000	$15,400
B.	$10,000	$11,400
C.	$15,000	$10,000
D.	$15,000	$11,400

Answer (D) is correct. *(Publisher, adapted)*
REQUIRED: The value of land for gift tax purposes and the donee's basis in the land.
DISCUSSION: The amount of a gift made in property is the fair market value of the property on the date of the gift [Sec. 2512(a)]. The fair market value of Sam's property on the date of the gift was $15,000.
The basis of property acquired by gift generally is the same as it was in the hands of the donor [Sec. 1015(a)], increased by the portion of the gift tax attributable to the appreciation in value of the property [Sec. 1015(d)(6)].

$$\frac{\$5,000 \text{ appreciation}}{\$15,000 \text{ taxable gift}} \times \$4,200 \text{ tax} = \$1,400$$

Stan's basis in the land is $11,400 ($10,000 basis of the donor + $1,400 of gift tax attributable to the appreciation of the property).
Answer (A) is incorrect. The amount Stan received for the land is $14,000. Also, Stan's basis was not $15,400. Answer (B) is incorrect. The amount Sam paid for the land 7 years ago is $10,000. Answer (C) is incorrect. Stan's basis was not $10,000.

21.2.2. Joe is contemplating retirement and decided to simplify his financial situation by disposing of some assets. He had the following transactions during 2017:

1. Sold his business to his son for $100,000. The fair market value of the business at the time of the sale was $175,000.

2. Paid college tuition of $17,000 for his brother's child.

3. Gave stock valued at $15,000 to his alma mater.

4. Paid $20,000 of the medical expenses of his sister who had no insurance.

What is the total amount of gifts (before exclusion) that should be reported on his gift tax return for 2017?

A. $75,000
B. $92,000
C. $107,000
D. $127,000

Answer (A) is correct. *(SEE, adapted)*
REQUIRED: The total amount of gifts reported.
DISCUSSION: Section 6019 provides that a gift tax return must be filed for almost all taxable gifts. Specifically excluded from the requirement for filing are transfers that qualify for and do not exceed the $14,000 annual exclusion of Sec. 2503(b), the Sec. 2503(e) exclusion for educational or medical expenses, or the charitable gifts provision of Sec. 6019(3). In addition, transfers to a spouse that qualify for the unlimited marital deduction do not require the filing of a gift tax return. However, a gift tax return must be filed for a transfer that exceeds the annual exclusion even if no tax will be paid because the donor's spouse agrees to gift-splitting. The $75,000 gift on the sale of the business is the only gift that is not excluded from the filing requirement.
Answer (B) is incorrect. Transfers for educational expenses are excluded from the requirement for filing. Answer (C) is incorrect. Transfers for educational expenses and charitable contributions are excluded from the requirement for filing. Answer (D) is incorrect. Transfers for educational expenses, charitable contributions, and medical expenses are excluded from the requirement for filing.

21.2.3. When her father died, Mary, age 25, inherited an income interest for life in a $100,000 trust. When she dies, her brother Steve, age 18, will receive the remainder interest. Under the regulations in effect at her father's death, what are the values of Mary's and Steve's interests (assuming a 9.60% interest rate is specified by the IRS for the month in which Mary's father died)?

	Mary's Interest	Steve's Interest
A.	$0	$100,000
B.	$97,518	$2,482
C.	$2,482	$97,518
D.	$100,000	$0

Answer (B) is correct. *(Publisher, adapted)*
REQUIRED: The values of the life and remainder interests in a trust.
DISCUSSION: Annuity interests are valued from actuarial tables that were promulgated in IRS Notice 89-60. The actuarial tables must be used regardless of the actual earnings rate of the annuity. Section 7520 added in 1988 calls for the actuarial tables to be revised periodically. These tables incorporate an interest rate, rounded to the nearest 0.2% that is 120% of the Federal midterm rate applicable for the month of the transfer. These tables were revised to take into account the most recent mortality experience.
Based on the annuity Table S, Mary's age, and a 9.6% interest rate, the income interest is calculated by multiplying the total trust assets by a factor of 0.97518. The value of Steve's interest is determined by multiplying the total trust assets by the remainder interest factor for Mary's age (0.02482). Thus, the values of the two interests are $97,518 for Mary and $2,482 for Steve.
Answer (A) is incorrect. Mary's interest has a value, and Steve's interest must be multiplied by the remainder interest factor. Answer (C) is incorrect. Mary has the majority interest, and Steve has the remainder interest. Answer (D) is incorrect. Steve's interest has a value, and Mary's interest is reduced by an annuity table factor, her age, and the IRS-specified interest rate.

21.2.4. On May 24, 2017, David gave his brother Larry one share of ABC stock, which was traded on an exchange. May 27 was a Saturday, and Monday, May 29, was Memorial Day. These were the quoted prices on Friday and Tuesday:

	Sales Price		
Date	High	Low	Closing
May 26	100	93	97.5
May 28	100.5	95.5	97

What is the fair market value of David's gift?

- A. $96.50
- B. $97.00
- C. $97.50
- D. $98.00

Answer (B) is correct. *(Publisher, adapted)*
    REQUIRED: The fair market value of the donor's gift.
    DISCUSSION: If there is a market for stocks on a stock exchange, the mean between the highest and lowest quoted selling prices on the date of the gift is the fair market value per share. If there were no sales on the date of the gift, the fair market value is determined by taking a weighted average of the means between the highest and lowest sales on the nearest date before and the nearest date after the date of the gift. The average is to be weighted inversely by the respective number of trading days between the selling dates and the date of the gift [Reg. 25.2512-2(b)].
    The mean sales price on May 26, 1 trading day before the date of David's gift, was $96.5, and the mean sales price on May 28, 2 trading days after the date of the gift, was $98. The fair market value of David's gift is determined as follows:

$$\frac{(2 \text{ days} \times 96.5) + (1 \text{ day} \times 98)}{3 \text{ days}} = \$97 \text{ per share}$$

    Answer (A) is incorrect. The mean sales price on May 26 is $96.50. Answer (C) is incorrect. The closing price on May 26 is $97.50. Answer (D) is incorrect. The mean sales price on May 28 is $98.

21.2.5. For federal gift tax purposes, the value of a gift is the fair market value of the property on the date of the gift or at the alternate valuation date.

- A. True.
- B. False.

Answer (B) is correct. *(SEE, adapted)*
    DISCUSSION: The amount of a gift made in property is the fair market value of the property at the date of the gift (Reg. 25.2512-1). The fair market value is that which would occur in an arm's-length transaction between a willing buyer and a willing seller in the normal market. An alternative valuation date of 6 months after the date of death may be elected for property transfers subject to the estate tax (Sec. 2032).

21.2.6. In valuing closely held stock, the nature and history of the business are two factors that are usually considered.

- A. True.
- B. False.

Answer (A) is correct. *(Publisher, adapted)*
    DISCUSSION: Factors taken into consideration in valuing stock when selling prices or bid and asked prices are unavailable include the company's net worth, prospective earning power and dividend paying capacity, and other relevant factors. Revenue Ruling 59-60 adds the nature and history of the business from its inception as important factors in valuing closely held stock.

21.3 Exclusions and Deductions from Gifts

21.3.1. During the current year, Mr. C, a U.S. citizen, made the following gifts:

- $17,000 cash to his son; $50,000 to his wife, also a U.S. citizen
- Equipment to his brother (fair market value $14,000, adjusted basis $10,000)
- $100,000 in cash to City W for construction of a new city park

Without considering gift-splitting, what is the total of Mr. C's exclusions and deductions for his current-year gift tax return?

- A. $164,000
- B. $174,000
- C. $178,000
- D. $181,000

Answer (C) is correct. *(SEE, adapted)*
    REQUIRED: The amount of exclusions and deductions for gifts.
    DISCUSSION: The first $14,000 of a gift of a present interest in property made to any person during the calendar year may be excluded [Sec. 2503(b)]. This provision allows Mr. C a total of $56,000 in exclusions (four gifts × $14,000). In addition, Sec. 2522(a)(1) provides that a gift to a city may be deducted as a charitable gift. The gift to the spouse of the taxpayer is eligible for a marital deduction under Sec. 2523. Both of these deductions are available for the balance of the gifts not excluded (Sec. 2524). The total of C's deductions and exclusions is therefore $178,000 ($56,000 in exclusions + $86,000 deduction for the gift to the city + $36,000 marital deduction for the gift to his wife).
    Answer (A) is incorrect. The $14,000 exclusion is allowed for the cash given to his son. This is in addition to the exclusion for the equipment to his brother, the cash given to his wife, and the cash given to City W. Answer (B) is incorrect. The exclusion for the gift to the brother is not the $10,000 adjusted basis. Answer (D) is incorrect. The gift to the son is limited to an exclusion amount.

21.3.2. In the current year, Jean Camp contributed to the National Wildlife Foundation a remainder interest in 100 acres of land with a fair market value of $100,000 and a basis of $20,000. The remainder interest has a 0.20994 actuarial factor. Jean only specified the property was to be used for "conservation purposes" in general. Her taxable gift in the current year is

A. $0

B. $4,199

C. $20,994

D. $100,000

Answer (A) is correct. *(Publisher, adapted)*
REQUIRED: The taxable gift that results from a gift of a remainder interest in real estate to a qualified organization in the current year.
DISCUSSION: Gifts of a remainder interest are valued at the actuarial factor times the fair market value, so Camp's gift amount is $20,994 ($100,000 × 0.20994). The actuarial factor is based on tables published by the IRS in TD 8819, the age of the donor, and the applicable interest rate for the month of the transfer. Gifts to a charity of less than an entire interest in property generally do not result in a charitable contribution deduction. However, a charitable contribution deduction is allowed for a gift of a remainder interest in real property made to a qualified organization after 1986 for any "conservation purposes" [Reg. 25.2522(c)-3(c)]. To receive the deduction, a charitable remainder trust cannot have a maximum payout percentage in excess of 50% of the trust's fair market value. In addition, the value of the charitable remainder must be at least 10% of the net fair market value of property transferred in trust on the date of its contribution to the trust. Camp's taxable gift is $0 ($20,944 gift amount − $20,944 charitable contribution deduction).
Answer (B) is incorrect. Jean's taxable gift in the current year is not $4,199. Answer (C) is incorrect. The gift amount is $20,994. Answer (D) is incorrect. The FMV of the land is $100,000.

21.3.3. In the current year, Blum, who is single, gave an outright gift of $50,000 to a friend, Gould, who needed the money to pay medical expenses. In filing the current-year gift tax return, Blum was entitled to a maximum exclusion of

A. $50,000

B. $20,000

C. $14,000

D. $0

Answer (C) is correct. *(CPA, adapted)*
REQUIRED: The maximum exclusion for a gift used to pay medical expenses.
DISCUSSION: The first $14,000 of gifts of present interest to each donee is excluded [Sec. 2503(b)]. In addition, an unlimited exclusion is available for amounts paid on behalf of the donee for medical care [Sec. 2503(e)]. However, the transfer for medical care must be made directly to the person who provides it (not the donee). Therefore, this exclusion is not available for Blum. Blum's maximum exclusion is the $14,000 per donee per year.
Answer (A) is incorrect. The $50,000 would have to be paid directly to the doctor (the medical care provider) in order for the entire amount to be excluded. Answer (B) is incorrect. The maximum exclusion amount was not $20,000. Answer (D) is incorrect. Blum was entitled to an exclusion amount.

21.3.4. During the current year, Nancy, who is single, made the following gifts:

- Paid $15,000 in medical bills for her friend. The payments were paid directly to her friend's doctor.
- Gave $18,000 to her mother to help her with rent and groceries.
- Gave $20,000 to her nephew Tom to get him started in business.
- Also made a $50,000 interest-free demand loan to her nephew James last year. The loan is still outstanding at the end of the current year. The applicable federal interest rate during the current year remained constant at 10%.

What is the amount of Nancy's taxable gifts in the current year?

A. $53,000

B. $10,000

C. $11,000

D. $6,000

Answer (B) is correct. *(SEE, adapted)*
REQUIRED: The correct amount of taxable gifts.
DISCUSSION: Under Sec. 2503, gifts are taxable to the extent that they exceed $14,000 unless they are made on behalf of any individual as tuition to an educational organization or as payment to someone who provides medical care to such individual. The payment must be made directly to the educational organization or person providing medical care.
The $15,000 Nancy paid directly to her friend's doctor is not a taxable gift. The gifts to her mother and to her nephew Tom are each taxable to the extent that they exceed the $14,000 exclusion of Sec. 2503(b). An interest-free loan generally results in a deemed transfer of interest between the borrower and the lender [Sec. 7872(a)]. The lender is deemed to have made a gift of the forgone interest to the borrower. The amount of Nancy's gift to her nephew James is deemed to be $5,000. Because the amount of deemed interest is less than the $14,000 exclusion, it is not a taxable gift.
Answer (A) is incorrect. Of the gifts listed, a total of only $10,000 qualifies as taxable gifts. Answer (C) is incorrect. The $15,000 paid to the doctor is entirely deductible. The amounts exceeding the $14,000 exclusion for her mother and her nephew represent taxable gifts. Answer (D) is incorrect. The $3,000 of the gift to help her mother in excess of the annual exclusion is also a taxable gift.

21.3.5. Donald is a tax return preparer. His client, Jody Black, told him that she had made several gifts during the current year. She asked whether she should file a gift tax return and, if so, how much tax she would owe. Jody has never given a taxable gift before. Donald reviewed Jody's gift transactions as follows:

1. Paid her parents' medical bills, $14,000 for her father and $10,000 for her mother

2. Bought a sports car for her son at a cost of $39,000

3. Gave $17,000 cash to her church

4. Prepared her will leaving her vacation cabin, valued at $75,000, to her sister

5. Sent a wedding gift of $1,000 to her niece

What is Donald's best answer to Jody's questions?

A. No return is due because gifts to family are excluded.

B. Jody must file a gift tax return and will owe tax on $25,000.

C. Jody must file a gift tax return, but she will not owe tax because of the unified credit.

D. None of the answers are correct.

Answer (C) is correct. *(SEE, adapted)*
    REQUIRED: The determination for filing a gift tax return and the amount of gift tax due.
    DISCUSSION: A tax return must be filed if there are any taxable gifts. After the $14,000 exclusion, Jody will have a taxable gift of $25,000 to her son. For gifts made in the current year, the applicable credit amount is $2,141,800, reduced by the amount allowable as an applicable credit amount for all preceding calendar years [Sec. 2505(a)].
    Answer (A) is incorrect. A return must be filed if there are any taxable gifts. Answer (B) is incorrect. No tax will be owed. Answer (D) is incorrect. A gift tax return must be filed, but no tax will be owed because of the applicable credit amount (unified credit).

21.3.6. Mary made the following gifts in the current year:

Gift	Donee	Value
Cash	Son	$16,000
6-month certificate of deposit	Daughter	8,000
Antique furniture	Sister	25,000
Stocks in trust		
Life estate	Brother	80,000
Remainder	Daughter	21,000

Mary's taxable gifts for the current year total

A. $142,000

B. $108,000

C. $100,000

D. $79,000

Answer (C) is correct. *(Publisher, adapted)*
    REQUIRED: The donor's taxable gifts for the current year.
    DISCUSSION: "Taxable gifts" means the total amount of gifts made during the calendar year reduced by the charitable and marital deductions [Sec. 2503(a)]. The first $14,000 of gifts of present interests made to each donee during the year is excluded [Sec. 2503(b)].
    Mary transferred $150,000 of property by gift during the year. The only gift not subject to the exclusion is the gift of the trust remainder, since it is a future interest. The exclusion for the gift to Daughter is limited to the $7,000 certificate of deposit.

Total amount of gifts	$150,000
Less exclusions:	
Son	(14,000)
Daughter	(8,000)
Sister	(14,000)
Brother	(14,000)
Taxable gifts	$100,000

    Answer (A) is incorrect. An exclusion is deducted for the son, the sister, and the brother. Answer (B) is incorrect. An exclusion is allowed for the gift to the daughter. The trust remainder is not subject to any exclusion from the gift tax because it is a future interest. Answer (D) is incorrect. The trust remainder of $21,000 is a taxable gift. It is not subject to any exclusion from the gift tax because it is a future interest.

21.3.7. Lanny won $10 million at a casino 2 years ago and invested in mutual funds. When he married Judy last year, they signed prenuptial agreements. Then, in the current year, Lanny decided to give away some of his money. He made the following gifts:

$100,000 cash to Judy
$50,000 to each of his three adult children
$50,000 to the Democratic Party

What are the total taxable gifts that Lanny made in the current year? (Assume no gift-splitting was elected.)

    A. $200,000

    B. $300,000

    C. $108,000

    D. $150,000

Answer (C) is correct. *(SEE, adapted)*
    REQUIRED: The total amount of taxable gifts assuming no gift splitting was elected.
    DISCUSSION: The total of the taxable gifts is the total gift amount of $250,000 minus exclusions for each gift and the marital deduction. The $50,000 transfer to the Democratic Party is not subject to gift tax, and it is not included in the total taxable gifts.

	Total Gifts	Exclusions and Deductions	Taxable Gifts
Judy	$100,000	$(100,000)	$ 0
Child 1	50,000	(14,000)	36,000
Child 2	50,000	(14,000)	36,000
Child 3	50,000	(14,000)	36,000
Total	$250,000	$(142,000)	$108,000

    Answer (A) is incorrect. The $50,000 transfer to the Democratic Party is not subject to gift tax, and each gift to the children is reduced by the annual exclusion. Answer (B) is incorrect. The total amount of money Lanny gave away is $300,000. Answer (D) is incorrect. The total amount of gifts is reduced by the $14,000 exclusion for each child.

21.3.8. During the current year, Blake transferred a corporate bond with a face amount and fair market value of $20,000 to a trust for the benefit of her 16-year-old child. Annual interest on this bond is $2,000, which is to be accumulated in the trust and distributed to the child on reaching the age of 21. The bond is then to be distributed to the donor or her successor-in-interest in liquidation of the trust. Present value of the total interest to be received by the child is $8,710. The amount of the gift that is excludable from taxable gifts is

    A. $20,000

    B. $6,000

    C. $8,710

    D. $0

Answer (D) is correct. *(CPA, adapted)*
    REQUIRED: The annual exclusion for a gift of a future interest.
    DISCUSSION: Section 2503(b) allows an annual exclusion of $14,000 to each donee. The exclusion is specifically limited to gifts of a present interest. A present interest in property is an unrestricted right to the immediate use, possession, or enjoyment of the property or the income from the property (Reg. 25.2503-3). Blake's child has no present right to the bond or income from it. A gift of a future interest does not qualify for the exclusion.
    Answer (A) is incorrect. The fair market value (without any exclusion) of the bond is $20,000. Answer (B) is incorrect. The fair market value of the bond reduced for the annual exclusion is $6,000. Answer (C) is incorrect. The present value of the future interest in the bond is $8,710.

21.3.9. When Jim and Nina became engaged in April of this year, Jim gave Nina a ring that had a fair market value of $50,000. After their wedding in July of the same year, Jim gave Nina $75,000 in cash so that Nina could have her own bank account. Both Jim and Nina are U.S. citizens. What was the amount of Jim's current-year gift tax marital deduction?

    A. $0

    B. $75,000

    C. $111,000

    D. $125,000

Answer (B) is correct. *(CPA, adapted)*
    REQUIRED: The marital deduction for the current year.
    DISCUSSION: Section 2503(b) allows an individual a $14,000 annual exclusion for gifts of present interests made to each donee during the calendar year.
    Section 2523 permits a marital deduction when a donor transfers property during the calendar year by gift to a donee who at the time of the gift is the donee's spouse. Section 2524 states that the deductible marital deduction amount may not exceed the includible gift; that is, the amount of the gift in excess of the annual exclusion. The fair market value of the ring would not qualify for the marital deduction because Nina was not Jim's spouse at the time she received the ring. However, $14,000 of the value of the ring would qualify for the annual exclusion. The $75,000 Jim gave Nina to open her own bank account would qualify for the marital deduction because Jim and Nina were married when the gift was made and the annual exclusion had been exhausted with the gift of the ring.
    Answer (A) is incorrect. Jim is entitled to a marital deduction for his gifts. Answer (C) is incorrect. The amount of $111,000 includes the FMV of the ring less its annual exclusion. Answer (D) is incorrect. The amount of $125,000 includes the FMV of the ring.

21.3.10. In March, Ted Thrifty created a trust for his son, Doug. Under the terms of the trust, Doug is to get for life the entire income from the property with the remainder going to Ted's grandson at Doug's death. The annual exclusion for gifts would apply to Ted's gift in trust to his son, Doug.

A. True.

B. False.

Answer (A) is correct. *(SEE, adapted)*
DISCUSSION: Section 2503(b) allows a donor to exclude the first $14,000 of each gift made in a calendar year. The exclusion applies only to gifts of present interests. Ted's gift in trust to his son qualifies for the exclusion because it is a present interest in the income of the trust. Under Reg. 25.2503-3, an unrestricted right to the immediate use, possession, or enjoyment of property or the income from property (such as a life estate) is a present interest in property and qualifies for the exclusion.

21.3.11. Gifts between spouses never generate taxable gifts.

A. True.

B. False.

Answer (B) is correct. *(Publisher, adapted)*
DISCUSSION: The marital deduction provided in Sec. 2523 is not available to a donor who is not a U.S. citizen. Furthermore, Sec. 2523(b) disallows the deduction in most cases if the interest passing to the spouse by gift is a terminable interest. A terminable interest is generally one that could end or terminate when some event occurs or a specified amount of time passes so that the property passes to someone else in such a way that the interest would not be included in the spouse's estate.

21.3.12. If a special election is made, a marital deduction can be taken for a transfer of a terminable interest.

A. True.

B. False.

Answer (A) is correct. *(Publisher, adapted)*
DISCUSSION: A donor is allowed a deduction for qualified terminable interest property (QTIP) if the donee spouse makes an election to treat it as such [Sec. 2523(f)]. The donee spouse must be entitled to all the income from the property, payable annually or at more frequent intervals, and no person may have a power to appoint any part of the property to any person other than the spouse [Sec. 2056(b)(7)(B)]. The result is that the donor is entitled to the marital deduction, but the donee spouse must include the entire value of the property in his or her estate (Sec. 2044). For transfers made after December 31, 1985, an election for this treatment must be made by the due date of the gift tax return, including extensions [Sec. 2523(f)(4)].

21.4 Gift-Splitting

21.4.1. During the current year, Mr. Jones made gifts to his son of the following items:

- A minivan with an adjusted basis of $13,000 and fair market value of $15,000.
- Bonds with an adjusted basis of $6,000 and fair market value of $18,000.
- Antique furniture with an adjusted basis of $12,000 and a fair market value of $35,000.
- An interest-free $10,000 loan on January 1, to buy a boat for his personal pleasure. His son repaid the loan in full on December 31. The applicable federal interest rate was 10%.

Mr. and Mrs. Jones elect gift-splitting. What is the total amount of their taxable gifts to their son in the current year?

A. $3,000

B. $32,000

C. $40,000

D. $68,000

Answer (C) is correct. *(SEE, adapted)*
REQUIRED: The total amount of taxable gifts by spouses who elect gift-splitting.
DISCUSSION: Gift-splitting allows spouses to treat each gift as made one-half by each. This allows each spouse to exclude the first $14,000 of each gift of a present interest to a third person in a calendar year, for a total exclusion of $28,000 per donee. Thus, Mr. and Mrs. Jones may exclude $28,000 of the total gifts made to their son in the current year.
The amount of a gift made in property is the fair market value of the property on the date of the gift. The gifts made to the son total $68,000 in the current year ($15,000 minivan + $18,000 bonds + $35,000 furniture). Applying the available exclusion to these gifts reduces the taxable gifts to $40,000 [$68 – (14 × 2)]. The interest-free loan does not qualify as a gift. Section 7872(c)(2) creates an exception for loans between individuals when the amount of the loan does not exceed $10,000. Accordingly, the imputed interest on the $10,000 interest-free loan does not result in a gift.
Answer (A) is incorrect. The amount of $3,000 is the total taxable gift if the adjusted basis (with the annual exclusion) was used to value the property. Answer (B) is incorrect. The amount of $31,000 is the adjusted basis (without any exclusion) of all property and $1,000 interest. Answer (D) is incorrect. The amount of $68,000 is the value of the taxable gifts before the annual exclusion.

678 SU 21: Wealth Transfer Taxes

21.4.2. All of the following statements concerning gift-splitting are true except

A. The annual gift tax exclusion allows spouses who consent to split their gifts to transfer up to $28,000 to any one person during any calendar year without gift tax liability, if the gift qualifies as a present interest.

B. To qualify for gift-splitting, a couple must be married at the time the gift is made to a third party.

C. For gift tax purposes, a husband and wife must file a joint income tax return to qualify for the gift-splitting benefits.

D. Both spouses must consent to the use of gift-splitting.

Answer (C) is correct. *(SEE, adapted)*
REQUIRED: The statement that is false for gift-splitting.
DISCUSSION: Section 2513 allows a gift to be treated as made one-half by the donor and one-half by the donor's spouse. There is no requirement that the spouses file a joint income tax return.
Answer (A) is incorrect. Gift-splitting allows spouses who consent to split their gifts to exclude the first $28,000 of each gift of a present interest. Answer (B) is incorrect. The donor must be married at the time of the gift to qualify for gift-splitting. Answer (D) is incorrect. Both spouses must consent to the use of gift-splitting.

21.4.3. Jack and Jill are married and agree to split the gifts that they made during the current year. Jack gives his nephew, James, $17,000, and Jill gives her niece, Janice, $15,000. Which statement is true regarding Jack and Jill's gifts?

A. Jack and Jill can combine their gifts of $32,000 on one gift tax return and take a $14,000 annual exclusion for each recipient.

B. Jack and Jill must file separate gift tax returns, and each may take a $14,000 annual exclusion for his or her gift.

C. Jack and Jill must file separate gift tax returns and report one-half of each gift on each return before applying the $14,000 annual exclusions.

D. None of the answers are correct.

Answer (C) is correct. *(SEE, adapted)*
REQUIRED: The true statement regarding gift splitting.
DISCUSSION: Gift-splitting allows spouses to treat each gift as made one-half by each. This allows each spouse to exclude the first $14,000 of each gift of a present interest to a third person in a calendar year, for a total exclusion of $28,000 per donee. Gift-splitting is not available to a couple if they legally divorce after the gift and one of the spouses remarries before the end of the calendar year.
Answer (A) is incorrect. Jack and Jill must file separate gift tax returns. Answer (B) is incorrect. Jack and Jill must treat each gift as made one-half by each. Answer (D) is incorrect. Jack and Jill must file separate gift tax returns and report one-half of each gift on each return before applying the $14,000 annual exclusions.

21.4.4. During the current year, Warren made the following gifts:

Cash to son Ronald	$ 44,000
Land to wife Laura	100,000
Cash to First Church	32,000
Painting to niece Suzie	20,000

Warren and Laura elect gift-splitting. Laura's only gift in the current year is a $56,000 cash gift to her mother. What is the amount of the taxable gifts to be reported by Warren in the current year?

A. $196,000

B. $48,000

C. $22,000

D. $8,000

Answer (C) is correct. *(Publisher, adapted)*
REQUIRED: The total taxable gifts after gift-splitting.
DISCUSSION: If both spouses consent, a gift made by one spouse to any person other than the other spouse is considered as made one-half by each spouse (Sec. 2513). In addition to his own gifts, Warren is treated as having made one-half of Laura's gift to her mother. By splitting the gifts, each spouse can take advantage of the $14,000 per donee exclusion.

Donee	Amount	Exclusion/ Deduction	Taxable
Ronald	$ 22,000	$ 14,000	$ 8,000
Laura	100,000	100,000	0
Church	16,000	16,000	0
Suzie	10,000	10,000	0
Laura's mother	28,000	14,000	14,000
Total taxable gifts			$22,000

Answer (A) is incorrect. The amount of $196,000 is the total of the gifts made by Warren without reduction for any annual exclusions or the gift splitting election. Answer (B) is incorrect. The amount of $48,000 fails to take into account Warren's portion of Laura's gift to her mother and the exclusions available for the gifts to Ronald, the church, Suzie, and Laura's mother. Answer (D) is incorrect. Warren's taxable gifts include $14,000 of Laura's gift to her mother.

21.4.5. Gift-splitting provisions are advantageous only if one spouse made no gifts during the tax year.

A. True.

B. False.

Answer (B) is correct. *(Publisher, adapted)*
DISCUSSION: When both spouses have made gifts but the gifts made by one spouse are much larger than those made by the other spouse, the progressive structure of the gift tax rates makes the election of gift-splitting advantageous. Furthermore, gift-splitting allows the $14,000 exclusion to be used by each spouse for each donee who receives a present interest.

21.5 Calculation of Gift Tax

21.5.1. Under the unified rate schedule,

A. Lifetime taxable gifts are taxed on a noncumulative basis.

B. Transfers at death are taxed on a noncumulative basis.

C. Lifetime taxable gifts and transfers at death are taxed on a cumulative basis.

D. The gift tax rates are higher than the estate tax rates.

Answer (C) is correct. *(CPA, adapted)*
REQUIRED: The true statement regarding the unified transfer tax rate schedule.
DISCUSSION: The same (unified transfer) tax rates of Sec. 2001 are applied to both the gift tax and estate tax bases. Any taxable gifts (other than gifts included in the estate tax base) made after 1976 are called adjusted taxable gifts, and such gifts are included in the donor's estate tax base. The addition of such taxable gifts to the estate tax base at their fair market value on the date of the gift results in the donor-decedent's estate being taxed at a higher marginal tax rate. These gifts are not taxed a second time when the donor dies because the gift taxes paid on the gifts reduce the amount of the estate tax that is owed.
Answer (A) is incorrect. Lifetime taxable gifts are taxed on a cumulative basis. Answer (B) is incorrect. Transfers at death are taxed on a cumulative basis. Answer (D) is incorrect. The same Sec. 2001 rates apply to compute both gift and estate tax.

21.5.2. Mr. C, who is single and a U.S. citizen, made the following gifts in the current year:

Cash to nephew	$1,924,000
Cash to sister	1,824,000
Property to brother (FMV)	1,824,000
Cash to the local university building fund	200,000

C had not made any gifts in prior years. What is C's net gift tax liability?

A. $16,000

B. $32,000

C. $2,141,800

D. $2,157,800

Answer (A) is correct. *(SEE, adapted)*
REQUIRED: The gift tax payable on gifts made to relatives and a university in the current year.
DISCUSSION: The total of the taxable gifts is the total gift amount minus annual exclusions for each gift and a deduction for the gift to the university.

	Total Gifts	Exclusions and Deductions	Taxable Gifts
Nephew	1,924,000	$ (14,000)	$1,910,000
Sister	1,824,000	(14,000)	1,810,000
Brother	1,824,000	(14,000)	1,810,000
University	200,000	(200,000)	0
Total	$5,772,000	$(242,000)	$5,530,000

The tax is calculated only on the $5,530,000 of taxable gifts for the current year since this is the first year in which taxable gifts have been made [Sec. 2502(a)]. The tax rates in Sec. 2001(c) are used. The tentative tax is $2,157,800 [$345,800 + ($5,530,000 − $1,000,000) ×.40]. This tax is reduced by the $2,141,800 applicable credit amount for the current year [Sec. 2505(a)], leaving a gift tax liability of $16,000. The Tax Relief Act of 2010 increased the applicable credit amount up to a $5 million exemption equivalent amount after 2009, indexed for inflation. The 2017 exemption is $5,490,000, providing a credit of $2,141,800 based on the tax rates in Sec. 2001(c). Additionally, the amount of the taxable gifts is reduced by $14,000 per recipient, the annual exclusion for gifts in 2017.
Answer (B) is incorrect. The applicable credit amount is not equal to $2,125,800 (the 2016 credit for the first $5,450,000). Answer (C) is incorrect. The applicable credit amount is $2,141,800. Answer (D) is incorrect. The tentative tax is $2,157,800.

21.5.3. In the current year, Rose made her first taxable gift when she gave her sister, Lily, stock with a fair market value of $6,500,000. What is Rose's gift tax due for the current year?

    A. [$345,800 + 40%($5,486,000)]

    B. [$345,800 + 40%($5,500,000)]

    C. [$345,800 + 40%($5,486,000)] – $2,125,800

    D. [$345,800 + 40%($5,486,000)] – $2,141,800

Answer (D) is correct. *(Publisher, adapted)*
    REQUIRED: The donor's gift tax payable for the current year.
    DISCUSSION: The donor's taxable gift is the $6,500,000 of stock transferred by gift reduced by the $14,000 exclusion under Sec. 2503(b), or $6,486,000. Since the donor has never made any other taxable gifts, the tax imposed is computed on the $6,486,000 of taxable gifts [Sec. 2502(a)]. The tax rates in Sec. 2001(c) are used. For taxable gifts in excess of $5,490,000, the tax is $2,141,800 plus 40% of the excess over $5,490,000. Furthermore, Sec. 2505(a) allows a credit equal to $2,141,800. Rose's gift tax due is $2,141,800, plus 40% of $996,000, minus the $2,141,800 applicable credit amount. The current-year applicable credit amount is $2,141,800. Effective for gifts made after December 31, 1998, the $10,000 annual exclusion for gifts is indexed for inflation and is $14,000 in the current year (2017).
    Answer (A) is incorrect. It does not subtract the applicable credit amount. Answer (B) is incorrect. It does not subtract the applicable credit amount, and the annual exclusion is not deducted. Answer (C) is incorrect. It subtracts the 2016 ($2,125,800) applicable credit amount.

21.5.4. In the current year, Spencer, a single taxpayer, made a $5.49 million taxable gift to his brother Tracy. The only other taxable gifts Spencer has made were a $2 million taxable gift to Tracy in 1980, and a $500,000 taxable gift to his sister Katharine in 1982. Spencer paid a total gift tax on the 1980 and 1982 gifts of $987,800. What is the gift tax due from Spencer for his current year gifts? The applicable credit for 1982 was $62,800.

    A. $54,200

    B. $117,000

    C. $1,062,800

    D. $3,141,800

Answer (B) is correct. *(Publisher, adapted)*
    REQUIRED: The donor's gift tax payable for the current year.
    DISCUSSION: The gift tax imposed is equal to the excess of a tentative tax on the sum of taxable gifts for the current year and for each preceding year, over a tentative tax computed on the sum of the taxable gifts for each preceding year [Sec. 2502(a)]. Section 2505 allows an applicable credit amount in 2017 equal to $2,141,800 reduced by the amounts allowable as credits to the individual for all preceding years. The 2017 applicable credit amount exempts up to $5.49 million. The taxpayer's last gift was in 1982, and the allowable applicable credit in that year was $62,800.

Tentative tax on $7,990,000	$ 3,141,800
Less: Tentative tax on $2,500,000	(945,800)
	$ 2,196,000
Less: Applicable credit amount ($2,141,800 – $62,800)	(2,079,000)
Gift tax payable	$ 117,000

    Answer (A) is incorrect. The estate credit must be reduced by the $62,800 taken previously. Answer (C) is incorrect. The tentative tax is also reduced by the tentative tax on $2,500,000. Answer (D) is incorrect. The tentative tax on $7,990,000 is $3,141,800.

21.5.5. Sharon made a gift of land with a fair market value of $5,504,000 to her daughter in 2017. She made no gifts in 1990-2016. In 1989, she used $155,800 of her applicable credit amount to offset gift tax otherwise due. What amount of applicable credit amount can Sharon use to offset gift tax due on the 2017 gift?

    A. $2,141,800

    B. $1,986,000

    C. $155,800

    D. $0

Answer (B) is correct. *(Publisher, adapted)*
    REQUIRED: The amount of applicable credit amount the donor may use to offset the gift tax in 2017.
    DISCUSSION: For gifts made in 2017, the applicable credit amount is $2,141,800 reduced by the amount allowable as an applicable credit amount for all preceding calendar years [Sec. 2505(a)]. Since Sharon used $155,800 of applicable credit amount in previous years, the amount of applicable credit amount she may use in 2017 is $1,986,000 ($2,141,800 – $155,800). The applicable credit amount exempts up to $5.49 million.
    Answer (A) is incorrect. The applicable credit amount is $2,141,800. Answer (C) is incorrect. The applicable credit amount for the gift in 1989 is $155,800. Answer (D) is incorrect. There is an applicable credit amount for the gift in 2017.

21.5.6. To calculate the tax due on the current year's taxable gifts, the tax paid on all prior years' taxable gifts is subtracted from the tax calculated using the current year's tax rates and cumulative lifetime taxable gifts.

A. True.

B. False.

Answer (B) is correct. *(Publisher, adapted)*
   DISCUSSION: To calculate the tax due on the current year's taxable gifts, the tentative tax (computed using current tax rates) on all taxable gifts in the preceding years is subtracted from the tentative tax (computed using current tax rates) on the sum of the current year's taxable gifts and the taxable gifts of all preceding years [Sec. 2502(a)].

21.5.7. The marginal tax rate on cumulative gifts in excess of $5.49 million is 40% for 2017.

A. True.

B. False.

Answer (A) is correct. *(Publisher, adapted)*
   DISCUSSION: The top unified tax rate in 2017 is 40% on taxable gifts over $5.49 million.

21.5.8. The applicable credit amount available to offset tax due on the current year's gifts is equal to the statutory credit for the current year and without regard to prior years. For 2017, that credit is $2,141,800.

A. True.

B. False.

Answer (B) is correct. *(Publisher, adapted)*
   DISCUSSION: The applicable credit amount available to offset tax due on the current year's gifts is equal to the statutory credit for the current year reduced by the sum of the amounts allowable as a credit to the individual for all preceding calendar years [Sec. 2505(a)]. For 2017, the statutory credit is $2,141,800.

21.6 Reporting Gifts

21.6.1. On July 1, Year 1, Vega made a transfer by gift in an amount sufficient to require the filing of a gift tax return. Vega was still alive in Year 2. If Vega did not request an extension of time for filing the Year 1 gift tax return, the due date for filing was

A. March 15, Year 2.

B. April 15, Year 2.

C. June 15, Year 2.

D. June 30, Year 2.

Answer (B) is correct. *(CPA, adapted)*
   REQUIRED: The date Form 709, *United States Gift Tax Return*, is due.
   DISCUSSION: Under Sec. 6075, gift tax returns are due on or before the 15th day of April following the close of the calendar year in which a gift was made. Since Vega made a gift in Year 1, Form 709 is due by April 15, Year 2.
   Answer (A) is incorrect. March 15, Year 2, was not the correct due date. Answer (C) is incorrect. June 15, Year 2, was not the correct due date. Answer (D) is incorrect. June 30, Year 2, was not the correct due date.

21.6.2. On February 4, Year 1, Mr. Smith made a gift in an amount sufficient to require the filing of a federal gift tax return. On October 5, Year 1, Mr. Smith died. No estate tax return will need to be filed for Mr. Smith. Assuming extensions have not been obtained, the gift tax return (Form 709) must be filed by (assuming none of the dates are Saturdays, Sundays, or holidays)

A. April 15, Year 1.

B. March 15, Year 2.

C. April 15, Year 2.

D. July 5, Year 2.

Answer (C) is correct. *(SEE, adapted)*
   REQUIRED: The date Form 709, *United States Gift Tax Return*, is due.
   DISCUSSION: Under Sec. 6075, gift tax returns are due on or before the 15th day of April following the close of the calendar year in which a gift was made. Since Mr. Smith made a gift in Year 1, Form 709 is generally due by April 15, Year 2.
   If the date falls on a weekend or holiday, the return is due the next business day.
   If an estate tax return were required of Mr. Smith's estate, this return would be due no later than 9 months after the date of death unless an extension was obtained [Sec. 6075(a)]. The due date for the gift tax return for the year of death is no later than the estate tax return due date [Sec. 6075(b)(3)]. Since an estate tax return is not being filed, this does not change the answer in this case.
   Answer (A) is incorrect. April 15, Year 1, is not the correct date by which the return must be filed. Answer (B) is incorrect. March 15, Year 2, is not the correct date by which the return must be filed. Answer (D) is incorrect. July 5, Year 2, is not the correct date by which the return must be filed.

21.6.3. For transfers by gift during the current year, a taxpayer must file a gift tax return for which of the following?

    A. A transfer of a present interest in property valued at $10,000, received as a gift from a foreign individual.

    B. A qualified transfer for educational or medical expenses.

    C. A transfer to one's spouse that qualified for the unlimited marital deduction.

    D. A transfer of $20,000 to a son for which one's spouse has agreed to gift-splitting.

Answer (D) is correct. *(SEE, adapted)*
    REQUIRED: The transfer for which a gift tax return must be filed.
    DISCUSSION: Section 6019 provides that a gift tax return must be filed for almost all taxable gifts. Specifically excluded from the requirement for filing are transfers that qualify for and do not exceed the $14,000 annual exclusion of Sec. 2503(b) or the Sec. 2503(e) exclusion for educational or medical expenses. In addition, transfers to a spouse that qualify for the unlimited marital deduction also do not require the filing of a gift tax return. However, a gift tax return must be filed for a transfer that exceeds the annual exclusion even if no tax will be paid because the donor's spouse agrees to gift-splitting.
    Answer (A) is incorrect. A transfer of a present interest in property that is not more than the annual exclusion is a gift that does not require a gift tax return to be filed. Answer (B) is incorrect. A qualified transfer for educational or medical expenses is a gift that does not require a gift tax return to be filed. Answer (C) is incorrect. A transfer to one's spouse that qualified for the unlimited marital deduction is a gift that does not require a gift tax return to be filed.

21.6.4. A U.S. citizen does not have to file a gift tax return for any year unless taxable gifts exceed $25,000.

    A. True.

    B. False.

Answer (B) is correct. *(SEE, adapted)*
    DISCUSSION: Section 6019 provides that a gift tax return must be filed unless all gifts made may be excluded under the $14,000 exclusion of Sec. 2503(b), the Sec. 2503(e) exclusion for transfers in payment of medical or tuition expenses, or the Sec. 6019(3) exclusion for charitable contributions, or unless they may be deducted under the marital deduction of Sec. 2523(a).

21.6.5. William makes a gift of land to charity in excess of the annual gift tax exclusion. William does not have to file a gift tax return if the entire value of the donated property qualifies for a gift tax charitable contribution deduction.

    A. True.

    B. False.

Answer (A) is correct. *(Publisher, adapted)*
    DISCUSSION: Effective for gifts made after August 5, 1997, gifts made to charity in excess of the annual exclusion do not necessitate the filing of a gift tax return if the entire value of the donated property qualifies for a gift tax charitable deduction [Sec. 6019(3)]. Gifts of partial interests in property, however, still require the filing of a gift tax return.

21.6.6. An extension of time to file an income tax return for any tax year that is a calendar year automatically extends the time for filing the annual gift tax return for that calendar year until the due date of the income tax return.

    A. True.

    B. False.

Answer (A) is correct. *(SEE, adapted)*
    DISCUSSION: A calendar-year taxpayer receiving an extension of time for filing his or her income tax return automatically receives an extension to that same extended due date for filing his or her gift tax return for that same year.

21.7 Inclusions in the Gross Estate

21.7.1. A decedent's gross estate includes the value of all property to the extent of the decedent's interest in the property at the time of death. Which one of the following items is not included in the gross estate?

A. Medical insurance reimbursements that were due the individual at death.

B. The value of the part of a deceased husband's real property allowed to his widow for her lifetime (dower interest).

C. Proceeds of life insurance on the decedent's life if the decedent possessed incidents of ownership in the policy.

D. Outstanding dividends declared to decedent after the date of death.

Answer (D) is correct. *(SEE, adapted)*
REQUIRED: The item not included in a decedent's gross estate.
DISCUSSION: Under Sec. 2033, the value of a gross estate includes the value at the time of death of all property in which the decedent had an interest at the time of death. A shareholder only has a right to or interest in dividends that have been declared by the directors. Since the dividends were declared after death, the decedent had no interest in them at the time of his or her death and they are not included in the gross estate. Note that, if the dividends had been declared (and the record date had passed) before the decedent's death but not paid, they would be includible in the gross estate.
Answer (A) is incorrect. Medical insurance reimbursements due the individual at death are considered property in which the decedent had an interest. Answer (B) is incorrect. Section 2034 provides that dower interests will not prevent the inclusion of such property in the decedent's gross estate. Answer (C) is incorrect. Section 2042 provides that the value of the gross estate includes proceeds of life insurance when the decedent possessed incidents of ownership in the policy.

21.7.2. Chester is preparing the estate tax return, Form 706, for his deceased brother John. John died December 15 of the current year. Which of the following will not be included in John's gross estate?

A. Real estate that will be passed to John when his parents die.

B. Stocks and bonds owned by John at his death.

C. Land that John had signed a contract to sell, but the sale of which was not completed.

D. Property jointly owned by John and his spouse.

Answer (A) is correct. *(SEE, adapted)*
REQUIRED: The item not included in a decedent's gross estate.
DISCUSSION: A decedent's gross estate includes the FMV of all property, real or personal, tangible or intangible, wherever situated, to the extent the decedent owned a beneficial interest at the time of death. Included in the GE are items such as cash, personal residence and effects, securities, other investments (e.g., real estate, collector items), other personal assets such as notes and claims (e.g., dividends declared prior to death if the record date had passed), and business interests (e.g., in a sole proprietorship, partnership interest). The GE includes the value of the surviving spouse's interest in property as dower or curtesy. John does not own the real estate at his death.
Answer (B) is incorrect. Stocks and bonds owned by John at his death are included in John's gross estate. Answer (C) is incorrect. Land that John had signed a contract to sell, but the sale of which was not completed, is included in John's gross estate. Answer (D) is incorrect. Property jointly owned by John and his spouse is included in John's gross estate.

21.7.3. Which of the following items of property would be included in the gross estate of a decedent who died in the current year?

1. Clothes and jewelry of the decedent.

2. Cash of $400,000 given to decedent's friend 3 years ago. No gift tax was paid on the transfer.

3. Land purchased by decedent and held as joint tenants with rights of survivorship with decedent's brother.

A. 1, 2, and 3.

B. 1 and 3.

C. 1 and 2.

D. 2 and 3.

Answer (B) is correct. *(Publisher, adapted)*
REQUIRED: The items of property included in the decedent's gross estate.
DISCUSSION: Under Secs. 2031 and 2033, a decedent's gross estate includes the value of all property, real or personal, tangible or intangible, wherever situated, to the extent the decedent owned a beneficial interest at the time of death. Clothes and jewelry of the decedent are included in the gross estate. Section 2040(a) provides for the inclusion of all property held as joint tenants with right of survivorship by the decedent and any other person, except the part of the property shown to have originally belonged to the other person and for which adequate and full consideration was not provided by the decedent. Therefore, the full value of the land is also included in the decedent's gross estate.
Answer (A) is incorrect. Cash of $400,000 given to a decedent's friend 3 years ago is not included in the gross estate. Answer (C) is incorrect. Cash given to a decedent's friend is not included in the gross estate; however, land purchased by a decedent is included. Answer (D) is incorrect. Clothes and jewelry of the decedent is included in the gross estate, while the cash given to the friend is not included.

21.7.4. Mr. C died on June 30 of the current year. Based on the following facts, compute Mr. C's gross estate.

- Last year, C gave cash of $50,000 to his friend. No gift tax was paid on the gift.

- C held property jointly with his brother. Each paid $30,000 of the total purchase price of $60,000. Fair market value of the property at date of death was $100,000.

- Two years ago, C purchased a life insurance policy on his life and gave it as a gift to his sister. C retained the right to change the beneficiary. Upon C's death, his sister received $150,000 under the policy.

- Ten years ago, C gave his son a summer home (fair market value when gifted - $125,000). C continued to use it until his death pursuant to an understanding with his son. Fair market value at date of death was $175,000.

    A. $200,000

    B. $250,000

    C. $375,000

    D. $425,000

Answer (C) is correct. *(SEE, adapted)*
REQUIRED: The gross estate of a decedent who died in the current year.
DISCUSSION: For decedents dying after 1981, gifts made prior to death are not included in the estate except for certain transfers such as those in which a life estate is retained or those involving life insurance [Sec. 2035(a)]. Therefore, the cash gift to a friend is not included in Mr. C's estate, but the life insurance is. The life insurance ($150,000) is also included because the right to change the beneficiary is an incident of ownership under Sec. 2042.
    The value of property owned jointly is included [Sec. 2040(a)]. To the extent it can be shown that consideration for the acquisition of the jointly held property was provided by the other joint tenant, a proportionate part is excluded (1/2). Thus, $50,000 of the fair market value of the property held with the brother must be included in the estate.
    Section 2036 requires inclusion in the gross estate of all property that the decedent transferred without full consideration while retaining for life its possession or enjoyment. Accordingly, the $175,000 fair market value of the summer home is included in C's gross estate. The gross estate therefore totals $375,000 ($50,000 + $150,000 + $175,000).
    Answer (A) is incorrect. The amount of $200,000 excludes the date-of-death value of the summer home. Answer (B) is incorrect. The amount of $250,000 includes the joint property at $100,000, not $50,000, and it excludes the date-of-death value of the summer home. Answer (D) is incorrect. The amount of $425,000 includes the $50,000 cash gift.

21.7.5. Mr. X died on September 24 of the current year. His will required the transfer of all possessions to his sister. At the date of death, the assets transferred were

	Adj. Basis	FMV
Apartment house	$275,000	$420,000
Stock	25,000	40,000
Dividends on above stock (declared September 30)	3,000	3,000
Medical insurance reimbursement (check received September 20 but not cashed)	5,000	5,000
Cash	50,000	50,000

The executrix did not elect the alternate valuation date. What is Mr. X's gross estate for purposes of an estate tax return, Form 706?

    A. $358,000

    B. $503,000

    C. $515,000

    D. $518,000

Answer (C) is correct. *(SEE, adapted)*
REQUIRED: The value of the decedent's gross estate for purposes of an estate tax return.
DISCUSSION: Under Sec. 2033, the value of a gross estate includes the value at the time of death of all property in which the decedent had an interest at the time of death. A shareholder has a right to, or an interest in, only those dividends that have been declared by the directors. Since the dividends were declared after death, the decedent had no interest in them at the time of his death, and they are not included in the gross estate. Note that, if the dividends had been declared (and the record date had passed) before the decedent's death but not paid, they would be includible in the gross estate. Medical insurance reimbursements due the individual at death are considered property in which the decedent had an interest. Here the reimbursements were actually received. Thus, the decedent's gross estate includes

Apartment house	$420,000
Stock	40,000
Medical insurance reimbursement	5,000
Cash	50,000
Gross estate	$515,000

    Answer (A) is incorrect. The property's total adjusted basis is $358,000, and it includes the dividends. Answer (B) is incorrect. The amount of $503,000 includes the dividends, and the stock is incorrectly valued at its adjusted basis. Answer (D) is incorrect. The amount of $518,000 includes the value of the dividends.

21.7.6. Mr. Good died on April 15 of the current year. His assets and their fair market value at the time of his death were

Cash	$ 10,000
Home	140,000
Life insurance payable to Mr. Good's estate	200,000
Series EE bonds	90,000
Municipal bonds	180,000

Mr. Good had borrowed $10,000 against the cash value of his life insurance policy. Mr. Good's estate is liable for the loan. What is the total amount of Mr. Good's gross estate for federal estate tax purposes?

A. $240,000

B. $420,000

C. $610,000

D. $620,000

Answer (D) is correct. *(SEE, adapted)*
REQUIRED: The value of the decedent's gross estate for federal estate tax purposes.
DISCUSSION: Under Sec. 2033, the value of a gross estate includes the value on the date of death of all property in which the decedent had an interest at the time of death. Section 2042 requires the inclusion of proceeds from life insurance policies where the proceeds are receivable by, or for the benefit of, the estate. U.S. savings bonds purchased by a decedent with his own funds are includible in his gross estate if registered in his own name or with another person as co-owner. The value of the municipal bonds is includible in the gross estate. The fact that the income generated by municipal bonds is tax exempt does not prevent them from being included in the gross estate. The federal estate tax is a tax upon the value of the property and not upon the income the property generates. The cash and the value of the home are also included in the gross estate. The estate's liability for the loan does not affect the amount of the gross estate unless the estate actually pays the loan.
Answer (A) is incorrect. The amount of $240,000 includes only the cash, the home, and the savings bonds. Answer (B) is incorrect. The amount of $420,000 excludes the life insurance. Answer (C) is incorrect. The amount of $610,000 includes a $10,000 reduction to the gross estate for the loan against the insurance policy.

21.7.7. In connection with a "buy-sell" agreement funded by a cross-purchase insurance arrangement, business associate Adam bought a policy on Burr's life to finance the purchase of Burr's interest. Adam, the beneficiary, paid the premiums and retained all incidents of ownership. On the death of Burr, the insurance proceeds will be

A. Includible in Burr's gross estate, if Burr owns 50% or more of the stock of the corporation.

B. Includible in Burr's gross estate only if Burr had purchased a similar policy on Adam's life at the same time and for the same purpose.

C. Includible in Burr's gross estate, if Adam has the right to veto Burr's power to borrow on the policy that Burr owns on Adam's life.

D. Excludable from Burr's gross estate.

Answer (D) is correct. *(CPA, adapted)*
REQUIRED: The life insurance proceeds in the gross estate.
DISCUSSION: The gross estate includes proceeds of insurance on the decedent's life under Sec. 2042 if either (1) the proceeds are payable to or for the estate or (2) the decedent had any incident of ownership in the policy at death.
Answer (A) is incorrect. The proceeds will not be includible in Burr's gross estate if Burr owns 50% or more of the stock of the corporation. Answer (B) is incorrect. The proceeds will not be includible in Burr's gross estate only if Burr had purchased a similar policy on Adam's life at the same time and for the same purpose. Answer (C) is incorrect. The proceeds will not be includible in Burr's gross estate if Adam has the right to veto Burr's power to borrow on the policy that Burr owns on Adam's life.

21.7.8. In December of Year 1, Ms. J assigned all rights under a life insurance policy in her name to another person. She did not receive any money or something of equal value in return. Ms. J was required to file a gift tax return. Ms. J died in February of Year 4. The proceeds of the life insurance policy are included in Ms. J's gross estate.

A. True.

B. False.

Answer (A) is correct. *(SEE, adapted)*
DISCUSSION: Although Ms. J no longer had an ownership interest in the life insurance policy at the time of her death, the value of the proceeds of the policy are included in her estate because she made a gift of the policy within 3 years of death [Sec. 2035(a)].

21.7.9. The gross estate, for purposes of the federal estate tax, includes one-half of the value of property owned by the decedent and spouse as tenants with right of survivorship if the decedent and spouse are the only joint tenants. This is true regardless of which spouse furnished the consideration for the property.

A. True.

B. False.

Answer (A) is correct. *(SEE, adapted)*
DISCUSSION: Under Sec. 2040(a), the decedent's estate normally includes the value of all property held as joint tenants with right of survivorship except to the extent it can be shown that any other joint tenants provided consideration for the property originally. But in the case of spouses owning property as joint tenants with right of survivorship, when one of the spouses dies, only one-half of the property is included in the decedent's estate regardless of who furnished consideration for the property [Sec. 2040(b)].

21.7.10. The gross estate will include the value of an annuity that a beneficiary is due to receive if the decedent possessed the right to receive such annuity either alone or with another person or persons during his or her lifetime.

A.   True.

B.   False.

Answer (A) is correct. *(SEE, adapted)*
   DISCUSSION: Under Sec. 2039, the gross estate includes the value of any annuity receivable by a beneficiary by reason of surviving the decedent if (1) the annuity was payable to the decedent or (2) the decedent possessed the right to receive such annuity or payment, either alone or in conjunction with another for his or her life or for any period not ascertainable without reference to his or her death, or for any period that does not end before his or her death.

21.7.11. Employer B carries a group life insurance policy on its employees. The employees own the right to change the beneficiaries and the right to terminate the policy. If an employee dies, the proceeds from the policy must be included in the decedent's gross estate.

A.   True.

B.   False.

Answer (A) is correct. *(SEE, adapted)*
   DISCUSSION: Section 2042 provides that proceeds from a life insurance policy under which the decedent possessed incidents of ownership must be included in the value of his or her gross estate. The right to change beneficiaries or to terminate the policy is each a sufficient incident of ownership to require the property to be included in the decedent's gross estate.

21.7.12. Rob is trustee of a trust established by Martha that gave the income interest to Bert for life. As trustee, Rob has the right to choose between Bert and Nan for the remainder interest. If Rob has that right to choose between Bert and Nan on the date of his death, the fair market value of the trust assets must be included in Rob's estate.

A.   True.

B.   False.

Answer (B) is correct. *(Publisher, adapted)*
   DISCUSSION: Section 2041 requires inclusion in the decedent's gross estate of the value of any property with respect to which the decedent had a general power of appointment created after October 21, 1942, at the time of his or her death. A general power of appointment is a power exercisable in favor of the decedent, his or her estate, his or her creditors, or the creditors of his or her estate [Sec. 2041(b)]. Since Rob could only choose to give the trust remainder to Bert or Nan, he only had a limited power of appointment and the value of the trust assets is not included in his gross estate.

21.7.13. Ike Hogg paid $4,000 of the $12,000 purchase price when he purchased property as joint tenants with his sister Ima. The property had a fair market value of $21,000 on the date of Ike's death, and his gross estate must include $7,000 of that value.

A.   True.

B.   False.

Answer (A) is correct. *(Publisher, adapted)*
   DISCUSSION: The decedent's gross estate includes the full value of property held as joint tenants with right of survivorship, except to the extent it can be shown the other joint tenant provided consideration [Sec. 2040(a)]. Since the decedent's sister provided two-thirds of the consideration to purchase the property, only one-third of the value of the property at the date of the decedent's death ($7,000) is included in his gross estate.

21.7.14. The gross estate includes the value of the surviving spouse's lifetime interest in the deceased spouse's real property.

A.   True.

B.   False.

Answer (A) is correct. *(SEE, adapted)*
   DISCUSSION: Under Sec. 2034, a decedent's gross estate includes any interest in property of the decedent's surviving spouse existing at the time of the decedent's death as dower or courtesy. Thus, the full value of property is included in the decedent's gross estate, without deducting the surviving spouse's interest.

21.8 Valuation of Estate Property

21.8.1. All of the following statements about the alternate valuation date for valuing property included in the decedent's gross estate are true except

A. The election applies to all of the property in the estate other than property for which the special use valuation applies.

B. Property affected by mere lapse of time is valued at date of death and includes those properties affected by the time value of money.

C. If the alternate valuation date is elected, property disposed of within 6 months after the decedent's death is valued as of the date of disposition.

D. Property not disposed of within 6 months after the decedent's death is valued as of 6 months after the decedent's death.

Answer (B) is correct. *(SEE, adapted)*
REQUIRED: The false statement concerning the alternate valuation date.
DISCUSSION: The alternate valuation method is to value the estate property as of 6 months after death, or when disposed of if earlier (Sec. 2032). However, property affected by mere lapse of time is valued as of the date of death with adjustments for differences in value 6 months after death that are not due to mere lapse of time. Properties affected by mere lapse of time do not include those due to time value of money, such as obligations of payment. They refer to property interests the value of which is based on years such as life estates, remainder interests, patents, etc.
Answer (A) is incorrect. The alternate valuation date election applies to all of the property in the estate other than property for which the special use valuation applies. Answer (C) is incorrect. If the alternate valuation date is elected, property disposed of within 6 months after the decedent's death is valued as of the date of disposition. Answer (D) is incorrect. Property not disposed of within 6 months after the decedent's death is valued as of 6 months after the decedent's death.

21.8.2. If the executor of a decedent's estate elects the alternate valuation date and none of the property included in the gross estate has been sold or distributed, the estate assets must be valued as of how many months after the decedent's death?

A. 3
B. 6
C. 9
D. 12

Answer (B) is correct. *(CPA, adapted)*
REQUIRED: The number of months after the decedent's death at which time the estate's assets are valued under the alternate valuation date.
DISCUSSION: Under Sec. 2032, if the executor of an estate elects the alternate valuation date, and the property in the gross estate has not been sold or distributed, the estate assets are valued as of the date 6 months after the decedent's death. If property is sold or distributed within the 6-month period, it is valued as of the date of sale or distribution.
Answer (A) is incorrect. The alternate valuation date under Sec. 2032 is not 3 months after the decedent's death. Answer (C) is incorrect. The alternate valuation date under Sec. 2032 is not 9 months after the decedent's death. Answer (D) is incorrect. The alternate valuation date under Sec. 2032 is not 12 months after the decedent's death.

21.8.3. Mr. Ash died on June 15 of the current year. The assets in his estate were valued on his date of death and alternate valuation date respectively as follows:

Asset	Date of Death Valuation	Alternate Valuation
Home	$ 2,250,000	$2,300,000
Stock	3,425,000	3,450,000
Bonds	200,000	125,000
Patent	100,000	95,000

The patent had 10 years of its life remaining at the time of Mr. Ash's death. The executor sold the home on August 1 of the current year for $2,275,000. If Mr. Ash's executor elects the alternate valuation date method, what is the value of Mr. Ash's estate?

A. $5,895,000
B. $5,945,000
C. $5,950,000
D. $5,970,000

Answer (C) is correct. *(SEE, adapted)*
REQUIRED: The correct value of the decedent's estate if the alternate valuation date is elected.
DISCUSSION: Under Sec. 2032, if the executor elects to use the alternate valuation date, the estate's assets are valued as of the date 6 months after the decedent's death. Assets that are sold or distributed within that 6-month period are valued as of the date of sale or distribution. Any asset that is affected by mere lapse of time is valued as of the date of the decedent's death but adjusted for any difference in its value not due to mere lapse of time as of the date 6 months after the decedent's death. Assets that are affected by mere lapse of time include patents, life estates, remainders, reversions, and other like properties.
Because the home was sold within the 6-month period after the decedent's death, it is valued as of the date of sale. Its value for estate tax purposes is therefore $2,275,000. The stock and the bonds are included in the estate at their alternate-valuation-date value. The patent is an asset that is affected by mere lapse of time. It is included in the estate at its date-of-death value since the $5,000 decline in value as of the alternate valuation date is apparently the value change associated with the passage of 6 months of time. The value of Mr. Ash's estate is $5,950,000 ($2,275,000 + $3,450,000 + $125,000 + $100,000).
Answer (A) is incorrect. The amount of $5,895,000 includes the house and the stock at the date-of-death value and the patent at the alternate-valuation-date value. Answer (B) is incorrect. The amount of $5,945,000 includes the patent at the alternate-valuation-date value. Answer (D) is incorrect. The amount of $5,970,000 includes the home and the patent at the alternate-valuation-date value.

21.8.4. With regard to the federal estate tax, the alternate valuation date

A. Is required to be used if the fair market value of the estate's assets has increased since the decedent's date of death.

B. If elected on the first return filed for the estate, may be revoked in an amended return provided that the first return was filed on time.

C. Must be used for valuation of the estate's liabilities if such date is used for valuation of the estate's assets.

D. Can be elected only if its use decreases both the value of the gross estate and the sum of the estate tax and the generation skipping transfer tax (reduced by any allowable credits).

Answer (D) is correct. *(CPA, adapted)*
REQUIRED: The correct statement about the alternate valuation date.
DISCUSSION: Section 2032 states the requirements for electing the alternate valuation date for property included in the decedent's gross estate. The effect of the election is to value all estate property on the date 6 months after death or when disposed of, if earlier. This election can only be made for estates of decedents dying after July 18, 1984, if the result is a reduction in both the value of the gross estate and the sum of the federal estate tax and the generation-skipping transfer tax (reduced by any allowable credits).
Answer (A) is incorrect. There is no requirement that the alternate valuation date be used if the fair market value of the estate's assets has increased since the decedent's date of death. Answer (B) is incorrect. The alternate valuation date election is irrevocable. Answer (C) is incorrect. There is no requirement that the alternate valuation date be used for valuation of the estate's liabilities.

21.8.5. The election of the alternate valuation date changes the rule that the gross estate includes property that the decedent owned or had an interest in on the date of death.

A. True.

B. False.

Answer (B) is correct. *(SEE, adapted)*
DISCUSSION: The alternate valuation date is only a method of placing a value on the property in an estate. It does not affect the property that must be included in the estate.

21.8.6. The gross estate for federal estate tax purposes includes the value of all property to the extent of the decedent's interest in the property at time of death. "Value" is the lesser of the decedent's adjusted basis or the fair market value of the property.

A. True.

B. False.

Answer (B) is correct. *(SEE, adapted)*
DISCUSSION: Under Sec. 2033, the gross estate includes the value of all property to the extent of the decedent's interest in the property at time of death. Under Sec. 2031 and the regulations, value is the fair market value of the property unless a special valuation rule (for example, Sec. 2032A) is used. Adjusted basis is irrelevant for gross estate purposes.

21.8.7. If certain conditions are met, the executor of an estate may elect to value real property devoted to farming or used in a closely held business on the basis of its current use as a farm or its use in the business, rather than its fair market value determined on the basis of its highest and best use.

A. True.

B. False.

Answer (A) is correct. *(SEE, adapted)*
DISCUSSION: Real and personal property is generally valued at its highest and best use. Section 2032A provides that, if certain conditions are met, qualified real property used in farming or real or personal property used in a closely held trade or business other than farming may be valued on the basis of its actual use. However, this applies only to qualified real and personal property and is available only if current-use valuation is elected on the first estate tax return filed.

21.9 Deductions from the Gross Estate

21.9.1. Which of the following is not an allowable deduction against a decedent's gross estate?

A. Administration and funeral expenses.

B. Claims against the estate.

C. Penalty incurred as the result of a late payment of the federal estate tax.

D. Casualty and theft losses.

Answer (C) is correct. *(SEE, adapted)*
REQUIRED: The item that is not an allowable deduction from the decedent's gross estate.
DISCUSSION: Sections 2053, 2054, 2055, and 2056 provide the allowable deductions from the gross estate. There is no provision allowing the deduction of a penalty incurred as the result of a late payment of the federal estate tax.
Answer (A) is incorrect. Administration and funeral expenses are allowable deductions against a decedent's gross estate. Answer (B) is incorrect. Claims against the estate are allowable deductions against a decedent's gross estate. Answer (D) is incorrect. Casualty and theft losses are allowable deductions against a decedent's gross estate.

21.9.2. Ordinary and necessary administration expenses paid by the fiduciary of an estate are deductible

A. Only on the fiduciary income tax return (Form 1041) and never on the federal estate tax return (Form 706).

B. Only on the federal estate tax return and never on the fiduciary income tax return.

C. On the fiduciary income tax return only if the estate tax deduction is waived for these expenses.

D. On both the fiduciary income tax return and on the estate tax return by adding a tax computed on the proportionate rates attributable to both returns.

21.9.3. Charlie Brownish is preparing the Form 706, *Estate Tax Return*, for his brother John, who died June 30, 2017. Charlie has identified gross estate items totaling $6,000,000. Considering the following potential deductions and other information, what will be John's estate?

Funeral expenses paid out of the estate	$ 10,000
Value of the residence owned jointly with John's spouse that will pass to the spouse (this property is included in the gross estate)	240,000
Mortgage on residence	20,000
Value of property given to charitable organizations per John's will	50,000

A. $5,730,000

B. $5,740,000

C. $5,720,000

D. None of the answers are correct.

21.9.4. Alan Curtis, a U.S. citizen, died on March 1 of the current year, leaving an adjusted gross estate with a fair market value of $2.4 million at the date of death. Under the terms of Alan's will, $375,000 was bequeathed outright to his widow. The remainder of Alan's estate was left to his mother. Alan made no taxable gifts during his lifetime. In computing the taxable estate, the executor of Alan's estate should claim a marital deduction of

A. $250,000

B. $375,000

C. $1,200,000

D. $2,025,000

Answer (C) is correct. *(CPA, adapted)*
REQUIRED: The deductibility of administration expenses.
DISCUSSION: Administration expenses (and debts of a decedent) are deductible on the estate tax return under Sec. 2053, and some may also qualify as deductions for income tax purposes on the estate's income tax return. Section 642(g), however, disallows a double deduction and requires a waiver of the right to deduct them on Form 706 in order to claim them on Form 1041.
Answer (A) is incorrect. They are deductible on Form 706. Answer (B) is incorrect. They are deductible on Form 1041. Answer (D) is incorrect. They are not deductible in full on both Form 706 and Form 1041.

Answer (C) is correct. *(SEE, adapted)*
REQUIRED: The taxable estate after deductions.
DISCUSSION: Deductions from the GE in computing the taxable estate (TE) include ones with respect to the following:

1. Administration and funeral expenses are deductible.

2. Unpaid mortgages on property are deductible if the value of the decedent's interest is included in the GE.

3. Bequests to qualified charitable organizations are deductible.

4. Outright transfers to a surviving spouse are deductible from the GE, to the extent the interest is included in the gross estate, the property passes in a qualifying manner, and interest conveyed must not be a nondeductible terminable interest.

John's estate is computed as follows:

GE items	$6,000,000
Funeral expenses	(10,000)
Marital transfer ($240,000 – $20,000 mortgage on residence)	(220,000)
Charitable contribution	(50,000)
Taxable estate	$5,720,000

Answer (A) is incorrect. The $10,000 of funeral expenses is deductible. Answer (B) is incorrect. The $20,000 unpaid mortgage is deductible. Answer (D) is incorrect. One of the answers is correct.

Answer (B) is correct. *(CPA, adapted)*
REQUIRED: The amount of the marital deduction.
DISCUSSION: A deduction from the gross estate is allowed for all property transferred in a qualified manner to the surviving spouse (Sec. 2056). Leaving it to the surviving spouse outright will qualify. Therefore, Alan's estate should claim a marital deduction of the entire $375,000 bequeathed to Alan's widow.
Answer (A) is incorrect. The amount of $250,000 does not include the full amount bequeathed to Alan's widow. Answer (C) is incorrect. The amount of $1,200,000 is half of Alan's estate, which does not fully qualify for a marital deduction. Answer (D) is incorrect. The amount left to Alan's mother is $2,025,000, which does not qualify for a marital deduction.

21.9.5. B died in the current year. The state of residence was not a community property state. From the items listed below, what are the allowable deductions from the gross estate?

Funeral expenses	$ 3,500
Executor and administrative fees	5,000
Mortgage on jointly held property, one-half purchase price paid by B	70,000
Transfers of cash to B's spouse	60,000
Expense of filing estate's income tax return	500

A. $68,500

B. $73,500

C. $103,500

D. $135,000

Answer (C) is correct. *(SEE, adapted)*
REQUIRED: The amount of allowable deductions from the gross estate.
DISCUSSION: Under Sec. 2053, deductions from the gross estate are allowed for funeral expenses, administration expenses, and claims against the estate for unpaid mortgages on property in which the value of the decedent's interest is included in the value of the gross estate. Only one-half of the mortgage may be deducted because only one-half the value of the property is included in B's estate. Section 2056 allows a marital deduction from the gross estate for most transfers to a surviving spouse. There are no provisions allowing the expense of filing the estate's income tax return to be deducted against the gross estate. Such amount can be deducted on the estate's income tax return (Form 1041). The allowable deductions are computed as follows:

Funeral expenses	$ 3,500
Executor and administrative fees	5,000
Mortgage ($70,000 × 1/2)	35,000
Cash to spouse	60,000
Allowable deductions	$103,500

Answer (A) is incorrect. The amount of $68,500 excludes B's half of the mortgage. Answer (B) is incorrect. The amount of $73,500 excludes executor and administrative fees and transfers of cash to B's spouse and includes the full amount of the mortgage. Answer (D) is incorrect. The amount of $135,000 excludes the funeral expenses and includes the full amount of the mortgage.

21.9.6. Medical expenses, if deducted only on the estate tax return, are fully deductible as administration expenses.

A. True.

B. False.

Answer (A) is correct. *(SEE, adapted)*
DISCUSSION: Section 2053 allows a deduction from the gross estate for claims against the estate. Medical expenses are deductible. Section 213(c) provides that medical expenses paid within 1 year of death may be deducted on either the estate tax return or the final income tax return of the decedent, but not on both returns.

21.9.7. Herman, as executor of the estate of his deceased father, must sell his father's house to make distributions to all beneficiaries. Herman pays $9,000 to paint and carpet the house to enhance its marketability. The $9,000 Herman pays is deductible from the gross estate to compute the taxable estate.

A. True.

B. False.

Answer (B) is correct. *(SEE, adapted)*
DISCUSSION: Expenses for selling property of an estate are deductible if the sale is necessary to pay the decedent's debts, expenses of administration, or taxes; to preserve the estate; or to affect a required cash distribution.

21.10 Calculation of Estate Tax

21.10.1. Form 706, *United States Estate (and Generation-Skipping Transfer) Tax Return*, was filed for the estate of John Doe in 2017. The gross estate tax was $250,000. All of the following items are credited against the gross estate tax to determine the net estate tax payable, except

A. Applicable credit amount.

B. Credit for gift taxes.

C. Marital deduction.

D. Credit for foreign death taxes.

Answer (C) is correct. *(SEE, adapted)*
REQUIRED: The credit that is not deductible in the determination of the estate tax payable.
DISCUSSION: There is no credit for a marital deduction. Instead the marital deduction is deductible in arriving at the taxable estate. The estate tax is then computed on the taxable estate.
Answer (A) is incorrect. Section 2010 allows an applicable credit amount of $2,141,800 for 2017 against the estate tax. Answer (B) is incorrect. Indirectly, there is a credit for gift taxes. This reduction occurs because the gross estate tax is computed on the taxable estate and all prior transfers. Subtracted from that is the amount of tax paid on prior transfers (gifts) based on current rates to arrive at the net estate tax. Answer (D) is incorrect. There is a credit for death taxes paid to to foreign governments.

21.10.2. What amount of a decedent's taxable estate is effectively tax-free in 2017 if the maximum applicable credit amount is taken?

- A. $0
- B. $14,000
- C. $2,141,800
- D. $5,490,000

Answer (D) is correct. *(CPA, adapted)*
REQUIRED: The amount of a decedent's taxable estate that is effectively tax-free.
DISCUSSION: In the case of decedents dying in 2017, the applicable credit amount allowed under Sec. 2010 is $2,141,800 [Sec. 2010(a)]. The applicable credit amount against the estate tax is not reduced by the applicable credit amount used against the gift tax during life. However, there is not a double benefit. Instead, the applicable credit amount used for lifetime gifts is taken into account in the initial computation of the estate tax, i.e., tax on the sum of the taxable estate plus prior gifts, less gift taxes imposed at current rates. The $2,141,800 applicable credit amount offsets the estate tax liability that would be imposed on a taxable estate of up to $5,490,000 computed at the rates in Sec. 2001(c).
Answer (A) is incorrect. The decedent is allowed an applicable credit amount. Answer (B) is incorrect. Although $14,000 is the annual amount of gifts excluded per donee in 2017, it does not directly limit the tax-free portion of a decedent's estate. Answer (C) is incorrect. The $2,141,800 applicable credit amount offsets the estate tax liability that would be imposed on a taxable estate of up to $5,490,000 computed at the rates in Sec. 2001(c).

21.10.3. Kary died in 2017 with a taxable estate of $7 million and adjusted taxable gifts of $1 million. She used $62,800 of applicable credit amount during her life and paid gift taxes of $283,000. Kary lived in a state that assesses a state death tax of $342,400 on this estate. The tax due on Kary's estate is

- A. $378,600
- B. $721,000
- C. $2,862,800
- D. $3,145,800

Answer (B) is correct. *(Publisher, adapted)*
REQUIRED: The tax due on the decedent's estate.
DISCUSSION: The tax due is equal to the tax imposed under Sec. 2001 reduced by allowable credits. The tax imposed under Sec. 2001 is equal to the excess of a tentative tax (computed on the sum of the taxable estate and the adjusted taxable gifts), over tax that would have been payable on gifts if the current rate schedule had been in effect at the time of the gifts [Sec. 2001(b)]. For decedents dying in 2017, the applicable credit amount against the estate tax is $2,141,800 (Sec. 2010).

Estate tax on $8,000,000		$3,145,800
Gift tax on $1,000,000	$345,800	
Applicable credit applied to gifts	(62,800)	
Gift taxes paid previously		(283,000)
Tentative estate tax		$2,862,800
Applicable credit amount		(2,141,800)
Estate tax payable		$ 721,000

Answer (A) is incorrect. The state death taxes are not allowed as a credit. Answer (C) is incorrect. The tentative estate tax is $2,862,800 before the applicable credit amounts. Answer (D) is incorrect. The figure of $3,145,800 is the estate tax on $8,000,000, which must be adjusted for the credit for gift taxes paid and applicable credit amounts.

21.10.4. Dinah Mite died in 2017 with a taxable estate of $5.99 million. She had made no taxable gifts during her lifetime. Her estate will pay a state death tax of $100,000. Her federal estate tax due is

- A. $100,000
- B. $2,241,800
- C. $200,000
- D. $2,341,800

Answer (C) is correct. *(Publisher, adapted)*
REQUIRED: The federal estate tax payable after credits in 2017.
DISCUSSION: The estate tax is imposed in Sec. 2001. For 2017, the credit for state death taxes is not allowed. Any state death taxes are taken as a deduction. For decedents dying in 2017, Sec. 2010 allows an applicable credit amount of $2,141,800.

Tax on $5,990,000	$2,341,800
Applicable credit amount	(2,141,800)
Estate tax payable	$ 200,000

Answer (A) is incorrect. The amount of $100,000 is the tax on $5.99 million reduced by the state death tax of $100,000, which was repealed for the years after 2004. Answer (B) is incorrect. The tax must be reduced by the applicable credit amount, not the state death tax. Answer (D) is incorrect. The amount of $2,341,800 is the tax on $5.99 million without reduction by the applicable credit amount of $2,141,800.

Questions 21.10.5 and 21.10.6 are based on the following information. John died in 2017 with a taxable estate of $5.49 million and adjusted taxable gifts of $1 million. During his life, he used applicable credit amounts of $79,300.

21.10.5. The applicable credit amount that his estate will subtract from tentative estate tax due is

A. $1,796,000

B. $1,875,300

C. $2,062,500

D. $2,141,800

Answer (D) is correct. *(Publisher, adapted)*
REQUIRED: The applicable credit amount available for the estate tax.
DISCUSSION: In the case of decedents dying in 2017, the ACA allowed is $2,141,800 [Sec. 2010(a)]. The applicable credit amount against the estate tax is not reduced by the amount of applicable credit amount used against the gift tax during life. There is not a double benefit; instead, the applicable credit amount used for lifetime gifts is taken into account in the initial computation of the estate tax, i.e., tax on the sum of the taxable estate plus prior adjusted taxable gifts, less gift taxes imposed at current rates.
Answer (A) is incorrect. The applicable credit amount that John's estate will subtract from the tentative estate tax due is equal to the full credit amount in 2017. Answer (B) is incorrect. Any gifts where the applicable credit amount was previously applied are added back to the taxable estate to compute the applicable credit amount. Answer (C) is incorrect. The applicable credit amount is equal to the full amount for decedents dying in 2017.

21.10.6. John paid gift taxes during his lifetime of $266,500. What is his estate tax due?

A. $133,500

B. $2,275,300

C. $400,000

D. $2,541,800

Answer (A) is correct. *(Publisher, adapted)*
REQUIRED: The amount of estate tax payable after credits.
DISCUSSION: Section 2001 imposes a tax equal to the excess of a tentative tax (computed on the sum of the taxable estate and the adjusted taxable gifts) over the tax that would have been payable on gifts if the current rate schedule had been in effect at the time of the gifts [Sec. 2001(b)]. The tax rate schedules are in Sec. 2001(c).

Estate tax on $6,490,000		$2,541,800
Gift tax on $1,000,000	$345,800	
Applicable credit applied to gifts	(79,300)	
Gift taxes paid previously		(266,500)
Tentative estate tax		$2,275,300
Applicable credit amount		(2,141,800)
Estate tax payable		$ 133,500

Answer (B) is incorrect. The tentative estate tax before the applicable credit amount is $2,275,300. Answer (C) is incorrect. The amount of $400,000 does not include the credit for the gift taxes paid previously. Answer (D) is incorrect. The estate tax is $2,541,800 before considering gift taxes paid previously and the applicable credit amount.

21.10.7. John Able gifted 40 acres of land to his son Jacob on August 15, 2010. The land was valued at $300,000 on a timely filed gift tax return. No gift tax was paid since this was John's first gift in excess of his annual exclusion. John died on August 1, 2015. The land was worth $2 million on the date of death. When reviewing the estate tax return, the IRS claimed that the value of the land gifted in 2010 should have been shown on the estate tax return as $1 million. No change in the value of the land on the gift tax return was requested by the IRS. John will be able to argue successfully that the IRS's revaluation of the land for estate tax return purposes was improper since the statute of limitations on the gift tax return had expired.

A. True.

B. False.

Answer (A) is correct. *(Publisher, adapted)*
DISCUSSION: In computing adjusted taxable gifts for estate tax purposes, the IRS may not revalue gifts made during life if the gift tax statute of limitations has expired. However, in order for this provision to apply, the gift in question must have been adequately disclosed. Since the 3-year statute of limitations had expired and the gift had been adequately disclosed, John will be able to argue successfully against the IRS's attempt at revaluation.

21.10.8. Alvin died in March of Year 1. Under the terms of his will, Alvin left $1 million in assets to his brother Bill. Bill died in December of Year 3. The assets inherited from Alvin were included in Bill's taxable estate. The amount of federal estate tax paid by Alvin's estate that was attributable to these assets was $100,000. The amount of tax paid by Bill's estate attributable to these assets was $75,000. Bill's estate can claim a credit of $100,000 for tax on the prior transfer.

A. True.

B. False.

Answer (B) is correct. *(SEE, adapted)*
DISCUSSION: Sec. 2013 allows a credit for taxes paid on prior transfers. The credit applies to a transfer of property by or from a person who died within 10 years before or within 2 years after the decedent's death. The credit serves to prevent an estate from being diminished by successive taxes on the same property within a brief period. The credit is subject to the limitations of Sec. 2013(c) and must be adjusted if the transferor predeceased the decedent by more than 2 years.
Under Sec. 2013(c), the credit is the lesser of (1) the estate tax paid by the transferor on the assets or (2) the amount by which the transferred assets increase the decedent's estate tax. Since the amount by which the transferred assets increased Bill's estate tax ($75,000) is less than the amount of estate tax paid by Alvin attributable to the assets ($100,000), the credit is $75,000.
Because Alvin predeceased Bill by more than 2 years, this credit must be adjusted. Sec. 2013(a)(1) allows the decedent to claim 80% of the credit if the transferor died within the third or fourth years before the decedent's death. Therefore, the credit allowable to Bill's estate for tax on the prior transfer is $60,000 ($75,000 × 80%).

21.11 Estate Tax Payment and Returns

21.11.1. An extension of time to pay the estate tax may be granted if the executor can show "reasonable cause" as to why the estate is unable to pay the tax in a timely manner. All of the following are illustrations of "reasonable cause" except

A. Since the estate includes a claim to substantial assets in a pending lawsuit, the gross estate cannot be determined when the tax is due.

B. The liquid assets of the estate are located in several jurisdictions and are not within the immediate control of the executor.

C. The estate would have to borrow funds at an interest rate higher than generally available to satisfy claims against the estate that are due and payable.

D. Payment of the estate taxes would require the liquidation of more than 50% of the assets of the estate.

Answer (D) is correct. *(SEE, adapted)*
REQUIRED: The cause for which it is not "reasonable" to grant an extension of time to pay estate tax.
DISCUSSION: Section 6161(a) provides that the time for payment of estate tax may be extended not in excess of 10 years for reasonable cause. Reasonable cause under Reg. 20.6161-1(a) might be based on a claim to substantial assets in a pending lawsuit, estate assets in other jurisdictions, estate assets consisting of rights to receive payment in the future, and payment of the tax requires borrowing at a higher interest rate than generally available. Liquidation of estate assets is a function of probate administration, and not reasonable cause for deferring payment of estate tax liability.
Answer (A) is incorrect. A situation in which the gross estate is undeterminable when the tax is due on account of the estate including a claim to substantial assets in a pending lawsuit is an example of reasonable cause to grant an extension of time to pay estate tax. Answer (B) is incorrect. The liquid assets of an estate being located in several jurisdictions not within the immediate control of the executor is an example of reasonable cause to grant an extension of time to pay estate tax. Answer (C) is incorrect. The estate having to borrow funds at an interest rate higher than generally available to satisfy claims against the estate that are due and payable is an example of reasonable cause to grant an extension of time to pay estate tax.

21.11.2. Which of the following rules does not apply to the filing of an estate tax return of a U.S. citizen?

A. Form 706 is the form that is used to file an estate tax return.

B. The return is due 9 months after the date of death unless an extension of time for filing has been granted.

C. The return is filed with the Cincinnati, Ohio, Service Center.

D. For 2017, the value of the gross estate must be over $5,000,000.

Answer (D) is correct. *(SEE, adapted)*
    REQUIRED: The rule not applicable for filing an estate tax return.
    DISCUSSION: Section 6018 provides that an estate tax return must be filed when the gross estate of a decedent exceeds $5,490,000 in 2017.
    Answer (A) is incorrect. Form 706 is the form that is used to file an estate tax return. Answer (B) is incorrect. The return is due 9 months after the date of death unless an extension of time for filing has been granted. Answer (C) is incorrect. The return is filed with the Cincinnati, Ohio, Service Center.

21.11.3. Charlie Grey died June 15, 2017. His taxable estate is $5,590,000. By what date is Form 706, *United States Estate Tax Return*, due?

A. Not due because taxable estate does not exceed the minimum taxable amount.

B. March 15, 2018.

C. April 15, 2018.

D. December 31, 2017.

Answer (B) is correct. *(SEE, adapted)*
    REQUIRED: The due date for Form 706, *United States Estate Tax Return*.
    DISCUSSION: The executor is required to file Form 706, *United States Estate Tax Return*, if the gross estate at the decedent's death exceeds $5,490,000 in 2017. Adjusted taxable gifts made by the decedent during his or her lifetime reduce the threshold. The estate tax return is due within 9 months after the date of the decedent's death. An extension of up to 6 months may be granted.
    Answer (A) is incorrect. The executor is required to file Form 706 if the gross estate at the decedent's death exceeds $5,490,000. Answer (C) is incorrect. April 15, 2018, is not the correct date by which Form 706 is due; it would be late. Answer (D) is incorrect. December 31, 2017, is not the due date for Form 706; it would be early.

21.11.4. The executor of an estate may request an extension of time to pay the estate tax. All of the following statements are true except

A. The usual extension of time to pay is up to 12 months.

B. When the executor applies for an extension, (s)he must show why the estate cannot pay the tax in full.

C. The IRS may extend the time for payment for up to 12 years.

D. A request for an extension of time to pay estate tax is filed on Form 4768.

Answer (C) is correct. *(SEE, adapted)*
    REQUIRED: The false statement regarding an extension of time to pay the estate tax.
    DISCUSSION: Under Sec. 6161(a)(1), the time for paying the estate tax may be extended by a reasonable period not to exceed 12 months. However, a satisfactory showing of undue hardship is required [Reg. 20.6161-1(b)]. The extension for filing the return is 6 months [Sec. 6081(a)]. The payment of the estate tax may be extended not in excess of 10 years for reasonable cause.
    Answer (A) is incorrect. The extension may be for a reasonable period not to exceed 12 months. Answer (B) is incorrect. A satisfactory showing of undue hardship is required [Reg. 20.6161-1(b)]. Answer (D) is incorrect. Form 4768 is filed to request an extension of time to pay estate tax.

21.11.5. Anna died January 20, 2017. Rick, the executor, filed Form 706, *United States Estate (and Generation-Skipping Transfer) Tax Return*, on June 30, 2017. Rick paid the tax due and distributed the assets on September 30, 2017. Generally, what is the last day the recipients could be assessed estate tax on the property received?

A. October 20, 2019.

B. September 30, 2020.

C. June 30, 2021.

D. October 20, 2021.

Answer (D) is correct. *(SEE, adapted)*
    REQUIRED: The period for assessment of estate tax when transfers from an estate are made.
    DISCUSSION: Although the general period for assessment of estate tax is 3 years after the due date for a timely filed Form 706, the assessment period is extended an additional (fourth) year for transfers from an estate.
    Answer (A) is incorrect. October 20, 2019, is not the last day by which recipients could be assessed estate tax on the property received. Answer (B) is incorrect. September 30, 2020, is not the last day by which recipients could be assessed estate tax on the property received. Answer (C) is incorrect. June 30, 2021, is not the last day by which recipients could be assessed estate tax on the property received.

21.11.6. On June 30 of the current year, Rita died with a gross estate of $5,665,000 and estate taxes payable of $70,000. Victor, the executor, filed the estate tax return on December 31 of that same year. He distributed all the assets of the estate without paying the estate tax liability. Dustin, one of several beneficiaries, received $40,000. What is the amount of taxes that may be assessed against Victor and Dustin?

	Victor	Dustin
A.	$70,000	$0
B.	$30,000	$40,000
C.	$70,000	$40,000
D.	$70,000	$70,000

Answer (C) is correct. *(SEE, adapted)*
REQUIRED: The liability of an executor and a beneficiary for estate tax due.
DISCUSSION: An executor is personally liable for unpaid estate taxes. An estate beneficiary is also personally liable but only to the extent of the value of assets (s)he received from the estate.
Answer (A) is incorrect. An amount of taxes may be assessed against Dustin. Answer (B) is incorrect. The executor is liable for the complete amount of estate tax due. Answer (D) is incorrect. The executor is liable for the complete amount of estate tax due, and the beneficiary is liable for up to the amount (s)he receives.

21.11.7. All of the following statements about the ability to pay estate taxes attributable to closely held businesses over an installment period are true except

A. The interest rate on the first $1 million of the taxable portion of the estate comprised of the closely held business is 2%.

B. The interest rate on any remaining portion of the estate tax attributable to a closely held business is 45% of the applicable rate for underpayments of tax.

C. The interest payments are deductible on the estate tax return.

D. Principal payments are not required under the installment plan until the fifth year.

Answer (C) is correct. *(Publisher, adapted)*
REQUIRED: The false statement regarding the provision for installment payment of estate taxes attributable to closely held businesses as modified by the Taxpayer Relief Act of 1997.
DISCUSSION: As modified by the Taxpayer Relief Act of 1997, the former 4% interest rate on the deferred estate tax attributable to the first $1 million in taxable value of the closely held business is reduced to 2%. The interest rate on the remaining deferred amount is reduced to 45% of the rate charged for underpayment of taxes. Also unmodified by the tax law changes in 1997, the principal payments are not required under the installment plan until the fifth year. The estate tax deduction, however, is no longer available for interest paid on the estate tax installment payments.
Answer (A) is incorrect. Regarding the ability to pay estate taxes attributable to closely held businesses over an installment period, the interest rate on the first $1 million of the taxable portion of the estate comprised of the closely held business is 2%. Answer (B) is incorrect. The interest rate on any remaining portion of the estate tax attributable to a closely held business is 45% of the applicable rate for the underpayments of tax. Answer (D) is incorrect. Regarding the ability to pay estate taxes attributable to closely held businesses over an installment period, the principal payments are not required under the installment plan until the fifth year.

21.11.8. Section 6166 contains provisions for extending the time for paying estate taxes when the estate consists largely of an interest in a closely held business. An interest in a closely held business does not include

A. An interest in a sole proprietorship.

B. An interest in a partnership carrying on a trade or business if 20% or more of the capital interest in such partnership is included in the gross estate or there are 15 or fewer partners.

C. Stock in a corporation carrying on a trade or business if 20% or more in value of the voting stock of such corporation is included in the gross estate or there are 15 or fewer shareholders.

D. Stock in an S corporation carrying on a trade or business if 15% or more in value of the voting stock of such corporation is included in the gross estate or there are 100 or fewer shareholders.

Answer (D) is correct. *(E. Fenton)*
REQUIRED: The interest that is not an interest in a closely held business for extensions of time to pay estate taxes.
DISCUSSION: Under Sec. 6166(a), estates that include a substantial interest in a closely held business may be allowed to delay payments of a portion of the estate tax due if the interest exceeds 35% of the adjusted gross estate. Section 6166(b) defines an interest in a closely held business to include a corporation carrying on a trade or business if 20% or more in value of the voting stock of such corporation is included in the gross estate or there are 15 or fewer shareholders. There are no separate requirements for S corporations.
Answer (A) is incorrect. A sole proprietorship is included as a closely held business. Answer (B) is incorrect. An interest in a partnership is included as a closely held business if the partnership is carrying on a trade or business and if 20% or more of the capital interest in the partnership is included in the gross estate or there are 15 or fewer partners. Answer (C) is incorrect. A closely held business does include stock in a corporation carrying on a trade or business if 20% or more in value of the voting stock is included in the gross estate or there are 15 or fewer shareholders.

21.11.9. During his lifetime, Mr. Grant, a United States citizen, made adjusted taxable gifts of $2,200,000. He died on March 15, 2017. At the time of his death, the fair market value of his assets were his home, $2,250,000; speed boat, $100,000; and investments, $990,000. None of Mr. Grant's gifts are included in his estate. Mr. Grant's executor is required to file Form 706, *United States Estate (and Generation-Skipping Transfer) Tax Return*.

    A. True.

    B. False.

Answer (A) is correct. *(SEE, adapted)*
    DISCUSSION: The executor of an estate is required to file Form 706, *United States Estate (and Generation-Skipping Transfer) Tax Return*, if the gross estate at the decedent's death in 2017 exceeds $5,490,000. Adjusted taxable gifts made by the decedent during his or her lifetime are added to the estate. Therefore, the adjusted taxable gifts of $2,200,000 are added to the value of the assets (which total $3,340,000). The $5,540,000 value of the estate exceeds the $5,490,000 threshold, and the executor will be required to file an estate tax return.

21.12 Generation-Skipping Transfers

21.12.1. Jennifer, age 55 years exactly, wants to provide for the financial security of her secretary, Sue, and other unrelated friends. She establishes a trust. Sue, age 65, will receive income from the trust for her life. On Sue's death, Sam, another friend who is currently 51, will receive income for his lifetime. Upon his death, the remainder interest will be divided equally between Kevin (age 39) and Stan (age 43). How many times will this trust be subject to a GSTT?

    A. None. No GSTT will be assessed.

    B. One.

    C. Two.

    D. Three.

Answer (A) is correct. *(Publisher, adapted)*
    REQUIRED: The number of times a GSTT will be assessed under the trust arrangement.
    DISCUSSION: A taxable termination is the termination of a nonskip person's interest held in trust, after which only a skip person has an interest [Sec. 2612(a)(1)]. An individual is a skip person if (s)he is assigned to a generation that is two or more generations below the generation assignment of the transferor. An individual who is not a lineal descendant (or married to a lineal descendant) of a grandparent of the transferor is assigned to a generation based on the date of such individual's birth. An individual born not more than 12 1/2 years after the transferor is assigned to the transferor's generation; an individual born 12 1/2 to 37 1/2 years after the transferor is assigned to the first generation younger than the transferor [Sec. 2651(d)].
    Since Sue is older than the transferor, she is not a younger generation beneficiary. Since Sam and Stan were both born within 12 1/2 years of the transferor's birth, they are assigned to the same generation as the transferor and are not younger generation beneficiaries. Since Kevin was born more than 12 1/2 years but not more than 37 1/2 years after the date of the birth of the transferor, he is assigned to the first generation younger than the transferor and is the only younger generation beneficiary under this trust.
    No one with an interest at any time in the trust is two or more generations younger than Jennifer, so no one is a skip person. With no skip person, there is no taxable termination, and no generation-skipping transfer tax is due.
    Answer (B) is incorrect. The trust will not be subject to the GSTT once. Answer (C) is incorrect. The trust will not be subject to the GSTT twice. Answer (D) is incorrect. The trust will not be subject to the GSTT three times.

21.12.2. The generation-skipping transfer tax is imposed

    A. Instead of the gift tax.

    B. Instead of the estate tax.

    C. As a separate tax in addition to the gift and estate taxes.

    D. On transfers of future interest to beneficiaries who are more than one generation above the donor's generation.

Answer (C) is correct. *(CPA, adapted)*
    REQUIRED: The applicability of the GSTT.
    DISCUSSION: The generation-skipping transfer tax (GSTT) is imposed, as a separate tax in addition to the gift and estate taxes, on generation-skipping transfers that are any taxable distributions or terminations with respect to a generation-skipping trust or direct skips [Sec. 2611(a)]. A taxable termination is the termination of a nonskip person's interest held in trust, after which only a skip person has an interest [Sec. 2612(a)(1)]. A skip person is a natural person assigned to a generation that is two or more generations below the transferor or a trust in which all interests are held by skip persons.
    Answer (A) is incorrect. The GSTT is a separate tax in addition to the gift tax. Answer (B) is incorrect. The GSTT is a separate tax in addition to the estate tax. Answer (D) is incorrect. The GSTT prevents tax avoidance by transferring property directly to a person more than one generation below the donee.

21.12.3. Which of the following is subject to the generation-skipping transfer tax?

A. Margaret wrote her will in 1985 establishing a generation-skipping trust. Her will was unchanged when she died in November 2017.

B. Sam wrote his will in 1960 but amended it in 1985 to add a generation-skipping trust. Sam was mentally incompetent from January 1986 until his death in February 2017.

C. Carol wrote a will in May 1986 that established a generation-skipping trust. She made no changes in her will before her June 2017 death.

D. Carlisle established in 1983 a generation-skipping trust by gift for the benefit of his descendants. The irrevocable trust was unchanged and no corpus was added prior to his death in 2017.

Answer (C) is correct. *(Publisher, adapted)*
REQUIRED: The trust subject to the generation-skipping transfer tax (GSTT).
DISCUSSION: Generally, the GSTT imposed by Sec. 2601 applies only to a generation-skipping transfer made after October 22, 1986. There are three exceptions: (1) The tax is not imposed on a generation-skipping transfer under a trust that was irrevocable on September 25, 1985, to the extent that the transfer is not made out of corpus added to the trust after September 25, 1985; (2) the tax is also not imposed on a transfer under a will executed before October 22, 1986, if the decedent dies before 1987; and (3) the tax is not imposed on the generation-skipping transfer of a decedent who was mentally incompetent on October 22, 1986, and remains such so as not to be able to change the disposition before death. Since Carol died in 2017, and the corpus was placed in the trust at that time, none of the exceptions apply, and her testamentary generation-skipping trust is subject to the GSTT.
Answer (A) is incorrect. The will was in existence on October 22, 1986; it was not amended after that date with respect to the generation-skipping transfer. Answer (B) is incorrect. Sam was mentally incompetent on October 22, 1986, and remained so until his death. Answer (D) is incorrect. The irrevocable generation-skipping trust was in existence on September 25, 1985, it was not amended after that date, and no corpus was added after September 25, 1985.

21.12.4. Which of the following is a true statement of the event(s) that may trigger a generation-skipping transfer tax?

A. A taxable termination only.

B. A taxable distribution only.

C. A taxable termination or a taxable distribution but not a direct skip.

D. A taxable termination, a taxable distribution, or a direct skip.

Answer (D) is correct. *(Publisher, adapted)*
REQUIRED: The event that may trigger a generation-skipping transfer tax.
DISCUSSION: A generation-skipping transfer is defined as a taxable termination, a taxable distribution, or a direct skip [Sec. 2611(a)]. A taxable termination is the termination of a nonskip person's interest held in trust, after which only a skip person has an interest [Sec. 2612(a)(1)]. A taxable distribution means any distribution from a trust to a skip person if it is not a taxable termination or a direct skip [Sec. 2612(b)]. A direct skip is a transfer subject to the estate tax or the gift tax of an interest in property to a skip person. A skip person is a natural person assigned to a generation that is two or more generations below the generation assignment of the transferor or a trust where all interests are held by skip persons [Sec. 2613(a)].
Answer (A) is incorrect. The generation-skipping transfer tax is triggered not only by a taxable termination. Answer (B) is incorrect. The generation-skipping transfer tax is triggered not only by a taxable distribution. Answer (C) is incorrect. The generation-skipping transfer tax may be triggered by a direct skip.

21.12.5. Thom (age 63) established a trust and named his second wife, Theresa (age 50), as income beneficiary for 20 years. After 20 years, Thom's son Trevor (age 40) and nephew Bob (age 25) are to receive lifetime income interests. Trevor died 22 years after the trust was established, and Bob died 34 years after the trust was established. After the deaths of both Trevor and Bob, the remainder passes equally to Thom's granddaughter Sara (age 20) and great-granddaughter Hope (age 1). Assuming both Sara and Hope were alive when Bob died, how many times is the generation-skipping transfer tax levied?

A. Never.

B. Once.

C. Twice.

D. Three times.

Answer (B) is correct. *(Publisher, adapted)*
REQUIRED: The number of times the generation-skipping transfer tax is levied.
DISCUSSION: The generation-skipping transfer tax (GSTT) is imposed on generation-skipping transfers that are any taxable distributions or terminations with respect to a generation-skipping trust or direct skips [Sec. 2611(a)]. A taxable termination is the termination of a nonskip person's interest held in trust, after which only a skip person has an interest [Sec. 2612(a)(1)]. A skip person is a natural person assigned to a generation that is two or more generations below the transferor or a trust in which all interests are held by skip persons. A nonskip person is any person who is not a skip person [Sec. 2613(b)].
Trevor and Bob are one generation below the transferor and are nonskip persons. There is no taxable termination on Trevor's death since Bob, a nonskip person, has an interest in the trust. Both Sara and Hope are skip persons, so there is a taxable termination on Bob's death.
Answer (A) is incorrect. The generation-skipping transfer tax is levied. Answer (C) is incorrect. The generation-skipping transfer tax is not levied twice. Answer (D) is incorrect. The generation-skipping transfer tax is not levied three times.

21.12.6. Thom (age 63) established a trust and named his second wife, Theresa (age 50), as income beneficiary for 20 years. After 20 years, Thom's son Trevor (age 40) and nephew Bob (age 25) are to receive lifetime income interests. After the deaths of both Trevor and Bob, the remainder passes equally to Thom's granddaughter Sara (age 20) and great-granddaughter Hope (age 1). How many younger generations are there in this trust arrangement?

A. 4
B. 3
C. 2
D. 1

Answer (B) is correct. *(Publisher, adapted)*
REQUIRED: The number of younger generations in the trust arrangement.
DISCUSSION: Younger generations refer to generations younger than the transferor's generation. An individual who is a lineal descendant of a grandparent of the grantor is assigned to that generation that results from comparing the number of generations between the grandparent and such individual with the number of generations between the grandparent and the transferor [Sec. 2651(b)(1)]. An individual who has been married to the transferor is assigned to the transferor's generation [Sec. 2651(c)(1)].
Since Theresa is married to the transferor, she is assigned to the same generation as Thom. Trevor and Bob are assigned to one generation below the transferor's generation. Sara is assigned to two generations below the transferor's generation. Hope is assigned to three generations below the transferor's generation.
Answer (A) is incorrect. There are not four younger generations involved in this trust arrangement. Answer (C) is incorrect. There are not two younger generations involved in this trust arrangement. Answer (D) is incorrect. There is not only one younger generation involved in this trust arrangement.

21.12.7. The transferor's child and the transferor's nephew are in different younger generations if their ages are more than 25 1/2 years apart.

A. True.
B. False.

Answer (B) is correct. *(Publisher, adapted)*
DISCUSSION: Since the transferor's child and nephew are both lineal descendants of a grandparent of the transferor, they are assigned to that generation that results from comparing the number of generations between the transferor's grandparent and themselves with the number of generations between the grandparent of the transferor and the transferor [Sec. 2651(b)(1)]. Since the number of generations between the transferor's child and the transferor's grandparent, and the transferor's nephew and the transferor's grandparent, is always the same, the transferor's child and nephew will always be assigned to the same generation.

21.12.8. Kay has an interest in a generation-skipping trust if she has only a future right to receive income or corpus from the trust.

A. True.
B. False.

Answer (B) is correct. *(Publisher, adapted)*
DISCUSSION: An interest in a trust exists if a person has a present (not future) right to receive income or corpus from the trust or is a permissible recipient of such income or corpus [Sec. 2652(c)].

21.12.9. Interests in a generation-skipping trust can pass between beneficiaries of the same generation without triggering the generation-skipping transfer tax.

A. True.
B. False.

Answer (A) is correct. *(Publisher, adapted)*
DISCUSSION: There must be a taxable distribution, termination, or direct skip for the tax to apply. A transfer is not a generation-skipping transfer if (1) the property transferred has already been taxed under the GSTT, (2) the transferee of that prior transfer was the same (or lower) generation as the transferee for the current event, and (3) the transfers do not have the effect of avoiding tax [Sec. 2611(b)(2)]. While interpretation of the third requirement is uncertain, requirements (1) and (2) could apply to the transfer from one skip person (Individual A) to another skip person (Individual B) of the same generation.

21.13 Taxable Amount and Taxpayer Identification

21.13.1. Which of the following is a true statement about the taxable amount of a generation-skipping transfer?

A. The taxable amount for a direct skip and a taxable termination are the same.

B. The taxable amount for a taxable termination is the value of the property received by the transferee reduced by expenses incurred by the transferee in connection with the determination, collection, or refund of the GSTT.

C. The taxable amount for a taxable distribution is the value of all property distributed less allowable expenses, debt, and taxes.

D. If a generation-skipping transfer tax on a taxable distribution is paid by the generation-skipping trust, an amount equal to the taxes paid by the trust will be treated as a taxable distribution.

Answer (D) is correct. *(Publisher, adapted)*
REQUIRED: The correct statement about the taxable amount of a generation-skipping transfer.
DISCUSSION: Under Sec. 2603, the transferee is liable for the GSTT on a taxable distribution. Therefore, if the GSTT on a taxable distribution is paid by the trust, the transferee is deemed to have received an additional taxable distribution equal to the amount of taxes paid by the trust [Sec. 2621(b)].
Answer (A) is incorrect. The taxable amount of a direct skip is the amount received by the transferee before taxes (Sec. 2623) but the taxable amount of a taxable termination (Sec. 2622) is the value of all property with respect to which the termination occurred reduced by deductions similar to those deductible against a gross estate under Sec. 2053 (taxes, debt, certain expenses). Answer (B) is incorrect. It describes the taxable amount of a taxable distribution (Sec. 2621) but not a taxable termination. Answer (C) is incorrect. The taxable amount of a taxable distribution is the value of property received by the transferee less any expense incurred by the transferee in connection with the determination, collection, or refund of the GSTT.

21.13.2. When Sam died, his property was placed in trust with his son David, and David's daughter Carole was eligible to receive principal and income at the trustee's discretion. When the property was placed in trust, its value was $5 million and the GSTT exemption was not allocated to this trust. Carole received a distribution of $8 million when the trust's value totaled $10 million. The appraisal to value trust assets cost $40,000 and was paid by the trust. What is the taxable amount of the generation-skipping transfer and who is responsible for the tax payment?

	Taxable Amount	Taxpayer
A.	$7,960,000	Trust
B.	$5,040,000	David
C.	$7,960,000	Carole
D.	$8,000,000	David

Answer (C) is correct. *(Publisher, adapted)*
REQUIRED: The taxable amount and identification of the taxpayer of a taxable distribution.
DISCUSSION: This is a taxable distribution because it is a distribution to a skip person (Carole) and a nonskip person (David) still has an interest in the trust. The amount of a taxable distribution is the value of property received by the transferee minus costs of determination, collection, and refund of the GSTT paid by the transferee (Sec. 2621). Since the trust paid the cost of appraisal, only $7,960,000 in assets remained to pass to Carole. The value of assets received by Carole is not further reduced since she incurred no additional costs associated with payment of the GSTT.
Carole is responsible for the tax payment as the transferee of a taxable distribution [Sec. 2603(a)(1)].
Answer (A) is incorrect. The trust is not responsible for the tax payment. Answer (B) is incorrect. Carole's distribution is reduced by the cost of the appraisal, and David is not responsible for the tax payment. Answer (D) is incorrect. Carole's total distribution is $8 million, and David is not responsible for the tax payment.

21.13.3. Tracy's will established a trust for his grandchildren solely to pay college tuition for the grandchildren. The distributions to pay the college tuition are generation-skipping transfers.

A. True.

B. False.

Answer (B) is correct. *(Publisher, adapted)*
DISCUSSION: A transfer that would not be a taxable gift if made inter vivos because of the exclusion for payment of medical expenses or tuition is not a generation-skipping transfer [Sec. 2611(b)(1)]. Tracy's payment of a grandchild's tuition would not be a taxable gift so the trust distribution to pay the tuition is not subject to the GSTT.

21.13.4. A generation-skipping transfer does not include a termination of a trust created by Sheila with income to her son and a remainder interest to her granddaughter if her son has power over the trust, which will cause the trust assets to be taxed in the son's estate.

A. True.

B. False.

Answer (A) is correct. *(Publisher, adapted)*
DISCUSSION: The transfer of property from the trust created by Sheila to her son and granddaughter is not a generation-skipping transfer. When trust property is subject to the gift tax or the estate tax, the donor or decedent that is taxed becomes the new transferor of the property for the GSTT [Sec. 2652(a)(1)]. Because Sheila's son must include the trust assets in his estate upon his death as a result of the power he holds over the trust, Sheila's son is considered the transferor for the income and remainder interests that are transferred. Any property transferred from the trust to the granddaughter is only transferred to the first generation below Sheila's son and is not a generation-skipping transfer.

21.14 Calculation of Generation-Skipping Transfer Tax

21.14.1. Several years ago, Jim's will established a trust for his son, Kevin, and grandsons. This year, a taxable termination occurred when Kevin died and trust assets were distributed to his grandsons, Mark and John. Jim's executor allocated $1,000,000 of his exemption to the trust, which had a value of $8,320,000 at that time. When the taxable termination occurred, trust assets had a value of $10,320,000. State death taxes attributable to trust property were $320,000. What is the inclusion ratio used to calculate the GSTT?

A. 1/10

B. 1/8

C. 7/8

D. 9/10

Answer (C) is correct. *(Publisher, adapted)*
REQUIRED: The inclusion ratio for a generation-skipping transfer with an exemption and death taxes.
DISCUSSION: The inclusion ratio multiplied by the maximum federal estate tax rate determines the tax rate for a generation-skipping transfer. The inclusion ratio is 1 minus a fraction whose numerator is the GSTT exemption allocated to the trust and whose denominator is generally the value of the property transferred into the trust reduced by the sum of (1) federal estate taxes or state death taxes attributable to the property and paid by the trust and (2) charitable deductions with respect to the trust property [Sec. 2642(a)]. Effective for transfers after December 31, 1998, the generation-skipping transfer tax exemption will be indexed for inflation. The inclusion ratio in this case is

$$1 - \frac{\$1,000,000}{\$8,320,000 - \$320,000} = 7/8$$

Answer (A) is incorrect. One-tenth was determined by using the trust assets' value this year and not subtracting it from 1. Answer (B) is incorrect. One-eighth should be subtracted from 1 when determining the inclusion ratio. Answer (D) is incorrect. The trust assets were incorrectly valued at $10,320,000 for the inclusion ratio.

21.14.2. For 2017, which of the following statements about the generation-skipping transfer exemption is false?

A. An individual (or his or her executor) can allocate a $5.49 million exemption to property with respect to which (s)he is the transferor.

B. All appreciation that occurs to trust property covered by the allocation of the $5.49 million exemption is also covered by the exemption up to a limit of $10.98 million.

C. If a married couple elects gift-splitting for a transfer, the transferred property may be allocated a GSTT exemption of up to $10.98 million.

D. The GSTT exemption may be allocated to an inter vivos transfer on a timely filed gift tax return or later statement of allocation filed with the IRS.

Answer (B) is correct. *(Publisher, adapted)*
REQUIRED: The false statement about the generation-skipping transfer exemption for 2017.
DISCUSSION: If all or part of the $5.49 million exemption is allocated to trust property, all appreciation that occurs after the allocation to the property covered by the exemption is also exempt from the GSTT. There is no $10.98 million limit.
Answer (A) is incorrect. An individual (or his or her executor) can allocate a $5.49 million exemption to property with respect to which (s)he is the transferor. Answer (C) is incorrect. If a married couple elects gift-splitting for a transfer, the transferred property may be allocated a GSTT exemption of up to $10.98 million. Answer (D) is incorrect. The GSTT exemption may be allocated to an inter vivos transfer on a timely filed gift tax return or later statement of allocation filed with the IRS.

21.14.3. Several years ago, Jim's will established a trust for his son, Kevin, and grandsons. This year, a taxable termination occurred when Kevin died and trust assets were distributed to grandsons, Mark and John. Jim's executor allocated $1,000,000 of his exemption to the trust, which had a value of $4,320,000 at that time. When the taxable termination occurred in Year 2, trust assets had a value of $8,320,000. State death taxes attributable to trust property were $320,000. What is the generation-skipping transfer tax due on the taxable termination?

A. $1,200,000

B. $1,296,000

C. $2,400,000

D. $2,496,000

Answer (D) is correct. *(Publisher, adapted)*
REQUIRED: The calculation of the generation-skipping transfer tax on a taxable termination.
DISCUSSION: The generation-skipping transfer tax is the product of the taxable amount times the applicable rate (Sec. 2602). The applicable rate is the maximum federal estate tax rate for the date of the taxable termination, taxable distribution, or direct skip (40%) times the inclusion ratio of 3/4 {1 − [$1,000,000 ÷ ($4,320,000 − $320,000)]} (Sec. 2641). The taxable amount of a taxable termination is the value of all property with respect to which the taxable termination has occurred ($8,320,000) reduced by expenses, deductions, and taxes that would be allowable under Sec. 2053 if this were an estate. State death taxes are not allowable deductions under Sec. 2053(c)(1)(B), so the taxable amount is $8,320,000. The generation-skipping transfer tax is $2,496,000 ($8,320,000 × 40% × 3/4), and the tax will be paid by the trustee from trust assets.
Answer (A) is incorrect. It uses the initial value of the trust reduced by the state death taxes as the tax base. Answer (B) is incorrect. It uses the initial value of the trust ($4,320,000) as the tax base. Answer (C) is incorrect. It deducts the state death taxes from the value of the trust property as the tax base.

STUDY UNIT TWENTY-TWO
PREPARER RULES

22.1 Coverage of Tax Return Preparer Rules

22.1.1. Preparers of which of the following returns are not covered by the preparer rules?

A. Individual income tax.

B. Corporate income tax.

C. Fiduciary income tax.

D. Information returns.

Answer (D) is correct. *(SEE, adapted)*

REQUIRED: The type of return for which preparers are not covered by the tax return preparer rules.

DISCUSSION: Section 7701(a)(36) defines a tax return preparer as any person who prepares or employs persons to prepare for compensation any return of tax or claim for refund under the IRC (Title 26).

Answer (A) is incorrect. Individual income tax is a tax covered by the Internal Revenue Code, and preparers of returns for this tax are subject to the preparer rules. Answer (B) is incorrect. Corporate income tax is a tax covered by the Internal Revenue Code, and preparers of returns for this tax are subject to the preparer rules. Answer (C) is incorrect. Fiduciary income tax is a tax covered by the Internal Revenue Code, and preparers of returns for this tax are subject to the preparer rules.

22.1.2. Which one of the following types of returns is not covered by the preparer rules?

A. Information returns.

B. Partnership returns.

C. C corporation returns.

D. S corporation returns.

Answer (A) is correct. *(SEE, adapted)*

REQUIRED: The type of return that is not covered by preparer rules.

DISCUSSION: Section 7701(a)(36) defines a tax return preparer as any person who prepares or employs persons to prepare for compensation any tax return or claim for refund under the IRC (Title 26).

Answer (B) is incorrect. Partnership returns are for a tax imposed by the IRC, and preparers are covered by the preparer rules. Answer (C) is incorrect. C corporation returns are for a tax imposed by the IRC, and preparers are covered by the preparer rules. Answer (D) is incorrect. S corporation returns are for a tax imposed by the IRC, and preparers are covered by the preparer rules.

22.1.3. Preparers of information returns such as Form 1099-DIV are not covered by the preparer rules.

A. True.

B. False.

Answer (A) is correct. *(SEE, adapted)*

DISCUSSION: Return preparers are those who prepare or employ others to prepare for compensation returns for tax imposed by the IRC (Title 26) [Sec. 7701(a)(36)]. Since information returns are required by Subtitle F, they are not covered by the preparer rules.

22.2 Identification of Tax Return Preparers

22.2.1. Which of the following is a tax return preparer according to the tax return preparer rules?

A. Mr. A engages a number of persons to prepare income tax returns on a commission basis but does not himself prepare returns.

B. Mr. B, controller of Corporation X, prepares and files X's corporate tax return.

C. Mr. C owns and operates a payroll service. Services provided to clients include the preparation of all employment tax returns.

D. Mr. D, an attorney, regularly advises clients in arranging future business transactions to minimize income tax.

Answer (A) is correct. *(SEE, adapted)*
REQUIRED: The tax return preparer as defined in the regulations.
DISCUSSION: Under Sec. 7701(a)(36), a tax return preparer is any person who prepares for compensation or employs others to prepare for compensation any tax return or claim for refund under the IRC (Title 26).
Answer (B) is incorrect. Section 7701(a)(36)(B)(ii) provides that a person who prepares a return for the employer by whom (s)he is regularly and continuously employed is not considered a tax return preparer. Answer (C) is incorrect. Employment tax returns are not considered income tax returns. Answer (D) is incorrect. Advising clients on specific issues of law with respect to the consequences of contemplated actions (rather than events that have already occurred) does not constitute tax return preparation.

22.2.2. Which of the following is a tax return preparer?

A. A neighbor who assists with preparation of depreciation schedule.

B. A son who enters income tax return information into a computer program and prints the return.

C. A woman who prepares income tax returns in her home during filing season and accepts payment for her services.

D. A volunteer at a local church who prepares income tax returns but accepts no payment.

Answer (C) is correct. *(SEE, adapted)*
REQUIRED: The person who is a tax return preparer.
DISCUSSION: Under Sec. 7701(a)(36), a tax return preparer is any person who prepares for compensation, or who employs others to prepare for compensation, any tax return or claim for refund under the IRC (Title 26).
Answer (A) is incorrect. A neighbor who assists with the preparation of a depreciation schedule is not a preparer. Answer (B) is incorrect. A person who merely furnishes typing, reproducing, or mechanical assistance is not a preparer. Answer (D) is incorrect. If no compensation is provided for a person to prepare a return or claim for refund, the person is not subject to the return preparer rules.

22.2.3. The duties in the preparation of XYZ Corporation's income tax return were assigned and completed as follows:

Joe
- The employee who obtained the information, applied the tax law to the information, and performed the necessary calculations.

Sue
- Joe's supervisor, who reviews Joe's work. In her review, Sue reviews the information provided and the application of the tax laws.

Company A
- A computer tax service that takes the information provided by Sue, verifies the mathematical accuracy, and prints the return form.

Pat
- A partner in the public accounting firm where Joe and Sue work. Pat reviews the return and the information provided and applies this information to XYZ's affairs. Pat also verifies that the partnership's policies have been followed and makes the final determination.

Who is the preparer of XYZ's return and is therefore required to sign it?

A. Joe.

B. Sue.

C. Company A.

D. Pat.

Answer (D) is correct. *(SEE, adapted)*
REQUIRED: The preparer of the tax return.
DISCUSSION: Regulation 301.7701-15(a) defines a tax return preparer as any person who prepares for compensation, or who employs one or more persons to prepare for compensation, any tax return or claim for refund of tax under the IRC (Title 26). Regulation 1.6694-1(b)(2) states that, if more than one income tax return preparer is involved in the preparation of a return or a claim for refund, the individual preparer who has the primary responsibility as between or among the preparers for the overall substantive accuracy of the preparation of the return or claim is considered to be the income tax return preparer for purposes of determining who is required to sign the return. Because Pat makes the final determination regarding the return, she is considered to be the preparer and must sign the return.
Answer (A) is incorrect. Joe does not have primary responsibility for the overall substantive accuracy of the return. Answer (B) is incorrect. Sue does not have primary responsibility for the overall substantive accuracy of the return. Answer (C) is incorrect. A person or company that merely furnishes typing, reproducing, or other mechanical assistance is not a tax return preparer [Sec. 7701(a)(36)(B)(i)].

22.2.4. All of the following are tax return preparers except

A. A person who prepares a substantial portion of the return for a fee.

B. A person who prepares a claim for a refund for a fee.

C. A person who gives an opinion about theoretical events that haven't occurred.

D. A person who prepares a United States return for a fee outside the United States.

Answer (C) is correct. *(SEE, adapted)*
    REQUIRED: The person who is not a tax return preparer.
    DISCUSSION: Under Sec. 7701(a)(36), a tax return preparer is any person who prepares for compensation or employs others to prepare for compensation any tax return or claim for refund under the IRC (Title 26). A person who gives an opinion about events that have not happened is not a tax return preparer.
    Answer (A) is incorrect. A person who prepares a substantial portion of the return for a fee is a tax return preparer under the regulations. Answer (B) is incorrect. A person who prepares a claim for a refund for a fee is a tax return preparer under the regulations. Answer (D) is incorrect. A person who prepares a United States return for a fee outside the United States is a tax return preparer under the regulations.

22.2.5. Joe is the trustee of a trust set up for his father. Under the Internal Revenue Code, when Joe prepares the annual trust tax return, Form 1041, he

A. Must obtain the written permission of the beneficiary prior to signing as a tax return preparer.

B. Is not considered a tax return preparer.

C. May not sign the return unless he receives additional compensation for the tax return.

D. Is considered a tax return preparer because his father is the grantor of the trust.

Answer (B) is correct. *(CPA, adapted)*
    REQUIRED: The correct statement about Joe regarding his preparation of the annual trust tax return.
    DISCUSSION: Joe is not considered a tax return preparer since he is a fiduciary who prepares the return for the trust.
    Answer (A) is incorrect. Since Joe is the trustee, he is not required to obtain the written permission of the beneficiary prior to signing as a tax return preparer. Answer (C) is incorrect. Compensation is not required for Joe to prepare the tax return. Answer (D) is incorrect. Joe is not considered a tax return preparer, as he is a fiduciary who prepares the return for the trust. The fact that his father is the grantor of the trust is irrelevant.

22.2.6. All compensated tax return preparers are required to have a PTIN for any such work performed on or after January 1, 2011.

A. True.

B. False.

Answer (A) is correct. *(Publisher, adapted)*
    DISCUSSION: Any individual who, for compensation, prepares, or assists in the preparation of, all or substantially all of a tax return or claim for refund after December 31, 2010, must have a PTIN. Failure to do so could result in the imposition of IRC Sec. 6695 penalties, injunction, referral for criminal investigation, or disciplinary action by the IRS Office of Professional Responsibility.

22.2.7. A reporting agent prepares Form 94X series returns for clients for compensation. The preparer occasionally assists clients with issues such as determining whether workers are employees or independent contractors for federal tax purposes. This preparer does not need a PTIN.

A. True.

B. False.

Answer (B) is correct. *(Publisher, adapted)*
    DISCUSSION: The PTIN regulations require all tax return preparers who are compensated for preparing, or assisting in the preparation of, all or substantially all of a tax return or claim for refund of tax to register and obtain a PTIN. The exemptions to this rule do not apply to reporting agents who render tax advice to any client.

22.2.8. Completion of a single schedule of a tax return will be considered a "substantial portion" if that schedule is the dominant portion of the entire tax return.

A. True.

B. False.

Answer (A) is correct. *(SEE, adapted)*
    DISCUSSION: Under Reg. 301.7701-15(b)(1), whether a schedule of a return is a substantial portion is determined by comparing the length and complexity of that portion to the return as a whole. A schedule that is the dominant portion of an entire tax return will usually be considered a substantial portion of the tax return.

22.2.9. Mr. C, a certified public accountant, prepared a claim for refund that resulted from an examination by the Internal Revenue Service. Mr. C is considered a tax return preparer.

A. True.

B. False.

Answer (B) is correct. *(SEE, adapted)*
    DISCUSSION: Under Sec. 7701(a)(36)(B)(iv), a person is not considered a tax return preparer merely because the preparation of a claim for refund is in response to a notice of deficiency issued by the IRS.

22.2.10. A person who prepares only a portion of a return will not be considered a preparer if that portion involves gross income, deductions, or the basis for determining tax credits of

1.   Under $10,000 or
2.   Under $400,000 and less than 20% of gross income (or 20% of adjusted gross income on an individual return) of the return as a whole.

A.   True.

B.   False.

Answer (A) is correct. *(SEE, adapted)*
  DISCUSSION: Regulation 301.7701-15(b)(3) provides that a schedule or portion of a return is not considered a substantial portion if it involves gross income, deductions, or amounts on the basis of which credits are determined that are (1) less than $10,000 or (2) less than $400,000 and also less than 20% of the gross income (or adjusted gross income if an individual) as shown on the return.

22.2.11. The preparer of a Form 1065, *U.S. Return of Partnership Income*, can be considered the preparer of a partner's individual income tax return if the entries on the partnership return that are reportable on the partner's return constitute a substantial portion of the partner's return.

A.   True.

B.   False.

Answer (A) is correct. *(SEE, adapted)*
  DISCUSSION: Under Reg. 301.7701-15(b)(3), a preparer of one return is not considered a preparer of another return just because entries may affect the other return, unless the entries (e.g., on a partnership return) are directly reflected on the other return (e.g., a partner's return) and constitute a substantial portion of the other return.

22.2.12. Mr. P, employed in the accounting department of Partnership T, prepares the partnership's income tax return. Mr. P is not considered a return preparer.

A.   True.

B.   False.

Answer (A) is correct. *(SEE, adapted)*
  DISCUSSION: Under Sec. 7701(a)(36)(B)(ii), a person who prepares a return or claim for refund of the employer by whom (s)he is regularly and continuously employed is not considered a tax return preparer. Since Mr. P is an employee of the partnership, he is not considered a return preparer.

22.2.13. Anyone who prepares a return or claim for a refund as a fiduciary is not covered by the preparer rules.

A.   True.

B.   False.

Answer (A) is correct. *(SEE, adapted)*
  DISCUSSION: Section 7701(a)(36)(B)(iii) provides that a person is not considered a tax return preparer merely because (s)he prepares a return or claim for refund as a fiduciary.

22.2.14. B is a college student working his way through school. During the tax season, he is paid to prepare his friends' tax returns. B was paid $250. B is not a tax preparer.

A.   True.

B.   False.

Answer (B) is correct. *(SEE, adapted)*
  DISCUSSION: Section 7701(a)(36) defines a tax return preparer as any person who prepares for compensation any return of tax or any claim for refund of tax imposed by the IRC (Title 26).

22.3 Activities of Tax Return Preparers

22.3.1. Under which of the following circumstances may a CPA charge fees that are contingent upon finding a specific result?

    A. For an examination of prospective financial statements.

    B. For an audit or a review if agreed upon by both the CPA and the client.

    C. For a compilation if a third party will use the financial statement and disclosure is not made in the report.

    D. If fixed by courts, other public authorities, or in tax matters if based on the results of judicial proceedings.

Answer (D) is correct. *(CPA, adapted)*
  REQUIRED: The circumstance in which a contingent fee arrangement is allowable.
  DISCUSSION: A contingent fee is established as part of an agreement under which the amount of the fee is dependent upon the finding or result. Fees are not deemed to be contingent if fixed by courts or other public authorities, or in tax matters, if they are based on the results of judicial proceedings or the finding of governmental agencies.
  Answer (A) is incorrect. The receipt of contingent fees by a member in public practice is specifically prohibited when the member performs an examination of prospective financial information. Answer (B) is incorrect. The receipt of contingent fees by a member in public practice is specifically prohibited when the member performs an audit or a review, whether or not the CPA and client agree upon it. Answer (C) is incorrect. The receipt of contingent fees by a member in public practice is specifically prohibited when the member performs a compilation that will be used by third parties and the report does not disclose the CPA's lack of independence.

22.3.2. Under the *Statements on Standards for Tax Services*, what is a CPA's responsibility for verifying information furnished by the taxpayer or third parties?

    A. A CPA need not make additional inquiries if the information furnished appears to be incorrect, incomplete, or inconsistent with other facts known to the CPA.

    B. A CPA need not consider implications of information furnished if the information comes directly from a third party.

    C. A CPA may rely in good faith on information furnished by the taxpayer or by third parties without verification.

    D. A CPA should not refer to the taxpayer's previous tax returns unless the returns report transactions that affect the current tax period.

Answer (C) is correct. *(CPA, adapted)*
  REQUIRED: The CPA's responsibility for client-provided information.
  DISCUSSION: A CPA may rely in good faith on information furnished by the taxpayer or by third parties without verification.
  Answer (A) is incorrect. Reasonable inquiries should be made if information appears to be incorrect, incomplete, or inconsistent on its face or on the basis of other known facts. Answer (B) is incorrect. A CPA should consider implications of information furnished by the taxpayer and third parties. Answer (D) is incorrect. A CPA may refer to the taxpayer's previous returns for verification of information that appears to be incorrect, incomplete, or inconsistent.

22.3.3. If, in good faith, a preparer reasonably takes the position that a revenue ruling does not accurately reflect the Internal Revenue Code, the preparation of a return by the preparer in conflict with the revenue ruling does not result in an understatement that is due to the taking of an unreasonable position.

    A. True.

    B. False.

Answer (A) is correct. *(SEE, adapted)*
  DISCUSSION: Under Sec. 6694(a), a preparer who takes a position contrary to a rule or regulation is not guilty of taking an unreasonable position if there was a realistic possibility of the position being sustained on its merits.

22.3.4. A tax return preparer may use the tax return information of a client to solicit from the client any additional current business, in matters not related to the IRS, which the preparer provides and offers to the public, provided the preparer has the client's written consent.

    A. True.

    B. False.

Answer (A) is correct. *(SEE, adapted)*
  DISCUSSION: A tax return preparer, with the consent of a taxpayer, may use the taxpayer's return information to solicit from him any additional current business, in matters not related to the IRS, which the preparer provides and offers to the public.

22.3.5. When preparing a return involving a deduction for travel and entertainment expenses, the return preparer must make reasonable inquiries to determine that the taxpayer's records are adequate to substantiate the deduction.

A. True.

B. False.

Answer (A) is correct. *(SEE, adapted)*
DISCUSSION: Regulation 1.6694-1(e)(1) provides that a return preparer should make appropriate inquiries of the taxpayer to determine the existence of facts and circumstances required by a Code section or regulations incidental to claiming a deduction. This applies to adequate documentation for travel and entertainment expenses and other deductions, even if the amount is minimal.

22.3.6. Generally, in preparing a return, the preparer may in good faith rely without verification upon information furnished by the taxpayer and need not make reasonable inquiries if the information as furnished appears to be incorrect or incomplete.

A. True.

B. False.

Answer (B) is correct. *(SEE, adapted)*
DISCUSSION: Regulation 1.6694-1(e)(1) requires a return preparer to make reasonable inquiries if the information as furnished appears incorrect or incomplete. The preparer may not ignore the implications of information furnished.

22.3.7. Mr. A, a partner in an accounting firm, discovers that one of his clients omitted a substantial amount of gross income. Mr. A should immediately notify his partners and the Internal Revenue Service.

A. True.

B. False.

Answer (B) is correct. *(SEE, adapted)*
DISCUSSION: Unless the understatement of gross income was done willfully or recklessly or was the result of a position that did not have a realistic possibility of being sustained on its merits, Mr. A will not be liable for a penalty (Sec. 6694). When a taxpayer's liability has been understated, there is no requirement that the tax return preparer notify the IRS.

22.4 Required Copies of Returns

22.4.1. Which of the following statements is true regarding records required to be maintained by return preparers?

A. Tax return preparers are required to maintain a complete copy of each return or claim for refund they have filed for 3 years after the return period.

B. Tax return preparers are required to maintain a list of the names, identification numbers, and tax years of taxpayers for whom returns are prepared and to keep this list for 3 years after the return period.

C. Preparers have a choice of maintaining a complete copy of each return or claim for refund they have filed for 3 years after the return period or a list of the names, identification numbers, and tax years of taxpayers for whom returns are prepared and to keep this list for 3 years after the return period.

D. Preparers are required to maintain a complete copy of each return or claim for refund they have filed for 3 years after the return period and a list of the names, identification numbers, and tax years of taxpayers for whom returns are prepared and to keep this list for 3 years after the return period.

Answer (C) is correct. *(SEE, adapted)*
REQUIRED: The true statement regarding the records that are required to be maintained by return preparers.
DISCUSSION: A return preparer is required to retain a completed copy of each return or claim prepared for 3 years after the close of the return period [Sec. 6107(b)], or a list may be kept that includes, for the returns and claims prepared, the following information: (1) the taxpayers' names, (2) taxpayer identification numbers, (3) their tax years, and (4) the types of returns or claims prepared. Additionally, this list must be kept for 3 years after the return period.
Answer (A) is incorrect. Tax return preparers are not required to maintain a complete copy of each return or claim for refund they have filed for 3 years after the return period. Answer (B) is incorrect. Tax return preparers are not required to maintain a list of the names, identification numbers, and tax years of taxpayers for whom returns are prepared and to keep this list for 3 years after the return period. Answer (D) is incorrect. The preparers are not required to maintain a complete copy of each return or claim for refund they have filed for 3 years after the return period and a list of the names, identification numbers, and tax years of taxpayers for whom returns are prepared and to keep this list for 3 years after the return period.

22.4.2. A tax return preparer does not meet the requirement of retaining a completed copy of returns and claims by using an electronic storage system.

A. True.

B. False.

Answer (B) is correct. *(Publisher, adapted)*
DISCUSSION: The preparer may either retain a paper or electronic copy of the completed return or refund claim to store and produce a copy of the return.

22.4.3. The preparer must furnish the taxpayer with a completed copy of the prepared return no later than the time the original return is presented for signing. The preparer must sign both the original and the copy.

    A. True.

    B. False.

Answer (B) is correct. *(SEE, adapted)*
    DISCUSSION: A return preparer is required to furnish a completed copy of the return or refund claim to the taxpayer no later than the time it is presented for the taxpayer's signature [Sec. 6107(a)]. The signature requirement may be satisfied by a photocopy of the signed copy of the return or claim. The preparer must retain the signed copy. The signature requirement can be met by a computer software program, rubber stamp, or mechanical device. Failure to provide a copy of the return is subject to a $50 penalty.

22.4.4. A tax return preparer who fails to furnish a copy of the return or claim for refund to the taxpayer shall be subject to a $50 penalty for the failure unless it is shown that the failure is due to reasonable cause and not due to willful neglect.

    A. True.

    B. False.

Answer (A) is correct. *(SEE, adapted)*
    DISCUSSION: Section 6695(a) provides that a tax return preparer with respect to any return or claim for refund who fails to furnish a copy of the return or claim for refund to the taxpayer when the return is presented for the taxpayer's signature must pay a penalty of $50, unless the failure is due to reasonable cause and not willful neglect.

22.4.5. Mr. B, a tax return preparer, prepared at different times during the tax season both Mr. X's individual and S corporation income tax returns. B was compensated for the preparation of both returns. Mr. B is only required to furnish a copy of his client's original income tax return at the time the second return is presented for signature.

    A. True.

    B. False.

Answer (B) is correct. *(SEE, adapted)*
    DISCUSSION: Section 6695(a) provides that a tax return preparer with respect to any return or claim for refund who fails to furnish a copy of the return to the taxpayer when the return is presented for the taxpayer's signature must pay a penalty of $50, unless the failure is due to reasonable cause and not willful neglect. Neither Sec. 6695 nor its regulations recognize as reasonable cause deferring furnishing a copy of one return until another return is presented for signature of the same individual.

22.4.6. A tax return preparer can satisfy the regulation requiring the preparer to retain a copy or record of each return prepared by retaining a photocopy of only the completed first page of each return prepared.

    A. True.

    B. False.

Answer (A) is correct. *(SEE, adapted)*
    DISCUSSION: The tax return preparer is required to keep either a copy of the return or some record that includes the name, taxpayer identification number, taxable year, and type of return or claim for refund filed [Reg. Sec. 1.6107-1(b)(1)]. The first page of the return includes the required information.

22.5 Signature, Identification, and Reporting Requirements

22.5.1. Which of the following is not true regarding the filing of information returns concerning employees who prepare tax returns?

    A. Annual listings of preparers, identification numbers, and place of work are required for preparers who employ others to prepare returns.

    B. The period for which the information return is required is a 12-month period beginning July 1 of each year.

    C. No information return is actually required to be submitted; a list is made and kept by the employing preparer.

    D. Information returns of income tax return preparers must be maintained by the preparer for 2 years.

Answer (D) is correct. *(SEE, adapted)*
    REQUIRED: The false statement regarding the filing of information returns concerning employees who prepare tax returns.
    DISCUSSION: Under Sec. 6060(a), a person who employs one or more income tax return preparers to prepare a return or claim for refund must file a return setting forth the name, identifying number, and place of work of each income tax return preparer employed by him or her. Section 6060(b) allows the IRS to approve an alternative method of reporting. Regulation 1.6060-1 states that the requirements of Sec. 6060 are satisfied by retaining a record of the name, identifying number, and principal place of work of each income tax return preparer employed, and making that record available for inspection upon request by the district director for the 3-year period following the close of the return period to which that record relates. The return period means the 12-month period beginning July 1 of each year [Reg. 1.6060-1(b)].
    Answer (A) is incorrect. Annual listings of preparers, identification numbers, and places of work are required for preparers who employ others to prepare returns. Answer (B) is incorrect. The period for which the information return is required is a 12-month period beginning July 1 of each year. Answer (C) is incorrect. No information return is actually required to be submitted; a list is made and kept by the employing preparer.

22.5.2. Mr. K employs X, Y, and Z to prepare income tax returns for taxpayers. X and Y collect the information from taxpayers and apply the tax laws. The return forms are completed by a computer service. One day, when certain returns prepared by X and Y were ready for their signatures, X was out of town for 2 weeks and Y was out of the office for the day. Which one of the following statements is correct?

A. Z may sign the returns prepared by X and Y, if Z reviews the information obtained by X and Y from the taxpayers and reviews the preparation of the returns.

B. Z may sign the returns prepared by X, if Z reviews the information obtained by X from the taxpayers and reviews the preparation of the returns.

C. Z may sign the returns prepared by Y if he reviews the information obtained by Y from the taxpayers and reviews the preparation of the returns.

D. X and Y must sign the returns that each one prepared.

Answer (B) is correct. *(SEE, adapted)*
REQUIRED: The correct statement about who may sign an income tax return.
DISCUSSION: Regulation 1.6695-1(b)(1) requires an individual who is a tax return preparer to sign the return after it has been completed and before it is presented to the taxpayer. If the preparer is unavailable for signature, another preparer must review the entire preparation of the return and then must sign the return. Z may sign the returns prepared by X, provided that Z reviews the information obtained by X relative to the taxpayer and Z reviews the preparation of each return prepared by X. Z may not sign the returns prepared by Y because Y is considered to be available.
Answer (A) is incorrect. Z may sign the return if he reviews the information obtained by X and the preparation of the returns. Z may not sign the returns prepared by Y because Y is considered to be available. Answer (C) is incorrect. Z may not sign the returns prepared by Y because Y is considered to be available. Answer (D) is incorrect. X and Y should not sign the returns that each one prepared.

22.5.3. Preparers are required to sign all the returns they prepare and include their identification numbers.

A. True.

B. False.

Answer (A) is correct. *(SEE, adapted)*
DISCUSSION: Regulation 1.6695-1(b) requires each individual tax preparer to sign each return or claim for refund after it is completed and before it is presented to the taxpayer for signature. Under Sec. 6109(a)(4), any return or claim for refund filed with the IRS prepared by a tax return preparer must include his or her identifying number.

22.5.4. A preparer is required to enter an identification number on the taxpayer's copy of the return.

A. True.

B. False.

Answer (B) is correct. *(SEE, adapted)*
DISCUSSION: A tax return preparer is not required to sign or affix an identification number to the taxpayer's copy of a federal income tax return (Rev. Rul. 78-317).

22.5.5. A signature stamp is sufficient to meet the return preparer signature requirement for an original return.

A. True.

B. False.

Answer (A) is correct. *(SEE, adapted)*
DISCUSSION: Regulation 1.6695-1(b)(1) requires an individual who is a tax return preparer to manually sign the return after it has been completed and before it is presented to the taxpayer. However, since 2004, three alternative methods, (1) computer software program, (2) rubber stamp, and (3) mechanical devices, have all been approved for original returns, amended returns, and extension requests.

22.5.6. Mr. V is a partner in DAV Tax Service and is responsible for the overall substantive accuracy of all income tax returns prepared by subordinates. Mr. V neither gathers the necessary information nor prepares the income tax forms. Mr. V is considered to be the preparer and should sign the returns as the preparer.

A. True.

B. False.

Answer (A) is correct. *(SEE, adapted)*
DISCUSSION: Regulation 1.6695-1(b)(2) states that, if more than one income tax return preparer is involved in the preparation of a return or claim for refund, the preparer who has primary responsibility for the overall accuracy of the preparation of such return or claim is required to manually sign the return.

22.5.7. A preparer who is employed by others or is a partner in a partnership must enter his or her identification number and the identification number of the employer or partnership.

A. True.

B. False.

Answer (A) is correct. *(SEE, adapted)*
DISCUSSION: Under Reg. 1.6109-2(a), a tax return preparer must include his or her identifying number. If there is a partnership or employment arrangement between two or more preparers, the identifying number of the partnership or employer must also be included.

22.6 Penalties on Tax Return Preparers

22.6.1. John is a tax return preparer. He prepares a tax return for a client and takes a position that he knows does not have a reasonable basis. He does not disclose this position on the tax return. The position John takes causes the client's tax liability to be substantially understated. John earns $150 for preparing the return. John is subject to a penalty of

A. $50

B. $100

C. $1,000

D. $5,000

Answer (C) is correct. *(Publisher, adapted)*
REQUIRED: The penalty for understatements due to unreasonable positions.
DISCUSSION: Section 6694(a) provides for a penalty of the greater of $1,000 or 50% of the income derived to be assessed against a tax return preparer who takes an unreasonable position with regard to a tax matter that produces an understatement of tax liability. The penalty is applicable if the return preparer knew, or reasonably should have known, that there was not a reasonable basis and the position was not disclosed as provided in Sec. 6662(d)(2)(B)(ii) or was frivolous. Section 6662(d)(2)(B)(ii) requires that the relevant facts affecting the item's tax treatment be adequately disclosed in the return or in a statement attached to the return, and that there be a reasonable basis for the position. The preparer may be relieved of the penalty if it can be shown that there is reasonable cause for the understatement and that the preparer acted in good faith. A position is reasonably based if based on one or more authorities set forth in Reg. 1.6662-4(d)(3)(iii).
Answer (A) is incorrect. The penalty for failure to retain a completed copy of the return, failure to sign a return as a preparer, or failure to furnish the needed identification number is $50. Answer (B) is incorrect. The penalty for not signing the prepared tax return and not providing his identifying number is $100. Answer (D) is incorrect. The penalty assessed against a return preparer whose willful or reckless conduct in preparing a return causes an understatement is the greater of $5,000 or 75% of the income derived.

22.6.2. Which of the following situations describes a disclosure of tax information by an income tax preparer that would subject the preparer to a penalty?

A. Ron died after furnishing tax return information to his tax return preparer. Ron's tax return preparer disclosed the information to Jerry, Ron's nephew, who is not the fiduciary of Ron's estate.

B. In the course of preparing a return for Duck Company, Jan obtained information indicating the existence of illegal kickbacks. Jan gave the information to Bill, an auditor in her firm, who was performing a financial audit of the company. Bill confirmed illegal kickbacks were occurring and brought the information to the attention of Duck Company officers.

C. Glade informed the proper federal officials of actions he mistakenly believed to be illegal.

D. Les, a return preparer, obtained information from Tom while selling Tom life insurance. The information was identical to tax return information that had been furnished to him previously. Les discussed this information with Mary, his wife, who was not an employee of any of his businesses.

Answer (A) is correct. *(SEE, adapted)*
REQUIRED: The situation in which a tax return preparer is subject to penalty for disclosure of tax information.
DISCUSSION: Section 6713 imposes a $250 penalty on an income tax return preparer who discloses information furnished in connection with preparation of any return, or uses the information for any purpose other than to prepare or assist in preparation of the return. Answer (A) is such a disclosure described in Sec. 6713 to which no exception applies. Section 7216 imposes criminal penalties for knowingly or recklessly making such disclosure.
Answer (B) is incorrect. A tax return preparer may disclose tax return information to another employee or member of the preparer's law or accounting firm who may use it to render other legal or accounting services to the taxpayer [Reg. 301.7216-2(e)(1)]. Answer (C) is incorrect. Disclosure made in a bona fide but mistaken belief that the activities constituted a violation of criminal law does not subject the preparer to liability under Secs. 6713 or 7216 [Reg. 301.7216-2(n)]. Answer (D) is incorrect. The information disclosed was obtained in a capacity other than as a return preparer [Reg. 301.7216-2(j)].

22.6.3. Which of the following situations describes a disclosure of tax return information by a tax return preparer that would subject the preparer to a penalty?

A. A tax return preparer discloses a grandfather's tax information to a granddaughter to inform her she will be claimed as a dependent on the grandfather's return.

B. An employee of the tax return preparer makes corporate return information available to shareholders.

C. After a client files for bankruptcy, the tax return preparer provides a copy of the last return filed to the court-appointed trustee, without written permission.

D. None of the answers are correct.

Answer (D) is correct. *(SEE, adapted)*
REQUIRED: The situation in which a tax return preparer is subject to penalty for disclosure of tax information.
DISCUSSION: Disclosing tax information to a granddaughter is permissible provided there has not been a specific prohibition by the grandfather. This rule also applies as to corporation and shareholder and between a bankruptee and a trustee.
Answer (A) is incorrect. A tax return preparer disclosing a grandfather's tax information to a granddaughter to inform her she will be claimed as a dependent on the grandfather's return would not subject the preparer to a penalty. Answer (B) is incorrect. An employee of the tax return preparer making corporate return information available to shareholders would not subject the preparer to a penalty. Answer (C) is incorrect. After a client files for bankruptcy, the tax return preparer providing a copy of the last return filed to the court-appointed trustee, without written permission, would not subject the preparer to a penalty.

22.6.4. Ralph is a tax return preparer. He obtains an important new client by implying that the returns he prepares always generate refunds. While preparing the client's return, Ralph learns that the client owes a substantial amount of tax. In order to produce a refund for the client, Ralph intentionally disregards rules and regulations. Ralph earns $1,000 for preparing the return. Ralph is subject to a penalty of

A. $100

B. $500

C. $1,000

D. $5,000

Answer (D) is correct. *(Publisher, adapted)*
REQUIRED: The penalty for willful or reckless conduct by a return preparer.
DISCUSSION: Section 6694(b) provides for a penalty of the greater of $5,000 or 75% of the income derived to be assessed against a return preparer whose willful or reckless conduct in preparing a tax return causes an understatement of liability. The penalty is applied if the understatement is due to either a willful attempt to understate the tax liability or to any reckless or intentional disregard of rules or regulations by the return preparer. The penalty is assessed against each return containing an understatement of liability caused by the return preparer's willful or reckless conduct.
Answer (A) is incorrect. The penalty for not signing the prepared tax return and not providing his identifying number is $100. Answer (B) is incorrect. The correct penalty amount is not $500. Answer (C) is incorrect. The penalty for a preparer who takes an unreasonable position with regard to a return or refund claim that produces an understatement is the greater of $1,000 or 50% of the income derived.

22.6.5. Which of the following statements about a tax return preparer's willful understatement of a tax liability is false?

A. A tax return preparer is considered to have willfully attempted to understate liability if the preparer disregards information furnished by the taxpayer and it results in an understatement of the taxpayer's tax liability.

B. Willful understatement of a taxpayer's tax liability by a tax return preparer will always result in a $5,000 penalty being imposed.

C. A tax return preparer will not be considered to have willfully attempted to understate liability if he relies in good faith upon information provided by a taxpayer without obtaining verification.

D. The willful understatement penalty upon a tax return preparer is abated when no understatement of the taxpayer's liability has occurred.

Answer (B) is correct. *(Publisher, adapted)*
REQUIRED: The false statement relating to the willful understatement penalty.
DISCUSSION: The greater of $5,000 or 75% of the income derived willful understatement penalty is not imposed in all situations involving a willful attempt to understate a taxpayer's tax liability. For example, Sec. 6694(d) permits abatement of the return preparer's penalty when it is established in final administrative determination or final judicial decision that the taxpayer's liability was not understated on his return or refund claim even though willful understatement on the part of the tax return preparer may have occurred (e.g., a willful overstatement of deductions that results in an underpayment is more than offset by a failure to exclude income that results in a larger overpayment).
Answer (A) is incorrect. A preparer may be considered to have willfully attempted to understate the liability if (s)he disregards information furnished by the taxpayer or other persons and it results in an understatement of the taxpayer's tax liability [Reg. 1.6694-1(e)]. Answer (C) is incorrect. A tax return preparer can in good faith rely upon information furnished by the taxpayer without having to obtain third-party verification [Reg. 1.6694-1(e)]. The tax return preparer, however, may not ignore the implications of information furnished by the taxpayer. Answer (D) is incorrect. The willful understatement penalty is abated when an understatement of a tax liability has not occurred [Reg. 1.6694-1(d)].

22.6.6. A penalty may be assessed against a tax return preparer who takes an unreasonable position that causes an understatement of liability on a return. For purposes of assessing the penalty, "understatement of liability" means

    A. Any understatement of tax liability greater than $100.

    B. Any understatement of the tax liability or overstatement of the amount to be refunded or credited.

    C. Any understatement that exceeds 10% of the tax liability shown on the return.

    D. Any overstatement of the amount refundable that exceeds 10% of the amount refundable shown on the claim for refund.

Answer (B) is correct. *(Publisher, adapted)*
    REQUIRED: The correct meaning of "understatement of liability."
    DISCUSSION: Section 6694(e) defines "understatement of liability" for purposes of assessing penalties against return preparers as any understatement of the net amount of tax payable under the IRC (Title 26) or any overstatement of the net amount creditable or refundable under the IRC (Title 26). Under Sec. 6694(d), penalties will not be assessed against tax return preparers unless there has been an understatement of liability.
    Answer (A) is incorrect. For purposes of assessing a penalty, "understatement of liability" does not mean any understatement of tax liability greater than $100. Answer (C) is incorrect. For purposes of assessing the penalty, "understatement of liability" does not mean any understatement that exceeds 10% of the tax liability shown on the return. Answer (D) is incorrect. For purposes of assessing the penalty, "understatement of liability" does not mean any overstatement of the amount refundable that exceeds 10% of the amount refundable shown on the claim for refund.

22.6.7. With respect to a penalty proposed pursuant to Sec. 6694 of the Internal Revenue Code, which of the following statements is true?

    A. The IRS must send a letter to the tax return preparer at least 30 days before the statute of limitations expires.

    B. After the IRS sends the tax return preparer a letter, that preparer has 10 days to request further consideration.

    C. If the IRS assesses either the Sec. 6694(a) or Sec. 6694(b) penalty, within 30 days the preparer can either pay the entire amount and then file for refund, or pay at least 15% of the entire amount and then file a claim for the amount paid.

    D. The preparer cannot bring suit in district court to determine liability for the penalty if the claim for refund is denied.

Answer (C) is correct. *(SEE, adapted)*
    REQUIRED: The true statement concerning Sec. 6694.
    DISCUSSION: The claim, which is made on Form 6118, *Claim for Refund of Income Tax Return Preparer Penalties*, must be filed with the service center that issued the statement of notice and demand to the preparer. Only a minimum of 15% need be paid.
    Answer (A) is incorrect. With respect to a penalty proposed pursuant to Sec. 6694, the IRS does not have to send a letter to the tax return preparer at least 30 days before the statute of limitations expires. Answer (B) is incorrect. With respect to a penalty proposed pursuant to Sec. 6694, after the IRS sends the tax return preparer a letter, the preparer does not have 10 days to request further consideration. Answer (D) is incorrect. With respect to a penalty proposed pursuant to Sec. 6694, the preparer can bring suit in district court to determine liability for the penalty if the claim for refund is denied.

22.6.8. Robert, a tax return preparer, intentionally disregards regulations in preparing a return for a client. As a consequence, the tax liability shown on the return is understated. The client is subsequently audited by the Internal Revenue Service and the penalty for willful or reckless conduct is assessed against Robert. Robert's client appeals the IRS's audit determination. An appeals officer determines that the client did not take several allowable deductions. These deductions eliminate the understatement produced by Robert's intentional disregard of regulations. Which of the following statements concerning the penalty assessed against Robert is true?

    A. Robert is still liable for the penalty.

    B. The penalty will be reduced in proportion to the reduction in the tax liability.

    C. The penalty will be abated and any amount Robert may have paid will be refunded.

    D. Robert may pay 15% of the penalty and bring an action in the United States district court for determination of his liability for the penalty.

Answer (C) is correct. *(Publisher, adapted)*
    REQUIRED: The true statement concerning the penalty assessed against a tax return preparer.
    DISCUSSION: Section 6694(d) states that the penalty for understatements due to unreasonable positions or the penalty for willful or reckless conduct will be abated if a final administrative determination or a final judicial decision is made that there was no understatement of liability. If the return preparer has paid any part of the penalty, the payment will be refunded. "Understatement of liability" means any understatement of the net amount of tax payable under the IRC (Title 26).
    Answer (A) is incorrect. Robert may not necessarily be liable for the penalty. Answer (B) is incorrect. The penalty will not be reduced in proportion to the reduction in the tax liability. Answer (D) is incorrect. The assessed penalty will be abated. Any part of the penalty paid will be refunded.

22.6.9. If a penalty is proposed against a preparer that the preparer does not agree with, what actions are available to the preparer?

    A. Request a conference with the agent and present additional information and explanations showing that the penalty is not warranted.

    B. Wait for the penalty to be assessed and for a notice and demand statement to be issued, then pay the penalty within 30 days and file a claim for refund.

    C. Wait for the penalty to be assessed and for a notice and demand statement to be issued, then pay at least 15% of the penalty within 30 days and file a claim for refund.

    D. All of the answers are correct.

Answer (D) is correct. *(SEE, adapted)*
    REQUIRED: The actions available to a preparer when (s)he does not agree with a proposed penalty.
    DISCUSSION: The first recourse a preparer has is to request a conference with the agent and present additional information and explanations. A return preparer who pays 15% or more of an assessed return preparer penalty after receipt of notice and demand may file a claim for a refund within 30 days of the notice [Sec. 6694(c)].
    Answer (A) is incorrect. The preparer may also (1) wait for the penalty to be assessed and for a notice and demand statement to be issued, then pay the penalty within 30 days and file a claim for refund; and (2) wait for the penalty to be assessed and for a notice and demand statement to be issued, then pay at least 15% of the penalty within 30 days and file a claim for refund. Answer (B) is incorrect. The preparer may also (1) request a conference with the agent and present additional information and explanations showing that the penalty is not warranted; and (2) wait for the penalty to be assessed and for a notice and demand statement to be issued, then pay at least 15% of the penalty within 30 days and file a claim for refund. Answer (C) is incorrect. The preparer may also (1) request a conference with the agent and present additional information and explanations showing that the penalty is not warranted; and (2) wait for the penalty to be assessed and for a notice and demand statement to be issued, then pay the penalty within 30 days and file a claim for refund.

22.6.10. In which of the following circumstances would a tax return preparer be prohibited from disclosing a client's tax return information?

    A. The information will be needed for a peer review.

    B. The information will be provided in response to a court order.

    C. The information will be provided to a section 501(c)(3) charity.

    D. The information will be used to prepare state or local tax returns.

Answer (C) is correct. *(CPA, adapted)*
    REQUIRED: The circumstance in which disclosure of tax return information is prohibited.
    DISCUSSION: There is no exception to the penalty for disclosure if the disclosure was made to a 501(c)(3) charity without the taxpayer's consent.
    Answer (A) is incorrect. A tax return preparer may disclose tax return information for the purpose of a quality or peer review to the extent necessary to accomplish the review. Answer (B) is incorrect. A tax return preparer may disclose tax return information pursuant to a court order. Answer (D) is incorrect. A tax return preparer may disclose tax return information for the purpose of preparing state or local tax returns provided that the other tax return preparer is in the same accounting firm.

22.6.11. During an interview conducted by the preparer, a taxpayer stated that he had paid $6,500 in doctor bills and $5,000 in deductible travel and entertainment expenses during the tax year, when in fact he had paid smaller amounts. On the basis of this information, the preparer properly calculated the deductions for medical expenses and for travel and entertainment expenses, which resulted in an understatement of tax liability. The preparer had no reason to believe that the medical expenses and the travel and entertainment expense information was incorrect or incomplete. The preparer did not ask for underlying documentation of the medical expenses but inquired about the existence of travel and entertainment expense records. The preparer was reasonably satisfied by the taxpayer's representations that the taxpayer had adequate records (or other corroborative evidence) for the deduction of $5,000 for travel and entertainment expenses. The preparer is not subject to a penalty under Sec. 6694.

    A. True.

    B. False.

Answer (A) is correct. *(SEE, adapted)*
    DISCUSSION: For purposes of Sec. 6694(a) and (b), a preparer may generally rely in good faith without verification on information furnished by the taxpayer, although the preparer may not ignore the implications of information furnished to the preparer or actually known to the preparer. Furthermore, the preparer must make appropriate inquiries to determine the existence of facts required by a Code section or regulation as a condition to claiming a deduction. The facts presented in this question are essentially the same as those in Example 2 of Reg. 1.6694-1(e), which concludes that the preparer is not subject to a penalty under Sec. 6694. The round dollar amounts of the two expenditures might be an indication, however, that the taxpayer was estimating his or her expenses. This might have led the preparer to make additional inquiries.

22.6.12. Mr. X, a taxpayer, engaged in a transaction that is adversely affected by a new statutory provision (the transaction occurred before the new law was enacted). Prior law supported a position favorable to Mr. X. Mr. Y, the tax return preparer, is taking a position that the new statute is inequitable as applied to the taxpayer's situation. The language of the new statute is unambiguous as it applies to the transaction engaged in by Mr. X. Mr. Y, the return preparer, would be subject to the penalty for understatement due to an unreasonable position.

A. True.

B. False.

Answer (A) is correct. *(SEE, adapted)*
    DISCUSSION: Section 6694(a) imposes a $1,000 or 50% of the income derived penalty on a preparer who takes an unreasonable position that causes an understatement of liability [Reg. 1.6694-2(b)(3)]. Example 2 of the previously cited Regulation describes the situation questioned and concludes that a position contrary to the statute does not satisfy the realistic possibility standard.

22.6.13. A preparer depreciated furniture and fixtures that the taxpayer purchased in the current year by using the wrong class life because (s)he did not understand the MACRS method. This position was not disclosed on the tax return, and it resulted in an understatement of tax. The preparer would be subject to the penalty for negligent or intentional disregard of rules and regulations.

A. True.

B. False.

Answer (A) is correct. *(SEE, adapted)*
    DISCUSSION: Section 6694(b) imposes a penalty of the greater of $5,000 or 75% of the income derived on a preparer if any part of any understatement of liability is due to reckless or intentional disregard of rules and regulations. Disclosure does not preclude the penalty. The IRS might assert the penalty for applying the wrong class life when the correct one is clearly set forth in rules and regulations.

22.6.14. Internal Revenue Code Sec. 6694(a) provides for a penalty against a return preparer for understatement of tax liability due to an unreasonable position. Section 6694(b) provides for a penalty if any part of the understatement is due to willful or reckless conduct. Both of these penalties may be assessed simultaneously on a given return but the total amount of the penalties cannot exceed the Sec. 6694(b) penalty.

A. True.

B. False.

Answer (A) is correct. *(SEE, adapted)*
    DISCUSSION: Under Sec. 6694(a), the penalty for understatements due to unreasonable positions is the greater of $1,000 or 50% of the income derived. Section 6694(b) provides a penalty of the greater of $5,000 or 75% of the income derived for willful or reckless conduct that results in an understatement of liability. Section 6694(b) further states that, if a person is subject to both penalties, the penalty for willful or reckless conduct must be reduced by the penalty imposed for understatements due to unreasonable positions. Thus, a tax return preparer subject to both penalties will pay a total penalty of the greater of $5,000 or 75% of the income derived.

22.6.15. Preparers who fail to properly sign the returns they prepared or who do not furnish the required tax preparer identification numbers may be fined $50 for each improper signature and an additional $50 for each identification number omitted.

A. True.

B. False.

Answer (A) is correct. *(SEE, adapted)*
    DISCUSSION: Section 6695(b) provides a penalty of $50 for each failure of a tax return preparer to sign a return prepared. Section 6695(c) also provides a penalty of $50 for each failure of an income tax return preparer to provide his or her identifying number.

22.6.16. A tax return preparer who fails to observe the requirements of the amount of the earned income credit may face a penalty of $510 in 2017.

A. True.

B. False.

Answer (A) is correct. *(Publisher, adapted)*
    DISCUSSION: A tax return preparer must follow the due diligence requirement when filing a return that claims the earned income credit. Failure to follow the due diligence requirements with respect to the credit will result in the imposition of a $510 penalty per failure.

22.6.17. The penalty for a preparer who fails to retain a copy or record of income tax returns and claims for refunds under Internal Revenue Code Sec. 6695(d) is $25 for each failure up to a maximum of $25,500 for a single return period.

    A. True.

    B. False.

Answer (B) is correct. *(SEE, adapted)*
    DISCUSSION: Section 6107(b) requires a tax return preparer to retain a completed copy of the return or claim for refund for 3 years after the close of the return period. Section 6695(d) imposes a penalty of $50 for each failure to retain a completed copy of the return or claim for refund for the required period, unless it is shown that the failure is due to reasonable cause and not due to willful neglect. Each Sec. 6695 penalty imposed on any preparer is limited to $25,500 for a single return period.

22.6.18. More than one preparer may be subject to the willful understatement of tax liability penalty on the same tax return.

    A. True.

    B. False.

Answer (A) is correct. *(SEE, adapted)*
    DISCUSSION: Regulation 1.6694-2(a)(1) provides that if an understatement of tax liability is due to a willful attempt by one or more income tax return preparers, each preparer who knew or reasonably should have known of the position will be subject to a separate penalty. Regulation 1.6694-1(b)(1) holds for documents prepared and advice given after December 31, 1991, that no more than one individual associated with a firm (e.g., as a partner or employee) is treated as a preparer with respect to a return or refund claim.

22.6.19. When the Internal Revenue Service assesses the return preparer a negligence penalty under Internal Revenue Code Sec. 6694, the preparer may, within 30 days, pay 15% of the penalty and file a claim for refund for the amount paid. If the claim is then denied, the preparer has 60 days to bring suit in the district court to determine the liability for the penalty.

    A. True.

    B. False.

Answer (B) is correct. *(SEE, adapted)*
    DISCUSSION: If a claim for refund filed by an income tax return preparer who has paid 15% of the assessed penalty is denied, the preparer has 30 days to bring suit in the district court to determine the liability for the penalty [Sec. 6694(c)(2)].

22.6.20. If a district court finds that a tax return preparer has continually or repeatedly engaged in guaranteeing the payment of tax refunds to his or her client-taxpayers, the court may enjoin such person from acting as a tax return preparer.

    A. True.

    B. False.

Answer (A) is correct. *(SEE, adapted)*
    DISCUSSION: Section 7407(b) states that if a court finds that a tax return preparer has (1) recklessly or intentionally disregarded rules or regulations or willfully understated tax liability, (2) misrepresented his or her eligibility to practice before the IRS, (3) guaranteed a tax refund or the allowance of a tax credit, or (4) engaged in other fraudulent or deceptive conduct that substantially interferes with the administration of the Internal Revenue laws, the court may enjoin such person from further engaging in such conduct. If the court finds that the preparer has continually or repeatedly engaged in such action, the court may enjoin the person from acting as an income tax return preparer.

22.6.21. A tax return preparer, who is not a preparer bank, who collects return preparation fees by endorsing and cashing income tax refund checks for clients and withholding the amount of the fee will be subject to a $510 penalty for each check negotiated in this manner.

    A. True.

    B. False.

Answer (A) is correct. *(SEE, adapted)*
    DISCUSSION: Section 6695(f) provides that any tax return preparer who endorses or otherwise negotiates any check made in respect of income taxes that is issued to a taxpayer will be subject to a penalty of $510 with respect to each such check. This does not apply to the deposit by a bank in the taxpayer's account.

☑ ≡
☐ ≡   Use **Gleim Test Prep** for interactive study and easy-to-use detailed analytics!
☐ ≡

STUDY UNIT TWENTY-THREE
FEDERAL TAX PROCESS AND PROCEDURE

23.1 Sources of Tax Law

23.1.1. Which of the following is a false statement regarding court cases, revenue rulings, and revenue procedures?

A. U.S. Supreme Court decisions on federal tax matters are published in Internal Revenue Bulletins.

B. Announcements concerning the Internal Revenue Service's acquiescence or nonacquiescence in Tax Court decisions (other than memorandum decisions) that are adverse to the government's position are published in Internal Revenue Bulletins.

C. The Internal Revenue Service does not publish decisions by United States District Courts or the United States Court of Federal Claims. To find these decisions one must look to publications issued by commercial printing houses.

D. The denial of a writ of certiorari by the U.S. Supreme Court is the equivalent of a reversal or disagreement.

Answer (D) is correct. *(SEE, adapted)*
REQUIRED: The false statement regarding court cases, revenue rulings, and revenue procedures.
DISCUSSION: The denial of a writ of certiorari by the U.S. Supreme Court is simply the Court's decision not to hear the case. The U.S. Supreme Court selects only those cases that it thinks are of sufficient public interest to warrant a U.S. Supreme Court hearing. The denial is neither a reversal nor a disagreement. Moreover, while the effect of the denial is to let stand the result in the court below, the denial does not signify agreement with the decision.
Answer (A) is incorrect. U.S. Supreme Court decisions on federal tax matters are published in Internal Revenue Bulletins. Answer (B) is incorrect. Announcements concerning the Internal Revenue Service's acquiescence or nonacquiescence in Tax Court decisions (other than memorandum decisions) that are adverse to the government's position are published in Internal Revenue Bulletins. Answer (C) is incorrect. The Internal Revenue Service does not publish decisions by United States District Courts or the United States Court of Federal Claims. To find these decisions one must look to publications issued by commercial printing houses.

23.1.2. Which of the following statements regarding Treasury Regulations is false?

A. Regulations are binding on all courts except the U.S. Supreme Court.

B. Interpretative regulations are issued under the general mandate of Sec. 7805(a).

C. Some Code sections specifically authorize regulations to provide the details of the meaning and rules for that particular Code section. These are called legislative regulations.

D. Temporary regulations are issued to provide guidance for the public and IRS employees until final regulations are issued.

Answer (A) is correct. *(SEE, adapted)*
REQUIRED: The false statement regarding Treasury Regulations.
DISCUSSION: Treasury Regulations explain the language of the Internal Revenue Code by giving explanations, definitions, examples, and rules that clarify the intent of Congress. They are not binding on any court if they conflict with the Code.
Answer (B) is incorrect. Interpretative regulations are issued under the general mandate of Sec. 7805(a). Answer (C) is incorrect. Some Code sections specifically authorize regulations to provide the details of the meaning and rules for that particular Code section. These are called legislative regulations. Answer (D) is incorrect. Temporary regulations are issued to provide guidance for the public and IRS employees until final regulations are issued.

23.1.3. All of the following statements relating to Treasury Regulations are true except

A. Temporary regulations are issued to provide guidance for the public and IRS employees until final regulations are issued.

B. Public hearings are always held on temporary regulations.

C. Final regulations supersede temporary regulations.

D. Proposed regulations are issued to solicit public written comments.

Answer (B) is correct. *(SEE, adapted)*
REQUIRED: The false statement about Treasury Regulations.
DISCUSSION: The Treasury Department issues regulations as interpretations of the Internal Revenue Code. Regulations are generally first issued to the public in proposed form. Practitioners and the public are invited to comment on the regulation and suggest changes before the regulation becomes final. The Treasury Department sometimes issues temporary regulations. These regulations give the public, practitioners, and IRS personnel guidance until appropriate final regulations are issued. Any temporary regulation issued after November 20, 1988, will expire within 3 years after the date of issuance and must also be issued as a proposed regulation [Sec. 7805(e)]. Because temporary regulations are also issued in proposed form, public hearings are not held on the temporary regulations. While in effect, temporary regulations have the same authority as final regulations.
Answer (A) is incorrect. Temporary regulations are issued to provide guidance for the public and IRS employees until final regulations are issued. Answer (C) is incorrect. Final regulations supersede temporary regulations. Answer (D) is incorrect. Proposed regulations are issued to solicit public written comments.

23.1.4. All of the following statements regarding revenue rulings and revenue procedures are true except

A. Revenue procedures are official statements of procedures that affect either the rights or duties of taxpayers or other members of the public.

B. The purpose of revenue rulings and revenue procedures is to promote a uniform application of the tax laws.

C. Taxpayers cannot appeal adverse return examination results that are based on revenue rulings to the federal courts.

D. IRS employees must follow revenue rulings and procedures.

Answer (C) is correct. *(SEE, adapted)*
REQUIRED: The false statement regarding revenue rulings and revenue procedures.
DISCUSSION: A revenue ruling sets forth the IRS's interpretation of the tax law. It is binding on IRS employees but not on the courts. Taxpayers may appeal adverse examination decisions whether or not based on a revenue ruling.
Answer (A) is incorrect. Revenue procedures are official statements of procedures that either affect the rights or duties of taxpayers or other members of the public. Answer (B) is incorrect. The purpose of revenue rulings and revenue procedures is to promote a uniform application of the tax laws. Answer (D) is incorrect. IRS employees must follow revenue rulings and procedures.

23.1.5. There are two types of income tax regulations, interpretive and legislative. These regulations provide explanations, definitions, examples, and rules that explain the language of the Code. Accordingly, your research of a particular Code section cannot be considered complete until you have read the regulations that interpret it.

A. True.

B. False.

Answer (A) is correct. *(SEE, adapted)*
DISCUSSION: Treasury regulations explain the language of the Internal Revenue Code by giving explanations, definitions, examples, and rules that clarify the intent of Congress. Interpretive regulations make the language of the statutes easier to understand and apply. Legislative regulations are those that are specifically authorized by Congress to provide the details of the meaning and rules for a particular Code section. Courts place great importance on the regulations and will follow them in rendering a decision unless they are plainly inconsistent with the Code. Regulations are also important because they state the government's position. Proper research of a particular Code section requires that the applicable provision in the regulations also be researched.

23.1.6. The courts give great importance to the literal language of the Internal Revenue Code, but they also consider, among other things, the history of a particular section of the Code, its relationship to other Code sections, and the reports of Congressional committees.

A. True.

B. False.

Answer (A) is correct. *(SEE, adapted)*
DISCUSSION: In applying the Internal Revenue Code to the facts of a case, the courts attempt to carry out the intent of Congress as expressed in the language of the Code. Therefore, they give great importance to the Code's literal language. The courts may also consider other sources that help explain or clarify the intent of a particular section. The reports of the Congressional committees, the history of the section, and the relationship to other Code sections may be considered by the courts in determining the intent of Congress.

23.1.7. The courts are bound by legislative regulations but not by interpretive regulations.

A. True.

B. False.

Answer (B) is correct. *(SEE, adapted)*

DISCUSSION: The two types of income tax regulations are interpretive and legislative (statutory). The Secretary of the Treasury is given the power to issue regulations by specific Code sections. These are called legislative or statutory regulations. Legislative regulations promulgated by the Treasury have the full force and effect of law unless they conflict with the Code, so they are not always binding.

Interpretive regulations are authorized by Sec. 7805(a), which empowers the Secretary to prescribe all needful rules and regulations for enforcement of the Code. Interpretive regulations also are not binding on a court. The weight given to an interpretive regulation by a court depends upon all the circumstances of a case.

23.1.8. All regulations are written by the Office of Chief Counsel. Internal Revenue Service employees and all courts, except the U.S. Supreme Court, are bound by these regulations.

A. True.

B. False.

Answer (B) is correct. *(SEE, adapted)*

DISCUSSION: Regulations are written by the Assistant Chief Counsels in the Corporate, Financial Institutions and Products, Income Tax and Accounting, Passthroughs and Specialized Industries, General Litigation, Employee Benefits and Exempt Organizations, and International areas. After being circulated, they are signed by the Chief Counsel and Commissioner of the IRS and the Assistant Secretary for Tax Policy of the Treasury Department. Courts generally give great importance to the regulations but are not bound by them. Courts may declare a regulation to be invalid if the regulation conflicts with, or is inconsistent with, the Internal Revenue Code.

23.1.9. Revenue rulings are the published conclusions of the IRS concerning the application of tax law to a specific set of facts.

A. True.

B. False.

Answer (A) is correct. *(SEE, adapted)*

DISCUSSION: A revenue ruling (abbreviated Rev. Rul.) is substantive, pertains to a specific set of facts, and sets forth the IRS's interpretation of the tax law and its application to those facts. IRS employees must follow published rulings.

23.1.10. The purpose of revenue rulings is to promote a uniform application of the tax law to an entire set of facts. Therefore, IRS employees must follow the rulings, while taxpayers may contest in court adverse return examination decisions based on these findings.

A. True.

B. False.

Answer (A) is correct. *(SEE, adapted)*

DISCUSSION: Revenue rulings are published in the Internal Revenue Bulletin (published weekly) and the Cumulative Bulletin (published semiannually). Each issue of the Internal Revenue Bulletin states that, in applying published rulings, the effect of subsequent legislation, regulations, court decisions, rulings, and procedures must be considered, and concerned persons are cautioned against reaching the same conclusions in other cases unless the facts and circumstances are substantially the same. Revenue rulings are interpretations by the IRS and therefore need not be followed in every instance if another interpretation is justified.

23.1.11. Revenue rulings, revenue procedures, and all U.S. Supreme Court decisions on federal tax matters are published in the Internal Revenue Bulletin (IRB).

A. True.

B. False.

Answer (A) is correct. *(SEE, adapted)*

DISCUSSION: The Internal Revenue Bulletin is published weekly and includes Treasury decisions, statutes, committee reports, U.S. Supreme Court decisions affecting internal revenue, lists of the acquiescences and nonacquiescences of the IRS to decisions of the courts, and administrative rulings.

23.1.12. In interpreting and applying the Internal Revenue Code to specific cases, courts are required to apply it in accordance with the law of the state in which the taxpayer and court are located.

A. True.

B. False.

Answer (B) is correct. *(Publisher, adapted)*

DISCUSSION: The Internal Revenue Code is federal law. The only courts in which a federal tax case may be brought are the U.S. Tax Court, U.S. District Court, and U.S. Court of Federal Claims. Each of these courts is a federal court and is not bound by state laws, except as the state law may affect or determine the underlying transactions which are the subject of taxation. Even then, generally only the decision of the highest court in the state will be followed with respect to the application of a state law.

23.1.13. Decisions of the courts other than the U.S. Supreme Court are binding on the Commissioner of Internal Revenue only for the particular taxpayer and for the years litigated.

A.   True.

B.   False.

Answer (A) is correct. *(SEE, adapted)*
   DISCUSSION: Decisions of courts other than the U.S. Supreme Court are binding on the Commissioner only for the particular taxpayer in question and only for the years litigated. Decisions of the U.S. Supreme Court are binding on the Commissioner for all taxpayers and also for future years.

23.2   Legislative Process

23.2.1. Prior to becoming law, a proposed statute is called a bill. A revenue bill is one that concerns taxation (the raising of revenue). Where must a revenue bill originate?

A.   The House of Representatives.

B.   The President.

C.   The Joint Committee on Taxation.

D.   The Senate.

Answer (A) is correct. *(Publisher, adapted)*
   REQUIRED: The government body that originates a revenue bill.
   DISCUSSION: Under the U.S. Constitution, a revenue bill must originate in the House of Representatives. This is a formality because a bill drafted by someone else, e.g., the administration, may be introduced onto the floor of the House by any Representative.
   Answer (B) is incorrect. The President can only introduce a revenue bill indirectly by persuading a Representative to introduce it on the floor of the House. Answer (C) is incorrect. The Joint Committee on Taxation is a permanent committee whose function is continually to review the operation and administration of the tax system and propose improvements. It too can introduce a revenue bill but only indirectly. Answer (D) is incorrect. A revenue bill does not reach the Senate until it has been approved by the House of Representatives.

23.2.2. When does a revenue bill go to the Senate Finance Committee?

A.   After approval by the House Ways and Means Committee.

B.   After approval by the Senate.

C.   After the President vetoes it.

D.   After it is referred to the Senate.

Answer (D) is correct. *(Publisher, adapted)*
   REQUIRED: The point at which a revenue bill goes to the Senate Finance Committee.
   DISCUSSION: The Senate Finance Committee operates similarly to the House Ways and Means Committee. Each studies a revenue bill after it has been introduced onto the floor of the House or Senate, holds hearings, and prepares a report for consideration by the entire legislative body. A revenue bill begins with its introduction onto the floor of the House, referral to the Ways and Means Committee, and return to the floor of the House for a vote. If the bill is approved by the House, it is referred to the Senate, which forwards it to the Senate Finance Committee. After the Senate Finance Committee, it goes back to the floor of the Senate for debate and a vote.
   Answer (A) is incorrect. A revenue bill must be approved by the House of Representatives after its review in the Ways and Means Committee. Answer (B) is incorrect. A revenue bill is not approved by the Senate until it goes through the Senate Finance Committee. Answer (C) is incorrect. If the President vetoes a revenue bill, it goes back to the Senate and House and becomes law if passed by two-thirds majority of each.

23.2.3. When or where are public hearings held on a revenue bill?

A.   On the floor of the House and the Senate.

B.   In the House Ways and Means Committee and the Senate Finance Committee.

C.   In the Joint Conference Committee.

D.   Upon first introduction to the House of Representatives.

Answer (B) is correct. *(Publisher, adapted)*
   REQUIRED: The time or place of public hearings held on a revenue bill.
   DISCUSSION: In both the House Ways and Means Committee and the Senate Finance Committee, public hearings are usually held on a revenue bill to allow the administration, taxpayers, and other groups to express their views.
   Answer (A) is incorrect. The members of Congress may debate a bill on the floor of the House and Senate, but that is not the place for public hearings. Answer (C) is incorrect. The Joint Conference Committee privately reconciles different versions of a bill passed by the House and Senate but does not usually hold public hearings. Answer (D) is incorrect. The first introduction to the House of Representatives is a mere formality before the bill is seriously considered.

23.2.4. As revenue bills go through Congress, they are usually approved in different versions since amendments are frequently made. Which committee is responsible for reconciling the House and Senate versions?

    A. Joint Conference Committee.

    B. Joint Committee on Taxation.

    C. House Ways and Means Committee.

    D. Senate Finance Committee.

Answer (A) is correct. *(Publisher, adapted)*
    REQUIRED: The committee that is responsible for reconciling House and Senate versions of a revenue bill.
    DISCUSSION: As revenue bills go through Congress, amendments are made. Thus, the Senate usually passes a different version of a bill from that approved in the House. The Joint Conference Committee includes members of both the Ways and Means Committee and the Finance Committee, who attempt to reconcile the differences. The new version goes to the House and Senate to be voted upon.
    Answer (B) is incorrect. The Joint Committee on Taxation provides only advisory assistance. Answer (C) is incorrect. The Ways and Means Committee merely reports to the House prior to initial approval. Answer (D) is incorrect. The Finance Committee performs the same function in the Senate as the Ways and Means Committee in the House.

23.2.5. A useful by-product of the legislative process is legislative history, which is used to help interpret the new law. Which of the following is the most useful part of the legislative history of a revenue bill?

    A. Testimony from committee hearings.

    B. Committee reports.

    C. Text from House and Senate floor debates.

    D. Explanation accompanying the introduction of a bill.

Answer (B) is correct. *(Publisher, adapted)*
    REQUIRED: The most useful part of the legislative history of a revenue bill.
    DISCUSSION: The committee reports usually contain a general explanation of the proposed legislation for the entire legislative body to consider. This explanation may contain reasons for the legislation, its potential impact, and its background. These reports come from the House Ways and Means Committee, Senate Finance Committee, and the Joint Conference Committee. They are frequently used to interpret new laws and are even cited by courts.
    Answer (A) is incorrect. Committee hearings only contain long testimony from various groups about what they think is important. Answer (C) is incorrect. Senate debates may provide the background of a new law but add little to its interpretation. Answer (D) is incorrect. Bills are dramatically changed by the time they are approved by the legislative body, so an original explanation is not extremely useful.

23.3 Return Examination

23.3.1. All of the following reasons are acceptable for transferring an examination from one IRS district to another except

    A. The place of examination is solely for the convenience of the taxpayer's representative (books and records are located at his or her client's office, which is located within the current IRS district).

    B. Books and records are located in another district.

    C. The place of examination is for the convenience of the Internal Revenue Service.

    D. The taxpayer's residence has changed since the return was filed.

Answer (A) is correct. *(SEE, adapted)*
    REQUIRED: The reason which is not acceptable for transferring an examination from one IRS district office to another.
    DISCUSSION: When a request is received to transfer a return to another district for examination, the district director having jurisdiction may transfer the case to the district director of such other district. The IRS will determine the time and place of the examination. In determining whether a transfer should be made, circumstances considered include the change of the taxpayer's domicile, discovery that the taxpayer's books and records are kept in another district, change of domicile of an executor or administrator to another district, and the effective administration of the tax laws [26 CFR 601.105(k)]. The convenience of the taxpayer's representative is not an acceptable reason to transfer an examination.
    Answer (B) is incorrect. Books and records being located in another district is a reason considered acceptable by the IRS in deciding whether to transfer an examination. Answer (C) is incorrect. The place of examination being for the convenience of the IRS is a reason considered acceptable by the IRS in deciding whether to transfer an examination. Answer (D) is incorrect. The taxpayer's residence having changed since the return was filed is a reason considered acceptable by the IRS in deciding whether to transfer an examination.

23.3.2. Before the initial in-person interview between the IRS and the taxpayer to determine or collect any taxes, a taxpayer should receive which one of the following publications from the IRS?

    A.   Publication 594, *The IRS Collection Process*.

    B.   Publication 5, *Your Appeal Rights and How to Prepare a Protest if You Don't Agree*.

    C.   Form 2848, *Power of Attorney and Declaration of Representative*.

    D.   Publication 1, *Your Rights as a Taxpayer*.

Answer (D) is correct. *(SEE, adapted)*
    REQUIRED: The correct publication a taxpayer should receive from the IRS before the initial in-person interview.
    DISCUSSION: Section 7521(b) provides that, prior to the initial in-person interview, an officer or employee of the IRS must provide to the taxpayer an explanation of the audit process and the taxpayer's rights under such process, or if the interview is related to the collection of any tax, an explanation of the collection process and the taxpayer's rights under such process. This explanation is provided in Publication 1, *Your Rights as a Taxpayer*.
    Answer (A) is incorrect. Publication 594 is received after the tax liability has been determined by the IRS. Answer (B) is incorrect. The taxpayer is not required to receive Publication 5 before the initial interview. Answer (C) is incorrect. The taxpayer is not required to receive Form 2848 before the initial interview.

23.3.3. An interview with the IRS must be suspended immediately if the taxpayer indicates a desire to consult with a representative.

    A.   True.

    B.   False.

Answer (A) is correct. *(Publisher, adapted)*
    DISCUSSION: Section 7521(b) requires the interview to be suspended in such a situation.

23.3.4. Jack and Jill Hill's return was selected for examination in Year 1. There was no change to the one issue examined -- medical expense. In Year 2, the Hills received a notice that their return was selected for examination and the issues were exemptions and contributions. Because they received a no-change in Year 1, they should contact the IRS to see if the examination should be discontinued in Year 2.

    A.   True.

    B.   False.

Answer (B) is correct. *(SEE, adapted)*
    DISCUSSION: If the same items were examined in either of the previous 2 years and the examination resulted in no change to the tax liability, the taxpayer should notify the person whose name and phone number appear in the appointment letter. The IRS will suspend but not cancel an audit (while reviewing its files to determine whether to proceed) so as to avoid repetitive examinations of the same items (Internal Revenue Manual 4.10.2.8.5).

23.3.5. Generally, a return is examined in the IRS district where the taxpayer lives. But if the return can be examined more quickly and conveniently in another district, such as where the books and records are located, the taxpayer can ask to have the case transferred.

    A.   True.

    B.   False.

Answer (A) is correct. *(SEE, adapted)*
    DISCUSSION: In most cases, an income tax examination is conducted in the Internal Revenue Service district office nearest the taxpayer's place of residence. The examination may be transferred to another IRS district office if the taxpayer's books and records are kept in another district, the taxpayer has changed domiciles, or an executor or administrator has moved to another district [26 CFR 601.105(k)]. The IRS has authority to determine the time and place of the examination.

23.3.6. Taxpayers or their authorized representatives may request a conference with the examining agent's supervisor if they are not in agreement with changes proposed by the examining agent as part of an office examination.

    A.   True.

    B.   False.

Answer (A) is correct. *(SEE, adapted)*
    DISCUSSION: If the taxpayer does not agree with the adjustments proposed, the examiner will fully explain the alternatives available. For office audits, these alternatives include an interview with a supervisor, immediately if practicable [26 CFR 601.105(c)(1)]. If a taxpayer wishes to take advantage of this alternative, (s)he should request such a conference. For field examinations, the next step is usually an Appeals office conference.

23.3.7. Mr. B owed an additional $5,000 tax as a result of the examination of his federal income tax return. The Internal Revenue Service gave this information, under an exchange agreement, to the state in which Mr. B lives. The Internal Revenue Service has violated Mr. B's right to privacy and may be sued for damages.

A. True.

B. False.

Answer (B) is correct. *(SEE, adapted)*
    DISCUSSION: Section 6103(d) allows returns and return information to be disclosed upon written request of the principal state tax official for the purpose of administering state tax laws. "Return information" includes data received or prepared by the IRS regarding a return, deficiency, or penalty. The IRS may disclose this information to the state in which B lives.

23.3.8. In any case in which a recognized representative is unable or unwilling to declare his or her own knowledge that the facts are true and correct, the Internal Revenue Service may require the taxpayer to make such a declaration under penalty of perjury.

A. True.

B. False.

Answer (A) is correct. *(SEE, adapted)*
    DISCUSSION: If a taxpayer's representative sends in the protest, (s)he must declare that (s)he prepared it and personally knows the statements of fact are true and correct (Publication 5). Alternatively, the taxpayer must make such a declaration under penalty of perjury (Publication 5 and Rev. Proc. 61-36).

23.3.9. If the Internal Revenue Service has selected your return for examination, you may make an audio recording of the examination interview if you follow certain procedures prescribed by the IRS.

A. True.

B. False.

Answer (A) is correct. *(SEE, adapted)*
    DISCUSSION: Section 7521(a) allows taxpayers to make audio recordings of the interview but with advance request and at the taxpayer's expense. IRS officers and employees are also permitted to make audio recordings of the interview. Advance permission of the taxpayer is required for IRS audio recordings, and a copy of the transcript or recording must be provided to the taxpayer.

23.3.10. The IRS can require the taxpayer to accompany a representative (attorney, CPA, enrolled agent, or person permitted to practice before the IRS) to an interview without issuing a summons.

A. True.

B. False.

Answer (B) is correct. *(Publisher, adapted)*
    DISCUSSION: The taxpayer need not accompany such representative to any interview unless the IRS issues a summons. Such a summons is subject to judicial review.

23.4 Power of Attorney and Tax Information Authorization

23.4.1. All of the following statements with respect to the Internal Revenue Service's Centralized Authorization File (CAF) are true except

A. The issuance of a CAF number does not indicate that a person is recognized or authorized to practice before the Internal Revenue Service.

B. Information from both powers of attorney and tax information authorizations is recorded onto the CAF system.

C. A tax information authorization or power of attorney will be rejected based on the absence of a CAF number.

D. Only documents that concern a matter(s) relating to a specific tax period that ends no later than 3 years after the date a power of attorney is received by the Internal Revenue Service will be recorded onto the CAF system.

Answer (C) is correct. *(SEE, adapted)*
    REQUIRED: The false statement concerning the CAF number.
    DISCUSSION: The purpose of the CAF number is to facilitate the processing of a power of attorney or a tax information authorization submitted by a recognized representative or an appointee. A recognized representative or an appointee should include the same CAF number on every power of attorney or tax information authorization filed. However, because the CAF number is not a substantive requirement, a tax information authorization or power of attorney which does not include such number will not be rejected based on the absence of a CAF number [26 CFR 601.506(d)(2)].
    Answer (A) is incorrect. The issuance of a CAF number does not indicate that a person is recognized or authorized to practice before the Internal Revenue Service. Answer (B) is incorrect. Information from both powers of attorney and tax information authorizations is recorded onto the CAF system. Answer (D) is incorrect. Only documents that concern a matter(s) relating to a specific tax period that ends no later than 3 years after the date a power of attorney is received by the Internal Revenue Service will be recorded onto the CAF system.

23.4.2. All of the following statements concerning the IRS's Centralized Authorization File (CAF) number are true except

A. The CAF number entitles the person to whom it is assigned to practice before any office of the Internal Revenue Service except a regional appeals office.

B. The CAF number allows IRS personnel to identify representatives and the scope of their authority and will automatically direct copies of notices and correspondence to the person authorized by the taxpayer.

C. A CAF number is a unique number that will be assigned to any person who files with the Service a power of attorney and a written declaration that (s)he is currently qualified to practice before the IRS and is authorized to represent the particular party on whose behalf (s)he acts.

D. A CAF number is a unique number that will be assigned to any person who files with the IRS a tax information authorization.

Answer (A) is correct. *(SEE, adapted)*
REQUIRED: The false statement concerning the CAF number.
DISCUSSION: The CAF number is the unique number that the Internal Revenue Service will assign to a representative after (s)he has filed a power of attorney or tax information authorization with an IRS office that is using the CAF system. The issuance of a CAF number does not indicate that a person is either recognized or authorized to practice before the IRS. That determination is made under the provisions of Circular 230 [26 CFR 601.506(d)].
Answer (B) is incorrect. The CAF number allows IRS personnel to identify representatives and the scope of their authority and will automatically direct copies of notices and correspondence to the person authorized by the taxpayer. Answer (C) is incorrect. A CAF number is a unique number that will be assigned to any person who files with the Service a power of attorney and a written declaration that (s)he is currently qualified to practice before the IRS and is authorized to represent the particular party on whose behalf he or she acts. Answer (D) is incorrect. A CAF number is a unique number that will be assigned to any person who files with the IRS a tax information authorization.

23.4.3. Which of the following would not be a proper execution of a power of attorney or tax information authorization?

A. For a corporation, by an officer having authority to bind the corporation.

B. For a deceased taxpayer, by the executor or administrator.

C. For a taxpayer with a court-appointed guardian, by the one appointed.

D. For a partnership, by any partner.

Answer (D) is correct. *(SEE, adapted)*
REQUIRED: The improper execution of a power of attorney or tax information authorization.
DISCUSSION: Rules for execution of a power of attorney and a tax information authorization are contained in 26 CFR 601.503 and .504. If the power of attorney is for a partnership, all partners must sign or a duly authorized member may sign, but not just any partner.
Answer (A) is incorrect. An officer having authority to bind the corporation has the proper authority to execute a power of attorney. Answer (B) is incorrect. The executor or administrator has the proper authority to execute a power of attorney for a deceased taxpayer. Answer (C) is incorrect. The court-appointed guardian has the proper authority to execute a power of attorney.

23.4.4. Which of the following is false with respect to powers of attorney?

A. The IRS will accept a facsimile (fax) copy of a power of attorney if the appropriate IRS office is equipped to receive it.

B. IRS Form 2848, *Power of Attorney and Declaration of Representative*, cannot be used by a taxpayer to appoint an unenrolled return preparer to act as the taxpayer's representative before revenue agents and examining officers of the Examination Division of the Internal Revenue Service.

C. A taxpayer's signature on a power of attorney does not have to be notarized or witnessed.

D. A taxpayer can execute a durable power of attorney that specifies that the appointment of the attorney-in-fact will not end due to the incapacity or incompetency of the taxpayer.

Answer (B) is correct. *(SEE, adapted)*
REQUIRED: The false statement with respect to powers of attorney.
DISCUSSION: Under 26 CFR 601.502, a recognized representative is defined as an individual appointed under a power of attorney, who files a declaration of representative, and is a member of certain specified categories. One category is an enrolled agent. An example of another category is an unenrolled return preparer. The unenrolled return preparer is limited in scope to appearing before revenue agents and examining officers. A properly completed Form 2848 satisfies the requirements of both a power of attorney and a declaration of representative [26 CFR 601.503(b)(1)]. A recognized representative is an individual who is recognized to practice before the IRS [26 CFR 601.501(b)(12)].
Answer (A) is incorrect. The IRS will accept a facsimile (fax) copy of a power of attorney if the appropriate IRS office is equipped to receive it. Answer (C) is incorrect. A taxpayer's signature on a power of attorney does not have to be notarized or witnessed. Answer (D) is incorrect. A taxpayer can execute a durable power of attorney that specifies that the appointment of the attorney-in-fact will not end due to the incapacity or incompetency of the taxpayer.

23.4.5. A power of attorney or tax information authorization should contain all of the following information except

    A. The taxpayer's intent as to the scope of authority of the representative.

    B. The divisions of the IRS that are involved in the matter covered by the power of attorney.

    C. Type of tax involved.

    D. The year(s) or period(s).

Answer (B) is correct. *(SEE, adapted)*
    REQUIRED: The information not required in a power of attorney or tax information authorization.
    DISCUSSION: A power of attorney or tax information authorization need not list the divisions of the IRS that are involved in the matter. Required information includes the taxpayer's intention as to the scope of the authority of the representative, the tax matter(s) to which the authority relates, and the year(s) or period(s) involved [26 CFR 601.503(a)].
    Answer (A) is incorrect. The taxpayer's intent as to the scope of authority of the representative is required in a power of attorney or tax information authorization. Answer (C) is incorrect. The type of tax involved is required in a power of attorney or tax information authorization. Answer (D) is incorrect. The year(s) or period(s) are required in a power of attorney or tax information authorization.

23.4.6. With regard to the declaration of the representative on a power of attorney, all of the following statements are true except

    A. A fiduciary is required to show his or her relationship.

    B. An attorney must indicate the state in which (s)he is admitted to practice.

    C. A CPA must include the state in which (s)he is licensed to practice.

    D. A full-time employee must show his or her title.

Answer (A) is correct. *(SEE, adapted)*
    REQUIRED: The false statement regarding the declaration of the representative on a power of attorney.
    DISCUSSION: A fiduciary stands in the position of a taxpayer and acts as the taxpayer. Therefore, a fiduciary does not act as a representative and should not file a power of attorney (Instructions for Form 2848).
    Answer (B) is incorrect. An attorney must enter the two-letter abbreviation for the state in which (s)he is admitted to practice in the jurisdiction column (Instructions for Form 2848). Answer (C) is incorrect. A certified public accountant must enter the two-letter abbreviation of the state in which (s)he is licensed to practice in the jurisdiction column (Instructions for Form 2848). Answer (D) is incorrect. A full-time employee must enter his or her title or position in the jurisdiction column (Instructions for Form 2848).

23.4.7. A power of attorney is required in all of the following circumstances except to

    A. Furnish information at the request of the IRS.

    B. Authorize the extension of the statute of limitations.

    C. Execute a closing agreement under Sec. 7121.

    D. Receive a refund check.

Answer (A) is correct. *(SEE, adapted)*
    REQUIRED: The circumstance in which a power of attorney is not required.
    DISCUSSION: A POA is a written authorization for one individual to act on behalf of another individual in tax matters. If the authorization is not limited, the individual can generally perform all acts that the taxpayer can perform. In general, a representative can do all of the following: represent the taxpayer before any office of the IRS; sign a waiver agreeing to a tax adjustment; sign a consent to extend the statutory time period for assessment or collection of a tax; sign a closing agreement under Sec. 7121 of the Internal Revenue Code; and receive, but not endorse or cash, a refund check. A power of attorney is not required to furnish information at the request of the IRS.
    Answer (B) is incorrect. A power of attorney is required to authorize the extension of the statute of limitations. Answer (C) is incorrect. A power of attorney is required to execute a closing agreement under Sec. 7121. Answer (D) is incorrect. A power of attorney is required to receive a refund check.

23.4.8. A taxpayer's representative who is recognized to practice before the Internal Revenue Service attends an estate tax case conference without the executor or administrator. No tax information authorization is necessary if the representative is the preparer of the estate tax return and the attorney of record for the executor or administrator before the court where the will is probated or the estate administered.

    A. True.

    B. False.

Answer (A) is correct. *(SEE, adapted)*
    DISCUSSION: Under 26 CFR 601.504(b)(2), a tax information authorization or power of attorney is not required at a conference concerning an estate tax case (even though the executor or administrator is not present at the conference) if the representative presents evidence that (s)he is recognized to practice before the IRS and is the attorney of record for the executor or administrator before the court where the will is probated or the estate is administered.

23.4.9. Form 2848, *Power of Attorney and Declaration of Representative*, properly executed by the taxpayer, permits the taxpayer's representative to make substitution of representatives without the taxpayer's specific grant of authority to do so.

A. True.

B. False.

Answer (A) is correct. *(SEE, adapted)*
DISCUSSION: A properly executed Form 2848, *Power of Attorney and Declaration of Representative*, permits the taxpayer's representative to make substitution of representatives without the taxpayer's specific grant of authority to do so. However, if the taxpayer wishes to authorize the taxpayer's representative to make substitution of representatives or delegate authority to other representatives, the power of attorney must state this intention [26 CFR 601.505(b)(2)].

23.4.10. To authorize the IRS to disclose information concerning the taxpayer's tax account(s) to an individual, whether or not the individual is authorized to practice before the IRS, or other party (such as a partnership or corporation), you may use Form 8821, *Tax Information Authorization*.

A. True.

B. False.

Answer (A) is correct. *(SEE, adapted)*
DISCUSSION: A tax information authorization is a document signed by the taxpayer authorizing any individual or entity (e.g., corporation, partnership, trust, or organization) designated by the taxpayer to receive and/or inspect confidential tax information in a specified matter [26 CFR 601.501(b)(15)]. Section 6103(c) authorizes the IRS to disclose return information to a person the taxpayer designates in a written request. The taxpayer's request must be in the form of a letter or other written document signed and dated by the taxpayer [Reg. 301.6103(c)-1(b)]. Form 8821, *Tax Information Authorization*, may be used.

23.4.11. A person possessing a tax information authorization can inspect or receive confidential information and advocate a taxpayer's position with respect to the federal tax laws.

A. True.

B. False.

Answer (B) is correct. *(SEE, adapted)*
DISCUSSION: A tax information authorization is a document signed by the taxpayer authorizing any individual or entity (e.g., corporation, partnership, trust, or organization) designated by the taxpayer to receive and/or inspect confidential tax information in a specified matter [26 CFR 601.501(b)(15)]. Section 6103(c) authorizes the IRS to disclose return information to a person whom the taxpayer designates in a written request. Such a person cannot advocate the taxpayer's position with respect to the federal tax laws.

23.4.12. A properly executed power of attorney can be used in connection with more than one particular type of tax.

A. True.

B. False.

Answer (A) is correct. *(SEE, adapted)*
DISCUSSION: The formal requirements for execution of a power of attorney are found in 26 CFR 601.503. A power of attorney may relate to more than one matter, as, for example, a power of attorney that relates to more than one particular type of tax. The specific type or types of tax should be stated on the power of attorney. A general reference to "all taxes" is not acceptable.

23.4.13. A fiduciary (trustee, executor, administrator, or receiver) is in effect recognized as the taxpayer, and a power of attorney is not required.

A. True.

B. False.

Answer (A) is correct. *(SEE, adapted)*
DISCUSSION: Under 26 CFR 601.504(a), a power of attorney must be filed with the IRS to authorize a recognized representative to represent a taxpayer. But a fiduciary of a taxpayer, such as the trustee of a trust, is treated as the taxpayer himself or herself. The fiduciary need not execute a power of attorney authorizing himself or herself to represent the taxpayer. The fiduciary should file Form 56, *Notice Concerning Fiduciary Relationship* [26 CFR 601.503(d)].

23.4.14. If a joint return is involved and the husband and wife are to be represented by the same representative, the power of attorney requires the signature of both husband and wife unless one spouse is duly authorized in writing to sign for the other spouse.

A. True.

B. False.

Answer (A) is correct. *(SEE, adapted)*
DISCUSSION: According to 26 CFR 601.503(c)(2), if a joint return is involved and the husband and wife are to be represented by the same representative, the power of attorney must be signed by both spouses unless one spouse is duly authorized in writing to sign for the other spouse.

23.4.15. If a joint return is involved, a power of attorney may be executed by either the husband or wife if they do not have the same representative; however, the representative cannot perform any act with respect to that joint return year that the represented spouse could not perform alone.

A. True.

B. False.

Answer (A) is correct. *(SEE, adapted)*
DISCUSSION: In the case of any matter concerning a joint return in which both husband and wife are not to be represented by the same recognized representative(s), the power of attorney must be executed by the spouse who is to be represented. However, the recognized representative of such spouse cannot perform any act with respect to a tax matter that the spouse being represented cannot perform alone [26 CFR 601.503(c)(2)].

23.4.16. If a court having jurisdiction over a debtor appoints a trustee, a receiver, or an attorney (designated to represent a trustee, a receiver, or a debtor in possession), then documents from the court attesting to this appointment preclude the necessity of a power of attorney or a tax information authorization.

A. True.

B. False.

Answer (A) is correct. *(SEE, adapted)*
DISCUSSION: Proof of appointment (of a trustee, receiver, or attorney) by a court having jurisdiction over the debtor is generally sufficient to authorize disclosure without a power of attorney or tax information authorization [26 CFR 601.504(b)(3)].

23.4.17. A power of attorney is not required to be submitted by an attorney of record in a case that is docketed in the Tax Court. However, a power of attorney is required to be submitted by an individual other than the attorney of record in any matter before the Internal Revenue Service concerning a docketed case.

A. True.

B. False.

Answer (A) is correct. *(SEE, adapted)*
DISCUSSION: A power of attorney or a tax information authorization is not required in cases docketed in the Tax Court (26 CFR 601.509). Counsel for a taxpayer must be admitted to practice before the Tax Court. When the taxpayer's petition to Tax Court is signed by counsel admitted to practice before the Tax Court, that counsel will be recognized as representing that party. A power of attorney is required to be submitted by an individual other than the attorney of record.

23.4.18. A tax information authorization is not required of a taxpayer's representative at a conference with IRS officials which is also attended by the taxpayer.

A. True.

B. False.

Answer (A) is correct. *(SEE, adapted)*
DISCUSSION: Submission of a tax information authorization to request disclosure of confidential tax information does not constitute practice before the IRS [26 CFR 601.504(b)(1)]. A tax information authorization is not required of a taxpayer's representative at a conference that is also attended by the taxpayer.

23.4.19. Either a tax information authorization or a power of attorney is required for a practitioner to receive a notice of deficiency under Sec. 6212.

A. True.

B. False.

Answer (A) is correct. *(SEE, adapted)*
DISCUSSION: The provisions of 26 CFR 601.504(a)(1) require a tax information authorization for a taxpayer's representative to receive a notice of deficiency under Sec. 6212. A tax information authorization is not required if the representative has filed a power of attorney for the same matters. Therefore, either a tax information authorization or a power of attorney will fulfill the requirements.

23.4.20. An attorney, a certified public accountant, or a person enrolled to practice before the Internal Revenue Service is not required to file a power of attorney in any form to receive or inspect confidential information about his or her clients' tax matters.

A. True.

B. False.

Answer (B) is correct. *(SEE, adapted)*
DISCUSSION: Any taxpayer representative must file either a power of attorney or a tax information authorization to receive or inspect confidential tax information. A representative who is recognized to practice before the IRS, such as an attorney, a CPA, or an enrolled agent, need only execute a declaration on the power of attorney that (s)he is so recognized. The declaration is in lieu of the general procedure of having two disinterested individuals witness the power of attorney [26 CFR 601.502(a)].

23.4.21. A taxpayer's representative is required to submit to the Internal Revenue Service a power of attorney properly executed by the taxpayer if the representative wishes to sign a waiver agreeing to a tax adjustment.

    A. True.

    B. False.

Answer (A) is correct. *(SEE, adapted)*
    DISCUSSION: Under 26 CFR 601.504(a)(2), a power of attorney is required for a taxpayer's representative to execute a waiver of restriction on assessment or collection of a deficiency in tax. The power of attorney must be in proper form and must be executed by the taxpayer.

23.4.22. A power of attorney is not required for a practitioner to sign a waiver of notice of disallowance of a claim for credit or a refund.

    A. True.

    B. False.

Answer (B) is correct. *(SEE, adapted)*
    DISCUSSION: A specific provision under 26 CFR 601.504(a)(2) states that a power of attorney is required for a taxpayer's representative to execute a waiver of notice of disallowance of a claim for credit or refund.

23.4.23. A taxpayer's representative is not required to submit to the Internal Revenue Service a power of attorney executed by the taxpayer if the representative wishes to execute a closing agreement under Sec. 7121 of the Internal Revenue Code.

    A. True.

    B. False.

Answer (B) is correct. *(SEE, adapted)*
    DISCUSSION: A specific provision of 26 CFR 601.504(a)(4) states that a power of attorney is required for a taxpayer's representative to execute a closing agreement under Sec. 7121.

23.4.24. A taxpayer's representative who is eligible to practice before the IRS must submit to the IRS a power of attorney (or in certain cases a proper copy) properly executed by the taxpayer if the representative wishes to extend the statutory period for assessment or collection of a tax on behalf of the taxpayer.

    A. True.

    B. False.

Answer (A) is correct. *(SEE, adapted)*
    DISCUSSION: Under 26 CFR 601.504(a)(3), a power of attorney is required for a taxpayer's representative to execute a consent to extend the statutory period for assessment or collection of a tax. The power of attorney must be in proper form and must be executed by the taxpayer.

23.4.25. A representative having a power of attorney is permitted to endorse a refund check if the taxpayer authorizes him to receive it.

    A. True.

    B. False.

Answer (B) is correct. *(SEE, adapted)*
    DISCUSSION: 26 CFR 601.504(a)(5) provides that a taxpayer's representative may receive a refund check if the taxpayer specifically authorizes this in IRS Form 2848, *Power of Attorney and Declaration of Representative*. However, the representative is not authorized to endorse and collect the refund check.

23.4.26. The right for a taxpayer's representative to receive refund checks must be specifically granted by the taxpayer in IRS Form 2848 or a general power of attorney.

    A. True.

    B. False.

Answer (A) is correct. *(SEE, adapted)*
    DISCUSSION: 26 CFR 601.504(a)(5) provides that for a taxpayer's representative to receive a refund check the taxpayer must specifically authorize this in IRS Form 2848, *Power of Attorney and Declaration of Representative*. But the representative is not authorized to endorse and collect the refund check.

23.4.27. A power of attorney is given for representation in tax matters. For acts to be performed, it lists, "in all tax matters." This is not a valid authorization.

    A. True.

    B. False.

Answer (A) is correct. *(SEE, adapted)*
    DISCUSSION: Use of technical language in the preparation of a power of attorney is not necessary, but the instrument should clearly express the taxpayer's intentions. It must clearly specify which acts the representative is authorized to perform [26 CFR 601.503(a)]. "In all tax matters" is not sufficient.

23.4.28. If a taxpayer has more than one representative in a matter and does not designate on the power of attorney which representative is to receive copies of notices and other written communication, it is the practice of the IRS to give such copies to the representative first named on the power of attorney with the latest date.

A. True.

B. False.

Answer (A) is correct. *(SEE, adapted)*
DISCUSSION: 26 CFR 601.506(a) states that if a taxpayer designates more than one representative to receive copies of notices and other written communications, the IRS will give copies of such communications to no more than two representatives so designated. It is the IRS's practice to give such copies to the representative first named on the power of attorney with the latest date unless the taxpayer lists the names of not more than two representatives to receive copies of written communications.

23.4.29. A corporate power of attorney must be signed by a witness attesting to its validity or have the corporate seal affixed in order for it to be valid.

A. True.

B. False.

Answer (B) is correct. *(SEE, adapted)*
DISCUSSION: It is not necessary that a power of attorney or a tax information authorization granted by a corporation be attested or that the corporate seal be affixed. Spaces provided on these authorization forms for affixing the corporate seal are for the convenience of the corporations required by charter or law to affix their corporate seals in the execution of instruments [26 CFR 601.503(c)(3)].

23.4.30. A single Form 2848, *Power of Attorney and Declaration of Representative*, may not cover more than one tax matter or more than 1 taxable year.

A. True.

B. False.

Answer (B) is correct. *(SEE, adapted)*
DISCUSSION: Under 26 CFR 601.503(a), a power of attorney or tax information authorization may relate to more than one matter (e.g., a taxpayer's income taxes for several different taxable years). The power of attorney must clearly express the taxpayer's intention as to the scope of the authority of the representative and must also clearly specify the tax matter(s) to which the authority relates.

23.4.31. If a power of attorney has been filed, a new power of attorney must be filed if the taxpayer changes the authority granted to a representative.

A. True.

B. False.

Answer (A) is correct. *(SEE, adapted)*
DISCUSSION: The effect of 26 CFR 601.503(a) and 505(a) is that a new power of attorney must be filed if a power of attorney has been filed and if, with respect to the same matter, the taxpayer desires to change the authority granted to a representative. Note that filing a new power of attorney does not automatically revoke a prior one under certain circumstances.

23.4.32. The filing of a Form 2848 terminates all previously filed tax information authorizations.

A. True.

B. False.

Answer (B) is correct. *(SEE, adapted)*
DISCUSSION: A new power of attorney (POA) is deemed to revoke a prior POA unless the new one contains a clause specifically stating that it does not revoke a prior POA.

23.4.33. A new power of attorney or tax information authorization is required if the taxpayer desires to add to or reduce the number of persons authorized to represent the taxpayer before the Internal Revenue Service in a tax matter.

A. True.

B. False.

Answer (A) is correct. *(SEE, adapted)*
DISCUSSION: The effect of 26 CFR 601.503(a) and 505(a) is that a new power of attorney must be filed if a power of attorney has been filed and if, with respect to the same matter, the taxpayer desires to change the authority granted to a representative, including changing the number of authorized representatives.

23.4.34. A taxpayer may revoke a power of attorney without authorizing a new representative by filing a statement of revocation with those offices of the Internal Revenue Service where the taxpayer has filed the power of attorney to be revoked.

A. True.

B. False.

Answer (A) is correct. *(SEE, adapted)*
DISCUSSION: A taxpayer may revoke a power of attorney without authorizing a new representative by filing a statement of revocation with those offices of the IRS where the taxpayer has filed the power of attorney to be revoked. The statement of revocation must indicate that the authority of the first power of attorney is revoked and must be signed by the taxpayer. Also, the name and address of each recognized representative whose authority is revoked must be listed, or a copy of the power of attorney to be revoked must be attached [26 CFR 601.505(a)(2)].

23.4.35. An Internal Revenue Service examiner cannot, under any circumstances, bypass a taxpayer's representative and contact the taxpayer directly if the representative holds a valid power of attorney from the taxpayer.

    A. True.

    B. False.

Answer (B) is correct. *(SEE, adapted)*
    DISCUSSION: Generally, an IRS examiner cannot bypass a taxpayer's representative and contact the taxpayer directly if the representative holds a valid power of attorney. However, if the representative has unreasonably delayed or hindered the examination by failing to furnish necessary nonprivileged information, an examiner may request permission from his or her immediate supervisor to contact the taxpayer directly [26 CFR 601.506(b)].

23.4.36. The purpose of a CAF number is to give IRS personnel quicker access to authorization information.

    A. True.

    B. False.

Answer (A) is correct. *(SEE, adapted)*
    DISCUSSION: The purpose of the CAF number is to facilitate the processing of a power of attorney or a tax information authorization submitted by a recognized representative or an appointee. A recognized representative or an appointee should include the same CAF number on every power of attorney or tax information authorization filed. However, because the CAF number is not a substantive requirement, a tax information authorization or power of attorney will not be rejected based on the absence of a CAF number [26 CFR 601.506(d)(2)].

23.5 Appeals within the IRS

23.5.1. With respect to preparation of a case for IRS appeals, the following statements are true except

    A. A brief written statement of the disputed issue(s) is required if the increase or decrease in tax, including penalties, or refund, determined by examination is more than $2,500 but not more than $10,000.

    B. If the proposed increase or decrease in tax, including penalties or claimed refund is more than $25,000, the taxpayer must submit a written protest of the disputed issues, including a statement of facts supporting the taxpayer's position on all disputed issues.

    C. A declaration that the statement of facts is true under penalties of perjury must be added and signed by the taxpayer.

    D. If a representative submits the protest for the taxpayer, (s)he must submit a declaration stating that (s)he submitted the protest and accompanying documents and whether (s)he knows personally that the statement of facts in the protest and accompanying documents is true and correct.

Answer (A) is correct. *(SEE, adapted)*
    REQUIRED: The false statement regarding the preparation of a case for IRS appeals.
    DISCUSSION: A formal written protest is required when the change exceeds $25,000 for any taxable period. The requirement of a brief written statement when the change exceeds $2,500 but is less than $10,000 was changed in 2000 (Publication 556, Rev. Nov. 2000).
    Answer (B) is incorrect. A formal written protest is required when the change exceeds $25,000 for any taxable period. Answer (C) is incorrect. A declaration that the statement of facts is true under penalties of perjury must be added and signed by the taxpayer when preparing a case for IRS appeals. Answer (D) is incorrect. If a representative submits the protest for the taxpayer, (s)he must submit a declaration stating that (s)he submitted the protest and accompanying documents and whether (s)he knows personally that the statement of facts in the protest and accompanying documents is true and correct.

23.5.2. In response to a preliminary (30-day) letter, a formal written protest discussing the facts and legal arguments must accompany a written request for an Appeals Conference in which of the following cases?

    A. A $2,000 tax increase was proposed.

    B. The tax return examination was made in an IRS office by a tax auditor.

    C. The tax return examination was made by correspondence.

    D. A disallowance of a $26,000 refund claim was proposed.

Answer (D) is correct. *(SEE, adapted)*
    REQUIRED: The situation that requires a formal written protest in a request for an Appeals Conference.
    DISCUSSION: A formal written protest is required when the appeal involves an amount greater than $25,000 (Publication 556). The statement must be filed within the 30-day period granted in the letter transmitting the report of examination.
    Answer (A) is incorrect. A small case request may be filed for changes not in excess of $25,000. Answer (B) is incorrect. An oral request is sufficient for examinations conducted in an IRS office by a tax auditor. Answer (C) is incorrect. An oral request is sufficient for examinations made by correspondence.

23.5.3. All of the following should be contained in a written protest letter except

A. A statement that the taxpayer wants to appeal the findings of the examiner to the appeals office.

B. The date and symbols from the letter showing the proposed adjustments and findings being protested.

C. Tax periods or years involved.

D. A statement indicating whether the examination was originally handled through correspondence, by a tax auditor, or by an IRS agent.

Answer (D) is correct. *(SEE, adapted)*
REQUIRED: The item that is not required in a written protest.
DISCUSSION: Publication 5, *Appeal Rights and Preparation of Protests for Unagreed Cases*, provides that a written protest should contain a statement that the taxpayer wants to appeal the findings of the examining officer, the date and symbols from the letter transmitting the proposed adjustments and findings protested, the taxpayer's name and address, the tax periods or years involved, an itemized schedule of the adjustments with which the taxpayer does not agree, a statement of facts supporting the taxpayer's position on any contested factual issue, and a statement outlining the law or authority relied upon. A statement indicating whether the examination was originally handled through correspondence, by a tax auditor, or by an IRS agent is not required.
Answer (A) is incorrect. A statement that the taxpayer wants to appeal the findings of the examiner to the appeals office should be contained in a written protest letter. Answer (B) is incorrect. The date and symbols from the letter showing the proposed adjustments and findings being protested should be contained in a written protest letter. Answer (C) is incorrect. The tax periods or years involved should be contained in a written protest letter.

23.5.4. Mr. K, who lives in Dallas, Texas, received a letter from the IRS stating that the result of a recent field examination is a tax deficiency of $15,000. The examination was handled by a revenue agent at Mr. K's place of business. The letter also states that Mr. K has a right to file a protest if he does not agree with the proposal. Generally, how many days does K have to file a small case request?

A. 15 days.

B. 30 days.

C. 60 days.

D. 90 days.

Answer (B) is correct. *(SEE, adapted)*
REQUIRED: The number of days granted to file a small case request.
DISCUSSION: A small case request must be filed within the 30-day period granted in the letter transmitting the report of examination. A small case request may be filed if the change is not more than $25,000 (Publication 556). A formal written protest is required when the change exceeds $25,000 for any taxable period.
Answer (A) is incorrect. Mr. K does not have 15 days to file a small case request since the change is the result of a field examination in which the tax deficiency does not exceed $25,000. Answer (C) is incorrect. Mr. K does not have 60 days to file a small case request since the change is the result of a field examination in which the tax deficiency does not exceed $25,000. Answer (D) is incorrect. Mr. K does not have 90 days to file a small case request since the change is the result of a field examination in which the tax deficiency does not exceed $25,000.

23.5.5. Gina disagreed with the results of an IRS examination of her tax return. She pursued the appeals procedures and disagreed with the appeals officer. If she wishes to appeal further, Gina may

A. Request a conference with a new appeals officer in a different district.

B. Wait for a notice of deficiency, not pay the tax, and petition the district court.

C. Wait for a notice of deficiency, not pay the tax, and petition the Tax Court.

D. Submit a revised written protest that outlines the issues and authority for the position taken.

Answer (C) is correct. *(SEE, adapted)*
REQUIRED: The true statement regarding an appeal of an IRS examination.
DISCUSSION: If there is no resolution of the tax dispute in appeals, the IRS will issue a 90-day letter (notice of deficiency) to the taxpayer. Within 90 days of receipt of the notice, the taxpayer may file a petition with the Tax Court.
Answer (A) is incorrect. Gina may not request a conference with a new appeals officer in a different district. Answer (B) is incorrect. Gina may not wait for a notice of deficiency, not pay the tax, and petition the district court. Answer (D) is incorrect. Gina may not submit a revised written protest that outlines the issues and authority for the position taken.

23.5.6. Only one level of appeal exists within the Internal Revenue Service. All appeals are made to the appeals office.

A. True.

B. False.

Answer (A) is correct. *(SEE, adapted)*
DISCUSSION: Other than a conference with the examining agent's supervisor, there is only one level of appeal within the IRS. All appeals are made to the appeals office in the taxpayer's region [26 CFR 601.105(c), (d) and 601.106].

23.5.7. Mr. V's income tax return was examined by an IRS tax auditor in an IRS office. The tax auditor proposed an additional tax liability of $12,000. Mr. V does not agree with the auditor's findings and wishes to schedule a conference with an IRS regional appeals office. V must file a formal written protest of the auditor's findings to obtain an appeals conference.

A. True.

B. False.

Answer (B) is correct. *(SEE, adapted)*
DISCUSSION: Under 26 CFR 601.105(d) and 601.106(a)(1)(iii), a formal written protest is required in a field examination case when the total amount of proposed change exceeds $25,000. If the examination was conducted by an IRS tax auditor in an IRS office, a written protest is not required regardless of the amount of proposed adjustment.

23.6 Deficiencies and Assessments

23.6.1. With regard to the statute of limitations, all of the following statements apply to requests to extend the statute. All of the statements are true except

A. If tax has been assessed within the 3-year limitation period, the IRS generally has 10 years following the assessment to begin a proceeding to collect the tax by levy or in a court proceeding.

B. Form 872-A, *Special Consent to Extend Time to Assess Tax*, extends the assessment period indefinitely.

C. The 10-year collection period may not be extended after it has expired, even if there has been a levy on any part of the taxpayer's property prior to the expiration and the extension is agreed to in writing before the levy is released.

D. Each time an extension is requested, the IRS must notify the taxpayer that the taxpayer may refuse to extend the period of limitations or may limit the extension to particular issues or to a particular period of time.

Answer (C) is correct. *(SEE, adapted)*
REQUIRED: The false statement regarding the statute of limitations.
DISCUSSION: The period of limitations on collection after assessment of any tax may be extended after the expiration thereof if there has been a levy on part of the taxpayer's property prior to such expiration and if the extension is agreed upon in writing prior to a release of the levy [Reg. 301.6502-1(a)(ii)].
Answer (A) is incorrect. It is a true statement with regard to the statute of limitations. Answer (B) is incorrect. Form 872-A indefinitely extends the time within which a tax may be assessed. Answer (D) is incorrect. The IRS is required to notify the taxpayer that (s)he may refuse to extend the statute of limitations.

23.6.2. Which of the following is usually required before taxes may be assessed?

A. A notice of deficiency must be issued.

B. The taxpayer must file a return.

C. A waiver of restrictions on assessment must be filed.

D. It must be 3 years after the return was filed.

Answer (A) is correct. *(Publisher, adapted)*
REQUIRED: The action that is usually required before taxes may be assessed.
DISCUSSION: The assessment of taxes is made by recording the liability of the taxpayer in the office of the Secretary of the Treasury (Sec. 6203). Taxes shown on a return filed by a taxpayer, overstatements of credits, and mathematical errors may be assessed immediately (Sec. 6201). However, in the case of a deficiency (the tax imposed in excess of the sum of the amount shown on the return plus amounts previously assessed), a notice of deficiency must be sent to the taxpayer prior to assessment [Sec. 6213(a)]. The taxpayer has 90 days after the notice of deficiency is mailed to file a petition in Tax Court (which prevents the assessment of taxes until the decision of the Tax Court is final). If a petition is not filed, taxes may be assessed 90 days after the notice of deficiency is mailed.
Answer (B) is incorrect. If the taxpayer does not file a return, the IRS may file a return for him or her, and an assessment may be made for any deficiency after the required procedures are followed. Answer (C) is incorrect. Although a waiver of restrictions on assessment will allow the taxes to be assessed immediately, they may also be assessed 90 days after a deficiency notice is mailed. Answer (D) is incorrect. An assessment of tax must generally be made within (not after) 3 years after the return was filed [Sec. 6501(a)]. The IRS has longer to assess if there is a substantial omission of gross income (in excess of 25%) or a willful attempt to evade tax.

23.6.3. Which of the following is not a situation in which taxes may be assessed without the issuance of a statutory notice of deficiency?

    A. Overstatement of a credit on a return.

    B. Mathematical error on a return.

    C. There is a waiver of restrictions on assessment.

    D. The taxpayer has not filed a return.

Answer (D) is correct. *(Publisher, adapted)*
    REQUIRED: The situation that does not allow taxes to be assessed without issuance of a notice of deficiency.
    DISCUSSION: There are several exceptions to the requirement that a notice of deficiency be mailed to the taxpayer (and 90 days elapse) before taxes may be assessed. However, the failure of a taxpayer to file a return does not allow the immediate assessment of taxes. A deficiency must be determined and a statutory notice of deficiency must be mailed.
    Answer (A) is incorrect. Section 6201(a)(3) provides that an overstatement of credits may be assessed without restriction. Answer (B) is incorrect. Section 6213(b) allows the assessment without restriction of additional amounts of tax owing because of mathematical or clerical errors in a return. Answer (C) is incorrect. A waiver of restrictions on assessment is formal permission by the taxpayer to the IRS to assess taxes without mailing a notice of deficiency [Sec. 6213(d)].

23.6.4. Ronald Raff filed his Year 1 individual income tax return on January 15, Year 2. There was no understatement of income on the return, and the return was properly signed and filed. The statute of limitations for Raff's Year 1 return expires (assuming no relevant day is a Saturday, Sunday, or holiday) on

    A. January 15, Year 5.

    B. April 15, Year 5.

    C. January 15, Year 8.

    D. April 15, Year 8.

Answer (B) is correct. *(CPA, adapted)*
    REQUIRED: The statute of limitations for a properly filed return.
    DISCUSSION: Under Sec. 6501(a), the general statute of limitations for assessment of a deficiency is 3 years from the date the return was filed. Under Sec. 6501(b), an income tax return filed before the due date for the return is considered to be filed on the due date for statute of limitations purposes. Since Raff's return was due April 15, Year 2, the statute of limitations will expire 3 years from that date.
    Answer (A) is incorrect. An income tax return filed before the due date is considered to be filed on the due date. Answer (C) is incorrect. The statute of limitations does not expire 6 years after the filing date, and not before the return's due date. Answer (D) is incorrect. The statute of limitations does not expire 6 years after the due date.

23.6.5. All of the following statements with regard to interest and penalties on agreed cases are true except

    A. Jan agreed to the proposed changes. She signed the agreement form and paid the additional tax. Jan will pay interest on the additional tax. Interest is figured from the due date of the return to the date she paid the additional tax.

    B. Joseph agreed to the proposed changes. He signed the agreement form, but he did not pay the additional tax. Joseph received a bill that included the interest. He paid the bill of $5,500 11 days after the billing date. He will not have to pay more interest or penalties.

    C. Jody agreed to the proposed changes. She signed the agreement form, but she did not pay the additional tax of $2,700. On June 5, Year 1, Jody received a bill dated June 2, Year 1, that included the interest. She paid the bill on June 21, Year 1. Jody will owe additional interest.

    D. Jane agreed to the proposed changes. She signed the agreement form on May 18, Year 1, but she did not pay the bill until October 3, Year 1. Jane will owe additional interest.

Answer (C) is correct. *(SEE, adapted)*
    REQUIRED: The false statement regarding interest and penalties on agreed cases.
    DISCUSSION: If the taxpayer does not pay the additional tax when (s)he signs the agreement, (s)he will receive a bill that includes interest. If the taxpayer pays the amount due within 10 business days of the billing date, (s)he will not have to pay more interest or penalties. This period is extended to 21 calendar days if the amount due is less than $100,000 (Publication 556, p. 4). Jody paid the bill within 21 days of the date of notice and demand and thus will owe no additional interest.
    Answer (A) is incorrect. Interest is charged from the due date of the tax return until the date the tax is paid. Answer (B) is incorrect. It is a true statement. If the taxpayer pays the total amount due within 21 days of the billing date, (s)he will not be billed for additional interest. If the taxpayer pays the amount due within 10 business days of the billing date, (s)he will not have to pay more interest or penalties. This period is extended to 21 calendar days if the amount due is less than $100,000 (Publication 556, p. 4). Answer (D) is incorrect. It is a true case. If the taxpayer does not pay the additional tax when (s)he signs the agreement, (s)he will receive a bill that includes interest. If the taxpayer pays the amount due within 10 business days of the billing date, (s)he will not have to pay more interest or penalties. This period is extended to 21 calendar days if the amount due is less than $100,000 (Publication 556, p. 4).

23.6.6. Harold Thompson, a self-employed individual, had income transactions for Year 1 (duly reported on his return filed in April Year 2) as follows:

Gross receipts	$400,000
Less cost of goods sold and deductions	(320,000)
Net business income	$ 80,000
Capital gains	36,000
Gross income	$116,000

In March Year 5, Thompson discovers that he inadvertently omitted some income on his Year 1 return. He retains Mann, CPA, to determine his position under the statute of limitations. Mann should advise Thompson that the 6-year statute of limitations would apply to his Year 1 return only if he omitted from gross income an amount in excess of

A. $20,000

B. $29,000

C. $100,000

D. $109,000

Answer (D) is correct. *(CPA, adapted)*
REQUIRED: The amount of gross income omission that would trigger the 6-year statute of limitations.
DISCUSSION: The normal statute of limitations is 3 years after the later of the due date of the return or the date the return was filed. A 6-year statute of limitations applies if gross income omitted from the return exceeds 25% of gross income reported on the return [Sec. 6501(e)(1)]. For a trade or business, gross income means the total of the amounts received from the sale of goods before deductions and cost of goods sold. The 6-year statute of limitations will apply if Thompson omitted from gross income an amount in excess of $109,000 [($400,000 + $36,000) × 25%].
Answer (A) is incorrect. The amount of $20,000 is 25% of the gross receipts less cost of goods sold and deductions. Answer (B) is incorrect. The amount of $29,000 is 25% of gross income. Answer (C) is incorrect. The amount of $100,000 is 25% of reported gross income without adding in capital gains.

23.6.7. Mr. Smith's Year 1 income tax return, which he filed on May 3, Year 2, was examined by the IRS. Smith did not have an extension of time to file. On October 20, Year 3, he signed a report agreeing to a deficiency of $10,000. He received a notice and demand showing additional tax, interest, and penalties. The notice was dated November 7, Year 3. If Mr. Smith paid the bill on November 12, Year 3, which of the following reflects the date interest starts accruing and the date it stops?

A. April 16, Year 2; November 7, Year 3.

B. April 16, Year 2; November 12, Year 3.

C. May 3, Year 2; November 7, Year 3.

D. October 20, Year 3; November 12, Year 3.

Answer (A) is correct. *(SEE, adapted)*
REQUIRED: The date interest on a deficiency starts accruing and the date it stops.
DISCUSSION: Under Sec. 6601(a), interest on any underpayment of tax begins to accrue on the date prescribed for payment, which is generally the due date of the return computed without regard to extensions. The interest generally continues to accrue until the date the tax is paid. However, Sec. 6601(c) provides that if a taxpayer files an agreement waiving the restrictions on assessment of deficiency, and notice and demand for payment are not made within 30 days after filing such waiver, interest will be suspended 30 days after signing of the waiver.
Once the demand for payment is made, interest does not accrue after the date of demand if the tax is paid within 21 days after the date of such demand [Sec. 6601(e)(3)].
Mr. Smith will be billed for interest from April 16, Year 2, through November 7, Year 3. The interest charge stops on the date the notice and demand for payment was made since such document was issued within 30 days of Smith's agreeing to the deficiency and payment was made within 21 days of the notice and demand. The interest rate charged for underpayments of tax by individuals is the short-term federal rate plus three percentage points (Sec. 6621).
Answer (B) is incorrect. November 12, Year 3, is not the correct date the interest stops accruing. Answer (C) is incorrect. May 3, Year 2, is not the correct date the interest starts accruing. Answer (D) is incorrect. October 20, Year 3, and November 12, Year 3, are not the correct dates the interest begins to accrue.

23.6.8. What is the statute of limitations on a return that was required to be filed but was never filed?

A. Indefinite.

B. 3 years.

C. 6 years.

D. 7 years.

Answer (A) is correct. *(M. Yates)*
REQUIRED: The statute of limitations on a return that was never filed.
DISCUSSION: When a return is not filed, the statute of limitations time period never begins and therefore never ends [Sec. 6501(c)(3)].
Answer (B) is incorrect. The correct statute of limitations on a return that was required to be filed but was never filed is not 3 years. Answer (C) is incorrect. The correct statute of limitations on a return that was required to be filed but was never filed is not 6 years. Answer (D) is incorrect. The correct statute of limitations on a return that was required to be filed but was never filed is not 7 years.

23.6.9. All of the following statements relating to the statutory notice of deficiency are true except

   A. If a taxpayer receives a notice of deficiency and sends money to the IRS without written instructions, the IRS will treat it as a payment and the taxpayer will not be able to petition the Tax Court.

   B. A notice of deficiency is not an assessment.

   C. If the taxpayer consents, the IRS can withdraw any notice of deficiency. However, after the notice is withdrawn, the taxpayer cannot file a petition with the Tax Court based on the withdrawn notice and the IRS may later issue a notice of deficiency greater or less than the amount in the withdrawn deficiency.

   D. The notice of deficiency provides the taxpayer 90 days (150 days if the taxpayer lives outside the United States) to either agree to the deficiency or file a petition with the Tax Court for a redetermination of the deficiency.

Answer (A) is correct. *(SEE, adapted)*
   REQUIRED: The false statement about the notice of deficiency.
   DISCUSSION: Normally, once a taxpayer pays the tax, the Tax Court does not have jurisdiction and the taxpayer must file a claim for a refund in U.S. District Court or the U.S. Court of Federal Claims. However, Sec. 6213(b)(4) provides that payment of additional tax due after the mailing of a notice of deficiency does not deprive the Tax Court of jurisdiction over the deficiency.
   Section 6213(a) provides that a taxpayer may file a petition with the Tax Court for a redetermination of the deficiency within 90 days (or 150 if the taxpayer lives outside the U.S.) after the notice of deficiency is mailed. If 90 days (or 150) pass and a petition is not filed, taxes may be assessed and the taxpayer must pay the tax and file a claim for refund.
   Answer (B) is incorrect. A notice of deficiency is not an assessment. Answer (C) is incorrect. If the taxpayer consents, the IRS can withdraw any notice of deficiency. However, after the notice is withdrawn, the taxpayer cannot file a petition with the Tax Court based on the withdrawn notice, and the IRS may later issue a notice of deficiency greater or less than the amount in the withdrawn deficiency. Answer (D) is incorrect. The notice of deficiency provides the taxpayer 90 days (150 days if the taxpayer lives outside the United States) either to agree to the deficiency or file a petition with the Tax Court for a redetermination of the deficiency.

23.6.10. Mr. P's current-year individual income tax return was examined, which resulted in a deficiency of $5,000. P signed an agreement form and paid the additional tax. The interest due from P will be figured from the due date of the return to the date of payment.

   A. True.

   B. False.

Answer (A) is correct. *(SEE, adapted)*
   DISCUSSION: Under Sec. 6601(a), interest on any underpayment of tax begins to accrue on the date prescribed for payment, which is generally the due date of the return computed without regard to extensions. The interest continues to accrue until the date the tax is paid, except in those cases where the taxpayer signs an agreement form without paying the tax and then pays the tax within 21 days of the date of the Notice and Demand for Tax. Since Mr. P paid the additional tax when he signed the agreement form, the interest will be figured from the due date of the return to the date of payment.

23.6.11. Mr. M was audited for the current year and agreed to the findings of the Internal Revenue Service examiner that he owed an additional $5,000. Mr. M did not pay the deficiency when he signed the agreement form. If Mr. M does not pay the amount due within 21 days of the billing date, he could be assessed more interest and/or penalties.

   A. True.

   B. False.

Answer (A) is correct. *(SEE, adapted)*
   DISCUSSION: Under Sec. 6601(a), interest on an underpayment of tax is figured from the date payment of the tax was due (generally, the due date of the return computed without regard to extensions) to the date the tax is paid. In cases in which a taxpayer agrees that additional tax is owed but does not pay the tax when the agreement form is signed, the taxpayer receives a Notice and Demand for Tax. Section 6601(e)(3) states that, if the additional tax is paid within 21 days of such notice, interest will cease to accrue as of the date of the notice rather than on the date of payment. However, if the additional tax is not paid within the 21-day period, Sec. 6601(e)(2) states that the general rule of Sec. 6601(a) takes effect and the interest will continue to accrue until the tax is paid.

23.6.12. The effect of a request for prompt assessment by a corporation in the process of dissolution is to limit the time in which an assessment of tax may be made or a proceeding in court without assessment for collection of tax may be begun. The assessment must be made or the proceeding started within 12 months from the date the request is filed.

   A. True.

   B. False.

Answer (B) is correct. *(SEE, adapted)*
   DISCUSSION: Under Sec. 6501(d), when a request for prompt assessment is made, the tax for which a corporation contemplating dissolution, a corporation in the process of dissolution, or a corporation that has undergone dissolution may be liable must be assessed (or the proceeding started) within 18 months from the date the request is filed.

23.7 IRS Collection Procedures

23.7.1. The collection process begins

A. At the IRS service center, where notices are generated requesting payment.

B. In an IRS Automated Collection Branch when a telephone contact is made with the taxpayer.

C. Only after the Problem Resolution Officer has acted upon the taxpayer's claim.

D. When a notice of federal tax lien is filed.

Answer (A) is correct. *(SEE, adapted)*
REQUIRED: The true statement concerning the IRS collection process.
DISCUSSION: Section 6301 authorizes the Internal Revenue Service, on behalf of the Secretary of the Treasury, to collect taxes imposed by the internal revenue laws. The collection process begins at the IRS service center, where notices are generated requesting payment. Regulation 301.6303-1 states that the district director or the director of the regional service center shall, after the making of a tax assessment, give notice to the person liable for the unpaid tax, stating the amount of the tax and demanding payment.
Answer (B) is incorrect. The collection process does not begin in an IRS Automated Collection Branch when a telephone contact is made with the taxpayer. Answer (C) is incorrect. The collection process does not begin only after the Problem Resolution Officer has acted upon the taxpayer's claim. Answer (D) is incorrect. The collection process does not begin when a notice of federal tax lien is filed.

23.7.2. The initial action required in the collection process is

A. The filing of a Notice of Levy.

B. An assessment.

C. The receipt of the fourth notice by certified mail.

D. A notification of a pending examination audit.

Answer (B) is correct. *(SEE, adapted)*
REQUIRED: The initial action required in the collection process.
DISCUSSION: Section 6201(a) authorizes the Internal Revenue Service to make a determination of all taxes. If the IRS makes a determination that a tax liability exists, the IRS has the authority under Sec. 6201(a) to assess the tax. The assessment of the taxes is the initial action required in the collection process.
Answer (A) is incorrect. The initial action required in the collection process is not the filing of a Notice of Levy. Answer (C) is incorrect. The initial action required in the collection process is not the receipt of the fourth notice by certified mail. Answer (D) is incorrect. A notification of a pending examination is part of the examination process, not the collection process.

23.7.3. During the period of an installment agreement,

A. All payments must be made timely, and interest and penalties continue to accrue.

B. Timely payments suspend the accrual of interest and penalties.

C. Payments can only be made by certified check.

D. A release of Notice of Federal Tax Lien is automatically filed.

Answer (A) is correct. *(SEE, adapted)*
REQUIRED: The true statement concerning an installment agreement.
DISCUSSION: Under Sec. 6159, the IRS is authorized to enter into written agreements with a taxpayer for the payment of a tax liability in installments. Once an installment agreement is made, the taxpayer must make each payment on time. Interest and penalties will continue to accrue. Failure to pay an installment can result in the termination of the agreement.
Answer (B) is incorrect. Timely payments during the period of an installment agreement do not suspend the accrual of interest and penalties. Answer (C) is incorrect. During the period of an installment agreement, payments do not have to be made only by certified check. Answer (D) is incorrect. During the period of an installment agreement, a release of Notice of Federal Tax Lien is filed upon taxpayer request.

23.7.4. All of the following statements with respect to a continuous levy are true except

A. A levy does not apply to property acquired by a taxpayer after the date of levy.

B. A levy applies to all property acquired prior to the date of levy.

C. A levy does not apply to wages and salaries received after the date of levy.

D. A levy of up to 15% may apply to all specified payments received after the date of levy.

Answer (C) is correct. *(Publisher, adapted)*
REQUIRED: The false statement with respect to a continuous levy.
DISCUSSION: A levy generally does not apply to property acquired after the date of levy. However, there is an exception for salaries and wages.
Answer (A) is incorrect. A levy does not apply to property acquired by a taxpayer after the date of levy. Answer (B) is incorrect. A levy applies to all property acquired prior to the date of levy. Answer (D) is incorrect. A levy of up to 15% may apply to all specified payments received after the date of levy.

23.7.5. Which of the following statements is false with respect to taxpayers' offers in compromise on unpaid tax liabilities?

- A. A compromise may be made only where there is doubt as to the liability for the amount owed.
- B. The Commissioner of Internal Revenue has the authority to compromise all taxes (including any interest, penalty, additional amount, or addition to the tax) arising under the revenue laws of the United States, except those relating to alcohol, tobacco, and firearms.
- C. Submission of an offer in compromise will usually extend the statute of limitations on collection of an account.
- D. Taxpayers have a right by law to submit an offer in compromise on their unpaid tax liability.

Answer (A) is correct. *(SEE, adapted)*
REQUIRED: The false statement regarding an offer in compromise.
DISCUSSION: Under Sec. 7122, the Commissioner of the Internal Revenue Service has the authority to compromise all taxes, interest, and penalties arising under the internal revenue laws, except those relating to alcohol, tobacco, and firearms. A compromise may be made on one or both of two grounds: (1) doubt as to the liability for the amount owed or (2) doubt as to the taxpayer's ability to make full payment [Reg. 301.7122-1(a)]. The doubt as to the liability for the amount owed must be supported by the evidence. In the case of inability to pay, the amount offered must exceed the total value of the taxpayer's equity in all his or her assets and must give sufficient consideration to present and future earning capacity. A compromise may be entered into by the IRS, whether a suit has been instituted or not, and may be entered into after a judgment has been rendered.
Answer (B) is incorrect. The Commissioner of Internal Revenue has the authority to compromise all taxes (including any interest, penalty, additional amount, or addition to the tax) arising under the revenue laws of the United States, except those relating to alcohol, tobacco, and firearms. Answer (C) is incorrect. During submission of an offer in compromise will usually extend the statute of limitations on collection of an account. Answer (D) is incorrect. Taxpayers have a right by law to submit an offer in compromise on their unpaid tax liability.

23.7.6. Which of the following is not a legal requirement that must be met before levy action can be taken?

- A. The taxpayer must have been audited by the IRS.
- B. An unpaid tax liability must exist.
- C. A notice and demand for payment must have been sent to the taxpayer's last known address.
- D. A Final Notice (Notice of Intent to Levy) must be given to the taxpayer at least 30 days in advance.

Answer (A) is correct. *(Publisher, adapted)*
REQUIRED: The event that is not a legal requirement that must be met before levy action can be taken.
DISCUSSION: Section 6331 authorizes the Internal Revenue Service to collect unpaid taxes by levying upon the taxpayer's property. Before levy action can be taken, it must first be determined that a tax liability exists. Within 60 days after making the assessment, the IRS is required to give a notice and demand for payment to the taxpayer. This notice must be left at the taxpayer's dwelling or usual place of business, or sent by mail to the taxpayer's last known address [Sec. 6303(a)]. If the taxpayer neglects or refuses to pay the tax within 10 days after notice and demand, a Final Notice (Notice of Intent to Levy) must be given to the taxpayer at least 30 days in advance [Sec. 6331(d)]. There is no requirement that a taxpayer first be audited.
Answer (B) is incorrect. An unpaid tax liability must exist before levy action can be taken. Answer (C) is incorrect. A notice and demand for payment must have been sent to the taxpayer's last known address before levy action can be taken. Answer (D) is incorrect. A Final Notice (Notice of Intent to Levy) must be given to the taxpayer at least 30 days in advance before levy action can be taken.

23.7.7. If the IRS seizes property that is not perishable, the IRS will

- A. Request sealed bids for the property.
- B. Advertise the sale for 90 days before the sale.
- C. Conduct the sale after the property has been held 60 days.
- D. Wait at least 10 days after seizure before conducting the sale.

Answer (D) is correct. *(SEE, adapted)*
REQUIRED: The time period for the sale of nonperishable seized property.
DISCUSSION: After seizure of property, the IRS gives notice of sale to the public and to the taxpayer from whom the property was seized. Under Sec. 6335(d), the time of sale must be not less than 10 days nor more than 40 days from the time of giving public notice. Section 6336 provides an exception to this rule in the case of perishable goods, which must be returned to the taxpayer if he pays the appraised value of the goods or posts a bond. If the taxpayer does not pay such amount or post a bond, the goods must be sold immediately.
Answer (A) is incorrect. The property may be sold by public auction as well as by public sale under sealed bids. Answer (B) is incorrect. The IRS may sell the property after 10 days of giving public notice. Answer (C) is incorrect. The sale must be conducted not more than 40 days from the time of giving public notice.

23.7.8. With regard to seizure of property in satisfaction of a tax liability, all of the following are true except

    A. Any real property used as a residence by the taxpayer may not be seized to satisfy a levy of $5,000 or less.

    B. The taxpayer's principal residence may not be seized without the written approval of a U.S. District Court judge or magistrate.

    C. Before the sale of property, the IRS will compute a minimum bid price. If the minimum is not offered at the sale, the IRS may buy the property.

    D. If the proceeds of a sale by the IRS are less than the total of the tax bill and the expenses of the levy and sale, the taxpayer will not have to pay the balance.

Answer (D) is correct. *(SEE, adapted)*
    REQUIRED: The false statement regarding the seizure of property in satisfaction of a tax liability.
    DISCUSSION: A levy is one method the IRS uses to collect tax that has not been paid voluntarily. A levy is the seizure of property in order to satisfy a tax debt. A levy cannot be made on a principal residence unless approval has been granted by a judge or magistrate of a district court. If the proceeds from the sale of the property seized are less than the total tax bill, the taxpayer is required to pay the balance.
    Answer (A) is incorrect. According to Code Sec. 6334(a)(13)(B), if the amount of a levy does not exceed $5,000, any real property used by a taxpayer as a residence is exempt from levy. Answer (B) is incorrect. A principal residence is exempt from levy unless a judge or magistrate of a federal district court approves the levy in writing [Sec. 6334(e)(1)(A)]. Answer (C) is incorrect. The government may, prior to the commencement of the selling process, decide to buy the property if the minimum bid price is not met or exceeded.

23.7.9. All of the following statements with respect to resolving tax problems involving the collection process are true except

    A. You may be entitled to a reimbursement for fees charged by your bank if the IRS has erroneously levied your account.

    B. You should first request assistance from IRS collection employees or their managers before seeking assistance from the Problem Resolution Officer.

    C. If you suffer a significant hardship because of the collection of the tax liability, you may request assistance from the IRS on Form 911, *Request for Taxpayer Advocate Service Assistance*.

    D. IRS collection division managers have the authority to issue a Taxpayer Assistance Order if a taxpayer is about to suffer a significant hardship because of the collection of the tax liability.

Answer (D) is correct. *(Publisher, adapted)*
    REQUIRED: The false statement about resolving tax problems involving the collection process.
    DISCUSSION: Under Sec. 7811(a), a Taxpayer Assistance Order (TAO) may be issued by the Office of the Ombudsman. A TAO may, among other things, order cessation of collection activity. Under Commissioner Delegation Order No. 232, Rev. No. 2 (dated 1/9/96), authority to issue and/or modify Taxpayer Assistance Orders is delegated to the Commissioner, Deputy Commissioner, or Taxpayer Ombudsman. No longer can Problem Resolution Officers modify TAOs. [The Taxpayer Ombudsman has been replaced by the Officer of Taxpayer Advocate in the Taxpayer Bill of Rights 2 (1996).] The order will be issued only if the Problem Resolution Officer determines that the taxpayer is suffering or is about to suffer a significant hardship as a result of the manner in which the internal revenue laws are being administered.
    Answer (A) is incorrect. A taxpayer has the right under the Taxpayer Bill of Rights to sue for actual economic damages if the IRS improperly maintains a lien (Sec. 7432). Answer (B) is incorrect. The IRS cautions that a taxpayer should apply for a TAO only if the problem persists after (s)he has requested assistance from IRS collection employees or their managers. Answer (C) is incorrect. A taxpayer applies for relief by filing Form 911, *Request for Taxpayer Advocate Service Assistance*.

23.7.10. All of the following statements with respect to a levy are true except

    A. A levy can be made on property in the hands of third parties or in the taxpayer's possession.

    B. Generally, court authorization is not required before levy action is taken.

    C. A Final Notice of Intent to Levy is not enforceable unless this notice is given to the taxpayer in person.

    D. The IRS must release a levy if the fair market value of the property exceeds the levy and its release would not hinder the collection of tax.

Answer (C) is correct. *(SEE, adapted)*
    REQUIRED: The false statement with respect to a levy.
    DISCUSSION: Section 6331 authorizes the IRS to collect unpaid taxes by levying upon the taxpayer's property. A tax liability must be assessed. Within 60 days after making the assessment, the IRS is required to give a notice and demand for payment to the taxpayer. This notice must be left at the taxpayer's dwelling or usual place of business or sent by mail to the taxpayer's last known address [Sec. 6303(a)]. If the taxpayer neglects or refuses to pay the tax within 10 days after notice and demand, a Final Notice (Notice of Intent to Levy) must be provided to the taxpayer at least 30 days in advance [Sec. 6331(d)]. This notice must be given in person, left at the taxpayer's dwelling or usual place of business, or sent by certified or registered mail to the taxpayer's last known address.
    Answer (A) is incorrect. The levy extends to all nonexempt property and rights to property belonging to the taxpayer. Answer (B) is incorrect. The courts have held that the IRS may levy upon a taxpayer's property without even a court hearing. Answer (D) is incorrect. Section 6343(a) directs the IRS to release a levy if the fair market value of the property exceeds the liability and release of the levy would not hinder collection of the tax.

23.7.11. Jeopardy levies may occur when the IRS waives the 10-day notice and demand period and/or Final Notice (Notice of Intent to Levy) 30-day period because

A. The taxpayer has filed for bankruptcy protection.

B. The seized property is perishable in nature.

C. The IRS is working in conjunction with the Drug Enforcement Administration.

D. A delay would endanger the collection of tax.

Answer (D) is correct. *(SEE, adapted)*
REQUIRED: The reason jeopardy levies may occur.
DISCUSSION: Under Sec. 6331(a), a taxpayer has 10 days to pay the tax after receiving a Notice and Demand for Tax. If the taxpayer neglects or refuses to pay the tax within that time, the IRS may issue a Final Notice (Notice of Intent to Levy) giving the taxpayer 30 days to pay the tax. If the tax is not paid within that period, the IRS may proceed to collect the tax by levy upon the taxpayer's property. If the IRS makes a finding that the assessment or collection of the tax deficiency is in jeopardy, the IRS may waive the 10-day Notice and Demand period and/or the Final Notice (Notice of Intent to Levy) 30-day period. Jeopardy levies may occur when delay would endanger collection of the tax, interest, penalties, etc. (Sec. 6861).
Answer (A) is incorrect. The taxpayer filing for bankruptcy protection is not a reason for jeopardy levies. Answer (B) is incorrect. Seizing property that is perishable in nature is not a reason for jeopardy levies. Answer (C) is incorrect. The IRS working in conjunction with the Drug Enforcement Administration is not a reason for jeopardy levies.

23.7.12. Once a Notice of Federal Tax Lien has been filed, all of the following are true except

A. The lien applies to all of the taxpayer's real and personal property and to all of his or her rights to property until the tax is paid or the lien is removed.

B. The IRS will issue a release of the notice of federal tax lien within 15 business days after the taxpayer satisfies the tax due (including interest and other additions) by paying the debt; by having it adjusted; or, if the IRS accepts a bond that the taxpayer submits, by guaranteeing a payment of the debt.

C. By law, a filed notice of tax lien can be withdrawn if withdrawal will speed collecting the tax.

D. The law requires the IRS to notify the taxpayer in writing within 5 business days after the filing of a lien.

Answer (B) is correct. *(SEE, adapted)*
REQUIRED: The situation that is false once a notice of federal tax lien has been filed.
DISCUSSION: The IRS may issue a Release of the Notice of Federal Tax Lien immediately after the tax due is satisfied if requested by the taxpayer. The tax due also includes all fees charged by the state or other jurisdiction for both filing and releasing the lien. The fees are added to the balance owed.
Answer (A) is incorrect. A federal tax lien attaches to all property and rights to property, whether real or personal, belonging to the taxpayer at the time the lien arises as well as to property subsequently acquired during the period of the lien. The lien can be removed before the payment of the tax. Sec. 6323(j) lists several items where the lien is removed before the payment of the tax. Answer (C) is incorrect. A filed notice of tax lien can be withdrawn if withdrawal will speed collection. Answer (D) is incorrect. The IRS must notify the taxpayer in writing within 5 business days after the filing of a lien.

23.7.13. Which of the following statements is false with respect to a Notice of Federal Tax Lien?

A. It is a public notice to the taxpayer's creditors that the government has a claim against all of the taxpayer's real, personal, and/or business property, including property acquired after the lien came into existence.

B. All fees charged by the state or other jurisdiction for both filing and releasing the lien will be added to the balance the taxpayer owes.

C. The IRS may issue a Release of the Notice of Federal Tax Lien immediately after acceptance of a bond guaranteeing payment of the liability if requested by the taxpayer.

D. A taxpayer cannot sue the federal government for damages if the IRS knowingly or negligently fails to release a Notice of Federal Tax Lien when a release is warranted.

Answer (D) is correct. *(SEE, adapted)*
REQUIRED: The statement that is false with respect to a Notice of Federal Tax Lien.
DISCUSSION: Section 6343 directs the IRS to release the levy on a taxpayer's property under certain circumstances. Section 6325 directs the IRS to issue a certificate of release of lien within 30 days after the tax liability is satisfied (or becomes unenforceable) or within 30 days after accepting a bond guaranteeing payment of the liability. The lien may be released immediately if requested by the taxpayer. Section 6326 provides for administrative appeal to the IRS for release of a lien. Section 7432(a) provides that a taxpayer may bring a civil action for damages against the U.S. if the IRS knowingly or negligently fails to release a lien under Sec. 6325.
Answer (A) is incorrect. A Notice of Federal Tax Lien is a public notice to the taxpayer's creditors that the government has a claim against all of the taxpayer's real, personal, and/or business property, including property acquired after the lien came into existence. Answer (B) is incorrect. All fees charged by the state or other jurisdiction for both filing and releasing the lien will be added to the balance the taxpayer owes. Answer (C) is incorrect. The IRS will issue a Release of the Notice of Federal Tax Lien within 30 days after acceptance of a bond guaranteeing payment of the liability.

23.7.14. All of the following statements with respect to the IRS seizure and sale of a taxpayer's property to satisfy his or her tax bill are true except

    A. A seizure may not be made on any property if the estimated cost of the seizure and sale exceeds the fair market value of the property to be seized.

    B. A taxpayer has the right to an administrative review of a seizure action when the IRS has taken personal property necessary to the maintenance of the taxpayer's business.

    C. A taxpayer does not have the right to redeem his or her property prior to sale by the IRS.

    D. After the sale, proceeds are applied first to the expenses of the levy and sale.

Answer (C) is correct. *(SEE, adapted)*
    REQUIRED: The false statement with respect to the IRS seizure and sale of a taxpayer's property.
    DISCUSSION: Section 6331(b) authorizes the seizure and sale of any property upon which the IRS may levy. Section 6337(a) provides a right of redemption by paying the amount due, together with expenses, at any time prior to sale of the property. For real property, the right of redemption continues until 180 days after the sale [Sec. 6337(b)].
    Answer (A) is incorrect. A seizure may not be made on any property if the estimated cost of the seizure and sale exceeds the fair market value of the property to be seized. Answer (B) is incorrect. A taxpayer has the right to an administrative review of a seizure action when the IRS has taken personal property necessary to the maintenance of the taxpayer's business. Answer (D) is incorrect. After the sale, proceeds are first applied to the expenses of the levy and sale.

23.7.15. The filing of bankruptcy may not eliminate tax debt; it may temporarily stop IRS enforcement action from collecting a debt related to the bankruptcy.

    A. True.

    B. False.

Answer (A) is correct. *(SEE, adapted)*
    DISCUSSION: Filing a petition in bankruptcy under Title 11 of the U.S. Code automatically stays assessment and collection of a tax. The stay remains in effect until the bankruptcy court discharges liabilities or lifts the stay.

23.7.16. Wage replacement payments are not subject to continuous levy under current law.

    A. True.

    B. False.

Answer (B) is correct. *(Publisher, adapted)*
    DISCUSSION: The decision to assess a levy must first be approved by a supervisor. Even though they are otherwise exempt from levy, the following payments are still generally subject to a levy of up to 15%: (1) any federal payment other than a payment for which eligibility is based on the income or assets or both of a payee; (2) unemployment benefits; (3) workers' compensation; (4) the minimum levy exemption amount for wages and like payments; (5) certain "means-tested" public assistance payments; and (6) certain railroad annuity, railroad pension, or railroad unemployment benefits.

23.7.17. A taxpayer's principal residence is exempt from levy by the IRS by federal law unless jeopardy exists or prior written approval of the IRS district director or assistant district director has been secured.

    A. True.

    B. False.

Answer (A) is correct. *(SEE, adapted)*
    DISCUSSION: Under Sec. 6334(a)(13), a taxpayer's principal residence is generally exempt from levy by the IRS. However, under Sec. 6334(e), levy is allowed on a taxpayer's principal residence if the district director or assistant district director personally approves such a levy in writing or if the collection of the tax is in jeopardy.

23.7.18. If at any step of the collection process a taxpayer does not agree with the recommendations of an IRS collection employee, the taxpayer has the right to discuss the matter with the employee's manager.

    A. True.

    B. False.

Answer (A) is correct. *(SEE, adapted)*
    DISCUSSION: When the Internal Revenue Service sends a Notice and Demand for Tax to a taxpayer, the notice is accompanied by a publication outlining the taxpayer's rights. One of these rights is the right to discuss the collection matter with the IRS collection employee's manager. If at any step of the collection process a taxpayer does not agree with the recommendations of the IRS employee, the taxpayer has the right to discuss the matter with the employee's manager.

23.7.19. If a person liable for tax neglects or refuses to pay the tax after demand has been made, a lien in favor of the government attaches to the taxpayer's property. The lien is automatically valid against all the taxpayer's creditors.

A. True.

B. False.

Answer (B) is correct. *(Publisher, adapted)*
    DISCUSSION: Section 6321 states that if a taxpayer neglects or refuses to pay a deficiency after demand, a lien attaches to all the taxpayer's property. Section 6323(a) states that this lien is not valid against any purchaser, holder of a security interest, holder of a mechanic's lien, or judgment lien creditor until the IRS files a Notice of Federal Tax Lien.

23.7.20. A levy is the taking of property to satisfy a tax liability.

A. True.

B. False.

Answer (A) is correct. *(SEE, adapted)*
    DISCUSSION: Section 7701(a)(21) defines a levy as the power of distraint and seizure by any means. Section 6331(a) authorizes the Internal Revenue Service to take (seize) property if a taxpayer neglects or refuses to pay a tax liability. The seized property can be sold to satisfy the unpaid liability.

23.7.21. According to Sec. 6334, unemployment benefits are the only property exempt from levy by federal law.

A. True.

B. False.

Answer (B) is correct. *(SEE, adapted)*
    DISCUSSION: Section 6334 lists various types of property that are exempt from levy. Unemployment benefits are one type of exempt property [Sec. 6334(a)(4)]. Among the other types of exempt property are wearing apparel, school books, workers' compensation, and undelivered mail.

23.7.22. A levy may no longer be in effect if it becomes unenforceable due to lapse of time.

A. True.

B. False.

Answer (A) is correct. *(SEE, adapted)*
    DISCUSSION: Section 6343(a)(1)(A) directs the IRS to release a levy when the liability for which the levy was made is satisfied or becomes unenforceable by reason of lapse of time.

23.7.23. Once served, a levy on salary or wages continues either for 90 days or until the tax liability is satisfied.

A. True.

B. False.

Answer (B) is correct. *(SEE, adapted)*
    DISCUSSION: Under Sec. 6331(e), a levy on salary or wages continues from the date the levy is first made until the levy is released. Under Sec. 6343, a levy must be released when the tax liability is satisfied or the levy becomes unenforceable due to lapse of time.

23.7.24. Submission of an offer in compromise by a taxpayer automatically suspends collection of an account.

A. True.

B. False.

Answer (B) is correct. *(SEE, adapted)*
    DISCUSSION: A taxpayer has the right to submit an offer in compromise. Section 7122 authorizes the Commissioner of the Internal Revenue Service to compromise taxes (including interest, penalties, additional amounts, or additions to the tax) arising under the internal revenue laws except those relating to alcohol, tobacco, and firearms. Regulation 301.7122-1(d)(2) states that the submission of an offer in compromise does not automatically operate to suspend collection of an account. Regulation 301.7122-1(f) states that an offer in compromise will not be accepted unless the taxpayer waives the running of the statutory period of limitations. If there is any indication that the filing of the offer is solely for the purpose of delaying collection of the tax or that delay would negatively affect collection of the tax, the IRS will continue collection efforts.

23.7.25. A Chapter 7 bankruptcy discharges all of the unpaid tax liability of a sole proprietor.

A. True.

B. False.

Answer (B) is correct. *(SEE, adapted)*
    DISCUSSION: Under Sec. 6871, upon the adjudication of bankruptcy, the IRS may immediately assess any tax deficiency (including interest, penalties, etc.) that has not previously been assessed. Filing a bankruptcy petition does not discharge a sole proprietor's unpaid tax liability. The IRS will file a proof of claim in the bankruptcy court and will attempt to satisfy the deficiency from the assets in the bankruptcy estate.

23.7.26. The recording of a Notice of Federal Tax Lien may restrict the taxpayer's ability to sell or transfer property during the existence of the lien.

A. True.

B. False.

Answer (A) is correct. *(SEE, adapted)*
DISCUSSION: The recording of a Notice of Federal Tax Lien serves to put potential purchasers of the taxpayer's property on notice that the government has a claim against the property. Such a recording may restrict the taxpayer's ability to sell or transfer the property during the existence of the lien.

23.7.27. The taxpayer must be informed of the filing of a tax lien and has the right to request a hearing before an impartial hearing officer.

A. True.

B. False.

Answer (A) is correct. *(Publisher, adapted)*
DISCUSSION: As a result of the IRS Restructuring and Reform Act of 1998, the taxpayer must be informed of the filing of a tax lien and has the right to request a hearing before an impartial hearing officer.

23.8 Claims for Refund

23.8.1. Elizabeth, a calendar-year taxpayer, filed her Year 1 individual return on March 15, Year 2. She did not pay her Year 1 income tax liability in full until March 30, Year 3. If Elizabeth discovers a mistake on her Year 1 return, what is the last day she may file a claim for refund?

A. March 15, Year 4.

B. March 15, Year 5.

C. March 30, Year 5.

D. April 15, Year 5.

Answer (D) is correct. *(SEE, adapted)*
REQUIRED: The date for filing an amended return to claim a refund.
DISCUSSION: Section 6511(b) states that a claim for refund must be made within the time limits specified in the statute of limitations on refunds. Section 6511(a) states that a refund may be paid 3 years from the time the return was filed or 2 years from the time the tax was paid, whichever is later. Under Sec. 6513(a), a return filed early is deemed filed on its due date. Therefore, Elizabeth must file a claim for refund no later than April 15, Year 5.
Answer (A) is incorrect. March 15, Year 4, is not the last day Elizabeth may file a claim for refund. Answer (B) is incorrect. March 15, Year 5, is not the last day Elizabeth may file a claim for refund. Answer (C) is incorrect. March 30, Year 5, is not the last day Elizabeth may file a claim for refund.

23.8.2. Richard Baker filed his Year 1 individual income tax return on April 15, Year 2. On December 31, Year 2, he learned that 100 shares of stock that he owned had become worthless in Year 1. Since he did not deduct this loss on his Year 1 return, Baker intends to file a claim for refund. This refund claim must be filed no later than April 15 of which year (assuming no relevant days are Saturdays, Sundays, or holidays)?

A. Year 3.

B. Year 5.

C. Year 8.

D. Year 9.

Answer (D) is correct. *(CPA, adapted)*
REQUIRED: The date for filing a refund claim for losses on worthless securities.
DISCUSSION: Section 6511(d) allows a 7-year period of limitation for filing a refund claim if the overpayment of tax is due to losses from worthless securities. The period of limitation is 7 years from the date prescribed for filing the return for the year with respect to which the claim is made.
Answer (A) is incorrect. Year 3 is not the latest year in which the claim for refund must be filed. Answer (B) is incorrect. Year 5 is not the latest year in which the claim for refund must be filed. Answer (C) is incorrect. Year 8 is not the latest year in which the claim for refund must be filed.

23.8.3. If a taxpayer and the IRS still disagree after an appeals conference, the taxpayer can take his or her case to

A. United States Tax Court.

B. United States Court of Federal Claims.

C. United States District Court.

D. All of the answers are correct.

Answer (D) is correct. *(SEE, adapted)*
REQUIRED: The court a taxpayer may take his or her case to when still disagreeing with the IRS after an appeals conference.
DISCUSSION: If a taxpayer and the IRS still disagree after an appeals conference, or the election was made to bypass the IRS appeals system, the case may be taken to the U.S. Tax Court, the U.S. Court of Federal Claims, or a U.S. District Court.
Answer (A) is incorrect. The taxpayer can also take his or her case to the U.S. Court of Federal Claims or a U.S. District Court. Answer (B) is incorrect. The taxpayer can also take his or her case to the U.S. Tax Court or a U.S. District Court. Answer (C) is incorrect. The taxpayer can also take his or her case to the U.S. Tax Court or the U.S. Court of Federal Claims.

23.8.4. If an individual paid income taxes in the current year through withholding but did not file a current-year return because his income was insufficient to require the filing of a return, the deadline for filing a refund claim is

A. 2 years from the date the tax was paid.

B. 2 years from the date a return would have been due.

C. 3 years from the date the tax was paid.

D. 3 years from the date a return would have been due.

Answer (A) is correct. *(CPA, adapted)*
　　REQUIRED: The deadline for filing a refund claim when no return is filed.
　　DISCUSSION: Section 6511(a) and (b) state that a claim for refund must be filed within 3 years from the time the return was filed or 2 years from the time the tax was paid, whichever is later. Section 6511(a) further states that if no return was filed, the claim for refund is due within 2 years from the time the tax was paid. For tax years ending after August 5, 1997, taxpayers who initially fail to file a return, but who receive a notice of deficiency and file suit to contest in Tax Court during the third year after the return due date, are permitted to obtain a refund of excessive amounts paid within the 3-year period prior to the deficiency notice.
　　Answer (B) is incorrect. The deadline for filing a refund claim is not 2 years from the date a return would have been due. Answer (C) is incorrect. The deadline for filing a refund claim is not 3 years from the date the tax was paid. Answer (D) is incorrect. The deadline for filing a refund claim is not 3 years from the date a return would have been due.

23.8.5. Ms. B filed her Year 1 Form 1040 on April 15, Year 2, but did not pay her tax liability of $3,000. On June 15, Year 3, she paid the tax in full. In Year 4, Ms. B discovered additional deductions for Year 1 that will result in a refund of $1,000. To receive her refund, Ms. B must file an amended income tax return by (assuming no relevant days are Saturdays, Sundays, or holidays)

A. April 15, Year 5.

B. June 15, Year 5.

C. April 15, Year 6.

D. June 15, Year 6.

Answer (B) is correct. *(SEE, adapted)*
　　REQUIRED: The date for filing a refund claim for taxes paid after the related return was filed.
　　DISCUSSION: Section 6511(b) states that a claim for a refund must be filed within the time limits established in the statute of limitations on refunds. Section 6511(a) provides that refunds may be made 3 years from the time the return was filed or 2 years from the time the tax was paid, whichever is later. Here, 2 years from the time the tax was paid is the later date, so B must file a claim before June 15, Year 5.
　　Answer (A) is incorrect. April 15, Year 5, is not the latest date by which an amended return must be filed. Answer (C) is incorrect. April 15, Year 6, is not the latest date by which an amended return must be filed. Answer (D) is incorrect. June 15, Year 6, is not the latest date by which an amended return must be filed.

23.8.6. Ms. Smith, a calendar-year taxpayer, made estimated tax payments of $1,000 and got an extension of time to August 15, Year 2, to file her Year 1 income tax return. She filed her return on November 1, Year 2, 2 1/2 months after the extension period ended and paid an additional $400 tax due on that date. On September 26, Year 5, Ms. Smith filed an amended return and claimed a refund of $800. The maximum refund she could receive is $400.

A. True.

B. False.

Answer (A) is correct. *(SEE, adapted)*
　　DISCUSSION: Section 6511(a) and (b) state that a claim for refund must be filed within 3 years from the time the return was filed or 2 years from the time the tax was paid, whichever is later. The limitation on the amount of refund that may be received if the claim was filed within the 3-year period is the portion of the tax paid within the 3 years prior to filing the claim plus any extension period for filing the return.
　　Ms. Smith filed the claim more than 2 years after paying the tax but less than 3 years from the time of filing the return. She may receive a refund only for the amount paid within 3 years plus 4 months (the extension was from April 15 to August 15) prior to September 26, Year 5. Since Ms. Smith paid only $400 during this period, her refund is limited to $400.

23.8.7. XYZ, Inc., a calendar-year corporation, reported a net operating loss on its Year 3 tax return. The NOL was carried back to the Year 1 tax return for a tax refund. The claim for refund was filed on July 15, Year 4. The refund was paid by the Internal Revenue Service on August 20, Year 4. XYZ will receive interest on the refund for the period March 15, Year 4, to July 15, Year 4.

A. True.

B. False.

Answer (B) is correct. *(M. Yates)*
　　DISCUSSION: Normally, interest on a refund is paid from the date of the overpayment (here, the date prescribed for filing the return) to a date preceding the date of the refund check by not more than 30 days [Sec. 6611(b)(2)]. However, Sec. 6611(e) provides that no interest will be paid on a refund of tax made within 45 days after the due date of the return or the date the return is filed, whichever is later. A claim for refund is a return. Since only 39 days passed between the date the refund claim was filed and the date of the refund, no interest will be paid on the refund.

23.8.8. If you are filing a claim for credit or refund based on contested income tax issues considered in previously examined returns and do not want to appeal within the IRS, you should request in writing that the claim be immediately rejected.

    A. True.

    B. False.

Answer (A) is correct. *(SEE, adapted)*
    DISCUSSION: A taxpayer may file a refund suit in the district court or the U.S. Court of Federal Claims only after the IRS rejects a refund claim. Thus, if you do not want to appeal within the IRS, you should request in writing that the claim be immediately rejected to enable jurisdictional requirements for court proceedings to be satisfied earlier.

23.8.9. Peter did not want to use the administrative appeal process within the IRS to contest income tax issues considered in the audit of his return. He filed a claim for refund and requested that the claim be immediately rejected. The IRS promptly sent him a notice of claim disallowance. Peter has 2 years from the date of the notice of disallowance to file a refund suit in a United States District Court or in the United States Court of Federal Claims.

    A. True.

    B. False.

Answer (B) is correct. *(SEE, adapted)*
    DISCUSSION: Generally, district courts and the Court of Federal Claims hear tax cases only after the tax has been paid and a claim for a refund has been filed. Claims for refund may be filed when a tax is deemed incorrect or excessive. The claim can be taken to court only if it is rejected or not acted on within 6 months from the date it is filed. Section 6532(a) indicates that the taxpayer must file suit no later than 2 years after the mailing of the rejected claim. The notice of disallowance must be sent by certified or registered mail.

23.8.10. Kevin and Keith are partners in a body shop business. Both of them had their individual returns examined and both disagreed with the IRS. Kevin decided to take his case to IRS appeals. After the conference, he and the IRS still disagreed. Keith decided to bypass IRS appeals. After satisfying certain procedural and jurisdictional requirements, both Kevin and Keith can take their cases to the following courts: the United States Tax Court, the United States Court of Federal Claims, or a United States District Court.

    A. True.

    B. False.

Answer (A) is correct. *(SEE, adapted)*
    DISCUSSION: If a taxpayer and the IRS still disagree after an appeals conference, or the election was made to bypass the IRS appeals system, the case may be taken to the U.S. Tax Court, the U.S. Court of Federal Claims, or a U.S. District Court.

23.8.11. In a civil proceeding against the U.S. in tax matters, a taxpayer as the prevailing party must prove his or her position is substantially justified in order to receive an award for litigation costs.

    A. True.

    B. False.

Answer (B) is correct. *(Publisher, adapted)*
    DISCUSSION: Section 7430 allows an award for litigation costs if the taxpayer is the prevailing party and the U.S. government cannot establish that its position was substantially justified.

23.8.12. A prevailing party who otherwise qualifies and does not unreasonably lengthen civil proceedings may receive an award for attorneys' fees limited to $180 per hour in 2017.

    A. True.

    B. False.

Answer (B) is correct. *(Publisher, adapted)*
    DISCUSSION: Litigation costs will be denied entirely to a prevailing party who unreasonably lengthens any portion of the civil proceedings. Section 7430 limits the amount of reasonable litigation costs to be paid for attorneys' services to $200 per hour for 2017.

23.9 Tax Court

23.9.1. The maximum amount of deficiency per tax year or tax period that may be heard by the Small Tax Case Division of the U.S. Tax Court is

A. $2,500

B. $10,000

C. $50,000

D. $75,000

Answer (C) is correct. *(SEE, adapted)*
REQUIRED: The maximum deficiency that may be handled by the Small Tax Case Division of the U.S. Tax Court.
DISCUSSION: The IRS Restructuring and Reform Act of 1998 increased the deficiency or overpayment limit for cases that may be heard by the Small Tax Case Division of the Tax Court. The limit is now $50,000 [Sec. 7463(a)]. It is the taxpayer's option (subject to agreement by the Tax Court) for the case to be heard by the Small Tax Case Division.
Answer (A) is incorrect. The IRS Restructuring and Reform Act of 1998 increased the maximum deficiency to an amount above $2,500. Answer (B) is incorrect. The maximum amount of deficiency was increased to an amount above $10,000 by the IRS Restructuring and Reform Act of 1998. Answer (D) is incorrect. The maximum amount of deficiency is below $75,000.

23.9.2. Nico wants his income tax case to be handled under the Tax Court's "small tax case procedure." All of the following statements regarding the "small tax case procedure" are true except that the

A. Amount in the case must be $50,000 or less for court proceedings begun after July 22, 1998.

B. Amount must be paid before going to Tax Court.

C. Tax Court must approve the request that the case be handled under the small tax case procedure.

D. Decision is final and cannot be appealed.

Answer (B) is correct. *(SEE, adapted)*
REQUIRED: The false statement regarding "the small tax case procedure."
DISCUSSION: The IRS Restructuring and Reform Act of 1998 increased the deficiency or overpayment limit for cases that may be heard by the Small Tax Case Division of the Tax Court. The limit is now $50,000 [Sec. 7463(a)]. It is the taxpayer's option (subject to agreement by the Tax Court) for the case to be heard by the Small Tax Case Division. Generally, the Tax Court hears cases before any tax has been assessed or paid. In order to petition, the taxpayer must first receive a notice of deficiency. Any case decided in the Small Tax Case Division of the Tax Court will not be reviewed by any other court.
Answer (A) is incorrect. The amount in the case must be $50,000 or less for court proceedings begun after July 22, 1998. Answer (C) is incorrect. The Tax Court must approve the request that the case be handled under the small tax case procedure. Answer (D) is incorrect. The decision is final and cannot be appealed.

23.9.3. The Tax Court has jurisdiction over all of the following taxes except

A. Income.

B. Employment.

C. Estate.

D. Gift.

Answer (B) is correct. *(SEE, adapted)*
REQUIRED: The type of tax over which the Tax Court has no jurisdiction.
DISCUSSION: The Tax Court is a court of limited jurisdiction. Section 7442 states that the Tax Court has such jurisdiction as is conferred on it by Title 26 of the U.S. Code; by Chapters 1, 2, 3, and 4 of the Internal Revenue Code of 1939; by Title II and Title III of the Revenue Act of 1926; or by laws enacted subsequent to February 26, 1926. The Tax Court's jurisdiction covers income, estate, gift, excise, and private foundation taxes. The Tax Court has no jurisdiction over employment taxes. The self-employment tax is an income tax, however, and thus is within the purview of the Tax Court.
Answer (A) is incorrect. Income tax is a tax over which the Tax Court has jurisdiction. Answer (C) is incorrect. Estate tax is a tax over which the Tax Court has jurisdiction. Answer (D) is incorrect. Gift tax is a tax over which the Tax Court has jurisdiction.

23.9.4. Which of the following statements is false with respect to the United States Tax Court?

A. It has jurisdiction over all federal taxes.

B. It is authorized by the Internal Revenue Code but is entirely separate from the Internal Revenue Service.

C. Its regular decisions are printed in bound volumes by the government.

D. It is based in Washington, D.C.

Answer (A) is correct. *(SEE, adapted)*
REQUIRED: The false statement about the operations of the Tax Court.
DISCUSSION: The Tax Court's jurisdiction is defined under Sec. 7442. In general, the Tax Court's jurisdiction covers income, estate, gift, excise, and private foundation taxes. The Tax Court does not have jurisdiction over employment taxes except for the self-employment tax, which has been classified by the Court as an income tax.
Answer (B) is incorrect. The Tax Court is authorized by Sec. 7441 and is operated and funded separately from the Internal Revenue Service. Answer (C) is incorrect. The Tax Court's regular decisions are printed in bound volumes twice each year by the U.S. Government Printing Office. Its memorandum decisions, on the other hand, are printed by private publishers. Answer (D) is incorrect. The Tax Court is based in Washington, D.C. Its judges ride "circuit" and hear cases in Washington and throughout the United States.

23.9.5. Johnny disagreed with the IRS examiner and her supervisor regarding his income tax case. His appeal rights were explained to him, and he wanted to go to Tax Court. Johnny must receive a notice of deficiency before he can go to Tax Court.

A. True.

B. False.

Answer (A) is correct. *(SEE, adapted)*
DISCUSSION: Generally, the Tax Court hears cases before any tax has been assessed or paid. In order to petition, the taxpayer must first receive a notice of deficiency.

23.9.6. Mr. W does not agree with the proposed tax deficiency of $20,000 resulting from an IRS examination of his income tax return. He has been unable to resolve his case within the administrative processes of the Internal Revenue Service. The United States Tax Court is the only court that he may petition without first making payment on the contested deficiency.

A. True.

B. False.

Answer (A) is correct. *(SEE, adapted)*
DISCUSSION: Under Sec. 6213(a), if a taxpayer files a petition with the Tax Court within 90 days after the notice of deficiency is mailed, a tax may not be assessed until the final decision of the Tax Court is rendered. If the taxpayer pays the tax and a claim for refund is disallowed by the IRS, the taxpayer may file a suit for refund in the U.S. District Court or in the U.S. Court of Federal Claims.

23.9.7. Correspondence in connection with cases docketed in the Tax Court will be addressed to counsel of record before the court in lieu of a power of attorney or tax information authorization.

A. True.

B. False.

Answer (A) is correct. *(SEE, adapted)*
DISCUSSION: Tax Court Rule 21(b)(2) states that, absent notice to the court that some other counsel is to receive correspondence, correspondence will be addressed to the counsel whose appearance was first entered of record.

23.9.8. With respect to docketed Tax Court cases, status solely as an enrolled agent or a CPA will not allow that person to practice before the Tax Court.

A. True.

B. False.

Answer (A) is correct. *(SEE, adapted)*
DISCUSSION: An individual, other than an attorney, must demonstrate his or her qualifications satisfactorily to the Tax Court by means of a written examination given by the Tax Court. In addition, the Tax Court may require that the individual give similar evidence by means of an oral examination (Rule 200).

23.9.9. Both the taxpayer and the government may appeal "small tax case procedure" decisions of the Tax Court to the appropriate court of appeals.

A. True.

B. False.

Answer (B) is correct. *(SEE, adapted)*
DISCUSSION: Section 7463(b) provides that a decision entered in any case in the Small Tax Case Division of the Tax Court shall not be reviewed by any other court.

23.9.10. The term "Practice before the Internal Revenue Service" includes the representation of clients in the United States Tax Court for cases being handled under the "small tax case procedure."

A. True.

B. False.

Answer (B) is correct. *(SEE, adapted)*
DISCUSSION: "Practice before the Internal Revenue Service" comprehends all matters connected with presentation to the Internal Revenue Service or any of its officers or employees relating to a client's rights, privileges, or liabilities under laws or regulations administered by the IRS. Such presentations include the preparation and filing of necessary documents; correspondence with and communication to the IRS; and the representation of a client at conferences, hearings, and meetings. It does not include the representation of clients in the United States Tax Court for cases being handled under the "small tax case procedure." The Tax Court of the United States has its own rules concerning who is allowed to practice before it in regular and small tax case matters (Sec. 7452).

23.9.11. The Commissioner of Internal Revenue will announce acquiescence or nonacquiescence only when the Tax Court's decision is adverse to the IRS's position.

A. True.

B. False.

Answer (A) is correct. *(SEE, adapted)*
DISCUSSION: The Commissioner is not required to endorse the general principles embodied in the decisions of the courts. (S)he may announce an acquiescence or nonacquiescence with regard to the regular, reported decisions of the Tax Court. The announcement relates only to the issue(s) decided adversely to the government. Beginning in 1991, the IRS expanded its acquiescence program to include other civil tax cases when guidance is helpful.

23.9.12. Whether or not the Commissioner of Internal Revenue decides to appeal an adverse Tax Court decision, (s)he may nonacquiesce in the case, which means that the Service does not accept the adverse decision and will not follow it in cases on the same issue.

A. True.

B. False.

Answer (A) is correct. *(SEE, adapted)*
DISCUSSION: The Commissioner may announce his or her acquiescence or nonacquiescence with regard to the regular, reported decisions of the Tax Court. Acquiescence is the Commissioner's public endorsement of a Tax Court decision. In some cases, only specific issues are acquiesced, or the agreement may be in result only.

23.9.13. The Commissioner of Internal Revenue may subsequently revise a nonacquiescence but not an acquiescence.

A. True.

B. False.

Answer (B) is correct. *(SEE, adapted)*
DISCUSSION: The Commissioner may at any time revise a nonacquiescence to a decision in a prior case. Likewise, an acquiescence may be withdrawn at any time with retroactive effect if the purpose is to correct a mistake in the application of tax law.

23.9.14. A Tax Court memorandum decision is a report of a Tax Court decision thought to be of little value as a precedent because the issue has been decided one or more times before.

A. True.

B. False.

Answer (A) is correct. *(SEE, adapted)*
DISCUSSION: Tax Court memorandum decisions have been considered to have very little value as precedents. These decisions generally concern routine matters for which the law has previously been determined but the facts are different.

23.9.15. The Tax Court exclusively hears tax cases nationwide. It decides cases consistently throughout the United States.

A. True.

B. False.

Answer (B) is correct. *(Publisher, adapted)*
DISCUSSION: While the Tax Court is the only forum that exclusively hears tax cases, it does not always decide similar cases in the same way. Under the decision in *Golsen*, 54 T.C. 742 (1970), the Tax Court will follow the rule adopted by the court of appeals to which the taxpayer would appeal an adverse decision. Thus, if the circuits are in conflict on a particular issue, the Tax Court may decide the issue differently depending upon the geographic origin of the case.

23.9.16. Although the Tax Court can decide a case in favor of the taxpayer, it has no authority to order the refund of overpayments made by the taxpayer.

A. True.
B. False.

Answer (B) is correct. *(Publisher, adapted)*
    DISCUSSION: The Technical and Miscellaneous Revenue Act of 1988 expanded the jurisdiction of the Tax Court. It allows the Tax Court to order the refund of overpayments determined in Tax Court [Sec. 6512(b)] as well as restrain assessments or collection of tax at issue before the Tax Court [Sec. 6213(a)].

23.9.17. The Tax Court has jurisdiction over credits that would offset the refund due to a taxpayer.

A. True.
B. False.

Answer (B) is correct. *(Publisher, adapted)*
    DISCUSSION: If an overpayment of tax is not refunded by the IRS within 120 days of the Tax Court's final decision, the order is appealable. However, the court does not have jurisdiction over credits that may reduce the refund due the taxpayer.

23.10 District Court and Court of Federal Claims

23.10.1. One difference between the Tax Court and a district court is that

A. The tax must be paid first to go to the Tax Court but not to a district court.
B. A trial by jury can be obtained in the Tax Court but not in a district court.
C. One can appeal an adverse decision of the Tax Court to the appropriate circuit court of appeals, while an appeal from a district court can be filed only with the U.S. Supreme Court.
D. A trial by jury can be had in a district court but not in the Tax Court.

Answer (D) is correct. *(M.J. Whiteman)*
    REQUIRED: The true statement about the differences between the Tax Court and a district court.
    DISCUSSION: Taxpayers who choose to have their cases heard before a district court may request a trial by jury. Cases heard before the Tax Court are decided by judges.
    Answer (A) is incorrect. The taxpayer must pay the deficiency and then sue for refund in his or her district court. The taxpayer need only receive a Notice of Deficiency to file a petition in the Tax Court. Answer (B) is incorrect. A trial by jury is available in the district courts but not in the Tax Court. Answer (C) is incorrect. Decisions of both the Tax Court and the district courts may be appealed to the circuit courts of appeal. Note that "small tax case procedure" decisions of the Tax Court may not be appealed.

23.10.2. Within 6 months from the date he filed it, Y received a formal notice from the IRS by certified mail disallowing his $10,000 tax refund claim. What is Y's appeal?

A. File a protest and request that the matter be referred to the IRS appeals office.
B. File suit in his U.S. District Court or the U.S. Court of Federal Claims no later than 2 years after the date of the notice.
C. File a petition with the U.S. Tax Court.
D. File a petition with the U.S. Tax Court and ask that it be handled under the "small tax case procedure."

Answer (B) is correct. *(SEE, adapted)*
    REQUIRED: The appeal for a taxpayer whose refund is disallowed.
    DISCUSSION: Section 6532(a)(1) provides the general rule that a suit must be brought within 2 years of the date of the notice. Appeal may be made to a U.S. District Court or the U.S. Court of Federal Claims. (The U.S. Claims Court was retitled the U.S. Court of Federal Claims effective November 1, 1992. No change in its basic function occurred at that time.)
    Answer (A) is incorrect. The IRS appeals office deals with appeals before proposed deficiencies are paid. Regulation Sec. 601.106 describes the IRS appeals office. Its purpose is to resolve tax controversies without litigation. Many situations involving the IRS appeals office have the district director issuing a preliminary (30-day) letter and the taxpayer requesting appeals consideration. Generally, when a tax payment has been made, the taxpayer's recourse lies within a U.S. District Court or the U.S. Court of Federal Claims. Answer (C) is incorrect. The Tax Court generally handles cases when the tax in dispute has not been paid. Its jurisdiction to handle overpayments does not extend to the issue described here [Sec. 6512(b)]. Answer (D) is incorrect. The Tax Court generally handles cases when the tax in dispute has not been paid. Its jurisdiction to handle overpayments does not extend to the issue described here [Sec. 6512(b)].

23.10.3. If the Internal Revenue Service has not acted upon your claim for refund within 6 months from the date you filed it, you can file suit for refund in your U.S. District Court or the U.S. Court of Federal Claims.

A. True.

B. False.

Answer (A) is correct. *(SEE, adapted)*
　　DISCUSSION: Section 6532(a)(1) states that a taxpayer cannot file a suit for refund before the IRS has acted on the claim or until 6 months have elapsed.

23.10.4. If a taxpayer wants to file a refund suit in a U.S. District Court having jurisdiction or in the U.S. Court of Federal Claims, based only on contested income tax or on estate tax or gift tax issues considered in previously examined returns, the taxpayer should file a claim for refund with the IRS and request that the claim be immediately rejected.

A. True.

B. False.

Answer (A) is correct. *(SEE, adapted)*
　　DISCUSSION: Before a taxpayer may file a refund suit in a U.S. District Court or the U.S. Court of Federal Claims, (s)he must first have paid the tax and filed a claim for refund with the Internal Revenue Service. Only after the IRS rejects the claim for refund may a taxpayer file a refund suit in a district court or Court of Federal Claims. If a taxpayer wishes to file such a suit, (s)he should file a claim for refund with the Internal Revenue Service and request in writing that the claim be immediately rejected.

23.10.5. The Commissioner of Internal Revenue does not file either acquiescence or nonacquiescence to adverse court decisions other than those regular, reported decisions of the Tax Court.

A. True.

B. False.

Answer (B) is correct. *(SEE, adapted)*
　　DISCUSSION: Until 1991, acquiescences and nonacquiescences were published only for certain regular decisions of the Tax Court, but the IRS has expanded its acquiescence program to include other civil tax cases when guidance is helpful.

23.11 Appeals

23.11.1. All of the following statements concerning court appeals and court petitions are true except

A. Both the taxpayer and the government may appeal decisions of the Tax Court or a district court to the appropriate circuit court of appeals.

B. The decisions of courts of appeal and some decisions of other federal courts may be reviewed by the U.S. Supreme Court.

C. For federal tax purposes, the most common type of case that the U.S. Supreme Court hears is one in which a federal tax statute is ruled to be invalid.

D. If a taxpayer's claim for refund is denied by the Internal Revenue Service or if no decision is made in 6 months, the taxpayer may petition either the U.S. Court of Federal Claims or the U.S. Circuit Court of Appeals.

Answer (D) is correct. *(SEE, adapted)*
　　REQUIRED: The false statement concerning court appeals and court petitions.
　　DISCUSSION: If a taxpayer's refund claim is denied by the Internal Revenue Service or if no decision is made in 6 months, the taxpayer may petition either the U.S. Court of Federal Claims or a district court. The U.S. Court of Appeals hears appeals from decisions of the Tax Court, a district court, and the U.S. Court of Federal Claims. Cases appealed from the Tax Court and a district court are heard in the Circuit Court of Appeals for the taxpayer's jurisdiction. Appeals from the U.S. Court of Federal Claims are heard by the Court of Appeals for the Federal Circuit. It is not a court of original jurisdiction.
　　Answer (A) is incorrect. Both the taxpayer and the government may appeal decisions of the Tax Court or a district court to the appropriate circuit court of appeals. Answer (B) is incorrect. The decisions of courts of appeal and some decisions of other federal courts may be reviewed by the U.S. Supreme Court. Answer (C) is incorrect. For federal tax purposes, the most common type of case that the U.S. Supreme Court hears is one in which a federal tax statute is ruled to be invalid.

23.11.2. Appeal from the U.S. Court of Federal Claims is to the

A. U.S. Circuit Court of Appeals.

B. U.S. Court of Appeals for the Federal Circuit.

C. U.S. Tax Court.

D. U.S. Supreme Court.

Answer (B) is correct. *(J.P. Trebby)*
  REQUIRED: The appellate court to which appeals from the U.S. Court of Federal Claims are taken.
  DISCUSSION: The U.S. Court of Appeals for the Federal Circuit is the appellate court to which appeals from the U.S. Court of Federal Claims are taken.
  Answer (A) is incorrect. The U.S. Circuit Court of Appeals is the appellate court that hears appeals from the U.S. District Court and the U.S. Tax Court. Answer (C) is incorrect. The U.S. Tax Court is a court of original jurisdiction, not an appellate court. Answer (D) is incorrect. In tax cases, there is no direct appeal to the U.S. Supreme Court from the U.S. Court of Federal Claims or from any other court of original jurisdiction.

23.11.3. All of the following statements are true.

- A petition to the U.S. Supreme Court to have a case that it is not obliged to review is by writ of certiorari.
- The writ of certiorari is initially requested by the appealing party.
- The writ of certiorari is issued by the U.S. Supreme Court to the lower appellate court requesting the record of a case for review.

A. True.

B. False.

Answer (A) is correct. *(SEE, adapted)*
  DISCUSSION: A petition to the U.S. Supreme Court to hear a case is by writ of certiorari requested by the appealing party. If the Court decides to hear the case, the writ is presented to the lower appellate court ordering the record of the case to be sent for review.

23.11.4. If one district court has rejected the Commissioner of Internal Revenue's position, the Commissioner cannot take that position before any other district court in the same court of appeals circuit.

A. True.

B. False.

Answer (B) is correct. *(SEE, adapted)*
  DISCUSSION: The Internal Revenue Service is not bound by the decisions of district courts. Therefore, if one district court has rejected the Commissioner of Internal Revenue's position, the Commissioner may take the same position before any other district court in the court of appeals circuit. However, if the court of appeals for the circuit has rendered a decision against the Commissioner of Internal Revenue's position, the other district courts in the circuit are bound by that decision.

☑ ≡
☐ ≡   Use **Gleim Test Prep** for interactive study and easy-to-use detailed analytics!
☐ ≡

APPENDIX A
SUBUNIT CROSS-REFERENCES
TO FEDERAL TAX TEXTBOOKS

This section contains the tables of contents of current federal tax textbooks with cross-references to the related subunits or study units in this study manual. The texts are listed in alphabetical order by the first author. As you study a particular chapter in your federal tax textbook, you can easily determine which subunit(s) to study in your Gleim EQE material.

Professors and students should note that, even though new editions of the texts listed below may be published as you use this study material, the new tables of contents usually will be very similar, if not the same. Thus, this edition of *Federal Tax Exam Questions and Explanations* will remain current and useful.

If you are using a textbook that is not included in this list or if you have any suggestions on how we can improve these cross-references to make them more relevant/useful, please submit your request/feedback at www.gleim.com/crossreferences/TAX or email them to TAXcrossreferences@gleim.com.

FEDERAL TAX TEXTBOOKS

CCH INCORPORATED, *Federal Taxation: Basic Principles (2018)*, 2018 Edition, CCH INC., 2017.

CCH INCORPORATED, *Federal Taxation: Comprehensive Topics (2018)*, 2018 Edition, CCH INC., 2017.

CCH INCORPORATED, *Principles of Business Taxation (2017)*, 2017 Edition, CCH INC., 2016.

Cruz, Deschamps, Niswander, Prendergast, and Schisler, *Fundamentals of Taxation 2017*, 10th Edition, McGraw-Hill, 2017.

Hoffman, Maloney, Raabe, and Young, *South-Western Federal Taxation 2018: Comprehensive*, 41st Edition, Cengage Learning, 2017.

Hoffman, Raabe, Young, Nellen, and Maloney, *South-Western Federal Taxation 2018: Corporations, Partnerships, Estates and Trusts*, 41st Edition, Cengage Learning, 2017.

Hoffman, Raabe, Young, Nellen, and Maloney, *South-Western Federal Taxation 2018: Individual Income Taxes*, 41st Edition, Cengage Learning, 2017.

Johnson, *Essentials of Federal Income Taxation for Individuals and Business (2017)*, 2017 Edition, CCH INC., 2016.

Jones, Callaghan, and Rhoades-Catanach, *Principles of Taxation for Business and Investment Planning*, 21st Edition, McGraw-Hill, 2017.

Murphy and Higgins, *Concepts in Federal Taxation 2018*, 25th Edition, Cengage Learning, 2017.

Pope, Rupert, and Anderson, *Pearson's Federal Taxation 2018: Comprehensive*, 31st Edition, Pearson, 2017.

Pope, Rupert, and Anderson, *Pearson's Federal Taxation 2018: Corporations, Partnerships, Estates & Trusts*, 31st Edition, Pearson, 2017.

Pope, Rupert, and Anderson, *Pearson's Federal Taxation 2018: Individuals*, 31st Edition, Pearson, 2017.

Pratt and Kulsrud, *Corporate, Partnership, Estate and Gift Taxation*, 2018 Edition, Van-Griner Publishing, 2017.

Pratt and Kulsrud, *Federal Taxation*, 2018 Edition, Van-Griner Publishing, 2017.

Pratt and Kulsrud, *Individual Taxation*, 2018 Edition, Van-Griner Publishing, 2017.

Raabe, Young, Nellen, and Maloney, *South-Western Federal Taxation 2018: Essentials of Taxation: Individuals and Business Entities*, 21st Edition, Cengage Learning, 2017.

Spilker, Ayers, Robinson, Outslay, Worsham, Barrick, and Weaver, *McGraw-Hill's Taxation of Business Entities*, 8th Edition, McGraw-Hill, 2016.

Spilker, Ayers, Robinson, Outslay, Worsham, Barrick, and Weaver, *McGraw-Hill's Taxation of Individuals*, 8th Edition, McGraw-Hill, 2016.

Spilker, Ayers, Robinson, Outslay, Worsham, Barrick, and Weaver, *McGraw-Hill's Taxation of Individuals and Business Entities*, 9th Edition, McGraw-Hill, 2017.

Whittenburg, Gill, and Altus-Buller, *Income Tax Fundamentals 2017*, 35th Edition, Cengage Learning, 2017.

FEDERAL TAX TEXTBOOKS

CCH INCORPORATED, *Federal Taxation: Basic Principles (2018)*, 2018 Edition, CCH INC., 2017.

Chapter   1 - Introduction to Federal Taxation and Understanding the Federal Tax Law - 23.1-23.2
Chapter   2 - Tax Research, Practice and Procedure - SU 23
Chapter   3 - Individual Taxation--An Overview - SU 7, 19.1-19.2
Chapter   4 - Gross Income - SU 1, 2.1, 2.8, 19.1-19.3, 19.8
Chapter   5 - Gross Income--Exclusions - SU 2
Chapter   6 - Deductions: General Concepts and Trade or Business Deductions - SUs 3-4, 5.1-5.4, 5.10, SU 10, 16.5, 21.3, 21.9
Chapter   7 - Deductions: Business/Investment Losses and Passive Activity Losses - 3.9, SU 4, 14.7, 16.9, 17.14
Chapter   8 - Deductions: Itemized Deductions - SU 6
Chapter   9 - Tax Credits, Prepayments and Special Methods - 7.6, SU 8
Chapter 10 - Property Transactions: Determination of Basis and Gains and Losses - SU 9
Chapter 11 - Property Transactions: Nonrecognition of Gains and Losses - SU 13
Chapter 12 - Property Transactions: Treatment of Capital and Section 1231 Assets - 9.7, SUs 11-12
Chapter 13 - Tax Accounting - 19.1-19.8
Chapter 14 - Deferred Compensation and Education Savings Plans - 1.8, 2.6, 5.5-5.12
Chapter 15 - Tax Planning for Individuals - SU 7
Chapter 16 - Partnerships, Corporations and S Corporations - SUs 14-16, 17.1-17.6, 17.10-17.18
Chapter 17 - Federal Estate Tax, Federal Gift Tax and Generation-Skipping Transfer Tax - SU 21
Chapter 18 - Income Taxation of Trusts and Estates - 7.8, 18.1-18.6

CCH INCORPORATED, *Federal Taxation: Comprehensive Topics (2018)*, 2018 Edition, CCH INC., 2017.

Chapter   1 - Introduction to Federal Taxation and Understanding the Federal Tax Law - 23.1-23.2
Chapter   2 - Tax Research, Practice and Procedure - SUs 22-23
Chapter   3 - Individual Taxation--An Overview - SU 7, 19.1-19.2
Chapter   4 - Gross Income - SU 1, 2.1, 2.8, 19.1-19.3, 19.8
Chapter   5 - Gross Income--Exclusions - SU 2
Chapter   6 - Deductions: General Concepts and Trade or Business Deductions - SUs 3-4, 5.1-5.4, 5.10, SU 10, 16.5, 21.3, 21.9
Chapter   7 - Deductions: Business/Investment Losses and Passive Activity Losses - 3.9, SU 4, 14.7, 16.9, 17.14
Chapter   8 - Deductions: Itemized Deductions - SU 6
Chapter   9 - Tax Credits, Prepayments, and Special Methods - 7.6, SU 8
Chapter 10 - Property Transactions: Determination of Basis and Gains and Losses - SU 9
Chapter 11 - Property Transactions: Nonrecognition of Gains and Losses - SU 13
Chapter 12 - Property Transactions: Treatment of Capital and Section 1231 Assets - 9.7, SUs 11-12
Chapter 13 - Tax Accounting - SU 19
Chapter 14 - Taxation of Corporations--Basic Concepts - SU 16
Chapter 15 - Corporate Nonliquidating Distributions - 17.1-17.4
Chapter 16 - Corporate Distributions in Complete Liquidations - 17.5-17.6
Chapter 17 - Corporate Reorganizations - 17.7
Chapter 18 - Accumulated Earnings and Personal Holding Company Taxes - 17.10-17.11

CCH INCORPORATED, *Principles of Business Taxation (2017),* **2017 Edition, CCH INC., 2016.**

Cruz, Deschamps, Niswander, Prendergast, and Schisler, *Fundamentals of Taxation 2017,* **10th Edition, McGraw-Hill, 2017.**

Part IV: Advanced Tax Practice Considerations
    Chapter 14 - Taxes on the Financial Statements - N/A
    Chapter 15 - Exempt Entities - 18.7
    Chapter 16 - Multistate Corporate Taxation - N/A
    Chapter 17 - Tax Practice and Ethics - SU 22, 23.3-23.10
Part V: Family Tax Planning
    Chapter 18 - The Federal Gift and Estate Taxes - SU 21
    Chapter 19 - Family Tax Planning - 1.9, 7.5, 11.8, 15.5, 18.4
    Chapter 20 - Income Taxation of Trusts and Estates - 7.8, 18.1-18.6

Hoffman, Raabe, Young, Nellen, and Maloney, *South-Western Federal Taxation 2018: Individual Income Taxes*, 41st Edition, Cengage Learning, 2017.

Part I: Introduction and Basic Tax Model
    Chapter 1 - An Introduction to Taxation and Understanding the Federal Tax Law - 23.1-23.2
    Chapter 2 - Working with the Tax Law - 23.1-23.2
    Chapter 3 - Tax Formula and Tax Determination; An Overview of Property Transactions - SU 7, 9.1, 9.8, 11.1-11.4, 11.7, 11.9
Part II: Gross Income
    Chapter 4 - Gross Income: Concepts and Inclusions - SU 1, 2.1, 2.8, 19.1-19.3, 19.8
    Chapter 5 - Gross Income: Exclusions - SU 2
Part III: Deductions
    Chapter 6 - Deductions and Losses: In General - SU 3, 19.1-19.3
    Chapter 7 - Deductions and Losses: Certain Business Expenses and Losses - SU 3, 4.1, 6.5, 11.5-11.7
    Chapter 8 - Depreciation, Cost Recovery, Amortization, and Depletion - SU 10
    Chapter 9 - Deductions: Employee and Self-Employed-Related Expenses - SU 3, 5.1-5.3, 6.6, 20.2
    Chapter 10 - Deductions and Losses: Certain Itemized Deductions - SU 6
    Chapter 11 - Investor Losses - 4.2-4.3
Part IV: Special Tax Computation Methods, Payment Procedures, and Tax Credits
    Chapter 12 - Alternative Minimum Tax - 7.6
    Chapter 13 - Tax Credits and Payment Procedures - SU 8
Part V: Property Transactions
    Chapter 14 - Property Transactions: Determination of Gain or Loss and Basis Considerations - SU 9
    Chapter 15 - Property Transactions: Nontaxable Exchanges - SU 13
    Chapter 16 - Property Transactions: Capital Gains and Losses - 9.7, SU 11
    Chapter 17 - Property Transactions: Section 1231 and Recapture Provisions - SU 12
Part VI: Accounting Periods, Accounting Methods, and Deferred Compensation
    Chapter 18 - Accounting Periods and Methods - SU 19
    Chapter 19 - Deferred Compensation - 1.8, 5.5-5.8
Part VII: Corporations and Partnerships
    Chapter 20 - Corporations and Partnerships - SUs 14-16, 17.1-17.6, 17.12-17.18

Johnson, *Essentials of Federal Income Taxation for Individuals and Business (2017)*, 2017 Edition, CCH INC., 2016.

    Chapter 1 - Overview of the Tax Structure - 23.1-23.2, 23.6
    Chapter 2 - Tax Determination, Payments and Reporting Procedures - SU 7, 23.3-23.11
    Chapter 3 - Gross Income Inclusions - SU 1, 2.1, 2.8
    Chapter 4 - Gross Income Exclusions and Deductions for AGI - SU 2
    Chapter 5 - Personal Itemized Deductions - SU 6
    Chapter 6 - Other Itemized Deductions - SU 6
    Chapter 7 - Self-Employment - 3.1, 4.4, 20.4
    Chapter 8 - Depreciation and Amortization - SU 10, 19.6
    Chapter 9 - Rental Activities - 3.7, 4.3
    Chapter 10 - Property: Basis and Nontaxable Exchanges - SU 9, SU 13
    Chapter 11 - Property: Capital Gains and Losses, and Depreciation Recapture - SUs 11-12
    Chapter 12 - NOLs, AMT, and Business Tax Credits - 4.1, 7.6, SU 8, 16.13
    Chapter 13 - Withholding, Payroll, and Estimated Taxes - 7.7, 16.15, 17.17, 18.5, SU 20
    Chapter 14 - C Corporations - SU 16, 17.1-17.3
    Chapter 15 - Partnerships and S Corporations - SUs 14-15, 17.12-17.18

Jones, Callaghan, and Rhoades-Catanach, *Principles of Taxation for Business and Investment Planning***, 21st Edition, McGraw-Hill, 2017.**

Part One: Exploring the Tax Environment
      Chapter   1 - Taxes and Taxing Jurisdictions - 23.1-23.2
      Chapter   2 - Policy Standards for a Good Tax - N/A
Part Two: Fundamentals of Tax Planning
      Chapter   3 - Taxes as Transaction Costs - 1.1
      Chapter   4 - Maxims of Income Tax Planning - N/A
      Chapter   5 - Tax Research - 23.1
Part Three: The Measurement of Taxable Income
      Chapter   6 - Taxable Income from Business Operations - 4.1, 16.9, 19.1-19.3
      Chapter   7 - Property Acquisitions and Cost Recovery Deductions - SUs 9-10
      Chapter   8 - Property Dispositions - SUs 11-12
      Chapter   9 - Nontaxable Exchanges - SU 13
Part Four: The Taxation of Business Income
      Chapter 10 - Sole Proprietorships, Partnerships, LLCs, and S Corporations - 1.2, 3.6, SU 14, 17.13
      Chapter 11 - The Corporate Taxpayer - 16.1, 16.10, 16.13
      Chapter 12 - The Choice of Business Entity - 14.1-14.3, 16.1
      Chapter 13 - Jurisdictional Issues in Business Taxation - 2.7, 8.7-8.8
Part Five: The Individual Taxpayer
      Chapter 14 - The Individual Tax Formula - SU 7, 8.1-8.7
      Chapter 15 - Compensation and Retirement Planning - 1.2-1.3, 2.2-2.5, 2.7, 5.5-5.8
      Chapter 16 - Investment and Personal Financial Planning - 4.3, SU 7, 8.5, SU 21
      Chapter 17 - Tax Consequences of Personal Activities - SUs 1-2, 6.1-6.5, SU 7
Part Six: The Tax Compliance Process
      Chapter 18 - The Tax Compliance Process - 23.1-23.2

Murphy and Higgins, *Concepts in Federal Taxation 2018***, 25th Edition, Cengage Learning, 2017.**

Part I: Conceptual Foundations of the Tax Law
      Chapter   1 - Federal Income Taxation-An Overview - SU 23
      Chapter   2 - Income Tax Concepts - 19.1-19.3, 19.8, 23.1-23.2
Part II: Gross Income
      Chapter   3 - Income Sources - SU 1, 2.1, 2.8
      Chapter   4 - Income Exclusions - SU 2
Part III: Deductions
      Chapter   5 - Introduction to Business Expenses - SU 3
      Chapter   6 - Business Expenses - SU 3, 5.1-5.8
      Chapter   7 - Losses-Deductions and Limitations - 3.9, SU 4
      Chapter   8 - Taxation of Individuals - SU 7
Part IV: Property Transactions
      Chapter   9 - Acquisitions of Property - SU 9
      Chapter 10 - Cost Recovery on Property: Depreciation, Depletion, and Amortization - SU 10
      Chapter 11 - Property Dispositions - SUs 11-12
      Chapter 12 - Non-recognition Transactions - SU 13
Part V: Income Tax Entities
      Chapter 13 - Choice of Business Entity-General Tax and Nontax Factors/Formation - N/A
      Chapter 14 - Choice of Business Entity-Operations and Distributions - N/A
      Chapter 15 - Choice of Business Entity-Other Considerations - N/A
Part VI: Tax Research
      Chapter 16 - Tax Research - 23.1

Pope, Rupert, and Anderson, *Pearson's Federal Taxation 2018: Comprehensive*, 31st Edition, Pearson, 2017.

Individuals

Chapter 1 - An Introduction to Taxation - 23.1-23.2
Chapter 2 - Determination of Tax - SU 7
Chapter 3 - Gross Income: Inclusions - SU 1, 2.1, 2.8
Chapter 4 - Gross Income: Exclusions - SU 2
Chapter 5 - Property Transactions: Capital Gains and Losses - SU 9, SU 11
Chapter 6 - Deductions and Losses - SU 3, SU 5, 11.7-11.8, 19.1-19.2
Chapter 7 - Itemized Deductions - SU 6
Chapter 8 - Losses and Bad Debts - 3.3, 3.9, SU 4, 6.5
Chapter 9 - Employee Expenses and Deferred Compensation - 3.6, 5.1, 5.5-5.8, 6.6-6.7
Chapter 10 - Depreciation, Cost Recovery, Amortization, and Depletion - SU 10
Chapter 11 - Accounting Periods and Methods - SU 19
Chapter 12 - Property Transactions: Nontaxable Exchanges - SU 13
Chapter 13 - Property Transactions: Section 1231 and Recapture - SU 12
Chapter 14 - Special Tax Computation Methods, Tax Credits, and Payment of Tax - 7.4, 7.6-7.7, SU 8

Corporations

Chapter 1 - Tax Research - 23.1
Chapter 2 - Corporate Formations and Capital Structure - 16.1-16.3
Chapter 3 - The Corporate Income Tax - 16.4-16.15, 17.8-17.11
Chapter 4 - Corporate Nonliquidating Distributions - 17.1-17.4
Chapter 5 - Other Corporate Tax Levies - 17.10-17.11
Chapter 6 - Corporate Liquidating Distributions - 17.5-17.6
Chapter 7 - Corporate Acquisitions and Reorganizations - 17.7
Chapter 8 - Consolidated Tax Returns - 17.8-17.9
Chapter 9 - Partnership Formation and Operation - SUs 14-15
Chapter 10 - Special Partnership Issues - 14.10, 15.1-15.2, 15.5, 15.7-15.8
Chapter 11 - S Corporations - 17.12-17.18
Chapter 12 - The Gift Tax - 21.1-21.6
Chapter 13 - The Estate Tax - 21.7-21.14
Chapter 14 - Income Taxation of Trusts and Estates - 7.8, 18.1-18.6
Chapter 15 - Administrative Procedures - SU 22, 23.3-23.11

Pope, Rupert, and Anderson, *Pearson's Federal Taxation 2018: Corporations, Partnerships, Estates & Trusts*, 31st Edition, Pearson, 2017.

Chapter 1 - Tax Research - 23.1
Chapter 2 - Corporate Formations and Capital Structure - 16.1-16.3
Chapter 3 - The Corporate Income Tax - 16.4-16.15, 17.8-17.11
Chapter 4 - Corporate Nonliquidating Distributions - 17.1-17.4
Chapter 5 - Other Corporate Tax Levies - 17.10-17.11
Chapter 6 - Corporate Liquidating Distributions - 17.5-17.6
Chapter 7 - Corporate Acquisitions and Reorganizations - 17.7
Chapter 8 - Consolidated Tax Returns - 17.8-17.9
Chapter 9 - Partnership Formation and Operation - SUs 14-15
Chapter 10 - Special Partnership Issues - 14.10, 15.1-15.2
Chapter 11 - S Corporations - 17.12-17.18
Chapter 12 - The Gift Tax - 21.1-21.6
Chapter 13 - The Estate Tax - 21.7-21.14
Chapter 14 - Income Taxation of Trusts and Estates - 7.8, 18.1-18.6
Chapter 15 - Administrative Procedures - SU 22, 23.3-23.11
Chapter 16 - U.S. Taxation of Foreign-Related Transactions - 2.7, 8.8

Pope, Rupert, and Anderson, *Pearson's Federal Taxation 2018: Individuals*, 31st Edition, Pearson, 2017.

Chapter   1 - An Introduction to Taxation - 23.1-23.2
Chapter   2 - Determination of Tax - SU 7
Chapter   3 - Gross Income: Inclusions - SU 1, 2.1, 2.8
Chapter   4 - Gross Income: Exclusions - SU 2
Chapter   5 - Property Transactions: Capital Gains and Losses - SU 9, SU 11
Chapter   6 - Deductions and Losses - SU 3, SU 5, 11.7-11.8, 19.1-19.2
Chapter   7 - Itemized Deductions - SU 6
Chapter   8 - Losses and Bad Debts - 3.3, 3.9, SU 4, 6.5
Chapter   9 - Employee Expenses and Deferred Compensation - 3.6, 5.1, 6.6
Chapter 10 - Depreciation, Cost Recovery, Amortization, and Depletion - SU 10
Chapter 11 - Accounting Periods and Methods - SU 19
Chapter 12 - Property Transactions: Nontaxable Exchanges - SU 13
Chapter 13 - Property Transactions: Section 1231 and Recapture - SU 12
Chapter 14 - Special Tax Computation Methods, Tax Credits, and Payment of Tax - 7.4, 7.6-7.7, SU 8
Chapter 15 - Tax Research - 23.1
Chapter 16 - Corporations - SU 16, 17.1-17.11
Chapter 17 - Partnerships and S Corporations - SU 14, 15.1-15.4, 17.12-17.18
Chapter 18 - Taxes and Investment Planning - 4.2-4.3, 5.2-5.3, 5.5-5.9, 7.8

Pratt and Kulsrud, *Corporate, Partnership, Estate and Gift Taxation*, 2018 Edition, Van-Griner Publishing, 2017.

Part I: Corporate Taxation
Chapter   1 - Income Taxation of Corporations - 16.12-16.15
Chapter   2 - Corporate Formation and Capital Structure - 16.5-16.11
Chapter   3 - Corporate Distributions: Cash, Property, and Stock Dividends - 17.1-17.2
Chapter   4 - Corporate Distributions: Stock Redemptions and Partial Liquidations - 17.3-17.4
Chapter   5 - Complete Liquidations - 17.5-17.6
Chapter   6 - Penalty Taxes on Corporate Accumulations - 17.10-17.11
Part II: Advanced Corporate Tax Topics
Chapter   7 - Corporate Reorganizations - 17.7
Chapter   8 - Consolidated Tax Returns - 17.8-17.9
Part III: Flow-Through Entities
Chapter   9 - Taxation of Partnerships and Partners - SU 14
Chapter 10 - Partnership Distributions, Dispositions of Partnership Interests, and Partnership Terminations - SU 15
Chapter 11 - S Corporations: General Rules Applicable to All S Corporations - 17.12-17.18
Chapter 12 - S Corporations, Former C Corporations, Sales and Purchases of Stock, Comparison of Entities - 14.2, 17.12-17.13
Part IV: Multijurisdictional Taxation
Chapter 13 - International Taxation - N/A
Chapter 14 - State and Local Taxation - N/A
Part V: Family Tax Planning
Chapter 15 - Estate and Gift Taxation - SU 21
Chapter 16 - Income Taxation of Estates and Trusts - 7.8, 18.1-18.6
Chapter 17 - Family Tax Planning - 1.8, 7.5, 11.8, 15.5, 18.4
Part VI: Tax Research and Tax Practice
Chapter 18 - Sources and Applications of Federal Tax Law - 23.1-23.2
Chapter 19 - Tax Practice and Procedure - 7.3, SU 22, 23.3-23.11

Pratt and Kulsrud, *Federal Taxation*, 2018 Edition, Van-Griner Publishing, 2017.

Part I: Introduction to the Federal Tax System
Chapter   1 - An Overview of Federal Taxation - 23.1-23.2, 23.6
Chapter   2 - Tax Practice and Research - 23.1-23.2
Chapter   3 - Taxable Entities; Tax Formula; Introduction to Property Transactions - 7.4, 7.8, 16.13
Chapter   4 - Personal and Dependency Exemptions; Filing Status; Determination of Tax for an Individual; Filing Requirements - SU 7
Part II: Gross Income
Chapter   5 - Gross Income - SU 1, 2.1, 2.8, 19.1-19.3, 19.8
Chapter   6 - Gross Income: Inclusions and Exclusions - SUs 1-2

Part III: Deductions and Losses
    Chapter   7 - Overview of Deductions and Losses - SU 3, 19.1-19.3
    Chapter   8 - Employee Business Expenses - 3.3-3.4, 3.6-3.7, 5.1, 6.6
    Chapter   9 - Capital Recovery: Depreciation, Amortization, and Depletion - SU 10
    Chapter 10 - Certain Business Deductions and Losses - SU 3, 4.1, 6.5, 11.5-11.7
    Chapter 11 - Itemized Deductions - SU 6
    Chapter 12 - Deductions for Certain Investment Expenses and Losses - 4.3, 5.2, 17.1-17.4
Part IV: Alternative Minimum Tax and Tax Credits
    Chapter 13 - The Alternative Minimum Tax and Tax Credits - 7.6, SU 8
Part V: Property Transactions
    Chapter 14 - Property Transactions: Basis Determination and Recognition of Gain or Loss - SU 9
    Chapter 15 - Nontaxable Exchanges - SU 13
    Chapter 16 - Property Transactions: Capital Gains and Losses - SU 9, SU 11, 12.1
    Chapter 17 - Property Transactions: Dispositions of Trade or Business Property - SU 12
Part VI: Employee Compensation and Retirement Plans
    Chapter 18 - Employee Compensation and Retirement Plans - 1.2, 2.3-2.5, 5.5-5.9
Part VII: Corporate Taxation
    Chapter 19 - Corporations: Formation and Operation - SU 16
    Chapter 20 - Corporate Distributions, Redemptions, and Liquidations - 17.1-17.6
    Chapter 21 - Taxation of Corporate Accumulations - 17.9-17.10
Part VIII: Flow-Through Entities
    Chapter 22 - Taxation of Partnerships and Partners - 14.1-14.5, 15.3
    Chapter 23 - S Corporations - 17.12-17.18
Part IX: Family Tax Planning
    Chapter 24 - The Federal Transfer Taxes - SU 21
    Chapter 25 - Income Taxation of Estates and Trusts - 7.8, 18.1-18.6
    Chapter 26 - Family Tax Planning - 1.8, 7.5, 11.8, 15.5, 18.4

Pratt and Kulsrud, *Individual Taxation*, 2018 Edition, Van-Griner Publishing, 2017.

Part I: Introduction to the Federal Tax System
    Chapter   1 - An Overview of Federal Taxation - 23.1-23.2, 23.6
    Chapter   2 - Tax Practice and Research - 23.1-23.2
    Chapter   3 - Taxable Entities; Tax Formula; Introduction to Property Transactions - 7.4, 7.8, 16.13
    Chapter   4 - Personal and Dependency Exemptions; Filing Status; Determination of Tax for an Individual; Filing Requirements - SU 7
Part II: Gross Income
    Chapter   5 - Gross Income - SU 1, 2.1, 2.8, 19.1-19.3, 19.8
    Chapter   6 - Gross Income: Inclusions and Exclusions - SUs 1-2
Part III: Deductions and Losses
    Chapter   7 - Overview of Deductions and Losses - SU 3
    Chapter   8 - Employee Business Expenses - 3.1-3.7, 5.1, 6.6
    Chapter   9 - Capital Recovery: Depreciation, Amortization, and Depletion - SU 10
    Chapter 10 - Certain Business Deductions and Losses - SU 3, 4.1, 6.5, 11.5-11.7
    Chapter 11 - Itemized Deductions - SU 6
    Chapter 12 - Deductions for Certain Investment Expenses and Losses - 4.3, 5.2, 17.1-17.4
Part IV: Alternative Minimum Tax and Tax Credits
    Chapter 13 - The Alternative Minimum Tax and Tax Credits - 7.6, SU 8
Part V: Property Transactions
    Chapter 14 - Property Transactions: Basis Determination and Recognition of Gain or Loss - SU 9
    Chapter 15 - Nontaxable Exchanges - SU 13
    Chapter 16 - Property Transactions: Capital Gains and Losses - SU 9, SU 11, 12.1
    Chapter 17 - Property Transactions: Dispositions of Trade or Business Property - SU 12
Part VI: Employee Compensation and Taxation of Business Forms
    Chapter 18 - Employee Compensation and Retirement Plans - 1.2, 2.3-2.5, 5.5-5.9
    Chapter 19 - Taxation of Business Forms and Their Owners - SU 14, SU 16, 17.12-17.18

Raabe, Young, Nellen, and Maloney, *South-Western Federal Taxation 2018: Essentials of Taxation: Individuals and Business Entities*, 21st Edition, Cengage Learning, 2017.

Part I: The World of Taxation
 Chapter 1 - Introduction to Taxation - 23.1-23.2, 23.4
 Chapter 2 - Working with the Tax Law - SU 22, 23.3-23.11
 Chapter 3 - Taxes on the Financial Statements - 16.12
Part II: Structure of the Federal Income Tax
 Chapter 4 - Gross Income - SUs 1-2
 Chapter 5 - Business Deductions - SU 3, 5.1-5.3, 6.4-6.5
 Chapter 6 - Losses and Loss Limitations - SU 4, SU 11
Part III: Property Transactions
 Chapter 7 - Property Transactions: Basis, Gain and Loss, and Nontaxable Exchanges - SU 9
 Chapter 8 - Property Transactions: Capital Gains and Losses, Section 1231, and Recapture Provisions - SU 9, SU 12, 16.10
Part IV: Taxation of Individuals
 Chapter 9 - Individuals as the Taxpayer - SU 7
 Chapter 10 - Individuals: Income, Deductions, and Credits - SU 1, SUs 5-6, SU 8
 Chapter 11 - Individuals as Employees and Proprietors - 1.2-1.3, 2.3, 3.6, 5.1
Part V: Business Entities
 Chapter 12 - Corporations: Organization, Capital Structure, and Operating Rules - 16.9-16.10
 Chapter 13 - Corporations: Earnings & Profits and Distributions - 16.9
 Chapter 14 - Partnerships and Limited Liability Entities - SUs 14-15
 Chapter 15 - S Corporations - 17.12-17.18
Part VI: Special Business Topics
 Chapter 16 - Multijurisdictional Taxation - N/A
 Chapter 17 - Business Tax Credits and Corporate Alternative Minimum Tax - 7.6, 16.13
 Chapter 18 - Comparative Forms of Doing Business - 14.2

Spilker, Ayers, Robinson, Outslay, Worsham, Barrick, and Weaver, *McGraw-Hill's Taxation of Business Entities*, 8th Edition, McGraw-Hill, 2016.

Part I: Business- and Investment-Related Transactions
 Chapter 1 - Business Income, Deductions, and Accounting Methods - SU 3, 16.5
 Chapter 2 - Property Acquisition and Cost Recovery - SUs 9-10
 Chapter 3 - Property Dispositions - SU 12
Part II: Entity Overview and Taxation of C Corporations
 Chapter 4 - Entities Overview - N/A
 Chapter 5 - Corporate Operations - SU 16
 Chapter 6 - Accounting for Income Taxes - 16.12
 Chapter 7 - Corporate Taxation: Nonliquidating Distributions - 16.9, 17.1-17.4
 Chapter 8 - Corporate Formation, Reorganization, and Liquidation - 11.6, 16.1, 17.3-17.9
Part III: Taxation of Flow-Through Entities
 Chapter 9 - Forming and Operating Partnerships - SU 14
 Chapter 10 - Dispositions of Partnership Interests and Partnership Distributions - SU 15
 Chapter 11 - S Corporations - 17.12-18
Part IV: Multijurisdictional Taxation and Transfer Taxes
 Chapter 12 - State and Local Taxes - N/A
 Chapter 13 - The U.S. Taxation of Multinational Transactions - N/A
 Chapter 14 - Transfer Taxes and Wealth Planning - SU 21

Spilker, Ayers, Robinson, Outslay, Worsham, Barrick, and Weaver, *McGraw-Hill's Taxation of Individuals*, 8th Edition, McGraw-Hill, 2016.

Part I: Intro to Taxation
 Chapter 1 - An Introduction to Tax - SU 23
 Chapter 2 - Tax Compliance, the IRS, and Tax Authorities - 23.1-23.2, 23.7
 Chapter 3 - Tax Planning Strategies and Related Limitations - N/A
Part II: Basic Individual Taxation
 Chapter 4 - Individual Income Tax Overview, Exemptions, and Filing Status - SU 7
 Chapter 5 - Gross Income and Exclusions - SUs 1-2
 Chapter 6 - Individual Deductions - SUs 5-6
 Chapter 7 - Investment - 4.2-4.3, 5.2-5.3
 Chapter 8 - Individual Income Tax Computation and Tax Credits - 7.4, 8.1-8.7, 8.13, 8.16

Part III: Business and Investment–Related Transactions
    Chapter   9 - Business Income, Deductions, and Accounting Methods - SU 3, 16.5
    Chapter 10 - Property Acquisition and Cost Recovery - SUs 9-10
    Chapter 11 - Property Dispositions - SU 12
Part IV: Specialized Topics
    Chapter 12 - Compensation - 2.2-2.3, 3.6, 5.1, 20.2-20.3
    Chapter 13 - Retirement Savings and Deferred Compensation - 5.5
    Chapter 14 - Tax Consequences of Home Ownership - 1.6, 3.7, 4.4, 6.3

Spilker, Ayers, Robinson, Outslay, Worsham, Barrick, and Weaver, *McGraw-Hill's Taxation of Individuals and Business Entities,* **9th Edition, McGraw-Hill, 2017.**

Part I: Intro to Taxation
    Chapter   1 - An Introduction to Tax - SU 23
    Chapter   2 - Tax Compliance, the IRS, and Tax Authorities - 23.1-23.2
    Chapter   3 - Tax Planning Strategies and Related Limitations - N/A
Part II: Basic Individual Taxation
    Chapter   4 - Individual Tax Overview, Exemptions, and Filing Status - SU 7
    Chapter   5 - Gross Income and Exclusions - SUs 1-2
    Chapter   6 - Individual Deductions - SUs 5-6
    Chapter   7 - Investments - 4.2-4.3, 5.2-5.3
    Chapter   8 - Individual Income Tax Computation and Tax Credits - 7.4, 7.8, 16.12
Part III: Business and Investment-Related Transactions
    Chapter   9 - Business Income, Deductions, and Accounting Methods - 3.4, 5.1-5.2, 6.6, 11.5-11.7
    Chapter 10 - Property Acquisition and Cost Recovery - SUs 9-10
    Chapter 11 - Property Dispositions - SUs 11-12
Part IV: Specialized Topics
    Chapter 12 - Compensation - 2.3, 3.6, 5.1, 8.10-8.12, 16.5, 20.2-20.3
    Chapter 13 - Retirement Savings and Deferred Compensation - 5.5-5.9
    Chapter 14 - Tax Consequences of Home Ownership - 6.3
Part V: Entity Overview and Taxation of C Corporations
    Chapter 15 - Entities Overview - N/A
    Chapter 16 - Corporate Operations - SU 16
    Chapter 17 - Accounting for Income Taxes - 16.12
    Chapter 18 - Corporate Taxation: Nonliquidating Distributions - 16.9, 17.1-17.4
    Chapter 19 - Corporate Formation, Reorganization, and Liquidation - 11.6, 16.1-16.8, 17.3-17.7, 17.9
Part VI: Taxation of Flow-Through Entities
    Chapter 20 - Forming and Operating Partnerships - SU 14
    Chapter 21 - Dispositions of Partnership Interests and Partnership Distributions - SU 15
    Chapter 22 - S Corporations - 17.12-17.18
Part VII: Multijurisdictional Taxation and Transfer Taxes
    Chapter 23 - State and Local Taxes - N/A
    Chapter 24 - The U.S. Taxation of Multinational Transactions - N/A
    Chapter 25 - Transfer Taxes and Wealth Planning - SU 21

Whittenburg, Gill, and Altus-Buller, *Income Tax Fundamentals 2017,* **35th Edition, Cengage Learning, 2017.**

    Chapter   1 - The Individual Income Tax Return - SU 7
    Chapter   2 - Gross Income and Exclusions - SUs 1-2
    Chapter   3 - Business Income and Expenses, Part I - 1.6, 3.1-3.3, 3.7, 4.1, 4.3, 5.2-5.3, 5.5-5.8
    Chapter   4 - Business Income and Expenses, Part II - 3.4-3.5, 4.4, 5.1, 5.10-5.12
    Chapter   5 - Itemized Deductions and Other Incentives - SU 6
    Chapter   6 - Credits and Special Taxes - SU 8
    Chapter   7 - Accounting Periods and Methods and Depreciation - 10.1-10.5, SU 19
    Chapter   8 - Capital Gains and Losses - SU 11
    Chapter   9 - Withholding, Estimated Payments, and Payroll Taxes - 7.7, 16.15, 17.17, 18.5, SU 20
    Chapter 10 - Partnership Taxation - SUs 14-15
    Chapter 11 - The Corporate Income Tax - 16.4-16.15, 17.8-17.11
    Chapter 12 - Tax Administration and Tax Planning - SU 23

INDEX